T0181078

Lecture Notes in Artificial Intelligence   12981

Subseries of Lecture Notes in Computer Science

Goreti Marreiros · Francisco S. Melo ·
Nuno Lau · Henrique Lopes Cardoso ·
Luís Paulo Reis (Eds.)

Progress in
Artificial Intelligence

20th EPIA Conference on Artificial Intelligence, EPIA 2021
Virtual Event, September 7–9, 2021
Proceedings

Springer

Editors
Goreti Marreiros (iD)
ISEP/GECAD
Polytechnic Institute of Porto
Porto, Portugal

Francisco S. Melo (iD)
IST/INESC-ID
University of Lisbon
Porto Salvo, Portugal

Nuno Lau (iD)
DETI/IEETA
University of Aveiro
Aveiro, Portugal

Henrique Lopes Cardoso (iD)
FEUP/LIACC
University of Porto
Porto, Portugal

Luís Paulo Reis (iD)
FEUP/LIACC
University of Porto
Porto, Portugal

ISSN 0302-9743   ISSN 1611-3349 (electronic)
Lecture Notes in Artificial Intelligence
ISBN 978-3-030-86229-9   ISBN 978-3-030-86230-5 (eBook)
https://doi.org/10.1007/978-3-030-86230-5

LNCS Sublibrary: SL7 – Artificial Intelligence

This Springer imprint is published by the registered company Springer Nature Switzerland AG
The registered company address is: Gewerbestrasse 11, 6330 Cham, Switzerland

Preface

This volume contains the papers presented at the 20th EPIA Conference on Artificial Intelligence (EPIA 2021), held during September 7–9, 2021, in Portugal. The EPIA Conference on Artificial Intelligence is a well-established European conference in the field of Artificial Intelligence (AI). Due to the COVID-19 pandemic, the 20th edition of the conference took place online.[1] As in previous editions, this international conference was hosted with the patronage of the Portuguese Association for Artificial Intelligence (APPIA).[2] The purpose of this conference is to promote research in all areas of AI, covering both theoretical/foundational issues and applications, and the scientific exchange among researchers, engineers, and practitioners in related disciplines.

As in previous editions, the program was based on a set of thematic tracks proposed by the AI community, dedicated to specific themes of AI. EPIA 2021 encompassed 12 tracks:

AIoTA	Artificial Intelligence and IoT in Agriculture
AIL	Artificial Intelligence and Law
AIM	Artificial Intelligence in Medicine
AIPES	Artificial Intelligence in Power and Energy Systems
AITS	Artificial Intelligence in Transportation Systems
ALEA	Artificial Life and Evolutionary Algorithms
AmIA	Ambient Intelligence and Affective Environments
GAI	General Artificial Intelligence
IROBOT	Intelligent Robotics
KDBI	Knowledge Discovery and Business Intelligence
MASTA	Multi-agent Systems: Theory and Applications
TeMA	Text Mining and Applications

The conference program included four invited talks:

Virginia Dignum (Umeå University, Sweden),
    with a talk on "Responsible AI: From principles to action";
Shimon Whiteson (University of Oxford, UK),
    with a talk on "Factored value functions for cooperative multi-agent reinforcement learning";
Lucia Specia (Imperial College London, UK),
    with a talk on "Multimodal simultaneous machine translation";

---

[1] The conference website can be found at http://www.appia.pt/epia2021/.
[2] http://www.appia.pt.

Fredrik Heintz (Linköping University, Sweden),
  with a talk on "Trustworthy human-centric AI: The European approach".

For this edition, 108 paper submissions were received from authors in 21 different countries (Afghanistan, Bangladesh, Brazil, Czech Republic, France, Germany, India, Iraq, Italy, Mexico, Morocco, the Netherlands, Norway, Portugal, Russia, Serbia, South Africa, Spain, Turkey, the UK, and the USA). After a careful review process, 62 papers were selected to be presented at EPIA 2021. The acceptance rate was thus circa 57%. All accepted papers were carefully revised by at least three reviewers from the Program Committee of the corresponding track.

We thank the thematic track organizing chairs, together with their respective Program Committee members, for their hard work. We would also like to express our gratitude to all the members of the EPIA International Steering Committee for their guidance regarding the scientific organization of EPIA 2021.

  Thank you all.

September 2021   Goreti Marreiros
                                                       Francisco S. Melo
                                                              Nuno Lau
                                               Henrique Lopes Cardoso
                                                       Luís Paulo Reis

Organization

Event and Program Chairs

Goreti Marreiros   GECAD, Polytechnic of Porto, Portugal
Francisco S. Melo   INESC-ID, Instituto Superior Técnico,
          University of Lisbon, Portugal
Nuno Lau   IEETA, University of Aveiro, Portugal
Henrique Lopes Cardoso   LIACC, University of Porto, Portugal
Luís Paulo Reis   LIACC, University of Porto, Portugal

Steering Committee

Ana Bazzan   Universidade Federal do Rio Grande do Sul, Brazil
Ann Nowe   Vrije Universiteit Brussel, Belgium
Catholijn Jonker   Delft University of Technology, The Netherlands
Ernesto Costa   University of Coimbra, Portugal
Eugénio Oliveira   University of Porto, Portugal
Helder Coelho   University of Lisbon, Portugal
João Pavão Martins   University of Lisbon, Portugal
José Júlio Alferes   NOVA University Lisbon, Portugal
Juan Pavón   Universidad Complutense Madrid, Spain
Luís Paulo Reis   University of Porto, Portugal
Paulo Novais   University of Minho, Portugal
Pavel Brazdil   University of Porto, Portugal
Virginia Dignum   Umeå University, Sweden

Track Chairs

Artificial Intelligence and IoT in Agriculture

José Boaventura Cunha   University of Trás-os-Montes and Alto Douro, Portugal
Josenalde Barbosa   Universidade Federal do Rio Grande do Sul, Brazil
Paulo Moura Oliveira   University of Trás-os-Montes and Alto Douro, Portugal
Raul Morais   University of Trás-os-Montes and Alto Douro, Portugal

Artificial Intelligence and Law

Pedro Freitas   Universidade Católica Portuguesa, Portugal
Paulo Novais   University of Minho, Portugal
Massimo Durante   University of Torino, Italy
Ugo Pagallo   University of Torino, Italy

Artificial Intelligence in Medicine

Manuel Filipe Santos	University of Minho, Portugal
Carlos Filipe Portela	University of Minho, Portugal
Allan Tucker	Brunel University London, UK
Manuel Fernandez Delgado	University of Santiago de Compostela, Spain

Artificial Intelligence in Power and Energy Systems

Zita Vale	Polytechnic of Porto, Portugal
Tiago Pinto	Polytechnic of Porto, Portugal
Pedro Faria	Polytechnic of Porto, Portugal
Elena Mocanu	University of Twente, The Netherlands
Decebal Constantin Mocanu	University of Twente, The Netherlands

Artificial Intelligence in Transportation Systems

Rosaldo Rossetti	University of Porto, Portugal
Alberto Fernandez	Universidad Rey Juan Carlos, Spain

Artificial Life and Evolutionary Algorithms

Ivo Gonçalves	University of Coimbra, Portugal
Mauro Castelli	NOVA IMS, Portugal
Luca Manzoni	University of Trieste, Italy
Leonardo Trujillo	Technical Institute of Tijuana, Mexico
Carlos Henggeler Antunes	University of Coimbra, Portugal

Ambient Intelligence and Affective Environments

Ana Almeida	Polytechnic of Porto, Portugal
Sara Rodriguez	University of Salamanca, Spain
Goreti Marreiros	Polytechnic of Porto, Portugal
Paulo Novais	University of Minho, Portugal
Peter Mikulecky	University of Hradec Kralove, Czech Republic

General Artificial Intelligence

Goreti Marreiros	Polytechnic of Porto, Portugal
Francisco S. Melo	University of Lisbon, Portugal
Nuno Lau	University of Aveiro, Portugal
Henrique Lopes Cardoso	University of Porto, Portugal
Luís Paulo Reis	University of Porto, Portugal

Intelligent Robotics

João Fabro   Universidade Tecnológica Federal do Paraná, Brazil
Reinaldo Bianchi   Centro Universitário da FEI, Brazil
Nuno Lau   University of Aveiro, Portugal
Luís Paulo Reis   University of Porto, Portugal

Knowledge Discovery and Business Intelligence

Paulo Cortez   University of Minho, Portugal
Albert Bifet   Université Paris-Saclay, France
Luís Cavique   Universidade Aberta, Portugal
João Gama   University of Porto, Portugal
Nuno Marques   NOVA University Lisbon, Portugal
Manuel Filipe Santos   University of Minho, Portugal

Multi-agent Systems: Theory and Applications

Ana Paula Rocha   University of Porto, Portugal
João Balsa   University of Lisbon, Portugal
Graçaliz Pereira Dimuro   Universidade Federal do Rio Grande, Brazil
Alberto Fernandez   Universidad Rey Juan Carlos, Spain

Text Mining and Applications

Joaquim Silva   NOVA University Lisbon, Portugal
Pablo Gamallo   University of Santiago de Compostela, Spain
Paulo Quaresma   University of Évora, Portugal
Irene Rodrigues   University of Évora, Portugal

Program Committee

Artificial Intelligence and IoT in Agriculture

Andrés Muñoz Ortega   Catholic University of Murcia, Spain
Aneesh Chauhan   Wageningen University and Research, The Netherlands
António Valente   University of Trás-os-Montes and Alto Douro, Portugal
Brett Whelan   University of Sydney, Australia
Bruno Tisseyre   University of Montpellier, France
Carlos Eduardo Cugnasca   University of São Paulo, Brazil
Carlos Serôdio   University of Trás-os-Montes and Alto Douro, Portugal
Dinos Ferentinos   Hellenic Agricultural Organization "Demeter", Greece
Eduardo Solteiro Pires   University of Trás-os-Montes and Alto Douro, Portugal
Emanuel Peres   University of Trás-os-Montes and Alto Douro, Portugal
Filipe Santos   University of Porto, Portugal

Javier Sanchis Sáez	Polytechnic University of Valencia, Spain
João Paulo Coelho	Polytechnic Institute of Bragança, Portugal
Joaquim Sousa	University of Trás-os-Montes and Alto Douro, Portugal
Jos Balendonck	Wageningen University and Research, The Netherlands
José António Sanz	Public University of Navarre, Spain
Kazuhisa Ito	Shibaura Institute of Technology, Japan
Laura Santana	Federal University of Rio Grande Do Norte, Brazil
Manoj Karkee	Washington State University, USA
Nieves Pávon-Pulido	Polytechnic University of Cartagena, Spain
Pedro Couto	University of Trás-os-Montes and Alto Douro, Portugal
Pedro Melo-Pinto	University of Trás-os-Montes and Alto Douro, Portugal
Tatiana Pinho	INESC-TEC, Portugal
Veronica Saiz-Rubio	Polytechnic University of Valencia, Spain
Yuxin Miao	University of Minnesota, USA

Artificial Intelligence and Law

Carlisle George	Middlesex University London, UK
Cinthia Freitas	Pontifical Catholic University of Paraná, Brazil
Clara Pereira	University of Oxford, UK
Federico Bueno de Mata	University of Salamanca, Spain
Flúvio Garcia	Pontifical Catholic University of Paraná, Brazil
Giovanni Sartor	European University Institute, Italy
Henrique Sousa Antunes	Catholic University of Portugal, Portugal
Isabel Pereira	University of Lisbon, Portugal
Luis Moniz Pereira	NOVA University Lisbon, Portugal
Manuel Masseno	Polytechnic Institute of Beja, Portugal
Pedro Oliveira	University of Minho, Portugal
Radboud Winkels	University of Amsterdam, The Netherlands
Serena Quattrocolo	University of Eastern Piedmont, Italy
Sofia Ranchordas	University of Groningen, The Netherlands
Vicente Julian	Polytechnic University of Valencia, Spain

Artificial Intelligence in Medicine

Álvaro Silva	Abel Salazar Biomedical Sciences Institute, Portugal
Andreas Holzinger	Medical University Graz, Austria
António Abelha	University of Minho, Portugal
António Manuel de Jesus Pereira	Polytechnic Institute of Leiria, Portugal
Barna Iantovics	Petru Maior University of Tîrgu-Mureş, Romania
Beatriz de la Iglesia	University of East Anglia, UK
Cinzia Pizzi	University of Padua, Italy
Filipe Pinto	Polytechnic Institute of Leiria, Portugal
Giorgio Leonardi	University of Piemonte Orientale, Italy
Göran Falkman	Universitet of Skövde, Sweden

Hélder Coelho	University of Lisbon, Portugal
Helena Lindgren	Umeå University, Sweden
Hugo Peixoto	University of Minho, Portugal
Inna Skarga-Bandurova	East Ukrainian National University, Ukraine
José Machado	University of Minho, Portugal
José Maia Neves	University of Minho, Portugal
Júlio Duarte	University of Minho, Portugal
Luca Anselma	University of Turin, Italy
Michael Ignaz Schumacher	University of Applied Sciences Western Switzerland, Switzerland
Miguel Angel Mayer	Pompeu Fabra University, Spain
Miriam Santos	University of Coimbra, Portugal
Panagiotis Bamidis	Aristotelian University of Thessaloniki, Greece
Pedro Gago	Polytechnic Institute of Leiria, Portugal
Pedro Pereira Rodrigues	University of Porto, Portugal
Radboud Winkels	University of Amsterdam, The Netherlands
Rainer Schmidt	Institute for Biometrics and Medical Informatics, Germany
Ricardo Martinho	Polytechnic Institute of Leiria, Portugal
Rui Camacho	University of Porto, Portugal
Salva Tortajada	Polytechnic University of Valencia, Spain
Teresa Guarda	Peninsula de Santa Elena University, Ecuador
Werner Ceusters	University at Buffalo, USA

Artificial Intelligence in Power and Energy Systems

Alfonso Briones	Complutense University Madrid, Spain
Amin Shokri Gazafroudi	Karlsruhe Institute of Technology, Germany
Ana Estanqueiro	National Laboratory of Energy and Geology, Portugal
Brígida Teixeira	Polytechnic Institute of Porto, Portugal
Bruno Canizes	Polytechnic Institute of Porto, Portugal
Bo Noerregaard Joergensen	University of Southern Denmark, Denmark
Catia Silva	Polytechnic Institute of Porto, Portugal
Dagmar Niebur	Drexel University, USA
Fernando Lezama	Polytechnic Institute of Porto, Portugal
Fernando Lopes	National Laboratory of Energy and Geology, Portugal
Germano Lambert-Torres	PS Solutions, Portugal
Goreti Marreiros	Polytechnic Institute of Porto, Portugal
Hugo Algarvio	National Laboratory of Energy and Geology, Portugal
Isabel Praça	Polytechnic Institute of Porto, Portugal
Jan Segerstam	Empower IM Ou, Finland
João P. S. Catalão	University of Porto, Portugal
João Peças Lopes	University of Porto, Portugal
Jose L. Rueda	Delft University of Technology, The Netherlands
Luís Gomes	Polytechnic Institute of Porto, Portugal
Olivier Boissier	Henri Fayol Institute, France

Peter Kadar   Obuda University, Hungary
Pierluigi Siano   Università degli Studi di Salerno, Italy
Roberto Casado   University of Salamanca, Spain
Ricardo Faia   Polytechnic Institute of Porto, Portugal
Rui Castro   University of Lisbon, Portugal

Artificial Intelligence in Transportation Systems

Ana L. C. Bazzan   Federal University of Rio Grande do Sul, Brazil
Ana Paula Rocha   University of Porto, Portugal
Carlos A. Iglesias   Polytechnic University of Madrid, Spain
Carlos Lisboa Bento   University of Coimbra, Portugal
Cristina Olaverri-Monreal   Johannes Kepler Universität Linz, Austria
Eduardo Camponogara   Federal University of Santa Catarina, Brazil
Eftihia Nathanail   University of Thessaly, Greece
Eugénio Oliveira   University of Porto, Portugal
Francesco Viti   University of Luxembourg, Luxembourg
Francisco Pereira   Technical University of Denmark, Denmark
Giuseppe Vizzari   University of Milano-Bicocca, Italy
Gonçalo Correia   Delft University of Technology, The Netherlands
Hilmi Celikoglu   Technical University of Istanbul, Turkey
Holger Billhardt   Rey Juan Carlos University, Spain
Javier J. Sanchez Medina   University of Las Palmas de Gran Canaria, Spain
João Jacob   University of Porto, Portugal
João Mendes-Moreira   University of Porto, Portugal
Josep-Maria Salanova   Centre for Research & Technology Hellas, Greece
Juergen Dunkel   Hanover University for Applied Sciences and Arts,
                               Germany
Luís Nunes   University Institute of Lisbon, Portugal
Marin Lujak   University Rey Juan Carlos, Spain
Rui Gomes   ARMIS Group, Portugal
Sascha Ossowski   Rey Juan Carlos University, Spain
Soora Rasouli   Eindhoven University of Technology, The Netherlands
Tânia Fontes   University of Porto, Portugal

Artificial Life and Evolutionary Algorithms

Arnaud Liefooghe   University of Lille, France
Carlos Henggeler Antunes   University of Coimbra, Portugal
Carlos M. Fonseca   University of Coimbra, Portugal
Colin Johnson   University of Kent, UK
Ender Özcan   University of Nottingham, UK
Eric Medvet   University of Trieste, Italy
Fernando G. Lobo   University of Algarve, Portugal
Francisco B. Pereira   Polytechnic Institute of Coimbra, Portugal
Gabriel Kronberger   University of Applied Sciences Upper Austria, Austria

Ivo Gonçalves	University of Coimbra, Portugal
James Foster	University of Idaho, USA
Jin-Kao Hao	University of Angers, France
Leonardo Trujillo	Technical Institute of Tijuana, Mexico
Luca Manzoni	University of Trieste, Italy
Luís Correia	University of Lisbon, Portugal
Luis Paquete	University of Coimbra, Portugal
Malcolm Heywood	Dalhousie University, Canada
Mauro Castelli	NOVA IMS, Portugal
Pablo Mesejo Santiago	Inria, France
Penousal Machado	University of Coimbra, Portugal
Petr Pošík	Czech Technical University in Prague, Czech Republic
Rui Mendes	University of Minho, Portugal
Stefano Cagnoni	University of Parma, Italy
Thomas Stützle	Université Libre de Bruxelles, Belgium
Ting Hu	Queen's University, Canada
William B. Langdon	University College London, UK

Ambient Intelligence and Affective Environments

Amílcar Cardoso	University of Coimbra, Portugal
Ana Paiva	University of Lisbon, Portugal
Ângelo Costa	Polytechnic University of Valencia, Spain
Antonio Caballero	University of Castilla-La Mancha, Spain
António Grilo	NOVA University Lisbon, Portugal
António Pereira	University of Aveiro, Portugal
Boon Kiat-Quek	National University of Singapore, Singapore
Bruno Fernandes	University of Minho, Portugal
Carlos A. Iglesias	Polytechnic University of Madrid, Spain
Carlos Ramos	Polytechnic Institute of Porto, Portugal
Cesar Analide	University of Minho, Portugal
Dalila Duraes	Polytechnic Institute of Porto, Portugal
Davide Carneiro	Polytechnic Institute of Porto, Portugal
Davy Preuveneers	KU Leuven, Belgium
Fábio Silva	University of Minho, Portugal
Fernando de la Prieta	University of Salamanca, Spain
Fernando Moreira	University Portucalense, Portugal
Florentino Fdez-Riverola	University of Vigo, Spain
Gianni Vercelli	University of Genoa, Italy
Grzegorz Napela	AGH University of Science and Technology, Poland
Guillaume Lopez	Aoyama Gakuin University, Japan
Hector Alaiz Moreton	University of Leon, Spain
Hoon Ko	Polytechnic Institute of Porto, South Korea
Ichiro Satoh	National Institute of Informatics Tokyo, Japan
Javier Bajo	Polytechnic University of Madrid, Spain
Javier Jaen	Polytechnic University of Valencia, Spain

Javier Prieto Tejedor	University of Salamanca, Spain
Jean Ilié	University Pierre et Marie Curie, France
João Carneiro	Polytechnic Institute of Porto, Portugal
João Ferreira	Lisbon University Institute, Portugal
João Ramos	Polytechnic Institute of Porto, Portugal
João Vilaça	Polytechnic Institute of Cávado and Ave, Portugal
José Machado	University of Minho, Portugal
José Molina	University Carlos III of Madrid, Spain
José Neves	University of Minho, Portugal
Juan Corchado	University of Salamanca, Spain
Juan Pavón	Complutense University Madrid, Spain
Javier Prieto Tejedor	University of Salamanca, Spain
Lino Figueiredo	Polytechnic Institute of Porto, Portugal
Luís Macedo	University of Coimbra, Portugal
Manuel Rodrigues	Polytechnic Institute of Porto, Portugal
Miguel Hornos	University of Granada, Spain
Pablo Chamoso	University of Salamanca, Spain
Penousal Machado	University of Coimbra, Portugal
Ricardo Santos	Polytechnic Institute of Porto, Portugal
Rui José	University of Minho, Portugal
Shin'Ichi Konomi	University of Tokyo, Japan
Tatsuo Nakajima	Waseda University, Japan
Tiago Oliveira	National Institute of Informatics, Japan
Vicente Julián	Polytechnic University of Valencia, Spain
Vitor Alves	University of Minho, Portugal

General Artificial Intelligence

Amílcar Cardoso	University of Coimbra, Portugal
Amparo Alonso-Betanzos	University of A Coruña, Spain
Ana Paiva	University of Lisbon, Portugal
Ana Paula Rocha	University of Porto, Portugal
Andrea Omicini	University of Bologna, Italy
Arlindo Oliveira	University of Lisbon, Portugal
Bernarde Ribeiro	University of Coimbra, Portugal
Carlos Lisboa Bento	University of Coimbra, Portugal
Carlos Ramos	Polytechnic Institute of Porto, Portugal
Cesar Analide	University of Minho, Portugal
Davide Carneiro	Polytechnic Institute of Porto, Portugal
Eric De La Clergerie	Inria, France
Ernesto Costa	University of Coimbra, Portugal
Gaël Dias	Normandy University, France
Goreti Marreiros	Polytechnic Institute of Porto, Portugal
João Balsa	University of Lisbon, Portugal
João Carneiro	Polytechnic Institute of Porto, Portugal
João Gama	University of Porto, Portugal

João Leite	NOVA University of Lisbon, Portugal
John-Jules Meyer	Utrecht University, The Netherlands
José Cascalho	University of Azores, Portugal
José Júlio Alferes	NOVA University of Lisbon, Portugal
José Machado	University of Minho, Portugal
Jose Molina	University Carlos III of Madrid, Spain
José Neves	University of Minho, Portugal
Juan Corchado	University of Salamanca, Spain
Juan Pavón	Complutense University Madrid, Spain
Luís Camarinha-Matos	NOVA University of Lisbon, Portugal
Luís Cavique	University Aberta, Portugal
Luís Correia	University of Lisbon, Portugal
Luís Macedo	University of Coimbra, Portugal
Luís Seabra Lopes	University of Aveiro, Portugal
Luísa Coheur	University of Lisbon, Portugal
Paulo Cortez	University of Minho, Portugal
Paulo Novais	University of Minho, Portugal
Paulo Quaresma	University of Évora, Portugal
Pedro Barahona	NOVA University of Lisbon, Portugal
Pedro Rangel Henriques	University of Minho, Portugal
Penousal Machado	University of Coimbra, Portugal
Ricardo Santos	Polytechnic Institute of Porto, Portugal
Rosaldo Rossetti	University of Porto, Portugal
Salvador Abreu	University of Évora, Portugal
Tatsu Naka	Waseda University, Japan
Vicente Julian	Polytechnic University of Valencia, Spain
Victor Alves	University of Minho, Portugal

Intelligent Robotics

André Conceição	Federal University of Bahia, Brazil
André Luís Marcato	Federal University of Juiz de Fora, Brazil
António J. R. Neves	University of Aveiro, Portugal
António Paulo Moreira	University of Porto, Portugal
Armando Pinho	University of Aveiro, Portugal
Armando Sousa	University of Porto, Portugal
Axel Hessler	DAI-Labor, TU Berlin, Germany
Brígida Mónica Faria	Polytechnic Institute of Porto, Portugal
Carlos Carreto	Polytechnic Institute of Guarda, Portugal
Cesar Analide	University of Minho, Portugal
Eurico Pedrosa	University of Aveiro, Portugal
Fei Chen	Advanced Robotics Department, Italy
Fernando Osorio	University of Sao Paulo, Brazil
Jorge Dias	University of Coimbra, Portugal
Josemar Rodrigues de Souza	Bahia State University, Brazil

Luís Correia	University of Lisbon, Portugal
Luis Moreno	University Carlos III of Madrid, Spain
Luís Seabra Lopes	University of Aveiro, Portugal
Marco Dorigo	Université Libre de Bruxelles, Belgium
Mikhail Prokopenko	The University of Sydney, Australia
Nicolas Jouandeau	Université Paris 8, France
Paulo Urbano	University of Lisbon, Portugal
Saeed Shiry	Amirkabir University of Technology, Iran
Urbano Nunes	University of Coimbra, Portugal

Knowledge Discovery and Business Intelligence

Agnes Braud	University of Strasbourg, France
Alberto Bugarin	University of Santiago de Compostela, Spain
Alípio M. Jorge	University of Porto, Portugal
Amílcar Oliveira	Portuguese Open University, Portugal
André Carvalho	University of São Paulo, Brazil
Antonio Tallón-Ballesteros	University of Huelva, Spain
Armando Mendes	University of Azores, Portugal
Carlos Ferreira	Polytechnic Institute of Porto, Portugal
Fátima Rodrigues	Polytechnic Institute of Porto, Portugal
João Moura-Pires	NOVA University of Lisbon, Portugal
José Alfredo Ferreira Costa	University Rio Grande Norte, Brazil
Karin Becker	University Rio Grande Norte, Brazil
Leandro Krug Wives	University Rio Grande Sul, Brazil
Manuel Fernandez Delgado	University of Santiago de Compostela, Spain
Marcos Aurélio Domingues	State University of Maringá, Brazil
Margarida Cardoso	University Institute of Lisbon, Portugal
Mark Embrechts	Rensselaer Polytechnic Institute, USA
Mohamed Gaber	Birmingham City University, UK
Murat Caner Testik	Hacettepe University, Turkey
Orlando Belo	University of Minho, Portugal
Pedro Castillo	University of Granada, Spain
Philippe Lenca	IMT Atlantique, France
Rita Ribeiro	University of Porto, Portugal
Roberto Henriques	NOVA University of Lisbon, Portugal
Rui Camacho	University of Porto, Portugal
Sérgio Moro	University Institute of Lisbon, Portugal
Ying Tan	Peking University, China

Multi-agent Systems: Theory and Applications

Adriana Giret	Polytechnic University of Valencia, Spain
Alberto Sardinha	University of Lisbon, Portugal
Alejandro Guerra-Hernández	University Veracruzana, Mexico

Andrea Omicini	University of Bologna, Italy
António J. M. Castro	University of Porto, Portugal
Carlos Carrascosa	Polytechnic University of Valencia, Spain
Carlos Martinho	University of Lisbon, Portugal
Daniel Castro Silva	University of Porto Portugal
Dave De Jonge	IIIA-CSIC, Spain
Diana Adamatti	University Federal of Rio Grande, Brazil
Francisco Grimaldo	Polytechnic University of Valencia, Spain
Henrique Lopes Cardoso	University of Porto, Portugal
Javier Carbo	University Carlos III of Madrid, Spain
João Leite	NOVA University of Lisbon, Portugal
John-Jules Meyer	Utrecht University, The Netherlands
Jordi Sabater Mir	IIIA-CSIC, Spain
Jorge Gomez-Sanz	Complutense University Madrid, Spain
Juan Carlos Burguillo	University of Vigo, Spain
Juan Corchado	University of Salamanca, Spain
Lars Braubach	University of Hamburg, Germany
Luis Correia	University of Lisbon, Portugal
Luis Macedo	University of Coimbra, Portugal
Luís Nunes	Lisbon University Institute, Portugal
Marin Lujak	University Rey Juan Carlos, Spain
Michael Ignaz Schumacher	University of Applied Sciences Western Switzerland, Switzerland
Paulo Leitão	Polytechnic Institute of Bragança, Portugal
Paulo Novais	University of Minho, Portugal
Rafael Cardoso	University of Manchester, UK
Ramon Hermoso	University of Zaragoza, Spain
Reyhan Aydogan	Delft University of Technology, The Netherlands
Rosa Vicari	Federal University of Rio Grande do Sul, Brazil
Viviane Silva	IBM Research Brazil, Brazil

Text Mining and Applications

Adam Jatowt	University of Kyoto, Japan
Adeline Nazarenko	University Sorbonne Paris Nord, France
Alberto Diaz	Complutense University Madrid, Spain
Alberto Simões	University of Minho, Portugal
Alexandre Rademaker	IBM, FGV, Brazil
Altigran Silva	Federal University of Amazonas, Brazil
Antoine Doucet	University of Caen, France
António Branco	University of Lisbon, Portugal
Béatrice Daille	University of Nantes, France
Bruno Martins	University of Lisbon, Portugal
Eric de La Clergerie	Inria, France
Fernando Batista	Lisbon University Institute, Portugal
Francisco Couto	University of Lisbon, Portugal

Gabriel Pereira Lopes	NOVA University of Lisbon, Portugal
Gaël Dias	Normandy University, France
Hugo Oliveira	University of Coimbra, Portugal
Iñaki Vicente	Elhuyar Foundation, Spain
Irene Rodrigues	University of Évora, Portugal
Jesús Vilares	University of A Coruña, Spain
Joaquim Ferreira da Silva	NOVA University of Lisbon, Portugal
Katerzyna Wegrzyn-Wolska	ESIGETEL, France
Luísa Coheur	University of Lisbon, Portugal
Manuel Vilares Ferro	University of Vigo, Spain
Marcos Garcia	University of A Coruña, Spain
Mário Silva	University of Lisbon, Portugal
Miguel Alonso	University of A Coruña, Spain
Pablo Gamallo	University of Santiago de Compostela, Spain
Patricia Martín-Rodilla	University of A Coruña, Spain
Paulo Quaresma	University of Évora, Portugal
Pavel Brazdil	University of Porto, Portugal
Renata Vieira	University of Évora, Portugal
Sérgio Nunes	University of Porto, Portugal

Additional Reviewers

Alexandre G. Lima	Francisco J. Ribadas-Pena
Alexandros Siomos	Louis Martin
André Monforte	Paulo Menezes
Brais Muñiz	Pedro Ruas
Brenda Salenave Santana	Rui Araújo
Diana Sousa	Sinan Oguz
Diógenes Araújo	Sylvia Chalencon
Diogo Freitas	Víctor Darriba

Abstracts of Invited Speakers

Abstracts of Invited Speakers

Responsible AI: From Principles to Action

Virginia Dignum

Umeå University, Sweden
virginia.dignum@umu.se

Abstract. Every day we see news about advances and the societal impact of AI. AI is changing the way we work, live and solve challenges but concerns about fairness, transparency or privacy are also growing. Ensuring AI ethics is more than designing systems whose result can be trusted. It is about the way we design them, why we design them, and who is involved in designing them. In order to develop and use AI responsibly, we need to work towards technical, societal, institutional and legal methods and tools which provide concrete support to AI practitioners, as well as awareness and training to enable participation of all, to ensure the alignment of AI systems with our societies' principles and values.

Ensuring the responsible development and use of AI is becoming a main direction in AI research and practice. Governments, corporations and international organisations alike are coming forward with proposals and declarations of their commitment to an accountable, responsible, transparent approach to AI, where human values and ethical principles are leading. In this area, the European Union has been a leading force, having just recently released a proposal for the regulation of AI, the AI Act[1].

Many of the AI risks, including bias, discrimination and lack of transparency can be linked to the characteristics of the data-driven techniques that are currently driving AI development, which are stochastic in nature and rely on the increasing size of datasets and computations. Such approaches perform well in accuracy but much worse in transparency and explanation. Rather than focus on the limitation of risks and safeguard of ethical and societal principles, AI governance should be designed as a stepping-stone for sustainable AI innovation. More than limiting options, governance can be used to extend and improve current approaches towards a next generation of AI: truly human-centred AI. This capacity must be nurtured and supported with strong support for research and innovation in alternative AI methods, that can combine accuracy with transparency and privacy, as well and multi-disciplinary efforts to develop and evaluate the societal and ethical impact of AI.

Responsible AI is fundamentally about human responsibility for the development of intelligent systems along fundamental human principles and values, to ensure human flourishing and well-being in a sustainable world. In fact, Responsible AI is more than the ticking of some ethical '"boxes' in a report, or the development of some add-on features, or switch-off buttons in AI systems. Enforcing responsibility and supporting accountability for AI and its outcomes is key.

---

[1] https://eur-lex.europa.eu/legal-content/EN/TXT/?uri=CELEX:52021PC0206.

Trustworthy Human-Centric AI – The European Approach

Fredrik Heintz

Linköping University, Sweden
fredrik.heintz@liu.se

Abstract. Europe has taken a clear stand that we want AI, but we do not want just any AI. We want AI that we can trust and that puts people at the center. This talk presents the European approach to Trustworthy Human-Centric AI including the main EU initiatives and the European AI ecosystem such as the different major projects and organizations. The talk will also touch upon some of the research challenges related to Trustworthy AI from the ICT-48 network TAILOR which has the goal of developing the scientific foundations for Trustworthy AI through integrating learning, optimisation, and reasoning.

To maximize the opportunities and minimize the risks, Europe has decided to focus on human-centered Trustworthy AI based on strong collaboration among key stakeholders. According to the High-Level Expert Group on AI, Trustworthy AI has three main aspects, it should be *Lawful*, ensuring respect for applicable laws and regulations; *Ethical*, ensuring adherence to ethical principles and values; and *Robust*, both from a technical and social perspective.

There are many technical research challenges related to these requirements, including *fairness*, *explainability*, *transparency*, and *safety*. To achieve these, we will most likely need to integrate learning and reasoning in a principled manner while retaining the explanatory power of more structured, often logical, approaches together with the adaptability, flexibility, and efficiency of data driven machine learning approaches.

To achieve its grand vision, Europe is establishing a growing ecosystem of AI initiatives. One key organization is CLAIRE, the pan-European Confederation of Laboratories for Artificial Intelligence Research in Europe based on the vision of European excellence across all of AI, for all of Europe, with a human-centred focus. Others are ELLIS, the European Laboratory for Learning and Intelligent Systems, and EurAI, the European AI Association. From the European commission some of the main initiatives are AI4EU, who is building a European AI On-Demand Platform; the four ICT-48 Networks AI4Media, ELISE, HumaneAI NET and TAILOR, plus the ICT-48 CSA VISION; and the public-private partnership (PPP) on AI, data and robotics between EU and Adra (the AI, Data, and Robotics Association), a new organization formed by BDVA, CLAIRE, ELLIS, EurAI and euRobotics.

Europe has a good position to take the lead on Trustworthy AI globally. We now need to consolidate and strengthen the European AI ecosystem so that we can accelerate towards a human-centric trustworthy future, together.

Multimodal Simultaneous Machine Translation

Lucia Specia

Imperial College London, UK
l.specia@imperial.ac.uk

Simultaneous machine translation (SiMT) aims to translate a continuous input text stream into another language with the lowest latency and highest quality possible. Therefore, translation has to start with an incomplete source text, which is read progressively, creating the need for anticipation. In this talk I will present work where we seek to understand whether the addition of visual information can compensate for the missing source context.

We analyse the impact of different multimodal approaches and visual features on state-of-the-art SiMT frameworks, including fixed and dynamic policy approaches using reinforcement learning. Our results show that visual context is helpful and that visually-grounded models based on explicit object region information perform the best. Our qualitative analysis illustrates cases where only the multimodal systems are able to translate correctly from English into gender-marked languages, as well as deal with differences in word order, such as adjective-noun placement between English and French.

Factored Value Functions for Cooperative Multi-agent Reinforcement Learning

Shimon Whiteson

University of Oxford, UK
shimon.whiteson@cs.ox.ac.uk

Cooperative multi-agent reinforcement learning (MARL) considers how teams of agents can coordinate their behaviour to efficiently achieve common goals. A key challenge therein is how to learn cooperative policies in a centralised fashion that nonetheless can be executed in a decentralised fashion. In this talk, I will discuss QMIX, a simple but powerful cooperative MARL algorithm that relies on factored value functions both to make learning efficient and to ensure decentralisability. Extensive results on the StarCraft Multi-Agent Challenge (SMAC), a benchmark we have developed, confirm that QMIX outperforms alternative approaches, though further analysis shows that this is not always for the reasons we expected.

Contents

Ambient Intelligence and Affective Environments

General AI

Intelligent Robotics

Knowledge Discovery and Business Intelligence

Multi-agent Systems: Theory and Applications

Text Mining and Applications

Artificial Intelligence and IoT
in Agriculture

Autonomous Robot Visual-Only Guidance in Agriculture Using Vanishing Point Estimation

José Sarmento[1]([⊠]), André Silva Aguiar[2]([⊠]), Filipe Neves dos Santos[2]([⊠]), and Armando Jorge Sousa[1,2]([⊠])

[1] Faculty of Engineering, University of Porto, 4200-465 Porto, Portugal
{up201909931,asousa}@fe.up.pt
[2] INESC TEC—INESC Technology and Science, 4200-465 Porto, Portugal
{andre.s.aguiar,fbsantos}@inesctec.pt

Abstract. Autonomous navigation in agriculture is very challenging as it usually takes place outdoors where there is rough terrain, uncontrolled natural lighting, constantly changing organic scenarios and sometimes the absence of a Global Navigation Satellite System (GNSS). In this work, a single camera and a Google coral dev Board Edge Tensor Processing Unit (TPU) setup is proposed to navigate among a woody crop, more specifically a vineyard. The guidance is provided by estimating the vanishing point and observing its position with respect to the central frame, and correcting the steering angle accordingly. The vanishing point is estimated by object detection using Deep Learning (DL) based Neural Networks (NN) to obtain the position of the trunks in the image. The NN's were trained using Transfer Learning (TL), which requires a smaller dataset than conventional training methods. For this purpose, a dataset with 4221 images was created considering image collection, annotation and augmentation procedures. Results show that our framework can detect the vanishing point with an average of the absolute error of 0.52° and can be considered for autonomous steering.

Keywords: Visual steering · Agriculture · Robotics · Deep learning

1 Introduction

Agricultural production differs from others in the sense that it is affected by uncontrolled inputs, such as climate, which affect the productivity of the system and constantly change the structures and characteristics of the environment. Humans are easily capable of identifying and working around these changing scenarios. Still, some of these jobs can be demanding and depending on the terrain and weather, it may be unsuitable or unpleasant for humans to do this work. The preceding factors lead to a decline in the agricultural workforce in well-developed countries as low productivity and hard, specialized work cannot justify the choice. Currently, there is a shift to more stable, well-paying jobs in

© Springer Nature Switzerland AG 2021
G. Marreiros et al. (Eds.): EPIA 2021, LNAI 12981, pp. 3–15, 2021.
https://doi.org/10.1007/978-3-030-86230-5_1

industry and services. Driven by rising labour costs, interest in automation has increased to find labour-saving solutions for crops and activities that are more difficult to automate [1]. An example is precision viticulture (PV), which aims to optimize vineyard management, reduce resource consumption and environmental impact, and maximize yield and production quality through automation, with robots playing a major role as monitoring tools, for example, as reviewed in [2]. This work aims to develop a vision-based guidance system for woody crops, more precisely for vineyards. This type of crops brings several challenges to autonomous robots. To automate them, the first step is the ability to navigate between vine rows autonomously, which requires taking into account the rough terrain that prevents the use of odometry for long periods of time, the dense vegetation and harsh landscape that can obstruct the GPS-GNSS signal, the outdoor lighting and the constantly changing appearance of the crops, and, depending on the season, the degree of noise added by loose vine whips and grass. In previous works, was approached the detection of vine trunk trees using Deep Learning models in an Edge-AI manner [3–5]. In this paper, we extend this work to estimate the Vanishing Point (VP) of the row of vines using a Neural Network (NN) model trained using transfer learning to detect the base of the trunks. The proposed system consists of a single camera and an edge Tensor Processing Unit (TPU) dev board (Coral) capable of deep-learning inference to detect the base of the vine trunk and perform a linear regression based on the positions of each row of detected base trunks. Then, by intersecting both row lines, our algorithm estimates the vanishing point located on the image that allows correcting the orientation of the robot inside the vineyard. The remainder of this paper is organized as follows. Section 2 contains a survey of related work. Section 3 details the hardware used and all the steps to obtain the vanishing point estimate. Section 4 presents the methodology used to evaluate the proposed solution and discusses the results. Finally, Sect. 5 concludes this work and discusses future work.

2   Related Work

To the best of our knowledge, Vanishing Point guidance has never been applied to vineyards. Nevertheless, there are many examples of autonomous guidance in vineyards. Also, when it comes to vanishing point navigation, most examples are applied to roads. One of the most common autonomous guidance techniques in vineyards is the use of a laser scanner, also called LiDAR. Laser scanner based guidance are proposed in [6] and [7]. The first one tracks only one of the vine rows and approximates all the laser measurements to a line. Results show that it is able to navigate a real vineyard (including performing U-turns) with the mean value of the error being less than 0.05 m. The second guides a robot in an orchard by tracking a center line obtained after acquiring the two rows from laser distance measures. The system has a maximum error of 0.5 m in the transverse direction and 1% of the row length in the longitudinal direction.

Reiser et al. [8] proposes a beacon localization system that estimates the position based on the received signal strength indication (RSSI). Results show an error of 0.6m using RSSI trilateration.

Vision-based guidance, the subject of this work, is complex and demands different approaches to the same problem. Stereo vision is one of them and differs from our proposed method by using two cameras instead of a single one. In [9] by using a density map that writes the depth information obtained by stereoscopic vision from the cameras into distance points. The robot was successfully guided along the rows at low speed ($\approx$1 km/h). In [10] the measured distance to objects is used and this information is encoded into the image. The system was able to perform autonomous navigation along the given paths with low resolution (640 × 480) in different vineyard rows but similar weather conditions. Another method of guidance is to use machine learning to observe the image from a single camera and classify areas of the image or identify specific objects through object recognition and extract the location. Sharifi et al. [11] uses a classification technique based on graph partitioning theory where the image is divided into terrain, trees and sky classes. Then, using Hough transform, the boundary lines are extracted and used to create a center line. The proposed approach is able to classify the orchard elements in the image (ground, trees, and sky), extract the boundary lines between terrain and trees, and generate the centerline for the robot to follow. Lyu et al. [12] applied a Naive Bayesian classification to detect the boundary between tree trunk and path, form the boundary lines and estimate the centerline. For the Vanishing Point detection some approaches rely on more traditional methods. For example, Gracia-Faura et al. [13] and Zhou et al. [14] propose a traditional algorithm that estimates the vanishing point using edge detection, followed by a RANSAC-based algorithm. Other approaches use machine learning techniques to estimate the VP. In this context, Chang et al. [15] proposes an AlexNet that treats the vanishing point as a Convolutional Neural Network (CNN) classification problem. The results show 99% accuracy in recovering the horizon line and 92% in locating the vanishing point within a range of ±5°. Liu et al. [16] presents D-VPnet, a single-shot Deep CNN-based network with a MobileNet as the backbone, for detecting dominant VPs in natural scenes. In [17] a vanishing point detection in orchards is proposed using a CNN. The algorithm proposed is a sliding window that is running along the image and inputs into the CNN the output of the network is the probability of path or tree for each window. Resulting in the averaged errors of 0.056 and 8.1° for lateral and angular difference in relation to the centerline, respectively.

3 Visual Steering on Agriculture: The Main Approach

The guidance system has two important requirements:

- To be able to execute an inference algorithm in real-time from a single camera input.
- To be able to execute the visual steering algorithm, by finding the vanishing point given the bounding boxes obtained from the inference algorithm, and converting the robot's displacement to the vanishing point into a velocity command and publish it.

3.1 Hardware

Considering the previously described requirements, the hardware chosen is a Google Coral Dev Board Mini that has a Accelerator Module capable of performing fast machine learning inference at the edge (4 trillion operations per second), avoiding the need for cloud computing and allowing inference to be performed in real time and locally. This module is placed in a single board computer with a quad-core CPU (MediaTek8167s), 2 GB RAM, 8 GB flash memory, a 24-pin dedicated connector for a MIPI-CSI2 camera and runs on Debian Linux. Thus, this device is not only able to run the inference algorithm, but also the visual steering. To do so, it receives images from a camera and uses the ROS2 framework to easily exchange between the distributed algorithms. In addition, everything previously described is possible on a small form factor device with low consumption.

3.2 Vanishing Point Detection

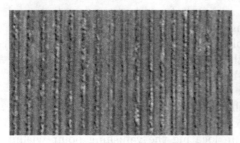 

(a) View from above of Qta. da Aveleda vines.

(b) Desired result from vanishing point extraction on Qta. da Aveleda vines.

Fig. 1. Vanishing point detection.

A vanishing point is the intersection of parallel lines in three-dimensional space when represented in two-dimensional space. As can be seen in Fig. 1a, it is possible to see that the lines are parallel when we look at them from the perspective of the "top view". When the image is viewed from inside the vineyard, Fig. 1b, the two vegetation lines converge to a single point called the vanishing point (VP).

Trunk Detection: To obtain the vine lines, the position of the vine trunks is determined. For this purpose, various neural networks are trained and then compared for object detection. The selected networks were MobileNet-V1, MobileNet-V2, MobileDets and Resnet50. Since the Google Coral Edge TPU has certain limitations in terms of compatible operations, not all NN architectures are ideal. Therefore, the selection was conditioned by already available trained networks supplied by Google and TensorFlow, which the TPU supports. To make the neural networks able to recognise the base of the trunks a dataset must be created. The dataset created consists of the annotation of 604 vineyard images recorded on-board of our agricultural robot [18] in two different stages of the year (summer and winter), Fig. 5. The annotation resulted in 8708 base trunk annotations (3278 in summer, 5430 in winter). In the summer images, the vineyard has more vegetation, and thus, the base of the vine trunks is sometimes occluded. For this reason, this set of images has fewer annotated trunks in comparison with the winter ones. To increase the size of the dataset, an augmentation procedure was performed (Fig. 2), which consisted in applying different transformations to the already annotated dataset, namely: A 15 and −15 rotation was applied to the images to simulate the irregularity of the vineyards, a varying random multiplication was performed to vary the brightness of the images, a random blur was applied, a flip transformation was also implemented and also a random combination of transformations selecting three out of seven transformations (scale, angle, translation, flip, multiplication, blur and noise) and applying them in random order. The final dataset consisted of 4221 labelled images.

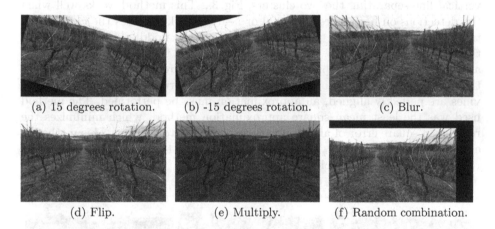

(a) 15 degrees rotation.   (b) -15 degrees rotation.   (c) Blur.

(d) Flip.   (e) Multiply.   (f) Random combination.

Fig. 2. Set of augmentation operations performed to create the final dataset.

The training method used was transfer learning, a technique that takes a previously trained model and re-trains either the final layers or the entire model with a new dataset considering the already established layers and weights trained by a previous dataset. In this case, the selected models were pre-trained using the COCO dataset, an object detection dataset trained to recognise 90 objects. The entire model was re-trained with the new base trunks detection dataset. During the training, an evaluation has to be performed for validation. For this purpose, the created dataset was divided as follows: 70% for the training, 15% for the validation and 15% for the benchmarking after the training, this last part will be explained later in Sect. 4.

To use the trained model in the Coral dev board mini, it must be fully quantized to 8-bit precision and compiled into a file compatible with the Edge TPU. To do this, the dataset that was in PASCAL VOC 1.1 was converted to TFRecord, TensorFlow's proprietary binary storage format. Binary data takes up less space on disk, requires less time to copy, and therefore makes the re-training process more efficient. Next, all models were trained using Google Colaboratory and the TensorFlow framework. If possible, the model was quantized during training, which is often better for model accuracy. Finally, the model must be compiled into a file compatible with the Edge TPU, as described previously. For this, the Edge TPU compiler is used, since this compiler requires TensorFlow Lite, which is a version optimized for mobile and edge devices, the model trained with TensorFlow is converted to TensorFlow Lite and then compiled.

Vanishing Point Estimation: Given the bounding box of the detected base trunk by the inference algorithm, two lines must be determined for the left and right rows. Since the detections are not assigned to a particular row, the clustering has to be done for this purpose. The method used was to sum and average all the x-values of the detection points, which gives the estimated mean vertical line separating the two clusters, Fig. 3a. This method works well when the detections on both sides are equal or nearly equal, which is the case for the trained models. Then, if a point is to the left of the middle line, it belongs to the left row and vice versa. After assigning the point to the corresponding row, a line must be drawn to approximate the respective row, Fig. 3b. Since neither the detections are exactly on the center of the base trunk nor the trunks of the vines are perfectly aligned, an approximation must be performed. The method used was the least mean square approximation method, which minimizes the root mean square error of all the points, in this case, to the line. This method is effective and not iterative. Then after obtaining the two lines, the intersection results in the Vanishing Point, Fig. 3c.

(a)   (b)   (c)

Fig. 3. Vanishing point estimation process. (a) Clustering step, the green line is the clustering threshold, yellow and red circles represent left and right row respectively. (b) Linear approximation step, the orange lines represent the best fit calculated for each row. (c) Intersection step, the blue line indicates the horizontal position of the estimated vanishing point. (Color figure online)

3.3 Autonomous Guidance

Figure 4a is a representation of a digital camera acquisition, and in Fig. 4b is shown the angle estimate obtained from the disparity between the horizontal distances from the center of the image and the VP estimate. For the guidance system to work, it needs to know how it is oriented in relation to the rows of vines. To obtain this information, the estimated position of the vanishing point is compared to the center of the image. Since the single camera is placed on the center frame of the system, the misalignment can be determined. So, to convert the displacement from the vanishing point to the center of the image (Δ_x) into an angle error, knowing that the distance in Fig. 4b is constant, we can obtain the following relation:

$$\hat{\theta} = \arctan\left(\frac{2\Delta_x \cdot \tan\left(f_w\right)}{\omega}\right),\tag{1}$$

where f_w represents the image horizontal field of view and ω its width.

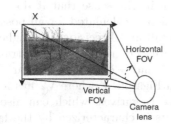

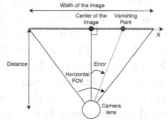

(a) Camera acquisition, vertical and horizontal perspective.

(b) Camera acquisition, only horizontal perspective.

Fig. 4. Illustration of angle estimation method.

4 Results

4.1 Methodology

To evaluate the base trunk detection, as referred in Sect. 3.2, a portion of the proposed dataset was reserved to later perform an unbiased benchmark of the detections using the most commonly used metrics (Precision, Recall, Average Precision (AP) and F1 Score) such in [19]. To evaluate the vanishing point estimation, a ground truth was created by manually labeling images extracted from a video recording of the vineyards in the winter and then in the summer. Then, by comparing the horizontal error between the ground truth and the obtained estimate, the error in pixels is obtained. Since the guidance system will deal with angles, it is interesting to evaluate the error in angles. To do that, Eq. 1 is used to obtain the angular error relative to the center of the image from the ground truth and also for the obtained estimate, then by subtracting both errors, the angular error between the two is obtained. Finally, the angle correction published by the visual steering algorithm and the error between the center frame and the vanishing point estimate was observed to evaluate the guidance system.

4.2 Base Trunk Detection

Since the metrics used depend on the terms True Positives (TP), False Positive (FP) and False Negative (FN), the concept of Intersection Over Union (IOU) is used, which, as the name suggests, is the ratio of the intersection of the detected and the ground truth bounding boxes with the respective union. The value can then be compared to a specific threshold t, and for example, if IOU $\geq$ t then is a TP, if IOU $\leq$ t then is a FP and if IOU $= 0$, then is FN. A brief explanation of the metrics follows. Starting with Precision, which is the percentage of true positives for a given validation threshold, i.e., if the number of FP is low for a given threshold, Precision is high. Recall is the percentage of true positives in agreement with all labeled data, i.e., if the number of FN is high, Recall is low. Average Precision differs from Precision in the sense that it does not refer to a specific threshold, i.e. Average Precision is calculated for all possible thresholds. The F1 score is calculated from Recall and Precision, the higher it is, the higher the Precision and Recall values are. The results of all re-trained models can be viewed in Table 1. Mobilenet V1 and V2 are very similar. The most noticeable difference can be seen between Figs. 5a–d, where V2 has fewer detections indicating a higher number of False Negatives, which can also be confirmed by the lower Recall value. Mobiledets is characterized by the large number of FP, as can be seen it has the lowest Precision. Although this number is very high, most of the cases are duplicate detections and unlabeled trunks detected by this model, as can be seen in Figs. 5e, f. Even though the second variant is beneficial, the duplicate detections can throw the clustering algorithm out of balance. From the vanishing point estimation perspective, this model is good because it has a higher number of detections. However, for the same reason, it requires more complexity to ensure that the set of harmful false positives can compensate the system. ResNet50 has very assertive results because it has a very small number of False Positives and thus has the highest Precision. On the other hand, it has a very high number of False Negatives, as shown by the Recall value, which is the lowest of all. So, for this application, it may not be the most interesting solution because, as can be seen in Figs. 5g and 5h, it has a very low number of detections, which may cause the linear regression algorithm not to approximate the vine line very well.

4.3 Vanishing Point Estimation

Figures 6a to c display vanishing point estimates by trained model in the winter. In Figs. 6d to i are shown the histograms of the Vanishing Point estimations error compared to the ground truth. Table 2 shows the average error and the maximum and minimum values in degrees by trained model and season. The average

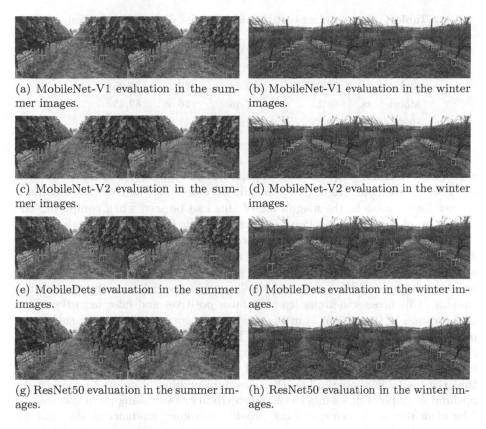

(a) MobileNet-V1 evaluation in the summer images.

(b) MobileNet-V1 evaluation in the winter images.

(c) MobileNet-V2 evaluation in the summer images.

(d) MobileNet-V2 evaluation in the winter images.

(e) MobileDets evaluation in the summer images.

(f) MobileDets evaluation in the winter images.

(g) ResNet50 evaluation in the summer images.

(h) ResNet50 evaluation in the winter images.

Fig. 5. Base trunk detections, in each image the left and right portions represent the detections and the ground truth respectively.

error was determined by summing all absolute error values and dividing by the total to evaluate the magnitude of the error rather than its relative position. For the winter annotations, the recorded error is so small that the error associated with the labeling of the images is relevant, which means that it is impossible to compare between the different models, although it also means that all models have good results and the vanishing point estimation algorithm is robust. In [15], vanishing point estimation is performed in the range ±5°. All previously mentioned models combined with the vine line estimation and intersection outperform the method proposed by [15], with the largest range recorded in the winter evaluation being ±2°, even tho having a considerately smaller dataset. It is also important to point out that there were a few outliers during the evaluation that are not currently filtered in the vanishing point estimation algorithm. These outliers are false positives that affect the line estimation algorithm, resulting in a false vanishing point estimate. For reference, in the winter evaluation there was only one instance of an outlier for the Mobilenet-v1 model. In contrast, the results for the summer annotations were not so satisfactory, although the

Table 1. Deep learning-based vanishing point detection evaluation.

Model	Precision (%)	Recall (%)	AP (%)	F1 score (%)
MobileNet-V1	94.55	77.36	77.08	85.10
MobileNet-V2	98.02	70.41	70.25	81.95
MobileDets	88.13	77.46	76.58	82.45
ResNet50	98.85	31.20	31.09	47.43

average error is not large, as seen in Table 2, the number of estimations with an error greater than 10px ($\approx$2°) is half or more than half of the annotated images for all models, the magnitude of this can be seen when comparing the dispersion of the Vanishing Point estimation error histograms from the winter (Figs. 6d to f) to the summer (Figs. 6g to i) where the range of values are [−20; 20]px and [−100; 100]px respectively. It was also observed that in some cases it was not possible to estimate a vanishing point. The reason for such results is the noise at the base of the trunk and the loose vines which sometimes cover the camera. This noise sometimes leads to false positives and false negatives. One of the causes of the outliers is in the clustering algorithm. Suppose a significant number of false positives are detected. In that case, this can throw the algorithm out of balance and lead to incorrect assimilation of row and subsequently incorrect line fitting and vanishing point estimation. The other main problem is that the model is unable to find the minimum number of points to produce an optimal fit (2 points), leading to the impossibility of vanishing point estimation. The algorithm as it stands will not provide as robust guidance in the summer as it does in the winter. A more complex clustering and filtering algorithm are needed to provide more reliable guidance, and, more importantly, a larger data set is also needed.

Table 2. Deep Learning-based vanishing point detection average absolute error and min and max range in degrees by time of the year. ResNet50 was not implemented due to the incapability of quantization.

Model	Winter		Summer	
	mean (°)	range (°)	mean (°)	range (°)
MobielNet-V1	0.52	[−1:2]	3.07	[−20:4]
MobielNet-V2	0.60	[−2:2]	2.94	[−20:10]
MobileDets	0.69	[−2:2]	2.89	[−20:3]

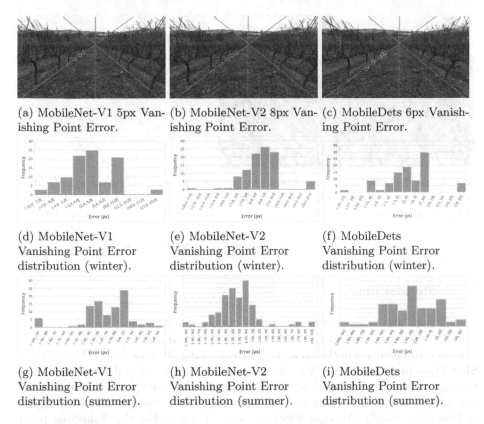

(a) MobileNet-V1 5px Vanishing Point Error.

(b) MobileNet-V2 8px Vanishing Point Error.

(c) MobileDets 6px Vanishing Point Error.

(d) MobileNet-V1 Vanishing Point Error distribution (winter).

(e) MobileNet-V2 Vanishing Point Error distribution (winter).

(f) MobileDets Vanishing Point Error distribution (winter).

(g) MobileNet-V1 Vanishing Point Error distribution (summer).

(h) MobileNet-V2 Vanishing Point Error distribution (summer).

(i) MobileDets Vanishing Point Error distribution (summer).

Fig. 6. Vanishing point estimation evaluation. In figs. (a) to (c) The vertical green and red lines are the vanishing point ground truth and estimation respectively. (Color figure online)

4.4 Autonomous Guidance Performance

As can be seen in Fig. 7a, there is a displacement between the centerline and the vanishing point, so to correct the system in this case, a positive angle correction was needed. In Fig. 7b the displacement error is plotted against the angular correction. When the red line (displacement) changes the sign, the blue line (angular correction) changes in the opposite sign, indicating that if there is a negative displacement, it will be corrected with a positive angular correction as it was intended. The controller currently has only an uncalibrated proportional gain, as there has been no method for evaluating controller performance. Future work will present a method for determining the response of the controller and investigate a possible Proportional Integrative Derivative (PID) controller implementation.

(a) 66px or 5.4° displacement between the vanishing point estimation and the center frame, blue and green line respectively.

(b) Relation between system displacement error and angle correction, blue and red line respectively.

Fig. 7. Visual steering evaluation. (Color figure online)

5   Conclusions

In this work was developed a Visual-only guidance system that makes use of the vanishing point to correct the steering angle. The vanishing point estimation is obtained by detection of the base of the trunks using Deep Learning. Four Single-Shot Detectors (MobileNet-V1, MobileNet-V2, MobilDets and ResNet50) were trained using transfer learning and built to be deployed on the Google coral dev mini with a built in-house dataset. The results were evaluated in terms of Precision, Recall, Average Precision and F1 Score. For the Vanishing point estimation, all trained models had a similar and good performance since the lowest average of the absolute error recorded was 0.52°. On the other hand, the performance on the summer proved that there is still progress to be made, being that the lowest average of the absolute error recorded was 2.89°. In future work, the dataset will be extended to improve the performance in the summer. Also, a PID controller will be implemented for guidance and tested in a novel 3D simulation created to emulate a vineyard.

Acknowledgements. The research leading to these results has received funding from the European Union's Horizon 2020 - The EU Framework Programme for Research and Innovation 2014–2020, under grant agreement No. 101004085.

References

1. Christiaensen, L., Rutledge, Z., Edward Taylor, J.: Viewpoint: the future of work in agri-food. Food Policy **99**(March 2020), 101963 (2021)
2. Ammoniaci, M., Paolo Kartsiotis, S., Perria, R., Storchi, P.: State of the art of monitoring technologies and data processing for precision viticulture. Agriculture (Switzerland) **11**(3), 1–21 (2021)

3. Silva Aguiar, A., Neves Dos Santos, F., Jorge Miranda De Sousa, A., Moura Oliveira, P., Carlos Santos, L.: Visual trunk detection using transfer learning and a deep learning-based coprocessor. IEEE Access **8**, 77308–77320 (2020)
4. Silva Pinto de Aguiar, A., Baptista Neves dos Santos, F., Carlos Feliz dos Santos, L., Manuel de Jesus Filipe, V., Jorge Miranda de Sousa, A.: Vineyard trunk detection using deep learning - an experimental device benchmark. Comput. Electron. Agric. **175**(March), 105535 (2020)
5. Silva Aguiar, A., et al.: Bringing semantics to the vineyard: an approach on deep learning-based vine trunk detection. Agriculture (Switzerland) **11**(2), 1–20 (2021)
6. Riggio, G., Fantuzzi, C., Secchi, C.: A low-cost navigation strategy for yield estimation in vineyards. In: Proceedings - IEEE International Conference on Robotics and Automation, pp. 2200–2205 (2018)
7. Bergerman, M., et al.: Robot farmers: autonomous orchard vehicles help tree fruit production. IEEE Robot. Autom. Mag. **22**(1), 54–63 (2015)
8. Reiser, D., Paraforos, D.S., Khan, M.T., Griepentrog, H.W., Vázquez-Arellano, M.: Autonomous field navigation, data acquisition and node location in wireless sensor networks. Precis. Agric. **18**(3), 279–292 (2017)
9. Rovira-Más, F., Millot, C., Sáiz-Rubio, V.: Navigation strategies for a vineyard robot. In: American Society of Agricultural and Biological Engineers Annual International Meeting, vol. 2015, no. 5, pp. 3936–3944 (2015)
10. Aghi, D., Mazzia, V., Chiaberge, M.: Local motion planner for autonomous navigation in vineyards with a RGB-D camera-based algorithm and deep learning synergy. arXiv, pp. 1–11 (2020)
11. Sharifi, M., Chen, X.: A novel vision based row guidance approach for navigation of agricultural mobile robots in orchards. In: ICARA 2015 - Proceedings of the 2015 6th International Conference on Automation, Robotics and Applications, pp. 251–255 (2015)
12. Kun Lyu, H., Ho Park, C., Hee Han, D., Woo Kwak, S., Choi, B.: Orchard free space and center line estimation using Naive Bayesian classifier for unmanned ground self-driving vehicle. Symmetry **10**(9), 355 (2018)
13. García-Faura, Á., Fernández-Martínez, F., Kleinlein, R., San-Segundo, R., Díaz-de María, F.: A multi-threshold approach and a realistic error measure for vanishing point detection in natural landscapes. Eng. Appl. Artif. Intell. **85**(August), 713–726 (2019)
14. Zhou, Z., Farhat, F., Wang, J.Z.: Detecting dominant vanishing points in natural scenes with application to composition-sensitive image retrieval. IEEE Trans. Multimedia **19**(12), 2651–2665 (2017)
15. Kai Chang, C., Zhao, J., Itti, L.: DeepVP: deep learning for vanishing point detection on 1 million street view images. In: Proceedings - IEEE International Conference on Robotics and Automation, pp. 4496–4503 (2018)
16. Bo Liu, Y., Zeng, M., Hao Meng, Q.: D-VPnet: a network for real-time dominant vanishing point detection in natural scenes. Neurocomputing **417**, 432–440 (2020)
17. Han, S.-H., Kang, K.-M., Choi, C.-H., Lee,D.-H., et al.: Deep learning-based path detection in citrus orchard. In: 2020 ASABE Annual International Virtual Meeting, page 1. American Society of Agricultural and Biological Engineers (2020)
18. Santos, L., et al.: Path planning aware of robot's center of mass for steep slope vineyards. Robotica **38**(4), 684–698 (2020)
19. Padilla, R., Netto, S.L., Da Silva, E.A.B.: A survey on performance metrics for object-detection algorithms. In: International Conference on Systems, Signals, and Image Processing, July 2020, pp. 237–242 (2020)

Terrace Vineyards Detection from UAV Imagery Using Machine Learning: A Preliminary Approach

Nuno Figueiredo[1,2]([✉]), Luís Pádua[2,3], Joaquim J. Sousa[2,3], and António Sousa[2,3]

[1] School of Management and Technology, P. Porto, Felgueiras, Portugal
nlf@estg.ipp.pt
[2] University of Trás-os-Montes e Alto Douro, Vila Real, Portugal
{luispadua,jjsousa,amrs}@utad.pt
[3] INESC Technology and Science (INESC-TEC), Porto, Portugal

Abstract. Alto Douro Wine Region is located in the Northeast of Portugal and is classified by UNESCO as a World Heritage Site. Snaked by the Douro River, the region has been producing wines for over 2000 years, with the world-famous Porto wine standing out. The vineyards, in that region, are built in a territory marked by steep slopes and the almost inexistence of flat land and water. The vineyards that cover the great slopes rise from the Douro River and form an immense terraced staircase. All these ingredients combined make the right key for exploring precision agriculture techniques. In this study, a preliminary approach allowing to perform terrace vineyards identification is presented. This is a key-enabling task towards the achievement of important goals such as production estimation and multi-temporal crop evaluation. The proposed methodology consists in the use of Convolutional Neural Networks (CNNs) to classify and segment the terrace vineyards, considering a high-resolution dataset acquired with remote sensing sensors mounted in unmanned aerial vehicles (UAVs).

Keywords: Precision agriculture · UAV sensors · Remote sensing · Terrace vineyards · Machine learning

1 Introduction

The majority of nations across the world are worried that the increasing population is bound to introduce more problems to food supplying. The predicted global scenario is critical, pointing to a considerable increase in the world population, while the scarcity of water and arable area are decreasing, due to climate change and global warming [1]. The production of local, seasonal and environmentally friendly products favors biodiversity, sustainable livelihoods and ensures healthy food. The region of Trás-os-Montes and Alto Douro stands out for having the largest area of vineyards, chestnut, almond, walnut and apple trees in Portugal, and for being the second region with the largest area of olive groves and cherry trees [2]. This region is bathed by the Douro River and has been producing wine for over 2000 years, including the world-famous Porto wine, representing

© Springer Nature Switzerland AG 2021
G. Marreiros et al. (Eds.): EPIA 2021, LNAI 12981, pp. 16–26, 2021.
https://doi.org/10.1007/978-3-030-86230-5_2

the main driving force behind technology, culture, traditions and the local economy. One of its main features is the terraces with vineyards, created through the division of leveled ramps. The technique requires a lot of labor and allows little mechanization, given the difficulty in using machines in steeper areas. The technological evolution that has occurred in the last two decades has allowed the development of equipment capable of manipulating, treating and analyzing a very high set of data.

The terms Artificial Intelligence (AI), Big Data, Machine Learning (ML), and Internet of Things (IoT) are under emphasis today, transforming all sectors of the economy and society [3]. After several other markets have been covered by digital transformation, it is now agriculture's turn. One of the technological systems that have recently been adopted in agriculture is the use of crop monitoring technology through unmanned aerial systems (UAS). This technology has been actively used by large-scale farmers in vineyards, chestnuts trees, flower plantations, and forestry to collect data relating to factors like the number of plants, vegetation cover, leaf and flower density, and other details that affect the production levels [4]. The data are utilized in the management of the vast plantations, particularly by highlighting issues that need to be addressed in the development of the crops. For instance, areas with limited leaf densities are inspected and the relevant treatments are applied [5]. Data acquired by sensors onboard UAVs are bound to enhance the ability of the farmers to respond to crop-related issues on a timely manner and to prevent losses often seen whenever there are phytosanitary issues [6]. Satellite data provides the actual synoptic view of large area at a time, the process of data acquisition and analysis is very fast through Geographic Information System (GIS) as compared to conventional methods and recent developments in UAVs platforms, sensors, and image processing techniques have resulted in an increasing uptake of this technology [7]. With UAV-based high-resolution imagery it is possible to detect tree and crop species, water deficiency identification, detection of diseases, and vegetation stress [8]. In addition to new machines, drones and precision farming equipment, artificial intelligence represents one of the last groundbreaking innovation that is already in use in crops and is becoming increasingly relevant [9]. Machine Learning is an AI technique that enables the training of algorithms for pattern recognition and decisions making, preferentially based on large amounts of data. ML techniques are often being applied in agriculture to exploit different sources of information, collected from RS or proximity sensors, so it can be applied throughout the cultivation and harvesting cycle [10, 11]. Thus, ML techniques allow the estimation of some parameters regarding the crop classification, the detection of diseases and the identification of objects in the images. ML usage makes agriculture more efficient and effective with the help of high precision algorithms, thus boosting the emerging concept of Intelligent Agriculture – Precision Agriculture (PA) [12].

Terrace vineyards towards viticultural zoning constitutes the preliminary step for significantly important activities such as cultures characterization and land use management and planning. In this study an automatic method that allows to perform terrace vineyards identification is presented. This is a key task towards the achievement of important goals such as production estimation and multi-temporal crop evaluation.

The proposed methodology consists on the use of CNN to classify and segment the terrace vineyards, considering a dataset of high-resolution aerial imagery acquired using a UAV in the Alto Douro region.

2 Background

Remote sensing helps farmers and other agricultural stakeholders observe the state of their crops and estimate productivity. Remote sensing is also used to monitor the crop growth rate and health, facilitating the prediction of yields which is essential in gauging and improving productivity for agricultural sustainability [13]. The following subsections present a brief introduction to the state of the art on the main topics used in this study.

2.1 UAV Sensors

The use of UAVs has contributed significantly to the progression of precision agriculture. These technologies are highly applicable in viticulture where they enhance remote sensing and facilitate efficient resource allocation and interventions to enhance productivity [14]. UAVs are becoming powerful sensing platforms that complement the techniques for remote sensing. The different sensors that can be coupled to an UAV allows to acquire high spatial and temporal resolution data that can assist in monitoring a diversity of characteristics of vegetation and field. The most widely used sensors in PA are: RGB, multispectral, hyperspectral, thermal infrared (TIR) and Light Detection and Ranging (LIDAR). RGB sensors (Fig. 1a) are good for creating orthophoto mosaics and to create digital elevation models (DEMs) through photogrammetric processing, and these sensors are also able to capture aerial videos. Multispectral sensors (Fig. 1b) can have multiple cameras, each one with a different filter, and can be used to calculate vegetation indices, which are correlated to plant biophysical parameters. Hyperspectral sensors (Fig. 1c) have a higher number of spectral bands to obtain the spectral signature for each pixel in the image and it's possible to identify, find and detect small changes in the physiology of the plants. TIR sensors (Fig. 1d) can detect less evapotranspiration on the plants, presented in the cases that are either dead or under stress. LiDAR (Fig. 1e) uses lasers to detect the distance of objects and are accurate at mapping landscape elevations [15, 16] and geometrical properties of vegetation [17]. Most of the data acquired by these sensors can be used in machine learning techniques to improve decision support in a precision agriculture context.

Fig. 1. Sensors used on UAVs. a) RGB sensor b) Multispectral sensor c) Hyperspectral sensor d) Thermal sensor e) LIDAR sensor.

2.2   Machine Learning in Agriculture

Machine learning can be used to enhance PA and improve productivity and cost-effectiveness in food production. The application of ML in agriculture involves enhancing the analysis of agricultural data comprising images gathered using remote sensing. Accordingly, analysts use ML techniques such as instance-based algorithms and artificial neural networks to develop capabilities in machines that enable them to enhance and segment images. Further, these techniques enable the machines to extract, fuse, and detect features in these images faster and more efficiently than the human eye which increases the accuracy of the analyses and their results [18].

Convolution Neural Network (CNN) has been adopted in crop farming to enhance precision agriculture. In most of the cases, the technology has shown effectiveness in plant image recognition and classification. Features of images from vegetation's are extracted, classified, segmented and finally fed into the model with high accuracy in the prediction [19]. Hyperspectral imaging with Support vector machines (SVM) and artificial neural networks (multilayer perceptrons, MLP) can be used to classify grapevine varieties with the prediction of a very large number of classes [20].

Disease prevention and detection is a priority in successful agriculture. The use of a SVM and spectral vegetation indices can differentiate healthy from diseased leaves with an accuracy of 97% in the classification [21].

Climate change affects all regions around the world. Sectors that rely strongly on certain temperatures and precipitation levels such as agriculture and forestry are particularly affected. RGB, multispectral and thermal infrared (TIR) imagery was acquired using UAV to study the vineyard status, vigor areas, potential water stress areas, and a multi-temporal vineyard characterization [22].

Regarding aerial vineyard images and ML, one work with UAV images and CNN classification was presented for early detection of diseased areas [23]. A standard deep convolutional neural network (CNN) to detect and segment vineyards is shown [24]. Vineyard yield estimation by combining remote sensing, computer vision and artificial neural network techniques is described [25]. A planner for autonomous navigation in vineyards with a RGB Camera and Deep Learning is explained [26] and an example of how the digitization of viticulture can be significantly supported by Deep Learning is shown [27]. A preliminary method for automatically detect vineyard parcels based on segmentation and morphological operations was presented [28] and a case study in vineyards to support multi-temporal analysis is proposed [29].

The state of the art for aerial vineyard images analysis is limited to flat vineyards with straight vine's row, without terrace vineyards with curvatures. One work with ML based approach to perform the vineyard segmentation from public satellite imagery it was presented, [30] a method to automatically detect vine rows in gray-scale aerial images is shown [31] and other approach based on A-star algorithm is proposed to reduce soil compaction in steep slope vineyards [32].

In this research a preliminary approach for curved terrace vineyards detection using machine learning and UAV RGB imagery is presented.

3 Materials and Methods

3.1 UAV Data Acquisition and Processing

A vineyard plot within the Douro Demarcated Region (41°08'11.6"N, 7°44'42.7"W, altitude 280 m) located in Quinta de Santa Eufémia (Viseu, Portugal) was used for this study. The data was acquired using a Phantom 4 (DJI, Shenzhen, China) with a 12.4 MP RGB sensor. Mission planning and the flight execution were carried using DroneDeploy installed on an Android smartphone. Flight height was set to 30 m from the UAV take-off position and imagery longitudinal and lateral overlap were set to 90% and 80%, respectively. A total of 192 images were captured at a nadiral perspective, covering an area of 2.44 ha with a spatial resolution of 2.19 cm.

The acquired images were processed in Pix4DMapper Pro (Pix4D SA, Lausanne, Switzerland) software to obtain an orthophoto mosaic (Fig. 2) of the surveyed area through photogrammetric processing.

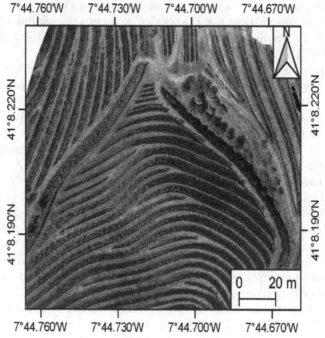

Fig. 2. Vineyard orthophoto mosaic used in this study.

3.2 Dataset

From the orthophoto mosaic, image with 7793 × 8537 pixels, Fig. 2, relevant information is gathered (features of each class) and it is used to build the training dataset. To optimize the building of the dataset, algorithmically, images are properly sliced into tiles of 26 ×

29 pixels with the objective of obtaining the most representative images from the two defined classes: one denoting background (eg. trees, ground, etc.) and another specifying terrace vineyard.

Having a large dataset is crucial for the performance of the machine learning model. However, the performance of training can be improved using data augmentation techniques. The training objective is to reduce the losses between the ground-truth and estimated results, as well as to reduce the presence of false positives in the final results [33]. Data augmentation consisted in synthetically replicating existing imagery with transformations that included different rotations, vertical/horizontal mirroring, zoom and scale variations.

The total of terrace vineyards images is higher than the background images and to avoid off-balance training, data augmentation was applied with Python's augmentor library. 725 images were selected per each class (dataset with total of 1450 images), 70% for training and 30% for test validation.

3.3 Machine Learning Approach

After imagery gathering, and dataset preparation, rough tiling and training/test a Machine Learning architecture was prepared to learn and predict the terrace vineyards. The whole process is depicted in Fig. 3. Several ML algorithms are analyzed to see which one has the best results in the classification process.

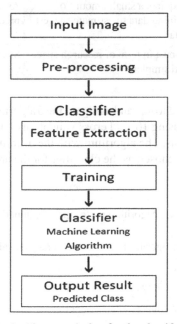

Fig. 3. Architecture design for the classification.

Programming activities were done in Python, with anaconda, Keras and Tensorflow backend.

3.4 Classifier

To choose the classifier, several types of architectures were analyzed, considering the most used in Machine Learning for image classification (Table 1) [34, 35]. Taking into account the principal advantages and disadvantages of architectures and analyzing the most used algorithms for binary classification, 6 algorithms have been implemented using the Python Scikit Learn library (Table 2).

Table 1. Comparison between classifiers.

Classifiers	Advantages	Disadvantages
Convolutional Neural Network (CNN)	Multiple features can be extracted simultaneously and robust to noise	High computation level and no generalization
Logistic Regression	Is easier to implement, interpret, and very efficient to train	Assumption of linearity between variables
Decision Tree	Requires less effort for data preparation during pre-processing	Often involves higher time to train the model
Support Vector Machine (SVM)	Great generalization potential with good robust	Complex algorithm structure
Gaussian Naive Bayes	Requires a small amount of training data to estimate the test data	Assumption of independent predictors
K-Nearest Neighbor (KNN)	Robust in term of research space and simplest	Susceptible to noise

The training data was used to test and compare the 6 algorithms. The training data was split, to prevent overfitting, using 10-fold cross validation (validation set) to evaluate the performance of the algorithms. The algorithm with the overall best performance was the CNN model (Table 2) being chosen as the classifier for the architecture of the proposed methodology.

Table 2. Algorithm performance comparison.

Classification algorithm	Accuracy on validation set
Decision Tree	69%
Gaussian Naive Bayes	72%
K-Nearest Neighbors	77%
Logistic Regression	85%
C-Support Vector Classification	88%
CNN model algorithm	**100%**

The architecture was built on the principle of convolutional neural networks. It consists of three parts: convolution, polling and flattening. The primary purpose of convolution is to extract features from the input image, so, a convolutional layer was added as the first layer (Conv2D) and 3 × 3 the size of the filter. The output of this layer corresponds to feature maps. An additional operation called rectified linear unit (ReLU) is used after every convolution operation. ReLU is an activation function and the output is used as input for the next neuron, and so on until the desired solution is obtained. Then the pooling is applied to reduce the dimensionality of each feature map and retains the essential information. It was used max pooling with a 2 × 2 filter. The filter will take the max values from each pool. After pooling comes flattening, the input layer for the neural network. A classic convolutional neural network has 3 convolutional blocks followed by a fully connected layer. It was created 2 layers neural network with a sigmoid function as an activation function for the last layer as it is needed to find the probability of the object being Terrace Vineyards or Background (others) (Fig. 4).

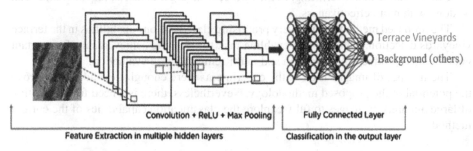

Terrace Vineyards

Background (others)

Convolution + ReLU + Max Pooling   Fully Connected Layer

Feature Extraction in multiple hidden layers   Classification in the output layer

Fig. 4. CNN network.

4 Results and Discussion

Training/test stage was set to perform during a maximum of 20 epochs in the CNN model with a 16 batch size and Adam optimizer. Adam optimization is a stochastic gradient descent method. Only two classes were considered for a binary problem: background and terrace vineyards, steps per epoch were set according to the ratio between the number of training images and batch size. Test steps were defined by the same rule. The training/test

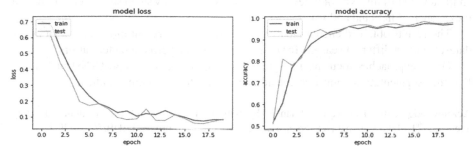

Fig. 5. CNN model training/test results.

plots of the learning stage seems to point out a convergence, even though there is still some space for loss and accuracy improvement (Fig. 5).

In the classification, with a new image of terrace vineyards, unknown by the classifier, the CNN model performed well, as can be seen in Table 3.

Table 3. Classification performance.

Class	Precision	Recall	F1-score
Terrace vineyards	100%	88%	93%
Background	100%	88%	93%

For the proposed methodology it was decided not to tune too much the algorithm since that could lead to overfitting. In the future, with larger datasets, the fine tuning can be done with more effectiveness.

The proposed method showed very promising classification capabilities in the terrace vineyards detection. This is a key-enabling task towards the achievement of important goals such as production estimation and multi-temporal crop evaluation.

The number of images used in the experiments were enough to validate and prove the potential of the proposed methodology. Nevertheless, there is a need for acquisition of large amounts of images to fully explore the classification capabilities of the current method.

5   Conclusions and Future Work

In this paper, a preliminary method for automatically detect terrace vineyards was proposed using machine learning. This work intended to constitute a starting point to address more complex cases regarding Douro's vineyards.

In comparison with other works carried out in the vineyards and terraces, limited to flat vineyards with straight vine's row, the model proposed in present work is a preliminary approach to detect terrace vineyards also with curvatures. Terrace vineyards constitutes the preliminary step for significantly important activities such as cultures characterization and land use management and planning; a great challenge due to the characteristics of this type of vineyards, a territory marked by steep slopes and the almost inexistence of flat land and water.

The results obtained encourage as a future work to carry out more tests with larger datasets and in different seasons for multi-temporal vineyard characterization.

Other approaches focusing fine-granularity segmentation – e.g. U-Net or Feature Pyramid segmentation – must be considered as well for upcoming studies.

Acknowledgments. This work is financed by National Funds through the Portuguese funding agency, FCT - Fundação para a Ciência e a Tecnologia, within project UIDB/50014/2020.

References

1. Gómez, M.I., Meemken, E., Verteramo Chiu, L.J.: Agricultural Value Chains and Social and Environmental Impacts: Trends, Challenges, and Policy Options – Background paper for The State of Agricultural Commodity Markets (SOCO) 2020. FAO, Rome (2020)
2. Instituto Nacional de Estatística - Recenseamento Agrícola. Análise dos principais resultados: 2019. INE, Lisboa (2021). https://www.ine.pt/xurl/pub/437178558. ISBN 978-989-25-0562-6
3. Eager, J.: Opportunities of Artificial Intelligence, Study for the committee on Industry, Research and Energy, Policy Department for Economic, Scientific and Quality of Life Policies. European Parliament, Luxembourg (2020)
4. Sylvester, G.: E-agriculture in Action: Drones for Agriculture. Food and Agriculture Organization of the United Nations and International Telecommunication Union, Bangkok (2018)
5. Balafoutis, A., et al.: Precision agriculture technologies positively contributing to GHG emissions mitigation, farm productivity and economics. Sustainability **9**, 1339 (2017)
6. Pádua, L., et al.: Multi-temporal analysis of forestry and coastal environments using UASs. Remote Sens. **10**(1), 24 (2018)
7. Pádua, L., et al.: UAS, sensors, and data processing in agroforestry: a review towards practical applications. Int. J. Remote Sens. **38**(8–10), 2349–2391 (2017)
8. Tsouros, D.C., Bibi, S., Sarigiannidis, P.G.: A review on UAV-based applications for precision agriculture. Information **10**(11), 349 (2019)
9. Jung, J., Maeda, M., Chang, A., Bhandari, M., Ashapure, A., Landivar-Bowles, J.: The potential of remote sensing and artificial intelligence as tools to improve the resilience of agriculture production systems. Curr. Opin. Biotechnol. **70**, 15–22 (2021)
10. Asokan, A., Anitha, J.: Machine learning based image processing techniques for satellite image analysis -a survey. In: IEEE International Conference on Machine Learning, Big Data, Cloud and Parallel Computing (COMITCon), pp. 1–6 (2019)
11. Liakos, K., Busato, P., Moshou, D., Pearson, S., Bochtis, D.: Machine learning in agriculture: a review. Sensors **18**(8), 2674 (2018)
12. Ponnusamy, V., Natarajan, S.: Precision agriculture using advanced technology of IoT, unmanned aerial vehicle, augmented reality, and machine learning. In: Gupta, D., Hugo C. de Albuquerque, V., Khanna, A., Mehta, P.L. (eds.) Smart Sensors for Industrial Internet of Things. IoT, pp. 207–229. Springer, Cham (2021). https://doi.org/10.1007/978-3-030-52624-5_14
13. Weiss, M., Jacob, F., Duveiller, G.: Remote sensing for agricultural applications: a meta-review. Remote Sens. Environ. **236**, 111402 (2020)
14. Adão, T., et al.: Hyperspectral imaging: a review on UAV-based sensors data processing and applications for agriculture and forestry. Remote Sens. **9**(11), 1110 (2017)
15. Daponte, P., et al.: A review on the use of drones for precision agriculture. In: IOP Conference Series: Earth and Environmental Science, vol. 275, p. 012022 (2019)
16. Hassler, S.C., Baysal-Gurel, F.: Unmanned aircraft system (UAS) technology and applications in agriculture. Agronomy **9**(10), 618 (2019)
17. Guimarães, N., Pádua, L., Marques, P., Silva, N., Peres, E., Sousa, J.J.: Forestry remote sensing from unmanned aerial vehicles: a review focusing on the data, processing and potentialities. Remote Sens. **12**(6), 1046 (2020)
18. Mavridou, E., Vrochidou, E., Papakostas, G., Pachidis, T., Kaburlasos, V.: Machine vision systems in precision agriculture for crop farming. J. Imaging **5**(12), 89 (2019)
19. Abdullahi, H., Sheriff, R., Mahieddine, F.: Convolution neural network in precision agriculture for plant image recognition and classification. In: INTECH 2017, pp. 1–3 (2017)

20. Gutiérrez, S., Fernández-Novales, J., Diago, M.P., Tardaguila, J.: On-the-go hyperspectral imaging under field conditions and machine learning for the classification of grapevine varieties. Front. Plant Sci. **9**, 1102 (2018)

21. Rumpf, T., Mahlein, A., Steiner, U., Oerke, E., Dehne, H., Plumer, L.: Early detection and classification of plant diseases with support vector machines based on hyperspectral reflectance. Comput. Electron. Agric. **74**(1), 91–99 (2010)

22. Pádua, L., et al.: Vineyard variability analysis through UAV-based vigour maps to assess climate change impacts. Agronomy **9**(10), 581 (2019)

23. Musci, M.A., Persello, C., Lingua, A.M.: UAV images and deep-learning algorithms for detecting flavescence doree disease in grapevine orchards. ISPRS – Int. Arch. Photogramm. Remote Sens. Spatial Inf. Sci. **XLIII-B3**, 1483–1489 (2020)

24. Jones, E.G., Wong, S., Milton, A., Sclauzero, J., Whittenbury, H., McDonnell, M.D.: The impact of pan-sharpening and spectral resolution on vineyard segmentation through machine learning. Remote Sens. **12**(6), 934 (2020)

25. Ballesteros, R., Intrigliolo, D.S., Ortega, J.F., Ramírez-Cuesta, J.M., Buesa, I., Moreno, M.A.: Vineyard yield estimation by combining remote sensing, computer vision and artificial neural network techniques. Precision Agric. **21**(6), 1242–1262 (2020)

26. Aghi, D., Mazzia, V., Chiaberge, M.: Local motion planner for autonomous navigation in vineyards with a RGB-D camera-based algorithm and deep learning synergy. Machines **8**(2), 27 (2020)

27. Franczyk, B., et al.: Deep learning for grape variety recognition. Procedia Comp. Sci. **176**, 1211–1220 (2020)

28. Adão, T., et al.: A pilot digital image processing approach for detecting vineyard parcels in Douro region through high resolution aerial imagery. In: Proceedings of the International Conference on Geoinformatics and Data Analysis - ICGDA 18 (2018)

29. Pádua, L., et al.: Very high resolution aerial data to support multi-temporal precision agriculture information management. Procedia Comp. Sci. **121**, 407–414 (2017)

30. Santos, L., Santos, F.N., Filipe, V., Shinde, P.: Vineyard segmentation from satellite imagery using machine learning. In: Moura Oliveira, P., Novais, P., Reis, L.P. (eds.) EPIA 2019. LNCS (LNAI), vol. 11804, pp. 109–120. Springer, Cham (2019). https://doi.org/10.1007/978-3-030-30241-2_10

31. Gay, P., Comba, L., Primicerio, J., Ricauda Aimonino, D.: Vineyard detection from unmanned aerial systems images. Comput. Electron. Agric. **114**, 78–87 (2015)

32. Santos, L., et al.: Path planning aware of soil compaction for steep slope vineyards. In: 2018 IEEE International Conference on Autonomous Robot Systems and Competitions (ICARSC), pp. 250–255, Torres Vedras (2018)

33. Zheng, Y., Kong, J., Jin, X., Wang, X., Zuo, M.: CropDeep: the crop vision dataset for deep-learning-based classification and detection in precision agriculture. Sensors **19**(5), 1058 (2019)

34. Azlah, M.A.F., Chua, L.S., Rahmad, F.R., Abdullah, F.I., Wan Alwi, S.R.: Review on techniques for plant leaf classification and recognition. Computers **8**(4), 77 (2019)

35. Koirala, A., Walsh, K.B., Wang, Z., Mccarthy, C.: Deep learning – method overview and review of use for fruit detection and yield estimation. Comput. Electron. Agric. **162**, 219–234 (2019)

Tomato Detection Using Deep Learning for Robotics Application

Tiago Cerveira Padilha[1,2], Germano Moreira[4],
Sandro Augusto Magalhães[1,3], Filipe Neves dos Santos[1(✉)],
Mário Cunha[1,4], and Miguel Oliveira[2]

[1] INESC TEC - Instituto de Engenharia de Sistemas e Computadores, Tecnologia e
Ciência, Campus da FEUP, Rua Dr. Roberto Frias, s/n 4200-465, Porto, Portugal
{tiago.padilha,sandro.a.magalhaes,fbsantos}@inesctec.pt
[2] Department of Mechanical Engineering, University of Aveiro, 3810 Aveiro, Portugal
{tiagopadilha,mriem}@ua.pt
[3] Faculty of Engineering, University of Porto, Rua Dr. Roberto Frias, s/n 4200-465,
Porto, Portugal
sandro.magalhaes@fe.up.pt
[4] Faculty of Sciences, University of Porto, Rua do Campo Alegre, s/n 4169-007,
Porto, Portugal
{up201608269,mccunha}@fc.up.pt

Abstract. The importance of agriculture and the production of fruits
and vegetables has stood out mainly over the past few years, especially
for the benefits for our health. In 2021, in the international year of fruit
and vegetables, it is important to encourage innovation and evolution
in this area, with the needs surrounding the different processes of the
different cultures. This paper compares the performance between two
datasets for robotics fruit harvesting using four deep learning object
detection models: YOLOv4, SSD ResNet 50, SSD Inception v2, SSD
MobileNet v2. This work aims to benchmark the Open Images Dataset
v6 (OIDv6) against an acquired dataset inside a tomatoes greenhouse
for tomato detection in agricultural environments, using a test dataset
with acquired non augmented images. The results highlight the benefit of using self-acquired datasets for the detection of tomatoes because
the state-of-the-art datasets, as OIDv6, lack some relevant characteristics of the fruits in the agricultural environment, as the shape and the
color. Detections in greenhouses environments differ greatly from the
data inside the OIDv6, which has fewer annotations per image and the
tomato is generally riped (reddish). Standing out in the use of our tomato
dataset, YOLOv4 stood out with a precision of 91%. The tomato dataset
was augmented and is publicly available (See https://rdm.inesctec.pt/
and https://rdm.inesctec.pt/dataset/ii-2021-001).

Keywords: Fruit detection · Machine learning · Computer vision ·
Agricultural robotics · Harvesting robotics

© Springer Nature Switzerland AG 2021
G. Marreiros et al. (Eds.): EPIA 2021, LNAI 12981, pp. 27–38, 2021.
https://doi.org/10.1007/978-3-030-86230-5_3

1   Introduction

The importance and benefits of fruit consumption are known to many and its production on a global scale has been a priority in the capacity for increased production. To ensure the conditions recommended by World Health Organization (WHO) [4], each person should consume at least 400 g of fruit and vegetables per day. The world production of fruits and vegetables in the year 2000 represented 306 g per day, in 2017 the production already represented 390 g [2]. An analysis of the growth of fruit primary production between 2000 and 2019, already represents an increase of approximately 65% according to FAOSTAT [1].

The various arduous tasks that sometimes the different stages of fruit cultivation represent, translate into a shortage of capable and specialized labor. This shortage of human resources is reflected in the difficult steps required to be taken in an agricultural process, from knowledge in analyzing products during their growth, such as harvesting, which in addition to being a stressful task is also time-consuming. The multiple problems associated with agriculture have opened the door to new technological solutions, including inspection and visual detection of fruits.

The implementation of automation in agricultural processes has been one of the most interesting solutions for companies looking to reduce costs and increase productivity. Robotic solutions have evolved and are increasingly suitable for environments in nature. They are usually composed of cameras and other sensors for the acquisition of images and detection of objects in real-time.

The visual detection of products in nature implies extra care in the unpredictability of events. Nature is unpredictable and an example of this is the heterogeneous characteristics that the same fruit can take, with respect to shape, color, size, branches, leaves, stems, as well as factors of variation in natural lighting.

Choosing the best descriptor for detecting or classifying a fruit is often a complex task, especially if we use traditional techniques. Deep Learning (DL) is based on non-linear models with a high capacity for learning data characteristics. The use of DL is a better approach in image processing than just using traditional methods. Computer image processing is one of the areas with the greatest application of artificial intelligence (AI) [16], but the quantity and quality of the dataset are essential for obtaining good results. In this context, the tomato dataset used presented Magalhães et al. [14], with improvements to annotations as well as the respective increase in the dataset.

The main goal of this study is to compare the training of DL model approaches using benchmark datasets against specific datasets. We can find different public datasets, which can be very useful for quick tests, training, and validating DL models. This approach can save several hours of acquiring and preparing a dataset, but we want to understand if it's enough to achieve the best results.

The following sections intend to illustrate how this research was conducted. Section 2 provides a review of the state of the art to understand how the researchers are conducting their work on this topic. Section 3 details the protocol used to conduct this works, as well as, the taken assumptions. Section 4 illustrates the results of the experience and performs a detailed analysis of them. Finally, Sect. 5 resumes the work and states some future work to improve the knowledge and technology in his topic.

2   State of the Art

This section reviews the most relevant contributions to this topic in the literature. This review focuses essentially on the deep learning applications for fruit detection.

The lighting conditions in the machine vision is an important issue to consider, in which there are several techniques used to increase the robustness in the detection of fruits, as proposed by Sa et al. [15] analyzes the same images with two different approaches: using RGB color and Near-Infrared (NIR). Its approach included the Deep Convolutional Neural Network (DCNN) architecture with the configuration of the VGG-16 network.

Analyzing in a more specific context in the detection of passion fruit, Tu et al. [18] proposed the use of Multiple Scale Faster Region-based Convolutional Neural Networks (MS-FRCNN) for using RGB color images combined with Depth (RGB-D). The proposed method was able to achieve greater accuracy despite not being the fastest to perform the detection. In a different approach to the detection of cherry tomatoes using regressive methods, Yuan et al. [19] chose to use the Single Shot multi-box Detection architecture (SSD), to compare four different neural networks, among which the Inception V2 was evidenced with an Average Precision (AP) of 98.85%.

The need to perform fruit detection in real-time, Bresilia et al. [6] resorted to the use of the YOLO neural network, with changes in the image input grid and elimination of some layers of the model, to obtain the best relationship between speed and accuracy. Its results were very promising with 95% of the detected fruits.

The approach of Liu et al. [13] based on the YOLOv3 model to create a new model YOLO-Tomato, dedicated specifically for the detection of tomatoes with greater precision. Even with influences caused by the variation of natural light, problems of occlusion, and overlap, they obtained results of approximately 94% of precision in the detection of tomatoes.

In a specific analysis in the apple detection, Briffis et al. [5] chose to use an Adaptative Training Sample Selection (ATSS) DL approach, based on the Resnet 50 and Feature Pyramid Network (FPN) as a backbone. The importance of testing the robustness of detecting fruit under different weather conditions, images with different types of noise and blur were considered for the evaluation. They obtained a maximum value of 94.6% of average precision. The use of deep learning for fruit detection has been widely used and the proof of this is the approach of Zhang et al. [20] which offers the adaptation of a DL architecture to detect different fruits. They proposed a new architecture based on the Multitask Cascaded Convolutional Network (MCCN) called Fruit-MCNN, as well as an augmentation method known as fusion augmentation (FA).

Aiming to detect mango fruit, Koirala et al. [11] compared the performance of six deep learning architectures: Faster R-CNN(VGG), Faster R-CNN(ZF), YOLOv3, YOLOv2, YOLOv2(tiny), and SSD. Also, a new architecture MangoYOLO was developed and trained using different datasets, to create the MangoYOLO models 's', 'pt', and 'bu'. MangoYOLO(pt) achieved an F1 score of 0.968 and Average Precision of 0.983, outperforming the other algorithms, with a detection speed of 8 ms per 512×512 pixel image and 70 ms per image (2 048 × 2 048 pixels). MangoYOLO(bu) achieved an F1 score of 0.89 on a daytime mango image dataset. This new model was robust when used with images of other orchards, cultivars, and lighting conditions.

Fruit detection in orchards can be quite challenging since there are a number of environment variances. That said, LedNet, a fast implementation framework of a deep-learning-based fruit detector for apple harvesting, was developed by Kang et al. [9]. The model adopts a feature pyramid network and atrous spatial pyramid pooling to improve its detection performance. LedNet achieved 0.821 and 0.853 on recall and accuracy, and its weights size and inference time were 7.4 M and 28 ms, respectively, proving its robustness and efficiency when performing real-time apple detection in orchards.

3　Materials and Methods

3.1　Data Acquisition and Processing

The fruit must be detected, or else it cannot be harvested. This sentence gives the motto for this work, whose main goal is to train and evaluate different Deep Learning (DL) models for tomato detection and classification, supporting the development of automatisms for robotic harvesting in a greenhouse. Since many DL models are characterized as supervised Machine Learning (ML) algorithms, it implies to be trained they must be provided with an annotated dataset. In this work we also seek to compare the performance of an existing public dataset, the Open Image Dataset (OID) [3], with a newly collected dataset, when training and evaluating these models.

Therefore, new images of tomato plants were collected in a greenhouse located in Barroselas, Viana do Castelo, Portugal (Fig. 1b) using a ZED camera[1]. The AgRob v16 robot (Fig. 1a), controlled by a human operator, was guided through the greenhouse inter-rows and captured images of the tomato plants, recording them as a video in a single ROSBag file.

The video recorded by the robot was converted into images by sampling a frame every 3 s, to reduce the correlation between images but ensuring an overlapping ratio of about 60%. This resulted in a dataset composed of 297 images with a resolution of 1280×720 px each.

---

[1] See https://www.stereolabs.com/zed/.

The images were manually annotated using the open-source annotation tool CVAT [17], considering only the class "tomato". After being annotated, the images were exported under Pascal VOC format [8], which resumes the annotations of each image in a single XML file.

(a)   (b)

Fig. 1. (a): Entrance of the greenhouse where the images were collected. (b): AgRob v16 robot.

High-resolution DL models are time and computationally-consuming. Besides, DL models already available in the state of the art consider the input of square images. Thus, the images had to be resized and split into a resolution of 720×720 px to avoid distortion. The dataset increased to 594 images.

To expand and add variability to the dataset, a process of augmentation was used, which allows various types of transformations that can be applied to an image. The transformations used were applied with a random factor and are as follows: Angle (a); Blur (b); Flip (c); Hue Saturation (d); Multiply (e); Noise (f); Combination1 (g), which applies a transformation randomly; Combination3 (h), which applies a combination of 3 transformations (a random combination of three of transformations with random values), Scale (i) and Translate (j) (Fig. 2). These changes expanded the dataset to 6055 annotated images.

To further train and validate the different models, the dataset was split into a training set and a validation set with a ratio of 3:1 (75% for training and 25% for validation). The training and validation sets contained 4541 and 1513 annotated images respectively.

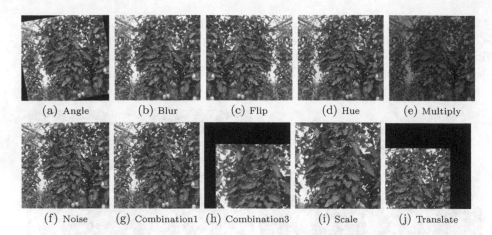

(a) Angle   (b) Blur   (c) Flip   (d) Hue   (e) Multiply

(f) Noise   (g) Combination1   (h) Combination3   (i) Scale   (j) Translate

Fig. 2. Different augmentation transformations applied to an image from the dataset.

To infer about the models, we used an independent test set, acquired under the same conditions as the dataset used for train and validation. The data of this set is the same for all the models, is composed of 304 images with a resolution of 720×720 px, as a result of the resized of 1280×720 px images, just as it was done for the other sets.

Regarding the OID v6 public dataset, we choose to use 15 different classes of fruits, including strawberry, tomato, apple orange, grape, lemon, banana, grapefruit, watermelon, pineapple, peach, pear, pomegranate, mango, melon. The training with the OID was proposing to compare a DL model with multiple classes fruits against specific datasets and was not used to training a class non-tomato.

3.2 Training and Evaluating DL Models

Four DL models were trained and evaluated for tomato identification and segmentation, in a greenhouse context, with the OID v6 dataset, and with an acquired dataset, as mentioned earlier.

We considered 3 pre-trained SSD models from the TensorFlow database and 1 pre-trained YOLO model from the Darknet database: SSD MobileNet v2; SSD Inception v2; SSD ResNet 50 and YOLO v4.

All the models were pre-trained with Google's COCO dataset [12]. Both training and inference scripts were run on Google Collaboratory (Colab) notebooks.

Through transfer learning, the pre-trained models were fine-tuned. Slight changes were made to the default training pipeline, most notably adjusting the batch-size for each model (Table 1) and to the optimizer, giving preference to the Adam optimizer for its ease of implementation, low memory requirements, for being computationally efficient, and well suited for problems with a large dataset and/or parameters [10].

Usually, the training sessions ran for 50,000 epochs, a reference value previously established by us. However, for some models this value was not enough to train these models successfully, in some cases, we used one of the training metrics, the "average loss", and stopped training when the curve, from the graph generated by this metric, converged. An evaluation session occurred every 50 epochs.

Table 1. Training batch size for each model.

DL model	Batch size
SSD MobileNet v2	24
SSD Inception v2	32
SSD ResNet 50	8
YOLO v4	64

To evaluate the models, we used the metrics defined by the Pascal VOC challenge [7] (Precision x Recall curve and Mean Average Precision), with the addition of the following metrics: Recall (1), which is the model's ability to detect all relevant objects, Precision (2), the model's ability to identify only relevant objects, and F1 Score (3), the first harmonic mean between Recall and Precision.

$$Recall = \frac{True\ Positives}{All\ groundtruths} \tag{1}$$

$$Precision = \frac{True\ Positives}{All\ detections} \tag{2}$$

$$F_1\ Score = 2 \times \frac{Precision \times Recall}{Precision + Recall} \tag{3}$$

When evaluating the 4 models, we used the OID v6 dataset and an independent dataset collected under the same conditions as the dataset used for training and validation, to identify tomatoes. Regarding the inference process, the Google Colab server was used in all cases with the Tesla T4 GPU and 12 GB VRAM.

4 Results and Discussion

In this section we intend to analyze and evaluate the result of artificial neural networks (ANN) in tomato detection, using two different datasets. The quality and robustness of a dataset in deep learning are essential to achieve the main goal of detecting and classifying an object. To understand its relevance in a real case of tomato detection, it is important to compare the use of a specific dataset against a public dataset with multiple classes. We carried out the model's evaluation as stated in Sect. 3.2.

To discuss the different results, the evaluation steps were divided into two phases, the first consists of the analysis of the results of the models trained with the acquired tomato dataset and the second with the same models but trained with OID v6. The main goal is to compare the two different datasets between the four neural networks, evaluating their performance using an inference algorithm. To obtain results, confidence greater than or equal to 30% was considered. The choice of this value is sustained according to the visual perception analysis of the validation data, with the objective of maximize the F1 score. It was also considered, a 50% IOU as default in obtaining the results shown in the Table 2.

Table 2. Results of the different SSD and YOLO models evaluation, considering a 30% predictions and IOU of 50%

Model	Dataset	mAP	Precision	Recall	F1
YOLO v4	Acquired tomato dataset	45.34%	91.03%	46.05%	61.16%
Resnet 50	Acquired tomato dataset	42.99%	90.39%	44.01%	59.20%
Inception v2	Acquired tomato dataset	36.23%	90.46%	37.32%	52.85%
Mobilenet v2	Acquired tomato dataset	32.07%	89.40%	33.08%	48.29%
YOLO v4	OID v6	0.0%	0.0%	0.0%	0.0%
Resnet 50	OID v6	0.33%	95.65	0.34%	0.68%
Inception v2	OID v6	0.49%	96.97%	0.49%	0.98%
Mobilenet v2	OID v6	1.18%	63.91%	1.67%	3.25%

Regarding our tomato dataset, Table 2 shows good results, namely, the precision obtained with the degree of confidence considered, with YOLOv4 standing out positively followed by Resnet50. Despite these results, the precision x recall ratio was lower than expected, caused essentially by false positives. This relationship can be seen in Fig. 3a. As is to be expected as high-value precision is due to the process of a degree of confidence. Despite the high-level values, the Mobilenet v2 obtained the worst performance followed by Inceptionv2, in which both remained below a 40% recall. Generally analyzing the various models using our tomato dataset, in the Table 2 the high precision values contrast with the low recall values and F1 score. Essentially, these results dues to various noise and false-positive predictions. In a visual comparison, directly between the ground truths and the detections, it is noticed that in conditions of the real environment, problems arise like tomatoes in the background and clustering problems.

In general, our tomato dataset can provide good accuracy vs recall in tomato detection, contrasting with the poor results of OID v6. In Fig. 3b it is possible to conclude that the use of YOLO v4 did not result in any tomato detection. However, Resnet50 can detect false positive fruits. It is important to remember that in the case of our tomato dataset, augmentation was made to increase their robustness, to decrease this typical problem. The purpose of using OID v6 was to understand whether it is a dataset capable of being used not only for validation but also for training deep learning models to detect tomatoes in greenhouses.

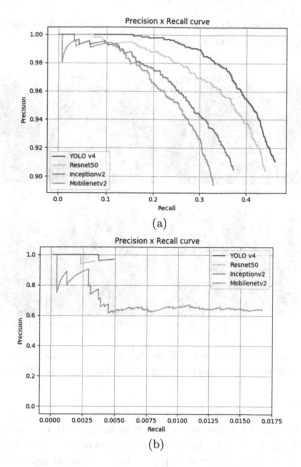

Fig. 3. Precision x Recall in the test dataset with 30% confidence; (a) curves using our tomato dataset; (b) curves using Open Image Datatset v6;

The use of several classes made the training of the respective models very difficult and time-consuming. The different classes can also be a problem, namely those that contain small datasets and with weak robustness. After inference with the test dataset, it was possible to understand that in the use of OID v6 several incorrect detections were made, namely the labels of bounding boxes with different fruits, among which included in the 15 classes, like grapes, banana, apple, lemon, etc. (Fig. 4). Among the various incorrect detections, we highlight the clustering of tomatoes as a single fruit and detections of leaves as a fruit.

The poor results of OID v6 are directly associated with the tomato class dataset, with images of ripe tomatoes (red) and with few tomatoes per image, contrasting with the images in which it is intended to detect tomatoes. Agricultural companies try to maximize their profits whenever possible and in the case of tomatoes in Portugal, they must be harvested at a relatively early stage of the crop. The reason is due to the speed of maturation of the fruit from its harvest until reaching the final customer.

(a) YOLO v4   (b) SSD Resnet 50   (c) SSD Inception v2   (d) SSD Mobilenet v2

(e) YOLO v4   (f) SSD Resnet 50   (g) SSD Inception v2   (h) SSD Mobilenet v2

Fig. 4. Results comparison with four DL models against two different datasets; (a, b, c, d) DL models with tomato dataset; (e, f, g, h) DL models with OID v6; (Color figure online)

In the analysis of the inference of the test images, it is possible to observe an example (Fig. 4) in which the four neural networks are compared. In the top zone (a, b, c, d) they represent the respective visual results of the models trained with our tomato dataset. It is possible to understand that in general tomato detections using our tomato dataset are very successful, even in cases of occlusion by leaves, variations in lighting, and clustering problems.

In another perspective of analysis, the bottom figures (e, f, g, h) represent the general results collected by the four neural networks trained by OID v6. In the case of YOLO v4, no objects were detected, unlike the other three models, with some objects detected, although they were detected as false positives.

5   Conclusion

Object detection is a crucial task in computer vision. The size and quality of the datasets are an important reason for the continuous improvement of the object detection algorithms, especially for deep learning-based techniques. As mentioned, to train four different neural networks, we compared a dataset of our own with a public and larger dataset with multiple classes, the OID v6 dataset.

Results demonstrate that all four models performed better when faced with the acquired tomato dataset. This could be explained by the divergence between the two datasets that were used. The OIDv6 is very varied in terms of the available classes, however, each of its classes offers different amounts of images, penalizing the training of certain classes. However, the wide variety of classes, many of the images have few annotations, as well as few cases in a real environment, such as in the greenhouse culture itself. Specifically, in the case of the tomato class, the dataset is mostly related to ripe tomatoes (red), contrasting with the color of the tomato that we intend to detect (green and sometimes reddish).

In addition, the set of images comes much closer to a real situation, which a harvesting robot would be exposed to, for example, with objects that are identical in terms of type, color, shape, texture in a similar background. In conclusion, it is important to highlight the proposal of this document to use YOLO v4 when using a dedicated dataset for the detection of tomatoes in the greenhouse, with a precision of 91%.

Some characteristics would still be important to address, which are sometimes limited by the amount of data not being sufficiently large and robust, as well as the analysis of situations in a real environment becomes complex with constant challenges. Therefore, the additional future work focus on:

1. Elaboration of a new dataset with the combination of our tomato dataset and the OID v6, for training evaluation;
2. Evaluate the performance of DL models on Field-programmable gate array (FPGA);
3. Evaluate the performance benchmark of the FPGA against GPU.

Acknowledgments. The research leading to these results has received funding from the European Union's Horizon 2020 - The EU Framework Programme for Research and Innovation 2014–2020, under grant agreement No. 101004085.

References

1. Food and Agriculture Organization of the United Nations (2021). http://www.fao.org/faostat/en/#data/QC
2. Fruit and Vegetables - Your Dietary Essentials: the international year of fruits and vegetables. Food & Agriculture org, S.l. (2021)
3. Open Images V6 (2021). https://storage.googleapis.com/openimages/web/index.html
4. World Health Organization (2021). https://www.who.int
5. Biffi, L.J., et al.: ATSS deep learning-based approach to detect apple fruits. Remote Sens. **13**(1), 54 (2020). https://doi.org/10.3390/rs13010054
6. Bresilla, K., Perulli, G.D., Boini, A., Morandi, B., Corelli Grappadelli, L., Manfrini, L.: Single-shot convolution neural networks for real-time fruit detection within the tree. Front. Plant Sci. **10**, 611 (2019). https://doi.org/10.3389/fpls.2019.00611
7. Everingham, M., Gool, L.V., Williams, C.K.I., Winn, J., Zisserman, A.: The PASCAL visual object classes (VOC) challenge. Int. J. Comput. Vis., 34 (2010). https://doi.org/10.1007/s11263-009-0275-4

8. Everingham, M., Van Gool, L., Williams, C.K.I., Winn, J., Zisserman, A.: The Pascal visual object classes (VOC) challenge. Int. J. Comput. Vis. **88**(2), 303–338 (2010). https://doi.org/10.1007/s11263-009-0275-4

9. Kang, H., Chen, C.: Fast implementation of real-time fruit detection in apple orchards using deep learning. Comput. Electr. Agric. **168**, 105108 (2020)

10. Kingma, D.P., Ba, J.: Adam: a method for stochastic optimization. arXiv:1412.6980 [cs] (January 2017)

11. Koirala, A., Walsh, K.B., Wang, Z., McCarthy, C.: Deep learning for real-time fruit detection and orchard fruit load estimation: benchmarking of 'MangoYOLO'. Precis. Agric. **20**(6), 1107–1135 (2019)

12. Lin, T.-Y., et al.: Microsoft COCO: common objects in context. In: Fleet, D., Pajdla, T., Schiele, B., Tuytelaars, T. (eds.) ECCV 2014. LNCS, vol. 8693, pp. 740–755. Springer, Cham (2014). https://doi.org/10.1007/978-3-319-10602-1_48

13. Liu, G., Nouaze, J.C., Touko Mbouembe, P.L., Kim, J.H.: YOLO-Tomato: a robust algorithm for Tomato detection based on YOLOv3. Sensors **20**(7), 2145 (2020). https://doi.org/10.3390/s20072145

14. Magalhães, S.A., et al.: Evaluating the single-shot multibox detector and Yolo deep learning models for the detection of tomatoes in a greenhouse. Sensors **21**(10) (2021). https://doi.org/10.3390/s21103569. https://www.mdpi.com/1424-8220/21/10/3569

15. Sa, I., Ge, Z., Dayoub, F., Upcroft, B., Perez, T., McCool, C.: DeepFruits: a fruit detection system using deep neural networks. Sensors **16**(8), 1222 (2016). https://doi.org/10.3390/s16081222

16. Saha, S.: A Comprehensive Guide to Convolutional Neural Networks - the ELI5 way (2018)

17. Sekachev, B., Manovich, N., Zhiltsov, M.: opencv/cvat: v1.1.0 (2020). https://doi.org/10.5281/zenodo.4009388. https://zenodo.org/record/4009388#.YHcbXD_OUkl

18. Tu, S., et al.: Passion fruit detection and counting based on multiple scale faster R-CNN using RGB-D images. Precis. Agric. **21**(5), 1072–1091 (2020). https://doi.org/10.1007/s11119-020-09709-3

19. Yuan, T., et al.: Robust Cherry Tomatoes detection algorithm in greenhouse scene based on SSD. Agriculture **10**(5), 160 (2020). https://doi.org/10.3390/agriculture10050160

20. Zhang, L., Gui, G., Khattak, A.M., Wang, M., Gao, W., Jia, J.: Multi-task cascaded convolutional networks based intelligent fruit detection for designing automated robot. IEEE Access **7**, 56028–56038 (2019). https://doi.org/10.1109/ACCESS.2019.2899940

Predicting Predawn Leaf Water Potential up to Seven Days Using Machine Learning

Ahmed A. Fares[✉], Fabio Vasconcelos, Joao Mendes-Moreira,
and Carlos Ferreira

INESC-TEC, Porto, Portugal
ahmed.a.fares@inesctec.pt
https://www.inesctec.pt

Abstract. Sustainable agricultural production requires a controlled usage of water, nutrients, and minerals from the environment. Different strategies of plant irrigation are being studied to control the quantity and quality balance of the fruits. Regarding efficient irrigation, particularly in deficit irrigation strategies, it is essential to act according to water stress status in the plant. For example, in the vine, to improve the quality of the grapes, the plants are deprived of water until they reach particular water stress before re-watered in specified phenological stages. The water status inside the plant is estimated by measuring either the Leaf Potential during the Predawn or soil water potential, along with the root zones. Measuring soil water potential has the advantage of being independent of diurnal atmospheric variations. However, this method has many logistic problems, making it very hard to apply along all the yard, especially the big ones. In this study, the Predawn Leaf Water Potential (PLWP) is daily predicted by Machine Learning models using data such as grapes variety, soil characteristics, irrigation schedules, and meteorological data. The benefits of these techniques are the reduction of the manual work of measuring PLWP and the capacity to implement those models on a larger scale by predicting PLWP up to 7 days which should enhance the ability to optimize the irrigation plan while the quantity and quality of the crop are under control.

Keywords: Precision agriculture · Leaf Water Potential · Machine Learning

1 Introduction

The best procedure for determining irrigation needs is to measure the crop evapotranspiration (Et), i.e., the amount of transpired water in the plant or its estimation. Several methods can be applied to estimate the Et but the most popular international method is described in FAO-56 Penman-Monteith (FAO-56) [14, 17–19]. It calculates evapotranspiration reference ETo, the Crop Coefficient

© Springer Nature Switzerland AG 2021
G. Marreiros et al. (Eds.): EPIA 2021, LNAI 12981, pp. 39–50, 2021.
https://doi.org/10.1007/978-3-030-86230-5_4

(Kc) and Water Stress Coefficient (Ks) when the plant culture diverges from its hydric comfort or it is subjected to deficit irrigation, as described in Eq. 1.

$$ET = ETo \times Kc \times Ks \tag{1}$$

Ks returns information about the water status inside the plant. This value is hard to calculate because it needs information about root morphology and soil surrounding the roots. To solve this difficulty, different methods to measure plant water status are being used nowadays [2]. The pressure chamber technique is considered the most accurate procedure available for plant water stress monitorization [6]. However, this technique requires manual work with a large pressure chamber. So, the implementation of this method on a large scale requires a large number of workers, each one equipped with a pressure chamber, which raises the financial cost of the technique. In vine, changes in water status have a direct effect on grape composition and quality. There is a growing interest in applying deficit irrigation strategies to reach a predetermined water stress level on the crop [7]. Therefore, this study aims to develop a stand-alone working model using Machine Learning techniques to predict the water stress inside the plant.

Section 2 presents the state of the art and related work in the same area; Sect. 3 shows a summary of the data, discussing the problem the client was facing and the experiments to predict Predawn Leaf Water Potential (PLWP); Sect. 4 explains the experiment; Sect. 5 shows the results of our models and the discussion about it; Sect. 6 concludes our work and describes future directions.

2   Background Concept

Knowing water status response is essential to obtain a balance between the quality of grapes and the yield [4]. Several indicators can be used to estimate this response. However, Leaf Water Potential (LWP) measured with a pressure chamber is a widely used indicator with an acceptable performance [8]. These measures can be taken along the day, but implementing it at predawn was favored as it is considered to represent soil water status more accurately since it minimizes the influence of environmental conditions, as shown in Fig. 1 and demonstrated in [5,20]. However, adverse environmental conditions can affect leaf stomatal opening, which leads to gaps between PLWP and Soil Water Potential(SWP) [3]. Figure 1 shows that Water Potential always has a negative value, where values closer to 0 Megapascal (MPa) indicate hydric comfort, while lower values represent water stress. According to [21], in Fig. 2, after bud burst phenological stage, it is not recommended to put the plant in water stress so it won't affect the bud growth. After Bloom, until Veraison, several restrictions of water can reduce the number of grapes. Between Veraison to Harvest, the water potential has a significant impact on grape size. A controlled reduction of grape size is related to the quality goal of the product. Therefore, it is essential to identify the periods when the crop is less sensitive and define the level of DI to be applied [25].

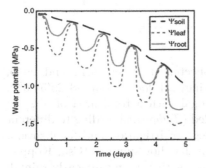

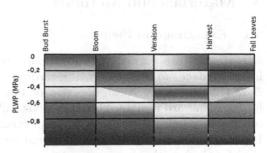

Fig. 1. Daily changes in the water potential (Represented as ψ) in the soil, leaf and root under normal conditions.

Fig. 2. The optimum PLWP range during different phenological stages. Green - Optimum; Yellow - unfavorable; Red - harmful [21]. (Color figure online)

Yang et al. [26] forecasted daily 7-day-ahead reference crop evapotranspiration (ETo) using the Penman-Monteith (PM) modeled public weather forecasts (including daily maximum and minimum temperatures, weather types, and wind scales, for six stations located in a wide range of climate zones of China were collected). Pelosi et al. [27] evaluate the performances of probabilistic daily ETo forecasts with lead times up to 5 days and a spatial resolution of 7 km, computed by using COSMO-LEPS outputs (provided by the European Consortium for small–scale modeling, COSMO). Brillante et al. [28] monitored weekly for three years leaf the water potentials Grapevines (Vitis vinifera L. cv Chardonnay) located in eight experimental plots (Burgundy, France). The water stress experienced by grapevine was modeled as a function of meteorological data (minimum and maximum temperature and rainfall, obtained from an on-site weather station) and soil characteristics (soil texture, gravel content, and slope) by a gradient boosting machine. The developed models reached outstanding prediction performance, comparable to the measurement accuracy.

The FAO-56 method [14] is being used for a long time to compute the crop water requirements and irrigation requirements based on soil, climate, and crop data. Recently, with the increasing availability of high-resolution Normalized Difference Vegetation Index (NDVI) time series, several authors are coupling the FAO-56 method with NDVI images [24,29]. For instance, the SAMIR (SAtellite Monitoring of IRrigation) tool [24] is based on the coupling of the FAO-56 dual crop coefficient model with time series of high-resolution NDVI imagery (Normalized Difference Vegetation Index) and can be used to compute spatially distributed estimates of ET and crop water budget at the regional scale. In [29] the SAMIR tool was used to estimate regional crop water consumption. In this work, the author explores time series images taken by the SPOT satellite, a commercial high-resolution optical imaging Earth observation satellite system operating from space. The target was to predict the actual basal crop coefficient (Kcb) and the vegetation fraction cover (fc).

3 Materials and Methods

3.1 Experimental Field

Experiments are carried out using data collected, between 2014 and 2016, from *Herdade do Esporão SA.* regarding vineyard located in 38°23′55.0″N 7°32′47.3″W, in the Alentejo region of Portugal with a total area of 452.865 ha. The vineyard is divided into 163 fields called (*Talhão*), according to different soil types, grape varieties (*Casta*), and strategy of irrigation and fertilization. Esporão vineyard is humid mesothermal with dry, hot summer (Csa, Koppen classification), with a mean annual temperature of 16.5 °C, mean yearly rainfall of 569 mm.

Usually, PLWP measures are collected using mature leaves located in the middle third of the plant using the pressure chamber method of Scholander [1]. In order to minimize the bias, each recorded measure is calculated by taking the average of 6 different samples picked from 6 neighbor plants in the same field. This process faces logistic difficulties such as the need for daily manual work done before dawn around 4:00 am to 6:00 am. The number of workers equipped with a Scholander chamber increases linearly with the area of the yard and number of measures.

EnviroScan capacitance sensor is a complete and stand-alone continuous soil moisture monitoring system. The system consists of a network of probes supporting an array of sensors that monitor changes in soil moisture, which could be installed at various depths [9]. In the current study, the yard has nine sensors distributed strategically, i.e., each set of homogeneous zones according to the soil type, altitude, and irrigation system has one sensor.

3.2 Data Visualization and Summarization

The first task was to normalize the data due to different timescales used in the recording process. Some of them were recorded every 15 min like humidity sensors; others were recorded daily like PLWP, while the rest have only one reading per year as grape variety (*Casta*) and soil characteristics. The inconsistent information collected from annual variables, i.e., Casta, Regime, Soil, Age, CC (Maximum moisture that the soil supports), CE (Minimum moisture that the soil needs before the plants start dying), TAW (Total Available Water), and vigor or the incoherent readings and missing humidity values are detected (see Table 1). PLWP readings recorded after the harvest date were removed because both showed irregular behavior, and there was no interest in collecting or calculating PLWP that late.

3.3 Problem Definition and Feature Engineering

The original idea is trying to predict PLWP for the next seven days. While 62.8% of PLWP reading was unknown, the first step was filling the unknown values, and then the predicted values can be passed as input variables to the future prediction models.

Table 1. Data summarization, where DOY- Day of the year; PLWP- Predawn Leaf Water Potential Measures (MPa); Hum.- Humidity Measures at 4 am. In the original dataset we had three variables, for different depths (20, 60 and 100 cm); Age- Age of the plant; W1- Amount of water irrigated on the previous day (mm); ETo- Evapotranspiration on the last day (mm); CC- Maximum moisture that the soil supports; CE- Minimum moisture that the soil needs before the plants start dying; TAW- Total Available Water.

	Min	1stQ	Median	Mean	3rdQ	Max	Missing values%
DOY	126	166	197	196.4	228	261	0%
PLWP	−0.98	−0.43	−0.32	−0.34	−0.22	−0.06	62.8%
Hum.	12.23	12.54	12.65	12.64	12.73	13.34	0.9%
Age	2	8	11	11.8	13	42	10.3%
W1	0	0	0	3.34	0	23.27	0%
ETo	1.6	5.6	6.2	6.131	6.9	8.6	0%
CC	0.26	0.28	0.31	0.31	0.33	0.39	1.6%
CE	0.11	0.15	0.16	0.16	0.18	0.23	1.6%
TAW	113.4	136.6	150.5	149.2	162.2	183.7	1.6%

There are several strategies to deal with unknown values. The simplest ways are either to delete the whole records with unknown values or to fill them with given statistics such as the average or the median for quantitative values. On the other hand, there are more complex strategies that normally lead to more accuracy; however, it requires more computing costs [16]. The five different Machine Learning methods from different regression families were applied to fill all the unknown values of PLWP that are Multivariate Linear Regression (MLR), Multivariate Adaptive Regression Splines (MARS), Support Vector Regression (SVR), Classification and Regression Trees (CART), and Random Forest (RF). The experiments were developed in R computing environment[1] by using *e1071* package [10] for SVR, *rpart* [11] for regression trees, *earth* [12] for MARS and *RandomForest* [13] for *RandomForest*. The SVR, MARS, and *RandomForest* are tuned using the function inside the respective package. The MLR and *rpart* are used with the standard hyper-parameters. The 10-fold cross-validation is used as a resampling method to evaluate each method by random partitioning. Each subset is used to evaluate the induced model, which has been trained using the

---

[1] https://www.r-project.org/about.html.

remaining nine subsets. This method was applied to data available from 2014. The performance measure is Root Mean Squared Error (RMSE), according to Eq. 2.

$$RMSE = \sqrt{\frac{1}{n} \sum_{t=1}^{n} Error_t^2} \tag{2}$$

Where "Error" is the difference between the predicted value of PLWP by model and the measured value of PWLP. The variable n is the number of samples. In a general sense, soil stores water; therefore, the water on the soil should be a continuous variable, so the variable "HWater" was created according to Eq. 3. Besides, the balance (BAL) variable was derived from the ideal balance of water inside the plant. Equation 4 shows the difference between irrigation and evapotranspiration.

$$HWater = \frac{\sum_{i=1}^{3} \frac{1}{i} \times Humidity_{t-i} \times W_{t-i}}{\sum_{i=1}^{3} \frac{1}{i}} \tag{3}$$

$$BAL = W_{t-1} - ETo_{t-1} \tag{4}$$

4   Experiments

4.1   Fill the Gaps

Variables Selection. The best variables were chosen using the *rfcv* function from *randomForest* package to perform a 10-fold cross-validation over the data from year 2014 with all the variables. Afterward, a cut point was chosen to select the most important variables to avoid overfitting and complexity of the system without compromising the accuracy.

The *varImpPlot* function from *randomForest* R package [13] has been used to know the variable importance, as it is shown in Fig. 3. DOY was the most important feature. According to the plant life cycle, the behavior of PLWP could differ during phenological stages. It can explain the importance of DOY since the dates of phenological stages were not available. Humidity in different depths also seems to be important, representing the absolute quantity of water in the soil. Since PLWP is a measure that represents the water inside the plant, the importance of this variable to the model makes sense. Other variables that seem to be important are *Casta*, Age, and W1. These are the variables that distinguish between plant characteristics and irrigation strategies. The ETo considers weather information to calculate the amount of water lost by the plant and seems to have some importance. The CE, CC, TAW, and Soil variables are correlated, and all of them are describing the soil characteristics. We can conclude that the soil type is important to predict PLWP, which is further supported since the available water is different for different types of soil [22]. According to this way of calculating variable importance, vigor and regime seem to be the least important variables.

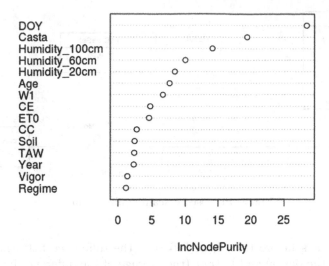

Fig. 3. Variable importance measures by *varImpPlot* function

Methodologies. The objective was to build a stand-alone working model to fill the gaps of PWLP for the previous agricultural cycles. This model will be used to train the prediction models on the one hand and also will be used to fill the gaps of the following agricultural cycles whenever needed.

Figure 4 shows the proposed cascading (CAS) technique to train a model for the prediction of PLWP and then predicted PLWP would be used as a variable for the prediction of the next day PLWP. To be able to do that, the algorithm was split into two different tasks: (1) fill the missing data, and (2) build model 2. So, instead of ignoring all the daily data with no values of PLWP, these values are predicted using model 1 afterward. These predictions are used as a variable to model 2. The big modification on the model 2 are the values of PLWP for the previous 3 days (T_i represents $P\hat{LW}P_{t-i}$; t is the current day and i the number of previous days) that are from model 1 and the respective modification of PLWP between two days ($C_i = P\hat{LW}P_{t-i} - P\hat{LW}P_{(t-1)-i}$).

4.2 Seven Days Prediction

Like filling the gaps models, the random forest was chosen to train seven models to predict PLWP for the next seven days, one model per day.

Variables Selection. The available variables were ETo, Field data, Irrigation, and PLWP of the previous seven days.

The variable $Mean7DaysCurrent$ was the most critical variable in all the seven models, which means the predicted value of a day is highly dependent on the weighted average of the seven days before that day, giving higher weights for closer days. Also, irrigation variables like Waterxxx (the average of the irrigation

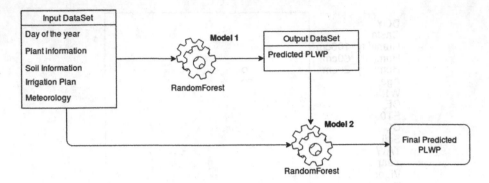

Fig. 4. Proposed cascading algorithm

of the three days before that day), EToWx (the difference between ETo and irrigation for the day x) and Balxxx (the average of the difference between ETo and irrigation of the three days before that day), were good candidates with moderate importance in predicting the following days.

Methodologies. The value of PLWP always depends on DOY, as mentioned in Sect. 4.1. We had split the experiment into two parts and compared the performance. (1) Creating one model for all phenological stages. (2) Creating three models (one model per phenological stage).

5 Results and Discussion

5.1 Algorithms Comparison and Variable Importance

Five different algorithms were used to choose the model that fits better with the year 2014. It was concluded that Support Vector Regression (SVR) with RMSE of 0.0812 and Random Forest with RMSE of 0.0791 obtained the best results, followed by MARS, RPart, and MLR with RMSE of 0.101, 0.105, and 0.110, respectively. Random Forest usually receives a good performance, and the induced models are of straightforward interpretation. Besides, we don't need to worry about tuning a large set of parameters that increase the computational costs [15]. Therefore, the random forest has been chosen as the best of the five algorithms tested for the current study while passing only two parameters *importance* is true and *nTrees* is 2000 trees for filling gaps model and 600 trees for each of the seven days models.

While *HWater* and *BAL* are calculated based on the amount of irrigation, it seems that there could be a chance to use them in understanding and control the performance of PLWP. The right panel depicts the previous values PLWP has of high significance, especially the previous day (T1). Moreover, the changes (C1 and C2) seem to have some importance.

5.2 Models Validation

Specialists from *Herdade do Esporão* agreed that an absolute error up to 0.2 Megapascal (MPa) is acceptable. An interesting observation is that all the algorithms seem to have very similar results, and all of them seem to have more accurate results when the measured values are higher than −0.7 MPa. At the same time, values smaller than −0.7 MPa are being predicted with values higher than their actual values. This situation can be explained by the limit between healthy and non-healthy plant behavior, supporting the idea of changing the plant behavior when the plant starts dying. Contrarily, PLWP above −0.2 MPa, the plant doesn't feel any limitation in water uptake [23], and it can be observed that our prediction is weak in this range.

Accepting a 0.2 MPa error, we can conclude that all the methods have around 98% of the predictions inside this range, except persistence. i.e. 98% of the predicted values have absolute error less than 0.2 MPa. Moreover, when we decrease the maximum acceptable error to 0.1 MPa, we got around 80% of accuracy.

5.3 Error Analysis

Fill the Gaps. This result shows that it exists a slight asymmetry in our predictions. In each day, it was collected more than one measure of PLWP. Thus it is possible to calculate RMSE/day. Also, it shows that cascading Random Forest has better results for all the scenarios, and all trials have beat the dummy persistence algorithm.

Predict Seven Days. To check the performance of the models, we have tested two different approaches. a) create one model per phenological stage, b) create only one model which covers the whole year. Then, Root Mean Square Error has been calculated as a validation metric. Also, the holdout methodology has been used as a validation technique. The idea was to keep the phenological stages consistent within a single year and across different years.

Tables 2 shows Root Mean Square Error when a single model was created for the whole year. It is understood that the accuracy of the models was decreasing while we tried to predict farther days. But at the same time, it was not reducing dramatically, and in the worst case to predict the 7th day, the Root Mean Square Error is higher than the error of predicting the current day by only 15%.

On the other side, Table 3 shows Root Mean Square Error when three models per year were created representing the three phenological stages. The results show a more extensive range of errors resulting from having different phenological stages in different years, especially in the transition from a stage to the following.

Table 2. Root Mean Square Error considering one model for all phenological stages

	Train 2014+2015	Train 2014+2016	Train 2015+2016
	Test 2016	Test 2015	Test 2014
T+1	0.084	0.086	0.084
T+2	0.083	0.087	0.084
T+3	0.083	0.088	0.084
T+4	0.085	0.089	0.085
T+5	0.086	0.091	0.087
T+6	0.087	0.092	0.088
T+7	0.089	0.092	0.089

Table 3. Root Mean Square Error considering 3 models (one model per stage)

	Train 2014+2015	Train 2014+2016	Train 2015+2016
	Test 2016	Test 2015	Test 2014
T+1	0.068 0.108 0.138	0.082 0.098 0.103	0.080 0.093 0.098
T+2	0.067 0.106 0.146	0.082 0.097 0.105	0.079 0.090 0.098
T+3	0.068 0.107 0.149	0.083 0.098 0.108	0.078 0.091 0.104
T+4	0.069 0.112 0.156	0.084 0.099 0.111	0.080 0.093 0.106
T+5	0.070 0.113 0.154	0.085 0.102 0.117	0.081 0.095 0.116
T+6	0.071 0.114 0.165	0.085 0.104 0.121	0.080 0.096 0.121
T+7	0.073 0.120 0.172	0.086 0.103 0.122	0.081 0.095 0.128

6 Conclusion and Future Work

In this project, several models were developed to predict PLWP at a specific time in the vineyard, from the flowering phenological stage until the maturation stage. An easy to collect information like grape varieties and soil type, moisture, and meteorological information was considered. The results showed the possibility to predict PLWP instead of physical examination that consumes time and money. Specialists from *Herdade do Esporão S.A.* defined the maximum acceptable error rate to be 0.2 MPa, so at this point, we conclude that the objective was accomplished by having around 98% of the predictions with error rates less than 0.2 MPa. Regarding different strategies, it seems that the cascading approach brings a slight improvement, so considering computational cost versus benefit does not seem to worth it.

Also, we have been able to forecast PLWP for the following seven days with an accuracy lower than predicting the current point of time by only 15%, which is considered an original work that should be followed by future enhancement.

6.1   Future Work

While the results look promising, we believe it could be even enhanced using more information regarding plagues, stomatal opening, root morphology, phenological stages, and NDVI (Normalized Difference Vegetation Index) information. Also, evolved models could improve themselves over time and include data from other vineyards to generalize these models.

As future work, we could focus on optimizing irrigation plans using our forecasting models once time and quantity of irrigation water are considered important decision variables.

Acknowledgments. This work is financed by National Funds through the Portuguese funding agency, FCT - Fundação para a Ciência e a Tecnologia, within project UIDB/50014/2020.

References

1. Scholander, P.F., Bradstreet, E.D., Hemmingsen, E.A., Hammel, H.T.: Sap pressure in vascular plants. Science **148**, 339–346 (1965)
2. Jones, H.G.: Monitoring plant and soil water status: established and novel methods revisited and their relevance to studies of drought tolerance. J. Exp. Bot. **58**, 119–130 (2007)
3. Tonietto, J., Carbonneau, A.: A multicriteria climatic classification system for grape-growing regions worldwide. Agric. For. Meteorol. **124**, 81–97 (2004)
4. Acevedo-Opazo, C., Ortega-Farias, S., Fuentes, S.: Effects of grapevine (Vitis vinifera L.) water status on water consumption, vegetative growth and grape quality: an irrigation scheduling application to achieve regulated deficit irrigation. Agric. Water Manag. **97**, 956–964 (2010)
5. Yamane, T., Shibayama, K., Hamana, Y., Yakushiji, H.: Response of container-grown girdled grapevines to short-term water-deficit stress. Am. J. Enol. Vitic. **60**, 50–56 (2009)
6. Acevedo-Opazo, C., Tisseyre, B., Guillaume, S., et al.: The potential of high spatial resolution information to define within-vineyard zones related to vine water status. Precision Agric. **9**, 285–302 (2008)
7. Acevedo-Opazo, C., Tisseyre, B., Ojeda, H., Ortega-Farias, S., Guillaume, S.: Is it possible to assess the spatial variability of vine water status? OENO One **42**, 203–219 (2008)
8. Améglio, T., et al.: Significance and limits in the use of predawn leaf water potential for tree irrigation. Plant Soil **207**, 155–167 (1999)
9. Wels, C., O'Kane, M., Fortin, S.: Assessment of water storage cover for Questa tailings facility, New Mexico. In: Proceedings of the 9th Annual Conference of the American Society for Surface Mining Reclamation, Albuquerque, New Mexico (2001)
10. Meyer, D., Dimitriadou, E., Hornik, K., Weingessel, A., Leisch, F., Chang, C.-C., Lin, C.-C.: "The e1071 package" in Misc Functions of Department of Statistics (e1071), TU Wien (2006)
11. Therneau, T., Atkinson, B.: rpart: recursive partitioning and regression trees. R package version 4.1-15 (2019)

12. Milborrow. S.: Derived from mda:mars by T. Hastie and R. Tibshirani., "earth: Multivariate Adaptive Regression Splines" (2011)
13. Liaw, A., Wiener, M.: Classification and regression by randomForest. R News **2**, 18–22 (2002)
14. Allan, R.G., Pereira, L.S., Raes, D., Smith, M.: Crop evapotranspiration - Guidelines for computing crop water requirements-FAO Irrigation and drainage paper 56, vol. 300, p. D05109. FAO, Rome (1998)
15. Chen, E.: Choosing a Machine Learning Classifier (2011)
16. Torgo, L.: Data Mining with R: Learning with Case Studies, 1st edn. Chapman and Hall/CRC (2016)
17. Suleiman, A.A., Hoogenboom, G.: Comparison of Priestley-Taylor and FAO-56 Penman-Monteith for daily reference evapotranspiration estimation in Georgia. J. Irrig. Drain. Eng. **133**, 175–182 (2007)
18. Mutziger, A.J., Burt, C.M., Howes, D.J., Allen, R.G.: Comparison of measured and FAO-56 modeled evaporation from bare soil. J. Irrig. Drain. Eng. **131**, 59–72 (2005)
19. de Jabloun, M., Sahli, A.: Evaluation of FAO-56 methodology for estimating reference evapotranspiration using limited climatic data: application to Tunisia. Agric. Water Manag. **95**, 707–715 (2008)
20. Ribeiro, A.C., Sá, A., Andrade, J.L.: Avaliação do stresse hídrico em videiras submetidas a diferentes regimes hídricos. In: VI Congreso Ibérico de Agro-Engenharia (2011)
21. Ojeda, H.: Riego cualitativo de precisión en la vid. Revista Enologia **1**, 14–17 (2007)
22. Cassel, D.K., Nielsen, D.R.: Field capacity and available water capacity. In: Methods of Soil Analysis: Part 1-Physical and Mineralogical Methods, pp. 901–926 (1986)
23. Van Leeuwen, C., et al.: Vine water status is a key factor in grape ripening and vintage quality for red Bordeaux wine. How can it be assessed for vineyard management purposes? OENO One **43**, 121–134 (2009)
24. Lepage, M., et al.: SAMIR a tool for irrigation monitoring using remote sensing for evapotranspiration estimate. Marrakech. Melia (2009)
25. Fernandes-Silva, A., Oliveira, M., Paço, T.A., Ferreira, I.: Deficit irrigation in Mediterranean fruit trees and grapevines: water stress indicators and crop responses. In Irrigation in Agroecosystems. IntechOpen (2018)
26. Yang, Y., et al.: Short-term forecasting of daily reference evapotranspiration using the Penman-Monteith model and public weather forecasts. Agric. Water Manag. **177**, 329–339 (2016)
27. Pelosi, A., Medina, H., Villani, P., D'Urso, G., Chirico, G.B.: Probabilistic forecasting of reference evapotranspiration with a limited area ensemble prediction system. Agric. Water Manag. **178**, 106–118 (2016)
28. Brillante, L., Bois, B., Mathieu, O., Lévêque, J.: Electrical imaging of soil water availability to grapevine: a benchmark experiment of several machine-learning techniques. Precision Agric. **17**(6), 637–658 (2016). https://doi.org/10.1007/s11119-016-9441-1
29. Saadi, S., et al.: Monitoring irrigation consumption using high resolution NDVI image time series: calibration and validation in the Kairouan Plain (Tunisia). Remote Sens. **7**(10), 13005–13028 (2015)

Artificial Intelligence and Law

Towards Ethical Judicial Analytics: Assessing Readability of Immigration and Asylum Decisions in the United Kingdom

Laura Scheinert[1](✉) and Emma L. Tonkin[2]

[1] University of Exeter, Exeter, UK
l.scheinert@exeter.ac.uk
[2] University of Bristol, Bristol, UK
e.l.tonkin@bristol.ac.uk

Abstract. Motivated by the broader issues of open justice and access to justice, this paper explores the ethical application of judicial analytics through the lens of an assessment of readability of written judicial decisions. To that end the paper aims 1) to review and reproduce for the UK context previous work that assesses readability of legal texts, and 2) to reflect critically on the ethical implications of applied judicial analytics. Focusing on the use case of assessing the readability of judicial Immigration and Asylum decisions in the UK, we put forward recommendations for ethical judicial analytics that aim to produce results that meet the needs of and are accepted by the stakeholders of the legal system.

Keywords: Readability · Judicial decisions · Immigration and Asylum · Ethical judicial analytics · Flesch Reading Ease · SMOG

1 Introduction

In recent years, calls for both open justice and accessible justice have led to an increased interest in leveraging the tools of machine learning (ML) and text/data mining for an exploration of the legal field and the various stakeholders, notably judges, within it. Focusing on the use case of assessing readability of written judicial decisions in the Immigration and Asylum jurisdiction in the United Kingdom (UK), we put forward recommendations for ethical judicial analytics that aim to produce results in service of the stakeholders of the legal system.

Suggestions to use so-called 'plain legal language', have been voiced since around the 1970s [43]. These link to readability – assessing the ease with which a text can be understood by its readers [32]. Assessing readability of legal texts, particularly judicial decisions, is important. It can be part of a wider project

This work was supported by the Economic and Social Research Council [ES/P000630/1]. We thank Gregory Tourte for his valuable technical contributions.

G. Marreiros et al. (Eds.): EPIA 2021, LNAI 12981, pp. 53–67, 2021.
https://doi.org/10.1007/978-3-030-86230-5_5

of assessing accessible justice – both in the sense of accessing dispute resolution and appeal processes as well as removing structural barriers to active legal participation more widely [28]. Broader issues of accessibility include access to legal representation, access to legal aid, a capacity to understand outcomes and procedures. These issues are, arguably, particularly pertinent for appellants in the Immigration and Asylum system, who, in the UK, face the challenges of the 'Hostile Environment' policy of the UK Home Office (HO), cuts to legal aid and therefore access to legal representation, and for whom English is often not a first language [6].

For context, persons wishing to appeal decisions (the 'appellant') by the HO – the UK government body responsible for Immigration and Asylum administration – can do so, in the first instance, to the First-tier Tribunal Immigration and Asylum Chamber (FtTIAC). FtTIAC decisions can be further appealed on points of potential errors of law, which is then decided by the Upper Tribunal Immigration and Asylum Chamber (UTIAC). UTIAC decisions are publicly available online.

The paper pursues two aims. The first is to review and replicate previous work that assesses readability of legal texts, applying readability formulas in the UK context of the Immigration and Asylum jurisdiction. Secondly, we reflect critically on the informative potential of an application of such formulas to judicial decisions. Ethical challenges arise in both the technical application, and the empirical case which is located in the judicial sphere where judicial independence is paramount and ML-driven approaches to assessing judicial performance might be seen as a threat. Through the lens of readability, we explore how ML and text/data mining can be leveraged responsibly to offer a constructive critique rather than destructive attack, a useful tool set rather than an instrument for blaming – but to present an accepted instrument for review and reflection on judicial practice.

The paper proceeds by reviewing the literature on readability of legal documents, reflecting on the pitfalls of judicial analytics, and replicating classic readability measures on a corpus of UTIAC decisions. We critique the readability formulas approach and discuss ethical issues in the use of ML and text/data mining on judicial written decisions, putting forward recommendations for what we call 'ethical judicial analytics'. The paper concludes by highlighting possible next steps and future work in assessing readability in such a way as to serve the stakeholders – appellants, lawyers, judges – of the legal system.

2   Assessing Readability, and Judicial Analytics

2.1   Development and Critique of Readability Formulas

The study of readability originated in the early-to-mid twentieth century and was originally concerned with assessing the appropriateness of reading materials for pupils in different (US) school grades. As such, accompanying formulas developed as part of a "broader effort to quantify student literacy" [30, p. 16], and to give teachers 'objective' measures at hand to match reading materials to students. This specific origin notwithstanding, definitions of readability have been quite broad from the onset. Dale and Chall [14, p. 23] define readability as "the sum total (including the interactions) of all those elements within a given piece of printed material that affects the success that a group of readers have with it", defining success as "the extent to which they understand it, read it at an optimum speed, and find it interesting". More recently, Pikulski [32, p. 1] defines readability as "the level of ease [...] with which text material can be understood by a particular reader who is reading that text for a specific purpose". A common denominator is conceptualising readability as depending on textual and reader-related factors.

Readability formulas aim to capture these factors by using "counts of language variables [...] to provide an index of probable difficulty for readers" [24, p. 64]. These usually include syntax (e.g. sentence length) and semantics (e.g. word length, number of difficult words) elements. Over 200 reading formulas have been developed. The most popular include the Flesch Reading Ease (FRE), Flesch–Kincaid, and (New) Dale–Chall formulas [see 4,24]. While using different parameter values, their unifying premise remains that readability can be calculated from a combination of easily quantifiable semantic and syntactic measures. From those 'classic' readability formulas, readability assessments have moved on to incorporate comprehension and cloze-testing (where texts are redacted such that a specified number of blanked-out words has to be filled by the reader, with readability assessed by the number of correct fillings), and to ML and natural language processing (NLP) methods [11]. The latter often go beyond mere syntactic/semantic measures and aim to model cognitive processes of reading [for an overview, see 40]. Developments in cognitive and NLP models aim to broaden the applicability of and refine the calculation of readability measures further [cf. 9,10,33].

These onward developments resulted from frequent critique to classic readability metrics. The standard formulas were seen by some to be too simple, to not take into account the complexity of the reading and comprehension processes, and to be inadequate [e.g. inappropriate as writing guidelines, see 4] [1], or even misleading and outright useless [15]. In the legal context, it has been pointed out that readability formulas might be skewed by the particular features of legal writing, i.e. the frequent use of long and complex words or sentences. Further critiques include that the classic formulas would provide only an indirect measurement of legal readability or yield even negative correlations, e.g. if plain language formats turn out to be longer than their originals, and would not provide specific guidance for legal drafters [1]. Put more concisely, standard readability formulas would not measure adult comprehension in a complex environment [25].

Another caveat needs to be raised, namely the observation that the question of whether or not classic readability formulas are applicable to the legal domain is complicated by the fact that legal texts have multiple audiences and multiple purposes [19, see]. What is at stake then is not just the extent to which a legal

---

[1] It should be noted, however, that readability formulas were never meant as a writing guide, though writing guidelines can be deduced accordingly [21].

text is readable *per se*, but the extent to which it is *readable by its different audiences*. Some hail the potential of 'plain legal language', convinced that "clients and citizens have a better chance of understanding it" [7, p. 186]. Others lament "the flawed methodology and insignificant statistical relevance of the empirical studies often presented to show the benefits of plain English" [3, p. 404]. While there is a suggestion to write for the most vulnerable when deciding which audience of legal texts to appeal to [38], an uncritical and sole focus on readability obscures other issues that need addressing to ensure full access to justice, such as legal representation [3]. As was discussed above, this is particularly pertinent for appellants in the Immigration and Asylum jurisdiction, for whom English is often not a first language, and who have been hard hit by cuts to legal aid funding [6].

2.2 Previous Work Assessing the Readability of Legal Texts

Legal statutes and judicial written decisions have received the particular attention of readability researchers. Martínez and Silva [26], for example, use FRE and average sentence length to measure readability of Brazilian tax law and conclude that understanding the tax code requires highly-educated readers. Martindale, Koch, and Karlinsky [25] investigate how the relationship between content and style complexity impacts comprehension of US tax legislation. They attest low reliability of the Flesch and Flesch–Kincaid formulas for adult texts, as they disagreed on text difficulty ranking of selected sections of US tax code and commentary. The 'Reading Complexity Evaluation Index' – a reader- rather than computer-rated Likert scale covering understanding, wordiness, clarity, and helpfulness – would be a more suited metric. In a similar vein, Alschner et al. [1] develop legislation-specific readability metrics, operationalising relevant plain language recommendations. Their computer-calculated metrics cover lexical, grammatical, stylistic, and structural aspects of legislative text. While the proposed metrics would need tailoring to different jurisdictions and further fine-tuning, the authors are confident that the metrics allow a more nuanced evaluation of statute readability than readability formula scores.

Critiques of readability formulas in general and words of caution against their application to the legal domain in particular notwithstanding (see Sect. 2.1), most reviewed work assessing the readability of judicial decisions interestingly quite happily uses precisely these classic readability formulas, or a combination of them. The FRE, Flesch–Kincaid and SMOG[2] formulas are the most frequently used single metrics for assessing judicial opinion readability [13,22,42]. Based on said scores, these studies find a decrease in opinion readability over time [13], inter- and intra-judge variation [42], and that the type of judicial retention system does not affect clarity of opinion [22]. Another approach is to use several classic readability measures and combine them into one readability index, using factor analysis/principal component analysis [19,30,36]. This index is then used either as a dependent variable (cf. Nelson [30] who finds that, on average, elected

---

[2] Short for 'Simple Measure of Gobbledygok' [see 42].

judges write more readable opinions than their non-elected counterparts[3]), or independent variable (where more readable judgments are more likely to prevail in court [36] or are more likely to be cited as precedent [19]). These studies highlight potentially interesting implications of a (however reliably measured) high/low readability of judicial opinions.

Only one reviewed study uses a custom metric to assess decision readability. Developing the 'Clarity Test' – a structured text assessment based on points for different elements of 'Start', 'Structure', and 'Style' of a judgment – for New Zealand Court of Appeal judgments, Campbell Pearson [8] finds an average increase in test scores with time.[4] The fact that the 'Clarity Test' is to be administered manually, however, poses challenges to automation and scalability.

2.3   Potential Pitfalls of Judicial Analytics

An exploration of readability in legal texts is perhaps the most straightforward use case for the increase in accessibility of published legal texts. As the previous section showed, such an exploration is well possible with the tools of ML and text/data mining. Yet, before jumping into any analysis that is *feasible*, we wish to pause and reflect on what is also *ethical* given the wider questions of judicial independence and public trust in the judiciary inherent in judicial analytics. An increasing interest in data-led legal studies, combined with the availability of relevant datasets and increasing levels of automating in text analysis, has resulted in increasing availability and commercialisation of applications such as predictive modelling of judicial decisions [34] and other more complex use cases. Judicial analytics frequently focuses on profiling and individual performance evaluation of judges, aggregating statistics on a variety of topics, such as average case length/time to completion, likely ruling, biases held by individual judges regarding gender or race, frequency of successful appeals against a judge and the type of language used in the courtroom that the judge is likely to find compelling [27].

Such judicial analytics applications, while powerful and increasingly popular as commercial services, raise ethical and practical concerns. Whilst these applications are not new [27], increased automation means that the costs are greatly reduced and hence broader analyses become financially practical. Wahlstrom et al. [41] remark that ethical problems in data mining arise when the data mined are of a personal nature, identifying privacy concerns and appropriate treatment of inaccurate data as key. Similarly, McGill and Salyzyn [27] identify data quality and limited data coverage as practical concerns, alongside the observation that some areas of law are less susceptible to automated analysis. Profiling may be viewed as invasive. In particular, some applications may involve inference of sensitive personal data.

Challenges of particular relevance to the UK legal context include the risk that an attempt at monitoring and publishing judges' performance may be seen

---

[3] Others do not find an effect of the type of judicial retention on opinion clarity [22].
[4] Note that others find decreasing readability over time [13,42].

– or indeed function – as a destructive attack on judicial independence, whilst only Upper Tribunal decisions are published, probably in part to protect data for appellants, resulting in limited availability of data. There is a risk that information drawn from data analytics, potentially based on inaccurate data or analytical tools, may decrease public trust in the judiciary. As such, this work may be viewed as potentially fuelling destructive critique, which may result in responses ranging from low engagement from judges to legal remedies that significantly limit the scope of work in this area. This risk is not merely theoretical. Following the introduction of statistical analysis tools designed to profile judges into the French market, the French government opted to revise Article 33 of the Justice Reform Act to prohibit data analytics on individual judicial behaviour [5, 27].

2.4   Lessons from the Literature

Our literature review shows four things. Firstly, readability formulas, in particular the FRE, and SMOG formulas, are still widely used in assessing the readability of legal texts, particularly in Anglo-American jurisdictions. The formulas' advantage is that they are easily quantifiable and machine-computable. Secondly, while studies that use classic readability formulas (or a combination of them) report interesting findings, custom metrics might provide more reliable results for the legal domain. It remains to be explored whether the rules-based metrics of Alschner et al. [1] or the 'Clarity' assessment framework of Campbell Pearson [8] are scaleable to jurisdictions other than the ones studied in the respective works. Thirdly, an assessment of legal readability would ideally take into account the different audiences of a given legal text and check comprehension for these various target readers [see approaches in 23, 29], while being mindful of the limitations of readability in ensuring the wider aim of accessible justice. Fourthly, it is important to apply judicial analytics, including in an assessment of readability of judicial decisions, in an ethical and responsible way that preserves both a constructively critical approach and judicial independence.

3   Ethical Judicial Analytics

3.1   Replicating Previous Work

In this section we look at the empirical replication of readability assessments and critical reflection on measures and approach. In a first step towards ethically assessing readability of judicial decisions, we present results of an exploration of written decisions of the UK's UTIAC, calculating FRE and SMOG scores for each of the decisions in the dataset. We were curious to see whether our results would replicate findings from previous studies of written judicial decisions in other Anglo-American jurisdictions. We also wanted to gain insight into the UTIAC decisions' readability over time as assessed by the classic formulas with a view to refining the assessment further in future work.

3.2   Dataset and Analysis

To build the corpus, we downloaded decision files from the UTIAC decision database (https://tribunalsdecisions.service.gov.uk/utiac) for all files dated between March 2000 and March 2021, using a scraper built in Python.[5] Decisions are available in both Word and PDF files. From the Word files, plain text was extracted and each decision file saved as a txt-file. The total of 33 627 files were read by a Python programme to extract the year information (using regex). The year information obtained from this procedure was compared against dates extracted from within document headers and the average difference was less than one year (mean $= -0.052$, std $= 0.756$). The readability measures FRE and SMOG were calculated using the 'readability project' (available at: https://pypi.org/project/readability/). To comply with the optimal input format for this application, core text was extracted from the plain text files (including only the 'reasons' sections but excluding headers and preliminaries) which was then tokenized using the 'ucto' tokenizer (available at: https://languagemachines.github.io/ucto/). Discarding 883 files where no core text could be extracted resulted in a corpus of a total of 32 744 decision files. The analysed dataset has decisions from the years 2000 to 2021, with the majority of cases written between 2014 and 2019 (see Fig. 1).

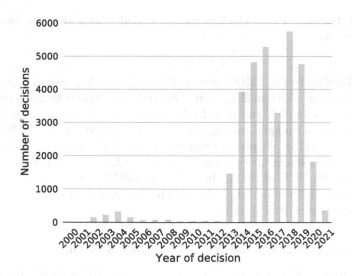

Fig. 1. Number of decisions per year

3.3   Results

Flesch Reading Ease. We first present results for FRE scores. Figure 2 shows that average FRE scores range from 53.65 (in 2000) to 63.13 (in 2018), with

---

[5] Checking the *robots.txt*-file revealed no restrictions on such scraping activity.

the average across all years being at 62.29 (std = 7.27). Pearson's r shows no significant or meaningful correlation between time (years) and FRE scores ($r = 0.079$, $p = 6.134$). A variation can be seen in the range of FRE scores which increases visibly for the years 2013 onward, although part of that may be due to the fact that a larger number of case files were published during those years (Fig. 1).

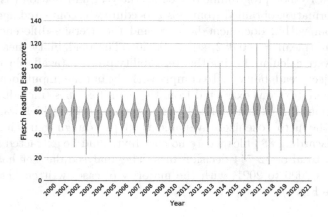

Fig. 2. Distribution of Flesch Reading Ease scores (all years). Higher values indicate higher readability.

SMOG. Turning to the SMOG scores, Fig. 3 shows that averages lie between 13.58 (in 2015) and 15.02 (in 2012), with the majority of years showing an average SMOG score of around 14 (mean = 13.74, std = 1.32). Again, Pearson's r shows no significant or meaningful correlation between time (years) and SMOG scores ($r = 0.009$, $p = 0.113$). We note an increase in the range between minimum and maximum SMOG scores for the years 2014 onward, though this trend is not as clear as with the FRE scores as the range of SMOG scores for the years 2002 and 2003 are equally quite large. Again, the unequal distribution of cases per year should be taken into account.

3.4 Interpretation and Critical Discussion of Results

The FRE scores can be interpreted to mean that the US grade levels associated with this readability measure are grades 8/9, 'plain English', to grades 11/12, meaning the text is assessed as 'fairly difficult to read'. The fact that some decisions were assessed as 'easily understood by 13- to 15-year-old students' (for FRE scores between 70 and 60) is somewhat surprising and perhaps even unexpected as previous works have found that judicial writing was more difficult to read (see Sect. 2.2; although even the highest average scores are close to 60 and therefore to grade levels 11/12). The SMOG score averages of around 14 indicate College-level difficulty. This is somewhat higher than what the FRE scores would suggest and similar to what was found by Whalen [42] where averages are reported to vary between SMOG scores of 13 and 14.5. Neither FRE nor SMOG scores seem to follow any temporal trends, while previous work has found increased readability difficulty of judicial decisions over time [13,42]. Another feature in the data is different to what was previously observed, namely the increasing range of the distribution of scores for each year.

The observed results could be brought about by a number of factors. The first set of factors is dataset-related: one the one hand, the dataset is skewed towards more recent years, with higher numbers of published decisions from 2014 onward (see Fig. 1), so a greater range of scores could simply be due to greater volumes of decisions. On the other hand, the increasing range for both FRE and SMOG scores could suggest a growing variation between a) different types of written decisions, and b) different judges. Disentangling these differences (e.g. controlling for length of decision and/ or identifying and mitigating for extreme values) and exploring such possible distinctions further could be in scope for future work.

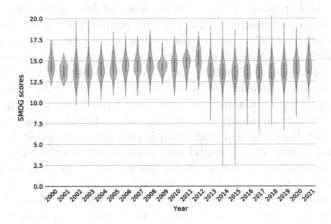

Fig. 3. Distribution of SMOG scores (all years). Higher values indicate lower readability.

The second set of factors are uncontrolled extraneous factors relating to the area of law and the (geographical) jurisdiction that limit the comparability of the results presented. For example, it could be that because previous literature has studied different areas of law (e.g. tax law, criminal law; [13,30]), and/ or different types of courts (mainly supreme courts; [19,22,42]), that these correlate with case complexity and therefore complexity of written decisions which in turn influences readability results. It might be that judges hearing immigration and asylum appeal are more aware of the need to write readable decisions because judicial training and/or frequently dealing with vulnerable appellants and parties for whom English is not a first language sensitises them to this need. The wider culture in the jurisdiction studied might also influence writing style and readability more generally. Rather than being generalisable to other jurisdictions and/or other areas of law, our study of readability of UK UTIAC decisions adds a contextualised piece to the puzzle of understanding readability of judicial written decisions.

3.5 Addressing Limitations of Standard Readability Formulas Through the Use of ML Approaches

Beyond the critical evaluation of specific results, reflections seem due on the analysis approach itself that produced the results. The critique directed at readability formulas both generally and for the legal domain specifically has been outlined in Sect. 2 and it is clear that the calculation and interpretation of standard readability metrics should be treated with caution. On the one hand, they might be unreliable in an application to complex texts. Custom metrics that take proper account of document structure and specific features, such as the quotation of legislation and case law, might be better suited [e.g. 1,8]. More advanced methods making use of NLP models and ML approaches could offer even more refined and reliable results [cf. 40]. Among the approaches proposed to better predict readability are the use of support vector machines [20,39], the inclusion of additional cohesion, coherence, and discourse relations measures [33], letter and word ngrams [12], and the development of theory-driven NLP models of human text comprehension and reading speed [9,10]. These studies suggest that combining classic readability formulas with NLP-derived measures and ML methods improve the reliability and accuracy of readability measures.

On the other hand, human evaluation is an important aspect in evaluating and validating approaches to readability assessment. Most of the above cited studies also involve an aspect of reader assessment of text readability. Such evaluation is vital to validate ML applications – with the caveat that reader-level factors such as literacy levels need to be taken into account to ensure texts classified as easier to read are indeed more easily accessible by all rather than aiding the already highly literate [35]. This harks back to the point on the importance of audience. We need to ask critically whether key stakeholder groups – here: appellants, lawyers, judges – have been involved in an assessment of readability (and they have not been in this study). Even if the scores suggest a decision can be 'easily understood' by teenage students, can it be as easily understood by someone whose first language is not English? Can a reader quickly grasp the outcome of the decision, or the relevant law cited therein? Gathering relevant stakeholder input would support suitable customisation of a readability assessment, as well as put its limitations into clearer focus [see 3], especially for a jurisdiction where the law is particularly complex and appellants are often particularly vulnerable.

3.6 Ethical Considerations in Judicial Analytics

Contemplating the bigger picture, ethical considerations of ML and text/data mining approaches analysing judicial output are important on at least two levels: at the technical application, and the substantive levels, meaning the real-world context within which analytics are applied. In terms of the former, data analytics should ideally be ethically assessed throughout their life cycle, including at the problem definition, data understanding and preparation, modelling, validation, and application stages [31]. Transparency, critical interpretation of results, explanation of underlying assumptions and qualifying limitations, and appropriate validation of methods and results that ensure fairness and replicability of approach are all essential in doing judicial analytics ethically and to an appropriate scientific standard [31]. Clearly identifying the assumptions and limitations underlying an approach supports accountability of the analytical work itself.

On the substantive level – the real-world context of the judicial sphere – the potential from social good from an analysis of readily machine-computable information (increased transparency, accountability and awareness-raising) stands in sharp contrast to the potential for harm (impeding judicial independence, undesirable strategic behaviour of stakeholders, inaccurate data and results; [27]). To some extent, finding an appropriate balance for judicial analytics (here applied to an assessment of readability of judicial decisions) may be approached similarly to analogous tasks in other fields. Compliance with relevant legislation in the respective jurisdiction is vital, and as the French example shows (see Sect. 2.3), these may vary significantly. Where judicial analytics involve collection of data about identifiable living individuals, such as judges or appellants, compliance with data protection legislation is equally key. Inaccuracy and ambiguity of data and results can be mitigated by ethical approaches to data analytics (cf. above).

Beyond compliance with relevant legislation and ethical implementation of analytics approaches, we identify the following steps as recommendations for future work: establishment and regular review of a solid ethics framework for judicial analytics applications, in readability and elsewhere; reference to available best practice guidance and frameworks, such as the 'European Ethical Charter on the Use of Artificial Intelligence (AI) in Judicial Systems and Their Environment' [16], the Legal and Privacy Framework [37], the UK Anonymisation Network guidelines [17] and the Association of Internet Researchers' ethical framework [2]; involvement of relevant stakeholders at each stage of the process; and appropriate privacy-by-design [18] engineering principles, notably the use of impact assessments to identify, track and mitigate risks.

By ensuring ethical considerations are given due space and place both within the life cycle of analytics approaches and within the wider context of their application, ML and text/data mining can be leveraged responsibly. Applications – be it an assessment of readability or a different task – that commit to ethical production and interpretation of results, transparent methods, and careful consideration of key stakeholders involved can harness the social good from judicial analytics. It can offer a constructive critique based on an accepted instrument for the review of and reflection on judicial practice.

4 Conclusions: Developing Ethical Judicial Analytics in Service of the Stakeholders of the Legal System

Motivated by the broader issues of open justice and access to justice, we explore the ethical application of judicial analytics through the lens of an assessment of readability of written judicial decisions of the UK Upper Tribunal Immigration and Asylum Chamber. Using a corpus of 32744 UTIAC decisions from the years 2000 to 2021, we calculate classic readability measures (Flesch Reading Ease, SMOG). Contrary to previous studies, our results indicate no trend of either increasing or decreasing readability over time, but show an increasing spread of scores with time. While slightly lower for FRE scores, grade levels associated with SMOG are similar to those reported in previous studies and indicate, on average, College-level difficulty for the texts in our dataset.

We situate our study within previous research on readability in the legal domain and current use cases for judicial analytics. Legal readability research ranges from applications of classic readability formulas to custom-made metrics. The premise that drives this research is that readable legal texts contribute to access to justice, which is, arguably, particularly pertinent for appellants in the Immigration and Asylum system. At the same time, a sole focus on readability might obfuscate other barriers to actively understanding and participating in the appeals process, and as such we highlight the works of scholars who maintain that legal representation remains key to accessible justice [3, 6].

An analysis of readability of judicial decisions using the tools of ML and text/ data mining also sits within the broader context of judicial analytics, which has expanded in recent years due to an increased accessibility of published legal texts. Such applications raise ethical and practical concerns. Used inappropriately, judicial analytics might hamper rather than bolster public trust in the judiciary and/or be seen to unduly attack judicial independence.

To ensure judicial analytics can serve – meet the needs of and be accepted by – the stakeholders of the legal system, including judges, we suggest that the development of judicial analytics tools can benefit significantly from an understanding of the context in which judges operate and the tools with which they work. Future work could take an assessment of readability as its starting point and expand it to apply custom metrics, include stakeholder input, and account for readers for whom English is not a first language. Used responsibly and with due regard to ethical guidelines as well as input from the stakeholders concerned, judicial analytics can serve as a tool set to support error detection and recovery, reinforce materials from judicial training or provide judges with an opportunity to re-frame, review and reflect on their work so they are optimally supported to administer accessible justice.

References

1. Alschner, W., D'Alimonte, D., Giuga, G.C., Gadbois, S.: Plain language assessment of statutes. In: Legal Knowledge and Information Systems: Proceedings of the 33rd JURIX Annual Conference, pp. 207–2010. IOS Press (2020). http://ebooks.iospress.nl/ISBN/978-1-64368-049-1
2. AoIR: The association of internet researchers ethics framework (2019). https://aoir.org/ethics/
3. Assy, R.: Can the law speak directly to its subjects? The limitation of plain language. J. Law Soc. **38**(3), 376–404 (2011). https://doi.org/10.1111/j.1467-6478.2011.00549.x
4. George Benjamin, R.: Reconstructing readability: recent developments and recommendations in the analysis of text difficulty. Educ. Psychol. Rev. **24**(1), 63–88 (2012). ISSN 1573-336X. https://doi.org/10.1007/s10648-011-9181-8
5. Bufithis, G.: Understanding the French ban on judicial analytics (2019). https://www.gregorybufithis.com/2019/06/09/understanding-the-french-ban-on-judicial-analytics/
6. Burridge, A., Gill, N.: Conveyor-belt justice: precarity, access to justice, and uneven geographies of legal aid in UK asylum appeals. Antipode **49**(1), 23–42 (2017). https://doi.org/10.1111/anti.12258
7. Butt, P.: The assumptions behind plain legal language. Hong Kong LJ **32**, 173 (2002)
8. Campbell Pearson, W.: Clarity in the Court of Appeal: measuring the readability of judgments. Bachelor thesis, law, University of Otago (2013)
9. Crossley, S.A., Skalicky, S., Dascalu, M., McNamara, D.S., Kyle, K.: Predicting text comprehension, processing, and familiarity in adult readers: new approaches to readability formulas. Discourse Process. **54**(5–6), 340–359 (2017). https://doi.org/10.1080/0163853X.2017.1296264
10. Crossley, S.A., Skalicky, S., Dascalu, M.: Moving beyond classic readability formulas: new methods and new models. J. Res. Read. **42**(3–4), 541–561 (2019). https://doi.org/10.1111/1467-9817.12283
11. Curtotti, M., McCreath, E.: Right to access implies right to know: an open online platform for research on the readability of law. J. Open Access Law **1**(1), 1–56 (2013)
12. Curtotti, M., McCreath, E., Bruce, T., Frug, S., Weibel, W., Ceynowa, N.: Machine learning for readability of legislative sentences. In: Proceedings of the 15th International Conference on Artificial Intelligence and Law, ICAIL 2015, New York, NY, USA, pp. 53–62, 2015. Association for Computing Machinery. ISBN 9781450335225. https://doi.org/10.1145/2746090.2746095
13. Daily, C.M., Dorsey, R.W., Kumar, G.: Readability of tax court opinions. In: Stock, T. (ed.) Advances in Taxation, vol. 19, pp. 171–183. Emerald Group Publishing Limited (2010). https://doi.org/10.1108/S1058-7497(2010)0000019009
14. Dale, E., Chall, J.S.: The concept of readability. Element. Eng. **26**(1), 19–26 (1949). ISSN 00135968. http://www.jstor.org/stable/41383594
15. Duffy, T.M.: Readability formulas: what's the use? In: Duffy, T.M., Waller, R. (eds.) Designing Usable Texts, chapter 6, pp. 113–143. Academic Press (1985). ISBN 978-0-12-223260-2. https://doi.org/10.1016/B978-0-12-223260-2.50011-6
16. European Commission for the Efficiency of Justice (CEPEJ): Cepej European ethical charter on the use of artificial intelligence (AI) in judicial systems and their environment (2019)

17. Elliot, M., Mackey, E., O'Hara, K.: The anonymisation decision-making framework 2nd edn. European practitioners' guide. UKAN (2020)
18. Everson, E.: Privacy by design: taking ctrl of big data. Cleveland State Law Rev. **65**, 27 (2017)
19. Fix, M.P., Fairbanks, B.R.: The effect of opinion readability on the impact of U.S. supreme court precedents in state high courts. Soc. Sci. Q. **101**(2), 811–824 (2020). https://doi.org/10.1111/ssqu.12752
20. François, T., Miltsakaki, E.: Do NLP and machine learning improve traditional readability formulas? In: Proceedings of the First Workshop on Predicting and Improving Text Readability for target reader populations, Montréal, Canada, pp. 49–57, June 2012. Association for Computational Linguistics (2012)
21. Fry, E.B.: Writeability: the principles of writing for increased comprehension. In: Zakaluk, B.L., Samuals, S.J. (eds.) Readability: Its Past, Present, and Future, chapter 5, Newark, Delaware, pp. 77–97. International Reading Association (1988)
22. Goelzhauser, G., Cann, D.M.: Judicial independence and opinion clarity on state supreme courts. State Politics Pol. Q. **14**(2), 123–141 (2014). https://doi.org/10.1177/1532440013520241
23. Horton, B.G., Thompson, L.R.: Jury instructions: are they too complicated for jurors to understand? Commun. Law Rev. **4**, 1–8 (2002)
24. Klare, G.R.: Assessing readability. Read. Res. Q. **10**(1), 62–102 (1974). ISSN 00340553. http://www.jstor.org/stable/747086
25. Martindale, B.C., Koch, B.S., Karlinsky, S.S.: Tax law complexity: the impact of style. J. Bus. Commun. (1973) **29**(4), 383–400 (1992). https://doi.org/10.1177/002194369202900405
26. Martínez, A., da Silva, R.: Tax law readability and tax complexity (2019)
27. McGill, J., Salyzyn, A.: Judging by numbers: how will judicial analytics impact the justice system and its stakeholders? Working paper, Ottawa Faculty of Law (2020)
28. Jerry McHale, M.: What does "access to justice" mean? UVic Ace (2016). http://www.uvicace.com/blog/2016/2/2/what-does-access-to-justice-mean
29. Mindlin, M.: Is plain language better a comparative readability study of court forms. Scribes J. Legal Writ. **10**, 55–66 (2005)
30. Nelson, M.N.: Elections and explanations: judicial retention and the readability of judicial opinions (2013). http://mjnelson.wustl.edu/papers/NelsonReadabilityAugust2013.pdf
31. Petrozzino, C.: Big data analytics: ethical considerations make a difference. Scitech Lawyer **16**(3), 14–21 (2020)
32. Pikulski, J.J.: Readability. Houghton Mifflin, Boston (2002)
33. Pitler, E., Nenkova, A.: Revisiting readability: a unified framework for predicting text quality. In: Proceedings of the Conference on Empirical Methods in Natural Language Processing, EMNLP 2008, USA, pp. 186–195. Association for Computational Linguistics (2008)
34. Samaha, A.M.: Judicial transparency in an age of prediction symposium: the future of judicial transparency - panel one: transparent virtues. Villanova Law Rev. **53**, 829 (2008)
35. Sikkema, T.: Does plain language only benefit the higher literate? avoiding the Matthew-effect in plain language revisions. Clarity J. **80**, 19–22 (2019). ISSN 2378-2056
36. Spencer, S.B., Feldman, A.: Words count: the empirical relationship between brief writing and summary judgment success. Legal Writ. J. Legal Writ. Inst. **22**, 61–108 (2018)

37. Stalla-Bourdillon, S., Knight, A.: Legal and privacy toolkit v1.0 (2017)
38. Sullivan, R.: The promise of plain language drafting. McGill LJ **47**, 97 (2001)
39. Sung, Y.-T., Chen, J.-L., Cha, J.-H., Tseng, H.-C., Chang, T.-H., Chang, K.-E.: Constructing and validating readability models: the method of integrating multi-level linguistic features with machine learning. Behav. Res. Methods **47**(2), 340–354 (2014). https://doi.org/10.3758/s13428-014-0459-x
40. Todirascu, A., François, T., Gala, N., Fairon, C., Ligozat, A.-L., Bernhard, D.: Coherence and cohesion for the assessment of text readability. In: Proceedings of 10th International Workshop on Natural Language Processing and Cognitive Science (NLPCS 2013), Marseille, France, pp. 11–19, October 2013. https://hal.archives-ouvertes.fr/hal-00860796
41. Wahlstrom, K., Roddick, J.F., Sarre, R., Estivill-Castro, V., deVries, D.: On the ethical and legal implications of data mining. School of Informatics and Engineering Flinders University (2006)
42. Whalen, R.: Judicial gobbledygook: the readability of Supreme Court writing. Yale Law J. Forum **125**(19), 200–211 (2015)
43. Williams, C.: Changing with the times: the evolution of plain language in the legal sphere. Revista Alicantina de Estudios Ingleses **28**, 183–203 (2015). https://doi.org/10.14198/raei.2015.28.10

A Comparison of Classification Methods Applied to Legal Text Data

Diógenes Carlos Araújo$^{(\boxtimes)}$, Alexandre Lima$^{(\boxtimes)}$, João Pedro Lima$^{(\boxtimes)}$, and José Alfredo Costa$^{(\boxtimes)}$

Universidade Federal do Rio Grande do Norte, Avenue Senador Salgado Filho 3000, Natal, Brazil

Abstract. The Brazilian judicial system is currently one of the largest in the world with more than 77 million legal cases awaiting decision. The use of machine learning could help to improve celerity through text classification. This paper aims to compare some supervised machine processing techniques. TF-IDF text representation was used. The paper discusses comparison among classification methods such as Random Forest, Adaboost using decision trees, Support Vector Machine, K-Nearest Neighbors, Naive Bayes and Multilayer Perceptron. The data set consists of 30,000 documents distributed among ten classes, which represent possible procedural movements resulting from court decisions. The classification results are quite satisfactory since some techniques were able to overcome a f1-score of 90%.

Keywords: Comparative · Machine learning · Natural language processing · Judicial · Law

1 Introduction

The world is facing the digital transformation in accelerated steps. Since computer revolution, which enabled information handling, the size and complexity of data sets is ever increasing. Digitalization has transformed economies and lives. The advances in computer and electronic instrumentation technologies and decreasingly cost of memory storage systems have been enabling large amounts of data to be available in many business, scientific, military and industrial applications. Such is the case of Judicial Systems. Some recent advances, such as Graphics Processing Unit wide usage had fastened the training of complex neural network models.

As said for Bhatt [2], innovation needs to have public value and be shaped to bring everyone into the digital age. Brazilian Court System is large and complex, with almost 80 million unconcluded cases [8]. Due to the strong judicial digitalization policy, most of these cases are processed entirely in a digital way, e.g., on the PJe platform, which is used by many Brazilian Courts. The application of machine learning techniques to judiciary system is highly desirable given the size and complexity of unstructured and unlabeled legal texts. The general idea is to

© Springer Nature Switzerland AG 2021
G. Marreiros et al. (Eds.): EPIA 2021, LNAI 12981, pp. 68–80, 2021.
https://doi.org/10.1007/978-3-030-86230-5_6

automatize some steps in the process, such as repetitive tasks, aiming the judicial effectiveness and celerity. Brazil already counts on various projects targeting the use of Artificial Intelligences (AI) in justice, with applications focusing on automatization and better information retrieval. Projects like Sinapses platform could lead to robust and easy to use artificial intelligence models [7]. Sinapses was initially developed by Court of Justice of Rondônia (TJRO) in collaboration with National Council of Justice (CNJ) with goals including to create a collaborative environment, which can condense and share machine learning models developed in several Brazillian courts. Another initiative is the Victor project from the Supreme Federal Court (STF), which was developed aiming machine learning models to analyze the legal appeal received by the STF in terms of general repercussion themes [13].

This paper aims to compare some classification methods applied to legal datasets, obtained from Court of Justice of Rio Grande do Norte (TJRN). The task relies on classification of movements for lawsuit cases based on its judicial sentence. Ten classes with 3,000 texts each were used, in a total of 30,000 sentences. The algorithms used in this study were Support Vector Machine (SVM), Random Forest (RF), Adaboost (AB), K-Nearest Neighbors (KNN), Naive Bayes (NB) and Multilayer Perceptron (MLP). The analysis is carried out on metrics of classification accuracy, interpretability and computational processing speed. The remainder of the paper is organized as follows. Section 2 describes related studies. Section 3 presents some theoretical background. Methodologies are presented in Sect. 4 and results and discussions are described in Sect. 5. Finally, Sect. 6 summarizes the paper with conclusions.

2   Related Work

The task of text classification aims to assign a label, or a class, to some piece of text (word, token, sentence or document). This simple objective enables the task to be applied on a broad range of natural language processing (NLP) applications like part-of-speech tagging, named entity recognition, topic assignment and sentiment analysis. In the legal domain, several works leverage text classification from which we cite a few.

About comparing multiple machine learning classifiers in law's texts, we have Neil [15] that used classifiers to assign the deontic modality (obligation, prohibition or permission) of sentences in regulatory texts from the financial domain, achieving F1 score values above 80%.

Another example is Lippi [12] that developed Claudette, a web application to automatically detect potential unconstitutional clauses in online terms of services. To achieve that, they experimented with several machine learning models (SVMs, Long short-term memory networks - LSTM, Convolutional neural networks - CNN and Hidden Markov models) and features (n-grams, part-of-speech tags, grammatical trees and word embeddings) to detect and classify such kinds of sentences.

An example of document classification is described by Chalkidis [6] which tackled the task of extreme multi-label classification (i.e., the tagging of documents with labels from a huge label set) upon documents of European Union legislation. They experimented with logistic regression and eight deep learning models, two of which were designed to deal with zero-shot learning tasks.

Howe [10] explored various machine learning models (SVM, CNN, ULMFit and pre-trained BERT) for classifying judgments into 31 legal areas. They evaluated the models' performance with three metrics (precision, F1 score and recall) and over three portions of the dataset (10%, 50% and 100%). The results were mixed, with the best models varying according to the tested scenario.

Bertalan [1], compares machine learning models (Logistic Regression, Latent Dirichlet Allocation, KNN, Regression Trees, Gaussian Naive Bayes and SVM) to predict the outcome of a lawsuit between Acquitted or Conviction, based on the analysis of sentence texts. The predictions are made for two specific cases of Simple Homicide and Active Corruption and the data was collected from the Judicial Court of São Paulo. Models are obtained through accuracy, precision, recall and F1-Score.

3 Theoretical Basis

3.1 Artificial Neural Networks

Artificial neurons were inspired by the biological processes that scientists were able to observe in the brain back in the 50s. An artificial neural network is composed of a group of interconnected artificial neurons and it uses a mathematical model for processing information through the modeling of complex nonlinear relationships between input variables without other information previously received. These networks are adaptable systems, where the flow of information changes its structure. Considered as a more conventional representation of artificial neural networks, the Multilayer Perceptron (MLP) is divided into three parts: input neurons (input layer), hidden neurons (hidden layer) and output neurons (output layer) [18].

3.2 Dropout

Dropout is a technique for regulating the neural network, capable of preventing overfitting and making it possible to combine several different architecture networks efficiently. The term "dropout" refers to removing some neurons temporarily, resulting in a network as shown in the Fig. 1. The choice of which neurons will be removed is made at random. A new network is drawn for each stage of the training. At the time of the test, the complete network is used with a correction factor so that the values are close to the training period [19].

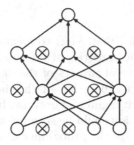

Fig. 1. Representation of the dropout function

3.3　Support Vector Machine

The SVM algorithm aims to find a hyperplane that divides space into the N dimensions of the data to differentiate all classes. There are several plans that can separate these classes and the goal is to find the plan that maximizes the distance between the border and the classes. This technique was proposed by Cortes [9]. For our example we will use the core as a radial basis function (RBF).

3.4　K-Nearest Neighbors

KNN is a memory-based method. The learning of memory-based algorithms consists only of storing training data. When a case needs to be tested, the training set is retrieved from memory for classification to be performed. A disadvantage with these types of algorithms is that their computational cost can be very high dependent on the amount of training data. Another negative point is that all attributes are considered in the classification, instead of considering only the most important ones [14]. Among the classification algorithms, KNN is one of the simplest and one of the best known for always obtaining good accuracy. It is considered a lazy learner because the algorithm waits for a query to generalize the model [5].

3.5　Naive Bayes

The Naive Bayes is a probabilistic classifier based on the application of the Bayes theorem, assuming that the variables are independent of each other (naive). For our study we will use the multinomial naive bayes, since we will use the TF-IDF to vectorize the text. With a multinomial event model, samples (feature vectors) represent the frequencies which certain events have been generated by a multinomial $(p_1, \ldots, p_n)$ where p_i is the probability that event i occurs (or K such multinomials in the multiclass case). A feature vector $x = (x_1, \ldots, x_n)$ is then a histogram, with x_i counting the number of times events i observed in a particular instance [17].

3.6 Decision Tree

The decision tree is a classifier that seeks to create a tree capable of dividing the data correctly through the statistics of information gain or purity between classes. For this, it creates several subsets of the data in a recursive way, in an attempt to obtain the perfect separation of the data. There are two popular techniques for calculating purity: gini and entropy. In this work we will use only entropy and the entropy equation could be seen below, with C being the possible classes, D being the database, p_i the probability of the element being of class i.

$$Entropy(D) = \sum_{i=1}^{C} p_i \log_2 p_i \qquad (1)$$

The information gain for the C4.5 algorithm that is used in this work will be obtained by the equation below, which will measure the difference between the entropy of the new subset in relation to the old one. This model was proposed by Quinlan [16] and is an improvement on the ID3 algorithm also developed by him.

$$IG(D, F) = Entropy(D) - \sum_{i=1} \frac{|D_i|}{|D|} Entropy(D_i) \qquad (2)$$

3.7 Random Forest

This estimator was presented by Breiman [4], which has demonstrated interesting properties and applications of the method. As with bagging, all bootstrap samples are equally distributed. The random forest classifier resembles bagging when considering different bootstrap samples for each classification tree. The crucial difference is due to the random selection of the predictor variables for the C4.5 algorithm [16].

The bias of the aggregate tree model will be equivalent to that observed in each tree. Thus, the random forest model aims to maintain the low bias of each individual classifier, as it reduces the variance. The procedure adds a step to the bagging algorithm. The variables that will be used to adjust C4.5 are selected randomly in each iteration. After being trained, the model will make a vote among the N trees to carry out the classification.

3.8 Adaboost

The adaboost of a decision tree will boost the algorithm, instead of choosing samples and random variables so that the trees are independent, it will do Boosting, which consists of adding weights to classes with a higher error rate in order to achieve a better model. The algorithm initially receives equal weights for all classes, then updates the weights using the exponential function.

In summary, Random Forest combines several trees with a high classification rate in parallel with low bias and high variance, while Adaboost combines several trees with low precision in a sequential manner with low variance.

3.9   Term Frequency - Inverse Document Frequency

TF-IDF (Term Frequency - Inverse Document Frequency) is a statistical metric widely utilized in information retrieval and data mining [11] as a way to assess the importance of words in a collection of texts. The importance of a word grows in proportion to the number of times the word appears in the text, but inversely by the frequency of the word in the collection of files.

TF-IDF is composed of the multiplication of two terms, which the first is the normalized term frequency (TF), calculated as the number of times the word appears in the document divided by the total words in that document. The second term is the inverse of the document frequency (IDF), computed as the logarithm of the number of documents in the collection divided by the number of documents in which that specific term appears.

4   Methodology

4.1   Type of Study

This work will perform a comparison between machine learning models in classifying legal textual data. Due to the confidentiality of the data it will not be possible to share the raw data. Instead, it is available a preprocessed version of it at Dataset_clear.csv[1] on which it has been removed names, lawsuits codes and personal identification numbers. The comparison between models will be made by observing the f1-score of each algorithm, the processing time and interpretability.

4.2   Dataset

The database was obtained from the database from TJRN and it refers to the lawsuit sentences which were divided according to the Management System of Unified Procedural Tables for each type of the workflow. In the experiment, we deal with ten selected classes (i.e., types of movements), each one consisting of three thousand samples. These classes are shown in Table 1, whose the mid column column shows the Portuguese word (expression) for the classes and the right one presents their English translation.

In order to clear up the concepts related to the classes, the following are adopted: (i) Class 196 - it is related to a sentence that finishes the trial or its execution. (ii) Class 198 - the judge accepted to review his own verdict due to a claim of absence, contradiction, clarification or even a formal error; (iii) Class 200 - the judge refused to review his own sentence since there's no reason related to Class 198 causes; (iv) 219 Class - the sentence full-fledges the claim; (v) Class 220 - the Court of Justice disclaimed the appeal; (vi) Class 339 - the judge granted a preliminary injunction; (vii) Class 458 - the lawsuit was abandoned

---

[1] https://raw.githubusercontent.com/dcada/machine-learning-text-law-portuguese/main/data_clear.csv.

Table 1. Selected types of movements that can be assigned to a lawsuit sentence.

Label	Name	Translation
196	*Extinção da execução ou do cumprimento da sentença*	Dismissal or judgement enforcement
198	*Acolhimento de Embargos de Declaração*	Acceptance of clarification motion
200	*Não Acolhimento de Embargos de Declaração*	Not acceptance of clarification motion
219	*Procedência*	Acceptance
220	*Improcedência*	Claim dismissed
339	*Liminar*	Preliminary injunction
458	*Abandono de Causa*	Abandonment of lawsuit
461	*Ausência das condições da ação*	Absence of condition for lawsuit
463	*Desistência*	Withdrawal
785	*Antecipação de tutela*	Early judicial decision

by the plaintiff for over 30 (thirty) days; (viii) Class 461 - the lawsuit conditions weren't fulfilled; (ix) Class 463 - the plaintiff renounced his undertaken claim; and (x) Class 785 - an early access to preliminary decision was granted.

4.3 Evaluation Measures

Given the various techniques pertaining to the machine learning field, the classification task consists of building a classifier model using known data in order to determine the class value for unlabeled instances. In order to contrast divergences and similarities among the utilized models, metrics and criterias were defined so that subsequent model development, performance and other additional aspects are analyzed. Some of these criteria, if not the most important ones, are set out below.

- **F1-Score:** It measures the ability the model to classify new instances correctly without recall.
- **Speed:** The computational processing time related to training and the use of the model (prediction).
- **Interpretability:** It refers to the condition of a model to be understandable either because they have a simple mathematical expression or because their representation allows users to understand their mathematical expression, like linear models and decision trees [3].

The f1-score is a harmonic average between precision and recall. The confusion matrix will also be used to observe which are the classes that the model has more difficulty in classifying. For the speed we will measure the training time and the prediction time of the model. The interpretability will be evaluated according to the possibility of an audit, an aspect that depends entirely on the nature of the model.

4.4 Machine Learning Pipeline

The pipeline comprises three stages: data pre-processing, data-processing and model evaluation. We adopted the Python programming language and nltk, scikit-learn and Tensorflow libraries.

Data Pre-processing. Data collection was carried out directly to the TJRN's database by court's employees, who extracted some examples at random, based on the movement code, from which files of the type .txt were obtained with the judicial sentences. With this data, we leveraged regular expressions to remove all characters that are not A-Z letters and to convert all letters to lowercase.

After that, the stopwords, that are words that do not add meaning to the text, were removed. The Portuguese applied stopwords list was the standard one in the nltk library.

Afterwards, the TF-IDF technique was applied to transform the texts into sparse vectors. It was adopted a minimum document frequency of 5% and a maximum of 90%, that is, the vocabulary will have the composition of words that appear in less than 90% of documents and more than 5%. To do this, the scikit learn library was used. The preprocessing code is available at Preprocessing.ipynb[2]. This resulted in a vocabulary of 850 words. Others techniques such as BERT and embeddings were tested but as no significant gain was observed and due to their computational cost, we decided to utilize just the TF-IDF vectors.

Data Processing. Data processing can be divided into four stages. The first stage is the data importing, responsible for reading the TF-IDF vectors and their labels so that it is possible to use them to train the models. The second stage is the division of the data, splitting the information in a training set and a testing set, with a ratio of 20% of the data for testing and 80% for training. This step is important to ensure that the testing and training are carried out with different data.

In the third stage, 6 different models were created: Random Forest, Adaboost based on the Decision Tree, Support Vector Machine, K-Nearest Neighbors, Naive Bayes and Multilayer Perceptron. The random forest parameters are: number of estimators: 100, criterion: entropy, maximum depth: 20, minimum sample for a division: 2, minimum sample per leaf: 1. For the Adaboost model the chosen parameters are: base estimator: Decision tree, criterion: entropy, divisor: best,

---

[2] https://raw.githubusercontent.com/dcada/machine-learning-text-law-portuguese/main/PreProcessing.ipynb.

maximum depth: 20, minimum sample for a division: 2, minimum sample per leaf: 1, number of estimators: 50.

The support vector machine has as parameters: regularization (C): 1, kernel: 'rbf', γ: 'scale'. K-nearest neighbors has the following parameters: number of neighbors: 5, weights: uniform. Naive bayes with α equals to 1. The MLP network is composed of hidden layers with relu as activation function and an output layer with softmax function. Dropout was applied in three of the hidden with a forgetting rate of 40%. The Adam optimizer with a learning rate of 0.002 was used as a function of cross entropy loss by sparse category. More details are presented in Table 2.

The fourth stage is to conduct the training using the training data. The jupyter notebook with the implementation of all machine learning models is available at Processing.ipynb[3]. All models with the exception of the neural network were implemented using scikit learn and the neural network was implemented in tensorflow.

Model Evaluation. In this stage, the confusion matrix will be generated and the metrics will be calculated from the test set.

Table 2. Multilayer perceptron structure

Layer	Number of neurons or dropout percentage	Type
First	850	Input
Second	400	Dense
Third	40%	Dropout
Fourth	160	Dense
Fifth	40%	Dropout
Sixth	120	Dense
Seventh	40%	Dropout
Eighth	60	Dense
Ninth	30	Dense
Tenth	10	Output

5   Results

The results presented below will be the best after five attempts of each algorithm. Our goal is to determine the best method for applying automated document classification to legal texts with the hope of facilitating legal experts in their classification of court documents. Besides the comparison among the achieved

---

[3] https://raw.githubusercontent.com/dcada/machine-learning-text-law-portuguese/main/Processing.ipynb.

metrics, we are also concerned with the interpretability of the models since there is a regulation about the utilization of AI in Brazilian legal system (CNJ resolution Nº 332). We are interested in the models' computational performance as well and so we compare their prediction and training times. As shown in the Table 3 some models got almost the same result. The ranking of f1-score is SVM, Random Forest draw with Adaboost, followed by MLP, Naive Bayes and KNN.

Table 3. F1-score results

Model	F1-score
Support Vector Machine	96.4%
Random Forest	95.1%
Adaboost	95.1%
Multilayer Perceptron	94.6%
K-Nearest Neighbors	92.2%
Naive Bayes	87.0%

Table 4 shows SVM performance on individual classes. The f1-scores has minimum of 94% and maximum of 98%, showing that the model was capable of distinguish the classes correctly. The worst classification for SVM was in label 198 "Acolhimento de Embargos de Declaração", followed by 200 "Não Acolhimento de Embargos de Declaração". The reason is that they are opposing classes, making the vocabulary for the texts to be very similar. Other models had shown the same difficulty in correctly classifying the labels 198 and 200, which was the case of Random Forest, Adaboost, MLP and KNN. The Naive Bayes model had the greatest errors for the classes 219 "Procedência" and 220 "Improcedência", achieving a f1-score of 80% and 75% respectively, but the Naive Bayes also had problem in label 461 "Ausência das condições da ação", achieving a f1-score of 80%, a difficulty that none of the others model had. Yet the f1-score got higher than expected for all models, showing that the dataset is not a hard one for a classification task.

The Table 5 presents the training time and the predicting time for all models. The model with shorter training time is the KNN as it was expected, since in the training step, the model only saves the train data to be used. Conversely, it entails in the second worst predicting time, due the fact of the highly dimension of the data and at predicting time it calculates the distance of the test data for all training data. The worst time in predicting was obtained by the SVM model due the highly dimension of the input data, making it harder to get the position of the data in relation to the borders. Additionally, this model also has the second worst training time. The worst training time was achieved by the Adaboost model, due to the fact that the created trees are sequentially connected and a full training is performed for each tree in every step. This model had the third predicting time because decision tree predicting is a sequence of conditions,

Table 4. SVM results

Class	Precision	Recall	F1-Score
196	97%	96%	97%
198	95%	95%	95%
200	94%	95%	94%
219	98%	96%	97%
220	97%	97%	97%
339	97%	96%	97%
458	97%	97%	97%
461	94%	96%	95%
463	99%	98%	98%
785	97%	98%	97%

what happens with Random Forest too that has the second fast predicting time and fourth training time. The fastest algorithm in predicting is Naive Bayes and second fastest in training. The Neural Network had regular performance in training and test being third and fourth respectively.

Table 5. Speed results

Model	Training time	Predicting time	Total time
Naive Bayes	50 ms	10 ms	60 ms
K-Nearest Neighbors	10 ms	23.4 s	23.4 s
Multilayer Perceptron	28.3 s	1.1 s	29.4 s
Random Forest	77.7 s	0.2 s	77.9 s
Support Vector Machine	177.5 s	83.7 s	261.2 s
Adaboost	1368.5 s	0.3 s	1368.8 s

The interpretability has high correlation due with the algorithm being used, which favors tree algorithms because they are just a sequence of conditions, which could be easier explained. The KNN is another explainable algorithm due the fact it will get the nearest texts for classifiers, which make possible an audit of texts. The Naive Bayes can be interpreted as a probability decision of that combination of words, which brings some degree of interpretability. However the neural network and SVM models have a high abstraction level, which makes almost impossible any interpretation or explanation for these classifications.

All comparisons resulted in the ranking presented in the Table 6, which gave a double of importance to the classification f1-score, since the classification performance is a essential point to the related application, followed by the interpretability degree, due the fact that this is a requirement established by the CNJ.

Table 6. Final ranking

Model	F1-score	Speed	Interpretability
Random Forest	2	4	1
Adaboost	2	6	1
K-Nearest Neighbors	5	2	3
Support Vector Machine	1	5	5
Multilayer Perceptron	4	3	5
Naive Bayes	6	1	4

Similar to previously mentioned works [1,6,10,12,15], there is slight better performance of all models, that could be explained by the different language and textual structure. There is a difference in the overall analysis, due this work evaluates interpretability and computational cost that isn't considered in others works.

6   Conclusions

This paper compared various machine learning models on a legal dataset acquired with the Judicial Court of Rio Grande do Norte. The classification results of all models were higher than expected, since the worst model achieved 87.0% and the best model 96.4%, even with a simple technique such as TF-IDF. Due to the necessity of auditing the classification, the best model to be used in Brazilian court system is the Random Forest with a 95.1% f1-score and such model was the best for interpretability and second in classification. Other models such as Adaboost with decision trees could be used too, the adaboost only loses to the Random Forest in the computational cost. If the computational cost is a big problem for any court that wants to use machine learning, another good alternative is the Naive Bayes or KNN that respectively had a f1-score of 87.0% and 92.2% and they had the lowest computational cost. If interpretability was not required, the MLP technique could be an alternative with a good accuracy and medium computational cost beyond some adaptations that could be made for a better performance.

References

1. Bertalan, V.G.F., Ruiz, E.E.S.: Predicting judicial outcomes in the Brazilian legal system using textual features. In: DHandNLP@ PROPOR, pp. 22–32 (2020)
2. Bhatt, G.: The Haves and Have-nots (2021)

3. Bibal, A., et al.: Impact of legal requirements on explainability in machine learning. arXiv preprint arXiv:2007.05479 (2020)
4. Breiman, L.: Random forests. Mach. Learn. **45**(1), 5–32 (2001)
5. Calvo-Zaragoza, J., et al.: Improving kNN multi-label classification in prototype selection scenarios. Pattern Recogn. **48**(5), 1608–1622 (2015)
6. Chalkidis, I., et al.: Extreme multi-label legal text classification: a case study in EU legislation. arXiv preprint arXiv:1905.10892 (2019)
7. CNJ - National Council of Justice: SINAPSES (2019)
8. CNJ - National Council of Justice: Justiça em Números: ano-base 2019 (2020)
9. Cortes, C., Vapnik, V.: Support-vector networks. Mach. Learn. **20**(3), 273–297 (1995)
10. Howe, J., et al.: Legal area classification: a comparative study of text classifiers on Singapore Supreme Court judgments. arXiv preprint arXiv:1904.06470 (2019)
11. Jones, K.S.: A statistical interpretation of term specificity and its application in retrieval. J. Documentation **60**, 493–502 (1972)
12. Lippi, M., et al.: CLAUDETTE: an automated detector of potentially unfair clauses in online terms of service. Artif. Intell. Law **27**(2), 117–139 (2019)
13. Maia, M., Junquilho, T.: Projeto victor: Perspectivas de aplicação da inteligência artificial ao direito. Revista de Direitos e Garantias Fundamentais **19**(3), 219–237 (2018)
14. Fernandes de Mello, R., Antonelli Ponti, M.: A brief introduction on Kernels. In: Machine Learning, pp. 325–362. Springer, Cham (2018). https://doi.org/10.1007/978-3-319-94989-5_6
15. Neill, J.O., et al.: Classifying sentential modality in legal language: a use case in financial regulations, acts and directives. In: Proceedings of the ICAIL, pp. 159–168 (2017)
16. Quinlan, J.R., et al.: Bagging, boosting, and c4.5. In: AAAI/IAAI, vol. 1, pp. 725–730 (1996)
17. Rish, I., et al.: An empirical study of the naive Bayes classifier. In: IJCAI 2001 Workshop on Empirical Methods in Artificial Intelligence, vol. 3, pp. 41–46 (2001)
18. Russel, S., Norvig, P.: Artificial Intelligence: A Modern Approach. Prentice Hall (2010)
19. Srivastava, N., et al.: Dropout: a simple way to prevent neural networks from overfitting. J. Mach. Learn. Res. **15**(1), 1929–1958 (2014)

Artificial Intelligence in Medicine

Aiding Clinical Triage with Text Classification

Rute Veladas[1](✉), Hua Yang[1,4], Paulo Quaresma[1](✉) (iD),
Teresa Gonçalves[1](✉) (iD), Renata Vieira[2](iD), Cátia Sousa Pinto[3],
João Pedro Martins[3], João Oliveira[3], and Maria Cortes Ferreira[3]

[1] Department of Informatics, University of Évora, Évora, Portugal
{rgv,huayang,pq,tcg}@uevora.pt
[2] CIDEHUS, University of Évora, Évora, Portugal
renatav@uevora.pt
[3] Serviços Partilhados do Ministério da Saúde, Lisboa, Portugal
{catia.pinto,joao.martins,joao.oliveira,
ricardo.vicente,maria.cortes}@spms.min-saude.pt
[4] Zhongyuan University of Technology, Zhenghou, China

Abstract. SNS24 is a telephone service for triage, counselling, and referral service provided by the Portuguese National Health Service. Currently, following the predefined 59 Clinical Pathways, the selection of the most appropriate one is manually done by nurses. This paper presents a study on using automatic text classification to aid on the clinical pathway selection. The experiments were carried out on 3 months calls data containing 269,669 records and a selection of the best combination of ten text representations and four machine learning algorithm was pursued by building 40 different models. Then, fine-tuning of the algorithm parameters and the text embedding model were performed achieving a final accuracy of 78.80% and F1 of 78.45%. The best setup was then used to calculate the accuracy of the top-3 and top-5 most probable clinical pathways, reaching values of 94.10% and 96.82%, respectively. These results suggest that using a machine learning approach to aid the clinical triage in phone call services is effective and promising.

Keywords: Machine learning · Text classification · Clinical triage · SNS24

1 Introduction

According to the EuroHealth Consumer Index, 17 European countries had some form of telephone clinical triage by 2018 [3]. SNS24 is a telephone service for triage, counselling and referral service provided by the Portuguese National Health Service. In 2018 SNS24 answered more than 1 million calls with an average duration of 7–8 min. Being of national scope, this is a service that promotes equity in the access to health care.

© Springer Nature Switzerland AG 2021
G. Marreiros et al. (Eds.): EPIA 2021, LNAI 12981, pp. 83–96, 2021.
https://doi.org/10.1007/978-3-030-86230-5_7

The SNS24 telephone service is provided by nurses and follows predefined clinical pathways. Triage is based on the selection of a clinical pathway by a nurse, considering the citizen's self reported symptoms and signs as well as relevant information provided on medical history. The choice of the most appropriate pathway is extremely important and relevant since it should ensure **high safety** (not failing to identify situations that require urgent medical contact) and have high **discriminatory capability** (do not send low clinical risk situations to Hospitals' Emergency). This is a quite complex problem because there are 59 possible clinical pathways, with five possible final referrals: self-care, observation at primary health care center, observation in hospital emergency, transference to the National Medical Emergency Institute or to the Anti-Poison Information Center.

During each shift, nurses log on to the platform and start answering incoming calls from a single queue. Each call begins with screening questions for emergency situations, in which case the call is redirected to National Medical Emergency Institute. For non-emergencies, the call ensures identification confirmation, specific protocol choice (that are elicited by a keyword search box) and free-text records for documentation purposes. Figure 1 illustrates this process.

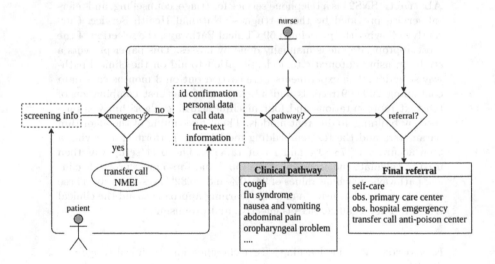

Fig. 1. SNS24 triage process

For each possible referral, there are different situations that need to be assessed. For instance, in a hospital ER there are several possible Manchester triage decisions and they should be analyzed and co-related with the SNS24 referral decision. Moreover, age and sex of the user and even other variables, such as date and time (e.g. day versus night situations) and clinical experience of the triage nurse should also be considered in this process.

Although promoting equity in access to health, SNS24 service can still accommodate many improvements such as allow a better and faster interaction between the citizens and SNS24 and decrease the duration of calls aiming to increase the quantity of handled and further improve the availability of the SNS24 service. Obviously, an improvement in the quality of the algorithm selection and a decrease of the average duration of the phone calls will have a major impact in the SNS24 service to citizens.

Therefore, it is important to support nurses in the selection of the most appropriate clinical pathway and optimize them through the analysis of post referral diagnosis made at primary care units and hospitals. This will improve the discriminatory capacity and clinical safety of the correspondent referrals, and allow SNS24 to improve quality of the existing services.

In this work, we focus on the task of selecting the most appropriate clinical pathway for clinical triage. The paper is organized as follows, in Sect. 2 we review related work; in Sect. 3 we describe the materials and methods used; in Sect. 5 we describe the experiments performed and analyse the results; and finally in Sect. 6 we draw conclusions.

2   Related Work

It is known that the use of clinical decision support systems improves the quality of telephone triage service [21] and the performance of care [9]. The current rate of adherence by citizens to recommendations is partial and reported as moderate, where rates of adherence to self-care, primary health care and hospital emergencies are 77.5%, 64.6% and 68.6% in Australia, respectively [30]. However, although these conclusions have not been consolidated [12], when the recommendations of these guidelines are followed, more suitable referrals to the Emergency Service are obtained [7] and a cost reduction can be achieved [20].

Machine Learning and Natural Language Processing techniques have been increasingly applied in clinical decision support systems, and there is a growing effort in applying these techniques to clinical narrations [11,14,17,19,25,26]. There is a wide variety of paradigms for classification problems (e.g. linear, probabilistic, neural networks) and, for each, there are several algorithms [1]. However, there is no classification algorithm that can be considered the best for all problems [8].

In the last years many conferences and evaluation tasks have focused on clinical decision support problems [10] and the overall performance of the best systems has improved with the use of the new machine learning approaches, such as Support Vector Machines and Deep Learning architectures [17,26,28]. Recent deep learning approaches typically use architectures based on bidirectional LSTM with attention mechanisms having as input word embedding vectors [25]. Current ongoing research tries to create hybrid systems, integrating pure Machine Learning algorithms with linguistic information, such as part-of-speech (POS) and syntactic and semantic information [32].

Mascio et al. [15] compared various word representations and classification algorithms for clinical text classification tasks. They experimented on four datasets and found that traditional word embeddings (Word2Vec, GloVe and

FastText) could achieve or exceed the performance of the ones based on contextual embeddings (BERT) when using the neural-network based approaches, while using traditional machine learning approaches (SVM), the contextual words embeddings achieved better performance. Topaz *et al.* [29] studied patients with high risk of hospitalization or emergency visits using clinical notes taken during home health care episodes. This study was experimented on a database which included 727,676 documents for 112,237 episodes and 89,459 unique patients; they used text mining and machine learning algorithms for the prediction, and feature selection techniques to find risk factors, and found that the using a Random Forest algorithm achieved the best performance with an F-measure of 0.83. Flores *et al.* [6] studied how to achieve the specified performance in biomedical text classification while reducing the number of labeled documents. They compared an active learning approach with Support Vector Machines, Naïve Bayes and a classifier based on Bidirectional Encoder Representations from Transformers (BERT) and experimented on three datasets with biomedical information in Spanish; the active learning approach obtained a AUC (area under the learning curve) performance greater than 85% in all cases. Mullenbach *et al.* [18] used a convolutional network and an attention mechanism to predict medical codes from clinical texts. Their method achieved a precision of 71% and a micro-F1 of 54%.

These related works give an idea of the technologies employed in the area. However there are no works to perform actual comparisons since the experimental setup, problem definition and datasets involved are particular for the demand of SNS24. Instead, we compared simple and more complex text representations as well as some of the classical text classification techniques adopted in these previous works for our problem.

3 Materials and Methods

This section details the materials and methods selected for the execution of the task, containing the description of the data set, the selection of the attributes and the set of experiments selected.

3.1 Available Data

The study protocol was approved by the competent ethics committee and the anonymized data was provided by SPMS (Serviços Partilhados do Ministério da Saúde). It has a total of 269,663 records with 18 attributes, corresponding to information collected during 3 months of calls received by the SNS24 phone-line (from January to March 2018). It includes personal data (age, gender, encrypted primary care unit) and call data (start and end date/time, initial intention, comments, contact reason, clinical pathway and final disposition, between others). The contact reason and comments are free text written in Portuguese by the technician who answered the respective call; the remaining are nominal attributes (except dates).

3.2 Task

With the available data, the task of selecting the most appropriate clinical pathway can be framed as a supervised multi-class classification problem where the attribute "Clinical pathway" is the class aiming to be predicted.

3.3 Dataset

From the 59 possible clinical pathways, in the provided data there was only examples of 53. The proportion of observations per class is diverse ranging from 14.006% for "Tosse/Cough" to 0.001% for "Problemas por calor/Heat-related problems"; 5 clinical pathways have proportions above 5% and 27 have less than 1%. Table 1 presents the five clinical pathways with more and less observations.

Table 1. The five clinical pathways with more and less observations.

Clinical pathway (class)	Examples	%
Tosse/Cough	37930	14.066
Síndrome Gripal/Flu syndrome	34266	12.707
Prob. por náuseas e vómitos/Nausea and vomiting...	14453	5.360
Dor abdominal/Abdominal pain	14382	5.333
Problema da orofaringe/Oropharyngeal problem	13503	5.007
Problemas no cotovelo/Elbow problems	137	0.051
Problemas por sarampo/Measles related problems	98	0.036
Prob. adaptaçño situaçño de crise/... crisis situation	60	0.022
NA	5	0.002
Problemas por calor/Heat problems	4	0.001

The available attributes were analysed and the first one selected for the experiments was "Contact Reason", a medium length free text attribute containing simple and straight-forward information about the patient's problem. It has a total of 31,417 distinct words with each value composed by an average number of 8.15 words (and standard deviation of 3.64). Table 2 presents a few examples for the "Contact Reason".

For building the dataset, clinical pathways with less than 50 instances were removed from the original data, resulting in a dataset with 269,654 instances.

3.4 Text Representation

The "Contact Reason" text was pre-processed with simple word count and Term Frequency–Inverse Document Frequency (TF-IDF) methods, which determine the importance of a word in a corpus, and also with word embedding models, which map the words into a low dimensional continuous space encoding their semantic and syntactic information (by assuming that words in similar context should have similar meaning) [13].

Table 2. Examples of the contact reason field

Febre desde esta manhã
Fever since this morning
Dor no ouvido esquerdo com tonturas associadas por 4 dias
Left ear pain with associated dizziness for 4 days
Tosse produtiva, congestño nasal e febre há 7 dias
Productive cough, nasal congestion and fever for the last 7 days
Dor de garganta desde Sexta e 38.7 °C de febre
Sore throat since Friday and 38.7 °C fever
Dor de cabeça, mialgias e tosse com expetoração verde
Headache, myalgias and cough with green expectoration
Laceração do couro cabeludo há 5 minutos
Scalp laceration 5 min ago
Dor no pescoço e garganta após biópsia à tiróide há 18h
Pain in neck and throat after thyroid biopsy 18 h ago

3.5 Experiments

A first set of experiments was done on the validation set to determine the combination of the machine learning algorithm and the text representation that produced the best results over the dataset. The algorithms tested were Support Vector Machines (with linear and rbf kernels), Random Forest and Multinomial Naïve Bayes; the "Contact Reason" text was processed to build the following text representations: word n-grams ($n \in \{1, 2, 3, 4\}$) using word counts and TF-IDF and embeddings using BERT [5] and Flair [2] models. Both Flair and BERT used pre-trained models publicly available for the Portuguese language.

After selecting the best combination of representation and algorithm, by using statistical McNemar tests to compare the results, a fine-tuning of the embedding model was performed and tested on both validation and test sets. Finally the performance of the generated model using the most probable class along with the three (top-3) and five (top-5) most probable ones were calculated. This was done since the purpose of the classification is to help nurses to find the clinical pathway and offering the most probable ones may help in their decision.

3.6 Experimental Setup

For developing the models Python (v3.7.9) along with scikit-learn (v0.23.2), Transformers[1] (v3.4.0) and Flair[2] (v0.6.1) were used.

---

[1] https://huggingface.co/transformers/v3.4.0/.
[2] https://github.com/flairNLP/flair.

The language models employed were FlairBBP[3] and BERT Large (BERTimbau[4]). Flair embeddings are based on the concept of contextual string embeddings which are used for sequence labelling. The FlairBBP language model was developed on the basis of a raw text corpus of 4.9 billion words from contemporary Portuguese texts. It was previously evaluated for the NLP task of named entity recognition [22] and also in specific domains like geoscience [4], law [24], and health [23]. BERTimbau was trained on the BrWaC (Brazilian Web as Corpus), a large Portuguese corpus [31] and evaluated on several NLP tasks [27].

A stratified split of the dataset into train, validation and test sets was made with a distribution of 64%, 16% and 20%, respectively. The first set of experiments (Sect. 4.1) was evaluated over the full split of validation set with the test split being used for the final evaluation of the best model (Sect. 4.2).

The models were evaluated using accuracy and weighted average of F1-measure (we also present the weighted precision and recall values of each experiment). To support the choice of the best model(s) McNemar tests [16] were performed with a level of significance $\alpha = 0.05$; in the results' tables, the significantly best performing models are presented in bold-face.

4   Results

This section presents the results obtained for each set of experiments done: (1) selection of the "best" combination of the algorithm and representation, (2) fine-tune of the embedding model and (3) calculation of the selected model performance using the most probable class along with the three (top-3) and five (top-5) most probable ones.

4.1   Find the "Best" Algorithm and Representation

This stage corresponds to the development of the models previously mentioned using "Contact Reason" attribute (see Sub-sect. 3.5), totaling 40 models using 4 different machine learning algorithms and 10 different text representations. The performance results were calculated over the validation set and are organized by the machine learning algorithm.

After obtaining the 40 models with default parameters for each algorithm, a fine-tuning of parameters was performed for the best combination of algorithm and representation.

Support Vector Machines. Table 3 and Table 4 present the results using the Support Vector Machine algorithm using linear and RBF kernels, respectively.

When comparing SVMs for the same representation, the linear SVM model always has a better performance with the exception of the uni-grams with TF-IDF and RBF SVM model. It is possible to observe that when using word n-grams the performance decreases when increasing n and that TF-IDF consistently produced better results when compared to using a simple n-gram count.

---

[3] https://github.com/jneto04/ner-pt#flair-embeddings---flairbbp.
[4] https://github.com/neuralmind-ai/portuguese-bert.

Table 3. Linear SVM: performance for different representations.

		Acc.	Prec.	Rec.	F1
Uni-grams	Count	76.28	76.05	76.28	75.99
	TF-IDF	76.47	76.14	76.47	76.10
Bi-grams	Count	72.03	71.74	72.03	71.72
	TF-IDF	73.34	72.90	73.34	72.88
Tri-grams	Count	61.23	62.59	61.23	60.99
	TF-IDF	62.56	63.46	65.56	62.07
Quadri-grams	Count	43.77	54.17	43.77	44.64
	TF-IDF	44.75	54.78	44.75	45.31
Embeddings	BERT	76.39	76.16	76.39	76.04
	Flair	**77.96**	**77.49**	**77.96**	**77.51**

Table 4. RBF SVM: performance for different representations.

		Acc.	Prec.	Rec.	F1
Uni-grams	Count	76.15	76.89	76.15	76.10
	TF-IDF	**76.97**	**77.28**	**76.97**	**76.83**
Bi-grams	Count	68.07	68.74	68.07	67.40
	TF-IDF	70.27	70.48	70.27	69.60
Tri-grams	Count	51.63	62.12	51.63	51.63
	TF-IDF	55.80	63.72	55.80	55.15
Quadri-grams	Count	32.88	62.59	32.88	32.57
	TF-IDF	34.75	62.11	34.75	36.01
Embeddings	BERT	75.83	75.81	75.84	75.52
	Flair	76.58	76.78	76.59	76.30

Random Forest. The results obtained with Random Forest algorithm are presented in Table 5. As observed, the best performance was also obtained using word uni-grams with with TF-IDF, but SVMs consistently generated better models. The observations made about the n-grams performance and TF-IDF for SVMs are also true for Random Forest.

Table 5. Random Forest: performance for different representations.

		Acc.	Prec.	Rec.	F1
Uni-grams	Count	73.84	73.33	73.84	73.26
	TF-IDF	**74.93**	**74.55**	**74.93**	**74.40**
Bi-grams	Count	66.51	66.14	66.51	65.54
	TF-IDF	68.10	67.70	68.11	67.41
Tri-grams	Count	55.83	58.61	55.83	55.73
	TF-IDF	56.73	58.98	56.73	56.39
Quadri-grams	Count	39.67	58.15	39.67	44.67
	TF-IDF	39.82	57.61	39.82	44.65
Embeddings	BERT	69.39	68.94	69.39	68.16
	Flair	68.36	68.43	68.37	66.96

Multinomial Naïve Bayes. Table 6 presents the results obtained with Multi-nomial Naïve Bayes algorithm. As can be seen, it under-performs the previous algorithms and, unlike the results previously presented, count produces better results when compared to TF-IDF.

Table 6. Multinomial NB: performance for different representations

		Acc.	Prec.	Rec.	F1
Uni-grams	Count	**66.26**	**67.68**	**66.26**	**63.85**
	TF-IDF	57.83	63.10	57.83	53.59
Bi-grams	Count	60.09	64.85	60.09	57.32
	TF-IDF	52.58	65.96	52.58	49.35
Tri-grams	Count	51.35	62.37	51.35	49.35
	TF-IDF	42.70	66.43	42.70	40.55
Quadri-grams	Count	36.18	60.52	36.18	34.74
	TF-IDF	29.45	62.11	29.45	26.20
Embeddings	BERT	58.73	60.16	58.74	57.73
	Flair	47.78	55.54	47.78	45.77

Parameter Optimization. As can be seen from Tables 3, 4, 5 and 6 the top 3 most performing approaches were: Flair with linear SVM, BERT with linear SVM and uni-grams with TF-IDF and RBF SVM. These models were parameter fine-tuned to maximize the F1-measure. Models were built with values of $C \in \{0.01, 0.1, 1, 10, 100, 1000\}$. For Flair and uni-grams the best model was obtained with $C = 1$ (default value) and $C = 0.1$ for BERT representation. For the RBF kernel with uni-gram and TF-IDF, the γ (gamma) parameter was also fine-tuned with different values but the default parameter (inverse of number of features times attribute variance, $1/(nfeatures * var)$) generated the best model.

Table 7 summarizes the results. The only improvement observed was for BERT using linear SVM, but still being lower than the one obtained with Flair. For this reason Flair with linear SVM combination was selected for pursuing the following experiments.

Table 7. SVM performance summary.

	Acc.	Prec.	Rec.	F1
BERT w/ linear SVM	76.39	76.16	76.39	76.04
BERT w/ linear SVM ($C = 0.1$)	**77.10**	**76.54**	**77.10**	**76.61**
Flair w/ linear SVM	**77.96**	**77.49**	**77.96**	**77.51**
Uni-gram TF-IDF w/ RBF SVM	**76.97**	**77.28**	**76.97**	**76.83**

4.2 Fine-Tuning the Embedding Model

The approach selected for the experiments on this stage was Flair using Linear SVM. Aiming to improve the previously obtained results, the pre-trained Flair embedding model was fine-tuned to be adapted to the clinical domain using a corpus built from the "Contact Reason" texts of the SNS24 dataset.

This new embedding model was used to evaluate the performance over the validation set and also the test. The results can be seen in Table 8. According to the significance tests performed, the Flair fine-tuning produced a significant improvement on the performance over the validation set. When applying this model to the test set, an accuracy of 78.80% and F1 of 78.45% were achieved.

Table 8. SVM performance with fine-tuned Flair model

	Acc.	Prec.	Rec.	F1
Original Flair (validation set)	77.96	77.49	77.96	77.51
Fine-tuned Flair (validation set)	**78.59**	**78.18**	**78.59**	**78.21**
Fine-tuned Flair (test set)	78.80	78.42	78.80	78.45

4.3 Considering the Most Probable Clinical Pathways

This section presents the performance when considering the three (top-3) and five (top-5) most probable classes given by the prediction model. This experiment was done using the fine-tuned Flair model with linear SVM and uni-grams TF-IDF with RBF SVM (the two "best" models from stage 1; see Sub-sect. 4.1).

Accuracy results for the test set are shown in Table 9. Looking at the results, and despite the significant difference between models when using the most probable class (top-1), this is no longer true when considering the top-3 and top-5 classes.

Table 9. Accuracy for the top-1, top-3 and top-5 most probable classes.

	Top-1	Top-3	Top-5
Unigram TF-IDF w/ RBF SVM	76.97	94.08	96.77
Fine-tuned Flair w/ linear SVM	**78.80**	94.10	96.82

5 Discussion

The experiments performed on Sub-sect. 4.1 provided information on the setup of the best model for the problem at hand. The best result obtained was with Flair embeddings and linear SVM, with an accuracy of 77.96% and an F1 of 77.51%. In these experiments it is possible to observe that, for all algorithms using n-grams, as the n increases the performance decreases, so uni-grams generated the best models when using word n-grams; for this setup, the best performance was obtained with TF-IDF and RBF SVM with an accuracy of 76.97% and F1 of 76.83%.

For the Random Forest algorithm, uni-grams with TF-IDF generated the best models but it under-performs SVM for all text representations (accuracy of 74.93% and F1 of 74.40%). For the Multinomial Naïve Bayes, the representation with better results was also uni-grams but with count with an accuracy of 66.26% and F1 of 63.85%; this algorithm under-performs by large SVMs and Random Forests. To finalize the initial experiments a fine-tuning of the SVM parameters was performed for several text representations. A small improvement was obtained using BERT but it was still lower than Flair with linear SVM.

Still pursuing the goal of obtaining the best classification model, the pretrained Flair model was fine-tuned using a corpus composed by the "Contact Reason" text of the SNS24 dataset to be better adapted to the clinical domain. This fine-tuning provided an improvement of the performance, reaching an accuracy of 78.80% and F1 of 78.45% for the test set.

Finally, the accuracy of two prediction models (fine-tuned Flair with linear SVM and unigram TF-IDF with RBF SVM) was measured calculating the top-3 and top-5 most probable classes. The results showed that, despite the significant difference between both models when using the most probable class, it was no longer true when presenting the top-3 or top-5 most probable classes. Consequently, one can say that uni-grams TF-IDF with RBF SVM would be the final model choice to incorporate in a clinical tool since its computational cost is lower when compared with the Flair representation.

6   Conclusions

SNS24 is a telephone triage service provided by the Portuguese National Health Service, where nurses select the most appropriate clinical pathway given the information self-reported by citizens. This paper proposes to use an automatic text classification approach to aid the SNS 24 clinical triage service.

A group of experiments were conducted on 3 months data containing a total of 269,669 call records. Several machine learning algorithms (SVM with linear and RBF kernel, Random Forest and Multinomial Naïve Bayes) and text representations (TF-IDF and count n-grams and BERT and Flair embeddings) were combined to produce classification models. The experimental results show that a fine-tuned Flair embedding with a linear SVM classification model achieves an accuracy of 78.80% and F1 of 78.45%; additionally accuracies of 94.10% and 96.82% were obtained when using the top-3 and top-5 most probable classes. These results suggest that using Machine Learning is an effective and promising approach to aid the clinical triage of phone call services.

Acknowledgement. This research work was funded by FCT – Fundação para Ciência e Tecnologia, I.P, within the project SNS24.Scout.IA: Aplicação de Metodologias de Inteligência Artificial e Processamento de Linguagem Natural no Serviço de Triagem, Aconselhamento e Encaminhamento do SNS24 (ref. DSAIPA/AI/0040/2019).

References

1. Aggarwal, C.C., Clustering, C.R.D.: Algorithms and applications (2014)
2. Akbik, A., Blythe, D., Vollgraf, R.: Contextual string embeddings for sequence labeling. In: Proceedings of the 27th International Conference on Computational Linguistics, pp. 1638–1649. Association for Computational Linguistics, Santa Fe (2018). https://www.aclweb.org/anthology/C18-1139
3. Björnberg, A., Phang, A.Y.: Euro health consumer index 2018 report. In: Health Consumer Powerhouse Euro Health Consumer Index, pp. 1–90 (2019)
4. Consoli, B.S., Santos, J., Gomes, D., Cordeiro, F., Vieira, R., Moreira, V.: Embeddings for named entity recognition in geoscience Portuguese literature. In: Proceedings of the 12th Language Resources and Evaluation Conference, pp. 4625–4630 (2020)
5. Devlin, J., Chang, M.W., Lee, K., Toutanova, K.: Bert: pre-training of deep bidirectional transformers for language understanding (2018)
6. Flores, C.A., Figueroa, R.L., Pezoa, J.E.: Active learning for biomedical text classification based on automatically generated regular expressions. IEEE Access **9**, 38767–38777 (2021)
7. Gibson, A., et al.: Emergency department attendance after telephone triage: a population-based data linkage study. Health Serv. Res. **53**(2), 1137–1162 (2018)
8. Gómez, D., Rojas, A.: An empirical overview of the no free lunch theorem and its effect on real-world machine learning classification. Neural Comput. **28**(1), 216–228 (2016)
9. Kaakinen, P., Kyngäs, H., Tarkiainen, K., Kääriäinen, M.: The effects of intervention on quality of telephone triage at an emergency unit in Finland: nurses' perspective. Int. Emerg. Nurs. **26**, 26–31 (2016)

10. Kadhim, A.I.: Survey on supervised machine learning techniques for automatic text classification. Artif. Intell. Rev. **52**(1), 273–292 (2019). https://doi.org/10.1007/s10462-018-09677-1
11. Kavuluru, R., Rios, A., Lu, Y.: An empirical evaluation of supervised learning approaches in assigning diagnosis codes to electronic medical records. Artif. Intell. Med. **65**(2), 155–166 (2015)
12. Lake, R., et al.: The quality, safety and governance of telephone triage and advice services-an overview of evidence from systematic reviews. BMC Health Serv. Res. **17**(1), 1–10 (2017). https://doi.org/10.1186/s12913-017-2564-x
13. Li, Y., Yang, T.: Word Embedding for Understanding Natural Language: A Survey, vol. 26 (2017). https://doi.org/10.1007/978-3-319-53817-4
14. Marafino, B.J., Boscardin, W.J., Dudley, R.A.: Efficient and sparse feature selection for biomedical text classification via the elastic net: application to ICU risk stratification from nursing notes. J. Biomed. Inf. **54**, 114–120 (2015)
15. Mascio, A., et al.: Comparative analysis of text classification approaches in electronic health records. arXiv preprint arXiv:2005.06624 (2020)
16. McNemar, Q.: Note on the sampling error of the difference between correlated proportions or percentages. Psychometrika **12**(2), 153–157 (1947)
17. Mujtaba, G., et al.: Clinical text classification research trends: systematic literature review and open issues. Expert Syst. Appl. **116**, 494–520 (2019)
18. Mullenbach, J., Wiegreffe, S., Duke, J., Sun, J., Eisenstein, J.: Explainable prediction of medical codes from clinical text. arXiv preprint arXiv:1802.05695 (2018)
19. Mustafa, A., Rahimi Azghadi, M.: Automated machine learning for healthcare and clinical notes analysis. Computers **10**(2), 24 (2021)
20. Navratil-Strawn, J.L., Ozminkowski, R.J., Hartley, S.K.: An economic analysis of a nurse-led telephone triage service. J. Telemedicine Telecare **20**(6), 330–338 (2014)
21. North, F., et al.: Clinical decision support improves quality of telephone triage documentation-an analysis of triage documentation before and after computerized clinical decision support. BMC Med. Inf. Decis. Making **14**(1), 1–10 (2014)
22. Santos, J., Consoli, B., dos Santos, C., Terra, J., Collonini, S., Vieira, R.: Assessing the impact of contextual embeddings for Portuguese named entity recognition. In: Proceedings of the 8th Brazilian Conference on Intelligent Systems, pp. 437–442 (2019)
23. Santos, J., dos Santos, H.D.P., Vieira, R.: Fall detection in clinical notes using language models and token classifier. In: Proceedings of the 33rd International Symposium on Computer-Based Medical Systems, CBMS 2020, Rochester, MN, USA, 28–30 July 2020, pp. 283–288 (2020)
24. Santos, J., Terra, J., Consoli, B.S., Vieira, R.: Multidomain contextual embeddings for named entity recognition. In: Proceedings of the 35th Conference of the Spanish Society for Natural Language Processing, pp. 434–441 (2019)
25. Shao, Y., Taylor, S., Marshall, N., Morioka, C., Zeng-Treitler, Q.: Clinical text classification with word embedding features vs. bag-of-words features. In: 2018 IEEE International Conference on Big Data (Big Data), pp. 2874–2878. IEEE (2018)
26. Shickel, B., Tighe, P.J., Bihorac, A., Rashidi, P.: Deep EHR: a survey of recent advances in deep learning techniques for electronic health record (EHR) analysis. IEEE J. Biomed. Health Inf. **22**(5), 1589–1604 (2017)
27. Souza, F., Nogueira, R., Lotufo, R.: BERTimbau: pretrained BERT models for Brazilian Portuguese. In: Cerri, R., Prati, R.C. (eds.) BRACIS 2020. LNCS (LNAI), vol. 12319, pp. 403–417. Springer, Cham (2020). https://doi.org/10.1007/978-3-030-61377-8_28

28. Stein, R.A., Jaques, P.A., Valiati, J.F.: An analysis of hierarchical text classification using word embeddings. Inf. Sci. **471**, 216–232 (2019)
29. Topaz, M., Woo, K., Ryvicker, M., Zolnoori, M., Cato, K.: Home healthcare clinical notes predict patient hospitalization and emergency department visits. Nursing Res. **69**(6), 448–454 (2020)
30. Tran, D.T., et al.: Compliance with telephone triage advice among adults aged 45 years and older: an Australian data linkage study. BMC Health Serv. Res. **17**(1), 1–13 (2017). https://doi.org/10.1186/s12913-017-2458-y
31. Wagner Filho, J.A., Wilkens, R., Idiart, M., Villavicencio, A.: The brWaC corpus: a new open resource for Brazilian Portuguese. In: Proceedings of the Eleventh International Conference on Language Resources and Evaluation (LREC 2018). European Language Resources Association (ELRA), Miyazaki, Japan (2018). https://www.aclweb.org/anthology/L18-1686
32. Young, T., Hazarika, D., Poria, S., Cambria, E.: Recent trends in deep learning based natural language processing. IEEE Comput. Intell. Mag. **13**(3), 55–75 (2018)

A Web-based Telepsychology Platform Prototype Using Cloud Computing and Deep Learning Tools

Diego Pérez-Hernández, Nieves Pavón-Pulido(✉) ⓘ, J. A. López-Riquelme ⓘ, and J. J. Feliú Batlle ⓘ

Technical University of Cartagena, Campus Muralla del Mar, 30202 Cartagena, Spain
nieves.pavon@upct.es

Abstract. This paper describes a web-based telepsychology platform prototype, which enables patients and therapists to respectively follow and track psychological therapies remotely and asynchronously. The software architecture consists of two main modules: backend and frontend. The backend is designed by using several cloud tools, provided by Google, for processing and storing patients' data in a secure manner and ensuring the highest privacy standards. In addition, therapies defined by therapists can also be uploaded to the platform for their posterior usage. The frontend is developed as a web application, which can be accessed according to the role of the user (patient or therapist), through a compatible browser. The presented prototype also allows some biomedical hardware devices to easily feed the platform with measurements that helps to estimate the stress degree and mood. Furthermore, the frontend includes a Deep Learning-based component capable of detecting facial landmarks, useful for estimating emotional features, which are stored preserving patients' privacy. Finally, the results obtained after testing the prototype in a controlled environment are presented, together with a discussion about the advantages and drawbacks of such system.

Keywords: Cloud computing · Telemedicine · e-Health

1 Introduction

Although the concept of Telemedicine [1], understood as the application of ICTs (Information and Communications Technologies), for allowing health care professionals to remotely evaluate, diagnose and treat patients is well-known, the deployment of truly effective solutions is still a challenge, in national health systems [2, 3]. In the context of mental health care, systems capable of enabling therapists to evaluate and treat patients, at distance, is even hardly to find [4, 5]. Mental disorders fluctuate over time and, in general, only patients' assessment is considered by therapists, who often observes the mental state through subjective responses to questionnaires. The impact of including techniques based on AI (Artificial Intelligence), in psychiatry is currently being researched [6]; however, symptoms nature and the difficulty of objectively estimating the degree of such symptoms makes smart automation hard. The same troubles could

© Springer Nature Switzerland AG 2021
G. Marreiros et al. (Eds.): EPIA 2021, LNAI 12981, pp. 97–108, 2021.
https://doi.org/10.1007/978-3-030-86230-5_8

be extended to remote patients' attention by using Telemedicine platforms. On the other hand, Internet of Things (IoT), solutions which incorporate biomedical sensors that acquire health parameters related to mental disorders are really hard to find, except those which are already included in smartphones applications (or similar), focused on fitness or health state tracking, but without medical support. Furthermore, the COVID'19 pandemics has emphasized the problems of national health systems in many countries and the low development of ICTs-based platforms for attending population maintaining the necessary social distance [7]. This fact is more pronounced in mental health ambit [8], even when a huge increase of people suffering depression and anxiety disorders is being detected, including COVID's persistent effects related to mood.

Telepsychology is an open research line, where many contributions could be done. This paper presents a new platform prototype which joins Cloud Computing, AI and IoT techniques, with the aim of providing a solution to allow patients to remotely attend sessions designed by therapists in a secure and private environment, and to enable therapists to evaluate the results of such sessions, by analyzing not only the patients' subjective assessment, but several biomedical parameters acquired by specific sensors.

The outline of the paper is as follows. Section 2 describes the designed software architecture. Section 3 shows how the prototype has been validated, together with the analysis of the obtained results. Finally, Sect. 4 presents the main conclusions and the work expected to be carried out in the future.

2 Description of the System

This section details the set of modules that comprise the full software architecture. Such architecture follows a client-server model, where the software components executed in the server side are considered as backend elements and those ones executed in the client side (a browser), since they need the user interaction, are considered as frontend components. The proposed client-server model has been deployed in the Cloud by using several cloud tools provided by Google:

- Google App Engine (GAE) [9], Standard Environment, which offers a "fully managed, serverless platform for developing and hosting cloud-based web applications at scale", which run in a "secure and reliable sandboxed environment" independent of the hardware, Operating System (OS), or physical location of the server.
- Cloud Endpoints [10] for easily managing and protecting the API (Application Programming Interface), implemented as main component of the backend, which provides the set of services called by the web application's client side (frontend), hosted in the GAE Standard Environment.
- Google Cloud's Vision API [11], which enables assigning labels to images and classifying them into a great variety of categories, including face detection and emotional features estimation.

The web client (developed with HTML5 and JavaScript), is executed in a browser, allowing users to access the backend services by sending REST (Representational State Transfer), API requests. Such client also uses the TensorFlow.js library, which enables the application to directly use Machine Learning (ML), pre-trained, out of the box models, such as, the MediaPipe FaceMesh [12] (a lightweight package that predicts "486 3D facial landmarks to infer the approximate surface geometry of a human face"), useful for estimating emotional features and storing them, preserving patients' privacy. Figure 1 shows the set of modules that comprise the global system, including commons hardware devices that would be useful for acquiring biomedical data: for example, heart rate (HR), galvanic skin response (GSR), visual information or basic electroencephalographic (EEG) parameters related to meditation and attention.

2.1   Cloud-Based Backend Software Architecture

The application backend, hosted in Google Cloud, has been designed as a collection of services which can be called from a web client by using the REST paradigm, considered as an architectural style for APIs that uses HTTP (Hypertext Transfer Protocol), requests to access and process remote data.

Google Cloud Tools.
The server-side software architecture is implemented with GAE, which provides interesting benefits in comparison to a classic server solution. Such applications are automatically scaled (depending on the application traffic), and deployment is carried out without server management and configuration. Resources consumption depends on how often the code is run, so over or under provisioning is avoided. Thus, developers are only focused in software design and implementation, without the need of managing the underlying infrastructure. Moreover, each application is protected from security threats through firewall capabilities, IAM (Identity and Access Management) rules and SSL/TSL (Secure Sockets Layer/Transport Layer Security) certificates management.

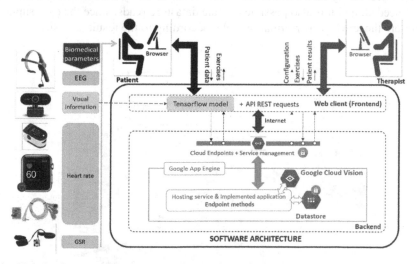

Fig. 1. Global software architecture including hardware devices that could be optionally included for measuring biomedical parameters.

The designed GAE application executes services implemented as Java methods in an Endpoint API, which are remotely called from the web client. With the aim of making the API development, deployment and management easier, Google Cloud Endpoints are used. This framework is defined as an API management system that helps developers to "secure, monitor, analyze and set quotas" on the designed APIs "using the same infrastructure that Google uses for its own APIs". The Cloud Endpoints Frameworks have been selected for providing the necessary tools and libraries that enable the REST API for the GAE application to be generated. These Endpoints Frameworks handle the low-level communication details of HTTP requests and responses sent and received by the GAE application. Thus, when the web client sends a request to the API, implemented as a part of such application, Endpoints Frameworks route the request's URL (Uniform Resource Locator), to the method that should process it. The value returned by the method is converted to JSON (JavaScript Object Notation), and sent it as response. Request parameters are also passed as JSON structures and automatically converted to Java objects, handled by the corresponding method. Regarding data storage that supports data encryption, Google Datastore is used, since it is a fully managed highly scalable NoSQL database, specifically designed for web applications, which allows ACID (Atomicity, Consistency, Isolation, Durability), transactions to be performed, thus ensuring data integrity. Figure 2 summarizes how the backend works.

Data Model.
As the telepsychology platform requires to manage structured data (personal data, exercises, treatments and therapies, among others), and time-series (from data provided by the biomedical sensors), the Google Datastore is the most appropriate storage option, since it "is designed to automatically scale to very large data sets, allowing applications to maintain high performances as they receive more traffic". Specifically, queries are served by previously built indexes; datastore writes scale by automatically distributing data, if needed; and it is also possible to scale datastore reads, since the only supported queries are those whose performance scales according to the result set's size.

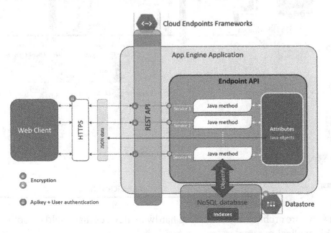

Fig. 2. Summary of how the GAE application (designed as backend), works.

Thus, the performance of a query that returns a number N of entities is the same when searches are carried out over a hundred entities or over thousands or millions of them. Figure 3 shows the ERD (Entity Relationship Diagram), used for modelling the proposed system's data warehouse, because, although Datastore-based databases are not managed by a RDBMS (Relational Database Management System), they share many of the same features as those that are relational:

- The category of object is implemented as a table in a relational database, however, it is a kind in the Datastore.
- Each kind can have different properties corresponding to columns of a single row in a table.
- Each row is equivalent to an entity, which could be defined as an individual object. Different rows could represent entities of the same kind, but with different values in their properties.

According to the data model, information is stored and processed according to the following rules:

- A patient is treated by only one therapist, though a therapist could attend a set of different patients.
- Each patient could remotely assist to a session scheduled by his/her therapist at a given time. Such session could be defined as synchronous or asynchronous (that is, in presence or absence of the therapist).
- In each session, a specific therapy is applied, and the patient should carry out the collection of exercises defined by the therapist for such therapy, according to the programmed session.
- Each exercise could include different kind of contents: reading a text, watching a video or a set of pictures, listening a record or any other defined by the therapist.
- Therapies could also include the use of drugs, whose doses' scheduling would be defined by the therapist. As different drugs could interact with each other, this fact is modelled by using the relationship *Interact*.
- Doses are modelled by two different entities: *Prescribed dose* and *Dose*. The first one allows the therapist to define how often the patient should take the drug. The last one enables the system to store information about how the patient is following the treatment by saving the taken doses along time.
- In each session, the patient could wear biomedical sensors for measuring several relevant parameters related to stress and emotional condition. It is necessary to save information about each connected sensor and the set of data acquired while a session is attended. Such data are stored as time-series.

Objectify Implementation of the Data Model.
Each entity which needs to be persisted is implemented as a POJO (Plain Old Java Object), Java class by using Objectify annotations, since Objectify is a Java data access API specifically designed for the Google Cloud Datastore.

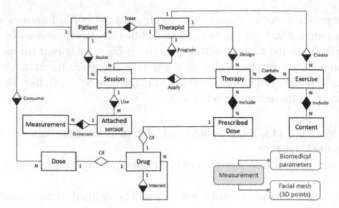

Fig. 3. ERD that defines the data model used in the telepsychology platform prototype. Specific properties for each entity are not shown for diagram simplification.

Available operations in the Datastore are *put()*, *get()*, *delete()* and *query()*, corresponding to the Objectify operations *save()*, *delete()* and *load()* for getting or querying data. While *save()* and *delete()* work with whole entities, *load()* allows the system to retrieve entities according to some defined criteria.

Objectify makes data inserting and retrieving easier, because it is not necessary to know SQL (Structured Query Language). Furthermore, join operations are not used, since one-to-one, one-to-many and many-to-many relationships between entities are defined by using a reference or a list of references to those objects that implement the related entities. Figure 4 illustrates how two entities *Patient* and *Therapist*, together with its relationship *Treat* is implemented by using Java classes annotated with Objectify.

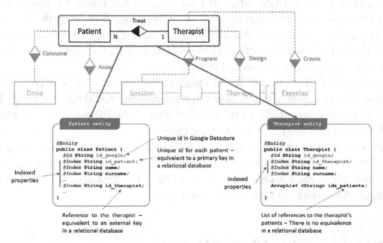

Fig. 4. Patient and *Therapist* entities and how the *Treat* relationship is implemented by using Objectify annotations. Note that, the list of patients treated by a specific therapist is saved as a class member and each patient also has a member referencing to his/her therapist. This double relationship (useful for accessing information easier), is not possible in a relational database.

Endpoint API.
The endpoint API developed as a part of the backend has been implemented as a Java class whose methods allow specific tasks to be carried out, such as properly storing and processing data-model's entities, among others. Such tasks are grouped according to their function (see Fig. 5). Each method corresponds to a service, which can be called from the web client through the REST API provided by the Cloud Endpoints Frameworks. All the methods are protected, since an API key is required to get a valid response when a method is called. Such API key is sent to the web client when the user (in the role of therapist or patient), accesses to the system by using a login-password pair. The API key is also protected, because its usage is limited to the designed GAE application, among other restrictions.

2.2 Web Client as Frontend

As GAE is mainly focused on enabling scalable mobile backends to be developed, the frontend of the telepsychology platform prototype has been designed as a web client, running in a browser, using HTML5 and JavaScript, and taking Material Design as metaphor. Thus, users use a familiar and usable interface similar to other known applications, such as, web-based clients for e-mail or social networks (see Fig. 6).

Patients use the same interface but with different options, according to his/her role. The therapist is responsible of creating an account for each patient. This is a simple process, because, the therapist should only fill same basic data and the system automatically sends an e-mail with a link that allows the patient to modify his/her personal data, user name and password. When the patient follows the link and accepts the account, the system attaches him/her to the therapist's list of patients.

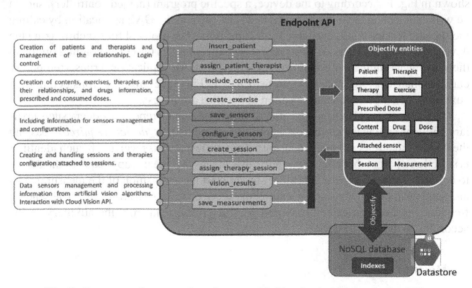

Fig. 5. Summary of groups of services provided by the designed endpoint API.

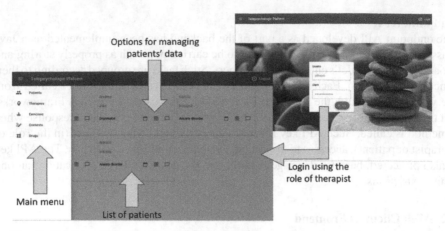

Fig. 6. User interface. Example of therapist screen when the option *Patients* is selected.

Therapist is also responsible of scheduling the sessions and assigning treatments, both pharmacological and psychotherapeutic (through specific exercises). Such schedule is shown to the patient by selecting the corresponding option, after accessing with the patient role. Figure 7 shows the main board from which the patient can access each session.

2.3 Biomedical Parameters Acquisition

Biomedical data can be optionally acquired by using compatible devices similar to those shown in Fig. 1. According to the device, a specific program (named controller), should be written to obtain the measurements and send them to the GAE application by calling the specific service that is available for this purpose. The protocol for synchronizing the device with a specific session starts when the patient selects the corresponding option in the web client running in his/her browser. Then, the GAE application writes a temporary entity in the Datastore (not shown in the ERD, at Fig. 3, because it is considered as an auxiliary one), with unique information about the current session.

The device controller triggered after turning it on, should repeatedly query such auxiliary entity by calling the corresponding Endpoint method "*is_device_required*" (passing the device's identifier as parameter), until a proper response is received. If such identifier is stored as a part of the temporary entity, that means that the therapy requires the device to be used. Then, the device controller should start the acquisition of the measurements and send them to the Datastore by calling the service "*save_measurement*". The sending frequency is an empirically configured parameter also read from the auxiliary entity, according to the type of device.

3   Results

The proposed telepsychology platform is in a prototype stage, consequently, it has not been tested in a real environment (a medical clinic, for example), yet. However, it has

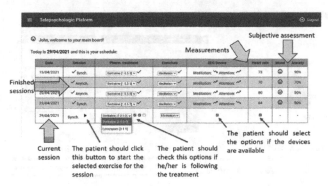

Fig. 7. Main board that helps the patient to follow the programmed sessions and the treatment.

been validated from a technical point of view through a set of trials typically used in the context of Software Engineering. First, the performance of the backend has been tested considering issues related to functionality, latency, security and privacy. Then, the whole system has been validated by accessing to the backend through the web application both, in the roles of therapist and patient. In addition, two devices have been selected for proving the process of biomedical sensors integration: The NeuroSky MindWave Mobile EEG Sensor, consisting of a wireless headset capable of monitoring attention, meditation and detecting raw-brainwaves; and the Apple Watch Series 2 for heart-rate measuring. The application that acts as the headset's controller is a program (under Windows 10), which should be previously installed in the patient's personal computer. On the other hand, an iOS application also specifically designed for interacting with the platform and running in an iOS smartphone, enables the use of the smartwatch and the connection with Google Cloud. A webcam has been used in the process of acquiring images needed for facial landmarks detection. Finally, the system has been validated, in an informal manner, by a female potential user with a real diagnose of anxious depression, pharmacologically treated with Sertraline and Lorazepam and psychologically treated with a cognitive behavioral therapy, whose exercises have been uploaded to the platform. These exercises are mainly focused on allowing the patient to listen to a set of audio files for helping her to practice meditation and introspection.

For instance, in one of the sessions, the patient has used the platform for carrying out an exercise based on the body-scan mindfulness technique, consisting of listening an audio file with instructions about paying attention to breath and different parts of the body during, approximately, 11 min. Figure 8 shows how the platform works while the patient is listening the audio for accomplishing the exercise.

Before starting, the webcam is activated and the TensorFlow model is locally loaded. Then, the patient's face is automatically detected and the facial landmarks are applied over the face. Such process is fully run in the browser and the facial landmarks are uploaded every 30 s to the Cloud, by calling the suitable Endpoint service. Both, facial landmarks and biomedical values start to be sent only when the Start button is clicked.

Before starting, it is necessary to turn on the biomedical devices and execute their controllers. As measuring heart rate through the smartwatch involves the use of an external application provided by Apple, the patient has to trigger it, before starting

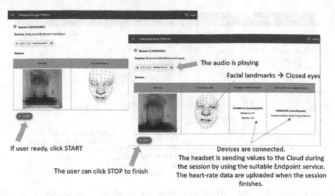

Fig. 8. The patient makes an exercise, listening an audio file.

the mentioned specific application that runs in the smartphone. The patient manually stops the session by clicking the Stop button; then, the devices receive a notification in the response of the last request that they did. Thus, the devices are aware when they should stop measuring. The iOS application queries if the session is stopped by calling the appropriate Endpoint service each 30 s. When the response is affirmative, the iOS application queries the Apple Health Center and downloads the information about heart rate in the time interval that happens between the start and stop of the session. Then, this information is uploaded to the platform by sending a request to the suitable Endpoint service. The facial landmarks are also shown as a 3D point cloud. In fact, only the landmarks (not the photograms), are stored in the cloud, thus preserving the patient's privacy during all the time. Additionally, the Google Cloud Vision API has been used to detect emotions. For doing this, the system takes a photogram, it reduces it and it sends a request to this API, including the image as a base64 encoded string in the body of the such request. The response includes information about four different emotions (joy, sorrow, anger and surprise), in terms of labels related to probability ("unknown", "very unlike", "unlike", "possible", "likely", "very likely"), and only this information is persisted in the Cloud. The results obtained after finishing the session, available for both, the patient and his/her therapist, are shown in Fig. 9. In the test, meditation and attention are registered together with the heart rate. The results can be downloaded in a CSV (Comma Separated Values) file, which makes posterior data analysis easier, since it is compatible with most statistical and spreadsheet software. Moreover, facial landmarks can be displayed with the corresponding time stamp, and the timestamped information about emotions acquired by using the Google Cloud Vision API is also available. Figure 10 graphically shows some results obtained during the session for the meditation and attention parameters and heart rate. Moreover, all the detected emotions for each photogram, sent to Google Cloud Vision every minute, are also displayed. It should be highlighted that the detected emotions do not correspond to real mood as correctly as expected. The patient checked such results and compared them to her own feelings, and she found several detected emotions were wrong.

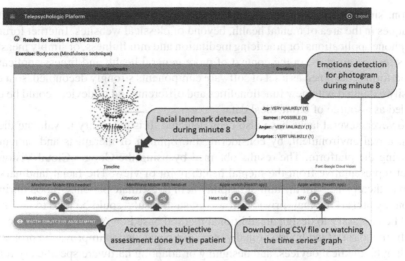

Fig. 9. Web user interface that shows the results of the exercise carried out in a specific session.

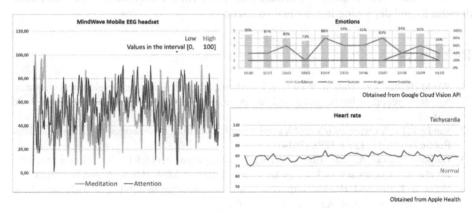

Fig. 10. Some biomedical data measured during the session.

4   Conclusions and Future Work

The telepsychology platform prototype presented in this paper paves the way to deploy a full Cloud-based solution for improving the communication between therapists and patients in real environments. The proposed platform provides a method for enhancing the adherence to treatments, mainly those related to psychological therapies, since it helps patient to follow the sessions at distance. It is also possible to measure biomedical parameters to estimate how the therapy is objectively acting and to analyze such results.

The system has been currently validated in a laboratory controlled scenario, mainly using trials that allow the validation of the system from a technical point of view. However, the tests undertaken during the development of the prototype have demonstrated the benefits and drawbacks of the system. The platform provides a novel full Cloud-based solution, since there hardly exist similar solutions focused on applying telemedicine techniques in the area of mental health, beyond of classical websites, Internet forums or smartphone applications for practicing meditation and mindfulness, or simply measuring some stress parameters, in the context of more general health and fitness applications. The platform is designed as a set of software components strongly decoupled, so it could be easily extended with new functionalities and different kind of devices could be easily included as a source of biomedical data.

However, several lacks have also been detected. It is necessary to validate the system in a real environment, by considering the opinion of therapists and patients for improving the platform. The results obtained by using the Google Cloud Vision API are not representative from the mental health point of view. The facial landmarks are shown to therapists, with the aim of helping them to estimate patients' mood during the session, by preserving their privacy. However, such results could be hard to interpret. It would be necessary to design an additional method based on AI to reliably detect emotions from the set of landmarks. Finally, it would be needed to improve the protocol for including biomedical devices, and designing or adapting hardware specifically focused on acquiring those biomedical parameters relevant in the context of mental health.

The future work is aimed to enhance the platform for overcoming the mentioned drawbacks and deploying it in several real scenarios.

References

1. World Health Organization (WHO): Telemedicine: opportunities and developments in member states: report on the second global survey on eHealth. Glob. Observ. eHealth Ser. **2**, 1–96 (2009)
2. van Dyk, L.: A review of telehealth service implementation frameworks. Int. J. Environ. Res. Public Health **11**, 1279–1298 (2014)
3. Barberan-García, A., et al.: Effects and barriers to deployment of telehealth wellness programs for chronic patients across 3 European countries. Respir. Med. **108**(4), 628–637 (2014)
4. What Is Telemental Health? https://www.nimh.nih.gov/health/publications/what-is-telemental-health/index.shtml. Accessed 30 Apr 2021
5. Fairburna, C.G., Patelb, V.: The impact of digital technology on psychological treatments and their dissemination. Behav. Res. Ther. **88**, 19–25 (2017)
6. Lovejoy, C.A.: Technology and mental health: The role of artificial intelligence. Eur. Psychiatry **55**, 1–3 (2019)
7. Bashshur, R., Doarn, C.R., Frenk J.M., Kvedar, J.C., Woolliscroft, J.O.: Telemedicine and the COVID-19 pandemic, lessons for the future. Telemed. e-Health **26**(5), 571–573 (2020)
8. Usher, K., Durkin, J., Bhullar, N.: The COVID-19 pandemic and mental health impacts. Int. J. Ment. Health Nurs. **29**, 315–318 (2020)
9. Google App Engine website: https://cloud.google.com/appengine. Accessed 30 Apr 2021
10. Cloud Endpoints website: https://cloud.google.com/endpoints. Accessed 30 Apr 2021
11. Google Cloud Vision website: https://cloud.google.com/vision. Accessed 30 Apr 2021
12. Kartynnik, Y., Ablavatski, A., Grihchenko, I., Grundmann, M.: Real-time facial surface geometry from monocular video on mobile GPUs. arXiv, 15 Jul 2019

Detecting, Predicting, and Preventing Driver Drowsiness with Wrist-Wearable Devices

Cláudia Rodrigues[1,3], Brígida Mónica Faria[1,2(✉)], and Luís Paulo Reis[1,3]

[1] LIACC – Artificial Intelligence and Computer Science Laboratory, Porto, Portugal
[2] ESS/P.Porto - School of Health, Polytechnic of Porto, Porto, Portugal
btf@ess.ipp.pt
[3] FEUP – Faculty of Engineering, University of Porto, Porto, Portugal
{up201508262,lpreis}@fe.up.pt

Abstract. Insufficient sleep is a prominent problem in modern society with several negative effects and risks. One of the most serious consequences is traffic accidents caused by drowsy driving. Current solutions are focused on detecting drowsiness, where individuals need to reach a certain drowsiness level to receive an alarm, which may be too late to react. In this context, it is relevant to develop a wearable system that integrates the prediction of drowsiness and its prevention. By predicting the drowsy state, the driver can be warned in advance while still alert. To minimize further incidents, the reason why a state of drowsiness occurs must be identified, caused by a sleep disorder or sleep deprivation. The contribution of this work is to review the main scientific and commercial solutions, and perform automatic sleep staging based on heart rate variability. Results show that, although promising, this approach requires a larger dataset to consider a user-dependent scenario.

Keywords: Drowsiness prediction · Biometric data · Non-intrusive system · Machine learning

1 Introduction

Driving is a highly complex activity that requires considerable perceptual, physical, and cognitive demands to be effective [1]. As the driver must remain aware of the environment, active attention plays a crucial role in safe driving. It is estimated by the World Health Organization that vehicle collisions cause approximately 1.35 million deaths worldwide and an even greater number of non-fatal injuries each year [2]. One of the leading contributors to this public health problem is drowsy driving, which accounts for 10–30% of all road accidents, and is a major cause of traffic fatalities [3].

Several factors can contribute to driver drowsiness. The most frequent causes include sleep disorders and behavioral factors such as sleep deprivation or shift work [4]. Long driving hours and time of day are also identified to increase

© Springer Nature Switzerland AG 2021
G. Marreiros et al. (Eds.): EPIA 2021, LNAI 12981, pp. 109–120, 2021.
https://doi.org/10.1007/978-3-030-86230-5_9

accident risk [5]. Professional drivers are therefore more susceptible to crashes. In a Portuguese study, more than 8 out of every 10 truck drivers reported to drive while feeling sleepy [6]. In addition to the high levels of driving exposure, many drivers work long hours, sometimes irregular and in conflict with natural circadian rhythms [7]. As a result, a considerable sleep debt can be accumulated. The working schedule also poses challenges in adopting a healthy lifestyle, including a balanced diet and regular exercise [8]. They are identified as a high-risk group for health conditions such as obesity and sleep apnea.

In order to reduce the chances of accidents, technology has a key role. Driving monitoring and assistance systems have been progressively integrated into vehicles to assist drivers for a safe and comfortable driving experience [9]. Several commercial products are also available in the market, considering different measurement methods [10]. However, most current approaches focus on the detection of an impaired state of the driver rather than on its prediction [11]. Thus, it is relevant to distinguish these two terms. The ideal goal should be to predict the onset of drowsiness since, at the detection point, drowsy driving may already have led to a potentially dangerous situation or even an accident [12].

These systems can be seen as a reactive approach to drowsiness events during driving. However, a preventive one can also be considered when identifying their underlying cause. Sleep deprivation has increased globally in today's fast-paced lifestyle, with sleep disorders reaching a substantial number of people [13]. In particular, insomnia affects approximately 10–15% of the general adult population [14], and obstructive sleep apnea 9–38% [15]. In this context, consumer products such as wearable devices are becoming widely available, and can automatically analyze sleep patterns. However, these new systems are rarely validated against polysomnography, considered the gold-standard method to assess sleep, to ensure their reliability and validity [16].

The proposed solution to increase road safety is to develop a wrist-worn wearable device that can detect and predict drowsiness when the user is driving, and continuously identify a potential chronic sleep deprivation or sleep disorder. A flowchart of the system is shown in Fig. 1. Towards the final goal, this work uses a public dataset for sleep staging based on heart rate variability (HRV) measured from electrocardiogram (ECG) signals. The preliminary results obtained will serve as a starting point for analyzing future wearable data.

Fig. 1. Representation of the proposed system.

The remainder of this paper is organized as follows: in Sect. 2 a comprehensive analysis of the literature is made; Sect. 3 describes the methodology used for sleep staging, with the results presented in Sect. 4; Sect. 5 provides the conclusions to the work developed, and future directions.

2   Related Work

2.1   Measurement of Driver Drowsiness

Several techniques to estimate driver drowsiness have been proposed in the literature. According to the source of information, these methods can be classified into the following measures: subjective, behavioral, vehicle-based and physiological [17]. A hybrid approach that combines several methods can also be used.

Subjective measures include self-assessment and observer ratings [18]. The driver's personal estimation is evaluated through scales such as the commonly used Karolinska sleepiness scale (KSS) [19], represented by a nine-point scale that ranges from "extremely alert" to "very sleepy" as shown in Fig. 2. During an experiment, the considered questionnaire is presented to the subject repeatedly, with either a time interval or certain conditions. In terms of observer ratings, experts or trained individuals observe the driver in real-time or by watching video recordings, with scales that focus on behavioral changes. As these measures are not practical to be applied in real driving conditions, they are mainly used as ground truth for drowsiness detection systems.

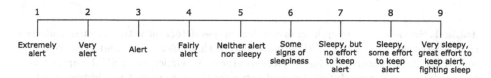

Fig. 2. Karolinska sleepiness scale (KSS).

Alternatively, behavioral measures use a camera and image processing techniques to monitor the driver. These methods evaluate mainly three parameters: facial expression, eye movements and head position. Vehicle-based systems assess driving performance, with features such as steering wheel movement and deviation of lane position. The last category involves using physiological signals, that include the following [10]:

– Brain activity: captured by electroencephalography (EEG);
– Ocular activity: measured by electrooculography (EOG);
– Muscle tone: recorded using electromyography (EMG);
– Cardiac activity: monitored through electrocardiography (ECG) and photoplethysmography (PPG) signals.
– Skin conductance: measured by electrodermal activity (EDA);

All of the different methods present some limitations [11,20]. Behavioral measures can be affected by the environment and driving conditions, such as changes in lighting and the use of glasses. Vehicle-based systems are highly dependent upon road geometry, and are often not effective in conditions with substantial variation. Finally, physiological methods involve the intrusive nature of sensors.

Nevertheless, this kind of data is considered reliable and accurate to measure the driver's functional state. It starts to change in the early stages of drowsiness and is, therefore, more suitable to provide an alert on time. Thus, non-invasive monitoring strategies for recording signals are required.

Over the years, the usage of wearables has been gradually growing. According to the International Data Corporation, global shipments of wearable devices reached 444.7 million units in 2020, which marks a 28.4% increase compared to the previous year [21]. In this market, prevails particularly the trend of fitness tracking and health monitoring with wrist-worn devices, such as smartwatches and fitness trackers [18]. The wide user acceptance is associated with advantages such as low cost, comfort, and continuous recording of several physiological signals. These can be considered suitable for the task of detecting driver drowsiness, and will be further assessed in the following sections.

2.2 Drowsiness Detection

The use of wrist-worn wearable devices for driver drowsiness detection has been explored by previous work. Table 1 summarizes existing studies, comparing the methodology adopted in terms of measures, algorithms and evaluation.

Table 1. Summary of research on driver drowsiness detection with measures collected from a wrist-wearable device. MVT–movement with accelerometer and gyroscope sensors; TMP–temperature; C–classes; Acc–accuracy; N–participants; SVM–support vector machine; CNN–convolutional neural network; KNN–k-nearest neighbors; and DS–decision stump. (*) detects drowsiness, stress and fatigue.

| Ref. | Measures | | | | Segments | Labeling | Model | C | Validation | Acc. | N |
	MVT	PPG	EDA	TMP							
[22]	x				1 min + 1 s	Video: KSS (1 min)	SVM	5	70/30 split	98.15%	20
[23]	x	x	x	x	10 s + 8 s	Video: 1–5 scale (5 min)	SVM	4 (*)	5-fold CV	98.3%	28
									LOSO CV	68.3%	
[24]		x			2 min	Video (1 min)	CNN	2	10-fold CV	64%	6
[25]		x			2 min + 2 s	KSS (5 min)	KNN	2	10-fold CV	99.9%	30
[18]		x			5 min + 2 s	Video: 1–6 scale (5 min)	KNN	2	10-fold CV	92.1%	30
							DS		LOSO CV	73.4%	

To record driver state, studies are conducted in simulated environments. The scoring is obtained with subjective metrics, whose levels are typically grouped to a reduced number of classes. The collected signals are divided mainly using a sliding window strategy and the model performance is evaluated with different forms of cross-validation (CV). Because physiological signals within persons can differ to a great extent, tests that consider the split among subjects are crucial to evaluate the ability to generalize for new users.

The majority of studies use PPG sensors to derive HRV features. This analysis refers to the variation in time between successive heart beats, called inter-beat intervals (IBIs), and represents a non-invasive measure of the autonomic nervous system [26]. Another commonly used description for IBIs is RR intervals, which is the time between two R-peaks of the QRS complex on the ECG. HRV can be described in 24 h, short-term ($\sim$5 min), and ultra-short-term (<5 min) measurement periods, using time-domain, frequency-domain, and non-linear parameters [27]. Time-domain indices measure the amount of HRV that was observed. Frequency-domain values estimate the distribution of absolute or relative power into component bands. Finally, non-linear metrics quantify the unpredictability and complexity of the time series. Although multi-lead ECG devices are established as the gold standard for computing HRV, wearable devices based on single-lead ECG and PPG are considered a viable and popular alternative. The main drawback is that this type of sensing is more affected by motion artefacts, pressure disturbances and skin pigmentation [28]. Nevertheless, noise and artifact reduction techniques can be used to improve signal quality. An overview of the typical methodology of HRV analysis for drowsiness detection systems is presented next, in Fig. 3.

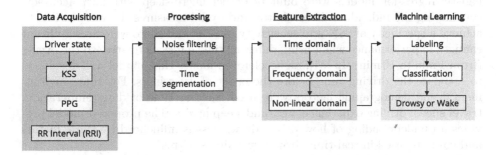

Fig. 3. Overview of the typical methodology used for drowsiness detection, when performing heart rate variability (HRV) analysis on photoplethysmogram (PPG) signals collected from wrist-worn wearable devices.

Results show that high accuracies can be achieved, but the employed datasets can introduce some conditioning factors. In HRV recordings, important subject variables that can affect measurements include age, sex, and health status [27]. Moreover, the association between measured signals and driver alertness is often performed at unknown circadian phase and wake duration [10]. The influence of inter-driver variance is reflected in lower values of accuracy, which indicates challenges that still need to be investigated to develop a robust, yet comfortable and cost-effective commercial drowsiness warning system. In this context, market products based on physiological signals present low progress compared to driving and driver behavioral technologies [10]. Apart from research, a wrist-wearable device is not yet available at the moment.

2.3   Drowsiness Prediction

For the task of predicting driver drowsiness, current research is still limited as there are no studies that consider wearable devices.

In [11], two independent models were developed using neural networks. Every minute, a detection model identifies the level of drowsiness, and a prediction model indicates the time required to reach a certain level of drowsiness (1.5 on a 0–4 scale). For that, physiological, behavioral, and vehicle-based indicators were investigated. The best performance was obtained with behavioral measures and additional information, namely, driving time and participant data. These models were able to detect and predict drowsiness with a mean square error of 0.22 and 4.18 min, respectively. However, inter-individual variability was only considered in [29]. To find a compromise between generalized and individual models, adaptive learning was used. The improvement in performance was significant from the first 3 min up to 15 min of input data, reaching about 40% in detection and 80% in prediction. Nevertheless, intra-individual variability was not addressed, that is, how regularly this adaptation would be necessary.

In order to predict the drowsy state, the time remaining until a target level is reached was used. However, other studies consider different approaches. In [30], logistic regression models were built to detect micro-sleep with 93% accuracy, considering the individual driver factor and eyelid measures. It was possible to achieve a specificity of 98% and sensitivity of 67%, and there were no significant changes in performance when using different time intervals relative to the events (from 1 min to 10 min). In [31], an accelerated failure time model was developed to estimate the driving time before the onset of drowsiness. For that, environmental and demographic factors were used, such as time of day, temperature, travel speed, driving experience, age, and sleep habits. The proposed model provides an understanding of how driver drowsiness is influenced by these factors and could be used in real-time drowsy warning systems.

In these studies, physiological measures were mainly collected in an intrusive manner, i.e., using electrodes. Therefore, a relevant direction is to investigate if similar results can be obtained in a simple and non-invasive way.

2.4   Sleep Staging

Sleep staging is essential to assess sleep and diagnose sleep disorders. This process involves segmenting a sleep period into 30 s epochs and assigning a sleep stage to each epoch [32]. According to the American Academy of Sleep Medicine (AASM) manual, sleep is divided into five stages: wake (W), rapid eye movement (REM), and three levels of non-REM (NREM) corresponding to N1, N2, and N3. Traditionally, sleep staging is performed by experts based on visual inspection of polysomnographic (PSG) recordings, which include multiple physiological parameters. Although it remains the gold standard for clinical assessment of sleep, PSG has some drawbacks: the scoring procedure is expensive, time-consuming, and prone to human errors [33]. Therefore, alternative methods and algorithms capable of accurately estimating sleep stages are needed.

To assess long-term sleep, actigraphy can be a useful tool [34]. This technique relies on a wrist-worn device that infers wake and sleep states by measuring movement through an accelerometer. Although it has some advantages, the cost and requirement of specialized technicians are among the main factors leading to the consideration of consumer wearables. These devices use multi-sensor data acquisition, and are not limited to binary sleep classification. Despite their widespread use, validation studies show that they tend to underestimate sleep disruptions and overestimate sleep efficiency, i.e., prioritize sensitivity to specificity [35]. In particular, these measures ranged from 95–97% and 39–62%, respectively, in four commercial solutions analyzed [36]. It is important to note that the algorithms implemented in these self-tracking devices are not public, and raw sensor data is not accessible for external use. As a result, although promising for understanding of sleep health, their application in sleep research and clinical sleep medicine is still limited [34]. Some recent studies are summarized in Table 2, considering different scoring resolutions.

Table 2. Summary of research of sleep staging with measures collected from a wrist-wearable device. Classification is divided in two-stages (wake/sleep), three-stages (wake/NREM/REM), four-stages (wake/light sleep(N1+N2)/deep sleep(N3)/REM), and five-stages (wake/N1/N2/N3/REM). Results are presented in a accuracy/kappa format. N–participants; LDA–Linear Discriminant Analysis; BLSTM–Bidirectional Long Short-Term Memory; ANN–Artificial Neural Network.

	Measures								
Ref.	MVT	PPG	Model	Validation	2-stage	3-stage	4-stage	5-stage	N
[37]	x	x	LDA	2 datasets	91.5%/0.55	72.9%/0.46	59.3%/0.42	-	101+51
[38]	x	x	LDA	LOSO CV	-	-	69%/0.52	-	60
[39]	x	x	BLSTM	LOSO CV	-	-	-	67.7%	39
[40]		x	BLSTM	4-fold CV	-	-	-	74.7%/0.63	292+60
[36]	x	x	ANN	2 datasets	80%/0.53	68.6%/0.4	-	-	31+188
[41]		x	SVM	LOSO CV	-	73%/0.43	60%/0.38	54%/0.35	18
[42]	x	x	LDA	LOSO CV	-	85%/0.67	77%/0.58	-	50

Despite the differences among studies, classifiers achieve a lower performance when the number of classes increase. A sequential model that considers the temporal dependencies of sleep is trained in [39] and [40]. These type of algorithms have also recently shown good results when the HRV analysis is performed using single-lead ECG data [43]. The influence of factors like demographics and environmental conditions on the signals recorded by the worn devices, and thus their capability in accurately staging sleep, should not be underestimated [34]. Except in [40], datasets are limited to healthy adults, without additional validation for other age groups or sleep disorders.

3　Methodology

For the sleep staging task based on HRV from ECG signals, the public dataset "EEG/EOG/EMG data from a cross sectional study on psychophysiological insomnia and normal sleep subjects" [44] was used. The data consists in recordings of 8h from 22 subjects, aged between 18 and 63 years. Table 3 shows the epoch distribution of the normal subjects by sleep stage. For the experiments, this data is classified into Wake, REM, and NREM (grouping N1, N2 and N3). Data processing was performed with the Python programming language, and scikit-learn and pyhrv [45] libraries.

Table 3. Distribution of segments by sleep stage. Stages N3 and N4 were merged into stage N3 according to the AASM manual.

Condition	Wake	REM	N1	N2	N3+N4	Total
Normal (11)	1272 (12%)	708 (7%)	3749 (36%)	2286 (22%)	2379 + 26 (23%)	10420

The ECG signal was initially synchronized in time with PSG results, and the segments classified as movement were removed. For HRV analysis, the signal was divided into segments of 1.5 min, 2.5 min, 3.5 min, and 4.5 min, centered in each 30 s interval, with the goal of evaluating the impact of segment length in performance. After extracting the RR interval time series, segments were processed in time, frequency, and non-linear domains, obtaining a total of 34 features. The approach considered applies two types of validation, namely, stratified 10-fold CV and LOSO-CV. In each iteration, training data was first normalized at each attribute, to a mean of zero and standard deviation of one. Then, after selecting the best subset of features using the Pearson's correlation coefficient with a threshold of 0.9, data was over-sampled with the SVM-Smote technique. Finally, performance measures were calculated as the average of all iterations, in particular the accuracy and sensitivity of each class. Figure 4 illustrates the process described. The four classification algorithms tested were support vector machine (SVM), linear discriminant analysis (LDA), k-nearest neighbors (KNN) with 15 neighbors, and random forest (RF) with a maximum depth of 20. The remaining parameters were set to the default values.

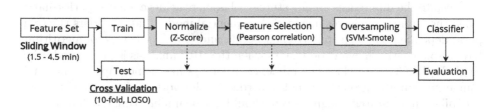

Fig. 4. Methodology adopted for sleep staging.

4   Results

The results of sleep classification are presented in Table 4. In the first validation test (10-fold CV), it is possible to observe that, except for the LDA algorithm, a larger segment dimension increases the accuracy. Using a 4.5 min window, RF obtained the best performance with a sensibility to Wake, REM, and NREM of 81%, 71%, and 93%, respectively. Regarding the subject-dependent test (LOSO-CV), this approach proved not sufficient to deal with individual variability. In the same setting, RF decreases the sensitivity of REM to 18%. This problem can be justified by a significant difference in class distribution between subjects. In particular, the REM stage ranges from 1 to 118 instances, and Wake from 7 to 331 instances. Therefore, to evaluate this type of scenario, a more comprehensive dataset is required.

Table 4. Results of the classification of 3 classes (accuracy and standard deviation), with different algorithms and window length.

10-fold CV				
Model	1.5 min	2.5 min	3.5 min	4.5 min
SVM	0.75 (0.01)	0.77 (0.01)	0.79 (0.01)	0.79 (0.01)
LDA	0.74 (0.01)	0.72 (0.01)	0.71 (0.01)	0.7 (0.01)
KNN	0.69 (0.02)	0.7 (0.02)	0.72 (0.01)	0.73 (0.01)
RF	0.84 (0.01)	0.87 (0.0)	0.89 (0.01)	0.9 (0.01)

LOSO-CV				
Model	1.5 min	2.5 min	3.5 min	4.5 min
SVM	0.69 (0.1)	0.67 (0.17)	0.68 (0.18)	0.67 (0.19)
LDA	0.63 (0.07)	0.58 (0.26)	0.6 (0.21)	0.57 (0.24)
KNN	0.63 (0.09)	0.56 (0.14)	0.56 (0.13)	0.55 (0.14)
RF	0.74 (0.12)	0.75 (0.12)	0.75 (0.14)	0.76 (0.14)

5   Conclusion

The impact of drowsy driving is of recognized severity. This work reviews current solutions to address this problem, with a focus on wrist-wearable devices, which allow continuous long-term monitoring of multiple signals. In this context, a system that can detect, predict, and prevent driver drowsiness is proposed. Towards the final solution, sleep staging was performed with HRV analysis on ECG signals, using traditional machine learning algorithms.

Results show that a broader dataset is essential to improve the performance on subject-dependent tests. Future work will explore deep learning architectures, and the inclusion of new signals.

Acknowledgements. This work was supported by the European Regional Development Fund through the programme COMPETE by FCT (Portugal) in the scope of the project PEst-UID/CEC/00027/2015 and Sono ao Volante 2.0 - Information system for predicting sleeping while driving and detecting disorders or chronic sleep deprivation - NORTE-01-0247-FEDER-039720, supported by Norte Portugal Regional Operational Programme (NORTE 2020), under the PORTUGAL 2020 Partnership Agreement. This research was partially supported by LIACC (FCT/UID/CEC/0027/2020).

References

1. Collet, C., Musicant, O.: Associating vehicles automation with drivers functional state assessment systems: a challenge for road safety in the future. Front. Hum. Neurosci. **13**, 131 (2019)
2. Global status report on road safety 2018. World Health Organization (2018)
3. Gonçalves, M., et al.: Sleepiness at the wheel across Europe: a survey of 19 countries. J. Sleep Res. **24**(3), 242–253 (2015)
4. Bioulac, S., et al.: Risk of motor vehicle accidents related to sleepiness at the wheel: a systematic review and meta-analysis. Sleep **40**(10) (2017)
5. Thiffault, P., Bergeron, J.: Monotony of road environment and driver fatigue: a simulator study. Accid. Anal. Prev. **35**(3), 381–391 (2003)
6. Catarino, R., Spratley, J., Catarino, I., Lunet, N., Pais-Clemente, M.: Sleepiness and sleep-disordered breathing in truck drivers. Sleep Breathing **18**(1), 59–68 (2014)
7. Anne, T., John, M., Rohrbaugh, W., Hammer, M.C., Fuller, S.Z.: Factors associated with falling asleep at the wheel among long-distance truck drivers. Accid. Anal. Prev. **32**(4), 493–504 (2000)
8. Greenfield, R., et al.: Truck drivers' perceptions on wearable devices and health promotion: a qualitative study. BMC Public Health **16**(1), 1–10 (2016)
9. Khan, M.Q., Lee, S.: A comprehensive survey of driving monitoring and assistance systems. Sensors **19**(11), 2574 (2019)
10. Doudou, M.., Bouabdallah, A.., Berge-Cherfaoui, V..: Driver drowsiness measurement technologies: current research, market solutions, and challenges. Int. J. Intell. Transp. Syst. Res. **18**(2), 297–319 (2019). https://doi.org/10.1007/s13177-019-00199-w
11. de Naurois, C.J., Bourdin, C., Stratulat, A., Diaz, E., Vercher, J.-L.: Detection and prediction of driver drowsiness using artificial neural network models. Accid. Anal. Prev.**126**, 95–104 (2019)
12. Kircher, A., Uddman, M., Sandin, J.: Vehicle control and drowsiness. Statens väg- och transportforskningsinstitut (2002)
13. Jaiswal, S.J., Owens, R.L., Malhotra, A.: Raising awareness about sleep disorders. Lung India Official Organ Indian Chest Soc. **34**(3), 262 (2017)
14. Tobaldini, E., et al.: Sleep, sleep deprivation, autonomic nervous system and cardiovascular diseases. Neurosci. Biobehav. Rev. **74**, 321–329 (2017)
15. Senaratna, C.V., et al.: Prevalence of obstructive sleep apnea in the general population: a systematic review. Sleep Med. Rev. **34**, 70–81 (2017)
16. Ameen, M.S., Cheung, L.M., Hauser, T., Hahn, M.A., Schabus, M.: About the accuracy and problems of consumer devices in the assessment of sleep. Sensors **19**(19), 4160 (2019)
17. Sahayadhas, A., Sundaraj, K., Murugappan, M.: Detecting driver drowsiness based on sensors: a review. Sensors **12**(12), 16937–16953 (2012)

18. Kundinger, T., Sofra, N., Riener, A.: Assessment of the potential of wrist-worn wearable sensors for driver drowsiness detection. Sensors **20**(4), 1029 (2020)

19. Shahid, A., Wilkinson, K., Marcu, S., Shapiro, C.M.: Karolinska sleepiness scale (kss). In: STOP, THAT and One Hundred Other Sleep Scales, pp. 209–210. Springer (2011). https://doi.org/10.1007/978-1-4419-9893-4

20. Awais, M., Badruddin, N., Drieberg, M.: A hybrid approach to detect driver drowsiness utilizing physiological signals to improve system performance and wearability. Sensors **17**(9), 1991 (2017)

21. Consumer enthusiasm for wearable devices drives the market to 28.4% growth in 2020, according to idc (2021)

22. Lee, B.-L., Lee, B.-G., Chung, W.-Y.: Standalone wearable driver drowsiness detection system in a smartwatch. IEEE Sensors J. **16**(13), 5444–5451 (2016)

23. Choi, M., Koo, G., Seo, M., Kim, S.W.: Wearable device-based system to monitor a driver's stress, fatigue, and drowsiness. IEEE Trans. Instrum. Meas. **67**(3), 634–645 (2017)

24. Lee, H., Lee, J., Shin, M.: Using wearable ECG/PPG sensors for driver drowsiness detection based on distinguishable pattern of recurrence plots. Electronics **8**(2), 192 (2019)

25. Kundinger, T., Yalavarthi, P.K., Riener, A., Wintersberger, P., Schartmüller, C.: Feasibility of smart wearables for driver drowsiness detection and its potential among different age groups. Int. J. Pervasive Comput. Commun. **16**, 1–23 (2020)

26. Sztajzel, J., et al.: Heart rate variability: a noninvasive electrocardiographic method to measure the autonomic nervous system. Swiss Med. Wkly **134**(35–36), 514–522 (2004)

27. Shaffer, F., Ginsberg, J.P.: An overview of heart rate variability metrics and norms. Front. Public Health **5**, 258 (2017)

28. Kamišalić, A., Fister, I., Turkanović, M., Karakatič, S.: Sensors and functionalities of non-invasive wrist-wearable devices: a review. Sensors **18**(6), 1714 (2018)

29. de Naurois, C.J., Bourdin, C., Bougard, C., Vercher, J.-L.: Adapting artificial neural networks to a specific driver enhances detection and prediction of drowsiness. Accid. Anal. Prev. **121**, 118–128 (2018)

30. Liang, Y., et al.: Prediction of drowsiness events in night shift workers during morning driving. Accid. Anal. Prev. **126**, 105–114 (2019)

31. Wang, J., Sun, S., Fang, S., Ting, F., Stipancic, J.: Predicting drowsy driving in real-time situations: using an advanced driving simulator, accelerated failure time model, and virtual location-based services. Accid. Anal. Prev. **99**, 321–329 (2017)

32. Radha, M., et al.: Sleep stage classification from heart-rate variability using long short-term memory neural networks. Sci. Rep. **9**(1), 1–11 (2019)

33. Aboalayon, K.A.I., Faezipour, M., Almuhammadi, W.S., Moslehpour, S.: Sleep stage classification using EEG signal analysis: a comprehensive survey and new investigation. Entropy **18**(9), 272 (2016)

34. De Zambotti, M., Cellini, N., Goldstone, A., Colrain, I.M., Baker, F.C.: Wearable sleep technology in clinical and research settings. Med. Sci. Sports Exerc. **51**(7), 1538 (2019)

35. Ibáñez, V., Silva, J., Cauli, O.: A survey on sleep assessment methods. PeerJ **6**, e4849 (2018)

36. Walch, O., Huang, Y., Forger, D., Goldstein, C.: Sleep stage prediction with raw acceleration and photoplethysmography heart rate data derived from a consumer wearable device. Sleep **42**(12), zsz180 (2019)

37. Fonseca, P., et al.: Validation of photoplethysmography-based sleep staging compared with polysomnography in healthy middle-aged adults. Sleep **40**(7), zsx097 (2017)
38. Beattie, Z., et al.: Estimation of sleep stages in a healthy adult population from optical plethysmography and accelerometer signals. Physiol. Meas. **38**(11), 1968 (2017)
39. Zhang, X., et al.: Sleep stage classification based on multi-level feature learning and recurrent neural networks via wearable device. Comput. Biol. Med. **103**, 71–81 (2018)
40. Radha, M., Fonseca, P., Ross, M., Cerny, A., Anderer, P., Aarts, R.M.: LSTM knowledge transfer for HRV-based sleep staging. arXiv preprint arXiv:1809.06221 (2018)
41. Molkkari, M., Tenhunen, M., Tarniceriu, A., Vehkaoja, A., Himanen, S.-L., Räsänen, E.: Non-linear heart rate variability measures in sleep stage analysis with photoplethysmography. In: 2019 Computing in Cardiology (CinC), p. 1. IEEE (2019)
42. Fedorin, I., Slyusarenko, K., Lee, W., Sakhnenko, N.: Sleep stages classification in a healthy people based on optical plethysmography and accelerometer signals via wearable devices. In: 2019 IEEE 2nd Ukraine Conference on Electrical and Computer Engineering (UKRCON), pp. 1201–1204. IEEE (2019)
43. Wei, Y., Qi, X., Wang, H., Liu, Z., Wang, G., Yan, X.: A multi-class automatic sleep staging method based on long short-term memory network using single-lead electrocardiogram signals. IEEE Access **7**, 85959–85970 (2019)
44. Rezaei, M., Mohammadi, H., Khazaie, H.: EEG/EOG/EMG data from a cross sectional study on psychophysiological insomnia and normal sleep subjects. Data in brief **15**, 314–319 (2017)
45. Gomes, P., Margaritoff, P., Silva, H.: pyHRV: development and evaluation of an open-source python toolbox for heart rate variability (HRV). In: Proceedings of International Conference on Electrical, Electronic and Computing Engineering (IcETRAN), pp. 822–828 (2019)

The Evolution of Artificial Intelligence in Medical Informatics: A Bibliometric Analysis

Bruno Elias Penteado[1]([⊠]) (iD), Marcelo Fornazin[2] (iD), and Leonardo Castro[2] (iD)

[1] Fiocruz Strategy for the 2030 Agenda, Oswaldo Cruz Foundation,
Rio de Janeiro, Brazil
[2] National School of Public Health, Oswaldo Cruz Foundation, Rio de Janeiro, Brazil
{marcelo.fornazin,leonardo.castro}@ensp.fiocruz.br

Abstract. Artificial intelligence (AI) and medical informatics research fields have considerable overlap, with technologies supporting different health issues in different contexts. In this work, we aimed to map out and understand the contributions of AI in medical informatics over time. To that, we applied bibliometric analysis with scientific literature since the 1970s. The production of papers exponentially increased over time, and we found periods with similar characteristics of the content. We also identified different clusters of technologies and applications varying according to the periods and related keywords. We hypothesized some future directions for the use of AI in medical informatics.

Keywords: Bibliometric analysis · Artificial intelligence · Medical informatics

1 Introduction

Artificial intelligence (AI) was first conceived in the 1950s, with the essays of Alan Turing on the use of computers to simulate intelligent behavior. The term itself was coined at the Dartmouth College conference in 1956, describing it as the science and engineering of making intelligent machines. Since then, AI has evolved dramatically over the last five decades, addressing multiple dimensions of informational and algorithmic issues. Current predictive models create opportunities for personalized medicine, being used for the diagnosis of diseases, the prediction of therapeutic responses, and potentially preventive medicine [1]. In addition, AI is considered the main driver for the 4th Industrial Revolution [2], which impacts our economies and societies [3].

Early on, healthcare was identified as one of the most promising applications of AI. The first AI systems were knowledge-based decision support systems that presented good performance but were never used routinely on actual patients for two main reasons: i) these were stand-alone systems, not connected to empirical

This study was supported by the Fiocruz Strategy for 2030 Agenda.

G. Marreiros et al. (Eds.): EPIA 2021, LNAI 12981, pp. 121–133, 2021.
https://doi.org/10.1007/978-3-030-86230-5_10

data, such as EHR; ii) due to subjectivity of the expertise expressed in those rules, the systems were not accepted, being more useful for teaching than for clinical practice [4]. Some of the limitations were only overcome with the advent of machine learning in the 2000s. Algorithms that learn from data offered a more practical approach than previous expert systems, which crafted medical knowledge into decision rules.

In the earlier prediction algorithms, there was a need for a feature selection and engineering process to make the models useful. Deep learning provided some advance on this since it learns complex features from the raw data rather than leaning on manual feature engineering. Such AI algorithmic advancements raised the debate about the usefulness of data-driven instead of theory-driven models [17]. However, a famous counterexample of the pure data-driven AI application is the Google Flu Trends, an AI-based tool that used aggregated search data to estimate flu activity in certain regions. In practice, Google's algorithm predicted more than double the proportion of doctor visits for influenza-like illness than the Centers for Disease Control and Prevention (CDC), which bases its estimates on surveillance reports from laboratories across the United States [5]. As pointed in [6], incorporating AI into clinical practice remains a challenge because of methodological flaws and underlying biases present in the study design.

In this work, we sought to understand how AI technologies and methods have evolved along with healthcare, understand the paths taken so far and discuss possible trends for the area's future. We do that with bibliometric analysis that helped us extract interesting patterns out of the scientific literature from this field of research. In particular, we aimed to answer the following research questions: RQ1) how were different periods organized around AI and how are different countries associated with key terms? This question is essential to understand waves of technological impact on the field; RQ2) how different topics have evolved over the years? This question is relevant to understand which bodies of knowledge were predominant at a specific time.

2   A Brief History of AI in Healthcare

As stated in the Introduction, AI was first introduced in the 1950s, and the earliest works in medicine have been reported almost two decades later. Some early developments of AI, such as the first industrial robot arm (Unimate in 1961), the first chatbot (Eliza, in 1964), and the first electronic person (Shakey, in 1966), were important milestones for AI but not directly applied to medical informatics.

The first generation of AI systems may be considered from the 1960 and 1970 decades, where the intention was to curate medical knowledge by experts and formulate robust decision rules [9]. Early AI in medicine researchers had discovered the applicability of AI to life sciences, especially in the Dendral experiments [8] in the late 1960s. This project gathered scientists from different areas in collaborative work that demonstrated the ability to represent and use expert knowledge in symbolic form. During the 1970s, there was a growing interest in biomedical applications, using the ARPANET and the SUMEX-AIM [12] infrastructure, promoting AI applications to biological and medical problems, and the collaboration and resource sharing within a national community of health research projects. Projects such as CASNET [10] and MYCIN [11] were developed. The late 1970s was known as the first "AI Winter", which showed reduced funding and interest in the field due to the perceived limitations of AI. In 1986, a decision support system - DXplain [14] - used symptoms to generate differential diagnoses on approximately 500 diseases. In 1991, the field was still consolidating amid a second "AI winter" because of the high cost of developing and maintaining expert systems and databases [1]. In this time, the popularization of personal computers and high-performance workstations enabled new types of AI in medical research and new models for technology dissemination [18]. Technological developments in the late 2000s and early 2010s, such as the IBM Watson [19] and Apple's Siri, have brought natural language processing and machine learning methods to analyze data over unstructured content to generate probable answers, being easier to build, maintain, and supported diverse applications [20,21]. IBM Watson was an open-domain question-answering system that used natural language processing and various searches to analyze data over unstructured content to generate probable answers, in particular from patients' electronic medical records. It showed success in some medical areas (e.g. [13]) and failures in others [26]. With the availability of larger health datasets, cloud computing, and improved computing power in these years, there was an important advancement in deep learning, with relevant applications in medical image analysis. Arterys [22] was the first deep learning cloud-based application approved by the US Food and Drugs Administration (FDA) in 2017. The application analyzed cardiac magnetic resonance images, and it was further expanded to liver, lung, chest, and musculoskeletal X-ray images.

3   Related Work

We list in this section some of the works that described the development of AI in medical informatics and healthcare, with different strategies and analytical tools.

In [9], the authors present a high-level overview of AI in medicine, dividing it into two significant successful periods: i) the early adoption, in the 60s–70s, with the development of expert systems and the codification of medical knowledge in explicit conditional rules and ii) the recent (from 2012 thus far) development of machine learning and deep learning techniques which showed a big improvement in image-based diagnosis, genome interpretation, biomarker discovery, patient monitoring, clinical outcome prediction, and robotic surgery.

In [24], the authors reviewed all the papers published in the AIME (Artificial Intelligence in MEdicine) conference from 1985 to 2013 and identified 30 research topics across 12 themes. The authors adopted a mixed-method approach, creating a taxonomy of themes using topic analysis and then counting the number of citations to identify the most impacting papers for the community. Knowledge engineering topics dominated in the first decade, and then machine learning and data mining prevailed after that. Both themes contributed to 51% of all papers produced in that period.

In [1], the authors presented a historical perspective and divided the adoption of AI technologies into three periods: i) 1950–1970, focusing on machines with the ability to make inferences that only a human could make; ii) 1970–2000, the 'AI winter', a period of reduced funding and interest[1], where some expert systems prototypes were successfully developed, and iii) the 1990s–2020s, where machine learning and deep learning gained momentum to provide personalized medicine, supported by infrastructural developments for the collection and storage of data and processing power.

The authors in [18] listed topics and themes compiled from the Artificial Intelligence in Medicine Europe (AIME) proceedings for 16 years (1991–2007). Topics included clinical data mining, knowledge discovery from databases, ontologies, text and image processing, feature selection, workflow, visualization.

Other systematic reviews were done for AI in medicine but limited to some niches, such as applications of deep learning in healthcare [28], surveillance in public health [29], consumer health [30], AI education for health professionals [25,27], AI adoption in healthcare [31], and economic impact [32]. In our previous work [33] we mapped out all the production medical informatics, emphasizing the importance of AI for developing the area.

This work extends the literature by providing an exploratory and empirical vision of AI applications in medical informatics, analyzing scientific literature developed since the 1990s through bibliometric techniques, having more than 15 thousand papers collected.

4   Methodology

We used the standard bibliometric workflow as defined in [23], consisting of five phases: study design, data collection, data analysis, data visualization, and interpretation. The study design consists of the research questions posed in Sect. 1 and the search strategy delimited in this section.

The data was collected from the Web of Science (WoS) Core Collection database, used here as a proxy for the science production as a whole. First, we defined a search string limited to papers categorized as "medical informatics" in the database, limiting research to those related to this area. Next, we filtered for papers written English and published in journals, conferences, or reviews. Finally, we expanded the query string using terms related to AI, using similar terms from the MeSH (Medical Subjects Heading[2]) taxonomy and other terms extracted from conferences' calls for papers. The final query string is made explicit in Table 1 and it was executed on April 2021. The results were exported

---

[1] In fact, the authors suggest two 'AI Winters', in the late 1970s and in the late 1980s and early 1990s.

[2] https://www.ncbi.nlm.nih.gov/mesh/?term=artificial+intelligence.

Table 1. Query string used for the search.

TS=("artificial intelligence" OR "computer heuristics" OR "expert system*" OR "fuzzy logic" OR "knowledge base" OR "ontolog*" OR "machine learning" OR "deep learning" OR "natural language processing" OR "NLP" OR "neural network" OR "cnn" OR "rnn" OR "lstm" OR "robotics" OR "computer vision" OR "knowledge representation" OR "machine intelligence" OR "computer reasoning" OR "data mining" OR "kdd" OR "knowledge acquisition" OR "agent" OR "case-based reasoning" OR "cbr" OR "knowledge engineering" OR "image recognition" OR "image interpretation" OR "intelligent device" OR "autonomous system" OR "intelligent system" OR "smart") AND SU=("medical informatics") AND DT= (Article OR Proceedings Paper OR Review) AND LA=("English")

from the WoS platform and imported into CorText (www.cortext.net) tool for further analysis.

The data analysis and visualization are carried out in Sect. 5. For RQ1, we performed a period detector over the authors' keywords of the papers in the dataset. The algorithm works by creating bag-of-words with the frequency of the top 500 keywords for each year. It then calculates the degree of similarity between each vector of keyword frequencies and determines cutting points in sequential years, generating clusters of years with similar occurrences of keywords. With that, it is possible to visualize how topic shifts occur over time. We focused on keywords since they are considered the basic elements of representing knowledge concepts and have been used to reveal research domains [7]. The associations of the countries and the key terms were answered by applying contingency matrices. It encodes the correlation of the elements of two dimensions, showing the joint distribution of two fields - in this case, countries of the first authors and the most frequent keywords. The contingency matrix shows the degree of correlation between any pair of items drawn from each field. The chi-squared metric is used for the correlation measurement, and a p-value of 0.05 is used to detect spurious relations. With that, it is possible to determine which elements of each dimension presented more correlation than the expected value for that pair of items. Thus, we can determine which countries contributed more to which topics in the whole dataset.

To address RQ2, we explored the co-occurrence of keywords in two levels: dividing by the periods detected and an overall clustering of subjects. We applied a network mapping of keyword co-occurrences for each of the periods detected. It is a bibliometric approach to visualize a knowledge structure from a research field [15]. For a paper containing a pair of keywords, an edge was created between both keywords (the nodes), conditioned, in this case, to the period to which the edge occurred. We limited it to the top 100 keywords to make the visualization cleaner. This leads to the definition of clusters around these pairs of keywords. The keyword clusters are formed using the Louvain algorithm [16] for community detection in graphs. Finally, we analyzed how each cluster evolved in each of the periods. As a result, we can identify how different topics are often connected and their predominance in general over the periods detected in RQ1. As the last step of the methodology, the interpretation is performed in Sect. 6, discussing the results obtained.

5   Results

The search strategy resulted in 15566 papers from 1973 to 2021. However, papers until 1989 did not present keywords, and this number fell to 15484 papers from 1990 to 2021. This is a limitation of our study in offering a historical perspective before that date. Figure 1 shows how the number of papers published has evolved over the years due to our search strategy. We can see consistent growth over the years, in particular in the 2010s.

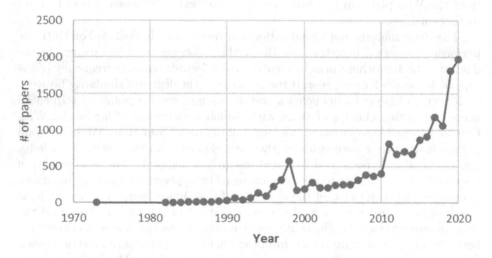

Fig. 1. The evolution on the number of papers published AI in medical informatics.

The period detector was executed with data from these years. Figure 2 illustrates the four periods detected: 1990–1996, 1997–2003, 2004–2015, and 2016–2021, as illustrated in the upper triangle of the matrix. The lower triangle illustrates the similarity between each pair of years.

The number of countries that produced works in this area also increased over the periods. In the first period, authors from 45 countries produced at least one paper; in the second period, 63; in the third, 95; the last period showed contributions from 115 countries. The five countries with the most contributions (USA, China, UK, Germany, and France) accounted for 53% of all authors.

Figure 3 presents the contingency matrix correlating countries' production and the most frequent keywords. The redder the cell, the more it deviates positively from its expected value; on the other hand, the bluer the cell, the more it deviates negatively from its expected value. We can notice the prevalence of some

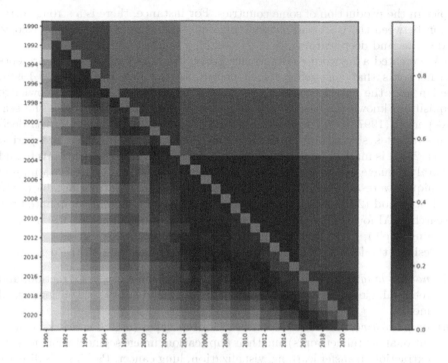

Fig. 2. The four periods detected for our dataset.

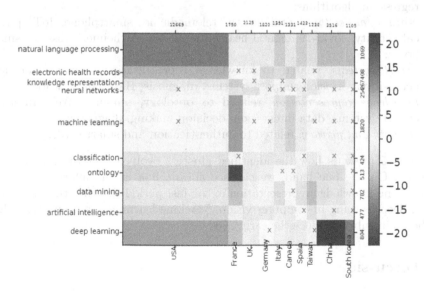

Fig. 3. The contingency matrix between countries and top keywords. Correlations statistically significant are marked by 'X'.

topics in the production of some countries. For instance, there is a strong correlation between the USA and natural language processing, France and ontology, and China and deep learning.

We created a keyword co-occurrence graph over the years. Figure 4 presents the networks that emerged for each period. In the first period (1990–1996), we can note the prevalence of expert systems and concepts such as knowledge acquisition, knowledge-based systems, and computer-aided diagnosis. The second period (1997–2003) includes knowledge representation, the Internet, decision support systems, fuzzy logic, and case-based reasoning. The third period (2004–2015) is marked by ontologies for interoperability, the Semantic Web, and natural language processing for information extraction from texts. Data mining techniques were also very used to discover new knowledge from databases. In the last period (2016–2021), deep learning and machine learning dominated the research in AI for medical informatics, together with mobile health, the Internet of Things (IoT), EHR, and the big data collected from these sources.

Besides, the following clusters were identified, considering all the periods:

i) *natural language processing*, related to information storage, extraction, and retrieval, electronic health records, UMLS, named entity recognition, social media;

ii) *deep learning*, related to computer vision, its types (neural networks, convolutional neural networks) and their application: image segmentation, feature extraction, transfer learning, visualization, lung cancer, Parkinson's disease;

iii) *machine learning*, related to data mining, feature selection, medical diagnosis, ECG, EEG, medical diagnosis, epilepsy, CDSS, and classification/regression algorithms;

iv) *e-health/m-health*: digital health, telemedicine, smartphone, IoT, physical activity, covid-19, mental health, dementia, Alzheimer's disease, smart home;

v) *expert systems*, related to knowledge representation, management, and acquisition, decision support systems, diagnosis, Bayesian networks;

vi) *knowledge representation*, related to ontology, semantic Web, Internet, expert systems, data integration, decision making, diagnosis; and

vii) *security and privacy*, related to authentication and smart cards.

Figure 5 presents how the identified clusters evolved over the four periods detected. On the one hand, we can see the decline in the interest in expert systems and knowledge representation in the last period. On the other hand, the rise of deep learning in computer vision. Machine learning has been established as the main sub-field since the early 2000s.

6   Discussion

Our RQ1 showed four distinct periods since the 1990s, namely: 1990–1996, 1997–2003, 2004–2015, and 2016–2021. In the first period (1990–1996), research was dedicated to expert systems to support physicians in clinical decision-making.

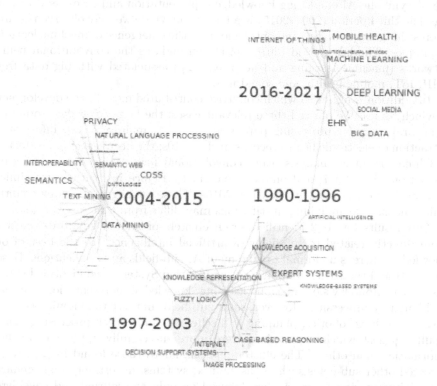

Fig. 4. The four clusters of keyword co-occurrences in each period detected in our dataset.

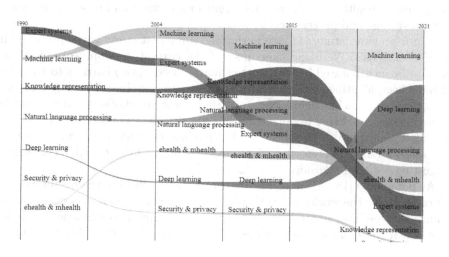

Fig. 5. The evolution in cluster distribution over the four periods.

Second period (1997–2003), we may observe the expansion of the Internet and the use of Symbolic AI employing knowledge representation and case-based reasoning. The third period (2004–2015) is a transition where we may observe research interest in interoperability and ontologies and the emergence of machine learning techniques. The last period (2016–2021) consolidates the convolutional neural networks (machine learning and deep learning) associated with big data from EHR, IoT, mobile health, and social media.

In addition, we showed which countries contributed most to the development of which topics. We noticed three relevant cases: the large scientific production of natural language processing papers in the USA, mainly for the information extraction of electronic health records in the 2010s; the deep learning production in China for image analysis using convolutional neural networks and feature extraction, since 2017; and ontology papers by France institutions for clinical decision support systems in the early 2010s. These are aggregations by country, which means that individual institutions may differ from that distribution.

Our results for RQ2 identified seven clusters of related keywords, most of them directly related to sub-fields of artificial intelligence. To the best of our knowledge, there is no formal taxonomy of AI sub-fields and applications. Based on MeSH and the ACM Computing Classification System[3], we identified expert systems, computer vision, machine learning, knowledge representation, and natural language processing. However, some sub-fields in these taxonomies were not covered, such as robotics, planning and schedule, and speech processing. These results suggest which applications were more successfully applied in medical informatics than others. The clusters are similar to those found in [24], which detected other sub-fields such as distributed systems, uncertainty management, and bioinformatics; however, they focused on only one journal and considered looser criteria - at least five papers mentioned. Besides, two other clusters not directly related were found in our work: i) mobile health/e-health, mobile phones, social, public health; and ii) security, regarding privacy and other issues based on data storage and processing.

In our previous study [34], we performed a forecast study with specialists in medical diagnosis. We found that most of the current developments in AI are likely to be incorporated in the next ten years. Besides, two barriers to adopting AI have been identified: the difficulty of incorporating clinical practice and the regulation of AI technologies. We argue that these are challenges that must be researched and are likely to appear in the next decade. In another study [33], we identified digital health as a new trend in medical informatics, heavily based on new sensors (smartphones, wearables, IoT, social media) and AI technologies, suggesting a digital transformation for healthcare.

As pointed by [18], AI in healthcare cannot be set off from the rest of medical informatics nor the world of health planning and policy. Realistic expectations require that we draw upon AI as only one of the many methodological domains from which good and necessary ideas can be derived. It is the ultimate applica-

---

[3] https://dl.acm.org/ccs.

tion in healthcare that must drive our work, oriented by policy and socio-cultural realities avoiding a new 'AI Winter'.

7   Conclusion

This work presented a bibliometric analysis of AI development in the area of medical informatics. We sought to understand how the research field of AI has been supporting medical informatics over time. The results may be related to [1], where the authors divide the history of AI in healthcare into three periods. The bibliometric analysis of this work fits in the last period (1990–2020) but extends that work by showing empirical results in fine-grained detail.

We identified four AI periods in healthcare development associated with respective technologies and applications (1990–1996, 1997–2003, 2004–2015, and 2016–2021). We argue that technological innovations such as the popularization of the Internet in the 1990s, the use of smartphones in the 2000s, the development of cloud computing in the 2010s for storage and computing power, and algorithmic innovations like deep learning techniques enabled and drove these shifts. Besides, the shift of data sources for algorithm learning is noteworthy. In the beginning, the data came from medical experts who were interviewed or watched to obtain explicit algorithmic rules. As more data was collected and made available, for instance, with the Web and social media development and the digitization of hospital records (EHR, mainly), more robust algorithms that learn from data were applied, showing promising results.

This paper presents some limitations. First, a lack of qualitative analysis to present a detailed analysis of specific papers that may represent the periods or clusters - this would require more space in this paper and will be used for future work in a journal paper. Second, the search strategy consisted of papers under medical informatics for journals and conferences in WoS. It may have caused false negatives in the results, although it also overlaps with other research areas such as computer science, information science, and engineering. The keywords were used as the source of information for the analysis, but papers before 1990 did not present this information.

Future works could draw on the association between countries and topics to understand AI developments' social and geopolitical aspects. Emergent topics, e.g., data quality issues such as missing and imbalanced data, and racial and gender biases issues, will be important for future research in healthcare. The regulation of AI will also play a key role for new applications and additional research must be done to avoid inequality and harmful issues.

References

1. Kaul, V., Enslin, S., Gross, S.A.: History of artificial intelligence in medicine. Gastrointest. Endosc. **02**(4), 807 812 (2020). https://doi.org/10.1016/j.gie.2020.06.040
2. Schwab, K.: The Fourth Industrial Revolution. Currency, New York (2017)

3. Greenhill, A.T., Edmunds, B.R.: A primer of artificial intelligence in medicine. Tech. Innovations Gastrointest. Endosc. **22**, 85–89 (2020). https://doi.org/10.1016/j.tgie.2019.150642

4. Hollis, K.F., Soualmia, L.F., Séroussi, B.: Artificial intelligence in health informatics: hype or reality? Yearb. Med. Inf. **28**(1), 3–4 (2019). https://doi.org/10.1055/s-0039-1677951

5. Lazer, D., Kennedy, R., King, G., Vespignani, A.: The parable of Google flu: traps in big data analysis. Science **343**(6176), 1203–1205 (2014). https://doi.org/10.1126/science.1248506

6. Roberts, M., et al.: Common pitfalls and recommendations for using machine learning to detect and prognosticate for COVID-19 using chest radiographs and CT scans. Nature Mach. Intell. **3**, 199–217 (2021). https://doi.org/10.1038/s42256-021-00307-0

7. Chen, G., Xiao, L.: Selecting publication keywords for domain analysis in bibliometrics: a comparison of three methods. J. Informetrics **10**, 212–223 (2016)

8. Lindsay, R.K., Buchanan, B.G., Feigenbaum, E.A., Lederberg, J.: Applications of Artificial Intelligence for Organic Chemistry: The DENDRAL Project. McGraw-Hill, New York (1980)

9. Yu, K.H., Beam, A.L., Kohane, I.S.: Artificial intelligence in healthcare. 2018. Nature Biomed. Eng. **2**, 719–731 (2018). https://doi.org/10.1038/s41551-018-0305-z

10. Weiss, S.M., Kulikowski, C.A., Amarel, S., Safir, A.: A model-based method for computer-aided medical decision making. Artif. Intell. **11**, 145–7 (1978)

11. Shortliffe, E.H.: Computer-based Medical Consultations: MYCIN. Elsevier, New York (1976)

12. Freiherr, G.: The seeds of artificial intelligence: SUMEX-AIM. U.S. G.P.O., DHEW publication no. (NIH) 80–2071. Washington, D.C.; U.S. Dept. of Health, Education, and Welfare, Public Health Service, National Institutes of Health (1980)

13. Bakkar, N., Kovalik, T., Lorenzini, I., et al.: Artificial intelligence in neurodegenerative disease research: use of IBM Watson to identify additional RNA-binding proteins altered in amyotrophic lateral sclerosis. Acta Neuropathol **135**(227–47), 19 (2018)

14. Barnett, G.O., Cimino, J.J., Hupp, J.A.: DXplain: an evolving diagnostic decision-support system. J. Am. Med. Assoc. **258**(1), 67–74 (1987). https://doi.org/10.1001/jama.1987.03400010071030

15. Su, H., Lee, P.: Mapping knowledge structure by keyword co-occurrence: a first look at journal papers in technology foresight. Scientometrics **85**, 65–70 (2010). https://doi.org/10.1007/s11192-010-0259-8

16. Blondel, V.D., Guillaume, J.L., Lambiotte, R., Lefebvre, E.: Fast unfolding of communities. J. Statist. Mech. Theor. Exper. (2008). https://doi.org/10.1088/1742-5468/2008/10/P10008

17. Anderson, C.: The End of Theory: The Data Deluge Makes the Scientific Method Obsolete (2008). https://www.wired.com/2008/06/pb-theory/. Accessed 24 Apr 2021

18. Patel, V.L., et al.: The coming of age of artificial intelligence in medicine. Artif. Intell. Med. **46**, 5–17 (2009)

19. Ferrucci, D., Levas, A., Bagchi, S., Gondek, D., Mueller, D.T.: Watson: beyond jeopardy! Artif. Intell. **200**, 93–105 (2013). https://doi.org/10.1016/j.artint.2012.06.009

20. Comendador, B., Francisco, B., Medenilla, J., et al.: Pharmabot: a pediatric generic medicine consultant chatbot. J. Autom. Control Eng. **3**, 137–40 (2015)

21. Ni, L., Lu, C., Liu, N., Liu, J.: MANDY: towards a smart primary care chatbot application. In: Chen, J., Theeramunkong, T., Supnithi, T., Tang, X. (eds.) KSS 2017. CCIS, vol. 780, pp. 38–52. Springer, Singapore (2017). https://doi.org/10.1007/978-981-10-6989-5_4

22. Arterys: medical imaging cloud AI. Available at: http://www.arterys.com

23. Zupic, I., Cater, T.: Bibliometric methods in management and organization. Organ. Res. Methods **18**(3), 429–472 (2015)

24. Peek, N., Combi, C., Marin, R., Bellazzi, R.: Thirty years of artificial intelligence in medicine (AIME) conferences: a review of research themes. Artif. Intell. Med. **65**(1), 61–73 (2015). https://doi.org/10.1016/j.artmed.2015.07.003

25. Sapci, A.H., Sapci, H.A.: Artificial intelligence education and tools for medical and health informatics students: systematic review. JMIR Med. Educ. **6**(1), e19285 (2020)

26. Topol, E.J.: High-performance medicine: the convergence of human and artificial intelligence. Nature Med. **25**, 44–56 (2019). https://www.nature.com/articles/s41591-018-0300-7

27. Masters, K.: Artificial intelligence in medical education. Med. Teach. **41**(9), 976–980 (2019). https://doi.org/10.1080/0142159X.2019.1595557

28. Ravì, D., et al.: Deep learning for health informatics: IEEE J. Biomed. Health Inf. **21**(1), 4–21 (2017). https://doi.org/10.1109/JBHI.2016.2636665

29. Thiébaut, R., Cossin, S.: Section editors for the IMIA yearbook section on public health and epidemiology informatics. Artificial intelligence for surveillance in public health. Yearb. Med. Inf. **28**(1), 232–234 (2019). https://doi.org/10.1055/s-0039-1677939

30. Lau, A.Y.S., Staccini, P.: Section editors for the IMIA yearbook section on education and consumer health informatics. Artificial intelligence in health: new opportunities, challenges, and practical implications. Yearb. Med. Inf. **28**(1), 174–178 (2019). DOI: https://doi.org/10.1055/s-0039-1677935

31. Alhashmi, S.F.S., Alshurideh, M., Al Kurdi, B., Salloum, S.A.: A systematic review of the factors affecting the artificial intelligence implementation in the health care sector. In: International Conference on Artificial Intelligence and Computer Vision. Advances in Intelligent Systems and Computing, vol. 1153 (2020)

32. Wolff, J., Pauling, J., Keck, A., Baumbach, J.: The economic impact of artificial intelligence in health care: systematic review. J. Med. Internet Res. **22**(2), e16866 (2020). https://doi.org/10.2196/16866

33. Fornazin, M., Penteado, B.E., Castro, L., Freire, S.: From medical informatics to digital health: a bibliometric analysis of the research field. In: Americas Conference on Information Systems (AMCIS), paper n. 1567 (2021)

34. Mota, F.B., et al.: Aplicações de inteligência artificial em diagnósticos médicos: expectativas para os próximos dez anos (2020–2030). Research Report - Fiocruz Strategic Study Center. Unpublished report

Artificial Intelligence in Power
and Energy Systems

Optimizing Energy Consumption of Household Appliances Using PSO and GWO

Inês Tavares, José Almeida, João Soares[✉], Sérgio Ramos, Zita Vale,
and Zahra Foroozandeh

GECAD - Research Group on Intelligent Engineering and Computing for Advanced
Innovation and Development, Polytechnic of Porto, Porto, Portugal
{ivtav,jorga,jan,scr,zav,zah}@isep.ipp.pt

Abstract. Due to the increasing electricity consumption in the residential sector, new control systems emerged to control the demand side. Some techniques have been developed, such as shaping the curve's load peaks by planning and shifting the electricity demand for household appliances. This paper presents a comparative analysis for the energy consumption optimization of two household appliances using two Swarm Intelligence (SI) algorithms: Particle Swarm Optimization (PSO) and Grey Wolf Optimizer (GWO). This problem's main objective is to minimize the energy cost according to both machines' energy consumption, respecting the restrictions applied. Three scenarios are presented: changing the energy market price during the day according to three types of energy tariffs. The results show that the user in the cheapest periods could switch on both machines because both techniques presented the highest energy consumption values. Regarding the objective function analysis, PSO and GWO obtained the best (more economical) values for the simple tariff due to its lower energy consumption. The GWO technique also presented more diverging values from the average objective function value than the PSO algorithm.

Keywords: Energy consumption · Grey Wolf Optimizer ·
Optimization · Particle Swarm Optimization · Swarm Intelligence

1 Introduction

Nowadays, electricity consumption is substantially increasing, and it is transforming the global energy mix framework [1]. The residential sector represents a large part of the total energy consumption worldwide due to the growing usage of modern electronic devices and appliances. The fast growth of urbanization and the actual global environmental situation has lead to several initiatives to promote the use of clean energy [2,3].

New control systems and appropriate methodologies such as demand-side management (DSM) and demand response (DR) must be developed and adopted,

© Springer Nature Switzerland AG 2021
G. Marreiros et al. (Eds.): EPIA 2021, LNAI 12981, pp. 137–150, 2021.
https://doi.org/10.1007/978-3-030-86230-5_11

allowing the participation of consumers through the use of flexibility from home appliances [3,4]. The scheduling usage of loads can be useful for energy management in residential buildings [5]. From a residential point of view, this flexibility consists of modifying the consumption profiles of domestic appliances through reducing or shifting their loads over different periods [3]. This flexibility allows to shave the curve's load peaks by planning and shifting the electricity demand of household appliances. The shaping of the load curve also ensures lower costs for consumers and improves environmental sustainability. The better matching of demand and supply saves the building of additional generation capacity and, consequently, reduces greenhouse emissions [4]. Also, these modifications on the amount of load (either shifted or decreased over time) can avoid some concerns such as the balance or congestion of distribution networks [3].

With an overall control algorithm optimizing domestic appliances' behavior, high-efficiency levels can be achieved [6]. The optimization of household appliances' use can be accomplished through meta-heuristic optimization techniques. Meta-heuristic techniques have been broadly used due to their simplicity, flexibility, derivation-free mechanism, and local optima avoidance. They can be divided into two main groups: single-solution-based and population-based. Swarm Intelligence (SI) is an interesting branch of population-based meta-heuristics [7].

A vast majority of SI algorithms focus on swarm's members' behavior, and their way of living beside the interactions and relations among them to locate their food sources [8]. Two popular SI algorithms are the Grey Wolf Optimizer (GWO) and Particle Swarm Optimization (PSO). PSO is the most popular in recent time, and GWO is the most recently developed method. In this problem, the accuracy of the chosen method is way more important than the computational flexibility of that method [9].

This paper presents an optimization of two household appliances' energy consumption, namely the dishwasher and the washing machine, for the first Saturday of January. The problem is the minimization of the energy price according to the required consumption of both machines. A PSO and GWO optimization algorithms are used to find suitable solutions for the re-schedule of the two domestic appliances on that day. The main objective of this paper is to analyze and compare the optimization results of these two algorithms.

This paper is structured as follows. The following section reviews some different approaches to the use of PSO and GWO. In Sect. 3, the methodology used in this paper is proposed, and the two SI optimization algorithms used are described as well as the mathematical optimization model. Section 4 characterizes the case studies and the respective scenarios, and Sect. 5 shows the experimental results and a discussion. Finally, Sect. 6 concludes this work.

2   Related Work

Several articles propose different methodologies and also other approaches related to the use of the PSO and GWO.

[10] suggests a multi-objective hybrid PSO-GWO method for system optimization. The main objective is to find the optimal size of the different system components to minimize the total cost of freshwater production and CO_2 emissions. The results show that the proposed PSO-GWO hybrid has a better performance than the same optimization methods used separately to reduce computational time and achieve the best function values.

In [11] it is proposed a new hybrid algorithm fusing the exploitation capability of the PSO with the exploration skill of GWO. This way, this combination aims to prevent the PSO from falling into local minimums by exploring GWO. The results show that this hybrid approach performs better than all methods employed in the comparisons (artificial bee colony and social spider algorithm) and indicates that it converges to more optimal solutions with fewer iterations.

The paper [12] presents a comparative analysis for selective harmonic elimination technique using PSO and GWO for Pulse Width Modulation inverters. It has been observed that the harmonics elimination by the GWO is better than PSO. The authors concluded that GWO can be used efficiently and works better for the scheme presented in this work.

The objective of [13] is to draw a fair comparison among eminent Nature-Inspired Algorithms in solving benchmark test functions. Among these methods, GA is the pioneer method for optimization, PSO is the most popular, and GWO is the most recent method developed. Results show that GWO is the overall best optimization technique, and PSO is still propitious to solve benchmark functions. Also, GWO is capable of solving a function successfully with a small number of populations and iterations.

3   Proposed Methodology

This section introduces a straightforward approach to the concept of PSO and GWO, and it is provided the mathematical formulation of the optimization problem.

3.1   Swarm Intelligence Optimization Algorithms

The original PSO algorithm was inspired by the social behavior and nature patterns, specifically the ability of groups of some species of animals to work together in locating desirable positions in a given area. This seeking behavior was associated with an optimization search for solutions to non-linear equations in a real-valued search space [14,15].

PSO is initialized with a population of random particles and placed in some problem or function search space. Each of them evaluates the objective function and its current location. Then, each particle determines its movement through the search space by combining some aspects of the history of its current and the best location (fitness) achieved so far with those of one or more members of the swarm, with some random perturbations (acceleration). The best solution of each particle is called *pbest*, and the best global value and its location, obtained by any particle in the population, is called *gbest*. The PSO concept consists of, at each time step, changing the velocity (accelerating) of each particle towards its *pbest* and *gbest* locations. Eventually, the swarm as a whole is likely to move close to an optimum of the fitness function. On each iteration of the algorithm, the current position is evaluated as a problem solution [14,16].

The GWO algorithm is a swarm intelligence technique, and it is inspired in nature by the social intelligence of grey wolves in leadership and hunting preys [7]. Grey wolves are social animals with a rigid dominant hierarchy shown in Fig. 1. They are divided into four levels, namely α, β, δ, and ω, and their dominance decreases from top to bottom. Group hunting is another interesting social activity of grey wolves, besides their social hierarchy [7].

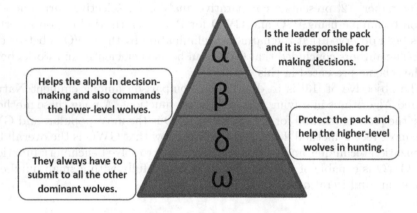

Fig. 1. Hierarchy of grey wolves [6].

According to this, the mathematical modeling of GWO is based on these two characteristics: social hierarchy and hunting behavior of grey wolves. Thus, the mathematical models resemble grey wolves' hunting process: searching for prey, encircling prey, and attacking prey [7].

Like other Swarm Intelligence algorithms, the GWO search process starts with creating a random population of grey wolves. After that, the four wolf groups and their locations are established, and the distances to the prey are measured. Each wolf is a candidate solution and is updated through the searching process. Besides, GWO uses powerful operations managed by two parameters to maintain the exploration and exploitation because it is prone to stagnation in local solutions [8].

Compared with PSO, which has two vectors (position and velocity), GWO has only one position vector, requiring less memory. GWO saves three best solutions while PSO only saves one best solution for each particle [8].

The optimizing energy consumption of household appliances problem was performed using PSO and GWO techniques to compare both. These two techniques were simulated, as the flowchart of Fig. 2 shows. It demonstrates the entire procedure performed by the optimization algorithms developed to find satisfactory results for each period's energy consumption for the two machines in the analysis.

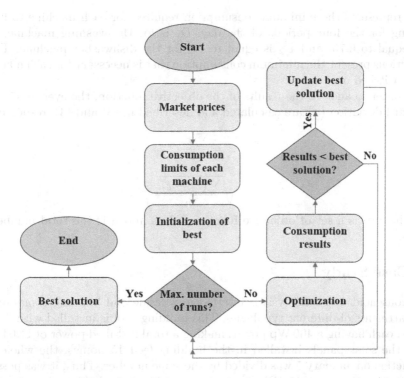

Fig. 2. Optimization based simulation to obtain the energy consumption of the two domestic appliances.

3.2 Mathematical Model

Since PV power production does not satisfy the consumer's energy consumption, the optimization problem's objective is to minimize the cost of the energy to be purchased according to the energy consumption of flexible appliances. The optimization problem consists of eight decision variables related to the four periods of the two washing machines.

The optimization problem can be formulated as follows:

$$Minimize Z = \sum_{t} \sum_{r} C_t \cdot P_{(r,t)} \tag{1}$$

Where C_t is the energy cost in period t and $P_{(r,t)}$ represents the energy consumption of machine r in period t and $t = 1, 2, 3, 4$ and $r = 1, 2$. The washing machine corresponds to $r = 1$ and the dishwasher corresponds to $r = 2$.

The constraints of the optimization problem are:

$$\sum_t P_{(r,t)} \geq D_r, \forall r \tag{2}$$

D represents the minimum consumption required for each machine to begin working for the four periods of the day. D_1 is for the washing machine, and it is equal to 0.75, and D_2 is equal to 1.5 for the dishwasher machine. These restrictions present the minimum consumption that is necessary for each machine to be switched on.

In order to analyse the results of the objective function, the average ($\bar{x}$) and standard deviation (σ) are calculated and described in (3) and (4), respectively.

$$\bar{x} = \frac{\sum x_i}{n} \tag{3}$$

$$\sigma = \sqrt{\frac{\sum (x_i - \bar{x})^2}{n}} \tag{4}$$

Where x_i is a set of objective function values and n is the total number of values.

4   Case Study

The household under analysis is inserted in a residential building composed of 15 apartments of different typologies. This building roof is installed with 28 PV panels, each having a 400 Wp power, making a total installed power of 11.04 kW. Since the solar panels installed in the building feed 15 homes, the whole PV production on January 5 was divided by the same number. Thus, it was possible to determine the amount of PV energy consumed by household appliances of one consumer. The household's energy consumption and the energy market prices on January 5 of 2019 are also taken into account.

When energy consumption is higher than the PV generation, it is necessary to buy energy from the market. Therefore, from the data obtained, it was necessary to analyze energy consumption and production to understand the amount of energy required to buy.

Before starting the optimization algorithm, a survey was conducted on household appliances. First, devices were divided into two categories: non-flexible and flexible. In the non-flexible group, appliances have no flexibility regarding the time when they can be switched on/off. On the other hand, machines that have higher hourly flexibility belong to the flexible group. Figure 3 shows the appliances that belong to each group.

Since the washing machine and the dishwasher belong to the group of flexible home appliances, these will be the variables to use in the optimization algorithm. The daily consumption of the devices on January 5 totals an energy consumption of 23.8 kWh.

For a better understanding of the problem, the day was divided into four periods, which comprise the following periods:

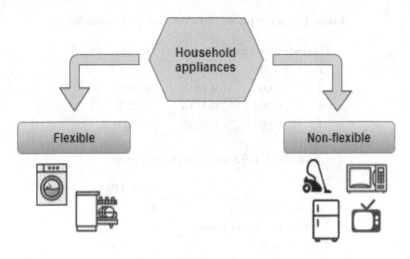

Fig. 3. Two categories of home appliances: rigid and flexible.

- **Period 1:** 0 h–07 h;
- **Period 2:** 07 h–12 h;
- **Period 3:** 12 h–18 h;
- **Period 4:** 18 h–24 h.

The study case is divided into three scenarios that analyze the energy consumption, and all of the three consist of changing the energy market price. Each situation's energy price varies according to the time of day and the type of energy tariff used by the consumer. There are, therefore, three types of energy tariff corresponding to each scenario.

Scenario 1 corresponds to the simple tariff, scenario 2, the bi-hourly tariff's energy price, and scenario 3 to the tri-hourly tariff. The characteristics of each tariff are as follow:

- **Simple tariff**: the energy price is the same during all day;
- **Bi-hourly tariff**: the energy price is lower in off-peak hours and higher in peak hours;
- **Tri-hourly tariff**: the energy price is more expensive at peak times, cheaper at off-peak times and an intermediate price at half peak hours.

According to this, the energy prices for each tariff are represented on Table 1.

Table 2 presents the PSO and GWO parameters used in the simulations. The population size, number of iterations, and maximum velocity were tested and adjusted to obtain better results. GWO was simulated using only two parameters (population size and iteration number) were applied.

All these simulations made for the three scenarios were performed using the R language in the RStudio program. The used system has 16 GB RAM and a Ryzen 5 3500U 2.10 GHz processor running Windows 10.

Table 1. Energy prices (€/kWh) for each scenario

Period	Scenario 1	Scenario 2	Scenario 3
1	0.066	0.0958	0.0958
2	0.066	0.1815	0.1639
3	0.066	0.1815	0.2215
4	0.066	0.0958	0.1639

Table 2. PSO and GWO parameters

	PSO	GWO
Inertia Weight (w)	0.7	
Maximum velocity (vmax)	5	
Population size		40
Acceleration constants (cg, ci)	1.49	
Iteration number		200

5   Results and Discussion

The methodology presented in Sect. 3 was applied to the three case studies of Sect. 4.

In scenario 1, for PSO, the best value through the 500 runs performed to the algorithm was obtained in run 437 and run 132 for GWO.

Table 3 presents the energy consumption of each machine in the four periods and the total consumption of both devices after implementing PSO and GWO techniques. The GWO algorithm obtained the highest total consumption compared to PSO. Since the energy price is the same all day long, this variable does not influence the results. Both machines could switch on at any time since the price is the same during all periods.

Table 3. Energy consumption (kWh) of both machines in scenario 1 obtained with PSO and GWO

	PSO		GWO	
	Machine 1	Machine 2	Machine 1	Machine 2
Period 1	0	0	0.287	0.553
Period 2	0.750	1.281	0.529	0.480
Period 3	0.422	0.134	0.697	0.792
Period 4	0.114	0.253	0.070	0.516
Total	1.286	1.668	1.583	2.341
	2.954		3.924	

Figure 4 shows the graph of the energy consumption of the two machines during the day. It can be observed that both devices registered the highest consumption value in period two and the lowest in period 1 with PSO optimization. Regarding GWO, the two machines reach their maximum energy consumption in period 3. About the minimum consumption values, machine 1 achieve it in period four and machine 2 in period 2.

In scenario 2, for PSO, the best value through the 500 runs performed to the algorithm was obtained in run 231 and run 132 for GWO.

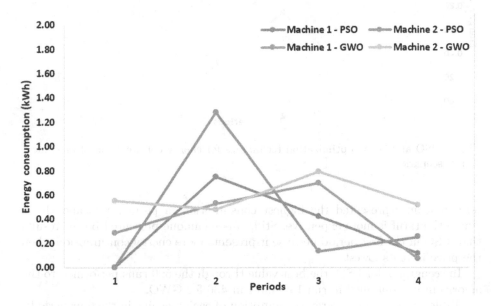

Fig. 4. PSO and GWO optimization techniques for energy consumption of machine 1 and 2 (scenario 1).

Table 4 presents the energy consumption of each machine in the four periods. On the opposite of scenario 1, the PSO registered the highest value of total energy consumption. Still, in this case, the values were much more competitive in comparison to the previous point.

Figure 5 presents the graph of both devices' energy consumption on that day, using PSO and GWO techniques. In period 4, machine 2 showed the highest energy consumption value for the PSO algorithm. This situation is expected because, according to Table 1, period 4 corresponds to one of the cheapest energy prices. This way, machine two will be switched on in period 4, when the price is lowest. Regarding machine 1, it presents its maximum value in period 2 with the PSO algorithm, but it corresponds to a more expensive energy price period. This way, machine one could also be switched on in period 4, since the consumption values are very close to period 2. It is also possible to observe that both lines of the optimization values of PSO are very similar. Regarding the GWO algorithm,

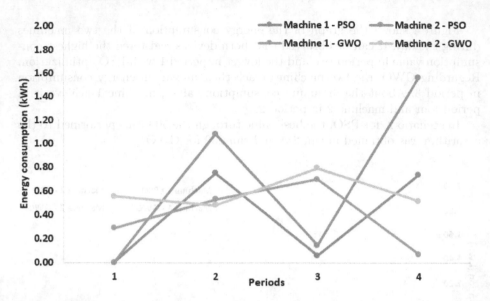

Fig. 5. PSO and GWO optimization techniques for energy consumption of machine 1 and 2 (scenario 2).

both machines presented the highest consumption in periods two and three, where the tariff is more expensive. Still, this technique presented better results than PSO in the first period because it presents more energy consumption when the price is at its lowest.

In scenario 3, for PSO, the best value through the 500 runs performed to the algorithm was obtained in run 139 and run 430 for GWO.

Table 5 presents the energy consumption of each machine in the four periods, using PSO and GWO. Like the previous scenario, PSO demonstrated the highest value of total energy consumption for both devices than GWO.

Table 4. Energy consumption (kWh) of both machines in scenario 2 obtained with PSO and GWO

	PSO		GWO	
	Machine 1	Machine 2	Machine 1	Machine 2
Period 1	0	0	0.287	0.553
Period 2	0.750	1.078	0.529	0.480
Period 3	0.059	0.145	0.697	0.792
Period 4	0.736	1.562	0.070	0.516
Total	1.545	2.785	1.583	2.341
	4.330		3.924	

Table 5. Energy consumption (kWh) of both machines in scenario 3 obtained with PSO and GWO

	PSO		GWO	
	Machine 1	Machine 2	Machine 1	Machine 2
Period 1	0.750	1.819	0.023	1.167
Period 2	0.750	0.972	0.622	0.724
Period 3	0.014	0.426	0.382	0.066
Period 4	0.127	0.141	0.066	0.384
Total	1.641	3.358	1.093	2.341
	4.999		3.433	

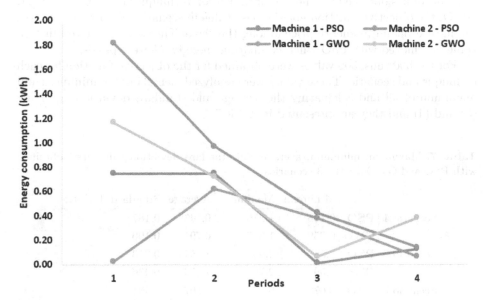

Fig. 6. PSO and GWO optimization techniques for energy consumption of machine 1 and 2 (scenario 3).

The graph represented in Fig. 6 shows the energy consumption of the two machines for the day. It illustrates that device 2 presents the highest energy consumption on period 1 for both techniques as expected, because the cheapest energy prices correspond to period 1, in conformity with Table 1. At period 1, machine two could be switched on by the residents to minimize energy costs. Regarding machine 1, periods 1 and 2 registered the same and highest energy consumption values, using the PSO algorithm. Considering that period one is cheaper than period 2, the user could switch on machine one at the first period. In period three, when the price is the most expensive, the GWO presents the better results for machine 2, and the PSO for machine one with GWO presents the best overall results.

Table 6. Objective function values (€) for PSO and GWO

	PSO	GWO
Scenario 1	0.195	0.259
Scenario 2	0.589	0.590
Scenario 3	0.670	0.507

The optimization problem is to minimize the energy cost that depends on the two machines' energy consumption regarding the objective function. So, the lower the value of the objective function, the better. Table 6 exhibits the objective function values obtained for the two optimization techniques used. For PSO and GWO, the objective function got the best value in scenario one because it gives the most economical energy price among the three. The best objective function value is achieved with PSO when comparing these two lowest prices.

For the 500 runs, 500 values were obtained for the objective function for each technique and scenario. These values were analyzed, achieving the minimum and maximum of all and calculating the average and standard deviation, applying (3) and (4) and they are presented in Table 7.

Table 7. Maximum, minimum, average and standard deviation values (€) obtained with PSO and GWO for the 3 scenarios

		Minimum	Maximum	Average	Standard deviation
Scenario 1	**PSO**	0.195	1.276	0.746	0.187
	GWO	0.259	1.317	0.791	0.196
Scenario 2	**PSO**	0.589	2.599	1.554	0.373
	GWO	0.590	2.769	1.676	0.436
Scenario 3	**PSO**	0.670	3.136	1.807	0.431
	GWO	0.507	3.136	1.963	0.477

By analyzing each scenario's standard deviation, the values of scenario 1 are less dispersed among themselves, approaching the average cost presented. On the contrary, scenario 3 shows a more significant standard deviation, which means that the values obtained in the 500 runs are quite dispersed, diverging from the average value obtained. Taking both techniques into account, the table results are quite competitive between the two SI algorithms. The exception is for the standard deviation results with the GWO algorithm that keep presenting worse outcomes than the PSO technique. This situation means that the obtained values from GWO diverge more from the calculated average objective function value.

6   Conclusions

With the increasing energy consumption in households, the control and optimization of domestic appliances' behavior have become crucial to achieve high-efficiency levels.

This paper presented an optimization approach regarding the energy consumption of two washing machines. The main objective is to implement two different Swarm Intelligence optimization algorithms (PSO and GWO) to minimize energy cost according to the machines' energy consumption, respecting the restrictions applied. This optimization approach was divided into three scenarios, in which the energy price differed during the day.

When the energy price is low, the energy consumption should be the highest and the user is allowed to switch the washing machines. In scenario 1, the residents could switch on the machines at any time since the energy price is always the same all day. Regarding scenario 2, both machines could be switched on by the user in period four because the PSO algorithm values were higher than GWO. For scenario 3, they should turn on both washing devices in period one as it is the most economical and registered the highest use for both optimization methods.

Then, the objective function was analyzed. The lowest value, i.e., the lowest energy price to be paid by the user, was obtained in scenario 1 for PSO and GWO. In this scenario, the smallest amount of energy consumption was registered for both machines using PSO, so it was expected that the objective function's value would also be the most economical.

Note that both SI algorithms were used because of their simplicity of implementation and performance. Due to the simplicity of the optimization problem that is proposed, deterministic methods could be more suitable to solve this problem. This situation is because they could guarantee a better solution than the one obtained with heuristics. Since the complexity is low, this type of algorithm's optimization time and computation would not be an issue. For future work, implementing this type of method and comparing it with heuristics could be something interesting.

Acknowledgment. This work has received funding from FEDER Funds through COMPETE program and from National Funds through FCT under the project BENEFICE–PTDC/EEI-EEE/29070/2017 and UIDB/00760/2020 under CEECIND/02814/2017 grant.

References

1. Soares, J., Pinto, T., Lezama, F., Morais, H.: Survey on complex optimization and simulation for the new power systems paradigm. Complexity **2018**, 1–32 (2018). https://doi.org/10.1155/2018/2340628
2. Padhee, M., Pal, A.: Effect of solar PV penetration on residential energy consumption pattern. In: 2018 North American Power Symposium (NAPS) (2019). https://doi.org/10.1109/NAPS.2018.8600657

3. Lezama, F., Soares, J., Canizes, B., Vale, Z.: Flexibility management model of home appliances to support DSO requests in smart grids. Sustain. Urban Areas **55**, 102048 (2020). https://doi.org/10.1016/j.scs.2020.102048
4. Mangiatordi, F., Pallotti, E., Del Vecchio, P., Leccese, F.: Power consumption scheduling for residential buildings. In: 2012 11th International Conference on Environment and Electrical Engineering (EEEIC), pp. 926–930 (2012). https://doi.org/10.1109/EEEIC.2012.62215087
5. Foroozandeh, Z., Ramos, S., Soares, J., Vale, Z.: Energy management in smart building by a multi-objective optimization model and Pascoletti-Serafini scalarization approach. Processes **2021**(9), 257 (2021). https://doi.org/10.3390/pr9020257
6. Molderink, A., Bakker, V., Bosman, M., Hurink, J., Smit, G.: Domestic energy management methodology for optimizing efficiency in smart grids. In: 2009 IEEE Bucharest PowerTech, pp. 1–7 (2009). https://doi.org/10.1109/PTC.2009.5281849
7. Mirjalili, S., Mirjalili, S., Lewis, A.: Grey wolf optimizer. Adv. Eng. Softw. **69**, 46–61 (2014). https://doi.org/10.1016/j.advengsoft.2013.12.007
8. Faris, H., Aljarah, I., Al-Betar, M.A., Mirjalili, S.: Grey wolf optimizer: a review of recent variants and applications. Neural Comput. Appl. **30**(2), 413–435 (2017). https://doi.org/10.1007/s00521-017-3272-5
9. Rostami, M., Berahmand, K., Nasiri, E., Forouzandeh, S.: Review of swarm intelligence-based feature selection methods. Eng. Appl. Artif. Intell. **100** (2021). https://doi.org/10.1016/j.engappai.2021.104210
10. Abdelshafy, A., Hassan, H., Jurasz, J.: Optimal design of a grid-connected desalination plant powered by renewable energy resources using a hybrid PSO-WO approach. Energy Convers. Manag. **173**, 331–347 (2018). https://doi.org/10.1016/j.enconman.2018.07.083
11. Şenel, F.A., Gökçe, F., Yüksel, A.S., Yiğit, T.: A novel hybrid PSO–GWO algorithm for optimization problems. Eng. Comput. **35**(4), 1359–1373 (2018). https://doi.org/10.1007/s00366-018-0668-5
12. Suman, S., Chatterjee, D., Mohanty, R.: Comparison of PSO and GWO techniques for SHEPWM inverters. In: 2020 International Conference on Computer, Electrical & Communication Engineering (ICCECE) (2020). https://doi.org/10.1109/ICCECE48148.2020.9223108
13. Islam, M., Tanveer, M., Akhand, M.: A comparative study on prominent nature inspired algorithms for function optimization. In: 2016 5th International Conference on Informatics, Electronics and Vision (ICIEV), pp. 803–808 (2016). https://doi.org/10.1109/ICIEV.2016.7760112
14. Bratton, D., Kennedy, J.: Defining a standard for particle swarm optimization. In: 2007 IEEE Swarm Intelligence Symposium (SIS), pp. 120–127 (2007). https://doi.org/10.1109/SIS.2007.368035
15. Eberhart, R.C., Shi, Y.: Particle swarm optimization: developments, applications and resources. In: Proceedings of the 2001 Congress on Evolutionary Computation (ICEC), pp. 1:81–86 (2001). https://doi.org/10.1109/cec.2001.934374
16. Poli, R., Kennedy, J., Blackwell, T.: Particle swarm optimization. Swarm Intell. **1**, 33–7 (2007). https://doi.org/10.1007/s11721-007-0002-0

Metaheuristics for Optimal Scheduling of Appliances in Energy Efficient Neighbourhoods

Amaia Alfageme[1,2] (ID), Iker Esnaola-Gonzalez[1(✉)] (ID), Francisco Javier Díez[1], and Eduardo Gilabert[1]

[1] TEKNIKER, Basque Research and Technology Alliance (BRTA), C/Iñaki Goenaga 5, 20600 Eibar, Spain
iker.esnaola@tekniker.es
[2] Faculty of Informatics, University of the Basque Country (UPV/EHU), Paseo Manuel Lardizabal 1, 20018 Donostia-San Sebastián, Spain

Abstract. As a consequence of the continuous growth in the world-wide electricity consumption, supplying all customer electrical requests is becoming increasingly difficult for electricity companies. That is why, they encourage their clients to actively manage their own demand, providing several resources such us their Optimal Demand Profile (ODP). This profile provides to users a summary of the demand they should consume during the day. However, this profile needs to be translated into specific control actions first, such as the when each appliance should be used. In this article a comparison of the performance of two metaheuristic optimisation algorithms (Tabu Search and Estimation of Distribution Algorithm (EDA)) and their variants for the calculation of optimal appliance scheduling is presented. Results show that Tabu Search algorithm can reach better feasible solutions at faster execution times than EDA does.

Keywords: Appliance scheduling optimisation · Optimal Demand Profile · Tabu Search · Estimation of Distribution Algorithm

1 Introduction

Electricity demand is globally increasing as the different sectors require more energy to carry out their tasks. According to the International Energy Agency[1], in 2018, the industry sector was the sector with the highest consumption, followed by the residential sector. However, the tendency for the residential sector is to increase its electricity consumption more sharply than the rest of the sectors, reaching the industrial sector amounts by 2050.

Balancing electricity supply and demand is currently a reality among electric companies, who aim to improve these optimisation techniques, and this is

---

[1] https://www.iea.org/.

© Springer Nature Switzerland AG 2021
G. Marreiros et al. (Eds.): EPIA 2021, LNAI 12981, pp. 151–162, 2021.
https://doi.org/10.1007/978-3-030-86230-5_12

why different methods have been proposed, including Demand Side Management (DSM) activities. DSM includes the reduction of electricity usage and shifts of energy usage to other off-peak periods in order to match energy demand with energy supply side [7]. In this regard, Demand Response (DR) [13] programs are introduced into the smart grids as a mechanism for active demand management which implies that the price of energy rises or falls based on a series of circumstances, such as the amount of energy demanded, transport costs, etc.

Some electricity companies encourage their customers to actively manage their demand by providing them a customised Optimal Demand Profile (ODP). This indicates customers how much electricity they should consume at any given time, in order to ensure that they contribute to the energy demand peak reductions and maximisation of renewable energies, among others. The definition of ODP takes into account different features of the electricity grid as a whole, such as the energy price, customer energy production availability, energy storage capacity, and their consumption habits. However, ODPs need to be translated into specific control actions, for instance, by determining the optimal scheduling of appliances.

This article solves the neighbourhood appliances scheduling optimisation problem to adapt households real consumption to neighbourhood ODP. Section 2 analyses the related work, Sect. 3 defines the problem to be solved and the model proposed, and Sect. 4 presents the different variants to be tested. Obtained results are compared and discussed in Sect. 5 and, finally, conclusions are shown in Sect. 6.

2 Related Work

Residential users are expected to play a key role in improving the efficiency of the network through the adoption of intelligent mechanisms for managing the energy demand. This type of networks motivates users to actively manage their daily demand, evaluating energy prices and being participants in the production and storage of electricity [6,11]. In fact, the most current lines of research regarding the generation of ODP consider customers capacity to produce renewable energy [1] (photovoltaic generally) and its subsequent storage through batteries.

In [2] the ODP is generated through the prediction of photovoltaic (PV) energy production, user consumption habits according to their electrical appliances, and the electricity taxes. The goal is to minimise the cost on the end users bill. There are different studies about the methods to solve the problem of obtaining the ODP for one or more households. The most applied method is through linear optimisation algorithms, where demand and production flow are defined as linear functions [9]. Also distributed algorithms [5] are considered. The generation of the ODP can be generated for a single household or for several (a neighbourhood), where balancing and coordinating the demand of all households and their joint capacity for electricity production is important.

The most common representation of appliances scheduling solution is by defining the use of each appliance from the solution as $a[t]$ vector where each position takes 1 value if a has to run at t, and 0 otherwise. Some research distinguishes the running mode (k) of appliances [5], where appliances solutions are represented as $a[t, k]$ matrix.

Some models are defined for a single household [10], and others manage residential electricity demand [12] coordinating all households appliances in real-time. In [4] a model for off-grid neighbourhoods is defined, where the ODP is generated through electricity production and storage capability.

The planning problem for the use of household appliances in a neighbourhood can be posed as an NP-hard problem with a discrete number of solutions if the ODP is discretised in units of time. One resolution technique is through heuristic methods and derivatives, where algorithms capable of reaching near-optimal solutions are proposed when evaluating some of the feasible solutions of the problem. In [14] an hybrid algorithm of Ant Colony and Simulated Annealing algorithms is proposed for a two-stage scheduling optimisation.

3   Problem Definition

As mentioned before, the goal of households is to adjust their demand to their personalised neighbourhood ODP, so that they achieve a reduction in their consumption bill and they contribute to a more sustainable environment by maximising the exploitation of renewable energies. Towards that goal, customers provide their appliances information to the method proposed in this article, specifying the mean consumption by unit of time and the duration of each one. They also indicate the aimed availability, that is, the time range customers would like the appliance to operate. As a result, the proposed method returns the moments of the day when each appliance should be used if the given ODP is aimed.

3.1   Representation of the Solution and Objective Function

Solution representation is given as X, which is a two dimensional matrix $(I_u x T)$ whose values can be 0 or 1 as shown in Eq. 1.

$$X = \{(x_{1_1}^1, ..., x_{1_U}^1, ..., x_{I_U}^1, ..., x_{I_U}^T) \mid x_{i_u}^t \in \{0, 1\}, \forall u = 1, ..., U \wedge \forall i = 1, ..., I \wedge \forall t = 1, ..., T\} \tag{1}$$

$$X_1 \rightarrow \begin{pmatrix} x_{1_1}^1 & \cdots & x_{1_1}^T \\ \vdots & \ddots & \vdots \\ x_{I_1}^1 & \cdots & x_{I_1}^T \end{pmatrix} ... X_U \rightarrow \begin{pmatrix} x_{1_U}^1 & \cdots & x_{1_U}^T \\ \vdots & \ddots & \vdots \\ x_{I_U}^1 & \cdots & x_{I_U}^T \end{pmatrix}$$

$$x_{i_u}^t = \begin{cases} 0 \rightarrow i_u \text{ off at } t \\ 1 \rightarrow i_u \text{ on at } t \end{cases}$$

The objective is to solve the appliances scheduling optimisation problem minimizing the difference between optimal (o) and real (r) demand, that is, the absolute value of the difference between these two metrics for each instant of time (t).

Optimal demand is unique for all household of the neighbourhood, but real demand is calculated as the sum of the individual fixed (z) and variable demand of each household, where variable demand is composed by the consumption (p_i) of all its appliances (i) as shown in Eq. 2.

$$\min_{X} f_{obj} = \sum_{t=1}^{T} | \left(\sum_{u=1}^{U} \left(\sum_{i_u=1}^{I_u} (p_{i_u} \times x_{i_u}^t) + z_{t,u} \right) - o_t \right) | \tag{2}$$

3.2 Constraints

Problem constraints are divided into two. On the one hand, the format constraints, which indicate where the 0's and 1's can be located on the solution, and on the other, the value limit constraints, which limit demand values.

The formulated format constraints are:

– Running time of i_u appliance is known and must be equal to y_{i_u}:

$$\forall i_u \left(\sum_{t=1}^{T} x_{i_u}^t = y_{i_u} \right) \tag{3}$$

This condition is achieved if the sum of all elements of the solution matrix is equal to the value y_{i_u}.

– Running time of i_u appliance is consecutive:

$$\forall i_u (\exists t_1 = min(t \mid x_{i_u}^t = 1), t_2 = max(t \mid x_{i_u}^t = 1) \mid t_2 - t_1 = y_{i_u} - 1) \tag{4}$$

This condition is achieved if the difference between highest and lowest instants of time with 1 value (t_2 and t_1) for each appliance i_u is equal to the number of instants of time that i_u must run (y_{i_u}) minus 1.

– Running time of each appliance i_u is inside a known time range ($w_{i_u} = w_{i_u}^{max} - w_{i_u}^{min} + 1$):

$$\forall x_{i_u}^t = 1 \rightarrow t > w_{i_u}^{min} \wedge t < w_{u i}^{max} \tag{5}$$

This condition is achieved if all 1 values of each appliance i_u are set at t higher than $w_{i_u}^{min}$ and lower than $w_{i_u}^{max}$.

The formulated value limit constraints are:

– For each instant of time, real demand is below a given d_{max} parameter value:

$$r_t = \sum_{u=1}^{U} (z_{t,u} + \sum_{i_u=1}^{I_u} (p_{i_u} \times x_{i_u}^t)) \leq d_{max,u} \forall t = 1, ..., T \tag{6}$$

This condition is achieved adapting the variable demand (appliances consumption).

– For each instant of time, absolute difference between optimal and real demand is below a given v_{max} parameter value:

$$\mid \sum_{u=1}^{U}(z_{t,u} + \sum_{i_u=1}^{I}(p_{i_u} \times x_{i_u}^t)) - o_t \mid = \mid r_t - o_t \mid \leq v_{max} \forall t = 1, ..., T \quad (7)$$

This condition is achieved adapting the variable demand (appliances consumption).

3.3 Search Space

The set of possible solutions of the problem is composed by all three dimensional matrices limited by the number of households, appliances and instants of time, where format constraints are fulfilled:

$$X = \{(x_{1_1}^1, ..., x_{1_U}^1, ..., x_{I_U}^1, ..., x_{I_U}^T) \mid x_{i_u}^t \in \{0,1\}, \forall u = 1, ..., U \wedge \forall i = 1, ..., I \wedge \forall t = 1, ..., T$$

$$\wedge \forall u \forall i (\sum_{t=1}^{T} x_{i_u}^t = y_{i_u}) \wedge \forall u \forall i (\exists t_1 = min(t \mid x_{i_u}^t = 1), t_2 = max(t \mid x_{i_u}^t = 1)$$

$$\mid t_2 - t_1 = \sum_{t=1}^{T} x_{i_u}^t = y_{i_u} - 1)\}$$

$$\wedge \forall x_{i_u}^t = 1 \rightarrow t > w_{i_u}^{min} \wedge t < w_{i_u}^{max}\}$$

$$(8)$$

The size of the solution search space is obtained by multiplying the number of positions that each appliance from the solution can take for all neighbourhood households:

$$\sigma = \prod_{u=1}^{U} \prod_{i=1}^{I} (w_{i_u}^{max} - w_{i_u}^{min} - y_{i_u} + 2) = \prod_{u=1}^{U} \prod_{i=1}^{I} (w_{i_u} - y_{i_u} + 1) \quad (9)$$

3.4 Algorithms for Solving the Problem

Metaheuristic methods are high-level heuristic methods, that is, methods that look for a sub-optimal solution, or in other words, a solution close to the optimal but at reasonable computational cost. This way, they try to overcome the inconveniences from heuristic algorithms, avoiding cycling on local optimas and searching for sub-optimal solutions in a more efficient way.

Considering the model definition, the number of possible solutions of the problem is finite. Dozens or even millions of feasible solutions (with high parameters) can be generated, but there is always possible to determine a discrete amount, that is, the size of the search space is calculable. Therefore, two different metaheuristics techniques have been used for the problem resolution: Tabu Search and Estimation of Distribution Algorithm algorithms. The reason for selecting these two algorithms, is that historically they have had a very scarce presence in problems related to the DSM.

Tabu Search Customization: Tabu Search is an algorithm which uses memory and tabu constraints. The objective is to get closer to the optimal solution of the problem avoiding getting stuck in local optimas by the use of memory. The algorithm stores the movements it has made, and gives priority to other movements that might ease the algorithm to move through other areas of the solutions search space.

- **Initial solution**: two configurations are defined for the calculation of the initial solution, either *randomly*, or through *greedy* heuristic method, starting the execution of the algorithm from a suboptimal solution.
- **Neighbourhood system**: a strategy is defined to represent the neighbourhood system of a solution, composed by all those feasible solutions in which the starting runtime moment of an appliance from the current solution has been modified. A secondary neighbourhood system is defined as a strategy to get out of local optimas when the algorithm gets stuck. So that, it is composed of all feasible solutions in which the operating moment of two or more household appliances are updated.
- **Tabu list**: two configuration are defined. The *right/left* method stores the direction in which the operation of an appliance has moved, that is, *left* if it is executed at lower time, *right* otherwise, updating the restriction value on direction column of the corresponding appliance. The *position* method stores the specific start time of the new operation of an appliance, that is, the restriction value is added to the column that indicates the unit of time for the new start time.
- **Additional configurations**: a secondary objective function is defined which determines neighbour solution objective value by updating current solution objective value to reduce computational complexity of the problem resolution. Also, the algorithm accepts not feasible solutions in order to widely move throughout solutions search space and to avoid get stuck in local optimas.

Estimation of Distribution Algorithm Customization: Estimation of Distribution Algorithm (EDA) is a derivative of the evolutionary algorithms, based on the probabilistic models learned from a set or population of individuals, to generate new individuals based on mentioned probability distribution. Initially, a population of candidate individuals is generated, then an estimation of the distribution is done from a reduced selection of the population, and finally a new candidate population is generated.

- **Initial population**: the random method is used, that is, N individuals (or solutions) are randomly selected from the set of feasible solutions of the problem.
- **Selection method**: *Tournament Selection* and *Rank Selection* are compared.
- **Probabilistic model, population distribution and sampling**: *UMDA (Univariate Marginal Distribution Algorithm)* probabilistic model adapted to problem variables dependency is applied.

– **Additional configurations**: an additional technique is applied to control premature convergence, through which a small percentage of cases from sampling process has been reserved to generate solutions that are not feasible in value. Three configurations of the algorithm are defined regarding this percentage of reserved probability $(0, 0.01, 0.05, 0.1\%)$.

4   Experimental Setup

Different variants of both algorithms have been configured based on the customisation of their hyperparameters as shown in Table 1. For the Tabu Search algorithm variants, the list type (which can take right/left (R/L) and position values) and tabu tenure (which can take values 10, 100 and 500) hyperparameter have been combined. As for the EDA, first of all, the UMDA (Univariate Marginal Distribution Algorithm) model has been selected for the generation of new individuals. Then, the selection method (which can take the rank or tournament values) and % of reserved probability (which can take values 0, 0.01, 0.05 and 0.1) hyperparameters have been combined. The performance of all these variants for both algorithms has been calculated and compared between them.

Table 1. Algorithms variants used in the experiments.

Algorithm	List type	Tabu tenure	ID
Tabu Search	R/L	10	TS1
		100	TS2
		500	TS3
	Position	10	TS4
		100	TS5
		500	TS6
Algorithm	*Selection method*	*% reserved probability*	*ID*
EDA-UMDA	Rank	0	EDA1
		0.01	EDA2
		0.05	EDA3
		0.1	EDA4
	Tournament	0	EDA5
		0.01	EDA6
		0.05	EDA7
		0.1	EDA8

All the algorithm variants have been evaluated with pseudo-random data. This pseudo-random consumption data has been generated for a variable number of households and based on the real consumption data and use of household appliances from a group of dwellers of the Aran Islands (Ireland), Aarhus (Denmark) and Madrid (Spain) who participated in the RESPOND project[2]. This algorithm clusters real appliance consumption data to determine appliance mean consumption, duration and aimed available time range.

More specifically, 30 problem instances have been generated for 10, 100 and 200 households, each one with 1 to 10 appliances with real simulated appliances. Each problem instance has been evaluated 10 times for each algorithm variant, and the execution time and reached suboptimal values have been stored. Then, a comparison has been made between all the variants regarding their performance in terms of execution time and precision on the achieved optimal values, where performance profile and accuracy profile [3, 8], have been used to evaluate these metrics.

5   Results and Discussion

The following tables show the results of execution time and optimal values achieved by the objective function after testing both algorithms by its variants.

Table 2 shows the results of the performance obtained by the Tabu Search variants, while Table 3 shows the results of the performance of the EDA variants.

Table 2. Performance of Tabu Search algorithm variants.

| Number of households | ID | Time | | | | Optimal value | | | |
		Min	Max	Mean	SD	Min	Max	Mean	SD
10	TS1	$2e^{-3}$	17.7	4.31	1.76	0	2838	235	269
10	TS4	$2.79e^{-3}$	24.7	6.03	5.51	0	1703	141	161
10	TS2	0	15.6	4.74	1.79	0	840	133	73.9
10	TS5	$5e^{-3}$	17.4	3.96	1.94	**0**	**882**	**123**	**60.3**
10	TS3	$2.99e^{-3}$	**13.5**	**2.91**	**1.24**	0	927	181	89.8
10	TS6	$4.99e^{-3}$	22.4	4.84	2.07	0	662	130	64.1
100	TS1	7.5	779	254	83.8	2	5778	1099	565
100	TS4	10.5	1090	355	117	1.2	3467	659	339
100	TS2	7.42	1827	475	188	6	3388	779	371
100	TS5	10.1	1716	420	150	**8**	**2788**	**627**	**384**
100	TS3	**4.84**	**1127**	**93**	**108**	6	4178	891	462
100	TS6	8.06	1878	489	179	4	2984	637	330
200	TS1	**21.3**	**3854**	**1007**	**393**	6	5646	1142	589
200	TS4	29.8	5396	1409	550	4	3388	814	354
200	TS2	22.5	6786	1896	662	4	5278	816	502
200	TS5	20.1	8869	1847	739	**6**	**4212**	**744**	**440**
200	TS3	10.5	5421	1431	666	12	5900	1244	718
200	TS6	17.5	5875	1800	632	8	4126	956	434

---

[2] http://project-respond.eu/.

Table 3. Performance of EDA algorithm variants.

Number of households	ID	Time				Optimal value			
		Min	Max	Mean	SD	Min	Max	Mean	SD
10	EDA1	**8.53**	**43.8**	**24.9**	**1.87**	0	3458	1349	390
10	EDA5	8.41	41.6	25.8	0.89	0	3730	752	382
10	EDA2	8.03	150	55.5	18.2	0	1034	498	126
10	EDA6	7.63	118	39.2	10.7	**0**	**630**	**272**	**82.9**
10	EDA3	8.32	126	36.7	12.5	0	3098	1393	224
10	EDA7	8.67	132	45.3	13.6	0	1262	494	106
10	EDA4	9.98	151	44.1	15	0	3718	1672	269
10	EDA8	10.3	105	41.5	12.4	0	2584	1044	168
100	EDA1	101	788	304	47.8	120	13042	6338	717
100	EDA5	97.3	509	310	7.85	**130**	**4640**	**2019**	**454**
100	EDA2	86.5	707	314	73.2	350	14000	7508	745
100	EDA6	138	1241	495	156	125	7366	3347	483
100	EDA3	**74.3**	**381**	**205**	**7.86**	1950	24564	11541	1626
100	EDA7	90.9	551	272	61.1	1078	20048	10692	834
100	EDA4	89.2	457	246	9.43	2600	29477	13849	1951
100	EDA8	81	349	229	15.6	2588	26066	12165	1745
200	EDA1	175	904	498	85.5	1450	20902	11377	1547
200	EDA5	208	1108	661	22.4	**274**	**7088**	**2780**	**746**
200	EDA2	151	816	475	63	1590	21512	11782	1428
200	EDA6	213	1049	618	84.8	522	16592	8299	627
200	EDA3	**149**	**606**	**391**	**4.93**	3482	25826	14117	2239
200	EDA7	164	681	474	26.2	3198	27654	14795	2367
200	EDA4	179	727	469	5.92	4178	30991	16940	2687
200	EDA8	159	674	434	3.93	3904	32860	16109	2026

Regarding the performance of the Tabu Search algorithm variants, less time is required when using the R/L instead of position for the tabu list hyperparameter. As a matter of fact, when R/L is used, the minimum performance values are reached, specifically when 500 value is used as tabu tenure (TS3). In contrast, when position is set for the tabu list hyperparameter, the algorithm is able to reach more accurate suboptimal values, reaching the best results with a tabu tenure hyperparameter value of 10 (TS4).

As for the EDA algorithm variants, when the rank selection method is set, more accurate optimal values are obtained compared with the tournament selection method. Furthermore, execution times are also lower for the rank selection method. Regarding the performance, the minimum execution time values have been obtained using the rank selection method using the parameter 0.1 (mostly) as percentage of reserved probability (EDA1). Moreover, when tournament selection method has been used, the minimum optimal values have been reached with no probability reserved (EDA5).

Figure 1 shows best mentioned algorithms variants according to their performance and accuracy. A complex scenario is proposed where the EDA4 method is the one that achieves the best execution times for 58% of the problems (TS3 do so in the remaining 42%), but for the remaining percentage of problems is only able to be second best algorithm for an additional 7.5%. In the remaining 34.5%, TS3 is placed as the second best variant, that is, from the 58% of problems that TS3 does not lead, it is the second best method in a ≈33% of the problems.

According to optimal values accuracy, TS4 method stands out above the rest, since it obtains a maximum precision value (≈5 points) in 83% of the executions, while TS3 does so in 17% and EDA algorithm variants are not able to reach this value.

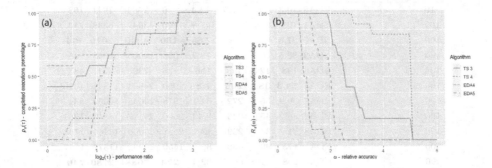

Fig. 1. Best variants execution time performance (a) and optimal values accuracy (b) comparison.

Tabu Search algorithm is the one that has obtained the best results both in terms of performance at execution time and precision of reached optimal values from all different problems. TS3 variant (tabu list R/L and tabu tenure of 500) is the best when execution time is prioritised, and TS4 variant (position tabu list and tabu tenure of 10) has highlighted in obtaining the lowest possible optimal values. Since the values of any parameter of the methods do not match, it is observed that the average performance values of TS4 method are 128.82% greater than those shown by TS3, while TS3 presents optimal values 38.76% higher. Thus, TS3 method is selected as the best variant of Tabu Search algorithm and for the hole comparison.

This algorithm applied to organise the use of household appliances can lead to a considerable decrease in the final bill. Users with electricity price of 0.10€/kWh who are able to produce and store their own electrical energy through renewable sources, and whose home is 100% electric could save more than 35% of his final bill, depending on the optimal conditions of electricity production.

6   Conclusion

The ODP represents the optimal amount of electrical demand to be consumed by customers in order to, on the one hand, help electric companies balance energy supply and demand, and on the other, help customers reduce their monthly bills and contribute to a more sustainable environment. To do so, users adapt the use of their appliances to approximate their total consumption to the target ODP, although it can sometimes be difficult for users to make this approximation.

This paper analyses two metaheuristic algorithms for neighbourhood appliances scheduling optimisation problem by comparing several variants for each of them. The algorithms are applied for neighbourhood scenario with various households, where each one pretends to adapt its appliances uses to adjust the demand to an optimal demand profile previously provided by its electricity supplier. When ODPs are defined to maximise the use of the energy produced by neighbourhoods, the defined algorithms organise the use of household appliances in such a way that the use of the energy produced by the users is maximised, thus reducing the cost of purchasing and transporting electricity. In addition, the energy prices provided by the supplier company are taken into account, trying to balance the cheapest prices with users consumption habits.

After evaluating all algorithms variants through 30 problem instances, Tabu Search algorithm variants have performed better results than EDA both for execution time and reached optimal values. When R/L tabu list and 500 tabu tenure are used, fastest execution time values are obtained, but lowest optimal values are reached when position tabu list is selected. However, this second variant gets very high computational time values, so the best algorithm for neighbourhood appliances use optimisation problem guided by ODP is Tabu Search, in particular when it is customised with R/L tabu list and 500 tabu tenure.

Acknowledgements. This work was supported by the SPRI-Basque Government's project 3KIA [grant number KK-2020/00049] of the ELKARTEK program.

References

1. Ata, M., Erenoğlu, A.K., Şengör, İ, Erdinç, O., Taşcıkaraoğlu, A., Catalão, J.P.: Optimal operation of a multi-energy system considering renewable energy sources stochasticity and impacts of electric vehicles. Energy **186**, 115841 (2019)
2. Barbato, A., Capone, A., Carello, G., Delfanti, M., Merlo, M., Zaminga, A.: House energy demand optimization in single and multi-user scenarios. In: 2011 IEEE International Conference on Smart Grid Communications (SmartGridComm), pp. 345–350. IEEE (2011)
3. Beiranvand, V., Hare, W., Lucet, Y.: Best practices for comparing optimization algorithms. Optim. Eng. **18**(4), 815–848 (2017). https://doi.org/10.1007/s11081-017-9366-1
4. Bouakkaz, A., Haddad, S., Gil Mena, A.J.: Optimal peak power shaving through household appliance scheduling in off-grid renewable energy system. In: 2019 IEEE International Conference on Environment and Electrical Engineering and 2019 IEEE Industrial and Commercial Power Systems Europe (EEEIC/I CPS Europe), pp. 1–6 (2019). https://doi.org/10.1109/EEEIC.2019.8783662
5. Chavali, P., Yang, P., Nehorai, A.: A distributed algorithm of appliance scheduling for home energy management system. IEEE Trans. Smart Grid **5**(1), 282–290 (2014)

6. Dorahaki, S., Dashti, R., Shaker, H.R.: Optimal energy management in the smart microgrid considering the electrical energy storage system and the demand-side energy efficiency program. J. Energy Storage **28**, 101229 (2020)
7. Esnaola-Gonzalez, I., Jelić, M., Pujić, D., Díez, F., Tomasevic, N.: An AI-powered system for residential demand response. Electronics **10** (2021). https://doi.org/10.3390/electronics10060693
8. Gould, N., Scott, J.: A note on performance profiles for benchmarking software. ACM Trans. Math. Softw. (TOMS) **43**(2), 1–5 (2016)
9. Huang, L., Walrand, J., Ramchandran, K.: Optimal demand response with energy storage management. In: 2012 IEEE Third International Conference on Smart Grid Communications (SmartGridComm), pp. 61–66. IEEE (2012)
10. Jamil, A., Javaid, N., Aslam, S.: An efficient home energy optimization by using meta-heuristic techniques while incorporating game-theoretic approach for real-time coordination among home appliances. In: 2018 5th International Multi-Topic ICT Conference (IMTIC), pp. 1–6 (2018). https://doi.org/10.1109/IMTIC.2018.8467218
11. Lorestani, A., Aghaee, S.S., Gharehpetian, G.B., Ardehali, M.M.: Energy management in smart home including PV panel, battery, electric heater with integration of plug-in electric vehicle. In: 2017 Smart Grid Conference (SGC), pp. 1–7 (2017). https://doi.org/10.1109/SGC.2017.8308855
12. Mirabbasi, D., Beydaghi, S.: Optimal scheduling of smart home appliances considering PHEV and energy storage system. In: 2015 4th International Conference on Electric Power and Energy Conversion Systems (EPECS), pp. 1–6 (2015). https://doi.org/10.1109/EPECS.2015.7368510
13. Nan, S., Zhou, M., Li, G.: Optimal residential community demand response scheduling in smart grid. Appl. Energy **210**, 1280–1289 (2018)
14. Yu, Y., Wang, W., Kuang, H.: A two-stage scheduling on household appliances including electric vehicles. In: 2016 3rd International Conference on Systems and Informatics (ICSAI), pp. 258–262 (2016). https://doi.org/10.1109/ICSAI.2016.7810964

Multitask Learning for Predicting Natural Flows: A Case Study at Paraiba do Sul River

Gabriel Dias Abreu[1]([✉])(iD), Leticia F. Pires[1]([✉])(iD),
Luciana C. D. Campos[1]([✉])(iD), and Leonardo Goliatt[2]([✉])(iD)

[1] Department of Computer Science, Federal University of Juiz de Fora,
Juiz de Fora, MG, Brazil
{gabrieldiasabreu,leticia1,luciana.campos}@ice.ufjf.br
[2] Computational Modeling Program, Federal University of Juiz de Fora,
Juiz de Fora, Brazil
leonardo.goliatt@ufjf.edu.br

Abstract. Forecasting the flow of rivers is essential for maintaining social well-being since their waters provide water and energy resources and cause serious tragedies such as floods and droughts. In this way, predicting long-term flow at measuring stations in a watershed with reasonable accuracy contributes to solving a range of problems that affect society and resource management. The present work proposes the MultiTask-LSTM model that combines the recurring model of Deep Learning LSTM with the transfer of learning MultiTask Learning, to predict and share information acquired along the hydrographic basin of Paraíba do Sul river. This method is robust for missing and noisy data, which are common problems in inflow time series. In the present work, we applied all 45 measurement stations' series located along the Paraíba do Sul River basin in the MultiTask-LSTM model for forecasting the set of these 45 series, combining each time series's learning in a single model. To confirm the MultiTask-LSTM model's robustness, we compared its predictions' results with the results obtained by the LSTM models applied to each isolated series, given that the LSTM presents good time series forecast results in the literature. In order to deal with missing data, we used techniques to impute missing data across all series to predict the 45 series of measurement stations alone with LSTM models. The experiments use three different forms of missing data imputation: the series' median, the ARIMA method, and the average of the months' days. We used these same series with imputing data in the MultiTask-LSTM model to make the comparison. This paper achieved better forecast results showing that MultiTask-LSTM is a robust model to missing and noisy data.

Keywords: Multitask Learning · Forecasting hydrological time series · Deep learning · Long short-term memory (LSTM) · Paraiba do Sul River · Brazil

© Springer Nature Switzerland AG 2021
G. Marreiros et al. (Eds.): EPIA 2021, LNAI 12981, pp. 163–175, 2021.
https://doi.org/10.1007/978-3-030-86230-5_13

1   Introduction

The flow forecast is necessary due to the dependence and fixation of societies around river basins throughout history. It is fundamental for the civilization to maintain its essential activities, such as agriculture, livestock, basic sanitation, hydroelectric power generation, industry, and tourism. Keeping water available implies developing techniques to identify and predict the behavior of these basins. Besides, it is possible to avoid tragedies such as those resulting from floods, droughts, rupture of dams, and disease vectors [14]. From a current perspective of society, the improvement of these techniques is in line with the water resources' growth management and environmental preservation. It is negatively impacted by the accelerated urban expansion, enabling sustainable development and enabling decision-making and long-term risk planning competent bodies [10].

Historical records contained in time series of water phenomena are often costly and difficult to measure, in addition to presenting noises and missing data, which impairs the performance of forecasting these time series [6]. The case study of this work, the river basin's Paraíba do Sul, has 45 flow measurement stations with many missing data in all stations resulting from the station shutdown or the like activities. In addition to hydro-geomorphological modifications or even failures in sensors that result in noise in the time series.

The hydro-geomorphological variables present in a basin present correlated variations temporally and also spatially. That indicates possible events, such as changes in the records measured by an upstream flow measurement station, which influence the forecast of the downstream measurement station[1]. Therefore, it is necessary to consider these phenomena to improve predictive capacity. For example, if a dam is installed in a river basin region, the entire flow downstream of that dam will be affected, so the time series forecasts of stations downstream from the dam need to consider this phenomenon.

The flow time series is susceptible to exogenous and uncertain factors, such as the measuring station's maintenance, probably because of measurement failures in sensors, which require its shutdown. Also, the relationships present in the time series distributed along the river basin, when not appropriately used, constitute a reneged potential for forecasting and wasting resources spent on flow measurements. Therefore, forecasting with robust methods for missing data and noise inflow time series is necessary.

MultiTask Learning is an approach to inductive learning transfer that increases generalization using information from related tasks. This is done by learning in parallel using a shared representation which can help to improve the learning of the others as defined in [4]. The MultiTask Learning method can be resilient to missing and noisy data since it considers the temporal and spatial relationships present in the river basin's flow time series. As a result,

---

[1] Downstream is the side where is directed the water flow and upstream is the part where the river is born. So, the mouth or outfall of a river is the most downstream point of this river, and the source is its most upstream point.

missing data or noise that would impair the model's performance has its negative effect diminished by the relationships present in the data, combining each time series's learning in a single model. The learning transfer method Multi-Task Learning still captures information implicit in the relationships between all flow time series along the river basin, providing better use of the available data concerning the forecast models' application separately in each measuring station. The motivation of this work consists of combining these characteristics of the transfer of learning MultiTask Learning with the LSTM model of recurrent neural networks.

The literature presents promising results in several applications. Jin and Sun [7] showed that multi-task learning (MTL) has the potential to improve generalization by transferring information in training signals of extra tasks. Ye and Dai [15] developed a multi-task learning algorithm, called the MultiTL-KELM, for multi-step-ahead time series prediction. MultiTL-KELM regards predictions of different horizons as different tasks. Knowledge from one task can benefit others, enabling it to explore the relatedness among horizons. Zhao and collaborators [17] introduced a multi-task learning framework that combines the tasks of self-supervised learning and scene classification. The proposed multi-task learning framework empowers a deep neural network to learn more discriminative features without increasing the parameters. The experimental results show that the proposed method can improve the accuracy of remote sensing scene classification. Cao et al. [3] proposed a deep learning model based on LSTM for time series prediction in wireless communication, employing multi-task learning to improve prediction accuracy. Through experiments on several real datasets, the authors showed that the proposed model is effective, and it outperforms other prediction methods.

The prediction of flow time series is widely used for the planning and management of water resources, as evidenced by the work in [13]. This paper presents the classic models such as ARIMA and Linear Regression, which are unable to capture the non-stationarity and non-linearity of the hydrological time series. This study also points to the growth of attention given to data-driven models such as neural networks that progress in predicting non-linear time series, capturing water time series's complexity. Aghelpour and Varshavian, [1] compare two stochastic and three artificial intelligence (AI) models in modeling and predicting the daily flow of a river. The results showed that the accuracy of AI models was higher than stochastic ones, and the Group Method of Data Handling (GMDH) and Multilayer Perceptron (MLP) produced the best validation performance among the AI models.

In comparison to several hydrological models, deep learning has made significant advances in methodologies and practical applications in recent years, which have greatly expanded the number and type of problems that neural networks can solve. One of the five most popular deep learning architectures is the long short-term memory (LSTM) network, which is widely applied for predicting time series [11]. LSTM is a specific recurrent neural network architecture that can learn long-term temporal dependencies and be robust to noise. This feature makes it efficient in water resource forecasting problems as explored in the works at [9], which showed the LSTM model as an alternative to complex models. Such models can include prior knowledge about inflows' behavior and the study at [16] which showed LSTM 's ability to predict water depth for long-term irrigation, thereby contributing to water management for irrigation. However, both works clarify the need for a considerable amount of data for LSTM to present satisfactory results.

The Paraíba do Sul River basin is of great importance for Brazilian economic development and supplies 32 million people [8]. This basin has 45 measurement stations whose captured time series have missing and noisy data, so forecasting this basin's flow is difficult. The work on [2] showed the efficiency of the LSTM model for the flow forecast in the Paraíba do Sul River basin compared to other classic models such as ARIMA and also pointed out the importance of the long flow forecast in this basin. This work used a subset of 4 of the 45 flow measurement stations on the Paraíba do Sul River.

To applying a Machine Learning technique to forecast time series, it is common to optimize an error measure by training a single forecast model of the desired time series. However, it is sometimes necessary to explore latent information from related series to improve forecasting performance, resulting in a learning paradigm known as Multi-Task Learning (MTL). According to Dorado-Moreno et al. [5] the high computational capacity of deep neural networks (DNN) can be combined with the improved generalization performance of MTL, designing independent output layers for each series and including a shared representation for them. The work of Shireen and collaborators [12] showed that models using MTL could capture information from several time-series simultaneously, with robustness to missing data and noise, making inferences about all historical data and their relationships within the scope photovoltaic panels.

This work proposes a robust forecasting model for missing and noisy data to make long-term flow predictions from information present in the time series of measuring stations located along a hydrographic basin. We have used the time series of measuring stations located along the Paraíba do Sul river basin as a case study for this work. The proposed model combines Deep Learning techniques, such as LSTM, with the transfer of learning MultiTask Learning - MTL, to take advantage of the implicit relationships between the time series of each measurement station, making the model robust to missing and noisy data to improve forecast performance.

2   Materials and Methods

2.1   Study Area and Data

The set of series used in this work consists of daily records collected, from 1935 to 2016, at 45 flow measurement stations along the Paraíba do Sul River basin, provided by the National Water Agency (ANA)[2]. Some measurement stations

---

[2] www.ana.gov.br.

present missing or noisy data in their collected historical series, as can be seen in Fig. 1. The missing data in the series come from failures of sensors present in the measuring station or similar problems, which resulted in their shutdown for maintenance. In red are non missing data from a measurement station.

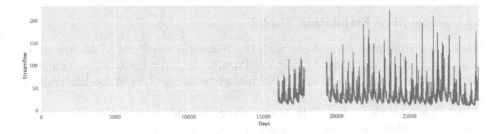

Fig. 1. Streamflow time series with missing data.

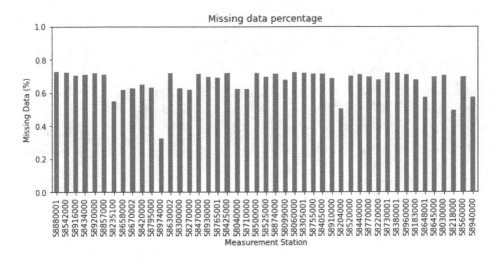

Fig. 2. Percentage of missing data per measurement station.

Missing data and noise are the problem for the time series' prediction since noise imply errors in learning the time series's behavior. On the other hand, missing data inhibits the model from understanding what happened when the data was unwilling. They, therefore, affect the continuity of the model forecast.

Figure 2 shows the number of records missing in the series of flow measurement stations along the basin, whether due to shutdown, maintenance, or defects present in the measurement stations in some period. The series' median, the ARIMA method, and the average of the months' days were some data imputations techniques to treat the missing data in these work's series. Simultaneously, the MTL-LSTM model, which combines two robust techniques for dealing with noisy data, MultiTask Learning and LSTM, was used to deal with noises. As the imputing values' process in the missing data creates noises, the learning characteristics were from the correlation of the imputed time series in the MTL-LSTM model.

2.2 Streamflow Estimation Model

The experiments were carried out with the historical series' set of 45 flow measurement stations distributed along the Paraíba do Sul river basin to compare the forecast made by the MTL-LSTM models with the LSTM models trained with each isolated series.

As shown in Fig. 3, the E time series are provided as input to the model. They are divided into rolling windows of size j and steps of size 1. Each step of these time series is concatenated with the E measuring station, forming a E rows matrix and j columns and a y vector with size E. These data are then provided to the LSTM, which learns to predict the time series's future behavior.

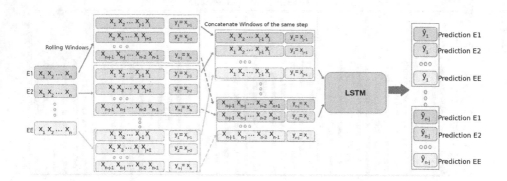

Fig. 3. MultiTask-LSTM model

The experiments were retrieved in the Google Colab[3] environment with 12 GB of RAM in GPUs using the Keras[4], NumPy[5] and Tensorflow libraries[6] in Python. All results were chosen about the average of 30 runs. The MAPE metric was chosen to compare the results, defined by the Eq. 1:

$$MAPE = \frac{100\%}{n} \sum_{t=1}^{n} \mid \frac{A_t - F_t}{A_t} \mid \qquad (1)$$

---

[3] colab.research.google.com.

[4] keras.io.

[5] numpy.org.

[6] www.tensorflow.org.

where A_t is the historical time series value in time t, F_t is the value predicted in time t, and n is the size of the time series.

The LSTM applied in the MTL-LSTM model had hyper-parameters as suggested by Campos et al. [2]. These hyperparameters were used to build a single-task learning LSTM (STL-LSTM) to separately model each time series collected on the 45 measurement stations.

The MTL-LSTM model uses 14-day windows as in the work of Campos et al. [2], with 45 reference stations and is written as:

$$Q_{1,t+14} = F(Q_{1,t}, Q_{1,t-1}, \cdots, Q_{1,t-13})$$
$$Q_{2,t+14} = F(Q_{2,t}, Q_{2,t-1}, \cdots, Q_{2,t-13})$$
$$\vdots$$
$$Q_{k,t+14} = F(Q_{k,t}, Q_{k,t-1}, \cdots, Q_{k,t-13})$$
$$\vdots$$
$$Q_{45,t+14} = F(Q_{45,t}, Q_{45,t-1}, \cdots, Q_{45,t-13})$$

where $Q_{k,t+14}$ is the streamflow at station k predicted $14\,\text{d}$ ahead.

We trained the model using a training set with the first 75% data of the time series, and the 10% of the followed data in the validation set to verify the hyperparameters, and the last 15% of data for the test set. Each experiment was performed 30 times, from which we calculated the average of the MAPE metric to assess the final performance of the model.

3   Computational Experiments

Figure 4 shows us that the MTL-LSTM model performs considerably better than the LSTM model when the median metric was applied in the imputation of missing data in the times series presented to the models, except for the station 58218000. The results evidence the MTL-LSTM model's capacity to learn hydro-geomorphological relations in the basin, ignoring the noise added by a constant median imputation.

When ARIMA or Mean of days per month are applied to impute missing values as in the Figs. 5 and 6, MTL-LSTM performs considerable better than LSTM in all measurement stations. This behavior shows the robustness of the MTL-LSTM model to learn series relations in the basin when data is more accurate with two imputation methods that preserve the seasonality and variability of the time series. This behavior indicates that MTL-LSTM would perform better than LSTM with no missing data.

The Table 1 summarizes the results found in the experiments. We can observe that the MultiTask-LSTM model obtains averaged percentage errors around half of the errors achieved with the individual LSTM models. Note that while the LSTM models achieved percentage errors above 40%, the MultiTask-LSTM model achieved MAPEs below 22%. As shown in Fig. 7, the MultiTask-LSTM has the advantage of having your training time faster as it places all flow measurement stations in the same model. On the other hand, the model containing only LSTM is considerably slower to train each time series separately.

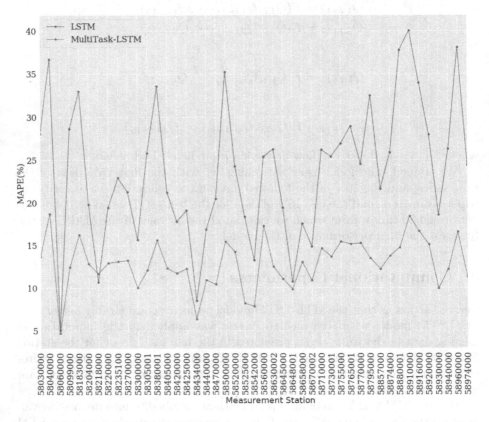

Fig. 4. MultiTask-LSTM and LSTM comparison with median missing data imputation

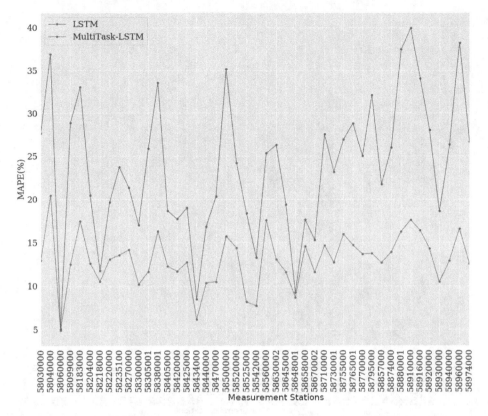

Fig. 5. MultiTask-LSTM and LSTM comparison with ARIMA missing data imputation

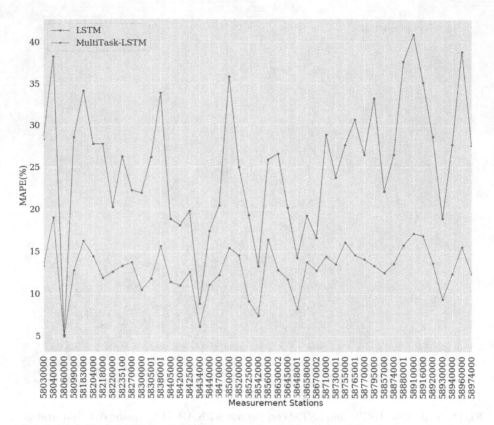

Fig. 6. MultiTask-LSTM and LSTM comparison with mean of days per month missing data imputation

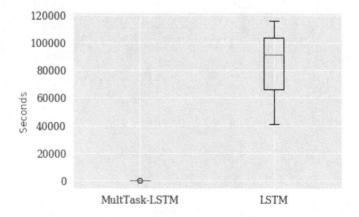

Fig. 7. Time comparison between MultiTask-LSTM and LSTM

Table 1. MAPE's mean for each streamflow measurement station by imputation method and model.

Stations (gauges)	ARIMA imputation		Mean imputation		Median imputation	
	LSTM	MultiTask-LSTM	LSTM	MultiTask-LSTM	LSTM	MultiTask-LSTM
58030000	27.67	**12.91**	28.31	**13.25**	28.04	**13.64**
58040000	36.90	**20.44**	38.25	**19.01**	36.72	**18.71**
58060000	5.03	**4.87**	5.08	**4.92**	5.04	**4.67**
58099000	28.87	**12.48**	28.56	**12.75**	28.65	**12.43**
58183000	33.03	**17.46**	34.11	**16.23**	33.01	**16.26**
58204000	20.42	**12.58**	27.70	**14.41**	19.77	**12.83**
58218000	11.71	**10.49**	27.71	**11.85**	**10.70**	11.66
58220000	19.61	**13.06**	20.22	**12.56**	19.44	**12.91**
58235100	23.70	**13.54**	26.23	**13.28**	22.89	**13.09**
58270000	21.30	**14.16**	22.22	**13.71**	21.23	**13.22**
58300000	16.99	**10.19**	21.90	**10.46**	15.65	**10.03**
58305001	25.85	**11.65**	26.15	**11.76**	25.80	**12.08**
58380001	33.53	**16.29**	33.81	**15.63**	33.56	**15.60**
58405000	18.66	**12.25**	18.84	**11.38**	21.23	**12.32**
58420000	17.70	**11.69**	18.10	**10.97**	17.80	**11.70**
58425000	19.01	**12.75**	19.75	**12.56**	19.09	**12.24**
58434000	8.48	**6.14**	8.85	**6.14**	8.48	**6.35**
58440000	16.84	**10.37**	17.41	**11.06**	16.86	**10.91**
58470000	20.31	**10.50**	20.45	**12.22**	20.45	**10.40**
58500000	35.10	**15.74**	35.79	**15.41**	35.24	**15.45**
58520000	24.18	**14.39**	24.95	**14.53**	24.26	**14.23**
58525000	18.39	**8.17**	19.32	**9.13**	18.33	**8.16**
58542000	13.27	**7.72**	13.26	**7.40**	13.25	**7.83**
58560000	25.30	**17.58**	25.85	**16.42**	25.38	**17.25**
58630002	26.27	**13.07**	26.56	**12.82**	26.23	**12.49**
58645000	19.35	**11.60**	20.17	**11.74**	19.40	**11.04**
58648001	9.23	**8.67**	14.27	**8.20**	10.73	**9.86**
58658000	17.61	**14.57**	19.22	**13.74**	17.56	**13.02**
58670002	15.29	**11.58**	16.61	**12.77**	14.84	**10.85**
58710000	27.51	**14.65**	28.81	**14.38**	26.16	**14.64**
58730001	23.15	**12.69**	23.74	**13.49**	25.37	**13.65**
58755000	26.90	**15.94**	27.61	**16.09**	26.92	**15.41**
58765001	28.78	**14.68**	30.62	**14.56**	28.93	**15.14**
58770000	24.99	**13.65**	26.46	**14.06**	24.53	**15.24**
58795000	32.11	**13.73**	33.19	**13.29**	32.50	**13.45**
58857000	21.70	**12.67**	22.11	**12.47**	21.62	**12.21**
58874000	25.99	**13.90**	26.48	**13.57**	25.86	**13.75**
58880001	37.45	**16.27**	37.59	**15.75**	37.78	**14.73**
58910000	39.96	**17.59**	40.88	**17.12**	40.07	**18.41**
58916000	34.03	**16.38**	35.11	**16.85**	33.98	**16.63**
58920000	28.03	**14.31**	28.63	**13.63**	27.95	**15.06**
58930000	18.59	**10.46**	18.93	**9.36**	18.58	**9.91**
58940000	26.32	**12.89**	27.66	**12.34**	26.27	**12.19**
58960000	38.23	**16.54**	38.84	**15.55**	38.10	**16.57**
58974000	26.63	**12.53**	27.54	**12.35**	24.38	**11.28**

4   Conclusion

Flow forecasting in the river basin is an essential issue for well-being and social development. To ensure adequate environmental, social and economic conditions, the study of models that provide the improvement of long-term flow forecasting is necessary, especially in time series with a lot of missing data, noise, and hydrogeomorphological changes such as flow time series.

Using the MultiTask Learning technique together with the Deep Learning model, LSTM, allows absorbing the information present in the data of all the time series of the measuring stations of a basin. In other words, it reuses the knowledge learned in a time series of a measuring station in the learning of the other series of that basin. The Paraíba do Sul River Basin, located in Brazil, was used as a case study for this work. However, the model can be applied to forecasting other basins where multiple flow measurement stations collect data, especially if these measuring stations have time series with noise or missing data.

The study used three missing data imputation techniques to verify robustness against noisy data of the MTL-LSTM model. As can be seen in Figs. 4, 5 and 6 the MTL-LSTM model achieved considerably better percentage errors in all missing data imputation scenarios. The LSTM models were applied in long-term forecasts in each series of flow measurement stations located along the Paraíba do Sul river basin. The MTL-LSTM model also presented a shorter training time when compared to the LSTM models, as seen in Fig. 7.

The learning transfer approach present in the MTL-LSTM model allowed the improvement of long-term forecasts. Results from all measuring stations in the hydrographic basin demonstrated the robustness of the data imputation procedure, maintaining a stable performance with the different imputations.

References

1. Aghelpour, P., Varshavian, V.: Evaluation of stochastic and artificial intelligence models in modeling and predicting of river daily flow time series. Stoch. Environ. Res. Risk Assess. **34**, 33–50 (2020). https://doi.org/10.1007/s00477-019-01761-4
2. Campos, L.C.D., Goliatt da Fonseca, L., Fonseca, T.L., de Abreu, G.D., Pires, L.F., Gorodetskaya, Y.: Short-term streamflow forecasting for Paraíba do Sul River using deep learning. In: Moura Oliveira, P., Novais, P., Reis, L.P. (eds.) EPIA 2019. LNCS (LNAI), vol. 11804, pp. 507–518. Springer, Cham (2019). https://doi.org/10.1007/978-3-030-30241-2_43
3. Cao, K., Hu, T., Li, Z., Zhao, G., Qian, X.: Deep multi-task learning model for time series prediction in wireless communication. Phys. Commun. **44**, 101251 (2021)
4. Caruana, R.: Multitask learning. Mach. Learn. **28**(1), 41–75 (1997)
5. Dorado-Moreno, M., et al.: Multi-task learning for the prediction of wind power ramp events with deep neural networks. Neural Netw. **123**, 401–411 (2020)
6. Herschy, R.W.: Streamflow Measurement. CRC Press, Boca Raton (2014)
7. Jin, F., Sun, S.: Neural network multitask learning for traffic flow forecasting. CoRR abs/1712.08862 (2017). http://arxiv.org/abs/1712.08862
8. Kelman, J.: Water supply to the two largest Brazilian metropolitan regions. Aquatic Procedia **5**, 13–21 (2015). At the Confluence Selection from the 2014 World Water Week in Stockholm

9. Kratzert, F., Klotz, D., Brenner, C., Schulz, K., Herrnegger, M.: Rainfall–runoff modelling using long short-term memory (LSTM) networks. Hydrol. Earth Syst. Sci. **22**(11), 6005–6022 (2018). https://doi.org/10.5194/hess-22-6005-2018
10. Rezende, O.M., Miguez, M.G., Veról, A.P.: Manejo de águas urbanas e sua relação com o desenvolvimento urbano em bases sustentáveis integradas: estudo de caso dos Rios Pilar-Calombé, em Duque de Caxias/RJ. Revista Brasileira de Recursos Hídricos **18**(2), 149–163 (2013)
11. Sherstinsky, A.: Fundamentals of recurrent neural network (RNN) and long short-term memory (LSTM) network. Physica D Nonlinear Phenomena **404**, 132306 (2020)
12. Shireen, T., Shao, C., Wang, H., Li, J., Zhang, X., Li, M.: Iterative multi-task learning for time-series modeling of solar panel PV outputs. Appl. Energy **212**, 654–662 (2018)
13. Yaseen, Z.M., El-shafie, A., Jaafar, O., Afan, H.A., Sayl, K.N.: Artificial intelligence based models for stream-flow forecasting: 2000–2015. J. Hydrol. **530**, 829–844 (2015)
14. Yassuda, E.R.: Gestão de recursos hídricos: fundamentos e aspectos institucionais. Revista de Administração pública **27**(2), 5–18 (1993)
15. Ye, R., Dai, Q.: Multitl-KELM: a multi-task learning algorithm for multi-step-ahead time series prediction. Appl. Soft Comput. **79**, 227–253 (2019)
16. Zhang, J., Zhu, Y., Zhang, X., Ye, M., Yang, J.: Developing a long short-term memory (LSTM) based model for predicting water table depth in agricultural areas. J. Hydrol. **561**, 918–929 (2018)
17. Zhao, Z., Luo, Z., Li, J., Chen, C., Piao, Y.: When self-supervised learning meets scene classification: remote sensing scene classification based on a multitask learning framework. Remote Sens. **12**(20), 3276 (2020)

PV Generation Forecasting Model
for Energy Management in Buildings

Brígida Teixeira[1,2]([✉]), Tiago Pinto[1,2], Pedro Faria[1,2], and Zita Vale[2]

[1] GECAD - Research Group on Intelligent Engineering and Computing for Advanced Innovation and Development, Porto, Portugal
[2] Institute of Engineering, Polytechnic of Porto (ISEP/IPP), Porto, Portugal
{bccta,tcp,pnf,zav}@isep.ipp.pt

Abstract. The increasing penetration of renewable energy sources and the need to adjust to the future demand requires adopting measures to improve energy resources management, especially in buildings. In this context, PV generation forecast has an essential role in the energy management entities by preventing problems related to intermittent weather conditions and allowing participation in incentive programs to reduce energy consumption. This paper proposes an automatic model for the day-ahead PV generation forecast, combining several forecasting algorithms with the expected weather conditions. To this end, this model communicates with a SCADA system, which is responsible for the cyber-physical energy management of an actual building.

Keywords: Energy management system · Forecast · PV generation

1 Introduction

Currently, sustainability is one of the biggest challenges in the energy sector. In an environment where the use of electronic devices and the internet is increasingly significant in the daily routine, studies show that the demand will more than double in the coming years, conducting to the need to produce more energy [4]. European Commission also says that the energy consumed in buildings corresponds to 40% of the total energy demand [2].

In order to deal with current and future demand requirements and considering the urgency of significantly reducing the environmental impact of fossil fuels, there is an investment in the penetration of renewable energy sources worldwide through the creation of new technologies, models, and legislation [3]. However, the intermittency of energy sources based on weather conditions raises several

This work was supported by the MAS-Society Project co-funded by Portugal 2020 Fundo Europeu de Desenvolvimento Regional (FEDER) through PO CI, and under Grant UIDB/00760/2020. Brígida Teixeira was supported by national funds through Fundação para a Ciência e a Tecnologia (FCT) PhD studentship with reference 2020.08174.BD.

G. Marreiros et al. (Eds.): EPIA 2021, LNAI 12981, pp. 176–182, 2021.
https://doi.org/10.1007/978-3-030-86230-5_14

challenges due to their uncertainty to satisfy the demand. In this way, forecasting has an essential role in providing energy management systems with information to better use energy, allowing them to take full advantage of renewable energy sources while decreasing cost and waste of energy.

This paper presents an automatic PV generation forecast model for Anonymous building energy management. The proposed methodology aims to improve the solar forecast results, supported by different data models and four forecast methods, namely Neural Artificial Networks (ANN), Support Vector Machines (SVM), Random Forest, and ARIMA. It is connected to a SCADA system, which ensures the cyber-physical energy management of the building. The Forecasting process executes in five main phases: data selection and transformation, creation of data models, model hyperparameters, forecast, and evaluation.

2   SCADA System

In order to monitor and manage GECAD research group energy resources, this section presents the implemented SCADA system [1] in Building N facilities located in Porto, Portugal. This building has twelve offices, a meeting room, a server room, two laboratories, two toilets, a kitchen, and three corridors. These rooms are equipped with several sensors and energy meters, which communicate with Programmable Logic Controllers (PLCs) connected to a central PLC to monitor and control the building. The communications are via TCP/IP protocol. The visualization and control of these resources are available from a touch panel installed in the hall or an internal web page. The sensors collect real-time data of the building's environment, allowing the observation of several indicators, such as external temperature, internal temperature, brightness, humidity, CO_2 levels, air quality, generation, and consumption.

The building has three-phase meters, which allows to analysis separately the consumption by type of resource. Phase 1 allows monitoring the loads in the area where the energy meter is installed; phase 2 observes the consumption of the air conditioning systems; phase 3 reads the consumption of the lights. Besides, this building has a PV system with a maximum 7.5 KW capacity installed on the rooftop. The energy generated by the PV satisfies part of the energy demand, and if there is a surplus of energy, it is injected into the network.

Furthermore, GECAD also has access to the Institute of Engineering of Polytechnic of Porto meteorological station (meteo@isep)[1], which enables to access real-time weather information (i.e., feel temperature, real temperature, wind speed, radiation, atmospheric pressure, humidity, and rain), and consult forecasts for the next three days.

3   Solar Forecasting Model

In building energy management and smart grids, having information on the estimated consumption and generation is essential for the optimization of energy

---

[1] meteo@isep - https://meteo.isep.ipp.pt/gauges.

resources, taking advantage of grid incentives to reduce electricity consumption, namely by participating in demand response programs. However, the weather conditions variation represents a significant challenge in forecasting renewable energy since they can harm the results, especially when the frequency is less than an hour. For example, the passage of a cloud causes a decrease in radiation, originating an error that will have more impact in a 15-min time interval forecast than a 1-h frequency.

This paper proposes a methodology to forecast the day-ahead PV generation, with a 15-min time interval, which corresponds to a total of 96 periods. The model is implemented in Python, and it contains four different artificial intelligence techniques to forecast PV generation, namely ANN, SVM, and Random Forests from scikit-learn library, and ARIMA from pmdarima library. The model's architecture is based on five phases. The selection of these techniques is based on previous works presented in the current literature.

The first phase is related to selecting and preparing the necessary historical data for the learning process of forecasting algorithms. This data is imported from SCADA's database and consists of the last 20 days of PV generation. Rain, radiation, and outside temperature are imported from the meteo@isep API as additional features for the learning process. After this, cleaning data occurs by detecting and replacing missing data, incorrect data, and outliers. The strategy for replacing corrupt or inaccurate data consists of an estimation based on the average between the last recorded value and the next.

The second phase is the generation of data models (or scenarios). For this purpose, the historical PV generation is used as a basis of the data model. Next, it will be added new information to this dataset, according the combination of several data transformations. The use of different data models helps to identify which type of information helps the most in the algorithms' training process. This are the considered transformations:

- Separation of the timestamp into the four columns (month, day, hour and minute);
- Insert a new column with the distance between the entry and the first value of forecast $t(0)$. For example, if the forecast starts at 00:00h, the train entry that corresponds to the previous period 23:45 h $t(-1)$ will have the value of -1, 23:30 h $t(-2)$ will have the value of -2, and so on. This strategy helps the algorithm to identify how old the entry is compared to the forecast;
- Insert three new columns with the values of the three periods of the previous day, at the same time $t(-96)$, $t(-97)$, $t(-98)$;
- Insert five new columns with the values of the five periods of the previous day, at the same time $t(-96)$, $t(-97)$, $t(-98)$, $t(-99)$, $t(-100)$;
- Insert seven new columns with the values of the seven periods of the previous day, at the same time $t(-96)$, $t(-97)$, $t(-98)$, $t(-99)$, $t(-100)$, $t(-101)$, $t(-102)$;
- Exclusion of night time periods, from 23:00 h to 05:00 h of the next day;
- Insert three new columns with the information of additional features (radiation, rain, and outside temperature).

Then, the data is split, where 80% is for training the model and 20% is for testing, following the normalization process.

The third phase is the tuning of the hyperparameters and training of the forecasting algorithms. For each algorithm, several configurations of the hyperparameters are tested to identify which one achieves more precise results. In the case of ANN, different solvers, activation functions, layers, and the number of nodes are tested. For the SVM, different kernels and gammas are tested. For the random forest, the studied parameters are the number of estimators and the criterions. In Arima, since it is a timeseries algorithm, its configuration is adjusted to the data frequency. Each hyperparameters setup is combined with all generated models to train the forecast algorithms.

The fourth phase is forecast execution. Once a week, this process runs in parallel with the previous phase, as the parameters are tested together with the forecast. In the remaining days, it is used only the algorithm that had the best performance in the training process. Instead of historical data, to perform the forecast, the algorithms require the forecast of additional features for the next day, obtained through access to the meteo@isep platform. This data is transformed according to the model with the best results (if used).

The fifth phase is the evaluation phase. The scenario that presented the best results is selected, namely the forecasting algorithm, the hyperparameters, and the model that most improved the learning process. The results obtained by combining these three factors are evaluated by calculating several error metrics: Minimum Error (MinE), Maximum Error (MaxE), Mean Absolute Error (MAE) (Eq. 1), Mean Absolute Percentage Error (MAPE) (Eq. 2), Root Mean Squared Error (RMSE) (Eq. 3) and Root Mean Squared Percentage Error (RMSPE) (Eq. 4). The scenario with the lowest MAPE value is selected.

$$MAE = \frac{1}{n} \sum_{t=1}^{n} |A_t - F_t| \tag{1}$$

$$MAPE = \frac{1}{n} \sum_{t=1}^{n} \left| \frac{A_t - F_t}{A_t} \right| \tag{2}$$

$$RMSE = \sqrt{\frac{\sum_{t=1}^{n}(F_t - A_t)^2}{n}} \tag{3}$$

$$RMSPE = \frac{\sqrt{\frac{\sum_{t=1}^{n}(F_t - A_t)^2}{n}}}{\frac{\sum A_t}{n}} \tag{4}$$

where n is the number of error entries, A_t is the real value and F_t is the forecasted value, for the PV generation at period t.

4   Case Study

This section presents a practical case study in order to demonstrate the proposed model. This case study aims to forecast the PV generation for 21 April 2020 and analyze the behavior of the different forecast methods. In this way, the selected historical dataset is from 01 April 2020 to 20 April 2020, and it is composed by PV generation, radiation, rain, and outside temperature. Table 1 presents the best results obtained for the April 21 2020 forecast.

Table 1. Top 10 best results for solar forecast

	Study	Model	MinE	MaxE	MAE	MSE	RMSE	MAPE	RMSPE	Feat.	Alg.
1	1308	30	0.0000	0.3099	0.0333	0.0048	0.0694	0.1868	0.3453	True	ann
2	2718	56	0.0000	0.2293	0.0290	0.0035	0.0590	0.1893	0.3500	True	ann
3	1391	31	0.0000	0.3114	0.0321	0.0048	0.0690	0.1909	0.353	True	ann
4	1254	29	0.0000	0.3251	0.0336	0.0056	0.0746	0.1935	0.3607	True	ann
5	1385	31	0.0004	0.2578	0.0307	0.0038	0.0614	0.2006	0.3624	True	ann
6	1315	30	0.0000	0.3607	0.0392	0.0067	0.0820	0.2008	0.3641	True	ann
7	1411	32	0.0000	0.3637	0.0378	0.0064	0.0800	0.2050	0.3714	True	ann
8	1389	31	0.0001	0.3422	0.0347	0.0055	0.0740	0.2059	0.3621	True	ann
9	1252	29	0.0000	0.3436	0.0360	0.0060	0.0776	0.2062	0.3786	True	ann
10	1393	31	0.0000	0.3664	0.0389	0.0068	0.0825	0.2073	0.3726	True	ann

Regarding the table above, it is possible to observe that the best results were obtained using the ANN method (indicated in the Alg. column), using the additional features (indicated in the Feat. column). The other algorithms had a worse performance and are below the tenth position. SVM presents the best results after the ANN, in the 31st position. This variation uses the transformations of the timestamp division, count of the distance from the entries to the initial instant of the forecast, and uses the data from the periods $t(-96)$, $t(-97)$ and $t(-98)$ of the previous day. In this case, the MAPE value is 18.68%. It is also possible to see that this model appears more than once (studies/scenarios 1308 and 1315). The difference between them relies on the used hyperparameters to configure the forecasting algorithm. Study 1308 uses the 'adam' solver, the activation function 'relu', and three layers with 100, 50 and 25 nodes. Study 1315 uses the 'lbfgs' solver, 'logistic' activation function three layers with two nodes each $(2, 2, 2)$, as parameters. The results of study 1308 can be seen in Fig. 1.

The graph in Fig. 1 shows that in the days before the forecast, the values of PV generation were higher than those that occurred on the forecast day (represented by the green line). However, the forecast line (shown in red) can detect the current weather changes and adjust to the actual values, analyzing the forecast of the additional features. Model 5, which corresponds to the same study but does not include features, has a MAPE value of 35.59%, representing an increase in the error of 16.91%.

Moreover, another critical factor that influences the error is the forecast of values near sunrise or sunset, where the sensitivity of the error is higher than in other periods. In other words, when the real value is 0, if the forecast value is greater than 0, the error is calculated with a large penalty. This penalty can be greater than 100% if the forecasted value is much higher or much lower than the

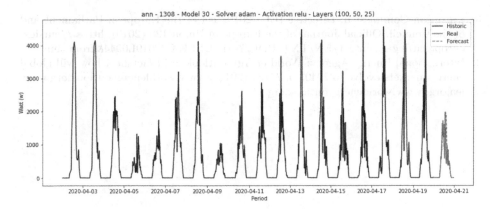

Fig. 1. Solar forecast results. (Color figure online)

real value, punishing the analysis of the model's error. In this specific case, the adjustment of these cases was made to consider a 100% error. However, the most appropriate solution in the future will be to use more suitable metrics to deal with these situations, as is the case of Mean Absolute Scaled Error (MASE).

5 Conclusions

This paper proposes an automatic PV generation forecasting model for building energy management. Thus, the model performs the forecast for the next day, with a 15-min interval, having at its disposal four different forecasting methods: ANN, SVM, Random Forest, and ARIMA. The one with the best results is selected after an exhaustive study of the intersection of the several forecasting methods, their hyperparameters, and data models that include features that help in the learning process. A case study was presented of the application of this model by using data collected in a real building. The results show that the model achieves promising results despite the intermittency of the weather.

As future work, it is suggested to use the error metric MASE for a more precise analyzes. Furthermore, a longer period of history may also be included, and other dataset transformations may be considered.

References

1. Abrishambaf, O., Faria, P., Vale, Z.: SCADA office building implementation in the context of an aggregator. In: Proceedings - IEEE 16th International Conference on Industrial Informatics, INDIN 2018, pp. 984–989 (2018). https://doi.org/10.1109/INDIN.2018.8471957
2. European Commission: Energy efficiency in buildings. Technical report (2020). https://ec.europa.eu/info/news/focus-energy-efficiency-buildings-2020-feb-17_en

3. European Commission: Directive (EU) 2019/944 of the European Parliament and of the Council. Official Journal of the European Union 125 (2019). https://eur-lex.europa.eu/legal-content/EN/TXT/PDF/?uri=CELEX:32019L0944&from=en
4. International Energy Agency: World energy outlook 2014 factsheet how will global energy markets evolve to 2040? p. 75739 (2015). www.worldenergyoutlook.orgwww.iea.org, www.worldenergyoutlook.org

Automatic Evolutionary Settings of Machine Learning Methods for Buildings' Thermal Loads Prediction

Gisele Goulart Tavares$^{(\boxtimes)}$, Priscila V. Z. Capriles , and Leonardo Goliatt

Federal University of Juiz de Fora, Juiz de Fora, Brazil
{giselegoulart,capriles,goliatt}@ice.ufjf.br

Abstract. Due to climate change, buildings can consume 30% more energy by 2040, with energy performance being the critical element for achieving sustainable development in the civil construction sector. One way to solve this evaluation problem is by applying Machine Learning Methods that can assist specialists in civil construction in analyzing scenarios even in the initial phase of the project. The present work evaluates the application of the Elastic Net, Extreme Learning Machine, and Extreme Gradient Boosting models for the prediction of heating and cooling loads in residential buildings. The database used has 768 samples, with eight geometric input variables and two thermal output variables. Differential Evolution optimization algorithm was applied to select method parameters to find the sets of hyperparameters that reinforce the predictive capabilities of the models. The comparisons of the results occurred using the metrics MAE, MAPE, RMSE, and R^2. The results showed that the Extreme Gradient Boosting method obtained a better performance among the tested methods than the literature, presenting the lowest values for the error metrics and significant differences in the statistical tests. Thus, combining Differential Evolution and Extreme Gradient Boosting methods, thermal loads can be predicted, assisting projects that aim at energy savings and sustainability

Keywords: Energy efficiency · Heating and cooling loads · Extreme Gradient Boosting · Load forecast

1 Introduction

The increase in population and the growing use of new technologies have resulted in the emergence of greater energy demands, leading to a rise in consumption of around 30% by 2040 [1]. In Brazil, only in the residential sector, it is estimated that the possession of air conditioning by families has more than doubled between 2005 and 2017, arousing interest in strategies aimed at reducing energy consumption coupled with the maintenance of environmental comfort [2]. In this context, energy savings are increasingly necessary to reduce their generation's environmental and social impacts.

© Springer Nature Switzerland AG 2021
G. Marreiros et al. (Eds.): EPIA 2021, LNAI 12981, pp. 183–195, 2021.
https://doi.org/10.1007/978-3-030-86230-5_15

The energy performance of buildings is highlighted as a key element for achieving sustainable development since it can reduce about 20% of greenhouse gas emissions and 20% of primary energy savings [3]. In commercial buildings, due to the negative influence that an uncomfortable environment causes on users' performance, the search for thermal comfort associated with low energy consumption has resulted in an increase in research in this field [4]. The continued use of electronic equipment and the high density of people in offices increase the challenge of maintaining these thermally comfortable environments.

To obtain the best performance of construction, three factors must be considered: architectural design, heating, cooling systems, and occupation. The architectural project is developed iteratively, with a team that reviews all aspects of the building and rethinks about decisions related to architecture. With a highly optimized project in hand, specialists in civil construction can reduce cooling and heating systems' capacity and minimize the need for this set of services.

However, despite the architectural design being an essential aspect of the building's performance, determining materials and configurations that optimize consumption and comfort in the structure is not easy. Considerations about the location, ventilation strategies, lighting, and materials to be used, increase the complexity of designing an energy-efficient project.

In this scenario, studies that consider computer simulations of models that deal with buildings' consumption are becoming more and more present. Several approaches are proposed for computational models of buildings, such as:

- The use of neural networks and support vector machines to predict the use of electricity in home heating systems [5];
- The generation of a database through residence parametrization to use machine learning algorithms to forecast heating and cooling loads [6];
- The application of genetic algorithms to minimize energy consumption and discomfort hours in a typical Italian residence simulated in different climatic zones [7].

The literature presents a diversity of works that carried out the modeling and simulation of different scenarios with various architectural types. However, the alternatives are often tested one by one, separately, and the results refer to comparisons between generated outputs. This process requires numerous tests and considerable execution time, turning to analyze many variables simultaneously, unviable. Thus, the combination of optimization methods and intelligent algorithms has shown promise [8]. The integration of these methods can improve the predictions related to the energy market, helping service providers understand different consumers' and users' demands to save energy by knowing their usage habits. Predicting the building's behavior based on design parameters can assist in decision-making by specialists, so manual and operationally costly analysis is unnecessary.

The present work aims to propose a combined method of machine learning and evolutionary algorithms to predict thermal loads (heating and cooling loads) in civil construction. The maximization of the regression methods' predictive performance is sought by optimizing hyperparameters of the Elastic-Net

Regression (NET), Extreme Learning Machine (ELM), and Extreme Gradient Boosting (XGB) techniques.

2   Methods

2.1   Dataset

The dataset used in this paper can be found in [9]. The dataset is composed by eight input variables and two output variables. The input variables are: relative compactness (RC), surface area, wall area, roof area, overall height, orientation, glazing area and glazing area distribution. The output variables are the heating loadings (HL) and cooling loadings (CL). Heating/cooling loads refer to the amount of thermal energy that would need to be added/removed from a space to keep the temperature in an acceptable range. To generate different building shapes, eighteen such elements were used according to Fig. 1(A). A subset of twelve shapes with distinct RC values was selected for the simulations as can be seen in Fig. 1(B).

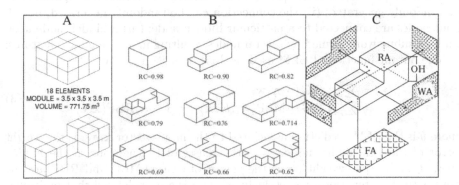

Fig. 1. A: Generation of shapes based on eighteen cubical elements [9]. B: Examples of building shapes [10]. C: Generic definition of building areas, where OH is the Overall Height, RA is the Roof Area, WA is the Wall Area and FA is the Floor Area. Adapted from [11].

2.2   Machine Learning Methods

Elastic Net Regression. The Elastic Net technique is an extension of the LASSO method, robust to correlations between the predictors [12]. Elastic Net uses a mix of $L1$ (LASSO) and $L2$ (Ridge) penalties and can be formulated as:

$$\hat{\beta}(enet) = \left(1 + \frac{\lambda_2}{n}\right)\left\{arg\min_{\beta} \|\mathbf{y} - \mathbf{X}\beta\|_2^2 + \lambda_2 \|\beta\|_2^2 + \lambda_1 \|\beta\|_1\right\} \qquad (1)$$

By setting $\alpha = \lambda_2/(\lambda_1 + \lambda_2)$, the estimator is equivalent to minimizing:

$$\hat{\beta}(enet2) = arg\min_{\beta} \|\mathbf{y} - \mathbf{X}\beta\|_2^2, \text{ subject to } P_\alpha(\beta) = (1-\alpha)\|\beta\|_1 + \alpha\|\beta\|_2^2 \leq s \text{ for some s} \quad (2)$$

where $P_\alpha(\beta)$ is the penalty Elastic Net [13]. The method is simplified to a Ridge regression when $\alpha = 1$ and to a LASSO regression when $\alpha = 0$. The $L1$ penalty, part of the NET method, makes the automatic selection of variables. In contrast, the $L2$ part encourages the grouped selection and stabilizes the solution paths about random sampling, thus improving the forecast. By inducing a grouping effect during the selection of variables, the method can select groups of correlated characteristics when the groups are not known in advance.

Extreme Learning Machine. Extreme Learning Machine (ELM) [14] is a feedforward artificial neural network, which has a single hidden layer. Compared with the Artificial Neural Network, the Support Vector Machine and other traditional prediction models, the ELM model retains the advantages of fast learning, good ability to generalize and convenience in terms of modeling. In ELMs there are three levels of randomness [15]: (i) fully connected, hidden node parameters are randomly generated; (ii) the connection can be randomly generated, not all input nodes are connected to a particular hidden node; (iii) a hidden node itself can be a subnetwork formed by several nodes resulting in learning local features;

The output function of ELM used in this paper is given by

$$\begin{aligned}\hat{y}(\mathbf{x}) &= \sum_{i=1}^{L} \beta_i G(\alpha, \gamma, \mathbf{w}_i, b_i, \mathbf{c}, \mathbf{x}) \\ &= \sum_{i=1}^{L} \beta_i G(\alpha\text{MLP}(\mathbf{w}_i, b_i, \mathbf{x}) + \gamma(1-\alpha)\text{RBF}(\mathbf{x}, \mathbf{c}))\end{aligned} \quad (3)$$

where $\hat{y}$ is the ELM prediction associated to the input vector $\mathbf{x}$, $\mathbf{w}_i$ is the weight vector of the i-th hidden node, b_i are the biases of the neurons in the hidden layer, β_i are output weights, $\mathbf{c}$ is the vector of centers. MLP and RBF are the input activation functions, respectively, while α is a user-defined that multiplies MLP($\cdot$) and RBF($\cdot$) terms. $G(\cdot)$ is the nonlinear output activation function and L is the number of neurons in the hidden layer. The output activation functions $G(\alpha, \mathbf{w}_i, b_i, \mathbf{c}, \mathbf{x})$ with the hidden nodes weights $(\mathbf{w}, b)$ are presented in Table 1.

Table 1. ELM activation functions.

#	Name	Activation function G
1	Identity	$G(x) = x$
2	ReLU	$G(x) = \max(0, x_i; i = 1, \cdots, D)$
3	Swish	$G(x) = x/(1 + exp(-x))$
4	Gaussian	$G(x) = exp(-x^2)$
5	Multiquadric	$G(x) = \sqrt{x^2 + b^2}$
6	Inverse multiquadric	$G(x) = 1/(x^2 + b^2)^{1/2}$

The parameters $(\mathbf{w}, b)$ are randomly generated (normally distributed with zero mean and standard deviation equals to one), and weights β_i of the output layer are determined analytically, while MLP and RBF are written as

$$\mathrm{MLP}(\mathbf{w}_i, b_i, \mathbf{x}) = \sum_{k=1}^{D} w_{ik} x_k + b_i \quad \text{and} \quad \mathrm{RBF}(\mathbf{x}, \mathbf{c}) = \sum_{j=1}^{D} \frac{x_j - c_{ij}}{r_i} \quad (4)$$

where D is the number of input features, the centers c_{ij} are taken uniformly from the bounding hyperrectangle of the input variables and $r = \max\left(\|\mathbf{x} - \mathbf{c}\|\right)/\sqrt{2D}$.

The output weight vector $[\beta_1, ..., \beta_L]$ can be determined by minimizing the approximation error [15]

$$\min_{\beta \in \mathbb{R}^L} \|\mathbf{H}\beta - \mathbf{y}\| \quad (5)$$

where $\mathbf{y}$ is the output data vector, $\mathbf{H}$ is the hidden layer output matrix

$$\mathbf{H} = \begin{bmatrix} G_1\left(\alpha, \gamma, \mathbf{w}_1, b_1, \mathbf{c}, \mathbf{x}_1\right) & \cdots & G_L\left(\alpha, \gamma, \mathbf{w}_L, b_L, \mathbf{c}, \mathbf{x}_1\right) \\ \vdots & \ddots & \vdots \\ G_1\left(\alpha, \gamma, \mathbf{w}_1, b_1, \mathbf{c}, \mathbf{x}_N\right) & \cdots & G_L\left(\alpha, \gamma, \mathbf{w}_L, b_L, \mathbf{c}, \mathbf{x}_N\right) \end{bmatrix} \quad \text{and } \mathbf{y} = \begin{bmatrix} y_1 \\ \vdots \\ y_N \end{bmatrix} \quad (6)$$

is the output data vector with N the number of data points. The optimal solution is given by

$$\beta = (\mathbf{H}^T\mathbf{H})^{-1}\mathbf{H}^T\mathbf{y} = \mathbf{H}^\dagger\mathbf{y} \quad (7)$$

where $\mathbf{H}^\dagger$ is the pseudoinverse of $\mathbf{H}$.

Gradient Boosting Machines. In several problems the goal is, using a training set $\{(x_i, y_i)\}_{i=1}^{N}$ with N samples, to find an approximation $\hat{f}(x)$ to a function $f(x)$ that minimizes the expected value of the loss function

$$L(y, \hat{f}(x)) = \sum_{i}^{N} [y_i - \hat{f}(x_i)]^2. \quad (8)$$

GB approximates f by an additive expansion of the form $\hat{f} = \sum_{m=1}^{M} \beta_m h(x, a_m)$ where the functions $h(x, a)$ are $h(x, a_m)$ is an K-node regression tree and the parameters $\{\beta, a\}$ are jointly fit to the training data in a forward stage wise manner [16]. At each iteration m, a regression tree partitions the variable space into disjoint regions $\{R_{km}\}_{k=1}^{K}$ at the mth iteration. A constant γ_{jm} is assigned to each such region and the predictive rule is $x \in R_{jm} \Rightarrow f(x) = \gamma_{jm}$. Using the indicator notation, the output of h for input x can be written as

$$h(x, \{R_{km}\}_{k=1}^{K}) = \sum_{k=1}^{K} \gamma_{km} I(x \in R_{km}), \quad I(\cdot) = 1 \text{ if } x \in R_{km} \text{ else } 0 \quad (9)$$

with parameters $\{R_{km}, \gamma_{km}\}$, $k = 1, 2, \ldots, J$, $m = 1, \ldots, M$, where γ_{km} is the value predicted in the region R_{km}.

As the model (9) predicts a constant value in each region R_{km}, the solution reduces to

$$\gamma_{km} = \arg\min_{\gamma} \sum_{x_i \in R_{km}} L(y_i, f_{m-1}(x_i) + \gamma), \quad \gamma \text{ constant.} \tag{10}$$

The current approximation $f_{m-1}(x)$ is then updated following the rule

$$\hat{f}_m(x) = \hat{f}_{m-1}(x) + \lambda \sum_{k=1}^{K} \gamma_{km} I(x \in R_{km}) \tag{11}$$

where parameter $0 < \lambda \leq 1$ is called the learning rate.

A substantial improvement in Gradient Boosting's accuracy can be achieved when at each iteration of the algorithm the base learner is fitted on a subsample of the training set drawn at random without replacement. Subsample size is some constant fraction of the size of the training set. Smaller values of subsample introduce randomness into the algorithm and help prevent overfitting [17]. The algorithm also becomes faster, because regression trees have to be fit to smaller datasets at each iteration.

The XGB method follows the same principles as the GB, with some differences in details of the modeling that perform more accurate approximations using the second-order derivative of the loss function (in the case of the logistic function), L1, and L2 regularization and parallel computing. XGB is the most regularized form of GB, using regularization similar to those of the Elastic Net method, which improve the generalization capabilities of the model. It presents better computational performance due to being able to perform faster training that can be distributed through different cores [18]. Uses improved data structures for better utilization of the processor's cache memory, which makes it faster.

2.3   Model Selection Based on Differential Evolution

Setting the parameters of an estimator is usually a difficult task. Often, these parameters are defined empirically, by testing different settings by hand. An alternative is the use of population-based evolutionary algorithms, such as Differential Evolution (DE) [19]. DE is one of the most efficient evolutionary algorithms (EAs) [20]. The basic strategy of DE consists in applying weighted and stochastic vector operations between the candidate solutions set [21]. Given a population of NP vectors $\{\theta_i | i = 1, 2, \ldots, NP\}$, at each iteration J $(J = 1, 2, ..., J_{max})$ of the DE, the following operations will be performed on such vectors:

1. Mutation: For each vector θ_i, a mutant vector $\mathbf{v_i}$ is generated according to

$$\mathbf{v_i} = \theta_{\mathbf{r_1}} + \mathbf{F}(\theta_{\mathbf{r_2}} - \theta_{\mathbf{r_3}}) \tag{12}$$

where r_1, r_2 and $r_3 \in \{1, 2, \ldots, NP\}$ are randomly chosen indexes, mutually different and different from i, and $F \in (0, 2)$ is a user-defined parameter.

2. Crossover: In this step, the D-dimensional trial vector μ_i will be generated by a stochastic operation given by

$$\mu_{i,j} = \begin{cases} v_{i,j}, & \text{if rand}(j) \leq CR \text{ or } j = \text{rand}(i) \\ \theta_{i,j}, & \text{if rand}(j) > CR \text{ and } j \neq \text{rand}(i) \end{cases} \tag{13}$$

where $j = 1, 2, ..., D$, $v_{i,j}$ is the value of j-th variable of vector v_i produced by Eq. (12), rand(j) is the j-th random value in the range $[0, 1]$, rand(i) $\in \{1, 2, ..., D\}$ is a random integer value produced for each solution and CR is a user-defined parameter in the range $[0, 1]$.

3. Selection: If vector μ_i is better than θ_i, then θ_i will be replaced by μ_i in the set (population). Otherwise, the old value θ_i will be maintained.

DE was applied here to find the best hyperparameters for NET, ELM, and XGB models for predict thermal loads in buildings. Each candidate solution θ_i encodes an estimator. Each vector θ_i is composed by 2 variables to NET ($D = 2$), 4 variables to ELM ($D = 4$), and 6 variables to XGB ($D = 6$), that correspond to the total of parameters to be adjusted (Table 2). Considering the DE approach, the goal is to find a candidate solution so that the method generates computed outputs that match the outputs of the training data.

Table 2. Hyperparameters sets used in model selection step.

NET		ELM		XGB	
Parameters	Sets	Parameters	Sets	Parameters	Sets
ll_ratio	[0,1]	n_hidden	1, 2, 3, ... , 500	learning rate	[0,1]
alpha	[0.1,1]	rbf_width	[0.01, 10]	n_estimators	10, 11, 12, ..., 900
max_iter	1000	activation_func	identity, relu, swish, gaussian, multiquadric, inv_multiquadric	colsample_bytree	[0,1]
tol	0.0001	alpha	[0, 1]	min_child_weight	1, 2, 3, ..., 10
normalize	false			subsample	[0,1]
				max_depth	1, 2, 3, ..., 30
				objective	squared_error

3   Computational Experiments

In this section, we present the results obtained for the regressions models described in Sect. 2. We ran each experiment 30 times using 10-fold cross-validation with shuffled data generated by different random seeds. The K-fold validation reduces the variation in estimating the model's performance for different data samples. Because of this, the performance becomes less sensitive to the partitioning of the data.

The experiments were conducted in Python language (3.5 version) and using scikit-learn framework [22] and XGBoost library [18]. The experiments were conducted on computers with the following specifications: Intel (R) Xeon (R) E5620 CPU (8 cores of 2.40 GHz and 2 MB cache memory), 8 GB RAM, and Linux Ubuntu 14.04 LTS operating system. In order to evaluate the predictive performance of each model we have used the evaluation metrics shown in Table 3.

Table 3. Performance metrics: $\hat{y}_i$ is the estimated target output, y_i is the corresponding target output, N is the number of samples, p is the number of model parameters, and $\bar{y}$ is the mean of the vector $[y_1, ..., y_N]$.

Metric	Expression
R^2	$1 - \frac{\sum_{i=0}^{N-1}(y_i-\hat{y}_i)^2}{\sum_{i=0}^{N-1}(y_i-\bar{y})^2}$
RMSE	$\sqrt{\frac{1}{N}\sum_{i=0}^{N-1}(y_i-\hat{y}_i)^2}$
MAPE	$100 \times \frac{1}{N}\sum_{i=0}^{N-1}\frac{|y_i-\hat{y}_i|}{|y_i|}$
MAE	$\frac{1}{N}\sum_{i=0}^{N-1}|y_i-\hat{y}_i|$

Figure 2 illustrates the values of the four statistical measures averaged in 30 runs for the predicted heating loads and cooling loads. In each bar, the vertical black line indicates the standard deviation. In the MAE, RMSE, and MAPE metrics, the lower values indicate better performance, and for the coefficient R^2, the best models should present their value closer to 1. By observing the metrics, it is possible to verify that the XGB method achieved better results, both for heating and cooling loads. The ELM method's heating loads obtained values slightly close to those achieved by the XGB in the metrics MAE, RMSE, and R^2. For all the metrics presented, it is possible to notice a common behavior among the three tested methods, which is the best average performance in predicting heating loads.

Table 4. Parameter distribution - heating loads.

Model	Hyperparameters	Min.	Median	Max.	Average	DP
NET	alpha	0.114	0.189	0.193	0.186	0.014
ELM	n_hidden	190.000	259.500	314.000	254.867	38.684
	rbf_width	0.010	0.021	0.067	0.028	0.018
	alpha	0	0.001	0.534	0.129	0.163
XGB	learning_rate	0.043	0.159	0.422	0.183	0.100
	n_estimators	259.000	720.500	879.000	654.633	204.629
	colsample_bytree	0.630	0.719	0.867	0.728	0.065
	subsample	0.915	0.976	0.999	0.928	0.022

Table 4 shows the distributions of some hyperparameters of the methods tested over the 30 runs to predict heating loads. For NET, alpha values were

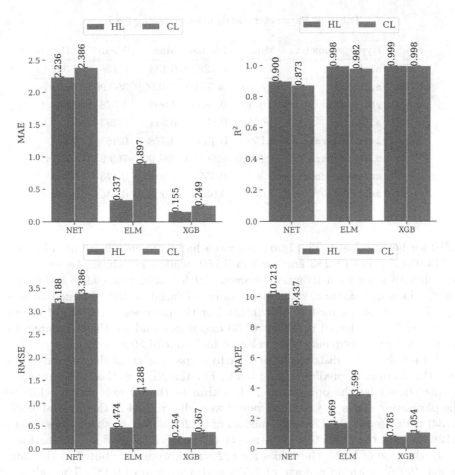

Fig. 2. Barplots for the statistical measures (averaged over 30 runs) for HL and CL. The performance metrics are Mean Absolute Error (MAE), Coefficient of Determination (R^2), Root Mean Square Error (RMSE) and Mean Absolute Percentage Error (MAPE).

distributed in the interval [0.114, 0.193] with mean 0.186, standard deviation 0.014, and median 0.189, and ll_ratio=1 was selected in 29 out of 30 runs.

For the ELM method, it is possible to notice that the parameter alpha varied in the range [0; 0.53] while the parameter rbf_width, despite having a larger range of possibilities ([0.01, 10]) varied only between the values [0.010, 0.067], indicating that the interval used in the optimization algorithm can be reduced and thus consequently decrease the search space. The number of neurons in the hidden layer of ELM varied between 190 and 314, with an average of 254.87 and a median of 259.5. The most frequent activation function was gaussian, being selected in 20 out of 30 executions.

In the case of the XGB method, the hyperparameter colsample_bytree presented values in the range [0.630, 0.867], with a mean of 0.728 and a median of

Table 5. Parameter distribution - cooling loads.

Model	Hyperparameters	Min.	Median	Max.	Mean	DP
NET	`alpha`	0.124	0.128	0.134	0.128	0.002
ELM	`n_hidden`	304.00	365.500	410.00	360.967	25.026
	`rbf_width`	0.064	0.182	9.996	1.378	2.884
	`alpha`	0.001	0.122	0.941	0.293	0.337
XGB	`learning_rate`	0.150	0.439	0.978	0.463	0.261
	`n_estimators`	189.000	829.500	894.000	769.933	161.142
	`colsample_bytree`	0.382	0.452	0.604	0.475	0.069
	`subsample`	0.812	0.956	0.995	0.945	0.046

0.719 for heating loads. The `learning_rate` had its values distributed between [0.043, 0.422], mean 0.183 and median 0.159, while the `subsample` had values very close to 1, with a distribution between [0.915, 0.999], mean 0.968 and median 0.976. The `n_estimators`, which has a range of variation [10] obtained an average of 654.633 and a median of 720.500. For the parameter `min_child_weight` the value 1 was selected in 29 out of 30 executions and for the `max_depth` the value 7 was more frequent, being selected in 16 out of 30 executions.

Table 5 shows the distribution of some hyperparameters of the methods tested over the 30 runs to predict cooling loads. For the NET method, `l1_ratio = 1` it was chosen by the optimization algorithm in the 30 executions, while for the parameter `alpha` the assigned values were distributed in the interval [0.124, 0.134] with a mean of 0.128 and a median of 0.128, indicating that values close to 0.128 improve the predictive performance of the NET method for cooling loads.

In the case of ELM, the values for `rbf_width` were distributed in the range [0.064, 9.996], with an average of 1.378 and a median of 0.182. The values of `alpha` were distributed in [0.001, 0.941], with an average of 0.293 and a median of 0.122, covering most of the range of possibilities [0, 1]. In the XGB method, the parameter `colsample_bytree` presented distribution in the interval [0.382, 0.604], with a mean of 0.475 and a median of 0.452. The `subsample` had distribution in the range [0.812, 0.995], with a mean of 0.475 and a median of 0.452, while the `learning_rate` was distributed in the range [0.150, 0.978], with a mean of 0.463 and a median of 0.439. The `n_estimators` showed a distribution concentrated in values close to the upper limit used by the evolutionary algorithm, with values in the range [189.000, 894.000], with an average of 769.933 and a median of 829.500. For `min_child_weight` the value 2 presented a higher frequency, being returned in 17 out of 30 executions, while for `max_depth` the frequencies were distributed in the interval [6], with the highest frequency occurring at value 7 in 6 out of 30 runs.

Table 6. Comparison between the results obtained from the best model of this study.

	(a) Heating Loads				(b) Cooling Loads			
Reference	MAE (kW)	RMSE (kW)	MAPE (%)	R^2	Reference	MAE (kW)	RMSE (kW)	MAPE (%)	R^2
[9]	0.510	–	2.180	–	[9]	1.420	–	4.620	–
[23]	0.340	0.460	–	1.000	[23]	0.680	0.970	–	0.990
[10]	0.236	0.346	–	0.999	[10]	0.890	1.566	–	0.986
[24]	0.380	–	**0.430**	–	[24]	0.970	–	3.400	–
[11]	0.315	**0.223**	1.350	0.998	[11]	0.565	0.837	2.342	0.991
[25]	0.262	0.404	1.395	0.998	[25]	0.486	0.763	1.924	0.994
[26]	0.224	0.341	1.114	0.999	[26]	0.491	0.722	1.973	0.994
[27]	0.175	0.265	0.913	0.999	[27]	0.307	0.461	1.197	0.998
DE+NET	2.202	3.178	10.157	0.901	DE+NET	2.384	3.387	9.416	0.873
DE+ELM	0.329	0.329	1.573	0.998	DE+ELM	0.861	1.222	3.434	0.986
DE+XGB	**0.150**	0.243	0.753	**0.999**	DE+XGB	**0.231**	**0.327**	**0.983**	**0.999**

Table 6 present the statistical measures for the best models (along 30 runs) found in this paper. To provide a comparison with other models in the literature, we also show the results collected from other studies that used the same dataset employed in this paper. Reference [9] implemented random forests, while [23] developed multivariate adaptive regression splines and gaussian processes were used in [25]. Reference [10] implemented a linear combination of two or more machine learning models. The results presented [24] were obtained by genetic programming, an automated learning of computer programs using a process inspired by biological evolution. The results in [11] were obtained using Random Forests and Multilayer Perceptron Neural Networks. Reference [26] implemented Gradient Boosting Machines and [27] used Extreme Gradient Boosting. As can be seen in Table 6 for the heating loads, DE+XGB obtained competitive results. For cooling loads, DE+XGB model reaches the best average performance for all statistical measures reflecting its ability to learn highly nonlinear relationships from data.

4   Conclusion

This paper evaluated the prediction of heating and cooling loads in buildings. For it, NET, ELM, and XGB models were used, coupled to the Differential Evolution algorithm to optimize the hyperparameters of the models. The use of the evolutionary algorithm in conjunction with the machine learning methods showed satisfactory results compared to the data in the literature. The XGB model achieved the best results for all the metrics tested, considering the three models tested in HL and CL. In addition, it obtained competitive results with recent works in the literature for heating loads and better performance in all metrics when approaching cooling loads. As future work, for the XGB model, which presented a better overall performance, it is proposed to apply dimensionality reduction methods to analyze the importance of each of the input variables, making it possible to improve the computational performance. Also, we purpose to test the DE + ELM method with a greater number of iterations for optimization to analyze the convergence of the method and check if it is possible to find lower error values.

References

1. Pérez-Lombard, L., Ortiz, J., Pout, C.: A review on buildings energy consumption information. Energy Buildings **40**(3), 394–398 (2008)
2. Ministério de Minas e Energia do Brasil: Uso de ar condicionado no setor residencial brasileiro: Perspectivas e contribuições para o avanço em eficiência energética. Technical report (2018)
3. Boermans, T., Grözinger, J.: Economic effects of investing in EE in buildings - the beam2 model. Background paper for EC Workshop on Cohesion policy (2011)
4. Touzani, S., Granderson, J., Fernandes, S.: Gradient boosting machine for modeling the energy consumption of commercial buildings. Energy Buildings **158**, 1533–1543 (2018)
5. Wang, Z., Srinivasan, R.S., Shi, J.: Artificial intelligent models for improved prediction of residential space heating. J. Energy Eng. **142**(4), 04016006 (2016)
6. Jihad, A.S., Tahiri, M.: Forecasting the heating and cooling load of residential buildings by using a learning algorithm "gradient descent", morocco. Case Stud. Thermal Eng. **12**, 85–93 (2018)
7. Ascione, F., Bianco, N., Mauro, G.M., Napolitano, D.F.: Building envelope design: Multi-objective optimization to minimize energy consumption, global cost and thermal discomfort. application to different italian climatic zones. Energy **174**, 359–374 (2019)
8. AlFaris, F., Juaidi, A., Manzano-Agugliaro, F.: Intelligent homes' technologies to optimize the energy performance for the net zero energy home. Energy Buildings **153**, 262–274 (2017)
9. Tsanas, A., Xifara, A.: Accurate quantitative estimation of energy performance of residential buildings using statistical machine learning tools. Energy and Buildings **49**, 560–567 (2012)
10. Chou, J.S., Bui, D.K.: Modeling heating and cooling loads by artificial intelligence for energy-efficient building design. Energy Buildings **82**, 437–446 (2014)
11. Duarte, G.R., Fonseca, L., Goliatt, P., Lemonge, A.: Comparison of machine learning techniques for predicting energy loads in buildings. Ambiente Construído **17**(3), 103–115 (2017)
12. Friedman, J., Hastie, T., Tibshirani, R.: Regularization paths for generalized linear models via coordinate descent. J. Stat. Softw. **33**(1), 1 (2010)
13. Zou, H., Hastie, T.: Regularization and variable selection via the elastic net. J. Roy. Stat. Soc. Ser. B (Statistical Methodology) **67**(2), 301–320 (2005)
14. bin Huang, G., yu Zhu, Q., kheong Siew, C.: Extreme learning machine: a new learning scheme of feedforward neural networks, pp. 985–990 (2006)
15. Huang, G., Huang, G.B., Song, S., You, K.: Trends in extreme learning machines: A review. Neural Netw. **61**, 32–48 (2015)
16. Hastie, T., Tibshirani, R., Friedman, J.: The elements of statistical learning: data mining, inference, and prediction, springer series in statistics (2009)
17. Friedman, J.H.: Stochastic gradient boosting. Comput. Stat. Data Anal. **38**(4), 367–378 (2002)
18. Chen, T., Guestrin, C.: Xgboost: a scalable tree boosting system. In: Proceedings of the 22nd ACM Sigkdd International Conference on Knowledge Discovery and Data Mining, pp. 785–794. ACM (2016)
19. Storn, R., Price, K.: Differential evolution-a simple and efficient heuristic for global optimization over continuous spaces. J. Global Optim. **11**(4), 341–359 (1997)

20. Kachitvichyanukul, V.: Comparison of three evolutionary algorithms: GA, PSO, and DE. Ind. Eng. Manage. Syst. **11**(3), 215–223 (2012)
21. Zhu, Q.Y., Qin, A., Suganthan, P., Huang, G.B.: Evolutionary extreme learning machine. Pattern Recogn. **38**(10), 1759–1763 (2005)
22. Pedregosa, F., et al.: Scikit-learn: machine learning in Python. J. Mach. Learn. Res. **12**, 2825–2830 (2011)
23. Cheng, M.Y., Cao, M.T.: Accurately predicting building energy performance using evolutionary multivariate adaptive regression splines. Appl. Soft Comput. **22**, 178–188 (2014)
24. Castelli, M., Trujillo, L., Vanneschi, L., Popovič, A.: Prediction of energy performance of residential buildings: a genetic programming approach. Energy Buildings **102**, 67–74 (2015)
25. Goliatt, L., Capriles, P., Duarte, G.R.: Modeling heating and cooling loads in buildings using gaussian processes. In: 2018 IEEE Congress on Evolutionary Computation (CEC), pp. 1–6. IEEE (2018)
26. Goliatt, L., Capriles, P.V.Z., Goulart Tavares, G.: Gradient boosting ensembles for predicting heating and cooling loads in building design. In: Moura Oliveira, P., Novais, P., Reis, L.P. (eds.) EPIA 2019. LNCS (LNAI), vol. 11804, pp. 495–506. Springer, Cham (2019). https://doi.org/10.1007/978-3-030-30241-2_42
27. Al-Rakhami, M., Gumaei, A., Alsanad, A., Alamri, A., Hassan, M.M.: An ensemble learning approach for accurate energy load prediction in residential buildings. IEEE Access **7**, 48328–48338 (2019)

Artificial Intelligence in Transportation Systems

Minimising Fleet Times in Multi-depot Pickup and Dropoff Problems

Martin Damyanov Aleksandrov[✉]

Technical University Berlin, Ernst-Reuter-Platz 7, 10587 Berlin, Germany
martin.aleksandrov@tu-berlin.de

Abstract. We look at multi-depot pickup and dropoff problems (MDPDPs) where a fleet of vehicles services commuting requests. We thus investigate minimising the fleet total/maximum travel, waiting, tour, and arrival times. For these objectives, we give a template that implements genetic algorithms (GAs) and evaluate their performance on new instances. The results indicate that there is a trade-off between minimising the waiting times and minimising the tour times, and minimising the arrival times lies somehow in the middle of it. Also, we measure how often commuters share rides, i.e. the sharing rate. For example, minimising the waiting times achieves the greatest sharing rate but the longest vehicle travel time compared to minimising any of the other times. Finally, the GAs reduce the number of running vehicles.

Keywords: Waiting time · Tour time · Arrival time

1 Introduction

Let us consider future mobility applications where a number of (human/robot) drivers run a fleet of *vehicles* and service a number of *customer requests*. Examples of such applications are autonomous, connected, subsidised, healthcare, and garbage vehicles. In such applications, drivers do not have preferences for the requests. This allows us to focus on managing the fleet in a manner that is optimal for customers. Two measures that capture such optimality criteria are service efficiency and service fairness [21]. We study these two criteria in problems where each vehicle has *begin/end depot locations* and *capacity*, and each request has *pick-up/drop-off service locations* and *demand* (i.e. MDPDPs).

Service efficiency is particularly important in such applications. It is often measured in terms of the total travel time of the fleet: totTRAVEL. However, a questionnaire reveals that customers rank the time they wait for a vehicle, the time they tour in a vehicle, and the time they arrive by a vehicle among the most important criteria for service quality [12]. In response, we also study the fleet waiting, tour, and arrival times. For a given customer, the *waiting time* is the time they wait for a car, the *tour time* is the time they travel between their locations, and the *arrival time* sums up these two times. Thus, we look at minimising the overall fleet service times: totWAIT; totTOUR; totARR.

© Springer Nature Switzerland AG 2021
G. Marreiros et al. (Eds.): EPIA 2021, LNAI 12981, pp. 199–210, 2021.
https://doi.org/10.1007/978-3-030-86230-5_16

Service fairness is another important measure. The most studied objectives are the minimisation of the range between the maximum and minimum workloads, as well as the maximum workload, where the workload is measured by the vehicle travel time. However, the range exhibits some problems. For example, the range could be zero but the vehicles may still have very large and equal workloads [9]. For this reason, we look at minimising the maximum travel workload: maxTRAVEL. Unlike such studies, we also measure workloads by means of the waiting, tour, and arrival times and, thus, minimise the associated maximum workloads of any vehicle: maxWAIT; maxTOUR; maxARR.

Although the proposed objectives are very natural in practice, Silva et al. [19] noted that important and practical problems with customer-oriented incentives have not been studied sufficiently even in the special case of minimising just the total waiting time. Indeed, we could not find any source that reports on research methods for the proposed new objectives in the context of our MDPDPs. In response, we propose to use approximate genetic algorithms (GAs) [10]. The reason for this choice is simple. GAs have been used successfully and extensively in the past. For example, according to the NEO website, GAs is the most-cited method for solving VRPs approximately, followed by Tabu Search.

We thus present a genetic template for minimising the proposed objectives in MDPDPs. The template has a number of parameters (e.g. population size, reproduction size, etc.) and a fitness function. As the objectives are unexplored, our main goal is to use the template in a way that offers a fair comparison between them. For this reason, we fix the template parameters and implement eight GAs with fitness functions totTRAVEL, maxTRAVEL, totWAIT, maxWAIT, totTOUR, maxTOUR, totARR, and maxARR. At the same time, we choose these parameters carefully in order to guarantee termination in a reasonable time (i.e. less than 10 minutes) for large-scale MDPDPs (i.e. 1 000 requests).

Further, we evaluate the performance of these GAs. For this purpose, we generate new datasets by using existing distributions from the CVRPLIB website and real-world distributions from the city of Berlin. We look at Berlin for two simple reasons. First, there are more than 300 000 in-commuters there per day and more than 90 000 of them travel by their own vehicle [1]. Second, the city has some of the most congested roads in the world [2]. Through experiments, we confirm that the number of commuting vehicles can be decreased significantly whenever their owners share rides among them. This could potentially lead to a significant reduction in their associated CO_2 emissions.

We also measure the objective values, sharing rates, and fleet busyness, that are induced by the GAs. In summary, there is a trade-off between minimising totWAIT/maxWAIT and totTOUR/maxTOUR, whilst minimising totARR/maxARR lies in the middle of it. Also, minimising totWAIT/maxWAIT achieves a high sharing rate but it induces a long travel time, whereas minimising totTOUR/maxTOUR achieves a short travel time but it induces a low sharing rate. We next outline the paper. We discuss related work in Sect. 2 and preliminaries in Sect. 3. Sections 4 and 5 contain details about the datasets and the template, respectively. We give results in Sect. 6 and conclude in Sect. 7.

2   Related Work

In the MDPDP, vehicles might have different begin and end depot locations. As a consequence, it generalises the vehicle routing problem (VRP) from [4], the capacitated VRP (CVRP) from [17], and the pickup and delivery problem (PDP) from [8,18]. Two good surveys of PDPs are [13] and [14]. For the same reason, the MDPDP also generalizes the multiple depot VRP, where firstly the customers are clustered among a number of depots and secondly the routing is solved for each depot: check the NEO website for a formulation of this problem. Recently, Vidal, Laporte, and Matl [21] discussed the need for deeper research on objectives based on customer waiting, tour, and arrival times. In the context of using GAs for minimising totTRAVEL in VRPs, two existing approaches are often adopted: (1) cluster-first route-second (C1R2) [6] and (2) route-first cluster-second (R1C2) [3]. Approach (1) has been studied for a long time [15] whereas approach (2) has proven promising in recent years [16]. We give a novel R1C2 approach for minimising totWAIT, maxWAIT, totTOUR, maxTOUR, totARR, and maxARR in MDPDPs with 1 000 requests. We are not familiar with any other method for doing so in such large problems. Thus, we hope that our contribution motivates future research in this direction.

3   Preliminaries for MDPDPs

For $p \in \mathbb{N}_{>0}$, we let $[p]$ denote $\{1, \ldots, p\}$. We also let $L \subset \mathbb{R}^2$ denote a finite set of locations. We consider a fleet of *vehicles* $V = \{v_i | i \in [n]\}$, where v_i has *begin/end* depot location $b_i \in L/e_i \in L$ and *capacity* $q_i \in \mathbb{N}_{>0}$. In practice, each $q_i \leq Q$ for some $Q \in \mathbb{N}_{>0}$. We also consider a set of *customer requests* $R = \{r_j = (p_j, d_j, m_j) | j \in [m]\}$, where r_j has *pick-up/drop-off* service location $p_j \in L/d_j \in L$ and *demand* $m_j \in \mathbb{N}_{>0}$. We suppose that $\max_{r_j \in R} m_j \leq \max_{v_i \in V} q_i$ holds. Otherwise, we can split each request r_j with $m_j > \max_{v_i \in V} q_i$ into a number of indivisible requests of smaller demands.

The locations from L form a network (i.e. graph). Each such location is represented as a pair of coordinates from some grid within $\mathbb{R}^2$. On top of this network, we consider vehicle travel times between pairs of locations. Thus, for $v_i \in V$, we write $t^i(l, l') \in \mathbb{R}_{\geq 0}^{\leq \infty}$ for the shortest travel time between $l, l' \in L$, and D_i for the matrix $[t^i(l, l')]_{|L| \times |L|}$. The value of $t^i(l, l')$ can account for features such as vehicle velocities, traffic volume, road closures, road constructions, intersection delays, etc. This can be computed by querying Google Maps.

We let $\mathcal{I}$ denote a MDPDP instance. We suppose that all requests in it are submitted at the same time. Thus, each given b_i and e_i could denote service locations of past requests or predicted locations of future requests. For this reason, we insist that each vehicle v_i starts from b_i and returns to e_i. Similarly, each q_i could denote the available capacity and not the total capacity of v_i. Also, each given m_j could denote the number of people or packages to be transported between p_j and d_j. These parameters allow us to control the fleet in a dynamic manner. However, as a first step, we focus on the static model in this paper.

3.1 Routing Plans

For a given subset of requests $R' \subseteq R$, a route $\mathcal{R}' = (s_1, \ldots, s_{2|R'|})$ is a sequence of the service (i.e. pick-up/drop-off) locations of the requests from R'. We associate each location s_l in $\mathcal{R}'$ with some request $r_j \in R'$ and weight $cap_l = +m_k$ if $s_l = p_j$ and $cap_l = -m_j$ if $s_l = d_j$. Thus, a plan $\mathcal{P} = \{\mathcal{R}_1, \ldots, \mathcal{R}_n\}$ is a set of routes, where $\mathcal{R}_i$ is assigned to $v_i \in V$. We let $R_i \subseteq R$ denote the set of requests associated with v_i. We write $\mathcal{R}_i = (s_1^i, \ldots, s_{2|R_i|}^i)$ and cap_l^i for each s_l^i. For a given $r_j \in R_i$, we also write $p_j = s_{k_j}^i$ and $d_j = s_{h_j}^i$. Let us consider plan $\mathcal{P}$. We consider four types of constraints for such plans.

Completeness constraints ensure that each request is serviced once by some vehicle: (a) $\forall r_j \in R, \exists v_i : r_j \in R_i \wedge m_j \leq q_i$. *Disjointness* constraints require that the requests cannot be split across multiple vehicles: (b) $\forall r_j \in R, \forall v_i : r_j \in R_i \Rightarrow \forall v_k, k \neq i : r_j \notin R_k$. *Ordering* constraints ask that the pickup of a given request is serviced before its corresponding dropoff: (c) $\forall v_i, \forall r_j \in R_i : k_j < h_j$ if $s_{k_j}^i \neq s_{h_j}^i$, else $k_j = h_j - 1$. *Capacity* constraints enforce that the capacity of any vehicle cannot be exceeded while servicing any request: (d) $\forall v_i, \forall r_j \in R_i : \sum_{l=k_j}^{h_j-1} cap_l^i \leq q_i$. We say that $\mathcal{P}$ is *feasible* iff (a–d) hold.

3.2 Fleet Objectives

Let us consider feasible plan $\mathcal{P}$. We study minimising the total travel time of all vehicles - totTRAVEL (left below) - and minimising the maximum travel time per vehicle - maxTRAVEL (right below). These are common in VRPs.

$$\underset{\mathcal{P}: \text{ feasible}}{\arg\min} \sum_{v_i \in V} \sum_{j=1}^{2|R_i|-1} t^i(s_j^i, s_{j+1}^i) \qquad \underset{\mathcal{P}: \text{ feasible}}{\arg\min} \max_{v_i \in V} \sum_{j=1}^{2|R_i|-1} t^i(s_j^i, s_{j+1}^i) \quad (1)$$

Pick $r_j \in R_i$. As v_i is at b_i when r_j has been submitted by customers, their *waiting time* is the time travelled by v_i between b_i and the pick-up location p_j: $w_{ij} = t^i(b_i, s_1^i) + [\sum_{l=1}^{(k_j-1)} t^i(s_l^i, s_{l+1}^i)]$. We note that $w_{ij} \geq 0$ holds.

$$(\text{totWAIT}): \underset{\mathcal{P}: \text{ feasible}}{\arg\min} \sum_{v_i \in V} \sum_{r_j \in R_i} w_{ij} \qquad (\text{maxWAIT}): \underset{\mathcal{P}: \text{ feasible}}{\arg\min} \max_{v_i \in V} \sum_{r_j \in R_i} w_{ij} \quad (2)$$

The *tour time* of the customers of r_j is the time travelled by v_i between the pick-up location p_j and the drop-off location d_j: $t_{ij} = \sum_{l=k_j}^{h_j-1} t^i(s_l^i, s_{l+1}^i)$. We note that $t_{ij} \geq 0$ holds.

$$(\text{totTOUR}): \underset{\mathcal{P}: \text{ feasible}}{\arg\min} \sum_{v_i \in V} \sum_{r_j \in R_i} t_{ij} \qquad (\text{maxTOUR}): \underset{\mathcal{P}: \text{ feasible}}{\arg\min} \max_{v_i \in V} \sum_{r_j \in R_i} t_{ij} \quad (3)$$

As v_i is at b_i when r_j has been submitted by customers, their arrival time is the time travelled by v_i between b_i and the drop-off location d_j: $a_{ij} = w_{ij} + t_{ij}$. We note that $a_{ij} \geq 0$ holds.

$$(\text{totARR}): \underset{\mathcal{P}: \text{ feasible}}{\arg\min} \sum_{v_i \in V} \sum_{r_j \in R_i} a_{ij} \qquad (\text{maxARR}): \underset{\mathcal{P}: \text{ feasible}}{\arg\min} \max_{v_i \in V} \sum_{r_j \in R_i} a_{ij} \quad (4)$$

4   New Datasets for MDPDPs

We solve multi-depot PDPs and not single-depot VRPs. We could not find such large instances. In response, we generated new instances. Each instance has a grid $[1\,000] \times [1\,000]$ with $n = 1\,000$ available vehicles and $m = 1\,000$ requests. We set the capacity of each vehicle to $c = 4$ (i.e. cars). We sampled each demand d uniformly at random from $D = \{1, 2, 3, 4\}$. We also sampled $4\,000$ locations within the grid (i.e. $1\,000$ begin depots, $1\,000$ end depots, $1\,000$ pickups, $1\,000$ dropoffs) and initialised each travel time with the associated distance. Thus, we produced four new datasets, each of two hundred instances: two *zoned* datasets (Z1 and Z2); *random* and *clustered* datasets (R and C). The sampling for Z1 and Z2 was guided by distributions about the number of private-car owners per $1\,000$ citizens in the city of Berlin [1] whereas the one for R and C was guided by distributions from Uchoa's dataset [20].

Datasets Z1 and Z2. The city of Berlin has three transport zones: A, B and C. Zone A surrounds the city center, zone B surrounds zone A, and zone C surrounds zone B. The zoned datasets provide simple models of this topology. Each instance contained A, B, and C where the radius of A was 100, B was 300, and C was 500. Using distributions of the number of private-car owners per $1\,000$ citizens in Berlin [1], we thus generated requests as follows: 200 in A, 300 in B, and 500 in C. In dataset Z1 (Z2), we sampled uniformly at random each drop-off (pick-up) location in A. Thus, each request required the transport of up to four commuters from A, B, and C to A (A to A, B, and C). The intuition is that dataset Z1 (Z2) could capture the morning (evening) rush hour in Berlin when many commuters need a ride from home to downtown (downtown to home).

Datasets R and C. The random dataset (R) was also guided by Uchoa's dataset. Basically, we first sampled locations from instances in the dataset until the number of such locations reached $2\,000$, and we then paired location 1 with $1\,001$, location 2 with $1\,002$, and so on until all locations were paired, thus forming $1\,000$ requests. The clustered dataset (C) was guided by Uchoa's dataset. Firstly, we partitioned the grid into four clusters (e.g. north-east, north-west, south-each, south-west Berlin). Then, within each cluster, we sampled, exponentially with a decay of 500, locations for 250 requests. Similar techniques were used for some existing instances [20].

5   Genetic Template for MDPDPs

We give a genetic template for the implementation of GAs for approximating optimal solutions to MDPDPs, see Algorithm 1. The algorithm initialises a population of K chromosomes that develops through N iterations, and it returns the best chromosome w.r.t. fitness function f. Within a given iteration, the population is evaluated w.r.t. f. Thus, the best P chromosomes do crossovers with the rest $(N - P)$ chromosomes until the population size reaches K. The population then mutates and gives offspring. Thus, the iteration ends.

Algorithm 1. A genetic template.

1: **procedure** GA-MDPDP(size K, number N, split P, fitness f, instance $\mathcal{I}$)
2:     $Pop \leftarrow$ INITIALISE($K, \mathcal{I}$)   ▷ a population of K chromosomes for $\mathcal{I}$
3:     **for** i from 1 to N **do**
4:         $Best \leftarrow$ pick the best P chromosomes from Pop w.r.t. f
5:         $Rest \leftarrow$ pick the rest $(N - P)$ chromosomes from Pop
6:         $Pop \leftarrow$ CROSSOVER($Best, Rest, K$, SELECTION(f))
7:         $Pop \leftarrow$ MUTATION(Pop)
8:     **end for**
9:     **return** the best chromosome from Pop w.r.t. f
10: **end procedure**

We next describe the sub-routines in Algorithm 1. INITIALISE($K, \mathcal{I}$): The population size is set to K. Each chromosome is initialised with a route through all the request locations in $\mathcal{I}$. This is done uniformly at random, subject to constraints (a) and (c). Thus, each chromosome induces a strict request ordering over the pickup locations. Then, the sub-routing picks some fixed vehicle ordering and clusters each route greedily into sub-routes by letting each vehicle in this ordering pick available requests according to the request ordering, subject to constraints (b) and (d). SELECTION(f): It does tournament selection based on the fitness function f of the chromosomes in the current iteration. CROSSOVER($Best, Rest, K$, SELECTION(f)): It does partially-mapped crossover [7] until the population size reaches K. MUTATION(Pop): It does inverse sequence mutation [11].

We refer to Algorithm 1 as "Alg totWAIT", "Alg maxWAIT", "Alg totTOUR", "Alg maxTOUR", "Alg totARR", "Alg maxARR", "Alg totTRAVEL", and "Alg maxTRAVEL" whenever the fitness function f is totWAIT, maxWAIT, totTOUR, maxTOUR, totARR, maxARR, totTRAVEL, and maxTRAVEL, respectively. Our goal was to compare these GAs in a fair manner. For this purpose, we fixed the remaining parameter values. For $K = 10\,000$, $N = 1\,000$, and $P = 1\,000$, the running time of GA-MDPDP($10\,000, 1\,000, 1\,000, f, \mathcal{I}$) was less than 10 minutes for any fitness function f and any given instance $\mathcal{I}$ in our datasets. However, we submit that an interesting future direction is parameter tuning. Algorithm 1 was implemented by using DEAP because this library offers plenty of genetic operators [5].

6   Experiments for MDPDPs

6.1   Objective Values

Let us consider datasets Z1 and Z2. Given the returned feasible plan (i.e. the best chromosome) per instance from Z1 (Z2), we calculated the objective (i.e. fitness) values of totWAIT, maxWAIT, totTOUR, maxTOUR, totARR, maxARR, totTRAVEL, and maxTRAVEL. We averaged these values across the instances from Z1 (Z2). Figure 1 depicts the results for the datasets Z1 and Z2. We next make a number of observations about these results.

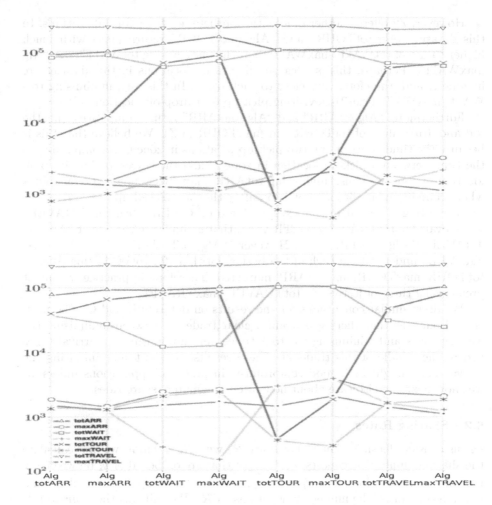

Fig. 1. Objective values: (top) dataset Z1; (bottom) dataset Z2.

First of all, the values of totWAIT, totARR, and totTRAVEL are one or two magnitudes (i.e. $\times 10^1 - 10^2$) above the values of maxWAIT, maxARR, and maxTRAVEL, respectively. These gaps are somehow preserved across the algorithms. We feel that the existence of these gaps supports a rather intuitive expectation because the former objectives are sums over vehicle times whereas the latter objectives are maximums over vehicle times.

By comparison, the values of totTOUR and maxTOUR indicate more counter-intuitive trends. For instance, "Alg totWAIT" and "Alg maxWAIT" return plans with much higher values of totTOUR/maxTOUR than "Alg tot-TOUR" and "Alg maxTOUR" in each of Z1 and Z2. At the same time, "Alg tot-TOUR" and "Alg maxTOUR" return plans with values of totWAIT/maxWAIT that are comparable to the ones of "Alg totWAIT" and "Alg maxWAIT" in Z1.

However, Z2 offers another differentiation between these four algorithms. In this dataset, "Alg totTOUR" and "Alg maxTOUR" return plans with much higher values of totWAIT/maxWAIT than the ones of "Alg totWAIT" and "Alg maxWAIT". Perhaps, this is because all pick-up locations in this dataset are in zone A and, therefore, very close to each other. In this way, minimising totWAIT/maxWAIT prioritises visiting pick-up over drop-off locations.

Furthermore, "Alg totARR" and "Alg maxARR" return competitive (i.e. the 3rd and 4th) values of totTOUR and maxTOUR in Z1. We believe that this is because the time between any two pick-up locations in zone C is comparable to the time between a pick-up location in zone C and the corresponding drop-off location in zone A. Thus, minimizing totARR/maxARR tends to prefer routes where commuters are dropped off soon after they are picked up.

Interestingly, each algorithm except "Alg totTRAVEL"/"Alg maxTRAVEL" gives a value of totTRAVEL/maxTRAVEL that is similar to the one of "Alg totTRAVEL"/"Alg maxTRAVEL". However, "Alg totTRAVEL" and "Alg maxTRAVEL" underperform each of the best algorithms for totWAIT/maxWAIT, totTOUR/maxTOUR, and totARR/maxARR. Therefore, in practice, we might prefer using these objectives to totTRAVEL/maxTRAVEL.

We drew similar conclusions for the results on datasets R and C. The most crucial one was that there was again a clear trade-off between minimising the waiting times and minimising the tour times, and minimising the arrival times lied in the middle of this trade-off. These results suggest that minimising the arrival times might be a good compromisis in practical applications unless, as we show next, we also care about how often commuters share rides.

6.2   Sharing Rates

Let us consider feasible plan $\mathcal{P}$. For route $\mathcal{R}_i$ with $R_i \neq \emptyset$ in it, we first calculate the sharing number of requests $n_i(s_j^i, s_{j+1}^i)$ that are on board of v_i between any pair of consecutive locations s_j^i and s_{j+1}^i. We then sum up these numbers and normalise them by the number of locations in $\mathcal{R}_i$. We call this the *sharing rate* of vehicle v_i in $\mathcal{P}$, labelled as $\mathrm{SR}(\mathcal{P}, v_i)$. We finally divide the sum of all vehicle rates over the number of running vehicles $N = |\{v_i \in V | |R_i| > 0\}| \in (0, n]$. We call this the *sharing rate* of $\mathcal{P}$, labelled as $\mathrm{SR}(\mathcal{P})$.

$$\mathrm{SR}(\mathcal{P}, v_i) = \sum_{j=1}^{2|R_i|-1} \frac{n(s_j^i, s_{j+1}^i)}{2|R_i|} \quad \mathrm{SR}(\mathcal{P}) = \sum_{v_i \in V} \frac{\mathrm{SR}(v_i)}{N}$$

Theoretically, the minimum value of the plan sharing rate is $\frac{1}{2}$. To see this, consider a plan where the drop-off location of each request is serviced immediately after the pick-up location. In such a plan, the sharing number is 1 between any pick-up and drop-off locations, and 0 between any drop-off and pick-up locations. At the same time, the maximum value of the rate approaches the capacity c, i.e. 4. This happens when there are only requests of unit demands and each running vehicle transports 4 requests along its entire route. Thus, rate values close to $\frac{1}{2}/4$ indicate less/more sharing.

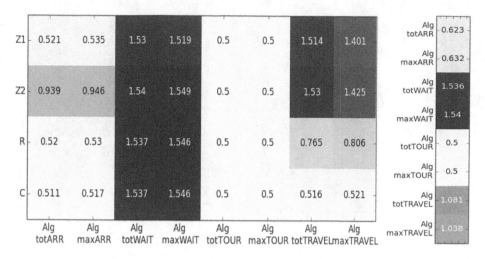

Fig. 2. Average sharing rate per running vehicle: (left) per dataset; (right) all datasets.

We give empirical results in Fig. 2. "Alg totWAIT" and "Alg maxWAIT" achieve average rate values of at least 1.5. As we sample demands uniformly at random, the average demand in the instances is around 2.5. Hence, the average number of requests per vehicle is $4/2.5 = 1.6$. For this reason, we feel that performance above 1.5 is quite competitive. "Alg totTOUR" and "Alg maxTOUR" achieve the theoretical lower bound. "Alg totARR" and "Alg maxARR" perform poorly on Z1, R, and C, but better on Z2. "Alg totTRAVEL" and "Alg maxTRAVEL" perform quite well on Z1 and Z2, but not so well on R and C.

6.3 Fleet Busyness

We next measured the busyness per vehicle in the feasible plan returned by each of the algorithms in each instance (i.e. the best chromosome). The busyness is given by means of the average travelled time per running vehicle across all instances in datasets. This time across all algorithms was the longest on R, followed by the time on C. We believe that this is a promising result because it suggests that the travel time might reduce in practical settings such as those modelled by Z1 and Z2.

In Fig. 3, "Alg totWAIT" and "Alg maxWAIT" give the greatest mean value ($\approx 1\,500$). Thus, they achieve the longest average travelled time. However, they divert vehicles towards pickups more often than dropoffs and, thus, give a high sharing rate (Fig. 2). Notably, "Alg totTOUR", "Alg maxTOUR", "Alg totARR", and "Alg maxARR" give means that are comparable to the lowest mean value of "Alg totTRAVEL" and "Alg maxTRAVEL" ($\approx 1\,100$). Unfortunately, these algorithms give a low sharing rate (Fig. 2).

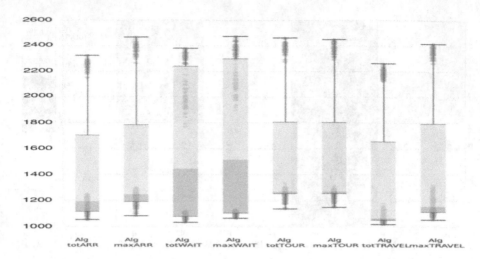

Fig. 3. Average travelled time per running vehicle across all datasets.

6.4   Fleet Size

We further calculated the number of dispatched vehicles in the feasible plan returned by each of the algorithms in each instance (i.e. the best chromosome). Each such vehicle serviced at least one request. We thus computed the minimum and maximum numbers of running vehicles across all instances per dataset. These numbers were quite similar and, for this reason, we report the minimum and maximum numbers of running vehicles across all datasets; see Table 1.

Table 1. Number of running vehicles from 1 000 available vehicles across all datasets.

	Z1	Z2	R	C
Alg totARR	min. 358, max. 375			
Alg maxARR	min. 328, max. 345			
Alg totWAIT	min. 355, max. 368			
Alg maxWAIT	min. 352, max. 365			
Alg totTOUR	min. 310, max. 334			
Alg maxTOUR	min. 315, max. 339			
Alg totTRAVEL	min. 354, max. 369			
Alg maxTRAVEL	min. 350, max. 366			

As $c = 4$ in our setup, the minimum number of vehicles that could be used is 250. This could happen if each of all 1 000 requests had demand 1 and each of 250 vehicles serviced 4 requests. However, as we sampled demands uniformly at random, the average demand in the instances is about 2.5. We thus expected that the average number of running vehicles would be around $1 000/2.5 = 400$. Surprisingly, all algorithms used 25–90 (i.e. 6.25%–22.5%) fewer vehicles.

They further used around 33% of all 1 000 available vehicles, i.e. ≈ 3 people per vehicle. To put this in a perspective, let us consider again the commuting setting in Berlin, where there are at least 90 000 commuting vehicles per day [1]. Suppose that we motivate the owners of such vehicles to use our system. Then, "Alg totTOUR" and "Alg maxTOUR" force them to wait longer time (Fig. 1) but travel shorter time (Fig. 3) whereas "Alg totWAIT" and "Alg maxWAIT" force them to share rides (Fig. 2) but travel longer time (Fig. 3). In both cases, the number of commuting vehicles is likely to decrease by around 67% (Table 1). Alternatively, this number could be around 30 000. This would lead to a significant reduction in their associated CO_2 emissions.

7   Conclusions

We considered multi-depot PDPs where vehicles service commuting requests. For this model, we consider minimising fleet objectives such as the total/maximal travel, waiting, tour, and arrival time. We proposed genetic algorithms for them and ran extensive experiments measuring their induced objective value, sharing rate, fleet busyness, and fleet size. The empirical results suggested that there is a tension between the objectives. Indeed, we observed a trade-off between minimising the waiting times and minimising the tour times, whereas minimising the arrival times is more or less in the middle of it. Also, minimising the waiting times achieved the highest sharing rate but the longest travelled time per vehicle whereas minimising the tour times achieved the lowest sharing rate but shorter travelled time per vehicle. The algorithms reduced significantly the number of vehicles used by one thousand commuters. This can potentially lead to a large reduction of their associated CO_2 emissions in practice. In our future work, we will run the genetic template with some more objectives, we will tune its parameters, and we will turn attention to the dynamic model. Finally, we would like to thank the reviewers of EPIA 2021 for their valuable feedback.

References

1. Broschüre Mobilität der Stadt - Berliner Verkehr in Zahlen (2017). https://www.berlin.de/sen/uvk/verkehr/verkehrsdaten/zahlen-und-fakten/mobilitaet-der-stadt-berliner-verkehr-in-zahlen-2017. Accessed 15 May 2021
2. NewStatesman - Berlin has biggest rise in public transport use and traffic congestion among world cities (2020). https://www.newstatesman.com/2020/05/berlin-has-biggest-rise-public-transport-use-and-traffic-congestion-among-world-cities. Accessed 15 June 2021
3. Beasley, J.: Route first-cluster second methods for vehicle routing. Omega **11**(4), 403–408 (1983). https://doi.org/10.1016/0305-0483(83)90033-6
4. Dantzig, G.B., Ramser, J.H.: The truck dispatching problem. Manage. Sci. **6**(1), 80–91 (1959). https://doi.org/10.1287/mnsc.6.1.80
5. Fortin, F.A., De Rainville, F.M., Gardner, M.A.G., Parizeau, M., Gagné, C.: DEAP: evolutionary algorithms made easy. J. Mach. Learn. Res. **13**(70), 2171–2175 (2012). http://jmlr.org/papers/v13/fortin12a.html

6. Gillett, B.E., Miller, L.R.: A heuristic algorithm for the vehicle-dispatch problem. Oper. Res. **22**(2), 340–349 (1974). https://doi.org/10.1287/opre.22.2.340

7. Goldberg, D.E., Lingle, R.: Alleles, loci, and the traveling salesman problem. In: Proceedings of the 1st International Conference on Genetic Algorithms, pp. 154–159. L. Erlbaum Associates Inc., USA, July 1985. https://dl.acm.org/doi/10.5555/645511.657095

8. Irnich, S.: Multi-depot pickup and delivery problem with a single hub and heterogeneous vehicles. Eur. J. Oper. Res. **122**(2), 310–328 (2000). https://doi.org/10.1016/S0377-2217(99)00235-0

9. Matl, P., Hartl, R.F., Vidal, T.: Workload equity in vehicle routing problems: a survey and analysis. Transp. Sci. **52**(2), 239–260 (2018). https://doi.org/10.1287/trsc.2017.0744

10. Mitchell, M.: An Introduction to Genetic Algorithms. MIT Press, Cambridge (1998). https://dl.acm.org/doi/10.5555/522098

11. Otman, A., Jaafar, A.: A comparative study of adaptive crossover operators for genetic algorithms to resolve the traveling salesman problem. Int. J. Comput. Appl. **31**(11), 49–57 (2011). https://www.ijcaonline.org/archives/volume31/number11/3945-5587

12. Paquette, J., Bellavance, F., Cordeau, J.F., Laporte, G.: Measuring quality of service in dial-a-ride operations: the case of a Canadian city. Transportation **39**(3), 539–564 (2012). https://doi.org/10.1007/s11116-011-9375-4

13. Parragh, S., Doerner, K., Hartl, R.: A survey on pickup and delivery problems: Part i: transportation between customers and depot. Journal für Betriebswirtschaft **58**, 21–51 (2008). https://doi.org/10.1007/s11301-008-0033-7

14. Parragh, S., Doerner, K., Hartl, R.: A survey on pickup and delivery problems: Part ii: transportation between pickup and delivery locations. Journal für Betriebswirtschaft **58**, 81–117 (2008). https://doi.org/10.1007/s11301-008-0036-4

15. Prins, C., Labadi, N., Reghioui, M.: Tour splitting algorithms for vehicle routing problems. Int. J. Prod. Res. **47**(2), 507–535 (2008). https://doi.org/10.1080/00207540802426599

16. Prins, C., Lacomme, P., Prodhon, C.: Order-first split-second methods for vehicle routing problems: a review. Transp. Res. Part C, Emerg. Technol. **40**, 179–200 (2014). https://doi.org/10.1016/j.trc.2014.01.011

17. Ralphs, T.K., Kopman, L., Pulleyblank, W.R., Trotter, L.E.: On the capacitated vehicle routing problem. Math. Program. **94**(2–3), 343–359 (2003). https://doi.org/10.1007/s10107-002-0323-0

18. Savelsbergh, M.W.P., Sol, M.: The general pickup and delivery problem. Transp. Sci. **29**(1), 17–29 (1995). https://doi.org/10.1287/trsc.29.1.17

19. Silva, M.M., Subramanian, A., Vidal, T., Ochi, L.S.: A simple and effective metaheuristic for the minimum latency problem. Eur. J. Oper. Res. **221**(3), 513–520 (2012). https://doi.org/10.1016/j.ejor.2012.03.044

20. Uchoa, E., Pecin, D., Pessoa, A.A., Poggi, M., Vidal, T., Subramanian, A.: New benchmark instances for the capacitated vehicle routing problem. Eur. J. Oper. Res. **257**(3), 845–858 (2017). https://doi.org/10.1016/j.ejor.2016.08.012

21. Vidal, T., Laporte, G., Matl, P.: A concise guide to existing and emerging vehicle routing problem variants. Eur. J. Oper. Res. **286**(2), 401–416 (2020). https://doi.org/10.1016/j.ejor.2019.10.010

Solving a Bilevel Problem with Station Location and Vehicle Routing Using Variable Neighborhood Descent and Ant Colony Optimization

Marcos R. C. O. Leite$^{(\boxtimes)}$ ⓘ, Heder S. Bernardino ⓘ,
and Luciana B. Gonçalves ⓘ

Federal University of Juiz de Fora, Juiz de Fora, MG 36036-900, Brazil
{heder,lbrugiolo}@ice.ufjf.br

Abstract. With the grown of global concern with environmental issues and incentives on the part of governments, the use of electric vehicles (EVs) by companies has increased. By joining the interest of governments on minimizing the costs of building the recharging infrastructure and of companies on minimizing their transport costs with the adoption of electric vehicles in their fleet, a bilevel optimization problem arises. An approach that combines the Variable Neighborhood Search (VND) with an Ant Colony Optimization (ACO) to solve this bilevel model is proposed here. The results of the computational experiments using different benchmark instances indicate the superior performance of the proposed approach, mainly in the allocation of the charging infrastructure (objective of the leader). Also, the proposal found better solutions than those from the literature while maintains the percentage of electric vehicles that compose the fleet above the required limit.

Keywords: Ant Colony Optimization · Variable Neighborhood Descent · Multilevel optimization · Vehicle routing · Electric vehicles

1 Introduction

The use of electric vehicles is increasing in various sectors, from personal use (customers) to commercial use (companies). As electric vehicles use a battery as a power source, they have a driving range limitation. Thus, it is necessary to plan the construction of a charging infrastructure ensuring that users can use them without worrying about they battery become uncharged during the journey.

In most cases, this construction is done by the government as a way to encourage the use of electric vehicles by consumers and companies. The budget for the construction of this recharge infrastructure is often limited and, therefore, reducing the construction cost becomes one of the government's objectives. The company in turn uses the charging infrastructure built by the government to increase

The authors thank the support provided by CAPES, FAPEMIG, CNPq, and UFJF.

© Springer Nature Switzerland AG 2021
G. Marreiros et al. (Eds.): EPIA 2021, LNAI 12981, pp. 211–223, 2021.
https://doi.org/10.1007/978-3-030-86230-5_17

the percentage of electric vehicles in its fleet and reduce its operating costs, since the government often offers subsidies for the use of electric vehicles, making them more attractive than conventional combustion vehicles. Consequently, the government must decide in which of the available locations the charging stations will be built and the company must define its composition of the fleet (respecting the minimum percentage required by the government of electric vehicles in its fleet) and its routes. It's possible to notice that this process is composed of two different problems, each with its own restrictions and objectives. These problems can be organized into levels, making multilevel optimization a good option to solve both problems simultaneously.

Thus, a bilevel approach combining Variable Neighborhood Descent (VND) and Ant Colony Optimization (ACO) is proposed here. VND is applied at the upper level to solve the problem of allocation of charging stations by the government, while ACO is applied at the lower level to solve the problem of the composition of the fleet and its routes by the company. Also, ACO is equipped with local search procedures and a route selection model. The proposal was applied to benchmark instances and the results obtained are better than those from the literature at both levels.

2   Related Work

The problem of allocating charging stations in conjunction with the vehicle routing problem makes it necessary to build an adequate charging infrastructure attending to budget limits and minimizing the costs. Therefore, the bilevel approach comes as a good option to address both problems simultaneously. In most cases, the upper level is responsible for the allocation problem of the charging stations and the lower level for the vehicle routing problem, as in [17].

In most cases, the government is responsible for building the recharge infrastructure and aims to reduce its construction cost as in [10,12,15] and in some cases the cost of construction must be less than the budget limit as in [18]. However, in some cases, companies may also be responsible for the construction as in [16] and in other cases the objectives may be different as in [6], where the objective in the upper level is to maximize the number of the served users and the objective in the lower level is to minimize the charging time. The objective of the lower level in [18] is to minimize the travel time of users of EVs. In [5,18] the same bilevel approach presented in [18] is used. A literature review of bilevel formulations involving this two problems and containing the objectives, restrictions and methods of solving each level is presented in [9].

There are several bilevel problems that involve the allocation of charging stations and vehicle routing, however there are few problems that consider the possibility of using a mixed fleet [10], although this option is more attractive to both the government and the company [7] since the cost of construction of the charging stations can be lower with the use of combustion vehicles. This bilevel model formulation is proposed in [10,12].

3   Bilevel Problem: Station Location and Vehicle Routing

The problem addressed is formed by two decision-making agents: the government and the company. The government is responsible for the allocation plan of charging stations aiming to achieve with this allocation the minimum percentage of electric vehicles in the fleet. The company is responsible for determining the composition of its fleet (EVs and CVs) and its routes using the stations built by the government. These two problems are combined in a bilevel model as in [10].

At the upper level, the problem of allocating charging stations is addressed, where the cost of building the charging stations should be minimized requiring a minimum percentage of electric vehicles in the fleet. An allocation is considered feasible when this required percentage of electric vehicles in the fleet composition is met. The elements of the bilevel model are presented in Table 1.

The allocation problem of charging stations (upper level) can be defined as

$$\min \sum_{s \in S} F_s z_s, \quad \text{subject to} \quad \sum_{k \in K} y_k \geq \alpha |K|, \quad z_s \in \{0,1\} \ \forall s \in S, \quad (1)$$

where one desires to minimize the total construction cost of charging stations, subject to the constraint that ensures a minimum percentage of EVs in the fleet. The design variables (z_s) are binary values. The construction cost F_s of a station is composed of a fixed and a variable costs, as $F_s = A + B \cdot N_s$ where A and B are coefficients, and N_s is the number of consumers in the neighborhood of the station. Thus, the more consumers in the neighborhood of a station, the higher its construction cost. A consumer is in the neighborhood of a given station when the energy needed to go from that station to the consumer is smaller than $Q/3$.

At the lower level, the problems of defining the composition of the fleet and its routes are addressed. Both are the performed by the company, which seeks to minimize the operating costs of its vehicles. The company has a single fixed deposit, from which vehicles must start their routes and serve all the company's customers. Each customer must be served only once. The company has two types of vehicles: electric (EVs) and combustion (CVs). It is considered that CVs always have enough fuel to visit consumers, and there is no need to fuel during the route. On the other hand, EVs can visit the charging stations due to the limitations of their batteries. Whenever a vehicle leaves a station or the depot, its battery is considered fully charged. The energy consumption of the battery is given by a linear function of the distance traveled by the vehicle. The lower level model of the company's fleet composition and routing plan can be formulated as

Table 1. Notation of the sets, parameters, decision variables (DVs) and non-decision variables (NDVs) used in the formulation of the bilevel problem. The NDVs are defined in the descriptions of the instances.

	Symbol	Description
Sets	$\{o\}$	the single depot
	C	set of customers indexed by c
	S	set of candidate charging infrastructures indexed by s
	V	set of nodes; $V = C \cup S \cup \{o\}$
	K	set of vehicles indexed by k
NDVs and parameters	d_{gh}	the distance from node g to node h
	U	the load capacity
	u_c	the demand of customer c
	Q	the battery power capacity of EV
	r	the power consumption rate (per unit distance)
	p^1_{gk}	the remaining battery power when vehicle k arrives at node g
	p^2_{gk}	the remaining battery power when vehicle k leaves node g
	F_s	the construction cost of the charging infrastructure s
	α	the desired EV adoption percentage
	CI	the unit operating cost of CV (per unit distance)
	CE	the unit operating cost of EV (per unit distance)
	TD^{EV}_k	the total travel distance of EV's
	TD^{CV}_k	the total travel distance of CV's
	M	a large number
DVs	x_{ghk}	$\begin{cases} 1, \text{ if vehicle k goes from node g to node h} \\ 0, \text{ otherwise} \end{cases}$
	y_k	$\begin{cases} 1, \text{ vehicle k is EV} \\ 0, \text{ vehicle k is CV} \end{cases}$
	z_s	$\begin{cases} 1, \text{ candidate charging infrastructure s is chosen} \\ 0, \text{ otherwise} \end{cases}$

$$\min f_C = CE \sum_{k \in K} TD_k^{EV} + CI \sum_{k \in K} TD_k^{CV} \tag{2}$$

subject to

$$\sum_{g \in V, g \neq c} \sum_{k \in K} x_{gck} = 1 \; \forall c \in C \tag{3}$$

$$\sum_{h \in V, h \neq o} x_{ohk} \leq 1 \; \forall k \in K \tag{4}$$

$$\sum_{g \in V, g \neq v} x_{gvk} = \sum_{h \in V, h \neq v} x_{vhk} \; \forall v \in V, \forall k \in K \tag{5}$$

$$\sum_{c \in C} u_c \sum_{v \in V} x_{cvk} \leq U \; \forall k \in K \tag{6}$$

$$p_{hk}^1 \leq p_{gk}^2 - r \cdot d_{gh} x_{ghk} + \tag{7}$$
$$M(2 - x_{ghk} - y_k) \; \forall g, h \in V, k \in K$$

$$p_{ok}^2 = Q \; \forall k \in K \tag{8}$$

$$p_{sk}^2 = Q \cdot z_s \; \forall s \in S, \forall k \in K \tag{9}$$

$$p_{ck}^2 = p_{ck}^1 \; \forall c \in C, \forall k \in K \tag{10}$$

$$p_{vk}^1 \geq 0 \; \forall v \in V, k \in K \tag{11}$$

$$\sum_{g \in V} \sum_{h \in V} d_{gh} x_{ghk} \leq TD_k^{EV} + M(1 - y_k) \tag{12}$$

$$\sum_{g \in V} \sum_{h \in V} d_{gh} x_{ghk} \leq TD_k^{CV} + M \cdot y_k \; \forall k \in K \tag{13}$$

$$TD_k^{EV}, TD_k^{CV} \geq 0 \; \forall k \in K \tag{14}$$

$$x_{ghk}, y_k \in \{0,1\} \; \forall g, h \in V, k \in K \tag{15}$$

The objective function (2) is to minimize total operating costs which are related to travel distance and vehicle's fuel type. The total travel distance is divided into two variables TD_k^{EV} and TD_k^{CV} that represents and stores the distance covered by the EVs and CVs respectively. Constraints (3) ensure every customer must be visited once and only once. Constraints (4) represent that each vehicle is assigned to one route at most. Constraints (5) are flow balance constraints that ensure that the number of arrivals at a node is equal to the number of departures. Constraints (6) ensure that the total customer demands of each vehicle don't exceed the load capacity. Constraints (7) are to calculate the vehicle's remaining power based on node sequence: if node h is visited after node g by an EV, the battery's remaining power at node h is reduced by the power consumption between nodes g and h, but if node h is not visited after node g or the vehicle is CV, constraints (7) are relaxed. Constraints (8) and (9) reset the battery power to its maximum value (Q) when EV leaves a chosen charging infrastructure or the depot. Constraints (10) ensure that the battery power remains the same while EV visits a customer node. Constraints (11) ensure that EVs have sufficient battery power to visit customers or charging infrastructures and return to the depot. Constraints (8)–(11) deal with the limited driving range of EVs but they do not affect the driving range of CVs, as constraint (7) is relaxed in case of CVs. Restrictions (12) and (13) ensure that the values of TD_k^{EV} and TD_k^{CV} should not be less than the total traveled by each type of vehicle, with restriction (12) being applied to EVs and relaxed for CVs and in a similar way, the restriction (13) applied to the CVs and relaxed for the EVs. Constraints (14) ensures that the values of TD_k^{EV} and TD_k^{CV} are non-negative. The binary decision variables x_{ghk} and y_k are presented in (15).

A limitation of the bilevel model addressed here is that a single company is considered. As the government pays for building the recharging infrastructure, more companies could use it. To deal with this new scenario, it is necessary to modify the model so that it considers other issues such as the simultaneous use of the charging infrastructure by more than one company and the interests of each company in planning the construction of the charging infrastructure.

4   Proposed Bilevel Approach

To solve the bilevel model, a technique that combines VND and ACO was proposed. VND is used at the upper level to solve the problem of allocating charging stations. ACO in conjunction with three local search procedures(Change, Remove and Exchange) and the route selection model is used at the lower level to solve the problems of defining the composition of the fleet and vehicle routing: the ACO defines the composition of the fleet and its routes. The solutions founded by the ACO are improved by applying local search procedures. At the end, the best solution is chosen based on the route selection procedure. A pseudo-code of the proposed approach is presented in Algorithm 1 and both search techniques of the proposal, namely VND and ACO, are described in the following sections.

Algorithm 1: Pseudo-code of the proposed bilevel approach.

---

1 $S_{best} \leftarrow$ generateInitialAllocation();
2 **repeat**
3   **repeat**
4   S' $\leftarrow$ Switch(S_{best}) ;   // Solving upper-level
5          $P_{ev} \leftarrow$ ACO(S') ;   // Solving lower-level
6   **if** $P_{ev} >= \alpha$ **then** $S_{best} \leftarrow$ S' ;
7   **until** *improvement*;
8   **repeat**
9   S" $\leftarrow$ Swap(S_{best}) ;   // Solving upper-level
10         $P_{ev} \leftarrow$ ACO(S") ;   // Solving lower-level
11   **if** $P_{ev} >= \alpha$ **then** $S_{best} \leftarrow$ S" ;
12   **until** *improvement*;
13 **until** *stop condition is met*;

4.1 Variable Neighborhood Descent for Station Allocation

The VND is a search heuristic that explores the search space in a deterministic way, through the use of different neighborhood structures that are explored in a pre-established order. Usually, different neighborhood structures have different local optimum, so this change of neighborhood structures can prevent the search process from getting trapped in a local optimum and being able to explore more of the search space, finding better solutions [3]. The proposed VND is based on that presented in [10]. The proposal uses the same binary vector structure to represent the allocations of charging stations, where each position represents a station available to be built, and the same switch operator. We propose here a simplified version of the swap operator from [10].

The switch operator selects a station to be closed in the current best solution (S_{best}). If the solution obtained (S') is feasible, then an improvement occurs as the construction cost is reduced. An allocation is feasible when the minimum percentage of electric vehicles (α) is met. This condition is verified considering the fleet (P_{ev}) obtained when the lower level problem is solved. The switch operator is applied to all stations chosen to be built in the current solution.

The swap operator proposed here selects one station to be built and another to be closed as long as the cost of building the selected unchosen station is smaller than the gain for closing the other one. Similar to switch, a better solution is found when the generated solution (S'') is feasible. Swap is applied to every unchosen stations in the current solution.

This process is repeated until the current solution remains unchanged after two consecutive iterations or until a maximum number of iterations is reached.

4.2 Ant Colony Optimization for Routing Planning

The proposed ACO is that presented in [12]. Each ant construct a complete solution of the problem and the choice of the type of vehicle that will be used on the route is made at the beginning of each route respecting the minimum percentage of electric vehicles in the fleet. All routes start at the depot and the next location to be visited is chosen according to the probability

$$P_{ij}^h = \begin{cases} \frac{[\tau_{ij}]^\alpha [\eta_{ij}]^\beta}{\sum_{l \in \mathcal{N}_i^k} [\tau_{il}]^\alpha [\eta_{il}]^\beta}, & \text{if } j \in \mathcal{N}_i^h \\ 0, & \text{otherwise} \end{cases} \tag{16}$$

where, for an ant h, i and j are current and destination locations respectively, τ_{ij} is the pheromone level, η_{ij} is the heuristic information, $\mathcal{N}_i^h$ is the set of possible destinations from i, and α and β are parameters used to control the influence on destination choice process of the pheromone and heuristic values. The heuristic value is calculated according to $\eta_{ij} = 1/d_{ij}$, where d_{ij} is the distance between locations i and j. To prevent electric vehicles from running out of battery during their routes, the algorithm performs a verification in advance to confirm whether it is possible for the vehicle to reach its destination and from there, whether it is possible for the vehicle to reach any station or depot. This ensures that the vehicle will not run out of battery during its route, as it will always have a place to recharge or return to the depot. In the case of combustion vehicles, this verification is not necessary as it is considered that they always have fuel to reach their destinations, not needing to recharge. Thus, the construction of the $\mathcal{N}_i^h$ set is done differently for each type of vehicle and the depot is assumed to be the destination when $\mathcal{N}_i^k = \emptyset$.

In the process of selecting the destination, with probability $(1 - q_0)$ the ant h uses the probabilistic rule defined in Eq. 16 to choose the next destination and with probability q_0 the ant h choose the location with the highest probability $j = \arg\max_{l \in \mathcal{N}_i^h} \{P_{il}^h\}$. The pheromone values start with τ_0 for all locations and is calculated as $\tau_0 = 1/\rho C^{nnh}, \forall (i,j) \in L$, where $L = \{(i,j) \mid i,j \in N\}$ is the set of arcs connecting the locations, ρ $(0 \leq \rho \leq 1)$ is the pheromone evaporation rate and C^{nnh} is the cost of the solution generated by the Nearest Neighbor Heuristic. The pheromone is evaporated in the end of each iteration according to $\tau_{ij} = (1 - \rho)\tau_{ij} \ \forall (i,j) \in L$ and the best ant deposits an amount of pheromone as $\tau_{ij} = \tau_{ij} + \Delta\tau_{ij}^{best}, \forall (i,j) \in L^{best}$, where L_{best} is the set of paths used by the best ant, $\Delta\tau_{ij}^{best} = 1/C^{best}$ is the amount of pheromone that the best ant deposits, and C^{best} is the cost of the solution found by the best ant.

The pheromone is updated using the best ant of each iteration as default and the best ant found so far is used only at each f_{req} iterations. The maximum and minimum values are imposed for pheromones in according to the Min-Max Ant System strategy [14]. The maximum pheromone value (τ_{max}) starts with τ_0 and is updated by $1/C^{best}$ when the best ant found so far is modified. The minimum pheromone value is calculated as $\tau_{min} = \tau_{max}(1 - \sqrt[n]{0.05})/((avg - 1)(\sqrt[n]{0.05})$, where avg is the average number of different locations available at each step of destination selection of each ant and n is the total number of customers. This allows the algorithm to run for a longer time and make a better exploration of the search space, being able to find better solutions.

In order to avoid premature stagnation in the search process due to the electist characteristic of the algorithm, two mechanisms were implemented to control the levels of pheromones during the search process, which are the λ-branching scheme [4] and the smoothing of trails [13]. Using the lambda mechanism, whenever the search process enters a process of stagnation, the levels of pheromones are adjusted according to the smoothing mechanism. In this way the algorithm is able to escape from great locations and explore new solutions without completely losing information about the best solutions found. This allows the algorithm to run for a longer time and make a better exploration of the search space, being able to find better solutions.

4.3   Local Search Procedures and Route Selection

To improve the solutions obtained at the lower level by the ACO, four local search procedures were implemented: the 2-opt heuristic [4] and the tree local search procedures proposed in [12], that are the Change, Remove and Exchange procedures. In the Change procedure, it is checked for each route whether it is possible to change the stations used by others that are available and in the Remove procedure it is checked whether it is possible to remove the stations used. In the exchange procedure, it is checked whether it is possible to exchange two consumers belonging to different routes. All procedures are executed in the order in which they were presented at the end of each ACO iteration and performed so that the cost of the solution is reduced and without losing its viability.

A set-based partitioning formulation procedure [1] was also implemented to improve the quality of the solutions found at the lower level through the selection of routes that will compose the solution. All routes found by ants during the execution of the ACO are stored in a set R without repeating. After the execution of the ACO, this set is applied to the route selection model. A commercial solver is used to solve the proposed route selection model and at the end of its execution, the composition of the fleet and the selected routes is returned by it. This is done respecting the required percentage of electric vehicles in the fleet and the other restrictions of the bilevel model.

5   Computational Experiments

Computational experiments were performed to comparative evaluate the proposal (labeled here as VND*+ACO) using benchmark instances from [11]. The proposal was implemented using Python and the source code is public available[1]. The results obtained in [10] and [12] were used in the comparisons.

The parameters used by VND are the same defined in [10,12]: $A = 500$ and $B = 100$. The ACO parameters were set to typical values: $\alpha = 1$ and $\beta = 5$ [10,12–14]. The other parameters used by ACO are the same used in [12]: $\rho = 0.8$, $q_0 = 0.8$, $f_{req} = 25$ and the number of ants $m = \frac{0.4}{q_0 \log(1-\rho)}$ as in [2]. The maximum number of ACO iterations was defined as 1,000 and to solve the routing select model the Gurobi[2] with its standard parameters was used. The stopping criteria was defined as 10,000 iterations and 10 independent runs were performed as in [10,12]. A Kruskal-Wallis test [8] based on the processing time was performed and with the result (p-value= 0.96034) we concluded that the stopping criteria is fair for the comparisons concerning the defined scenarios and instances.

5.1   Analysis of the Results

The results obtained by VND*+ACO were compared with those achieved by [10] and [12]. [10] uses a combination of VND and Scatter Search (VND+SS) and [12] uses a combination of VND and ACO (VND+ACO). Table 2 presents the results with lower α values (0%, 20%, 40%) and Table 3 shown those with higher α values (60%, 80%, 100%), where "CC" denotes the total construction

---

[1] https://www.dropbox.com/sh/f188599zra37s4f/AABoV7GeiRoti_6GAc-aASfEa?
dl=0.
[2] http://www.gurobi.com.

cost at the upper level, and "CV" and "EV" represent the costs of the routes of CVs and EVs, respectively, and "Total" denotes the sum of the EVs and CVs routing costs. The results in Tables 2 and 3 for the VND+SS approach refer to our implementation of the algorithm presented in [10] while the results of VND+ACO are those presented in [12].

According to the results presented in Tables 2 and 3, one can notice that the proposed approach performed better than the other methods in all the scenarios evaluated in each of the instances at upper level. This shows that VND*+ACO can find solutions with a lower construction cost and meet the constraint (percentage of electric vehicles in the fleet). In some cases the cost is 0 as the construction of stations is not necessary. The good results obtained by the proposal is due to the efficiency of routing at the lower level, which can obtain solutions with more efficient routes with fewer visits to charging stations and with a larger number of customers visited per route, making the number of vehicles used equal or close to the minimum necessary for each instance.

Table 2. Results for lower alpha values. The best values are in boldface.

Inst.	CI:CE	Costs	VND+SS			VND+ACO			VND*+ACO		
			0%	20%	40%	0%	20%	40%	0%	20%	40%
X-n351-k40	4:2	CC	0	0	0	0	0	0	0	0	0
		Total	121227.5	121227.5	121227.5	119277.36	119277.36	119277.36	**118994.73**	**118994.73**	**118994.73**
		CV	67636.2	67636.2	67636.2	**65476.48**	**65476.48**	**65476.48**	66434.92	66434.92	66434.92
		EV	53591.3	53591.3	53591.3	53800.88	53800.88	53800.88	**52559.08**	**52559.08**	**52559.08**
	4:1	CC	0	0	0	0	0	0	0	0	0
		Total	97820.45	97820.45	97820.45	81097.12	81097.12	81097.12	**80983.25**	**80983.25**	**80983.25**
		CV	68401.5	68401.5	68401.5	64047.96	64047.96	64047.96	**60058.00**	**60058.00**	**60058.00**
		EV	29418.95	29418.95	29418.95	**17049.16**	**17049.16**	**17049.16**	20925.25	20925.25	20925.25
	4:0.5	CC	0	0	0	0	0	0	0	0	0
		Total	78068.85	78068.85	78068.85	**74751.07**	**74751.07**	**74751.07**	76562.43	76562.43	76562.43
		CV	62657.2	62657.2	62657.2	60480.72	60480.72	60480.72	**60020.32**	**60020.32**	**60020.32**
		EV	15411.65	15411.65	15411.65	**14270.35**	**14270.35**	**14270.35**	14730.75	14730.75	14730.75
X-n685-k75	4:2	CC	0	0	0	0	0	0	0	0	0
		Total	306779.12	306779.12	306779.12	296885.2	296885.2	296885.2	**288685.53**	**288685.53**	**288685.53**
		CV	108317.92	108317.92	108317.92	122318.72	122318.72	122318.72	**107998.32**	**107998.32**	**107998.32**
		EV	198461.2	198461.2	198461.2	**174566.48**	**174566.48**	**174566.48**	180687.21	180687.21	180687.21
	4:1	CC	0	0	0	0	0	0	0	0	0
		Total	205826.25	205826.25	205826.25	188803.55	188803.55	188803.55	**172177.22**	**172177.22**	**172177.22**
		CV	102965.96	102965.96	102965.96	**85081.56**	**85081.56**	**85081.56**	93302.92	93302.92	93302.92
		EV	102860.29	102860.29	102860.29	103721.99	103721.99	103721.99	**78874.3**	**78874.3**	**78874.3**
	4:0.5	CC	0	0	0	0	0	0	0	0	0
		Total	153498.16	153498.16	153498.16	**144645.67**	**144645.67**	**144645.67**	145579.85	145579.85	145579.85
		CV	100235.6	100235.6	100235.6	92470.24	92470.24	92470.24	94567.46	94567.46	94567.46
		EV	53262.56	53262.56	53262.56	52175.44	52175.44	52175.44	**51012.39**	**51012.39**	**51012.39**
X-n819-k171	4:2	CC	0	0	0	0	0	0	0	0	0
		Total	303710.18	303710.18	303710.18	303289.56	303289.56	303289.56	**302998.24**	**302998.24**	**302998.24**
		CV	110064.84	110064.84	110064.84	**109361.64**	**109361.64**	**109361.64**	109586.37	109586.37	109586.37
		EV	193645.34	193645.34	193645.34	193927.92	193927.92	193927.92	**193411.87**	**193411.87**	**193411.87**
	4:1	CC	0	0	0	0	0	0	0	0	0
		Total	380465.64	380465.64	380465.64	375027.16	375027.16	375027.16	**335929.55**	**335929.55**	**335929.55**
		CV	247633.28	247633.28	247633.28	**241530.6**	**241530.6**	**241530.6**	293437.31	293437.31	293437.31
		EV	132830.36	132830.36	132830.36	133496.56	133496.56	133496.56	**42492.24**	**42492.24**	**42492.24**
	4:0.5	CC	0	0	0	0	0	0	0	0	0
		Total	154528.39	154528.39	154528.39	**143821.53**	**143821.53**	**143821.53**	147322.11	147322.11	147322.11
		CV	102149.08	102149.08	102149.08	**94647.76**	**94647.76**	**94647.76**	96334.50	96334.50	96334.50
		EV	52379.31	52379.31	52379.31	**49173.77**	**49173.77**	**49173.77**	50987.61	50987.61	50987.61

Table 3. Results for higher alpha values. The best values are in boldface.

Inst.	Cl:CE	Costs	VND+SS			VND+ACO			VND*+ACO		
			60%	80%	100%	60%	80%	100%	60%	80%	100%
X-n351-k40	4:2	CC	133800	133800	172100	0	0	145000	0	0	92300
		Total	86563.06	86563.06	86276.5	119277.36	119277.36	**83033.62**	118354.67	118354.67	**81357.96**
		CV	**15979.88**	**15979.88**	0	65476.48	65476.48	0	66768.24	66768.24	0
		EV	70583.18	70583.18	86276.5	53800.88	53800.88	83033.62	**51586.43**	**51586.43**	81357.96
	4:1	CC	0	155700	190600	0	0	127900	0	0	92300
		Total	97820.45	44445.91	43818.24	81097.12	**41740.33**	**41740.33**	80983.25	93435.85	60731.82
		CV	68401.5	5181.0	0	64047.96	**25934.96**	0	60058	59631.28	0
		EV	29418.95	39264.91	43818.24	**17049.16**	**35411.98**	41740.33	20925.25	3804.57	60731.82
	4:0.5	CC	167300	167300	192800	0	0	157600	0	0	92300
		Total	23492.49	**23492.49**	21333.4	74751.07	74751.07	20284.98	72463.45	72463.45	20186.09
		CV	**3410.96**	**3410.96**	0	60480.72	60480.72	0	58467.21	58467.21	0
		EV	20081.53	20081.53	21333.4	14270.35	14270.35	20284.98	**13996.24**	**13996.24**	20186.09
X-n685-k75	4:2	CC	0	345100	373900	0	324000	355400	0	0	278900
		Total	306779.12	**235045.78**	237586.98	296885.2	240129.24	215119.34	302709.24	238987.09	213939.17
		CV	**108317.92**	**26125.12**	0	122318.72	40873.08	0	123135.84	42994.41	0
		EV	198461.2	208920.66	237586.98	174566.48	199256.16	215119.34	179573.4	**195992.68**	213939.17
	4:1	CC	0	335600	364200	0	319200	301900	0	0	278900
		Total	205826.25	**135837.41**	109575.83	188803.55	157900.61	**103479.76**	172177.22	172177.22	143257.96
		CV	102965.96	**33591.0**	0	**85081.56**	65375.04	0	93302.92	93302.92	0
		EV	102860.29	102246.41	109575.83	103721.99	92525.57	**103479.76**	**78874.3**	**78874.3**	143257.96
	4:0.5	CC	0	329000	329000	0	319600	342700	0	0	278900
		Total	153498.16	121928.65	53550.99	144645.67	77917.63	**53542.16**	144645.67	**75170.14**	55215.92
		CV	100235.6	74573.2	0	92470.24	28835.44	0	92470.24	**27984.01**	0
		EV	53262.56	47355.45	53550.99	52175.44	49082.19	**53542.16**	52175.44	**47186.13**	55215.92
X-n819-k171	4:2	CC	362100	396700	396700	0	0	361600	0	0	154700
		Total	**242433.7**	**223826.7**	223826.7	303289.56	303289.56	215369.42	306232.79	303289.56	213567.96
		CV	110064.84	42814.4	0	109361.64	0	0	**108456.78**	0	0
		EV	199619.3	223826.7	223826.7	**193927.92**	193927.92	215369.42	197776.01	193927.92	213567.96
	4:1	CC	0	398300	398300	0	353200	353200	0	154700	154700
		Total	380465.64	182828.75	182828.75	375027.16	**181582.28**	**181582.28**	335929.55	221430.72	221430.72
		CV	247633.28	0	0	**241530.6**	0	0	293437.31	0	0
		EV	132830.36	182828.75	182828.75	133496.56	**181582.28**	**181582.28**	42492.24	221430.72	221430.72
	4:0.5	CC	0	370500	359200	0	0	359200	0	0	154700
		Total	154528.39	70094.67	56534.93	143821.53	143821.53	52415.51	**142975.88**	**142975.88**	51984.45
		CV	102149.08	18183.48	0	**94647.76**	0	0	96711.56	96711.56	0
		EV	52379.31	51911.19	56534.93	49173.77	52415.51	52415.51	**46264.32**	**46264.32**	51984.45

The proposal is simpler and more effective. It is also possible to note that the proposed approach performs better at the lower level in some of the scenarios, however in some cases the use of CVs is greater by the proposed approach. This is due to the decrease in the number of charging stations available at the top level and, in some cases, there is no station available which makes it necessary to use more CVs to serve all customers. Consequently, there is also an increase in total cost, since the operational cost of CVs is higher than that of EVs.

In general, the proposed approach presents good results in all tested scenarios, being superior in all at the upper level and most of them at the lower level, showing the efficiency of the proposed approach when compared with the approaches present in the literature. Although in some scenarios the total operational cost of the proposed approach is higher due to the greater use of combustion vehicles, the proposed approach manages to be better in other scenarios and always achieve at least the minimum percentage of electric vehicles required by the government in the fleet, showing that the proposed approach manages to solve the proposed bilevel model efficiently and with good results.

6   Concluding Remarks and Future Works

We proposed here a combination of VND and ACO for solving a bilevel optimization problem concerning the allocation of charging stations at the upper
level and vehicle routing at the lower level. A VND from the literature was modified, making it simpler and faster with the modification of the neighborhood
structures used in the search for new allocations of charging stations.

The proposed approach was compared with two other approaches found in the
literature using three benchmark instances from [11]. For comparison, six values
were used for the required percentage of electric vehicles (α), ranging from 0% to
100% and three different proportions were also used for vehicle operating costs
(CI: CE), which are 4:1, 4:2 and 4:0.5, totaling 36 scenarios. The analysis of the
results shows that the proposed approach achieves good results and surpasses
those presented by the literature in several of the scenarios tested at the lower
level and in all at the upper level. The proposed approach allocates the charging
stations more efficiently, reducing the government's construction cost while the
minimum required percentage of electric vehicles in the fleet is not violated.

As future work, we intend to apply the proposed approach to other instances.
Also, improving the bilevel model with the simultaneous use of the charging
infrastructure by more than one company is an interesting research avenue.

References

1. Balinski, M.L., Quandt, R.E.: On an integer program for a delivery problem. Oper.
   Res. **12**(2), 300–304 (1964)
2. Dorigo, M., Gambardella, L.M.: Ant colony system: a cooperative learning approach to the traveling salesman problem. IEEE Trans. Evol. Comput. **1**(1), 53–66
   (1997)
3. Duarte, A., Sánchez-Oro, J., Mladenović, N., Todosijević, R.: Variable neighborhood search. In: Burke, E.K., Kendall, G. (eds.) Search Methodologies, pp. 341–
   367. Springer, Boston (2018). https://doi.org/10.1007/0-387-28356-0_8
4. Gambardella, L.M., Dorigo, M.: Ant-q: a reinforcement learning approach to the
   traveling salesman problem. In: Prieditis, A., Russell, S. (eds.) Machine Learning
   Proceedings 1995, pp. 252–260. Morgan Kaufmann, San Francisco (1995)
5. Guo, F., Yang, J., Lu, J.: The battery charging station location problem: impact
   of users' range anxiety and distance convenience. Transp. Res. Part E: Logistics
   Transp. Rev. **114**, 1–18 (2018)
6. He, J., Yang, H., Tang, T.Q., Huang, H.J.: An optimal charging station location
   model with the consideration of electric vehicle's driving range. Transp. Res. Part
   C Emerging Technol. **86**, 641–654 (2018)
7. In, J., Bell, J.E.: Alternative fuel infrastructure and customer location impacts on
   fleet mix and vehicle routing. Transp. J. **54**(4), 409–437 (2015)
8. Kruskal, W.H., Wallis, W.A.: Use of ranks in one-criterion variance analysis. J.
   Am. Stat. Assoc. **47**(260), 583–621 (1952)
9. Leite, M.R., Bernandino, H.S., Gonçalves, L.B., Soares, S.: Optimization in Multi-
   level Green Transportation Problems with Electrical Vehicles, chap. 9, pp. 203–228.
   John Wiley & Sons, Ltd. (2019)

10. Li, Y., Zhang, P., Wu, Y.: Public recharging infrastructure location strategy for promoting electric vehicles: a bi-level programming approach. J. Clean. Prod. **172**, 2720–2734 (2018)
11. Mavrovouniotis, M., Menelaou, C., Timotheou, S., Panayiotou, C., Ellinas, G., Polycarpou, M.: Benchmark set for the IEEE WCCI-2020 competition on evolutionary computation for the electric vehicle routing problem. Technical report, University of Cyprus, Dept. of Electrical and Computer Engineering, Nicosia, Cyprus (2020)
12. de Oliveira Leite, M.R.C., Bernardino, H.S., Gonçalves, L.B.: A variable neighborhood descent with ant colony optimization to solve a bilevel problem with station location and vehicle routing (2021)
13. Sttzle, T., Hoos, H.H.: Improving the ant system: A detailed report on the max-min ant system. Technical report, Technical University of Darmstadt, Darmstadt, Germany (1996), AIDA 96–12
14. Stützle, T., Hoos, H.H.: Max-min ant system and local search for the traveling salesman problem. In: Proceedings of 1997 IEEE International Conference on Evolutionary Computation (ICEC 1997), vol. 16, pp. 309–314, May 1997
15. Xiong, Y., Gan, J., An, B., Miao, C., Bazzan, A.L.C.: Optimal electric vehicle fast charging station placement based on game theoretical framework. IEEE Trans. Intell. Transp. Syst. **19**(8), 2493–2504 (2018)
16. Yang, J., Sun, H.: Battery swap station location-routing problem with capacitated electric vehicles. Comput. Oper. Res. **55**(C), 217–232 (2015)
17. Zhang, G., Yang, H., Dong, J.: Electric vehicle charging stations layout research based on bi-level programming. In: International Conference on Electric Utility Deregulation and Restructuring and Power Technologies (DRPT), pp. 609–614 (2015)
18. Zheng, H., He, X., Li, Y., Peeta, S.: Traffic equilibrium and charging facility locations for electric vehicles. Netw. Spat. Econ. **17**(2), 435–457 (2017)

Artificial Life and Evolutionary Algorithms

Genetic Programming for Feature Extraction in Motor Imagery Brain-Computer Interface

Gabriel Henrique de Souza[1]([✉]) [iD], Heder Soares Bernardino[1] [iD],
Alex Borges Vieira[1] [iD], and Helio José Corrêa Barbosa[1,2] [iD]

[1] Universidade Federal de Juiz de Fora, Juiz de Fora, Brazil
gabriel.souza@engenharia.ufjf.br
[2] Laboratório Nacional de Computação Científica, Petrópolis, Brazil

Abstract. Brain-Computer Interfaces (BCI) have many applications, such as motor rehabilitation in post-stroke situations. In most cases, the BCI captures brain signals and classifies them to determine a command in an electronic system. Given a large number of BCI applications, many models are improving signal classification accuracy. For instance, we proposed the Single Electrode Energy (SEE) to classify motor imagery and won the Clinical BCI Challenge 2020. However, this method uses a single electrode to extract the brain characteristics. Here, we propose a new method, named single feature genetic programming, to create a function for feature extraction in BCI. Our approach assembles more than one electrode in a unique characteristic value. Moreover, we tested the use of a bank of band-pass filter and wavelet to preprocess the data. We evaluate the new approach using the Clinical BCI Challenge 2020 data and compare it with SEE. Our results show that When Single Feature Genetic Programming has a kappa coefficient 18% better than SEE.

Keywords: Evolutionary computation · Stroke rehabilitation ·
Clinical BCI challenge · Brain-machine interface

1 Introduction

One can use non-invasive Brain-Computer Interfaces (BCI) to control electronic devices without surgical procedures. One of the most common types of equipment for non-invasive BCI is the Electroencephalogram (EEG) [13]. EEG-BCI can have many applications such as robot control [2,3], smart home control [6,11], and stroke motor rehabilitation [5,16,17].

EEG-BCI classifies brain signals using an EEG and its output determines a command in an electronic system. One can also use signal preprocessing and

The authors thank the financial support provided by CAPES, CNPq (grants 312337/2017-5, 312682/2018-2, 311206/2018-2, and 451203/2019-4), FAPEMIG, FAPESP, and UFJF.

© Springer Nature Switzerland AG 2021
G. Marreiros et al. (Eds.): EPIA 2021, LNAI 12981, pp. 227–238, 2021.
https://doi.org/10.1007/978-3-030-86230-5_18

feature extraction to enhance signal classification. Due to the wide range of BCI applications, there are several methods to classify EEG signals nowadays. For example, the Sigmoid Single Electrode Energy (Sigmoid-SEE) [1] was proposed to classify motor imagery. Sigmoid-SEE includes a band-pass filter, a function of feature extraction, and a logistic classifier.

Periodically, there are competitions worldwide to assess the quality of the different classification techniques. For example, the Clinical BCI Challenge[1] competition, held during the 2020 IEEE World Congress on Computational Intelligence, aimed at classifying imagined movements in patients with stroke. The Sigmoid-SEE method achieved the best results of the competition.

During the last years, Genetic Programming (GP) has been used in many procedures related to brain signals classification, such as feature extraction [7, 12] and classification [15]. Its main advantage is the ability to create different functions or classifiers. Also, GP allows for a specific structure for each subject.

We propose here the single feature genetic programming (SFGP) to create a function for feature extraction in BCI. Sigmoid-SEE uses only a single electrode, but GP can use many electrodes to extract the characteristic value. The proposed SFGP method uses the characteristic value function of Sigmoid-SEE in all electrodes and combines these values in a new one using GP. SFGP finds out the characteristic value function during the training phase. Then, it assembles more than one electrode in a unique characteristic value. Moreover, the proposed method considers a bank of band-pass filter and wavelet to preprocess the data.

We evaluate the proposed SFGP using the Clinical BCI Challenge 2020 dataset. When compared to SEE, the Single Feature Genetic Programming has a kappa coefficient 18% better.

2   The Clinical Brain-Computer Interface Dataset

The Clinical Brain-Computer interface was part of the IEEE World Congress on Computational Intelligence in 2020. The competition's goal was to classify the data collected from 10 hemiparetic stroke patients during a motor imagery task. We only use eight subjects' datasets, because two subjects did not have their labels available, and then we cannot use their data for supervised learning.

Two data files are available to each one of the first eight subjects. The first file contains the training set, and the second file contains the data that the competitors should classify. Only the first file of each subject has its available classes, and for this reason, we only use this file in this work.

Figure 1 presents the experiment sequence of activities. The task performed during the first phase (first file) is: (i) the subject sees the phrase "get ready" for 3 s; (ii) after 2 s from the beginning, a beep sounds; and (ii) after 3 s from the beginning, a cue in form of a hand is shown on the screen for 5 s while the subject imagined the movement indicated [1]. The movements indicated on the screen were "left motor attempt" and "right motor attempt". Each file has 80

---

[1] https://sites.google.com/view/bci-comp-wcci/.

executions of this sequence of activities (40 of each class). The experiments use the window from 3 to 4.5 s.

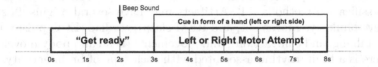

Fig. 1. Description of the activity sequence of the experiment.

The data were collected with electroencephalogram equipment and electrodes positioned in F3, FC3, C3, CP3, P3, FCz, CPz, F4, FC4, C4, CP4, and P4 according to the international 10-10 system. One can see the position of these electrodes on the head in Fig. 2. The equipment was configured for 512 Hz acquisition, a band-pass filter between 0.1 and 100 Hz, and 50 Hz notch filter.

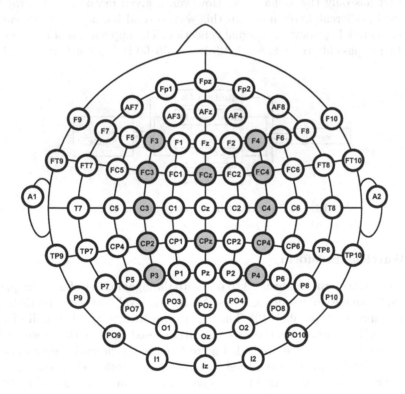

Fig. 2. International 10-10 system. The electrodes provided on the dataset are highlighted in green. (Color figure online)

3　Data Preprocessing

The signal collected by the electroencephalogram has several types of artifacts. These artifacts are a problem both for interpretation by a clinician and for automatic classification methods [14]. Artifacts may have several origins [9] such as ocular (eye blink, eye movement, and REM sleep), cardiac (ECG pulse), muscle (sniffing, talking, and contraction), and movements (head and body movements). Also, there is a brain rhythm associated with each type of brain activity. These rhythms can be divided into frequency bands such as delta, theta, alpha, beta, and Gamma [9]. The preprocessing of the signal allows for the proper signal separation according to the band of interest, such as alpha rhythms (8–13 Hz). Preprocessing techniques include the band-pass filter and the wavelet transform.

3.1　Band-Pass Filter

The band-pass filter maintains only the frequencies within a certain range. For example, the application of a band-pass filter between 8 and 13 Hz generates a signal that has only the alpha wave. However, a given motor activity, may be expressed in different frequencies. In this way, several band-pass filters can be applied in parallel, generating a signal collection. The application of a filter bank with 14 band-pass filters (4–8, 8–12, 12–16, ..., 56–60 Hz) is illustrated in Fig. 3.

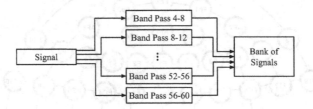

Fig. 3. Bank of 14 band-pass filters in Hz.

3.2　Wavelet Transform

The wavelet transform can be used to separate the signal into different frequency windows. It can have one or more levels. At the first level, low-pass and high-pass filters are applied in parallel [12]. The signals are then reduced to half of their original size. The signal from the low-pass filter is used again in the process when there are more levels to be applied. Figure 4 shows a schematic representation of a 3-level wavelet. In this case, there are four output series, three coming from high pass filters (D1, D2, and D3) and one coming from a low pass filter (A3).

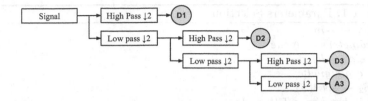

Fig. 4. 3-level wavelet. Each low and high band pass splits the band domain by half.

4 Sigmoid Single Electrode Energy

The Sigmoid Single Electrode Energy (Sigmoid-SEE) is the method used by the winners of the Clinical BCI Challenge 2020 [1]. This method has been designed to classify the signal from a single electrode into two motor imagery classes. The classification is divided into three stages: (i) application of a band-pass filter (optional); (ii) extraction of the characteristic value; and (iii) classification using logistic regression.

In the first stage, a band-pass filter is applied to the signal as $Z = G_{a,b}(S)$, where $S \in \mathbb{R}^N$ is the electrode signal and $G_{a,b}(\cdot)$ is the a-b Hz band-pass filter. In the second step, the characteristic value of the filtered signal is extracted as

$$f = F(Z) = \log \left(\sum_i^N \frac{|Z_i|}{N} \right). \tag{1}$$

Finally, the characteristic value is used to decide which class the signal belongs to as

$$p = \frac{1}{1 + e^{-(\alpha + \beta f)}} \tag{2}$$

where p is the probability that the signal belongs to the first class, and α and β are parameters of the model. The parameters α and β are estimated by the Limited-memory Broyden–Fletcher–Goldfarb–Shanno algorithm (LBFGS) [4] using the training data. Usually, a threshold equals to 0.5 is adopted to separate the classes, i.e., the signal is classified as belonging to class 1 when $p < 0.5$, and class 2, otherwise. In this work, classes 1 and 2 are the movement imagination of left and right hands, respectively.

For this method, one must define the electrode to be used and the band-pass filter window. A parameter selection approach is described in Algorithm 1, where values for both parameters are analyzed. In this procedure, the training set S is split into two: (i) $S1$: data used for calculating α and β (regression); and (ii) $S2$: data for choosing the parameters (validation).

5 Genetic Programming

Genetic Programming (GP) [10] is an evolutionary algorithm for generating programs in an arbitrary language. A program can represent a function, a classifier,

---

Algorithm 1. Parameters Selection

$best\_value \leftarrow -inf$
$best\_parameters \leftarrow None$
for e in *electrodes* **do**
$\quad S \leftarrow eeg\_signal[e]$
$\quad S_1, S_2 \leftarrow split(S)$
$\quad$ **for** j in *band_pass_filters* **do**
$\quad\quad$ see $\leftarrow$ fit(S_1, e, j)
$\quad\quad$ **if** fitness(see, S_2) > $best\_value$ **then**
$\quad\quad\quad best\_parameters \leftarrow [e, j]$
$\quad\quad$ **end if**
$\quad$ **end for**
end for
return $best\_parameters$

---

a circuit design, and others artifacts. Here, GP is used to generate a function that minimizes an error $E : \mathbb{R}^Q \to \mathbb{R}$. GP is composed of the following steps: (i) creation of an initial population; (ii) generating of a new population from the current one; (iii) evaluation and choice of individuals for the next generation; and (iv) verification of the stopping criterion. The process returns to step (ii) while the stop criterion is not met. We used a maximum number of generations to limit the search. One can see the pseudocode of the GP in Algorithm 2.

Algorithm 2. Pseudocode of Genetic Programming.

Create the initial population
Evaluate the initial population
while stop criterion is not met **do**
$\quad$ Select and copy the parents
$\quad$ Apply crossover and mutation
$\quad$ Evaluate the new individuals
$\quad$ Select the individuals for next generation and save the best individual
end while
return Best individual

The tree structure is a common way of representing the candidate functions in GP. This structure was chosen here to facilitate the manipulation of the population. The operators are the internal nodes of the trees, and the variables are found in the leaves. One can see an example of a function represented by a tree in Fig. 5. The population is initialized with trees randomly generated with depth smaller than or equals to 3.

New individuals are created on each generation applying crossover and mutation operators on selected individuals. The individuals to be recombined are chosen here using a tournament selection. Each pair of selected parents are recombined using One-Point Crossover, which swaps a randomly chosen subtree from

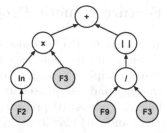

Fig. 5. Function $V(F) = (\ln(F2) \times F3) + |F9/F3|$ represented using a tree.

the parents. Figure 6 illustrates the crossover. The crossover is applied with a probability θ. Otherwise, the selected individuals are cloned. In both cases, the mutation is applied to the resulting individuals with a probability γ. The uniform mutation was chosen to bring variability to the individuals. This mutation operator replaces a subtree of the individual with another randomly generated subtree.

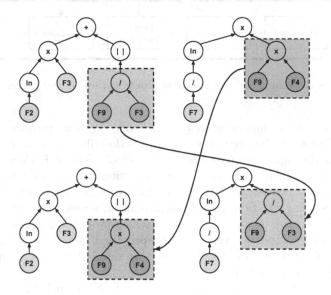

Fig. 6. Illustration of one-point crossover.

The individual with the best fitness value in each generation is stored during the evolution and, thus, the best solution so far can be obtained. These steps are repeated until a stopping criteria is met.

6   Proposed Single Feature Genetic Programming

The single feature genetic programming (SFGP) also uses only one character-istic value, like Sigmoid-SEE. Sigmoid-SEE only uses data from one electrode. However, SFGP uses data from multiple electrodes to generate its characteris-tic value. One can see the training and use phases in Fig. 7. The use phase of SFGP is performed by the following steps: (i) preprocessing; (ii) application of the characteristic value function; and (iii) classification using logistic regression. The training phase is performed by: (i) preprocessing; (ii) function fit (GP); and (iii) classifier training.

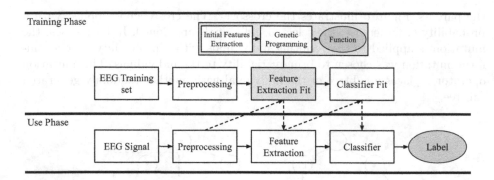

Fig. 7. Steps of training and use phases of single feature genetic programming.

One can use many functions as preprocessing, such as wavelet and band-pass filter. Therefore, the preprocessing step is described as $Z = P(S)$, where $S \in \mathbb{R}^{E \times N}$ is the signal composed by N values of a set of E electrodes. $P(\cdot)$ is the preprocessing function (an identity function can be used when no fil-ter/transformation is used), $Z \in \mathbb{R}^{M \times N}$ is the processed signal, and M depends on the preprocessing function used. Bandpass filter, wavelet, and identity func-tion are analyzed experimentally as preprocessing procedures in Sect. 7.

The initial characteristics values in the proposed model are obtained with the function of extraction of the characteristic value of SEE. This function is applied to each Z signal as in Eq. 1.

The characteristic value v is computed as $v = V(F)$, with $V : \mathbb{R}^M \to \mathbb{R}$ being found by the Genetic Programming technique. The error function used here is the cross-entropy function.

Finally, the classification of the characteristic value is performed using Eq. 2 in the same way as in the SEE model.

7   Computational Experiments

We compare the performances of SFGP and Sigmoid-SEE using the Clinical BCI Challenge data [1]. We choose the Sigmoid-SEE because it has shown the best overall score in this competition. The preprocessing step is optional in SFGP, and one can use any of the functions presented in Sect. 3. Pre-processing is indicated at the beginning of the algorithm's name, as follows: (i) SFGP: without preprocessing; (ii) FBSFGP: with band-pass filter bank; and (iii) WLSFGP: with wavelet transform.

The experiments were carried out using 5×5-fold cross-validation for each proposed method. The 5×5-fold cross-validation is composed of 5 balanced fold cross-validation. A stratified k-fold is used to guarantee that each fold contains the same number of trials for each class as the dataset is balanced.

The fitness function used in this optimization was cross-entropy. The non–parametric Kruskal-Wallis statistical test and the Dunn post-hoc test were used to verify the existence of a statistically significant difference between the results obtained by the methods. We implemented SFGP using the DEAP library [8], and the developed code is available[2].

We used Sigmoid-SEE as a means of comparison with other methods. When choosing the electrodes, we considered all 12 electrodes for optimization. The band-pass filters in the optimization were $[a, b] \ \forall \ a, b \ \in [4, 8, 12, ..., 60]$. Also, we considered situations without a band-pass filter. In Algorithm 1, the data are split into 3/4 for training and 1/4 for validation to prevent overfitting.

SFGP, WLSFGP, and FBSFGP were run with 100 generations and 300 individuals. The probabilities of crossover and mutation were $\theta = 0.85$, $\gamma = 0.15$. For the internal nodes of the tree in GP, 8 operators are considered: $a \times b$, $a + b$, $\ln(|a|)$, a/b, $a - b$, $|a|$, $-(a)$, and $\sqrt{|a|}$, where a and b are operands. The operators $\ln(|a|)$ and a/b are protected, as a in the first operator and b in the second one must be different from zero. These protected operators return zero when an invalid parameter is used. The max depth is 3 for the initial population and 2 for the subtrees used in mutation. All operators in GP are not allowed to generate individuals with a depth larger than 6. We performed the tournaments in GP with three individuals. The filter bank used in FBSFGP consists of filters in the following form: $[a, b] \ \forall \ a, b \ \in [4, 8, 12, ..., 60]$. We performed the wavelet transform used in WLSFGP with five levels (6 created waves per electrode).

One can see the kappa values of the experiments and the result of the statistical significance test in Table 1. We separated the results per subject due to the physiological difference between them. One can observe that SFGP and WLSFGP presented results better than those found by Sigmoid-SEE in most cases. The average of the subjects' median kappa for the SFGP was 0.609. This represents an improvement of 18% when compared to the Sigmoid-SEE. For WLSFGP, the improvement was 15% when compared to Sigmoid-SEE. The statistical test presents a statistically significant difference between the methods (p-value < 0.05) in comparing Sigmoid-SEE and SGFP or WLSFGP. The FBS-FGP approach obtained a value 9% smaller than Sigmoid-SEE but without a statistically significant difference.

The SFGP method obtained the highest median kappa value among all the methods evaluated for five of the eight subjects (1, 2, 3, 7, and 8). Also, the SFGP

---

[2] https://github.com/ghdesouza/bci.

Table 1. Median Kappa values of 5×5-fold cross-validation (80 trials for each subject). The best value is shown in **boldface** and $^{+\,+}$ indicates the results that are different with statistical significance (p-value < 0.05) when compared with Sigmoid-SEE.

Subject	Sigmoid-SEE	SFGP	FBSFGP	WLSFGP
1	0.625	$^+$**0.875**$^+$	0.500	0.625
2	**1.000**	**1.000**	$^+$0.500$^+$	**1.000**
3	0.250	$^+$**0.625**$^+$	$^+$0.500$^+$	$^+$**0.625**$^+$
4	0.250	0.500	$^+$**0.625**$^+$	0.375
5	0.375	0.250	$^+$**0.500**$^+$	0.375
6	**0.500**	0.375	**0.500**	**0.500**
7	**0.750**	**0.750**	$^+$0.250$^+$	**0.750**
8	0.375	$^+$**0.500**$^+$	0.375	$^+$**0.500**$^+$
Average	0.516	$^+$**0.609**$^+$	0.469	$^+$**0.594**$^+$

was statistically better than other methods in 3 of 8 subjects (1, 3, and 7). No subject gets a lower result than Sigmoid-SEE with p-value < 0.05, despite SFGP showing a lower kappa value for subjects 5 and 6 when compared to Sigmoid-SEE. In addition, SFGP presented a result 18% better than Sigmoid-SEE. From the results obtained by SFGP, one can conclude that the introduction of the new electrode and GP improves the classification result when compared to the use of a single electrode.

The proposed FBSFGP presented the best kappa value for 3 of the eight subjects (4, 5, and 6) and obtained a lower value than Sigmoid-SEE in 3 other ones (1, 2, and 7). Overall, Sigmoid-SEE obtained an average of the median kappas among subjects equal to 0.516 while FBSFGP reached a value equal to 0.469. This difference occurs mainly due to the results found for the second subject. For the second subject, there is a 50% drop in the median kappa found. A characteristic that may have caused this difference is the fact that FBSFGP does not consider frequencies greater 60 Hz in this experiment. The FBSFGP approach is the only method used here, in which this frequency range was not considered and was the only method that did not obtain a median kappa of 1,000 for subject 2. The inclusion of this frequency range in the initial characteristics of FBSFGP may cause an improvement in the results of this subject. In general, it is concluded that FBSFGP has a larger variation among the subjects in the experiments. That can be caused by the dimension size of the FBSFGP, and it is more detailed in Sect. 7.1.

The proposed WLSFGP has shown the best kappa value for five of the eight subjects (2, 3, 6, 7, and 8) with a $p - value < 0.05$ for 2 of them (7 and 8) when compared with Sigmoid-SEE. Also, it was the only model that obtained kappa values larger than or equal to those found by Sigmoid-SEE in all eight subjects. The WLSFGP proved to be the method with the lowest deviation between the subjects and obtains an average kappa of 0.594.

Comparing the results of SFGP and WLSFGP, one can notice that SFGP performed better in 2 subjects (1 and 4), WLSFGP obtained better results in two other subjects (5 and 6), and they obtained similar results for the remaining four subjects. The average of the results obtained by SFGP is 1.03% better than the average of those achieved by WLSFGP. Overall, SFGP presented the best results among all the methods considered here.

7.1 Dimension of the Problem

Each preprocessing technique creates a different number of initial characteristics. For SFGP, which does not have a preprocessing step, there are 12 initial characteristics to be used by GP. For FBSFGP, 14 initial characteristics are created per electrode, totaling 168 characteristics. For WLSFGP, six initial characteristics are created for each electrode, totaling 72 characteristics. The same computational resources were given to all methods (100 iterations with a population of 300 individuals). However, given the difference in the size of the search space for each method, the choice of the best model among them may vary with the use of a higher or lower computational budget.

The change in the maximum depth of GP individuals also influences the size of the search space. Thus, this is a parameter that affects the quality of the solution. The use of a smaller depth reduces the number of possible solutions, making it possible to exclude solutions with good results. On the other hand, the use of larger depths increases the search space. It causes a larger computational budget required to find the solutions.

8   Conclusions

EEG-BCI can be used for post-stroke rehabilitation. For this, it must be able to classify the EEG signal correctly. We proposed the single feature genetic programming (SFGP) model. We compared its efficiency with that of the Sigmoid Single Electrode Energy (Sigmoid-SEE). This comparison was made using data from the Clinical BCI Challenge, a competition won with SEE in 2020.

The use of Genetic Programming to create a function for extraction of characteristics for the Brain-Machine Interface presented good results for the Motor Imagery classification problem. It showed an 18% improvement in the kappa coefficient when compared to Sigmoid Single Electrode Energy (Sigmoid-SEE). At first, the use of the Filter Bank did not significantly improve Single Feature Genetic Programming (SFGP). The use of Wavelet for preprocessing with SFGP proved to be quite consistent, being better or equal to Sigmoid-SEE for all subjects. With the use of Wavelet or the filter bank, the number of possible models (search space) increases. Experiments with a larger computational budget tend to improve the results, as the GP search had not stabilized considering the computational budget allowed for the GP techniques. In addition, the inclusion of spatial filters may bring improvements to the process.

References

1. Andreu-Perez, Chowdhury, A., Prasad, M.: Clinical BCI Challenge-WCCI2020. https://sites.google.com/view/bci-comp-wcci/
2. Barbosa, A.O., Achanccaray, D.R., Meggiolaro, M.A.: Activation of a mobile robot through a brain computer interface. In: IEEE International Conference on Robotics and Automation, pp. 4815–4821 (2010)
3. Bell, C.J., Shenoy, P., Chalodhorn, R., Rao, R.P.: Control of a humanoid robot by a noninvasive brain-computer interface in humans. J. Neural Eng. **5**(2), 214 (2008)
4. Broyden, C.G.: The convergence of a class of double-rank minimization algorithms 1. general considerations. IMA J. Appl. Math. **6**(1), 76–90 (1970)
5. Buch, E., et al.: Think to move: a neuromagnetic brain-computer interface (BCI) system for chronic stroke. Stroke **39**(3), 910–917 (2008)
6. Edlinger, G., Holzner, C., Guger, C.: A hybrid brain-computer interface for smart home control. In: Jacko, J.A. (ed.) HCI 2011. A hybrid brain-computer interface for smart home control, vol. 6762, pp. 417–426. Springer, Heidelberg (2011). https://doi.org/10.1007/978-3-642-21605-3_46
7. Emigdio, Z., Trujillo, L., Legrand, P., Faïta-Aïnseba, F., et al.: Eeg feature extraction using genetic programming for the classification of mental states. Algorithms **13**(9), 221 (2020)
8. Fortin, F.A., De Rainville, F.M., Gardner, M.A., Parizeau, M., Gagné, C.: DEAP: evolutionary algorithms made easy. J. Mach. Learn. Res. **13**, 2171–2175 (2012)
9. Islam, M.K., Rastegarnia, A., Yang, Z.: Methods for artifact detection and removal from scalp EEG: a review. Neurophysiologie Clinique/Clin. Neurophysiol. **46**(4–5), 287–305 (2016)
10. Koza, J.R.: Genetic Programming: On the Programming of Computers by Means of Natural Selection. The MIT Press (1992)
11. Lee, W.T., Nisar, H., Malik, A.S., Yeap, K.H.: A brain computer interface for smart home control. In: IEEE International Symposium on Consumer Electronics, pp. 35–36 (2013)
12. Miranda, Í.M., Aranha, C., Ladeira, M.: Classification of EEG signals using genetic programming for feature construction. In: Proceedings of the Genetic and Evolutionary Computation Conference, pp. 1275–1283 (2019)
13. Nicolas-Alonso, L.F., Gomez-Gil, J.: Brain computer interfaces, a review. Sensors **12**(2), 1211–1279 (2012)
14. O'Regan, S., Faul, S., Marnane, W.: Automatic detection of EEG artefacts arising from head movements using EEG and gyroscope signals. Med. Eng. Phys. **35**(7), 867–874 (2013)
15. Poli, R., Salvaris, M., Cinel, C.: Evolution of a brain-computer interface mouse via genetic programming. In: Silva, S., Foster, J.A., Nicolau, M., Machado, P., Giacobini, M. (eds.) EuroGP 2011. LNCS, vol. 6621, pp. 203–214. Springer, Heidelberg (2011). https://doi.org/10.1007/978-3-642-20407-4_18
16. Silvoni, S., et al.: Brain-computer interface in stroke: a review of progress. Clin. EEG Neurosci. **42**(4), 245–252 (2011)
17. de Souza, G.H., Bernardino, H.S., Vieira, A.B., Barbosa, H.J.C.: Differential evolution based spatial filter optimization for brain-computer interface. In: Proceedings of the ACM Genetic and Evolutionary Computation Conference, pp. 1165–1173 (2019)

FERMAT: Feature Engineering with Grammatical Evolution

Mariana Monteiro[1], Nuno Lourenço[1]([✉]), and Francisco B. Pereira[1,2]

[1] CISUC – Centre for Informatics and Systems, University of Coimbra, Coimbra, Portugal
{naml,xico}@dei.uc.pt
[2] Polytechnic Institute of Coimbra, ISEC, Coimbra, Portugal

Abstract. Feature engineering is a key step in a machine learning study. We propose FERMAT, a grammatical evolution framework for the automatic discovery of an optimal set of engineered features, with enhanced ability to characterize data. The framework contains a grammar specifying the original features and possible operations that can be applied to data. The optimization process searches for a transformation strategy to apply to the original dataset, aiming at creating a novel characterization composed by a combination of original and engineered attributes. FERMAT was applied to two real-world drug development datasets and results reveal that the framework is able to craft novel representations for data that foster the predictive ability of tree-based regression models.

Keywords: Feature engineering · Grammatical evolution · Drug development

1 Introduction

When building a supervised Machine Learning (ML) pipeline, an accurate characterization of data is crucial. In fact, it is widely recognized that the accuracy and generalization ability of a computational model is deeply rooted in the quality of the data that was used to train it.

Data pre-processing is an important step before training a model. In simple terms, it usually starts by data cleaning, aiming at removing/correcting erroneous or missing information. Afterwards, the data is transformed to enhance its quality and discriminating ability. Arguably, the most important transformation is feature engineering, a process that seeks for the best representation for data. These methods may focus on determining the optimal subset of the original attributes, or, conversely, may promote the creation of novel descriptors. Principal Component Analysis is a classical approach to create novel attributes resulting from a linear combination of the original features [9], but, over the years, many ideas have been proposed to build new predictors based on the application of mathematical operations or other transformations to the original data.

© Springer Nature Switzerland AG 2021
G. Marreiros et al. (Eds.): EPIA 2021, LNAI 12981, pp. 239–251, 2021.
https://doi.org/10.1007/978-3-030-86230-5_19

Manual feature engineering works by carefully choosing features and crafting how they can be combined into novel attributes, with enhanced information gain. However, this requires specialized knowledge and has proven to be a subjective task, error-prone and time consuming. This situation justifies the appearance of automated tools, removing the burden of feature engineering from the data analysis team [2,10,15,16,18].

In this work we propose FERMAT, an automated Genetic Programming (GP) feature engineering tool. GP comprises a suite of stochastic optimization algorithms, able to build variable length solutions, composed by a combination of pre-determined building blocks. FERMAT is based on Structured Grammatical Evolution (SGE) [11,12], a grammar-based GP variant that effectively addresses low-locality and redundancy issues. At start, it considers the original features and a suite of mathematical operations as building blocks. Then, it searches for the optimal data transformation that fosters the development of robust supervised models. Throughout the process, it simultaneously selects a subset of original features and combines them, engineering novel attributes with enhanced discriminating power.

FERMAT was applied to two pharmacokinetics problems, the prediction of human oral bioavailability (%F) and plasma-protein binding levels (%PPB) [1]. Results show that the framework is effective in discovering strategies that can build enhanced representations of data, composed by a combination of original and engineered features. The transformed datasets increase the predictive ability of regression models in the two problems addressed in this study.

The remainder of the paper is organized as follows: in Sect. 2 we review some related work and briefly describe SGE. Section 3 comprises a detailed presentation of FERMAT. In Sect. 4 we provide some experimental settings and describe the two datasets, whereas in Sect. 5 we present and analyse the results obtained in the experiments. Finally, in Sect. 6 we gather the main conclusions and suggest possible directions for future work.

2   Related Work

When developing ML approaches, practitioners usually follow a predefined number of steps that can be described as a pipeline, namely (i) data acquisition and data cleaning, (ii) feature selection and engineering, (iii) selection and tuning of an adequate ML model and (iv) training and validation. Even though they are sequentially described, these steps are interconnected: e.g., model selection has to consider the type of features engineered in step (ii). In this pipeline, even expert ML practitioners, with deep insight into model development and training, are faced with the tedious and somehow subjective task of selecting and engineering the most informative attributes.

2.1   AutoML - Automated Machine Learning

AutoML aims at overcoming the challenges caused by the large number of decisions that have to be made before deploying a model. The most common form of AutoML is finding the optimal hyper-parameters for a ML model, with grid search [8] and Bayesian optimization [19] being some of the most widely used methods. However, the end game for AutoML is to fully automate the entire pipeline: from the data pre-processing to model deployment, without the need of human intervention.

In recent years, we have witnessed an increase on AutoML frameworks, such as the Auto-WEKA [20], Auto-Sklearn [6], Tree-based Pipeline Optimization Tool (TPOT) [16], Resilient Classification Pipeline Evolution (RECIPE) [18] and AutoML-DSGE [2]. These last 3 are of particular interest to this work, since they are based on evolutionary approaches. TPOT is a GP-based framework that searches both for the best primitives (e.g., data pre-processors or ML models) that will compose the pipeline and also for the best settings for each of those primitives. RECIPE and AutoML-DSGE are grammar-based GP methods that generate pipelines of fixed size. The adoption of grammars simplifies the definition of the search space and the inclusion of domain-knowledge. Additionally, these frameworks can be easily extended by including new production rules in the grammar. RECIPE uses a Context-Free Grammar GP (CFG-GP) [23], whereas AutoML-DSGE relies on SGE [11].

The success of ML models is largely dependent on the features that characterize a given problem. As such, being able to select and/or engineer adequate features is of the utmost importance [3]. However, this is a hard task, requiring specialized knowledge [7]. In [10], the authors argue that evolutionary methods, such as GP, can be used to automatically engineer features, thus alleviating the burden of the human developer. Along this line, there are a few works that rely on GP to create an engineered feature set [14, 15].

2.2 Structured Grammatical Evolution

SGE is a GE variant that allows for the evolution of programs in an arbitrary language using a Context-Free Grammar. A grammar is defined by a quadruple $G = (N, T, S, P)$, where N and T are non-empty sets of non-terminal and terminal symbols, respectively, S is an element of N called axiom, and P is a set of productions $A ::= \alpha$, with $A \in N$ and $\alpha \in (N \cup T)^*$, where N and T are disjoint sets. An example of a grammar is depicted in Fig. 1.

The distinctive characteristic of SGE is related to how each solution is encoded, which allows for a one-to-one mapping between each genotype and a non-terminal symbol of the grammar. This genotypic organization ensures that a change in one of the genes does not affect other non-terminals, narrowing the modifications that can occur at the phenotypic level, thereby improving the locality of the representation (consult [11, 12] for additional details).

2.3 Drug Development

In drug development, the main goal of pharmaceutical companies is to create compounds with the least possible noxious effects. To minimize the expensive *in vivo* assays to select candidate compounds, studies in pharmacokinetics are

$$N = \{< start >, < expr >, < term >, < op >\}$$

$$T = \{+, -, /, *, (,), x_1, 0.5\}$$

$$S = \{< start >\}$$

And the production set P is:

```
<start> ::= <expr><op><expr>    (0)
        |   <expr>              (1)

<expr>  ::= <value><op><value>      (0)
        |   (<value><op><value>)    (1)

<op>    ::= +   (0)
        |   -   (1)
        |   /   (2)
        |   *   (3)

<value> ::= x₁   (0)
        |   0.5  (1)
```

Fig. 1. Example of a grammar that creates polynomial expressions. N is the set of non-terminal symbols, T is the set of terminal symbols and S is the grammar's axiom. Adapted from [11].

adopting *in silico* strategies. Over the last few years, ML algorithms are increasingly being used in all stages of drug discovery and development [21]. Besides being simpler and cheaper, ML has proven to be efficient in lowering the development process failure rate.

In a study from 2006, Archetti *et al.* [1] proposed the application of GP methods to the prediction of oral bioavailability, median oral lethal dose and plasma-protein binding levels. The results obtained where encouraging, revealing that this optimization method compared well with the more traditional ML approaches. Later, in [4,22], the authors explored the application of geometric semantic evolutionary approaches to tackle the same problems, obtaining even better results. Finally, Dick *et al.* performed an overall comparison on the GP-based and ML methods used, until the time of writing, on the oral bioavailability data [5]. The work highlighted that the best method for this dataset was a regression Random Forest.

3   FERMAT

In this section we detail FERMAT, our SGE-based approach for feature selection and engineering. Figure 2 presents a general overview of the framework. The first step, Data Preparation, randomly splits the input data in two different datasets. The first one, Search, is used to guide the feature engineering process. The Test dataset is kept aside, and will be used to evaluate the generalization ability of the solutions proposed by FERMAT.

The second step, Search, is the most important component of the framework. It relies on SGE to search for an enhanced feature characterization of the problem being addressed. During evolution, FERMAT will use a grammar composed

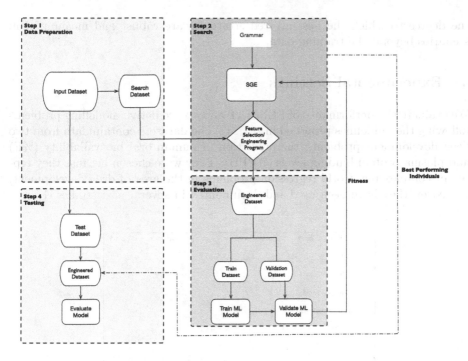

Fig. 2. FERMAT: proposed architecture

by derivations that consider original features and a set of possible operations. The grammar will guide the creation of feature engineering programs. These solutions can then be used to obtain novel engineered feature sets by selecting and combining original attributes. Using a grammar promotes a simple and flexible definition of the search space.

Step 3 comprises the Evaluation phase and is directly connected to the Search step, since all individuals generated by SGE require a fitness assignment. In the proposed framework, evaluation is straightforward. Each individual is applied to the Search Dataset to perform feature selection and/or engineering. This leads to the creation of a new *Engineered* dataset, where its attributes are composed by a mixture of original and engineered features (according to the rules specified in the program encoded in the individual). The engineered dataset is divided into Train and Validation. The first one is used to train a supervised ML model that aims to solve the problem at hand. After training, the Validation dataset is used to estimate the predictive ability of the model. The value obtained in validation is returned to the SGE as feedback to assign the quality of the solution.

The last step, Testing, is performed when the evolution of solutions is completed and it consists in estimating the generalization ability of the best programs discovered. To prevent contamination of information, generalization is assessed on a subset of the data never seen before. This is a crucial step, as it estimates the degree to which the best evolved strategies are robust and meaningful in scenarios beyond the training data.

4   Experimental Settings

We evaluate the performance of FERMAT on two predictive modelling problems following the guidelines proposed in [13, 24]. The datasets contain data from two drug development problems: the prediction of human oral bioavailability (%F) and plasma-protein binding levels (%PPB). They were chosen because they represent complex real-world regression problems in the area of drug development. Moreover, they have been used and documented in several past studies [1, 4].

$$N = \{< start >, < featureset >, < expr >, < features >, < op >\}$$

$$T = \{+, -, /, *, (,), x_1, ..., x_{max\_features}\}$$

$$S = \{< start >\}$$

And the production set P is:

```
<start> ::= <featureset>

<featureset> ::= < expr > | < expr >,< expr >
              |   [...]
              |   < expr >, [...] , < expr >

<expr> ::= <expr><op><expr>
        |   (<expr><op><expr>)
        |   < features >

<op> ::= +
      |   -
      |   /
      |   *

<features> ::= x_1 | x_2 | ... | x_{max_features}
```

Fig. 3. Grammar used to evolve programs for feature selection and engineering. The non-terminal <featureset> corresponds to the resulting feature engineering program, and <features> represents all the original features available in the dataset.

The BIO dataset contains data about the fraction of an administered drug that goes to the systemic blood circulation, reaching its therapeutic site of action. It is composed by 359 drugs, each one characterized by a set of 241 molecular descriptors and 1 target %F. The goal is to predict the value of %F, using the molecular descriptors of each drug. In the second dataset, the aim is to predict the protein-plasma binding level, %PPB. This value corresponds to the percentage of a drug's initial dose that reaches the blood circulation and binds to plasma proteins. It comprises 131 drugs, each one characterized by 625 molecular structures, depicted as SMILES codes (Simplified Molecular Input Line Entry Specification), and 1 target representing the known %PPB value for that entry.

Initially, each dataset is randomly split in two: 80% of the samples are selected to the Search Dataset, whereas the remaining 20% are put apart to the Test dataset (Step 1 from Fig. 2). The parameter settings used by the SGE were selected according to the guidelines proposed in [11]: {Number of Runs: 30; Population Size: 1000; Generations: 50; Crossover Rate: 0.9; Mutation Rate: 0.1; Elistim: 10%; Tournament Selection with size 3; Maximum Tree Depth: 10}.

The grammar used by FERMAT is depicted in Fig. 3, where the axiom is the <start> symbol. The non-terminal <featureset> consists on the set of original and transformed features that will be derived. When the derivation ends, it will correspond to a program that can be used to perform feature engineering on the Search dataset. To avoid any bias, the maximal cardinality of this set is identical to the number of original features. Finally, <features> represents all the original features that describe the problem being addressed.

Each generated engineering strategy is evaluated according to the procedure described in Sect. 3. A regression decision tree is trained using the default hyper-parameters proposed by sklearn[1] and then it is applied to the validation subset. Its performance is estimated using the Root Mean Squared Error (RMSE) and this value is returned to the SGE to be used as the quality of the solution.

At the end of the optimization, FERMAT delivers a set of strategies to engineer attributes. Performance validation is done in the final Testing step. Here, we rely on the engineered datasets to build regression Random Forest (RF) models, using the default configuration proposed by sklearn[2].

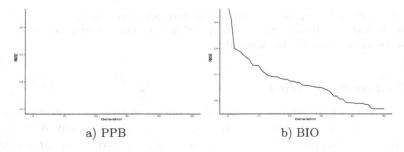

a) PPB   b) BIO

Fig. 4. Evolution of the RMSE. Values are averages of the best individual found in each of the 30 runs. Panels a) and b) refer, respectively, to the PPB and BIO datasets.

5   Results

The evolution of the best individual RMSE over the 50 generations performed by SGE is displayed in Fig. 4. Panel a) displays the results obtained with the PPB dataset, whereas panel b) contains the outcomes of the BIO dataset. Results presented are averages of the 30 runs. A brief overview of the curves reveals that FERMAT is gradually discovering better solutions, proposing strategies

---

[1] DecisionTreeRegressor configuration details.

[2] RandomForestRegressor configuration details.

that select and engineer features with enhanced predictive ability. The trend is similar for both problems addressed in this study, suggesting that the framework is robust and might be applied to different supervised scenarios.

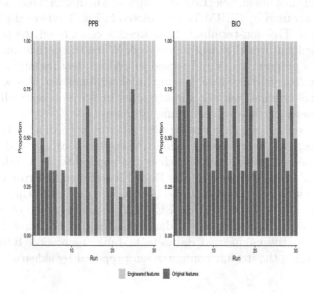

Fig. 5. Proportion of original and engineered features occurring in the best solutions obtained by the SGE framework in each one of the 30 runs. Results are presented for the two datasets considered in this study.

5.1   Feature Engineering

We analysed the best solutions obtained in each run to investigate the composition of the discovered attributes. In concrete, we aim to verify if FERMAT concentrates on feature selection by choosing the best features from the original set, while discarding redundant or irrelevant information, or, on the contrary, promotes the creation of novel attributes.

The 2 charts from Fig. 5 illustrate the proportion of attributes from the best solutions discovered by FERMAT that are either original or engineered features. We present the distribution for the 30 runs in each of the 2 problems. There is a natural diversity of combinations, but, in general, the best solutions tend to combine both original and engineered features. Solutions comprising only a subset of original features are extremely rare. On the other hand, in the PPB dataset, several best solutions are composed exclusively by engineered features. The diversity of strategies confirms that the framework is able to discover novel descriptions of the instances, suited for the situation being addressed.

Going one step further, we examined if the engineered features appearing in the best solutions are a simple combination of original attributes, or, on the contrary, are the result of successive combinations performed by the SGE (*i.e.*, if the resulting features are obtained by combining already engineered attributes).

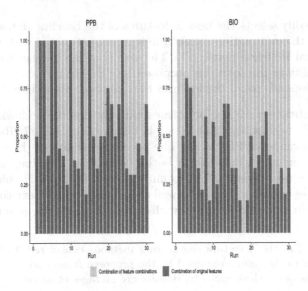

Fig. 6. Proportion of engineered features that result from combinations of original attributes or from the merging of already engineered features. Results are presented individually for the best individual appearing in each one of the 30 runs and for the two datasets considered in this study.

Figure 6 highlights this distribution. A brief perusal of the results confirms that engineered features can be either a simple merging of two original attributes or the result of several hierarchical combinations. The same general trend is visible in both problems. As a general rule, these results show that the dataset characterization promoted by FERMAT is the result of a combination of original attributes with engineered features exhibiting a variable hierarchical degree.

5.2   Absolute Performance

The absolute performance of the strategies created by FERMAT can be assessed with the Test dataset. The best transformation strategies were applied to the original features describing the test dataset and then the modified descriptors were used to build RF models. The RMSE obtained corresponds the predictive ability of the approach. In the tests we consider the best strategy found in each of the 30 runs. To estimate how effective this absolute performance is, we compare the results obtained by FERMAT with 3 other variants. Each one of them adopts an alternative strategy to select the attributes that best describe the datasets:

FERMAT refers to the features obtained by applying the engineering strategies proposed by the framework.

FERMAT-Sel simplifies the solutions proposed by FERMAT by discarding engineered features. The final result just comprises original features, thus being similar to a straightforward feature selection method.

Best-Sel greedily selects the best K features of the baseline dataset. Selection is based on the information gain of the features, estimated with the RReliefF (Regressional ReliefF) metric [17]. The size K of the dataset corresponds to the cardinality of the solutions proposed by FERMAT.
Baseline corresponds to all the features that compose the original datasets.

Thirty repetitions were also performed with the described alternatives[3]. The average RMSE obtained in all the tests is displayed in Table 1. Results clearly show the effectiveness of FERMAT. The predictive ability of the solutions proposed by the framework outperform both the original Baseline, as well as the two feature selection variants. This confirms that FERMAT is able to perform both an effective feature selection, as well as an engineering of existing attributes aiming at creating novel descriptors with enhanced predictive potential.

Table 1. RMSE of the 4 feature engineering methods considered. Column labelled FERMAT refers to the results obtained by the proposed framework. Consult the text for details on the other three variants. Results are averages of 30 runs.

Dataset	FERMAT	FERMAT-Sel	Best-Sel	Baseline
PPB	23.01	36.96	40.13	39.52
BIO	25.68	27.37	36.39	34.18

We applied the non-parametric Kruskal-Wallis test to confirm the statistical significance of the results ($\alpha = 0.05$). The test was applied to the results obtained in each dataset. When statistical differences were detected at the group level, we used the Mann-Whitney post-hoc test, with Bonferroni correction, to investigate all pairwise comparisons. In both datasets, FERMAT statistically outperformed the other three variants. In the PPB dataset, no other significant differences were identified. As for the BIO dataset, the FERMAT-Sel variant outperformed both the Best-Sel and Baseline variants.

6   Conclusions

In this paper we proposed FERMAT, an SGE-based framework for feature engineering. This approach departs from the original dataset for a given problem and creates strategies to select and combine attributes leading to an enhanced characterization of the instances. The transformations are guided by a grammar specifying both the original features and the transformation operations.

FERMAT was applied to two real-world predictive pharmacokinetics and drug development problems. Results show that the framework is effective in discovering strategies to enhance the characterization of datasets. In both problems,

---

[3] Some of the best solutions are composed just by engineered features. In these runs, it is not possible to design a solution for FERMAT-Sel. Accordingly, the number of repetitions for this variant is lower than for the remaining alternatives.

FERMAT was able to propose a novel set of features that help regression models to achieve a lower predictive error, when compared to the original baseline representation and to two simple feature selection methods. A detailed analysis revealed that the crafted datasets comprise a combination of original and novel features, confirming that the automatic framework is able to simultaneously perform feature selection and feature engineering.

Given the reported results, FERMAT proved to be a reliable alternative to the tedious and subjective task of feature selection and engineering. The framework architecture allows its application to a wide range of supervised problems. In the near future, we plan to confirm its effectiveness on regression and classification problems from different domains. We will also investigate the possibility to include additional components to the grammar, aiming at verifying if the novel ingredients further enhance the discriminating ability of the engineered datasets. Examples of components that could be considered include domain specific knowledge regarding the problem being addressed or tools that allow for a detailed exploratory data analysis.

Acknowledgments. This work was funded by FEDER funds through the Operational Programme Competitiveness Factors- COMPETE and national funds by FCT - Foundation for Science and Technology (POCI-01-0145-FEDER-029297, CISUC - UID/CEC/ 00326/2020) and within the scope of the project A4A: Audiology for All (CENTRO-01-0247-FEDER-047083) financed by the Operational Program for Competitiveness and Internationalisation of PORTUGAL 2020 through the European Regional Development Fund.

References

1. Archetti, F., Lanzeni, S., Messina, E., Vanneschi, L.: Genetic programming for computational pharmacokinetics in drug discovery and development. Genetic Program. Evolvable Mach. **8**(4), 413–432 (2007)
2. Assunção, F., Lourenço, N., Ribeiro, B., Machado, P.: Evolution of Scikit-learn pipelines with dynamic structured grammatical evolution. In: Castillo, P.A., Jiménez Laredo, J.L., Fernández de Vega, F. (eds.) EvoApplications 2020. LNCS, vol. 12104, pp. 530–545. Springer, Cham (2020). https://doi.org/10.1007/978-3-030-43722-0_34
3. Bengio, Y., Courville, A., Vincent, P.: Representation learning: a review and new perspectives. IEEE Trans. Pattern Anal. Mach. Intell. **35**(8), 1798–1828 (2013)
4. Castelli, M., Manzoni, L., Vanneschi, L.: An efficient genetic programming system with geometric semantic operators and its application to human oral bioavailability prediction. arXiv preprint arXiv:1208.2437 (2012)
5. Dick, G., Rimoni, A.P., Whigham, P.A.: A re-examination of the use of genetic programming on the oral bioavailability problem. In: Proceedings of the 2015 Annual Conference on Genetic and Evolutionary Computation, pp. 1015–1022 (2015)
6. Feurer, M., Klein, A., Eggensperger, K., Springenberg, J.T., Blum, M., Hutter, F.: Auto-sklearn: efficient and robust automated machine learning. In: Hutter, F., Kotthoff, L., Vanschoren, J. (eds.) Automated Machine Learning. TSSCML, pp. 113–134. Springer, Cham (2019). https://doi.org/10.1007/978-3-030-05318-5_6

7. Foster, D., Karloff, H., Thaler, J.: Variable selection is hard. In: Conference on Learning Theory, pp. 696–709. PMLR (2015)
8. Jiménez, Á.B., Lázaro, J.L., Dorronsoro, J.R.: Finding optimal model parameters by deterministic and annealed focused grid search. Neurocomputing **72**(13–15), 2824–2832 (2009)
9. Jolliffe, I.T.: Principal components in regression analysis. In: Principal component analysis, pp. 129–155. Springer, New York (1986). https://doi.org/10.1007/978-1-4757-1904-8_8
10. La Cava, W., Moore, J.: A general feature engineering wrapper for machine learning using ε-Lexicase survival. In: McDermott, J., Castelli, M., Sekanina, L., Haasdijk, E., García-Sánchez, P. (eds.) EuroGP 2017. LNCS, vol. 10196, pp. 80–95. Springer, Cham (2017). https://doi.org/10.1007/978-3-319-55696-3_6
11. Lourenço, N., Assunção, F., Pereira, F.B., Costa, E., Machado, P.: Structured grammatical evolution: a dynamic approach. In: Ryan, C., O'Neill, M., Collins, J.J. (eds.) Handbook of Grammatical Evolution, pp. 137–161. Springer, Cham (2018). https://doi.org/10.1007/978-3-319-78717-6_6
12. Lourenço, N., Pereira, F.B., Costa, E.: Unveiling the properties of structured grammatical evolution. Genetic Program. Evolvable Mach. **17**(3), 251–289 (2016). https://doi.org/10.1007/s10710-015-9262-4
13. McDermott, J., et al.: Genetic programming needs better benchmarks. In: Proceedings of the 14th Annual Conference on Genetic and Evolutionary Computation, pp. 791–798 (2012)
14. Muharram, M.A., Smith, G.D.: The effect of evolved attributes on classification algorithms. In: Gedeon, T.T.D., Fung, L.C.C. (eds.) AI 2003. LNCS (LNAI), vol. 2903, pp. 933–941. Springer, Heidelberg (2003). https://doi.org/10.1007/978-3-540-24581-0_80
15. Muharram, M.A., Smith, G.D.: Evolutionary feature construction using information gain and Gini index. In: Keijzer, M., O'Reilly, U.-M., Lucas, S., Costa, E., Soule, T. (eds.) EuroGP 2004. LNCS, vol. 3003, pp. 379–388. Springer, Heidelberg (2004). https://doi.org/10.1007/978-3-540-24650-3_36
16. Olson, R.S., Moore, J.H.: TPOT: a tree-based pipeline optimization tool for automating machine learning. In: Hutter, F., Kotthoff, L., Vanschoren, J. (eds.) Automated Machine Learning. TSSCML, pp. 151–160. Springer, Cham (2019). https://doi.org/10.1007/978-3-030-05318-5_8
17. Robnik-Šikonja, M., Kononenko, I.: Theoretical and empirical analysis of ReliefF and RReliefF. Mach. Learn. **53**(1), 23–69 (2003)
18. de Sá, A.G.C., Pinto, W.J.G.S., Oliveira, L.O.V.B., Pappa, G.L.: RECIPE: a grammar-based framework for automatically evolving classification pipelines. In: McDermott, J., Castelli, M., Sekanina, L., Haasdijk, E., García-Sánchez, P. (eds.) EuroGP 2017. LNCS, vol. 10196, pp. 246–261. Springer, Cham (2017). https://doi.org/10.1007/978-3-319-55696-3_16
19. Shahriari, B., Swersky, K., Wang, Z., Adams, R.P., De Freitas, N.: Taking the human out of the loop: a review of Bayesian optimization. Proc. IEEE **104**(1), 148–175 (2015)
20. Thornton, C., Hutter, F., Hoos, H.H., Leyton-Brown, K.: Auto-WEKA: combined selection and hyperparameter optimization of classification algorithms. In: Proceedings of the 19th ACM SIGKDD International Conference on Knowledge Discovery and Data Mining, pp. 847–855 (2013)
21. Vamathevan, J., et al.: Applications of machine learning in drug discovery and development. Nat. Rev. Drug Discov. **18**(1), 463–477 (2019). https://doi.org/10.1038/s41573-019-0024-5

22. Vanneschi, L., Silva, S., Castelli, M., Manzoni, L.: Geometric semantic genetic programming for real life applications. In: Riolo, R., Moore, J.H., Kotanchek, M. (eds.) Genetic Programming Theory and Practice XI. GEC, pp. 191–209. Springer, New York (2014). https://doi.org/10.1007/978-1-4939-0375-7_11
23. Whigham, P.A., et al.: Grammatically-based genetic programming. In: Proceedings of the Workshop on Genetic Programming: from Theory to Real-World Applications, vol. 16, pp. 33–41 (1995)
24. White, D.R., et al.: Better GP benchmarks: community survey results and proposals. Genetic Program. Evolvable Mach. **14**(1), 3–29 (2013)

Ambient Intelligence and Affective Environments

A Reputation Score Proposal for Online Video Platforms

David Garcia-Retuerta[1]([✉]) [iD], Roberto Casado-Vara[1] [iD],
Diego Valdeolmillos[1] [iD], and Juan M. Corchado[1,2] [iD]

[1] University of Salamanca, Patio de Escuelas Menores, 37008 Salamanca, Spain
`dvid@usal.es`
[2] Air Institute, IoT Digital Innovation Hub (Spain), Calle Segunda 4,
37188 Salamanca, Spain
`https://bisite.usal.es/en/group/team/David`

Abstract. Boosting the engagement of users and content creators is of critical importance for online video platforms. The success of an online platform can be defined by the number of active users and the amount of time they spend on it, as they will probably take the best advantage of all the available functionalities and spread the word about it. The goal of this research is to propose effective algorithms to create a reputation system capable of generating trust among users and increasing engagement. The algorithm rewards users and content creators for their actions, in addition to motivating them through considerable increases in their reputation during their initial iterations with the platform. The growth is modelled by three basic reputation functions: exponential, logarithmic and lineal mappings. The Noixion TV platform has been used to develop the use case and its data has been gathered to analyse the behaviour of the proposed system.

Keywords: Reputation system · Trust score · Video platform

1 Introduction

In 2020, over four and a half billion people world-wide were considered active Internet users, accounting for almost 60% of the total population [1]. Such a vast

This research has been supported by the project "Intelligent and sustainable mobility supported by multi-agent systems and edge computing (InEDGE-Mobility): Towards Sustainable Intelligent Mobility: Blockchain-based framework for IoT Security", Reference: RTI2018-095390-B-C32, financed by the Spanish Ministry of Science, Innovation and Universities (MCIU), the State Research Agency (AEI) and the European Regional Development Fund (FEDER). The research was partially supported by the project "Computación cuántica, virtualización de red, edge computing y registro distribuido para la inteligencia artificial del futuro", Reference: CCTT3/20/SA/0001, financed by Institute for Business Competitiveness of Castilla y León, and the European Regional Development Fund (FEDER).

© Springer Nature Switzerland AG 2021
G. Marreiros et al. (Eds.): EPIA 2021, LNAI 12981, pp. 255–265, 2021.
https://doi.org/10.1007/978-3-030-86230-5_20

penetration rate has changed many aspects of our daily lives, revolutionising human interaction and dramatically changing several markets [2]. Personal communication is now possible among individuals, regardless of time and location, social interaction has extended from the regional to the global scope (resulting in a mixing of traditional cultures as people with similar ideas meet each other online), new forms of expression, such as memes, have emerged and corporate communications greatly benefit from tools such as email, video-conferences and online sales.

One of the many revolutions brought about by the Internet refers to trust. Online marketplaces like BlaBlaCar, eBay and Vinted have developed methods of transmitting trust online, which makes it possible for millions of users to share rides, purchase items and sell clothes. Digital trust allows peers who have never interacted before to trust each other instantly and to start collaborating thanks to innovative tools [4]. One of the most used methods of representing how much a user can be trusted is by defining a reputation score.

Several metrics can be used to measure the extent to which users are trustworthy. Early e-commerce companies based their models on "trust authorities" and "agreement frameworks" (*centralised trust*) [5]. However, the growth of the collaborative economy has shifted the focus towards *distributed trust* [6]. This modern concept of trust is based on reviews, profile pictures, social network connections, past activity and so on. All of these measurements can then be combined to assign a score to each user.

As reputation scores became more common, system developers added a new function to them—increasing user engagement. Members of the community gain greater influence on a platform through their actions and their fidelity. The goal of this work is to achieve both tasks successfully, providing users with rewards when they use the app as well as information about the trust they can have in each other [8].

This article is structured as follows: Sect. 2 provides a review of the state of the art on reputation systems and the most important proposals. Section 3 describes the methodology and materials, which are then used in Sect. 4 to carry out the use case. Lastly, Sect. 5 presents the conclusions drawn from the conducted study.

2   Related Works

Several reputation systems have been proposed over the last years. Most of them are rather context-dependent. This is due to the fact that each solution is designed for a specific use case and, in most cases, a generic solution is not sufficient. Applying specific proposals to different problems undermines performance and, frequently, adaptations of past solutions are required when the use case is new. Nevertheless, most context-dependent proposals found in the state of the art perform better than the more generic ones [9].

Academic and commercial proposals researching reputation algorithms are presented below.

2.1 Commercial Proposals

At the moment, commercial applications have developed the most important reputation algorithms. In general, the commercial proposals are mainly focused on directly assigning a reputation to their users within a commercial system. The particular systems which stand out are of: Amazon, Waze, BlaBlaCar, Research-Gate and TripAdvisor.

A review of the state of the art shows that all such existing reputation algorithm proposals focus mainly on their context, disregarding context-free metrics [10]. Only a small number of desirable features of the reputation systems can be found, while most of the system implementation is greatly related to each use case [7]. Thus, specific algorithms need to be designed to obtain good results on new systems. In order to achieve this, it is very important to pinpoint the factor and its weight in determining the reliability of a user, making it account for the suitable amount of the created reputation score. For example, eBay shows the number of positive, neutral and negative comments a seller received in total; as well as in the past 7 days, past month and past 6 months. It also shows the total number of votes, the percentage of positive votes, the number of 5-stars ratings related to "the article suits its description", "communication", "delivery time" and "delivery cost". From this it can be gathered that this reputation system is hardly extrapolable to other platforms besides online commerce.

Similarly, it is necessary to analyse how the occurrence of a parameter evolves over time. Commercial platforms are characterised by not being static, as the users and the platform evolve over time. Therefore, the set metrics must be updated regularly to avoid inaccuracies.

In addition, most of the commercial proposals inform the user of the highest reputation level which they can achieve. This motivates them to achieve it and understand how much their actions are contributing to their score.

2.2 Academic Proposals

Two of the most outstanding scientific proposals found in the state of the art are PageRank and EigenTrust.

PageRank is the most popular of the reputation systems, developed in 1999 [11]. It was used by Google in its early years to sort the websites presented in the search engine in a mechanical and objective way. In 2006 another algorithm was proposed for reputation management in P2P (*peer-to-peer*) networks, it was EigenTrust [12]. It was used to decrease the impact of malignant peers on the performance of a P2P system.

Furthermore, PathTrust [9] is a system based on the graph of relationships created among the participants of virtual organisations. This proposal is based on the previous two systems (PageRank and EigenTrust), and seems particularly well suited to resist the major threats within a large system.

Each of the algorithms' strengths and weaknesses are described below:

- **PageRank**: One of the main advantages of this algorithm is that it usually converges in about 45 iterations. Moreover, its scaling factor is approximately linear in $\log(n)$, it uses graph theory to link pages, and its computational process can be personalized. In addition, PageRank is able to predict backlinks and to estimate web traffic.

Nevertheless, random walks on graphs cause some problems. Users are assumed to behave as a "random surfer", which may not be the case in a real-world scenario. That is to say, the algorithm considers that the user randomly gets bored and shifts to a new random webpage, even though it is known that many users make use of the same websites in a loop without ever getting bored.

- **EigenTrust**: It became one of the most successful and better know reputation system. It has successfully solved a wide variety of problems common to P2P networks, which can be considered to be the context of the algorithm. However, its main downside is its strong reliance on a group of pre-trusted peers. As a result, the nodes distributed around them (setting them as a centre) and some peers obtain low scores despite behaving optimally [13].

- **PathTrust**: It makes use of trust relationships between the participants, and it is meant to be resistant against false positive feedback. In an attack involving false positive feedback, a set of users cooperate to increase their own reputation by publishing false positive reviews for each other. To prevent that situation, the exchange would only increase the trust relationship between those users, not affecting the path from an honest inquirer to the attacker, resulting in no reputational change from the point of view of honest inquirers. Moreover, this graph-based approach also has the ability to form long-term relationships.

However, this approach has some significant drawbacks. As the trust between two users is based on their past iterations with each other, the first-day reputation is considered unreliable. Users leave ratings for each other after each iteration, when such ratings accumulate, they create a relationship value. Furthermore, a single user can be responsible for a big change in reputation with a single positive or negative review.

3   The Platform

This study aims to create the theoretical basis for a future reputation score systems. Several configurations have been tested and subtle modifications carried have been made until the resulting system was fully created. In order to test the proposed ideas, the video platform noixion.io was used as a model.

Noixion (Fig. 1) is a decentralized media platform for sharing videos, streaming, creating TV channels, etc. It is powered by TRON, a blockchain-based decentralized operating system based on a cryptocurrency native to the system, known as TRX. Its design is very similar to Ethereum, with which it has no fundamental differences.

Fig. 1. Interface of the used video platform (Noixion).

The methodology used was to analyse the potential flaws of every proposal, and overcome them so that the system is resilient and resistant. When all the postulated tests were passed, several inputs were fed into the system and the results were analysed. If the reputation of the synthetic data was considered abnormal, further iterations were carried out.

4 Implementation

The algorithm which assigns a reputation score to each user is described in this section. The goal is to obtain a mapping function which receives the most important characteristics of a user as input, and transforms them into an appropriate score value. The reputation system rewards users for their activity and for the positive feedback from other users. Prizes are awarded in the form of TRX20 tokens (NoixionDividends, hereafter ND) every 24 h. The greater the reputation achieved during the previous 24 h, the greater the number of awarded tokens. To calculate the reputation of each user, a series of relevant factors have been identified, each of which has been given a certain weight within the algorithm. A summary of the work flow is shown in Fig. 2.

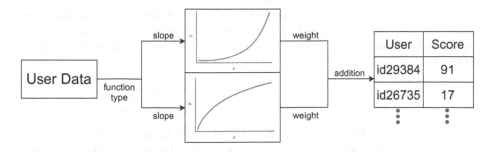

Fig. 2. Workflow on the reputation system of the platform. The user data is retrieved, the corresponding mathematical function applied to each of the variables, and their addition assigns a reputation score to each of the users.

The section is divided as follows: firstly, the factors that are considered essential when determining reputation are outlined. Afterwards, the mapping functions are described and each of the obtained metrics is described. Then, the metrics defined for the use case are presented.

4.1 Essential Factors

Several factors can be considered to measure how trust-worthy a user is. However, a balance must be reached between considering too many inputs (obtaining a high accuracy) and considering too little inputs (obtaining a high performance). In this case, the most essential factors have been selected, therefore obtaining a good equilibrium between performance, accuracy and explicability.

The following factors have been selected:

- **Logins**. Accessing the platform on a daily basis is rewarded as a means of boosting engagement.
- **Content consumption**. A user who passively makes full use of the multimedia content on the platform is rewarded. This includes the consumption of videos, movies, streaming, series, documentaries, stories, comments and subscriptions.
- **Content creation**. A user who takes full active advantage of the platform's features related to content-creation is rewarded. The rewards are associated with uploads, videos, stories, streaming, chatting in streaming channels and comments.
- **Purchases**. Whenever the user purchases an item, they are given a reward, encouraging the spending of the cryptocurrency.
- **Coindrops**. The amount of captured coindrops is used to reward users who are active during streaming sessions.

4.2 Mapping Functions

The reputation system is based on two basic functions: a logarithmic function (Eq. 1), an exponential function (Eq. 2) and a linear function (Eq. 3). Different metrics are defined for each of the identified factors by adapting the weights of the basic functions. As a result, each metric calculates the reputation score achieved by its corresponding factor, and each factor has its own metric. User reputation is then calculated in a process equivalent to the weighted average of all the factors' score.

$$scoreParameter_i = y_{maximum} * \frac{\log(slope * \frac{x}{x_{maximum}} + 1)}{\log(2 + slope)} \tag{1}$$

Equation (1) is the previously mentioned logarithmic equation. It is used in cases where the slope should be greater in the initial instances and then gradually decreases in subsequent instances. For example, to encourage new users to upload videos, the first few videos the user uploads will have a considerable effect on their reputation, however, the user will not be able to continue gaining reputation at the same rhythm after producing a considerable number of videos. Instead, further uploads will have a smaller impact on the reputation of the user. Logarithmic growth is regulated by the *slope* variable of the equation, whereas the maximum number of instances is regulated by $x_{maximum}$. This factor is dynamic due to the usage characteristics of the social network. So, in this case for example, the maximum score $x_{maximum}$ can take a value of 200, meaning that a user with more than 200 uploaded videos obtains a 100% score, which will greatly contribute to the final score. Moreover, the factor $y_{maximum}$ can reach a value up to 1, so that each factor has a score between 0 and 1.

$$scoreParameter_j = y_{maximum} * \left(\frac{x}{x_{maximum}}\right)^{slope} \qquad (2)$$

Equation (2) shows the mentioned exponential function. It is defined to be used to map inputs in which the importance of low values is small and it becomes more important as the value of the factor grows. For instance, an user that has 3 viewers while streaming will receive small rewards, but a user who had 1,000 viewers is considered a successful user and therefore obtains a high reputation.

$$scoreParameter_j = slope * x \qquad (3)$$

Equation (3) shows the mentioned linear function. It is defined to be used to map inputs in which the importance of values is constant over time. For instance, the thumbs-up/thumbs-down ratio provides a reward which does not need to vary depending on the ratio values.

The exponential and logarithmic functions are represented in Fig. 3. As it can be observed, the slope and the parameter $x_{maximum}$ can be modified and it will affect to the limits.

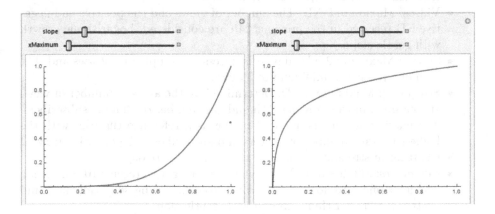

Fig. 3. Exponential and logarithm.

4.3 Defined Metrics

The default growth of the rewards, specifically the identity function, is set as linear. The factors are detailed below, as well as the assigned weight and limit for each of them:

- **Login**: 1 ND the first time you access the platform every day.
- **Content consumption**: This category can add up to 13 ND / day.
  - Videos: Maximum 1 ND/day if the user views at least one video.
  - Movies: Maximum 1 ND/day if the user views at least one film.
  - Streaming: Maximum 1 ND/day if the user views at least one live streamed video.
  - Series: Maximum 1 ND/day if the user views at least one episode.
  - Documentaries: Maximum 1 ND/ day the user views a documentary.
  - Stories: Maximum 1 ND/day the user views at least one story.
  - Comments: Maximum 2 ND. It is necessary to receive at least 10 positive ratings, determined on the basis of the received scores. Each negative score cancels a positive one. Exponential growth with gentle slope.
  - Subscriptions: Maximum 5 ND. The user receives ND depending on the number of channels to which he/she is subscribed. The reward for each user will be calculated taking as reference the channel of the user with the largest number of subscribers. In case of being banned from a channel, the user will not be rewarded. Logarithmic growth.
- **Content creation**: It is considered the most important factor as it encourages the use of the platform and its improvement. Quantity is rewarded, but above all quality. This category can add up to 45 ND/day.
  - Uploads: Maximum 30 ND. It is necessary to upload 5 videos (the next video uploads are not considered to prevent creators from fragmenting their videos too much). Logarithmic growth.
  - Videos: Maximum 5 ND. The number of views and the positive and negative ND received in the previous 24h are considered. Logarithmic growth with gentle slope.
  - Stories: Maximum 2 ND/ day. It is necessary to upload 2 stories and that each one receives a minimum of 50 views.
  - Streaming: Maximum 5 ND. Determined by the average number of viewers obtained in the previous 24 h and the number of channel subscribers. The maximum limit is updated taking as a reference the user with the highest average number of viewers and subscribers. Exponential growth.
  - Chatting in streaming channels: Maximum 1 ND/ day.
  - Comments: Maximum 10 ND. It will be necessary to receive 10 comments. The next ones are not considered to avoid favouring sensationalism and controversy. Logarithmic growth with gentle slope.
- **Purchases made**: Maximum 1 ND/ day. The spending of currency is encouraged.
- **Coindrops in streaming chats**: No limit. The amount of ND received will be proportional to the amount of NXN spent on coindrops.

The previous metrics are expected to encourage user engagement as well as finding a good balance between quality content and quantity. Moreover, other important aspects upon which the metrics have been defined are

- The number of comments of videos should not be used, as it would reward polarising videos. Instead, the like/dislike ratio should be used.
- Rewards are given each day according to the behaviour of the user on the previous day, in order to maximise the simplicity.
- To set maximums in order to avoid users getting rich using bots/repetitive behaviour which does not contribute in any way to the platform.
- To use a logarithmic function for the number of uploaded videos (on the last day) because the reward for uploading an excessively high number of videos is similar to uploading just 2 videos. As a result, a "normal" behaviour of users is encouraged.
- To use a soft logarithmic function for the amount of posted comments (on the last day) because the reward for posting an excessively high number of videos is similar to just posting 5 comments. As a result, a "normal" behaviour of users is encouraged.

4.4 Generalisation Potential and Risks

The definition of three core functions allows the reputation system to be extrapolated to other use cases beyond online video platforms. For example, such core functions have been previously used in a public transport application [3]. The most relevant factors of the considered use case must be identified, each factor weight must be decided and the suitable core function for each variable chosen. As a result, any developer of a platform without experience in reputation systems can use these principles and their expertise to assign trust-worthy scores to the users.

It is expected that some users will try to understand the working of the reputation system in order to falsely attain greater influence. This possibility must be considered as most online platforms suffer from this issue, with a particular incidence in the case of the dating app "Tinder" [14]. In this particular case, most users want to achieve a visibility as high as possible using all alternatives available which allow them to stand out.

The developed system prevents this malicious usage by adapting the weight of each variable to their relative importance. In this regard, users would need to make a wide ranging usage of the platform to obtain a high score (just the behaviour which is meant to be encouraged). Therefore, the cheaters are cheated into using the platform properly.

The only successful fraud they could perform would be related to knowing which variables make use of a sharp logarithmic function and which of the exponential or linear functions. It would result in them focusing their efforts on achieving a maximum score for each action. The researchers consider that it would not be an undeserved reward as they would need to make extensive usage of the platform and to get involved in all of its sections.

5   Conclusions and Future Work

A versatile mapping function to create a reputation system has been developed, and its adaptation for a video platform has been proposed. The created system is expected to boost user engagement as it provides various forms of reward and recognition of the users' actions. Many common aspects and problems of such systems have been considered and overcome during the design phase, resulting in a robust system.

The proposal is scalable, trust-worthy and adaptable, making it perfect for new video platforms and other programs which need to have a built-in reputation system.

The webpage has recently been released and the number of active users is expected to grow gradually in the following months. Once a sufficient amount of data has been gathered, the algorithms will be re-evaluated and the weights fine-tuned to attract more users.

References

1. Digital 2021: Global Overview Report—DataReportal–Global Digital Insights (2021). Retrieved 6 April 2021 from https://datareportal.com/reports/digital-2021-global-overview-report
2. Corchado, J.M., et al.: Deepint.net: a rapid deployment platform for smart territories. Sensors **21**(1), 236 (2021)
3. García-Retuerta, D., Rivas, A., Guisado-Gámez, J., Antoniou, E., Chamoso, P.: Reputation system for increased engagement in public transport oriented-applications. Electronics **10**(9), 1070 (2021)
4. Wang, Y.D., Emurian, H.H.: An overview of online trust: concepts, elements, and implications. Comput. Hum. Behav. **21**(1), 105–125 (2005)
5. Manchala, D.W.: E-commerce trust metrics and models. IEEE Internet Comput. **4**(2), 36–44 (2000)
6. Seidel, M.D.L.: Questioning centralized organizations in a time of distributed trust. J. Manag. Inquiry **27**(1), 40–44 (2018)
7. Busom, N., Petrlic, R., Sebé, F., Sorge, C., Valls, M.: A privacy-preserving reputation system with user rewards. J. Netw. Comput. Appl. **80**, 58–66 (2017)
8. García-Retuerta, D., Rivas, A., Guisado-Gámez, J., Antoniou, E., Chamoso, P.: Reputation algorithm for users and activities in a public transport oriented application. In: Novais, P., Vercelli, G., Larriba-Pey, J.L., Herrera, F., Chamoso, P. (eds.) ISAmI 2020. AISC, vol. 1239, pp. 213–223. Springer, Cham (2021). https://doi.org/10.1007/978-3-030-58356-9_21
9. Kerschbaum, F., Haller, J., Karabulut, Y., Robinson, P.: PathTrust: a trust-based reputation service for virtual organization formation. In: Stølen, K., Winsborough, W.H., Martinelli, F., Massacci, F. (eds.) iTrust 2006. LNCS, vol. 3986, pp. 193–205. Springer, Heidelberg (2006). https://doi.org/10.1007/11755593_15
10. Resnick, P., Zeckhauser, R.: Trust among strangers in Internet transactions: empirical analysis of eBay's reputation system. In: The Economics of the Internet and E-commerce. Emerald Group Publishing Limited (2002)
11. Page, L., Brin, S., Motwani, R., Winograd, T.: The PageRank citation ranking: bringing order to the web. Stanford InfoLab (1999)

12. Kamvar, S., Schlosser, M., Garcia-Molina, H.: The EigenTrust algorithm for reputation management in P2P networks. In: Proceedings of the 12th International Conference on World Wide Web, pp. 640–651 (2003)
13. Kurdi, H.A.: HonestPeer: an enhanced EigenTrust algorithm for reputation management in P2P systems. J. King Saud Univ. Comput. Inf. Sci. **27**(3), 315–322 (2015)
14. Garda, M.B., Karhulahti, V.M.: Let's Play Tinder! aesthetics of a dating app. Games Cult. **16**(2), 248–261 (2021)

A Reinforcement Learning Approach to Improve User Achievement of Health-Related Goals

Diogo Martinho[1](✉) (iD), João Carneiro[1] (iD), José Neves[2] (iD), Paulo Novais[2] (iD),
Juan Corchado[3] (iD), and Goreti Marreiros[1] (iD)

[1] Research Group on Intelligent Engineering and Computing for Advanced Innovation and
Development (GECAD), Institute of Engineering, Polytechnic of Porto, Porto, Portugal
{diepm,jrc,mgt}@isep.ipp.pt
[2] ALGORITMI Centre, University of Minho, Guimarães, Portugal
jneves@di.uminho.pt
[3] BISITE Digital Innovation Hub, University of Salamanca.
Edificio Multiusos, Salamanca, Spain
corchado@usal.es

Abstract. The demand and interest for personalized, efficient, and inexpensive healthcare solutions has significantly increased over the last decade to overcome the major limitations of existing traditional healthcare approaches. This new trend relies on the definition of intelligent mechanisms that can persuade the end-user to achieve health-related outcomes and ultimately improve his health condition and well-being. In this sense, the work here proposed explores a Multi-Agent System composed by personal agents that follow user preferences and a coaching agent which relies on a reinforcement learning approach to identify the most impactful messages to persuade a certain agent to follow established health-related goals. To validate the proposed system, a set of simulations were performed considering different types of persuasive messages and we were able to identify the most adequate sequence of messages that can persuade different users to achieve health-related goals based on their preferences.

Keywords: Reinforcement learning · Healthcare systems · Multi-agent systems

1 Introduction

We are currently witnessing a shift in the healthcare paradigm with all the noticeable advancements in technology. In a world where the costs of living are increasing at a daunting rate derived from increasing taxes, lower and lower incomes, pandemic effects, etc. [1–3], and at the same time we observe a significant burden of the healthcare providers [4], the reality is that the quality of traditional healthcare methods fall short of required to correctly support patients and their needs during their daily lives [5]. We think less and less about disease-centered solutions and the focus has diverged towards a patient-centered reality where the patient and the underlying needs and preferences become key factors to treat and manage his/her own health condition effectively [6]. In this sense, we observe strong efforts in the literature to develop personalized healthcare solutions that

© Springer Nature Switzerland AG 2021
G. Marreiros et al. (Eds.): EPIA 2021, LNAI 12981, pp. 266–277, 2021.
https://doi.org/10.1007/978-3-030-86230-5_21

can support patients during their daily lives and in return improve their health condition and well-being. Such solutions rely on the intelligent use of both novel technological features and successful engagement strategies that can persuade the patient to be an active player and in return guide him/her to follow healthier behaviors [7–9].

We observe several works in this area already combining engagement strategies such as Persuasion and Behavior Change Theories [10–12] with Artificial Intelligence methods such as Natural Language Processing [13, 14], Computer Vision [15], Fuzzy Logic [16, 17], Reinforcement Learning (RL) [18], etc. Among these works, we highlight the use of Reinforcement Learning as one of the most effective approaches to draw healthier outcomes. In the work of [18], the authors identified several domains of application of RL in the area of Healthcare. They referred to works done in dynamic treatment regimens which includes treatment and management of chronic diseases such as diabetes, depression, and cancer, or diseases that require critical care such as anesthesia or sepsis. They also referred to the use of RL to process both structured and unstructured data which can range from medical image processing to free text analysis. Finally, the authors also pointed towards other interesting and general domains such as using RL for healthcare resource scheduling, use of RL in surgery procedures, and use of RL in the healthcare management with the inclusion of healthcare plans to manage physical activities. In the work of [19] the authors also discussed the many domains of application of RL in the area of healthcare and suggested the use of RL in the development of dialogue systems which includes the development of multi-agent systems with conversational agents that can rely on RL mechanisms to identify the best way to interact with the patient.

In this work we follow the conceptual ideas first discussed in [20] and propose a Multi Agent System which considers both agents that support the patient and follow his/her preferences and needs and a coaching agent which persuades other agents to accomplish health-related goals by using a RL strategy to identify the best sequence of messages to exchange with those agents (based on their preferences and needs). To validate our proposed model, we selected different simulation scenarios which include different types of messages that can be exchanged with the user (by the personal agent) and we observed how easily the coaching agent was able to identify the best sequence of action compared to a "normal" coaching agent that did not make use of this approach and attempted to persuade other agents with random sequences of messages. We were able to observe significant advantages over the use of RL for this purpose and we also identified other benefits of our proposal more related with the generic structure that was applied in the RL process.

2 Proposed Model

The main goal of the proposed work is to identify the most impactful sequence of interactions that should happen between the healthcare system and a certain patient based on his preferences and needs. As such we introduce a Multi-Agent System composed by two main entities which will interact with each other and understand how to interact with a patient. These entities are referred as Personal Agent and Coaching Agent (Fig. 1).

It is important to note that this interaction happens always between one PA, that represents a patient, and the CA. For several patients, a new instantiation for both PA and CA specific for that patient would be necessary.

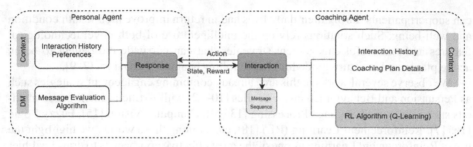

Fig. 1. Multi-agent system architecture

2.1 Personal Agent

The first entity of the proposed system is the Personal Agent (PA), and as the name refers this agent will interact with the person (patient) and exchange messages throughout the day to motivate him/her to follow health-related goals. To do so, the PA will follow patient preferences regarding context variables (for example, preferences regarding which types of messages are most suited at a certain time of the day, which days of the week the person prefers to do physical activities, which days of the week the person prefers to rest, previously accepted or rejected goals based on the messages that were sent to that person, etc.). Besides that, the PA will also have its own internal Message Evaluation algorithm to decide whether the person is more or less likely to accept or reject a certain message to follow a health-related goal (also combining the information from the context). This evaluation algorithm can be configured to be as simple as to follow a set of preferences to a more complex and intelligent process that can combine these preferences and other information obtained from the context and past interactions with the user to better judge whether a certain interaction is more likely to succeed or not. In the case of this study and as explained in more detail in the Discussion section, the first case was considered.

2.2 Coaching Agent

The second entity of the proposed system is the Coaching Agent (CA) and has the main task of selecting the most appropriate messages to send to the patient. To do so, the CA will process context information which also includes details from all previous interactions with that patient (information related to goals that were achieved, how many messages were exchanged before the patient achieved a new goal, how many goals were achieved during the current week/month, etc.) and details related with the current coaching plan given to the user. The structure of a coaching plan has been previously introduced in [21] and the main idea is to establish health-related goals that can be improved depending on the patient progress. This information is then combined with the execution of the RL algorithm to identify the best sequence of messages to exchange with a certain patient. This process is iterative and depending on the response obtained from the PA side, the RL algorithm will be improved for the next iteration until a correct sequence of action is identified for a certain patient. Below we introduce the general definition of RL as well as the model-free implementation of RL with the Q-Learning algorithm that is used by the CA.

Reinforcement Learning. Reinforcement learning is a machine learning process in which an *agent* has different goals related to a specific *environment* and must decide which *action* is the most adequate to achieve a goal according to a given *state* of the environment. This goal can be represented by a value (*reward*) and the agent should attempt to maximize this value when choosing which actions to take (*policy*) given a state signal. Over the long run the agent will identify the optimal policy which corresponds to the policy that provides the highest reward value.

In this work, each action is represented as a set of n messages, or in other words, as $M = \{m_1, m_2, \ldots, m_n\}$, that can be sent to a certain patient before he achieves (or not) an established health-related goal. An interaction history will be stored with the result of the interaction after sending M at certain time (or stage) and the corresponding reward value (which in this case indicates whether the patient achieved or not and established health-related goal). This flow corresponds to a Markov Decision Process, in which the CA and the environment (in our case the environment equivalent to the PA) interact with each other during a set of Y stages. At a stage $y \in Y$, the CA is presented with a state $s_y \in S$ from a set of states and must select an action $a_y \in A(s_y)$ from a set of possible actions available for that state. After selecting that action, the CA receives a reward r_{y+1} resulting from the action taken and is then presented with a new state s_{y+1}. With this result, the CA may change (or not) the preferred policy for the next interaction, and over the long run the RL problem will be "solved" with the CA finding the policy that achieves the highest reward value. The expected return (the sum of rewards) for the CA starting in state s, taking action a, and then following policy ρ thereafter is called as the action-value function for policy ρ. In the context of Q-learning, this function is also called as Q-function and is denoted as:

$$Q_y^\rho(s, a) \doteq E_\rho \left[\sum_{j=y}^{Y} r_{j+1} \middle| s_y = s, a_y = a \right]$$

It should be noted that we opted to use Q-Learning method in the proposed work, in comparison to other RL methods such as SARSA because of the off-policy characteristics of the Q-Learning method. As a result, it is possible to evaluate and improve policies that are different from the selected policy in each stage and therefore it is possible to maintain a continuous exploration process in which the CA can select different policies while learning what is the optimal policy in a certain environment.

3 Results and Discussion

To validate the proposed model, we defined 3 different simulation scenarios and compared the results according to 3 different levels of complexity. In the first scenario we tested our model by considering 2 different types of persuasive messages; in the second scenario 4 different persuasive messages were considered; and in the third scenario 6 different persuasives messages were considered. For simulation purposes we do not define each persuasive message but instead refer as Message 1, Message 2, Message 3, etc., but these message could be easily adapted to refer to some of the most known and used persuasive models that were mentioned in the introduction of this study, such as the six principles of persuasion by Cialdini [22, 23] or the Transtheoretical Model of Behavior Change [24], among others [10].

Each scenario was tested with a time length of 30 days and we studied both the accuracy of each set of messages and corresponding interactions as well as the total number of health-related goals that were achieved after accepting (or not) the messages sent to the PA. Furthermore, 10 simulations were performed for each scenario and the results were compared in terms of average values obtained.

To validate our model, we compared the approach here proposed in which the CA uses the RL algorithm to decide what messages should be sent to the PA with an approach where the CA does not use the RL algorithm and instead attempts to send a random set of messages to the PA.

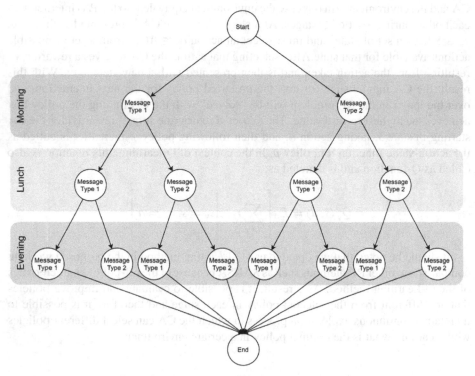

Fig. 2. Message flow example (2 message types)

For all the scenarios simulated, we considered that the maximum number of inter-actions between the CA and PA would be of three messages per day, and that a goal would be achieved only after the PA accepted all three messages exchanged. We chose this number specifically with given evidence on the literature [25] that recommends the exchange of messages at certain periods of the day, such as morning, lunch, and early evening, and these interactions would represent those moments of the day. Furthermore, the CA was also allowed to exchange repeated types of messages during a day. To exemplify this, in Fig. 2 it is shown the total number of possible combinations of messages that can be sent during a day when two types of messages are considered.

For this example, the total number of combinations corresponds to 8 possible outcomes, and for the remaining scenarios corresponds to a total of n^3 possible outcomes, with n being the number of different types of persuasive messages considered.

The evaluation algorithm defined for the PA was simplified to only select a random sequence of types of messages as the most impactful, which in turn would persuade the patient to achieve a health-related goal. This simplification of the evaluation process was considered since the main goal of this work is to test the performance of the CA using the RL algorithm and, as such, the way the PA could be modeled to evaluate each received message in a more or less intelligent way falls out of the scope of this study.

The average results obtained regarding the number of accepted goals and messages exchanged are presented in Table 1.

After performing all simulations in each scenario, it is possible to observe that the use of RL compared to a Random approach obtained far better results regarding both the total number of messages exchanged and the total number of goals completed after 30 days.

Table 1. Simulation results

Day	Scenario 1 – 2 Messages				Scenario 2 – 4 Messages				Scenario 3 – 6 Messages			
	Goals – RL	Goals – RA	Msgs – RL	Msgs – RA	Goals – RL	Goals – RA	Msgs – RL	Msgs – RA	Goals – RL	Goals – RA	Msgs – RL	Msgs – RA
1	0,1	0,2	1,5	1,7	0	0	1,2	1,1	0	0	1.2	1.2
2	0,6	0,3	4,2	3,5	0	0	2,9	2,5	0	0	2.5	2.5
3	1,3	0,3	7,2	4,9	0,3	0	5,1	4	0.1	0	4.4	3.7
4	2,3	0,4	10,2	6,4	0,9	0	7,8	5,5	0.2	0	7	4.8
5	3,3	0,5	13,2	8,1	1,6	0	10,7	6,8	0.6	0	9.8	6
6	4,3	0,6	16,2	10	2,4	0	13,6	8,1	1	0	12.7	7.2
7	5,3	0,7	19,2	11,7	3,2	0	16,6	9,7	1.6	0	15.6	8.2
8	6,3	0,8	22,2	13,2	4,1	0	19,6	10,7	2.2	0	18.6	9.2
9	7,3	1	25,2	15	5	0	22,6	12,2	3.1	0	21.6	10.2
10	8,3	1	28,2	16,2	6	0	25,6	13,6	4	0	24.6	11.6
11	9,3	1	31,2	17,6	7	0	28,6	14,8	4.9	0	27.6	12.9
12	10,3	1,2	34,2	19,6	8	0	31,6	15,8	5.8	0	30.6	14
13	11,3	1,5	37,2	21,4	9	0	34,6	17	6.8	0	33.6	15.6
14	12,3	1,6	40,2	22,8	10	0	37,6	18,3	7.8	0	36.6	16.6
15	13,3	1,6	43,2	24,4	11	0	40,6	19,8	8.8	0	39.6	17.7
16	14,3	1,6	46,2	25,6	12	0	43,6	21,1	9.8	0	42.6	18.7

(*continued*)

Table 1. (*continued*)

Day	Scenario 1 – 2 Messages				Scenario 2 – 4 Messages				Scenario 3 – 6 Messages			
	Goals – RL	Goals – RA	Msgs – RL	Msgs – RA	Goals – RL	Goals – RA	Msgs – RL	Msgs – RA	Goals – RL	Goals – RA	Msgs – RL	Msgs – RA
17	15,3	1,7	49,2	27,3	13	0	46,6	22,4	10.8	0	45.6	19.9
18	16,3	1,9	52,2	29,1	14	0	49,6	23,6	11.8	0	48.6	21
19	17,3	2	55,2	30,4	15	0	52,6	25,2	12.8	0	51.6	22.2
20	18,3	2	58,2	32,1	16	0	55,6	26,3	13.8	0	54.6	23.2
21	19,3	2,3	61,2	34,4	17	0	58,6	27,3	14.8	0	57.6	24.3
22	20,3	2,4	64,2	36,5	18	0,1	61,6	28,5	15.8	0	60.6	25.5
23	21,3	2,6	67,2	38,2	19	0,1	64,6	29,5	16.8	0.1	63.6	26.7
24	22,3	2,7	70,2	39,8	20	0,2	67,6	30,8	17.8	0.1	66.6	28
25	23,3	3	73,2	41,5	21	0,2	70,6	32	18.8	0.1	69.6	29.2
26	24,3	3,3	76,2	43,5	22	0,2	73,6	33,1	19.8	0.1	72.6	30.7
27	25,3	3,5	79,2	45,4	23	0,2	76,6	34,6	20.8	0.1	75.6	31.9
28	26,3	3,7	82,2	47,4	24	0,2	79,6	35,8	21.8	0.2	78.6	33.4
29	27,3	3,8	85,2	48,9	25	0,2	82,6	37,2	22.8	0.2	81.6	34.7
30	28,3	3,9	88,2	50,6	26	0,2	85,6	38,4	23.8	0.2	84.6	35.7

Looking at the total number of achieved goals, in the first scenario, both agents achieved the highest average values compared to the remaining scenarios. However, while the Random Agent was only able to obtain an average of 4 goals accepted at the end of 30 days, the RL Agent was able to obtain an average exceeding 28 goals accepted. In the second and third scenario, the Random Agent obtained even worse results and was only able to persuade the PA to achieve a health-related goal in two simulations for each scenario. On the other hand, the RL Agent still obtained very satisfactory results and only had a slight decrease in the total number of achieved goals to an average of 26 goals accepted in the second scenario and nearly 24 goals in the third scenario. Regarding the number of messages exchanged to persuade the PA to achieve a goal during each day, both the RL Agent and Random Agent also obtained the best results in the first scenario, with an average of nearly 88 messages exchanged between the PA and the RL Agent and 51 Messages between the Random Agent and the PA. In the second and third scenarios, a significant decrease was observed for the Random Agent (only nearly 39 messages exchanged after 30 days in the second scenario and only nearly 36 messages exchanged in the third scenario). A less significant decrease was observed in the case of the RL Agent (nearly 86 messages exchanged after 30 days in the second scenario and 85 messages exchanged in the third scenario). These results show a clear superior performance between the RL Agent and the Random Agent, however it still was not clear if the accuracy of all the interactions performed between the CA and the PA were also superior in the case of the interactions between the RL Agent and the PA and the Random Agent and the PA. Therefore, the system was also evaluated regarding the number of messages that were exchanged per day between each of these two entities and the number of messages that were actually successful to persuade the PA to achieve a health-related goal. These results are shown in Fig. 3, Fig. 4 and Fig. 5 respectively.

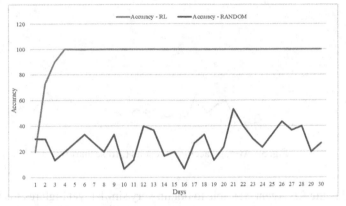

Fig. 3. Average accuracy results (1st scenario)

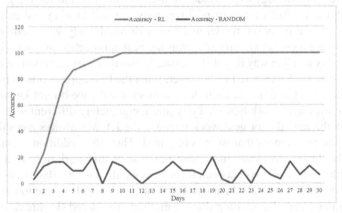

Fig. 4. Average accuracy results (2nd scenario)

A linear increase on the accuracy value was observed from the interactions between the RL Agent and PA in each of the three scenarios with a peak of 100% accuracy achieved by the 4th day in the first scenario, 10th day in the second scenario and 13th day in the third scenario. This accuracy value is supported by the fact of how the Message Evaluation Algorithm was configured for the PA in this study. Since we are only considering a set of Messages the RL Agent learns which set and sequence of messages is most persuading and then repeats the same set for the remaining days in each scenario. On the other hand, the highest accuracy value obtained from the interactions between the Random Agent and PA was of slightly over 55% in the first scenario. In the remaining scenarios, the peak observed had a value lower than 20%. These results also reveal a clear performance with the use of the RL method. In fact, despite the scenario complexity it was still possible

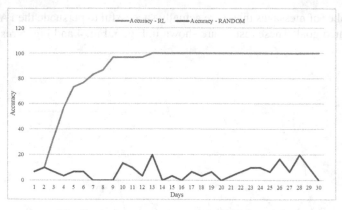

Fig. 5. Average accuracy results (3rd scenario)

to observe that the RL Agent was able to obtain very similar, yet high results in terms of accuracy, number of accepted goals and number of messages exchanged. These numbers are even more significant if we compare them with a less intelligent approach such as the use of a random strategy to persuade the user to follow health-related goals.

Although these results are very positive, they are still lacking and can be further improved. First, the proposed model and the performed study was made on the sole basis that we were trying to identify what was the best approach to interact with a certain user during a day and that way be able to persuade him to achieve a certain health-related goal. This approach does not tell us however, what the best approach is to interact with a certain user, over the time, on each day. In other words, we do not know whether a certain set of messages work best on a day and a completely different set of messages work best on the next day or next week because the PA was always modelled to keep the same initial preferences that were configured. Therefore, additional improvements could and should be considered in the continuation of this work to have a model that can learn with the interactions between the user not only during a day but also take into account the context to make a better judgement of the ideal interaction at any given moment in time. Second, regarding the RL method considered (in this case and as we explained, it was opted to use the Q-Learning method), it could and should also be improved to support scenarios of even higher complexity. Even though we were able to obtain very fast results in each simulation, we are aware that the algorithm performance will decrease significantly as the complexity of the scenario increases and in a scenario with dozens of different types of messages consider, this would force to incorporate a different approach to measure the ideal set of messages to exchange with the user. Such approach could consider the use of deep Q-Learning with neural networks to approximate the Q-Function that was presented. Third, the proposed model should be further evaluated considering users with different preferences and ways of living (or in other words, improve the current Evaluation Algorithm). Our goal is to have a system that is prepared to deal with any type of user, whether they like to perform physical exercise during the day or work out on weekends or after eating a more indulging meal, etc. By doing so, the system will be prepared to interact with any user regardless of age or gender and correctly support the user during his/her daily life. Finally, although the proposed Multi-Agent approach currently considers only two types of agents, we intend to incorporate a third agent (Checker Agent) that will monitor the user progress in real time and acquire health inputs from devices such as Smart Bands. By doing so, we will be able to evaluate the accuracy of each interaction even more precisely and understand how easily (or not) a health-related goal was achieved after exchanging a set of messages.

4 Conclusions and Future Work

The rising costs of living and the overall demand for answers to relieve the healthcare burden has led towards a reality in which traditional healthcare no longer is adequate and instead new solutions are being developed to support people throughout their daily lives from a patient-centered perspective in which the person himself/herself becomes the key factor to manage and improve his/her health condition. Personalizing and enhancing the support provided based on the preferences, needs and the way people behave is essential to accomplish this goal, and as such, emerging healthcare systems must be able to understand what the best approach is when interacting with the patient to lead him/her towards improving his/her health condition. The work here presented explores a Reinforcement Learning approach to identify the best way to interact with a patient based on his/her preferences and needs, experience from previous interactions under a perspective of motivating the patient to accomplish health-related goals. To do we incorporated this approach in a Multi-Agent System in which we consider agents that represent patients and their preferences and an agent that attempts to persuade those agents using a combination of messages that best fits the preferences of those patients. To validate our model, we can a set of simulations with different scenarios and levels of complexity and obtained better results compared to a less intelligent approach. As future work we intend to improve the proposed model according to different points that were discussed in this study and which are mostly related with the ability to consider higher complexity scenarios and patients with more complex behaviors and ways of living. Additionally, the inclusion of additional agents that can monitor the health condition of the patient will be ideal to measure the accuracy and the impact of each interaction performed between the proposed system and the patient. With these points in mind, it will be possible to present an intelligent approach that correctly support the patient despite of his/her age, gender, or any demographical aspects but instead operate based on how that person behaves throughout his/her daily life and at the same time lead him/her to accomplish health-related goals result in healthier lifestyles.

Acknowledgments. The work presented in this paper has been developed under the EUREKA - ITEA3 Project PHE (PHE-16040), and by National Funds through FCT (Fundação para a Ciência e a Tecnologia) under the under the project UIDB/00760/2020 and by NORTE-01-0247-FEDER-033275 (AIRDOC - "Aplicação móvel Inteligente para suporte individualizado e monitorização da função e sons Respiratórios de Doentes Obstrutivos Crónicos") by NORTE 2020 (Programa Operacional Regional do Norte).

References

1. Li, Y., Mutchler, J.E.: Older adults and the economic impact of the COVID-19 pandemic. J. Aging Soc. Policy **32**, 477–487 (2020)
2. Clarke, L.: An introduction to economic studies, health emergencies, and COVID-19. J. Evid. Based Med. **13**, 161–167 (2020)
3. Laborde, D., Martin, W., Vos, R.: Impacts of COVID-19 on global poverty, food security, and diets: Insights from global model scenario analysis. Agri. Econ. (2021)
4. Papoutsi, E., Giannakoulis, V.G., Ntella, V., Pappa, S., Katsaounou, P.: Global burden of COVID-19 pandemic on healthcare workers. Eur. Respir. Soc. (2020)
5. Miller, I.F., Becker, A.D., Grenfell, B.T., Metcalf, C.J.E.: Disease and healthcare burden of COVID-19 in the United States. Nat. Med. **26**, 1212–1217 (2020)
6. Chawla, N.V., Davis, D.A.: Bringing big data to personalized healthcare: a patient-centered framework. J. Gen. Intern. Med. **28**, 660–665 (2013)
7. Costa, A., Heras, S., Palanca, J., Jordán, J., Novais, P., Julián, V.: Argumentation schemes for events suggestion in an e-Health platform. In: International Conference on Persuasive Technology, pp. 17–30. Springer, Cham (2017). https://doi.org/10.1007/978-3-319-551 34-0_2
8. Costa, A., Heras, S., Palanca, J., Novais, P., Julián, V.: A persuasive cognitive assistant system. In: International Symposium on Ambient Intelligence, pp. 151–160. Springer, Cham (2016). https://doi.org/10.1007/978-3-319-40114-0_17
9. Costa, A., Heras, S., Palanca, J., Novais, P., Julián, V.: Persuasion and recommendation system applied to a cognitive assistant. ADCAIJ: Adv. Distrib. Comput. Artif. Intell. J. Salamanca **5**, (2016). (ISSN: 2255–2863)
10. Alkiş, N., Findik-Coşkunçay, D.: Use of persuasion strategies in mobile health applications. In: Sezgin, E., Yildirim, S., Yildirim, S.Ö., Sumuer, E. (eds.) Current and Emerging mHealth Technologies, pp. 9–21. Springer, Cham (2018). https://doi.org/10.1007/978-3-319-73135-3_2
11. Qasim, M.M., Ahmad, M., Omar, M.: Persuasive strategies in mobile healthcare: a systematic literature review. Literatures **87**, 7 (2017)
12. de Vries, R.A.J., Truong, K.P., Zaga, C., Li, J., Evers, V.: A word of advice: how to tailor motivational text messages based on behavior change theory to personality and gender. Pers. Ubiquit. Comput. **21**(4), 675–687 (2017). https://doi.org/10.1007/s00779-017-1025-1
13. Donadello, I., Dragoni, M., Eccher, C.: Explaining reasoning algorithms with persuasiveness: a case study for a behavioural change system. In: Proceedings of the 35th Annual ACM Symposium on Applied Computing, pp. 646–653 (2020)
14. Anselma, L., Mazzei, A.: Building a persuasive virtual dietitian. In: Informatics, p. 27. Multidisciplinary Digital Publishing Institute (2020)
15. Leo, M., Carcagnì, P., Mazzeo, P.L., Spagnolo, P., Cazzato, D., Distante, C.: Analysis of facial information for healthcare applications: a survey on computer vision-based approaches. Information **11**, 128 (2020)
16. Sengan, S., Kamalam, G., Vellingiri, J., Gopal, J., Velayutham, P., Subramaniyaswamy, V.: Medical information retrieval systems for e-Health care records using fuzzy based machine learning model. Microprocess. Microsyst. 103344 (2020)
17. Mardani, A., et al.: Application of decision making and fuzzy sets theory to evaluate the healthcare and medical problems: a review of three decades of research with recent developments. Expert Syst. Appl. **137**, 202–231 (2019)
18. Yu, C., Liu, J., Nemati, S.: Reinforcement learning in healthcare: a survey. arXiv preprint arXiv:1908.08796 (2019)

19. Coronato, A., Naeem, M., De Pietro, G., Paragliola, G.: Reinforcement learning for intelligent healthcare applications: a survey. Artif. Intell. Med. **109**, 101964 (2020)
20. Martinho, D., Carneiro, J., Novais, P., Neves, J., Corchado, J., Marreiros, G.: A conceptual approach to enhance the well-being of elderly people. In: Moura Oliveira, P., Novais, P., Reis, L.P. (eds.) EPIA 2019. LNCS (LNAI), vol. 11805, pp. 50–61. Springer, Cham (2019). https://doi.org/10.1007/978-3-030-30244-3_5
21. Martinho, D., Vieira, A., Carneiro, J., Martins, C., Almeida, A., Marreiros, G.: A definition of a coaching plan to guide patients with chronic obstructive respiratory diseases. In: Rocha, Á., Adeli, H., Reis, L.P., Costanzo, S., Orovic, I., Moreira, F. (eds.) WorldCIST 2020. AISC, vol. 1161, pp. 54–64. Springer, Cham (2020). https://doi.org/10.1007/978-3-030-45697-9_6
22. Cialdini, R.B.: The Psychology of Persuasion. New York (1993)
23. Cialdini, R.B., Cialdini, R.B.: Influence: The Psychology of Persuasion. Collins, New York (2007)
24. Prochaska, J.O., DiClemente, C.C.: Stages and processes of self-change of smoking: toward an integrative model of change. J. Consult. Clin. Psychol. **51**, 390 (1983)
25. Bidargaddi, N., et al.: To prompt or not to prompt? A microrandomized trial of time-varying push notifications to increase proximal engagement with a mobile health app. JMIR mHealth uHealth **6**, e10123 (2018)

Urban Human Mobility Modelling and Prediction: Impact of Comfort and Well-Being Indicators

Luís Rosa[1(⊠)], Fábio Silva[1,2], and Cesar Analide[1]

[1] Centro ALGORITMI, Department of Informatics, University of Minho,
Braga, Portugal
id8123@alunos.uminho.pt, analide@di.uminho.pt
[2] CIICESI, ESTG, Politécnico do Porto, Felgueiras, Portugal
fas@estg.ipp.pt

Abstract. There are increasingly more discussions on and guidelines about different levels of indicators surrounding smart cities (e.g., comfort, well-being and weather conditions). They are an important opportunity to illustrate how smart urban development strategies and digital tools can be stretched or reinvented to address localised social issues. Thus, multi-source heterogeneous data provides a new driving force for exploring urban human mobility patterns. In this work, we forecast human mobility using indoor or outdoor environment datasets, respectively, Metropolitan Transportation Authority (MTA) Wi-Fi and LinkNYC kiosks, collected in New York City to study how comfort and well-being indicators influence people's movements. By comparing the forecasting performance of statistical and Deep Learning (DL) methods on the aggregated mobile data we show that each class of methods has its advantages and disadvantages depending on the forecasting scenario. However, for our time-series forecasting problem, DL methods are preferable when it comes to simplicity and immediacy of use, since they do not require a time-consuming model selection for each different cell. DL approaches are also appropriate when aiming to reduce the maximum forecasting error. Statistical methods instead have shown their superiority in providing more precise forecasting results, but they require data domain knowledge and computationally expensive techniques in order to select the best parameters.

Keywords: Human mobility patterns · Device network datasets · Deep learning methods · Statistical methods

1 Introduction

Recent studies about human mobility, comfort and well-being and social interactions evaluated impacts on the perceptions of citizens [11,12,20,21]. The match between human activities in city and urban infrastructures may be the main

© Springer Nature Switzerland AG 2021
G. Marreiros et al. (Eds.): EPIA 2021, LNAI 12981, pp. 278–289, 2021.
https://doi.org/10.1007/978-3-030-86230-5_22

contributor for these works. Additionally, human mobility is associated with a large personal and societal cost, with problems being attributed to a combination of individual factors (physical, cognitive and psychological) combined with environmental conditions [6]. As an example, the relationship between human mobility behavior and climate—namely, weather and environmental conditions when travel planning decisions are made. Meteorological effects could influence travel demand and route choices in various ways, including diversion to other trip modes or paths, or deferring and cancelling trips [23].

On the other hand, smartphones and embedded sensor systems have given researchers unprecedented access to new and rich datasets, recording detailed information about how people live and move through urban areas. We can select a number of examples that highlight how datasets generated from these devices are lending insight into individuals lives and urban analysis. For example, in [13], embedded sensors were used to measure the spatio-temporal patterns of an entire city's usage of a shared-bicycle scheme. Other approaches used Bluetooth sensors to measure social interactions [10] or GPS sensors to show urban planning and design [5]. Lastly, [8] uses the dataset from public transport automated fare collection systems which was previously used to investigate travellers' perceptions.

In this paper, we study mobility patterns evaluating and comparing the performance of classical and modern Machine Learning (ML) methods based on two approaches, univariate and multivariate, using two sets of time series forecasting datasets, which provide the temporal variations of census over time. The traditional methods considered are Autoregressive Integrated Moving Average (ARIMA) model, Autoregressive Integrated Moving Average model with exogenous variables (ARIMAX), Seasonal Autoregressive Integrated Moving Average (SARIMA) model and Seasonal Autoregressive Integrated Moving Average model with exogenous variables (SARIMAX). These are types of traditional time series models most commonly used in time series forecasting. DL models such as Long Short-Term Memory (LSTM), Convolutional Neural Network (CNN), hybrid CNN-LSTM and Bi-Directional LSTM were the ML techniques explored. These ML methods are capable of identifying structure and pattern of data such as non-linearity and complexity in time series forecasting. Each model must be studied and understood in a parameterized way so that the integration with any data set does not cause any problem. In fact, experimental results confirm the importance of performing a parametric grid search when using any forecasting method, as the output of this process directly determines the effectiveness of each model.

All this is possible thanks to the availability of data describing long-term human behaviour on mobile phones. The available data is based on a few years of network traffic generated by LinkNYC Kiosk devices, MTA Wi-Fi Locations, based on the city of New York, and context reactions of citizens via their smartphones. Basically, in a modern society where smartphones are widely used, understanding the impact of environmental factors, comfort and well-being indicators has both theoretical and practical implications in understanding and modelling human behaviour.

The rest of the paper is planned as follows: Sect. 2 focuses on a study about crowdsensed data from mobile devices and different human mobility forecasting methods such as DL and statistical models. In the next section, we execute an experimental case study that covers the benefits of Neural Network (NN) and statistical techniques in human mobility. In Sect. 4, we discuss the results of the case study. In Sect. 5, the conclusion summarizes the article's arguments before extending the debate further by offering trajectories for future investigation on the prediction of human mobility.

2 State of the Art

For the realization of this project some concepts should be defined. In order to clarify their meaning and guarantee the quality of the project, the next sub-chapters introduce two crowdsensing infrastructures and indicators which are crucial to the understanding of the present work.

2.1 Crowdsensing Infrastructures

Contributing to this literature, this article investigates the human mobility that is captured with the development of the new public Wi-Fi infrastructure which is gradually making an appearance in cities across the world; such an infrastructure is growing steadily across New York City in recent times, and is called LinkNYC or Link [14]. This network infrastructure has been adapted and deployed to provide a free Wi-Fi service. It has transformed the way information is delivered in city streets, and supporting civic engagement has become a core part of our research. With thousands of screens encouraging New Yorkers to interact and offering helpful resources, it can provide strong participation of citizens in this work. As we see in Fig. 1, there are more than 1,800 LinkNYC kiosks around the city, including hundreds in Brooklyn.

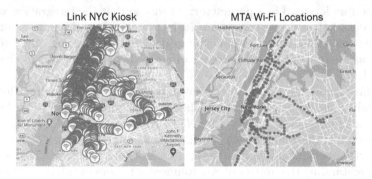

Link NYC Kiosk   MTA Wi-Fi Locations

Fig. 1. Map of LinkNYC kiosk and MTA Wi-Fi locations.

In its turn, Transit Wireless' mission keeps millions of New York City subway riders connected, safe and informed via Wi-Fi network connectivity [7]. Figure 1 shows the 282 stations more than 100 ft below ground, and 109 stations above ground with endless miles of tunnels and bustle [3]. It only contains stations that are considered Wi-Fi-ready.

In both infrastructures, wireless network availability along with crowding in streets or public transport provides crowdsensing research opportunities based on people flow or passenger volume. Because rush hour (peak) is characterised by big spikes of demand concentrated in rather short time periods, leaving the transport network under-utilised before and after such spikes, it presents a real opportunity to understand human movements.

2.2 Well-Being and Comfort

The advances in mobile computing and Artificial Intelligence (AI) techniques enable people to probe the dynamics of human movements in a city. We can analyse the impact of well-being and comfort indicators in these dynamics using crowd sensing with the two datasets proposed in this paper.

Elena Alatarsteva and Galina Barysheva [1] argue that the modern man can be defined with regard to two levels of well-being: internal (subjective) and external (objective). In the external strand, well-being could be characterized by wage levels, residence conditions, educational opportunities, the environment, safety and civil rights. In its turn, the internal strand is conceptualized only as an internal state of an individual. However, other authors from different branches specify the definition of this concept. Their articles categorized it into different classes: Community Well-being [2], Economic Well-being [15], Emotional Well-being [22], Physical Well-being [18], Development and activity [17], Psychological Well-being [19] and Work Well-being [4]. Although these classes categorize well-being in multiple ways, they have common points.

On the other hand, regarding comfort, it is difficult to reach a consensus from literature on its definition. Some papers show factors that influence comfort. One of them shows that different activities can influence comfort, concluding that characteristics of the environment and the context can change how people feel [24]. Although it is often considered a synonym for well-being, it classifies the atmosphere that surrounds the human being. However, a mental health organization in the UK has argued that "it is important to realize that well-being is a much broader concept than moment-to-moment happiness" [9]. In other words, the comfort indicator is characterized by an extensive variety of factors, which associates it with a long-term context, e.g. a person may find himself comfortable but unhappy (and vice versa).

As we see, comfort and well-being are distinct terms, but we believe that from them our experimental case study can allow understanding the mechanism hidden in human mobility that affects New York City both at community and individual levels.

3   Experimental Case Study

This experimental case is particularly useful in investigating "how" and "why" questions concerning human mobility behaviours. As a qualitative research methodology, this case study focuses on understanding these phenomena in broader circumstances than those in which it is located. Our study aims to investigate the comfort, well-being and motivation through questionary-based online surveys, and further understand a complex social phenomenon in human mobility: how citizens react in indoor and outdoor environments, and why.

3.1   Data Collection

We designed and conducted this study involving LinkNYC kiosk data contributed by one hundred thousand of users, while MTA Wi-Fi Locations captured fifty thousand interactions with smartphones in subway locations. In order to enrich our dataset, well-being and comfort metrics were gathered via questionnaire-based mobile applications [20,25]. In these individual forms, users were asked about their comfort and well-being voluntarily based on the environment they were in. In order to collect respondents' attitudes and opinions, these works adapted a response scheme like Likert scale, commonly used in opinion polls.

Other information can be considered, like the weather. We used an API so that the information gathered was even wider. This includes, for example, the Meteostat API that enables the collection of a vast amount of data associated with weather conditions such as date, temp, heating degree, cooling degree, precipitation, snowfall and snow/ice depth. Archived data is provided for many legacy weather stations.

3.2   Data Pre-processing

This study involved the daily participation of citizens that connected to LinkNYC Kiosks and Wifi Metro Stations and used the application with the questions stated above during the period from 1 January 2017 to 31 December 2019. The collected dataset contains 1054 lines and a total of 23 features. But because data is taken from multiple sources which are in different formats, it is simply unrealistic to expect that the data will be perfect. Therefore, first of all, the following steps of data processing were done:

- Elimination of irrelevant variables: Some variables like the wifi status, tablet status, phone status, which is not relevant to the prediction, were deleted;
- Duplicate values: Some rows were duplicate data. We removed them to not give to data object an advantage or bias, when running machine learning algorithms;
- Handling of missing values: In the treatment of missing values, we replaced these values by the preceding value, due to the fact the data is captured sequentially. This method results in less introduction of variability in the dataset;

- Handling non-numerical data: Since DL models only accept numbers, we applied One Hot Encoder method to perform pre-processing in several features represented by strings;
- Target encoding: Since the target presents values in a certain way sorted from 1 to 5, a label encoding technique was used to normalize these values (thus transforming these values into classes 0 to 4);
- Splitting the dataset: We split the dataset into a 70:30 ratio. This means that you take 70% of the data (2 years) for training the model while leaving out the rest 30% (1 year);
- Cross-validation: 10-fold cross-validation to divide the model tests 10 times.

The data preprocessing transforms the data to bring it to such a state that the machine can easily parse it. In other words, the features of the data can be easily interpreted by ML algorithms. In this case, we wanted to study if the treated data was relevant to the prediction of physical well-being. Therefore, we used NN and dynamic regression models where the order of the treated data is quite relevant, although no shuffle has been done. In addition to pre-processing, other special precautions regarding the way data had to be processed were taken, which we will detail in the next subsection.

3.3   Building the Models

This step is the most important and most meticulous requirement of the entire research. With this, the aim of this work was to relate univariate and multivariate analysis in daily census in different environments (indoor and outdoor). In univariate time series dataset is generally provided as a single column of data, in this study, it's "census" column. On the other hand, a multivariate time series covers several variables such as census, temperature, heating degree, cooling degree, comfort, social interaction, physical, financial life, work, psychology, satisfaction that are recorded simultaneously over time.

In DL predictions and being a multiclass classification problem, the loss function is therefore categorical_crossentropy. Furthermore, in the final layer, a softmax activation function was used. Here we have to take into account the type of this activation function and the loss function, as the incorrect use of these can lead to false results. With the use of values in MinMaxScaler technique, the final step was validating and tuning the models. In these approaches, the objective was to experiment with some combinations in order to find a good fit. The number of layers, the number of neurons, the windows size, epochs, batch size, among other, in DL models, were tested together.

In the case of auto-regression, components are specified in the model as a parameter. The notations used by ARIMA and ARIMAX models are number of delayed observations, number of times that gross observations are differentiated, size of the moving media window and, besides these, the SARIMA and SARIMAX models add the number of iterations for each seasonal period parameter.

3.4 Results

Since we want to classify the number of people some precautions have to be taken when we use DL (or NN models) and auto-regression models (or statistical models). Given that we are studying two datasets, Root Mean Squared Error (RMSE) and Mean Absolute Error (MAE) errors were computed for each them. Essentially eight approaches are presented in Table 1.

Using the four NN models, besides building a predictive model that returns a minimization in error, we also adopt another data mining strategy based on the loss functions [16]. Basically, these two-fold approaches enable (i) presenting performance bounds of MAE, and (ii) demonstrating new properties of MAE that make it more appropriate than Mean Squared Error (MSE) as a loss function for Deep Neural Network (DNN).

Table 1. RMSE and MAE for Deep Learning and statistical models with univariate and multivariate time series.

| | | MTA Wi-Fi | | | | LinkNYC Kiosks | | | |
| | | Univariate | | Multivariate | | Univariate | | Multivariate | |
Model	Algorithm	RMSE	MAE	RMSE	MAE	RMSE	MAE	RMSE	MAE
Deep learning	CNN	519.4	411.2	1145.7	970.4	659.3	532.1	1716.7	1407.4
	LSTM	969.5	742.3	1014.6	798.4	1375.4	752.9	1348.7	1143.3
	CNN-LSTM	1054.0	859.5	825.5	639.5	1173.0	968.4	1145.7	970.4
	Bi-Dir LSTM	32.3	24.6	131.4	101.9	1287.3	1104.8	256.9	203.7
Statistical	ARIMA	1111.6	899.4	-	-	1559.2	1201.6	-	-
	ARIMAX	-	-	1333.6	905.4	-	-	1617.0	1290.7
	SARIMA	1496.9	1186.1	-	-	1659.7	1388.9	-	-
	SARIMAX	-	-	1696.2	1211.0	-	-	1796.9	1441.0

Based on the above tables, we can draw two different perceptions concerning the experimental results. In this study, the whole experiment is carried out in two phases. The first phase of the experiment includes the eight models in the indoor environment dataset and then studying the outdoor environment dataset. Then, the models' performance is analyzed with metrics such as RMSE and MAE. Globally, these metrics show different performances between proposed types of models in study. In two datasets, the RMSE and MAE values are higher in autoregressive models than in DL models. However, we can find approximate values, for example, between the hybrid CNN-LSTM model and ARIMA models applied on MTA Wi-Fi dataset, using univariate time series. Or comparing accuracy between the LSTM and SARIMAX models applied on LinkNYC Kiosks dataset with all variables. But then we can find extreme values, in the case of MTA Wi-Fi dataset, between the Bi-Directional LSTM and SARIMA models using unique variable and, in LinkNYC Kiosks dataset, the Bi-Directional LSTM and ARIMAX models when applied in multivariate time series. Although each metric has its own pros and cons, they are useful to address problems such as underfitting and overfitting which can lead to a poor performance on the final model despite the accuracy value. The quality assurance of results was only possible based on the loss functions.

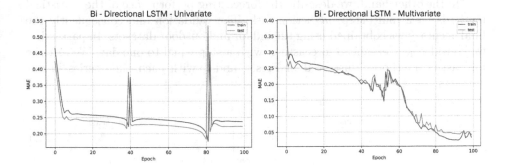

Fig. 2. Loss functions with lowest score based on MTA Wi-Fi dataset.

First of all, we choose the functions based on the number of variable (i.e., univariate and multivariate), and lowest score. In MTA Wi-Fi dataset, either with one or several variables, the Bi-Directional LSTM model presented the loss functions with lowest score. Figure 2 shows that, initially, the model has good performance, after 30 epochs it tends to converge, then it degrades. Taking Table 1 into account, CNN model for univariate model or hybrid CNN-LSTM model for multivariate also presents reasonable values and acceptable to be used for prediction and forecasting human mobility. They can be a good alternative for predictive modelling of human mobility.

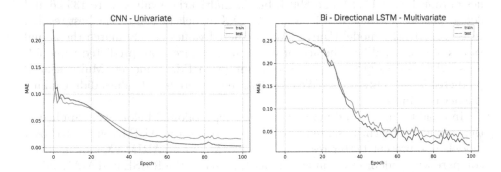

Fig. 3. Loss functions with lowest score based on LinkNYC Kiosks dataset.

As shown in Fig. 3, when LinkNYC Kiosks dataset only has a variable the lines of function in CNN model until 20 epoch seems to be converging, then it tends to degrade. Whereas in the Bi-Directional LSTM model with multivariate (or multi variables) the lines of testing and training data never converge, the distance between them is decreasing over time. Additionally, we can see in Table 1 that the RMSE and MAE values in remaining models are worse than these models, making it hard to choose an alternative model.

On the other hand, we describe the forecasting performance of the statistical methods for a multi-step prediction task. The validation and consequently the final accuracy was obtained using the indoor and outdoor datasets. In particular, we consider 30-step-ahead forecasting, with a step equal to one day. We test the forecasting methods illustrated in Figs. 4 and 5 with each time series in our datasets.

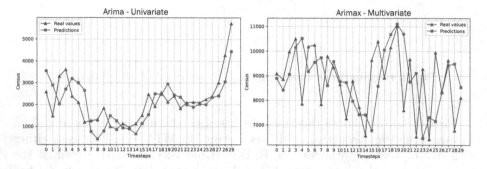

Fig. 4. Autoregression models for time series forecasting based on MTA Wi-Fi dataset.

As ours is a multi-step forecasting process, we also compute the forecasting error represented in Table 1. Based on them, when we applied Autoregression models on indoor dataset with a univariate, the lowest RMSE and MAE values obtained were 1111.6 and 899.4, but in multivariate values were 1333.6 and 905.4. This means that ARIMA and ARIMAX models presented the best results. In Fig. 4, ARIMA model (Univariate) predicted values closely match the actual values of Census. When the actual value changes direction, predicted value follows, which seems great at first sight. But in ARIMAX model (Multivariate), predicted values were worse. We can observe that predicted values didn't mimic the actual values.

In a bid to find a good model the same steps followed before were applied in the second approach presented in Fig. 5. Although, the ARIMA and ARIMAX models also present better results than SARIMA and SARIMAX models, if we compare with indoor environment dataset, globally, the RMSE and MAE values are worse. In other words, while ARIMA and ARIMAX have value pairs 1559.2 & 1201.6 and 1617.0 & 1290.7, respectively, the SARIMA is 1659.7 & 1388.9 and SARIMAX is 1796.9 & 1441.0, which means the first pair of statistical models presents a better performance.

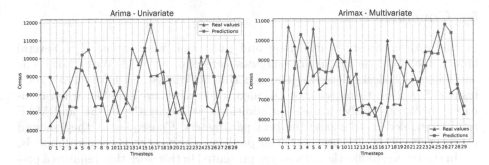

Fig. 5. Autoregression models for time series forecasting based on LinkNYC Kiosks dataset.

Figure 5 also compares predicted and actual census. We can observe that while the model outputs predicted values, they are not so close to actual values than occur in another dataset. But when it starts to generate values, the output almost resembles the sine wave. Later, in the last timestamp, values are similar.

4 Discussion

Something we can infer after the results is that the proposed DL techniques (especially Bi-Directional LSTM) may work better than statistical methods. In other words, experimental results of the proposed work show an improvement in the neural network over the statistical methods. Even changing the number of variables (i.e., change univariate to multivariate or vice-versa) and correct parameters, the performance of the neural network presents satisfactory results. Therefore, a neural network is fully modular. With Autoregressive Models, we forecast "only" on prior events, but these models are computationally intensive, more than NN models.

Models were trained to predict the Census of the next 30 days based on historical data. The census is a spatial-temporal popularity metric of human mobility. This metric captures the specifics of life within a human movements phenomena, and it is an empirical metric for people mobility of that particular area and time in the city. However, we can go further and based on the same datasets reach other interesting results. Adding other human mobility metrics such as displacement, perturbation and duration we can refine knowledge about people's movements. As we mentioned, there are peaks of mobility, where there is variability in the density of people in an area of the city that may correspond to a smaller or greater collection of data in the interaction with the different infrastructures proposed in this paper. Thus, taking their effects into consideration in predicting human mobility will not only make it possible to improve the prediction accuracy but also many actions can be supported by the use of these metrics that may provide improvements to the planning in New York City.

5   Conclusions

In this article the study modelling and prediction were extended to several human mobility phenomena. It evaluates census using MTA Wi-Fi Locations and LinkNYC kiosks datasets. The experiments carried out have shown good results. Based on them, selected DL algorithms are more suitable, when compared to Autoregressive models. In addition, evaluating the RMSE and MAE results, enabled us to choose the best parameters. Consequently, they showed neural networks models provide better prediction accuracy than statical models.

In the future, unlike the data source presented in this work that requires a pre-connectivity to wi-fi, we hope to measure population using only device signals. They can give a better understanding of human mobility mainly based on census data and, consequently, stakeholders may be able to provide suitable responses to citizens (especially vulnerable ones), building and maintaining quality socially inclusive services and facilities. It means, planning and managing of pedestrian spaces should take into consideration the correct design of paths (also cycle paths), streets, common places, recognizing that the roads are both a social space and a space for mobility.

Acknowledgments. This work has been supported by FCT - Fundacao para a Ciencia e Tecnologia within the R&D Units Project Scope: UIDB/00319/2020. It has also been supported by national funds through FCT – Fundação para a Ciência e Tecnologia through project UIDB/04728/2020.

References

1. Alatartseva, E., Barysheva, G.: Well-being: subjective and objective aspects. Procedia - Soc. Behav. Sci. **166**, 36–42 (2015). https://doi.org/10.1016/j.sbspro.2014.12.479, www.sciencedirect.com
2. Atkinson, S., et al.: Review team: What is Community Wellbeing? Technical report (2017)
3. Authority, M.T.: Transit Wireless Wifi: Product Reviews, Howtos & Buying Advice (2021). https://transitwirelesswifi.com/
4. Bartels, A.L., Peterson, S.J., Reina, C.S.: Understanding well-being at work: Development and validation of the Eudaimonic workplace well-being scale. PLoS One (2019). https://doi.org/10.1371/journal.pone.0215957
5. Blečić, I., Congiu, T., Fancello, G., Trunfio, G.A.: Planning and design support tools for walkability: a guide for Urban analysts (2020). https://doi.org/10.3390/su12114405
6. De Nadai, M., Cardoso, A., Lima, A., Lepri, B., Oliver, N.: Strategies and limitations in app usage and human mobility. Sci. Rep. **9**, 10935 (2019). https://doi.org/10.1038/s41598-019-47493-x
7. Department, M.R.E.: MTA Wi-Fi Locations (2021). https://data.ny.gov/Transportation/MTA-Wi-Fi-Locations/pwa9-tmie
8. Fadeev, A., Alhusseini, S., Belova, E.: Monitoring public transport demand using data from automated fare collection system (2018)
9. of Health, D.: What works well to improve wellbeing (2020). http://whatworkswell.schoolfoodplan.com/

10. Katevas, K., Hänsel, K., Clegg, R., Leontiadis, I., Haddadi, H., Tokarchuk, L.: Finding dory in the crowd: Detecting social interactions using multi-modal mobile sensing. In: SenSys-ML 2019 - Proceedings of the 1st Workshop on Machine Learning on Edge in Sensor Systems, Part of SenSys 2019 (2019)

11. Lawal, O., Nwegbu, C.: Movement and risk perception: evidence from spatial analysis of mobile phone-based mobility during the COVID-19 lockdown, Nigeria. GeoJournal, 1–16 (2020). https://doi.org/10.1007/s10708-020-10331-z

12. Lee, K., Sener, I.N.: Emerging data for pedestrian and bicycle monitoring: sources and applications. Transp. Res. Interdisciplinary Perspect. **4**, 100095 (2020). https://doi.org/10.1016/j.trip.2020.100095

13. Loaiza-Monsalve, D., Riascos, A.P.: Human mobility in bike-sharing systems: structure of local and non-local dynamics. PLoS One **14**(3), e0213106 (2019)

14. NYC Department of Information Technology & Telecommunications: Find a Link (2021). https://www.link.nyc/find-a-link.html

15. Publishing, O.E.C.D.: OECD Framework for Statistics on the Distribution of Household Income, Consumption and Wealth. OECD, June 2013

16. Parmar, R.: Common loss functions in machine learning (2018). https://towardsdatascience.com/common-loss-functions-in-machine-learning-46af0ffc4d23

17. PBS: Public Broadcasting Service: Physical Well-Being and Motor Development (2019). https://www.pbs.org/pre-school-u/pre-school-u-domains/physical-well-being-and-motor-development/

18. Rath, T., Harter, J.: The Economics of Wellbeing. Gallup Press, New York (2010)

19. Ruggeri, K., Garcia-Garzon, E., Maguire, Á., Matz, S., Huppert, F.A.: Well-being is more than happiness and life satisfaction: a multidimensional analysis of 21 countries. Health and Quality of Life Outcomes (2020)

20. Sousa, D., Silva, F., Analide, C.: Learning user comfort and well-being through smart devices. In: Analide, C., Novais, P., Camacho, D., Yin, H. (eds.) IDEAL 2020. LNCS, vol. 12489, pp. 350–361. Springer, Cham (2020). https://doi.org/10.1007/978-3-030-62362-3_31

21. Thornton, F., et al.: Human mobility and environmental change: a survey of perceptions and policy direction. Popul. Environ. **40**(3), 239–256 (2018). https://doi.org/10.1007/s11111-018-0309-3

22. Trudel-Fitzgerald, C., Millstein, R.A., Von Hippel, C., Howe, C.J., Tomasso, L.P., Wagner, G.R., Vanderweele, T.J.: Psychological well-being as part of the public health debate? Insight into dimensions, interventions, and policy. BMC Public Health (2019). https://doi.org/10.1186/s12889-019-8029-x

23. Vanky, A.P., Verma, S.K., Courtney, T.K., Santi, P., Ratti, C.: Effect of weather on pedestrian trip count and duration: city-scale evaluations using mobile phone application data. Preventive Medicine Reports (2017)

24. Vink, P., Hallbeck, S.: Editorial: comfort and discomfort studies demonstrate the need for a new model (2012). https://doi.org/10.1016/j.apergo.2011.06.001

25. Woodward, K., Kanjo, E., Brown, D., McGinnity, T.M., Inkster, B., MacIntyre, D., Tsanas, T.: Beyond mobile apps: a survey of technologies for mental well-being. IEEE Trans. Affect. Comput. (2020). https://doi.org/10.1109/TAFFC.2020.3015018

Comparison of Transfer Learning Behaviour in Violence Detection with Different Public Datasets

Dalila Durães[1](✉) ⓘ, Flávio Santos[1] ⓘ, Francisco S. Marcondes[1] ⓘ, Sascha Lange[2], and José Machado[1] ⓘ

[1] Centre Algoritmi, University of Minho, 4710-057 Braga, Portugal
{dalila.duraes,flavio.santos,
francisco.marcondes}@algoritmi.uminho.pt, jmac@di.uminho.pt
[2] Bosch Car Multimedia, 4705-820 Braga, Portugal
sascha.lange@pt.bosch.com

Abstract. The detection and recognition of violence have been area of interest to research, mainly in surveillance, Human-Computer Interaction and information retrieval for video based on content. The primary purpose of detecting and recognizing violence is to automatically and in real-time recognize violence. Hence, it is a crucial area and object of several studies, as it will enable systems to have the necessary means to contain violence automatically. In this sense, pre-trained models are used to solve general problems of recognition of violent activity. These models were pre-trained with datasets from: hockey fight; movies; violence in real surveillance; and fighting in real situations. From this pre-training models, general patterns are extracted that are very important to detect violent behaviour in videos. Our approach uses a state-of-the-art pre-trained violence detection model in general activity recognition tasks and then tweaks it for violence detection inside a car. For this, we created our dataset with videos inside the car to apply in this study.

Keywords: Deep learning · Violence detection · Video recognition · Inside car

1 Introduction

Let us look at the concept of violence and the definition of the World Health Organization (WHO). Violence is the threat or intentional use of physical force or power against oneself, another person or against a group or community, which can result or is likely to result in injury, death, or psychological harm [1]. Furthermore, traditional video surveillance systems with a human operator monitoring the system are traditional forms of violence detection. However, human errors can quickly occur many times due to the lack of perception of violence, making these systems very weak in terms of detecting violence.

The main objective of intelligent systems is to detect violence, automatically and effectively verifying whether or not violence occurs in a short time. Furthermore, there

© Springer Nature Switzerland AG 2021
G. Marreiros et al. (Eds.): EPIA 2021, LNAI 12981, pp. 290–298, 2021.
https://doi.org/10.1007/978-3-030-86230-5_23

have been several studies on the automatic recognition of human actions in videos in recent years. These studies allow the evolution of several applications such as video surveillance and human-computer interaction [2, 35].

In the last years, it was published several previous surveys about specific areas, namely: i) abnormal human behaviour recognition [3–5]; ii) human detection behaviour [6, 7]; iii) crowd behaviour [8]; iv) datasets human recognition [9–11]; and v) foreground segmentation [12]. Additionally, there is some research of fast violent detection [13–17], multi-features descriptors for human activity tracking and recognition [18], segmentation [12], and vision enhanced colour fusion techniques [18].

It is challenging to capture practical and detailed features to detect violence on video due to variations in the human body [20, 34]. The errors that can occur are essentially due to scale, point of view, mutual occlusion, and dynamic scenes. When detecting violence takes place inside a vehicle, the problem increases since there is little literature on the subject [19, 20], and there was no public data set available.

Accordingly, the remainder of the paper is organized as follows. Section 2 presents a preliminary state-of-art. Section 3 exhibits the methodology and methods, with the architecture's networks, the dataset, and the training setting used in the analysis. Section 4 discusses research directions and open problems that we gathered and distilled from our analysis. Finally, Sect. 5 concludes this paper.

2 State of Art

This section explains the different types of architectures that can be applied to detecting video violence. To detect video violence, we must consider the two standard dimensions (x, y) and a third dimension (t), where t is the variation in time-space. This third dimension is crucial as it allows to observe changes in orientation over time. These changes may not be equivalent or symmetrical with temporal variation and may need space and time to be treated asymmetrically. So, three techniques can be applied: (i) Based on RGB [21]; (ii) Key Points [22]; and (iii) Dynamic Image [23]. In this paper, we only use the RGB Based technique.

2.1 RGB Based

This technique is based on the RGB colour detection algorithm to detect the foreground of video sequences. The algorithm procedure eliminates all objects that do not contain the colour requirements. The change map and blob's area are computed. A change map showing the pixel's temporal variation between two consecutive binary frames, percentage area increase, or decrease characterizes a fire property for swinging [21].

To use this technique, we can apply several different architectures, which depend on accuracy and performance. In this case, we want an architecture with a good relation between accuracy/performance, especially with lower computational performance.

C2D – Resnet 50
C2D is a usual 2D convolution network [24]. The Residual Network (ResNet) was

conceived to explore a neural network depth [25, 26]. It aims to handle the vanishing/exploding gradient problem that worsens according to the number of layers raises because of a network difficulty in learning identity functions [27]. The numeral 50 denotes the network depth, i.e., the number of layers.

SlowFast Network

Globally, we can describe a SlowFast network architecture as a single stream architecture that operates at two different temporal rates (Slow pathway and Fast pathway), which are fused by lateral connections. The concept is to model two tracks separately, working at low and high temporal resolutions. One of the paths is set to capture fast-moving movements but little spatial details (fast path). The other path is lighter and more focused on the spatial and semantic domain (slow path) [28].

Inflated 3D ConvNet (I3D)

This architecture results from adding one dimension into a C2D architecture, a C3D [29]. This architecture is not a simple C3D, but a C2D architecture with was inflating. What is normally done is pre-trained the models in C2D and whose kernels are extended into a 3D shape. The result is growing the network by adding a layer, usually temporal, dimension [26]. This is an I3D stand for a two-stream inflated 3D convolution network [26]. Therefore, I3D is a composition of an inflated C2D with optical flow information [26, 29].

Non-local Block

In computer vision, non-local networks are an efficient, generic, and straightforward component for capturing long-range dependencies with deep neural networks. Intuitively, a non-local operation determines the response at a location as a weighted sum of features at all locations in the input feature maps. The collection of positions can be in space, time or space-time, which indicates that the operations are appropriate for image, sequence and video problems [30].

X3D

The X3D architecture is low-computation management regarding computation/accuracy trade-off for violence detection on video. Additionally, X3D extends a tiny base 2D image architecture toward a spatiotemporal one by extending multiple potential axes. The resulting architecture is X3D (Expand 3D) to extend from the 2D space into the 3D spacetime field. The architecture describes a basic set of extension operations used for sequentially extending X2D from a short spatial network to X3D, a spatiotemporal network, by implementing the following operations on temporal, spatial, width and depth dimensions [31].

Flow Gated Network

This network consists of cascaded 3D CNNs, and they have consistent structures so that their output could be fused. This network uses the idea of depth-wise separable convolutions to adjust the 3D convolutional layers in the network, which can significantly reduce the network parameters without performance loss. The joining block is also composed of elementary 3D CNNs, which process information after self-learned temporal pooling. Finally, the fully connected layers generate output [21].

3 Methodology and Methods

3.1 Architecture Networks

The model used in this work was based on a flow gated network. This model has been changed slightly, and we use a convolutional based neural network. The model is composed of 14 convolutional layers. However, between every two convolutional layers, we use a MaxPooling layer. After the last convolutional layer, we apply two consecutive fully connected layers. It is important to note that we use the ReLU activation function in all layers. Our model was based on the architecture proposed in [31] and is presented in Fig. 1.

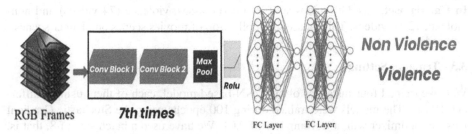

Fig. 1. Model architecture based on flow gated.

The idea is to have a reduced network, which has reduced the model parameters significantly and without losing performance.

3.2 Dataset

In this section, we describe all datasets used in the experiments. We have used four datasets, Hockey Fights (HF), Movies, Real Life Violence Recognition (RLVS), and Real World Fight (RWF). Then we have applied it to our dataset In Car dataset.

Hockey Fights (HF) dataset [32] is a violence recognition dataset composed of 1,000 videos divided into two classes, fight, and no-fight, wherein 500 videos there are fights and 500 videos there are non-fight. All the videos extracted from the games of the National Hockey League (NHL)

Movies dataset was introduced in [33], it is composed of 200 videos grouped in 2 classes: fight and non-fight. Each class has 100 videos, so it is a balanced dataset. All fight videos were extracted from movie scenes, and the non-fights videos were extracted from public action recognition datasets.

Real Life Violence Recognition (RLVS) dataset [1] was proposed to mitigate the weakness of the previous dataset, such as low resolution and few numbers of videos. RLVS is composed of 2,000 videos, where 1,000 are violent videos and 1,000 non-violent videos. The violent video clips are extracted from many different environments such as streets, prison, and schools. In comparison, the non-violent videos are human activities such as playing football and basketball, tennis, swimming, eating. Unlike previous benchmarks, this dataset includes videos with a wide variety of gender, race, and age collected from different categories. Also, the RLVS benchmark is used to fine-tuning the proposed model and makes it more reliable in real-life situations [1].

Such as the RLVS, the **Real Word Fight (RWF) dataset** also has 2,000 videos splitted in two classes, violence (1,000 videos) and non-violence (1,000 videos). The major difference between RWF and all others dataset is that their videos are all from surveillance cameras [21]. The RWF 2000 solve insufficient high-quality data from real violence activities. This dataset has a large scale with 2,000 clips extracted from surveillance videos from the YouTube website, consisting of 2,000 trimmed video clips captured by surveillance cameras from real-world scenes. That was cut video into a 5-s clip with 30 FPS. In the end, it deleted the noisy clips which contain unrealistic and non-monitoring scenes and annotate each clip as Violence or Non-Violence [21].

In Car dataset, has 340 videos split into two classes, violence (74 videos) and non-violence (266 videos). This dataset is a collection of movies scenes and Huber scenes.

3.3 Training Settings

We have trained four instances of our CNN-based model, each of them using a different dataset. The models were trained during 100 epochs using the Stochastic Gradient Descent optimizer with a learning rate of 0.01. We have used a batch size of 8, that is, eight videos for iteration. To evaluate our model in the test set, we have selected the best model in the validation set of the 100 epochs. The validation set is 20% of the training set. In the next section, we present and discuss the results obtained from these experiments.

4   Results and Discussion

Table 1 presents all the accuracy and f-measure results obtained from the experiments. We have presented the results on the test set of each dataset and our In Car data. As expected, the test data results with the Hockey Fights and Movies benchmarks are better

Table 1. Train data, accuracy and F-Measure for the three datasets.

Setting		Accuracy		F-Measure
Model	Train data	Test data	P30 data	In car dataset
Flow Gated RGB	Hockey Fights	93,00	21,17	8,11
Flow Gated RGB	Movies	90,00	32,64	32,51
Flow Gated RGB	VFCF	82,00	56,47	60,27
Flow Gated RGB	RWF	81,00	50,00	53,46
Flow Gated RGB	RLVS	87,25	**75,00**	**75,51**

than RWF and RLVS because Hockey Fights and Movies have few and simple videos. Besides, they have videos with a very closed scenario.

From Table 2, we can see the cross-entropy loss obtained from all datasets. We have computed the cross-entropy loss for the training and test set for each dataset. Besides, we also have computed it for the In Car dataset. The loss function is essential because it represents the function, we want to minimize in the optimization process. The results show that the RWF has the lowest loss value in the In Car dataset.

Table 2. Train and testing loss for the three datasets.

Setting		Loss		
Model	Train data	Train data	Test data	In car dataset
Flow Gated RGB	Hockey Fights	0,089	**0,405**	12,64
Flow Gated RGB	Movies	0,117	0,925	2,947
Flow Gated RGB	VFCF	0,031	1,008	1,912
Flow Gated RGB	RWF	0,577	0,543	**1,138**
Flow Gated RGB	RLVS	**0,012**	0,849	1,447

Based on the four training dataset, we have the training loss, the test loss for each dataset. When the transfer learning is making for the In Car dataset, we can observe the results for our dataset (Fig. 2).

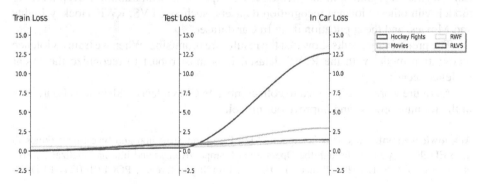

Fig. 2. Comparison between the four public dataset and In Car dataset.

The confusion matrix presented in Fig. 3 can be seen as a description of the model decisions in a dataset. Metrics such as Accuracy, Misclassification error, True positive rate, False positive rate, True negative rate, Precision, and Relevance can all be computed from the confusion matrix. Due to its importance, we have computed the confusion matrix of all trained models in the In Car dataset.

The results presented in the confusion matrix of Fig. 3 shows that the models trained from Movies, Hockey Fights, and RWF make bad decisions in the in-car scenario. They

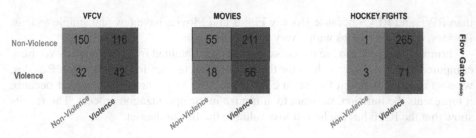

Fig. 3. Confusion matrix obtained from all models in Car dataset.

almost always predict non-violence for the videos. Thus, the robustness power of the models trained with those datasets can be limited to the same data distribution. However, the confusion matrix obtained from the model trained with the RLVS dataset has better decisions, although it is not perfect.

5   Conclusion and Future Work

First of all, we have found four public datasets for detecting violence. Then we have created our dataset based on movies and uber films published on YouTube. All the videos from our dataset have been cut in order to have a duration of 20 s. Then we have analyzed all the models applied to violence detection. We have chosen the model with fewer parameters in order to have faster processing. Then, we have applied transfer learning to solve In Car Violence Recognition. Since there is no dataset specific for In Car Violence recognition in the literature, we experiment with training a deep learning model with others violence recognition datasets, such as RLVS, RWF, Hockey Fights and Movies, and the application in an In Car dataset.

The preliminary results show that the results are promising. When we train a violence recognition model with the RLVS dataset, it is most robust to recognize the in-car violence scenes.

As future works, we intended to collect more In Car violence videos to validate data in the training process and improve our model.

Acknowledgement. This work is supported by: European Structural and Investment Funds in the FEDER component, through the Operational Competitiveness and Internationalization Programme (COMPETE 2020) [Project nº 039334; Funding Reference: POCI-01–0247-FEDER-039334].

References

1. Soliman, M.M., Kamal, M.H., Nashed, M.A.E.M., Mostafa, Y.M., Chawky, B.S., Khattab, D.: Violence recognition from videos using deep learning techniques. In: 2019 Ninth International Conference on Intelligent Computing and Information Systems (ICICIS), pp. 80–85. IEEE, December 2019

2. Poppe, R.: A survey on vision-based human action recognition. Image Vis. Comput. **28**(6), 976–990 (2010)
3. Mabrouk, A.B., Zagrouba, E.: Abnormal behavior recognition for intelligent video surveillance systems: a review. Expert Syst. Appl. **91**, 480–491 (2018)
4. Lopez-Fuentes, L., van de Weijer, J., González-Hidalgo, M., Skinnemoen, H., Bagdanov, A.D.: Review on computer vision techniques in emergency situations. Multimedia Tools Appl. **77**(13), 17069–17107 (2017). https://doi.org/10.1007/s11042-017-5276-7
5. Wang, P., Li, W., Ogunbona, P., Wan, J., Escalera, S.: RGB-D-based human motion recognition with deep learning: a survey. Comput. Vis. Image Underst. **171**, 118–139 (2018)
6. Gowsikhaa, D., Abirami, S., Baskaran, R.: Automated human behavior analysis from surveillance videos: a survey. Artif. Intell. Rev. **42**(4), 747–765 (2012). https://doi.org/10.1007/s10462-012-9341-3
7. Afsar, P., Cortez, P., Santos, H.: Automatic visual detection of human behavior: a review from 2000 to 2014. Expert Syst. Appl. **42**(20), 6935–6956 (2015)
8. Maheshwari, S., Heda, S.: A review on crowd behavior analysis methods for video surveillance. In: Proceedings of the Second International Conference on Information and Communication Technology for Competitive Strategies, pp. 1–5, March 2016
9. Dubuisson, S., Gonzales, C.: A survey of datasets for visual tracking. Mach. Vis. Appl. **27**(1), 23–52 (2015). https://doi.org/10.1007/s00138-015-0713-y
10. Zhang, J., Li, W., Ogunbona, P.O., Wang, P., Tang, C.: RGB-D-based action recognition datasets: a survey. Pattern Recogn. **60**, 86–105 (2016)
11. Singh, T., Vishwakarma, D.K.: Video benchmarks of human action datasets: a review. Artif. Intell. Rev. **52**(2), 1107–1154 (2018). https://doi.org/10.1007/s10462-018-9651-1
12. Komagal, E., Yogameena, B.: Foreground segmentation with PTZ camera: a survey. Multimedia Tools Appl. **77**(17), 22489–22542 (2018)
13. Zhou, P., Ding, Q., Luo, H., Hou, X.: Violence detection in surveillance video using low-level features. PLoS One **13**(10) (2018)
14. Deniz, O., Serrano, I., Bueno, G., Kim, T.K.: Fast violence detection in video. In: 2014 International Conference on Computer Vision Theory and Applications (VISAPP), vol. 2, pp. 478–485. IEEE, January 2014
15. De Souza, F.D., Chavez, G.C., do Valle Jr, E.A., Araújo, A.D.A.: Violence detection in video using spatio-temporal features. In: 2010 23rd SIBGRAPI Conference on Graphics, Patterns and Images, pp. 224–230. IEEE, August 2010
16. Gao, Y., Liu, H., Sun, X., Wang, C., Liu, Y.: Violence detection using oriented violent flows. Image Vis. Comput. **48**, 37–41 (2016)
17. Hassner, T., Itcher, Y., Kliper-Gross, O.: Violent flows: real-time detection of violent crowd behavior. In: 2012 IEEE Computer Society Conference on Computer Vision and Pattern Recognition Workshops, pp. 1–6. IEEE, June 2012
18. Jalal, A., Mahmood, M., Hasan, A.S.: Multi-features descriptors for human activity tracking and recognition in Indoor-outdoor environments. In: 2019 16th International Bhurban Conference on Applied Sciences and Technology (IBCAST), pp. 371–376. IEEE, January 2019
19. Mahmood, S., Khan, Y.D., Khalid Mahmood, M.: A treatise to vision enhancement and color fusion techniques in night vision devices. Multimedia Tools Appl. **77**(2), 2689–2737 (2017). https://doi.org/10.1007/s11042-017-4365-y
20. Marcondes, F.S., Durães, D., Gonçalves, F., Fonseca, J., Machado, J., Novais, P.: In-vehicle violence detection in carpooling: a brief survey towards a general surveillance system. In: International Symposium on Distributed Computing and Artificial Intelligence, pp. 211–220. Springer, Cham, June 2020

21. Cheng, M., Cai, K., Li, M. RWF-2000: an open large scale video database for violence detection. In: 2020 25th International Conference on Pattern Recognition (ICPR), pp. 4183–4190). IEEE, January 2021
22. Mabrouk, A.B., Zagrouba, E.: Spatio-temporal feature using optical flow based distribution for violence detection. Pattern Recogn. Lett. **92**, 62–67 (2017)
23. Senst, T., Eiselein, V., Kuhn, A., Sikora, T.: Crowd violence detection using global motion-compensated Lagrangian features and scale-sensitive video-level representation. IEEE Trans. Inf. Forensics Secur. **12**(12), 2945–2956 (2017)
24. Goodfellow, I., Bengio, Y., Courville, A., Bengio, Y.: Deep learning, vol. 1, No. 2, MIT press, Cambridge
25. He, K., Zhang, X., Ren, S., Sun, J.: Deep residual learning for image recognition. In: Proceeding of the IEEE Conference on Computer Vision and Pattern Recognition, pp. 770–778 (2016)
26. Huang, G., Liu, Z., Van Der Maaten, L., Weinberger, K.Q.: Densely connected convolutional networks. In: Proceedings of the IEEE Conference on Computer Vision and Pattern Recognition, pp. 4700–4708 (2017)
27. Hochreiter, S., Bengio, Y., Fransconi, P., Schmidhuber, J.: Gradient flow in recurrent nets: the difficulty of learning long-terms dependencies (2001)
28. Feichtenhofer, C., Fan, H., Malik, J., He, K.: Slowfast networks for video recognition. In: Proceedings of the IEEE International Conference on Computer Vision, pp. 6202–6211 (2019)
29. Carreira, J., Andrew, Z.: Quo vadis, action recognition? A new model and the kinetics dataset. In: Proceedings of the IEEE Conference on Computer Vision and Pattern Recognition, pp. 6299–6308 (2017)
30. Wang, X., Girshick, R., Gupta, A., He, K.: Non-local neural networks. In Proceedings of the IEEE Conference on Computer Vision and Pattern Recognition, pp. 7794–7803 (2018)
31. Feichtenhofer, C.: X3d: Expanding architectures for efficient video recognition. In: Proceedings of the IEEE/CVF Conference on Computer Vision and Pattern Recognition, pp. 203–213 (2020)
32. Gracia, I.S., Suarez, O.D., Garcia, G.B., Kim, T.K.: Fast fight detection. PLoS One **10**(4), e0120448 (2015)
33. Serrano Gracia, I., Deniz Suarez, O., Bueno Garcia, G., Kim, T.-K.: Fast fight detection. PLoS ONE **10**(4), e0120448 (2015). https://doi.org/10.1371/journal.pone.0120448
34. Durães, D., Marcondes, F. S., Gonçalves, F., Fonseca, J., Machado, J., & Novais, P. (2020, June). Detection Violent Behaviors: A Survey. In International Symposium on Ambient Intelligence (pp. 106–116). Springer, Cham.
35. Costa, A., Castillo, J.C., Novais, P., Fernández-Caballero, A., Simoes, R.: Sensor-driven agenda for intelligent home care of the elderly. Expert Syst. Appl. **39**(15), 12192–12204 (2012). https://doi.org/10.1016/j.eswa.2012.04.058

General AI

Deep Neural Network Architectures for Speech Deception Detection: A Brief Survey

Andrey Lucas Herchonvicz[(✉)] and Rafael de Santiago

Department of Computer Science and Statistics, Federal University
of Santa Catarina, Florianópolis, Brazil
andrey.lh@posgrad.ufsc.br, r.santiago@ufsc.br

Abstract. The task of detecting deception has a long history since using the polygraph. In contrast, spot deception in conversational speech has been proved to be a current complex challenge. The use of this technology can be applied in many fields such as security, cybersecurity, human resources, psychology, media, and also for suspect interrogation. Due to the difficulty of detecting lies through speech, many approaches are applying deep learning combining audio of speech and textual characteristics from audio transcription. Many techniques have been developed to spot deceit through speech, and the purpose of this paper is to discuss in more detail these approaches. We discuss deep learning-based techniques and also other aspects such as available datasets and metrics. Finally, we argue about the limitations and examine promising and future works.

Keywords: Speech deception detection · Lie detection · Voice stress · Deep learning

1 Introduction

Deception detection has a long human history. It starts with the invention of the polygraph, a device that uses a set of sensors to retrieve a person's measures, such as blood pressure, pulse, respiration, and perspiration. This technology is not available for the general public and was applied by some governments to interrogate criminal suspects [17]. If this technology were accessible, many fields could benefit. Human Resources (HR) could spot deceit speech from candidates in a job interview. Financial institutions and insurance companies could use this technology as an auxiliary tool to catch deceit statements before providing a loan or to register claims. Finally, computer applications could use this technology as an authentication method.

In the last few years, deep learning-based approaches have been using to classify deceptive or truth statements. Such methods are evolving and achieving better results as the computing power will become more accessible [13]. Another important aspect is the features used to spot lies through speech. There are many

G. Marreiros et al. (Eds.): EPIA 2021, LNAI 12981, pp. 301–312, 2021.
https://doi.org/10.1007/978-3-030-86230-5_24

different types such as Mel-frequency Cepstral Coefficients (MFCC) [11], Zero-Crossing Rate (ZCR) [4], Fundamental Frequency (F0), acoustic and prosodic features [16]. Another possibility is to transcribe the speech and extract text features [10].

However, the most challenging task in deception detection is the lack of data. The most common reasons that lead a person to hide the truth are to gain something or get rid of something [22]. So, it is hard to produce a synthetic dataset with the same characteristics as real life.

In this paper, we aim to explore such methods in order to understand the latest achievements in deep neural networks to detect deception, to the best of our knowledge. Moreover, we intend to compare these techniques to figure out what are the most suitable approaches. Features have a huge impact on the results and we propose a comparison between these features.

Our main contributions are:

- Survey the most relevant speech deception detection using deep learning papers;
- Describe the steps of how the research was conducted in these works;
- Compare these works and discuss the main contributions;
- Describe the current challenges and opportunities for future work.

The rest of this paper is divided as follows. In Sect. 2, we describe the steps we took to conduct this work. An overview of Deep Learning features and methods applied to the deception detection task in speech are presented in Sects. 3 and 4. We discuss and compare the presented methods in Sect. 5. Finally, we present our conclusion in Sect. 6.

2   Methodology

The search strategy considered published conference papers and articles that contains the follow queries in the title, abstract or keywords:

- "neural network" OR "deep learning" AND;
- ("voice" OR "speech" OR "lexical") AND ("deception" OR "deceit" OR "lie" OR "stress") AND "detection".

The search process was conducted in ACM Digital Library, IEEE Xplore, Scopus, and Web of Science corpus, which are some of the largest indexers of articles available. In addition, the Google search tool focused on researching academic works, Google Scholar, was used. Finally, the article repository of Cornell University, arXiv.org, was also used.

The research of detecting deception is a field presented in many fields, such as computer science, psychology, and medicine. The search strategy focused on documents published only in computer science and discard research of other fields because we are interested in automatic deception detection. Furthermore, some criteria was used, and the process to select papers were as follows:

1. Search for papers in indexers;
2. Remove duplicates;
3. Remove invalid articles;
4. Discard papers published before 2010;
5. Remove articles with the words "video", "image", "twitter" or "tweet" in the title;
6. Discard papers not related to computer science;
7. Research to spot lie using other techniques, rather than only speech and speech and text was rejected;
8. Consider only papers that are using deep learning or neural network methods;
9. Discarded multi-class classification problems;
10. Remove papers that are not focusing only on deep learning;
11. Remove papers not related to this research.

3 Speech Deception Detection Features

There are several types of features that can be extracted from audio signal. Such features can be acoustic where the speech data is processed by an algorithm in order to describe characteristics of a signal. According to [20], the most suitable features to emotion recognition are MFCCs, Preceptual linear prediction cepstral coefficients (PLP), and Linear Prediction Cepstral Coefficients (LPCC). This suggests that these features types can be applied to deception detection since the both tasks are closely related [24].

4 Deep Learning Methods to Speech Deception Detection

With expanding computing power, new approaches emerged in the last few years to detect deception. One of the most promising fields is deep learning. In this section we will describe methods to detect deception that are using deep learning. The Subsect. 4.1 describes methods to spot lies thought speech using LSTM networks. Subsection 4.2 shows approaches to speech deception detection using hydrid networks.

4.1 Long Short-Term Memory

Long short-term memory (LSTM) is a type of recurrent neural network (RNN) where each cell has the input, the previous state, and the memory. Because of this architecture, LSTM is useful to process sequences of data. [7] develop a cross-language MLP model, using English and Hebrew speeches. Due to lack of data, the authors created a dataset through a card game where the subjects are forced to bluff to win the game.

After collecting the audio, the authors pre-processed the data by removing silence periods of speeches (trim). Next, a spectrogram was extracted from each audio segment. At this point, each audio sequence was ready to input in the model.

The LSTM model was trained on the English speeches and tested on Hebrew and vice-versa. The authors used an LSTM with 64 hidden neurons and mini-batches of 64 samples. The training process was made using 300 epochs. The authors also used a cross-validation technique with 5 k-fold.

Table 1 presents the result of the work in terms of accuracy, precision, recall, and f1-score. The model was trained with three different input features, mixed trained and tested language, trained in English and tested in Hebrew, and trained in Hebrew and tested in English.

Table 1. Comparison of models performance according with training and testing set

Train language	Test language	Accuracy	Precision	Recall	F1-Score
English	Hebrew	56%	36%	29%	32.12%
Hebrew	English	58%	50%	34%	40.47%
Mixed	Mixed	**60%**	**52%**	**42%**	**46.47%**

Marcolla proposes a work to spot lies using voice stress [12]. Their method uses only voice and the features are a set of MFCC characteristics extracted from audio. The model using to detecting voice stress is an LSTM neural network. Thus, in their work, the authors tested several variations of deep neural architectures and hyperparameters.

The dataset was collected through a set of interviews in the Brazilian Portuguese language, where the subjects were instructed to answer questions with true and false statements.

In their method, the authors applied a pre-processing phase by first, splitting the audio into many files. Next, all silence periods were removed before and after the statements. Forward, the features were extracted and the vectors were padded with zeros based on the largest sequence. Finally, the model was trained.

In their work, the authors tested several LSTM models until you reach the best performance in terms of accuracy. The best model was a 3 layer LSTM with 300 hidden neurons each and a batch size of 64 samples. Furthermore, the loss function was binary cross-entropy with softmax as the activation function. The model was trained using Adam optimizer with 150 epochs and 0.01 as the learning rate. Finally, the number of MFCCs was 13. The accuracy of this model was 72.5%.

4.2 Hybrid Networks

The architecture proposed by [2], which is an ensemble of a Bidirectional LSTM (BLSTM) with dense layers and an attention mechanism. The idea of BLSTM is that memory can be propagated through the sequence as-is and in the reverse order. The gives more context to the network.

In their work, the authors used the Daily Deceptive Dialogues Corpus of Mandarin (DDDM) [9] dataset. The DDDM was recorded in Mandarin through a game where the subjects were convinced to lie about their own experiences to win opportunities.

There are two different sets of features used in this work. The first group of features has 988 features and were extracted from the answer of subjects. The main features of the first group are F0, energy, loudness, MFCC, probability of voicing, 8 line spectral frequencies (LSF), Zero-crossing rate, and delta regression coefficients.

The second group of features was extracted using the interaction between questions of the interviewer and answers by the interviewee. This group consists of 20 features such as duration, duration difference, duration addition, duration ratio, utterance-duration ratio, silence-duration ratio, silence-utterance ratio, hesitation time, backchannel times, and silence times.

The model used in this work consists of five layers. The first and fourth layers are fully connected with 16 hidden units using Rectified Linear Unit (ReLU) as the activation function. These layers also have a dropout of 0.5. The second layer is a BLSTM with 8 hidden units and a dropout of 0.5. Next, is the Attention layer with 0.5 of dropout. Finally, the last layer is the output layer with 1 hidden unit.

For training, the authors used a batch size of 32, a learning rate of 0.0005, and an early stopping strategy to stop model training when the performance stops to improve. Furthermore, a cross-validation technique was used with a k-fold of 10. The Adamax optimizer was used and the model was training with 300 epochs.

Table 2 shows the results of the proposed method. As we can see the best performance in terms of accuracy was achieved by using both, acoustic and temporal set of features.

Table 2. Comparison of models performance according with training and testing set

Input features set	Accuracy	Precision	Recall	F1-Score
Acoustic	70.85%	70.53%	70.31%	70.03%
Temporal	66.02%	68.37%	66.02%	64.87%
Acoustic + Temporal	**74.71%**	**75.52%**	**74.71%**	**74.39%**

A recurrent neural network is combined with a convolution operation in the work of [23]. The proposed method consists of using ConvBLSTM, BLSTM, and fully connected layers. ConvBLSTM is like a regular LSTM where the internal multiplications are replaced by convolutions operations.

In this work, two models were trained using different datasets. The first dataset was created by the authors where the subjects were convinced to take a makeup test to get a job opportunity. After the test, teachers of the university interviewed the subjects and they are forced to lie, in order to not lose a job opportunity and not be suspended from university for cheating. This dataset was recorded in Chinese. The second dataset using in this work was the Columbia-SRI-Colorado (CSC) corpus which was recorded in English [8].

The models were trained using acoustic features. The feature set consists of Zero-crossing rate, Root mean square of the frame energy, F0, Spectral centroid, Spectral spread, Spectral entropy, Spectral flux, Spectral roll-off, MFCCs, Delta MFCCs, second-order delta MFCCs, and LPCC.

Once the speech waveform was collected, the authors removed the silent segments. Next, features were extracted and normalization was applied. The normalization consists of zero-padding the audio sequences into the same dimension. Finally, the audio sequences are passed to the model for training.

The first two layers of the model are a ConvBLSTM 60 hidden units and kernel shape of (60,2,4). The next two layers are BLSTM with 1024 and 512 hidden units. Following, a fully connected layer comes next with 512 cells and another fully connected with 2 cells. After the second ConvBLSTM and the second BLSTM, the authors used a batch normalization and a dropout of 0.6. A skip connection was used after the first batch normalization and dropout through the first fully connected layer. Excessive abstraction can cause information loss and gradient diffusion, and one way to prevent that from happening in the top feature, is using skip connections.

The training was performed through 60,000 steps with a learning rate of 0.0001, batch size of 128, and clipping of 32. The model obtained 80.85% of accuracy in the research dataset and 68.4% in CSC. The authors also compared the ConvBLSTM+Skip with another two models. The first was training by replacing the ConvBLSTM layers with regular BLSTM. The accuracy was 74.9% in the research dataset and 66.4% in CSC. The second was trained using the proposed model but without the skip connection. The accuracy was 76.75% in the research dataset and 65.45% in CSC.

Audio is not limited to acoustic features. Through speech, we can transcribe the audio into text, extract textual features, and combined acoustic and textural features. That is the proposed of the authors in [13]. In their work, the authors proposed a hybrid neural network model using fully connected layers with a BLSTM.

In their work, the authors used the Columbia X-Cultural Deception (CXD) Corpus [11], recorded in English by native American English and Mandarin Chinese. In CXD, the subjects answered bibliography questions, and they were convinced to lie in order to a financial incentive.

The first type of features were acoustic-prosodic features. This set was composed by low-level descriptor (LLD) from ComParE Challenge baseline feature set [19]. This set contains different types of features such as pitch, F0, energy, spectral, MFCC, duration, voice quality, spectral harmonicity, and psychoacoustic spectral sharpness. Emotion features act as clues to detect deception [1]. That is why the authors used the Interspeech 2009 (IS09) emotion challenge feature set [18]. Finally, the authors also extracted MFCCs generating 13 cepstral coefficients by each window of 256 frames with a step of 100 frames.

The second group of features used in their work was lexical. This group of features is composed of unigrams, bigrams, and trigrams between deceptive and truthful speeches. Thus, Word Embeddings (WE) was extracted from audio transcriptions using GloVe [15] pre-trained word vectors.

In their work, the authors tested 4 different deep learning models using different features set. The model with the best performance in terms of f1-score was an ensemble of two models. The first is a BLSTM with 256 hidden units and a softmax as activation functions, using the pre-trained word embeddings as features. The second model is an MLP with 6 layers and 1095 hidden units each and was trained using the Interspeech 2009 (IS09) emotion challenge feature set. The activation function was ReLu and a batch normalization was applied. It was also used a dropout of 0.497 with L2 regularization of 0.2. Finally, the MLP was trained using the Stochastic Gradient Descent (SGD) optimizer and learning rate of 0.00134. To balance the weights of the two networks, the authors applied an auxiliary softmax prediction layer to the BLSTM.

Table 3 compare the results of the hybrid model with other tested approaches. The performance of the models was calculated in terms of precision, recall, and F1-score. The hybrid approach achieved 67.32%, 60.80%, and 63.90%, respectively. Besides the deep learning models, the authors also compared with baseline classifiers trained with Logistic Regression (LR) and Random Forest (RF).

Table 3. Comparison of models performance. Table taken from [11].

	Features	Precision	Recall	F1-Score
Hydrid	WE + IS09	67.32%	60.80%	**63.90%**
BLSTM	WE	60.46%	60.45%	60.46%
BLSTM	MFCC	54.19%	55.10%	54.64%
MLP	IS09	65.87%	59.84%	62.71%
MLP	IS13	63.65%	58.03%	60.71%
LR	Trigrams	58.67%	**63.95%**	61.19%
RF	IS09	72.67%	50.44%	59.54%
RF	IS09 + Trigrams	**76.11%**	46.99%	58.10%

One of the main problems to detect deception is the lack of data. There are a few datasets available on the internet, but every corpus has different characteristics. Besides, deep neural networks achieve the best results with a huge amount of data. On the other hand, we have a huge amount of data, but these data are unlabeled. To address this problem, [4] proposed an approach using a semi-supervised technique composed of an encoder, a decoder, and a classifier.

In their work, the authors chose to use two different datasets. The first one is the CSC corpus which was recorded in English, where 5411 samples were used. The second dataset was created by the authors using the audio from two popular role-playing games in China: the werewolf game and the killer game.

Essentially, the audios were extracted from the videos, cut, and labeled as truth and lies. At last, the dataset is composed of 468 deceitful statements and 519 true statements.

Table shows 4 the features used in this research. The feature set used in their work was selected from INTERSPEECH 2009 Emotion Challenge [18]. The feature set is composed of 16×2 low-level descriptors (LLD) which consist of ZCR, harmonics-to—noise (HNR), MFCC 1–12, root mean square (RMS), and 12 description functions with mean, maximum and minimum, mean. Furthermore, the total feature vector per chunk contains $16 \times 2 \times 12 = 384$ attributes.

Table 4. LLDs and functionals. Table taken from [4].

LLDs (16×2)	Functionals(12)
(Δ)RMS Energy	Standard deviation
(Δ)F0	Kurtosis, skewness
(Δ)MFCC 1–12	Linear regression: offset, slope, MSE
(Δ)ZCR	Mean
(Δ)HNR	Extremes: value, rel, position, range

The semi-supervised additive noise autoencoder (SS-ANE) is a variation of the semi-supervised autoencoder (SS-AE), which was proposed by [3], and is used for speech emotion recognition. The idea of this model is to combine supervised learning and unsupervised learning where each part is composed of several layers B. Each of layers B contains weights, batch normalization process to accelerate training, Elu as activation functions which is a variation of the ReLu that prevents 0 as output, and a dropout to avoid over-fitting. The encoder components are used to extract high-order features of original data. Finally, the decoder is divided into two parts, the first one is responsible to maps the features to the output to reconstruct the data. The second part classifies the information into the coded features.

Table 5 compare the accuracy results of the proposed model with other tested approaches in CSC corpus and proposed killer game dataset, respectively. Tested approaches are Support Vector Machine (SVM), Deep Neural Networks (DNN) [6], StackedAutoencoder (SDAE) + SVM [21], SS-AE [3], Deep Boltzmann Machines (DBM) [5], and Deep Belief Network (DBN) [14]. The proposed model achieved the highest accuracy in relation to other approaches in both datasets, regardless of the number of labeled samples. Thus, the performance in the killer dataset with 200 out of 519 labeled data was 63.89%, which is better than all other approaches, even using all labeled data. Also in the CSC dataset, the accuracy of 62.78% with 1000 out of 5411 labeled data was the best results, except in comparison with DBN with all labeled data.

Table 5. Average accuracy rate with 500, 1000 and all labelled examples. Table taken from [4].

Model	CSC corpus			Proposed corpus		
	Labelled examples					
	500	1000	All	500	1000	All
SVM	56.04%	58.57%	59.40%	57.82%	59.48%	60.04%
DNN [6]	56.87%	59.46%	60.48%	58.34%	60.35%	61.08%
SDAE+SVM [21]	57.75%	60.58%	61.63%	59.96%	61.10%	62.13%
SS-AE [3]	58.01%	60.89%		60.09%	61.48%	
DBM [5]	57.61%	60.75%	61.86%	58.83%	60.59%	61.40%
DBN [14]	58.44%	61.03%	**62.88%**	60.09%	61.62%	**63.64%**
SS-ANE	**59.52%**	**62.78%**		**61.81%**	**63.89%**	

Table 6. Comparison between deep neural network methods to detect deception.

Paper	Method	Corpus	Features types	Best Acc	Best F1
[7]	LSTM	Own	Acoustic	60%	46.47%
[12]	LSTM	Own	Acoustic	72.5%	-
[2]	BLSTM with Attention	DDDM	Acoustic + Temporal	74.71%	**74.39%**
[23]	ConvBLSTM + BLSTM with Skip connection	Own CSC	Acoustic	**80.85%** 62.71%	- -
[13]	BLSTM + MLP	CXD	Acoustic + Lexical	-	63.90%
[4]	SS-ANE	Own CSC	Acoustic	63.89% 62.78%	- -

5 Discussions

Table 6 presents a comparison between the methods presented in this work. Relevant deep neural network methods to detect deception using audio data, are LSTM or hybrid networks based approaches.

As we can see, the best accuracy was achieved by using a combination of ConvBLSTM and BLSTM with skip connection. The model was trained using its own dataset. However, in the same work, the authors used the CSC dataset and in this case, the accuracy was almost 18% lower. This difference could be related to many factors including how data was collected. In the dataset created by the researchers, the subjects were forced to lie to get away from disciplinary measurements. On the other hand, in the CSC dataset, the subjects are convinced to lie in order to fit the top entrepreneurs in America profile. This indicates that the emotions expressed by the participants may have been quite different and leading to different speech characteristics. Other factors that can contribute to the difference in accuracy are languages and cultures (English and Chinese), amount of data, data quality.

We can compare the ConvBLSTM and BLSTM with a skip connection model with SS-ANE due to both approaches are using the CSC dataset. The results in terms of accuracy were very similar, with a small advantage of 0.07% for the SS-ANE: 62.71% to ConvBLSTM and 62.78% to SS-ANE. However, the results of the SS-ANE were achieved used only 1000 out of 5411 labeled data, which corresponds to approximately 18% of labeled data.

In terms of F1-Score, the best result was 74.39% achieved by BLSTM with an Attention mechanism. The approach achieved an improvement by using temporal features such as duration, silence, and hesitation times, in conjunction with acoustic features. The last paper achieved 63.90% of F1-Score. This work applied acoustic and lexical features. However, the last work used a dataset with native English and Chinese speaking in English. This could be more challenging to spot lies in comparing to a dataset where all subjects speak the native language.

The first two approaches used an LSTM network. The accuracy was 60% and 72.5%, respectively. Each of these works created its own dataset. The first proposed a card game where subjects had to lie in order to win the game. In the second approach, subjects were instructed to tell the truth or lie to answer the question. It is hard to compare because emotions can be a clue to spot lies.

Although we have some good results, there are some concerns that we need to address in order to compare these studies. All of the approaches presented in this work are using synthetic data. This means that these works can successfully detect deception in their specific context proposed by the respective experiments, but in the real-world is different. There is no evidence that an automatic lie detector that works for lies to gain advantages, also works for lies to get rid of something. None of these presented works are considering this scenario.

Another concern is that there is no consensus on which corpus to use, only two of these studies used the same dataset. Because of this is hard to figure out what has the best results overall. If these researches were using the same corpus, we could compare the deep neural network architectures for speech deception detection. We could also reproduce these methods more easily and investigate what happened if we change something. Thus, we could compare the feature sets in order to collect the best of each work.

6 Conclusions and Future Works

The focus of this work was to present and compare relevant methods to detect deception using deep neural networks. This is challenging because the lack of data and the quality of data can have a huge impact to determine success. Moreover, methods that work in one dataset may have not work for another. We can address this to a large number of variables such as language and culture and conditions that the data was collected.

This work showed that the current approaches to detect deception with deep neural networks have promising results. The best accuracy was 80.85% achieved by a deep neural network using ConvBLSTM and BLSTM with a skip connection [23]. This results was accomplish using their own dataset. In terms of F1-Score, a BLSTM with Attention mechanism had the best result with 74.39% [2]. In this case, the deep neural network was trained using the DDDM dataset. Furthermore, the work using a semi-supervised approach showed interesting results with 62.78% of accuracy on CSC corpus with only 18% of labeled data [4].

We also have researchers using different types of features set, which can imply that there is no consensus regarding which features set has the best results. Thus, it is hard to determine if one work can be applied in real worlds scenarios because all of these works were performed in synthetic data. In addition, despite that a few works used more than one language, there is no a strong evidence that one model trained in one language can have similar results in other languages. In this case, cultural differences and multiple accents can influence the results.

Despite, the field to detect deception has many challenges, there are also many opportunities for future works. An opportunity that meets the problems identified in this work is the need for more data, as was pointed out by [12]. Another topic that can be explored is the feature set. There is a possibility to include behavioral attributes and the personality of the person, as indicated by [2]. To validate the robustness of the deception detection systems, [13] identified improvements by testing their approach in different datasets. Finally, [4] suggested model improvement through the combination of other deep neural network approaches.

Although the field to detect deception has many opportunities, there are also many open challenges to explore, and mitigating these challenges can be explored as new opportunities. One of these challenges is deception detection systems applied to different languages. Another field that can be explored is to detect if a speech lie detector can be applied in situations of lies to benefit and to get rid of something. Finally, we can explore if deception detection systems can help in real-world situations by comparing these systems with the polygraph.

References

1. Amiriparian, S., Pohjalainen, J., Marchi, E., Pugachevskiy, S., Schuller, B.W.: Is deception emotional? an emotion-driven predictive approach. In: INTERSPEECH, pp. 2011–2015 (2016)
2. Chou, H.C., Liu, Y.W., Lee, C.C.: Joint learning of conversational temporal dynamics and acoustic features for speech deception detection in dialog games. In: 2019 Asia-Pacific Signal and Information Processing Association Annual Summit and Conference (APSIPA ASC), pp. 1044–1050. IEEE (2019)
3. Deng, J., Xu, X., Zhang, Z., Frühholz, S., Schuller, B.: Semisupervised autoencoders for speech emotion recognition. IEEE/ACM Trans. Audio, Speech Lang. Process. **26**(1), 31–43 (2017)
4. Fu, H., Lei, P., Tao, H., Zhao, L., Yang, J.: Improved semi-supervised autoencoder for deception detection. PloS One **14**(10), e0223361 (2019)
5. Goodfellow, I.J., Mirza, M., Courville, A., Bengio, Y.: Multi-prediction deep Boltzmann machines. In: Proceedings of the 26th International Conference on Neural Information Processing Systems-Volume 1, pp. 548–556 (2013)

6. Han, K., Yu, D., Tashev, I.: Speech emotion recognition using deep neural network and extreme learning machine. In: Fifteenth Annual Conference of the International Speech Communication Association (2014)
7. Hershkovitch Neiterman, E., Bitan, M., Azaria, A.: Multilingual deception detection by autonomous agents. Companion Proc. Web Conf. **2020**, 480–484 (2020)
8. Hirschberg, J.B., et al.: Distinguishing deceptive from non-deceptive speech (2005)
9. Huang, C.H., Chou, H.C., Wu, Y.T., Lee, C.C., Liu, Y.W.: Acoustic indicators of deception in mandarin daily conversations recorded from an interactive game. In: INTERSPEECH, pp. 1731–1735 (2019)
10. Kopev, D., Ali, A., Koychev, I., Nakov, P.: Detecting deception in political debates using acoustic and textual features. In: 2019 IEEE Automatic Speech Recognition and Understanding Workshop (ASRU), pp. 652–659. IEEE (2019)
11. Levitan, S.I., et al.: Cross-cultural production and detection of deception from speech. In: Proceedings of the 2015 ACM on Workshop on Multimodal Deception Detection, pp. 1–8 (2015)
12. Marcolla, F.M., de Santiago, R., Dazzi, R.L.: Novel lie speech classification by using voice stress. In: ICAART (2), pp. 742–749 (2020)
13. Mendels, G., Levitan, S.I., Lee, K.Z., Hirschberg, J.: Hybrid acoustic-lexical deep learning approach for deception detection. In: INTERSPEECH, pp. 1472–1476 (2017)
14. Mohamed, A.R., Hinton, G., Penn, G.: Understanding how deep belief networks perform acoustic modelling. In: 2012 IEEE International Conference on Acoustics, Speech and Signal Processing (ICASSP), pp. 4273–4276. IEEE (2012)
15. Pennington, J., Socher, R., Manning, C.D.: Glove: global vectors for word representation. In: Proceedings of the 2014 Conference on Empirical Methods in Natural Language Processing (EMNLP), pp. 1532–1543 (2014)
16. Pérez-Rosas, V., Abouelenien, M., Mihalcea, R., Xiao, Y., Linton, C., Burzo, M.: Verbal and nonverbal clues for real-life deception detection. In: Proceedings of the 2015 Conference on Empirical Methods in Natural Language Processing, pp. 2336–2346 (2015)
17. Place, V.: The Guilt Project: Rape, Morality, and Law. Other Press, LLC, New York (2010)
18. Schuller, B., Steidl, S., Batliner, A.: The interspeech 2009 emotion challenge. In: Tenth Annual Conference of the International Speech Communication Association (2009)
19. Schuller, B., et al.: The interspeech 2013 computational paralinguistics challenge: social signals, conflict, emotion, autism. In: Proceedings INTERSPEECH 2013, 14th Annual Conference of the International Speech Communication Association, Lyon, France (2013)
20. Sharma, G., Umapathy, K., Krishnan, S.: Trends in audio signal feature extraction methods. Appl. Acoust. **158**, 107020 (2020)
21. Vincent, P., Larochelle, H., Lajoie, I., Bengio, Y., Manzagol, P.A., Bottou, L.: Stacked denoising autoencoders: learning useful representations in a deep network with a local denoising criterion. J. Mach. Learn. Res. **11**(12), 3371–3408 (2010)
22. White, L.: Telling more: lies, secrets, and history. Hist. Theory **39**(4), 11–22 (2000)
23. Xie, Y., Liang, R., Tao, H., Zhu, Y., Zhao, L.: Convolutional bidirectional long short-term memory for deception detection with acoustic features. IEEE Access **6**, 76527–76534 (2018)
24. Zloteanu, M.: The role of emotions in detecting deception. In: Deception: An Interdisciplinary Exploration, pp. 203–217. Brill (2015)

3DSRASG: 3D Scene Retrieval and Augmentation Using Semantic Graphs

Sharadha Srinivasan, Shreya Kumar[✉], Vallikannu Chockalingam, and Chitrakala S.

College of Engineering Guindy, Anna University, Chennai, India
shreyakumar603@gmail.com , chitras@annauniv.edu

Abstract. Computer Vision, encompassing 3D Vision and 3D scene Reconstruction, is a field of importance to real-world problems involving 3D views of scenes. The goal of the proposed system is to retrieve 3D scenes from the database, and further augment the scenes in an iterative manner based on the user's commands to finally produce the required output 3D scenes, in the form of a suggestive interface. The process is done recursively to facilitate additions and deletions, until the desired scene is generated. In addition to synthesizing the required 3D indoor scenes from text, a speech recognition system has been integrated with the system that will enable the users to choose from either modes of input. The application includes the projection and rendering of 3D scenes which will enable a 360-° view of the scene. The robustness of scene generation and quick retrieval of scenes will promote the usage of this work in avenues such as story telling, interior designing, and as a helpful educational tool for autistic children.

Keywords: Gaussian Mixture Model · Natural Language Processing · Reinforcement learning · Scene Synthesis · Semantic Scene Graph · Speech Processing

1 Introduction

There is a profuse amount of ongoing research in 3D scene reconstruction and modeling. The proposed system deals with an approach to model 3D scenes that is designed to achieve a combination of 2 tasks: speech-based scene retrieval from scene database, and progressive editing to evolve the scene to accommodate the modifications given as input by the user. Users have the ability to utilize English language statements as commands to produce and edit 3D indoor scenes. 3D scene reconstruction takes as input depth scans or a few images, and then generates the required scene. Natural Language Processing converts the textual inputs in context to scene-related descriptions, and scene editing based on the input speech.

S. Sharadha, K. Shreya, C. Vallikannu—Contributed equally to this paper.

© Springer Nature Switzerland AG 2021
G. Marreiros et al. (Eds.): EPIA 2021, LNAI 12981, pp. 313–324, 2021.
https://doi.org/10.1007/978-3-030-86230-5_25

Scene editing is done by initially parsing the command given by the user and then converting it into a Semantic Graph. The Semantic Graph is utilized to obtain sub-scenes from databases that matches the command given by the user. The pith of this work is the Semantic Scene Graph (SSG), which is essentially a scene depiction that indicates details about the objects in the scene. Semantic scene graph is built for every scene which is used to map object relationships. This is used to retrieve sub-scenes, which also aids in object detection and segmentation. A new 3D scene is created after incorporating augmented scenes within existing scenes wherein the new objects are seamlessly merged with the existing environment. The process is done recursively to facilitate additions and deletions, until the desired scene is generated. This approach also helps to generate complex scenes from any 3D scene dataset, thus providing richer spatial and semantic contexts, with improved versatility. This work could be used in areas ranging from education to interior designing [2,4,6]. The hassle-free usage and quick retrieval of scenes will promote the usage of this work in various avenues. This work could provide favorable models in the prototyping stage for architecture and interior design. Other designing softwares currently being used for the this purpose involve the user to pick and drop objects, which could be an arduous task. The major issues of the related work include object classification loss and predicate classification loss, encodes only a small set of relationships, the problem of less robust post-processing in GAN-based methods and no quantitative metrics to precisely compare the expressive power of generation methods.

The benefit of this work is that is that it deals with information-driven scene demonstration. This work aims to improve the scene generation process and also enhances and augments scenes as and when required by the user. Since the recovered sub-scenes are retrieved from the database or further augmented 3D scenes, the information and semantics that are reflected by the placement and object occurrence inside these scenes would directly be incorporated into the new scene. They need not be recreated or re-examined for such fallacies, thus improving the speed and efficiency. This model is compared to prior work by a series of parameters that will showcase the robustness of the system's ability to generate plausible 3D scenes. All the existing systems lack an interactive user-friendly interface which includes a Speech Recognition and Processing module which would be integrated with this system to enable a better experience for the user. This work enables the novice users to engage with the system efficiently.

The following section would focus on the System Design where the Block Diagram and the overall flow of the system will be explained, followed by other sections including the module-wise design, the experimental analysis, and results. Finally, the paper is concluded.

2   3DSRASG: System Design

2.1   Block Diagram

In the preprocessing stage, the 3D Scene Processing module consists of a 3D scene dataset, scene annotations and learning model. These 3D models are converted into synthetic scenes. These are given as a input to the Semantic Scene Graph Generation module. The user gives input either in the form of text or the speech signal is converted into text, which is then parsed to obtain the entities, the objects and the relationships. After the textual processing, the entities and relationships are fed into the Semantic Scene Graph generation model. The information from the outputs of 3D Scene Processing and the Textual processing steps are utilized to create a Semantic Scene Graph. Following this, the required sub-scene is generated. Further scene augmentation and editing can be done recursively. The flow of the proposed system is shown in Fig. 1. Firstly, an SSG for the given input sentence is created. This Text-SSG is then matched with the closely available scene from the database, in this case, a table and a chair. The missing objects are then added in the Scene Extraction and Enhancement stage where the coffee mug and open book are added to the User-SSG, and the scene is then displayed as a part of the preview.

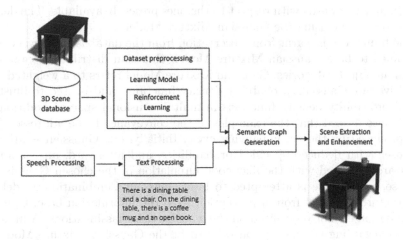

Fig. 1. Architecture diagram

2.2 Dataset Preprocessing

A profuse amount of annotated 3D scenes are collected and are utilized as references for scene synthesis and develop semantic scene graphs for all 3D scenes in the dataset. The 3D scenes which have been utilized are SceneNN, consisting of 80 scenes and SceneSynth, consisting of 133 scenes. For scene enhancement, indoor scenes models are taken from 3D scenes in the dataset by displaying the relative dispersion and co-occurrence. The progression includes connecting the nodes generated from the 3D model and text, by forming cogent annotations for each model present in the database. The annotations are obtained from ShapeNetSem to give labels corresponding to the arrangements and orientations (Ex: "front"). To ease the learning process, all real-world scenes from the SceneNN dataset are converted into a synthetic scenes after extraction from SceneSynth depending on the item labels or annotations in SceneNN.

2.3   Reinforcement Learning Using Gaussian Mixture Model

Reinforcement Learning is a process in which a representative is made to become familiar with an activity by interacting with the activity's environment. The result of a Markov decision process, is the one where at each step the representative keeps track of the present condition of the environment, s_t, and picks an appropriate action based on a particular action policy $a_t = \Pi(s_t)$ [5]. As a result, there is a change in the state of the environment s_{t+1} and it results in the production of $r_t = r(s_t, a_t)$, considered as the reward. The representative then investigates to determine a strategy that will intensify the expected total of discounted rewards, described as

$$R = \sum_{n=1}^{\infty} \gamma^t r_t \tag{1}$$

where γ is the discount rate, with values in [0,1], that regulates the significance of the subsequent rewards with respect to the ones presently available. The density estimation is done using the Gaussian Mixture Model.

The framework is learnt from observation from the database and every scene is assumed to be a Gaussian Mixture Model. Gaussian distribution cannot be used in all object categories. Gaussian Mixture Model refers to a weighted total of multivariate Gaussian probability density functions, and is used to illustrate general probability density functions in multidimensional spaces. Additionally, there is also a need that the examples of the conveyance to be addressed have been produced by the accompanying cycle. Initially, one Gaussian is arbitrarily chosen with deduced specified probabilities, and afterward, an example is haphazardly created with the likelihood circulation of the chosen Gaussian. In any case, every scene is attempted to be a Gaussian Combination Model and the structure is gained from a perception from the information base. Gaussian dissemination cannot be utilized on the whole article classifications. A limit has been set regarding the perception tally to fit the Gaussian Mixture Model. In the event that the perceptions are lesser than the limit, the tuples are recorded for every scene and it is found a way into a discrete likelihood circulation. P is the discrete arrangement probability. It is defined as $P = 1$, when a new item is placed close to an observation that has been saved inside a spatial threshold, otherwise $P = 0$. From the scene database, a relationship model is used to encipher object relationships (either group wise or pair relationships) for a specified textual description. The relationship model consists of an arrangement model A, which keeps track of the spatial arrangements of objects with reference to the anchor object, and an object occurrence model O, which explains the existence of independent items and the co-occurrence of items in a group. Pairwise relationships [3]: When subjected to a pairwise relationship, the score [5] of the pairwise arrangement model is defined as

$$A(o_{act}, o_{anchor}, r) = P(x, y, z, \Theta) \tag{2}$$

where o_{anchor} the anchor object, o_{act} is the active object, and r is the relationship between them. P(x, y, z, θ) is the probability distribution of the relative location [x, y, z] and orientation θ between the anchor object and the active object. Every arrangement model is considered to be a Gaussian Mixture Model and the variables from observations in the database scenes are learnt. Group relationships [3]: The occurrence of objects occurring in groups is defined through the probability

$$O(o_i^m, r) = C(o_i^m, r)/C(s, r) \tag{3}$$

where $C(o_i^m, r)$ is the number of scenes annotated with relationship r which are observed with m instances of o_i. $C(s,r)$ is the total number of scenes, s annotated with r. The co-occurrence probability of an object [3] pair in a group is computed using

$$O(o_i^m, o_j^n, r) = C(o_i^m, o_j^n, r)/maxC(o_i^m, r), C(o_i^n, r) \tag{4}$$

where $C(o_i^m, o_j^n, r)$ is the observation count of two objects with specified instance numbers co-occurring in a group with relationship r. For group relationships, the arrangement model [3] is represented as the total of weighted pairwise arrangement scores:

$$A(O, r) = \sum_{o_i, o_j \in O} \omega A(o_i^m, o_j^n, r) \tag{5}$$

where O is the set of objects in the group; ω is the weight for the corresponding pairwise model $A(o_i^m, o_j^n, r)$ which equals to 1, if one object in the pair is the anchor, otherwise ω is set to $O(o_i, o_j, r)$, i.e., the co-occurrence probability of object instance o_i and o_j in the group.

2.4   Speech Processing

For speech processing, the acoustic model is used. Acoustic model [7] takes the input features and produces characters or separate units. The language models are trained on various large text corpora, and the decoder merges input from acoustic models and language models to produce the resulting transcriptions. The speech recognition system includes data preprocessing, feature extraction, acoustic modeling, and language modeling. The speech is converted to a text which is ultimately given as an input to the system. The Automatic Speech Recognition [7] problem is a statistical classification problem. Classes are defined as sequence of words W, from a closed vocabulary and the parametric representation of the input speech signal defined as X. The classification problem [7] is stated as figuring out the sequence of words W that optimizes the quantity, P (W | X), given as

$$P(W|X) = P(X|W)P(W)/P(X) \tag{6}$$

P (W) is referred to as the language model that depends on linguistic knowledge and high-level constraints of word strings for specific tasks. P(X| W) is a quantity that is the acoustic model.

2.5 Text Processing

The Stanford CoreNLP framework is used in Parts of Speech tagging. This framework is also used to convert the input statements and commands to a dependency tree. The obtained dependency tree [9] assigns an annotation label and parent token to every token present in a sentence. The low-level dependency [10] representation is converted to a list of entities with relationships and attributes, and a list of verbs present in the command. This is the Entity-Command Representation (ECR) [3] of a given sentence. A scene entity contains Category (Ex. "desk"), Attributes (Ex. "oval"), Count (Ex. "many"), Relationships (Ex. "on desk"), and Entities. The verbs are considered as commands. After the seed tokens are identified for the scene entities and commands, pattern matching takes place. The Standford Core NLP output is augmented into the dependency parser. There are 4 special classes: Spatial nouns (Ex. "left"), Counting adjectives (Ex. "some"), Group nouns (Ex. "stack"), and Adjectival verbs (Ex. "messy") [3]. The entity-command representation is converted to a Semantic Scene Graph.

2.6 Semantic Scene Graph Generation

The Semantic Scene Graph (SSG) [1,4,8] encodes the items, their characteristics and co relations onto a graph. SSGs are the intermediate between the input text and the output scene. SSGs correspond to non-oriented graphs. These graphs have 3 components: named edges, nodes and co-relations. The nodes are used to illustrate characteristics like "rectangular" from "rectangular table" and co-relations are used to depict relationships like spatial, corresponding to "above", "below" etc. The named edges connects the co-relations and characteristics.

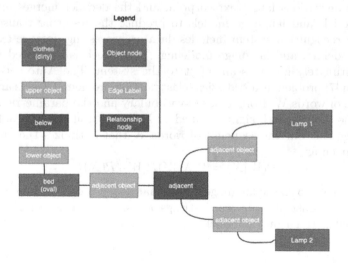

Fig. 2. There is an oval bed with 2 adjacent lamps and dirty clothes on top of it

Algorithm 1. SSG Algorithm

Ensure: Textual Processing has been completed.
  Initialize aligned nodes N as empty set
  Initialize aligned words W as empty set
  for o in object nodes of G(s)/ N **do**
    for w in s/ W **do**
      if o implies w according to WBS **then**
        $Add(o, w); N = N \cup \{o\};$
        $W = W \cup \{w\};$
      end if
    end for
  end for
  for a in attribute nodes of G(s)/ N **do**
    for w in s / W **do**
      if a implies w according to WBW or SYN and a's object is in N **then**
      Add(a,w); N= N $\cup \{a\} W = W \cup \{w\}$
      end if
    end for
    for r in relation nodes of G(s) / N **do**
      for w in s / W **do**
        if r implies w according to WBW or SYN and r's subject and object nodes
        are both in N **then**
        Add(r,w); N=N $\cup \{r\}; W = W \cup \{w\};$
      end if
    end for
    end for
  end for

To fabricate a semantic graph, an object node is first created. Objects are assumed as pivots in this work, as this permits direct retrieval. Then, the connections among objects are realized and are displayed in the graph. The initial object is perceived as the pivot, according to which the other objects are placed and the co-relations are identified. For each object type, the forward facing object is extracted, after which it is rotated relative to the other objects and how it would be aligned realistically. When disposed with a number of objects, one is considered as active and the other as anchor [3].

Then the location of the active object with respect to the anchor object is perceived and stored. For every connection (pairwise or group wise), a correlation node is generated, and associated with the appropriate objects. Names are associated with the edges depending on whether the associated object is an active or anchor item.

The same is illustrated using Fig. 2. The input being "There is an oval bed with 2 adjacent lamps and dirty clothes on top of it", is analyzed and the object nodes, Edges and Relationship nodes are identified.

2.7   Scene Extraction and Enhancement

A Semantic Scene Graph is developed from a textual input. The framework has two modes [3] for advancing the client connected with the scene. If the graphs do not contain a verb node, the framework adjusts Text-SSG to Semantic Scene Graphs of the 3D dataset scenes and searches for a subgraph that matches the given sentence. Nodes that are not aligned from the text are added to the user graph as nodes. Each enhanced subgraph is adjusted and consolidated to User-SSG and supplement the missing objects to the current scene, in view of their relationship to the existing objects. Though for graphs with verb nodes, the aligned nodes to objects in the current scene were directly adjusted, and the scene synthesis functions were executed denoted by the verb. By iterating this process, intricate and logical scenes could be produced by using a set of sentences. A node in T_g is a relationship or an object that needs to be available in the synthesized scene [3]. The nodes of each D_g are aligned to search for the matches that compare accurately to the corresponding scenes. A node in D_g is lined up with one node in T_g. For a group relation node, the content makes reference to the anchor object to address a gathering, the node is said to be adjusted when its relationship and associated anchor object are coordinated. To find the best coordinated scene from D_g for a given T_g, alignment is ranked based on the following metric [3]:

$$\alpha(T_g, D_g) = \sum \alpha(N_i, N_j) \tag{7}$$

Here, N_i and N_j are the nodes from T_g and D_g, respectively; $\alpha(N_i, N_j)$ equals to 1 if N_i and N_j are aligned, and 0 otherwise. The stored scene concept from the scene database is used to enhance the sub-scenes acquired from the Sub-scene graph. The new objects that are inserted come with the same arrangements as in the original database scenes. They need to be updated to satisfy the relationships in the updated U_g. A transformation matrix [3] is computed to align position and orientation of the objects in the S_g and its counterpart in U_g, and this is set as the pre-assigned transformation matrix for objects from the retrieved scene. The objects added by graph enhancement from T_g do not have an initial position with respect to the retrieved scene. Hence, the placement of the newly added objects is determined based on the relationship to the anchor object and its underlying relations with the pre-existing objects in the scene.

3   Results

The results obtained through this speech based scene enhancement method is exhibited, in order to examine the performance. The user can interact with the system through a user interface created using Qt 5.0 software, where the user will be given the option to provide input through speech or text. If the user has entered the input using speech, the speech gets converted to text and each sentence is separated by a "." to distinguish from each other. The speech processing module takes advantage of this iterative enhancement module, by using the group relationships model and incorporating attributes from scene databases, a great level of efficacy was achieved for scene modeling compared to the attempts made previously to achieve scene synthesis through text. A sample scene generation and enhancement scenario is presented in Fig. 3.

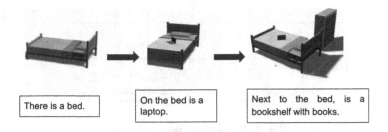

| There is a bed. | On the bed is a laptop. | Next to the bed, is a bookshelf with books. |

Fig. 3. Step-by-step scene development and augmentation

This plausibility test contains 10 test cases of generating 3D scenes from a given input text. The study employed 50 participants in the field of computer science and related fields, with each of them rating a total of 10 scenes each, resulting in a total of $10 \times 50 = 500$ results. Scores are given by the users on the following parameters:

1. Naturalness: How realistic the scenes are to real-life scenarios.
2. Symmetry: Object symmetry with respect to other objects existing in the scene as expected in the input text.
3. Placement: Spatial arrangement of the objects as mentioned in the input text.
4. Coherence: If logical relations present in the input text are present in the output scene.
5. Appeal: Overall visual appeal, Eg: color coding, object dimensions, aesthetics, etc.

Scores are to be given on a scale of 1 (very unsatisfied) to 5 (extremely satisfied). The plots of the variance and averages for each of the factors from the responses of the 50 candidates for each of the parameters: naturalness, symmetry, placement, coherence, appeal were drawn as shown in Fig. 4 and Fig. 5 respectively. Equation 8 and Eq. 9 give the formulas for calculating the average and variance respectively.

$$A = \frac{1}{n}\sum_{i=1}^{n} a_i = \frac{a_1 + a_2 + \cdots + a_n}{n} \tag{8}$$

where A is the Average, n is the total number of items, a_i is value of each item.

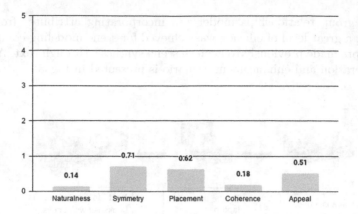

Fig. 4. Plausibility test variance

$$S^2 = \frac{\sum (x_i - \bar{x})^2}{n - 1} \tag{9}$$

where S^2 is the Sampled Variance, x_i is the value of a single variation, $\bar{x}$ is the average of all observations, n is the total number of observations.

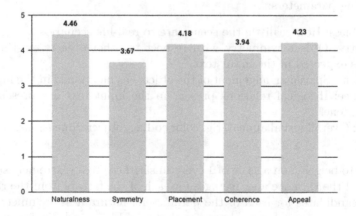

Fig. 5. Plausibility test average

The mean of all the scores obtained across all factors is 4.09. Now naturalness value is compared, as done in the Plausibility Test against Chang et al. (PTC) [3] where it is seen that the naturalness score 4.46 of the proposed system 3DSRASG is better than 1.56 of Chang et al. [10]. This can be credited to improvements in areas like handing relationships, particularly those that occur in groups, the translation to scene graph representations, and the scene enhancement feature. The variance value for every parameter is shown in Fig. 4 is very less, especially for the parameters Naturalness and Coherence. This also provides validation that the proposed procedure has a great performance score and performs with great robustness.

4   Conclusion

The proposed system was achieved as desired. The speech subjected to the system is converted to text through the speech processing module. The description of the scenes intended, either text from speech or through direct text input is subjected to the text processing module. This module focuses on parts of speech tagging. It identifies the entities and commands too. The Semantic Scene Graph Generation module then illustrates the relationships and attributes among the objects in the scene in the form of a graph. The subsequent and final module is the Scene Extraction and Enhancement module, which focuses on extracting the most similar scenes from the database. This scene is further augmented until it fits the need of the user. Then the interface is provided to the user with the five options, ranked from the most similar to least similar. Therefore, the relational model has proved sufficient in providing the user with the 3D indoor scene. The Semantic Scene Graphs were able to successfully link the texts and 3D Scenes. In addition to this, it was also able to concentrate on information regarding the arrangements and positions of the objects in the 3D Scenes. Moreover, the proposed system 3DSRASG supports scene editing and the required 3D indoor scene was extracted from given text in just a few seconds.

Future Work. Aside from 3D scene retrieval and augmentation, issues such as inappropriate object placement, unrealistic object retrieval, retrieved object dimension issues where the objects are sometimes placed inappropriately or the inability to change the dimensions, can be solved by further training the learning model. Eg. "There is food on the dining table". In this situation, sometimes, the objects are partially placed on the table. Such uncertainty in object placement and symmetry could be significantly improved by assisting the existing learning models to better understand the user's intent.

References

1. Wald, J., Dhamo, H., Navab, N., Tombari, F.: Learning 3D semantic scene graphs from 3D indoor reconstructions. In: 2020 IEEE/CVF Conference on Computer Vision and Pattern Recognition (CVPR)
2. Wang, K., Lin, Y.-A., Weissmann, B., Savva, M., Chang, A.X., Ritchie, D.: PlanIT: planning and instantiating indoor scenes with relation graph and spatial prior networks. ACM Trans. Graph. **38**(4), 1–15 (2019)
3. Ma, R., et al.: Language-driven synthesis of 3D scenes from scene databases. ACM (2018)
4. Balint, J.T., Bidarra, R.: A generalized semantic representation for procedural generation of rooms. In: Proceedings of the 14th International Conference on the Foundations of Digital Games (2019)
5. Agostini, A., Celaya, E.: Reinforcement learning with a Gaussian mixture model. In: The 2010 International Joint Conference on Neural Networks (IJCNN) (2010)

324   S. Srinivasan et al.

6. Jiang, Y., Lim, M., Saxena, A.: Learning object arrangements in 3D Scenes using human context. In: 29th International Conference on Machine Learning 2012 (2012)
7. Sarma, K.K., Sarma, M.: Acoustic modeling of speech signal using artificial neural network: a review of techniques and current trends. Intelligent Applications for Heterogeneous System Modeling and Design, ASASEHPC series (2015)
8. Wald, J., Dhamo, H., Navab, N., Tombari, F.: Learning 3D semantic scene graphs from 3D indoor reconstructions. arXiv (2020)
9. Chang, A.X., Eric, M., Savva, M., Manning, C.D.: SceneSeer: 3D scene design with natural language. arXiv (2017)
10. Chang, A., Savva, M., Manning, C.D.: Learning spatial knowledge for text to 3D scene generation. In: Proceedings of the 2014 Conference on Empirical Methods in Natural Language Processing (EMNLP) (2014)

Revisiting "Recurrent World Models Facilitate Policy Evolution"

Bernardo Esteves[1] and Francisco S. Melo[1,2(✉)]

[1] INESC-ID, Lisbon, Portugal
bernardo.esteves@tecnico.ulisboa.pt, fmelo@inesc-id.pt
[2] Instituto Superior Técnico, University of Lisbon, Lisbon, Portugal

Abstract. This paper contributes a detailed analysis of the architecture of Ha and Schmidhuber [5]. The original paper proposes an architecture comprising 3 main components: a "visual" module, a "memory" module; and a controller. As a whole, such architecture performed well in challenging domains. We investigate how each of the aforementioned components contributes individually to the final performance of the system. Our results shed additional light on the role of the different components in the overall behavior of the agent, and illustrate how the different design options affect the behavior of the resulting agent.

Keywords: Deep reinforcement learning · Model-based learning · Ablation study

1 Introduction

In recent years, reinforcement learning (RL) has been the focus of increasing interest, largely due to the impressive successes in video games [11], classical games [13] and control [10], among others. RL algorithms can roughly be categorized as *model-free* and *model-based* [15]. While most of the aforementioned success stories rely on model-free approaches, it is a well-known fact that model-based approaches exhibit better sample efficiency and are more transferable [18].

In a recent work, Ha and Schmidhuber [5] propose a model-based approach inspired by human mental models that attained competitive performance in two difficult tasks [5]. The proposed approach includes two key modules (see Fig. 1): a *visual processing module V* that, in abstract terms, translates the perceptual information of the agent to an internal representation; and a *memory module M* that corresponds to the agent's internal model of the world's dynamics. Based on the information from these two modules, the paper goes on to show that a simple controller is able to attain state-of-the-art results in these two tasks.

This work was supported by national funds through Fundação para a Ciência e a Tecnologia (FCT) with ref. UIDB/50021/2020. BE acknowledges a research grant from Fundação Calouste Gulbenkian under program "Novos Talentos em IA."

© Springer Nature Switzerland AG 2021
G. Marreiros et al. (Eds.): EPIA 2021, LNAI 12981, pp. 325–337, 2021.
https://doi.org/10.1007/978-3-030-86230-5_26

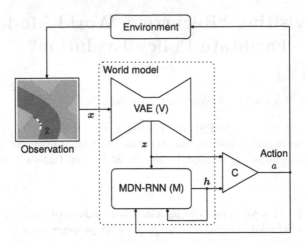

Fig. 1. The model of Ha and Schmidhuber [5] (adapted from the original). The model comprises a world model and a controller C. The world model, in turn, comprises a visual processing component (V) and a memory component (M).

In this paper, we depart from the work of Ha and Schmidhuber [5] and investigate the impact of the different model components in the observed performance of the agent. Our analysis focuses on one of the domains considered in the original paper—the carRacing-v0 domain from Open AI gym [2], depicted in Fig. 1, on the left—and considers how different design choices contributed (positively or negatively) to the results from the original paper.

Notation

We use upright symbols (such as a or x) to denote random variables, and tilted symbols (such as a or x) to denote instances thereof. We use boldface symbols (such as **x** or $\boldsymbol{x}$) to denote vectors and matrices.

2   Background

This section provides an overview of the different modules used in the model of Ha and Schmidhuber [5].

2.1   Variational Autoencoders

Variational autoencoders (VAEs) are generative models originally proposed in the work of Kingma and Welling [8]. A VAE is a latent variable model, assuming that the data of interest, hereby denoted as **x**, can be explained by some set of non-observed (latent) variables **z**. In other words,

$$p(\boldsymbol{x}) = \int_{\mathcal{Z}} p_\phi(\boldsymbol{x} \mid \boldsymbol{z}) p(\boldsymbol{z}) \mathrm{d}\boldsymbol{z},$$

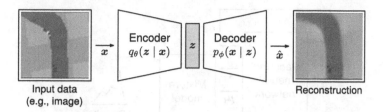

Fig. 2. The variational autoencoder [8].

Fig. 3. Example reconstruction results using the trained VAE.

where $p(z)$ is some prior distribution over the latent variables. Training a VAE thus consists in computing $p_\phi(x \mid z)$.

A standard VAE has the structure depicted in Fig. 2 and includes two main parts: an *encoder* and a *decoder*. The encoder is a neural network that, given an input x, outputs a distribution $q_\theta(z \mid x)$ over the space of latent variables. In a sense, it "encodes" the input x as a low-dimensional representation z. The decoder, in turn, is a neural network that, given a latent vector z, outputs the distribution $p_\phi(x \mid z)$. The, given a dataset $\{x_n, n = 1, \dots, N\}$, the whole encoder-decoder network is trained to minimize the loss

$$\mathcal{L}(\theta, \phi) = -\sum_{n=1}^{N} \mathbb{E}_{z \sim q_\theta(x_n)} \left[\log p_\phi(x_n \mid z) \right] + \mathrm{KL}[q_\theta(x_n) \| p].$$

The first term measures the reconstruction error—the ability of the model to reconstruct x_n given a code z sampled from $q_\theta(\cdot \mid x_n)$. The second works as a regularization term, keeping q_θ as close as possible to the prior p.

Figure 3 illustrates the reconstruction ability of the VAE trained with the data from the carRacing-v0 scenario. In the model of [5], the VAE is responsible for processing the visual inputs x and encoding them as a low-dimensional representation, z. Specifically, the output of the encoder is an input-conditioned Gaussian distribution $q_\theta(\cdot \mid x)$ over latent variables, where the parameters θ correspond to the mean μ and variance σ of the distribution.

2.2 MDN-RNN

A *mixture density network* (MDN) is a probabilistic model originally proposed in the work of Bishop [1]. In an MDN, we model a conditional distribution $p(y \mid x)$ as a *Gaussian mixture*, i.e., we assume that

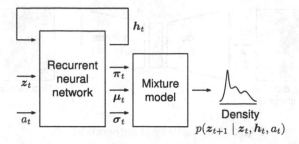

Fig. 4. Mixture density network [1] in the model of Ha and Schmidhuber [5].

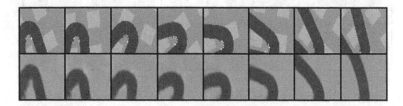

Fig. 5. Predictions using the trained RNN. In each column, an input image x_t is passed through the VAE to get a code, z_t. The pair (z_t, a_t) is used in the MDN-RNN to generate z_{t+1} which is then turned into an image $\hat{x}_{t+1}$ using the VAE decoder. The top row shows the image x_{t+1}, while the bottom row shows $\hat{x}_{t+1}$.

$$p(\boldsymbol{y} \mid \boldsymbol{x}) = \sum_{m=1}^{M} \pi_m(\boldsymbol{x}) \mathcal{N}(\boldsymbol{y} \mid \mu_m(\boldsymbol{x}), \sigma_m(\boldsymbol{x})),$$

where the scalars π_m are the *mixture coefficients*, and $\boldsymbol{\mu}_m$ and σ_m are the parameters of the mixture's mth component. Given a dataset $\{(\boldsymbol{x}_n, \boldsymbol{y}_n), n = 1, \ldots, N\}$, the MDN is trained to minimize the negative log-likelihood of the data.

In the model of Ha and Schmidhuber [5], the MDN takes as input, at each time step, the latent vector z_t coming out of the VAE and the action vector $\boldsymbol{a}_t$ of the agent, and the output is the next latent vector, z_{t+1}. In other words, the MDN learns the distribution $p(z_{t+1} \mid z_t, \boldsymbol{a}_t)$. Since the role of the MDN in the overall model is to capture the temporal dynamics of z_t, the neural network in Fig. 4 is actually a *recurrent neural network*—namely an LSTM [7]—computing a prediction for the next latent vector, z_{t+1}, as a function of the current latent vector, z_t, the agent's current action, a_t, and the history up to time t, encoded in the RNNs hidden state $\boldsymbol{h}_t$. A similar MDN-RNN architecture has been previously used for successful sequence modeling and generation [4]. Figure 5 illustrates the predictions from the trained MDN-RNN in the carRacing-v0 scenario.

2.3 Controller

The model comprising the VAE and the MDN-RNN network are used to determine the action to be executed by the agent. Namely, the VAE provides in z_t a compact representation of the present perception of the agent, while the MDN-RNN hidden state, h_t, provides a compact representation of the *history* of the agent. The two are then used in a controller C to compute

$$a_t = \sigma(\boldsymbol{K}\boldsymbol{f}(\boldsymbol{z}_t, \boldsymbol{h}_t; \boldsymbol{w}) + b), \tag{1}$$

where σ is a squashing function, $\boldsymbol{f}$ is a non-linear function parameterized by $\boldsymbol{w}$, $\boldsymbol{K}$ is a gain matrix and b is a bias term. The parameters $\boldsymbol{w}$, gains and bias are determined using CMA-ES [6], an approach widely used in RL and robotics [14].

In the remainder of the paper we investigate the impact of each component and its several design choices in the overall performance of the agent:

- In the original paper, the visual model outputs a distribution $q_\theta(\cdot \mid \boldsymbol{x})$, and the latent vector $\boldsymbol{z}$ is sampled from this distribution. We also consider the alternative of having the visual module return the *mean* of the distribution $q_\theta(\cdot \mid \boldsymbol{x})$. We denote these two alternatives as V_{sampled} and V_{mean}.
- Tallec et al. [16] provided empirical evidence that the performance of Ha and Schmidhuber [5] can be replicated by using an *untrained* MDN-RNN. Therefore, in our analysis, we look at the performance of the agent with trained and untrained memory models (i.e., where the MDN-RNN weights are random). We denote these two alternatives as M_{trained} and $M_{\text{untrained}}$.
- In terms of the controller, we consider three distinct possibilities of increasing complexity. In the simplest controller, the action $\boldsymbol{a}_t$ considers that both σ and $\boldsymbol{f}$ correspond to the identity function. The action is, therefore, an affine function of $\boldsymbol{z}_t$ and $\boldsymbol{h}_t$. The second controller, corresponding to the one of Ha and Schmidhuber [5], considers only $\boldsymbol{f}$ to be the identity function. The last controller considers only σ to be the identity function. We denote the three alternatives as C_{linear}, C_{squash} and $C_{\text{nonlinear}}$.

We report the results obtained by considering different combinations of V, M and C, as described above. To avoid disrupting the presentation, we omit the description of the network architectures used and training methods, and refer to the appendix for details. In the upcoming discussion, HS denotes the model of Ha and Schmidhuber [5], corresponding to $V_{\text{sampled}} + M_{\text{trained}} + C_{\text{squash}}$.

3   Comparative Analysis

In this section we report the results of our empirical analysis of the model proposed by Ha and Schmidhuber [5]. We start, in Table 1, by presenting the results of HS and several variations thereof, as well as those of other approaches from the literature. For the sake of comparison, we also present the results of two baselines: the performances of an untrained HS agent and a controller optimized to work directly on images from the game. It is worth mentioning that variation $V_{\text{mean}} + M_{\text{untrained}} + C_{\text{linear}}$ was previously studied by Tallec et al. [16], while $V_{\text{mean}} + M_{\text{trained}} + C_{\text{linear}}$ was investigated by Risi and Stanley [12]. In the continuation, we discuss some additional variations.

330   B. Esteves and F. S. Melo

Table 1. Performance of different approaches in the carRacing-v0 domain. A policy clears the game if the average score is above 900 (entries in bold).

Method	Avg. score
Prieur et al.[†]	343 ± 18
Guan et al.[††]	893 ± 41
Jang et al.[‡]	591 ± 45
Gaier and Ha [3]	893 ± 74
Tang et al. [17]	$\mathbf{914 \pm 15}$
CEOBillionaire (gym leaderboard)	838 ± 11
HS [5]	$\mathbf{906 \pm 21}$
$V_{\mathrm{mean}} + M_{\mathrm{untrained}} + C_{\mathrm{linear}}$	852 ± 110
$V_{\mathrm{mean}} + M_{\mathrm{trained}} + C_{\mathrm{linear}}$	$\mathbf{901 \pm 43}$
Untrained HS	95 ± 81
Controller on image	735 ± 139

[†] https://tinyurl.com/y73377bq.
[††] https://github.com/AMD-RIPS/RL-2018.
[‡] https://goo.gl/VpDqSw.

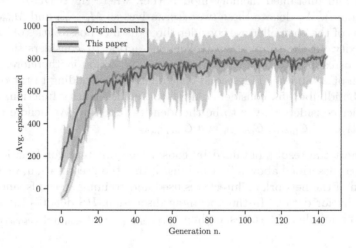

Fig. 6. Comparison between the original results of HS and ours.

3.1   Replicating HS

We started by replicating the results of Ha and Schmidhuber [5]. In the original work, the model was trained for $1,800$ generations. In our results, the model was trained for only 140 generations. The differences between our and the original HS implementation are depicted in Fig. 6: our performance is similar to the original paper, although with a larger variance in the task returns.

Table 2. Comparison of the average score of several variations of HS, differing in the visual information available to the agent.

Method	Cropped	Full
HS	853 ± 83	881 ± 40
$V_{mean} + M_{trained} + C_{squash}$	869 ± 86	$\mathbf{900 \pm 35}$
$V_{sampled} + M_{trained} + C_{linear}$	801 ± 163	835 ± 93
$V_{mean} + M_{trained} + C_{linear}$	$\mathbf{901 \pm 43}$	$\mathbf{920 \pm 29}$

Table 3. Comparison of the average score obtained by removing components from HS.

Method	Avg. score
$V_{sampled} + C_{squash}$	629 ± 102
$V_{mean} + C_{linear}$	826 ± 117
$V_{mean} + C_{nonlinear}$	872 ± 72
$V_{mean} + M_{untrained} + C_{linear}$	852 ± 110
$M_{trained} + C_{linear}$	852 ± 113
$M_{untrained} + C_{linear}$	754 ± 143

3.2 Perceptual Model

We compare in Table 2 the performance obtained when using the *mean* of q_θ against that obtained using *samples* of q_θ. Our results clearly show that the use of the mean leads to better performance of the agent, which is to be expected. In fact, considering the mean of q_θ—rather some potentially low-probability sample thereof—will generally improve the agent's ability to select a better action.

We also compare the performance obtained when we change the way the visual information is used—a linear vs a squashed controller C. Interestingly, if q_θ is sampled, C_{squash} leads to better performance, while in the case of the mean of q_θ, C_{linear} performs best. This suggests that the squashing function in the output of the controller attenuates the noise coming out from sampling q_θ.

Finally, in the original work of Ha and Schmidhuber [5], a bar at the bottom of the screen containing information about speed and acceleration is cropped from the model's visual input. We compare the performance obtained when using such cropped images against that obtained from the game's full image. As seen in our results, the use of the lower bar does improve the performance of the agent. Most approaches in the upper part of Table 1 use the full game image.

3.3 Ablation Study

We now report in Table 3 the performance obtained by removing different components from the model in Fig. 1. We start by considering only the visual module.

Table 4. Comparison of the average score obtained by considering a visual module that processes a stacked sequence of 4 frames, instead of a single frame. $V_{\text{mean, k-skip}}$ indicates the 4 stacked frames are obtained by skipping k frames in the real game.

Method	Avg. score
$V_{\text{mean, 0-skip}} + C_{\text{linear}}$	**900 ± 54**
$V_{\text{mean, 1-skip}} + C_{\text{linear}}$	885 ± 48
$V_{\text{mean, 3-skip}} + C_{\text{linear}}$	734 ± 159
$V_{\text{mean, 0-skip}} + C_{\text{nonlinear}}$	**902 ± 31**

Table 5. Comparison of the average score obtained when the model is trained with data from a good driving policy.

Method	Avg. score
$V_{\text{mean}} + C_{\text{linear}}$	836 ± 78
$V_{\text{mean}} + M_{\text{trained}} + C_{\text{linear}}$	**910 ± 34**

The first result ($V_{\text{sampled}} + C_{\text{squash}}$) corresponds to the configuration of HS without the memory module, and is the worst performing configuration. Following our conclusions from Sect. 3.2, we again observe that the use of the mean of q_θ and of a full game image both contribute to an improved performance. Finally, we note that none of the memoryless configurations solved the game.

We also consider the impact of the memory module. Following Tallec et al. [16], we analyze both the impact of considering only the memory module and the performance obtained with an *untrained* memory module. The results suggest that the memory module provides the agent with the temporal information that is lacking in the visual information.

To confirm such interpretation, we considered a variation of the original model, where the vision module is trained not with single frame but with *stacked sequence of frames*, thus (implicitly) including temporal information in the visual perception. The results are reported in Table 4.

Our results show that, in fact, by including the multiple frames in the visual module, the agent is again able to complete the game, confirming the intuition that, in fact, the role of the memory module is to complement the visual perception with temporal information.

3.4   Training Policy

To conclude our analysis, we note that the HS model is trained with a batch of images from the game obtained with a random driving policy. We thus conducted an experiment to assess the impact that the policy used to sample the environment has in the model learned by the agent and, consequently, in the performance of the agent. The results are reported in Table 5. Our results show that, by simply considering a better policy, the performance considerably improves.

4   Conclusion and Future Work

In this paper we conducted an empirical analysis of the architecture of Ha and Schmidhuber [5]. Our results highlight the role of each component of the model in the overall performance of the agent. Our contributions suggest that modifying the original architecture with a mean distribution of the visual model and a linear controller leads to a better and faster learning performance of the agent. Another improvement suggested by our results is with respect with the policy used to sample the data used to train the model. We refer to the appendix for additional discussions.

A   Full Comparative Results

For completeness, we provide in this appendix some additional results not reported in the main body of the paper.

A.1   Ablation Study Additional Results

We include, in Table 6, a comparison between the average score obtained when using the full image and a cropped image. The results complements those portrayed in Table 2, but suggest essentially the same conclusions.

Table 6. Average score on both the game's cropped and full image

Method	Cropped	Full
$V_{\text{mean}} + C_{\text{linear}}$	836 ± 78	877 ± 44
$V_{\text{sampled}} + C_{\text{squash}}$	629 ± 102	813 ± 102
$V_{\text{mean}} + C_{\text{nonlinear}}$	872 ± 72	881 ± 79
$M_{\text{trained}} + C_{\text{linear}}$	852 ± 113	894 ± 25
$M_{\text{untrained}} + C_{\text{linear}}$	754 ± 143	702 ± 121
$V_{\text{mean}} + M_{\text{untrained}} + C_{\text{linear}}$	852 ± 110	886 ± 55

Table 7. Average score obtained with V_{mean} trained with images from different sampling methods on the game's full image.

Method	Cropped	Full
$V_{\text{mean}} + C_{\text{linear}}$	826 ± 117	877 ± 44
$V_{\text{mean}} + C_{\text{linear}}$ (*Improved sample*)	836 ± 78	$\mathbf{906 \pm 51}$

Table 8. Average score and steps to reach 900-score, training the VAE and MDN-RNN components with images obtained using different sampling methods.

Method	Avg. score	900 in step
$V_{mean} + M_{trained} + C_{linear}$ (Full)	920 ± 29	72
$V_{mean} + M_{trained} + C_{linear}$ (Crop)	901 ± 43	119
$V_{mean} + M_{trained} + C_{linear}$ (Full) (*Improved sample*)	913 ± 34	36
$V_{mean} + M_{trained} + C_{linear}$ (Crop) (*Improved sample*)	910 ± 34	35

A.2   Improved Sample Policy

The VAE and MDN-RNN components are trained with a batch of images from the game sampled with a random driving policy. However, it is also important to understand the impact that the policy used to sample the batch of images used to train these components has on the performance of the system as a whole. We thus considered training these components with a mix of images sampled with both a random policy and an expert policy. Results obtained with such a mix sample are denoted as *improved sample*.

Table 7 shows the performance obtained when the visual component is trained with images from a mixed policy, in contrast with the performance obtained with images from a random policy. We can observe an improvement both in the cropped and the full image cases.

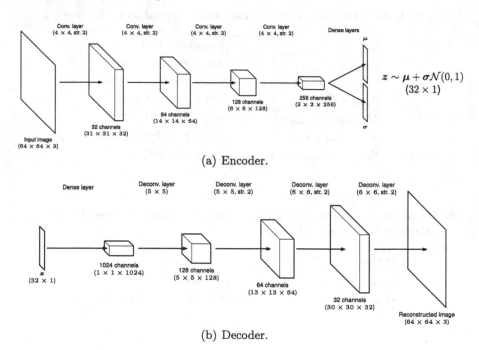

(a) Encoder.

(b) Decoder.

Fig. 7. VAE architectural details from the original World Models implementation [5]

In Table 8 reports the results obtained when we include a memory component. We report both the average score and the time step at which the agent attained a score of 900. Using a better sampling method for training the "visual" and "memory" components, the system as a whole tends to achieve better results— mostly when using cropped images—and reach a high score faster.

B   Model details

In this section we provide the details of the architectures used in the different experiments. The overall structure of the neural networks used closely follow those of the original HS paper [5], and we refer to that work for further details.

B.1   VAE

We start by presenting the details for the VAE. The encoder and decoder are represented in Fig. 7. The encoder comprises 4 convolutional layers where, in each layer, the filter size is always 4, and the stride is 2. The dimension of the latent space is $N_z = 32$. The decoder, in turn, comprises 4 deconvolution layers that reconstruct a $64 \times 64 \times 3$ image $\hat{x}$ from a code z. The VAE is trained using gradient descent with a dataset of previously gathered environment frames.

B.2   MDN-RNN

The memory module consists of a recurrent neural network (RNN) followed by a mixture density network (MDN) like represented on Fig. 4. The RNN is a single LSTM [7] layer with a hidden size of 256 and the MDN is composed by a single linear fully-connected layer with 5 gaussians per latent unit of z. The MDN-RNN is trained with gradient descent, by using the previous learned VAE and trying to sequentially reconstruct the sequences from the same previously garthered environment dataset.

B.3   Controller

The original controller presented by Ha et al. [5] consists of a single fully-connected layer with an custom environment specific activation function defined in Table. 9. In this work, we also analyzed different architecture choices like removing the squashing activation function and adding a hidden layer with 24 hidden units and with Tanh activation function. The controller is trained with CMA-ES [6] by interacting with the environment.

Table 9. Custom activation function from Ha et al. [5] implementation

Controller output action	Value
Steering wheel direction	$tanh\,(output\,[0])$
Accelerator	$sigmoid\,(output\,[1])$
Brake	$max(0,\,tanh\,(output\,[2]))$

B.4   Hyperparameters

(See Table 10)

Table 10. Hyperparameters used for training the World Models agent

Parameter	VAE	MDN-RNN
Learning rate	0.001	0.001
Optimizer	Adam [9]	RMSprop [4]
Adam betas/RMSprop alpha	$(0.9, 0.999)$	0.9
eps	10^{-8}	10^{-8}
Learning rate scheduler	ReduceLROnPlateau	
ReduceLROnPlateau factor	0.5	0.5
ReduceLROnPlateau patience	5	5
Early stopping patience	3	3
Image transformations	[ResizeImage, RandomHorizontalFlip]	–
Batch size	32	16
Sequence length	–	32
Parameters for training the controller with CMA-ES		Value
Population size		64
Number of samples		16
Initial standard deviation		0.1
Total iterations		140

References

1. Bishop, C.: Mixture density networks. Technical Report NCRG/94/004, Neural Computing Research Group, Aston University, February 1994
2. Brockman, G., et al.: OpenAI Gym. CoRR abs/1606.01540 (2016)
3. Gaier, A., Ha, D.: Weight agnostic neural networks. Adv. Neural Inf. Process. Syst. **32**, 5365–5378 (2019)
4. Graves, A.: Generating sequences with recurrent neural networks. CoRR abs/1308.0850 (2013)
5. Ha, D., Schmidhuber, J.: Recurrent world models facilitate policy evolution. Adv. Neural Inf. Process. Syst. **31**, 2450–2462 (2018)
6. Hansen, N., Ostermeier, A.: Completely derandomized self-adaptation in evolution strategies. Evol. Comput. **9**(2), 159–195 (2001)

7. Hochreiter, S., Schmidhuber, J.: Long short-term memory. Neural Comput. **9**(8), 1735–1780 (1997)
8. Kingma, D., Welling, M.: Auto-encoding variational Bayes. In: Proceedings 2nd International Conference on Learning Representations (2014)
9. Kingma, D.P., Ba, J.: Adam: a method for stochastic optimization. CoRR abs/1412.6980 (2014)
10. Lillicrap, T., et al.: Continuous control with deep reinforcement learning. In: Proceedings of the 4th International Conference Learning Representations (2016)
11. Mnih, V., et al.: Human-level control through deep reinforcement learning. Nature **518**, 529–533 (2015)
12. Risi, S., Stanley, K.: Deep neuroevolution of recurrent and discrete world models. In: Proceedings of the 2019 Genetic and Evolutionary Computation Conference, pp. 456–462 (2019)
13. Silver, D., et al.: A general reinforcement learning algorithm that masters chess, Shogi, and go through self-play. Science **362**, 1140–1144 (2018)
14. Stulp, F., Sigaud, O.: Path integral policy improvement with covariance matrix adaptation. In: Proceedings of the 29th International Conference Machine Learning, pp. 1547–1554 (2012)
15. Sutton, R., Barto, A.: Reinforcement Learning: An Introduction. MIT Press, Cambridge (2018)
16. Tallec, C., Blier, L., Kalainathan, D.: Reproducing "World Models": Is training the recurrent network really needed? (2018). https://ctallec.github.io/world-models/
17. Tang, Y., Nguyen, D., Ha, D.: Neuroevolution of self-interpretable agents. CoRR abs/2003.08165 (2020)
18. Wang, T., et al.: Benchmarking model-based reinforcement learning. CoRR abs/1907.02057 (2019)

Deep Neural Networks for Approximating Stream Reasoning with C-SPARQL

Ricardo Ferreira, Carolina Lopes, Ricardo Gonçalves, Matthias Knorr[✉],
Ludwig Krippahl, and João Leite

NOVA LINCS and Departamento de Informática, Universidade Nova de Lisboa,
Caparica, Portugal
mkn@fct.unl.pt

Abstract. The amount of information produced, whether by newspapers, blogs and social networks, or by monitoring systems, is increasing rapidly. Processing all this data in real-time, while taking into consideration advanced knowledge about the problem domain, is challenging, but required in scenarios where assessing potential risks in a timely fashion is critical. C-SPARQL, a language for continuous queries over streams of RDF data, is one of the more prominent approaches in stream reasoning that provides such continuous inference capabilities over dynamic data that go beyond mere stream processing. However, it has been shown that, in the presence of huge amounts of data, C-SPARQL may not be able to answer queries in time, in particular when the frequency of incoming data is higher than the time required for reasoning with that data. In this paper, we investigate whether reasoning with C-SPARQL can be approximated using Recurrent Neural Networks and Convolutional Neural Networks, two neural network architectures that have been shown to be well-suited for time series forecasting and time series classification, to leverage on their higher processing speed once the network has been trained. We consider a variety of different kinds of queries and obtain overall positive results with high accuracies while improving processing time often by several orders of magnitude.

1 Introduction

Large amounts of data are constantly being produced, whether by newspapers, blogs and social networks, or by monitoring systems (such as traffic sensors, financial market prediction, weather forecasting, etc.) [22]. For such data streams, it is often necessary to be able to infer new information with high efficiency in real time. For example, observing data about a patient's health status, diet and physical activity can help to anticipate health problems and request medical support in case of an emergency. Also monitoring traffic in a city area can help react to problems, such as traffic jams or accidents, in real time allowing to reroute traffic to improve travel time and reduce environmental impact.

Data Stream Management Systems (DSMS) and Complex Event Processors (CEP) tackle this problem [7], where the former allow continuous querying over

© Springer Nature Switzerland AG 2021
G. Marreiros et al. (Eds.): EPIA 2021, LNAI 12981, pp. 338–350, 2021.
https://doi.org/10.1007/978-3-030-86230-5_27

a data stream and the latter aim at identifying patterns of events that occur in a data stream. However, these systems cannot handle situations when the data is heterogeneous and it is necessary to integrate background knowledge, such as the patient's record, data on medication, or general medical knowledge expressed in an ontology, and perform more complex reasoning tasks.

Stream reasoning aims at overcoming these limitations [8,9,22] and one of the more prominent approaches is C-SPARQL (Continuous SPARQL) [1,2], a language for continuously querying over streams, that combines the features of DSMS and CEP, and the ability to incorporate background knowledge. C-SPARQL builds on language standards for the Semantic Web whose development has been driven by the World Wide Web Consortium (W3C), namely, on the Resource Description Framework (RDF) [23], a standard model of data exchange on the Web which has led to the development of Linked Open Data [16] with a large amount of structured and interconnected data,[1] and SPARQL the query language for querying over RDF data [14]. In more detail, C-SPARQL is able to process queries over various RDF streams simultaneously, employing so-called windows that focus only on a limited (recent) portion of the stream, taking into account background knowledge in the form of RDF graphs. Query answers can be variable bindings or again RDF graphs, and both of these even in the form of streams, thus C-SPARQL is capable of updating knowledge bases as new information arrives.

While C-SPARQL is thus in principle well-suited to perform stream reasoning, these advanced reasoning capabilities come at a price [27]. It has been shown that there is a limit on the amount of triples the system is capable of processing per second, which varies depending on the complexity of the considered query, and which may be prohibitive in real world scenarios. In fact, at higher rates where the amount of triples per second is superior than the limit, C-SPARQL provides erroneous answers.

It has been argued that in the face of huge amounts of data, sound and complete reasoning can be considered as a gold standard, but for obtaining answers in a timely fashion, approximate methods need to be applied [18]. These approximate methods include approaches based on machine learning, such as Neural Networks (NNs) [15], which are able to learn and generalize patterns from a given data set, making them, once trained, applicable to unseen situations with a considerably higher processing speed and robust to noisy data [17]. These methods have gained further interest with the advent of Deep Neural Networks [13], which are behind a variety of substantial recent advances in Artificial Intelligence, for example, in speech and visual recognition oe vehicle control, and which allow to detect considerably more sophisticated patterns in a data set.

A few solutions to such deductive reasoning using Deep Learning have appeared within the field of neural-symbolic integration [3,17]. Namely, Makni and Hendler [21] propose noise-tolerant reasoning for RDF(S) knowledge graphs [5], Hohenecker and Lukasiewicz [20] introduce Recursive Reasoning Networks for OWL 2 RL reasoning [24], and Ebrahimi et al. [10] tackle learning of simple

---

[1] https://lod-cloud.net/.

deductive RDFS reasoning. However, none of these approaches takes streaming data into account, making them unsuitable in the scenarios where reacting to temporal sequences of events is required.

In this paper, we investigate whether reasoning with C-SPARQL can be approximated using Deep Learning. We consider Recurrent Neural Networks (RNNs) [26] and Convolutional Neural Networks (CNN) [28], two neural network architectures that have been shown to be well-suited for time series forecasting and time series classification [4,11]. Using a data set containing sensor data on traffic, pollution and weather conditions, we consider different kinds of queries aiming to cover different features within the expressiveness C-SPARQL offers, and we generate the target labels for the training set using C-SPARQL itself to avoid the cost of manually labeling the data. We are able to show that such approximate reasoning is indeed possible and obtain overall positive results with high accuracies while improving processing time often by several orders of magnitude. We also provide considerations on which of the two arquitectures is more suitable in which situation.

2 Background

In this section, we recall relevant notions to facilitate the reading of the remaining material, namely on C-SPARQL, and the two kinds of neural networks we consider, recurrent and convolutional neural networks.

2.1 C-SPARQL

C-SPARQL (Continuous SPARQL) [1,2] is a declarative query language that combines the features of DSMS and CEP to continuously query over streams of data taking into account background knowledge. C-SPARQL builds on the Resource Description Framework (RDF) [23], a standard model of data exchange on the Web and SPARQL the query language for querying over RDF data [14].

To represent continuous streams of data, RDF streams are introduced [1]. An *RDF stream* is an ordered sequence of pairs, where each pair consists of an RDF triple $\langle subject, predicate, object \rangle$ and its timestamp τ. Subsequent timestamps τ_i and τ_{i+1} are monotonically non-decreasing ($\tau_i \leq \tau_{i+1}$), i.e., any (unbounded, though finite) number of consecutive triples can have the same timestamp, but they still occur sequentially according to the given order.

To be able to process such streaming data, C-SPARQL applies *windows* to delimit a finite amount of triples to be considered, which aligns with the idea that we cannot consider the entire stream when reasoning (nor store it). Such windows can be *physical*, i.e., a specific number of triples is selected, or *logical*, i.e., the triples that occur in a certain interval of time are selected. The latter can be *sliding* windows, when they are progressively advancing with a time step smaller than their interval, or *non-overlapping* (also called *tumbling*) when they are advancing with exactly their time interval at each iteration [2].

Continuous queries in C-SPARQL extend SPARQL queries [14] with the necessary features to handle streams of data. More concisely, a C-SPARQL query starts with a registration statement to be able to produce continuous output in the form of variable bindings, tables or graphs, also indicating at which frequency the query is processed. A basic C-SPARQL query then contains *SELECT*, *FROM* and *WHERE* statements, where the *SELECT* statement indicates the variables one is interested in, the *FROM* statement the IRI of the stream considered, including the definition of the kind of applied window, and the *WHERE* statement a condition for the query. In addition, C-SPARQL queries also permit the usage of the following advanced characteristics:

- Aggregate functions, namely, count, sum, average, minimum and maximum, which additionally allow grouping results as well as subsequent filters on the aggregated data;
- Incorporation of static background knowledge in the form of external RDF documents that can be referred to in the query (optionally introduced in the prefix statement);
- Usage of the timestamp function to be able to compare the time of occurrence of different events in the window of the stream;
- Querying various streams simultaneously;
- Stream the results of the continuous query, in addition to returning the variable bindings and graphs.

For the concise description of the syntax of SPARQL queries, and their formal semantics based on mappings we refer to [2].

It should be noted that, as shown in [27], the query execution time depends on the complexity of the query and increases linearly with the growth of the window size and the size of the static background knowledge, effectively limiting the number of triples that can be processed per unit of time, resulting in wrong answers if this threshold is passed.

2.2 Neural Networks for Time Series Classification

We assume a basic understanding of (deep) neural networks and how they can be trained using supervised learning [13,15]. Here, we provide an overview on the two network architechtures particularly well-suited for time series classification.

Recurrent Neural Networks. Recurrent neural networks (RNNs) are a type of deep neural networks specially designed for sequence modelling, that have received a great amount of attention due to their flexibility in capturing nonlinear relationships [26]. An RNN is very similar to a feedforward neural network with the exception that, in RNNs, the output of the recurrent layer is passed as input to that same layer in the next time step. At each time step, the neurons receive an input vector and the output vector from the previous time step. RNNs have had great success in forecasting and classifying time series. However, they suffer from the vanishing gradient problem [25], which causes the RNN to lose the ability to "learn more" at a certain point and results in difficulties capturing long-term dependencies. To overcome both problems, more sophisticated architectures were introduced such as Long Short-Term Memory Units (LSTM) [19], and Gated Recurrent Units (GRU) [6], which are a simplified version of LSTM, aimed at being useful for smaller datasets.

Convolutional Neural Networks. Convolutional Neural Networks (CNNs) have first been applied very successfully in the context of image recognition, and have shown impressive results when dealing with Time Series Classification [11]. Their distinguishing characteristic is the usage of convolutional and pooling layers for detecting patterns [28].

A convolutional layer aims at recognizing patterns that exist in the data. This layer applies a finite number of filters to the input, creating as output, for each filter, a feature map with the patterns detected by that filter. The values of the kernel matrix used in the convolution operation for each filter are adjusted during training, so that the network can learn the patterns it needs to find. Pooling layers then allow us to reduce the dimensions of such data by joining the outputs from a portion of the neurons in the previous layer into a single neuron of the following layer, using, e.g., *Max pooling* where the highest value is selected. This way, the data is compressed, simplifying the result without losing the most relevant information. Combining these layers leads to a gradual reduction in the amount of information to be processed along the network and requires fewer parameters than an equivalent fully connected network.

3   Methodology

In order to test our hypothesis that stream reasoning with C-SPARQL can be approximated using RNNs and CNNs, we designed and executed a series of experiments, whose rationale is explained in this section.

In general, each experiment consists of performing the following two steps.

1. Formulate a C-SPARQL query using different combinations of features (mentioned in Sect. 2) and execute this query using C-SPARQL to obtain the correct query answers;
2. Use an encoding of the original data together with the stream reasoner's answers for developing, training, and testing various models for RNNs and CNNs to determine, for each of them, the one with the best performance in terms of approximation of reasoning.

Both steps are detailed next after introducing the test data we have used.

3.1   Dataset

To perform our experiments, we chose a publicly available dataset[2] that gathers data on traffic, pollution and weather conditions by 449 sensors distributed

---

[2] http://iot.ee.surrey.ac.uk:8080/datasets.html.

throughout the city of Aarhus in Denmark. The data collected by the sensors is diverse, including average speed, number of vehicles detected, measurements of, for example, carbon, sulfur, ozone, nitrogen, as well as data on temperature, pressure and humidity.

To aid our experiments, we created an event processor that returns discretized events from the data in the dataset. The benefits of this are two-fold. Given the known limitations in terms of capacity of processing large amounts of data of C-SPARQL, we can perform simple event detection a-priori to reduce the amount of data to be processed with C-SPARQL and at the same time avoid that it be applied for simple event detection where it would not be necessary in the first place. Such pre-processing also facilitates encoding the streaming data as input for the neural networks, and, thus, in addition allows for a fairer comparison of processing time, as both use the same pre-processed set of input data.

This event processor is a Python script[3] that creates certain events based on the present data, namely *movement, no_movement, normal air, low carbon, high carbon, low nitrogen, high nitrogen, low sulfure* and *high sulfure*. For example, if a sensor does not detect any vehicles at a given time instant, the event detector would return the *no_movement* event, and if the carbon values are above normal (based on average values), the *high_carbon* event. In addition, to allow for more interesting queries involving advanced reasoning, we divided the city (and thus the sensors) into 10 sectors with the aim to allow comparisons between different areas. To balance the amount of data per sector, we only considered 15 sensors per sector, and condensed the time step in the original dataset from 5 min to 1 min. Thus, all computed events are associated with their sector and a timestamp, given in minutes. The dataset resulting from this process contains 17532 samples of sliding windows (with a time step of 1 min) of size 5 corresponding to 5 min.

3.2 C-SPARQL Queries

The queries we designed aim to leverage the expressive features C-SPARQL offers. In our experiments, we thus created queries of varying complexity using different combinations of the features, most notably aggregations, background knowledge and time comparisons, incorporating combinatorics over the different sectors, which is not easily coverable by a stream processor.

Considering that Neural Networks are not able to straightforwardly provide RDF triples as answers, we only took into account queries that return answers that can be encoded into a constant number of neurons, i.e., queries that return a Boolean answer (ASK operator) or a fixed number of answers. For similar reasons, we also abstained from considering C-SPARQL queries that return a stream of RDF data. This is not a major limitation and the queries we present in Sect. 4 are expressive and showcase a wide variety of possible use cases.

To process C-SPARQL queries we have used the Ready-To-Go Pack.[4] When processing a query, time and memory usage were measured. To avoid that

---

[3] https://github.com/CarolinaMagLopes/Deep-Neural-Networks-for-C-SPARQL.

[4] http://streamreasoning.org/resources/c-sparql.

C-SPARQL starts giving wrong answers when passing the threshold of processable amount of data per time step, we added sufficient delay to the query processing (as determined in prior tests and higher than any processing times), without affecting the measured processing times themselves.

3.3 Training RNNs and CNNs

The result of running the queries are windows of data together with the corresponding query result. To be able to train a neural network with this data, we needed to encode the data accordingly. To cover the 9 events in 10 sectors, a matrix of size (9×10) has been used. For the case of RNNs, a window of 5 min thus results in an input of 5 such matrices, whereas for CNNs an additional dimension of 5 is added, hence each window corresponds to a matrix of size $(9 \times 10 \times 5)$.

Then for each query, varying architectures with different numbers (and kinds) of layers and neurons were designed, trained, and tested for both CNNs as well as LSTM and GRU architectures, the RNNs, we considered here, using also Dropout and Gaussian Noise to avoid overfitting of the networks. The quality of their reasoning approximation has been measured using the accuracy (the fraction of correct answers) obtained with the test set and from training.

From the 17532 samples, 1532 were reserved for testing and 16000 were used for training and validation, typically with 10% of these being used in the validation set. The number of epochs used for training varies depending on the used network and the query, corresponding in all cases to the best results achieved while avoiding overfitting. For RNNs, this varies between 100 and 1000 epochs, for CNN, 50 epochs provided the best results.

The networks were developed and tested using Python3, namely using *TensorFlow*[5], *Keras*[6] and *SciKit-Learn*[7], where Keras in particular provides implementations of CNNs, LSTM and GRU architectures.

4 Experiments and Results

In this section, we present the different experiments carried out with the aim of assessing to what extent neural networks are able to approximate reasoning with C-SPARQL. Among the many different queries that we tested, we have chosen several representatives of certain combinations of the features of C-SPARQL (cf. Sect. 2), and grouped them together in subsections according to the chosen features to facilitate the reading.[8]

In each case, we indicate the representative queries and the processing times of C-SPARQL, RNNs and CNNs, as well as the resulting accuracy for the test

---

[5] https://www.tensorflow.org/.

[6] https://keras.io/.

[7] https://scikit-learn.org/stable/.

[8] An extended version of the paper contains the exact encoding of the queries, final configurations of the networks, and plots of the learning phase [12].

set for both network architectures. Please note that w.r.t. RNNs, we often refer directly to LSTM in this section, as they turned out to provide better results than GRU for all the tests of RNNs.

The experiments were run on a computer with an Intel Core i3-3240T processor with 2.90 GHz and 4 GB of RAM.

As this is common to all experiments, we remark here that running the event processor to create the data set of events only required on average a few milliseconds per sample, meaning that this is irrelevant for the overall processing time of windows covering 5 min, i.e., it is insignificant for ensuring whether processing queries is possible in real-time. We also note that our experiments when processing with C-SPARQL have shown overall that, even for more complicated queries, memory consumption does nor surpass a few hundred MB, which does not constitute a bottle-neck for processing or running the tests, which is why we do not report it individually. Finally, we also report here that training the networks took on average between 45 min to 4.5 h for RNNs and 4 to 10 min for CNNs, depending on the query and the number of epochs to achieve the best results. While this adds to the time necessary to use a neural network instead of C-SPARQL, it only needs to be done once before applying the network for approximating reasoning. Hence, once the network is trained, this does not affect the usage in real time either.

4.1 Queries with Temporal Events

For the first set of queries, we tested the identification of sequences of temporal events for RDF triples with the timestamp function, which is one of the fundamental characteristics of C-SPARQL.

Here, we wanted to determine within a window the occurrence, in a sector, of the complex event composed of

$$t_1 : normal\_air\&no\_movement \qquad t_2 : high\_carbon\&movement$$
$$t_3 : high\_sulfure$$

where t_1, t_2 and t_3 are timestamps such that $t_1 < t_2 < t_3$.

For this event, we created different kinds of queries to cover the expressiveness of C-SPARQL. Query 1 selects the sectors where the complex event occurred (using the SELECT operator), while Query 2, tests whether the event occurred in all ten sectors (using the ASK operator). Query 3 is considerably more complex than the previous two since aggregation is added in the form of COUNT and MAX, aiming to determine the sector with the highest number of occurrences of this complex event. The obtained results are reported in the following table.[9]

---

[9] C-SPARQL processing times vary depending on the number of tuples per window.

Results	C-SPARQL Time	LSTM Train Acc	Test Acc	Time	CNN Train Acc	Test Acc	Time
Query 1	10–25 min	0.9801	0.9780	180 μs	0.9832	0.9976	280 μs
Query 2	10–15 min	0.8760	0.8695	210 μs	0.9898	0.9852	450 μs
Query 3	15–30+ min	0.9350	0.9311	700 μs	0.9324	0.9222	240 μs

We can see that CNNs provide excellent results for both Queries 1 and 2, whereas LSTMs provide excellent results as well for Query 1, but only good results for Query 2 (ASK), which is already observed during training. Such difficulties can be circumvented though by counting the results of Query 1, for which the results are excellent and obtain the correct answer with high precision. For Query 3, which is considerably more complex with the aggregations, very good results are achieved for both kinds of networks.

Overall, we conclude that detecting temporal sequences in stream reasoning using neural networks is feasible with, in general, very good results even for more complex queries. At the same time, processing with any of the trained networks is at least 6 orders of magnitudes faster than reasoning with C-SPARQL. In particular, for the queries considered here, C-SPARQL could not be used with the considered data in real time as the processing time is far higher than the admitted processing time of 1 min (each window captures 5 min, but the time step of the sliding window is 1 min), thus resulting in incorrect answers in such a setting, unlike the networks that easily permit processing in real time.

4.2 Queries with Background Knowledge

In the second part, we introduced an additional layer of complexity by adding background knowledge in the form of an ontology containing information about the type of sectors (*school_area*, *urban_area*, etc.), events, called infractions, not allowed in the various types of sectors (for example, the *high_carbon* event should not happen in *school_area*) and information about adjacency between sectors. Here, we did not consider temporal comparisons between events, but made use of various aggregation functions.

Query 4 consists in selecting the sectors where more infractions occurred than the average of infractions in the adjacent sectors, thus making use of the topological knowledge, whereas Query 5 asks if the number of sectors, where more infractions occurred than the average of infractions in the adjacent sectors, is greater than or equal to 4, requiring aggregations within an aggregation.

For Query 6, we further increased the complexity of the query and made use of the Property Paths Operators that C-SPARQL provides, namely, among them the '/' operator, where $pred_1/pred_2$ corresponds to the sequence path of $pred_1$ followed by $pred_2$. This allows to query for sectors where more infractions occurred than the average of infractions in the sectors adjacent to adjacent sectors. To allow for more meaningful answers, for this query, we increased the number of sectors to 15 choosing sensors in the same way as described in Sect. 3, since with the initial 10 sectors, any sector would be close to almost all the others.

Results	C-SPARQL Time	LSTM Train Acc	Test Acc	Time	CNN Train Acc	Test Acc	Time
Query 4	20–40 ms	0.9810	0.9775	1 ms	0.9797	0.9799	545 μs
Query 5	20 ms	0.9130	0.8930	1 ms	0.9180	0.9066	460 μs
Query 6	30 ms	0.9840	0.9771	1 ms	0.9795	0.9728	700 μs

Both LSTMs and CNNs perform similarly, showing excellent results for both queries 4 and 6, and only good results for Query 5 (using ASK). Similar to the solution for Query 2 for LSTMs, we can circumvent this and take advantage of the excellent performance for Query 4 and simply count the results there. We observe that C-SPARQL reasoning involving ontologies can be captured with LSTMs and CNNs as well. Notably, for this kind of queries C-SPARQL provides very good processing times that allow its usage in real time, but using the trained networks is still at least 30 and 60 times faster for LSTMs and CNNs, resp.

4.3 Combining Temporal Events and Background Knowledge

In the final set of queries, we combine comparisons of temporal events with background knowledge and aggregations to obtain highly sophisticated queries for testing our hypothesis. We reuse the complex event from Sect. 4.1 and the ontology from Sect. 4.2 for the two final queries. Namely, with Query 7 we determine those sectors that have more occurrences of the complex event than the average in the adjacent sectors, and with Query 8, similar to Query 6, those sectors that have more occurrences of the complex event than in the close, but not immediately adjacent sectors.

Results	C-SPARQL Time	LSTM Train Acc	Test Acc	Time	CNN Train Acc	Test Acc	Time
Query 7	20–30+min	0.8990	0.8864	1 ms	0.8310	0.8317	460 μs
Query 8	25–30+min	0.8860	0.8718	1 ms	0.8584	0.8555	555 μs

We can observe that both kinds of networks achieve good results. Given the observed results also from training, where our tests with more advanced models would result in overfitting, we believe that this may be due to the fact that for such complicated queries more training data would be necessary, and leave this for future work. We also note that, here, LSTMs show a slightly better performance. We conjecture that this could be related to the fact that for a CNN the entire input is presented as a matrix possibly somewhat obfuscating the temporal aspect, whereas for LSTMs the temporal component of the input is separated, and thus possibly easier to distinguish. In any case, similar to Sect. 4.1, C-SPARQL cannot be applied in real time, as the processing time by far exceeds the limit, whereas the networks are again six orders of magnitude faster. Thus, even though there is still space for improvement here in terms of resulting precision for the approximation, given the unsuitability of using C-SPARQL in real time for such queries, our approach is also very promising for such highly complex queries.

5   Conclusions

We have investigated whether expressive stream reasoning with C-SPARQL can be approximated using Recurrent and Convolutional Neural Networks, since for more sophisticated queries with higher quantities of data to be processed, C-SPARQL does not process the data fast enough to provide timely answers.

Our experiments on a real data set containing among others data on traffic and air pollution show that both RNNs and CNNs are well-suited for this task, as their processing time is vastly superior compared to C-SPARQL, in particular when relative comparisons of temporal events are required, and in many cases, they show excellent or very good results of approximation of reasoning, even when utilizing more complex combinations of C-SPARQL's features.

When comparing both architectures, we noted slightly better results for RNNs ,i.e., LSTMs, when approximating highly complex queries in particular including many temporal comparisons (Query 7 and 8). On the other hand, CNNs performed a bit better for ASK queries (notably Query 2), which requires counting globally, and training them is notably faster. Our preliminary conclusion is that CNNs could be more suitable where space perception is more important, while RNNs seem preferable for queries more oriented towards temporal aspects.

Still, C-SPARQL remains more suitable if the frequency of incoming data is below its processing capabilities and when obtaining the correct result is mandatory, or where ad-hoc variants of a query are needed, which would require retraining the network, as well as in situations when returning answer substitutions where the domain is not previously limited and known, or when returning constructed graphs (as streams).

In terms of future work, it would be interesting to further explore the situations where the networks were not providing excellent results. This could be tackled by trying to use larger datasets and further test the combinations of features of C-SPARQL that proved more difficult when approximating reasoning. Another option would be to consider, e.g., Echo-State Networks (ESN), that have shown promising results in term series classification as well [4].

Acknowledgments. We thank the anonymous reviewers for their helpful comments and acknowledge support by FCT project RIVER (PTDC/CCI-COM/30952/2017) and by FCT project NOVA LINCS (UIDB/04516/2020).

References

1. Barbieri, D.F., Braga, D., Ceri, S., Della Valle, E., Grossniklaus, M.: Incremental reasoning on streams and rich background knowledge. In: Aroyo, L., et al. (eds.) ESWC 2010. LNCS, vol. 6088, pp. 1–15. Springer, Heidelberg (2010). https://doi.org/10.1007/978-3-642-13486-9_1
2. Barbieri, D.F., Braga, D., Ceri, S., Valle, E.D., Grossniklaus, M.: C-SPARQL: a continuous query language for RDF data streams. Int. J. Semant. Comput. 4(01), 3–25 (2010)
3. Besold, T.R., et al.: Neural-symbolic learning and reasoning: a survey and interpretation. CoRR abs/1711.03902 (2017)
4. Bianchi, F.M., Scardapane, S., Løkse, S., Jenssen, R.: Reservoir computing approaches for representation and classification of multivariate time series. IEEE Trans. Neural Netw. Learn. Syst. 32(5), 2169–2179 (2021)
5. Brickey, D., Guha, R. (eds.): RDF Schema 1.1. W3C Recommendation, 23 February 2014
6. Cho, K., et al.: Learning phrase representations using RNN encoder-decoder for statistical machine translation. In: EMNLP, pp. 1724–1734. ACL (2014)
7. Cugola, G., Margara, A.: Processing flows of information: from data stream to complex event processing. ACM Comput. Surv. (CSUR) 44(3), 1–62 (2012)
8. Della Valle, E., Ceri, S., Van Harmelen, F., Fensel, D.: It's a streaming world! reasoning upon rapidly changing information. IEEE Intell. Syst. 24(6), 83–89 (2009)
9. Dell'Aglio, D., Della Valle, E., van Harmelen, F., Bernstein, A.: Stream reasoning: a survey and outlook. Data Sci. 1(1–2), 59–83 (2017)
10. Ebrahimi, M., Sarker, M.K., Bianchi, F., Xie, N., Doran, D., Hitzler, P.: Reasoning over RDF knowledge bases using deep learning. CoRR abs/1811.04132 (2018)
11. Fawaz, H.I., Forestier, G., Weber, J., Idoumghar, L., Muller, P.A.: Deep learning for time series classification: a review. Data Mining Knowl. Discov. 33(4), 917–963 (2019)
12. Ferreira, R., Lopes, C., Gonçalves, R., Knorr, M., Krippahl, L., Leite, J.: Deep neural networks for approximating stream reasoning with C-SPARQL. CoRR abs/2106.08452 (2021)
13. Goodfellow, I., Bengio, Y., Courville, A.: Deep Learning. MIT Press, Cambridge (2016)
14. Harris, S., Seaborne, A., Prud'hommeaux, E. (eds.): SPARQL 1.1 Query Language. W3C Recommendation, 21 March 2013
15. Haykin, S.: Neural networks: a comprehensive foundation. Prentice Hall PTR, Hoboken (1994)
16. Heath, T., Bizer, C.: Linked Data: Evolving the Web into a Global Data Space. Morgan & Claypool Publishers, Synthesis Lectures on the Semantic Web (2011)
17. Hitzler, P., Bianchi, F., Ebrahimi, M., Sarker, M.K.: Neural-symbolic integration and the semantic web. Semant. Web 11(1), 3–11 (2020)
18. Hitzler, P., van Harmelen, F.: A reasonable semantic web. Semant. Web 1(1–2), 39–44 (2010)
19. Hochreiter, S., Schmidhuber, J.: Long short-term memory. Neural Comput. 9(8), 1735–1780 (1997)
20. Hohenecker, P., Lukasiewicz, T.: Ontology reasoning with deep neural networks. J. Artif. Intell. Res. 68, 503–540 (2020)
21. Makni, B., Hendler, J.A.: Deep learning for noise-tolerant RDFS reasoning. Semant. Web 10(5), 823–862 (2019)

22. Margara, A., Urbani, J., Van Harmelen, F., Bal, H.: Streaming the web: reasoning over dynamic data. J. Web Semant. **25**, 24–44 (2014)
23. Miller, E.: An introduction to the resource description framework. D Lib. Mag. 4(5), 15–19 (1998)
24. Motik, B., Grau, B.C., Horrocks, I., Wu, Z., Fokoue, A., Lutz, C. (eds.): OWL 2 Web Ontology Language Profiles. W3C Recommendation, 11 December 2012
25. Pascanu, R., Mikolov, T., Bengio, Y.: Understanding the exploding gradient problem. CoRR abs/1211.5063 (2012)
26. Qin, Y., Song, D., Chen, H., Cheng, W., Jiang, G., Cottrell, G.W.: A dual-stage attention-based recurrent neural network for time series prediction. In: IJCAI, pp. 2627–2633. ijcai.org (2017)
27. Ren, X., Khrouf, H., Kazi-Aoul, Z., Chabchoub, Y., Curé, O.: On measuring performances of C-SPARQL and CQELS. In: SR+SWIT@ISWC. CEUR Workshop Proceedings, vol. 1783, pp. 1–12. CEUR-WS.org (2016)
28. Wang, Z., Yan, W., Oates, T.: Time series classification from scratch with deep neural networks: a strong baseline. In: IJCNN, pp. 1578–1585. IEEE (2017)

The DeepONets for Finance: An Approach to Calibrate the Heston Model

Igor Michel Santos Leite[1]([⊠]) [iD], João Daniel Madureira Yamim[1]([⊠]) [iD],
and Leonardo Goliatt da Fonseca[2]([⊠]) [iD]

[1] Graduate Program in Computational Modelling, Federal University of Juiz de Fora,
Juiz de Fora, MG, Brazil
igor.leite@ice.ufjf.br
[2] Department of Applied and Computational Mechanics,
Federal University of Juiz de Fora, Juiz de Fora, MG, Brazil
leonardo.goliatt@engenharia.ufjf.br
https://www.ufjf.br/pgmc/, https://www.ufjf.br/mac/

Abstract. The Heston model is the most renowned stochastic volatility function in finance, but the calibration input parameters is a challenging task. This contest grows up because the instantaneous volatility is unobservable or market quotes are absent/unviable to agents, remaining the asset time-series as tangible. Moreover, these conditions are unfit to approach based on Maximum Likelihood Estimation or optimisation of the differences in Pricing models and quotes in the real market. Today, neural networks are a well-known tool with malleable and powerful features to map accurately any nonlinear continuous operator in complex systems. This work adopts the deep operator networks (DeepONets) to learn the Heston parameters based on observed time series. We perform simulations of trajectories following the Heston model with a truncated Euler discretization scheme and randomised inputs parameters. The five parameters are estimated by Stacked and Unstacked DeepONets and compared with GJR-GARCH and standard neural network with the Tukeys' test. The results indicated the improvement in accuracy of the Unstacked model. However, the statistical test indicates some similarity between the Unstacked model and standard neural network.

Keywords: Neural networks · Parameter estimation · Calibration · Heston model · Monte carlo simulation

1 Introduction

The stochastic models are attractive ways to describe dynamic systems evolution where the behaviour does not follow a strict deterministic law. These characteristics make the stochastic models a natural choice for modelling complex systems

Supported by Coordenação de Aperfeiçoamento de Pessoal de Nível Superior-CAPES, Fundação de Amparo à Pesquisa do Estado de Minas Gerais-FAPEMIG (grant TEC-APQ-00334/18) and Conselho Nacional de Desenvolvimento Científico e Tecnológico-CNPq (grant 429639/2016-3).

© Springer Nature Switzerland AG 2021
G. Marreiros et al. (Eds.): EPIA 2021, LNAI 12981, pp. 351–362, 2021.
https://doi.org/10.1007/978-3-030-86230-5_28

under uncertainty. In [13] is listed a wide of application for stochastic models as follows: Protein Kinetics, Hydrology, Finance, Structural Mechanics and others.

In the scope of financial application, Heston [10] developed one of the most popular stochastic volatility models of financial literature. The Heston model is more realistic and the favourite choice of the agents to consider the dynamic of volatility as uncertain, being more accurate than others model in pricing derivatives in the real market, besides being mathematically treatable.

However, the Heston model parameters estimation poses substantial challenges. Since there is no closed joint transition probability function of the two-dimensional diffusion process, making the Maximum Likelihood Estimation (MLE) method and other estimation tools limited or challenging to be implemented [27][1]. In other words, the calibration parameters step is a crucial process to adopt any stochastic models in fullness.

Nowadays, the Multilayer Perceptron (MLP) is classified as the most common application of Artificial Neural Networks (ANN or NN) architectures [7]. The main characteristic of MLP is the existence of multiple layers, called hidden layers, that associate inputs with outputs without recurrence and can extracts increasingly abstract features. The sophistication of these networks lies in the grouping of layers that can imitate any continuous function, following the universal approximation theorem[2].

The advances in research about ANN to learn mathematics operators resulted in deep operator networks (DeepONets) [16,17]. In contrast with other neural networks, DeepONet is the combination of two deep neural networks to approximates linear and nonlinear operators simultaneously. This network showed promising results in chemistry [19] and electroconvection [2].

Hence, this paper examines the application of DeepONet to learn the parameters in the Heston model. For this purpose, we simulate the times-series paths based on the Heston Model wherein the parameters are known (dataset). These trajectories are the neural network's input, while the targets/outputs are the original parameters used to generate the respective path. The validation and significance of results are inferred by the mean squared error (MSE) comparison of DeepONet with fully-connected networks (Fully-NN) and GJR-GARCH in Tukey's Test.

Given the broad applications, data limitation, and interest in the Heston model, this paper contributes to enriches the literature with novel parameter estimation tools based solely on historical time-series, more details will introduce in Sect. 2.1. The DeepONet has flexibility enough to allows modification and extension for other stochastic models. However, this paper is limited in exploring the DeepONet to learn the relation of parameters in the Heston Model.

The rest of this paper is organised as follows. Section 2 introduces a Literature Review, describes the Heston Model and the DeepONet. Section 3 presents the

---

[1] The problem of parameter estimation for stochastic processes is not limited to the Heston model. This gap is shown in [21] with exemplification for interest rates.

[2] See [7, Chapter 6.4.1].

general methodology adopted in this work. Section 4 shows the results, compares the estimations tools. The conclusion of this paper is presented in Sect. 5.

2 Problem Formulation

2.1 Related Work

Heston [10] published the notorious stochastic volatility equation, being called the Heston model. This model tries to reflect the intrinsic nature of markets and their derivatives, drawing on the limitations of other models in not match with stylised features observable in empirical studies. Despite the advances, the Heston model suffers from a problem in input parameters estimation

The literature describes two possible ways to calibrate the parameters: the assumption of known volatilities and the unknown volatilities case. In the first case, the literature is sparse because the volatilities are generally unobservable in the real market. These constraints narrow the application of traditional approaches based on MLE; see [25] for more details.

For the unknown volatilities case, the surveys suggest alternatives tools: Gallant and Tauchen [5] with the Generalised Method of Moment (GMM) algorithm, which depends on selecting an auxiliary model. Jacquier et al. [12] proposed the Markov Chain Monte Carlo (MCMC) method based on Bayesian inference to estimate the log volatility parameters. Cape et al. [3] applied in Heston and Bates models while [20] notes that the variance process by MCMC estimation has limitations and distortions. The major drawback is the need for prior knowledge of parameter distributions for implementing this algorithm and the high computational cost.

Rouah [24] also showed another approach to estimate the parameter under unknown volatilities. The approach is based on minimising a loss function between quoted market prices and Pricing models or between market prices and *implied volatilities*[3]. More recently, Mrázek and Pospíšil [23] calibrate Heston stochastic volatility model to actual market data (DAX options). However, the major limitation of this methodology is the feasibility of access to information about future negotiations/contracts. Notwithstanding, this methodology is improper when the agent has an observable time series due to practical constraints, making metaheuristics improper due to the absence of a specific evaluation function.

Considering the situations where just a time-series is known, Engle and Lee [4] described a methodology to estimate the parameter in the Heston Model (except correlation) based in [8] to adopt a Generalised Autoregressive Conditional Heteroscedastic (GARCH) model to approximate the parameters that govern the data. Lewis [14] avoided the absence in correlation term adopting the GJR-GARCH to estimates the main parameters, but with some limitations[4].

---

[3] See [11][Chapter 15, Sect. 11] for more details about implied volatilities.

[4] The GJR-GARCH model also captures the stylised facts in finance, like the GARCH model, but appends the relation between negative shocks returns at last observation as positive shocks. This asymmetry is known as the leverage effect.

The calibration of the Heston model by ANN was studied in [26], the cited work followed a similar way introduced in [9] with the addition of option prices and considering the Heston, Bergomi and rough Bergomi models for estimation. Liu [15] develop a generic calibration framework to calibrate the Heston and Bates models by a complex schema involving training an ANN to return the option prices and implied volatility and posteriorly invert the already trained neural network conditional on certainly known input.

However, the cited works with the ANN approach have the same assumption, the access of market data and, consequently, the likewise issues aforementioned earlier. This situation restrains the adoption of these tools in some scenarios, such as the real options approach where some assets do not have complete information/negotiation in the market.

On the other hand, Xie et al. [28] compared different architectures for MLP based solely on time-series for a simplified stochastic model. The authors concluded that the MLP provides a robust parameter estimation approach for simplified models but is limited in scenarios with high diffusion levels and few samples. Moysiadis et al. [22] considered convolution and recurrent neural networks to calibrate the speed of mean reversion in the Hull-White model. Unfortunately, the cited authors also recognise that few works attempted have been made to address the calibration problem in finance by neural networks with a similar approach.

2.2   The Heston Model

The Heston model assumes that the dynamic of the asset price X_t, follows a Geometric Brownian Motion (GBM) and the instantaneous volatility, v_t, is governed by a mean-reverting square root stochastic process or simply CIR model[5]. The Eq. (1) shows the stochastic differential equations (SDE) for the Heston model.

$$dX_t = \alpha X_t dt + X_t \sqrt{v_t} dZ_X^1$$
$$dv_t = \eta(\overline{v} - v_t)dt + \sqrt{v_t}\sigma_v dZ_v^2 \qquad (1)$$
$$\mathbb{E}\left[dZ_X^1 \, dZ_v^2\right] = \rho \cdot dt$$

where α the drift/trend of the process, $\eta > 0$ the mean reversion speed for the variance; $\overline{v} > 0$ the mean reversion level for the variance or the long run mean variance; $\sigma_v > 0$ the volatility of volatility (vol of vol); $dZ = \sqrt{dt} \cdot N(0,1)$ the Wiener process with $N(0,1)$ being the standard normal distribution; $\rho \in [-1,1]$ the correlation between dZ_X^1 and dZ_v^2; $\mathbb{E}$ the mathematical expectation and $[0,T]$ is the time interval.

Set the distance between two sequential points how $\Delta t = t_i - t_{i-1} = \frac{T-t_0}{N}$: $\{i \leq N \mid N \in \mathbb{N}\}$, the Eq. (2) introduces the discrete version of Heston model

---

[5] CIR is a short-form of Cox, Ingersoll, and Ross (the original authors), see [6, Chapter 2, pg. 15].

by Euler scheme, where $f(v_t) = \max(v_t, 0)$ represents the truncation rule to satisfy the constrain $v_t > 0$[6].

$$v_{t+\Delta t} = f_1(v_t) + \eta(\overline{v} - f_2(v_t))\Delta t + \sigma_v \sqrt{f_3(v_t) \cdot \Delta t} \cdot N_1(0,1)$$
$$\theta = (\alpha - v_{t+\Delta t}/2)\Delta t + \sqrt{\Delta t \cdot v_{t+\Delta t}} \left(\rho \cdot N_1(0,1) + (1 - \rho^2) \cdot N_2(0,1)\right) \quad (2)$$
$$X_{t+\Delta t} = X_t \cdot \mathrm{EXP}(\theta)$$

Hence, the parameters α, η, $\overline{v}$, σ_v and ρ are always unknown. To adopt the Heston model in practical applications, one should estimate these parameters firstly. Considering the indirect inference with CJR-GARCH(1,1), henceforth just GARCH, introduced in [14], following the Eq. (3), where $r_t = \log\left(X_t/X_{t-1}\right)$ is the one-period log return, the I_{t-1} is a dummy variable, z_t is a sequence of independent and identically distributed (i.i.d.) random variables with zero-mean and unit variance, while μ, β and γ need been estimated based in observable time-series.

$$r_t = \mu + \varepsilon_t, \qquad \varepsilon_t = z_t \sqrt{h_t}$$
$$h_t = \omega + (\beta_1 + \gamma I_{t-1})\varepsilon_{t-1}^2 + \beta_2 h_{t-1}$$
$$I_{t-1} = \begin{cases} 0, & \text{if } r_{t-1} \leq 0 \\ 1, & \text{otherwise} \end{cases} \quad (3)$$

The relation between Eq. (1) and Eq. (3) is showed in Eq. (4).

$$\alpha = \mu, \quad \eta = \frac{1}{\Delta t}\left(1 - \beta_1 - \beta_2 - \frac{1}{2}\gamma\right), \overline{v} = \frac{\omega}{\Delta t\left(1 - \beta_1 - \beta_2 - \frac{1}{2}\gamma\right)},$$
$$\sigma_v = \sqrt{\frac{1}{\Delta t}(2\beta_1^2 + 2\beta_1\gamma + \frac{5}{4}\gamma^2)} \quad \text{and} \quad \rho = -\frac{\gamma}{\sqrt{\pi(\beta_1^2 + \beta_1\gamma + \frac{5}{8}\gamma^2)}} \quad (4)$$

2.3 The Deep Operator Networks - DeepONets

The application of Neural networks as universal approximators of continuous functions is well-known in several fields with notorious and high accurate results. However, new researches are feasible and required to supply the remaining gaps. In this context, Lu et al. [16] proposed DeepONets learn operators accurately and efficiently by neural networks. Despite the model is recent, the application still now demonstrates significant results in different application, see [2,19].

A DeepONet was developed around two sub-networks. The first one encoding the input function as a standard ANN and called the branch net, while the trunk net (second branch) decoding the locations for the output functions. Additionally, Lu et al. [16] also introduce two different topologies as showed in Fig. 1. The

---

[6] Mrázek and Pospíšil [23] describes some discretization and truncation schemes with richness of details.

Stacked form (Fig. 1a) with lots of branch networks stacked parallel where each branch return one value of b_k. The Unstacked net (Fig. 1b) merge the parallel branches into one single branch network.

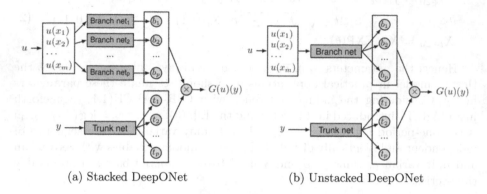

(a) Stacked DeepONet   (b) Unstacked DeepONet

Fig. 1. Illustrations of DeepONets

In all forms the DeepONet, the input $u \in \mathbb{R}^d$, with d as the number of features, feeds the branch net and generate a vector out of branch net $[b_1, b_2, \cdots, b_p]^T \in \mathbb{R}^p$, while $y \in \mathbb{R}$ feeds the trunk net and generate the vector out of $[t_1, t_2, \cdots, t_p] \in \mathbb{R}^p$. Hence, the desired outputs G is mapped as $G(u)(t) \approx \sum_{k=1}^{p} t_k \cdot b_k + b_0$, where b_0 is bias and can be suppressed. Note than y have the same dimension of the output problem, i.e., y is just a scalar for problems where the outputs dimension is one.

3   Method

The Heston Model has five parameters $(\alpha, \eta, \overline{v}, \sigma_v, \rho)$ that needs to be estimated, as previously described, being theses the outputs/target of this work whereas the input data is the simulated time-series. Considering the DeepONets for such application, we assume that each parameter is a priori independent and have its network without links between her, so we have 5 networks. Thus, the network can optimise the weights of the connections independently, allowing the one-to-one analysis.

Initially the Heston time-series dataset, with 5000 paths/lines/trajectories and 200 steps/columns, was generated by MCS with parameters seeded randomly following a uniform distribution with interval $X_0 = [300; 1000]$, $v_0 = [0, 0.07]$, $\overline{v} = v_0 * [0.9, 1.1]$, $\alpha = [-0.05, 0.05]$, $\sigma_v = [0.001, 0.0501]$, $\eta = [0.005, 2]$, $\rho = [-.8, 0]$, $T = 20$ and $\Delta t = 0.1^7$. This data was divided in 80% to train and 20% to test, being the test data used to compare the results.

---

[7] These interval was choice to comprise the values observed in literature. However, the plenty combinations of parameters are feasible depending of the market considered.

Figure 2 introduces an overview of the steps adopted in this work. The training step starts with the return time-series[8] feed the branch net while we do a feature extraction by TSFEL [1] combined with Principal Component Analysis (PCA) to find one component and feed the trunk net. We considered the same learning condition in DeepONet and Fully-NN with Training epochs = 1000, Hidden layers for both branch and trunk nets in DeepONet: 2 40, Activation = Linear to α and ρ and ReLU to other, Objective function = MSE, Optimiser = Adam and Learning rate = 0.001. The topology in Fully-NN was $[25 - 20 - 15 - 10 - 1]$ with Sigmoid activation to all nodes[9]. We highlight that just the test data is used to compare the DeepONet approach with Fully-NN and GARCH estimation.

All the experiments were carried out on Ubuntu 20.04 operating system running Python 3.8.5 with Tensorflow version 2.0.0, tsfel 0.1.4, numpy 1.16.0, pandas 1.0.5, statsmodels 0.12.2, arch 4.10 to GJR-GARCH approach and DeepXDE[10] 0.11.0 to all versions of DeepONets [18].

4   Results and Discussion

Figure 3 shows the evolution of Loss in training and test data to the cases of DeepONets. We highlight that just in η (Fig. 3d) was observed the potential of the model to overfitting. Hence, we considered the network with 200 training epochs to α, ρ, $\overline{\sigma}$ and σ_v, while to η the best results was the Unstacked model with 400 epochs and Stacked with 250 epochs.

Figure (4) shows the MSE for all parameter in four approaches. Note then error in α estimation reveals a little variation with manifold outliers in methodologies based on neural network, Fig. 4a. The equivalence situation did not astonish because the drift parameter is directly observable in the return times series, can be calculated without significant complications. Tukey's test indicated differentiation between GARCH and Unstacked Model only.

In ρ, Fig. 4e is observable the distortion in GARCH results, while Tukey's test classifies just the NN based estimators as equals. The MSE to η, Fig. 4d, shows the outliers just in DeepONet estimators. However, the statistical test indicated the equivalence between Unstacked, Fully-NN and GARCH models. Unlike α, these variables are more complex to calibrate because of the possible relationship with other estimated parameters, such as showed in the Eq. 4 where exists a link between the estimators.

---

[8] The price time-series is convert in return time-series, it is a common procedure in finance and can be interpreted as the standardisation step.

[9] Linear activation was considered in output node to α and ρ. The values inside brackets indicate the number of neurons in each layer. Other topologies were tested, but without significant gain.

[10] A Python library designed for scientific machine learning (https://github.com/lululxvi/deepxde).

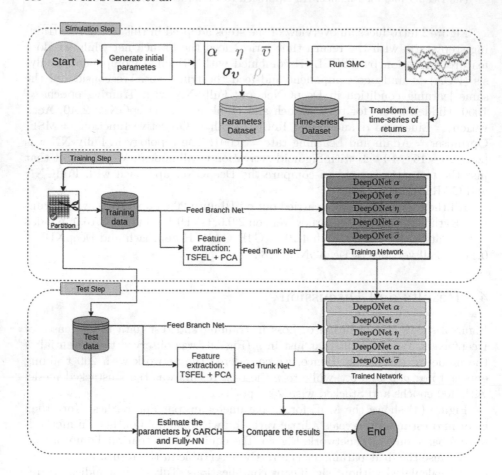

Fig. 2. Flowchart of the experiment

One unanticipated finding was the error in ρ calibration by GARCH why this occurrence rate, Fig. 4e. This discrepancy could be attributed to the numerical aspect's borderline situation, where the estimated GARCH values are close to zero. This condition is sufficient to degenerate the results, such as model misspecification, highlighting the complexity to calibrate correlation over endogeneity. Although the data rescale has adopted to avoid convergence issues.

The variable $\overline{v}$, Fig. 4c, shows the clear advantage of the Unstacked model in the comparison with the others, being the Stacked model with less accurate, while GARCH and Fully-NN are not statistically different by Tukey's test. The last case, σ_v, is showed in Fig. 4b, the superiority of the Unstsacked model is notorious but followed by Fully-NN closely. Hence, the statistical test did not indicate differentiability between Unstacked and Fully-NN models whereas the other comparisons were statistically distinct.

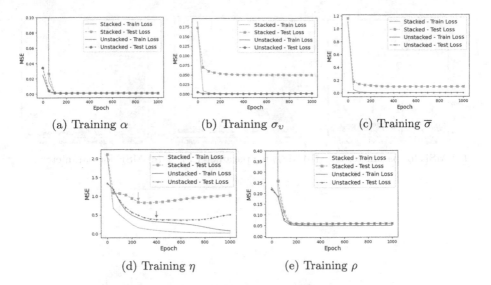

(a) Training α (b) Training σ_v (c) Training $\overline{\sigma}$

(d) Training η (e) Training ρ

Fig. 3. Training evolution of Loss in DeepONets

Overall, these results indicate that the Unstacked and Fully-NN models are equivalent and return a similar result, the exception to $\overline{v}$ case. Another situation matches those observed in [28], where the increase in the number of hidden layers and neurons does not improve the performance. We test different combinations with the number of hidden layers and did not find results with significant differences.

The observation about the hidden layers suggests an essential insight into the limitation around the number of hidden layers in NN approaches for calibrating the Heston Model parameters. We believe that pass the time-series and just one feature may not enough for the DeepONets and Fully-NN to extract all pertinent information about the data to then estimates values.

This hypothesis is reinforced by the observation introduced in [26] about the over-parametrisation of the Heston model. This remark implies in restriction of some model from learning the nuances map around the parameters' values. In other words, the intricacy of sophisticated stochastic models requires an upscale in the relation of input and output data, and two or more combinations of parameters may lead to similar values, making the optimiser stuck at a local minimum.

The main trade-off is the limitation around the size of the time series since the time length represents the number of features that feed the network and this condition restrains. In other words, we need to retrain the neural networks with different time series sizes if the data have more than 200 observations or less.

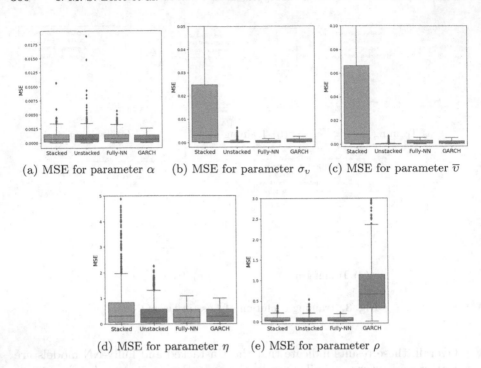

(a) MSE for parameter α (b) MSE for parameter σ_v (c) MSE for parameter $\overline{v}$

(d) MSE for parameter η (e) MSE for parameter ρ

Fig. 4. Estimation error with different methodologies

5   Conclusion

This study investigated the feasibility of parameter estimation in stochastic differential equations by the novel DeepOnets based solely on discrete time-series and one feature. We showed that the approach by NN is feasibility calibrate the Heston Model parameter, but with caveats. The Unstacked model is equivalent with the Fully-NN to calibration in three of five parameters, despite the differences in the network, and obtained the minimal error in two parameters ($\overline{v}$ and σ_v). The error reduction is significant because in real options applications each 1% improved in accuracy reflect in thousands of dollars saved depending on the business model and scale. For instance, considering the option pricing every 1% of accuracy, on average(each parameter shows a different impact in outlay), represent 0.19$ saved every 30 dollars invested.

The results of this research reiterate and reinforce the observation of other researchers about the low variation for the modification in the number of hidden layers. In other words, the improvement in topologies complexities could not reflect in precision gain directly. This is an important issue for future research because several questions remain unanswered at present. Further research should be done to investigate the relation of endogeneity and adjustment of network inputs to increase accuracy.

Future works should analyse (i) the workableness of connections between the branch outputs (recurrence), like form, to induce the endogeneity. (ii) Consider the feature extractor for time-series to create a "fingerprint" of the data to mitigate, simplify the analysis and improve the inferences about the volatility stochastic in observable series. (iii) Adopting the Long short-term memory (LSTM) or another recurrent neural network (RNN) to tries learn the relation between the time-series and the parameters of the Heston Model.

References

1. Barandas, M., et al: Tsfel: Time series feature extraction library. SoftwareX **11**, 100456 (2020). https://doi.org/10.1016/j.softx.2020.100456
2. Cai, S., Wang, Z., Lu, L., Zaki, T.A., Karniadakis, G.E.: Deepm&mnet: inferring the electroconvection multiphysics fields based on operator approximation by neural networks. J. Comput. Phys. **436**, 110296 (2021). https://doi.org/10.1016/j.jcp.2021.110296
3. Cape, J., Dearden, W., Gamber, W., Liebner, J., Lu, Q., Nguyen, M.L.: Estimating heston's and bates' models parameters using Markov chain monte carlo simulation. J. Stat. Comput. Simul. **85**(11), 2295–2314 (2015). https://doi.org/10.1080/00949655.2014.926899
4. Engle, R.F., Lee, G.G.J.: Estimating diffusion models of stochastic volatility. In: Rossi, P. (ed.) MODELLING STOCK MARKET VOLATILITY: Bridging the Gap to Continuous Time, vol. 1, chap. 11, pp. 333–355. Academic Press Inc, 525 B Street, Suite 1900, San Diego, California 92101–4495, USA (1996)
5. Gallant, A.R., Tauchen, G.: Which moments to match? Econometric Theor. **12**(4), 657–681 (1996). https://doi.org/10.1017/S0266466600006976
6. Gatheral, J.: The volatility surface : a practitioner's guide. Wiley (2012). https://doi.org/10.1002/9781119202073
7. Goodfellow, I., Bengio, Y., Courville, A.: Deep Learning. Adaptive Computation and Machine Learning Series. MIT Press, Cambridge (2017)
8. Gourieroux, C., Monfort, A., Renault, E.: Indirect inference. J. Appl. Econ. **8**, S85–S118 (1993). http://www.jstor.org/stable/2285076
9. Hernandez, A.: Model calibration with neural networks (2015). https://doi.org/10.2139/ssrn.2812140
10. Heston, S.L.: A closed-form solution for options with stochastic volatility with applications to bond and currency options. Rev. Finan. Stud. **6**(2), 327–343 (2015). https://doi.org/10.1093/rfs/6.2.327
11. Hull, J.: Options, Futures, and Other Derivatives. 10th edn, Pearson Prentice Hall, Upper Saddle River (2017)
12. Jacquier, E., Polson, N.G., Rossi, P.E.: Bayesian analysis of stochastic volatility models. J. Bus. Econ. Stat. **12**(4), 371–389 (1994). http://www.jstor.org/stable/1392199
13. Kloeden, P.E., Platen, E.P.: Stochastic Modelling and Applied Probability, Applications of Mathematics, 2 edn. vol. 1. Springer, Berlin (1992)
14. Lewis, A.L.: Option Valuation Under Stochastic Volatility: With Mathematica Code, chap. Appendix 1.1 - Parameter Estimators for the GARCH Diffusion Model. Finance Press, Newport Beach, California, USA (2000)

15. Liu, S., Borovykh, A., Grzelak, L.A., Oosterlee, C.W.: A neural network-based framework for financial model calibration. J. Math. Ind. **9**(1), 9 (2019). https://doi.org/10.1186/s13362-019-0066-7

16. Lu, L., Jin, P., Karniadakis, G.E.: Deeponet: Learning nonlinear operators for identifying differential equations based on the universal approximation theorem of operators (2020). https://arxiv.org/abs/1910.03193

17. Lu, L., Jin, P., Pang, G., Zhang, Z., Karniadakis, G.E.: Learning nonlinear operators via deeponet based on the universal approximation theorem of operators. Nature Mach. Intell. **3**(3), 218–229 (2021). https://doi.org/10.1038/s42256-021-00302-5

18. Lu, L., Meng, X., Mao, Z., Karniadakis, G.E.: DeepXDE: a deep learning library for solving differential equations. SIAM Rev. **63**(1), 208–228 (2021). https://doi.org/10.1137/19M1274067

19. Mao, Z., Lu, L., Marxen, O., Zaki, T.A., Karniadakis, G.E.: Deepm & mnet for hypersonics: Predicting the coupled flow and finite-rate chemistry behind a normal shock using neural-network approximation of operators (2020). https://arxiv.org/abs/2011.03349

20. Márkus, L., Kumar, A.: Modelling joint behaviour of asset prices using stochastic correlation. Method. Comput. Appl. Probab. **23**(1), 341–354 (2021). https://doi.org/10.1007/s11009-020-09838-2

21. Monsalve-Cobis, A., González-Manteiga, W., Febrero-Bande, M.: Goodness-of-fit test for interest rate models: an approach based on empirical processes. Comput. Stat. Data Anal. **55**(12), 3073–3092 (2011). https://doi.org/10.1016/j.csda.2011.06.004

22. Moysiadis, G., Anagnostou, I., Kandhai, D.: Calibrating the mean-reversion parameter in the hull-white model using neural networks. In: Alzate, C., et al. (eds.) MIDAS/PAP-2018. LNCS (LNAI), vol. 11054, pp. 23–36. Springer, Cham (2019). https://doi.org/10.1007/978-3-030-13463-1_2

23. Mrázek, M., Pospíšil, J.: Calibration and simulation of heston model. Open Math. **15**(1), 679–704 (2017). https://doi.org/10.1515/math-2017-0058

24. Rouah, F.D.: The Heston model and its extensions in Matlab and C#, Wiley finance series, 1 edn, vol. 1. Wiley, Hoboken (2013)

25. Tang, C.Y., Chen, S.X.: Parameter estimation and bias correction for diffusion processes. J. Econ. **149**(1), 65–81 (2009). https://doi.org/10.1016/j.jeconom.2008.11.001

26. Tomas, M.: Pricing and calibration of stochastic models via neural networks. Master's thesis, Department of Mathematics, Imperial College London (2018). https://www.imperial.ac.uk/media/imperial-college/faculty-of-natural-sciences/department-of-mathematics/math-finance/TOMAS_MEHDI_01390785.pdf

27. Wang, X., He, X., Bao, Y., Zhao, Y.: Parameter estimates of heston stochastic volatility model with mle and consistent ekf algorithm. Sci. China Inf. Sci. **61**(4), 042202 (2018). https://doi.org/10.1007/s11432-017-9215-8

28. Xie, Z., Kulasiri, D., Samarasinghe, S., Rajanayaka, C.: The estimation of parameters for stochastic differential equations using neural networks. Inverse Prob. Sci. Eng. **15**(6), 629–641 (2007). https://doi.org/10.1080/17415970600907429

Faster Than LASER - Towards Stream Reasoning with Deep Neural Networks

João Ferreira, Diogo Lavado, Ricardo Gonçalves[(✉)], Matthias Knorr, Ludwig Krippahl, and João Leite

NOVA LINCS & Departamento de Informática, Universidade Nova de Lisboa, Caparica, Portugal
rjrg@fct.unl.pt

Abstract. With the constant increase of available data in various domains, such as the Internet of Things, Social Networks or Smart Cities, it has become fundamental that agents are able to process and reason with such data in real time. Whereas reasoning over time-annotated data with background knowledge may be challenging, due to the volume and velocity in which such data is being produced, such complex reasoning is necessary in scenarios where agents need to discover potential problems and this cannot be done with simple stream processing techniques. Stream Reasoners aim at bridging this gap between reasoning and stream processing and LASER is such a stream reasoner designed to analyse and perform complex reasoning over streams of data. It is based on LARS, a rule-based logical language extending Answer Set Programming, and it has shown better runtime results than other state-of-the-art stream reasoning systems. Nevertheless, for high levels of data throughput even LASER may be unable to compute answers in a timely fashion. In this paper, we study whether Convolutional and Recurrent Neural Networks, which have shown to be particularly well-suited for time series forecasting and classification, can be trained to approximate reasoning with LASER, so that agents can benefit from their high processing speed.

1 Introduction

We are witnessing a huge increase on data production in various domains, such as the Internet of Things (IoT), Industry 4.0, Social Networks and Smart Cities. In order to deal with this highly dynamic data, to extract implicit relevant information from such data streams and be able to react to it in a timely fashion, agents need the ability to process, query and perform complex reasoning over such huge amounts of time-annotated data in real time. For example, in an assisted living scenario, a robot designed to help elderly people who live alone should be able to use the data produced by several sensors to detect potential risk situations momentarily and react by calling for assistance in case of an emergency. Also, the data from different sensors in a Smart City scenario, such as traffic and pollution information, can help an agent to detect or even anticipate

© Springer Nature Switzerland AG 2021
G. Marreiros et al. (Eds.): EPIA 2021, LNAI 12981, pp. 363–375, 2021.
https://doi.org/10.1007/978-3-030-86230-5_29

problems, and react to these by, for example, rerouting traffic to prevent traffic jams, specially on those areas with high levels of pollution, thus having an impact on the flow of traffic and the pollution footprint.

To deal with this highly dynamic data and their limited storage capacity for such data, agents can rely on stream processing systems [8], i.e., Data Stream Management Systems (DSMS), which allow to continuously query on only a snapshot of a data stream, and Complex Event Processors (CEP), which focus on the identification of temporal patterns occurring in a data stream. These systems cannot, however, perform complex reasoning tasks that require the integration of heterogeneous sources and background knowledge, such as, for example in the assisted living scenario, a database with the patient's records, a set of action policy rules, or a biomedical health ontology with information about diseases, their symptoms and treatments.

Stream Reasoning aims at overcoming these limitations, by bridging the gap between reasoning and stream processing [9,10]. One of the state of the art stream reasoners is LASER [3], a system based on LARS [4], which is a rule-based logical language extending Answer Set Programming (ASP) [17], designed to analyse and perform complex reasoning over streams of data. LASER allows one to declaratively encode a query as a set of logic programming rules, extending the language of ASP with temporal operators, such as $\Diamond$ (at some time instance) and $\Box$ (at every time instance) and $@_t$ (at a specific time t), together with window operators, which allow focusing on portions of the data stream. Empirical results [3] show that LASER has considerably better runtime results than other state-of-the-art stream reasoners, such as C-SPARQL [2] or CQELS [25].

Although LASER takes efficient computation into account while supporting expressive reasoning, such expressiveness necessarily imposes bounds on what can be computed efficiently. In fact, for high levels of data throughput and depending on the complexity of the considered queries, namely when the frequency of incoming data is higher than the time required for reasoning with that data, in particular when requiring to compute large combinatorics, LASER is not able to answer queries in time. This is prohibitive in real world scenarios where the timely detection and reaction to problematic situations cannot be compromised.

Whereas Stream Reasoning systems, such as LASER, provide expressive sound and complete reasoning, it has been argued [22] that, for huge amounts of data, approximate methods need to be considered for obtaining answers in real time. Machine Learning approaches, such as Neural Networks [20], have been successfully applied in a variety of domains for their ability to learn from examples, and generalize to unseen situations. Once trained, and since the computation of Neural Networks is only based on the manipulation of real-valued vectors and matrices, their processing speed is constant on the size of the input and usually extremely fast. Recent advances in Deep Learning [18] and its successful applications in several complex problems such as image, video, or speech recognition, led to the development of sophisticated Neural Networks capable of learning highly complex patterns from the data. This raised the interest of using such techniques to approximate formal deductive reasoning.

Within the field of neural-symbolic integration [5,21] the problem of approximating logical reasoning with Neural Networks has been considered. Early work on using neural networks for deductive reasoning opened the door for representing several propositional non-classical logics [16], building on systems that translate symbolic representations directly into neural networks [15,19]. Neural-symbolic approaches based on logic tensor networks [11] learn sub-symbolic vector representations from training facts in a knowledge base. Other neural-symbolic approaches focusing on first-order inference include, e.g., CLIP++ [14], lifted relational neural networks [27], TensorLog [7], and recent work on approximating ontology reasoning [21]. Yet, none of these solutions considers reasoning with and reacting to time-annotated, streaming data.

In this paper, we investigate the feasibility of using Deep Neural Networks to approximate stream reasoning with LASER, to take advantage of their high processing speed. We explore two types of neural networks, namely Convolutional Neural Networks (CNN) [29] and Recurrent Neural Networks (RNNs) [26], which have been shown to obtain good results when applied to time-annotated data problems, such as time series forecasting and classification [6,12]. For our experiments, we consider a real dataset with time-annotated sensor data on traffic, pollution and weather conditions, and explore different types of LASER queries, in order to cover different expressive features of its language. We obtain promising results, showing that it is indeed possible for agents to approximate reasoning with LASER with high levels of accuracy, and with significant improvements of the processing time. We also discuss the differences between the results obtained by the two types of neural networks considered.

In the remainder, we recall, in Sect. 2, the necessary material on LASER and the two types of neural networks. Then, in Sect. 3, we describe the methodology used for the experiments and, in Sect. 4, the obtained results. Finally, in Sect. 5 we present a discussion of the results and draw some conclusions.

2   Background

In this section, we recall some useful notions for the remainder of the paper, namely those related to the stream reasoner LASER, and the two types of neural networks we consider, convolutional and recurrent neural networks.

2.1   Laser

LASER [3] is a stream reasoning system based on LARS [4], a rule-based logical language extending Answer Set Programming (ASP) [17] with stream reasoning capabilities. The concept of data stream is modelled in LARS as a sequence of time-annotated atoms, more precisely, as pairs $S = \langle T, v \rangle$, where T is a closed time interval timeline of natural numbers, and $v : \mathbb{N} \rightarrow 2^A$ is an evaluation function, that indicates which atoms are true at each time point in T. The language of LARS contains the usual boolean operators, but offers also temporal operators such as $\Diamond$ and $\Box$ to express that a formula holds, respectively, at some time or at every time of a given stream. The operator $@_t$ allows us to express that a formula holds at a specific time t within a stream. An essential component of stream reasoning is the concept of *window*, since it allows restricting the focus only to a portion of the stream, usually to the most recent elements. In LARS, tuple-based and time-based windows are considered. A time-based window of size n, represented as $\boxplus^n$, restricts the focus only to those atoms that are true in the last n time points of the stream, whereas a tuple-based window of size n, represented as $\boxplus^{\#n}$, restricts the focus to the last n atoms of the stream.

To address the trade-off between expressiveness and efficiency, LASER considers a tractable fragment of LARS, called Plain LARS. In more detail, given a set $\mathcal{A}$ of *atoms*, the set $\mathcal{A}^+$ of *extended atoms* is defined by the grammar

$$a \mid @_t a \mid \boxplus^w @_t a \mid \boxplus^w \Diamond a \mid \boxplus^w \Box a$$

where $a \in \mathcal{A}$, $t \in \mathbb{N}$ is a time point, and w can be either n or $\#n$. Then, a Plain LARS program over $\mathcal{A}$ is a set of rules of the form $\alpha \leftarrow \beta_1, \ldots, \beta_m$ where α is either a or $@_t a$, with $a \in \mathcal{A}$, and each β_i is an extended atom.

The resulting language is highly expressive allowing sofisticated queries for reasoning with streaming data as well as the direct encoding of rich background knowledge to be taken into account in the reasoning process.

The semantics of Plain LARS programs is rooted in the notion of *answer stream*, an extension of the answer set semantics for logic programs [3].

A fundamental feature of LASER is the implementation of an incremental evaluation procedure, which, by annotating formulae and efficiently propagating and removing such annotations, avoids many unnecessary re-computations.

2.2 Neural Networks

We now present a brief overview of the two types of neural networks considered here, for which we assume familiarity with the basic notions on supervised learning with Artificial Neural Networks [18,20].

Recurrent Neural Networks. Recurrent Neural Networks (RNNs) form a class of Artificial Neural Networks that have shown the ability to detect patterns in sequential data [26]. RNNs have been successfully applied to speech recognition and synthesis and time-series prediction and classification. The key distinguishing feature of this type of architecture is how the information passes through the network. They have a feedback mechanism, in which the output of the recurrent layer gets transmitted back into itself in the next step. This allows the network to take into account previous inputs, besides the current one. Long Short Term Memory (LSTM) [24] networks are a type of RNN built from gated cells, structured blocks that allow for a better control of the information flow over the network. These gated cells receive as input the data from the current time step, the hidden state and cell state from the previous time step. The new hidden state will depend on these three inputs after nonlinear transformations with activation functions. The new cell state, however, will only be subject to linear transformations. This helps preventing the vanishing gradients problem [23] and preserving long-term information through the network, improving the identification of patterns extendning over longer periods of time.

Convolutional Neural Networks. Convolutional Neural Networks (CNNs) are well-known for their successful application in processing data with positionally invariant patterns, such as images, where CNNs are the state of the art methods, or time series, which can be seen as one-dimensional grids of data organized along the time axis [1]. CNNs include convolutional layers in which kernels are applied to the input data in order to produce feature maps capable of detecting useful patterns. These patterns are then fed into subsequent layers to help identify increasingly complex features [1,28]. In addition, CNNs include pooling layers that aggregate patches of feature maps to help abstract from the position of detected features in the input and reduce the dimension of the data. The use of these two kinds of layers leads to a significant decrease in the number of trainable parameters compared to using only fully connected layers. Nevertheless, CNNs used for classification problems generally include a small set of fully connected layers at the end, after convolution and pooling layers extracted useful features form the data. Dropout layers can also be used for regularization. Dropout layers randomly set to zero outputs from the previous layer at each batch during training. This helps reduce overfitting by forcing the network to avoid relying too much on specific inputs instead of broader patterns.

3   Methods

In this section, we present the experiments we designed to test whether stream reasoning with LASER can be approximated by RNNs and CNNs.

In general terms, each experiment consisted of *i*) the development of a LASER query, considering different aspects of the expressiveness of its language as detailed in Sect. 2.1, and its execution in order to obtain the results according to LASER; *ii*) the use of such labeled data (an encoding of the input data stream and the corresponding output according to LASER) to train and test different RNN and CNN models, to be able to choose, for each of these types, the best model in terms of approximating stream reasoning with LASER.

Before we detail these two steps, we introduce the considered dataset.

3.1   Dataset

The dataset we used in our experiments is a publicly available dataset[1] containing time-stamped information about road traffic, pollution, and weather reports

---

[1] http://iot.ee.surrey.ac.uk:8080/datasets.html.

obtained from 449 sensors distributed throughout the city of Aarhus in Denmark. The dataset includes, for example, *pollution* events, such as ozone, carbon monoxide, sulfure dioxide and nitrogen dioxide measures, on average 1942 pollution events per timestamp of five minutes, *traffic* events such as vehicle count and average speed, on average 700 traffic events per timestamp, and *weather* events such as wind speed and direction, temperature, humidity and pressure measures, on average 2 weather events per timestamp.

To allow for more complex queries involving advanced reasoning, we grouped the sensors into sectors, according to their geographic position, thus enabling comparisons between sectors and the sensors within these. We also considered rich background knowledge, namely the definition of static notions such as city, town and suburbs of cities, and relations between these, such as adjacency.

Taking into account the mentioned limitation of LASER to process large amounts of data, we reduced the number of sensors to be considered from 499 to 273, which also allowed for a more even distribution of sensors per sector. The data from the dataset provided in .csv was encoded as facts indicating the occurrence of an event in a sector, associated to the time interval as natural numbers, where each time step corresponds to five minutes. The resulting data set contains a total of 17569 time steps that was used as input for Laser.

3.2 LASER Queries

We developed a set of queries to systematically explore different aspects of LASER's expressive language, namely the usage of combinations of window operators ⊞ and temporal operators $\Box$, $\Diamond$, and $@_t$. For part of these queries, we enriched the reasoning process with background knowledge, i.e., knowledge that is not derived from the stream, including notions such as adjacency, an ontology over the concepts of city, town and suburb, and topological information, such as which towns are suburbs of which cities. Given that neural networks can only provide answers through a fixed number of output neurons, we only considered LASER queries with a fixed number of answers, i.e., boolean or discrete. For boolean queries, we took into account the overall balance between positive and negative outputs, since highly unbalanced scenarios could impose unwanted bias in the training process of the neural networks. For queries with discrete output, the final count was obtained by a simple post-processing step, as LASER does not include aggregation functions. To construct and process LASER queries, we built on the available prototype of LASER[2] extended with means to represent factual background knowledge more straightforwardly and with additional operators to facilitate the comparison of strings and numeric values.[3]

3.3 Training and Testing CNNs and RNNs

For each query, the neural networks considered receive an encoding of the input stream, just as the query, and produce an output of the same type as the out-

---

[2] https://github.com/karmaresearch/Laser.
[3] https://github.com/jmd-ferreira/approx_laser.

put of the query. Such outputs are sequences of time steps, similar to streams, containing the query results, and are used as labels to train the neural networks. To encode the input data for the neural network, we use an array of fixed size corresponding to the sensor readings that are relevant to the query, structured w.r.t. sectors and events. In the case of LSTMs, the RNNs considered here, an input is a sequence of size w, where w is the window size used for the query, and each element of that sequence is an array containing the features per sector. For CNNs, the input is a matrix of size $w \times n$, corresponding to the entire sequence of w arrays, each of size n. We also used standardization, to account for range differences between features, to prevent a slow or unstable learning processes.

For each query, we designed, trained and tested different architectures, both for CNNs and LSTMs, varying, for example, the number and type of layers, the number of neurons in each layer, or the kernel size for CNNs. We also used Dropout layers after dense layers to avoid overfitting. The training and test set accuracy (the fraction of correct answers) of these neural networks were used as a measure to assess their ability to approximate LASER. In real applications, one must often consider that different errors have different consequences and so other metrics may be useful, such as confusion matrices, AUC, precision and recall or the F-score. However, since our goal is to assess how well the networks approximate LASER in a range of hypothetical scenarios chosen to span different types of queries and problems, we decided to focus on accuracy.

The available 17569 samples were divided into 80% used for training (with either 30% or 20% reserved for training validation depending on the query) and 20% for testing. The number of epochs for training varies for the queries, namely, for LSTMs, between 100 and 200 and, for CNNs, between 50 and 200.

The design, training and testing of our CNNs and RNNs models was done using the Python library Tensorflow[4] and Keras[5], a high-level API for Tensorflow that provides implementations of CNNs and LSTM architectures.

4 Description of Experiments and Results

In this section, we present the experiments done to assess whether LASER can be approximated by RNNs and CNNs. We considered a set of queries exploring different aspects of LASER's expressive language (cf. Section 2.1), along with different types of problems, such as classification or regression, and the use of background knowledge, and we present representatives for such different queries. For each experiment, we present the considered query and discuss the results in terms of approximation obtained by the CNNs and LSTMs, the considered type of RNNs. To ease readability, we opted to present just a natural language description of each query, instead of its formal representation in LASER. [6]

---

[4] https://blog.tensorflow.org/2019/09/tensorflow-20-is-now-available.html.
[5] https://www.tensorflow.org/guide/keras.
[6] An extended version of the paper contains the exact encoding of the queries, final configurations of the networks, and plots of the learning phase [13].

The experiments were run on a computer with an Intel i7 8th gen hexa-core processor, with GPU Nvidia 1050 Ti, and 8GB of RAM. We note that pre-processing the input data (for LASER) as well as encoding the input for the networks took only a few milliseconds per time step, which is why it is not reported individually, and that training the networks required on average not more than ten minutes for both kinds of networks, which is only once before applying the network, and, once trained, neural networks never required more than 300 μs to produce the output for one time step in any of the experiments.

4.1   Test Case 1

The first experiment aimed at considering a complex temporal boolean query, leveraging on LASER's expressive temporal language. This query considers intermediate notions of industrial, urban and highway events, defined using different temporal patterns of pollution and traffic events. A metropolitan event occurs in a sector within a given time window if at least one industrial event, one urban event, and one highway event are detected in that sector in that time window. The results for the following query are reported in the subsequent table:
"Are there any metropolitan events in the last 9 time steps?"

	LSTM Train Acc	LSTM Test Acc	CNN Train Acc	CNN Test Acc
Query 1	0.9667	0.9107	0.9951	0.9996

During the training phase, we observed that LSTM models showed considerable levels of overfitting and some inconsistency in terms of accuracy and loss, which did not occur with CNNs, whose performance was more stable. Still, regarding the test set, both types of networks showed excellent results, with those of CNNs being slightly better than those of RNNs.

Overall, the results obtained allow us to conclude that it is indeed feasible to consider both CNNs and RNNs to approximate the complex temporal reasoning of LASER on boolean queries. Moreover, the gain in terms of processing time is impressive, as the reported limit of $300\mu s$ to produce the output for each time step, is several orders of magnitude faster than LASER's average of 89 s per time step. Also note that LASER's processing time here becomes prohibitive when the data in this scenario arrives with a frequency of less than a minute.

4.2   Test Case 2

In the second experiment, we considered a classification problem that involves temporal reasoning and complex comparisons between sectors. The aim was to test whether neural networks are able to approximate stream reasoning when the problem is not just a binary classification problem, as in the previous test case, but rather a complex multi-label classification problem.

This query involves temporal concepts such as high and low traffic and pollution, which depend on different traffic and pollution measures given by the sensors. Two sectors are then called conflicting with respect to traffic and pollution if they consistently differ on the registered traffic and pollution events within a window of three time steps, meaning that one of the sectors always registered high traffic and high pollution, and the other always low traffic and low pollution. The query and the obtained results are given as follows:

"Are there any pairs of conflicting sectors within the last 3 time steps?"

	LSTM Train Acc	LSTM Test Acc	CNN Train Acc	CNN Test Acc
Query 2	0.9997	0.9896	0.9956	0.9951

During the training phase, and contrarily to CNNs, RNNs showed slight signs of overfitting on the last epochs. Nevertheless, we can see that both CNNs and RNNs present excellent results for this query. Hence, multi-label classification problems in stream reasoning can also be approximated with CNNs and LSTMs. Here, LASER requires on average 10 s per time step, which is still slower than processing with neural networks by a large margin.

4.3   Test Case 3

In this experiment, we considered a problem involving temporal reasoning and complex classification of sectors. The aim was to test if neural networks can approximate stream reasoning for complex multiclass classification problems.

This query considers complex temporal conditions on pollution and traffic, to define urban, work, rural and industrial events. Then, for a given time window, a sector is classified as rural if at least one rural event was registered during that time window; as a living sector if only urban events were registered during that time window; as an office sector if both urban and working events were registered during that time window, and no other type of event was registered; and as a factory sector if industrial events were registered in that time window, but no rural events. The query and the results are as follows:

"Based on the last 3 timestamps, what is the classification of each sector?"

	LSTM Train Acc	LSTM Test Acc	CNN Train Acc	CNN Test Acc
Query 3	0.9996	0.9962	0.9974	0.9933

This query, which defines a multiclass classification problem, makes extensive use of LASER's expressive power. Since the classification of each sector is independent of the others, we trained ten neural networks, one per sector, each providing the classification for one sector, which resulted in much better approximation results than considering just one neuronal network for all sectors.

We can see that both CNNs and RNNs present excellent results for this query, thus allowing us to conclude that CNNs and RNNs can also approximate stream reasoning for the case of multiclass classification problems. Processing with LASER took on average 30 s per time step which is again much slower than processing with Neural Networks.

4.4 Test Case 4

In this experiment, we considered a problem that involves temporal reasoning, complex classification and counting of sectors. The aim was to test whether neural networks are able to approximate stream reasoning when the problem is a complex regression problem. This query considers the notion of rural event, which is detected in a sector if, in a given time window, that sector registers low and decreasing measurements of traffic and pollution. The considered query is: *"In the last four time steps, how many sectors registered a rural event?"*

For this regression problem, we considered the mean squared error as a measure of approximation, and the results are reported in the following table.

	LSTM Train Loss	LSTM Test Loss	CNN Train Loss	CNN Test Loss
Query 4	0.05	0.13	0.01	0.006

We can observe very goods results for LSTMs, and excellent ones for CNNs. This is as clear indication that both CNNs and RNNs can approximate stream reasoning for the case of regression problems. In this experiment, LASER required on average 7 s per time step for answering the query, which is again a lot slower than network processing.

4.5 Test Case 5

In this experiment, we considered a problem that involves the combination of temporal reasoning with background knowledge. The aim was to test whether neural networks are able to approximate stream reasoning when temporal reasoning over the stream is enhanced with rich background knowledge.

For this query we considered LASER's ability to define and reason with background knowledge, and defined concepts such as city and town, with towns being suburbs of a city, and a proximity relation between suburbs based on whether these are suburbs of the same city. In addition, we defined a notion of anomaly occurrence in a sector in a given time window, if such sector is a city (static classification) and it is classified as an industrial sector (based on the occurrence of temporal events), together with two of its suburbs. To cope with the extra complexity of this query, and to obtain a balanced training set, we only considered the measures given by a subset of 100 sensors. The query and the obtained results are the following:
"In the last four timestamps, in which sectors an anomaly has been detected?"

	LSTM Train Acc	LSTM Test Acc	CNN Train Acc	CNN Test Acc
Query 5	0.9628	0.9418	0.9519	0.9341

We can see that both types of networks present excellent results, again showing clear benefits in terms of processing time for the networks. This experiment further strengths the hypothesis that both CNNs and RNNs can be successfully used to approximate stream reasoning with LASER, even when complex temporal reasoning over the stream is combined with rich background knowledge.

5 Conclusions

In this paper, we have investigated the viability of using Recurrent and Convolutional Neural Networks to approximate expressive stream reasoning with LASER, so that agents can leverage on their fast processing time, which would make them suitable for scenarios where, due to the velocity and size of data to be processed, LASER cannot be used to provide answers in a timely fashion.

Our experiments on a real dataset with time-annotated sensor data on traffic, pollution and weather conditions, show that both RNNs and CNNs provide excellent approximations to stream reasoning with LASER, even for different types of complex queries exploring LASER's expressive language, providing at the same time incomparably better performance in terms of processing time.

In terms of comparing CNNs and RNNs results, we could not observe a significant difference between the two in terms of approximation. During the training phase, however, we observed that, contrarily to the case of CNNs, RNNs were usually more prone to overfitting and their accuracy would sometimes significantly oscillate between epochs. In general terms, however, we could not conclude that one of the architectures is better suited than the other for approximating stream reasoning, despite the small advantages of CNNs on queries 1 and 4.

We should note that LASER, which has shown promising results in terms of processing time and expressiveness when compared with other state-of-art stream reasoners, is still useful in scenarios where agents need certain answers, or when the low size and velocity of the incoming data allows LASER to present answers in time, or where not enough training data is available or is imbalanced.

For future work, it would be interesting to experiment with larger datasets, to see if it is possible to improve on those cases where the results were not excellent. Lastly, we have focused on the approximation of stream reasoning with neural networks to leverage on their high processing speed, but it would also be interesting to investigate, in a stream reasoning scenario, how agents can benefit from neural networks' natural ability to cope with noisy data.

Acknowledgments. We thank the anonymous reviewers for their helpful comments and acknowledge support by FCT project RIVER (PTDC/CCI-COM/30952/2017) and by FCT project NOVA LINCS (UIDB/04516/2020).

References

1. Albawi, S., Mohammed, T.A., Al-Zawi, S.: Understanding of a convolutional neural network. In: ICET, pp. 1–6 (2017)
2. Barbieri, D.F., Braga, D., Ceri, S., Valle, E.D., Grossniklaus, M.: C-SPARQL: a continuous query language for RDF data streams. Int. J. Seman. Comput. **4**(01), 3–25 (2010)
3. Bazoobandi, H.R., Beck, H., Urbani, J.: Expressive stream reasoning with laser. In: d'Amato, C., et al. (eds.) ISWC 2017. LNCS, vol. 10587, pp. 87–103. Springer, Cham (2017). https://doi.org/10.1007/978-3-319-68288-4_6
4. Beck, H., Dao-Tran, M., Eiter, T.: LARS: A logic-based framework for analytic reasoning over streams. Artif, Intell. **261** 16–70 (2018)
5. Besold, T.R., et al.: Neural-symbolic learning and reasoning: A survey and interpretation. CoRR arXiv:1711.03902 (2017)
6. Bianchi, F.M., Scardapane, S., Løkse, S., Jenssen, R.: Reservoir computing approaches for representation and classification of multivariate time series. arXiv preprint arXiv:1803.07870 (2018)
7. Cohen, W.W., Yang, F., Mazaitis, K.: Tensorlog: a probabilistic database implemented using deep-learning infrastructure. J. Artif. Intell. Res. **67**, 285–325 (2020)
8. Cugola, G., Margara, A.: Processing flows of information: from data stream to complex event processing. ACM Comput. Surv. (CSUR) **44**(3), 1–62 (2012)
9. Della Valle, E., Ceri, S., Van Harmelen, F., Fensel, D.: It's a streaming world! reasoning upon rapidly changing information. IEEE Intel. Sys. **24**(6), 83–89 (2009)
10. Dell'Aglio, D., Della Valle, E., van Harmelen, F., Bernstein, A.: Stream reasoning: a survey and outlook. Data Sci. **1**(1–2), 59–83 (2017)
11. Donadello, I., Serafini, L., d'Avila Garcez, A.S.: Logic tensor networks for semantic image interpretation. In: IJCAI, pp. 1596–1602 (2017) ijcai.org
12. Ismail Fawaz, H., Forestier, G., Weber, J., Idoumghar, L., Muller, P.-A.: Deep learning for time series classification: a review. Data Min. Knowl. Dis. **33**(4), 917–963 (2019). https://doi.org/10.1007/s10618-019-00619-1
13. Ferreira, J., Lavado, D., Gonçalves, R., Knorr, M., Krippahl, L., Leite, J.: Faster than LASER - towards stream reasoning with deep neural networks. CoRR arXiv:2106.08457 (2021)
14. França, M.V.M., Zaverucha, G., d'Avila Garcez, A.S.: Fast relational learning using bottom clause propositionalization with artificial neural networks. Mach. Learn. **94**(1), 81–104 (2013). https://doi.org/10.1007/s10994-013-5392-1
15. d'Avila Garcez, A.S., et al.: Neural-symbolic learning and reasoning: Contributions and challenges. In: AAAI Spring Symposia, AAAI Press (2015)
16. d'Avila Garcez, A.S., Lamb, L.C., Gabbay, D.M.: Neural-Symbolic Cognitive Reasoning. Springer, Berlin (2009). https://doi.org/10.1007/978-3-540-73246-4
17. Gelfond, M., Lifschitz, V.: Classical negation in logic programs and disjunctive databases. New Gener. Comput. **9**(3/4), 365–386 (1991)
18. Goodfellow, I., Bengio, Y., Courville, A.: Deep Learning. MIT Press, Cambridge (2016)
19. Hammer, B., Hitzler, P. (eds.): Perspectives of Neural-Symbolic Integration, Studies in Computational Intelligence, vol. 77. Springer, Berlin (2007)
20. Haykin, S.: Neural networks: a comprehensive foundation. Prentice Hall PTR, Upper Saddle River (1994)
21. Hitzler, P., Bianchi, F., Ebrahimi, M., Sarker, M.K.: Neural-symbolic integration and the semantic web. Seman. Web **11**(1), 3–11 (2020)

22. Hitzler, P., van Harmelen, F.: A reasonable semantic web. Seman. Web **1**(1–2), 39–44 (2010)
23. Hochreiter, S.: The vanishing gradient problem during learning recurrent neural nets and problem solutions. Int. J. Uncertain. Fuzziness Knowl. Based Syst. **6**(2), 107–116 (1998)
24. Hochreiter, S., Schmidhuber, J.: Long short-term memory. Neural Comput. **9**(8), 1735–1780 (1997)
25. Le-Phuoc, D., Dao-Tran, M., Xavier Parreira, J., Hauswirth, M.: A native and adaptive approach for unified processing of linked streams and linked data. In: Aroyo, L., et al. (eds.) ISWC 2011. LNCS, vol. 7031, pp. 370–388. Springer, Heidelberg (2011). https://doi.org/10.1007/978-3-642-25073-6_24
26. Qin, Y., Song, D., Chen, H., Cheng, W., Jiang, G., Cottrell, G.W.: A dual-stage attention-based recurrent neural network for time series prediction. In: IJCAI, pp. 2627–2633 (2017) ijcai.org
27. Sourek, G., Aschenbrenner, V., Zelezný, F., Schockaert, S., Kuzelka, O.: Lifted relational neural networks: efficient learning of latent relational structures. J. Artif. Intell. Res. **62**, 69–100 (2018)
28. Tu, F., Yin, S., Ouyang, P., Tang, S., Liu, L., Wei, S.: Deep convolutional neural network architecture with reconfigurable computation patterns. IEEE Trans. Very Large Scale Integr. (VLSI) Syst. **25**(8), 2220–2233 (2017)
29. Wang, Z., Yan, W., Oates, T.: Time series classification from scratch with deep neural networks: a strong baseline. In: IJCNN, pp. 1578–1585. IEEE (2017)

Using Regression Error Analysis and Feature Selection to Automatic Cluster Labeling

Lucia Emilia Soares Silva[1]([✉]), Vinicius Ponte Machado[1],
Sidiney Souza Araujo[1], Bruno Vicente Alves de Lima[2],
and Rodrigo de Melo Souza Veras[1]

[1] Departamento de Computação, Universidade Federal do Piauí, Teresina, Brazil
{luciaemilia,vinicius,sidiney,rveras}@ufpi.edu.br
[2] Instituto Federal do Maranhão, Timon, Brazil
brunovicente.lima@ifma.edu.br

Abstract. Cluster Labeling Models apply Artificial Intelligence techniques to extract the key features of clustered data to provide a tool for clustering interpretation. For this purpose, we applied different techniques such as Classification, Regression, Fuzzy Logic, and Data Discretization to identify essential attributes for cluster formation and the ranges of values associated with them. This paper presents an improvement to the Regression-based Cluster Labeling Model that integrates to the model an attribute selection step based on the coefficient of determination obtained by regression models in order to make its application possible in large datasets. The model was tested on the literature datasets Iris, Breast Cancer, and Parkinson's Disease, evaluating the labeling performance of different dimensionality. The results obtained from the experiments showed that the model is sound, providing specific labels for each cluster representing between 99% and 100% of the elements of the clusters for the datasets used.

Keywords: Clustering · Cluster interpretation · Labeling · Unsupervised learning · Feature selection · Dimensionality reduction

1 Introduction

The clustering problem is one of the most significant among those in the area of unsupervised learning, a subarea of Machine Learning (ML), considering its many real-life applications, as there is typically a large amount of unlabeled data available [4]. Thus, research has been developed to analyze clusterings, based on the idea that attribute data describe intrinsic characteristics of entities, a task called Cluster Labeling [5,7,8]. The label of a cluster summarizes its common elements' characteristics facilitating the understanding and interpretation of the data through the values of essential characteristics of their elements [6], so the labeling problem is defined as follows.

© Springer Nature Switzerland AG 2021
G. Marreiros et al. (Eds.): EPIA 2021, LNAI 12981, pp. 376–388, 2021.
https://doi.org/10.1007/978-3-030-86230-5_30

Given a set X of elements represented by an attribute vector defined in $\mathbb{R}^m$ and expressed by $\vec{x} = (x_1, ..., x_m)$, such as $X = \{\vec{x}_{i,j}|_{i,j=0}^{i=n,j=m}$, and partitioned into a subset of clusters $C = \{c_a\}|_{a=1}^b$, let $c_a \cap c_{a'} = \{\emptyset\} \; \forall \; 1 \le a \le b$ and $a \ne a'$; the goal is to present a set of labels $L = \{l_{c_a}\}|_{a=1}^b$, where each specific label is provided by a set of pairs of attributes and their respective ranges, so that $l_{c_a} = \{(attr_j, [p_j, q_j])\}|_{j=1}^{m^{(c_a)}}$ can better express the associated cluster c_a, where l_{c_a} is the label of the cluster c_a, $attr_j$ is an attribute of the problem, $[p_j, q_j]$ is the range of the attribute $attr_j$, where p_j is the lower limit and q_j the upper limit, and $m^{(c_a)}$ is the number of attributes in the label of c_a.

As it is a research area under development, different Cluster Labeling models have been proposed, observing the adaptability and limitations of the models in the literature. Thus, this paper presents improvements on a Cluster Labeling model that relies on the use of regression to perform a multivariate analysis of the clusters identifying the attributes ranges of values with minimum influential data points, revealed by the regressions prediction error, to indicate the most significant attributes for each cluster's definition [11]. In this model, the authors highlight the limitation of dealing with a large amount of data, a problem that we propose to solve by adding an intermediate step in the model to select attributes based on the determination coefficient of the regressions since the following steps of the proposed model prioritize attributes in which the regression residuals are minimal. In this way, selecting the attributes whose regressions have the lowest coefficient of determination optimizes execution time and memory resources, making the labeling of large datasets feasible.

The sequence of this paper is subdivided as follows: the models for cluster labeling in the literature are covered in Sects. 2; the improvements on the proposed model are presented in Section 3, followed by the methodology in Sect. 4. The experimental results for labeling clusters of some datasets from the literature are discussed in Sect. 5. Finally, Sect. 6 discusses the conclusions obtained by this research.

2   Related Works

The concept of labeling problem as we presented in the Introduction was proposed for the first time in Lopes et al. [7], and defines as its objective to provide the specialist a clear cluster identification through a label that describes the common features of its elements. The authors proposed identifying the significant features of each cluster's composition and their associated values through a combination of data discretization and supervised learning.

Their proposed model, the Automatic Labeling Model (ALM), starts by grouping the data using the K-means algorithm. The dataset is discretized to delimit ranges of values for the features in parallel, generating a discrete auxiliary dataset. The discretized dataset is submitted to a set of Multilayer Perceptrons (MLP) to identify the relationships between the features. Each MLP is trained to predict one feature per cluster, using the other features as inputs. The attributes whose MLP are the most successful are selected for the composition of the labels, and their associated ranges are those represented by the most frequent value of the cluster in the discrete dataset.

The experiments carried out with ALM obtained satisfactory results, in which the pairs of attributes represented, on average, 90% of the cluster samples. In addition, the ALM has been applied to different problems [7], obtaining satisfactory results in all. Although efficient, the ALM has limitations, such as the use of ranges of values previously established for the composition of the labels, resulting from the discretization process and the complexity and computational cost linked to the use of one MLP for each attribute per cluster.

As alternatives to the ALM, other models of cluster labeling can be found in the literature. A second model of cluster labeling, proposed by Machado et al. [8], uses the output of the Fuzzy C-means algorithm to delimit the ranges of values of the attributes, selecting as relevant those within no intersection between clusters until a certain distance from the centroid. The model was evaluated by the percentage of elements in the clusters that their respective labels can represent, ac hiving 92.7% in the experiment carried out with the Iris dataset. This model's main limitation is its dependence on the Fuzzy C-means algorithm that provides the degree of relevance of the elements. Considering this, the labeling model in Imperes et al. [5] includes a method for calculating each element's degree of relevance based on the distance to the centroid of the clusters, applicable to any clustering algorithm based on distance. In experiments, the obtained labels represented between 90% and 98.68% of the cluster's elements.

Based on the limitation of these works, the labeling model proposed by Silva et al. [11] aimed to dispense with the discretization step through regression, making the delimitation of value ranges part of the process of analyzing attribute relevance. Furthermore, the model ensures that excluding any part of the value range considers only the elements that compose it. The detailed operation of the model is described in the next section. Despite the results obtained, the authors highlight the model's limitation in labeling large datasets, given that the model steps are performed for each attribute or each attribute by group, making the problem complex. Thus, to contribute to research development, this work includes in the proposed model an attribute selection step based on the coefficient of determination of the model regressions, making the model feasible for labeling large datasets.

3 Cluster Labeling Model

The labeling model illustrated in Fig. 1 shows the aggregation of Feature Selection in the model proposed by Silva et al. [11]. The model uses regression in Step I to obtain the function that describes the prediction error of the attribute in their respective domains per cluster. The proposal is to use the coefficient of determination from these regressions to select the best attributes to continue the labeling process. The resulting model workflow is described above using as an example the Iris [2] dataset, which is composed of 150 instances described by 4 attributes: *Sepal Length* (SL), *Petal Length* (PL), *Sepal Width* (SW) and *Petal*

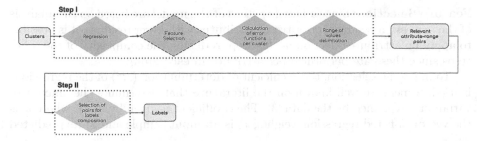

Fig. 1. Flowchart of the custer labeling model.

Width (PW), divided into three clusters, as suggested by the number of classes, using the K-means cluster algorithm [9].

3.1 Step I—Definition of Attribute–Range Pairs

Regression: To determine each attribute's relevance–range pair on cluster labeling, the first step of the labeling model uses a set of m regression models, where m is the number of characteristics of the problem. Each model is trained to predict an attribute, using the rest of the attributes as input. To avoid problems related to different scales between attributes, the elements are normalized using the MinMax method with a range of $[0, 1]$.

As a result, all elements are predicted by the regression models generating a set X' of elements $\vec{x}'_{i,j}$ represented by an attribute vector $\vec{x}' = (x'_1, ..., x'_m)$ and partitioned according to the clusters information. Table 1 illustrates the Sepal Length attribute prediction in a sample of 10 elements of the Cluster 1. The column X_{sl} presents the attributes original values, and the column X'_{sl}, the predicted values for each element.

Table 1. Prediction of the sepal length attribute.

#	X_{sl}	X'_{sl}	Cluster
0	0.22	0.2	1
1	0.17	0.11	1
2	0.11	0.13	1
3	0.08	0.14	1
4	0.19	0.22	1
5	0.31	0.31	1
6	0.08	0.17	1
7	0.19	0.2	1
8	0.03	0.09	1
9	0.17	0.15	1

Feature Selection: Since all further steps of the model are based on the analysis of the regression residues, prioritizing attributes with lower residues, it is possible to apply an attribute selection in this step, reducing the complexity of the other steps since these are performed per attribute in each group.

To make the selection, the coefficient of determination (R^2) of the regressions is used, a measure well known on the literature that determines the amount of variability explained by the data [3]. The coefficient is given by Eq. 1, where w is the vector of fitted regression weights, x_i is an input sample and x_i' its predicted value.

$$R^2 = \frac{w_1 \sum_{i=1}^{n}(x_i - \bar{x})x_i'}{\sum_{i=1}^{n}(x_i' - \bar{x}')^2}, \tag{1}$$

For attributes with high explained variability, the residues of the regressions will be smaller, and therefore, will be prioritized in the following steps. So that, given an input hyperparameter r_{min}, only the attributes whose regressions present a coefficient of determination above r_{min} will be considered in the other steps of the model.

In the Iris database experiment, all regressions show R^2 above 0.6, used as a threshold, and all attributes are kept. To wit, the R_j^2 obtained were: $R_{SL}^2 = 0.87$, $R_{SW}^2 = 0.65$, $R_{PL}^2 = 0.98$, and $R_{PW}^2 = 0.95$.

Calculation of Error Functions: Seeking to identify for each cluster which ranges of attributes provided the smallest possible prediction error, we calculate the average prediction error for each distinct value of each attribute in each cluster, that we can represent as $\vec{\xi}_j^{c_a} = (\overline{x}_{d,j})$, where $x_{d,j}$ a distinct value of the attribute j, and $\overline{x}_{d,j}$ is it's average prediction error. As an example, for the Cluster 1 in the Table 1, there are 7 distinct values: 0.03, 0.08, 0.11, 0.17, 0.19, 0.22, and 0.31, for which we have the average prediction errors as $\vec{\xi}_{SL}^{c_1} = (0.07, 0.085, 0.02, 0.025, 0.02, 0.02, 0.01)$.

Then, we can calculate an function to describe the predicted error for the entire domain of an attribute per cluster using a polynomial approximation [10]: $(x, y) = (x_{d,j}, \vec{\xi}_{x_{d,j}})$, generating a set of functions $F = f_j^{c_a}$, as exemplifies the Fig. 2a.

Determination of the Intervals of Values: From the polynomial approximations, it is possible to estimate the prediction error for any range by the Area Under the Curve (AUC) given by the integration of the function $f_j^{c_a}$.

Since the objective is to identify the most relevant attribute ranges for each cluster, that is, the intervals for which the prediction error is as small as possible, we calculate the AUC for each possible range of each function in $f_j^{c_a}$. At first, the initial ranges are determined using as limits the starting and ending points of the functions and the intersection points between them, as shown in Fig. 2b.

For each of those ranges, we calculate the estimated error for all functions $f_j^{c_a}$ with domain in the range using the minimum and maximum points as limits.

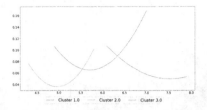
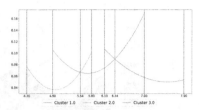

(a) Polynomial approximation of the mean error functions of the predictions.

(b) Delimitation of initial ranges

Fig. 2. Polynomial functions and ranges delimitation for the sepal length attribute per group.

The defined intervals are assigned to the clusters with the lowest estimated error. If consecutive intervals are assigned to the same cluster, they are concatenated to form more extensive ranges, as shown in Fig. 3.

A range can be relevant to defining more than one cluster since the difference between the error estimated by the functions in the range can be small or equal to zero. In this case, the range is assigned to the clusters whose estimated error is limited to a threshold of $t\%$ from the minimum error, with t being an hyperparameter of the model.

The t parameter also allows to extend the intervals beyond the intersection points, as long as the condition defined by the parameter is true, so the ranges are not limited to the initial limits (notice the extension of the ranges beyond the intersections in the Fig. 3). Thus, to each cluster c_a we associate a set of attribute–range pairs $R_{c_a} = \{(attr_j, [p_j, q_j])\}|_{j=1}^m$, where the estimated error $\xi_{[p_j,q_j]}^{c_a}$ is limited by Eq. 2.

$$\xi_{[p_j,q_j]}^{c_a} \leq min(\{\xi_{[p_j,q_j]}^{c_a}\}|_{a=1}^b) + t * min(\{\xi_{[p_j,q_j]}^{c_a}\}|_{a=1}^b) \tag{2}$$

In the SL attribute example, for which $t = 0.3$, the ranges $[4, 3 - 5, 46]$, $[5, 46 - 6, 07]$ and $[6, 07 - 7, 9]$ are assigned to Clusters 1, 2 and 3, respectively, as shown in Fig. 3.

At the end of this step, we have a set $R = \{r_{c_a}\}|_{a=0}^b$ of attribute-range pairs associated with each cluster c_a. Table 2 shows the ranges associated with each attribute by cluster for the Iris dataset, composing the set R of the problem.

3.2   Step II

Step II of the labelling consists of selecting attribute–range pairs for the composition of the cluster labels that represent the largest possible number of elements in the cluster, ensuring that each label represents specifically and exclusively one cluster.

To this end, the pairs are assigned to the cluster labels (l_{c_a}) iteratively using as criteria the rate of elements $\vec{x}_{i,j}$ in the cluster c_a that are within the range

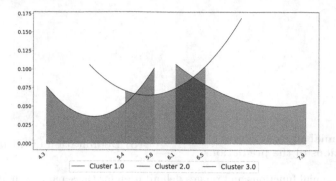

Fig. 3. Assignment of ranges of sepal length attribute to the clusters.

Table 2. Ranges associated with each attribute per cluster for iris dataset.

Cluster	Attribute	Range
1	PL	4,9–6,9
	SL	6,1–7,9
	PW	1,77–2,5
	SW	2,76–3,27
2	PL	1,0–1,9
	SL	4,30–5,8
	PW	0,1–0,6
	SW	3,15–4,40
3	PL	3,0–5,1
	SL	5,4–6,5
	PW	1,0–1,87
	SW	2,00–2,89

defined in the previous step, $[p_j, q_j]$. This measure is denoted by precision (P_j) and is given by Eq. 3.

$$P_j = \frac{n^{(c_a|p_j \leq x_{i,j} \leq q_j)}}{n^{(c_a)}} \tag{3}$$

To determine the number of attribute–range pairs of a label, we use a hyper parameter E as a threshold for the percentage of elements of another cluster a label can represent and still be considered sufficiently specific for it cluster, adding as many pairs as necessary so this percentage, calculated by a measurement Error Rate ER, to be bellow E.

$$ER_{l_{c_a}} = \frac{n^{(\overline{c_a}|p_j \leq x_{i,j} \leq q_j \forall (attr_j, [p_j, q_j]) \in l_{c_a})}}{n^{(\overline{c_a})}} \tag{4}$$

In the example of the Iris dataset, the attribute's precision–range pairs in each cluster, shown in Table 3, determines the order of inserting the pairs in the labels.

Table 3. Precision of attribute–range pairs of each cluster in Iris dataset.

Cluster	Attribute	Range	Precision
1	SL	6,1–7,9	1,0
	PL	4,9–6,9	1,0
	PW	1,77–2,5	0,89
	SW	2,76–3,27	0,68
2	PL	1,0–1,9	1,0
	SL	4,30–5,8	1,0
	PW	0,1–0,6	1,0
	SW	3,15–4,40	0,74
3	PL	3,0–5,1	1,0
	PW	1,0–1,87	0,9
	SL	5,4–6,5	0,81
	SW	2,0–2,89	0,61

Table 4. Cluster 1 labeling.

Iteration	l_{c1}	$ER_{l_{c1}}$
1	(SL, [6,1 - 7,9])	0,21
1	(PL, [4,9 - 6,9])	0,12

If there is more than one pair with the same precision, we select the one that will produce the lowest ER. So, in the first iteration of the Cluster 1 labelling, it is possible to add any of the pairs of higher precision: (SL, [6,1–7,9]) and (PL, [4,9–6,9]). So we verify the Error Rate produced by adding any of those pairs in the label, as shown in Table 4. By setting $E = 0.2$, the pair (PL, [4,9–6,9]) can result in a satisfactory label, with ER bellow E, without the need to add other components, so the label for Cluster 1 is given by $l_{c1} = \{(PL, [4, 9 - 6, 9])\}$.

The Cluster 2 labeling considers the addition of pairs (PL, [1,0–1,9]), (PW, [0,1–0,6]), or (SL, [4,30–5,8]) in the first iteration, according to Table 3, since they all show the same precision. So, we verify the ER of adding those pair to the labels, and as the pairs of the attributes CP and LP produce the equal ER, as shown in Table 5, we add both pairs to the label at once. As the ER is bellow E no other iteration is necessary, given $r_{g2} = \{(PL, [1, 0 - 1, 9]), (PW, [0, 1 - 0, 6])\}$.

For Cluster 3, the E threshold is satisfied in the first iteration, as shown in Table 6, resulting in the cluster label provided by $r_{g3} = \{(PL, [3, 0 - 5, 1])\}$.

After defining the labels, we calculate the representativeness of each label, or the Agreement Rate (AR), according to the rate of elements within the ranges of all attributes of the label in relation to the number of elements in the cluster, as is presented in Eq. 5.

$$AR_{l,c_a} = \frac{n^{(c_a | p_j \leq x_{i,j} \leq q_j \, \forall (attr_j, [p_j, q_j]) \in l)}}{n^{(c_a)}} \tag{5}$$

Table 5. Cluster 2 labeling.

Iteration	l_{c2}	$ER_{l_{c2}}$
1	(PL, [1,0–1,9])	0,0
1	(PW, [0,1–0,6])	0,0
1	(SL, [4,30–5,8])	0,3

Table 6. Cluster 3 labeling.

Iteration	l_{c3}	$ER_{l_{c3}}$
1	(PL, [3,0–5,1])	0,05

At the end of Step II, the labeling model results in a set of labels $L = \{\{(PL, [4, 9 - 6, 9])\}, \{(PL, [1, 0 - 1, 9]), (PW, [0, 1 - 0, 6])\}, \{(PL, [3, 0 - 5, 1])\}\}$ so each label l_{c_a} is able to better explain the associated group c_a, as shows Table 7.

Table 7. Labels for Iris dataset clusters.

Cluster	# Elemements	Label		AR	ER
		Attribute	Range		
1	38	PL	[4,9–6,9]	1,0	0,12
2	50	PL	[1,0–1,9]	1,0	0,0
		PW	[0,1–0,6]		
3	62	PL	[3,0–5,1]	1,0	0,05

4 Experimental Methodology

In the experiments, three datasets from the literature were used: Iris, Parkinson, and Breast Cancer. Iris labeling was presented on the proposed model, the other two experiments are discussed on the section bellow. The choice of those datasets was due to its presence in at least one of the related works, allowing a comparison with the proposed model's performance with the literature. For each data set, the number of clusters is determined by the number of classes provided, setting the value of k for the K-means algorithm. All the datasets can be found in the UCI repository [1].

The regressions from Step I where performed by a Support Vector Regressor with a RBF kernel [12]. In each experiment, ten regressions were performed per attribute using the k-folds method, so we could guarantee that all elements were predicted to construct the X' set.

We evaluated the parameter t in each problem by varying it between 0.1 and 1.0, picking as the best value the one that resulted in labels with the highest average Agreement Rate (Average Agreement - AA) and the lowest number of attribute–range pairs in the composition of the clusters labels. The variance of this metric for all experiments are presented in Table 8. The parameter E was set as $E = 0.2$ in all experiments. The r_{min} threshold for attribute selection in Step I was set to 0.6, seeking to exclude only the attributes with the lowest R^2 values, with the exception of the *Parkinson* datasets which, due to its size of 754 attributes, required adjusting the threshold to 0.9.

Table 8. Variation of the parameter t for all datasets.

Dataset	Average agreement	Pairs per label
Iris	0.97 ± 0.08	5.6 ± 0.7
Breast Cancer	0.95 ± 0.38	6.1 ± 1.1
Parkinson	1.0 ± 0.0	14 ± 0.0

5   Results

Breast Cancer: In identifying Breast Cancer, the experiments were repeated varying the parameter t. The results obtained, presented in Table 8, show an average Agreement Rate of 0.95 with a standard deviation of ± 0.38. The best label is obtained for a $t = 0.9$, yielding five attributes–range pairs that represent an average of 99% of the elements of the clusters. Table 9 describes the cluster labels of this experiment.

Table 9. Labels for breast cancer dataset clusters.

Cluster	# Elem.	Label		AR	ER
		Attribute	Range		
1	232	UCS	[1,0–5,0]	0,99	0,05
		MA	[1,0–10,0]		
		BN	[1,0–5,97]		
2	451	SECS	[2,0–10,0]	0,99	0,17
		UCS	[1,9–10,0]		

Cluster 1 is described by a label with three attributes–range pairs. The more significant number of components of the label is due to the intersection of the ranges of the attribute Uniformity of Cell Size (UCS) in both cluster's labels, and the fact that the range of the attribute AM also represents more than 20% of the elements on the other cluster, although it's precision on Cluster 2 does not outperforms the other attributes, therefore it does not appear on the label. Table 9 also shows that the label agreement rates for the opposite clusters are a maximum of 0.17, that is, less than 20% of the elements have similar characteristics described by labels of both clusters.

Finally, the label provides an interpretation of the clusters: (1) Cluster 1 is composed of elements that, in 99% of the cases, have a measured uniformity of cell size between 1.0 and 5.0, marginal adhesion between 1.0 and 10.0, bare nuclei between 1. and 5.97; (2) Cluster 2 presents, for 99% of the cases, single epithelial cell size from 2.0 to 10 and uniformity of the cell size between 1.9 and 10.0.

Parkinson Disease: For the Parkinson Disease dataset, the result for the cluster labeling of varying t, Table 8, show an Average Agreement of 1.00, a result shown in Table 10, where for all labels the selected attributes are output from the WT algorithm and refer to entropy measures, being the coefficient values of the Shannon entropy measure (coefficients from 7 to 10) and the logarithmic basis (coefficients from 7 to 9).

Table 10. Labels for Parkinson dataset clusters.

Cluster	# Elem.	Label		AR	ER
		Attribute	Range		
1	278	Shannon	[(−1.356.650.945,0) − (−171.785.758,4)]	1,0	0,0
			[(−2.653.531.661,0) − (−324.289.685,9)]		
			[(−5.533.806.774,0) − (−679.106.796,3)]		
			[(−11.518.567.429) − (−1.399.384.344)]		
		Log	[210,2833−243,0695]		
			[220,8377−253,4672]		
			[231,3445−263,868]		
2	478	Shannon	[(−741.3860.397,0) − (−1.364,961.909,0)]	1,0	0,0
			[(−14.399.805.778,0) − (−2.676.653.063,0)]		
			[(−29.918.736.773,0) − (−5.582.147.455,0)]		
			[(−62.062.235.037) − (−11.621.821.092)]		
		Log	[243,2066−267,0312]		
			[253,6039−277,4293]		
			[264,0013−287,8304]		

The attributes selected in the labeling of this dataset have no intersecting intervals between groups, so their accuracy are 1.0 across all groups, and they are added to the labels in a single iteration. Thus, the evaluation measures are 1.0 for the Agreement Rate and 0.0 for the Error Rate, indicating that the labels assigned to the clusters are specific to them.

Comparison Between Models: The results obtained by labelling the clusters of the datasets were compared with the models proposed by Machado et al. [8], Lopes et al. [6], and Imperes Filho et al. [5], considering the Average Agreement of the labels and the number of attribute–range pairs that compose them. Table 11 shows the achieved results.

The proposed model obtained better results than the cluster labelling models taken from the literature, providing more representative and cohesive labels, and, consequently, more accurate interpretations of the groups.

Table 11. Comparison between the labeling models.

Model	Iris		Parkinson		Breast Cancer	
	Average agreement	# Pairs	Average agreement	# Pairs	Average agreement	# Pairs
Machado, 2015	0.92	4	–	–	–	–
Lopes, 2016	0.91	7	–	–	–	–
Imperes, 2020	0.93	4	0.98	6	0.93	6
Proposed model	**1.00**	4	**1.00**	14	**0.99**	5

6   Conclusion

The labeling models proposed in the literature are based on using different artificial intelligence techniques to determine the most relevant attributes for the composition of the clusters and the ranges of values associated with them. This paper provides an improved cluster labeling model based on regression residual analysis with an attribute selection step that makes the model applicable to large datasets.

The results obtained in the experiments show that the model helps label the clusters, with an average agreement rate between 0.99 and 1.00 for the datasets used, exceeding the results in the literature. Also, the model guarantees the specificity of the labels, that is, that all labels obtained are exclusive to their groups.

Some limitations can be pointed out to motivate the continuation of this research in the future; for example, the use of the predictive models requires numerical data, which means that the inclusion of other types of data in the labels of the groups is still not feasible. Thus, in future research, it is intended to study approaches that can solve this problem.

References

1. Dua, D., Graff, C.: UCI machine learning repository (2017). http://archive.ics.uci.edu/ml
2. Fisher, R.A.: The use of multiple measurements in taxonomic problems. Ann. Eugenics **7**(7), 179–188 (1936)
3. Hair, J., Black, W., Babin, B., Anderson, R., Tatham, R.: Análise multivariada de dados - 6ed. Bookman (2009). https://books.google.com.br/books?id=oFQs_zJI2GwC
4. Hu, H., Wen, Y., Chua, T.S., Li, X.: Toward scalable systems for big data analytics: a technology tutorial. IEEE Access **2**, 652–687 (2014)
5. Imperes Filho, F., Machado, V.P., Veras, R.M.S., Aires, K.R.T., Silva, A.M.L.: Group labeling methodology using distance-based data grouping algorithms. Revista de Informática Teórica e Aplicada **27**(1), 48–61 (2020)

6. Lopes, L., Machado, V.P., Rabêlo, R.A.L., Fernandes, R., Lima, B.V.A.: Automatic labelling of clusters of discrete and continuous data with supervised machine learning. Knowl.-Based Syst. **106** (2016). https://doi.org/10.1016/j.knosys.2016.05.044
7. Lopes, L.A., Machado, V.P., Rabêlo, R.A.L.: Automatic cluster labeling through artificial neural networks. In: International Joint Conference on Artificial Neural Networks (IJCNN), pp. 762–769 (2014)
8. Machado, V.P., Ribeiro, V.P., Rabelo, R.A.L.: Rotulacao de grupos utilizando conjuntos fuzzy. In: XII Simposio Brasileiro de Automacao Inteligente-SBAI. No. 12 (2015)
9. MacQueen, J.: Some methods for classfication and analysis of multivariate observations, vol. 1. University of California Press (1967)
10. Muller, J.M.: Elementary Functions. Springer, Berlin (2006) https://doi.org/10.1007/b137928
11. Silva, L.E.S., Machado, V.P., Araújo, S., Lima, B.V.A., Veras, R.M.S.: Automatic cluster labeling based on regression error analysis. In: 28th International Conference on Systems, Signals and Image Processing (IWSSIP), Bratislava, Slovakia (2021)
12. Vapnik, V.N.: The Nature of Statistical Learning Theory. Springer, New York (1995). https://doi.org/10.1007/978-1-4757-2440-0

A Chatbot for Recipe Recommendation and Preference Modeling

Álvaro Mendes Samagaio[1,2](✉) ⓘ, Henrique Lopes Cardoso[1,3] ⓘ,
and David Ribeiro[2] ⓘ

[1] Faculdade de Engenharia, Universidade do Porto, Porto, Portugal
hlc@fe.up.pt
[2] Fraunhofer Portugal, Porto, Portugal
david.ribeiro@fraunhofer.pt
[3] Laboratório de Inteligência Artificial e Ciência de Computadores (LIACC),
Porto, Portugal

Abstract. This paper describes the main steps and challenges in building a chatbot for a nutritional recommendation system addressed to the elderly population. We identified 4 main components: Natural Language Understanding (NLU), Dialogue Management, Preference Modeling and Ingredient Matching and Extraction. To address the specific challenges of a chatbot for this domain we have tested transformer-based models both in the development of the NLU component and the Dialogue Management component. Moreover, we explored word embeddings and nutritional knowledge bases combined with sentiment analysis for user preferences modeling. The sentiment analysis algorithms used to model food preferences showed to correctly match the real feeling of the users. Each one of these components were evaluated individually using appropriate metrics. Moreover, the developed chatbot was successfully tested by users and its opinions were recorded by means of usability and user experience questionnaires. The results of usability tests show that the components were well integrated. The scores obtained were higher than the benchmark values for both the System Usability and the User Experience Questionnaires.

Keywords: Chatbot · Knowledge base · Natural Language Processing

1 Introduction

According to a report from the World Health Organization [22], nutrition is defined as one of the key factors that influence Healthy Aging. In fact, elderly people are more affected by malnutrition than other social groups. Nutritional smart assistants may play an important role in preventing malnutrition and contributing to healthier dietary habits [19] by leveraging the potential of artificial intelligence to create appropriate meal recommendations [5]. An important

G. Marreiros et al. (Eds.): EPIA 2021, LNAI 12981, pp. 389–402, 2021.
https://doi.org/10.1007/978-3-030-86230-5_31

requirement of such smart assistants is their ability to understand human language, which entails understanding user input and take into account the discourse context [4]. Furthermore, being able to consider past interactions and personal information will enable engaging in multi-turn conversations.

This paper describes the construction and validation of a chatbot for recipe recommendation, encompassing ingredient retrieval, preference modeling, and sentiment analysis, with the aim of providing a human-like experience. This work addresses the challenges of creating and combining the chatbot's modules. The developed system is able to communicate and understand domain-specific requests and appropriately act upon them. The system was evaluated following user experience benchmark tests.

2   Background

Chatbots are conversational agents that use Artificial Intelligence (AI) methodologies in order to communicate with people using human language. These applications make use of Natural Language Processing (NLP) and Machine Learning (ML) techniques. These aim at equipping the chatbot with Natural Language Understanding (NLU) capabilities, which includes determining the user intent and extracting named entities from user input. Chatbots use this information to infer how to respond to user input, namely by providing generated or selected answers.

Retrieval-based methods rely on a set of rules that define the next response, which may be a good solution for simple, closed domain and task-oriented chatbots [2]. On the other hand, machine learning based models can learn patterns from large amounts of data in order to select a response from a set of possible answers [24]. Lommatzsch et al. [15] explore an information retrieval methodology to build a chatbot that helps users to find information in large knowledge bases. The match between user input and the text containing the answer may follow different approaches, such as inverted index methods (e.g. TF-IDF [15]), pretrained word embeddings or language models [8]. Response prediction is often realized by machine learning models that take the current state of the conversation as input (current and past intents and entities). Recurrent Neural Networks are among the most used architectures for these tasks [17]. Transformer-based models [20] have also been used for response prediction [21] in chatbots. Usually, these models are connected to external knowledge bases that provide information for specific actions or answers of the chatbot.

According to Montenegro et al. [16], counseling and coaching agents are the two modalities of health-related conversational agents. Counseling agents are used in cases where social engagement is necessary, so that the user is encouraged to alter his habits towards healthier ones [12]. Also, they can be used as support tools for patients that suffer from emotional health disorders [10] Fadhil [6] studies the challenges of developing a chatbot for meal recommendation, highlighting user engagement as a core concept in applications that deal with lifestyle habits. The humanness of the agent is a crucial characteristic that

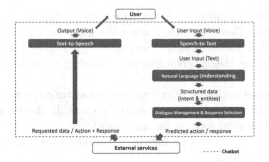

Fig. 1. Chatbot structure and components

can be improved through generative algorithms, both in speech synthesis and response generation. In this context, accurately tracking the context of the dialog is an important characteristic. Abd-alrazaq et al. [1] report that rule-based chatbots have wider adoption in health contexts, since this technology is more reliable and avoids unpredictable errors still present in generative approaches to response creation. On the other hand, rule-based approaches are not flexible enough to conduct a conversation, which is important in user engagement. In nutritional recommender systems, it is important to integrate information about food. LanguaL [11] is a faceted knowledge base about ingredients that comprehends a very specific description of each ingredient. Among others, it includes: Facet A, indicating the food group (such as Poultry or Fruits) in 33 classes; Facet B, presenting the food source (such as Chicken or Lemon) in 213 classes; and Facet C, specifying the part of animal or plant (such as Skeletal Meat Part or Fruit, Peel Removed) in 79 classes.

3   Methodology

We have developed a chatbot for recipe recommendation using the Rasa Open Source[1] framework. The chatbot includes four main components: (i) Intent Classification and Entity Recognition (encapsulated in Rasa's NLU module); (ii) Preference Modeling; (iii) Food Matching; and (iv) Dialogue Management, as seen in Fig. 1.

NLU and Dialogue Management of the chatbot were fully developed using Rasa. This required the collection of two datasets for training and testing the models. Food preferences were approached using sentiment analysis to extract and calculate the intensity and the polarity of the sentiment towards a given ingredient/dish. Based on the user preferences, ingredients/dishes are retrieved from a database. These last two tasks are not integrated in the Rasa framework and pose a real challenge to the development of the chatbot. The use cases that the chatbot is able to perform deal with different aspects of the meal planning system:

---

[1] https://www.rasa.com/.

1. UC.1 Meal Plan Creation – Generating a meal plan for a set of parameters
2. UC.2 Meal Plan Deletion – Removing the plan for a given week
3. UC.3 Meal Plan Visualization – Seeing the previously created plan
4. UC.4 Alternative Meals Visualisation – Seeing a list of alternatives for a given meal
5. UC.5 Meal Substitution – Selecting and substituting a meal from the plan
6. UC.6 - UC.9 Check nutritional content – Consult the nutritional value for a day, a meal, a meal part or an ingredient
7. UC.10 and UC.11 Express preference – Convey user tastes towards either a recipe or an ingredient
8. UC.12 Personal Information Collection – Inquire user details to enable tailored meals
9. UC.13 Personal Information Visualisation – Seeing personal details
10. UC.14 Personal Information Alteration – Updating personal details

3.1 Intent Classification and Entity Recognition

The first task that must be addressed in the development of the NLU part of the chatbot is creating a model that is able to classify user utterances into one of the recognizable intents. In the Rasa framework, the processes included in the NLU component require annotated data, consisting of several examples for each intent, with annotated entities. Due to the closed and specific domain of this work, a crowd-sourced dataset based on the previously defined use cases was collected to bootstrap the NLU module. In total, 124 volunteers completed the form; 81 answers were taken as valid. Each volunteer was asked to write several English samples for each intent. The use cases that had a larger range of variability were selected for collection in the form: plan creation and visualization with time indication (UC.1 and UC.3), meal alteration (UC.4), nutritional composition consultation (UC.6 - UC.9), preferences indication (UC.10 and UC.11), and personal information visualization and alteration (UC.12 and UC.13).

The final dataset for the NLU training phase contains 1502 samples, divided by 19 intents and 1513 instances for 15 different entity types. Intent classification is a multi-class classification task with 19 classes, such as "Show Personal Information", "Create Meal Plan", "Delete Plan" or "Show Alternative Meal". Moreover, the extraction of entities from user utterances is also a part of the NLU pipeline. This is a sequence labeling problem with 15 classes, such as "Ingredient", "Meal", "Day of Week" or "Person Name". It is important to mention that the Rasa framework enables the use of the DIET classification model [3], which is based on a transformer architecture and allows for combined intent classification and entity recognition, using a combined loss function. The performance of the two processes is improved if trained together. Several approaches were tried, grouped according to the type of features that they use. The models were trained and tested 3 times with stratified and randomly selected 80/20 train-test ratios. The pipelines are resumed in Table 1.

Table 2 (average scores with standard deviation) shows that IE.A4, which uses the combination of both sparse and dense features, generated the worst

Table 1. Pipelines for joint intent classification and entity recognition

Approach	Tokenizer	Featurizers
IE.A1: Baseline	spaCy	Sklearn Count Vectors + Lexical and Syntactic Featuriser
IE.A2: Pre-trained Word Embeddings	spaCy	GloVe word vectors
IE.A3: Language Model	BERT	BERT embeddings
IE.A4: Mixed	BERT	Sklearn Count Vectors + Lexical and Syntactic Featuriser + BERT embeddings

Table 2. Joint entity extraction and intent classification results using DIET

	Model	Precision	Recall	F1
Intent	IE.A1	76.5 ± 6.1	70.7 ± 4.3	72.4 ± 4.6
	IE.A2	72.9 ± 1.9	73.2 ± 3.4	72.4 ± 2.5
	IE.A3	**78.7 ± 4.8**	**75.6 ± 4.9**	**75.5 ± 4.1**
	IE.A4	68.3 ± 7.5	62.3 ± 10.2	63.2 ± 9.2
Entity	IE.A1	89.0 ± 1.4	**87.4 ± 4.4**	**87.5 ± 2.4**
	IE.A2	87.8 ± 2.5	**87.0 ± 0.6**	86.7 ± 2.1
	IE.A3	86.1 ± 1.3	71.5 ± 6.4	76.7 ± 3.9
	IE.A4	87.9 ± 3.9	80.0 ± 2.4	81.9 ± 3.8

results, regarding intent classification. These results may have been caused by the extra sparse feature set for entity recognition that the model has to deal with. This may increase the size of feature space and hence favor overfitting, therefore decreasing the baseline (IE.A1) performance. Contextual embeddings prove to be better for intent classification (IE.A3), where more variation may be present and context plays a more important role. GloVe vectors have shown to be the best set of features for entity recognition. This may be due to the unchanging values that the vectors assume, which is favorable for a closed domain such as the scope of this work. This means that there is not enough variation in word meaning for the contextual embeddings to make a difference in entity recognition. Comparing entity extraction results for IE.A1 and IE.A3 reinforces the premise that, in this closed domain, these less changing features provide better results, since there is only a small improvement from the sparse features to contextual embeddings. Looking at these results, it becomes clear that even though the dataset is rather small, the joint task allows for good performance.

3.2 Preference Modeling

One of the advantages of using Natural Language is the increased facility of expressing preferences and opinions. Preference expression use-cases require the implementation of an algorithm capable of transforming qualitative preferences into a quantitative values. A dataset was collected using volunteers. They were asked to give three examples of sentences that indicate a like or a dislike towards a meal element. However, in order to correctly model the preference as a numeric value, volunteers were also required to evaluate the intensity of the preference on a scale from 0 (extremely negative) to 5 (extremely positive). More examples were added manually to the ones extracted from the form, namely other minor intents not collected in the form.

In this work, the VADER NLTK Sentiment Analyser[2] was used, which produces a magnitude score regarding the intensity of the sentiment. VADER was tested against the ground-truth collected in the Volunteer Form. The distribution of answers is the following: 0 (57 samples), 1 (34 samples), 2 (26 samples), 3 (27 samples), 4 (29 samples), and 5 (64 samples). Taking into account that VADER's ratings range from 0 to 1, a linear transformation was applied to the form values, in order to match them to this range. Moreover, a rating of 0 will prevent the system from including that element in future meal plans. However, it is very hard to achieve a 0 rating using VADER. For that reason, inferior and superior thresholds were defined to map some predictions to either 0 or 1, so that these extreme values are also possible to achieve. The used thresholds were the median of the extremity classes from Table 3 (1 and 4).

The first metrics that were calculated were both the Spearman's and Person's coefficients. The values obtained were respectively 0.67 and 0.68, which shows that the model can correctly scale the intensity of the sentiments. The Mean Absolute Error (MAE) was also calculated for both the normal and the thresholded models, which was 0.85 and 0.86, respectively. This suggests that the applied threshold has a small influence in the error value. Also, on average, the predictions are always one unit above or below the real value. Moreover, the extremity classes have more weight in the error value since they have the largest number of samples and the errors represent a higher variation. This means that a missed classification in these classes produces a larger error value. Table 3 shows the mean, median and standard deviation for each label (with and without thresholding). The largest differences from the prediction median and the value of the class happen at the extremities. This may be explained by the fact that there are no more classes before 0 and after 5, concentrating all the possible values in the nearest bin. Also, it is very hard to have a prediction exactly at the extremes since it would represent the most negative or positive sentiment that one can express using text. On the contrary, the predictions for the classes 1 to 4 have central metrics that are closer to the real value, also having a lower standard deviation. For these intervals, the model actually has a good predicting power. When analysing the thresholded model, it is possible to note that the median and mean values for each class become more accurate.

3.3 Food Matching

Another crucial challenge that appeared while trying to model dietary preferences supported by a dataset of ingredients and recipes was the matching

---

[2] https://www.nltk.org/howto/sentiment.html.

Table 3. Central tendency per class, for each classifier (thresholded or not)

Class	VADER			VADER thresholded		
	Mean	Median	Std. Dev	Mean	Median	Std. Dev
0	1.68	1	0.85	1.19	0	1.34
1	1.68	2	0.73	1.24	2	1.18
2	2.15	2	0.73	2.04	2	0.96
3	2.81	3	0.92	2.89	3	1.19
4	3.76	4	0.58	4.14	4	0.88
5	3.42	4	1.04	3.95	5	1.61

algorithm that mapped the entities captured by the NLU module from the user sentence to the correct entries in the dataset. A simple word matching-based method would often leave several correct options unretrieved, such as food groups. For that reason, the implemented algorithm is capable of discerning between individual ingredients and food groups, requiring semantic information that can be found both in word embeddings and knowledge graphs or ontologies. Furthermore, the information provided by *LanguaL* facets (A, B and C) on each ingredient created an interesting way to classify the ingredients and then extract them from the database. This approach is based on the work of Wu et al. [23], which uses embeddings for several extraction and ranking tasks.

A new set of pre-trained embeddings was created through retrofitting [7] the ConceptNet Numberbatch [18] (CNET) pre-trained embeddings with LanguaL information, so that they better represent the semantic interactions between ingredients. Ingredient naming includes cooking or preservation methods, which are not relevant for ingredient classification according to *LanguaL* facets and should be ignored in the retrofitting task. Here are some examples of ingredients that share some wording: "Pineapple, canned in juice"; "Pasta, plain, fresh, raw"; "Tuna, canned in brine, drained"; "Cheese, Edam"; "Peppers, capsicum, green, boiled in salted water". Taking this into account, a weighting mechanism, based on a TF-IDF representation of the ingredient names, was used to address the irregular naming pattern present in the ingredients database, assigning less weight to shared words between several ingredients.

Using this method it was possible to classify each ingredient with a label from each LanguaL facet. The created embeddings were used to retrieve the correct ingredients from the dataset, given a query entity extracted from user input. The entity may point to a group of ingredients, to a specific ingredient, or even to a group of ingredients that do not match the *LanguaL* labels exactly. After creating embeddings for each ingredient and descriptor, we classified them and measured the accuracy per class. Table 4 resumes the results obtained for two sets of pre-trained embeddings: GloVe (no ontology information) and ConceptNet Numberbatch (retrofitted with ontology information), as well as for the retrofitted version of the Numberbatch embeddings with and without TF-IDF

Table 4. Ingredient facet classification accuracy results

Model	Facet A	Facet B	Facet C
GloVe 400k vocabulary	0.281	0.315	0.087
ConceptNet Numberbatch	0.420	0.399	0.092
CNET Retrofitted (no TF-IDF)	0.648	0.505	0.402
CNET Retrofitted (w/ TF-IDF)	0.692	0.595	0.451

weighting, that incorporates the LanguaL knowledge. The tests were performed using K-Fold cross validation with 6 folds, which was the maximum number of folds that allowed to have at least one ingredient per class for each LanguaL facet in each fold.

As it is evident in the Table 4, the Numberbatch embeddings, even without retrofitting with LanguaL information, provide a better source of semantic knowledge, which comes from the general knowledge graph on which it has been trained. Furthermore, retrofitting does in fact incorporate semantic knowledge into the embeddings. Moreover, the employed TF-IDF weighting mechanism helps improve the accuracy by giving increased importance to the words that are important for ingredient classification. Facet C shows the largest margin of improvement, whereas facet A denotes the best classification accuracy. The improvements obtained as compared to using generic pre-trained embeddings show that we were able to incorporate food semantic information available in *LanguaL* into the word vectors.

3.4   Dialogue Management

Bearing in mind that there are not public datasets for this specific case, we had to collect a set of possible paths that the chatbot can take (stories) through simulated conversations. After obtaining a satisfactory amount of data, the model was trained so that it would be able to make some initial predictions, while alleviating the annotation process and increasing collection speed. Furthermore, some actions were mapped to immediately trigger specific intents. The dataset consisted of 87 manually collected stories, that correspond to a variety of paths that the conversation may take.

Rasa provides several mechanisms for response prediction, based on predicition policies[3]. Three different approaches were tested regarding the response prediction algorithm: a rule-based approach to obtain a baseline score, a Recurrent Neural Network (LSTM) based approach, and a Transformer based approach. These approaches correspond to the Memoization Policy, to the Keras Policy and to the TED Policy, respectively. These policies are the models that Rasa provides for response prediction. The combinations tested are shown in Table 5 and correspond to: DM.1 – Rule-based, Memoization Policy; DM.2 – Recurrent

---

[3] https://rasa.com/docs/rasa/policies/.

Table 5. Dialogue Management pipelines that test different policies for response prediction

Approach	Policies
DM.1: Baseline – Rule-Based	Fallback Policy, Mapping Policy and Memoization Policy
DM.2: Recurrent Neural Network	Fallback Policy, Mapping Policy and Keras Policy
DM.3: Transformer	Fallback Policy, Mapping Policy and TED Policy

Table 6. Results on the Dialogue Management approaches

Model	F1	Accuracy
DM.1	0.741 ± 0.018	0.586 ± 0.027
DM.2	0.859 ± 0.016	0.754 ± 0.025
DM.3	$\mathbf{0.899 \pm 0.013}$	$\mathbf{0.815 \pm 0.025}$

Neural Network, Keras Policy; and DM.3 – Transformer, TED Policy. The first pipeline is expected to produce the worst results, since it is less flexible, while the last one is expected to be the best due to the capability of learning the important factors that allow response prediction.

A similar methodology to the one used in NLU validation was taken: the models were tested three times for a 80/20 train/test ratio. The F1 score and accuracy results are shown in Table 6. A correct story corresponds to predicting every single action/response correctly for the whole story. As it is possible to observe, the Memoization Policy has the worst performance of the three configurations, owing to the fact that it does not generalize well for unseen data. When comparing TED Policy with Keras Policy, it is clear that the former has a better performance demonstrating the superiority of transformer architectures. The attention module allows the model to select what is effectively important without needing a huge dataset to learn what to ignore, which is the case of the Recurrent architecture of Keras Policy. The model selected for the chatbot was the TED Policy. Ideally, the training data would contain every possible path that the agent can take.

4   User Validation

A full evaluation of an interactive system requires also human judgment. Based on the work of Holmes et al. [9] two well established questionnaires were used: User Experience Questionnaire (UEQ) [13] and the System Usability Scale (SUS) [14]. Additionally, Holmes et al. have created a Chatbot Usability Questionnaire (CUQ) that followed the scheme of the SUS. The full test is composed by three parts: (1) volunteers completed 5 tasks and evaluated its predicted and real easiness before and after each task through a Single Ease Question (SEQ) on a scale from 1 (very hard) to 7 (very easy); (2) they then went through a questionnaire answering step (SUS, UEQ and CUQ); and (3) tried out and evaluated the ingredient retrieval algorithm.

Test Tasks: The first part of the test is composed by the following 5 tasks: (1) Chatbot's welcoming process - Create a user profile; (2) Generate a meal plan and see the ingredients; (3) Check the plan and express preference; (4) Create a plan, check the meals and ask an alternative and (5) Check the plan and ask for nutritional content. The tasks have increasing difficulty and are composed by sub-tasks that repeat from task to task, so that it is possible to understand the learning curve of using the chatbot.

Food Matching Validation: After the surveys, the volunteer must suggest an ingredient (different from the ones already chosen). Both the results obtained through the ingredient retrieval algorithm (based on embeddings) and the results using the search function implemented in the API (fuzzy matching based in the name) are shown to the volunteer who has to answer three questions: (1) The scale of correctness of the options retrieved by the embeddings algorithm from "totally incorrect" to "totally correct", including "mostly incorrect" and "mostly correct"; (2) If there is any option on the search results that should also be in the embeddings results list. The answers range from "none missing" to "all missing", including "a few missing" and "many missing" and (3) Indicate the preferred option for ingredient retrieval. This way it is possible to evaluate the developed algorithm from a user standpoint, using approximate recall and precision metrics.

4.1 Results

A total of 22 volunteers performed the test, where most of them had already used a conversational agent or a smart assistant at least once.

Single Ease Question: Regarding the preconceived and real difficulty of the tasks, it is possible to see in Fig. 2 that, on average, the tasks were thought to be less easy than their real easiness. Excluding Task 1, which is not plan-related, Task 4 presented the lowest average difference. However, this task is the one that requires the most steps and even though it is the most complex one, the learning curve is fast enough that volunteers feel as confident as when performing Task 2, which is the user's first contact with plan-related requests. Furthermore, looking at the absolute values of real easiness, they are close to the maximum of 7 for three of the tasks. The differences between pre and post easiness values are statistically significant, with $p < 0.05$ (T-Student).

System Usability Score: The final average SUS score for the system was 84.7 ± 8.4, which is higher than the benchmark score: "Excellent" in the SUS adjective grading system and "Acceptable" in the acceptability scale. The lower score was 67.5 and the highest was 97.5 (see Fig. 3, Left). Hence, this system has a high degree of usability when considering traditional SUS scores, although these benchmark scores have not included usability scores from conversational agents.

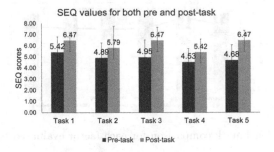

Fig. 2. Average values for pre-task and post-task difficulty assessment question

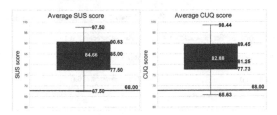

Fig. 3. System usability scale (left) and chatbot usability questionnaire (right) scores

User Experience Questionnaire: This questionnaire produces 6 different metrics according to the factor that it measures. The scores were normalized to the range [−3, 3] and the values were also compared against the benchmark for each factor, as shown in Fig. 4. The chatbot was classified with high scores in all factors, when compared to the benchmarks.

The factors that received the worst results were *Efficiency* and *Dependability*, even though the latter is still considered as Excellent. Regarding *Efficiency*, this lower score may be due to the increased time that some requests to the API take to process (bottleneck of task duration). Dependability analyzed indicators such as predictability, given support, security and expectations. These scores may be increased by improving the failing scenarios and responses of the chatbot, which are very important to prevent user confusion. For instance, predictability and support may be improved with clear and adequate feedback when the chatbot fails to understand a request. On the other hand, the best value is achieved for *Perspicuity* which takes into account system understandability, easiness, complexity and clarity. These results reinforce the observations from SEQ. This property is highly desirable for the elderly population to adopt and engage with this technology.

Chatbot Usability Questionnaire: The results obtained for this questionnaire were normalized to the same interval used by SUS (0–100), so that it is possible to compare between them and with the benchmarks. The average score for CUQ was 82.9 ± 8.6, as shown in Fig. 3 (right). Once again, it is well above

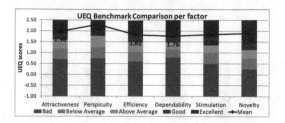

Fig. 4. Benchmark comparison for each factor evaluated by UEQ

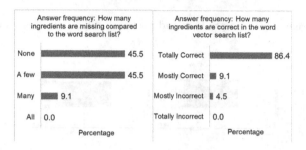

Fig. 5. Response frequency for food matching: precision (left) and recall (right)

the benchmark value of 68.0 and positions the chatbot in the same categories as the SUS score.

Food Matching: The validation of the food matching algorithm was performed through a user questionnaire. The questions tried to assess the recall and precision of the developed algorithm. Figure 5 (left) shows the answer distribution for the question that addressed the correctness (precision) of the shown results by the embeddings-based search algorithm. The results show that the developed algorithm has a high level of precision. The largest part of the query outputs are totally correct, meaning that the ingredients retrieved are in fact related to the query term. Figure 5 (right) shows the answer frequency regarding the comparison made between the existing word-based search and the developed algorithm. The goal was to identify items that were correctly present in the former and missing in the latter. This would not calculate the true recall of the model, since this would require a list of all correct items per query. Nonetheless, it is a good comparison to detect missing items. Results show that the vast majority of the answers were positive, meaning that recall is also high. However, it is possible to affirm that the model shows increased precision when compared to recall. Regarding user preference, 77% of the users preferred the embeddings-based method as extraction algorithm, when considering a rating scenario. This shows that, even though the algorithm does not always gather all ingredient samples from the dataset and bearing in mind the use case of expressing food preferences, users prefer to have the preference rating applied only to correct ingredients.

5 Conclusions

This work describes some of the components and challenges of building a chatbot for a nutritional recommender system. A set of different tools must be applied together in order to accomplish the final objective. Furthermore, considering the user-based results, the implementation and integration of the actions proved to be well adapted to user needs, even though there is still room for improvements.

Possible improvements include collecting more data and preferably with real users for further training and model refinement (threshold tuning, parameter definition), creating a proper dataset to evaluate the ingredient extraction algorithm, and implementing failing mechanisms that make the experience more natural and human-like. The collection of more data will allow further model training and refining, namely in the variability of available answers and possible conversation flows. Moreover, the tests explained in Sect. 4 should be performed with a set of people from the target population. Another option would be to design proper tests that more precisely assess the chatbot's user experience. This would allow to assess the general acceptance of the chatbot in between the target population. Regarding the human like experience, some psychology and conversational principles addressing elderly care may be incorporated into the speech tone and style of the chatbot. The inclusion of chitchat possibilities for Dialogue Management also increases the humanness of the chatbot. Furthermore, a speech-to-text and text-to-speech module may be added at both ends of the chatbot to complete the experience and increase the immersive feeling.

Acknowledgments. This research is partially supported by LIACC (FCT/UID /CEC/0027/2020), funded by Fundação para a Ciência e a Tecnologia (FCT).

References

1. Abd-alrazaq, A.A., Alajlani, M., Alalwan, A.A., Bewick, B.M., Gardner, P., Househ, M.: An overview of the features of chatbots in mental health: a scoping review. Int. J. Med. Inf. **132**, 103978 (2019)
2. Arsovski, S., Osipyan, H., Oladele, M.I., Cheok, A.D.: Automatic knowledge extraction of any chatbot from conversation. Expert Syst. Appl. **137**, 343–348 (2019)
3. Bunk, T., Varshneya, D., Vlasov, V., Nicho, A.: DIET: Lightweight language understanding for dialogue systems (2020). https://github.com/RasaHQ/DIET-paper
4. Dale, R.: The return of the chatbots. Nat. Lang. Eng. **22**(5), 811–817 (2016)
5. Devi, K.: Personalized nutrition recommendation for diabetic patients using improved k-means and krill-herd optimization (2020) www.ijstr.org
6. Fadhil, A.: Can a Chatbot Determine My Diet?: Addressing Challenges of Chatbot Application for Meal Recommendation (2018). http://arxiv.org/abs/1802.09100
7. Faruqui, M., Dodge, J., Jauhar, S.K., Dyer, C., Hovy, E., Smith, N.A.: Retrofitting word vectors to semantic lexicons. In: NAACL HLT 2015–2015 Conference of the North American Chapter of the Association for Computational Linguistics: Human Language Technologies, Proceedings of the Conference, pp. 1606–1615 (2015). https://doi.org/10.3115/v1/n15-1184, http://nlp.stanford.edu/

8. Gu, J.C., et al.: Speaker-Aware BERT for Multi-Turn Response Selection in Retrieval-Based Chatbots. Technical Report (2020)

9. Holmes, S., Moorhead, A., Bond, R., Zheng, H., Coates, V., McTear, M.: Usability testing of a healthcare chatbot: can we use conventional methods to assess conversational user interfaces? In: ECCE 2019 - Proceedings of the 31st European Conference on Cognitive Ergonomics: "Design for Cognition", pp. 207–214. Association for Computing Machinery Inc, New York (9 2019)

10. Hudlicka, E.: Virtual training and coaching of health behavior: Example from mindfulness meditation training. Patient Educ. Couns. **92**(2), 160–166 (2013). https://doi.org/10.1016/j.pec.2013.05.007

11. Ireland, J.D., Møller, A.: Langual food description: a learning process. Eur. J. Clin. Nutr. **64**, S44–S48 (2010). https://doi.org/10.1038/ejcn.2010.209

12. Johnson, W.L., Labore, C., Chiu, Y.C.: A Pedagogical Agent for Psychosocial Intervention on a Handheld Computer. Technical Report (2004)

13. Laugwitz, B., Held, T., Schrepp, M.: Construction and Evaluation of a User Experience Questionnaire. In: Holzinger, A. (eds) HCI and Usability for Education and Work. USAB 2008. Lecture Notes in Computer Science, vol. 5298, pp. 63–76. Springer, Berlin (2008). https://doi.org/10.1007/978-3-540-89350-96

14. Lewis, J.R., Sauro, J.: The Factor Structure of the System Usability Scale. Technical Report

15. Lommatzsch, A., Katins, J.: An Information Retrieval-based Approach for Building Intuitive Chatbots for Large Knowledge Bases. Technical report https://dialogflow.com/

16. Montenegro, J.L.Z., da Costa, C.A., da Rosa Righi, R.: Survey of conversational agents in health. Expert Syst. Appl. **129**, 56–67 (2019)

17. Sordoni, A., Bengio, Y., Vahabi, H., Lioma, C., Simonsen, J.G., Nie, J.Y.: A Hierarchical recurrent encoder-decoder for generative context-aware query suggestion. In: Ccs 2015, pp. 158–169 (7 2015). http://arxiv.org/abs/1507.02221

18. Speer, R., Chin, J., Havasi, C.: ConceptNet 5.5: An Open Multilingual Graph of General Knowledge (12 2016). http://arxiv.org/abs/1612.03975

19. Trattner, C., Elsweiler, D.: Food Recommender Systems Important Contributions, Challenges and Future Research Directions (11 2017). http://arxiv.org/abs/1711.02760

20. Vaswani, A., et al.: Attention is all you need. In: Guyon, I. (eds.) Advances in Neural Information Processing Systems. vol. 30. Curran Associates, Inc. (2017)

21. Vlasov, V., Mosig, J.E.M., Nichol, A.: Dialogue Transformers (10 2019). http://arxiv.org/abs/1910.00486

22. World Health Organization: World report on ageing and health. Technical report, World Health Organization, Geneva, Switzerland (2015)

23. Wu, L., Fisch, A., Chopra, S., Adams, K., Bordes, A., Weston, J.: StarSpace: Embed all the things! In: 32nd AAAI Conference on Artificial Intelligence, AAAI 2018, pp. 5569–5577. AAAI press (9 2018)

24. Yan, Z., et al.: DocChat: An information retrieval approach for chatbot engines using unstructured documents. In: 54th Annual Meeting of the Association for Computational Linguistics, ACL 2016 - Long Papers. vol. 1, pp. 516–525. Association for Computational Linguistics (ACL) (2016)

Intelligent Robotics

Exploiting Symmetry in Human Robot-Assisted Dressing Using Reinforcement Learning

Pedro Ildefonso[1]([✉]), Pedro Remédios[1], Rui Silva[1,2], Miguel Vasco[1], Francisco S. Melo[1], Ana Paiva[1], and Manuela Veloso[2]

[1] INESC-ID/Instituto Superior Técnico, University of Lisbon, Lisbon, Portugal
{pedro.ildefonso,pedroremedios,miguel.vasco}@tecnico.ulisboa.pt,
{fmelo,ana.paiva}@inesc-id.pt
[2] Carnegie Mellon University, Pittsburgh, PA, USA
mmv@cs.cmu.edu

Abstract. In this work, we address the problem of symmetry transfer in human-robot collaborative tasks, i.e., how certain actions can be extended to their symmetrical by exploiting symmetries in their execution. We contribute an approach capable of considering the symmetry inherent to a given task, such as the human or robot's lateral symmetry, abstracting them from the robot's decision process. We instantiate our approach in a robot-assisted backpack dressing scenario. A two-manipulator Baxter robot assists a human user in sequentially putting on both straps of a backpack. We evaluate the proposed symmetry-transfer approach in two complementary perspectives: the quality of the agent's learned policy in a simulated environment and the efficiency of the complete system in a real-life scenario with a robotic platform. The results show that our approach allows the extension of the execution of single-side trained collaborative tasks to their symmetrical with no additional training and minimal performance loss.

Keywords: Symbiotic autonomy · Robot assistance · Reinforcement learning

1 Introduction

Current demographic transitions in western societies have brought about increased life expectancy and, along with it, the need for long-term care [1]. Healthcare systems need to leverage the opportunities offered by technological advances in artificial intelligence and robotics, an area known as *assisted living*. Personal assistant robots and bots can thus contribute significantly to improve life quality in elder and disabled people. Close to our work, recent works in this area have considered tasks where a robot assists a human user in dressing up a jacket [5], a shoe [6], a hat [7], or even a backpack [16,17].

© Springer Nature Switzerland AG 2021
G. Marreiros et al. (Eds.): EPIA 2021, LNAI 12981, pp. 405–417, 2021.
https://doi.org/10.1007/978-3-030-86230-5_32

The latter works, in particular, rely on the concept of *symbiotic autonomy*. Symbiotic autonomy explores the idea of using human assistance as a mechanism for augmenting the abilities of a robot. A robot endowed with symbiotic autonomy explicitly considers its limitations and plans to ask the assistance of (human) bystanders when necessary. These assistance requests usually consist of voice commands, such as asking a nearby human to call the elevator [14,20], or to move to a more convenient position so the robot can better operate [16,17].

While the concept of symbiotic autonomy helped robots overcome some of their limitations, we expect robots to perform increasingly complex tasks. Learning approaches have been applied successfully to these tasks and are now common [9,15]. However, these learning approaches require significant training and data, which typically require a human to perform the collaborative task with the robot. Considering the time and sample complexity involved in learning complex tasks, the need for human intervention implies a significant human effort in the training and data collection process [13]. To alleviate this effort, some works have considered approaches for transfer learning [2,4], allowing an agent to learn policies robust to different domains.

In this work, we exploit the *symmetry structure* inherent to many human-robot collaboration tasks to reduce the training effort required to teach the robot to jointly work with the human. We consider a dressing task, where a robot assists a human in putting on a backpack. We follow previous work that proposes a symbiotic autonomy approach to this scenario [16]. In our task, symmetry occurs both in terms of the task's target and the robot's execution. We contribute a novel approach to symmetry transfer that allows the robot to address a collaborative task in a way that is independent/invariant to existing symmetries in the task. The use of symmetry in this fashion abstracts the collaborative task, and the robot uses symmetry only at execution time to resolve its actuation.

In our robot-assisted dressing scenario, we exploit the lateral symmetry in the robot frame and the user's body. By exploiting the task's symmetry we can make the learning process more efficient since the robot requires fewer interactions with the human user to learn and perform the same task. We argue that our use of symmetry can be extended to different application domains beyond that considered in this paper, such as those featured in [5–7].

2   Background

In reinforcement learning [19], an agent interacts with a stochastic environment in a sequence of steps. At each step, the agent observes the state X_t of the environment and performs an action A_t. As a result, it incurs a cost C_t and the environment transitions to a new state X_{t+1}. The interaction between the agent and the environment can be described as a *Markov decision process* (MDP) and represented as a tuple $(\mathcal{X}, \mathcal{A}, P, c, \gamma)$, where $\mathcal{X}$ is the set of the possible states of the environment, $\mathcal{A}$ is the set of actions available to the agent, P is a state transition kernel, where $P(y \mid x, a)$ is the probability of moving from state x to state y upon executing action a. The function c is the instantaneous cost and is such that $\mathbb{E}\left[C_t \mid X_t = x, A_t = a\right] = c(x, a)$. The constant γ is a discount factor.

A *policy* is a function $\pi : \mathcal{X} \to \mathcal{A}$ that maps each state to an action. The goal of the agent is to select the actions that minimize the *total discounted cost*,

$$TDC = \mathbb{E}\left[\sum_{t=0}^{\infty} \gamma^t C_t\right]. \tag{1}$$

When at state x the expected total discounted cost for selecting action a and then selecting actions in the best possible way can be captured by the *optimal Q-value*, $Q^*(x, a)$. *Q-learning* [21] is a reinforcement learning method that allows an agent to learn Q^* in an online, incremental manner, from observed trajectories. After experiencing a transition (x, a, c, x'), Q-learning performs the update

$$\hat{Q}(x, a) \leftarrow \hat{Q}(x, a) + \alpha(c + \gamma \min_{a' \in \mathcal{A}} \hat{Q}(x', a') - \hat{Q}(x, a)), \tag{2}$$

where $\hat{Q}$ is the agent's estimate of Q^* and α is a scalar step-size. The optimal policy, π^*, can be computed for each state $x \in \mathcal{X}$ as $\pi^*(x) = \mathrm{argmin}_{a \in \mathcal{A}} Q^*(x, a)$. The algorithm can be made more efficient by storing the transitions experienced by the agent and, at each step, performing multiple Q-learning updates by reusing these stored transitions—an approach known as Dyna-Q [18].

3 Problem Formulation with Symmetry Based-Approach

This section instantiates the problem of a human-robot collaboration scenario where a two manipulator BAXTER robot assists a human user putting on both straps of a backpack. We assume the straps are placed sequentially, one at a time, and that the robot can either put the first strap on the right or the left shoulder of the human user, given the symmetry inherent to a human body. Additionally, we assume the robot can request assistance before placing each of the straps. We start by describing the robot's decision process as an MDP.

3.1 MDP Model

Following the principles of symbiotic autonomy [16], we allow the robot to indirectly control the user's target pose by voicing specific requests. These requests may come at a cost, in order to penalize disturbing the user. The goal of the robot is to execute a sequence of motions that successfully completes the task. The execution of a motion also comes at a cost, depending on whether the motion was successful or not. The goal of the agent is, therefore, to determine the actions it should perform at each time step (either a motion or a voice request to the user) that maximize the probability of successful completion of the task while at the same time minimizing the cost associated with the actions executed.

The challenge associated with this problem regards the uncertainty in the user's response and the execution success. In order to plan over this uncertainty, we represent the problem using a Markov decision process. The MDP operates over state and action spaces. For our scenario in particular, we instantiate these

(a) First strap.   (b) Second strap.

Fig. 1. The collaborative approach for robot-assisted backpack dressing, in its BASE-LINE execution. (a) The motion to place the first strap on the right arm of the user; (b) Placing the second strap on the left arm.

spaces to those of the task of first placing the *right strap* of the backpack, and then the left one. We refer to this as the *baseline task*. In contrast, *mirror task* refers to the symmetrical task of first placing the *left strap* of the backpack, and then the right one. The MDP elements $(\mathcal{X}, \mathcal{A}, P, c, \gamma)$ are specified as follows:

- *State space $\mathcal{X}$*: The backpack assistance task requires the robot to pass each strap of the backpack through the corresponding hand and arm of the user, up to the shoulder level, and drop it there. Since the task involves placing both straps, we model the target pose as depending on the position of the right and left hands, elbows and shoulders of the user. We consider the 3D position of these joints, resulting in a 18-dimensional real-valued vector. Additionally, the state vector also includes a Boolean variable indicating if the first strap is placed. A state x is thus a tuple (t, f), where t contains the pose information and f flags the successful placement of the first strap.
- *Action space $\mathcal{A}$*: The robot is provided with both communication and execution actions. The latter actions consist in the execution of one of two possible types of motions by the robot, corresponding to the placement of either the first or second strap of the backpack. Figure 1 depicts the differences between each type of motion. These motions are taught to the robot by demonstration, as described in Sect. 4.2. The communication actions, on the other hand, allow the robot to voice one of six possible requests to the human user—MOVE FORWARD, MOVE BACKWARDS, MOVE LEFT, MOVE RIGHT, RAISE ARM (for placing of the first strap) and GIVE ARM (for placing of the second strap). Finally, the robot is also provided with a QUIT action to be used when the robot believes the costs associated with placing the user in a convenient pose are too large, and it is better to stop immediately.
- *Transition probabilities P*: The transition probabilities model the human response to the robot commands. We do not define these explicitly, since the response of the human to the robot's actions are not available beforehand.

The use of a reinforcement learning method such as Q-learning or Dyna-Q relieves us from the requirement of an explicit transition model.

- *Cost function* c: The cost function asserts the "effort" of executing an action a in each state x. As the goal is to minimize the total effort of putting the backpack, we adopt the following cost function:
  - Successful executions correspond to a cost of 0: these are considered when the placement of both straps is successful.
  - Assistance requests require effort from the user and thus have an associated cost. We assign a cost of 1 for each assistance request performed.
  - Quitting the task is penalized with a cost of 9. The rationale for this value is that if the total cost of all assistance requests is too large, the robot should instead quit the task execution. This might happen, for example, if the human user is unable to perform a certain action. Experimentally, in initial trials, the average number of requests performed in successful trials was 6, which would suggest a cost of 6. The cost of quitting must be higher, so that the agent is able to perform successfully without subjecting the human to a large number of requests.
  - Unsuccessful executions are penalized with a cost of 7: since the agent should try to execute the placement of either the first or the second strap at least once, the cost corresponding to a failed execution has to be lower than the aforementioned cost of quitting without trying.

Solving the MDP yields an optimal policy π^* that ensures that the robot incurs as little cost as possible. Different methods can be used for solving this MDP [11]. However, since we do not have an explicit model for the human response, we adopt a reinforcement learning approach, as discussed next.

3.2   Reinforcement Learning

Reinforcement learning (RL) is commonly used to learn the optimal policy for an MDP from experience without requiring an explicit model of that MDP. In our scenario, we do not have a model of how humans respond to the robot's actions and, as such, RL is the natural approach to optimize the robot's action selection. However, each iteration of the algorithm requires actual interactions with human users that are expensive to get. We thus adopt a Dyna-Q approach [18], given its superior data efficiency. Specifically,

- We build estimates of P and c using data from the interaction with the user.
- Those estimates are used to generate additional synthetic data. Real and synthetic data are used to estimate Q^* using Q-learning updates.
- The estimated Q^* is further refined through additional user interactions.

During learning, the agent tries to complete the task by experimenting different initial and intermediate user poses, different voicing requests, and different execution motions. Such experiments provide the data used to compute Q^*.

The standard Q-learning update in (2) updates the individual components of Q^*, which is not possible in our scenario, since the state space is continuous.

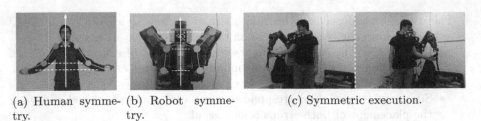

(a) Human symme- (b) Robot symme-   (c) Symmetric execution.
try.   try.

Fig. 2. (a) Symmetry of the target pose in terms of the human body; (b) Symmetry of the two-manipulator robot; (c) Symmetry inherent to our collaborative task. The robot can place the backpack from the right or the left. This work considers the blue line as the BASELINE execution, and the orange line as MIRROR execution. (Color figure online)

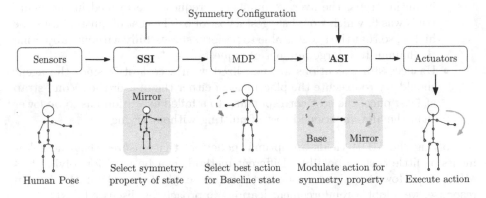

Fig. 3. Proposed architecture for symmetry-transfer in collaborative tasks. The sensors detect the human's pose to determine the state of the world. A *State Symmetry Implementer* (SSI) module detects the symmetry configuration of the state (BASELINE or MIRROR). The robot then selects the MDP action to take, irrespectively of the specific symmetry configuration of the state. The *Action Symmetry Implementer* (ASI) module then resolves the MDP action into a specific movement that again takes into consideration the specific symmetry configuration of the state.

We thus adopt an approximate representation for Q^* as the linear combination of a predefined set of state features $\phi_i, i = 1, \ldots, p$, i.e.,

$$Q^*(x, a) \approx \sum_{i=1}^{p} \phi_i(x)\theta_{i,a} = \phi^T(x)\boldsymbol{\theta}_a, \tag{3}$$

where $\boldsymbol{\theta}_a$ are the weights of the linear combination for action a. In our implementation, the state features correspond to radial kernels defined using the *random kitchen sinks* method [12].

3.3   Extending MDPs with Symmetry

We are interested in exploiting the symmetry inherent to many human-robot collaboration tasks to reduce the training effort required to learn such tasks. We consider two specific types of symmetry. First, we consider *symmetry on the target pose*. In this type of symmetry the target pose is typically a function of the human's body, which exhibits a lateral symmetry nature (Fig. 2(a)). Second, we consider *symmetry on the robot execution*. Many robots are designed in a way that displays intrinsic symmetry (for example, due to their human-like shape). A two-arm manipulator such as Baxter can execute symmetric trajectories according to a given longitudinal plane (Fig. 2(b)).

These two types of symmetry define *symmetrical tasks*—tasks that can be completed through similar motions, possibly mirrored with respect to some reference frame. We address symmetric tasks by abstracting the aforementioned types of symmetry and considering these only at execution time to resolve the robot's action. We follow the pipeline depicted in Fig. 3. Initially, given the position of the user, the robot determines the current symmetry configuration—BASELINE or MIRROR—using the following spatial criteria: when the user is closer to the left side of the robot, we assume a BASELINE task. Conversely, if the user is closer to the right side of the robot, we assume a MIRROR task (Fig. 2(c)).

Once the symmetry configuration is determined, the pose of the human is projected (using symmetry) to the baseline execution, and the MDP optimal action is computed for the projected pose. This projection is computed by a module dubbed *state symmetry implementer* (SSI, see Fig. 3). Given the current task, τ, and state of the world, $x = (t, f)$—where t is the 18-dimensional vector containing the 3D joint positions (x, y, z) of the right and left hand, elbow, and shoulder of the user, and f is a Boolean variable indicating if the first strap has been successfully placed—the SSI module computes

$$\bar{x} = \mathrm{SSI}(x, \tau) = \begin{cases} (t, f) & \text{if } \tau = \text{BASELINE}; \\ (t_{\mathrm{sym}}, f) & \text{otherwise}, \end{cases}$$

where t_{sym} is similar to t, but with mirrored coordinates with respect to the robot's reference frame. The projection of x allows us to consider an MDP operating in a single symmetry configuration. The features $\phi(\bar{x})$ match the MDP state representation and are independent of the user's symmetry configuration.

Given the state representation, we use the optimal MDP policy to select an optimal action to execute, which is independent of the symmetry configuration of the user. The *action symmetry implementer* (ASI, see Fig. 3) takes the optimal MDP action and maps it back to the correct symmetry configuration. When in MIRROR task, the abstract action is replaced with its symmetrical counterpart for both voice commands (MOVE RIGHT, MOVE LEFT, RAISE ARM, GIVE ARM) and motion commands.

The advantage of our symmetry-aware architecture is that the robot can perform both the baseline and mirror tasks using the same MDP. This abstract MDP is significantly smaller than one that simultaneously described both tasks.

The smaller size of the abstract MDP, in turn, leads to faster convergence of the reinforcement learning method.

4   Experimental Procedure

We now describe the experimental setup used to evaluate the proposed approach, using the Baxter robot to put a backpack on a human user.

4.1   Experimental Setup

The Baxter robot is a humanoid robotic platform with two symmetric manipulators, each having 7 degrees of freedom and an end gripper to hold the backpack. To obtain the human pose, we use both the Microsoft Kinect v2 RGBD camera and a human pose estimation algorithm, TFPose tracker [3]. Furthermore, we employ the AprilTag system [10]: using an Augmented Reality Quick Response code (AR code), aligned with the robot symmetry axis, we are able to compute a symmetry-aligned reference frame to which we transform the positions of the human joints, taken in the camera reference frame (see Fig. 2(b)).

4.2   Kinesthetic Learning

The robot movements necessary to place the backpack are taught via human demonstration. We represent trajectories using *cooperative probabilistic motion primitives* (CoProMPs) [8]—one primitive to put the first strap of the backpack on one arm and a second primitive to put the second strap on the other arm. Both can easily be learned from human demonstrations through kinesthetic teaching. We demonstrated the movements needed to place the two straps of the backpack for different poses of the human. We considered 10 different poses for the first strap and 7 different poses for the second strap.

4.3   Probabilistic Human Displacement Model

To build the transition model for Dyna-Q, the robot interacts with the human user, voicing different requests and observing the user's response. This data is then used to build a transition model that describes the user's motion in the baseline task. For each voice request a, we model the change in the user's pose as a function $d(a_t) = t_{t+1} - t_t$. We model this pose difference as an action-specific Gaussian distribution p_a, considering 30 sample pairs of poses, (t_t, t_{t+1}). To learn the distributions, we resort to a Gaussian kernel density estimator, with bandwidths selected through grid-search with 5-fold validation.

4.4   Cost Estimation

To estimate the cost function for Dyna-Q, the robot must be able to determine whether the task can be successfully completed, given the pose of the human user. To do so, we train a support vector machine (SVM) classifier that determines, for each pose, whether each of the two straps can be placed successfully. We train two classifiers using a data-set comprising pairs (pose, success) obtained experimentally. For the first-strap classifier, we record 24 9-dimensional samples, considering the 3-dimensional positions of the right arm joints. Similarly, we record 25 samples of the position of the left arm joints for the left-strap classifier.

5   Evaluation and Results

We evaluate our proposed approach in terms of the quality of the agent's policy, resorting to a simulation environment [16], and of the performance of the whole system in a real-life scenario with a robotic platform.

5.1   Policy Learning in Simulation

To evaluate the robot's policy in the backpack task, we first consider only the BASELINE task. This evaluation is a quality indicator for the baseline policy, on which our proposed approach builds. In this initial evaluation we resort to a simulated environment, using the learned models for human motion and successful placement described in Sects. 4.3 and 4.4. We run Q-learning for $300,000$ episodes on synthetic data generated by our models, considering an ϵ-greedy strategy with $\epsilon = 0.1$. We evaluated the performance of the algorithm for different numbers of basis functions.

Figures 4(a) and 4(b) present the performance of the agent in terms of total reward and number of assistance requests. The algorithm is robust to changes to the number of basis functions. Also, the number of assistance requests tends to slowly increase as the training advances, since the agent stops failing and starts executing successfully.

5.2   Real-World Evaluation with a Robotic Platform

We also evaluated our approach in an actual robotic platform operating in a real-life scenario. In this scenario, the robot can perform both the BASELINE and MIRROR tasks, taking into consideration the pose of the human user.

We consider two distinct metrics: a "safety-oriented" metric and a "task-oriented" metric. The first metric aims at evaluating the performance of the robot for applications that require no physical contact with the human user. To be considered successful under such metric, the interaction must follow the following criteria:

– The robot must be able to put both straps of the backpack on the user.
– The robot must not touch the user during any moment of the interaction.

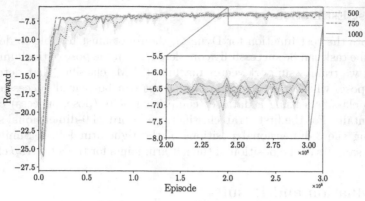

(a) Average reward convergence.

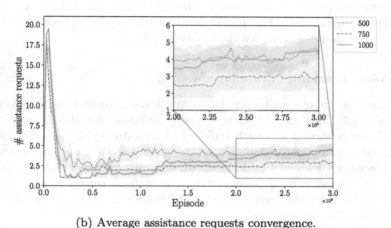

(b) Average assistance requests convergence.

Fig. 4. Obtained for 3×10^5 episodes. We report the performance every $2,500$ episodes. We report results obtained for 500, 750 and $1,000$ state basis functions. The results are averaged over 10 runs with the shaded areas representing the standard error.

- At the end of each trajectory, the straps must be placed on the user's shoulder without any assistance from the user.

The task-oriented metric in turn considers a more cooperative interaction, removing the criterion of human user assistance during the task. With this metric, we wish to evaluate the performance of the robot in a regular collaborative setting of putting a backpack on the user. For the execution of such task to be considered successful, the interaction must respect the following criteria:

- The robot must be able to put both straps of the backpack on the user.
- User assistance is allowed during execution (although ideally kept to a minimum). For example, the user can adjust the strap to be stable on its shoulder.
- The robot may gently touch the user during the interaction.

We evaluated the previous criteria by annotating recordings of the interactions between the robot and users. We recorded 60 interactions, of which 30 are BASE-LINE tasks, and 30 are MIRROR (non-trained) tasks. The interactions were evaluated by 4 independent annotators and the average results from such evaluation are presented in Table 1.

Table 1. Performance on the backpack task in a real-world scenario.

	Safety-oriented metric		Task-oriented metric	
	BASELINE	MIRROR	BASELINE	MIRROR
Single-task success rate (%)	66.7	42.5	100.0	85.8
Total success rate (%)	54.6		92.9	

As expected, the performance of the robot considering the stricter safety-oriented metric is lower in comparison with the more cooperative task-oriented metric, with an increase from 54.6% successful rate in the former to 92.9% success rate in the latter. This increase clearly shows the importance of the human user's collaboration for the completion of the backpack putting task. The decrease in performance from the BASELINE task to the MIRROR task is quite less significant. The robot is able to complete the latter with a success rate of 85.8%, which results in a 14.2% decrease in success rate according to the task-oriented metric in the BASELINE task. With no additional training of the robot, the proposed symmetry-transfer system allows a robotic agent to perform the collaborative task on both sides, with minimal performance loss.

6   Conclusions

In this paper, we presented a novel approach that explores the symmetry structure of human-robot collaborative tasks. In this approach, we consider the inherent symmetry of the task execution, abstracting it from the robot decision process itself. By considering the symmetrical properties of the task solely at sensing and execution time, we are able to naturally extend typical single-sided tasks to their symmetrical side, with no additional training.

We instantiated our approach in a robot-assisted backpack dressing scenario, in which a robot assists the human in putting on both straps of the backpack. We evaluated the quality of the single-side policy in a simulation environment and the efficiency of the approach in a real-life scenario, using the symmetrical two-manipulator robotic platform BAXTER.

Given the dressing-like nature of such tasks, becomes inescapable that the way these are performed becomes unique for each human with its own physical features. The training made for one human can only be extended for those with similar physical features. Therefore the results, despite being obtained for the same human subject that trained the agent, show that our approach allows for an efficient extension of the execution of single-side trained collaborative tasks to their symmetrical, with minimal loss in performance. As future work a study on the generalization of such tasks being performed for different human users with distinct physical features is mandatory. By training the agent for several distinct human subjects the model would be evaluated in its ability to perform for such broad set of human shapes.

Acknowledgements. This work was partially supported by national funds through the Portuguese Fundação para a Ciência e a Tecnologia under project UIDB/50021/ 2020 (INESC-ID multi-annual funding) and the Carnegie Mellon Portugal Program and its Information and Communications Technologies Institute, under project CMUP-ERI/HCI/0051/2013. R. Silva acknowledges the PhD grant SFRH/BD/113695/ 2015. M. Vasco acknowledges the PhD grant SFRH/BD/139362/2018.

References

1. Average life expectancy by country. https://www.worlddata.info/life-expectancy. php#by-world
2. Barrett, S., Taylor, M., Stone, P.: Transfer learning for reinforcement learning on a physical robot. In: AAMAS Workshop on Adaptive Learning Agents (2010)
3. Cao, Z., Hidalgo, G., Simon, T., Wei, S., Sheikh, Y.: OpenPose: realtime multi-person 2D pose estimation using part affinity fields. IEEE Trans. Pattern Anal. Mach. Intell. **43**(1), 172–186 (2021)
4. Christiano, P., et al.: Transfer from simulation to real world through learning deep inverse dynamics model. CoRR abs/1610.03518 (2016)
5. Gao, Y., Chang, H., Demiris, Y.: User modelling for personalised dressing assistance by humanoid robots. In: Proceedings of 2015 IEEE/RSJ International Conference Intelligent Robots and Systems, pp. 1840–1845 (2015)
6. Jevtić, A., et al.: Personalized robot assistant for support in dressing. IEEE Trans. Cognitive Developmental Syst. **11**(3), 363–374 (2019)
7. Klee, S., Ferreira, B., Silva, R., Costeira, J., Melo, F., Veloso, M.: Personalized assistance for dressing users. In: Proceedings of 7th International Conference Social Robotics (2015)
8. Maeda, G., Ewerton, M., Lioutikov, R., Amor, H., Peters, J., Neumann, G.: Learning interaction for collaborative tasks with probabilistic movement primitives. In: Proceedings of the 2014 IEEE-RAS International Conference Humanoid Robots, pp. 527–534 (2014)
9. Mahler, J., Goldberg, K.: Learning deep policies for robot bin picking by simulating robust grasping sequences. In: Proceedings of 1st Annual Conference Robot Learning (2017)
10. Olson, E.: AprilTag: a robust and and flexible visual fiducial system. In: Proceedings of 2011 IEEE International Conference Robotics and Automation, pp. 3400–3407 (2011)
11. Puterman, M.: Markov Decision Processes: Discrete Stochastic Dynamic Programming. John Wiley & Sons (2014)
12. Rahimi, A., Recht, B.: Weighted sums of random kitchen sinks: Replacing minimization with randomization in learning. In: Advances in Neural Information Processing Systems 22, pp. 1313–1320 (2009)

13. Roh, Y., Heo, G., Whang, S.: A survey on data collection for machine learning: a big data-AI integration perspective. IEEE Trans. Knowl. Data Eng. **33**(4), 1328–1347 (2019)
14. ce Rosenthal, S., Biswas, J., Veloso, M.: An effective personal mobile robot agent through symbiotic human-robot interaction. In: Proceedings of 9th International Conference Autonomous Agents and Multiagent Systems, pp. 915–922 (2010)
15. Rusu, A., Večerik, M., Rothörl, T., Heess, N., Pascanu, R., Hadsell, R.: Sim-to-real robot learning from pixels with progressive nets. In: Proceedings of 1st Annual Conference Robot Learning (2017)
16. Silva, R., Faria, M., Melo, F., Veloso, M.: Adaptive indirect control through communication in collaborative human-robot interaction. In: Proceedings of 2017 IEEE/RSJ International Conference Intelligent Robots and Systems, pp. 3617–3622 (2017)
17. Silva, R., Melo, F., Veloso, M.: Adaptive symbiotic collaboration for targeted complex manipulation tasks. In: Proceedings of 22nd Eur. Conf. Artificial Intelligence (2016)
18. Sutton, R.: Integrated architectures for learning, planning, and reacting based on approximating dynamic programming. In: Proceedings of 7th International Conference Machine Learning, pp. 216–224 (1990)
19. Sutton, R., Barto, A.: Reinforcement Learning: An Introduction. MIT Press (2018)
20. Veloso, M., Biswas, J., Coltin, B., Rosenthal, S.: CoBots: robust symbiotic autonomous mobile service robots. In: Proceedings of 24th International Joint Conference Artificial Intelligence, pp. 4423–4429 (2015)
21. Watkins, C.: Learning from delayed rewards. Ph.D. thesis, King's College, Cambridge University (1989)

I2SL: Learn How to Swarm Autonomous Quadrotors Using Iterative Imitation Supervised Learning

Omar Shrit[✉] and Michèle Sebag

Université Paris Saclay, Rue Joliot Curie, 91190 Gif-sur-Yvette, France
{omar.shrit,michele.sebag}@universite-paris-saclay.fr

Abstract. In this paper, a decentralized controller for a quadrotor swarm is presented following the leader-follower principle. The quadrotors embedding the decentralized controller follow a remotely controlled leader. The controller, governing the behavior of a set of followers is learned using an Iterative Imitation supervised learning approach. The novelty of this approach is to build complex policies supporting the flocking behavior for a set of quadrotors while requiring only COTS (Commercial Of The Shelf) wireless sensors. In the first iteration, a set of trajectories is generated using the well-known Reynolds flocking model (adapted by Schilling et al., 2018, to add a migration term); the logs are exploited to enable the follower quadrotor controller to achieve the migration function. In the further iterations, the learned controller is exploited in combination with the Reynolds model; the logs generated are then exploited to learn a follower quadrotor controller achieving both the migration and the flocking functions, as robust as the Reynolds model. The validation of the approach using a Software In The Loop (SITL) environment relying on the Gazebo simulator, confirms that the learned controller enables the followers to accurately follow the leader while collectively satisfying the swarm properties.

Simulation Videos

Available at https://tinyurl.com/7b2f7mcz

1 Introduction

It is well known that animals, e.g., insects, birds or mammals [1], can be organized in various ways, having either one leader [2], a hierarchy of leaders [3], or no leader at all [4]. The objective of this organization is to create emergent behaviors. By monitoring these behaviors, an observer can deduce that these animals are trying to achieve a synchronous movement also known as collective motion in order to force back the danger from a predator [5] or to migrate from one zone to another [6]. The collective motion itself is a result of a collective behavior [7], in which this complex behavior is composed of simple interactions

© Springer Nature Switzerland AG 2021
G. Marreiros et al. (Eds.): EPIA 2021, LNAI 12981, pp. 418–432, 2021.
https://doi.org/10.1007/978-3-030-86230-5_33

between the agents. While collective behavior aims to fulfil a common goal, this goal depends on the context. For example, a school of fishes can change their direction immediately if they face an instant danger; a group of bees can attack directly the predators in order to save the nest and the group. Flocking and swarming behaviors are not limited to mammals and birds. It is well observed at the micro-biological level, as it is the case for cells [8] and bacteria [9]. Overall, a swarm can be defined as a group of similar agents interacting with each other in order to create emergent behavior.

Related Works. The above observation is at the root of analytical models, enabling us to understand and mimic the behaviors of animals and insects. Several flocking models have been developed in the last decades such as the Reynolds model [10], the Vicsek model [11] or the Olfati-Saber model [12]. When tuned correctly, these models can achieve the flocking behavior perfectly. The issue with these models arises when deploying them directly on a multi-agent system such as quadrotors. These models rely on precise localization which is rarely possible in real-life scenarios. Therefore, several adaptations are required. Viragh et al. [13] adapt the Viscek model by adding several parameters such as the inner noise of sensors, inertia, time delay, and communication constrained in order to enhance the behavioral law. They test this model on a set of quadrotors while using GNSS as a localization system [14]. To improve their outdoor swarms, they use an evolutionary algorithm to find the best flocking parameters for an outdoor swarm of 30 quadrotors [15].

Another approach relies on the use of vision onboard sensors instead of GNSS systems. Vision-based swarms can follow a true decentralized controller for a set of quadrotors, that is not based on external localization systems. Schilling et al. [16] embed six cameras on each quadrotor in order to provide 360° vision of the environment. They adapt the Reynolds flocking model by adding a migration term. Their method, deployed on real quadrotors in indoor [17] and outdoor [18] environments, relies on the prediction of the velocity command using supervised learning.

However, it is challenging to deploy these methods on small and nano quadrotors [19] because 1) they require the use of heavy sensors, such as a complete set of cameras, or expensive GNSS; 2) the addition of these sensors will require a considerable amount of onboard computation which is rarely available on nano quadrotors; 3) the outdoor performance is related to the weather condition, since GNSS improves performance on sunny days, and similarly, vision sensors perceive better their neighbors with good lighting conditions.

Contributions. In this paper, we present I2SL (*Iterative Imitation Supervised Learning*), a supervised iterative imitation learning method that is inspired from [16,20,21]. The contributions of this method can be described in two perspectives. From the control perspective: this method addresses the challenge of the design of a decentralized swarm controller for small quadrotors using imitation learning. The use of imitation learning is favored in this case since the existence of an oracle demonstrator (flocking model), eliminating the need for reinforcement learning since it requires the design of a specific reward function that can used for all agents. In addition, several researchers [22,23] have demonstrated that imitation learning can be combined successfully in the case of multi-agent system in order to learn a specific policy. From the perception perspective: our aim is to learn a decentralized controller using only one wireless sensor on each quadrotor, with very limited computation on-board. The approach has been validated on MagicFlock[1], a home-made SITL framework based on RotorS [24] and extended to model a swarm (as RotorS supports only one quadrotor). The choice of developing this framework is related to the limited access to real quadrotors hardware.

The presented work extends the IL4MRC method [21], which likewise aims to achieve a decentralized controller with cheap embedded wireless sensors. The contribution is based on the combination of IL4MRC with Dagger, along with an iterative approach, gradually refining the controller learned in the former iteration, thereby exploring only the necessary information rather than exploring the entire environment. In the first iteration, the leader is assigned a random model to simulate a human pilot, while the followers are using a flocking model, and each quadrotor generates logs describing its state as a vector of sensor values. The controller learned from these logs immediately enforces the following of the leader, i.e. it supports the *migration* function. But does not enforce the *Cohesion* and *Separation* rules in order to avoid one another. In the second iteration, the former controller is used in alternation with the flocking policy following the Dagger approach. The obtained trajectories thus alternate between avoiding any possible collision and following the leader. After several iterations, while each quadrotor is controlled from its embedded controller, they collectively 'swarm' around the (remotely controlled) leader, i.e. they satisfy the main swarm properties: i) following the leader, ii) avoiding collision and preventing separation of the neighbor followers.

Formally, the presented approach makes the following contributions:

- The learning procedure combines agile iterative imitation learning with a multi-agent system in order to create a decentralized swarm controller for quadrotors;
- It learns a decentralized controller, that requires only one cheap wireless sensor and very limited computational on-board resources.

This paper is organized as follows. Section 2 introduces the formal definition of the flocking model and presents an overview of I2SL. Section 3 gives a proof of concept for the accuracy of the proposed method. Sections 4 and 5 respectively present the experimental setting and the experimental validation of I2SL. Section 6 concludes the paper with some perspectives for further research.

---

[1] https://github.com/shrit/MagicFlock.

2 Methodology

This section introduces the flocking model used in the paper for the sake of self-contentedness and presents the I2SL approach.

2.1 Flocking Algorithm

This subsection presents the adaptation of the Reynolds flocking model, as described in [16], except for its ability to handle the leader-follower mechanism. Specifically, the considered swarm comprises a *piloted* leader and a set of followers that follow the leader. The leader is remotely controlled and is not aware of the followers. The followers' objective is to migrate toward this leader. Similar to [16], we omit the velocity matching term since the quadrotors do not communicate with one another, and do not have additional sensors to estimate neighbors' velocity reactively. Most generally the flocking model involves three terms, known as *cohesion, separation,* and *migration*. Let $\mathcal{N}_i$ denote the set of neighbor follower quadrotors of the quadrotor i, with

$$\mathcal{N}_i = (follower\ j : j \neq i \wedge \|\mathbf{r_{ij}}\| < r^{max}) \tag{1}$$

where $\|.\|$ is the euclidean norm. $\mathbf{r_{ij}} \in \mathbb{R}^3$, $\mathbf{r_{ij}} = \mathbf{p}_j - \mathbf{p}_i$ denotes to the relative position of quadrotor j with respect to follower i. Only one set of quadrotors is considered at a time; they can not divide themselves into several sets as they all need to stay close to the leader. Formally, the swarm is said to be valid as long as $d_{ij} < 30$ m. The three terms cohesion, separation, and migration work together to produce the flocking behavior; the separation term pushes away agents that are close to each other to avoid a collision; inversely the cohesion term moves far away quadrotors toward their nearest neighbors. Both terms work together in order to provide a consistent swarm behavior.

$$\mathbf{v_i}^{sep} = -\frac{k^{sep}}{\mathcal{N}_i} \sum_{j \in \mathcal{N}_i} \frac{\mathbf{r}_{ij}}{\|\mathbf{r_{ij}}\|^2} \tag{2}$$

$$\mathbf{v_i}^{coh} = \frac{k^{sep}}{\mathcal{N}_i} \sum_{j \in \mathcal{N}_i} \mathbf{r}_{ij} \tag{3}$$

Where k^{sep} is the separation gain, k^{coh} is the cohesion gain. The sum of two velocities (Cohesion and Separation) produce the Reynolds velocity $\mathbf{v_i}^{rey} = \mathbf{v_i}^{sep} + \mathbf{v_i}^{coh}$. In addition to the above terms, the migration terms allows the followers quadrotors to move toward the leader quadrotor permanently. The migration point is not fixed: it is the position of the leader itself. The migration term is given by:

$$\mathbf{v_i}^{mig} = k^{mig} \frac{\mathbf{r}_{ij}}{\|\mathbf{r_{ij}}\|} \tag{4}$$

Where k^{mig} is the migration gain and $\mathbf{r}_{ij} \in \mathbb{R}^3$ is the relative position of the migration point w.r.t. the i-the quadrotor, with $\mathbf{r}_i^{mig} = \mathbf{p}^{leader} - \mathbf{p}_i^{follower}$. In order to achieve the flocking behavior, the controller embedded on each follower uses the sum of the tree velocity commands $\mathbf{v_i} = \mathbf{v_i}^{sep} + \mathbf{v_i}^{coh} + \mathbf{v_i}^{mig}$. The leader is normally operated by a human pilot, with a limited velocity (racing tasks are not considered in the following). In simulation, the maximum speed of the flocking model is bounded to a maximum final velocity command, set to $v_{max} = 2\,\mathrm{m/s}$, and the velocity of each follower $\mathbf{v_i}$ is accordingly bounded as:

$$\mathbf{v_i} = \min(\|\mathbf{v_i}\|, v_{max}) \tag{5}$$

2.2 Iterative Imitation Supervised Learning

The proposed approach takes inspiration from [21]. The extension aims to relieve the simplifying assumptions of discrete action space and a good initial condition of the swarm. We show that using the flocking policy to generate the logs that will serve to the imitation-based controller learning relieves the need for such simplifying assumptions. Formally, the proposed iterative imitation approach uses a 3-step process inspired from the Dagger algorithm [20].
At the iteration i:

- The trajectory executed by each quadrotor is logged, defined as a sequence of states s_t and actions a_t. This trajectory is generated after controller π_i using the Dagger mechanism:

$$\pi_i = \beta_i \pi^* + (1 - \beta_i)\hat{\pi}_{i-1} \tag{6}$$

Where π^* is the flocking policy, and $\hat{\pi}_{i-1}$ is the policy learned in the last iteration. β is decayed exponentially from 1 to 0 over time as $\beta = e^{-\lambda i}$ where $\lambda = 0.69314$ is a constant.
- The trajectories generated in the above are logged to form a training dataset $\mathcal{E}_i$:

$$\mathcal{E}_i = \{(s_t, a_t), t = 1, \dots T\} \tag{7}$$

and the datasets are stacked:

$$\mathcal{E} \leftarrow \mathcal{E}_i + \mathcal{E}_{i-1} \tag{8}$$

- The model $\mathcal{F}_i$ is trained from $\mathcal{E}$ to learn the best action to execute based on the sequence of the last states:

$$\mathcal{U} = \mathcal{F}_i(\mathcal{Y}) \tag{9}$$

The state of each quadrotor is defined as a vector of the signal strength the azimuth and the elevation angles perceived from neighbors $i = 1, \dots, n$. Therefore, at each time step t the state of the quadrotor j is given as $s_t^j = (rss_1, \phi_1, \theta_1, rss_2, \phi_2, \theta_2, \dots, rss_n, \phi_n, \theta_n)$. While the action a_t^j is the velocity vector $\mathbf{v}$.

3 A Proof of Principle of I2SL: Application to Quadrotors Control

This section presents a proof of principle of I2SL,[2] applied to the control of a set of quadrotors. After describing the position of the problem, the algorithmic pipeline (data acquisition phase, training of the model, exploitation of the model) is detailed.

3.1 Position of the Problem

Considering a set of quadrotors with one leader and several followers, the goal is to gradually build an independent controller for each follower, knowing that each follower has very minimal sensing capabilities, such as measuring the distance to its neighbors, and receive the azimuth and elevation angles of its neighbors. The objective of this controller is to achieve the flocking behavior known as swarming for the followers' quadrotors, where the leader quadrotor is manually controlled by a human pilot.

Following [21], the main goal of the proposed approach is to achieve some trade-off between efficiency and computational and other resources. On the one hand, the cost of sophisticated sensors is an issue. On the other hand, quadrotors consume a considerable amount of energy when carrying heavy sensors, not to mention the algorithmic complexity to analyze the perceived data from the environment.

In the simulation, Gazebo provides a generic wireless sensor that can be added to each quadrotor, we have integrated 3 antennas on each robot. The wireless sensor considers obstacles in the nearby of each robot which affect the value of the Received Signal Strength (RSS) according to the number and density of the obstacles. The proposed method does not require sharing information, which means there are no communications between the agents. Therefore, the wireless channel is not used only RSS values are perceived from neighbors. In addition, for the only sake of simulation, we add a ray sensor on each quadrotor to provide angle estimation (azimuth and elevation) to neighbors. During simulation as provided by the link in the abstract to experiment videos, we have turned off ray visualization to remove heavy computations from GPU. However, in a real-life scenario, one can use COTS quadrotors that have an embedded WiFi card such as Intel 5300 with 3 antennas allowing to estimate Angle of Arrival (AoA) of signals and the RSS values from neighbors, more details are discussed in Sect. 6.

Each robot is capable of mapping distances and angles to its neighbors. In this case, one might argue that robots can create a polar coordinate system thus constructing gradually a relative localization system. Indeed, this system can be used directly by the flocking model and remove the need for imitation learning. Arguably this is true. However, there are two disadvantages to this method. First, this will require more computation from each robot, since it

---

[2] https://github.com/shrit/MagicFlock.

needs to calculate the relative position of neighbors in each time step and then apply the calculations related flocking model. Second, the sensor noise needs to be estimated before the flight, and proper modifications have to be applied to the flocking model accordingly. However, imitation learning alleviates the need for such a calibration as the noise is embedded inside the data. The learned controller has a better estimation of its neighbors allowing it to perform as well as the oracle flocking model as demonstrated in Sect. 5.

Quadrotor Settings: Formally we have defined one setting of quadrotors to train and test the models on the quadrotors. We have a set of 7 quadrotors, in which there are one leader and 6 followers. The goal is to embed the **same** trained controller on all the followers to *follow* the leader without having any collision with the neighbor quadrotors.

3.2   Data Acquisition

During the data acquisition, the state of each follower is recorded along with a set of episodes. Each follower registers two data sets simultaneously. The first data set registers the states of the leaders along with the migration velocity as given by the flocking model. The second data set registers the state of the other followers' neighbors along with the Reynolds velocity as given by the flocking model.

First Iteration: Each episode starts with quadrotors taking off. Once the taking off has finished, the leader chooses a direction randomly and moves in this direction for 80 s. The follower quadrotors use the flocking model and start following the leader. The max velocity of the leader is equal to 0.7 m per second which are slightly lower than the followers equal to 1.0 m per second. This small variation allows the followers to catch up with the leader. The episode ends once the followers are close to the leader and there is no longer any change in their distances. To ensure the diversity of the collected data set, all the quadrotors are reset into a new position at the end of each episode, allowing each quadrotor to have a different set of neighbors.

Second Iteration. Similar to the first episode, the episode starts by taking off, and then the leader moves before the other quadrotors. The main difference is that the value of β is reduced from 1 to 0.5 in this iteration allowing alteration between the flocking model and model trained in the first iteration.

Third and Further Iterations. The following iterations follow the same principle in the second iteration while continuing to reduce β as described in Sect. 2.

3.3   Forward Model

The data set is exploited to learn a forward model. The forward model uses the last states in order to predict the action to execute at this time step. Formally, the data set is decomposed as a set of the last five states, that are trained to predict the action a_t.

$$(X = (s_{t-4}, s_{t-3}, s_{t-2}, s_{t-1}, s_t); Z = a_t) \tag{10}$$

We use a mainstream supervised learning algorithm to train a function $\mathcal{F}$ such that $\mathcal{F}(X) = Z$ from 80% of the data.

During the training, the quality of the model $\mathcal{F}$ is estimated by applying the model on the validation set which comprises 20% of the data set.

3.4   I2SL Controller

At production time, model $\mathcal{F}$ is used as the decentralized controller that is embedded on each quadrotor. The model is composed of two submodels, the first model is trained on the data set that is based on sensor value received from the leader while the second model is trained on data set received from the neighbors followers.

$$a_t = \mathcal{F}(s_{t-4}, s_{t-3}, s_{t-2}, s_{t-1}, s_t) \tag{11}$$

The quadrotors are operated at production time very similarly as in the data acquisition phase. In each episode, the quadrotors take off, the leader is randomly operated. The leader starts moving 5 s before the followers, in order to allow for the followers to accumulate a decent amount of states from the sensor in order to predict the good action. The episode runs as long as the flocking behavior is maintained and neither collision nor separation is noticed. As said, we consider that the flocking is maintained as long as the distance between two quadrotors $d_{ij} < 30$ m.

4   Experimental Setting

This section describes the goal of experiments and the experimental setting used to validate the I2SL approach.

4.1   Goals of Experiments

As said, an episode starts with the swarm taking off. Once the taking off has finished the leader starts moving 5 s before the followers. We create a ZigZag experiment that allows testing if the learned models are capable of imitating the flocking behavior, and how the followers are behaving when the leader changes its direction from time to time.

Such experiments aim to simulate a human pilot flying the leader quadrotor through a specific trajectory while the followers keep appropriate distances among all of them.

The straightforward performance indicator is to measure the minimum and the maximum distance between the follower quadrotors during the flight; these indicators reflect the consistency of the learned flocking behavior. The distance metric is given by:

$$d^{min} = \min_{i,j \in \mathcal{N}} \|\mathbf{r}_{ij}\| \tag{12}$$

$$d^{max} = \max_{i,j \in \mathcal{N}} \|\mathbf{r}_{ij}\| \tag{13}$$

Where $\mathcal{N}$ if the set of follower quadrotors and d^{min}, d^{max} is respectively the minimum and the maximum distance observed in the follower quadrotors swarm. In addition to the indicators, we show the trajectory executed by the leader and the followers for each iteration and each experiment.

4.2   Baseline

To assess the performance of I2SL we used the flocking model that uses the absolute positioning system. The flocking model (oracle) delivers the perfect flocking behavior when knowing the exact position of all the neighbor followers. The gain of the flocking model have been chosen as described in [16], since they modulate the strength of the cohesion and the separation of the swarm.

The behavior in each iteration is compared with the behavior obtained in the former iteration, and with the flocking model.

4.3   Simulation Platform

In the experiments, the system includes seven robots of the same type, the IRIS quadrotor designed by 3DR[3], with height 0.11 m, width 0.47 m, and weight 1.5 kg. The quadrotors are simulated using the software in the loop simulation (SITL) [24] integrating the Gazebo simulator[4]. Each quadrotor uses PX4[5] as an autopilot software.

The maximum velocity that a quadrotor can reach is 1 m/s, The take-off altitude is 45 m.

4.4   Learning of the Flocking Model

The total training data set for all the iterations records at least 24h of flying time. The flocking model is implemented as a neural net, using mlpack [25], while the linear algebra library is Armadillo [26]. The neural architecture is a 2-hidden layers, with 256 neurons on each layer and Sigmoid as activation function. The training uses Glorot initialization [27], with .5 Dropout and batch size 32; the hyper-parameters are adjusted using Adam [28] with $\beta_1 = 0.9$, $\beta_2 = 0.999$, $\varepsilon = 10^{-8}$, and initial learning rate $\alpha = 0.001$.

---

[3] https://3dr.com/.
[4] http://gazebosim.org/.
[5] https://px4.io/.

5   Empirical Validation

5.1   Zigzag Experiment

The zigzag experiment aims to assess whether the followers are capable to imitate the flocking behavior. The experiment runs as follows: all the quadrotors take off, the leader follows a random trajectory for 5 s and then follows the zigzag trajectory that is already embedded on the leader. The followers do not know about their leader's trajectory, their objective is to follow the leader and avoid collision and dispersion. The same experiment is executed on each iteration, allowing us to validate the learned model in each iteration.

We compare the first and the second iteration in Figs. 1 and 2. In both iterations, the trained controller uses the data perceived by the wireless sensor. The first iteration uses the classic imitation learning algorithm, while the second iteration applies the Dagger approach. The result Fig. 1 (left) shows the trajectory executed by each quadrotor, while the inter-quadrotor distances is shown in Fig. 2 (left). In the first iteration, we observe that the quadrotors learn how to follow the leader. However, they do not learn how to respect distances among them, resulting in several minor collisions between the quadrotors and distortion in the executed trajectory; this is confirmed in Fig. 2 for this experiment. In the second iteration (right) quadrotors start to learn how to avoid each other, but their behavior is very aggressive, and not refined yet to be similar to the flocking model. In addition, in both iterations, no collision was observed between the followers.

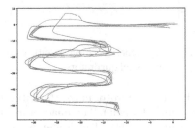 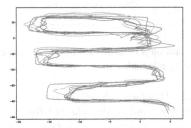

(a) Iteration 1 (sensor based): trajectories exe-   (b) Iteration 2 (sensor based): trajectories executed by all quadrotors   cuted by all quadrotors

Fig. 1. This figure compares the trajectories executed during the zigzag experiment by the quadrotors in both the first and the second iteration. All the quadrotors take off from the (0,0) coordination, and they land at (11, −55) in the first iteration, and at (5, −44) in the second iteration. The leader quadrotors labeled in blue have an integrated embedded trajectory to simulate a human pilot, while all the followers use the learned controller based on a cheap wireless sensor. This figure shows an improved trajectory in the second iteration. This is due to the usage of the iterative learning technique over the basic imitation supervised learning represented in the first iteration.

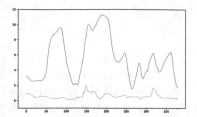 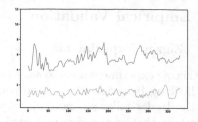

(a) Iteration 1 (sensors based): max and min inter-quadrotor distances

(b) Iteration 2 (sensor based): max and min inter-quadrotor distances

Fig. 2. This figure shows the inter-quadrotors distances among the followers for both trajectories executed in iteration 1 (left) and iteration 2 (right). The blue line shows the maximum inter-quadrotor distances while the orange one shows the minimum distance. We observe a considerable improvement in the second iteration comparing it the first one, as the decentralized controller has learned the cohesion and separation policy in the second iteration. The quadrotors remain collision-free in the second iteration and do not disperse. Knowing that in the first iteration we observe minor collisions but non of these collisions were not critical allowing us to complete the experiment. (Color figure online)

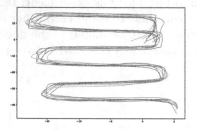 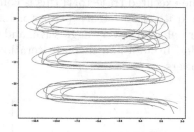

(a) Iteration 3 (sensor based): trajectories executed by all quadrotors

(b) Flocking model (position-based): trajectories executed by all quadrotors

Fig. 3. This figure shows the trajectory executed by the quadrotor in the third iteration (left) compared to the adapted Reynolds flocking model (right). The quadrotors start their trajectory at coordination $(0, 0)$ and end at $(5, -44)$. The leader is labeled in blue in both cases. By comparing the two trajectories, we can observe a similar performance between the flocking model (position-based) and the third iteration of the learned controller (wireless sensors-based).

We continue to train the controller iteratively, resulting in a third iteration with a performance similar to the flocking model in Fig. 3. The controller uses the wireless sensor data, while the flocking model using the absolute position acting as ground truth for swarming behavior. We observe that the followers' quadrotors respect distances among each other in a similar manner compared to the flocking model in Fig. 4.

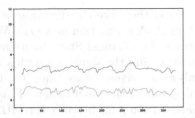 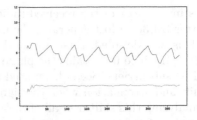

(a) Iteration 3 (sensor based): max and min inter-quadrotor distances

(b) Flocking model (position based): max and min inter-quadrotor distances

Fig. 4. Results of inter-agent distances when executing the zigzag trajectory by the quadrotors. The controller from the third iteration shows a similar performance compared to the flocking model. The quadrotors do not disperse nor collide with one another. These results show that the controller can be improved iteratively in order to achieve a performance compared to the flocking model.

6 Discussion and Future Work

In this paper, we presented I2SL, an Iterative Imitation Supervised Learning method used in order to resolve the challenge of decentralized controller design for a set of quadrotors with no computational power and endowed with a single wireless sensor. The objective of this method is to resolve the optimization issue offline rather than during the flight and to learn the flocking behavior for follower quadrotors while following the remotely controlled leader. This approach demonstrated the feasibility of a leader-followers swarm using MagicFlock, a Software In the Loop (SITL) simulation framework that is based on RotorS.

Wireless antennas are often intended to be used as a communication tool using the radio channel. One might consider this usage in order to share state information and leader commands between quadrotors. This method might work when the number of quadrotors is small. However, when the number of the agent increases, the communication channel tends to saturate, with a high loss of the packets sent between the transmitter and receiver. A possible solution would be is a re-transmission, but this might increase the communication delay. In both cases, the power consumption increases due to the frequent treatment of the sent or the received packets. Therefore, it is easier to have only one pilot that communicates with only the leader quadrotor, while the followers use the trained embedded controller and the wireless sensor to swarm around the leader.

When reading this work, one might question the type of wireless sensor that can be used with these robots. To this end, any available wireless communication tools that allow the estimation of Angle of Arrival (AoA) and signal strength can be used, such as Bluetooth, Zigbee, Ultra-Wideband (UWB). Among these wireless tools, we have considered using WiFi for several reasons, First, most commercial quadrotors are already embedded WiFi antennas, removing the cost for additional sensors that need to be embedded on each robot. Second, most integrated WiFi cards have several antennas installed on these robots allowing to estimate AoA of the received radio signal and therefore the direction of the emitter [29,30]. Most generally, the method for AoA estimation on COTS WiFi cards is well detailed. First, we need to extract the Channel State Information (CSI) [31] since it contains the phase information and the signal strength for all OFDM subcarriers. Second, we need to analyze the signal phase since it suffers a shift and attenuation when the signal propagates in the environment. Finally, by analyzing this shift over all of these subcarriers using for instance the MUSIC algorithm [32], one can easily deduce the AoA of the signal. This method can be used with a commodity WiFi card such as Intel 5300 since it has several antennas that can be arranged to a uniform antennas array.

To demonstrate the capacity of precise AoA estimation. Several researchers went even further by analyzing and smoothing the CSI values to create a decimeter localization systems [33,34] or even a system that has a similar performance to the ground truth [35]. However, the goal of future work is not to create a localization system for quadrotors nor to use fixed Access Points (AP) that act as beacons but instead is to use AoA estimation techniques and integrate them directly on real quadrotor platforms that are equipped with such antennas.

Finally, our further research will focus on transfer learning, from simulation to real quadrotors. Besides, we will adapt the designed method and find a suitable AoA estimation technique for real pico-quadrotors. In the medium term, our goal is to achieve outdoor swarms entirely based on wireless antennas acting as bearing and heading sensors.

References

1. Lebar Bajec, I., Heppner, F.: Organized flight in birds. Animal Behaviour **78**, 777–789 (2012)
2. Couzin, I., Krause, J., Franks, N., Levin, S.: Effective leadership and decision-making in animal groups on the move. Nature **433**, 513–516 (2005)
3. Nagy, M., Akos, Z., Biro, D., Vicsek, T.: Hierarchical group dynamics in pigeon flocks. Nature **464**(7290), 890–893 (2010)
4. Aoki, I.: A simulation study on the schooling mechanism in fish. Nippon Suisan Gakkaishi **48**(8), 1081–1088 (1982)
5. Beauchamp, G.: Group-size effects on vigilance: a search for mechanisms. Behavioural processes **63**, 141–145 (2003)
6. Grossman, D., Aranson, I.S., Jacob, E.B.: Emergence of agent swarm migration and vortex formation through inelastic collisions. New J. Phys. **10**(2), 023036 (2008). https://doi.org/10.1088
7. Vicsek, T., Zafeiris, A.: Collective motion. Phys. Rep. **517**(3), 71–140 (2012)
8. Trepat, X., et al.: Physical forces during collective cell migration. Nature Phys. **5**, 426–430 (2009)
9. Wu, Y., Kaiser, A.D., Jiang, Y., Alber, M.S.: Presented at the (2009)
10. Reynolds, C.W.: Flocks, herds and schools: a distributed behavioral model. SIGGRAPH Comput. Graph. **21**(4), 25–34 (1987). http://doi.acm.org/10.1145/37402.37406
11. Vicsek, T., Czirók, A., Ben-Jacob, E., Cohen, I., Shochet, O.: Novel type of phase transition in a system of self-driven particles. Phys. Rev. Lett. **75**(6), 1226 (1995)

12. Olfati-Saber, R.: Flocking for multi-agent dynamic systems: algorithms and theory. IEEE Trans. Autom. Control **51**(3), 401–420 (2006)
13. Virágh, C., et al.: Flocking algorithm for autonomous flying robots, vol. 9, 10 2013
14. Vásárhelyi, G., et al.: Outdoor flocking and formation flight with autonomous aerial robots. CoRR **abs/1402.3588** (2014)
15. Vásárhelyi, G., Virágh, C., Somorjai, G., Nepusz, T., Eiben, A.E., Vicsek, T.: Optimized flocking of autonomous drones in confined environments. Science Robotics, vol. 3, no. 20 (2018)
16. Schilling, F., Lecoeur, J., Schiano, F., Floreano, D.: Learning vision-based cohesive flight in drone swarms. CoRR, vol. abs/1809.00543 (2018). http://arxiv.org/abs/1809.00543
17. Schilling, F., Lecoeur, J., Schiano, F., Floreano, D.: Learning vision-based flight in drone swarms by imitation, CoRR, vol. abs/1908.02999 (2019). http://arxiv.org/abs/1908.02999
18. Schilling, F., Schiano, F., Floreano, D.: Vision-based flocking in outdoor environments (2020)
19. Mulgaonkar, Y., Kumar, V.: Towards open-source, printable pico-quadrotors (2014)
20. Ross, S., Gordon, G.J., Bagnell, J.A.: A reduction of imitation learning and structured prediction to no-regret online learning (2011)
21. Shrit, O., Filliat, D., Sebag, M.: Iterative Learning for Model Reactive Control: Application to autonomous multi-agent control. In: ICARA, Prague, Czech Republic, February 2021. https://hal.archives-ouvertes.fr/hal-03133162
22. Bhattacharyya, R.P., Phillips, D.J., Wulfe, B., Morton, J., Kuefler, A., Kochenderfer, M.J.: Multi-agent imitation learning for driving simulation. In: IEEE/RSJ International Conference on Intelligent Robots and Systems (IROS) 2018, pp. 1534–1539 (2018)
23. Le, H.M., Yue, Y., Carr, P., Lucey, P.: Coordinated multi-agent imitation learning. In: International Conference on Machine Learning. PMLR, 2017, pp. 1995–2003 (2017)
24. Furrer, F., Burri, M., Achtelik, M., Siegwart, R.: RotorS—a modular Gazebo MAV simulator framework. In: Koubaa, A. (ed.) Robot Operating System (ROS). SCI, vol. 625, pp. 595–625. Springer, Cham (2016). https://doi.org/10.1007/978-3-319-26054-9_23
25. Curtin, R.R.: Mlpack: a scalable c++ machine learning library. J. Mach. Learn. Res. **14**(1), 801–805 (2013). http://dl.acm.org/citation.cfm?id=2502581.2502606
26. Sanderson, C.: Armadillo: C++ template metaprogramming for compile-time optimization of linear algebra. Computational Statistics and Data Analysis **71** (2014)
27. Glorot, X., Bengio, Y.: Understanding the difficulty of training deep feedforward neural networks. In: Proceedings of the International Conference on Artificial Intelligence and Statistics (AISTATS 2010). Society for Artificial Intelligence and Statistics (2010)
28. Kingma, D.P., Ba, J.: Adam: a method for stochastic optimization (2014). arxiv:1412.6980. Comment: Published as a conference paper at the 3rd International Conference for Learning Representations, San Diego (2015). arxiv.org/abs/1412.6980
29. Paulraj, A., Reddy, V.U., Shan, T.J., Kailath, T.: Performance analysis of the music algorithm with spatial smoothing in the presence of coherent sources. In: MILCOM 1986 - IEEE Military Communications Conference: Communications-Computers: Teamed for the 90's, vol. 3, pp. 41.5.1–41.5.5 (1986)

30. Niculescu, D., Nath, B.: Vor base stations for indoor 802.11 positioning. In: Proceedings of the 10th Annual International Conference on Mobile Computing and Networking. In: MobiCom 2004, pp. 58–69. Association for Computing Machinery, New York (2004). https://doi.org/10.1145/1023720.1023727

31. Halperin, D., Hu, W., Sheth, A., Wetherall, D.: Tool release: gathering 802.11n traces with channel state information. SIGCOMM Comput. Commun. Rev. **41**(1), 53 (2011). https://doi.org/10.1145/1925861.1925870

32. Schmidt, R.: Multiple emitter location and signal parameter estimation (1979)

33. Kotaru, M., Joshi, K., Bharadia, D., Katti, S.: Spotfi: decimeter level localization using wifi. In: ser. SIGCOMM '15, New York, NY, USA (2015). https://doi.org/10.1145/2785956.2787487

34. Xiong, J., Jamieson, K.: Arraytrack: a fine-grained indoor location system. In: 10th USENIX Symposium on Networked Systems Design and Implementation (NSDI 13). Lombard, IL: USENIX Association, pp. 71–84, April 2013. https://www.usenix.org/conference/nsdi13/technical-sessions/presentation/xiong

35. Kotaru, M., Katti, S.: Position tracking for virtual reality using commodity wifi (2017)

Neural Network Classifier and Robotic Manipulation for an Autonomous Industrial Cork Feeder

André Salgueiro[1], Sofia Santos[1(✉)], Artur Pereira[1], Bernardo Cunha[1],
Eurico Pedrosa[1], José Luis Azevedo[1], Nuno Lau[1], Paulo Lopes[2],
and Tiago Gomes[3]

[1] Department of Electronics, Telecommunications and Informatics,
University of Aveiro, Aveiro, Portugal
{andre.salgueiro,m.sofia}@ua.pt
[2] Department of Physics, University of Aveiro, Aveiro, Portugal
[3] Azevedos - Industria, Maquinas e Equipamentos Industriais S.A, Lourosa, Portugal

Abstract. This paper presents a solution for an autonomous cork puncher feeder with a robotic arm using image processing techniques and a convolutional neural network. Due to the need for cork strips to be inserted into the puncher with a specific orientation, to produce high quality cork stoppers, the identification of the orientation of each cork strip on the conveyor belt is a necessity. In response to this problem a convolutional neural network is used to analyse images processed with subtracted background, to create a robust solution for cork strips classification. In the tests carried out, a classification accuracy of 100% was obtained in a test data set with 12 different cork strips.

Keywords: Cork · Deep learning · Convolutional neural network · Universal Robots · Computer vision

1 Introduction

This paper describes the design and implementation of an autonomous system with the objective of analysing and efficiently feeding cork strips to a cork puncher for the creation of cork stoppers. The cork industry has a large representation in Portugal with 642 companies producing over 40 million cork stoppers per day [1]. Portugal is the largest exporter of cork in the world, with cork representing 2% of its exported goods. The high demand of the wine industry for cork stoppers, which utilises 70.5% of the produced cork, requires innovation and automation of the production line to increase the overall productivity while minimising cork waste.

The created system addresses the productive aspect of feeding cork punchers with cork strips transported in a moving conveyor belt, where they are randomly placed, and, in order to produce the best quality cork stoppers, the strips have to be inserted with their belly side down, as this is where the cork is of the

© Springer Nature Switzerland AG 2021
G. Marreiros et al. (Eds.): EPIA 2021, LNAI 12981, pp. 433–444, 2021.
https://doi.org/10.1007/978-3-030-86230-5_34

highest quality and the puncher used for this project is manufactured to punch from the side and near the bottom. The solution for this problem consists in a combination of a robot arm, which performs the delivery movement of the cork strip to the puncher, and the acquisition, analysis and classification of images of the cork strip using a convolutional neural network, to identify its orientation (Back, Belly, Side with Belly Upwards and Side with Belly Downwards, examples in Fig. 1) and position on the conveyor belt.

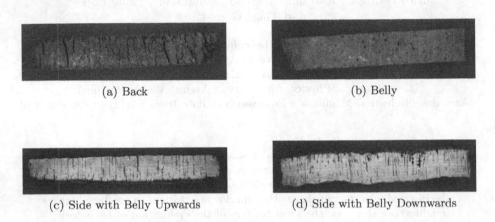

(a) Back

(b) Belly

(c) Side with Belly Upwards

(d) Side with Belly Downwards

Fig. 1. The four different classes of classification of the cork strip's orientation

Currently there are three types of cork punchers presented in the market: manual where the operator places the cork strip and handles the puncher through a pedal to extract the cork stopper; semi-manual where the puncher is always moving and the operator only places the cork strip to punch; automatic where the operator only feeds the machine with the cork strip making sure the strip is facing the correct way. All these three methods constantly require an operator. This paper proposes a solution to fully automate the system workflow in order to increase the quantity and speed of production of cork stoppers.

Previous works related to the analysis and classification of cork images are focused on analysing the texture [2,3], pattern recognition [4] or defect detection [5] either by using image processing or machine learning techniques. The created system is presented as an autonomous solution for the manipulation of cork strips, in which the analysis and classification of the images refers to the identification of the position and orientation of the cork strips. The paper is structured as follows, Sect. 2 presents an overview of the components that make up the system and a detailed description of the work done. The obtained results and conclusions are presented in Sects. 3 and 4, respectively.

2   Implementation

2.1   System Overview

The system can be divided into two phases, firstly the acquisition and analysis of cork strip images and secondly the manipulation, pick up and delivery of the cork strip to the puncher. The first phase comprises two components, a conveyor belt and an inspection tunnel with a camera, and the second phase is composed of a robot arm and a gripper.

The entire system (represented in Fig. 2) is managed by a computer that controls two units, the cork detection and classification unit (CDC unit) where the cork strip images, acquired by the camera, are processed and passed through the convolutional neural network for classification and the robot movement control unit (RMC unit) that controls all the movements of the robot.

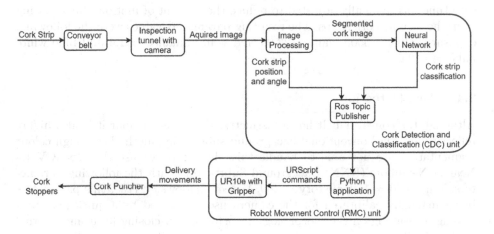

Fig. 2. Structural representation of the system

2.2   Conveyor Belt and Inspection Tunnel

To provide the computer vision system with a constant flow of new cork strips a conveyor belt is used, allowing for the transport of the cork strips at an adjustable speed. The belt is made on a uniform green colour to contrast with the cork strips.

The cork industry is prone to a lot of dirt and dust and considering the system uses a camera, its exposure to dust would interfere with the image classification, therefore an enclosed detection system was necessary. An illuminated box with a camera was placed on top of the conveyor belt to serve as an inspection tunnel where all cork strips go through to be detected and classified. This inspection tunnel has two LED strips placed on opposite ends to provide a controlled light environment so that the image acquisition is always carried out with the same lighting conditions.

2.3   Computer Vision

To properly detect and classify every cork strip going through the conveyor belt a single PointGrey BlackFly camera is placed on the top of a closed illuminated box (inspection tunnel) aiming down providing a bird's-eye view of the conveyor belt. This camera placement creates a perspective problem, as two cork strips, when on top of each other, will be detected as a single strip which could lead to an erroneous classification and create issues in the pick up of the cork piece. Therefore, in the scope of this project, it is guaranteed that the cork strips are separated when placed in the conveyor belt.

The conveyor belt material is reflective and the light of the inspection tunnel creates white spots on the captured camera images, however the positioning of the LED strips minimises the amount of reflection and allows for a clean image when the left and right borders of the raw capture are discarded.

The camera parameters were calibrated to reduce distortion and the exposure time was manually adjusted to reduce the amount of motion blur resulting from the moving cork strips. The resulting parameters values were the following: exposure value = 5000, gain = 23.95, red white balance = 1.4 and blue white balance = 2.6.

2.4   Cork Detection

Although the conveyor belt has a distinctive dark green colour it is also highly reflective and the conventional background subtraction methods through colour segmentation are not able to handle this. Therefore we use the OpenCV K-Nearest Neighbors (KNN) Background Subtractor (with the following parameters: Threshold = 150, History = 300, Detect shadows = True, this parameters being manually calibrated for the camera used) followed by a quick post processing, consisting on the morphology transformation closing [6] using a kernel of size (7, 7) to remove the noise caused by the cork texture providing a clear mask of the cork strips. Using this mask we extract the contours using OpenCV function *findContours* [7] and sort them by size while discarding the ones with very small areas belonging to leftover dust and cork particles presented in the conveyor belt as well as imperfections detected. When one or more cork strips arrive at the inspection tunnel and are within the camera's field of view the detected cork strip is extracted by finding the minimum rectangle involving the max contour using the OpenCV function *minAreaRect* [8]. This rectangle is then cropped and placed vertically using the OpenCV function *warpPerspective*. This is done to simplify the preparation of the image for the classifier. Each detected cork strip is tracked throughout the inspection tunnel and reported to the classifier for a temporary classification of the upwards face. When the cork strip passes through the camera's centre, its relative position on the belt, length and angle are calculated, through measurement of the pixel distance between the corners of the cork strip. The relation between the pixels and real distance was previously calibrated using a chess board with a known cell size, placed on the conveyor belt, by finding the corners of the cells and calculating their euclidean distance giving us a pixel to millimetre ratio. The neural network classifier is prompted for a final result which is an average of all the previous temporary classifications for the cork strip (Fig. 3).

In a first approach, the data set creation algorithm would start saving the images of the cork strips from the moment they appeared in the camera's field of view until they were no longer visible, providing a growing view of the entire cork strip, and to feed the Convolutional Neural Network (CNN) these images were scaled down to a fixed size. In order to avoid this scaling, which consequently loses a lot of small details from the texture of the cork, and avoid multiple similar images of the same cork strip (this happens when cork strip is too long), a fixed Region of Interest (ROI) is created and while the cork strip is moving through the inspection tunnel this ROI is constantly seeing a new part of the cork strip, providing a moving view of the cork strip.

Cropped images of a cork strip are grouped together and assigned a unique identifier while the conveyor belt is moving, giving us a collection of different pictures of the same cork strip to further improve the data set.

A total of three data sets are required, one for the training, one for validation and another for testing of the neural network. Building the data sets was done semi-manually, each cork strip being manually placed at the start of the conveyor belt one side at a time and assigned a label corresponding to the upwards face (Belly, Back, Side with Belly Upwards, Side with Belly Downwards) making sure all four sides of a single cork strip are used and not repeated. A total of 56 cork strips were used. The cork collection was split into the three required data sets using the unique cork strip identifiers to make sure two images of the same cork do not end up in different data sets. The amount of cork strips for each data set is 60% for the training data set, 20% for validation and the last 20% for testing, this being done for all four possible cork faces.

2.5   Neural Network

When handing over the cork strip to the cork puncher the robotic arm must guarantee that the belly side (the inner layer of the cork strip) is facing down, this is important because the puncher starts punching near the bottom of the strip, and the belly side is where the best quality cork is located. If the robotic arm delivers the cork strip with the belly side up, most of the cork stoppers produced will be unusable. If the cork stripped is handled on its side it would cause the cork puncher to jam and stop production. Given these situations, it is of the utmost importance to make sure that the classification is always correct and there is no room for mistakes. The approach chosen to tackle this was a Convolutional Neural Network (CNN), considered at the moment the state of art in image classification. This algorithm gives us a confidence value where we can fine tune and discard any classification that is not certain.

The chosen CNN architecture was inspired by the VGG16 model for its simple but effective classification. The VGG model was the winner of the ImageNet Large Scale Visual Recognition Challenge 2014 (ILSVRC2014) [9]. The network input is an RGB segmented image of the cork strip, scaled to a fixed size of

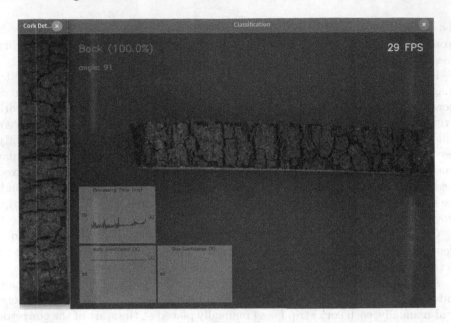

Fig. 3. Cork detection result

50×200 pixels. The hidden layers were fine tuned to our specific problem and, through a series of tests of multiple architectures, the best network architecture emerged (results of the different architectures in Fig. 8). The network is composed of a convolutional layer with a kernel size of 3×3 and 32 filters followed by a dropout of 25%, followed by a 2×2 max pooling layer with a stride of 2, it then goes through 2 fully connected dense layers with 128 filters, followed by a 50% dropout, and 64 filters followed by another 50% dropout. The dropouts were added to prevent over-fitting and a Rectified Linear Unit activation was added to all hidden layers. Finally, for the output, a dense softmax layer with 4 filters is added to predict one of the four possible faces of the cork strip. A graphical representation of the neural network is presented in Fig. 4.

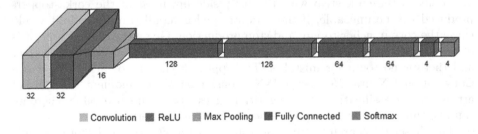

Fig. 4. Neural network architecture

2.6 Robot Arm

The pickup and transport of the cork strips from the conveyor belt to the puncher is performed by a robot arm that is placed at the end of the conveyor belt, beside the puncher, in a table of the same height. The selected robot was the collaborative manipulator UR10e from Universal Robots, presented in Fig. 5, which configures a robotic solution with great work capacity, high safety requirements and capacity for collaborative work. The UR10e robot arm has 6 degrees of freedom (DoF), a reach of 1300 mm and all joints have a 360 degree amplitude [10].

Fig. 5. Universal Robot UR10e robot arm

2.7 Gripper

Regarding the manipulation of the cork strips, the gripper should be capable of grasping the strips without damaging them. The selected gripper was a servo-electric GRIPKIT-E2 from Weiss Robotics, due to its integrated controller with the Universal Robots system.

2.8 Robot Arm Movement Controller

The RMC unit consists of a Python application that communicates directly with the UR10e robot through an Ethernet TCP socket and sends scripts in URScript language to execute movements. URScript is the robot programming language [11], which includes built-in variables and functions for motion and action control of the robot at the script level. As the gripper is integrated in the UR10e robot system it is possible to control it at the script level. This method allows communication without delays or interpolation of movements. The communication of this system unit with the CDC unit is made through a ROS Topic [12] using a message with the information of the position, in Cartesian coordinates, and rotation of the cork strip on the conveyor belt as well as the label of classification of the cork strip orientation.

Simulated Environment. To analyse and test the most efficient and safe movements, a simulated environment was developed using the Gazebo simulator. Accurate 3D models of the necessary equipment (conveyor belt, cork puncher and the robot arm) were modelled as a way to represent the real system (see Fig. 6).

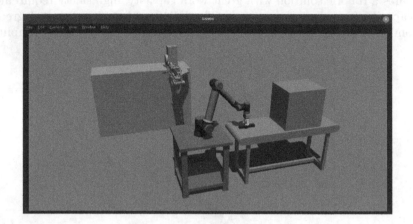

Fig. 6. Simulated environment

Delivery Motion. After passing the inspection tunnel, the CDC unit publishes the message and the application starts the sequence of the delivery movements, which can be divided into three phases. The first phase corresponds to the grasping of the cork strip from the conveyor belt, a combination of a relative Cartesian movement of UR10e Tool Center Point (TCP) to the pick point of the strip (the coordinates of this point were set to 10 cm from the tip of the strip), and a rotation of the TCP between 0 and 90° to match the angle of the cork strip.

The second phase, depending on the cork strip orientation (back, belly, side with belly upwards or side with belly downwards), triggers one of the 4 different sequences. These sequences consist of movements to well-defined positions that depend on the position of the puncher. For safety reasons, there are intermediate movements that guarantee a safe positioning of the robot, avoiding collisions when making the necessary rotations to deliver the cork strip with its belly side facing downwards.

The last phase is the insertion of the cork strip in the puncher entrance. The puncher has a small conveyor belt and pneumatic lever that grabs the cork strip and pulls it inside the puncher (see Fig. 7). To prevent the strip from falling or colliding with the puncher, the robot performs a small Cartesian movement in the direction of the puncher entrance and when the puncher closes the lever the gripper releases the cork strip and the robot returns to the starting position to initiate the grasp of another cork strip.

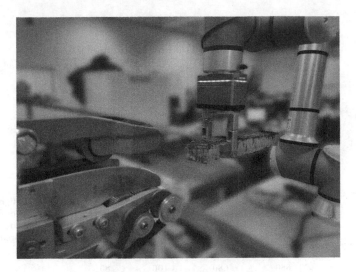

Fig. 7. Delivery of a cork strip

3   Results and Analysis

The overall data set was divided into three unique data sets with the composition presented in Table 1. In order to obtain the best possible classification accuracy, multiple architectures were tested following the same pattern of a convolutional layer followed by a ReLU activation and finally the max pooling. Then a series of fully connected layers (dense layers) leads to the final layer with a filter size of 4 (one for each class) with a softmax activation for the result. Multiple configurations were tested, consisting of conv-relu-maxpool blocks (1, 2 or 3) with varying filter sizes (32, 64 or 128), followed by a series of fully connected layers (0, 1 or 2) with varying filter sizes (64, 128 or 256). The best performing architectures are represented in the validation loss in Fig. 8. These networks were put through an accuracy test with never seen before cork strips to classify, saving the data from all predictions, including the confidence level of each prediction to manually analyse metrics such as number of correct predictions, lowest confidence level of a correct prediction and the highest confidence level of a wrong prediction.

To validate the performance of the classification a test data set, previously created with random cork strips that would not appear in the training or validation data sets, comprised of 12 unique cork strips of each side (Back, Belly, Side with belly upwards and Side with belly downwards) was used. The classifier was tested by predicting each image of the 12 cork strips on all 4 sides (48 total unique strips) for a total o 2491 images, managing to correctly predict all 2491 images. Since the algorithm provides us with a confidence level for each prediction, this metric was analysed and a minimum value of 51% and 54% was seen on two single frames of the same cork strip and since each cork strip is analysed an average of 52 times, the final classification does not take these values into account and ignores them (see Table 2).

Table 1. Composition of the data sets

	Training	Validation	Testing
Back	32	12	12
Belly	32	12	12
Side belly upwards	32	12	12
Side belly downwards	32	12	12
Total	128	48	48

Table 2. Neural network classification results

	Correct predictions	Total predictions	Accuracy	Lowest confidence correct prediction	Highest confidence wrong prediction
Back	589	589	100	51	0
Belly	680	680	100	85	0
Side belly upwards	629	629	100	100	0
Side belly downwards	593	593	100	99	0
Total	2491	2491			

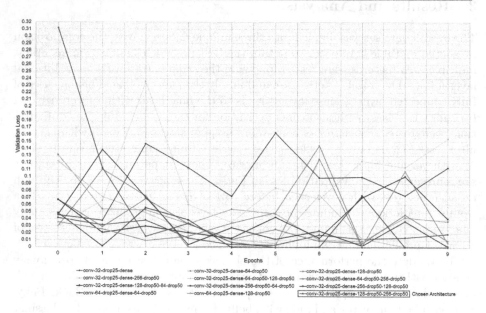

Fig. 8. Validation loss for each epoch in different network architectures

4   Conclusion and Future Work

This paper presents a solution to the cork stopper industry of an automatic feeder of cork strips to a puncher. The neural network used shows positive results since it was able to correctly identify, 100% of the time, cork strips that it had never seen before. This result is due to the fact that multiple pictures of a single cork strip are analysed and the final result is an average of the classification of all the images (Table 2), so even if some misclassification occurs the end result will be correct. This project was created for an industrial environment where there is no margin for error, as a misclassification could jam the machine and stop production.

The entire data sets were composed of cork strips that were production ready straight from the factory, meaning they would be used to produce cork stoppers. Initially we considered that, to increase the robustness of the system, there were some factors that could have been taken into account such as the humidity of the cork, which could potentially influence its colour and texture. However to add this factor all the cork strips would have to be soaked in water and if there were any changes they would be permanent. We were unsure of the influence of this factor in the real case because of the process that cork goes through before it is cut into strips [13], so we did not include it in our data sets.

The handling of the cork strips was carried out successfully but some cases were detected that may present an extra challenge to the delivery. Very convex or concave cork strips need to be picked up at a different point so that their insertion in the puncher can be performed without collisions. This implies that the curvature of the cork strip is detected, but as the inspection tunnel only has one vertical camera, it is impossible to identify the curvature in certain orientations of the cork strip. These cases are special and uncommon, but to increase the robustness of the system, a solution could be created with more cameras in the inspection tunnel.

Acknowledgments. This work was funded by ANI (POCI-FEDER) in the context of the Project XtremeCork POCI-01-0247-FEDER-033140.

References

1. Cortiça, A.P.: Cork yearbook 19/20 (2019). https://www.apcor.pt/wp-content/uploads/2019/12/boletim_estatistico_apcor_2019.pdf
2. Paniagua, B., Vega-Rodríguez, M.A., Gómez-Pulido, J.A., Sánchez-Pérez, J.M.: Automatic texture characterization using gabor filters and neurofuzzy computing. Int. J. Adv. Manuf. Technol. **52**(1–4), 15–32 (2011). https://doi.org/10.1007/s00170-010-2706-3
3. Paniagua, B., Vega-Rodríguez, M.A., Bustos-García, P., Gómez-Pulido, J.A., Sánchez-Pérez, J.M.: Advanced texture analysis in cork quality detection. 2007 5th IEEE International Conference on Industrial Informatics, pp. 311–315 (2007). https://doi.org/10.1109/indin.2007.4384775
4. Georgieva, A., Jordanov, I.: Intelligent visual recognition and classification of cork tiles with neural networks. IEEE Trans. Neural Networks **20**(4), 675–685 (2009). https://doi.org/10.1109/tnn.2008.2011903
5. Lima, J.L., Costa, P.G.: Modular approach to real-time cork classification using image processing. In: 2005 IEEE Conference on Emerging Technologies and Factory Automation 2, pp. 361–368 (2005). https://doi.org/10.1109/etfa.2005.1612701

444   A. Salgueiro et al.

6. Open Source Computer Vision Library: Morphological Transformations, 4.1.0 edn. https://docs.opencv.org/4.1.0/d9/d61/tutorial_py_morphological_ops.html
7. Open Source Computer Vision Library: Contours, 4.1.0 edn. https://docs.opencv.org/4.1.0/d4/d73/tutorial_py_contours_begin.html
8. Open Source Computer Vision Library: Creating bounding rotated boxes and ellipses for contours, 4.1.0 edn. https://docs.opencv.org/4.1.0/de/d62/tutorial_bounding_rotated_ellipses.html
9. Simonyan, K., Zisserman, A.: Very deep convolutional networks for large-scale image recognition. International Conference on Learning Representations (2015)
10. Robots, U.: Ur10e user manual. https://s3-eu-west-1.amazonaws.com/ur-support-site/77195/99405_UR10e_User_Manual_en_Global.pdf
11. Robots, U.: URScript API reference. https://s3-eu-west-1.amazonaws.com/ur-support-site/32554/scriptManual-3.5.4.pdf
12. Conley, K., Thomas, D.: Robot operating system - topics. http://wiki.ros.org/rostopic, version ROS Melodic Morenia
13. Cortiça, A.P.: Production of natural cork stoppers. https://www.apcor.pt/en/cork/processing/industrial-path/natural-cork-stoppers/

NOPL - Notification Oriented Programming Language - A New Language, and Its Application to Program a Robotic Soccer Team

João Alberto Fabro[✉], Leonardo Araujo Santos, Matheus Diniz de Freitas, Adriano Francisco Ronszcka, and Jean Marcelo Simão

UTFPR-Federal University of Technology - Paraná, Curitiba, Brazil
{fabro,jeansimao}@utfpr.edu.br

Abstract. This paper presents the development of NOPL (Notification Oriented Programming Language) Version 1.2, and its compiler, to implement a complete solution for a team of robotic soccer players. The NOPL language implements the concepts proposed by the Notification Oriented Paradigm (NOP), that evolves together concepts from both declarative and imperative programming paradigms. At first, a prototypical version of the language and compiler (version 1.0), was developed to evaluate the feasibility of programming within this new paradigm. Although successful, this first version had some limitations, which made difficult the development of complex applications that solve real problems. In this sense, this paper introduces version 1.2 of the NOPL language and compiler, in which is possible to create complex applications in an easier and direct way. This new version is then evaluated in the development of a complete control software for robot soccer matches (Robocup), using a simulator for the Small Size League (SSL) category. The control program developed in NOPL V1.2 was then compared, in terms of code complexity and maintenance level, with functionally equivalent solutions developed with NOPL 1.0 and a previously developed control system, in C++ programming language from the Imperative Paradigm (Object Oriented). Experiments realized with NOPL 1.2 showed its easy of use, allowing for a much more concise expression of rules for a team of 6 robots, when compared to NOPL 1.0 (61% fewer lines of code for the same functionalities).

Keywords: Notification Oriented Paradigm · Rule-Oriented Programming Language · Robot soccer · Small Size League (SSL)

1 Introduction

The main currently used programming techniques, such as Object Oriented Programming (OOP) of the Imperative Paradigm (IP) and Rule Based Systems (RBS) of the Declarative Paradigm (DP), lead to the development of applications

© Springer Nature Switzerland AG 2021
G. Marreiros et al. (Eds.): EPIA 2021, LNAI 12981, pp. 445–455, 2021.
https://doi.org/10.1007/978-3-030-86230-5_35

with strong coupling of causal expressions and unnecessary evaluations [1, 2]. Aimed at solving such deficiencies present in these programming paradigms, the Notification Oriented Paradigm (NOP) was proposed.

In NOP, all the decision making is performed by rules, that receive notifications only when a change happens in the value of any variable. Rule entities present a new way of performing inferences in terms of evaluations of logical-causal expressions. The inferences are accomplished through small, reactive and decoupled computational entities that collaborate with each other through very precise and decoupled notifications, which compose a collaborative notification chain [3].

Since each component of NOP is smartly reactive, precisely connected to other components in a 'notification graph', and only propagates notifications when it is actually needed, this paradigm is diverse of other approaches to programming and software development [4], In NOP there are no explicit redundant loops like in an imperative programming, or implicit redundant loops like in monolithic inference engines of declarative programming, and every logic-causal decision is explicit in the definitions of rule entities, in a rule-oriented way. Also, NOP is different from "event" based approaches, since every change in the value of any variable can start a notification chain.

The first NOP implementations where in the form of frameworks over usual imperative languages (such as C++, Java and C#), naturally providing to them new meaning and connotation by means of the notification orientation. Even if the results achieved with these NOP frameworks were proper, they would not be as proper as those obtained from a NOP specific programming language, so the Notification Oriented Programming Language (called NOPL 1.0) was developed [5]. Despite bringing good results in terms of performance for the applications, NOPL 1.0 did not represent a major advancement in ease of programming. This is mainly due to some limitations of the language and its compiler, which causes the programmer to have to explicitly write every rule for the application, which, on several occasions, lead to the creation of several, very similar rules. In this sense, this paper presents a new NOPL language and compiler, version 1.2, which allows the development of NOP applications in a more concise way, enabling an easier design of software under this paradigm. This new version is compared, in terms of code complexity and maintainability level, using as test-bench a robot soccer control software developed in both NOPL 1.2, and NOPL 1.0, and also with a functionally identical approach developed in C++, using IP/OOP (Imperative Paradigm/Object Oriented Programming). NOPL is proposed as a general use language, and although applicable to robotic programming, does not qualify as a "robot programming language" [6].

The remainder of the paper is organized as follows. Section 2 presents the concepts of the Notification Oriented Paradigm for software development. In Sect. 3, the NOPL programming language is presented, and the application of this technique and language to develop a complete control program for a team of soccer playing robots is presented in Sects. 4 and 5. Finally, in Sect. 6, some conclusions and possibilities of future work are also presented.

2   Notification Oriented Programming

Although it takes advantage of IP (Imperative) and DP (Declarative) Paradigms concepts, NOP presents a new way of structuring and executing the logic of computational programs, a fact that would justify its classification as a paradigm [2]. NOP allows the expression of software dynamics and its cause-and-effect logic by means of notifications, which promotes a high level of decoupling and then can be executed in parallel [2]. This characteristic differentiates it from the behavior of IP programs, in which the logic of the program is totally dependent on the execution sequence, and from the RBS (Rule Based Systems), where the execution sequence is abstracted and dependent on the used monolithic inference mechanism [2].

In NOP, computational entities being generically called FBEs (Fact Base Elements). By means of their Attribute Entities (related to data or facts) and Method Entities (related with functionalities or services), FBEs are subject of logical-causal correlation through Rule entities, which are also fundamental elements of NOP.

Actually, the Attributes of FBEs are capable of precisely notifying the concerned Rules which evaluate their states. If the Rule approves itself, it can instigate Methods of FBEs to execute. However, all that happens by means of sub-entities concerned to the Rules, which compose a notifications chain. Namely, each Rule has a Condition Entity and an Action Entity. Still, each Condition is related to one or more Premise Entities, whereas each Action is related to one or more Instigation Entity. Figure 1 presents a complete example of a *Rule*, composed of all its sub-entities.

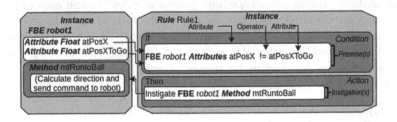

Fig. 1. Example of *Rule* in NOP.

3   The Notification Oriented Programming Language

A first attempt to develop a complete programming language for NOP (NOPL 1.0), was presented in [5]. In general, the source code of an application developed using NOPL follows a declarations pattern, where the FBEs that make up the application are first declared, then the instances of FBEs that will be used are declared, and finally the set of Rules that govern the behavior of the system is declared. First, the developer needs to define the FBEs of his program. Then the developer needs to declare the instances of such FBEs. Subsequently, the Rules must be defined, in order to specify each causal logical evaluation of the states of the instances of FBEs, that occur automatically through notifications. Finally, it is possible to add specific code in the target language of the compiler (*main* code block), that can be chosen during the compilation process (both C or C++ can be selected as target language) [5]. It is important to make clear the most fundamental aspect of this new programming paradigm: all decisions are specified in the form of rules. In NOP *Methods*, there is only the execution of mathematical calculations, call to external functionalities, and change of *Attributes* states, but decision commands such as "if" and "switch/case" are not allowed, leaving all the decisions to be modelled as NOP rules. Thus, programming in NOP is much more "declarative", with the difference that all the inferences are made over "object-like" entities called FBEs, with their encapsulated *Attributes* and *Methods*, providing a new way of thinking about software development.

One of the main motivations behind the development of NOP and NOPL was the increase in execution efficiency that could be obtained by avoiding re-evaluations of comparison statements that occur even when the variable (or variables) compared haven't changed their values. This re-evaluation is common in any loop inside every source code, but it is even more present in robotics applications, such as the robot soccer application presented in this paper. But a secondary advantage, in the opinion of the authors, is the higher level of organization that NOP brings to source code. Since *Attributes* and *Methods* are defined in the same *FBE*, some of the advantages of the object oriented approach are maintained (such as encapsulation and information hiding). On the other hand, *Methods* can only execute calculations/external access, and thus all the decision making process (also known as "business rules" in the area of software engineering) are declared, together, in an specific area of the source code (the *Rules* section). Thus, an explicit separation is created between *Methods*, that only perform actions or calculations, and "decisions", that are explicit taken by notification of *Rules*. Listing 1.1 present a simplified example of a complete program in NOPL.

```
fbe  Robot
      attributes
          float  atRobotPosX  0.0
      end  attributes
      methods
          method  mtRunToBall  ( ... )
      end  methods
end  fbe

fbe  Ball
      attributes
          float  atBallPosX  0.0
      end  attributes
      methods
          ...
      end  methods
end  fbe

inst  Robot  robot1
inst  Ball  ball
```

```
rule rlRunToBallRobot1
    condition
        subcondition condRobot1NotBallPos
            premise prRb1NotBallPos robot1.atRobotPosX != ball.
                atBallPosX
        end subcondition
    end condition
    action
        instigation inRb1Move robot1.mtRunToBall();
    end action
end rule
```

Listing 1.1. NOPL Source Code Example

When developing NOP applications using NOPL 1.0, it is noticeable that there is the need to write very similar lines of code along the source code. Since each of the Rules present in the source code is related to a specific instance of a FBE, if there are 2 or more instances of one FBE, it is necessary to replicate the rule for each instance. This need is error prone, and significantly difficulties maintenance, since any change in a rule has to be manually replicated. Also, the number of Rules to be declared is directly proportional to the number of instances of FBEs. Because of this, when developing NOP applications using NOPL 1.0, it is noticeable the need to write lines of code very similar throughout the source code. For each new instance of FBE created, new Rules and consequently new lines of code must be added to the system, resulting in increased size and complexity of the source code.

In order to exemplify the presented problem, a robotic soccer game, such as those proposed by Robocup [7], was selected. The Small Size League (SSL) is a Robocup league in which two teams of small robots (of cylindrical shape, with no more than 180 mm of diameter, and 150 mm of height) compete in an arena with a vision system positioned from the top, providing a complete view of the field, its robots and the ball. In this category, 8 vs 8 robots (subcategory A) or 6 vs 6 robots (subcategory B) have to play autonomously, usually controlled by a central computer for each team, that receives the position of each robot and the ball, and defines actions for each robot player to execute. The complete rulebook is available at the category website[1]. The behavior of each robot depends on the position (function) assigned to it.

A robot can be either a goalkeeper, a defender, a midfield, an attacker, or any other role specified by the programmer. Usually, only when changing the role of goalkeeper it is necessary to ask for permission from the referee, otherwise robots can change their roles. It is common that some robots stop working during the game (due to electronic or mechanical failure), so it is also possible to exchange players from the bench to the game, or otherwise exchange roles between two robot players during the match. Thus, each robot could be modeled as an FBE that has only its Attributes, such as position in the field, its number, role, status (playing or in the bench, for instance), battery status, and so on. With only one robot (R1) present at the start, the control system could be created with the following Rules:

---

[1] http://ssl.robocup.org.

– *Rule* 1: If R1's position is 'defender' then execute the method 'defend'.
– *Rule* 2: If R1's position is 'attacker' then execute the method 'attack'.

However, if it is necessary to expand this application in order to control two robots (R1 and R2), using version 1.0 of NOPL, it would be necessary to double the number of Rules that govern the behavior of the system in order for both to operate correctly. In this case, the system would present the following Rules:

– *Rule* 1: If R1's position is 'defender' then execute the method 'defend'.
– *Rule* 2: If R1's position is 'attacker' then execute the method 'attack'.
– *Rule* 3: If R2's position is 'defender' then execute the method 'defend'.
– *Rule* 4: If R2's position is 'attacker' then execute the method 'attack'.

In order to facilitate the development of NOP applications with multiple instances of FBEs and multiple Rules, a new concept has been inserted in NOPL 1.2, presented here, for programming NOP: FBE Rule applications. A FBE Rule is defined as a Rule that, instead of being related to an instance of FBE, is related to an FBE. Thus, for each new instance, the entire set of FBE Rules associated with the FBE will be created automatically. This new concept reduces the need for code redundancy in the Rules declaration, making the number of Rules to be declared independent of the number of instances of FBEs.

4   Case Study - Control of 6 Robots for the Small Size League (SSL) Category - In Simulation

In order to compare more effectively the real benefits of using the FBE Rules concept in the development of NOP applications, the development of a known complex application was chosen as a case study 1. The application referred to in this article is within the scope of robot control of robots according to Robocup's SSL category.

In order to allow software development without relying on real robots, a SSL simulator was used. This environment consists of two applications: *GrSim Simulator* [8] and *RefereeBox*. GrSim Simulator is a functional simulator of the Robocup SSL game environment. Simulated robots have characteristics very close to real ones, such as dimensions, maximum speed, inertia and acceleration. In addition, this application is responsible for sending information about objects in the field for the robot control system. Figure 2 presents a screenshot with both applications running, that allow for simulated soccer matches to be executed. Only 2 robots from one team appear, but a complete match comprises 2 teams of 6 robots each.

Upon receiving such information, the application that controls the robots reads the data for each one of them, processes them, and sends specific commands to each of the robots to grSim Simulator. The simulator will execute the received commands, update the actions using the simulated physics and obtain the new perceptions of the environment.

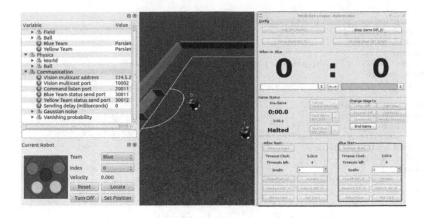

Fig. 2. GrSim Simulator (left) and RefereeBox (right). (Color figure online)

The Referee Box application, in turn, is a simple program that allows a neutral operator to send orders issued by the referee directly to the software of the competing teams. In addition to sending the referee commands, Referee Box also acts as an auxiliary utility for the referee, in which it is possible to keep track of the time of play, goals scored and the yellow and red cards.

In this context, based on three variables, namely cmdReferee, lastCmd and teamColor, the control system must be able to evaluate and determine the behavior of each of the robots being controlled. The variable cmdReferee represents the last command sent by the Referee Box application. The variable lastCmd, in turn, represents the predecessor value sent by the Referee Box application, that is, the penultimate command received. The variable TeamColor represents the color of the team being controlled, being able to assume the value Yellow (Yellow) or Blue (Blue).

Using NOPL, each robot to be controlled was represented by an instance of *FBE Robot*. As already mentioned, in the current version of NOPL each *Rule* is associated with an instance of *FBE*, as presented in Listing 1.2. In analyzing the code presented, it is possible to observe that the two are very similar in their statements. The only real difference between them is the instance of *FBE Robot* with which each of them relates. In this sense, it is clear the code redundancy for the construction of *Rules* in this initial version of NOPL. In Listing 1.3 the same behaviour is attained by using a *fbeRule*, that is a rule declared internally to the *Robot* FBE, that is very similar to 'classes' in object oriented code. But in NOPL 1.2, in addition to the attributes and methods, this 'class definition' also has templates for rules. Each time this FBE is instantiated, the compiler would create the correspondent rules, using the specific attributes of this instance, avoiding the necessity for the programmer to explicit declare all the rules for all instances of each FBE.

```
rule rlMoveRobot1
  condition
    subcondition condition1
```

```
        premise robot1.atPos != robot1.atPosToGo
      end_subcondition
    end_condition
    action
      instigation inMoveRobot1 robot1.mtExecuteMove();
    end_action
  end_rule

rule rlMoveRobot2
  condition
    subcondition condition2
      premise robot2.atPos != robot2.atPosToGo
    end_subcondition
  end_condition
  action
    instigation inMoveRobot2 robot2.mtExecuteMove();
  end_action
end_rule
```

Listing 1.2. *Rules* developed with NOPL 1.0.

```
fbe Robot
  attributes
    int atPosX;
    int atPosToGoX;
  end_attributes
  methods
    mtExecuteMove();
  end_methods
  fbeRule rlRobotMove
    condition
      subcondition condition1
        premise prRobotMoveX Robot.atPosX != Robot.atPosToGoX
      end_subcondition
    end_condition
    action
      instigation inMoveX Robot.mtExecuteMove();
    end_action
  end_fbeRule
end_fbe
```

Listing 1.3. *FBE Rule* created with NOPL 1.2.

5   Experimental Results

In order to verify the benefits of using FBE Rules in NOP applications, two control systems for a simulated soccer match of NOP robots, according to rules and characteristics of the SSL category, were developed. The first was developed using NOPL 1.0, the second used the new version of NOPL, with support for *FBE Rules*. Both systems were compared, in terms of code complexity, with a functionally equivalent solution built on the IP/OOP by other developer, which was used as a basis for comparison as being considered standard in the software development industry. The metrics used for comparisons of source code were the number of lines of code (LOC) and number of tokens. For the maintainability level, the metric used was the time taken to add a new functional requirement to the application in question.

For counting the amount of tokens present in the source code, a lexical analyzer was created with the well known *flex* tool [9] to generate lexical analysers.

Table 1 displays the measured data (number of lines of code and amount of tokens) present in each of the developed source codes.

Table 1. Results from comparing code size

	IP/OOP(C++)	NOPL 1.0	NOPL 1.2
Lines of code	3.649	8.578	3.357
Tokens	24.173	40.813	19.254

The observed difference between NOL 1.0 and NOPL 1.2 in Table 1 is due to the fact that, in NOPL 1.0, the developer has to declare the same set of *Rules* for each of the 6 instances of the *FBE* Robot, thus generating much more source code. In addition, using the concept of *FBE Rules*, thereby redundancy in the *Rules* declaration is mitigated and causes the number of lines of code and tokens to be even smaller than the results obtained by the solution developed in C++ under IP/OOP.

In order to compare the maintenance level of the NOP application source code and the IP/OOP application, an adaptive maintenance activity was proposed. A new functional requirement should be added in each of these *programs*. The functional requirement chosen for this comparison determines that, when the command received from the application '*Referee Box*' is '*halt*' (i.e. suspending the match), two robots must move to near the ball and perform successive change of passes until the matc,h is restarted. This requirement was proposed only as a way of assessing maintainability, and not as a real rule of robot soccer.

The comparison metrics used to measure the maintainability level were the time taken to develop the code required for the new requirement and the number of lines changed in the source code. The time used for maintenance is directly linked to the cost of the maintenance process of a software and therefore defines the feasibility of the maintenance to be performed [10].

In order to make the comparison fair and impartial, two developers of the original control systems, authors of the control solution developed under the IP/OOP, were invited to contribute to this activity, developing the new requirement in C++ (each one its own version). Thus, a possible learning curve for understanding the existing source code would not interfere with the comparison.

After about 4 h of activities, it was verified that the solutions developed by both developers approached the behavior expected by the new requirement. When the '*Halt*' command is received, the *kicker* robot moves toward the ball. However, the pass does not run towards the other robot (*partner*). In addition, after the first pass, the robots begin to move to positions different from the expected ones. Thus, both solutions developed under the IP/OOP were not able to meet the proposed new functional requirement.

Both developers reported that the main difficulty of programming this new behavior is in the dynamics necessary for the robots to execute the pass and, in the sequence, to position themselves to receive the pass of their companion.

Using IP/OOP, the programmer must explicitly state the action that must be performed and when it should be sequentially executed. However, robot soccer is a dynamic environment in which it is difficult to predict the sequence in which different situations will occur.

On the other hand, the addition of the new requirement was easily performed in the two NOP applications (NOPL 1.0 and NOPL 1.2). This is mainly due to the way in which the behavior of the robots is expressed through *Rules* in the NOP applications, facilitating the activity of identifying the parts of the architecture that should be changed to accommodate the new requirement.

In this way, work on adding the new requirement to the system focused on creating *Rules* that would be able to perform the action described by the requirement. Because it is a dynamic behavior, involving both the spatial perception of the field and movements, three new *Rules* for each of the two robots were created. These rules aim to position each of the robots next to the ball and make the robot that is closest to the ball move to the ball and make the pass to a teammate.

The time taken to complete the solution, that is, to code the *Rules* that should be added to the system and implement them, was approximately one hour for both NOPL 1.0 and NOPL 1.2. Altogether, about 80 new lines of code were added to the source code of the application developed using version 1.2 of NOPL and 534 new lines in the solution developed using NOPL 1.0.

6 Conclusions

The results show that the use of the FBE Rules concept allowed to create a functionally identical application as developed from version 1.0 of NOPL using 61% fewer lines of code and 52% less *tokens*. This directly influences in the easiness of application development in NOPL by allowing the source code to be More concise, pragmatic, and structured, presenting a number of tokens and line numbers close enough to those presented by the solution developed in PI/OOP, however with the difference of a rule-oriented approach with decision well organized and easily understandable and changeable by any developer.

In order to evaluate the maintainability of NOPL code, a new functional requirement was implemented in both NOPL 1.0 and 1.2, as well as in the previous equivalent PI/OOP C++ solution.

When comparing the process of adding a new requirement in applications developed from NOPL it is possible to observe that NOPL 1.0 needs many more lines of code to solve the same problem when compared to version 1.2. By using the concept of *FBE Rule*, introduced in NOPL 1.2, it was possible to solve the problem with only 80 new lines of code against the 534 required in the 1.0 version of NOPL. This represents an economy of approximately 85% of lines of code and has a direct impact on the speed of development and the maintainability level of the application.

In addition to the presented results, before the control of the robotic soccer team, only small applications had been developed using NOPL in order to validate distinct functionalities of this new programming language and paradigm.

The main reason for this is the bureaucracy that the developer has, using NOPL version 1.0, to create and organize the source code when it presents multiple instances of *FBEs* and a large set of *Rules*. However, using the concept of *FBE Rule* presented in this paper, it was possible to develop a robot soccer control application of known complexity. This opens up new horizons for NOP and demonstrates that it can be used to solve problems that require more complex *software* solutions.

As future works, the research team is interested in how to better evaluate the advantages in performance, and code organization, between NOPL 1.2 and IP/OOP C++ code, and thus new software for other leagues of robots would be developed by several programmers, aiming to obtain quantitative data about productivity and maintainability of both NOPL and C++ source code.

References

1. Simão, J.M.: A contribution to the development of a HMS simulation tool and proposition of a meta-model for holonic control. Ph.D. thesis, School in Electrical Engineering and Industrial Computer Science (CPGEI) at Federal University of Technology - Paraná (UTFPR, Brazil) and Research Center For Automatic Control of Nancy (CRAN) - Henry Poincaré University (UHP, France) (2005)
2. Linhares, R.R., Simão, J.M., Stadzisz, P.C.: NOCA - a notification-oriented computer architecture. IEEE Lat. Am. Trans. **13**(5), 1593–1604 (2015)
3. Simão, J.M., et al.: Notification oriented and object oriented paradigm comparison via sale system. J. Softw. Eng. Appl. **5**(09), 695–710 (2012). ISSN 1945–3116. https://doi.org/10.4236/jsea.2012.56047
4. Banaszewski, R.F., Stadzisz, P.C., Tacla, C.A., Simão., J.M.: Notification oriented paradigm (NOP): a software development approach based on artificial intelligence concepts. In: Proceedings of Logic Applied to Technology, Santos/Brazil, 21–23 November, pp. 216–222. Citeseer (2007)
5. Ronszcka, A.F., Ferreira, C.A., Stadzisz, P.C., Fabro, J.A., Simão, J.M.: Notification-oriented programming language and compiler. In: 2017 VII Brazilian Symposium on Computing Systems Engineering (SBESC), pp. 125–131 (November 2017)
6. Wang, X., Zhang, J.: Rpl: A robot programming language based on reactive agent. In: Proceedings of the 2017 2nd International Conference on Electrical, Automation and Mechanical Engineering, EAME 2017, pp. 250–255. Atlantis Press (April 2017)
7. Asada, M., Veloso, M., Kraetzschmar, G.K., Kitano, H.: RoboCup: today and tomorrow. In: Experimental Robotics VI, vol. 250, p. 369 (1999)
8. Monajjemi, V., Koochakzadeh, A., Ghidary, S.S.: grSim – RoboCup small size robot soccer simulator. In: Röfer, T., Mayer, N.M., Savage, J., Saranlı, U. (eds.) RoboCup 2011. LNCS (LNAI), vol. 7416, pp. 450–460. Springer, Heidelberg (2012). https://doi.org/10.1007/978-3-642-32060-6_38
9. Paxson, V.: Flex, version 2.5 (1990). http://www.gnu.org/software/flex
10. Arthur, L.J.: Software Evolution: The Software Maintenance Challenge. Wiley-Interscience, New York (1988)

Compound Movement Recognition Using Dynamic Movement Primitives

Ali H. Kordia[1,2]([✉]) and Francisco S. Melo[1,2]

[1] INESC-ID, Lisbon, Portugal
`fmelo@inesc-id.pt`
[2] Instituto Superior Técnico, University of Lisbon, Lisbon, Portugal
`ali.kordia@tecnico.ulisboa.pt`

Abstract. This paper proposes a method for recognizing compound trajectories. Given a library of pre-learned movements described using dynamic movement primitives, our approach is able to break down an observed trajectory into its individual components, each of which is a segment of one of the movements in the library. We build on previous work that uses critical points for movement recognition and prediction, and extend it to handle trajectories comprising multiple segments from possibly different movements. Our approach assumes that each segment in the observed trajectory is either the initial segment of a new primitive or the continuation of the previous segment. Then, given a partial trajectory, our method is able to predict the most likely next target—i.e., the end-point of the movement currently being executed, if the latter is executed to the end. By using an effective search tree, our approach is able to run at execution time and provide an efficient way for action recognition and prediction, which has applications in human-robot interaction scenarios. We validate our approach both in simulation and in a human-robot interaction scenario involving the Baxter robot.

Keywords: Movement recognition · Movement prediction · Compound movements · Dynamic movement primitives

1 Introduction

The interaction between humans and robots has become more widespread. Robots act to cooperate with humans in all areas of our daily life. The ability of a robot to understand humans and respond quickly during the interaction is, therefore, a fundamental skill that everyday robotic platforms should have. Towards the development of such skills, robots should recognize and understand

This work was partially supported by national funds through FCT, Fundação para a Ciência e a Tecnologia, under projects UIDB/50021/2020 and PTDC/CCI-COM/7203/2020. The first author acknowledges the Ph.D. grant from the Global Platform for Syrian Students. The authors thank Miguel Vasco for useful discussions and revisions of the document.

G. Marreiros et al. (Eds.): EPIA 2021, LNAI 12981, pp. 456–468, 2021.
https://doi.org/10.1007/978-3-030-86230-5_36

the actions of humans, even if they are complex and comprise several different movements.

During infancy, humans build a "library" of new movements by learning to combine simpler movements [5]. This method of learning complex movements allows humans to learn how to carry out complex tasks. The ability to combine simple motions into more complex ones has also been a topic of intense research in the robotics community [6,8,14,15].

In this paper, we look at the converse problem: can we recognize a complex movement as the combination of several simpler movements and, if so, which? The ability to break down a movement into its simpler components is fundamental not only for recognition purposes but also if the robot wants to replicate the observed movement: instead of having to learn the new movement from scratch, it can use simpler movements it already knows (and which were recognized by observation) and compose them to perform a more complex one [6].

There is a significant volume of work on movement recognition and prediction. For example, some works propose the use of *hidden Markov models* (HMM) to recognize motions [1,9,16,19,20] or to compute a probability distribution over a set of pre-learned trajectories [2]. Yoon et al. [20] and Kordia and Melo [7] use specific features of the observed trajectory to facilitate recognition. However, all previous works assume that the observed trajectory is atomic and corresponds (or is close) to one of a set of pre-learned trajectories. Such methods are not designed to deal with compound trajectories.

Some works do address complex movement recognition, assuming that the observed movement is obtained as the combination of *complete* simpler motions [3]. Maeda et al. [12] use a probabilistic model (I-ProMPs) to distinguish movements, whereby the observed path is approached with the closest human action to it. Ma et al. [11] work at the task level: the observed movements of the human body are divided into parts that may overlap. An algorithm is built to capture these parts by extracting them from video frames. A bag-of-words representation is then used to distinguish the partial movements, using the temporal and spatial relationship between the parts.

In this work, we do not assume that the observed motion is composed of full atomic movements. Instead, we accommodate the case where the observed movement arises as the composition of several *movement segments*, possibly coming from different movement primitives. We assume that each such segment is either the initial segment of a new movement primitive or the continuation of the previous segment. We build on an existing method for movement recognition that overcomes movement alignment problems by using *critical points* [7], and discover the simplest representation of the observed movement as the combination of segment from pre-learned movement primitives. We use *dynamic movement primitives* (DMP) [4] as our preferred movement representation.

Our method identifies the observed movement, whether it is new or compound, and predicts its most likely target, should the current movement be executed all the way to the end. The recognition of the observed movement as the combination of simpler movements can then be used in a framework for movement combination and optimization [8,10,17,18].

2   Recognition and Prediction Using Critical Points

In this section, we go over our previous recognition framework [7] upon which our approach is built. In our previous work, we used the difference in change ratios of both linear velocity and angle at critical points to match previously learned trajectories with a trajectory being observed. The use of critical points alleviates the need for time aligning the trajectories, while the use of change ratios makes the recognition robust to transformations of the trajectory such as scaling or rotation.

2.1   Motion Recognition

A movement in the library is denoted as a trajectory $\mathbf{y}_{0:T} = \{y(t), t = 0, \ldots, T\}$. A *critical point* [13] is any local minimum of the function $h(t)$ defined as[1]

$$h(t) = \|\dot{y}(t)\|^2 + \|\ddot{y}(t)C_t\|^2. \tag{1}$$

Let $\tau_0, \ldots, \tau_{M+1}$ denote the critical points of the observed trajectory. Following Kordia and Melo [7], to match a segment m of the observed trajectory $\mathbf{y}_{0:t}$ with a movement $\mathbf{y}_n$ in the library, we compute the difference in ratios of velocity change between the segment m of $\mathbf{y}_{0:t}$ and the corresponding segment of $\mathbf{y}_n$, i.e.,

$$\epsilon_v^{(m)}(\mathbf{y}_{0:t}, \mathbf{y}_n) = \bar{\delta}_v^{(m)}(\mathbf{y}_n) - \bar{\delta}_v^{(m)}(\mathbf{y}_{0:t}).$$

Similarly, we compute the difference in ratios of angle change in the segments m of $\mathbf{y}_{0:t}$ and $\mathbf{y}_n$ as

$$\epsilon_\theta^{(m)}(\mathbf{y}_{0:t}, \mathbf{y}_n) = \bar{\delta}_\theta^{(m)}(\mathbf{y}_n) - \bar{\delta}_\theta^{(m)}(\mathbf{y}_{0:t}).$$

The local error at the mth critical point with the nth DMP in the library is a function of both differences, and given by

$$\epsilon^{(m)}(\mathbf{y}_{0:t}, \mathbf{y}_n) = \|\epsilon_v^{(m)}(\mathbf{y}_{0:t}, \mathbf{y}_n)\| + \|\epsilon_\theta^{(m)}(\mathbf{y}_{0:t}, \mathbf{y}_n)\|. \tag{2}$$

Finally, the accumulated error for the nth DMP in the library is

$$E(\mathbf{y}_{0:t}, \mathbf{y}_n) = \sum_{m=1}^{M_*} \epsilon^{(m)}(\mathbf{y}_{0:t}, \mathbf{y}_n), \tag{3}$$

where M_* is the total number of critical points observed so far.

The error $E(\mathbf{y}_{0:t}, \mathbf{y}_n)$ is calculated for the complete set of N movements in the library. From such computation, it is possible to build a recognition matrix with the accumulated error as each new critical point is observed. The movement selected (recognized) is the one with smallest accumulated error.

---

[1] C_t is a time-dependent weighting factor. In our experiments, we used $C_t = 1$.

2.2 Motion Prediction

Motion prediction employs the recognition results to predict the endpoint of the observed trajectory. The original paper proposes two approaches to predict the endpoint of an observed trajectory, but in this paper we consider only one of the two, which is also based on extrapolating the trajectory beyond the observed critical points using change ratios—much like those considered for recognition [7].

To predict the end point of a partial movement recognized as being y_n in the library, we assume that the ratio of change between the current critical point (say m) and the end of the trajectory and between the current critical point and the beginning of the trajectory should be constant in the two executions of the movement—i.e., the one being observed and the one in the library. In other words,

$$\frac{y_n(\tau_{M+1}) - y_n(\tau_m)}{y_n(\tau_m) - y_n(\tau_0)} = \frac{y(\tau_{M+1}) - y(\tau_m)}{y(\tau_m) - y(\tau_0)}. \tag{4}$$

Rearranging the terms, we can compute the predicted endpoint $\hat{y}_n(\tau_{M+1})$ as

$$\hat{y}_n(\tau_{M+1}) = y(\tau_m) + \frac{y(\tau_m) - y(\tau_0)}{y_n(\tau_m) - y_n(\tau_0)} \cdot (y_n(\tau_{M+1}) - y_n(\tau_m)). \tag{5}$$

3 Recognition and Prediction of Compound Movements

We address the problem of movement recognition, when the observed movement is possibly a compound trajectory comprising segments from multiple simpler movements. We henceforth refer to these simpler movements as *primitive movements*. The purpose of our approach is to recognize the individual components forming the observed movement, out of a library of pre-learned (primitive) movements. We assume that each segment in the trajectory is either (i) the initial segment of a possibly different primitive movement; or (ii) the continuation of the previous primitive movement. We consider a segment to be the part of a trajectory lying between two critical points.

Besides recognition, we are also interested in predicting the endpoint of the observed trajectory. Unfortunately, since the trajectory can be formed by an arbitrary number of segments coming from different primitive movements, it is not possible to predict, beforehand, the endpoint of the movement—unless if we know exactly how many and which segments compose the trajectory. As such, we instead predict *the most likely end-point for the current primitive movement*, assuming that it is performed all the way to the end.

Our approach builds on the recognition and prediction framework of Kordia and Melo [7], summarized in Sect. 2.2, extending such work to consider partial trajectory recognition and prediction. Much like in that work, our method relies on the identification of the critical points extracted from the observed trajectory, comparing them with the corresponding critical points in the trajectories in the library.

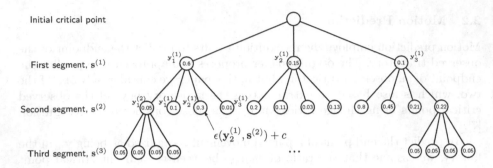

Fig. 1. Example of a search tree. Each node is associated with a segment of a primitive movement in the library, and contains the error associated when comparing the current segment with the primitive movement segment corresponding to that node (the numbers in the nodes).

3.1   Motion Recognition

We can interpret the approach of Kordia and Melo [7] as deploying a "sequence search": at each critical point, the current "sequence of segments" is compared with each movement in the library, and recognition thus consists of identifying the movement in the library that best matches the observed "sequence".

   In our proposed approach, we instead build a *search tree*. The depth of the tree corresponds to the number of observed segments, and each node corresponds to a primitive movement in the library. The search tree is built as follows:

- Each node of the tree has as many children as there are primitive movements in the library plus one.
- The children corresponding to the primitive movements in the library represent the situation where the current segment is the initial segment of the respective primitive movements.
- The additional child represents the situation where the current segment is a continuation of the current primitive movement.
- Each node in the tree is associated with a segment error, as defined in (2).

   Figure 1 shows an example of a possible search tree for the case where the movement library contains only 3 primitive movements. By using the search tree, we can now determine the sequence of primitives that minimizes the total cost. After each new critical point is discovered, the tree grows a level in depth and the node values are computed.

   Note that our approach considers the several possible cases: that the current segment corresponds to the beginning of a new primitive movement; or that the current segment is the continuation of the previous primitive movement. Additionally, to discourage the search process from excessively switching between movement primitives, we add a small cost of c to all the nodes corresponding to changes in the movement primitives.

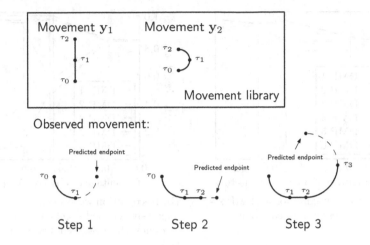

Fig. 2. Example of what the prediction process looks like. After observing a segment and recognizing to which primitive movement such segment "belongs", we predict the endpoint as the endpoint of the corresponding primitive movement.

To render searching the tree a more efficient process, in our approach we do not grow the complete tree simultaneously. Instead, we expand only the nodes corresponding to the path with the smallest average cost per node. While this heuristic for growing the tree still leads to the expansion of some unnecessary nodes, it is significantly more efficient than performing a full breadth-first search.

3.2 Motion Prediction

As previously discussed, the observed trajectory can be formed by an arbitrary number of segments coming from different primitive movements. As such, it is not possible to predict, beforehand, the endpoint of the complete movement. In our approach, we predict *the most likely end-point for the current primitive movement*, assuming that it is performed all the way to the end.

The prediction process uses the basic approach described in Sect. 2.2. At each critical point, after associating the most recent segment with a segment from one of the primitive movements in the library, we compute the endpoint of such primitive movement as the predicted endpoint of the trajectory, using (5). The process is illustrated in Fig. 2.

4   Experiments and Results

This section describes the experiments conducted to test the proposed work. We conducted four experiments, each of which is intended to show the effectiveness, accuracy, and features of the proposed approach.

The first experiment illustrates the recognition process during the discovery of new critical points and the accuracy of the prediction of the target point.

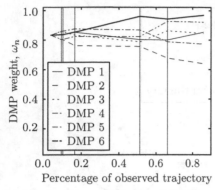
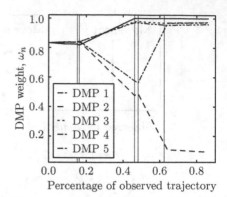

(a) Recognition weights for all DMP sequences at successive critical points.

(b) Recognition weights for each DMP at successive critical points when one DMP matches the observed trajectory (from [7]).

Fig. 3. Weights evolution during the recognition process, as larger portions of the trajectory are observed.

The second experiment showcases the ability of our method to recognize the components forming the observed trajectory, and how these are used to predict the endpoint of the trajectory. The third experiment illustrates the scalability of our approach when the library contains a large number of primitive movements. Finally, the fourth experiments showcases the application of our approach in a real world scenario featuring the Baxter robot.

In the first three experiments, we use a 2D simulation environment. The library contains trajectories stored in the form of DMPs. A trajectory is gradually observed, and our approach performs recognition and prediction in runtime.

4.1   Recognition

We start by illustrating the ability of our approach to perform recognition when the observed trajectory comprises segments from multiple primitive movements and when it contains segments from a single movement. The results are in Fig. 3.

We notice in Fig. 3a that for some DMPs the recognition weights may first decrease, as the system identifies another primitive as the most likely, and then increase, because the system decides that better recognition is attained by switching to that particular primitive movement. The converse is also observed: the weight of some primitives first increases, as that primitive is the best to explain the observed movement, and then decrease, as switching to another primitive offers better recognition.

To facilitate the analysis of the performance, we depict in Fig. 4 the evolution of the entropy in the recognition weights. We immediately note that the recognition process is slower if the observed trajectory is the composition of more than one movement, compared with a trajectory comprising a single movement. In

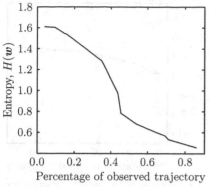

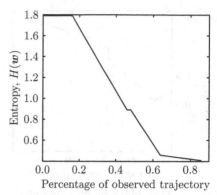

(a) Entropy of the prediction with the observation of new critical points.

(b) Entropy of the prediction with the observation of new critical points when one DMP matches the observed trajectory (from [7]).

Fig. 4. Entropy evolution during the recognition process, as larger portions of the trajectory are observed.

fact, comparing the results in Fig. 4a with the results of the recognition using a single trajectory, in Fig. 4b, we note that the entropy decreases more slowly in Fig. 4a. This is due to the fact that, after the currently observed trajectory, we still consider the possibility that the current trajectory may not yet be over and, as such, there may be new primitive movements following the current trajectory. Hence, as we observe new critical points, there is always some level of uncertainty regarding the prediction that is only resolved as the trajectory concludes.

4.2 Prediction

We also tested the ability of our approach to predict the target point of the observed trajectory. We depict in Fig. 5 the evolution of our prediction as more critical points are observed.

Note how the prediction approaches towards the target point, and the uncertainty decreases with the discovery of new critical points. Also, as seen in Fig. 4a, the entropy decreases lowly, which affects the prediction. The prediction process needs to observe the last part of the monitored trajectory to reach the last DMP in the chosen configuration and obtain a correct prediction, so slower convergence is to be expected.

4.3 Accuracy

We now test the ability of our approach to deal with large movement libraries. We compute the recognition error, given by $|\omega_{\max} - \omega_*|$, with $\omega_{\max}$ is the weight associated with the most likely DMP sequence, and ω_* is the weight for the *real* DMP sequence corresponding to the observed trajectory. We also compute the

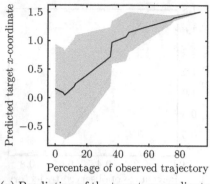
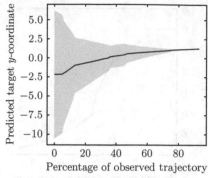

(a) Prediction of the target x coordinate.   (b) Prediction of the target y coordinate.

Fig. 5. Uncertainty in the prediction of the target for the two dimensions of the trajectory. The solid line corresponds to the mean predicted target, $\hat{y}(\tau_{M+1})$, while the shaded area corresponds to the variance in the prediction.

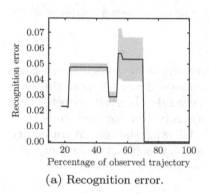
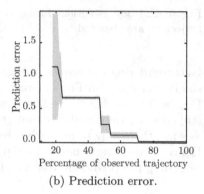

(a) Recognition error.   (b) Prediction error.

Fig. 6. The errors in recognition and prediction for the 25 observed trajectories, as a function of the observed trajectory. The solid lines depict the mean error values, while the shaded area depicts the variance in these errors.

prediction error, given by $\|\hat{y}(\tau_{M+1}) - y(\tau_{M+1})\|$, where $\hat{y}(\tau_{M+1})$ is the predicted endpoint and $y(\tau_{M+1})$ is the actual endpoint.

In Fig. 6 we can see the average prediction and recognition errors averaged over 25 different trajectories, composed from segments of movements from a library of 85 primitive movements.

It is apparent from the figure that, while the prediction error decreases steadily (the trajectory approaches its endpoint, so the prediction errors tend to decrease), the recognition error fluctuates significantly, due to the fact that when a new segment is observed, the cost for changing the primitive motion generating a segment leads the search algorithm to, sometimes, "delay" the shift to a different primitive.

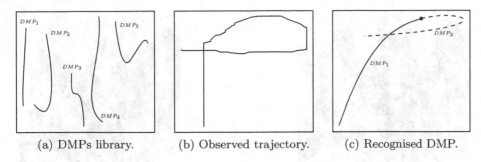

(a) DMPs library.   (b) Observed trajectory.   (c) Recognised DMP.

Fig. 7. Recognizing the "P" letter using two of learned DMPs in the DMPs library, where the trajectory in 7b is constructed using the first DMP and the second one.

4.4   Improving the Knowledge of the Robot

We illustrate a practical application of our approach, where we recognize the letter "P" using a library of number trajectories (or parts thereof). Note, for example, that "P" can be formed by composing the movement for number "1" and part of the movement for number "3" (see Fig. 7). Similarly, the output resulting from observing the trajectory for "B" would be three consecutive partial paths: "1" followed by half of "3" twice.

4.5   Experiment with Robot

In this experiment, Baxter is initially shown the movements of the Pawn (one step forward in the board) and the King (one step sideways in the board) in chess. Baxter then observes a human user performing the movement of the Knight (two steps forward and one step sideways). The Knight's movement can be seen as a composition of two consecutive movements from the Pawn and one of the King, and Baxter successfully recognizes the movement as the composition of the two simpler movements. Baxter could now use the identified sequence of movements to replicate the Knight's movement using, for example, the framework of Kordia and Melo [6] (Fig. 8).

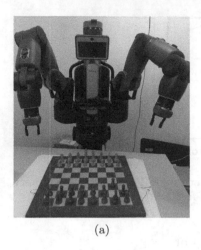

(a)   (b)

Fig. 8. Illustration of the human-interaction scenario considered in the paper, where BAXTER succeed in anticipation to the user complex motion.

5   Conclusion

In this work we presented a simple, effective, and robust way to observe a trajectory, predict its goal, and identify the sub-trajectories that compose it. Our method works without training or prior knowledge of the observed trajectory, and relies only on the movements in its library. The library serves as an initial knowledge base of the robot, but can be improved as more trajectories are observed, following, for example, the approach in [6].

Our approach follows on our previous work [7], using critical points for efficient and effective trajectory identification, alleviating the need for time alignment. Our approach assumes that each segment in the observed trajectory is either the initial segment of a movement in its library or the continuation of the previous movement. Then, given a partial trajectory, our method is able to predict the most likely next target—i.e., the end-point of the movement currently being executed, if the latter is executed to the end. By using an effective search tree, our approach is able to run at execution time and provide an efficient way for action recognition and prediction.

References

1. Black, M.J., Jepson, A.D.: A probabilistic framework for matching temporal trajectories: condensation-based recognition of gestures and expressions. In: Burkhardt, H., Neumann, B. (eds.) ECCV 1998. LNCS, vol. 1406, pp. 909–924. Springer, Heidelberg (1998). https://doi.org/10.1007/BFb0055712
2. Black, M., Jepson, A.: Recognizing temporal trajectories using the condensation algorithm. In: Proceedings of the 3rd IEEE International Conference on Automatic Face and Gesture Recognition, pp. 16–21 (1998)

3. Dermy, O., Paraschos, A., Ewerton, M., Peters, J., Charpillet, F., Ivaldi, S.: Prediction of intention during interaction with iCub with probabilistic movement primitives. Front. Robot. AI **4**, 45 (2017)
4. Ijspeert, A., Nakanishi, J., Hoffmann, H., Pastor, P., Schaal, S.: Dynamical movement primitives Learning attractor models for motor behaviors. Neural Comput. **25**(2), 328–373 (2013)
5. Kelso, J.: Dynamic Patterns: The Self-Organization of Brain and Behavior. MIT Press, Cambridge (1995)
6. Kordia, A., Melo, F.: An end-to-end approach for learning and generating complex robot motions from demonstration. In: Proceedings of the 16th IEEE International Conference on Control, Automation, Robotics and Vision, pp. 1008–1014 (2020)
7. Kordia, A., Melo, F.: Movement recognition and prediction using DMPs. In: Proceedings of the 2021 IEEE International Conference on Robotics and Automation (2021)
8. Kulvicius, T., Ning, K., Tamosiunaite, M., Worgötter, F.: Joining movement sequences: modified dynamic movement primitives for robotics applications exemplified on handwriting. IEEE Trans. Robot. **28**(1), 145–157 (2012)
9. Lee, D., Ott, C., Nakamura, Y.: Mimetic communication model with compliant physical contact in human-humanoid interaction. Int. J. Robot. Res. **29**(13), 1684–1704 (2010)
10. Loshchilov, I.: A computationally efficient limited memory CMA-ES for large scale optimization. In: Proceedings of the 2014 Annual Conference on Genetic and Evolutionary Computation, pp. 397–404 (2014)
11. Ma, S., Zhang, J., Ikizler-Cinbis, N., Sclaroff, S.: Action recognition and localization by hierarchical space-time segments. In: Proceedings of the IEEE International Conference on Computer Vision, pp. 2744–2751 (2013)
12. Maeda, G., Neumann, G., Ewerton, M., Lioutikov, R., Kroemer, O., Peters, J.: Probabilistic movement primitives for coordination of multiple human-robot collaborative tasks. Auton. Robot. **41**(3), 593–612 (2017)
13. Meier, F., Theodorou, E., Schaal, S.: Movement segmentation and recognition for imitation learning. In: Proceedings of the 15th International Conference on Artificial Intelligence and Statistics, pp. 761–769 (2012)
14. Mulling, K., Kober, J., Peters, J.: Learning table tennis with a mixture of motor primitives. In: Proceedings of the 2010 IEEE-RAS International Conference on Humanoid Robots, pp. 411–416 (2010)
15. Nemec, B., Tamosiunaite, M., Woergoetter, F., Ude, A.: Task adaptation through exploration and action sequencing. In: Proceedings of the 9th IEEE-RAS International Conference on Humanoid Robots, pp. 610–616 (2009)
16. Oliver, N., Rosario, B., Pentland, A.: A Bayesian computer vision system for modeling human interactions. IEEE Trans. Pattern Anal. Mach. Intell. **22**(8), 831–843 (2000)
17. Stulp, F., Sigaud, O.: Path integral policy improvement with covariance matrix adaptation. In: Proceedings of the 29th International Conference on Machine Learning, pp. 1547–1554 (2012)
18. Stulp, F., Sigaud, O.: Robot skill learning: from reinforcement learning to evolution strategies. PALADYN J. Behav. Robot. **4**(1), 49–61 (2013)

19. Tanaka, Y., Kinugawa, J., Sugahara, Y., Kosuge, K.: Motion planning with worker's trajectory prediction for assembly task partner robot. In: Proceedings of the 2012 IEEE/RSJ International Conference on Intelligent Robots and Systems, pp. 1525–1532 (2012)
20. Yoon, H., Soh, J., Bae, Y., Yang, H.: Hand gesture recognition using combined features of location, angle and velocity. Pattern Recogn. **34**(7), 1491–1501 (2001)

Metaheuristics for the Robot Part Sequencing and Allocation Problem with Collision Avoidance

Marco Croucamp[✉] and Jacomine Grobler[✉]

Department of Industrial Engineering, Stellenbosch University,
Stellenbosch, South Africa

Abstract. Warehouse efficiency has a significant impact on a supply chain's efficiency. The purpose of this paper is to develop an algorithm that can sequence products to be picked or binned, allocate the products to robots, and optimise the routing of the robots through a warehouse. The algorithm incorporates collision avoidance since the aisle width does not allow two robots to pass each other. Both alternative routing heuristics and metaheuristics for the sequencing and allocation are investigated by means of an empirical analysis conducted on a number of real world problems of different sizes. A return routing heuristic outperformed the s-shape, largest gap and midpoint heuristics with a significant margin. The results for the sequencing and allocation problem showed that an evolutionary strategy algorithm outperformed other benchmarked metaheuristics.

Keywords: Picking and binning · Automated guided vehicles · Metaheuristics

1 Introduction

The efficiency of a supply chain is measured by the time and costs of warehouse activities, amongst other factors. Benefits of optimising warehouse activities include a decrease in order picking and binning time, cost savings on correct part picking, a decrease in incorrect shipments, and an overall increase in customer satisfaction.

Costs related to order picking can be as high as 45 to 55% of all operational costs [21]. Automated warehousing solutions have been conceptualised since 2009 [2], yet businesses struggle with the implementation of automatic warehouse systems due to inexperience, capital expenses and technological gaps. Kiva robots were introduced by Amazon in 2009, but nobody knew that it would eventually change the face of automated warehousing. Amazon, for example, is using over 30 000 of the Kiva robots in their facilities to perform picking and binning tasks [2]. The routing and sequencing of robots is thus an important problem when optimising the efficiency of a warehouse.

© Springer Nature Switzerland AG 2021
G. Marreiros et al. (Eds.): EPIA 2021, LNAI 12981, pp. 469–481, 2021.
https://doi.org/10.1007/978-3-030-86230-5_37

The purpose of this paper is to develop an algorithm that can sequence parts to be picked and binned, allocate the parts to their respective picking or binning robots, and optimise the routing strategy through the warehouse. The objective of the algorithm is to minimise the total time needed to pick and bin all parts, given the number of robots available to perform the picking and binning functions. The algorithm also incorporates collision avoidance since the aisle width of the warehouse does not allow two robots to pass each other. Collisions inside the warehouse will decrease the overall warehouse efficiency, cause physical damage to the robots, and also result in time consuming congestion.

A number of metaheuristics were tested including a covariance matrix adaptation evolution algorithm (CMA-ES), a genetic algorithm, particle swarm optimisation (PSO) and a differential evolution (DE) algorithm. In addition to the metaheuristics listed, different routing heuristics were tested to solve the robot routing problem. A routing heuristic consists of predefined rules to guide the robot through the warehouse, considering the robot's sequence of parts to be picked or binned. These heuristics include the midpoint heuristic, the s-shape heuristic, the return heuristic, and the largest gap heuristic.

The robot routing problem was solved before the sequencing and allocation problem because the best performing routing heuristic was used in the part sequencing and allocation algorithm. The return heuristic outperformed the other routing heuristics over five real world datasets of different sizes. On the part sequencing and allocation problem the CMA-ES statistically outperformed the other metaheuristics.

To the best of the authors' knowledge, this paper is the first where these four metaheuristics have been tested for solving the robot picking and binning problem, given that all collisions must be avoided.

The rest of the paper is organised as follows: Sect. 2 describes related literature. Section 3 provides a description of the part sequencing and allocation problem. The problem is solved in a two-step process, namely routing heuristic selection (described in Sect. 4) and solving the actual part sequencing and allocation problem (described in Sect. 5). Section 6 describes a sensitivity analysis performed on the number of robots in the system. Finally, the paper is concluded in Sect. 7.

2   Related Literature

Automated mobile transporters in warehouses are called automated guided vehicles (AGV). The purpose of implementing AGVs is to increase the efficiency of warehouse operations and reduce warehouse costs [22]. Schulze et al. [19] also mentions that automation of transportation in the production, trade and service industries is critical when optimising logistic processes. AGVs provide several benefits when implemented, costs and reliability being two of the main advantages. AGVs also provide unmatched flexibility when integrated into an existing or changing environment. The use of AGVs can be found throughout industry, including the automotive, printing, pharmaceutical, metal, food, aerospace industries and port facilities.

De Ryck et al. [5] provide an overview of the most recent AGV control algorithms and techniques. They divide AGV control tasks into five main areas namely, task allocation, localisation, path planning, motion planning, and vehicle management. This paper focuses mainly on task allocation and path planning. Task allocation is concerned with determining which robot performs which tasks e.g. the picking and binning of parts at certain locations. Path planning is concerned with generating the shortest obstacle free path from the point of origin to destination and back.

Another important distinction to make is the difference between centralised and decentralised AGV architectures. Centralised systems make use of global information to find an optimal or near optimal solution for the AGVS. This optimisation is typically performed before initiation of the first tasks and is static in nature. An example is allocating tasks and planning the best paths for all robots in the system. A decentralised system makes use of local information and the individual robots have built in intelligence to make their own decisions as the system changes dynamically [4,5,7]. This paper focuses on the centralised case where the system needs to be re-optimised each time a significant change occurs. Furthermore, the problem considered in this paper can be classified as a SR-ST-IA (single robot tasks-single task robots-instantaneous assignment) system since a robot can only pick or bin one part at a time, only one robot is required per part, and the picking and binning of parts are independent of each other.

An investigation into existing research related to centralised AGV architectures showed that the requirement for collision avoidance adds significant complexity to the problem. A number of researchers have investigated robot path planning [13,15,17], but far fewer papers address path planning and task allocation in a warehouse environment. In a warehouse the aisle and shelf layout needs to be considered and collisions need to be avoided between multiple robots.

Algorithms already utilised for path planning and task allocation in warehouses include the A* shortest path method [10], Dijkstra's algorithm [24], simulated annealing [16], and ant colony optimisation [14,16]. It is, however, evident that there is a definite opportunity for research into more metaheuristic-based algorithms considering task allocation, path planning, and the avoidance of moving obstacles.

3   The Part Sequencing and Allocation Problem

In a warehouse with N number of parts, all the parts need to be picked and binned on a daily basis. The picking and binning is done using a robot from a set of robots. A robot cannot carry more than one part at a time. A robot enters the warehouse through the entrance gate, completes the job (picking or binning), and then exits through the exit gate. The time it takes a robot to pick or bin a part is equal to the standard moving time plus the delay time for collision avoidance, the physical picking or binning time, and the time to travel to the exit gate.

The objective of the model is to minimise the total time it takes all the robots to complete their picking and binning processes by optimising the sequence and allocation of parts to be picked and binned. The sequence has a significant influence on the total picking and binning time. Each sequence has different collision avoidance scenarios that must be incorporated. Changing the sequence affects the number of collisions to avoid and also influences the total picking and binning time. Furthermore, the allocation of picking/binning tasks to robots also need to be addressed.

The following symbols need to be denoted for the mathematical model of the problem:

$$I \triangleq \text{The number of parts in the warehouse; and}$$

$$K \triangleq \text{The number of robots in the system.}$$

$$x_{ijk} = \begin{cases} 1 \text{ if robot } k \text{ is binning or picking part } i \text{ immediately before part} \\ \quad j \text{ where } i, j \in \{1, ..., I\} \text{ are the parts to be picked and} \\ \quad i, j \in \{I+1, ..., 2I\} \text{ are the parts to be binned,} \\ 0 \text{ otherwise} \end{cases}$$

$w_{ijk} \triangleq$ Time added to avoid collision if part i is picked or binned immediately before part j by robot k

$t_i \triangleq$ The travel time without delays for part i from the entrance to the exit

$n_i \triangleq$ Starting time of new task for part i from the entrance gate

$p \triangleq$ Process time for picking or binning incurred for all parts

The model can be formulated as follows:

$$\text{Minimise } Z = \max_{1 \leq i \leq 2I} \{n_i\} \tag{1}$$

Subject to:

$$\sum_{i=1}^{2I} \sum_{k=1}^{K} x_{ijk} = 1 \quad \forall j \in \{1, ..., 2I\} \tag{2}$$

$$\sum_{j=1}^{2I} \sum_{k=1}^{K} x_{ijk} = 1 \quad \forall i \in \{1, ..., 2I\} \tag{3}$$

$$\sum_{i=1}^{2I} x_{ipk} - \sum_{j=1}^{2I} x_{pjk} = 0 \quad \forall p \in \{1, ..., 2I\}, k \in \{1, ..., K\} \tag{4}$$

$$\sum_{k=1}^{K} \sum_{i=1, i \neq j}^{2I} x_{ijk}(n_i + p + w_{ijk} + t_i) \leq n_j \quad \forall j \in \{1, ..., 2I\} \tag{5}$$

$$t_i, n_i, p, w_{ijk} \in \{0, R\}$$
$$x_{ijk} \in \{0, 1\}$$

The objective of the model (Eq. 1) is to minimise the maximum time it takes to complete all the picking and binning jobs for all the robots and Eqs. 2 and 3 ensure that all parts are picked and binned. Each robot can only pick and bin one part at a time.

Equation 4 enforces continuity in the model, so that the next part is picked or binned. The different delay times that can be incurred, depending on the number of robots on the same route, is calculated using Eq. 5. If there are robots on the route the equation will add the respective delay time given the position of the other robot. This constraint is used to avoid collisions in the warehouse.

4   Solving the Routing Problem

The strategy for solving the part sequencing and allocation problem can be seen in Fig. 1. Regardless of the sequence in which parts need to be picked or binned, each time a robot enters the warehouse it needs to use a routing heuristic to determine its actual path through the warehouse. The strategy thus consists of two parts namely: determining the actual path by solving the routing problem (by means of any one of four routing heuristics) and solving the part sequencing and allocation strategy (by means of a metaheuristic algorithm). This two part strategy is executed sequentially with the best routing heuristic first being determined and then used as input to the part sequencing and allocation problem, which is solved by means of a metaheuristic algorithm.

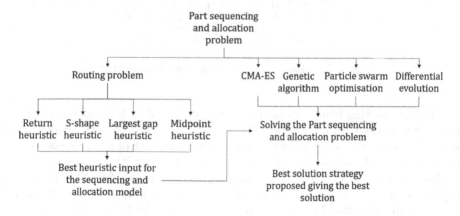

Fig. 1. Part sequencing and allocation problem solution strategy

Four routing heuristics were considered (Fig. 2) [6]:

- **S-shape**: For each aisle with a part to be picked, the robot enters the aisle at one side and exits at the opposite side of the aisle [8], it then returns in the opposite direction in the next aisle so that it moves in the form of an 's', until all the products have been picked.
- **Midpoint**: The heuristic separates the warehouse into two horizontal sections, creating a hypothetical midline between the two sections [20]. The midpoint heuristic then allows for all the products in the first section to be picked before the robot can move into the second section.
- **Largest gap**: The largest gap heuristic follows the same methodology as the midpoint heuristic. The only difference is that the robot follows an aisle until it reaches the largest gap in the respective aisle. The robot then returns to the aisle's starting position and moves on to the next aisle. The largest gap is the largest part of an aisle where no parts need to be picked.
- **Return**: The robot will enter each aisle, pick all the items in the aisle, turn around and return to the starting point of that aisle [8].

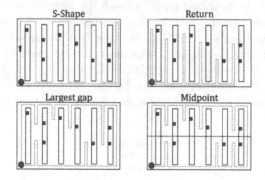

Fig. 2. Examples of the different routing heuristics

The four routing heuristics are compared as described in Algorithm 1. Each heuristic was tested with the same 30 randomly generated sequences to pick and bin in the same warehouse layout, which is representative of the warehouse used for this study. The robot routing heuristics were tested with two robots.

Table 1 shows the average minimum value obtained for all 30 random sequences, over five datasets of different sizes, ranging from 8 to 40 parts, based on real customer data. The table also shows the standard deviations (σ) of the minimum values for the 30 sequences.

Algorithm 1: Robot routing algorithm

1 Initialise a warehouse with i number of storage spaces per aisle and j number of aisles
2 Distribute parts evenly between the number of robots
3 **for** *each heuristic* **do**
4   **for** *each sequence* **do**
5   Pick and bin parts as per sequence
6   Calculate time used
7   **end**
8   Return results
9 **end**

Table 1. Routing heuristics results

		Return heuristic	S-shape heuristic	Largest gap heuristic	Midpoint heuristic
8 Parts	Average	**217.97**	267.57	267.37	294.83
	σ	7.00	1.98	8.86	12.97
16 Parts	Average	**439.43**	533.17	522.70	582.70
	σ	13.88	2.12	13.11	16.74
24 Parts	Average	**680.97**	797.70	803.30	888.13
	σ	18.51	2.26	11.81	17.80
32 Parts	Average	**903.33**	1062.33	1072.10	1176.13
	σ	27.40	2.37	17.48	24.13
40 Parts	Average	**1060.23**	1328.83	1281.73	1374.90
	σ	27.31	3.41	24.66	31.63

The results of the statistical comparison in Table 2 were obtained by comparing, for each dataset, the result of a heuristic's performance to each of the other heuristics' performance. For every comparison, a Mann–Whitney U test at 5% significance was performed (using the two sets of 30 sequences of the two heuristics under comparison) and if the first heuristic outperformed the second heuristic statistically significantly, a win was recorded. If no statistical difference could be observed, a draw was recorded. If the second heuristic outperformed the first heuristic, a loss was recorded for the first heuristic. The total number of wins, draws and losses were then recorded for all datasets of the heuristic under evaluation. As an example, (5-0-0) in row 1 column 2, indicates that the return heuristic significantly outperformed the s-shape heuristic 5 times over the 5 datasets. No draws and losses were recorded.

Table 2. Routing heuristic hypothesis testing results

	Return heuristic	S-shape heuristic	Largest gap heuristic	Midpoint heuristic	Total
Return heuristic	–	5-0-0	5-0-0	5-0-0	**15-0-0**
S-shape heuristic	0-0-5	–	2-1-2	5-0-0	**7-1-7**
Largest gap heuristic	0-0-5	2-1-2	–	5-0-0	**7-1-7**
Midpoint heuristic	0-0-5	0-0-5	0-0-5	–	**0-0-15**

From the results it is clear that the return heuristic outperformed the other heuristics by a significant margin and is thus used for the routing of robots when solving the part sequencing and allocation problem.

5   The Parts Sequencing and Allocation Metaheuristic Algorithm

The problem representation of the algorithm consists of n_x continuous variables, where $n_x/3$ is the number of parts to be picked and binned. The n_x variables are divided into three sets equal in size. The first set of variables define the sequence in which the picking takes place. The second set is the sequence in which the binning takes place, and the third set is the allocation of parts to a robot in the system. The sequencing variables of dimensions 1 to $2n_x/3$ are then sorted from largest to smallest to give the sequence in which the parts are to be picked or binned. The process used for robot allocation (dimensions $2n_x/3 + 1$ to n_x) is shown below in Fig. 3 and the pseudocode of the fitness function evaluation procedure is provided in Algorithm 2.

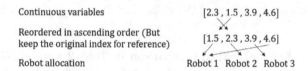

Fig. 3. Robot allocation process

The fitness function evaluation procedure was then used in conjunction with four metaheuristics namely:

- CMA-ES [1].
- A GA with a floating point representation, tournament selection, blend crossover [9] and Gaussian mutation [18].
- The guaranteed convergence particle swarm optimization algorithm [3].
- The self-adaptive neighbourhood based (SaNSDE) algorithm of [23].

These algorithms were selected based on their previous successful application to scheduling problems [12] and the metaheuristic parameters are shown in Table 3 and were selected based on the work done in [11]. The notation $x \rightarrow y$ is used to indicate that the associated parameter is decreasing or increasing linearly from x to y over 95% of the maximum number of iterations. The same five datasets from the routing problem were used to evaluate the alternative metaheuristics.

Table 3. Metaheuristic parameters

Parameter	Value used
General parameters	
Population size	100
Max iterations (Size $= 8, 16, 24, 32, 40$ parts)	500, 500, 750, 900, 1250
GCPSO parameters	
Acceleration constant (c_1)	$2.0 \rightarrow 0.7$
Acceleration constant (c_2)	$0.7 \rightarrow 2.0$
Inertia weight	$0.9 \rightarrow 0.4$
SaNSDE parameters	
Probability of reproduction	$0.75 \rightarrow 0.25$
Scaling factor	$0.75 \rightarrow 0.125$
GA parameters	
Probability of crossover	$0.6 \rightarrow 0.4$
Probability of mutation	0.1
Blend crossover parameter	0.4
CMA-ES parameters	As specified in [1]

The results are summarised in Table 4, which shows the average minimum value obtained over 30 runs for each dataset. The table also shows the standard deviations (σ) of the minimum values for the 30 runs.

The hypothesis testing procedure applied to the routing heuristic results (shown in Table 2) was also used to compare the metaheuristics i.e. pairwise Mann-Whitney U tests between each two sets of 30 algorithm runs. In Table 5 (4-1-0) in row 1 column 2, indicates that the CMAES significantly outperformed the GCPSO algorithm four times over the five datasets. One draw and no losses were recorded.

The results from the hypothesis tests conclude that the CMA-ES outperformed the other metaheuristics on the sequencing and allocation problem with the most number of wins. The CMA-ES algorithm had a total of eight wins, six draws, and one loss. The second best performing metaheuristic was the SaNSDE with six wins, seven draws, and two losses. The GA was the third best metaheuristic and had a total of four wins, eight draws, and three losses. The worst performing metaheuristic was the GCPSO with zero recorded wins, three draws, and twelve losses.

6   Sensitivity Analysis

Finally, a sensitivity analysis was conducted using the same experimental setup as described in Sects. 4 and 5 on the number of robots. The number of robots was increased from two (original setting) to a number where no significant improvement could be identified. The maximum number of robots identified was seven.

Algorithm 2: Part allocation and sequencing fitness function evaluation procedure

---

1 Divide the n_x-dimensional candidate solution into 3 sets
2 **for** *The first set → picking sequence* **do**
3 $\quad|\quad$ Arrange the first set in ascending order → part picking sequence ($\boldsymbol{p}$)
4 **end**
5 **for** *The second set → binning sequence* **do**
6 $\quad|\quad$ Arrange the second set in ascending order → part binning sequence ($\boldsymbol{b}$)
7 **end**
8 **for** *The third set → robot allocation* **do**
9 $\quad|\quad$ Given the number of robots (K) in the system do allocation according to Figure 3.
10 **end**
11 Assign each robot → next destination node
12 **for** *All the parts in the warehouse* **do**
13 $\quad|\quad$ Route each robot to their destination using the routing heuristic
14 $\quad|\quad$ **if** *the next node is occupied* **then**
15 $\quad|\quad\quad|\quad$ WAIT
16 $\quad|\quad$ **end**
17 $\quad|\quad$ **else**
18 $\quad|\quad\quad|\quad$ Move along the path
19 $\quad|\quad$ **end**
20 **end**
21 **if** *robot is done with picking and binning* **then**
22 $\quad|\quad$ state = **DONE**
23 **end**
24 **else**
25 $\quad|\quad$ state = **ACTIVE**
26 **end**
27 **if** *all robot states = DONE* **then**
28 $\quad|\quad$ return Fval = Count time steps used
29 **end**

Table 4. Metaheuristics results

		CMA-ES	GCPSO	GA	SaNSDE
8 Parts	**Average**	187.37	**187.03**	**187.03**	186.23
	σ	1.67	1.52	1.96	1.45
16 Parts	**Average**	**374.97**	378.27	375.27	375.20
	σ	2.58	3.12	2.55	1.63
24 Parts	**Average**	**593.33**	602.67	595.60	591.73
	σ	3.28	6.33	4.88	1.95
32 Parts	**Average**	**783.47**	803.93	787.70	788.43
	σ	3.88	7.88	5.18	3.06
40 Parts	**Average**	**929.53**	965.37	935.83	936.17
	σ	7.99	7.52	5.41	3.12

The algorithm was run five times for each of the number of robots considered and the results of the median run were used to compare the scenarios.

When increasing the number of robots from two robots to three robots an improvement of 28.2% on the fitness value could be seen. The improvement from three robots to four showed an improvement of 20.8%. The percentage improvement decreases further to 11.9% when introducing a fifth robot. Introducing

Table 5. Hypothesis testing results

	CMA-ES	GCPSO	SaNSDE	GA	Total
CMA-ES	–	4-1-0	2-2-1	2-3-0	**8-6-1**
GCPSO	0-1-4	–	0-1-4	0-1-4	**0-3-12**
SaNSDE	1-2-2	4-1-0	–	1-4-0	**6-7-2**
GA	0-3-2	4-1-0	0-4-1	–	**4-8-3**

another robot to make a total of six, improves the fitness value by only 5.2%. The maximum number of robots shows a slight improvement of 1.8%.

7   Conclusion

The robot part sequencing and allocation problem was solved in two parts. The return heuristic, the s-shape heuristic, the midpoint heuristic and the largest gap heuristic were evaluated for solving the robot routing problem. The return heuristic was the best routing heuristic for this application. After the best routing heuristic was determined, the part sequencing and allocation problem was solved with the covariance matrix adaptation evolution strategy (CMA-ES) algorithm, a genetic algorithm (GA), the guaranteed convergence particle swarm optimisation (GCPSO) algorithm and the self-adaptive differential evolution algorithm with neighbourhood search (SaNSDE). The CMA-ES statistically outperformed the other metaheuristics in solving the part sequencing and allocation problem. Overall the CMA-ES, along with the return routing heuristic, was shown to be effective and applicable for solving the part sequencing and allocation problem.

A number of opportunities for future research exist and include the use of alternative metaheuristics, reformulating the problem as a multi-objective optimisation problem, investigating whether the return heuristic is also best when considering more than two robots, using different routing strategies for each robot, and allowing the batching of parts.

Acknowledgements. This work is based on the research supported in part by the National Research Foundation of South Africa (Grant Number: 129340).

References

1. Auger, A., Hansen, N.: A restart CMA evolution strategy with increasing population size. In: 2005 IEEE Congress on Evolutionary Computation, vol. 2, pp. 1769–1776. IEEE (2005)
2. Banker, S.: Warehouse 2025. ARC Advisory Group, Technical report (2009)
3. Van den Bergh, F., Engelbrecht, A.P.: A new locally convergent particle swarm optimiser. In: IEEE International Conference on Systems, Man and Cybernetics, vol. 3, pp. 6–12. IEEE (2002)

4. Chen, H., Wang, Q., Yu, M., Cao, J., Sun, J.: Path planning for multi-robot systems in intelligent warehouse. In: Xiang, Y., Sun, J., Fortino, G., Guerrieri, A., Jung, J.J. (eds.) IDCS 2018. LNCS, vol. 11226, pp. 148–159. Springer, Cham (2018). https://doi.org/10.1007/978-3-030-02738-4_13
5. De Ryck, M., Versteyhe, M., Debrouwere, F.: Automated guided vehicle systems, state-of-the-art control algorithms and techniques. J. Manuf. Syst. **54**, 152–173 (2020)
6. Dekker, R., De Koster, M., Roodbergen, K.J., Van Kalleveen, H.: Improving order-picking response time at Ankor's warehouse. Interfaces **34**(4), 303–313 (2004)
7. Draganjac, I., Petrović, T., Miklić, D., Kovačić, Z., Oršulić, J.: Highly-scalable traffic management of autonomous industrial transportation systems. Robot. Comput.-Integr. Manuf. **63**, 101915 (2020)
8. Dukic, G., Oluic, C.: Order-picking methods: improving order-picking efficiency. Int. J. Logist. Syst. Manag. **3**(4), 451–460 (2007)
9. Eshelman, L.J., Schaffer, J.D.: Real-coded genetic algorithms and interval-schemata. Found. Genetic Algorithms **2**, 187–202 (1993)
10. Gochev, I., Nadzinski, G., Stankovski, M.: Path planning and collision avoidance regime for a multi-agent system in industrial robotics. Mach. Technol. Mater. **11**(11), 519–522 (2017)
11. Grobler, J.: The heterogeneous meta-hyper-heuristic: from low level heuristics to low level meta-heuristics. Ph.D. thesis, University of Pretoria (2015)
12. Grobler, J., Engelbrecht, A.P.: Hyper-heuristics for the flexible job shop scheduling problem with additional constraints. In: Tan, Y., Shi, Y., Li, L. (eds.) ICSI 2016. LNCS, vol. 9713, pp. 3–10. Springer, Cham (2016). https://doi.org/10.1007/978-3-319-41009-8_1
13. Jabbarpour, M.R., Zarrabi, H., Jung, J.J., Kim, P.: A green ant-based method for path planning of unmanned ground vehicles. IEEE Access **5**, 1820–1832 (2017)
14. Kulatunga, A., Liu, D., Dissanayake, G., Siyambalapitiya, S.: Ant colony optimization based simultaneous task allocation and path planning of autonomous vehicles. In: 2006 IEEE Conference on Cybernetics and Intelligent Systems, pp. 1–6. IEEE (2006)
15. Lee, H.Y., Shin, H., Chae, J.: Path planning for mobile agents using a genetic algorithm with a direction guided factor. Electronics **7**(10), 212 (2018)
16. Liu, D., Kulatunga, A.: Simultaneous planning and scheduling for multi-autonomous vehicles. In: Dahal, K.P., Tan, K.C., Cowling, P.I. (eds.) Evolutionary Scheduling. SCI, vol. 49, pp. 437–464. Springer, Heidelberg (2007). https://doi.org/10.1007/978-3-540-48584-1_16
17. López-González, A., Campaña, J.M., Martínez, E.H., Contro, P.P.: Multi robot distance based formation using parallel genetic algorithm. Appl. Soft Comput. **86**, 105929 (2020)
18. Olorunda, O., Engelbrecht, A.P.: An analysis of heterogeneous cooperative algorithms. In: 2009 IEEE Congress on Evolutionary Computation, pp. 1562–1569 (2009)
19. Schulze, L., Behling, S., Buhrs, S.: Automated guided vehicle systems: a driver for increased business performance. In: Proceedings of the International Multiconference of Engineers and Computer Scientists, vol. 2, pp. 1–6 (2008)
20. Theys, C., Bräysy, O., Dullaert, W., Raa, B.: Towards a metaheuristic for routing order pickers in a warehouse. In: Evolutionary Methods for Design, Optimization and Control, pp. 385–390 (2007)
21. Tompkins, J., White, J., Bozer, Y., Frazelle, E., Tanchoco, J.: Trevino. Facilities planning 9 (1996)

22. Vivaldini, K.C., et al.: Robotic forklifts for intelligent warehouses: routing, path planning, and auto-localization. In: 2010 IEEE International Conference on Industrial Technology (ICIT), pp. 1463–1468. IEEE (2010)
23. Yang, Z., Tang, K., Yao, X.: Self-adaptive differential evolution with neighborhood search. In: 2008 IEEE Congress on Evolutionary Computation (IEEE World Congress on Computational Intelligence), pp. 1110–1116. IEEE (2008)
24. Zhang, Z., Guo, Q., Chen, J., Yuan, P.: Collision-free route planning for multiple AGVs in an automated warehouse based on collision classification. IEEE Access **6**, 26022–26035 (2018)

Knowledge Discovery and Business Intelligence

Generalised Partial Association in Causal Rules Discovery

Ana Rita Nogueira[1,2]([✉]), Carlos Ferreira[1], João Gama[1], and Alberto Pinto[1,2]

[1] LIAAD - INESC TEC, Rua Dr. Roberto Frias, 4200-465 Porto, Portugal
ana.r.nogueira@inesctec.pt
[2] Faculdade de Ciências da Universidade do Porto, Rua do Campo Alegre 1021/1055,
4169-007 Porto, Portugal

Abstract. One of the most significant challenges for machine learning nowadays is the discovery of causal relationships from data. This causal discovery is commonly performed using Bayesian like algorithms. However, more recently, more and more causal discovery algorithms have appeared that do not fall into this category. In this paper, we present a new algorithm that explores global causal association rules with Uncertainty Coefficient. Our algorithm, CRPA-UC, is a global structure discovery approach that combines the advantages of association mining with causal discovery and can be applied to binary and non-binary discrete data. This approach was compared to the PC algorithm using several well-known data sets, using several metrics.

Keywords: Causality · Causal association rules · Generalised Cochran-Mantel-Haenszel · Uncertainty coefficient

1 Introduction

Causal discovery aims to study the possible cause-and-effect relationships between variables in a data set [9]. These causal relationships can be found through several methods, with the most commonly applied algorithms based on Bayesian networks. Despite being the most widely used algorithms for searching for causal relationships in observational data, more and more causal discovery algorithms that do not fall into this category have appeared in recent years.

Association Rule Mining or ARM is a technique that can find correlations between variables in data [11]. Within the association rules algorithms, we have the causal association rules that apply independence tests to determine if there is a causal relationship between two or more variables [10]. Approaches like these have the advantage of being able to create causal hypotheses when dealing with large amounts of data [6]. There are already a few approaches that combine association rule mining and causal discovery. However, they have some restrains/limitations: (1) it is only possible to apply these algorithms to binary data sets and (2) only to one variable (local structure discovery) [7]. Besides this, (3) they apply a naive approach as an orientation method since they assume that

© Springer Nature Switzerland AG 2021
G. Marreiros et al. (Eds.): EPIA 2021, LNAI 12981, pp. 485–497, 2021.
https://doi.org/10.1007/978-3-030-86230-5_38

all the rules are *variable => target*, which is not always true. These limitations mean that it is not possible to apply these types of algorithms to, for example, non-binary discrete data. This data can be binary (gender), or it can encode stages ($\{normal, risk, failure\}$). This fact implies the need to binarise the data to be able to apply these causal association rules, leading to a data set size increase and, consequently, a run-time increase. Another critical issue presented by previous methodologies is that it is impossible to infer causal direction [5]. With these methodologies, it is only possible to create and evaluate the undirected relations of the variables with a chosen target, implying the necessity of having a clear idea of what variable is the target to apply these methodologies. However, in some instances, the study (and evaluation) of the entire environment is the objective and not a specific outcome. In such cases, these approaches cannot be applied.

To deal with these limitations, we propose CRPA-UC. This approach applies the Generalised Cochran-Mantel-Haenszel (GCMH) test, combined with the χ^2 so that it is possible to apply this method in any discrete data set. Finally, and since both independence tests are symmetrical, we propose using the Uncertainty Coefficient (UC) [16] that will act as an orientation method. We also provide an extensive evaluation of this approach using several public data sets, where the proposed approach outperforms the state-of-the-art method (in this case, PC [15]).

This paper is organised as follows: Sect. 2 describes some essential definitions. Section 3 describes the proposed approach, and Sect. 4 the results obtained in the tests.

2 Background

In this section, we introduce some important notations that will be used through the document.

2.1 Association Rule Mining

Association rule mining is inserted in the field of *data mining/machine learning*. The algorithms that fall into this category create *If/Then* rules (*if => then*) and are designed to handle categorical data. Related to rule mining, there is a set of measures that quantify the effectiveness of a rule. These metrics are **support**, which measures the historical data support (how much the data supports the proposed rule) the rule has, **confidence**, which measures how confidant the algorithm is in the rule, and **lift**, which is the ratio between confidence and support. One of the best-known association rules algorithm is the *apriori*, which was proposed by Agrawal et al. [1], being that several authors have applied it in their research. This is the case of Manimaran and Velmurugan [11] who applied association rule mining, specifically the *apriori* algorithm, to find relationships between medical diagnosis tests for oral cancer.

Within the association rule mining, we have a special case: causal association rule mining. In this category of association rules algorithms, we are not interested in searching for rules $\{attribute = value\} \rightarrow \{attribute = value\}$, but instead $\{variable\} \rightarrow \{variable\}$. The change from the traditional definition of an association rule is that, in this type of algorithm, the objective is to find supposed causal connections between a target and the remaining variables and not between the attributes' values. This is evident given the definition of causal rule: *"Association rule $x \rightarrow z$ is a causal rule if there exists a significant partial association between variables X and Z"* [10]. What this means is that, unlike the traditional association rules, in these algorithms, the rule $A \rightarrow B$ can be considered as a causal rule if: (1) A and B are directly associated[1], (2) the support of the association $A \rightarrow B$ is greater than the minimum support and (3) the partial association [10] (*i.e.*, to test if two variables are dependent from one another it is necessary to find a set of covariates with similar distribution to control the effects of those control variables in the tested ones) between A and B is different from zero. One possible example is the work of Jin et al. [6]: CR-PA. This algorithm searches for potentially causal rules for a target variable through the application of two conditional independence tests: χ^2 and the Cochran-Mantel-Haenszel (CMH) test. The χ^2 test is applied to determine if two variables are related to each other. If they are not, it is not necessary to apply the second conditional independence test. To the variables selected in this phase, the CMH to contingency tables of type $K \times 2 \times 2$. The authors of CR-PA have also proposed a similar algorithm: CR-CS [9]. This approach exchanges the conditional independence tests for retrospective cohort studies (odds ratio) to find causal rules. To create these cohort studies, the algorithm selects two types of samples (exposure samples and control samples) and tries to match them so that the distribution of the control variables of the two groups is as similar as possible. The association of two variables is defined by a support threshold and a minimum odds ratio.

Both these approaches can only be applied to binary data and to one variable each time (local structure discovery) [7]. Besides this, these algorithms have the disadvantages of applying a naive approach as an orientation method since they use the results from the conditional independence test to direct, always directing as $variable => target$. Moreover, since these tests are symmetric, it is impossible to assume one direction, considering that the test result only hints that there is a dependence between the variables.

2.2 Cochran-Mantel-Haenszel Test

The Cochran-Mantel-Haenszel (CMH) test [3] is a test of independence, which differs from others like χ^2, because it tests if the relationship between two variables is maintained when influenced by the remaining variables, instead of only testing if two variables are related. There are two distinct versions of this test:

---

[1] Two variables are directly associated if a statistical test (for example χ^2) finds them associated.

the binary version and its generalised version [8], which can be used in every categorical data. The binary version is given by Eq. (1).

$$CMH = \frac{(|\sum_{k=1}^{r} \frac{n_{11k}n_{22k}-n_{21k}n_{12k}}{n_{..k}}| - \frac{1}{2})^2}{\sum_{k=1}^{r} \frac{n_{1.k}n_{2.k}n_{.1k}n_{.2k}}{n_{..k}^2(n_{..k}-1)}} \tag{1}$$

In the previous equation, the values n represent the cells of contingency tables identical to Table 1 (each cell of this table represent how many cases there are given the values of the studied variables and their supposed confounders), being that n_{11k} represents the first cell in the first row of table k, n_{12k} the second cell in the first row, n_{21k} the first cell in the second row and n_{22k} the second cell in the second row, $n_{1.k}$, $n_{2.k}$, $n_{.1k}$, $n_{.2k}$ and $n_{..k}$ represent the sum of the cell in the first row, the sum of the cell in the second row, the sum of the cell in the first column, the sum of the cell in the second column and the sum of all the cells, of a table k.

As explained previously, this version of the CMH test can only be applied to binary data. However, other categorical non-binary data in which the application of this type of algorithms can be relevant. To those cases, the **GCMH test** is applied instead. This variant was designed to be used in contingency tables of size $I \times J \times K$ (instead of $2 \times 2 \times K$, as in the binary version) and is given by Eq. (2) [8]. In the equations previously presented, B_h represents the product of Kronecker between C_h and R_h (these values are obtained from the partial contingency table, as showed in Table 2), Var the co-variance matrix, $(nh-mh)$ the difference between the observed and the expected and H_0 as the null hypothesis.

$$Q_{CMH} = G'Var\{G|H_0\}^{-1}G \qquad G_h = B_h(n_h - m_h) \qquad G = \sum_h G_h$$

$$Var\{G|H_0\} = \sum_h Var\{G_h|H_0\} \qquad B_h = C_h \bigotimes R_h. \tag{2}$$

Table 1. Example of a partial contingency table used in CMH test (in which $c_k = \{A = a1, B = b1\}$)

$c_k = \{A, B\}$	$C = c_1$	$C = c_2$	Total
$D = d_1$	n_{11k}	n_{12k}	$n_{1.k}$
$D = d_2$	n_{21k}	n_{22k}	$n_{2.k}$
Total	$n_{.1k}$	$n_{.2k}$	$n_{..k}$

Table 2. Example of a partial contingency table used in GCMH test (in which $c_h = \{A = a1, B = b1\}$)

$c_h = \{A, B\}$	$C = c_1$	$C = c_2$	$C = c_3$	$\cdots$	$C = c_n$	Total
$R = r_1$	n_{11h}	n_{12h}	n_{13h}	$\cdots$	n_{1nh}	$n_{1.h}$
$R = r_2$	n_{21h}	n_{22h}	n_{23h}	$\cdots$	n_{2nh}	$n_{2.h}$
$R = r_3$	n_{31h}	n_{32h}	n_{3nh}	$\cdots$	n_{3nh}	$n_{3.h}$
$\cdots$	$\cdots$	$\cdots$	$\cdots$	$\cdots$	$\cdots$	$\cdots$
$R = r_n$	n_{n1h}	n_{n2h}	n_{n3h}	$\cdots$	n_{nnh}	$n_{n.h}$
Total	$n_{.1h}$	$n_{.2h}$	$n_{.3h}$	$\cdots$	$n_{.nh}$	$n_{..h}$

2.3   Uncertainty Coefficient

The uncertainty coefficient is as measure of entropy used for discrete variables, that measures how much a variable x can explain a variable y and is given by the first formula in Eq. (3) [17]. This dependence is obtained by combining the entropy from y ($H(y)$) and the entropy of y given x ($H(y|x)$) (Eq. (3)). This coefficient has values comprehended between 0 and 1, being 0 the representation of no relation between the variables (x does not explain y) and 1 a full relation (x completely explains y).

$$U(y|x) \equiv \frac{H(y) - H(y|x)}{H(y)} \quad H(y) = -\sum_j p_j \ln p_j \quad H(y|x) = -\sum_{i,j} p_{ij} \ln \frac{p_{ij}}{p_i}$$

$$(3)$$

This measure has already been used in causal discovery-related tasks. For example, Zhang et al. [19] applied this dependence measure to test the conditional independence of variables in the IC algorithm. In the work of Samothrakiset al. [14], the uncertainty coefficient is used as an asymmetric dependence feature that is used to train two Gradient Boosting Machines to detect a causal relationship between a pair of variables.

Given its asymmetric property, the uncertainty coefficient is a candidate to be used as an orientation method since it can assign the dependence of the relationship orientation and states its degree.

3   Causal Association Rules with Partial Association and Uncertainty Coefficient

In this section, we present CRPA-UC, a causal association rules algorithm. This approach can be used for both binary and non-binary categorical data. As conditional independence tests, it applies two tests: χ^2 and GCMH. Besides this, and since it is a global structure discovery algorithm, to direct the dependencies found by the conditional independence tests accordingly, the UC is applied. It is important to note that in this approach, testing a pair {A,B} and {B,A} will produce the same result. Hence each pair of variables is only tested once.

CRPA-UC (Algorithm 1) starts by searching, for each variable, for frequent itemsets (s_1, a) (with user-defined support) in which they are present and selects every variable a that meets this criterion. This pruning is performed because the objective is to generate rules that represent the data's frequent behaviours. Since infrequent itemsets only generate more infrequent supersets, these relations can be discarded. It is important to note that at this point, the algorithm only takes into account the frequency of the variables and not the values they can take. Next, CRPA-UC applies the χ^2 test (line 4). It defines that two variables are associated if the value resulting from the test is greater than or equal to its critical value ct, with significance level α. If the two variables are not dependent, then the second and third tests are ignored. In this case, χ^2 acts as a pre-processing method, in a way that CMH is more computationally demanding and if the algorithm determines *apriori* that two variables are not related, there is no need to apply it. In line 5, to variables selected by χ^2, the Generalised CMH test is applied. As explained earlier, this test checks if two variables remain dependent, given the other variables' influence. After determining all the potential partial associations, the UC is applied to determine the associations' direction (lines 7 and 8). The direction is obtained by testing both options ($A => B$ and $B => A$), with the selected option being the one with the highest coefficient (for the sake of consistency, the chosen value must also be higher than a minimum user-defined coefficient).

3.1 An Illustrative Example

To explain in more detail how this approach works, we will use as an example a data set[2] with three discrete variables (A, B and C), with 10 000 instance and values comprehended in $\{0, 1, 2\}$. This data set can be represented as $B \leftarrow A \rightarrow C$, meaning that A is a common cause of B and C. In this example, we will set the minimum support and α as 1% (being the correspondent critical value 6.64 for one degree of freedom), and the minimum accepted coefficient as 0.60. As we are looking for causal rules for all variables of the data set (in this case A, B and C), this algorithm will have three iterations: one to search for the rules of A, another to find the rules of B and a third for the rules of C. Since both GCMH test and χ^2 tests are symmetric, searching for the direction of the relation between A and B (when A is the target), and B and A (when B is the target) will have the same result (i.e. we will have $A \rightarrow B$ or $B \rightarrow A$ duplicated). To solve this duplication of results, the already tested variables are discarded, meaning that A is tested with B and C, B is only tested with C and C is not tested at all (as mentioned in the previous section).

We will start with variable A: in the first phase, the algorithm looks for the frequent itemsets in which the variable A is present. In this case, the method does not remove any variables since the minimum support is 100 (*number of instances* × *support*). Both B and C have higher support (4039 and 3653 respectively) and therefore are not removed. In the second phase (line 3 in the algorithm), the χ^2 test is applied. In this case, the value obtained for B and C are 1104.83 and 2758.66 respectively. Since we set α as 1% (with the correspondent critical being 6.64), this means that there is a (still undirected) dependence between B, C and A. Because of this, these two variables are selected to the next step: the GCMH test. The values obtained from this test are: 985.30 for A-B and 2690.41 for A-C. Since they are both higher than the critical value, this means that again B and C are associated with A. Finally, the UC is applied to B and C. As we can see in Table 3, the rules $A => B$ and $A => C$ are selected since the coefficient in both of these rules is the highest and is higher than the minimum acceptable coefficient. After the discovery A's rules, the same process is repeated for B. First, the algorithm looks for frequent itemsets with

---

[2] The data set is available in https://tinyurl.com/gitbub.

Algorithm 1: Causal Rules with Partial Association and Uncertainty Coefficient: CRPA-UC

Input: Let **D** be a data set with a set of variables $S = \{s_1, s_2, ..., s_n\}$. Let α be the significance level for the conditional independence tests and **ct** the correspondent critical value. Let $\mathbf{m}_{supp}$ be the minimum support. Let $\mathbf{u}_{coef}$ be the minimum accepted coefficient.

Output: R, a set of cause rules

1 **for** *each variable s_1 in D* **do**
2   Search for frequent itemsets in D containing s_1, with support higher than m_{supp}, and save them in F
3   **for** *each pair $\{s_1, s_2\}$ in F, with distribution $d = dist(s_1, s_2)$* **do**
4   **if** $\chi^2(d) \geq ct$ *verifies* **then**
5   **if** $Generalised_C MH(d) \geq ct$ *verifies* **then**
6   Verify $\{s_1, s_2\}$ direction using the uncertainty coefficient (UC)
7   **if** *the coefficient is higher than u_{coef}* **then**
8   Save rule in R

9 **return** R

Table 3. UC for variable A

Variable	$A \rightarrow Variable$	$Variable \rightarrow A$
B	<u>0.70</u>	0.60
C	<u>0.78</u>	0.70

variable B and scores the variables accordingly. In this case, and as stated before, the algorithm ignores variable A and only tests variable C. Being that this variable has the support of 3863 is not removed. After that, the first test is applied between variables B and C, and the correspondent value is 106.46, meaning that these two variables are dependent. This means that this variable is selected to be tested with the GCMH test, which returns the value 4.21. Since this value is inferior to the critical value (6.64) so B and C are independent. Since there are no variables to test with C (since after testing, the variables are removed), the algorithm ends with the following rules: $A \Longrightarrow B$ and $A \Longrightarrow C$.

4   Results and Discussion

To evaluate the proposed approach and make a comparative study, we design the following configuration of experiments: we compare the models generated by our approach with the PC algorithm and the real network in four distinct data sets, using pattern metrics [18]. We also compare the same models' performance in the classification, using several public data sets.

PC algorithm is a constraint-based bayesian causal algorithm and was proposed by Spirtes et al. [15]. It relies on the *faithfulness* assumption, which means that all the independencies in a DAG need to be under the d-separation criterion.

It can be divided into two distinct phases: the skeleton phase and the orientation phase. The algorithm starts with a fully connected graph in the first phase and removes an edge if the two nodes are not dependent. In the second phase, the algorithm orients the edges by first searching for v-structures and applying a set of rules [15]. This algorithm was selected instead of the algorithms presented in Sect. 2.1 because they are both local structure discovery algorithm (it only searches for the relations of a given variable) it is not possible to compare them with the proposed approach (at least not without modifying them).

A sensitivity analysis was performed to choose the optimal parameters for the approaches presented in the following sections. This analysis consisted of obtaining the error (*1 - accuracy*) for the presented data sets (by dividing them into 70% train, 30% test). In the case of PC, this test was repeated for significance levels 1% and 5%. In the case of CRPA-UC, the combination of significance level (1% and 5%), minimum support (1% and 5%) and uncertainty coefficient (0.1, 0.2, 0,3, 0,4, 0,5, 0,6, 0,7 and 0.8) were tested. In these tests, we concluded that the algorithm's error in the three data sets did not change much when the parameters were changed. For this reason, for all the data sets, we selected a significance level and minimum support of 1% and a minimum accepted coefficient of 0.6 (since this coefficient represents the strength of the relation, with this value we can find relationships that are moderately strong and avoid the weak ones). For easier comparison, in the tests presented in the following sections, only simple rules (*A => B*) will be considered for CRPA-UC.

4.1   Pattern Metrics Evaluation

To evaluate causal discovery algorithms, more specifically, graphical models, there is a set of metrics commonly used [18]. These metrics are: missing relationships, extra relationships, correct directed edges, incorrect directed edges Structural Hamming Distance (SHD) and Structural Intervention Distance (SID) [13]. To implement these measures it is necessary to have a network that represents the true relationships present in the data set. We have selected four public networks to test the approaches: asia[3], cancer (See footnote 3), sachs (See footnote 3) and lucas[4].

If we analyse Table 4, we can see that in general, CRPA-UC tends to have more edges that are correctly directed when compared with PC and less misdirected edges. Despite this, our approach tends to have more extra relations than PC (except in the case of *sachs* data set). If we analyse Fig. 1, that represents the comparison of the networks generated by PC and CRPA-UC with the true network for data set sachs, we can see that PC did not direct any edges and found a lower number of edges, when compared with CRPA-UC, that directed almost every edge it found correctly. This difference can be explained by the fact that these algorithms apply different independence tests (PC usually applies the

---

[3] Data set with 10 000 instances generated based on the network available in http://www.bnlearn.com/.

[4] http://www.causality.inf.ethz.ch/data/LUCAS.html.

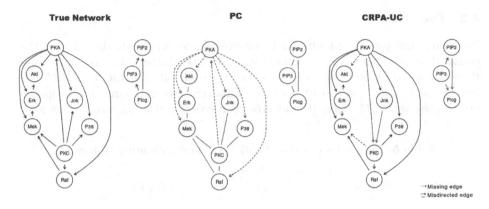

Fig. 1. True networks and graphs generated by PC and CRPA-UC for data set *Sachs*

Table 4. Pattern Metrics for Asia(8 edges), Cancer(4 edges), Sachs(17 edges) and Lucas(12 edges) data set

Dataset	Sachs		Cancer		Asia		Lucas	
Algorithm	PC	CRPAUC	PC	CRPAUC	PC	CRPAUC	PC	CRPAUC
Missing edges	7	2	0	0	3	4	0	0
Extra edges	0	0	0	0	0	1	0	1
Correct adjacencies	10	15	4	4	5	4	12	12
Incorrect adjacencies	0	0	0	0	0	1	0	1
Correct directed edges	0	10	2	2	2	2	7	9
Incorrect directed edges	10	5	2	2	3	2	5	3
SHD	17	7	2	2	6	7	5	4
SID	60	54	10	10	30	33	41	38

G^2, which is similar to χ^2), which means that in theory, they can obtain different dependencies. The orientation method is also different: PC applies a set of orientation rules [15], whereas CRPA-UC applies a coefficient that explains how a variable can predict another, and that is why it transmits more information about the relationship, such as its strength. Besides this, and if we analyse the data itself, we can see that asia, cancer and lucas data sets are binary, while sachs has non-binary categorical data (three categories per variable). From this, we can conclude that, while both approaches work similarly in binary data, while CRPA-UC appears to find more correct relations than PC in non-binary data. This number of correct relationships might happen because, in the binary data sets, it is impossible to presume any order. In Sachs case, the change in category is intrinsically connected with the changes in other variables (for example, if one gene takes the value of high, another gene can go low) [12]. Analysing now the two measures also presented in Table 4 (*SHD* and *SID*), it is possible to see that CRPA-UC in general has a better performance than PC (only having worse performance in *asia* data set).

4.2   Prediction

To better understand our approach, we now demonstrate another side of the causal discovery: prediction. To do that, and since all the rules are simple and there are no cycles between them, we converted each rule generate by CRPA-UC into an edge of the equivalent network. This time, we compared the proposed approaches with PC using 10-fold cross-validation in the following data sets:

Table 5. Error rates of PC and CRPA-UC in classification problems

Data set	PC	CRPA-UC
1 asia	15.18 ± 1.47	15.18 ± 1.47
2 cancer	1.05 ± 0.28	1.00 ± 0.25
3 coronary	14.13 ± 2.43	14.13 ± 2.43
4 earthquake	0.77 ± 0.33	0.67 ± 0.33
5 gmb	37.34 ± 4.92	+26.50 ± 5.07
6 lucas	20.02 ± 3.38	18.15 ± 4.02
7 monica	44.48 ± 3.35	+14.50 ± 0.67
8 mux6	61.86 ± 9.66	+45.26 ± 14.94
9 pre sex	24.64 ± 3.90	23.84 ± 3.32
10 sachs	39.61 ± 1.23	+34.49 ± 1.34
11 survey	43.95 ± 0.91	44.17 ± 1.12
12 titanic	24.16 ± 7.28	22.64 ± 3.45
13 youth risk 2009	40.80 ± 7.07	40.40 ± 6.31
Average Mean	25.385	20.602
Geometric Mean	17.594	14.709
Average Ranks	1.769	1.077
Average Error Ratio	1	0.842
Wicoxon test		0.00872
Win/Losses		10/1
Significant win/losses		4/0

asia, cancer, sachs, lucas, monica[5], earthquake (See footnote 3), survey (See footnote 3), coronary (See footnote 3), titanic (See footnote 5), youth risk 2009 (See footnote 5), gmB[6], mux6[7] and pre-sex[8]. Since PC produces a partially directed acyclic graph (PDAG), to be able to use the models for prediction, these models were extended to directed acyclic graphs (DAG) [4]. These algorithms' performance was compared in terms of error rate (Table 5). This comparison was performed using the PC algorithm as a reference. The performance of CRPA-UC in each data set was compared to the reference using the Wilcoxon signed ranked-test. The sign $+/-$ indicates that the algorithm is significantly better/worse than the reference with a p-value of less than 5%. Besides this, the algorithms are also compared in terms of the average and geometric mean of the errors, average ranks, average error ratio, win/losses, significant win/losses (number of times that the reference was better or worse than the algorithm, using signed ranked-test) and the Wilcoxon signed ranked-test. For the Wilcoxon signed ranked-test, we also consider a p-value of 5%.

If we analyse Table 5, it is possible to see that, in general, the CRPA-UC has a better performance than PC since the value obtained in the Wilcoxon test is 0.00873 or 0.873% (less then the p-value of 5%), which means that the difference between the performance is significant. This difference can also be seen in the values of the average and geometric ranks. More specifically, if we look at the average ranks, we can see that CRPA-UC has lower ranks (on average) than PC (1.077 against 1.769). The result obtained in these tests reinforces what was demonstrated in the previous section: the combination of *independence test-orientation method* has a beneficial impact on performance. This fact can be explained in two ways: first, by the difference in the way G^2 and GCMH calculate the dependencies. While G^2 is based on the GCMH likelihood-ratio, GCMH is a generalisation of the McNemar test [2]. This can explain the difference in the found relationships. Second, we use an orientation method that, besides orienting the relationships, can also find dependence between the variables (eliminating the weaker relations) to obtain more information about them.

5   Conclusion

Causality has become an increasingly studied topic in machine learning/data mining. Although Bayesian networks are among the favourite algorithms for applying causal discovery in observational data, more and more causal discovery algorithms have appeared that do not fall into this category in recent years. One example is the causal rule discovery algorithms. There are already a few approaches that combine causality with association rules. However, these methods have some disadvantages: they can only be used for local structure discovery in binary data and apply a naive approach has orientation method. This paper

---

[5] http://vincentarelbundock.github.io/Rdatasets/.

[6] https://rdrr.io/cran/pcalg/man/gmB.html.

[7] https://www.openml.org.

[8] https://cran.r-project.org/web/packages/vcd/index.html.

proposes a global causal association discovery algorithm for both binary and non-binary discrete data: CRPA-UC. In this method, we apply a combination of two independence tests, as well as the UC as a direct method. In the experiments, we compared this approach with PC, using public data sets. From these results, we can conclude that applying a more powerful independence test with an orientation method that also gives information about the variables' dependency positively impacts the method's performance. In the future, we are planning to study orientation in more depth and try to understand its overall impact on the discovery of causal relationships.

Acknowledgments. This research was carried out in the context of the project Fail-Stopper (DSAIPA/DS/0086/2018) and supported by the *Fundação* para a Ciência e Tecnologia (FCT), Portugal for the PhD Grant SFRH/BD/146197/2019.

References

1. Agrawal, R., Srikant, R., et al.: Fast algorithms for mining association rules. In: Proceedings of the 20th International Conference on Very Large Data Bases, VLDB, pp. 487–499 (1994)
2. Agresti, A.: Categorical Data Analysis, vol. 482. Wiley, Hoboken (2003)
3. Cochran, W.G.: Some methods for strengthening the common χ 2 tests. Biometrics **10**(4), 417–451 (1954)
4. Dor, D., Tarsi, M.: A simple algorithm to construct a consistent extension of a partially oriented graph. Technicial report R-185, Cognitive Systems Laboratory, UCLA (1992)
5. Ehring, D.: Causation and Persistence: A Theory of Causation. Oxford University Press, Oxford (1997)
6. Jin, Z., Li, J., Liu, L., Le, T.D., Sun, B., Wang, R.: Discovery of causal rules using partial association. In: Proceedings - IEEE International Conference on Data Mining, ICDM, pp. 309–318 (2012). https://doi.org/10.1109/ICDM.2012.36
7. Korb, K.B., Nicholson, A.E.: Bayesian Artificial Intelligence. CRC Press, Boca Raton (2010)
8. Landis, J.R., Heyman, E.R., Koch, G.G.: Average partial association in three-way contingency tables: a review and discussion of alternative tests. Int. Stat. Rev. **46**(3), 237 (2006). https://doi.org/10.2307/1402373
9. Li, J., et al.: From observational studies to causal rule mining. ACM Trans. Intell. Syst. Technol. (TIST) **7**(2), 14 (2016)
10. Li, J., Liu, L., Le, T.D.: Causal rule discovery with partial association test. In: Practical Approaches to Causal Relationship Exploration. SECE, pp. 33–50. Springer, Cham (2015). https://doi.org/10.1007/978-3-319-14433-7_4
11. Manimaran, J., Velmurugan, T.: Implementing association rules in medical diagnosis test data, December 2015
12. Mantel, N.: Chi-square tests with one degree of freedom; extensions of the Mantel-Haenszel procedure. J. Am. Stat. Assoc. **58**(303), 690–700 (1963)
13. Peters, J., Bühlmann, P.: Structural intervention distance for evaluating causal graphs. Neural Comput. **27**(3), 771–799 (2015)

14. Samothrakis, S., Perez, D., Lucas, S.: Training gradient boosting machines using curve-fitting and information-theoretic features for causal direction detection. In: Guyon, I., Statnikov, A., Batu, B.B. (eds.) Cause Effect Pairs in Machine Learning. TSSCML, pp. 331–338. Springer, Cham (2019). https://doi.org/10.1007/978-3-030-21810-2_11

15. Spirtes, P., Glymour, C., Scheines, R.: Causation, Prediction, and Search, vol. 81. Springer, New York (1993). https://doi.org/10.1007/978-1-4612-2748-9

16. Theil, H.: On the estimation of relationships involving qualitative variables. Am. J. Sociol. **76**(1), 103–154 (1970)

17. Theil, H.: Statistical decomposition analysis; with applications in the social and administrative sciences. Technical report (1972)

18. Yu, K., Li, J., Liu, L.: A review on algorithms for constraint-based causal discovery, pp. 1–17 (2016)

19. Zhang, X., Baral, C., Kim, S.: An algorithm to learn causal relations between genes from steady state data: simulation and its application to melanoma dataset. In: Miksch, S., Hunter, J., Keravnou, E.T. (eds.) AIME 2005. LNCS (LNAI), vol. 3581, pp. 524–534. Springer, Heidelberg (2005). https://doi.org/10.1007/11527770_69

Dynamic Topic Modeling Using Social Network Analytics

Shazia Tabassum[1]([✉]), João Gama[1], Paulo Azevedo[1], Luis Teixeira[2],
Carlos Martins[2], and Andre Martins[2]

[1] INESC TEC, University of Porto, Rua Dr. Roberto Frias, Porto, Portugal
shazia.tabassum@lnesctec.pt
[2] Skorr, Lisbon, Portugal
https://www.inesctec.pt/
https://skorr.social/

Abstract. Topic modeling or inference has been one of the well-known problems in the area of text mining. It deals with the automatic categorisation of words or documents into similarity groups also known as topics. In most of the social media platforms such as Twitter, Instagram, and Facebook, hashtags are used to define the content of posts. Therefore, modelling of hashtags helps in categorising posts as well as analysing user preferences. In this work, we tried to address this problem involving hashtags that stream in real-time. Our approach encompasses graph of hashtags, dynamic sampling and modularity based community detection over the data from a popular social media engagement application. Further, we analysed the topic clusters' structure and quality using empirical experiments. The results unveil latent semantic relations between hashtags and also show frequent hashtags in a cluster. Moreover, in this approach, the words in different languages are treated synonymously. Besides, we also observed top trending topics and correlated clusters.

Keywords: Topic modelling · Social network analysis · Hashtag networks

1 Introduction

Social media applications such as Twitter, Facebook, Instagram, Google, Linkedin have now become the core aspect of people's lives. Consequently, these are growing into a dominant platform for businesses, politics, education, marketing, news and so forth. The users are interested in which of such topics or products is one of the primary questions of research in this area. Inferring topics from unstructured data has been quite a challenging task.

Typically, the data gathered by the above applications is in the form of posts generated by the users. Posts can be short texts, images, videos, messy data such as concatenated words, URLs, misspelled words, acronyms, slangs and more. Classification of posts into topics is a complex problem. While topic modeling

© Springer Nature Switzerland AG 2021
G. Marreiros et al. (Eds.): EPIA 2021, LNAI 12981, pp. 498–509, 2021.
https://doi.org/10.1007/978-3-030-86230-5_39

algorithms such as Latent semantic analysis and Latent dirichlet allocation are originally designed to derive topics from large documents such as articles, and books. They are often less efficient when applied to short text content like posts [1]. Posts on the other hand are associated with rich user-generated hashtags to identify their content, to appear in search results and to enhance connectivity to the same topic. In [18] the authors state that hashtags provide a crowd sourcing way for tagging short texts, which is usually ignored by Bayesian statistics and Machine learning methods. Therefore, in this work, we propose to use these hashtags to derive topics using social network analysis methods, mainly community detection.

Moreover, the data generated from social media is typically massive and high velocity. Therefore, we tried to address the above issues by proposing an approach with the contributions stated below:

1. We propose fast and incremental method using social network analytics.
2. Unlike conventional models we use hashtags to model topics which saves the learning time, preprocessing steps, removal of stop words etc.
3. Our model categorises tags/words based on connectivity and modularity. In this way the tags/words are grouped accurately even though they belong to different languages or new hashtags appear.
4. We employ dynamic sampling mechanisms to decrease space complexity.

Rest of the paper is organised as follows: In Sect. 2 we presented a brief overview of the related works. Section 3 details the data set and some statistics about it. The methodology is described in Sect. 4. The experiments and results are discussed in Sect. 5. Finally, Sect. 6 summarizes conclusions and some potential future works.

2   Related Work

Research works focusing on topic modelling are mostly based on inferring abstract topics from long text documents. Latent dirichlet allocation [5] is one of the most popular techniques used for topic modelling where the topic probabilities provide an explicit representation of a document. However, it assumes fixed number of topics that a document belongs to. Other well known models include Latent semantic analysis [8], Correlated topic models [4], Probabilistic latent semantic indexing [10]. Word2Vec [13] is another popular word representation techniques. This model outputs a vector for each word, so it is necessary to combine those vectors to retrieve only one representation per product title or post, since there is the need to have the entire sentence representation and not only the values of each word. Word2Vec output dimensions can be configurable, and there is no ideal number for it since it can depend on the application and the tasks being performed. Moreover, these types of models are very common and can be expensive to train. However, traditional topic models also known as flat text models are incapable of modeling short texts or posts due to the severe sparseness, noise and unstructured data [11,18].

Recently, several researchers have focused on specifically hashtags clustering. In [14] the authors clustered hashtags using K-means on map reduce to find the structure and meaning in Twitter hashtags. Their study was limited to understanding the top few hashtags from three clusters. They found the top hashtags to be understandable as they are popular and while increasing the number of clusters the hashtags are dispersed into more specific topics. In another interesting work, multi-view clustering was used to analyse the temporal trends in Twitter hashtags during the Covid-19 pandemic [7]. The authors found that some topic clusters shift over the course of pandemic while others are persistent. Topic modelling was also applied on Instagram hashtags for annotating images [2]. In [3] the authors clustered twitter hashtags into several groups according to their word distributions. The model was expensive as Jensen-Shannon divergence was calculated between any two hashtags from the data. However, they considered a very small data set and calculated the probabilities for top 20 frequent hashtags while the structure and quality of clusters was not analysed.

While most of the models above were run on small-scale data sets crawled from one of the social media applications, we used a considerably large one which is composed of data from several micro blogging applications and also visualised the quality and structure of our clusters. Moreover, our approach is dynamic considering community detection for clustering tags.

3   Case Study

An anonymized data set is collected from a social media activity management application. The data set ranges from January to May 2020; comprises of 1002440 posts with 124615 hashtags posted by users on different social networking platforms (Twitter, Facebook, Instagram, Google). The content of posts is not available, instead the posts are identified with posts IDs and the users are identified with anonymous user IDs. Figure 2 displays the distribution of hashtags vs posts. A few hashtags are used by large number of posts and many different hastags are discussed by only some users. This satisfies a power law relation which is usually seen in most of the real world social networks [17]. Each post can include one or more hashtags or none. The number of posts per day is given in Fig. 1 which shows the seasonality of data. As one can observe there is decreased activity on weekends (Saturday and Sunday) compared to other days with the peaks on Fridays. The data in the last week of April had not been available which can be seen as an inconsistency in the curve with abnormally low activity close to zero. Figure 3 displays the top ten trending hashtags in the given data set. This type of analysis with the help of topic modelling or trending hashtags can be used to detect events. In the figure, the top two of frequent hashtags are relating to Covid19. What we need from our model is to cluster these hashtags and also the one's that are less frequent (such as covid, covid 19, corona etc.) to be classified as one topic relating to Covid19. Similarly, with the other tags and their related posts. In order to achieve this we followed the methodology briefed below.

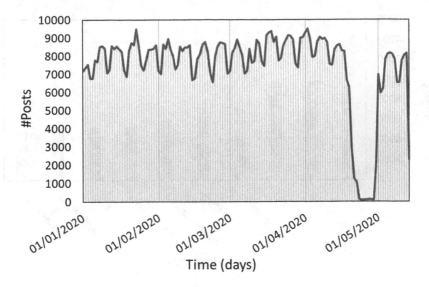

Fig. 1. Temporal distribution of posts per day

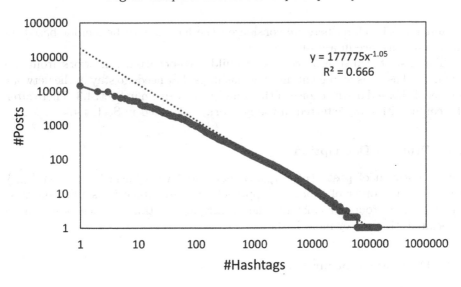

Fig. 2. Posts vs hashtags distribution (blue line). Power curve following given function (red) (Color figure online)

4   Methodology

Text documents share common or similar words between them, which is exploited in calculating similarity scores. However, topic modeling in hashtags is unlike

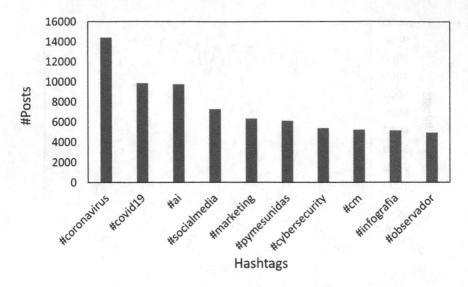

Fig. 3. Top ten trending hashtags distribution

documents. Therefore, here we considered the hashtags to be similar based on their co-occurrence in a post.

The first step in the process is to build a co-occurrence network from the streaming hashtags incrementally. The hashtags that needs to stay in the network are decided based on the choice of the sampling algorithm in Sect. 4.3. There after the communities are detected in the network as detailed in Sect. 4.4.

4.1 Problem Description

Given a stream of posts $\{p_1, p_2, p_3...\}$ associated with hashtags $\{h_1, h_2, h_3...\}$ arriving in the order of time, our approach aims to categorize similar posts or hashtags into groups or clusters called topics at any time t. Each post can be associated with one or more hashtags.

4.2 Hashtag Co-occurrence Network

In our graph based approach, we constructed the network of hashtags by creating an edge e between the ones that have been tagged together in a post. Therefore $e = (h_i, h_j, t)$ where $i, j \in \mathbb{N}$ and t is the time stamp when it occurred.

4.3 Stream Sampling

As posts are temporal in nature generating in every time instance, so are the hashtags. Also, there are new hashtags emerging over time. Moreover, the context for grouping hashtags may change over time. For example, hand sanitizers and face masks were not as closely related as with the onset of covid19. Therefore, we employed the approach of exploiting the relation between hashtags based on the recent events or popular events by using the real-time dynamic sampling techniques below.

Sliding Windows. Sometimes applications need recent information and its value diminishes by time. In that case sliding windows continuously maintain a window size of recent information [9]. It is a common approach in data streams where an item at index i enters the window while another item at index $i - w$ exits it. Where w is the window size which can be fixed or adaptive. The window size can be based on number of observations or length of time. In the later case an edge (h_i, h_j, t) enters window while an edge $(h_i, h_j, t - w)$ exits.

Space Saving. The Space Saving Algorithm [12] is the most approximate and efficient algorithm for finding the top frequent items from a data stream. The algorithm maintains the partial interest of information as it monitors only a subset of items from the stream. It maintains counters for every item in the sample and increments its count when the item re-occurs in the stream. If a new item is encountered in the stream, it is replaced with an item with the least counter value and its count is incremented.

Biased Random Sampling. This algorithm [16] ensures every incoming item m in stream goes into the reservoir with probability 1. Any item n from the reservoir is chosen for replacement at random. Therefore, on every item insertion, the probability of removal for the items in the reservoir is $1/k$, where k is the size of reservoir. Hence, the item insertion is deterministic but deletion is probabilistic. The probability of n staying in the reservoir when m arrives is given by $(1 - 1/k)^{(t_m - t_n)}$. As the time of occurrence or index of m increases, the probability of item n from time t staying in reservoir decreases. Thus the item staying for a long time in the reservoir has an exponentially greater probability of getting out than an item inserted recently. Consequently, the items in the reservoir are super linearly biased to the latest time. This is a notable property of this algorithm as it does not have to store the ordering or indexing information as in sliding windows. It is a simple algorithm with $O(1)$ computational complexity.

4.4   Community Detection

Community detection is very well known problem in social networks. Communities can be defined as groups, modules or clusters of nodes which are densely connected between themselves and sparsely connected to the rest of the network. The connections can be directed, undirected, weighted etc. Communities can be overlapping (where a node belongs to more than one community) or distinct. Community detection is in its essence a clustering problem. Thus, detecting

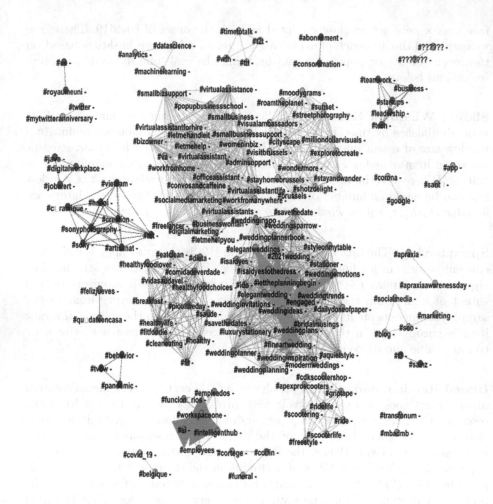

Fig. 4. Sliding window

communities reduces to a problem of clustering data points. It has a wide scope of applicability in real-world networks.

In this work, we applied the community detection algorithm proposed by Blondel et al. [6] on every dynamic sample snapshot discretely. However, an incremental community detection algorithm can also be applied on every incoming edge. Nevertheless, the technique mentioned above is a heuristic based on modularity optimization. **Modularity** is a function that can be defined as the number of edges within communities minus the number of expected edges in the same at random [15] as computed below.

$$Q = \frac{1}{2m} \sum [A_{ij} - \frac{k_i k_j}{2m}]\delta(c_i, c_j), \tag{1}$$

where m is the number of edges, k_i and k_j represent, respectively, the degree of nodes i and j, A_{ij} is the entry of the adjacency matrix that gives the number of edges between nodes i and j, $\frac{k_i k_j}{2m}$ represents the expected number of edges falling between those nodes, c_i and c_j denote the groups to which nodes i and j belong, and $\delta(c_i, c_j)$ represents the Kronecker delta. Maximizing this function leads to communities with highly connected nodes between themselves than to the rest of the network. However in very large networks the connections are very sparse and even a single edge between two clusters is regarded as strong correlation. Therefore, a resolution parameter is used to control high or low number of communities to be detected. Modularity is also used as a quality metric as shown in Table 1.

The above said algorithm has a fastest runtime of $O(n.log_2 n)$, where n is the number of nodes in the network. In our case n is very small compared to the total number of nodes in the network, for instance n is equal to the number of hashtags in a sliding window.

5   Experimental Evaluation

The experiments are conducted to evaluate the above method of detecting topic clusters in the data detailed in Sect. 3[1]. To facilitate visual evaluation and demonstration, the size of samples is fixed to be 1000 edges. In the case of sliding windows the window size is based on number of observations i.e. 1000 edges. However, a time window such as edges from recent one day/one month can also be considered. The resolution parameter in community detection for all the methods is set to 1.0. The detected clusters are shown in Figs. 4, 5, and 6. The figures represent sample snapshots in the end of stream. Each cluster with a different color in the figure represents a topic. Sliding windows and biased sampling considers repetitive edges as the frequency or weight of an edge which is depicted as thick arrows or lines in the figures. The thicker edge represents stronger connection between two hashtags. The hashtags with thicker edges are considered top hashtags in their cluster as they are most frequent.

The choice of sampling algorithm has different trade offs. For finding the most frequent or trending topics from the stream over time, space saving is a relevant choice; however, it is computationally expensive compared to the other two though it is space efficient and the fastest one of its genre. The one with least time complexity among the three is biased sampling but lacks in terms of structure in this case, with a very sparse graph.

5.1   Results Discussion

We see that the clusters in the figures clearly make sense in terms of synonymy and polysemy (for example in Fig. 5, synonyms such as covid, covid 19, etc., are

---

[1] Python code for algorithms is available at https://github.com/ShaziaTabassum/hashtagnetworkstream.

Fig. 5. Space saving

grouped in one blue cluster on the right and polysemy words are sharing two clusters green and orange in the center). The clusters formed by sliding windows are more denser than the other two. Quantitative metrics of these graphs are displayed in Table 1. The bias to low degree hashtags has increased the number of components and decreased the density. Nevertheless, a large cluster of the popular topic "covid19" can only be seen in space saving because sliding window and biased sampling collect data from the end of stream that is from the month of May, where it has low occurrence in our data. Moreover, the top trending hashtags from Fig. 3 in analysis are found inside communities of space saving (Fig. 5). However, they are also found in sliding window and biased sampling as we increase the sample size.

Fig. 6. Biased random sampling

The results also show correlated clusters that share common hashtags as seen in Fig. 5, the green and orange cluster. Another important feature is that tags in different languages (Portugues, Spanish or more) are still clustered semantically, such as in Fig. 5 "confinamiento" belongs to covid cluster. Moreover, acronyms such as "ai" belongs to artificial intelligence cluster.

The posts and users relating to these hashtags can be further investigated for numerous applications. Each post is associated with multiple hashtags, therefore each post can be assigned to a number of topics.

Table 1. Network properties

	Average degree	Avg. weighted degree	Density	Modularity	#Clusters
Sliding window	6.6	6.667	0.087	0.723	25
Space saving	3.413	3.413	0.022	0.806	33
Biased sampling	2.687	2.747	0.015	0.872	61

6   Conclusion and Future Work

In this work, we have presented a fast and memory efficient approach for incrementally categorising posts into topics using hashtags. We proved the efficacy of method over a large data set. We discussed how the different sampling algorithms can effect the outcome. Further, we considered their biases and trade offs. We analysed the seasonality and trending hashtags in the data. We compared their outcomes in terms of semantics and structure of clusters. To facilitate comprehensibility we preferred network visualisation layouts over the conventional presentation using tables.

There can be many potential applications as an advancement of this work. The users posting in particular topics can be classified accordingly to analyse their preferences for product marketing and identifying nano influencers to enhance their engagement. On the availability of posts text we can implement other topic models and improve them using our approach. Further, we intend to analyse the trend of topics overtime and the evolution of communities. Additionally, predicting hashtags for the missing ones using our topic model.

Acknowledgements. This work is financed by National Funds through the Portuguese funding agency, FCT - Fundação para a Ciência e a Tecnologia, within project UIDB/50014/2020.

References

1. Alash, H.M., Al-Sultany, G.A.: Improve topic modeling algorithms based on Twitter hashtags. J. Phys. Conf. Ser. **1660**, 012100 (2020)
2. Argyrou, A., Giannoulakis, S., Tsapatsoulis, N.: Topic modelling on instagram hashtags: An alternative way to automatic image annotation? In: 2018 13th International Workshop on Semantic and Social Media Adaptation and Personalization (SMAP), pp. 61–67. IEEE (2018)
3. Bhakdisuparit, N., Fujino, I.: Understanding and clustering hashtags according to their word distributions. In: 2018 5th International Conference on Business and Industrial Research (ICBIR), pp. 204–209. IEEE (2018)
4. Blei, D., Lafferty, J.: Correlated topic models. Adv. Neural. Inf. Process. Syst. **18**, 147 (2006)
5. Blei, D.M., Ng, A.Y., Jordan, M.I.: Latent Dirichlet allocation. J. Mach. Learn. Res. **3**, 993–1022 (2003)

6. Blondel, V.D., Guillaume, J.L., Lambiotte, R., Lefebvre, E.: Fast unfolding of communities in large networks. J. Stat. Mech. Theory Exp. **2008**(10), P10008 (2008)
7. Cruickshank, I.J., Carley, K.M.: Characterizing communities of hashtag usage on twitter during the 2020 covid-19 pandemic by multi-view clustering. Appl. Network Sci. **5**(1), 1–40 (2020)
8. Deerwester, S., Dumais, S.T., Furnas, G.W., Landauer, T.K., Harshman, R.: Indexing by latent semantic analysis. J. Am. Soc. Inf. Sci. **41**(6), 391–407 (1990)
9. Gama, J.: Knowledge Discovery from Data Streams. Chapman and Hall/CRC Data Mining and Knowledge Discovery Series, CRC Press (2010)
10. Hofmann, T.: Probabilistic latent semantic indexing. In: Proceedings of the 22nd Annual International ACM SIGIR Conference on Research and Development in Information Retrieval, pp. 50–57 (1999)
11. Hong, L., Davison, B.D.: Empirical study of topic modeling in twitter. In: Proceedings of the First Workshop on Social Media Analytics, pp. 80–88 (2010)
12. Metwally, A., Agrawal, D., El Abbadi, A.: Efficient computation of frequent and top-k elements in data streams. In: International Conference on Database Theory, pp. 398–412. Springer (2005)
13. Mikolov, T., Yih, W.t., Zweig, G.: Linguistic regularities in continuous space word representations. In: Proceedings of the 2013 Conference of the North American Chapter of the Association for Computational Linguistics: Human Language Technologies, pp. 746–751 (2013)
14. Muntean, C.I., Morar, G.A., Moldovan, D.: Exploring the meaning behind twitter hashtags through clustering. In: Abramowicz, W., Domingue, J., Węcel, K. (eds.) BIS 2012. LNBIP, pp. 231–242. Springer, Heidelberg (2012). https://doi.org/10.1007/978-3-642-34228-8_22
15. Newman, M.E.: Finding community structure in networks using the eigenvectors of matrices. Phys. Rev. E **74**(3), 036104 (2006)
16. Tabassum, S., Gama, J.: Sampling massive streaming call graphs. In: ACM Symposium on Advanced Computing, pp. 923–928 (2016)
17. Tabassum, S., Pereira, F.S., Fernandes, S., Gama, J.: Social network analysis: an overview. Wiley Interdisciplinary Rev. Data Mining Knowl. Discov. **8**(5), e1256 (2018)
18. Wang, Y., Liu, J., Huang, Y., Feng, X.: Using hashtag graph-based topic model to connect semantically-related words without co-occurrence in microblogs. IEEE Trans. Knowl. Data Eng. **28**(7), 1919–1933 (2016)

Imbalanced Learning in Assessing the Risk of Corruption in Public Administration

Marcelo Oliveira Vasconcelos[1]([✉]) [iD], Ricardo Matos Chaim[2] [iD], and Luís Cavique[3] [iD]

[1] Tribunal de Contas do Distrito Federal, Brasília, Brasil
mov@tc.df.gov.br
[2] Universidade de Brasília, Brasília, Brasil
ricardc@unb.br
[3] LASIGE, Universidade Aberta, Lisboa, Portugal
luis.cavique@uab.pt

Abstract. This research aims to identify the corruption of the civil servants in the Federal District, Brazilian Public Administration. For this purpose, a predictive model was created integrating data from eight different systems and applying logistic regression to real datasets that, by their nature, present a low percentage of examples of interest in identifying patterns for machine learning, a situation defined as a class imbalance. In this study, the imbalance of classes was considered extreme at a ratio of 1:707 or, in percentage terms, 0.14% of the interest class to the population. Two possible approaches were used, balancing with resampling techniques using synthetic minority oversampling technique SMOTE and applying algorithms with specific parameterization to obtain the desired standards of the minority class without generating bias from the dominant class. The best modeling result was obtained by applying it to the second approach, generating an area value on the ROC curve of around 0.69. Based on sixty-eight features, the respective coefficients that correspond to the risk factors for corruption were found. A subset of twenty features is discussed in order to find practical utility after the discovery process.

Keywords: Data enrichment · Imbalanced learning · Corruption · Public administration

1 Introduction

Corruption in public administration is a problem that could be addressed through machine learning to identify risk factors for mitigation by the supervisory body. This research explores this scenario in a Brazilian case study.

Corruption is a common problem in developing countries (Olken 2007), leading to an increase in the cost of public services, undermining economic growth (Mauro 1995), and impairing private business conduction.

Corruption is the abuse of the power entrusted to private gain (Transparency International, n.d.), and the cost of corruption is high. Part of that cost is the fee added to the contract value by charging the public budget. Another part of public administration

© Springer Nature Switzerland AG 2021
G. Marreiros et al. (Eds.): EPIA 2021, LNAI 12981, pp. 510–523, 2021.
https://doi.org/10.1007/978-3-030-86230-5_40

is poor public resources management that generates low-quality public service provision. There is also the devaluation of assets and losses of national and international investments (Padula & Albuquerque 2018).

This research sought to study and apply data mining techniques to create a predictive model for assessing the risk of the corruptibility of public servants in the Federal District, considering studies carried out on corruption and consultation with specialists on the subject.

This document contributes to the corruption data enrichment, the research of two classes of algorithms in imbalanced learning, and the impact of knowledge discovery in corruption literature.

The procedure used in this work can be summarized in three steps: (i) data enrichment and data cleansing, (ii) imbalance learning models, (iii) discussion of the findings. The proposed procedure can be presented in the following data pipeline: data pre-processing → learning models → findings discussion.

The remaining of the paper is organized as follows. Section 2 describes the data enrichment and data cleansing processes. Section 3 presents two imbalanced learning approaches. Section 4 provides computational results. The discussion of the results is reported in Sect. 5. Finally, in Sect. 6, the conclusions are drawn.

2 Data Enrichment and Data Cleansing

In the data mining process, data enrichment and data cleansing are essential stages to set a data frame. This section is handling the activities of these stages.

Data enrichment enhances collected data with relevant context obtained from additional sources (Knapp & Langill 2014). Data cleansing is the process of attempting to fill in missing values, smooth out noise while identifying outliers, and correct inconsistencies in the data (Han et al. 2012).

Data enrichment and data cleansing have activities occurring in parallel and are explained in this section.

A compilation of eight different databases from the Brazilian Federal Government and Federal District was used to compose the data frame. These data represent the information from 303,036 civil servants, militaries, and pensioners of the Federal District.

Federal District is a legal entity of internal public law, which is part of the political-administrative structure of Brazil, of a *sui generis* nature because it is neither a state nor a municipality. A unique entity accumulates the legislative powers reserved to the states and the municipalities, which gives it a hybrid nature of state and municipality.

The concept of corruption adopted in this research was described in Brazilian Law No. 8,429/92, which defines corruption as an act of improbity that, under the influence or not of the position, causes illicit enrichment, causes or not mandatory, will be used to the purse or violate Public Administration principles (Brasil 1992).

The attribute corresponding to this definition is represented by "C.CorruptionTG", which will be described with the independent attributes in Table 1.

The data obtained from these databases were outlined by their attributes classified by domains according to the following areas of knowledge: corruption (C), functional work (W), political (P), and Business (B), as defined below.

Table 1. Extract of attribute's description

Attribute name	Type	Brief description
Corruption domain (C)		
C.CorruptionTG	Boolean	Cases of dismission by corruption, this is the target
C.CEIS	Boolean	Cases of individuals or legal entities with restrictions on the right to participate in tenders or to contract with the Public Administration by sanctions
C.TCDFrestriction	Boolean	Cases of person who are not qualified to exercise a position in a commission or a trust function within the Public Administration of the Federal District for a period of up to eight years due to severe irregularities found by the TCDF
Functional work domain (W)		
W.Salary	Numeric	Salary of the civil servant or military that included the salary received by any of the databases (SIGRH and SIAPE) or the sum of salaries in the case of civil servants who accumulate public positions as permitted by the Federal Constitution
W.QtySIGRHOff	Int	Quantity of positions that the civil servant or military held until Nov/2020 into the SIGRH determined only with the SIGRH database
W.QtySIAPEOff	Int	Quantity of positions the civil servant or military held in Public Security until Nov/2020 at SIAPE (Public Security, SIAPE)
W.QtySIGRHfunc	Int	Quantity of functions that the civil servant occupied until Nov/2020 in the SIGRH (Servers, except Public Security, SIGRH)
W.QtySIAPEfunc	Int	Quantity of functions that the civil servant or military occupied until Nov/2020 in SIAPE (SIAPE Public Security)
Political domain (P)		
P.CandEducation	Categorical	Candidate's level of education can be defined as non-disclosable, reads and writers, incomplete or complete elementary school, incomplete or complete high school, and incomplete or complete higher education
P.CandMaritalSt	Categorical	The civil status situation of the candidate civil servant: single, married, non-disclosable, widowed, legally separated, or divorced
Business Domain (B)		
B.OwnershipPerc	Numeric	Percentage of share capital that the civil servant or military presents at Nov/2020
B.QtFirmAct	Int	Number of secondary activities registered by the company in which the civil servant or military is a partner

(continued)

Table 1. (*continued*)

Attribute name	Type	Brief description
B.CodFirmAct	Categorical	The main activity of the firm/company in which the civil servant or military is a partner
B.CodFirmSize	Categorical	Size of the company that can be Individual Micro entrepreneur (MEI), Microenterprise (ME), Small Business (EPP), medium or large depending on the gross annual turnover of the head office and its branches, or that is, the global gross revenue defined in the tax legislation
B.DaysOwnership	Numeric	This attribute informs the number of days that the server is a partner in the company until Nov/2020
B.CodFirmTaxOpt	Categorical	This attribute informs if the company opted for the simplified taxation system - Simples Nacional - which aims to help micro and small companies concerning the payment of taxes

For this research, a dataset was created after an ETL process (extract, transform and load) collected from these different data sources, as described below:

- Expulsion Registrations maintained by Comptroller General of the Federal District (Portal da Transparência DF);
- SIGRH - Integrated Resource Management System maintained by Federal District Government;
- SIAPE – Integrated Human Resources Administration System maintained by Federal Government;
- Persons that by sanction are not allowed for the exercise commission position or a trust function within the scope of the Public Administration of the Federal District maintained by TCDF;
- Private Non-Profit Entities Prevented from contracting with the Public Administration (CEPIM) maintained by Office of the Comptroller General (Controladoria-Geral da União—CGU);
- Registration of Unfaithful and Suspended Companies (CEIS) maintained by Office of the Comptroller General (Controladoria-Geral da União—CGU);
- Electoral Data maintained by Superior Electoral Court (TSE); and
- Personal and Legal Data maintained by Secretariat of the Federal Revenue of Brazil (SRF/ME).

In the present work, the dependent variable (C.CorruptionTG) is binary. In preparing the data, to obtain processed and prepared data to demonstrate the understanding of the business. Database integration work took place for the integrated Resource Management System (SIGRH) and the Integrated Human Resource Management System (SIAPE). There are two different databases for payment of the Federal District Government civil servant/military that separate Public Security servers (SIAPE) from other civil servants (Education, Health, and other areas).

Categorical attributes were transformed into binary, i.e., variables that describe categories or classifications; for binary attributes, variables with a value of 0 or 1 express the existence or absence of the binary attribute. This procedure is also known as an application for dummy variables.

Another perspective of attribute construction used was the transformation of categorical attributes into counting attributes. This procedure was performed because the attribute when expressing quantity has meaning in the context of business understanding. In contrast, the categorical value does not express benefit in the context of the investigation.

For example, a categorical attribute means that the civil servant or military man/woman occupied in Public Administration has no meaning for this investigation. However, several positions he/she had occupied could inform that this one does not have a stable condition and could represent an anomaly.

Initially, the data set comprised 28 attributes (numeric and categorical) list in Table 1, which after necessary transformations of the categorical resulted in 11 numeric attributes and 1,116 binaries attributes described in Table 2.

Moreover, to avoid bias of the numerical attributes in the algorithm, these numerical attributes were normalized as the last transformation. Finally, each value was subtracted from the lowest value of the attribute and divided by the amplitude (highest value subtracted from the lowest value of the attribute), resulting in values between zero and one.

Along with all these steps, missing values and outliers were treated properly; some attributes were built to generate relevant information for the business from the original data. After cleansing data and building attributes, analysis of variance and correlation was performed.

Regarding the assessment of correlation between variables, four attributes with Pearson's correlation above 0.9 and seven attributes with a correlation between 0.8 and 0.9 were identified and excluded.

After calculating the variance of the attributes, one of them presented a null value, 294 attributes showed a variance less than 0.00001, and 421 attributes registered a variance between 0.00001 and 0.0001.

After excluding these attributes in this condition, the dimensionality reduced from 1,127 attributes to 397 attributes.

Another measure that reduces the dimensionality was excluding predictors that cannot be concluded if there is a statistically significant association with the response variable (target), i.e., when the predictor has a p-value greater or equal to the significance level, 0.05. Excluding these attributes (predictors), the model generated was left with sixty-eight attributes, and all of the excluding attributes in the cleansing process in resume in Table 2.

Table 2. Data cleansing

	Types of attributes			
	Numeric	Categorical	Binary	Total
Original attributes	11	13	4	28
1 - Transformation of categorical attributes into binaries	11	0	1116	1127
2 - Exclusions of attributes with:				
2.1 - Correlation between > 0.8	8	0	1105	1112
2.2 - Variance < 0.0001	8	0	389	397
2.3 – p-value > 0.05	8	0	60	68

3 Imbalanced Learning

In this section, the research's theoretical for imbalanced learning is presented. In the context of actual data related to corruption or fraud, the number of examples of the interest data predominately represents a small percentage of the dataset. This characteristic is considered a class imbalance. Therefore, the class of interest is reduced concerning the dominant class.

Most machine learning algorithms assume that all misclassification errors made by a model are equal. However, it is often not the case for imbalanced classification problems. For example, missing a positive or minority class case is worse than incorrectly classifying an example from the negative or majority class. There are many real-world examples, such as detecting spam email, diagnosing a medical condition, or identifying fraud (Brownlee 2020).

Zhu et al. (Zhu et al. 2018) suggest solving imbalanced datasets by two possible solutions: data-level solutions and algorithm-level solutions. Table 3 presents a variant of the taxonomy presented in Vimalraj & Rajendran (Vimalraj & Rajendran 2018), showing the algorithms that handle imbalanced data for both methods.

Table 3. Methods and algorithms to handle imbalanced data

Data-level	Algorithmic-level
Over-sampling (smote)	One class learning
Under-sampling	Cost-sensitive learning
Feature selection	Logistic regression

The data-level solutions are resampling data as a pre-processing step to reduce the negative effect caused by class imbalance.

Two methods are considered usual to minimize class imbalance in the pre-processing data phase: under-sampling and over-sampling.

The first deals with the random exclusion of observations from the majority class, while the second deals with the multiple creations of copies of observations from the minority class. However, both methods have disadvantages. For example, under-sampling can discard potentially useful data instances, while oversampling can increase the probability of overfitting, which corresponds to the occurrence of a statistical model very well-adjusted to the set of data previously observed, but proves inefficient to predict new results.

A specific technique was created to minimize the effects of the previous techniques – synthetic minority oversampling technique (SMOTE), covered in detail in the next item.

The algorithm-level solutions aim to develop new algorithms or modify existing ones to deal with imbalanced datasets. For example, in Brownlee (Brownlee 2020), the author presents two approaches for modifying algorithms in Logistic Regression to apply for imbalanced classes: Weighted Logistic Regression Algorithm and Heuristic implementation for Logistic Regression.

3.1 Synthetic Minority Oversampling Technique (SMOTE)

SMOTE technique was presented by Chawla (Chawla et al. 2002). SMOTE combines the oversampling method of the minority class (abnormal), under-sampling of the majority class (standard), and the creation of synthetic examples of the minority class. As a result, this new dataset can better perform the classifier (in the ROC space) than merely sub-sampling of the majority class.

This technique is widely used. An indicator of this fact is that the SMOTE article (Chawla et al. 2002) was cited more than 6,300 according to Web of Science. Furthermore, after 15 years of the publication of this paper, more than 85 extensions of SMOTE have been proposed by specialized literature. (Alberto Fernandez et al. 2018).

3.2 Logistic Regression

Logistic Regression is a method developed under the leadership of the statistician Ronald Fisher. It involves estimating parameter β of a probability distribution of random variable X with a certain number of independent observations.

Logistic Regression is usual in situations where the dependent variable is of a binary or dichotomous nature, while the independent variables can be categorical or not. The Logistic Regression seeks to estimate the probability of a given event concerning a set of variables that explain the phenomenon.

In Logistic Regression, the probability of an event occurring can be estimated directly. The dependent variable can assume two states (0 or 1), and there is a set of p independent variables X1, X2,..., Xp according to the following equation.

$$P(Y = 1) = \frac{1}{1 + e^{-g(x)}}$$
(1)

Where g (x) = B_0 + $B_1 X_1$ + ... + $B_p X_p$. The coefficients B_0, B_1,... B_p are estimated from the dataset, using the maximum likelihood method, which determines the combination of coefficients that maximizes the probability.

The classic references of Logistic Regression are Cox & Snell and Hosmer & Lemeshow (Hosmer & Lemeshow 1999). Positive values for Logistic Regression coefficients represent an increase in the probability, i.e., a negative decrease in the probability.

An important concept was presented by Mandrekar (Mandrekar 2010), which defined as ROC curve a sensibility graph versus a test specificity, and the area above this curve expresses the model's measure performance. In this study, it is established that an area above the ROC – AUC curve (*Area Under Curve – AUC*) of 0.5 suggests no discrimination; 0.7 to 0.8 is considered acceptable; 0.8 to 0.9 is considered excellent, and over 0.9 is considered exceptional.

Logistic Regression is a powerful classifier by providing probabilities and by extending to multi-class classification problems. The advantages of using Logist Regression are that it has been extensively studied, and it does not make assumptions about the distribution of the independent variables (Maalouf & Siddiqi 2014).

In an imbalanced dataset context, there are implementations of Logistic Regression for algorithm-level solutions (Maalouf & Siddiqi 2014)(Maalouf & Trafalis 2011) (Brownlee 2020), and for data-level solutions (Torgo et al. 2013) (Brownlee 2020).

4   Computational Results

In this research, after pre-processing the dataset, two approaches were applied for Logistic Regression to obtain better performance: data-level solutions and algorithm-level solutions. In this section, both solutions will be detailed.

According to Brownlee (Brownlee 2020), an extreme imbalance is challenging for modeling that requires specialized techniques. Therefore, in this investigation, the two possibilities of data imbalance treatment were addressed.

4.1   Data-Level Solutions

This approach is the treatment of data to make the classes balanced. In the literature, the technique widely used for imbalanced data is SMOTE and its variations/extensions, as explained in item 3.2.

The values obtained as an application of the SMOTE technique and extensions are summarized in Table 4.

4.2   Algorithm-Level Solutions

In a different approach, without applying the sampling method, the Logistic Regression algorithm was employed with specific characteristics to deal with the imbalanced data. (Brownlee 2020) The performance was obtained concerning the area of the ROC curve (AUC).

Initials tests were executed using different machine learning techniques, but the low performance on AUC takes to abandon these approaches. For the Decision Tree, the result for AUC was 0.578. Applying Support Vector Machine, the AUC was 0.621. The neural network reveals the worst value, 0.500, and the better performance in this

Table 4. Data-Level Solutions - Results of the area on the ROC curve with SMOTE

Techniques	Area under ROC curve (AUC)	Package
SMOTE e random Under-sampling	0.658	from imblearn.over_sampling & from imblearn.under_sampling (Python)
SMOTE and Tomek Links sampling	0.534	imblearn.combine & imblearn.under_sampling (Python)
SMOTEENN	0.601	imblearn.combine (Python)
SMOTE	0.422	SmoteFamily (R)
DBSMOTE	0.534	SmoteFamily (R)
ADAS	0.548	SmoteFamily (R)
ANS	0.534	SmoteFamily (R)
SLS	0.491	SmoteFamily (R)

Source: Smote Family documentation available in https://cran.r-project.org/web/packages/smotef amily/smotefamily.pdf

test was for Logistic Regression, at least 0.647. All of the tests were applied by the same technique - Predefined Weights, and this type of approach will be detailed in the following paragraphs.

Two models were applied. The first was defining weight for the different classes, which is the proportion of cases of the minority class concerning the majority class.

In this approach, the focus is on modifying the classifier learning procedure.

An important property has to be addressed by the algorithm. Not all classification errors are equal. For this research, a false negative is worse or more costly than a false positive.

This issue is settled by cost-sensitive learning that takes the costs of prediction errors into account when training a machine learning model.

In cost-sensitive learning, each class is given a misclassification cost instead of each instance being either correctly or incorrectly classified. Thus, instead of optimizing the accuracy, the problem is then to minimize the total misclassification cost. Thus, a penalty associated with an incorrect prediction is named cost.

Weighted Logistic Regression implements cost-sensitive learning for Logistic Regression in Python (library Scikit-Learn), supporting class weighting.

This relation in target attribute (C.CorruptionTG) was 428 cases True and 302,608 cases False, the ratio value is $428/302,608 = 0.0014$. Adopting this value was employed as a class weight for the weighted Logistic Regression algorithm.t

The second model was a heuristic implementation of best practices used in the weighting of classes available in the library Scikit-Learn implemented in Python.

In this model, the weight assigned is dividing the population quantity by the product of the number of classes by the population quantity of the majority class, and the algorithm calculates it.

Both implementations were for Logistic Regression (LOGIT) through the Scikit-Learn library implemented in Python.

The results were calculated by averages of the AUC curve calculated using cross-validation with ten folders. That is, the partitions were remade three times to represent the most appropriate value for measurement.

For addressed adequately, the imbalanced classes were used as a library resource to ensure that the cross-validation partitions contain proportional samples from the minority class that is the class of interest in the research. Table 5 shows a summary of the algorithm-level computational results.

Table 5. Algorithm-level solutions

Model	Area under ROC curve (AUC)
I - Predefined weights	0.692
II - Heuristic weights	0.647

The best result for algorithm-level solutions was the Predefined Weights with a fixed weight assignment of 0.0014 according to the proportion of True and False cases of the target attribute.

The values obtained as an application of the Data-level solutions by applying SMOTE technique were not better than applying the Algorithm-level Solution. For example, the value range for AUC was from 0.491 to 0.658.

From this modeling result of Predefined Weights, the coefficients of the logistic regression attributes were established.

5 Discussion

The last section has presented the results of different approaches, and the best result, Predefined Weights, was used for modeling. Finally, the coefficients of the Logistic Regression attributes were established, and Table 6 lists the main attributes.

The coefficient ($b_\#$) is the estimated increase in the natural logarithm odds of the outcome per unit increase in the exposure value. In other words, the exponential function of the regression coefficient ($e^{b\#}$) is the odds ratio associated with a one-unit increase in exposure. (Szumilas 2010).

$P(Y = 1) = \frac{1}{1+e^{-g(x)}}$, Where g (x) $= -4.07 + 1.606\, X_1 + \dots - 1.230\, X_{68}$.

The value of the Intercept is - 4.07, so, for x = 0; g(0) $= -4.07$; P(Y = 1) = 0.01679, i.e., the meaning that the target outcome (e.g., a correct response - corrupt) was about 1.68%.

Observing the relatively low value of the Intercept constant and seeing several attributes with positive coefficients, we see that the model operates with a low risk of corruption increased by the attributes with the highest coefficient.

Table 6. Main attributes and coefficients of logistic regression in descending order

A#	Attribute	Coeff. (b#)	e(b#)	A#	Attribute	Coeff. (b#)	e(b#)
A1	W.QtySIGRHfunc	1.606	4.987	A13	B.CodFirmAct accounting	0.539	1.715
A2	C.CEIS	1.124	3.079	A14	P.CandMaritalSt.1	0.533	1.705
A3	B.CodFirmAct HighEducInst	0.827	2.287	A15	P.CandEducation.6	0.531	1.701
A4	B.CodFirmAct ClinicalLab	0.725	2.065				
A5	W.QtySIAPEOff	0.709	2.033				
A6	B.CodFirmAct legal Services	0.673	1.961	A62	W.Salary	(0.129)	0.879
A7	B.CodFirmAct furniture trade	0.657	1.929	A63	C.TCDFrestriction	(0.142)	0.867
A8	B.OwnershipPerc	0.625	1.869	A64	B.CodFirmSize.1	(0.224)	0.798
A9	B.CodFirmAct souvenir trade	0.615	1.850	A65	B.QtFirmAct	(0.229)	0.7951
A10	B.CodFirmTaxOpt.6	0.594	1.811	A66	B.DaysOwnership	(0.291)	0.746
A11	B.CodFirmAct technical	0.565	1.760	A67	W.QtySIAPEfunc	(0.363)	0.695
A12	B.CodFirmAct book edition	0.561	1.753	A68	W.QtySIGRHOff	(1.230)	0.292

However, an attribute with a negative coefficient, such as F.DaysOwnership, indicates that the lack of this attribute, the corporate bond of a civil servant/military, reduces corruption risk.

The simplest way to interpret the Logistic Regression coefficient is to understand that the e(x), odds ratio, represents the proportion of increasing or decreasing the attribute related to the target (C.CorruptionTG).

The attribute "W.QtySIGRHfunc"[A1] presents e(x) = 4.9870. If possible, to increase the target (binary attribute) for a specific value less than one, the attribute "W.QtySIGRHfunc" most increased by 498,7% in a proportion way. This idea is not precise due to the impossibility of the target increased by different values. However, it could explain how to interpret the behavior of the attributes related to the target.

Next, the main rules obtained by analyzing the final model's attributes and coefficients will be outlined. The effects were divided into an increased or decreased risk of corruption and increased or decreased probability.

The highest risk scenario would represent civil servants/military with the following characteristics. With the highest risk of corruption, the following characteristics were listed, whether cumulative or not:

- A civil servant with several functions changes, excluding Public Security workers (policemen and firefighters) (W.QtySIGRHfunc [A1]);
- Civil servant partner of a company present on the list of Registration of Unfaithful and Suspended Companies (C.CEIS [A2]) or that has a high percentage of share capital or that the company has cadastral activity in the specific areas of higher education institution [A3], clinical laboratories [A4], legal services [A6], furniture [A9] and souvenir trade [A10] technical [A11] and accounting activities [A13], and, book edition [A12];
- Civil servant that was a candidate for elective office (political office) [A14] e [A15].On the other hand, the scenario for civil servant/military with a low risk of corruption could be composed by these attributes:
- A civil servant with several positions changes, excluding Public Security workers (police and firefighters) (W.QtySIGRHOff [A68]);
- Policemen and firefighters (Public Security Workers) with several function changes positions (W.QtySIAPEfunc [A67]).

6 Conclusions

Data enrichment and data cleansing were applied in this study by integrating eight different databases that could be delt into four domains. It started with 28 attributes, some of them were transformed to meet business needs, and the final 68 attributes were set for the data mining process.

As a result, the dataset represents extremely imbalanced classes that could be challenging to create a better model at a ratio of 1:707 or, in percentage terms, 0.14% of the interest class to the population.

In the process of reducing the dimensionality without loss performance (Area under ROC), attributes with a correlation greater than 0.8, variances less than 0.0001, and with a p-value greater than 0.05 were excluded. As a result, the dimensionality reduces from 1,127 attributes to 68 attributes.

Two approaches were utilized: data-level solutions by SMOTE and extensions, and algorithm-level solutions, by Predefined Weights and Heuristic Weights. In this case, applying an algorithm-level solution resulted in a better performance than a data-level solution (area value on the ROC curve of around 0.69).

The impact of knowledge discovery in corruption literature was the Logistic Regression coefficients representing the risk factor for each attribute concerning the possibility of corruption. The numerical representativeness of this coefficient is related to the response variable or target attribute of the investigation.

These identified risk factors for corruption can assist in the definition of overseen planning on the most significant risk for Public Administration, so cases with a high probability of occurrence and a high financial or social impact.

It is difficult to obtain similarly published works with machine learning applications in corruption or fraud, possibly because of resistance from those who work with this activity. Furthermore, the high resilience and dynamics of fraudsters can be helped by the available publications.

Acknowledgments. L.Cavique would like to thank the FCT Projects of Scientific Research and Technological Development in Data Science and Artificial Intelligence in Public Administration, 2018–2022 (DSAIPA/DS/0039/2018), for its support.

References

Fernandez, A., Garcia, S., Herrera, F., Chawla, N.V.: SMOTE for learning from imbalanced data: progress and challenges, marking the 15th anniversary. J. Artif. Intell. Res. **61**, 863–905 (2018)

Brasil: Lei nº 8429, de 2 de julho de 1992, DOU (1992). http://www.planalto.gov.br/ccivil_03/leis/l8429.htm

Brownlee, J.: Imbalanced Classification with Python Choose Better Metrics, Balance Skewed Classes, and Apply Cost-Sensitive Learning. Machine Learning Mastery, vol. V1.2, pp. 1–22 (2020)

Chawla, N.V., Bowyer, K.W., Hall, L.O., Kegelmeyer, W.P.: SMOTE: synthetic minority over-sampling technique. J. Artif. Intell. Res. **16**(1), 321–357 (2002). https://doi.org/10.1613/jair.953

Han, J., Kamber, M., Pei, J.: Data Mining: Concepts and Techniques. Kaufmann, M., (ed.), 3 (2012)

Hosmer, D., Lemeshow, S.: Applied Survival Analysis - Regression Modeling of Time to Event Data, John Wiley, New York, pp. 386 (1999)

Knapp, E.D., Langill, J.T. Industrial network security: securing critical infrastructure networks for smart grid, SCADA, and other industrial control systems. In: Industrial Network Security: Securing Critical Infrastructure Networks for Smart Grid, SCADA, and Other Industrial Control Systems, Second Edition (2014). https://doi.org/10.1016/B978-0-12-420114-9.00018-6

Maalouf, M., Siddiqi, M.: Weighted logistic regression for large-scale imbalanced and rare events data. Knowl.-Based Syst. **59**, 142–148 (2014). https://doi.org/10.1016/j.knosys.2014.01.012

Maalouf, M., Trafalis, T.B.: Robust weighted kernel logistic regression in imbalanced and rare events data. Comput. Stat. Data Anal. **55**(1), 168–183 (2011). https://doi.org/10.1016/j.csda.2010.06.014

Mandrekar, J.N.: Receiver operating characteristic curve in diagnostic test assessment. J. Thorac. Oncol. **5**(9), 1315–1316 (2010). https://doi.org/10.1097/JTO.0b013e3181ec173d

Mauro, P.: Corruption and growth. Source: Q. J. Econ. **110**(3), 681–712 (1995)

Olken, B.A.: Monitoring corruption : evidence from a field experiment in Indonesia. J. Polit. Econ. **115**(2), 200–249 (2007)

Padula, A.J.A., Albuquerque, P.H.M.: Government corruption on Brazilian capital markets: a study on Lava Jato (Car Wash) investigation. Revista de Administração de Empresas **58**(4), 405–417 (2018). https://doi.org/10.1590/S0034-759020180406

Szumilas, M.: Explaining odds ratios. J. Can. Acad. Child. Adolesc. Psychiatry, **341**(19:3), 227–229 (2010). https://doi.org/10.1136/bmj.c4414

Torgo, L., Ribeiro, R.P., Pfahringer, B., Branco, P.: SMOTE for regression. In: Correia, L., Reis, L.P., Cascalho, J. (eds.) EPIA 2013. LNCS (LNAI), vol. 8154, pp. 378–389. Springer, Heidelberg (2013). https://doi.org/10.1007/978-3-642-40669-0_33

Transparency International. (n.d.).: Transparency International - What is Corruption?, 16 June 2019. https://www.transparency.org/what-is-corruption

Vimalraj, S., Rajendran, P.: A review on handling imbalanced data. In: International Conference on Current Trends towards Converging Technologies (ICCTCT), pp. 1–11. IEEE (2018)

Zhu, B., Baesens, B., Backiel, A., Vanden Broucke, S.K.L.M.: Benchmarking sampling techniques for imbalance learning in churn prediction. J. Oper. Res. Soc. **69**(1), 49–65 (2018). https://doi.org/10.1057/s41274-016-0176-1

Modelling Voting Behaviour During a General Election Campaign Using Dynamic Bayesian Networks

Patrício Costa[1,2,3,4](✉) [iD], Ana Rita Nogueira[5,6] [iD], and João Gama[1,6] [iD]

[1] Faculty of Economics, University of Porto, Porto, Portugal
pcosta@med.uminho.pt
[2] Life and Health Sciences Research Institute (ICVS),
School of Medicine, University of Minho, Braga, Portugal
[3] ICVS/3B's–P.T. Government Associate Laboratory, Braga/Guimarães, Portugal
[4] Faculty of Psychology and Education Sciences, University of Porto, Porto, Portugal
[5] Faculty of Sciences, University of Porto, Porto, Portugal
[6] LIAAD - INESC TEC, Porto, Portugal

Abstract. This work aims to develop a Machine Learning framework to predict voting behaviour. Data resulted from longitudinally collected variables during the Portuguese 2019 general election campaign. Naïve Bayes (NB), and Tree Augmented Naïve Bayes (TAN) and three different expert models using Dynamic Bayesian Networks (DBN) predict voting behaviour systematically for each moment in time considered using past information. Even though the differences found in some performance comparisons are not statistically significant, TAN and NB outperformed DBN experts' models. The learned models outperformed one of the experts' models when predicting abstention and two when predicting right-wing parties vote. Specifically, for the right-wing parties vote, TAN and NB presented satisfactory accuracy, while the experts' models were below 50% in the third evaluation moment.

Keywords: Machine learning · Voting behaviour · Dynamic Bayesian Networks · Causality

1 Introduction

The study of the determinants of voting behaviour is one of the main topics of research in the political science domain. The development of theoretical models to explain and predict voters' decisions started in 1940 at Columbia University, with a team of social scientists led by Paul Lazarsfeld. He applied sophisticated survey research methods to the study of electoral behaviour.

Nowadays, political scientists face new challenges, considering the declining voter turnout, the increasing volatility or the emergence of new political parties, which have introduced new electoral realignments, leading to the emergence of new theories. With the decline of the traditional (structural, class) determinants of voting, it becomes necessary to find new axes that explain voting behaviour.

© Springer Nature Switzerland AG 2021
G. Marreiros et al. (Eds.): EPIA 2021, LNAI 12981, pp. 524–536, 2021.
https://doi.org/10.1007/978-3-030-86230-5_41

With the decline of party identification and other traditional long-term anchors in voting decisions, short-term factors are being increasingly relevant [1]. These short-term factors include party leaders' traits, economic growth and campaign issues. Nowadays, party leaders are assuming a central role in contemporary Western Democracies, independently of their political system. However, strong empirical evidence is needed. This phenomenon, described as the personalisation of politics, accounts for the ascending importance of the politician as an individual actor [2], being an important determinant on voting decisions [3].

Langer [4] divides personalisation into three categories: *presidentialization* of power, leadership focus and politicisation of private persona. There is an inconsistent definition of the personalisation of politics phenomenon. It is considered the process of increasing the prominence of the politician as an individual [2]. Briefly, personalisation is changing the focus of politics from issues to people and from parties to politicians [5].

This new role of the party and political leaders enhances the need for political campaign staff and polls' companies to adapt to a new reality. It is also an opportunity to reflect on the boundaries of political marketing strategies, particularly political campaigns and their effects.

ML allows the researcher to drive new theory by uncovering hidden complexities, to elucidate blind spots between theory and reality, and it also leads to new measures for analytical modelling with smaller samples [6].

We seek to extend the traditional analytical tools/methodologies applied in the Political Science research domain. Accompanying the recent developments within other research areas, to predict voting behaviour, mainly turnout and main party choices (left-wing and right-wing parties). Our main goal is to develop and test different Bayesian Networks (BNs) based on the main predictors of voting behaviour collected during the Portuguese 2019 general election campaign. We explore the influence of political leaders' personality traits and campaign tone on implicit and explicit measures of voting behaviour longitudinally. Thus, we propose the use of Dynamic Bayesian Networks (DBNs) to explore the underlying causal mechanisms that drive voters' decisions in different situations during a campaign period.

Our primary research hypotheses consist in studying voting behaviour main determinants (sociodemographic characteristics such as sex, age and education), political attitudes (such as party identification and political interest), party leaders' traits and campaign tone perceptions. We also aim to test the stability of voting behaviour during the campaign period and what are the main drivers for change. We will test the campaign effects and how the mentioned variables affect voting behaviour. Finally, and the most relevant for this work, we aimed to compare the performance of voting behaviour predictions of the NB and TAN ML algorithms with the three different expert models using DBN. This paper is organised as follows: Sect. 2 describes some essential definitions. Section 3 describes data and the proposed approach, Sect. 4 the results obtained in the tests, and Sect. 5 contains the main conclusions and some limitations of this work.

2   Background

In this section, we briefly describe some of the Bayesian learning methods used in data mining for classification problems. We start by presenting the NB classifier. Then, we introduce BNs [23], emphasising the TAN [24], which is an extension of the NB classifier. Finally, we present DBNs, which are BNs that allow incorporating a temporal component, besides the causal model.

The NB classifier uses probabilistic methods and assumes that all the attributes' values are independent between them. This method allows calculating the conditional probability of the object belonging to the class C is given by the following expression (1) [9].

$$P(C|A_1, \ldots, A_n) = \alpha. \, P(C). \prod_{i=1}^{n} P(A_i|C) \tag{1}$$

The NB classifier learns from "training data the conditional probability of each attribute A_i given the class label C. Classification is then done by applying Bayes rule to compute the probability of C given the particular instance of $A_1, \ldots, A_n$, and then predicting the class with the highest posterior probability [8, pp. 131–132].

Furthermore, the described independence assumption is problematic to observe in real-world situations. In many cases, we cannot ignore the theoretically-supported relations between some relevant variable used for modelling.

Thus, a BN model consists of a directed acyclic graph of 'nodes', in which its values are defined in terms of different, mutually exclusive, 'states', and 'links' that conceptualise a system. The edges of the graph form a directed acyclic graph (DAG), which is a graph with no cyclic paths (no loops), allowing for efficient inference and learning [10].

The BNs rely on Bayes' theorem in the sense that it describes how prior knowledge about a given hypothesis H is updated by the observation of the evidence E.

The Bayesian networks are factored representations of probability distributions that generalise the NB classifier and allow to represent and manipulate independence assumptions effectively. Although, while BNs require space of all possible combinations of edges, TAN examine a restricted form of correlation edges, approximating the interactions between attributes by using a tree structure imposed on the NB [8]. TAN is based on the supposition that a classifier with less restrictive assumptions could outperform the NB classifier.

TAN classifiers allow to form a tree structure and consequently reduce the NB bias. The K-Dependence Bayesian Classifier (K-DBC) consists in a BN, containing the structure of an NB and allowing each feature to have a maximum of k-feature nodes as parents [11].

The BNs that allows incorporating a temporal component, besides the causal model, are called DBNs. These graphical model-based methods allow time-series modelling, and their static component (nodes, edges and probabilities) interpretation is similar to the one of BNs. They can find probabilistic models representing a system's causal structure [12] and allow for detailed voting behaviour predictions.

Some assumptions should be ensured when applying and analysing a constraint-based algorithm [13]:

a. Causal sufficiency: the set of observed variables satisfies the causal sufficiency assumption;

b. Faithfulness and Markov condition: the states of a DBN satisfy the (first-order) Markov condition (the state of a system at time t depends only on its immediate past, the state at time $t-1$): *the future is independent of the past given the present* [14, p. 2];
c. Reliable independence tests.

With DBNs, a dynamic system is modelled, and the underlying process is stationary (the assumption that the data are generated by a distribution that does not change with time; the structure and parameters of DBN are fixed over time). Different approaches have been proposed to relax this restriction [15, 16].On the other hand, the use of BNs has some substantial advantages such as:

a. It facilitates learning causal relationships between variables [17], and can easily be converted into decision support systems [18];
b. Its graphical capabilities display the links between different system components, thus facilitating the discussion of the system structure [19];
c. They may be interpreted as a causal model which generated the data. The arrows in the DAG can represent causal relations/dependencies between variables. However, to assume causality, association data is not enough [10].

In the next section, we explore the variables that will be modelled, and we implement the described learning algorithms.

3 Data

3.1 Data Collection

This project uses longitudinal data collected in four different moments concerning the Portuguese 2019 general election (t_0-approximately two weeks before the campaign period–selection study; t_1-pre-campaign; t_2-campaign; and t_3-post-election.

3.2 Participants

The study sample size comprises of 236 participants. From which 61% are female (n = 145), 13% (n = 31) aged between 18 and 24 y.o., 36% (n = 85) aged between 25 and 34 y.o., 33% (n = 77) aged between 35 and 44 y.o. and 18% (n = 43) older than 44 y.o. The majority of the participants have higher education (59%; n = 140).

3.3 Variables

Absolute frequencies and percentages for all the measured variables are presented in Table 1. Left-right ideology and party identification were only measured at the baseline since they can be considered long-term factors for voting behaviour prediction. The majority of our sample voters revealed not being identified with a particular party (58%), positioning themselves on the centre in the left-right ideology scale. The importance of voting, the interest in politics, the campaign tone and leaders' evaluations for left and right parties were collected in the four time points.

Table 1. Study population by political attitudes variables in different moments in time

Variables		t_0		t_1		t_2		t_3	
		N	%	N	%	N	%	N	%
Left–right ideology	Left	62	26.3%						
	Center	126	53.4%						
	Right	48	20.3%						
Party identification	No party identification	136	57.6%						
	Left parties	65	27.5%						
	Right parties	35	14.8%						
Importance of voting	It does not make any difference	52	22.0%	29	12.3%	36	15.3%	31	13.1%
	It does make the difference	184	78.0%	207	87.7%	200	84.7%	205	86.9%
Interest in politics	Not interested in politics	42	17.8%	28	11.9%	21	8.9%	19	8.1%
	Interested in politics	194	82.2%	208	88.1%	215	91.1%	217	91.9%
CT_left Left parties campaign tone	Negative	48	20.3%	49	20.8%	55	23.3%	62	26.3%
	Neutral	113	47.9%	123	52.1%	134	56.8%	118	50.0%
	Positive	75	31.8%	64	27.1%	47	19.9%	56	23.7%
CT_right Right parties campaign tone	Negative	118	50.0%	59	25.0%	79	33.5%	89	37.7%
	Neutral	62	26.3%	107	45.3%	93	39.4%	107	45.3%
	Positive	56	23.7%	70	29.7%	64	27.1%	40	16.9%
PL_left Left parties leaders	Low	50	21.2%	42	17.8%	56	23.7%	61	25.8%
	Medium	116	49.2%	139	58.9%	121	51.3%	112	47.5%
	High	70	29.7%	55	23.3%	59	25.0%	63	26.7%
PL_right Right parties leaders	Low	90	38.1%	77	32.6%	101	42.8%	103	43.6%
	Medium	89	37.7%	108	45.8%	84	35.6%	99	41.9%
	High	57	24.2%	51	21.6%	51	21.6%	34	14.4%
VOTE voting behaviour	Abstention	62	26.3%	59	25.0%	56	23.7%	28	11.9%
	Left parties	120	50.8%	125	53.0%	117	49.6%	131	55.5%
	Right parties	54	22.9%	52	22.0%	63	26.7%	77	32.6%

3.4   Data Modelling

The first approach for data modelling consisted of the application of the NB learning algorithm. The second algorithm was TAN. Finally, considering the temporal dependencies of our data, a third learning algorithm was applied, the DBN, which is a BN that relates variables to each other over adjacent time steps [20]. Three experienced PhD researchers and specialists in the political science research domain were invited to build connections between the variables following the assumption that the aim was to predict voting behaviour (abstention, left and right). The three conceptualised models were tested using DBN (EXP_1, EXP_2, and EXP_3).

3.5 Comparison of Models

To assess if there are significant differences in the performance of the five different approaches, we followed recommendations in the literature [21]. We had used the corrected Friedman test [22], followed by *Nemenyi* test or Friedman's Aligned Ranks test, with *Shaffer* procedure to correct the p-values [23, 24], when significant differences were found. The results from the *post-hoc* tests are presented with average rank diagrams.

4 Results and Discussion

For the importance of voting and interest in politics, we used Cochran's Q test to compare the proportion of voters considering that voting does make the difference and voters interested in politics across the four measurement moments. Significant differences were found in both variables (importance, $\chi 2(3) = 17.2$, p = .001; interest $\chi 2(3) = 30.1$, p < .001). Pairwise comparisons were then performed, and p-values were adjusted using the Bonferroni correction method. Regarding the importance of voting, significant differences were found between baseline (t_0) and measurement moments t_1 (p = .004) and t_3 (p = .001). No significant differences were observed between t_0 and t_2 (middle campaign period; p = .057) and all the other pairwise comparisons. As for the interest in politics, differences were found only between the baseline (t_0) and all the other measurement moments (p's < .05). No significant differences were detected for all the other pairwise comparisons. These results demonstrate that the proportion of voters considering that voting does make the difference and voters interested in politics changed significantly over time.

The majority of participants (54%) maintained their option from t_0 to t_3. For those who changed across the campaign period, 8% returned to their baseline option. The most relevant change occurred from abstention in t_0 to voting in a left party (12%).

The real 2019 election abstention was 51.4%. The reported abstention in the post-election poll was approximately 12%, which is significantly different from the real one ($\chi 2(1) = 148$, p < .001). The reported turnout rates are frequently higher than the real ones. On the one hand, people who vote and who are willing to answer surveys are likely to be correlated, leading to an under-representation of abstainers in surveys [25]. On the other hand, the pressure of social norms leads individuals to over-report voting in an attempt to conform to socially desirable behaviour [26], particularly when they are asked about voting in a survey. However, if we only consider turnout and the distribution of left and right parties, vote results from this study (63% and 37%, respectively) are similar to the real ones (62% and 38%, respectively; considering the same parties about whom were obtained voting intentions in the study), $\chi 2(1) = 0.183$, p = .669.

Before modelling data, it is crucial to capture the relations between the variables. Since we have dichotomous, polytomous, dichotomised and polytomized data, different coefficients were computed (Pearson's Phi, Cramer's V, tetrachoric and polychoric, respectively). Generally, the highest correlations observed were within the same variables across time (the highest observed value was between Interest t_1 and Interest t_3; .932). The campaign tone was also highly correlated with the party leaders' evaluations.

Regarding voting behaviour, the highest correlation was between Vote t_1 and Vote t_2 (Cramer's $V = .747$). The highest observed correlations were between time t and t-1, the immediate past. However, there are also considerable correlations between other moments in time. This might indicate that the assumption that $t + 1$ is independent of t-1 given that t is not fully accomplished. We performed a few multinomial logistic regressions and detected the violation of this assumption in some cases.

The correlation between the baseline and the reported vote after the election was only Cramer's $V = .399$, meaning that voting behaviour changes across time.

Next, NB, TAN and the DBN models and their main results are described. The estimated probabilities presented in Table 2 correspond to the model predicting the reported vote in t3 (post-election survey), using all the previous information. This estimation is the main outcome of this work. For NB and TAN, we do not have results for t0 to t2 because, in these cases, all the information was used to model t3. For the experts' models, since the DBN is the temporal component that is considered, the probabilities for all moments in time points are presented.

Table 2. Voting behaviour (temporal) probability distributions

Model	VOTE voting behaviour	t_0	t_1	t_2	t_3
NB	Abstention				0.120
	Left parties				0.554
	Right parties				0.326
TAN	Abstention				0.120
	Left parties				0.554
	Right parties				0.326
EXP_1	Abstention	0.260	0.198	0.181	0.176
	Left parties	0.490	0.515	0.522	0.524
	Right parties	0.250	0.287	0.297	0.301
EXP_2	Abstention	0.263	0.201	0.184	0.179
	Left parties	0.491	0.512	0.519	0.521
	Right parties	0.246	0.287	0.297	0.301
EXP_3	Abstention	0.271	0.194	0.169	0.161
	Left parties	0.450	0.526	0.547	0.555
	Right parties	0.278	0.280	0.284	0.285

NB and TAN models present similar class proportions for t3, which correspond to the obtained result in our sample. Regarding the experts' models, these models differ significantly from the observed proportions in t3 (for EXP_1 and EXP_2, $\chi 2(2) = 59.7$,

$p < .001$; and for EXP_3, $\chi 2(2) = 80.4$, $p < .001$). EXP_1 and EXP_2 revealed to be similar models. NB and TAN models predictions do not differ significantly from the real reported values ($\chi 2(2) = 5.79$, $p = .055$ and $\chi 2(2) = 2.82$, $p = .244$, respectively). Experts models tend to overestimate the abstention proportion and to underestimate the vote in the right parties. However, as shown in Table 2, there is a trend to diminish the abstention probabilities and to increase the vote for the right parties.

We developed and tested five different models (EXP_1, EXP_2, EXP_3, NB and TAN) for the prediction of a multiple class outcome (abstention, left and right) in three different predictions across time (predicting vote at time point 1 (t_1) using the information gathered in time point 0 (t_0); predicting vote at time point 2 (t_2) using the information gathered in t_0 and t_1; and, finally, predicting vote at time point 3 (t_3) using the information gathered in t_0, t_1 and t_2).

The method used in this project was the leave-one-out cross-validation (LOOCV), which is a particular case of k-fold cross-validation, where k is the number of samples [27]. The method consists of repeating the holdout method for the total sample size (N, where parameter k is equal to N). Basically, in each fold, the model trains with all participants except for the one (N-1) who is used to test (prediction). This approach has the advantage of using all participants for training and testing the model, which is particularly relevant, considering our study sample size.

For validation purposes three different models were performed. We develop a model:

1. in t_0 and predict for t1 (m1);
2. with t_0 and t_1 and predict for t_2 (m2);
3. with t_0, t_1 and t_2 and predict for t_3 (m3).

The obtained results for the LOOCV method, using DBNs, are presented in Table 3.

Considering the overall accuracy of the three predictions (vote at t_1, t_2 and t_3), no significant differences were found between the five models tested (corrected Friedman's $\chi 2(4, 8) = 2.93$, $p = .091$). Since we have a multiple class outcome (abstention, left and right), we also compared the accuracy for each outcome in the five models, and.

no significant differences were found for the vote in right-wing parties (corrected Friedman's $\chi 2(4, 8) = 3.47$, $p = .483$). The *Nemenyi* test, considering a 0.05 significance level, proves to be conservative, not identifying the obtained differences. The Friedman's Aligned Ranks test (with Shaffer correction) was applied, but the result also proves to be conservative. The solution was to use Friedman's Aligned Ranks test results with no p-value correction method, presented in the model graph in Fig. 1.

The models are the nodes, and if two nodes are linked, we cannot reject the null hypothesis of being equal. TAN and NB models perform significantly better than EXP_3 in predicting abstention behaviour.

Table 3. Performance measures

Outcome	Model	Measure	EXP_1	EXP_2	EXP_3	NB	TAN
Abstention	m1	Accuracy	0.720	0.720	0.653	0.775	0.763
		Precision	0.462	0.462	0.391	0.547	0.525
		Recall	0.729	0.729	0.695	0.593	0.525
		Specificity	0.718	0.718	0.638	0.836	0.842
		AUC	0.766	0.766	0.682	0.834	0.825
	m2	Accuracy	0.805	0.805	0.809	0.843	0.852
		Precision	0.561	0.561	0.562	0.651	0.714
		Recall	0.821	0.821	0.893	0.732	0.625
		Specificity	0.800	0.800	0.783	0.878	0.922
		AUC	0.858	0.858	0.893	0.900	0.888
	m3	Accuracy	0.725	0.725	0.695	0.847	0.873
		Precision	0.215	0.215	0.194	0.400	0.450
		Recall	0.500	0.500	0.500	0.571	0.321
		Specificity	0.755	0.755	0.721	0.885	0.947
		AUC	0.652	0.652	0.646	0.768	0.743
Left	m1	Accuracy	0.771	0.771	0.716	0.767	0.763
		Precision	0.820	0.820	0.796	0.792	0.785
		Recall	0.728	0.728	0.624	0.760	0.760
		Specificity	0.820	0.820	0.820	0.775	0.766
		AUC	0.807	0.807	0.782	0.877	0.880
	m2	Accuracy	0.843	0.843	0.856	0.839	0.839
		Precision	0.851	0.851	0.881	0.856	0.821
		Recall	0.829	0.829	0.821	0.812	0.863
		Specificity	0.857	0.857	0.891	0.866	0.815
		AUC	0.901	0.901	0.905	0.927	0.920
	m3	Accuracy	0.750	0.750	0.763	0.831	0.831
		Precision	0.795	0.795	0.832	0.864	0.827
		Recall	0.740	0.740	0.718	0.824	0.878
		Specificity	0.762	0.762	0.819	0.838	0.771
		AUC	0.824	0.824	0.855	0.917	0.895

(*continued*)

Table 3. (*continued*)

Outcome	Model	Measure	EXP_1	EXP_2	EXP_3	NB	TAN
Right	m1	Accuracy	0.881	0.881	0.860	0.881	0.847
		Precision	0.875	0.875	0.788	0.731	0.643
		Recall	0.539	0.539	0.500	0.731	0.692
		Specificity	0.978	0.978	0.962	0.924	0.891
		AUC	0.839	0.839	0.860	0.925	0.923
	m2	Accuracy	0.852	0.852	0.877	0.886	0.886
		Precision	0.850	0.850	0.947	0.790	0.781
		Recall	0.540	0.540	0.571	0.778	0.794
		Specificity	0.965	0.965	0.988	0.925	0.919
		AUC	0.872	0.872	0.847	0.933	0.927
	m3	Accuracy	0.746	0.746	0.763	0.839	0.839
		Precision	0.673	0.673	0.706	0.775	0.753
		Recall	0.429	0.429	0.468	0.714	0.753
		Specificity	0.899	0.899	0.906	0.899	0.881
		AUC	0.812	0.812	0.805	0.894	0.883

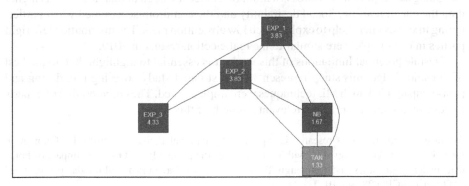

Fig. 1. Models average rankings and significant differences for the prediction of abstention

5 Conclusion

The present study aimed to develop an ML framework to predict voting behaviour during the Portuguese 2019 general election. Data was collected longitudinally in four moments in time, and two different modelling approaches were used, depending on the inclusion or not of the temporal dynamic component.

The majority of the participants (54%) maintained their opinions across data collection in different periods. The most relevant change occurred from abstention in the baseline for voting in a left-wing party (12%) in the post-election survey.

NB, TAN and DBN models were implemented. Three DBNs were developed considering the opinion of three experts in the Political Science research domain.

Interest in politics and party identification presented the most substantial influence on voting behaviour. The major influences detected were from party identification to ideology and campaign tone to party leaders' evaluations, mainly in the right-wing parties.

Despite not having significant differences in some performance comparisons, TAN and NB outperformed DBN experts' models. Generally, experts' models were less accurate predicting abstention, and the learned models outperformed EXP_3 predicting this outcome. No significant differences were found for left or right-wing parties vote prediction.

The participants who were responsible for the significant shift observed in our data (non-voters to voting left-wing parties) were also examined. They reveal to lack proximity to any particular party, and they ideologically position themselves in the centre; also, they present lower proportions of a higher education and report increasing positive evaluations of left-wing parties leaders and campaign tone during the campaign period. Younger voters present lower turnout rates and older people with higher education levels present a higher probability of voting in right-wing parties. The "education effect" [28] was also observed in our models. There was a positive effect of education on participation, suggesting additional evidence for a causal interpretation. It was also clear that age affects party identification, with young voters not identifying themselves with any particular party.

Using self-reported measures is a limitation since it was clear that turnout was higher than the one in real-life. Social desirability and the compromise assumed when participating in surveys may help to explain such low abstention rates. The distribution left-right parties in our sample were similar to the real election results in 2019.

Despite potential limitations of this work, it is essential to highlight that, to the best of our knowledge, this study represents the first panel study covering pre, during and post-campaign in which ML techniques were implemented. The collaboration of experts to develop the models is also a relevant strength of this work.

Acknowledgements. This research is supported by national funds through FCT - Foundation for Science and Technology, I.P., within the scope of the project PACTO – "The impact of Political leaders' Attributes and Campaign TOne on voting behaviour: a multimodal perspective" (PTDC/CPO-CPO/28886/2017).

References

1. Dalton, R.J., Wattenberg, M.P.: Parties Without Partisans: Political Change in Advanced Industrial Democracies. Oxford University Press, Oxford (2002)
2. Rahat, G., Sheafer, T.: The personalizations of politics: Israel, 1949–2003. Polit. Commun. **24**(1), 65–80 (2007). https://doi.org/10.1080/10584600601128739
3. Van Aelst, P., Sheafer, T., Stanyer, J.: The personalization of mediated political communication: a review of concepts, operationalizations and key findings. Journalism **13**(2), 203–220 (2012)

4. Langer, A.I.: A historical exploration of the personalisation of politics in the print media: the British prime ministers (1945–1999). Parliam. Aff. **60**(3), 371–387 (2007)
5. Adam, S., Maier, M.: Personalization of politics a critical review and agenda for research. Ann. Int. Commun. Assoc. **34**(1), 213–257 (2016). https://doi.org/10.1080/23808985.2010. 11679101
6. Spisak, B.R., Van Der Laken, P.A., Doornenbal, B.M.: Finding the right fuel for the analytical engine: expanding the leader trait paradigm through machine learning? Leadersh. Q. (2019). https://doi.org/10.1016/j.leaqua.2019.05.005
7. Pearl, J.: Probabilistic Reasoning in Intelligent Systems: Networks of Plausible Inference. Elsevier, San Francisco (2014)
8. Friedman, N., Geiger, D., Goldszmidt, M.: Bayesian network classifiers. Mach. Learn. **29**(2), 131–163 (1997). https://doi.org/10.1023/A:1007465528199
9. Gama, J., Ferreira, A.C.P.D.L., Carvalho, D., Faceli, K., Lorena, A.C., Oliveira, M.: Extração de conhecimento de dados: data mining. Edições Sílabo (2015)
10. Needham, C.J., Bradford, J.R., Bulpitt, A.J., Westhead, D.R.: A primer on learning in Bayesian networks for computational biology. PLoS Comput. Biol. **3**(8), 1409–1416 (2007). https:// doi.org/10.1371/journal.pcbi.0030129
11. Duan, Z., Wang, L.: K-dependence Bayesian classifier ensemble. Entropy **19**(12), 651 (2017). https://doi.org/10.3390/e19120651
12. Heintzman, N., Kleinberg, S.: Using uncertain data from body-worn sensors to gain insight into type 1 diabetes. J. Biomed. Inform. **63**, 259–268 (2016). https://doi.org/10.1016/j.jbi. 2016.08.022
13. Yu, K., Li, J., Liu, L.: A review on algorithms for constraint-based causal discovery, pp. 1–17 (2016). http://arxiv.org/abs/1611.03977
14. Murphy, K., Mian, S.: Modeling gene expression data using dynamic Bayesian networks. BT-Technical Report, Computer Science Division. University of California, Berkeley (1999)
15. Zhu, S., Wang, Y.: Hidden markov induced dynamic Bayesian network for recovering time evolving gene regulatory networks. Sci. Rep. **5**, 1–17 (2015). https://doi.org/10.1038/sre p17841
16. Jia, Y., Huan, J.: Constructing non-stationary dynamic Bayesian networks with a flexible lag choosing mechanism. BMC Bioinformatics **11**(Suppl. 6), 1–13 (2010). https://doi.org/10. 1186/1471-2105-11-27
17. Uusitalo, L.: Advantages and challenges of Bayesian networks in environmental modelling. Ecol. Model. **203**(3–4), 312–318 (2007). https://doi.org/10.1016/j.ecolmodel.2006.11.033
18. Marcot, B.G., Holthausen, R.S., Raphael, M.G., Rowland, M.M., Wisdom, M.J.: Using Bayesian belief networks to evaluate fish and wildlife population viability under land management alternatives from an environmental impact statement. For. Ecol. Manage. **153**(1–3), 29–42 (2001). https://doi.org/10.1016/S0378-1127(01)00452-2
19. Martín De Santa Olalla, F.J., Domínguez, A., Artigao, A., Fabeiro, C., Ortega, J.F.: Integrated water resources management of the hydrogeological unit 'Eastern Mancha' using Bayesian belief networks. Agric. Water Manag. **77**(1–3), 21–36 (2005). https://doi.org/10.1016/j.agwat. 2004.09.029.
20. Dagum, P., Galper, A., Horvitz, E.: Dynamic network models for forecasting. Uncertainty in Artificial Intelligent, pp. 41–48 (1992)
21. Demšar, J.: Statistical comparisons of classifiers over multiple data sets. J. Mach. Learn. Res. **7**, 1–30 (2006)
22. Iman, R.L., Davenport, J.M.: Approximations of the critical region of the fbietkan statistic. Commun. Stat. Methods **9**(6), 571–595 (1980)
23. García, S., Herrera, F.: An extension on 'statistical comparisons of classifiers over multiple data sets' for all pairwise comparisons. J. Mach. Learn. Res. **9**, 2677–2694 (2008)

24. Shaffer, J.P.: Modified sequentially rejective multiple test procedures. J. Am. Stat. Assoc. **81**(395), 826–831 (1986). https://doi.org/10.1080/01621459.1986.10478341
25. da Silva, F.F., Costa, P.: Do we need warm leaders? Exploratory study of the role of voter evaluations of leaders' traits on turnout in seven European countries. Eur. J. Polit. Res. **58**(1), 117–140 (2019). https://doi.org/10.1111/1475-6765.12273
26. Silver, B.D., Anderson, B.A., Abramson, P.R.: Who overreports voting? Am. Polit. Sci. Rev. **80**(2), 613–624 (1986). https://doi.org/10.2307/1958277
27. Kuhn, M., Johnson, K.: Applied Predictive Modeling, vol. 26, Springer, New York (2013). https://doi.org/10.1007/978-1-4614-6849-3
28. Henderson, J.A.: Hookworm eradication as a natural experiment for schooling and voting in the American South. Polit. Behav. **40**(2), 467–494 (2018)

ESTHER: A Recommendation System for Higher Education Programs

Bruno Mota da Silva and Cláudia Martins Antunes(✉)

Instituto Superior Técnico, Universidade de Lisboa, Lisbon, Portugal
claudia.antunes@tecnico.ulisboa.pt

Abstract. Automatic discovery of information in educational data has been broadening its horizons, opening new opportunities to its application. An open wide area to explore is the recommendation of undergraduate programs to high school students. However, traditional recommendation systems, based on collaborative filtering, require the existence of both a large number of items and users, which in this context are too small to guarantee reasonable levels of performance.

In this paper, we propose a hybrid approach, combining collaborative filtering and a content-based architecture, while exploring the hierarchical information about programs organization. This information is extracted from courses programs, through natural language processing, and since programs share some courses, we are able to present recommendations, not just based on the performance of students, but also on their interests and results in each of the courses that compose each program.

Keywords: Recommendation systems · Higher education programs · Educational data mining

1 Introduction

Nowadays, it is common to have teenagers applying to a higher education program after finishing their high school. Every year, new programs appear and thousands of candidates must choose which one is the best for them.

This type of problem is very well-known in Educational Data Mining and in Recommendation Systems community [3,11]. This past decade, many studies were made on creating engines that help students in choosing the courses that are suited for them, using different approaches, like content-based or collaborative filtering recommendation systems. The last type is the most used due to the large amount of data community can give.

Despite courses recommendation being a more studied problem, we want to apply these systems to programs recommendation that is not very researched yet. This brings an important challenge, since courses recommenders have already the

Supported by national funds by Fundação para a Ciência e Tecnologia (FCT) through project GameCourse (PTDC/CCI-CIF/30754/2017).

© Springer Nature Switzerland AG 2021
G. Marreiros et al. (Eds.): EPIA 2021, LNAI 12981, pp. 537–548, 2021.
https://doi.org/10.1007/978-3-030-86230-5_42

target user inside the system rating previous courses among the others students, and in our problem candidates did not rate anything to be compared to other users in first hand.

Considering all of these aspects, our work aims for creating a recommendation system that will receive candidates personal data and high-school academic records, with the proper consent given by them considering general data protection regulations (GDPR), and will output the programs that most fit to their profile, comparing to the current student community. The system will consider the personal characteristics of the students as a matching measure and the programs' courses, objectives and description to find keywords that define the corresponding programs. These keywords will allow to compute ratings for every program considering the academic marks of the students on their own program.

This paper is divided in four more sections. Literature review covers the basic aspects of recommendation systems, with special focus on their use for educational purposes. After this, we present the architecture of our system that can be applied at a common university structure. After system architecture, current results are shown, followed by the reached conclusions at this time.

2   Literature Review

Recommendation Systems (RS) are software tools and techniques that provide suggestions for items to be of use to a user [10]. A RS can be exploited for different purposes, such as, to increase the number of items sold, to better understand what the user wants or, in another point of view, to recommend a specific item to that user. A recommendation system is typically characterized by a set of users C, a set of items I and a rating function f that measures the utility of the item i to user c [5]. Hence, the aim of the RS is to recommend the item $i' \in I$ for each customer $c \in C$ that maximizes the user's rating.

There are two big tasks in a recommendation system. First, you need to gather all the data you need to make a proper suggestion, and then you must do the recommendation to the user. Considering these two tasks and all the subtasks each one has, Jariha and Jain proposed a general architecture for recommendation systems, as it can be seen on Fig. 1 [5].

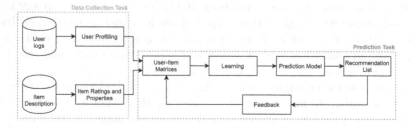

Fig. 1. Architecture of recommendation system, proposed by Jariha and Jain (2018).

Based on users' profiles, item properties and collected ratings, an user-item matrix is generated which is fed to the recommendation algorithms as input [5]. This matrix has the users' ratings for each item and it will be the main tool to do the recommendation process. During the data collection task, it can be gathered a high quantity of irrelevant data. Hence, some RS architecture have a Learning module that aims on finding which are the user's relevant features for recommendation. After that, using the most suited RS model for the problem, we predict top N recommended items for each active user. Since these systems are very dynamic, a feedback step can be implemented to enhance its performance.

There are two main types of recommendation engines, Content-based and Collaborative Filtering. The first one is focused on item similarities, as illustrated in Fig. 2, if someone likes the red item, and consequently the red item is similar to the blue item, then the content-based RS will recommend the blue item to the user [1]. In collaborative filtering approaches, we use past behaviors of users to recommend items to the active user. The main idea of collaborative filtering RS is represented on Fig. 3. If the blue user is similar to the purple user, and the blue user likes the red item, therefore the collaborative filtering RS will recommend the red item to the purple user [1].

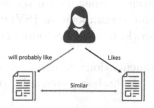

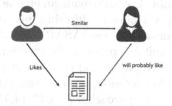

Fig. 2. Content-based scheme. (Color figure online)

Fig. 3. Collaborative filtering scheme. (Color figure online)

There is also a third type of recomendation systems, knowledge-based approaches where recommendations are given based on explicit specification of the kind of content the user wants. These systems are very similar to content-based ones, but with domain knowledge input. Finally, a hybrid recommendation system is constructed if there is a combination of two or more RS philosophies in order to improve the global performance.

2.1 Recommendation Systems in Education

Over the years, a large amount of educational data is being generated and there are being applied more collaborative filtering approaches than content-based methods in this area.

Morsomme and Alferez proposed a collaborative recommendation system that outputs courses to the target users, by exploiting courses that other similar students had taken, through k-means clustering and K-nearest neighbors techniques [2].

A recommendation system for course selection was developed in Liberal Arts bachelor of the University College Maastricht [6], using two types of data, students and courses. Student data consisted of anonymized students' course enrollments, and course data consisted of catalogues with descriptions of all courses, which allowed to find the topics of each one, using the Latent Dirichlet Allocation statistical model. Recurring to regression models of student data, the authors could predict his grade for each course. In the end, the system outputs 20 courses whose content best matches the user's academic interest in terms of Kullback-Leibler distance.

This content-based approach was applied as well in Dublin [8], where the authors used an information retrieval algorithm to compute course-course similarities, based on the text description and learning outcomes of each one.

In Faculty of Engineering of the University of Porto, it was created an engine to help students choosing an adequate higher education program to access a specific job in the future [13]. Therefore, it was implemented a recommendation system that uses the data from alumni and job offers and outputs a ranking of programs that could lead to the candidates' desired careers. The collaborative filtering approach can match the skills needed for that job and the skills given to the students of a specific degree.

Fábio Carballo made an engine that predicts students masters courses marks, using collaborative filtering methods, singular value decomposition (SVD) and as-soon-as-possible (ASAP) classifiers. With his work, he could recommend the more suitable program for students skills [4].

The topic around course and programs recommendations gained even more attention recently, with several published studies in the last years, following a variety of approaches [7, 9, 12, 14, 15].

3 Recommendation System for Higher Education Programs

ESTHER (rEcommendation SysTem for Higher Education pRograms) shall enlighten candidates about the degrees that are more compatible with their interests and that were successfully concluded by similar students, using a hybrid approach.

3.1 Requirements Specification

Our system must recommend higher education programs to a specific high-school student who wants to enroll at university. Usually, the candidate searches information about each program at universities webpages, such as courses or professional careers, or talks with students who are already enrolled at the programs he or she likes. The process of choosing a degree is very important to a high school student and it must be done analysing all the information available. Therefore, the main use case of our system focuses on candidates point of view.

As we can see on Fig. 4, when the candidate uses our system, he or she must be able to give personal data that will be considered during the recommendation process. After that, the system must output a ranking of the programs that are most suitable to the candidate. Candidate's personal data can be academic interests, high school grades, personal data, such age or gender, among others. Since we are collecting data, it must be made according to the GDPR, applying anonymization techniques when necessary.

Looking at the system from Admin point of view, there are several tasks he or she must be able to do, as we can see on Fig. 5. System Administrator is the one responsible for system updates: upload new students data every year, upload students grades at the end of each semester, and update programs and courses when necessary. All the essential data to relate the candidate to current students and to make proper recommendations must be inputted before the system launching.

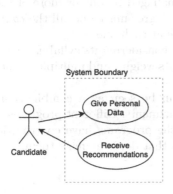

Fig. 4. Candidate use case.

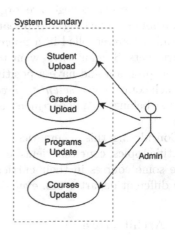

Fig. 5. Admin use case.

Finally, analysts staff can use this system when useful, to get a summary of student community and a characterization of new students.

3.2   Knowledge Domain

The creation of this recommendation system has several entities involved, systematized in a simplified Entity-Relation Diagram, shown in Fig. 6.

It starts with the student applying for higher education, the so-called *candidate*. This entity and current *students* are people with personal data. This composite attribute can contain variables related to several areas, such as age, gender, high-school grades, parents jobs, socio-economic background and motivations for choosing some specific school as their higher education school. Additionally, students also have a college enrollment identification number.

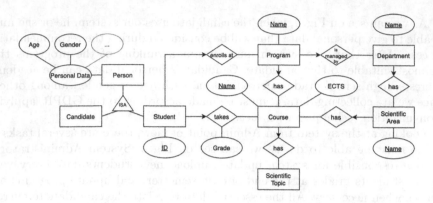

Fig. 6. Entity Relation Diagram for this Knowledge Domain.

Usually, every college are organized in scientific *departments*, which are responsible for teaching and research on some particular knowledge areas, and all students are enrolled in a *program* that is managed by one or more of these departments. Students who want to finish their degree must take all the *courses* of their program and have a positive final *grade* at each one.

Each course has a *scientific area* associated, considering its syllabus thematics, that belongs to a department as well, a credits weight, and multiple scientific topics.

Considering this schematics, a program can be seen as a combination of scientific topics, courses, scientific areas or departments. Different programs can share some courses in their curricula and all the programs have contributions from different departments, even from the ones that don't manage them.

3.3   Architecture

The overview of our system architecture can be seen on Fig. 7, where we can distinguish two main modules: Students Profiler and Programs Recommender.

Candidates start using our system by inputting their personal data that will be used to find their profile. Current students data allow us to compute candidate profiles that will feed the second module. Programs Recommender uses the previous output to estimate a program success measure considering estimated grades, returning in the end a ranking of the most suitable programs to the candidates.

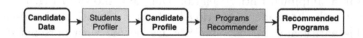

Fig. 7. Proposed architecture for this recommendation system.

Students Profiler. There is a major difference between our recommendation system and the common ones, where the target user is inside the system among the others. Here, the target user candidate is not in the system, since he or she is not enrolled at a higher education degree yet, and therefore can not rate programs or take courses. Hence, it must be developed a strategy where we can compare users.

Students Profiler, as it is shown diagrammatically in Fig. 8, computes the candidate profile as if he or she was inside the system, by comparing him with current students. Since candidates and students are both people, they share personal variables that can be used to compute the similarity between them. Therefore, the first step is to collect these data and build a students profiling model.

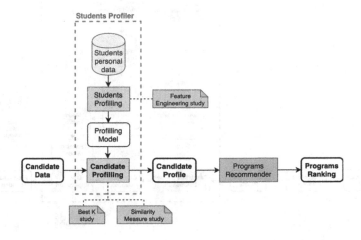

Fig. 8. Proposed architecture for Student Profiler module.

During this model building, we will perform data preparation and a feature engineering study. In this study, we create more informative variables useful for discriminate among different profiles, by combining existing to generate new ones.

A simple choice to implement student profiler is to apply the K Nearest Neighbors (KNN) method, after choosing the best similarity measure and number of neighbors, K.

To compute the similarity, we can make use of the euclidean distance that measures the distance between two points in "straight line", the cosine distance that measures the difference in orientation of two points, or the Jaccard index that measures the intersection between datasets, among others. Different measures must be studied and we should use the one that results in better outcomes. We also need to tune the KNN process as well by trying to find the optimal value for K, that is the one having the minimum error rate.

In the end, Students Profiler will return candidate profile that will be fed to the next module.

Programs Recommender. Programs Recommender module is a more complex one which aims at finding the ranking of the best programs to the candidates, considering their profile and interests. All the tasks and elements regarding Program Recommender module are shown in Fig. 9.

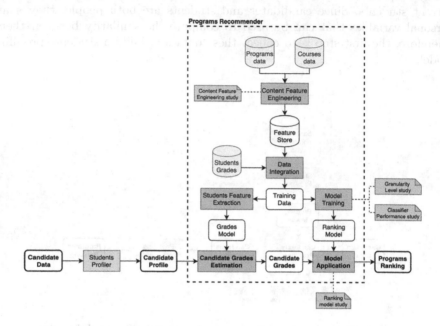

Fig. 9. Proposed architecture for Programs Recommender module.

In order to reach its goal, this module has to create two models. The first one, called Grades Model, for estimating the candidate performance in each possible academic units, and the second one, the Ranking Model, for mapping students to programs.

As usual, the Grades Model is constructed by following a collaborative filtering approach, meaning that it uses a singular value decomposition (SVD) matrix factorization. This factorization performs a feature extraction step, reducing the number of elements to the minimum required for estimating students grades. When in the presence of the candidate profile, received from the Students Profiler, the Grades Model is applied to estimate the candidate grades.

Using the candidate profile, instead of its original data, is the first difference in our approach, but there is more, achieved through the use of a content-based approach.

RS usually deal with a very large number of items, but the number of programs available in any university is just a few, when compared. Additionally, each student is enrolled on just one program, which means that our grades matrix would be very sparse, not contributing for a good recommendation. A third aspect is that programs share some courses (for example all engineering students study Physics and Maths, while all art students study Drawing and Geometry). But we can go a step further, and understand that courses cover some topics present in different areas. For example, several engineering courses study systems, their architecture and their dynamics.

Considering these aspects, we make use of the domain knowledge represented in Fig. 6, and perform a thorough information retrieval operation from the syllabus of all existing courses, contained on every program available. This analysis is done using natural language processing (NLP) usual techniques, which are able to identify the terms present on all courses syllabus. In this manner, instead of describing each program by its generic description, we do it through a bag of words (terms) and their importance on the course, and consequently program. These terms are then the new features stored in the Feature Store, which is a kind of a repository to save variables derived from some source, and the formula to derive them. These formulas, when applied to students grades stored, create new records, richer than the original ones, which feed the training of the Ranking Model.

The third proposal is the possibility of dealing with the academic units at different levels of granularity: we can aggregate everything to recommend programs, or we can simply identify a ranking of topics that are recommend for the candidate. This ability is very important to reach a new level of explainability, so needed in the field.

To summarize, our system architecture has all the tasks separated by the two modules. Note that most of them are done before the candidate uses our recommendation system, only the steps in bold are done during each system running. As it was mentioned in Sect. 3.1, every datasources must be updated when necessary.

4 Preliminary Results

A recommendation system validation is a hard task to take. In contexts, like education, where these systems can not be made available before being proved 'correct', this task is even harder.

In our case, we made use of students data collected at the time of their enrollment in the university, to mimetize candidates surveys. Then, we used students data from 2014 to 2018 for training and data from 2019 for evaluation purposes. Moreover, every model of the system has to be validated independently, in order to better estimate each component performance, and only after tuning each of them evaluate its global quality.

We started by evaluating the Students Module, which has the use of KNN to estimate candidate profile on its basis. As data sources for this phase, we had personal data from 7918 students and grades from 7302 students, that resulted in a dataset of 7300 instances by intersecting the first ones. This dataset is composed by 101 variables, where enrolled program is the only categorical one, all of the others are numeric. Note that, we had no missing values on the dataset.

In this module, we wanted to find the K students that are most similar to the candidate. Therefore, we made a study to find the best pair (K, similarity measure) mimetizing a KNN performance study, but without focusing on the classification task. First, we needed to define which condition must students achieve to have success on their program, based on their Grade Point Average (GPA), from a 0–20 scale. Hence, a histogram was made and it is shown at Fig. 10.

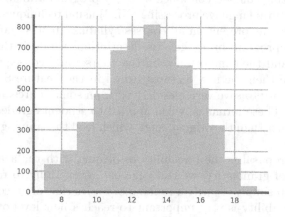

Fig. 10. Number of students by each GPA class.

Since the average of students GPA is 12.99, we labeled as having success students which GPA was equal to 13 or more, and not having success otherwise. This way we guaranteed a balanced dataset. After the labelling, we computed ten trials of data train-test split for five similarity measures (chebyshev, correlation, cosine, euclidean, and manhattan) and for K between 5 and 155 in multiples of 5. For each pair (K, similarity measure), we computed the average of KNN model accuracies, since 70% train and 30% test datasets are random in each trial. The results are shown in Fig. 11, and zoomed in Fig. 12.

Students Profiler module has five conditions that will be tested in the global system: (120, chebyshev); (100, correlation); (90, cosine); (30, euclidean) and (20, manhattan).

We implemented as well a simple recommendation system where we used the candidate profile, composed by the average grades of all neighbors for all courses taken by them, to predict the candidate grades for all available courses. In this component, four conditions were used for testing the system behaviour for all similarity measures: A) using SVD as matrix factorization technique with the K values mentioned above and considering all the variables from students data; B) same as A), but using K equals to 5; C) using SVD with the best K values predicted using a reduced students dataset with only academic records; and D) same as C) but using the Slope One prediction method.

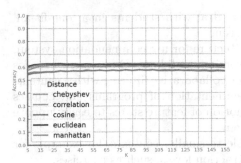
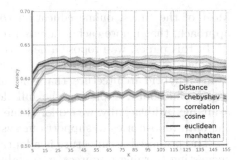

Fig. 11. K and similarity measure study.

Fig. 12. Zoom of K and similarity measure study.

After that, we used 1509 candidates to test the system, where we computed the GPA that each of them would have in each one of the available programs using their predicted course grades and ranked them by GPAs. Then, we computed the mean absolute error for those which first recommended program coincides with their current program in terms of GPA, and results are showed in Table 1.

Table 1. Mean Absolute Errors for each prediction method and for each similarity measure

Similarity measure	A	B	C	D
Chebyshev	2.065	2.378	2.139	2.289
Correlation	2.149	2.580	2.359	2.325
Cosine	2.153	2.583	2.430	2.451
Euclidean	2.538	2.497	2.153	2.289
Manhattan	2.313	2.488	2.376	2.451

The next steps will consist of improving the way we recommend the programs and its ranking model, considering different ensembles, namely random forests and gradient boosting. At this time, we are predicting GPA with almost 90% accuracy.

5   Conclusions

The current educational context, even more after the beginning of the pandemic situation, demands new educational systems. Systems able to address the difficulties inherent to distance learning contexts, where students are far from educators, and plenty of times try to follow their path without any guidance.

Most of the times, online education tools deal with students in a 'one-fit-all' approach, that ignore each students preferences.

In this paper, we propose a new architecture for a recommendation system, designed for suggesting programs to university candidates. Our system benefits from an hybrid architecture, that combines collaborative filtering with a content-based philosophy, exploring the full documentation of programs and courses available. Additionally, we explored the notion of feature stores to easily update the data repositories to support our system.

The proposed architecture is adaptable to smaller contexts, for example for suggesting learning resources at any abstraction levels, such as exercises.

References

1. Aggarwal, C.C.: Recommender Systems: The Textbook (2016)
2. Al-Badarneh, A., Alsakran, J.: An automated recommender system for course selection. Int. J. Adv. Comput. Sci. Appl. **7** (2016). https://doi.org/10.14569/IJACSA.2016.070323
3. Baker, R.S., Yacef, K.: The state of educational data mining in 2009: a review and future visions. J. Educ. Data Mining **1**(1), 3–17 (2009)
4. Carballo, F.O.G.: Masters' courses recommendation: exploring collaborative filtering and singular value decomposition with student profiling (2014)
5. Jariha, P., Jain, S.K.: A state-of-the-art recommender systems: an overview on concepts, methodology and challenges, pp. 1769–1774 (2018)
6. Morsomme, R., Alferez, S.V.: Content-based course recommender system for liberal arts education (2019)
7. MS, B., Taniguchi, Y., Konomi, S.: Course recommendation for university environments (July 2020)
8. O'Mahony, M.P., Smyth, B.: A recommender system for on-line course enrolment: an initial study, 133–136 (2007). https://doi.org/10.1145/1297231.1297254
9. Polyzou, A., Nikolakopoulos, A.N., Karypis, G.: Scholars walk: a Markov chain framework for course recommendation (May 2019)
10. Ricci, F., Rokach, L., Shapira, B.: Recommender Systems Handbook, pp. 1–35 (October 2010)
11. Rivera, A.C., Tapia-Leon, M., Lujan-Mora, S.: Recommendation systems in education: a systematic mapping study. In: Rocha, Á., Guarda, T. (eds.) ICITS 2018. AISC, vol. 721, pp. 937–947. Springer, Cham (2018). https://doi.org/10.1007/978-3-319-73450-7_89
12. Scherzinger, F., Singla, A., Wolf, V., Backenköhler, M.: Data-driven approach towards a personalized curriculum (July 2018)
13. de Sousa, A.I.N.A.: Market-based higher education course recommendation (2016)
14. Yu, R., Li, Q., Fischer, C., Doroudi, S., Xu, D.: Towards accurate and fair prediction of college success: evaluating different sources of student data (July 2020)
15. Zhao, Y., Xu, Q., Chen, M., Weiss, G.M.: Predicting student performance in a master of data science program using admissions data (July 2020)

A Well Lubricated Machine: A Data Driven Model for Lubricant Oil Conditions

Roney Malaguti[1,3]([✉])(iD), Nuno Lourenço[2](iD), and Cristovão Silva[3](iD)

[1] Stratio Automotive - R&D Department, Rua Pedro Nunes - Quinta da Nora, Ed.D,
3030-199 Coimbra, Portugal
roney@stratioautomotive.com
[2] CISUC, Department of Informatics Engineering, University of Coimbra, Coimbra,
Portugal
naml@dei.uc.pt
[3] CEMMPRE, Department of Mechanical Engineering, University of Coimbra,
Coimbra, Portugal
cristovao.silva@dem.uc.pt

Abstract. Diagnostic and predictive failure processes based on intelligent lubricant oil analysis are a important of the condition-based maintenance (CBM) approaches for diesel vehicle fleets. Companies are equipping each vehicle in the fleet with a large number of sensors, which allows the collection of vast amounts of data about the current state of each asset. With all this information now allows for the research and development of predictive models to help a fleet manager make informed decisions about the operating condition of the vehicles. This allows companies to accurately identify the state of wear and tear of a piece of equipment or system, making CBM more effective and reliable.

In this paper we present a supervised machine learning framework based on the Random Forest Classifier (RF) to determine the operating condition of lubricant oil in diesel engines based on data from 5 different vehicles. We describe the how practitioners should collect and process data, and which features can be engineered to help describe the state of the lubrication system. This data will then be used by a RF model to determine the operational condition of the lubricating oil.

The results presented show that the proposed approach is able to successfully identify the oil operating conditions, with the predictive model obtaining a Recall of 97.9%, a Precision of 99.5% and a F1-score of 98.7%. In addition, we evaluate the importance is the inclusion of new engineered features projected from raw data for better determination of the operating condition.

Keywords: Condition-based maintenance (CBM) · Lubricating oils · Diesel vehicle · Random forest classifier

© Springer Nature Switzerland AG 2021
G. Marreiros et al. (Eds.): EPIA 2021, LNAI 12981, pp. 549–560, 2021.
https://doi.org/10.1007/978-3-030-86230-5_43

1   Introduction

Fleet of vehicles are a key element in the operation of companies engaged in the transportation industry. When a vehicle comes to an halt due a failure it will impact the service and increase costs, making the preemptive identification of vehicle faults of paramount importance [10]. Modern industries that rely on maintenance techniques and methods to anticipate failure are increasingly focusing on the use lube oil testing as a key factor to identify the state of the vehicle conditions. Investments in research and development of diagnostic and fault prediction systems based on lubricant testing have increased, with the purpose of providing early warnings of machine malfunctions and extend the life of the equipment whilst reducing unnecessary oil change costs and waste [4,15]. Companies are gradually investing in systems and sensors to acquire information about the vehicles in real time, creating large data sets, allowing operators to make more informed decisions. However, the high sampling frequency, with some systems capturing information every second, and the large number of variables (i.e., sensors) being observed, create a challenging scenario for a human operator. To overcome this issue, practitioners and researchers are resorting to Artificial Intelligence and Machine Learning techniques to support operators in the analysis and help in the decision making process [15].

In this work we follow on this line of research, by proposing an data-driven approach to predict the operation condition of the lubricant oil in a fleet of heavy-duty passenger vehicles, using information about the condition of the vehicle (e.g., temperature, engine rotation) and features engineered to describe the current state of the oil. This information is then given to a Machine Learning (ML), namely, a Random Forest, which indicates if the oil is good or not to continue in operation. The obtained results show that the model is able to successfully predict the operating conditions using the information gathered from the vehicle, obtaining a Recall of 97.9%, a Precision of 99.5% and a F1-score of 98.7%. We also analyse the importance of the features used, and show that features engineered by us are important to the model accurately identify the oil conditions.

The remainder of the paper is structured as follows: Sect. 2 presents the related work; Sect. 3 details the data acquisition process. In Sect. 4 describes the experimental settings used in our study, and Sect. 5 discusses the main results. Finally, Sect. 6 gathers the main conclusions.

2   Related Work

Condition-Based Maintenance (CBM) is strategy for monitoring the current condition of assets, taking into account the evolution of certain indicators, which helps to determine when a given maintenance operation is required. These indicators result from regular check-ups to the machines and include non-intrusive measurements such as visual inspections, vehicle performance analysis, and scheduled tests (such as temperature and vibration measurements) [14]. The data can be collected at regular intervals or continuously through the use of embedded internal sensors. Some studies have proposed maintenance decision criteria to improve CBM using a detailed analysis of used oil data, in addition to observing the status of the equipment. On top of this, we can use the oil condition to determine whether the fluid in the system is healthy or requires maintenance. In the work presented in [10] the authors present an exponential smoothing model to determine the condition of diesel engine oil in urban buses. The model aims at monitoring the evolution of the state of the oil and its degradation. Applying the Lubrication Condition Monitoring (LCM) as baseline, the oil replacement intervals can be increased, which directly means an increase in availability and a reduction in maintenance costs [10]. [15] presents detailed method based on the latest research trends of the LCM-based method, which can be used for maintenance decision support and its application in equipment diagnosis and prognosis. The work studies the possibility of using physical, chemical, elemental, emission, and additive analysis as some of the LCM tests and criteria. The results show that it is possible to use a data-driven model to reliably describe the condition of a component or system.

Lubricants play an important role in a machine, and studying their conditions can help assess the rate at which equipment degrades. [8] details several physicochemical tests used in the study of oils for determining their state, and argues that the understanding of waste oil analysis is difficult due to the interdependence of the individual analyses. In recent years [4], oil aging or degradation research has become more reliable, providing accurate diagnosis of the remaining useful life of lubricant or impending breakdown in the systems or processes in which they are used. To evaluate lubricating oils, samples must be collected during and after service, and conditions that specify the lubricant's consistency and the state of the equipment must be considered [12]. According to [5], the main parameters related to oil degradation are: oxidation, nitration, viscosity, depletion of antioxidant additives, anti-wear, Total Acid Number (TAN), Total Base Number (TBN) and Remaining Useful Life (RUL). Another important parameter to take into account is the Oil Stress Factor (OSF), which has been used as an estimator of the potential stress suffered by the oil and correlates to its possible degradation as a function of engine condition [3,13]. To compute the OSF we can use two different ways: Oil_z [9], described in Eq. 1 and OSF_v3 [3] described in Eq. 2.

$$Oil_z = (1/V_{max}) \times (N_{Vmax}/N_{Pemax}) \times (Pe/V_h) \times (ODI/O_{vol}) \qquad (1)$$

Where:
V_{max} = Vehicle top speed (km/h);
N_{Vmax} = Engine top speed (RPM);
N_{Pemax} = Engine speed at maximum engine power (RPM);
Pe = Maximum engine power (kW);
V_h = Engine displacement (Litres);
ODI = Oil drain interval (km);
O_{vol} − Oil volume including top ups (Litres).

$$OSF\_v3 \; = \; (P/V_d \;) \times (C_e/V_s \;) \tag{2}$$

Where:
P = Power output (W);
V_d = Volume displaced by cylinder (m^3);
C_e = Number of engine combustion cycles;
V_s = Volume of oil in sump (m^3).

To find the OSF over the operating life cycle, Eq. 1 and Eq. 2 use engine characteristics such as power, maximum rotation, and whole lubricant volume, as well as details on speed and rotation in motion. Another essential variable to note is the oil viscosity under ideal working conditions, which reflects the fluidity of the oil at a specified temperature, where more viscous oils are thicker, while the less viscous ones are more fluid. Another important relationship that needs to be taken into account is the one between the oil temperature and viscosity, which is known to have a strong effect on engine friction. To compute the viscosity, one can use the formula for kinematic viscosity which is defined by:

$$\nu = \mu/\rho \tag{3}$$

where ρ is the specific mass of the fluid and μ is the dynamic viscosity.

3   Data Collection

Due to the complexity of diesel engines and the lubricant system, it is difficult to identify the conditions or faults from a single feature of the vehicle or the lubricant oil. Thus, to have a proper characterization of the vehicles we need to collect a large amount of variables. To do this, we use a proprietary real-time acquisition hardware, developed by Stratio Automotive [11]. This hardware allows for the collection of more than 200 parameters provided by the vehicle sensors.

After collecting the data, the first step is to clean and pre-process it. Due to the way that the acquisition hardware works, we need to identify the periods were the vehicle was making a trip, i.e. had the engine running. This step prevents the data entry of one trip from being extrapolated to another trip that took place long after the engine shutdown.

In the next step we analyse which variables are relevant to the identification of the oil conditions. We select the parameters that are directly linked to the vehicle lubrication system, namely: Engine Oil Temperature (°C), Coolant Temperature (°C), Engine Oil Pressure (mbar), Vehicle speed (km/h), Engine speed (rpm). Additionally, and to have a better characterisation of the current state of the oil, we computed 4 additional variables: Oil_z (Eq. 1), and OSF (Eq. 2), Kinematic Viscosity (Eq. 3) and Dynamic Viscosity (Eq. 3).

To characterize the condition of the oil, we relied on an oil slick test (Fig. 1), which is a fast and relatively inexpensive way of estimating the deterioration of the lubricant and look for the existence of pollutants. When using this test, we place a droplet of oil on a circular piece of paper which reacts to the elements present in the sample. After the reaction period defined by the test manufacturer, the oil stain is divided into 4 distinct zones of information: (i) the central zone of the stain is characterized by its uniform dark intensity and indicates the presence of sediments such as dust, abrasion particles, carbon and other insoluble deposits; (ii) the second zone indicates the condition of the oil sample by comparing the colour of the oil with the scale in the oil test; (iii) the boundary between the second and third zone, which indicates the presence of water in the oil sample, where peaks emerge around the edge of the second zone; (iv) and the last zone is called the fuel ring, that indicates if the oil sample is contaminated by fuel.

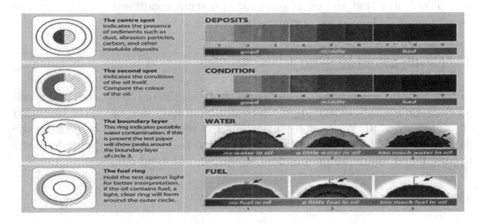

Fig. 1. Example of an oil slick text

It is important to mention that the lubricant analysis needs to be carried with great precautions to reduce the risk of contamination of the oil sample by external factors, which could lead to anomalies in the oil condition analysis. To address this issue, the following procedure was considered:

1. The person in charge of collecting the oil wears new gloves to avoid contamination of the sample by particles from the environment;
2. A drop of oil is collected through the dipstick and placed in the centre of the test;
3. A period of time of about 3 to 10 h is given for the oil drop to be absorbed and the cotton wool to separate the contaminants;
4. The test results are compared with the instructions sheet;
5. A picture of the test is taken and it is stored in a contamination free environment.

Table 1. Description of the vehicles selected to for the collection of the data

Brand	Model	Year	Engine	Oil
Mercedes	Citaro O530	2002	OM906h LA	GALP ULtra S3 10W40
Volvo	B7L	2004	D7E	GALP ULtra S3 10W40
MAN	12.240 HOCL NL	2007	D0836L OH56	GALP ULtra LS 10W40
MAN	14.240 HOCL NL	2009	D0836L OH56	GALP ULtra LS 10W40
Temsa	Avenue LF12	2017	ISBe6.7	GALP LD Supra 15W40
Temsa	Avenue LF12	2017	ISBe6.7	GALP LD Supra 15W40

Finally, the slick tests checks the oil for solid particle contamination and condition on a scale of 0 to 9 (Fig. 1). However, we convert this scale to a binary one: 0 indicates that the oil is good for operating conditions, and 1 indicates that the oil is not good for operating conditions.

4 Experimental Study

In this section we detail the experimental study conducted to evaluate the possibility of using a data-driven approach the automatically determine the condition of a lubricating oil. We start by describing the vehicles selected to perform the data collection. Then we describe the prediction model and the evaluation metrics used, and finally we present and discuss the obtained results.

4.1 Dataset

Following the procedure describe in Sect. 3 we contacted a company with a fleet of heavy duty vehicles for public transportation and performed the acquisition of data between January 1st 2020 and August 1st 2020 (Table 1). We selected vehicles of different manufactures, models, engines, oils in the lubricating system and with years of manufacturing ranging from 2002 to 2017. It is also important to refer that given the selected ranges of year of manufacturing our dataset will contain a diverse set of wear and tear of the engine and lubricating system, since the oldest vehicle has been running for 19 years. In total our dataset is composed of roughly 13M samples for the aforementioned period.

Since most of the time the oil is good for operating conditions, we have a highly imbalanced dataset. In concrete, only about 10% of the samples correspond to situations where the oil is not good for operating conditions. To address this issue, we applied a stratified data balancing strategy.

4.2 Prediction Model

When selecting a prediction algorithm one has to take into account the conditions in which it will be operating. Apart from having a model that can deal with the characteristics of the data we have, we also need to take into consideration the specific situations in which it will be deployed, namely assisting a human operator in the decision making process. As such, we have to select a model that, if needed, is able to provided the human expert with an explanation about the decision process. At the same time, we need to take into consideration the computational resources available to run the model. Given these requirements we selected Random Forests [1] as our prediction model.

Random Forests (RF) are an ensemble classifier that result from the combination of multiple Decision Trees (DT). In the standard RF model, we select a limited random number of features from the training set, and use this subset (i.e., a bootstrap) to create a full DT. This procedure is repeated for as many DT as we include in the RF. The RF decision is performed using the most popular class predicted by each DT. By limiting the number of features that can be selected for the bootstrap, and by not pruning the DTs, we reduce the computational load required allowing the RF model to be deployed in environments with modest computing capabilities [1].

In our experimental study we rely on the Python module scikit-learn (sklearn) [7] implementation of the RF classification algorithm[1], with 200 individual DTs of maximum size 4 and with 4 features in each bootstrap. For all the other remaining parameters we used the sklearn default values.

4.3 Evaluation Metrics

Evaluating a Machine Learning algorithm is an essential part of any project. A model may achieve satisfying results when evaluated using a specific metric, but otherwise could be not enough for application in real world. For this type of situation, it is necessary to select a group of evaluation metrics that are representative of the problem one is dealing with and that reflects the real conditions of the environment where the model will be deployed [12]. Given our specific situation, and the imbalanced nature of the problem at hand, we selected the following evaluation metrics to assess the performance:

1. **Precision score** is the number of correct positive results divided by the number of positive results predicted by the classifier [2];
2. **Recall score** is the number of correct positive results divided by the number of all relevant samples (all samples that should have been identified as positive) [2];
3. **F1-score** is the Harmonic Mean between precision and recall. This evaluation metric indicate how precise your classifier is (how many instances it classifies correctly), as well as how robust it is (it does not miss a significant number of instances). High precision but lower recall, show an extremely accurate, but it misses a large number of instances that are difficult to classify. The greater the F1 Score, the better is the performance of our model [2];

---

[1] Random Forest Classifier.

4. **Receiver Operating Characteristic (ROC) curve** is one of the popular metrics used in the industry to binary classification problems. ROC curves typically feature True Positive Rate on the Y axis, and False Positive Rate on the X axis. This means that the top left corner of the plot is the "ideal" point indicating a false positive rate of zero, and a true positive rate of one. The "steepness" of ROC curves is also important, since it is ideal to maximize the true positive rate while minimizing the false positive rate. Using this curve we can compute the **Area Under Curve (AUC)**, that show the probability of the classifier will rank a randomly chosen positive example higher than a randomly chosen negative example. This value of the AUC varies between 0 and 1, it does mean that a larger area under the curve is usually better and is close to the value 1 [2].

5   Results

The results obtained by the prediction model are summarised in Table 2. Each line shows the values obtained for Recall, F1-Measure and Precision. The results are averages of a 6-fold cross validation. A brief perusal of the table shows that the model is able to correctly identify all relevant instances, with a recall equal to 97.9%. A detailed inspection of how each instance is being classified by the model reveals that it is able to correctly identify all the instances where the oil is good for operating conditions (label 0). However, it fails to correctly classify a small number of instances with label 1, i.e., it is not able to identify some situations when the lubricating oil should be changed because it is no longer good for operating conditions. This is not a surprised when one takes the imbalanced nature of the problem at hand and the results presented in our previous works [16], which revealed that for some cases there is a small overlap between samples of the two classes.

Looking at the results obtained in the precision metric, we can see that they are slightly higher which confirms that the model is identifying most of the situations where a vehicle has an oil in the lubricating system that is not in good conditions. Finally, it is important to refer the low values of standard deviation for all the metrics, which are an indication of a robust model. In Fig. 2 we show the mean ROC curve obtained using a 6-fold cross-validation. This results confirm what we have discussed previously, showing that we have a high true positive rate. This is a remarkable results, given the nature of our problem, where accurately identifying the situations where the oil is gone bad is of the utmost importance to avoid catastrophic failures.

Table 2. Results obtained with the Random Forest model using 6-cross validation, with the standard deviation between parenthesis

Metrics	Value
Recall	97.9% (±0.9)
Precision	99.5% (±0.69)
F1-score	98.7% (±0.5)

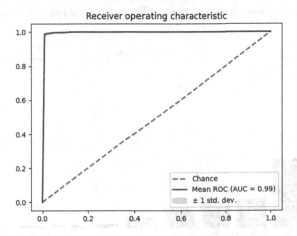

Fig. 2. Receiver Operating Characteristic (ROC) curve obtained by our model using a 6-fold cross-validation

We also conducted an analysis to understand which of the used features the most relevant to distinguish the operating conditions. This study will allows us to verify if the additional features that we developed (i.e., Oil_z, OSF, Kinematic Viscosity and Dynamic Viscosity) are useful. To compute the importance of the features, we used the normalized Gini importance metric [6]. Figure 3 depicts the results of the 9 most important features. Each bar in the figure represents the importance score, between 0 and 1, of the corresponding feature. For example, the Temperature of the Oil (°C) accounts for an importance score of roughly 0.4. The red line represents the cumulative sum of the importance of the different features. A brief perusal of the results confirm that the proposed features have an high importance score. In concrete, the Dynamic Viscosity accounts for almost 0.2 of importance, the Kinematic Viscosity for ∼0.15 and the OSF_v3 for about 0.10. Another interesting result is that the first 4 variables (Temperature of the Oil (°C), Dynamic Viscosity, Engine Coolant Temperature (°C) and Kinematic Viscosity) account for 0.9 of the importance. The temperature is used by the Centralina of the vehicle to compute the lubrification needs of the engine. Higher temperatures result smaller values of the kinematic and dynamic viscosity which decrease the lubrication power of the oil. Since viscosity control is one of the most important factors in determining the lubricant's operating condition, it is not a surprise that these variables play an important role in the model's decisions.

Despite not having an the same level of importance score as the temperatures and viscosities we can verify in the fifth position of importance, the calculated feature OSF_v3. This feature represents the operating conditions of the vehicle and although the selected vehicles are of different brands and models they tend to follow the same patterns of operation. Nevertheless, it is important to take this descriptor into account in the implementation of the model in a business environment where vehicles may have different operating conditions.

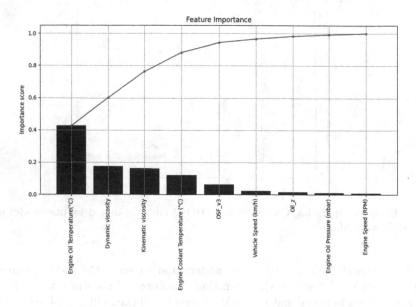

Fig. 3. Importance of selected features

6   Conclusion

Modern industries rely on maintenance techniques and methods to anticipate failures in their equipment. The transportation industry is not an exception, and nowadays they are investing more and more in the research and development of methodologies that will allow them to preemptively identify vehicles breakdown signatures, preventing catastrophic failures and large costs. One of such signatures is concerned with the engine maintenance, in which they want to establish the most economical oil change and overhaul intervals in terms of cost, wear and failure diagnosis efficiency.

In this paper, we propose an automated method for identifying lubricating oil conditions in diesel engines. We collected data from a fleet of heavy duty passenger vehicles, and using real-time information from sensors in the vehicles as well as engineered features, we build a Random Forests classifier model to predict if the oil is good for operating conditions. Given the reported results, the proposed model proved to be effective obtaining a Recall of 97.9% a Precision of 99.5% and a F1-score of 98.7%, which shows that it is able to identify most of the situations where the oil is not good for operating conditions and needs to be changed.

Finally, we performed an analysis on the importance of the features that were being used. The results show that the engineered features used are paramount to identify the conditions of the oil. In concrete, the Dynamic Viscosity and Kinematic Viscosity, two of the features engineered by us, account for roughly 35% of the importance score. The results obtained in this work are encouraging and are a step forward towards the automation of the condition monitoring of vehicle lubrication systems in real-time.

Acknowledgments. This work is partially funded by national funds through the FCT - Foundation for Science and Technology, I.P., within the scope of the project CISUC - UID/CEC/00326/2020 and by European Social Fund, through the Regional Operational Program Centro 2020 and by national funds through FCT - Fundação para a Ciência e a Tecnologia, under the project UIDB/00285/2020.

References

1. Breiman, L.: Random forests. Mach. Learn. **45**(1), 5–32 (2001)
2. Hanafy, M., Ming, R.: Machine learning approaches for auto insurance big data. Risks **9**(2), 1–23 (2021). https://doi.org/10.3390/risks9020042
3. Lee, P.M., et al.: The degradation of lubricants in gasoline engines: development of a test procedure to evaluate engine oil degradation and its consequences for Rheology. Tribol. Interface Eng. Ser. **48**, 593–602 (2005)
4. Lopez, P., Mabe, J., Miró, G., Etxeberria, L.: Low cost photonic sensor for in-line oil quality monitoring: methodological development process towards uncertainty mitigation. Sensors (Switzerland) **18**(7), 2015 (2018)
5. Macián-Martínez, V., Tormos-Martínez, B., Gómez-Estrada, Y.A., Bermúdez-Tamarit, V.: Revisión del proceso de la degradación en los aceites lubricantes en motores de gas natural comprimido y diesel. Dyna (Spain) **88**(1), 49–58 (2013)
6. Menze, B.H., et al.: A comparison of random forest and its Gini importance with standard chemometric methods for the feature selection and classification of spectral data. BMC Bioinf. **10**(1), 1–16 (2009)
7. Pedregosa, F., et al.: Scikit-learn: machine learning in Python. J. Mach. Learn. Res. **12**, 2825–2830 (2011)
8. Perić, S., Nedić, B., Grkić, A.: Applicative monitoring of vehicles engine oil. Tribol. Ind. **36**(3), 308–315 (2014)
9. Prasad, M.V., Lakshminarayanan, P.A.: Estimation of oil drain life of engine oils in new generation diesel engines in tropical conditions. SAE Int. J. Fuels Lubricants **5**(2) (2012). https://doi.org/10.4271/2011-01-2405
10. Raposo, H., Farinha, J.T., Fonseca, I., Ferreira, L.A.: Condition monitoring with prediction based on diesel engine oil analysis: a case study for urban buses. Actuators **8**(1), 1–15 (2019)

11. Homepage - stratio. https://stratioautomotive.com/. Accessed 19 Mar 2021
12. Sharma, B.C., Gandhi, O.P.: Performance evaluation and analysis of lubricating oil using parameter profile approach. Ind. Lubr. Tribol. **60**(3), 131–137 (2008)
13. Taylor, R.I., Mainwaring, R., Mortier, R.M.: Engine lubricant trends since 1990. Proc. Instit. Mech. Eng. Part J J. Eng. Tribol. **219**(5), 331–346 (2005)
14. Vališ, D., Žák, L., Pokora, O.: Failure prediction of diesel engine based on occurrence of selected wear particles in oil. Eng. Fail. Anal. **56**, 501–511 (2015)
15. Wakiru, J.M., Pintelon, L., Muchiri, P.N., Chemweno, P.K.: A review on lubricant condition monitoring information analysis for maintenance decision support. Mech. Syst. Signal Process. **118**, 108–132 (2019)
16. Malaguti, R., Lourenço, N., Silva, C.: Wear and tear: a data driven analysis of the operating condition of lubricant oils. In: Advances in Production Management Systems. Artificial Intelligence for Sustainable and Resilient Production Systems (APMS 2021), pp. 1–9. Springer Nature Switzerland AG (2021)

A Comparison of Machine Learning Methods for Extremely Unbalanced Industrial Quality Data

Pedro José Pereira[1], Adriana Pereira[2], Paulo Cortez[1(✉)], and André Pilastri[3]

[1] ALGORITMI Centre, Department of Information Systems, University of Minho,
Guimarães, Portugal
{id6927,a67662}@alunos.uminho.pt, pcortez@dsi.uminho.pt
[2] Bosch Car Multimedia, Braga, Portugal
adriana.pereira@pt.bosch.com
[3] EPMQ - IT Engineering Maturity and Quality Lab, CCG ZGDV Institute,
Guimarães, Portugal
andre.pilastri@ccg.pt

Abstract. The Industry 4.0 revolution is impacting manufacturing companies, which need to adopt more data intelligence processes in order to compete in the markets they operate. In particular, quality control is a key manufacturing process that has been addressed by Machine Learning (ML), aiming to improve productivity (e.g., reduce costs). However, modern industries produce a tiny portion of defective products, which results in extremely unbalanced datasets. In this paper, we analyze recent big data collected from a major automotive assembly manufacturer and related with the quality of eight products. The eight datasets include millions of records but only a tiny percentage of failures (less than 0.07%). To handle such datasets, we perform a two-stage ML comparison study. Firstly, we consider two products and explore four ML algorithms, Random Forest (RF), two Automated ML (AutoML) methods and a deep Autoencoder (AE), and three balancing training strategies, namely None, Synthetic Minority Oversampling Technique (SMOTE) and Gaussian Copula (GC). When considering both classification performance and computational effort, interesting results were obtained by RF. Then, the selected RF was further explored by considering all eight datasets and five balancing methods: None, SMOTE, GC, Random Undersampling (RU) and Tomek Links (TL). Overall, competitive results were achieved by the combination of GC with RF.

Keywords: Anomaly detection · Industrial data · Random forest

1 Introduction

The Industry 4.0 concept is increasing the pressure of companies to adopt data intelligence processes in order to remain competitive in the markets they operate

© Springer Nature Switzerland AG 2021
G. Marreiros et al. (Eds.): EPIA 2021, LNAI 12981, pp. 561–572, 2021.
https://doi.org/10.1007/978-3-030-86230-5_44

[12]. In particular, quality control is a crucial manufacturing process that can directly impact on productivity by reducing costs, defective products and complaints, among others [16]. In the past, several studies have explored Machine Learning (ML) algorithms to model quality control [2,6]. For instance, in 2016 there was a Kaggle challenge that addressed an industrial manufacturing quality prediction by using ML approaches [9,12,16].

Usually industrial quality ML prediction is addressed as a binary classification task, which is often a nontrivial task for two main reasons. Firstly, there is typically a lack of failures in modern manufacturing processes, thus the classification task is highly unbalanced [6]. For instance, there can be more than 99% of normal cases. Under such extreme unbalanced distribution, ML algorithms might produce misleading results due to the usage of standard loss functions (e.g., classification accuracy), which do not correctly measure the detection of faulty products. Secondly, industrial quality often involves big data, due to the volume and velocity of the produced data records, which increases the computational effort required by the ML algorithms.

In this paper, we address a relevant industrial manufacturing quality prediction task from a major automotive assembly company. The goal is to reduce the quantity of performed tests while maintaining the product quality, thus reducing inspection times and costs. The analyzed data includes millions of records but is extremely unbalanced, containing less than 0.1% of faulty products. This contrasts with related works, which handled a substantially higher number of failures (from 0.58% to 7%, as shown in Sect. 2). In particular, we handle eight extremely unbalanced datasets by exploring different ML algorithms and balancing training methods. Using a reduced set of two products, we first compare three supervised learning methods, Random Forest (RF) and two Automated ML (AutoML) approaches [8], and an unsupervised deep learning AutoEncoder (AE). Each ML is tested using three balancing strategies: no balancing (None), Synthetic Minority Oversampling Technique (SMOTE) [3] and Gaussian Copula (GC) [13]. Since RF provided interesting results in terms of both classification performance and computational effort, the RF algorithm was further selected as the base model for the remainder experiments, which considered all eight product datasets and five balancing training strategies: None, SMOTE, GC, Random Undersampling (RU) and Tomek Links (TL) [10].

This paper is organized as follows. The related work is presented in Sect. 2. Then, Sect. 3 describes the industrial data, ML methods and evaluation procedure. Next, Sect. 4 details the obtained results. Finally, Sect. 5 discusses the main conclusions and the future work.

2   Related Work

Several ML approaches have been proposed for industrial quality prediction tasks, which tends to produce unbalanced datasets. For instance, in [2] a semiconductor manufacturing test was modeled as a binary classification task that contained 7% of failures. In 2016, the "Bosch Production Line Performance" dataset, which included only 0.58% of failures, was made publicly available via a Kaggle competition [9]. Several studies explored this dataset by using the XGBoost algorithm [12,16]. However, none of the previous works explored training data balancing techniques, such as oversampling, undersampling, SMOTE or TL [3]. More recently, Fathy et al. [6] also addressed manufacturing quality prediction as binary classification task, exploring a dataset that contained 1.7% of faults. The authors used data augmentation techniques to balance the training data, namely SMOTE and Generative Adversarial Networks (GANs). In terms of ML algorithms, several supervised methods were compared, including Logistic Regression (LR), RF and XGBoost. While interesting results were achieved, no undersampling technique was explored in the comparison. Moreover, only a single dataset was used.

Regarding evaluation metrics, the related works used mostly measures based on class labels, such as: Matthew's Correlation Coefficient (MCC) [12,16]; a combination of the True Positive Rate (TPR) and True Negative Rate (TNR) [2]; and F1-Score [6]. However, when class decision scores or probabilities are available, is it possible to compute the Area Under the Curve (AUC) of the Receiver Operating Characteristic (ROC) curve [7]. The AUC measure provides several advantages over class label metrics [15]: it does not consider a single TPR to TNR trade-off; quality values are not affected if the classification data is unbalanced; and AUC values have an easy human interpretation (e.g., 50% is the performance of a random classifier, while 100% corresponds to a perfect discrimination). However, only one of industrial quality detection study has considered the AUC metric [12].

In this work, we analyse a manufacturing quality prediction task from a major automotive assembly company and that involves a tiny percentage of failure cases (less than 0.1%) that is much smaller than what has been handled in related works. Moreover, in contrast with [6], we handle eight different datasets and compare a larger set of balancing methods (including GC and two undersampling methods, RU and TL). Finally, since we handle big data, we consider both the classification performance (using the AUC metric) and the computational effort (in terms of time elapsed) when evaluating the ML methods, allowing to assess if they are feasible for a real industrial environment deployment.

3   Materials and Methods

3.1   Data

This work was developed within a larger R&D project set within the Industry 4.0 concept and that aims to design an Artificial Intelligence (AI) technological infrastructure to improve the manufacturing processes of a major automotive assembly company. The company provided a total of 8 datasets, each related with a distinct type of steering wheel angle sensor. Due to business privacy issues, the products are here denoted as P01, P02, ..., P08. Each product is assembled during the production line, either by robots, humans or a combination of both. Then, the products are subject to two different types of tests: functional, executed immediately after assembly, and torque, performed after the functional tests in order to measure the amount of torque being applied to an object.

The functional tests return a numeric value that measures a particular physical property. The measurements are compared with an acceptance interval set (composed of lower and upper bounds). In total, there are 10 functional tests, termed here as F01, F02, ..., F10. If a given product fails any of the functional tests, it is immediately considered as a faulty product and thus it is not evaluated by the final torque testing. Otherwise, the product is subject to a sequence of 4 torque tests, each returning also a numerical output that is compared with an acceptance interval. If any of the torque tests fails, the global quality status of the product is "fail", else it is labelled as "pass" (normal product).

Table 1 summarizes the analyzed data attributes. The ML goal is to predict the overall torque class label ($y \in \{$"fail", "pass"$\}$) based on the functional test values, which are used as the inputs of the ML algorithms. Our datasets only include the more challenging records, the products that passed all individual functional tests and have a final torque inspection value (y). A high performing ML method can potentially provide value to the company by reducing the amount of executed torque tests, which results in energy, time and other savings (e.g., torque instrumentation maintenance costs).

Table 1. Description of the industrial quality data attributes.

Attribute	Description	Range [min, max]
F01	Sensitivity	[0.999, 1.001]
F02	Hysteresis	[0.035, 2.500]
F03	Maximum nonlinearity (clockwise)	[0.100, 1.764]
F04	Minimum nonlinearity (clockwise)	[−1.778, −0.099]
F05	Maximum nonlinearity (anti-clockwise)	[0.090, 1.799]
F06	Minimum nonlinearity (anti-clockwise)	[−1.790, −0.090]
F07	Maximum K (clockwise)	[0.000, 0.188]
F08	Minimum K (clockwise)	[−0.180, 0.000]
F09	Maximum K (anti-clockwise)	[0.000, 0.184]
F10	Minimum K (anti-clockwise)	[−0.188, 0.000]
y	If a product passes a torque test	"Pass" or "Fail"

Nowadays, modern manufacturing lines produce high volumes of quality products, which results in a tiny fraction of failures. Indeed, our 8 datasets are extremely unbalanced, with the percentage of failures being below 0.1%. Table 2 presents the total number of records and percentage of failures for each product. The data records were collected in the years of 2019 and 2020. Excepting P07, all products have more than 100,000 records, with P06 containing almost 2 million examples. While we handle big data, there is a clear lack of minority class examples, with the percentage of failures ranging from 0.006% to 0.074%.

Table 2. Number of records and percentage of failures for each product.

Product	No. of records	Failures (%)
P01	610,380	0.013
P02	142,100	0.049
P03	714,816	0.006
P04	287,496	0.014
P05	219,860	0.022
P06	1,823,845	0.011
P07	33,897	0.074
P08	592,124	0.015

3.2 Balancing Methods

Data unbalancement can be quite harmful during the learning phase of classification algorithms. A common practice to solve this issue is apply data balancing techniques to the training data, which can be classified into two main approaches: undersampling and oversampling. The former consists on reducing the number of examples from the majority class, while the latter generates synthetic records from the minority class. Previous studies in smart manufacturing only considered oversampling techniques [6], namely SMOTE and GANs. In this work, we compare both undersampling and oversampling approaches. Given that we work with big data (Table 2), we do not explore the GAN method, since it requires a high computational effort during its training phase. Thus, we adopt faster balancing methods, namely two oversampling methods (SMOTE and GC) and two undersampling techniques (RU and TL). These methods are compared with the simpler no balancing method (None).

Concerning undersampling techniques, RU is quite easy to implement, it consists on randomly selecting only a few examples from the majority class, aiming to achieve balanced data. Given that our datasets have several hundred thousands records but only a few hundreds of failures, we did not to completely balance the data, since this would result in very small training set sizes. Instead, for RU we selected a more reasonable 25% random selection of the majority class records (resulting in a 75% reduction of the normal cases). As for the TL method, it performs a more sophisticated selection of positive examples. TL are pairs of examples from opposite classes that have high proximity, i.e., that are more similar. Such examples are noisy and make it difficult for the classifier to draw a borderline between classes. The TL technique tries to identify and remove the majority class records contained in these pairs, leaving the minority ones untouchable, aiming to create a consistent subset of data, thus, smoothing the modelling phase [10].

In terms of oversampling, SMOTE [4] is a popular data augmentation technique for the minority class. In the past, SMOTE has obtained interesting results for quality prediction data [6]. The synthetic data generation process starts by randomly selecting a minority class sample s_1 and searching for its k nearest neighbours, also belonging to minority class. In this work, we assumed $k = 5$, which is the default SMOTE implementation value, thus the neighbourhood samples are $s_2, s_3, \ldots, s_6$. Then, for each pair $(s_1, s_2), (s_1, s_3), \ldots, (s_1, s_6)$, a synthetic example is generated, considering the line segment that unites them [4]. This technique does not guarantee that generated data is realistic [6], which may be problematic for our datasets context. Considering that a torque test is only performed if all functional tests are within the acceptance intervals, it must be guaranteed that the synthetic data are also set within the same intervals. Therefore, after applying SMOTE for data augmentation, we replace values that are outside these intervals by the interval limit (lower or upper). For instance, considering the acceptance interval $[-1, 1]$ and a synthetic value $v = 1.5$ (>1), after applying our synthetic data treatment, we get $v = 1$. Lastly, GC is a model based on mathematical copula functions that converts all data columns distributions to a standard normal, aiming to remove any bias that might be induced [13]. The GC implementation used on this work allows to define a set of restrictions that must be fulfilled by new generated data to ensure its validity. Thus, unlike SMOTE, it is not necessary to perform any verification after the generation of the data. Instead, we define acceptance intervals for each column and GC guarantees that new data are within these intervals and valid. Both SMOTE and CG were set to generate balanced datasets with 50% of instances for each class.

In terms of implementation, all code was developed using the Python programming language. For SMOTE, RU and TL techniques, we used the *imbalanced-learn* library [11], while *sdv* [13] was used for GC. All methods were implemented with their default parameter values.

3.3 Machine Learning Algorithms

Product quality prediction is often modeled as a supervised learning binary classification task, where the purpose is to know in advance if a given product has enough quality to pass the next production step (e.g., "pass" or "fail"). When the number of failures is low, a popular ML approach is to assume an unsupervised Anomaly Detection (AD), which only uses normal records (thus one-class) during the training phase. In this paper, both one-class and binary classification strategies are compared. It should be noted that balancing methods (such as described in Sect. 3.2) can only be applied to binary classification, since they required labeled training data (with two or more classes).

Concerning the binary classification algorithms, we consider the RF algorithm and two AutoML implementations, namely H2O (https://www.h2o.ai/products/h2o-automl/) and AutoGluon (https://auto.gluon.ai/). In 2014, the RF tree ensemble algorithm was ranked favorably when compared with hundreds of classifiers for a large set of classification tasks [5]. As for the H2O and AutoGluon tools, they provided good results in a recent AutoML benchmark study [8]. AutoML automatically compares several algorithms with different parameter combinations, returning the best ML model for a given task. For both AutoML tools, the best ML model is set by randomly splitting the training data into fit

(2/3) and validation (1/3) sets. Then, the AUC metric computed on the validation set is used as the selection criterion. While automating the ML algorithm and parameter tuning, the AutoML approach tends to require more computational resources, since it requires the training of a larger number of ML algorithms. The two AutoML tools were set used with their default configurations, which assumes a search of the best within the following ML algorithms: H2O – Generalized Linear Model (GLM), RF, Extremely Randomized Trees (XRT), Gradient Boosting Machine (GBM), XGBoost, Deep Learning Neural Network (DLNN) and two Stacked Ensembles; AutoGluon – GBM, CatBoost Boosted Trees, RF, Extra Trees, k-Nearest Neighbors (k-NN), a DLNN and a Stacked Ensemble. All supervised ML methods (RF, H2O and AutoGluon) return a failure class probability ($p_i \in [0,1]$ for the i-th example) and that is used to compute the ROC curves [7]. When needed, class labels can be defined by using a decision threshold K, where it is considered a failure if $p_i > K$.

As for the one-class learning, we adopted an AE, which is a popular deep Learning architecture for AD [17]. An AE is composed by an encoder, a bottleneck layer (defining the latent space) and then a decoder. The model is trained only with normal data, aiming to generate outputs similar to the inputs. A well trained AE reconstructs normal examples with smaller errors, tending to produce larger reconstruction errors when faced with anomalous situations. After some preliminary experiments, conducted using product P01, the AE was set as fully connected feedforward deep neural network with: 4 hidden layers (each with 8 nodes) that defines the encoder; a bottleneck layer of 4 nodes; and a decoder component that is similar to the encoder. All nodes use the ReLu activation function and each transforming layer is coupled with a batch normalization layer. The AE is trained to minimize the reconstruction error, which was set as the Mean Squared Error (MSE). In each training iteration (epoch), 10% of the training data is randomly used as a validation set, allowing to monitor the reconstruction error and perform an early stopping. The Adam optimizer was used to adjust the AE weights, being stopped if there is no improvement after 25 epochs (early stopping) or after a maximum of 100 epochs. After the model is trained, we use the reconstruction error (MSE_i for the i-th example) to compute the failure probability, where the higher the error, the higher is the anomaly class probability (p_i is computed as the normalized MSE_i values, such that $p_i \in [0,1]$). Similarly to the supervised learning methods, a threshold K is used to assign class labels.

All ML algorithms were implemented using the Python programming language. For H2O and AutoGluon, we used the h2o and autogluon libraries, both of them with default parameter values that includes an execution time limit of 1 h. The RF assumes the scikit-learn [14] implementation, which uses a default of 100 trees. Finally, AE was implemented using tensorflow [1].

3.4   Evaluation

To evaluate methods, we use the AUC measure of the ROC curve [7]. The ROC represents the discrimination performance of a binary classifier when considering all possible K threshold values, plotting one minus the specificity (x-axis) versus the sensitivity (y-axis). The AUC is computed as $\int_0^1 ROCdK$. We also stored the computational effort, measured in terms of the time elapsed for training (in s) and predicting one example (in ms). Furthermore, to produce more robust results, for each product we apply five runs of a holdout training and test split, using 67% of the data records (random stratified selection) for training and the remaining 33% examples for testing. The data balancing techniques are applied only to the training data, thus, both validation and test subsets are kept unbalanced. We particularly note that validation sets are only used by the AutoML and AE algorithms. For the AutoML, it is used to set the leaderboard, which contains the best set of models and their hyperparameters. As for the AE, the validation set is used by the early stopping procedure and it only includes normal examples (one-class). All created subsets of data, either by splits or balancing techniques, were stored locally in order to ensure all models were evaluated using the same datasets (e.g., same test sets). All evaluation measures (AUC and computational effort) are aggregated by considering the average of the five runs.

4   Results

The experiments were executed in an Intel Xeon 1.70 GHz server. When using oversampling, the amount of records almost duplicates, which increases the execution time. Since five runs are applied for each dataset, it is computationally costly to apply all balancing techniques and ML algorithms to all products. Thus, we conducted an initial comparison study by considering two datasets (P01 and P02) and both SMOTE and GC oversampling techniques, aiming to select a reasonable performing ML algorithm for the remainder comparison scenarios.

Table 3 presents the average results for the first comparison study. For product P01, all models achieved a poor performance, with most AUC values being close to 50% (random classifier). In particular, AutoGluon performed worst on both synthetic data generators, H2O only had a slight AUC improvement when using SMOTE and AE obtained the second worst AUC value. As for the RF, it achieved the highest AUC value on P01 data when using the GC oversampling technique. Regarding P02 data, the AUC results are considerably better for all ML algorithms. Specifically, AutoGluon achieved the best AUC value (83.52%), followed by H2O (82.70%) and RF (81.51%), all using GC as the balancing data technique. AE presented the worst predictive performance on product P02 (65.72%). Overall, when considering both products, RF and AutoGluon obtained similar predictive performances. However, the RF training is much faster than AutoGluon (around ten/sixty times faster). For this reason, we selected RF for the remainder quality prediction experiments.

Table 4 presents the second quality prediction comparison results, which uses RF as the base ML model and explores five different balancing methods over all 8 datasets. An analysis to the table shows that GC is clearly the best data balancing technique, achieving the highest AUC values for 6 of the analyzed

Table 3. First quality prediction comparison results (**bold** denotes best average AUC).

Product	ML method	Balancing technique	AUC	Train time (s)	Prediction time (s)
P01	AutoGluon	None	57.81	2028	0.022
		GC	54.98	2197	0.069
		SMOTE	50.90	2137	0.016
	H2O	None	56.60	2988	0.007
		GC	53.00	3224	0.070
		SMOTE	56.75	3215	0.010
	RF	None	51.15	45	0.008
		GC	**59.23**	226	0.017
		SMOTE	50.98	242	0.012
	AE	None	53.72	78	0.036
P02	AutoGluon	None	83.32	1931	0.047
		GC	**83.52**	1930	0.084
		SMOTE	82.51	1922	0.033
	H2O	None	78.85	3210	0.021
		GC	82.70	3226	0.085
		SMOTE	80.82	3219	0.039
	RF	None	78.62	5	0.007
		GC	81.51	32	0.016
		SMOTE	79.41	34	0.009
	AE	None	65.72	27	0.034

8 products (P01, P02, P03, P04, P05 and P06). On the remainder datasets (P07 and P08), RF obtained the best predictive performance when using RU and SMOTE techniques, respectively. The last five rows of Table 4 show the average performance of each approach when considering all eight products. The average results also favor the GC oversampling technique, which produces a positive impact on the AUC values, presenting a difference of 7.19 and 10.08% points when compared with the RU (second best overall balancing method) and no balancing methods (None, the worst overall approach). In terms of the final quality prediction quality, the obtained AUC GC RF results reflect the difficulty of modeling extremely unbalanced datasets. For some products, a very good discrimination was achieved (e.g., 82% for P02 and P07, 73% for P04), but there are products that obtained a much lower AUC values (e.g., 50% for P08, 59% for P01). On average, the GC RF class discrimination performance is reasonable (around 67%). Regarding the training times, and as expected, both oversampling techniques (GC and SMOTE) require a larger computational effort. Nevertheless, the obtained GC RF models can still be achieved within a reasonable computational effort. In effect, it requires around 18 min of training

Table 4. Second quality prediction comparison results (**bold** denotes best average AUC).

Product	Balancing technique	AUC	Train time (s)	Prediction time (s)
P01	None	51.15	44.79	0.008
	GC	**59.23**	226.19	0.017
	SMOTE	50.98	242.24	0.012
	RU	53.08	9.91	0.009
	TL	50.35	45.73	0.008
P02	None	78.62	5.06	0.007
	GC	**81.51**	31.73	0.016
	SMOTE	79.41	34.08	0.009
	RU	81.22	1.25	0.007
	TL	78.18	5.24	0.007
P03	None	53.13	43.08	0.007
	GC	**62.18**	278.16	0.018
	SMOTE	53.82	341.49	0.010
	RU	54.57	8.78	0.007
	TL	52.47	43.57	0.008
P04	None	50.25	7.48	0.006
	GC	**73.07**	66.96	0.014
	SMOTE	59.45	96.52	0.008
	RU	53.63	1.97	0.008
	TL	51.01	7.65	0.006
P05	None	51.11	9.38	0.006
	GC	**68.53**	69.69	0.016
	SMOTE	55.63	87.34	0.009
	RU	57.97	1.99	0.006
	TL	53.00	9.31	0.006
P06	None	51.66	339.33	0.011
	GC	**61.87**	1104.61	0.029
	SMOTE	53.84	1164.85	0.014
	RU	54.85	52.74	0.011
	TL	51.51	354.12	0.011
P07	None	72.60	0.82	0.006
	GC	81.85	5.92	0.012
	SMOTE	76.53	6.02	0.008
	RU	**82.18**	0.27	0.006
	TL	72.59	0.87	0.006
P08	None	49.43	40.22	0.008
	GC	50.21	248.32	0.018
	SMOTE	**51.31**	225.06	0.011
	RU	50.37	9.64	0.009
	TL	49.41	43.78	0.009
Average	None	57.24	61.27	0.008
	GC	**67.31**	253.95	0.017
	SMOTE	60.12	274.70	0.010
	RU	60.98	10.82	0.008
	TL	57.32	63.78	0.008

effort for the largest dataset, which originally contains 1,8 million records (before the application of the GC method). As for the inference times, the GC RF predictions require 0.017 ms, which means that a trained model can be used to produce real-time industrial product quality predictions.

The obtained results were shown to the manufacturing company experts, who considered them very positive. In particular, the experts highlighted the GC RF discrimination results that were obtained for three of the analysed products (P02, P04 and P07). Moreover, they confirmed that required computational effort is adequate for a real industrial deployment of the ML models.

5   Conclusions

The Industry 4.0 revolution is transforming manufacturing companies, which are increasingly adopting data intelligence processes in order to remain competitive in the market. In the last years, several works used Machine Learning (ML) to enhance product quality control, which is a key manufacturing element. Currently, modern manufacturing companies tend to have a high quality production, which results in a tiny percentage of failures, thus originating extremely unbalanced data that is challenging for common ML algorithms.

In this paper, we analyze millions of records related with eight products assembled by a major automotive company. Only a tiny fraction (less than 0.07%) correspond to failures. To handle such extremely unbalanced data, we compared four ML algorithms and five balancing techniques. Overall, the best results were achieved by a Gaussian Copula (GC) oversampling technique when adopting a supervised Random Forest (RF) base learner. In particular, a very good class discrimination was achieved for three of the eight analyzed products. Moreover, the GC RF combination requires a computational effort (in terms of training and prediction times) that is feasible for the analyzed domain (e.g., it requires around 18 min to process 3.6 million records).

In future work, we intend to explore more datasets by testing the proposed GC RF model over a larger range of products. Also, we plan to deploy the ML algorithms and balancing methods in a real industrial setting, which would allow us to monitor the capability of the ML models through time and assess if they can provide productivity gains (e.g., by reducing the number of torque tests).

Acknowledgments. This work is supported by: European Structural and Investment Funds in the FEDER component, through the Operational Competitiveness and Internationalization Programme (COMPETE 2020) [Project n 39479; Funding Reference: POCI-01-0247-FEDER-39479].

References

1. Abadi, M., et al.: TensorFlow: large-scale machine learning on heterogeneous systems (2015). https://www.tensorflow.org/

2. Adam, A., Chew, L.C., Shapiai, M.I., Lee, W.J., Ibrahim, Z., Khalid, M.: A hybrid artificial neural network-naive Bayes for solving imbalanced dataset problems in semiconductor manufacturing test process. In: HIS, pp. 133–138. IEEE (2011)
3. Batista, G.E.A.P.A., Prati, R.C., Monard, M.C.: A study of the behavior of several methods for balancing machine learning training data. SIGKDD Explor. 6(1), 20–29 (2004). https://doi.org/10.1145/1007730.1007735
4. Chawla, N.V., Bowyer, K.W., Hall, L.O., Kegelmeyer, W.P.: SMOTE: synthetic minority over-sampling technique. J. Artif. Intell. Res. 16, 321–357 (2002)
5. Delgado, M.F., Cernadas, E., Barro, S., Amorim, D.G.: Do we need hundreds of classifiers to solve real world classification problems? J. Mach. Learn. Res. 15(1), 3133–3181 (2014). http://dl.acm.org/citation.cfm?id=2697065
6. Fathy, Y., Jaber, M., Brintrup, A.: Learning with imbalanced data in smart manufacturing: a comparative analysis. IEEE Access 9, 2734–2757 (2021)
7. Fawcett, T.: An introduction to ROC analysis. Pattern Recogn. Lett. 27, 861–874 (2006)
8. Ferreira, L., Pilastri, A., Martins, C.M., Pires, P.M., Cortez, P.: A comparison of AutoML tools for Machine Learning, Deep Learning and XGBoost. In: International Joint Conference on Neural Networks, IJCNN 2021, July. IEEE (2021)
9. Kaggle: Bosch production line performance. https://www.kaggle.com/c/bosch-production-line-performance. Accessed 27 Apr 2021
10. Kubat, M., Matwin, S.: Addressing the curse of imbalanced training sets: one-sided selection. In: ICML, pp. 179–186. Morgan Kaufmann (1997)
11. Lemaître, G., Nogueira, F., Aridas, C.K.: Imbalanced-learn: a Python toolbox to tackle the curse of imbalanced datasets in machine learning. J. Mach. Learn. Res. 18(17), 1–5 (2017). http://jmlr.org/papers/v18/16-365
12. Mangal, A., Kumar, N.: Using Big Data to enhance the Bosch production line performance: a Kaggle challenge. In: IEEE BigData, pp. 2029–2035. IEEE Computer Society (2016)
13. Patki, N., Wedge, R., Veeramachaneni, K.: The synthetic data vault. In: 2016 IEEE International Conference on Data Science and Advanced Analytics, DSAA 2016, Montreal, QC, Canada, 17–19 October 2016, pp. 399–410. IEEE (2016). https://doi.org/10.1109/DSAA.2016.49
14. Pedregosa, F., et al.: Scikit-learn: machine learning in Python. J. Mach. Learn. Res. 12, 2825–2830 (2011)
15. Pereira, P.J., Cortez, P., Mendes, R.: Multi-objective grammatical evolution of decision trees for mobile marketing user conversion prediction. Expert Syst. Appl. 168, 114287 (2021). https://doi.org/10.1016/j.eswa.2020.114287
16. Zhang, D., Xu, B., Wood, J.: Predict failures in production lines: a two-stage approach with clustering and supervised learning. In: IEEE BigData, pp. 2070–2074. IEEE Computer Society (2016)
17. Zhou, C., Paffenroth, R.C.: Anomaly detection with robust deep autoencoders. In: Proceedings of the 23rd ACM SIGKDD International Conference on Knowledge Discovery and Data Mining, Halifax, NS, Canada, 13–17 August 2017, pp. 665–674. ACM (2017). https://doi.org/10.1145/3097983.3098052

Towards Top-Up Prediction on Telco Operators

Pedro Miguel Alves[1], Ricardo Ângelo Filipe[2] , and Benedita Malheiro[1,3]([✉])

[1] Instituto Superior de Engenharia do Porto, Politécnico do Porto, Porto, Portugal
{1161571,mbm}@isep.ipp.pt
[2] Altice Labs, Aveiro, Portugal
ricardo-a-filipe@alticelabs.com
[3] Instituto de Engenharia de Sistemas e Computadores,
Tecnologia e Ciência, Porto, Portugal

Abstract. In spite of their growing maturity, telecommunication operators lack complete client characterisation, essential to improve quality of service. Additionally, studies show that the cost to retain a client is lower than the cost associated to acquire new ones. Hence, understanding and predicting future client actions is a trend on the rise, crucial to improve the relationship between operator and client. In this paper, we focus in pay-as-you-go clients with uneven top-ups. We aim to determine to what extent we are able to predict the individual frequency and average value of monthly top-ups. To answer this question, we resort to a Portuguese mobile network operator data set with around 200 000 clients, and nine-month of client top-up events, to build client profiles. The proposed method adopts sliding window multiple linear regression and accuracy metrics to determine the best set of features and window size for the prediction of the individual top-up monthly frequency and monthly value. Results are very promising, showing that it is possible to estimate the upcoming individual target values with high accuracy.

Keywords: Business intelligence · Business analytics · Data science · Linear regression · Sliding window · Telecom operator

1 Introduction

Pay-as-you-go services are a Telco business model used by millions around the globe on a daily basis. Achieving a fine-grained characterisation of these clients is a *must* have for Telecommunication Operators, to ensure better quality-of-service in an environment that is very challenging with a plethora of products and competitor companies. Additionally, in developed countries with market penetration around 100%, studies show that the cost to retain a client is lower that the cost to acquire a new one [11]. Hence, it is very appealing to identify patterns in these clients, and understand if a client will or not make a top-up in the near future. The possibility to predict top-up values is also interesting to understand the health and the growth of the business for market share.

© Springer Nature Switzerland AG 2021
G. Marreiros et al. (Eds.): EPIA 2021, LNAI 12981, pp. 573–583, 2021.
https://doi.org/10.1007/978-3-030-86230-5_45

The characterisation of pay-as-you-go clients is a hard task due to their volatility. We resorted to Recency, Frequency, and Monetary value (RFM) analysis [15] to better understand the data set from a Portuguese mobile network operator with around 200 000 clients and nine months of top-up events. To refine the individual profiles, we manufactured several new features based on the original ones and then selected the most promising subset of features. Finally, we implemented multiple linear regression, using the selected features, to predict individual top-up targets.

Results show that it is possible to characterise clients and predict the individual monthly top-up frequency and monetary value. Hence, with the help of appropriate algorithms, client historical data can provide useful information to Telco data analytics and marketing teams.

The rest of the paper is organised as follows. Section 2 describes the methodological approach, comprising the data set analysis, feature manufacturing and selection, predictive algorithm and evaluation. Section 3 presents the experiments and results. Section 4 concludes the paper and identifies future directions.

2   Methodological Approach

The methodological approach started by surveying the literature, analysing the data set, building and selecting the most most promising set of features, and implementing sliding window multiple linear regression (MLR).

The literature survey, which focused on the prediction of Telco customer behaviour, identified a large body of work on the prediction of mobile client churn [3, 5, 9] – a related but distinct task. Considering top-up frequency and value prediction, no contributions were found.

2.1   Data Set Analysis

Telco data sets can be poked with the help of marketing methodologies such as RFM analysis [15] to better understand client behaviour. RFM stands for Recency, Frequency, and Monetary value, where recency represents the engagement with the operator and frequency and monetary value characterise the overall top-up behaviour.

Another interesting approach related with the problem at hand is the Customer Lifetime Value (CLV). In business analysis, CLV is the general measure of the projected revenue that a client will bring over the lifespan of the established contract, and can be used to predict repeated client purchases. However, its main drawback is that, in most cases, it requires a decent-sized investment of time, coordination, and organisational alignment to determine and continue to analyse CLV [10]. This is aggravated when there is an extended time between purchases just like in the pre-paid pay-as-you-go telecommunications environment. Another drawback is the fact that CLV is no longer supported by Python development environments [2].

The data set analysis contemplated RFM, subscription age and distribution of top-up events per month.

2.2 Building and Selecting Features

The refinement of the individual profiles was performed by using the raw numeric features to create new individual features corresponding to frequency, average and standard deviation, total, maximum and minimum values.

Using the total number of features in regression tasks can result in high dimensionality which encumbers processing. The presence of too many features is a drawback to most inducers even when these attributes are relevant for the task, not to mention irrelevant or redundant features which can obscure existing patterns [6]. In previous Telco-related works, feature selection techniques are typically categorised as filters, wrappers and embedded approaches [4,16]. Filters use measures of association between each predictor variable and the target to examine its predictive power. Wrappers look for the optimal subset of features by using predictive or trained algorithms. Specifically, they use different combinations or subsets of attributes to find the best subset of features. The embedded approach explores the advantages of both wrappers and filters to identify the best features, using attribute subsets and checking the performance of the corresponding models [4].

To find the best combination of features for the prediction of the individual top-up monthly frequency and monthly value, several feature selection techniques were explored, including wrappers (Forward Selection, Backward Selection, Recursive Feature Elimination and Recursive Feature Elimination Cross Validation), a filter (Univariate Selection) and an embedded approach (Selection using Shrinkage) [1]. A brief description of these methods follows.

- Forward Selection is an iterative method which starts without features. In each iteration, it adds the feature which best improves the model until the addition of a new variable no longer improves the performance of the model.
- Backward Selection starts with all features and removes the least significant feature at each iteration which improves the performance of the model. This is repeated until no improvement is observed with the removal of features.
- Recursive Feature Elimination (RFE) is a greedy optimisation algorithm which aims to find the best performing feature subset. It repeatedly creates models and keeps aside the best or the worst performing feature after each iteration. Then, constructs the next model, using the remaining features, until all features have been eliminated. Finally, the features are ranked based on the order of their elimination.
- Recursive Feature Elimination Cross-Validation (RFECV) ranks features with the help of recursive feature elimination and cross-validated selection of the best number of features. Cross-validation is a technique for evaluating machine learning models by training and evaluating several models on subsets of the available input data, using the remaining data subset.
- Univariate Selection selects the best features based on univariate statistical tests, in this case, according to the k highest scores.
- Selection using Shrinkage applies, during the learning process, the least absolute shrinkage and selection operator to choose the features to include based on importance weights and cross-validation [12].

Several MLR experiments were made using these six feature selection methods to identify the most promising set of features, i.e., the subset of i independent variables to use in future regressions.

2.3   Sliding Window Regression

Model. Since this is a forecasting problem, multiple linear regression (MLR) was chosen to predict future client *monthly top-up frequency* and the *monthly top-up value*. MLR is a statistical technique, based on ordinary least squares, which predicts the value of a dependent variable based on a set of explanatory variables. It determines the linear relationship between the independent and the dependent variables. Equation 1 presents the general MLR expression where y_i represents dependent variable, $x_{i1}, x_{i2}, \cdots, x_{ij}$ the j independent explanatory variables, β_0 the intercept constant, $\beta_1, \beta_2, \cdots, \beta_j$ the slope coefficients of the j explanatory variables and ϵ_i the error.

$$y_i = \beta_0 + \beta_1 x_{i1} + \beta_2 x_{i2} + \cdots + \beta_j x_{ij} + \epsilon_i \tag{1}$$

The proposed method adopts a sliding window of size $n + 1$ months, where the first n window months are for training and the last window month to test. Specifically, the model is trained using the independent observations of the first $n - 1$ months and the target observations of month n, and is tested with the $n + 1$ month. The window then slides one month and repeats the process till the end of the data set. Considering a data set with m months of data, the sliding window MLR predicts a total of t months, where $t = m - n$. Figure 1 displays the adopted sliding window where $\vec{x_i} = \{x_{i1}, x_{i2}, \cdots, x_{ij}\}$ represents the set of j independent variables and y_i the target variable used for training, and $\hat{y_i}$ the target variable predicted during test.

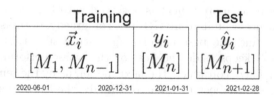

Fig. 1. Sliding window of size $n + 1$ months

Sliding Window. To determine the best sliding window dimension another set of MLR experiments was performed using, this time, different sliding window sizes together with the best set of features obtained. The sliding window is applied to the original features, whereas the manufactured features maintain the historical perspective.

Evaluation. In all experiments, the evaluation of both prediction models was based on the *Mean Absolute Error* (MAE) and *Root Mean Squared Error* (RMSE) predictive accuracy metrics. These metrics measure the closeness (error) between the predicted target features (dependent variables) and the observed values. Specifically, RMSE determines the standard deviation and MAE the average of these errors within the test partition. The calculated error values correspond to the weighted average error of the t tested months, where each weight w_i represents the number of top-up events of that month. Equation 2 and Eq. 3 present the MAE and RMSE of the sliding window regression.

$$MAE = \frac{\sum_{i=1}^{t} w_i MAE_i}{\sum_{i=1}^{t} w_i} \tag{2}$$

$$RMSE = \frac{\sum_{i=1}^{t} w_i RMSE_i}{\sum_{i=1}^{t} w_i} \tag{3}$$

Finally, the *Pearson Correlation Coefficient* (PCC) was calculated, using also the event-weighted average of the t tested months, to determine the correlation between the training and test months.

3   Experiments and Results

The experiments address the parameterization of the prediction of the individual top-up monthly frequency and monthly value. The aim is to determine:

1. The subset of features to select;
2. The window size to adopt.

The algorithm was implemented using Python with Jupyter Notebooks [7], and the Scikit-Learn library [8]. The visual analysis was performed with the Seaborn library [14]. To serve as reference, the hardware specification of the machines where the experiments were executed is 8.00 GB of RAM, Intel Core i5-4200M CPU @ 2.50 GHz processor, 297 GB of physical memory and Microsoft Windows 10 Enterprise operating system.

3.1   Data Set

The data set expands over a period of nine months, from the beginning of June 2020 to the end of February 2021, and includes information of 205 098 pre-paid clients and a total of 841 357 events (Fig. 2). All sensitive personal information was anonymized. The top-up data holds, apart the individual `card identification`, the categorical `type of top-up`, the `type of tariff`, the `date` of the top-up, `value` of the top-up, the `card balance` after top-up and the `age of subscription` in months. Table 1 presents the distribution of top-up events per month, which has an average of 93 484.11 events per month with a coefficient of variance c_v of 14.27. The mobile traffic data displays a tendency to have higher numbers in the middle and in the end of the year. This behaviour is expected in a Telco Operator, since the number of client events is higher during holiday seasons. Between these periods, client activity tends to reduce. As a consequence, the quantity of top-ups tends to follow the same trend.

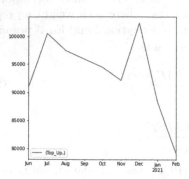

Fig. 2. Top-up data

Table 1. Events per month

Year	Month	Events
2020	June	90955
2020	July	100498
2020	August	97441
2020	September	95916
2020	October	94436
2020	November	92148
2020	December	102356
2021	January	88302
2021	February	79305

Figure 3a shows the range, in months, of the client subscription time, whereas Fig. 3b, Fig. 3c and Fig. 3d display the RFM visual analysis over the nine-month period. The displayed power loss RFM curves indicate that client activity, with the exception of few outliers, is infrequent and top-up values are low. Such evidence is common in pre-paid telecommunication subscriptions.

To have a better understanding of the data and how the clients behave, individual client profiles were built. Additional variables such as frequency, mean and standard deviation, maximum, minimum and total values were calculated from numerical top-up features. These derived features were calculated incrementally and monthly since the target features, i.e., the monthly frequency and monthly value of top-up are very sporadic. Moreover, the corresponding global variables were calculated, taking all clients into account, making use of cumulative calculus. The client profiling provided a better understanding of where clients stand globally, allowing a general client classification.

To be able to analyse the potential impact of all data set features on the dependent variables, the categorical features were converted to numeric features through One-Hot-Encoder [13]. Finally, all data were normalised. The resulting data set allows experimenting with window dimensions from 3 to 9, corresponding to 7 to 1 test months. The c_v of the number of events of the test months ranges from 10.95 with a six-month and 18.63 with an eighth-month window. In the end, the initial set of seven features grew to a total of 27, including the unique customer card identification.

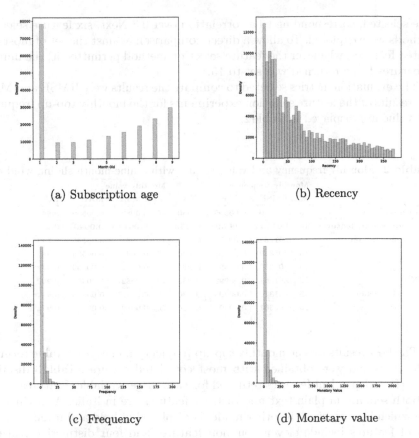

(a) Subscription age

(b) Recency

(c) Frequency

(d) Monetary value

Fig. 3. Subscription age and RFM analysis top-up

3.2 Parameterization

Two sets of experiments were performed to determine the best subset of features and dimension of the sliding window.

Feature Selection. The first set of experiments adopted a nine-month sliding window, holding the complete data set, which uses the first eight months of window data to train the model and the last window month to test the model. The predictions for the ninth month were then compared against the observed individual monthly recharge frequency and monthly value. To fulfil the purpose of predicting the both target variables, two MLR models were built. To that end, several feature selection techniques were explored to determine the best features to include with each MLR model.

Initially, the features with a correlation with the target feature over 0.5 were used as independent variables. This threshold proved to be too restrictive, resulting in just 8 features. To overcome this problem, the 15 most correlated features were selected, corresponding to a correlation over 0.3 Next, six feature selection methods were explored. To allow a direct comparison against the set of most correlated features, whenever the feature selection method permitted it, the number of features to be returned was set to 15.

The evaluation metrics selected to compare the results were RMSE and MAE. The results of the feature selection experiments for the monthly top-up frequency and value are displayed in Table 2.

Table 2. Monthly frequency and value results with a nine-month sliding window

	Monthly frequency				Monthly value			
	#	RMSE	MAE	PCC	#	RMSE	MAE	PCC
Forward selection	15	0.01370	0.00999	0.930	15	0.00827	0.00556	0.942
Most correlated features	15	**0.01165**	**0.00698**	**0.933**	15	**0.00740**	**0.00431**	**0.946**
Univariate selection	15	0.01287	0.00873	0.923	15	0.00810	0.00536	0.942
RFE	15	0.01370	0.00998	0.930	15	0.00828	0.00556	0.942
Shrinkage	15	0.01370	0.00998	0.930	15	0.00826	0.00556	0.942
RFECV	26	0.01367	0.00999	0.930	23	0.00827	0.00556	0.942
Backward selection	15	0.01370	0.00998	0.930	15	0.00827	0.00556	0.942
All features	26	0.01367	0.00999	0.930	26	0.00827	0.00556	0.942

The best results for the monthly top-up frequency and average value returned 15 features and were obtained with most correlated features. Table 3 discriminates the independent features returned for each target variable. Features shared by both sets are in plain text and distinct features are in italic. A distinct feature which is a target of the other model is displayed in bold and italic. The two sets of features include eleven common features and four distinctive features, including the other target.

Several of the chosen features are related with the types of top-up. This is expected since the operator forces clients to recharge after a predefined period of inactivity. Hence, different types of top-up influence the features selected for the prediction of both monthly top-up frequency and value.

Window Dimension. A second set of experiments was performed to analyse the impact of the sliding window size in the accuracy of the prediction results. These experiments were performed using the 15 most correlated features and window sizes of 3, 4, 5, 6, 7, 8 and 9 months (Table 4). The best results (lower errors) occurred with a four-month window for the individual monthly frequency and a nine-month window for the individual monthly value. This indicates that more historical data is required to predict accurately the individual top-up value than the individual top-up frequency.

Figure 4 shows the predicted and observed monthly frequency (Fig. 4a) and average monthly value (Fig. 4b) of the top-up events with a four-month sliding window and a nine-month sliding window, respectively. The linear relation between the predictions and observations displays low error and a close fit between data and trend line.

Table 3. Selected features by top-up target variable

	Monthly frequency	Monthly value
1:	Card balance	Card balance
2:	Maximum top-up value per day	Maximum top-up value per day
3:	Maximum number of top-ups per day	Maximum number of top-ups per day
4:	Minimum number of top-ups per day	Minimum number of top-ups per day
5:	Number of top-ups on last date	Number of top-ups on last date
6:	Std. deviation of the monthly top-up frequency	Std. deviation of monthly top-up frequency
7:	Std. deviation of monthly top-up value	Std. deviation of monthly top-up value
8:	Subscription age	Subscription age
9:	Tariff code	Tariff code
10:	Total number of top-ups made	Total number of top-ups made
11:	Total value of top-ups made	Total value of top-ups made
12:	*First Data Iberica top-up*	*Minimum top-up value per day*
13:	*Auchan top-up*	*Special services top-up*
14:	*PayShop top-up*	*Value of last top-up*
15:	*Monthly top-up value*	*Monthly top-up frequency*

Table 4. Results with different sliding window dimensions

Window size (months)	Monthly frequency			Monthly value		
	RMSE	MAE	PCC	RMSE	MAE	PCC
9	0.01165	0.00698	0.933	**0.00740**	**0.00431**	0.946
8	0.01052	0.00633	0.938	0.01754	0.00591	0.947
7	0.01048	0.00680	0.952	0.00992	0.00612	0.945
6	0.00996	0.00623	0.951	0.01027	0.00647	0.957
5	0.00951	0.00629	0.961	0.00972	0.00594	0.965
4	**0.00924**	**0.00595**	**0.972**	0.01036	0.00686	**0.976**
3	0.00979	0.00611	0.815	0.01023	0.00651	0.816

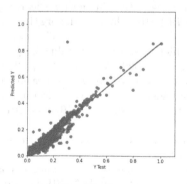   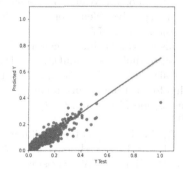

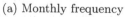

(a) Monthly frequency   (b) Monthly average value

Fig. 4. Trend and relation between predicted and observed values

4   Conclusion and Future Work

In a world with a plethora of products and services, it is a difficult task for a Telco Operator to predict client behaviour. Hence, in these complex environments, prediction systems play an important role as they are able to anticipate future client needs.

This paper explores a prediction system for client monthly top-up frequency and value, using real top-up data, from a Portuguese Telco Operator.

First, the data set was created from the original top-up data. Based on the raw data, new variables were calculated to refine client profiles. With a total of seven original and twenty derived features, the next step was to implement a sliding window multiple linear regression. To optimise the run-time performance of the system, several feature selection techniques and window sizes were explored to reduce the number of features and maintain low error metrics when compared to the results using all features. The experiments identified the most promising set of features and sliding window dimensions. The created predictive models use fifteen features and present the highest accuracy regarding the frequency and value of the individual top-ups with windows of four and nine months, respectively.

As future work, the intention is to use the selected set of features to predict the same targets, this time, using multivariate linear regression, followed by data stream regression, and compare results. In principle, the data stream implementation, with incremental model updating and prequential evaluation, should display improved performance.

Acknowledgements. This work was partially supported by National Funds through the FCT– Fundação para a Ciência e a Tecnologia (Portuguese Foundation for Science and Technology) as part of project UIDB/50014/2020.

References

1. Cai, J., Luo, J., Wang, S., Yang, S.: Feature selection in machine learning: a new perspective. Neurocomputing **300**, 70–79 (2018). https://doi.org/10.1016/j.neucom.2017.11.077
2. Davidson, C.: Github - camdavidsonpilon/lifetimes: Lifetime value in python. https://github.com/CamDavidsonPilon/lifetimes (2020) Accessed 16 Apr 2021
3. De Caigny, A., Coussement, K., De Bock, K.W.: A new hybrid classification algorithm for customer churn prediction based on logistic regression and decision trees. Eur. J. Oper. Res. **269**(2), 760–772 (2018). https://doi.org/10.1016/j.ejor.2018.02.009
4. E, V., Ravikumar, D.P.: Attribute selection for telecommunication churn prediction. Int. J. Eng. Technol. **7**(4.39), 506–509 (2018)
5. Jain, H., Khunteta, A., Srivastava, S.: Churn prediction in telecommunication using logistic regression and logit boost. Procedia Comput. Sci. **167**, 101–112 (2020). https://doi.org/10.1016/j.procs.2020.03.187. International Conference on Computational Intelligence and Data Science

6. John, G.H., Kohavi, R., Pfleger, K.: Irrelevant features and the subset selection problem. In: Cohen, W.W., Hirsh, H. (eds.) Machine Learning Proceedings 1994, pp. 121–129. Morgan Kaufmann, San Francisco (CA) (1994). https://doi.org/10.1016/B978-1-55860-335-6.50023-4

7. Jupyter: Project jupyter—home. https://jupyter.org/ (2021). Accessed 15 Apr 2021

8. scikit learn: scikit-learn: machine learning in python – scikit-learn 0.24.1 documentation. https://scikit-learn.org/stable/ (2021). Accessed 15 Apr 2021

9. Nie, G., Rowe, W., Zhang, L., Tian, Y., Shi, Y.: Credit card churn forecasting by logistic regression and decision tree. Expert Syst. Appl. **38**(12), 15273–15285 (2011). https://doi.org/10.1016/j.eswa.2011.06.028

10. Pratt, M.: Customer lifetime value 101—adroll blog. https://www.adroll.com/blog/customer-experience/customer-lifetime-value-101 (2019). Accessed 16 Apr 2021

11. PwC network: Analytical imperatives for telecom marketers in emerging markets. https://www.strategyand.pwc.com/m1/en/reports/hitting-the-target.pdf (2014). Accessed 15 Apr 2021

12. Tibshirani, R.: Regression shrinkage and selection via the lasso. J. Royal Stat. Soc. Ser. B (Methodological) **58**(1), 267–288 (1996). https://doi.org/10.1111/j.2517-6161.1996.tb02080.x

13. Vorotyntsev, D.: Benchmarking categorical encoders: Towards data science. https://towardsdatascience.com/benchmarking-categorical-encoders-9c322bd77ee8 (2019). Accessed 15 Apr 2021

14. Waskom, M.: seaborn: statistical data visualization – seaborn 0.11.1 documentation. https://seaborn.pydata.org/ (2020). Accessed 15 Apr 2021

15. Wei, J.T., Lin, S.Y., Wu, H.H.: A review of the application of RFM model. Afr. J. Bus. Manage. **4**(19), 4199–4206 (2010)

16. Yulianti, Y., Saifudin, A.: Sequential feature selection in customer churn prediction based on naive bayes. IOP Conf. Ser: Mater. Sci. Eng. **879**, 012090 (2020). https://doi.org/10.1088/1757-899X/879/1/012090

Biomedical Knowledge Graph Embeddings for Personalized Medicine

Joana Vilela[1,2] (ID), Muhammad Asif[1,2] (ID), Ana Rita Marques[1,2] (ID),
João Xavier Santos[1,2] (ID), Célia Rasga[1,2] (ID), Astrid Vicente[1,2] (ID),
and Hugo Martiniano[1,2(✉)] (ID)

[1] Instituto Nacional de Saúde Doutor Ricardo Jorge, Lisboa, Portugal
hugo.martiniano@insa.min-saude.pt
[2] BioISI - Biosystems and Integrative Sciences Institute, Lisboa, Portugal
https://insa.min-saude.pt, https://bioisi.pt

Abstract. Personalized medicine promises to revolutionize healthcare in the coming years. However significant challenges remain, namely in regard to integrating the vast amount of biomedical knowledge generated in the last few years. Here we describe an approach that uses Knowledge Graph Embedding (KGE) methods on a biomedical Knowledge Graph as a path to reasoning over the wealth of information stored in publicly accessible databases. We use curated databases such as Ensembl, DisGeNET and Gene Ontology as data sources to build a Knowledge Graph containing relationships between genes, diseases and other biological entities and explore the potential of KGE methods to derive medically relevant insights from this KG. To showcase the method's usefulness we describe two use cases: a) prediction of gene-disease associations and b) clustering of disease embeddings. We show that the top gene-disease associations predicted by this approach can be confirmed in external databases or have already been identified in the literature. An analysis of clusters of diseases, with a focus on Autism Spectrum Disorder (ASD), affords novel insights into the biology of this paradigmatic complex disorder and the overlap of its genetic background with other diseases.

Keywords: Knowledge Graph Embedding · Personalized medicine · Gene-disease associations

1 Introduction

1.1 Personalized Medicine

Personalized medicine is an emerging concept which has seen increased consolidation with the rapid evolution of technologies for analysis of molecular data, such as DNA sequencing, proteomics and imaging [19]. The large amount of inter-individual variation revealed by these techniques sustains the basilar principle of personalized medicine: individual disease context is unique and is shaped by

G. Marreiros et al. (Eds.): EPIA 2021, LNAI 12981, pp. 584–595, 2021.
https://doi.org/10.1007/978-3-030-86230-5_46

a person's molecular and physiological background in articulation with behavior and lifelong environmental exposures [11].

Understanding the genetic determinants of diseases is a central issue in personalized medicine and is a first step towards determining, on one hand, how genetic variability affects the health of an individual or group and, on the other hand, how different diseases can share similar genetic profiles and, thus, be amenable to intervention by similar therapeutic strategies.

It is increasingly recognized that a large number of genes is involved even in seemingly simple diseases [8], and that the same genes can play a central role in several apparently unrelated diseases. The implications of the former are that mutations in many different genes can contribute equally to a disease state, while the implications of the later are that the same mutation in the same gene can lead to different diseases [6]. This last phenomenon is termed "pleiotropy" and can be defined as the mechanism whereby a gene (or a mutation in a gene) affects multiple, sometimes seemingly unrelated diseases. There is ample experimental evidence indicating that pleiotropy is widespread in the human genome. The characterization of these pleiotropic mechanisms not only helps explain the shared genetic architecture among different diseases and traits, but also contributes to novel insights into the disruption of shared biological pathways. This has important implications in the context of personalized medicine, namely in that similar therapeutic approaches can be applied to different diseases.

A large amount of biological and biomedical knowledge has been collected in the past few years but several challenges remain in regard to collecting and integrating all the information scattered throughout different databases. In this work we explore the use of Knowledge Graph Embedding (KGE) methods [20] as a tool to model the relationships of biological entities such as genes and diseases, and gain valuable insights into their associations that can be of use in the area of personalized medicine.

For this purpose we produced a large-scale Knowledge Graph (KG) combining data from several curated biological and biomedical databases and applied Knowledge Graph Embedding (KGE) methods as a means to extract novel information from this KG. KGE methods have seen increased use in several domains, due to their broad applicability, scaling capabilities and good performance [20]. In the past few years KGs and KGE methods have been used for various purposes in the biological and biomedical domains, such as drug repurposing and prediction of gene-disease associations or drug side-effects [15,17].

A Knowledge Graph (KG) is a directed heterogeneous multi-graph $\mathcal{G}(\mathcal{V}, \mathcal{E})$, where each vertex ($v \in \mathcal{V}$) constitutes an entity (with a given entity type) and each edge ($e \in \mathcal{E}$) a relationship. Entities and relationships in a KG are organized in sets of triplets (h, r, t), where h is the head entity, r is the relationship and t is the tail entity, h and t are vertices in the graph, while r is an edge connecting h and t. Each triplet represents a fact, where the head entity (or subject) is related to the tail entity (or object) through the relationship.

Knowledge Graph Embedding (KGE) methods learn a representation of entities in $\mathbb{R}^d$, termed an embedding, such that the representation in the embedding space reflects their relationships with other entities in the KG. This is done by optimizing a score function: $f(h, r, t)$. Several methods have been proposed for this task, with different score functions, such as ComplEx [18], DistMult [21] and TransE [7]. The resulting embedding vectors can be used for downstream supervised or unsupervised machine learning tasks.

Here we report an application of KGE methods to a biological KG, relating entities such as genes, biological processes and diseases, and showcase it's application in the area of personalized medicine, namely in a) the prediction of gene-disease associations and in b) the identification of disease clusters.

Using this methodology we show that our approach a) identifies plausible gene-disease associations and b) affords useful insights into disease classification.

2   Methods

2.1   Knowledge Graph

As a first step, we built an integrated Knowledge Graph (KG) composed of a series of biological entities and their relationships, extracted from several established biological and biomedical databases. The KG contains 7 unique entity types: genes, diseases, phenotypes, disease groups, molecular functions, cellular components and biological processes. Entities are represented by their codes in the various databases: genes are represented by their Ensembl Gene IDs (https://ensembl.org), diseases, phenotypes and disease groups are represented by Concept Unique Identifiers (CUI) from the Unified Medical System (UMLS), as obtained from DisGeNET (https://disgenet.org), and Gene Ontology (GO) terms (https://geneontology.org) for biological processes, molecular functions and cellular components, represented by their respective GO IDs. The final KG has 1,785,464 triplets, composed of 99,525 unique entities and 31 relationship types. These entities comprise 25,450 genes, 21,623 diseases, 958 disease groups, 7,409 phenotypes, 11,153 molecular functions, 4,184 cellular components and 28,748 biological processes. Regarding relationships, the KG contains 901,472 gene-disease associations, 234,920 gene-phenotype associations and 160,867 gene-group associations, while the rest of the relationships comprise gene-GO annotations (397,763) and GO ontology relationships (90,442).

2.2   Knowledge Graph Embeddings

We applied Knowledge Graph embedding methods [2] to produce a vector representation (embedding) of each entity in the KG. For this application, we tested three KG embedding algorithms, ComplEx [18], DistMult [21] and TransE [7], as implemented in the DGL-KE package [22]. Training is performed through negative sampling by corrupting triplets (h, r, t) to create triplets of the form (h', r, t) or (h, r, t'), where h' and t' are randomly sampled from the sets of h and t. We apply filtered sampling, to ensure that the randomly generated triplets are not present in the KG.

Table 1. Methods used in this study and their respective scoring functions.

Method	Scoring function
ComplEx	$-\|\mathbf{h} + \mathbf{r} - \mathbf{t}\|_{\frac{1}{2}}$
DistMult	$\mathbf{h}^T diag(\mathbf{r})\mathbf{t}$
TransE	$Real(\mathbf{h}^T diag(\mathbf{r})\mathbf{t})$

Table 1 gives a summary of all KGE methods used and their respective scoring functions.

We performed a 80/10/10 split of the KG into training, test, and validation sets. The training and test sets were used for hyperparameter tuning. We used the Optuna optimization framework [2]. Optuna is a hyperparameter optimization software implementing several search strategies to achieve optimal coverage of high-dimensional hyperparameter spaces. We used the default settings for Optuna, setting the maximum number of evaluations to 30, and optimized the following parameter sets: max_step in {500, 1000, 2000, 5000, 10000, 20000, 50000}, hidden_dim in {100, 200, 300, 400, 500, 1000, 2000, 5000}, neg_sample_size in {100, 200, 300, 400, 500, 1000, 2000, 5000}, batch_size in {1000, 2000, 5000, 10000}, regularization_coef in {1e-5, 1e-6, 1e-7, 1e-8, 1e-9} and lr in {0.1, 0.01}. The gamma parameter was set to 12 and all other parameters were left at their default values.

For performance evaluation we calculated Mean Rank (MR), Mean Reciprocal Rank (MRR), HITS@1, HITS@3 and HITS@10 (the mean fraction of true results in the top 1, 3, and 10, respectively). MR was used as the optimization target for Optuna. Performance evaluation was done with a negative sample size of 16 and a batch size of 2048.

To avoid test set contamination, validation was performed with the training and validation set, withholding the test set used for hyperparameter tuning. Embedding generation for downstream tasks was performed using the full KG with the best hyperparameters found by the procedure described above.

2.3 Clustering

Clustering of disease embeddings was performed using Hierarchical Density-Based Spatial Clustering of Applications with Noise (HDBSCAN) [9]. Due to the high dimensionality of the embeddings, we applied a previous dimensionality reduction step using UMAP [14], with cosine distance as the distance metric. Using the Optuna library [2] we optimised the number of components for UMAP (in {2, 3, 4, 5, 6, 7, 8, 9, 10}) and, for HDBSCAN, the number of neighbors (in {10, 20, 30, 40, 50, 60, 70, 80, 90, 100}) and minimum cluster size (in {10, 20, 30, 40, 50, 60, 70, 80, 90, 100}). We selected the parameter set which maximized cluster validity, as evaluated by the Density-Based Cluster Validity (DBCV) [16] metric.

3 Results and Discussion

3.1 Knowledge Graph Embedding

Using the optimum hyperparameter set for each algorithm, identified as described in the methods section, we compared the performance of the KGE methods tested. The performance metrics on the validation set are displayed in Table 2. All methods exhibit good performance, with the TransE algorithm with l1-regularization showing the best results. On the basis of this comparison, we selected TransE (l1) and the embeddings produced by this method for use in subsequent steps.

Table 2. Performance metrics for each method.

Method	MRR	MR	HITS@1	HITS@3	HITS@10
ComplEx	0.92	1.24	0.86	0.98	**1.0**
DistMult	0.92	1.24	0.88	0.98	**1.0**
TransE (l1)	**0.95**	**1.15**	**0.92**	**0.99**	**1.0**
TransE (l2)	0.94	1.17	0.90	**0.99**	**1.0**

3.2 Use Case: Prediction of Gene-Disease Associations

Through link prediction is it possible to identify relationships among entities in the KG that were not present in the training dataset. Here, we apply this approach to the prediction of novel gene-disease associations. For this purpose, we used the TransE method, with l1 regularization and the optimum set of parameters (max_step = 20000, hidden_dim = 1000, neg_sample_size = 500, batch_size = 5000, learning rate = 0.01, regularization coefficient = 1e−05) determined through the testing procedure described in the methods section. We estimated the scores of all gene-disease associations, discarding those already present in the KG. The remaining gene-disease associations are considered as novel associations.

We display in Table 3 the top 20 novel predicted gene-disease associations. The new associations identified cover a broad spectrum of diseases, targeting a diversity of organs and pathways. Some of the diseases are related with abnormal muscular function (in e.g. Generalized amyotrophy and Peripheral motor neuropathy), or with ocular disturbances (in e.g. Rod-Cone Dystrophy and Strabismus), or brain alterations (in e.g. Pontoneocerebellar hypoplasia and Microcephaly).

We searched for these genes in two external databases: Online Mendelian Inheritance in Man (OMIM) and Orphanet. Several of the new associations are supported in these databases (see Table 3). In the cases where we don't find a sharp association in databases linking the gene to the disease, it is possible to establish an association between the gene and the organ affected (in e.g.

Table 3. Top 20 predicted gene-disease associations.

Gene symbol	Disease	DB accession
ACTA1	Generalized amyotrophy	OMIM:102610
AR	Gastrointestinal carcinoid tumor	–
CACNA1F	Cone dystrophy	OMIM:300476
CDK13	Byzanthine arch palate	–
CFC1B	Left atrial isomerism	OMIM:605194
CHL1-AS2	Scoliosis, Isolated, Suscecibility to, 3	–
COL17A1	Alopecia	–
HTR2A	Opiate addiction	–
IGHMBP2	Peripheral motor neuropathy	OMIM:182960
KCNJ1	Metabolic alkalosis	OMIM:241200
LMOD3	Pena-shokeir syndrome type I	
MYBPC3	Tachycardia, Ventricular	ORPHA:54260
NDUFAF5	Nicotinamide adenine dinucleotide coenzyme Q reductase deficiency	OMIM:618238
PIGN	Strabismus	–
PIGN	Microcephaly	–
POLR3A	Strabismus	–
PRPH2	Autosomal recessive retinitis pigmentosa	ORPHA:791
RLBP1	Rod-cone dystrophy	OMIM:607475
SEMA3E	Hirschsprung disease	–
TSEN2	Pontoneocerebellar hypoplasia	OMIM:612389

COL17A1/Alopecia), between the gene and a similar disease pathway (in e.g. HTR2A/Opiate Addiction), or a link of the gene to a syndrome that includes the associated phenotype or a similar phenotype (in e.g. PIGN/Microcephaly). The gene list that results from these type of association evidence is constituted by new candidate genes that can be addressed in future research in the context of the associated diseases.

Interestingly, the prediction algorithm identified a case of pleiotropy, as we have a gene that contributes to two different phenotypes (PIGN is associated to Microcephaly and Strabismus). The PIGN gene encodes a protein that is involved in glycosylphosphatidylinositol (GPI)-anchor biosynthesis. This gene is associated to Fryns syndrome (ORPHA: 2059) and Multiple Congenital Anomalies Hypotonia Seizures Syndrome (ORPHA: 280633, OMIM: 614080).

Our results suggest PIGN as a new candidate gene for Microcephaly. This is supported by several case studies reporting genetic alterations including this gene associated to syndromes with developmental abnormalities and congenital anomalies [13]. Regarding the new association of PIGN with Strabismus, case reports of congenital anomalies in the Multiple Congenital Anomalies Hypotonia Seizures Syndrome (MCAHS1)/*PIGN*-Related Epilepsy include cases with wandering eye movements and strabismus [10]. In addition, eye-related pathologies linked with eye rod and cone distrophy are associated with 2 genes in our analysis: Cone Dystrophy associated with *CACNA1F* and Rod-Cone Dystrophy associated with the *RLBP1* gene (see Table 3). We predict the involvement of these two genes in rod and cone affections. Both gene-disease associations were not present in the training dataset.

Concerning other top-scored novel gene-disease associations, the AR gene, associated in this study to Gastrointestinal Carcinoid Tumor, was already associated with prostate cancer [5]. The *CDK13* gene, here newly associated with a palate defect, the Byzanthine arch palate, was already linked to dysmorphic facial features that are part of a condition that includes congenital heart defects, dysmorphic facial features, and intellectual developmental disorder (OMIM:617360). Another novel gene-disease association encountered associates Alopecia with *COL17A1*, a gene involved in epidermal diseases as Epidermolysis bullosa, junctional, non-Herlitz type (OMIM:113811), an affection characterized by skin blistering with sparse axillary and pubic hair.

Our method also shows a good performance in the identification of diseases associated to RNA coding genes. The *CHL1-AS2* gene is an RNA gene that was already associated with Idiopathic Scoliosis. The prediction algorithm indicates this long non-coding RNA as being implicated in the susceptibility to Scoliosis (Scoliosis, Isolated, Susceptibility to, 3).

New candidate genes were also identified for opiate addiction (*HTR2A*) and Pena-Shokeir syndrome type I (*LMOD3*). The *HTR2A* gene is related with several psychiatric disorders (OMIM:182135) as alcohol dependence, Anorexia nervosa, Obsessive-compulsive disorder or Schizophrenia. Pena-Shokeir syndrome type I (ORPHA:994) is a rare genetic syndrome characterized by decreased fetal movements, intrauterine growth restriction, joint contractures or pulmonary hypoplasia. The new association of this disease with *LMOD3* can constitute an important clue for the study of these pathologies as this gene (OMIM:616112) is associated with Nemaline myopathy-10, an autosomal recessive severe congenital myopathy characterized by early-onset generalized muscle weakness and hypotonia, with respiratory insufficiency (OMIM:616165). Another novel gene-disease association resulting from this study is the association of the Hirschsprung Disease (OMIM:142623) to the *SEMA3E* gene. Hirschsprung Disease is characterized by congenital absence of intrinsic ganglion cells in the myenteric (Auerbach) and submucosal (Meissner) plexuses of the gastrointestinal tract, which causes the loss of motility. The *SEMA3E* gene is implicated in several abnormalities (OMIM:608166) as the ones that characterize the CHARGE syndrome (ORPHA:138), a multiple congenital anomaly syndrome, that also includes nerve dysfunction and is characterized by a variable combination of anomalies such as cranial nerve dysfunction.

Prediction of new genes associated to diseases is a valuable tool in the context of a Personalised Medicine approach. New case-control studies can be designed taking these new associations into account, and analysis of genetic mutations in

candidate genes resulting from these associations can yield better diagnosis and
therapeutics.

3.3 Use Case: Autism Spectrum Disorder (ASD) Disease Clusters

To investigate the relationships between diseases, we extracted all disease embeddings and performed clustering analysis to identify groups of related diseases.
Clustering as described in the methods yields 88 clusters, comprised of 13384
diseases, with 8051 being classified as outliers. Optimum parameters for the clustering (best DBCV value: 0.34) were 4 dimensions for the UMAP algorithm, and
for HDBSCAN, 10 neighbors and 50 minimum instances per cluster.

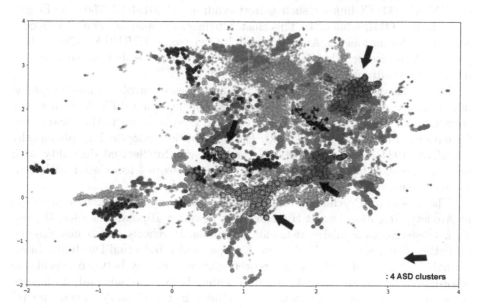

Fig. 1. Representation of 88 disease clusters. Highlighted clusters (arrows) correspond
to the ASD-related clusters.

A representation of the clusters in two of the UMAP-derived dimensions
is depicted in Fig. 1. Here, we focus our an analysis on the clusters related to
Autism Spectrum Disorder (ASD). ASD is a neurodevelopmental disorder with
a strong genetic component, characterized by communication deficits and repetitive behavioral patterns [1]. ASD can vary in the degree of clinical severity and in
the associated symptoms. The underlying genetic causes of ASD are unknown,
except in the cases associated with genetic syndromes. Given the diversity of
biological mechanisms that can be affected, the development of therapeutic
approaches is a complex task.

In the past few years we have developed several integrative approaches based
on machine learning methods to obtain insights into the genetic and phenotypic

complexity of ASD beyond what can be obtained with conventional analysis methods [3,4,12]. Here, we are particularly interested in assessing how much of the diversity underlying the ASD spectrum can be captured by this approach. Of the 88 clusters, we identified four clusters containing disease terms associated with ASD, (highlighted in Fig. 1): a cluster of 'Syndromic forms and congenital malformations'; a cluster of 'Brain alterations'; a cluster of 'Psychiatric disorders' and a cluster of 'Multi-systemic dysfunctions'.

The cluster of 'Syndromic forms and congenital malformations' integrates syndromic forms of ASD. Unlike other cases of autism, syndromic forms of the disorder are caused by mutations in single genes or chromosomal regions. These include two syndromic forms of ASD: a) AUTS2 deficiency (ORPHA:352490, OMIM: 615834) and b) susceptibility to Autism linked to the X chromosome (OMIM: 615834) (X-linked), such as Rett syndrome (OMIM: 312750) and Fragile X syndrome (OMIM: 300624). This cluster includes diseases associated with congenital malformations as Auriculo-condylar syndrome (ORPHA:137888), Blepharochalasis disease (MedGen UID: 14154), or Hyperphosphatasia with mental retardation syndrome (MedGen UID: 383800).

In the cluster of 'Brain alterations' we find diseases involving macrocephaly, microcephaly, cortical abnormal organization or involving difficulties in motor coordination. These include Complex Cortical Dysplasia with other brain malformations (MedGen UID: 832902), Early Infantile Epileptic Encephalopathy (ORPHA: 1934), Autism Spectrum Disorder and Intellectual disability with autism, speech delay, stereotyped behavior and seizures associated with neurodevelopmental disorders.

The cluster of 'Psychiatric disorders' integrates several psychiatric disorders as Anxiety, Attention Deficit Hyperactivity Disorder, Bipolar Disorder, Depression, Obsessive Compulsive Behavior, Paranoia, Psychosis and Schizophrenia, and other diseases such as Parkinson, Epilepsy and Intellectual Disability. Interestingly, our method captures the existence of comorbidity between psychiatric disorders and substance use disorders (cocaine, heroin, opioids and alcohol are some of the substance addictions also included in the cluster). Several neurotransmitter pathways, such as dopamine, serotonin, norepinephrine, GABA or glutamate pathways are involved in substance use disorders, as well as in other mental disorders including ASD. This cluster integrates the Atypical autism (ORPHA: 199627) and the Asperger Syndrome (MedGen UID: 68633).

Finally, the cluster of 'Multi-systemic dysfunctions' combines several multi-systemic dysfunctions as cardiomyopathies, cerebellar ataxia, encephalopathies, seizures, 3-methylglutaconic aciduria, inborn errors of the phospholipid metabolism, deficiencies in oxidative phosphorylation, liver disease, renal failure, testicular dysgenesis or optic atrophy. Several of these problems are often associated with mitochondrial disorders and it is recognized that some individuals with ASD have comorbid medical conditions consistently associated with mitochondrial dysfunction. Mitochondrial disorders are very heterogeneous and often involve several biological pathways and high-energy demanding systems, such as the central nervous, muscular and gastrointestinal systems.

These four clusters encompass a wide range of the diversity that exists in the ASD spectrum and identify the clinical aspects that can be regarded as separate entities and the traits that are common with other diseases included in the same clusters. These results can assist in developing therapeutic approaches targeting specific patient profiles.

4 Conclusions

We describe an approach to integrate biological information from several data sources through the construction of a KG and the application of KGE techniques to obtain entity embeddings for the entities in the KG. To showcase the usefulness of this approach in gaining insight into issues related to personalized medicine, we demonstrate the use of link prediction to identify novel gene-disease associations and cluster disease embeddings to explore relationships among diseases.

We show that this method is able to identify novel gene-disease associations (not present in the KG) and that these can be either confirmed by external data sources (OMIM and Orphanet) or are shown to be plausible given biological and medical considerations. We identified disease groups through clustering of disease embeddings and show that this approach captures known relationships between ASD and comorbid diseases, and between ASD and several psychiatric disorders, and can afford important insights regarding the genetic architecture of this complex disease.

In future studies, we plan to expand the KG with information from other biological and biomedical databases and explore other embedding methods, as well as focus on obtaining other biological insights that can be gleaned from this approach and applied in the field of genomics and personalized medicine.

Acknowledgements. The authors would like to acknowledge the support by the UID/MULTI/04046/2019 centre grant from FCT, Portugal (to BioISI), and the Med-PerSyst project (POCI-01-0145-FEDER-016428-PAC) "Redes sinapticas e abordagens compreensivas de medicina personalizada em doenças neurocomportamentais ao longo da vida" (SAICTPAC/0010/2015). This work used the European Grid Infrastructure (EGI) with the support of NCG-INGRID-PT/INCD (Portugal). This work was produced with the support of INCD funded by FCT and FEDER under the project 01/SAICT/2016 n° 022153.

References

1. Diagnostic and Statistical Manual of Mental Disorders: Dsm-5. Amer Psychiatric Pub Incorporated (2013), google-Books-ID: EIbMlwEACAAJ
2. Akiba, T., Sano, S., Yanase, T., Ohta, T., Koyama, M.: Optuna: a next-generation Hyperparameter Optimization Framework. In: Proceedings of the 25th ACM SIGKDD International Conference on Knowledge Discovery & Data Mining, KDD 2019, pp. 2623–2631. Association for Computing Machinery, New York (July 2019). https://doi.org/10.1145/3292500.3330701

3. Asif, M., Martiniano, H.F.M.C.M., Vicente, A.M., Couto, F.M.: Identifying disease genes using machine learning and gene functional similarities, assessed through Gene Ontology. PLoS One **13**(12), 1–15 (2018). https://doi.org/10.1371/journal.pone.0208626

4. Asif, M., et al.: Identification of biological mechanisms underlying a multidimensional ASD phenotype using machine learning. bioRxiv p. 470757 (2019)

5. Aurilio, G., et al.: Androgen receptor signaling pathway in prostate cancer: from genetics to clinical applications. Cells **9**(12) (2020). https://doi.org/10.3390/cells9122653

6. Autism Spectrum Disorders Working Group of The Psychiatric Genomics Consortium: Meta-analysis of GWAS of over 16,000 individuals with autism spectrum disorder highlights a novel locus at 10q24.32 and a significant overlap with schizophrenia. Mol. Autism **8**, 21 (2017). https://doi.org/10.1186/s13229-017-0137-9

7. Bordes, A., Usunier, N., Garcia-Duran, A., Weston, J., Yakhnenko, O.: Translating embeddings for modeling multi-relational data. In: Burges, C.J.C., Bottou, L., Welling, M., Ghahramani, Z., Weinberger, K.Q. (eds.) Advances in Neural Information Processing Systems, vol. 26, pp. 2787–2795. Curran Associates, Inc. (2013). http://papers.nips.cc/paper/5071-translating-embeddings-for-modeling-multi-relational-data.pdf

8. Boyle, E.A., Li, Y.I., Pritchard, J.K.: An expanded view of complex traits: from polygenic to omnigenic. Cell **169**(7), 1177–1186 (2017)

9. Campello, R.J.G.B., Moulavi, D., Sander, J.: Density-based clustering based on hierarchical density estimates. In: Pei, J., Tseng, V.S., Cao, L., Motoda, H., Xu, G. (eds.) PAKDD 2013. LNCS (LNAI), vol. 7819, pp. 160–172. Springer, Heidelberg (2013). https://doi.org/10.1007/978-3-642-37456-2_14

10. Fleming, L., et al.: Genotype-phenotype correlation of congenital anomalies in multiple congenital anomalies hypotonia seizures syndrome (MCAHS1)/PIGN-related epilepsy. Am. J. Med. Genet.. Part A **170A**(1), 77–86 (2016). https://doi.org/10.1002/ajmg.a.37369

11. Goetz, L.H., Schork, N.J.: Personalized medicine: motivation, challenges, and progress. Fertil. Steril. **109**(6), 952–963 (2018). https://doi.org/10.1016/j.fertnstert.2018.05.006

12. Martiniano, H.F.M.C., Asif, M., Vicente, A.M., Correia, L.: Network propagation-based semi-supervised identification of genes associated with autism spectrum disorder. In: Raposo, M., Ribeiro, P., Sério, S., Staiano, A., Ciaramella, A. (eds.) CIBB 2018. LNCS, vol. 11925, pp. 239–248. Springer, Cham (2020). https://doi.org/10.1007/978-3-030-34585-3_21

13. Maydan, G., et al.: Multiple congenital anomalies-hypotonia-seizures syndrome is caused by a mutation in PIGN. J. Med. Genet. **48**(6), 383–389 (2011). https://doi.org/10.1136/jmg.2010.087114

14. McInnes, L., Healy, J., Melville, J.: UMAP: Uniform Manifold Approximation and Projection for Dimension Reduction. arXiv:1802.03426 [cs, stat] (December 2018), http://arxiv.org/abs/1802.03426, arXiv: 1802.03426

15. Mohamed, S.K., Nounu, A., Nováček, V.: Biological applications of knowledge graph embedding models. Briefings Bioinform. **22**(2), 1679–1693 (2021)

16. Moulavi, D., Jaskowiak, P.A., Campello, R.J.G.B., Zimek, A., Sander, J.: Density-Based Clustering Validation. In: Proceedings of the 2014 SIAM International Conference on Data Mining, pp. 839–847. Proceedings, Society for Industrial and Applied Mathematics (April 2014). https://doi.org/10.1137/1.9781611973440.96, https://epubs.siam.org/doi/10.1137/1.9781611973440.96

17. Nicholson, D.N., Greene, C.S.: Constructing knowledge graphs and their biomedical applications. Comput. Struct. Biotech. J. **18**, 1414–1428 (2020). https://doi.org/10.1016/j.csbj.2020.05.017

18. Trouillon, T., Welbl, J., Riedel, S., Gaussier, E., Bouchard, G.: Complex embeddings for simple link prediction. In: Balcan, M.F., Weinberger, K.Q. (eds.) Proceedings of The 33rd International Conference on Machine Learning. Proceedings of Machine Learning Research, vol. 48, pp. 2071–2080. PMLR, New York (June 2016). http://proceedings.mlr.press/v48/trouillon16.html

19. Vicente, A.M., Ballensiefen, W., Jönsson, J.I.: How personalised medicine will transform healthcare by 2030: the ICPerMed vision. J. Transl. Med. **18**(1), 180 (2020)

20. Wang, Q., Mao, Z., Wang, B., Guo, L.: Knowledge graph embedding: a survey of approaches and applications. IEEE Trans. Knowl. Data Eng. **29**(12), 2724–2743 (2017). https://doi.org/10.1109/TKDE.2017.2754499

21. Yang, B., Yih, W.T., He, X., Gao, J., Deng, L.: Embedding Entities and Relations for Learning and Inference in Knowledge Bases. arXiv:1412.6575 [cs] (August 2015), http://arxiv.org/abs/1412.6575, arXiv: 1412.6575

22. Zheng, D., et al.: DGL-KE: Training Knowledge Graph Embeddings at Scale. In: Proceedings of the 43rd International ACM SIGIR Conference on Research and Development in Information Retrieval, SIGIR 2020, pp. 739–748. Association for Computing Machinery, New York (2020)

Deploying a Speech Therapy Game Using a Deep Neural Network Sibilant Consonants Classifier

William Costa[✉], Sofia Cavaco[✉], and Nuno Marques[✉]

NOVA LINCS, Department of Computer Science, Faculdade de Ciências e Tecnologia, Universidade NOVA de Lisboa, 2829-516 Caparica, Portugal
wd.costa@campus.fct.unl.pt, {scavaco,nmm}@fct.unl.pt

Abstract. Speech therapy games present a relevant application of business intelligence to real-world problems. However many such models are only studied in a research environment and lack the discussion on the practical issues related to their deployment. In this article, we depict the main aspects that are critical to the deployment of a real-time sound recognition neural model. We have previously presented a classifier of a serious game for mobile platforms that allows children to practice their isolated sibilants exercises at home to correct sibilant distortions, which was further motivated by the Covid-19 pandemic present at the time this article is posted. Since the current classifier reached an accuracy of over 95%, we conducted a study on the ongoing issues for deploying the game. Such issues include pruning and optimization of the current classifier to ensure near real-time classifications and silence detection to prevent sending silence segment requests to the classifier. To analyze if the classification is done in a tolerable amount of time, several requests were done to the server with pre-defined time intervals and the interval of time between the request and response was recorded. Deploying a program presents new obstacles, from choosing host providers to ensuring everything runs smoothly and on time. This paper proposes a guide to deploying an application containing a neural network classifier to free- and controlled-cost cloud servers to motivate further deployment research.

Keywords: Deep learning · Sibilant consonants · Speech and language therapy · Model deployment

1 Introduction

Children with speech sound disorders (SSD) may need to attend speech and language therapy sessions to surpass their speech difficulties. During the Covid-19 pandemic speech and language pathologists (SLP) faced new difficulties to provide speech therapy to these children due to the restrictions imposed on face-to-face interactions. In many cases, there was the need to change from physical to

© Springer Nature Switzerland AG 2021
G. Marreiros et al. (Eds.): EPIA 2021, LNAI 12981, pp. 596–608, 2021.
https://doi.org/10.1007/978-3-030-86230-5_47

online sessions. This led to an increased motivation on using tools that (1) promote more productive speech therapy sessions and (2) ensure that the patients can achieve speech improvements at a similar or higher rate than in face-to-face sessions.

Computer games and gamified tools for speech therapy have the potential to motivate children on practicing speech productions and can easily be used in online settings. While some such games and tools have been produced, only a few of them have an automatic speech recognition (ASR) system and can respond to the player's speech production without the assistance of an SLP. Some examples of such systems proposed in the literature include sPeAK-MAN [15] and VITHEA [3], which both perform automatic speech recognition. sPeAK-MAN is a game based on Pac-Man. Its main objective is to eat all the yellow circles on the map whilst running from the ghosts. The twist in this game is that to scare off the ghost, the player must correctly pronounce the word above the ghosts' head. This game was developed for Microsoft Kinect speech recognition but reports several issues regarding lag in speech recognition and accuracy. VITHEA, on the other hand, is based on the concept of a virtual session where a virtual therapist prompts the user to pronounce the visual or audible stimulus correctly. This tool uses the mature INESC-TEC Speech Language Recognition (SLR) [12] but game-play does not require real-time speech recognition. The player uses a button to start and end capturing the speech production and then waits while the whole speech production is sent and processed by an ASR. Another example is SpokeIt, which is a game that shows demonstrations of how to correctly pronounce the prompt words with animations of moving lips [7]. SpokeIt uses Pocketsphinx for offline speech recognition. These tools present an answer to help patients in their speech therapy needs, but there is still a lack of options available in production. This may be due to the reported lag in speech recognition that would be accentuated in production and/or the accuracy problems that could be increased when dealing with new situations, such as a variety of different accents and recording devices.

We have previously proposed a serious game for speech therapy that can be used to treat sigmatism, an SSD that consists of incorrectly producing the sibilant consonant [5]. This game focus on improving the production of the European Portuguese (EP) sibilant consonants and, its main goal is to improve the speech therapy process children go through by providing a fun environment that motivates children on practicing the production of these phonemes. The game has the potential to be used during online therapy sessions and also at home for more intensive practice.

The game uses a sibilant consonants automatic classifier to recognize the child's sibilant productions. This classifier runs in a server that receives the children's sibilant productions from the game and sends back the classification results to the game. Here, we propose some improvements to the data processing algorithm that allow time optimizations on the game's response to the child's speech productions. These consist of detecting silence portions of the signal, to avoid sending requests to the server that contain silence segments. In order to implement silence detection a sound level meter was implemented on the client.

While earlier and simpler versions of the classifier have been tested online, our latest classifier, implemented with convolutional neural networks (CNN), had only been tested locally, that is, with the server and game running on the same machine. Here, we report a study on the adaptation of the game for online therapy sessions, in which the server was installed in the cloud. Following this study, we propose guidelines for the deployment of CNN models in cloud servers providing free and controlled cost servers. Distinct key aspects are discussed: optimizing and reducing the number of useless requests to the server, adjusting and configuring computational resources, and classifier optimization. A specific Cython classifier is provided for models pre-trained and saved using Tensorflow. Final model adjustment is then applied to achieve the required response time.

2   Serious Game for Sigmatism and EP Sibilant Consonants

There are four different sibilant consonant sounds in EP: [z] as in zebra, [s] as in snake, [ʃ] as the *sh* sound in sheep, and [ʒ] as the *s* sound in Asia. The different sibilant phonemes are produced by using different points of articulation (Fig. 1). The alveolar sibilants, [z] and [s], are produced with the tongue nearly touching the alveolar region of the mouth. The palato-alveolar sibilants, [ʃ] and [ʒ], are produced by positioning the tongue towards the palatal region of the mouth. The sibilants can either be voiced or voiceless, depending on whether the vocal folds are used during the sound production or are not used. Both [z] and [ʒ] are voiced sibilants, and [s] and [ʃ] are voiceless sibilants.

Sigmatism, which consists of the distortion of sibilant consonants, is a common type of SSD among children with different native languages [10,16], including EP [8,14]. Most children with sigmatism cannot produce some sibilant sounds correctly either because they do not use the correct point of articulation or because they exchange the voiced and voiceless sounds [13].

SLPs frequently use the isolated sibilants exercise to assess and treat this type of speech errors. This exercise consists of producing the sibilant sounds with short or long duration.

We have previously proposed the BioVisualSpeech isolated sibilants game, which is a serious game for correction of distortion errors during the production of EP sibilant consonants that incorporates the isolated sibilants exercise. The game is aimed at children from five to nine years of age. It was implemented using Unity and was made available in Android using Flutter, an open-source framework to develop multiplatform applications.

The game includes a different scenario and character for each sibilant (Fig. 2). Following the suggestions of SLPs, we chose characters or themes whose names start with a sibilant consonant. Thus we have a bumblebee (*zangão* in EP) for [z], a serpent (*serpente* in EP) for [s], a ladybug (*joaninha* in EP) for [ʒ], and a boy running away from the rain (*chuva* in EP) for [ʃ].

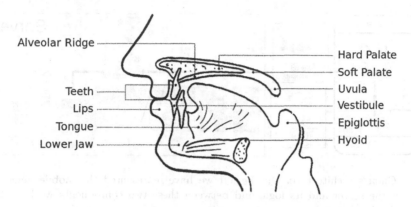

Fig. 1. Main places of articulation in the vocal tract (adapted from [9].)

Fig. 2. The BioVisualSpeech isolated sibilant game's four scenarios.

The game goal is to move the main character towards a target. In order to make the character move, the child needs to correctly produce the expected sibilant consonant.

Because the game is controlled by the child's voice, the game needs to classify the child's speech productions. For that, it uses a sibilant consonant classifier that runs in a server. Figure 3 shows the game's architecture, which consists of a server with the classifier, a (possible mobile) device where the game's graphical user interface (GUI) runs, and the built-in microphone to capture the child's speech productions.

The game's GUI captures the speech productions and sends them to the server for classification. The server then returns a classification result to the device. The game's main character will then progress towards the target if the classification result matches the expected sibilant consonant. Since this game is intended for real-time, usage time is one of the most important constraints So, we have defined 700 ms as the maximum response time for our application. Since

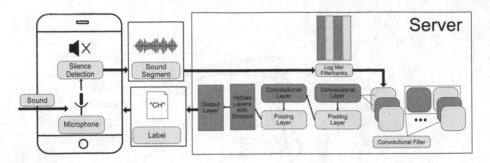

Fig. 3. Game's architecture. On the left we have represented the mobile device, on the right the server and its logic and between these two components we have their communication pattern.

a normal wireless connection takes on average 200 ms for server communication (as tested with simple get requests), our server code should at most take 500 ms.

3   Sibilants Classifier

In our previous work, we have developed classifiers of EP sibilant consonants [4–6]. We compared the performance of several different classifiers that used Mel frequency cepstral coefficients or log Mel filterbanks. These included support vector machines, simple one hidden layer artificial neural networks, and several different CNN architectures. In the present study, as seen in Fig. 3, we use log Mel filterbanks in a 2D CNN to learn an EP sibilants classifier model [6]. The input to our CNN are $f \times t$ log Mel filterbanks of children's sibilant productions recorder with a 44100 Hz sampling rate (for further details on the data set used to learn the model see [5]). We use the first $f = 80$ filters to represent the data, which were extracted with a 25 ms window and a 10 ms shift.

Our 2D CNN applies spectro-temporal convolutions across 80×8 input matrices. We use the $t = 9$ input columns as our width, and $f = 80$ filters as our height, with just one channel. The network has two convolutional layers, each followed by the corresponding pooling layer. The convolutional layers use 50, and 25 kernel filters respectively (which result in the same number of feature maps). The kernel filters are 10×2 for the first convolutional layer, and 10×2 for the second layer, with strides of 2×1 for the first layer and 1 for the second layer. The corresponding pooling layers have a size of 2×2, both with a stride of 1. The LeCun normal initializer was used with a max norm of 2 for the filters in both layers [11]. Afterward, the output from the convolutional layers was flattened and fed into the first out of four fully connected layers. These fully connected layers have 1000, 500, 100, and 10 neurons, respectively. We used the ReLU as the activation function of the convolutional and hidden layers. The 10 neurons fully connected output layer uses the softmax function. (For further architecture details see [4]).

4   Results for the Deployed Architecture

One of the requisites to deploy our architecture was to find a means to deploy our solution and study its usage. For this, we needed to find a low-cost host provider that supported the following requisites (1) run Python code for the distinct system components and (2) provide easy access to mobile devices (i.e., with an HTTPS certificate). Our final decision was Python Anywhere [2] free and web-dev plans, as those plans already provide a good set of web servers that can fulfill our requisites. In this section, we are going to describe how such deployment can be made. Several results and optimizations are presented.

4.1   Silence Detection

Currently, the classifier is implemented to classify the sound production as one of the 4 EP sibilants. When deployed the server may be asked to classify sound productions that contain data not related to one of the sibilants previously mention. Currently to mitigate miss-classifications a minimum confidence threshold was added in order to ensure only sibilants were being classified.

Since the main goal of the classifier is to help children better pronounce the EP sibilants the system's correctness is paramount. For this, it is important to focus only on the samples with a sound production as it not only alleviates the server load, reducing the total amount of requests but also, ensures a decrease of false positives presented to the player as there are fewer samples of noise that may be miss-classified.

To do this, we tested the implementation of a silence detector, as seen on the device present in Fig. 3, that uses the signal's intensity average (in the decibel scale) to determine if there is sound (non-silence) present in an audio sample. The audio sample, or waveform, consists of a sequence of samples, which here we call waveform samples to avoid confusion with the term audio sample. In more specific terms, the algorithm segments the audio sample after recording for at least 150ms and calculates the signal's intensity to. If the intensity is above the threshold the segment is sent to the server for classification otherwise it is discarded. This algorithm calculates the intensity average of the audio segments using the following expression

$$\begin{cases} SquaredSum = \dfrac{\sum\limits_{w_{sample} \in segment} w_{sample}^2}{|segment|} \\ Intensity_{avg} = 20 \times log_{10}\left(\dfrac{SquaredSum}{refValue}\right) \ , \end{cases} \tag{1}$$

where w_{sample} represents the value of every waveform sample in the segment, $|\,segment\,|$ represents the size of the audio segment array (that is, the number of waveform samples in the segment), and $refValue$ represents a unique reference value for each device that depends on the device's microphone and that can be defined in the game's settings. With this evaluation sounds with $Intensity_{avg}$ below or at 30 decibels (dB) are discarded, as they are considered silence, and sounds above this threshold are sent to the server for further classification.

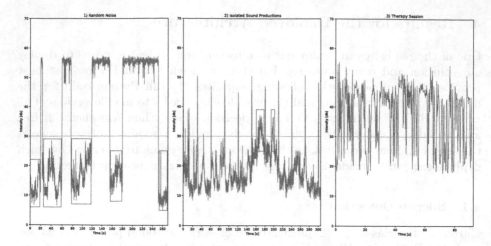

Fig. 4. Silence detection results. A) Represents an audio sample of silence with some noise. B) Represents an audio sample of a quiet room with the isolated sound productions [s] and [ʃ]. C) Represents an audio sample of a normal speech therapy session. Red rectangles represent areas where our silence detector considered silence and green squares represent areas where noise was categorized as a relevant audio sample. (Color figure online)

To test the usability of this algorithm three types of audio were used, (1) audio containing mostly silence with some intervals of random noise, (2) audio containing both sound productions of sibilants and silence, and (3) a recorded therapy session. Figure 4 represents graphs of the 3 cases mentioned above. In the first graph, random noise of varying size is added to a recording of silence which can be observed in the image. In this graph areas inside red squares are considered silent as they are below the yellow line and the other areas are considered as relevant audio samples as they are above the line. The second graph relates to a recording of audio inside a quiet room where productions of [s] and [ʃ] were inserted at every 30 s. Since this recording was not done in a controlled environment there are instances of noise present in the intervals of time classified between 30–40 dB, the areas inside the green squares. The productions can be seen in this graph in the areas that reach that are above the yellow line and outside the green squares (consisting of the values above 40 dB). The final graph relates to a recorded therapy session where the therapist and the patient are both talking, which leads to a graph where most of the recorded values are above the threshold. In these circumstances the detectors signal a higher area of time above the threshold but, even in these circumstances, there are several places where silence is detected.

4.2   PythonAnywhere Performance

To confirm the provider was fit to host our solution we decided to have a load test. We send 15 consecutive server requests (representing the average amount of requests needed to complete a stage of the game) with 4 different time intervals 5 min, 30 min, 60 min, and 120 min respectively. In this test our server was responsible for converting audio samples to log mel filterbanks and classify the sample as one of the sibilants mentioned before, returning this result.

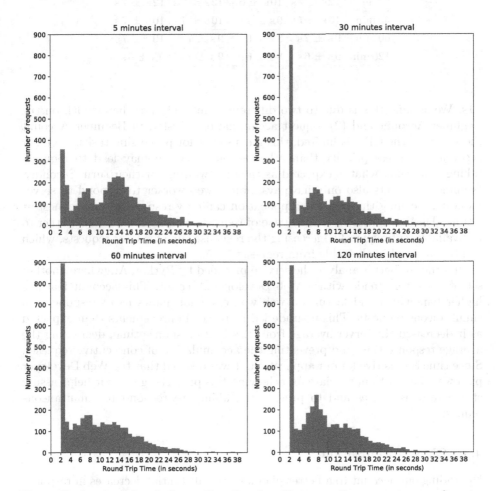

Fig. 5. PythonAnywhere's Stress Test Results. 15 consecutive requests were done to the server in intervals of time of 5, 30, 60 and 120 min and their respective response time was recorded.

Figure 5 and Table 1 present the results of our stress test. According to the histogram, a server request may arrive at an interval of time of 2–3 s but on average it will take more time than what is expected of a real-time application, what is further proved when looking at the previous table, as it shows that, on average, a request should expect a response time of 9 to 12 s. Another concern, in both the table and histogram alike, is that the standard deviation is substantially high, which means that our responses may take from as low as 2 s to as high as

Table 1. Average + Standart deviation for 15 server requests with the time intervals 5, 30, 60, 12

	Overall	0–5	5–10	10–15
5 min	12 s ± 7 s	10 s ± 6 s	12 s ± 7 s	12 s ± 7 s
30 min	10 s ± 7 s	9 s ± 7 s	10 s ± 7 s	10 s ± 7 s
60 min	9 s ± 7 s	8 s ± 6 s	9 s ± 7 s	10 s ± 7 s
120 min	9 s ± 6 s	8 s ± 6 s	9 s ± 7 s	9 s ± 6 s

19 s. We assume this is due to two different points, (1) Low bandwidth on the Beginner Account and (2) request accumulation. Firstly, in Beginner Account the access to the CPU is limited, this means that for processing tasks, beginner accounts have less priority than other accounts, which may lead to requests taking more than what is expected as they are waiting for their turn. Secondly, Beginner Accounts also only have available 1 web worker to respond to server requests, meaning that our web application can only respond to one request at a time. This limitation creates a queue of requests waiting for the web worker to be available, subsequently, increasing the response time for later requests, which can be observed in the table from requests 5–15.

In order to better analyze the service provided by Python Anywhere another set of tests were made with a Web Developer Account. This account features higher bandwidth and features 3 web workers what allows us to respond to 3 simultaneous requests. This upgrade led to bigger improvements than expected as it decreased the server average from 12 s to 2 s response time, decreasing the average response time and preventing the accumulation of consecutive requests. Since time is sensitive for our application, it was decided that the Web Developer plan was the most appropriate for achieving this projects' goal as it helps assure stable response times and to provide the ability to respond to simultaneous requests.

4.3   CNN Optimization

Upgrading our account to a better plan lead to substantial decreases in response time, but for real-time application, the response time and server resource usage were still too high. So we started working on optimizations to further decrease our times. The first optimization is Cython, as it promises *"both very fast program execution and tight integration with external C libraries, while keeping up the high programmer productivity for which the Python language is well known."* [1] to compile our code to C as it promises to create a very efficient C code that should perform better than our Python Code. After applying this change to our code and performing 100 requests, we were able to further decrease the time needed for our request, from 2.23 s to 1.77 s, as seen in Table 2. We also tested the effect of reducing the size of the first convolutional layer [4] to 1/5 of its original size. Although this change resulted in a decrease of 20% in response time such reduction was not needed as the initial network already achieves the needed response times. The final model needs an average of 0.7 s for each sound classification.

Table 2. Response times

	Python	Cython	Cython + Reduced layer
Mean	2.23 s	0.70s	0.57 s
Standard deviation	0.06 s	0.3 s	0.2 s

5 Discussion

As seen in Fig. 4 silence is easily detected by our algorithm. Our results showed silence detection was effective to reduce the amount the server workload during normal speech therapy sessions.

Our results show that the tasks of calculating log mels and classification pose themselves as time-consuming tasks. The results presented in Table 2 are only possible using a fast Cython implementation of our pre-trained CNN classifier[1]. Additionally, deployment on the PythonAnywhere cloud server required additional tuning of the algorithm, since for now only single thread support is provided in the low-cost access plans.

After cloud-server tuning and Cython optimization, classification model size was revealed as a relevant bottleneck task in our application. So, in the present setting, CNN pruning presents itself as a very relevant optimization. This is even more relevant since previous results (e.g. [4]) show us that most filters in the CNN are only contributing with minor accuracy gains for the binary classifier. For the present experiment, the features chosen for the final classifier were the first 10 out of the 50 available as the main motivation was to assess the decrease in time of such reduction.

The presented tasks are crucial to achieving our purpose of classifying sound productions promptly for our game, so project deployment should ensure a trade-off considering reduced computation time while keeping the correctness of the results.

6 Conclusions and Future Work

Here we present several challenges required for the deployment of a CNN-based model in the framework of a speech therapy game. Distinct lessons can be extracted from different components:

---

[1] Code repository is available in https://github.com/alTaWBC/custom_cnn.

Client-Based Silence Detection: As observed in the section before our silence detection works well but there are still some improvements that could be done to avoid sending unwanted audio samples to our server. Further improvements in this area could be noise detection to eliminate unwanted noises and voice detection to eliminate sound productions incoming from sources other than the player (Eg. If used in therapy sessions distinguish between the therapist and patient). Silence detection could simultaneously improve both classifier accuracy and server performance. Such improvements are also very relevant for supporting more simultaneous client sessions without increasing too much the number of cloud-based servers.

Cloud-Server: Currently the full classification time using the cloud-server process takes around 700 ms. This is enough for the reply time of the speech therapy game. The use of a cloud solution also provides an easy solution for improving the system if more simultaneous games are needed by simply upgrading the number of virtual servers contracted to python anywhere. Of course for reaching an effective production environment, a good cost-per-game model is required to acquire enough cloud resources for assuring enough simultaneous sessions.

Future classification speed improvements would be to further optimize our code with Cython and studying how to divide the Network between different servers while trying to maintain the current classification time and preserve the original architecture. In Cython the current optimizations are type assignments and the conversion of NumPy to a C version of NumPy. Just these small changes allow a decrease of around half a second from the initial time. Still, more optimizations can be done with this library such as further optimize by implementing memory views and C arrays. Future work would include a more thorough exploration of this library to implement such modifications. In regards to the pruning mentioned in the last paragraph of Subsect. 4.3, two routes can be followed, (1) Feature Extraction and/or (2) Parallel Distributed CNN. Further work regarding the trade-off between network size and classification speed is now relevant. This motivates the continuation of previous studies regarding the identification of the most relevant features for the CNN classifier, while still assuring a high enough classification accuracy (e.g. [4]). The second option, Parallel Distributed CNN, is to divide the current Network between servers (e.g. 5 servers where each contains 10 of the 50 filters) to keep the same accuracy as the original Network and to ensure response times below 700 ms. In such a parallel setting, additional cloud resources with distinct computational power could be used and configured. The Cython/C code being used for deploying the CNN classifier should enable access to a bigger set of providers and solutions. This paper proposes a guide to the deployment of a CNN model in a particular setting. We hope this example could help to motivate and inspire further deployment of research using deep-learning and CNN-based models.

Acknowledgements. This work was supported by the Portuguese Foundation for Science and Technology under projects BioVisualSpeech (CMUP-ERI/TIC/0033/2014) and NOVA-LINCS (PEest/UID/CEC/04516/2019).

References

1. Cython: C-extensions for python. https://cython.org
2. Host, run, and code python in the cloud: Pythonanywere. https://eu.pythonanywhere.com
3. Abad, A., et al.: Automatic word naming recognition for an on-line aphasia treatment system. Comput. Speech Lang. **27**(6), 1235–1248 (2013). Special Issue on Speech and Language Processing for Assistive Technology
4. Anjos, I., et al.: Detection of voicing and place of articulation of fricatives with deep learning in a virtual speech and language therapy tutor. In: Proceedings of Interspeech 2020, pp. 3156–3160 (2020). 10.21437/Interspeech. 2020–2821, http://dx.doi.org/10.21437/Interspeech.2020-2821
5. Anjos, I., Marques, N., Grilo, M., Guimarães, I., Magalhães, J., Cavaco, S.: Sibilant consonants classification with deep neural networks. In: Moura Oliveira, P., Novais, P., Reis, L.P. (eds.) EPIA 2019. LNCS (LNAI), vol. 11805, pp. 435–447. Springer, Cham (2019). https://doi.org/10.1007/978-3-030-30244-3_36
6. Anjos, I., Marques, N., Grilo, M., Guimarães, I., Magalhães, J., Cavaco, S.: Sibilant consonants classification comparison with multi- and single-class neural networks. Expert Syst. **37**(6), September 2020. https://doi.org/10.1111/exsy.12620, https://doi.org/10.1111/exsy.12620
7. Duval, J., Rubin, Z., Segura, E.M., Friedman, N., Zlatanov, M., Yang, L., Kurniawan, S.: Spokeit: Building a mobile speech therapy experience. In: MobileHCI 2018. Association for Computing Machinery (2018)
8. Figueiredo, A.C.: Análise acústica dos fonemas produzidos por crianças com desempenho articulatório alterado. Master's thesis, Escola Superior de Saúde de Alcoitão (2017)
9. Guimarães, I.: A Ciência e a Arte da Voz Humana. ESSA - Escola Superior de Saúde do Alcoitão (2007)
10. Honová, J., Jindra, P., Pešák, J.: Analysis of articulation of fricative praealveolar sibilant "s" in control population. Biomed. Papers **147**(2), 239–242 (2003), medical Faculty of the University Palacky, Olomouc, Czechoslovakia
11. LeCun, Y.A., Bottou, L., Orr, G.B., Müller, K.-R.: Efficient BackProp. In: Montavon, G., Orr, G.B., Müller, K.-R. (eds.) Neural Networks: Tricks of the Trade. LNCS, vol. 7700, pp. 9–48. Springer, Heidelberg (2012). https://doi.org/10.1007/978-3-642-35289-8_3
12. Pompili, A., Abad, A., Trancoso, I., Fonseca, J., Martins, I.P.: Evaluation and extensions of an automatic speech therapy platform. In: Quaresma, P., Vieira, R., Aluísio, S., Moniz, H., Batista, F., Gonçalves, T. (eds.) PROPOR 2020. LNCS (LNAI), vol. 12037, pp. 43–52. Springer, Cham (2020). https://doi.org/10.1007/978-3-030-41505-1_5
13. Preston, J., Edwards, M.L.: Phonological awareness and types of sound errors in preschoolers with speech sound disorders. J. Speech Lang. Hearing Res. **53**(1), 44–60 (2010)
14. Rua, M.: Caraterização do desempenho articulatório e oromotor de crianças com alterações da fala. Master's thesis, Escola Superior de Saúde de Alcoitão (2015)

15. Tan, C.T., Johnston, A., Ballard, K., Ferguson, S., Perera-Schulz, D.: Speak-man: towards popular gameplay for speech therapy. In: Proceedings of The 9th Australasian Conference on Interactive Entertainment: Matters of Life and Death, IE 2013. Association for Computing Machinery, New York (2013)
16. Weinrich, M., Zehner, H.: Phonetiche und Phonologische Störungen bein Kindern. Springer, Heidelberg (2005)

Data Streams for Unsupervised Analysis of Company Data

Miguel Carrega, Hugo Santos, and Nuno Marques[✉]

NOVA LINCS, Department of Computer Science, Faculdade de Ciências e
Tecnologia, Universidade NOVA de Lisboa, 2829-516 Caparica, Portugal
nmm@fct.unl.pt

Abstract. Financial data is increasingly made available in high quantities and in high quality for companies that trade in the stock market.
However, such data is generally made available comprising many distinct financial indicators and most of these indicators are highly correlated and non-stationary. Computational tools for visualizing the huge
diversity of available financial information, especially when it comes to
financial indicators, are needed for micro and macro-economic financial
analysis and forecasting. In this work we will present an automatic tool
that can be a valuable assistant on this process: the Ubiquitous Self-
Organizing Map (UbiSOM). The UbiSOM can be used for performing
advance exploratory data analysis in company fundamental data and
help to uncover new and emergent correlations in companies with similar company financial fundamentals that would remain undetected otherwise. Our results show that the generated SOM are stable enough to
function as conceptual maps, that can accurately describe and adapt to
the highly volatile financial data stream, even in the presence of financial shocks. Moreover, the SOM is presented as a valuable tool capable of
describing different technological companies during the period of 2003–
2018, based solely on four key fundamental indicators.

1 Introduction

Economic and Financial data indicators are frequently described as highly non-
stationary processes. Such non-stationarity has a non-deterministic trend even
when variations are not stochastic shocks and have permanent effects. Financial analysts study the correlations of market price movements with different
company fundamental indicators in an attempt to justify some of the more permanent variations. The 2007–2008 financial crisis has allowed the identification of
unique challenges in the traditional econometric analysis over time series. Recent
results showed that "even well after the crisis began and real-time information
about the collapse of the economy was available, these forecasters consistently
predicted a mild recession" [12]. Such outcome is believed to be a failure of traditional forecasting models to capture the severity of distinct shocks and their
correlated effect on the economy, severely restraining their ability to explain
major shifts in the economic trends. Both economists and financial analysts

© Springer Nature Switzerland AG 2021
G. Marreiros et al. (Eds.): EPIA 2021, LNAI 12981, pp. 609–621, 2021.
https://doi.org/10.1007/978-3-030-86230-5_48

need better and more intuitive new tools to help them address the increasingly high number of multi-dimensional aspects contained in financial data and accurately use the information made accessible from ever increasing sources of data streams. Indeed, the increasing availability of better and up-to-date information jointly with the recent results of artificial intelligence and deep neural networks provide financial analysts with a host of alternative powerful tools today.

The Self-organizing map (SOM) [6] is useful in providing financial analysts a means to visually analyze multi-dimensional financial data from companies in a conceptual feature map. By feeding the SOM with a dataset comprised of fundamental company data (i.e. fundamental indicators, such as *revenue, net income, debt ratio,* and so forth, for each company under analysis) spanning several consecutive quarterly financial reports, it is possible to visually locate in the map where companies with similar fundamentals cluster together and where they fall wide apart. For risk analysis, it is tremendously useful for a financial analyst to know whether a given company being analyzed is in financial distress and potentially headed for bankruptcy. By the same token, it also very useful to know whether the company's share price, given the evolution of the company's fundamental indicators expressed in its quarterly financial reports, will likely decrease within a year for instance.

Our two main contributions in this paper are: i) Explore a how financial information can be modeled through the use of the Ubiquitous self-organizing map (UbiSOM) [10]—a modern variant of the SOM more suited to the handling of data streams (as is the case in general of financial data), ii) the use of a conceptual feature map per economic sector to visually study company share price evolution, given the outcome of their fundamental indicators taken from the consecutive quarterly financial reports. In this paper, a dataset comprised of a number of relevant fundamental indicators from large US companies in the technological sector is selected as an illustrative proof of concept.

2   Non-supervised Data Analysis, Advanced Data Exploration and Visualization Tools

Successful knowledge extraction in complex and unstructured real domains is better accomplished when the data scientist has a good understanding of the problem being handled. Although subjective and dependent on the data analyst, such visual representation of the relations among patterns can uniquely combine the advantages of high-dimensional data visualization and machine learning [7]. A traditional unsupervised clustering algorithm like K-means could be used to separate data into different groups of similarity, or clusters. However, an algorithm more oriented towards data visualisation and interpretation as the SOM, should be first applied in this case. Indeed, SOM is a very natural and easy to use extension of the basic K-means method when we need to consider data visualization and the topological ordination of micro-clusters (e.g. [9]).

Similarly to K-means, the SOM also divides the data patterns into a predefined number of micro-clusters: the map units. Each micro-cluster is defined by the mean of the data points belonging to that micro-cluster (or prototype pattern). The SOM algorithm and its associated visualization methods are particularly useful for helping the data analyst in visualising high dimensional correlations among similar data due to the possibility of micro-clustering visualization as a conceptual map: a two dimensional representation of the input space.

The SOM can then be used as an objective clustering tool by further clustering its resulting prototypes (also known as units or micro-clusters) with a second clustering algorithm, however such analysis is beyond the scope of this paper and is left for future work. In this paper, the main purpose is to represent macro-clusters by its topological organization of units—which helps reduce high dimensional data—and to provide a different method for data exploration and visualization. Since financial data have a very volatile streaming nature, we used an extension of the SOM [6] particularly well suited for such an analysis: the UbiSOM algorithm [10].

The UbiSOM will be used to perform advanced exploratory data analysis. In SOM several data samples will be represented by a unit in the map and proper visualization tools could be used to analyse correlation and changes in the behavior of distinct financial indicators. Particularly useful will be the study of emergent patterns in changing areas or the analysis of map stability during distinct financial shocks and on the new trends detected by the algorithm's capability to adapt to concept drifts in the stream of financial data.

2.1 UbiSOM Concepts and Stream Learning Metrics

BMU: A difference between SOM and other artificial neural networks is that they apply competitive learning as opposed to error-correction learning. This means that the output nodes compete with each other to represent the input. The node that provides the highest activation, given a data point, is declared the winner (Best Matching Unit—BMU). This is calculated by using the Euclidean distance between the training example x and the output nodes, where the winning node is the one with the shortest distance. Each output node has a weight vector w_k with $k = 1, ..., K$, where K is the number of output nodes. The BMU c can be determined by the formula [6,10]:

$$c = \min_k |x - w_k|.$$

Training Process: After the BMU is calculated, it will shift its vector closer to the data point, by updating its weights. This is similar to the behaviour of the K-Means algorithm (when $K = $ Lines $\times$ Columns of neurons in the map). However the SOM also supports topological learning on its neuronal map, meaning the vectors of the nodes close to the BMU also shift in the same direction but by a smaller amount. The update to the weights of the output nodes closely follows the *Kohonen* learning rule [10]:

$$w_i(t + 1) = w_i(t) + \eta(t)h'_{ci}(t)|x_t - w_i(t)| , \tag{1}$$

where $\eta(t)$ is the learning rate, $h'_{ci}(t)$ is the neighbourhood function and t is the current iteration. So, in a data stream, x_t represents the current observation. Notice that neurons where $h'_{ci}(t)$ is below a threshold of 0.01 are not updated in UbiSOM [10]. The use of the *Kohonen* learning rule allows simultaneous update of BMU own weights and map learning. The topological organization of the units in the map is achieved since $h'_{ci}(t)$ also updates the vectors of the neighboring nodes close to the BMU (although by a smaller amount). UbiSOM [10] is used to automatically adjust the different training parameters ($\eta(t)$ and $h'_{ci}(t)$) according to how well the current model is describing the data.

Average Quantization Error: During BMU search the average quantization error is calculated by averaging the distance between the BMU $w_c(t)$ and observation x_t for the last T observations:

$$\overline{qe}(t) = \frac{1}{T} \sum_{t}^{t-T+1} |x_t - w_c(t)| \qquad (2)$$

Stream Learning and UbiSOM: To assess the "fit" of the map to the underlying stream distribution a sliding window of length T is used. Such window allows the continuous monitoring of the standard SOM quantization error and neuron utility as average measures. UbiSOM is able to maintain infinite plasticity by making $\eta(t)$ and $h'_{ci}(t)$ training parameters in Eq. 1 dependent of several average assessment metrics. Namely, in UbiSOM each neuron measures the time since it was lastly updated. This is used as an aging mechanism for computing a neuron utility (or ratio of updated neurons) over the sliding window T. A drift function is then used by weighted averaging $\overline{qe}(t)$ in Eq. 2 and this neuron utility. Such function is usually determined by $\overline{qe}(t)$ when most neurons are being updated and assures good neuron utility when the error is small enough [10]. Both $\eta(t)$ and $h'_{ci}(t)$ of Eq. 1 are control the learning of the traditional SOM. In UbiSOM this variation depends on the drift function. So, instead of a decreasing function dependent on t, the map now achieves the capability to adapt to the input in each iteration. Moreover, the UbiSOM learning is governed by a finite state-machine, using two states conform with Kohonen's proposal in SOM [6]: an ordering state and a convergence state. The ordering state is used as the initial state and when a abrupt change in underlying distribution is detected. In the convergence phase, the drift function is also used to smooth the η_f parameter. For additional information we recommend the original UbiSOM publications [10,11].

3   Experimental Setup

The dataset used in the current experiment is drawn from the financial data of the 37 largest cap US companies of the **technology sector** (part of the S&P500 index). The technology sector in the US has been historically very volatile with a surprising continuing uptrend in valuation since many years ago, which will best showcase our experiments. Quarterly financial data from these tech companies were taken from Morningstar[1] via the research and backtesting platform Quantopian[2]. The latter allows researchers to experiment and fiddle with company financial data in a friendly manner. The data collected spans 16 years in total (hence 64 quarters), ranging from 2003 to 2018. Such company financials are also called fundamental indicators in finance literature, as opposed to the so-called technical indicators. Both fundamental and technical indicators play a key role in finance for assessing a company's financial health and help draw some conclusions about a company's future outlook. In other words, they give investors and financial analysts tools which allow them to, more or less confidently, know whether an investment in a given company is a fairly good bet or not. Fundamental indicators base that assessment on the financial reports companies make public on a quarterly basis, where technical indicators look at the price fluctuations on the market to derive a future outlook for the company. Traditionally, long term investments tend to build their decisions and tooling around fundamental indicators. That being said, from the vast amount of company fundamental indicators there is in the financial literature, which not only comprise several of well known factors and ratios, such as "sales" and "profit" figures for the quarter and the quarterly "earnings-per-share" ratio, they also mention several additional obscure figures and ratios (at least for the non-financial experts), such as the "earnings yield" or the "minority interest", to name only two. The point is: there is a huge amount of fundamental indicators that can be found in the literature. Many of which are even downloadable from a website like Morningstar.

Based on earlier experiments with the same companies of the technology sector, but using decision trees instead, we've made a conscious decision to limit our study to 12 fundamental indicators. This decision was supported by advice of a financial advisor regarding a first filtering of the fundamental indicators by relevance in a typical investment decision making. Preliminary results show that among those 12 fundamental indicators, 4 stand out above all others in terms of relevance in the present study. The following indicators are therefore explored in more detail in the remaining sections:

- *cost of revenue*—the total expense the company incurs in salaries, energy, materials (supplies), marketing, etc. in order to ready the products or services it sells to customers in the quarter;
- *share issuance*—number of new shares issued during the quarter; a company typically issues more shares to the public to seek capital from investors to help fund its expansion plans;
- *total debt*—the total debt of the company, as it appears in the balance sheet statement report each quarter;
- *market cap*—means market capitalization; the end-of-quarter market price multiplied by the number of shares. I.e. how much investors value the company in the open market.

---

[1] https://www.morningstar.com/.
[2] https://www.quantopian.com/.

The dataset comprised of the tech companies with the 12 fundamental indicators collected on a quarterly basis was normalized in blocks of 4 years each, for a total of 16 years. This normalization was applied due to the growth of the companies over the years, allowing comparisons to be performed between companies from 2003 with companies on much later years. Moreover, each indicator was divided by the company's market capitalization (market cap) in the respective quarter in order to compare indicators from different companies regardless the size. In initial experiments, because a few companies were much larger than the rest, UbiSOM found an initial uninteresting cluster of companies. For this reason a logarithmic scale was applied to all indicators afterwards, which distributed more evenly this lower bracket of data. A final normalization step scaled all values to fit into the [0.0 .. 1.0] range, thus preparing the data to be trained by the multiSOM—a tool used to train and visualize the UbiSOM training procedure [8].

3.1 SOM Training

This sub-section analyses the SOM training process and its sensibility of the SOM map regarding yearly variations in the training data. For increased sensibility to variations, the parameter T was set to 300. This is a fairly low value for T, forcing the map to a very fast convergence. Despite eventual training problems, this value was selected since it allows the model to more easily detect abrupt variations among different years or among the map trained on the full 16 year dataset and each 2 year period (that has around 300 distinct patterns in our dataset). All the remaining patterns use the values recommended by UbiSOM sensibility analysis [11]. Figure 1 shows the average quantization error $\overline{qe}(t)$ during 30,000 iterations on the full dataset. A random order of presentation is used while selecting distinct patterns. This forces the model to avoid considering any eventual changes in the full 16 year period. Then the model is followed by 20,000 iterations for each biannual period separately.

From all the two year periods, only the 2005–2006 biannual (upper line in Fig. 1 labeled 0506) keeps (and even raises temporarily) the average quantization error from the full 16 year model. Also biannuals in the 2006–2010 range have comparatively higher values than biannuals from other periods. The two 2011–2012 and 2017–2018 biannuals have the smallest average quantization error. Most probably they have the least diverse patterns from quarterly data. All the remaining biannuals presented more regular patterns, allowing the model to better adjust to biannual data on the specific period. With the current parameters, all the adjustments require much more than the 300 iterations and in all cases the model didn't find the need to reset the SOM learning, by moving from the convergence to ordering state. Namely, the temporary raise in quantization error observed in the first 2000 iterations on the 2005–2006 biannual data block was not considered by UbiSOM as a relevant indication for a reset to order training state.

A similar test was done with the UbiSOM sensibility analysis recommend value of $T = 2,000$ (all the remaining UbiSOM parameters remain the same).

With such values the map has more time to find a stable configuration and eventual random year changes can be ignored. Results improved regarding map stability. Although there are longer convergence times in the two-year period, we found higher values for topological measures (standard SOM topological error was used [6]), confirming that $T = 2,000$ is indeed better for stable maps.

This result shows that a global and stable SOM representing the 16 year period can only be acquired by repeated training on all available years. The relatively high value of $0.21 < \overline{qe}(t) < 0.24$ for average quantization error, shows the levels of unpredictability or randomness that would be expected in the financial patterns of the dataset. However, the decrease of the $\overline{qe}(t)$ value by 0.15 after repeated presentation of patterns in stable biannual periods has two distinct meanings: the SOMs tuned for the biannual periods are not representative of the patterns in the 16 year dataset and can not be used for long term analysis and the convergence of UbiSOM when adjusting the map with new quarter data should be done by also resampling the other relevant year patterns in the dataset. Also, the dataset included the 2007–2008 financial crisis period, the relevant changes in resulting average quantization error for the maps trained including that biannual show that there is the capability of the SOM model trained the selected fundamental company data to detect the patterns occurring during such crises. A detailed future analysis of the individual SOM models between 2006 and 2009 seems very relevant from a econometric perspective, but it is considered outside the scope of this article.

3.2   SOM Analysis

Our ongoing study aims to find financial patterns in UbiSOM Self-organized Maps in order to help predict and describe factors that influence the stock market behaviour.

After the data was trained (we select the $T = 2000$ model trained for $30,000$ iterations on the full 16 year dataset), further analysis made it possible to observe patterns on the companies' behaviour over the different periods of time in this study.

Figure 2 presents a visualization of the result of our algorithm. We use the traditional U-Matrix and the yearly price variation of companies in each SOM unit to build a color-map. A U-matrix (unified distance matrix) is a heatmap representation of the SOM that visualizes the distance between the neurons/units. This distance is calculated by using the Euclidean distance between the neurons and is presented by using a gray scale. The scale goes from darker (for higher euclidean distances and higher variation) to white. This allows the identification of regions of the map with possible clusters with fairly uniform patterns (lighter areas) or regions with high variation among patterns (outliers, in darker areas [5]).

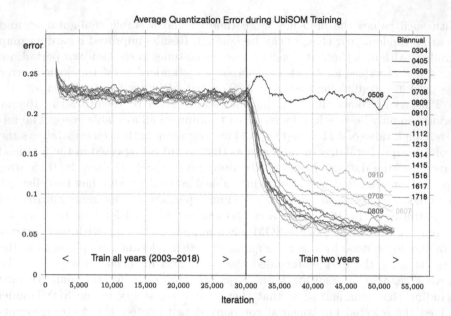

Fig. 1. Evolution of average quantization error per iteration when training the UbiSOM with $T = 300$. The full 16 year dataset is used for 30,000 iterations and then each biannual data block is used for training during more 20,000 iterations separately.

Figure 2a shows a representation of a risk analysis. Each colored rectangle on the map represents how each company for the quarter in that unit will be valued one year into the future, by comparing each to their respective current year's worth, as a percentage. There are few steps required for this calculation. First the companies' growth was calculated, by dividing the market cap of the next quarter by the current quarter, which results in a growth percentage for each quarter (100% indicates the company has the same value in the next full year quarter). Then there was a selection of the bottom 20% quarters for different patterns (i.e. company quarters) in each unit on the map. So the map represents the average of the worst quarters for each node.

Three distinct map regions were selected for analysis. Map region A corresponds to a stable area where most fundamental indicators usually have similar values. Most companies in this area are stable and don't present huge losses within one year. Map region B corresponds to a less stable area with more distinct patterns among distinct units and higher values in the U-Mat, however that area surrounds a more stable sub-region, B_1, that corresponds to a clear SOM cluster. In this area we found the units with less risky companies, but also some units with high risk (essentially when approaching the border between A and B regions) Some companies in this area seem to present a tendency to move from one area to the other as quarters follow one after another in a time sequence. An example of this changing behaviour is *Apple* (for simplicity, not represented in the figure), which moved from area A to area B in the first years, while it

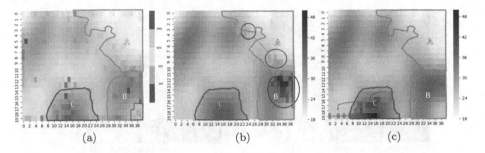

Fig. 2. Stable SOM result for the used dataset. (a) presents three selected areas based on the U-Matrix and the bottom 20% quarters of the future (1 year ahead) company's worth. Each colored rectangle on the map represents how much companies will be valued 1 year into the future: 100% green means bottom 20% companies' worth stay the same after one year, on average, given their quarterly data in the year) (b) presents the variation of quarterly data for company [CERN] in a good and stable region of the SOM and (c) presents quarterly data for company [JCS] that is inside a risky region of the SOM.

was growing the most, and later moved back to area A, where it still remains until at least 2018. The example in Fig. 2b demonstrates a similar behaviour where the company moves from area A to B. This same pattern could indicate a possible future trajectory back to area A. Both these regions seem to correspond to reasonably safe bets for a financial analyst. In contrast, we have also selected area C, a risky area with highly unstable patterns (i.e. with high distances in the SOM U-Matrix) in which companies have a higher chance in lowering their valuation in the future.

The component planes (CP) show the distribution of each attribute of the dataset on a gray scaled map grid. They can be seen as a sliced version of SOM, where each slice is the representation of a feature. Component plains are presented using a gray scale, where darker points in CP indicates higher feature values for patterns in that area (near 1.0 in the normalized scale). Whiter points in CP represent values near 0.0 in the normalized scale. Figure 3 presents component planes of 4 indicators: *cost of revenue, share issuance, total debt* and *market cap*. By analysing these CPs it is possible to identify differences in the indicators' values in different areas. Image 3a shows the CP for the cost of revenue. The lower values are concentrated on area B, increasing gradually as it moves towards area A. Area C has even higher values for this component with a fairly uniform value. Images 3b and 3d have both a similar behaviour, but with inverted values. The share issuance's values are low for both area A and B, while they are specially high in area C. The opposite happens with the market cap's value (high in areas A and B, low in area C). All the large companies in the dataset are located in either area A or B. These two indicators' similarities could be the reason for the clear separation of the *good* areas and the *bad* area. In image 3c, representing the total debt indicator, there is a fluid transition from area B to area C, with the values getting slightly higher as it gets closer

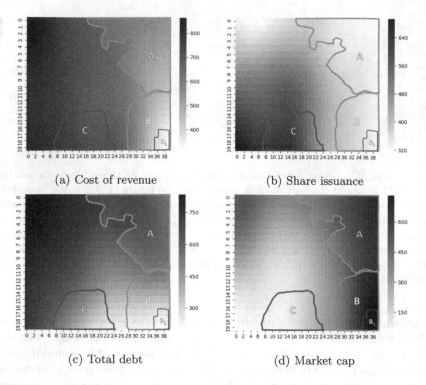

(a) Cost of revenue   (b) Share issuance

(c) Total debt   (d) Market cap

Fig. 3. Component planes with the three studied areas (A, B, C) for the selected SOM model.

to area C. On the other hand, there is a distinct difference between the values in areas A and B. This implies that companies in area A have higher debt than the companies in area B, which could be the distinguishing factor between the two areas.

Figure 2b and Fig. 2c show the trajectories of the companies in different shades of blue, where lighter blue represents the earlier years and darker the latest years. In Fig. 2b we have the representation of CERN (Cerner Corporation) over the U-Matrix. This company showed a growth of 1,450% over the 16 year period under study. It is possible to notice 3 major time intervals that express the behaviour of the company over the years. The first time interval moved from the top of area A to its bottom, where it stayed for around 2 years, moving then towards the area in between A and B. In Fig. 2c we have the representation of JCS (Communications System, Inc.) over the U-Matrix. This company decreased in value, being worth around only 33% of its value in 2003. There are no distinguishable time intervals (so no marks were added to the trajectory) but there is also a trajectory defined over the years. The company starts inside area C, where it stays for a period of around 10 years, and then moves out of area C only for one year. It ends up going back to the center of area C until 2018. This analysis shows the difference between two distinct companies. While, according to both companies fundamental indicators, CERN was a less risky bet and valuating stock, JCS was a company with less clear fundamentals and ended up being a high risk investment. Solely by comparing the selected fundamental indicators in distinct quarters, a SOM map can locate different companies in distinct areas of the map and similar companies in the same areas of the map. Over time, depending on the evolution of their fundamental indicators, companies move among distinct areas of the SOM. In this straightforward analysis, we already found two areas (A and B) where the companies that grew the most revealed an observable pattern. This analysis could indicate a clear trajectory of a successful company. Hence, it not only helps pinpoint promising companies to an investor, but also be an invaluable tool for a financial analyst to help him perceive macro-economic trends.

4   Related Work

For bankruptcy estimation, the Altman's Z-score [1] is widely recognized in the finance literature as the *de facto* standard for determining whether a company, notably in the manufacturing space, is hurtling for bankruptcy. It is a formula-driven estimation comprised of five financial ratios, that yields a score (called a Z-score) for each company being analysed. It has been revised over the years (see [2]) in an attempt to include more economic sectors beyond manufacturing companies and to adapt itself to more "modern" times. In any case, despite the need of revisions from time to time, the Altman's Z-score is still widely used by financial analysts when they want to assess how likely a company is in serious financial distress. Although standing the test of time, it is a product of the experienced hands of the US finance Professor Edward Altman, in which revisions must be carried with thorough analysis and through trial and error. In the work of [4, chap. 4], the SOM is used for analyzing failures of small and medium-sized enterprises without the need to manipulate financial ratios from experienced hands like Altman's inside a formula. The visualization here proposed is able to study companies that are likely to decrease in share price within a year. Such analysis presents some similarities with the previous use of SOM for risk analysis (e.g. [3,4]).

Several examples of applying the SOM in finance are available. Noticeable early results in [4] use these maps for the analysis of investment opportunities in emerging stock markets. A large dataset of 30 emerging markets is compressed into two-dimensional maps with 24 neurons (6 × 4) and with various attributes (e.g. returns, risks, market size, volume of transactions, price-earnings ratios, price book values, dividend yields). The article shows that SOM can be used to analyse similarities between different markets, highlighting that it can be a useful tool for improving asset allocation and for creating new benchmarks on emerging markets. However only the relative volatility between these emerging markets is analysed. In a more recent study [3], the authors use SOM to cluster and visualise the temporal progression of financial indicators, in order to help predict the development of companies over a period of time and calculate their risk of bankruptcy. The data used is composed of 29 financial ratios of 110,723 companies from 2003 to 2006, in which 2,792 of them went bankrupt by the year 2007. This data is labeled according to whether the companies went bankrupt or not by that year. The map generated is used to represent the bankruptcy risk of companies and for calculating trajectory vectors to identify trajectory patterns and for studying their influence on the bankruptcy risk. The results presented here were inspired by aspects in such previous studies and confirm the validity of the SOM as a tool for financial analysis. Notice however the presented results from this study are focused in financial analysis of a given sector of the economy and expand on the previous analysis by using the UbiSOM, a tool capable of continuous data stream analysis and of detecting changes in the underlying data.

5   Conclusions

More, better and more easily accessible data streams are becoming available. In particular financial data. The increase in data quality in platforms such as Quantopian and the ease-of-use computational framework it brings to a researcher can enable faster deployment of innovative AI techniques and tools. The Ubiquitous self-organizing map (UbiSOM) is one such tool. This paper shows that the Ubi-SOM is a very good approach for conducting risk analysis of companies in a given sector of the economy, as made clear by the illustrative examples just presented.

The stock market contains a large amount of data and many indicators reflect, even forecast, company share price valuation over time—some more than others. The UbiSOM can be a helpful tool for determining which companies would most likely decrease in share price in a relatively short timeframe (e.g. within a year), as it allows to visualize data and detect patterns in the resulting maps, adding meaningful insights that would be hard to get otherwise. Experimental analysis give evidence that this tool can provide alternative perspectives over the financial data by revealing companies which by similarity to others in the resulting maps can be attributed as being "bad" companies which are likely to decrease in price.

Experimental data in Sect. 2.1 shows that the stream model can also be applied to financial data streams. Indeed, the divergence observed in the average quantization errors between crisis and non-crisis periods suggest the simultaneous usage of crisis/non-crisis models is a possibility. In a future work we intend to study such possibility by improving the UbiSOM data stream processing model capability of detecting and adapting to financial shocks. The current model is already capable of providing to a SOM-aware financial analyst a tool to produce detailed sector-wise financial analysis in reports and the long term (2–16 years). In the near future we intend to provide our Industry partners with quarter reports based on SOM conceptual map analysis per sector. Such conceptual maps should prove to be a useful tool for politicians, economists or company managers but also can provide an important help for financial analysts to identify safe investments.

References

1. Altman, E.I.: Financial ratios, discriminant analysis and the prediction of corporate bankruptcy. J. Financ. **23**(4), 589–609 (1968)
2. Altman, E.I.: Predicting financial distress of companies: revisiting the Z-score and ZETA® models. In: Handbook of Research Methods and Applications in Empirical Finance, Edward Elgar Publishing (2013)
3. Chen, N., Ribeiro, B., Vieira, A., Chen, A.: Clustering and visualization of bankruptcy trajectory using self-organizing map. Expert Syst. Appl. **40**(1), 385–393 (2013)
4. Deboeck, G., Kohonen, T. (eds.): Visual Explorations in Finance with Self-Organizing Maps. Springer, London (1998) https://doi.org/10.1007/978-1-4471-3913-3
5. Gorricha, J.M.L.: Exploratory data analysis using self-organising maps defined in up to three dimensions. Ph.D. thesis, Universidade Nova de Lisboa (2015)
6. Kohonen, T.: Self-Organizing Maps. Springer Series in Information Sciences. 3 edn. Springer, Berlin (2001) https://doi.org/10.1007/978-3-642-56927-2
7. Kovalerchuk, B.: Visual Knowledge Discovery and Machine Learning. ISRL, vol. 144. Springer, Cham (2018). https://doi.org/10.1007/978-3-319-73040-0
8. Marques, N.C., Silva, B., Santos, H.: An interactive interface for multi-dimensional data stream analysis. In: 20th International Conference Information Visualisation (IV), pp. 223–229. IEEE, Lisbon, Portugal (July 2016). https://doi.org/10.1109/IV.2016.72
9. Qian, J., et al.: Introducing self-organized maps (SOM) as a visualization tool for materials research and education. Results Mater. **4**, 100020 (2019)
10. Silva, B., Marques, N.C.: The ubiquitous self-organizing map for non-stationary data streams. J. Big Data **2**(1), 1–22 (2015). https://doi.org/10.1186/s40537-015-0033-0
11. Silva, B.M.N.d.: Exploratory Cluster Analysis from Ubiquitous Data Streams using Self-Organizing Maps. Ph.D. thesis, Universidade Nova de Lisboa (2016). https://run.unl.pt/handle/10362/19974
12. Stock, J.H., Watson, M.W.: Twenty years of time series econometrics in ten pictures. J. Econ. Perspect. **31**(2), 59–86 (2017)

Multi-agent Systems: Theory and Applications

One Arm to Rule Them All: Online Learning with Multi-armed Bandits for Low-Resource Conversational Agents

Vânia Mendonça[1,2](✉) ⓘ, Luísa Coheur[1,2] ⓘ, and Alberto Sardinha[1,2] ⓘ

[1] INESC-ID, Lisbon, Portugal
[2] Instituto Superior Técnico, Lisbon, Portugal
{vania.mendonca,luisa.coheur,jose.alberto.sardinha}@tecnico.ulisboa.pt

Abstract. In a low-resource scenario, the lack of annotated data can be an obstacle not only to train a robust system, but also to evaluate and compare different approaches before deploying the best one for a given setting. We propose to dynamically find the best approach for a given setting by taking advantage of feedback naturally present on the scenario in hand (when it exists). To this end, we present a novel application of online learning algorithms, where we frame the choice of the best approach as a multi-armed bandits problem. Our proof-of-concept is a retrieval-based conversational agent, in which the answer selection criteria available to the agent are the competing approaches (arms). In our experiment, an adversarial multi-armed bandits approach converges to the performance of the best criterion after just three interaction turns, which suggests the appropriateness of our approach in a low-resource conversational agent.

Keywords: Online learning · Multi-armed bandits · Conversational agents

1 Introduction

State of the art on several Natural Language Processing tasks is currently dominated by deep learning approaches. In the particular case of conversational agents, such deep approaches have been applied to either generate an answer from scratch - *generation-based* - or to find the best match among a collection of candidate answers - *retrieval-based* -, with some works combining both approaches. Focusing on retrieval-based conversational agents, current

This work was supported by: Fundação para a Ciência e a Tecnologia (FCT) under reference UIDB/50021/2020 (INESC-ID multi-annual funding), as well as under the HOTSPOT project with reference PTDC/CCI-COM/7203/2020; Air Force Office of Scientific Research under award number FA9550-19-1-0020; P2020 program, supervised by Agência Nacional de Inovação (ANI), under the project CMU-PT Ref. 045909 (MAIA). Vânia Mendonça was funded by an FCT grant, ref. SFRH/BD/121443/2016.

© Springer Nature Switzerland AG 2021
G. Marreiros et al. (Eds.): EPIA 2021, LNAI 12981, pp. 625–634, 2021.
https://doi.org/10.1007/978-3-030-86230-5_49

approaches often make use of large amounts of annotated data and/or heavy computations [8,29][1], which may not be viable in real world *low-resource* scenarios (i.e. scenarios that are scarce in datasets annotated with the appropriateness of each answer to a certain input). An alternative that could be more appropriate to a low-resource scenario would be an agent based on shallow criteria (e.g., similarity measures [3]) to select an answer.

Consider an agent equipped with an arbitrary number of answer selection criteria (either shallow or pre-trained). Assuming that we do not know in advance which criterion is going to be the best for a given setting (i.e., domain and/or language), how can the agent dynamically prioritize the best criterion (if such criterion exists) without a previous evaluation on an annotated dataset? One way to tackle this challenge is to take advantage of user feedback at each interaction to assess which criterion is doing the best job, using, for instance, online learning. We thus frame the problem of choosing a selection criterion at each interaction as a *multi-armed bandits* problem. Under this online learning framework, each selection criterion is an *arm*, and our goal is to converge towards the performance of the best criterion. Each selection criterion is evaluated in an online fashion, by taking advantage of human feedback available at each user interaction.

Existing similar proposals frame the choice of a selection criterion at each interaction as a problem of prediction with expert advice [18,19]. Unlike multi-armed bandits, this framework assumes that there is a single optimal outcome based on which the competing approaches (experts) are evaluated. However, in a conversational agent scenario, there is no single appropriate answer; moreover, the user is not expected to give feedback to all the experts, as only the agent's final answer will be presented to the user.

Thus, to the best of our knowledge, our work is the first to frame the problem of converging to the best answer selection criteria as a multi-armed bandits problem in a retrieval-based conversational agent scenario, keeping a low-resource setting in mind. Our experimental results show that an adversarial multi-armed bandits approach is able to converge towards the performance of the best individual expert after just three interaction turns, suggesting that this may be adequate for a low-resource setting.

2   From Prediction with Expert Advice to Multi-armed Bandits

A problem of prediction with expert advice can be seen as an iterative game between a *forecaster* and the *environment*, in which the forecaster consults different sources (*experts*) to provide the best forecast [7]. At each time-step t, the forecaster consults the predictions made by a set of K experts (each associated with a weight ω_k), in the decision space $\mathcal{D}$. Considering these predictions, the forecaster makes its own prediction, $\hat{p}^t \in \mathcal{D}$. At the same time, the environment reveals an outcome y^t in the decision space $\mathcal{Y}$ (which may not be exactly the same as $\mathcal{D}$).

---

[1] See Boussaha *et al.* [5] for a review of recent retrieval-based systems.

Prediction with expert advice works under the assumption that the forecaster learns its own loss, ℓ^t, and the loss of each expert, ℓ_k^t, after the environment's outcome is revealed. In our conversational agent scenario, this assumption does not hold, since there is no single optimal outcome (i.e., a single appropriate answer), but instead there may be several appropriate outcomes (or none at all) among the candidate answers. Moreover, in a real world scenario, the user is not expected to give feedback to all the experts' answers, as only the agent's final answer will be presented to the user. Thus, we consider a related class of problems, *multi-armed bandits*, in which the environment's outcome is unknown, and only the forecaster learns its own loss [12,21]. In this class of problems, one starts by attempting to estimate the means of the loss distributions for each expert (here called *arm*) in the first iterations (the exploration phase), and when the forecaster has a high level of confidence in the estimated values, one may keep choosing the prediction with the smallest estimated loss (the exploitation phase).

A popular online algorithm for *adversarial* multi-armed bandits is Exponential-weighting for Exploration and Exploitation (EXP3) [2]. At each time step t, the forecaster's prediction is randomly selected according to the probability distribution given by the weights $\omega_1^{t-1}, \ldots, \omega_K^{t-1}$ of each arm k:

$$p_k^t = \frac{\omega_k^{t-1}}{\sum_{k'=1}^{K} \omega_{k'}^{t-1}} \tag{1}$$

Since only the arm selected by the forecaster knows its loss, only the weight of that arm is updated, as follows:

$$\omega_k^t = \omega_k^{t-1} e^{-\eta \hat{\ell}_k^t} \tag{2}$$

where η is the learning rate, and $\hat{\ell}_k^t = \frac{\ell_k^t}{p_k^t}$, (with ℓ_k^t being the loss obtained by the chosen arm k).

As for *stochastic* multi-armed bandit problems, i.e., problems where the loss is randomly sampled from an unknown underlying distribution, a popular algorithm used is Upper Confidence Bound (UCB) [1]. At each time step t, UCB estimates the average loss for each prediction, as well as a confidence interval, and selects the arm k with the lowest confidence bound (rather than the prediction with lowest estimated loss), as follows:

$$k^t = \underset{k}{\operatorname{argmin}} \{ \hat{Q}(k) - \sqrt{\frac{2 log(t)}{N(k)}} \} \tag{3}$$

where $N(k)$ is the counter for how many times the arm k was selected by UCB, and $\hat{Q}(k)$ is the estimated cost associated with the arm k. $\hat{Q}(k)$ is updated whenever k corresponds to the arm selected by the forecaster, k^t, as follows:

$$\hat{Q}(k) = \hat{Q}(k) + \frac{1}{N(k)+1}(\ell_k^t - \hat{Q}(k)) \tag{4}$$

3   Related Work

Online learning, and particularly the multi-armed bandits framework, has been relatively under-explored in conversational agents and dialog systems, despite the interactive nature of this field. Several works have applied some form of online learning to conversational agents or dialog systems, most of them based on the Reinforcement Learning (RL) framework [4]. RL has been mostly applied to task-oriented dialog systems [9,13,24,25], but it has also been proposed in the context of non-task oriented systems: Yu *et al.* [28] use RL to select a response strategy among a fixed set of available strategies; Serban et al. [23] use RL to select a response from an ensemble of both retrieval and generation-based dialog systems.

More recently, online frameworks based on bandits have also been used in conversational agents and dialog systems. Genevay *et al.* [10] applied multi-armed bandits for user adaptation in a task-oriented spoken dialog system, using the UCB algorithm to choose the best source user from which to transfer relevant information to a target new user. Upadhyay *et al.* [26] applied contextual bandits [27] to select a skill to respond to a user query, in a virtual assistant scenario. Liu *et al.* [15] used contextual bandits to select an answer from a pool of candidates at each turn, given the conversation context, in a retrieval-based conversational agent. The work with the closest goal to ours is that of Mendonça *et al.* [18,19], who combine multiple answer selection criteria under the framework of prediction with expert advice. This framework assumes that there is a single optimal outcome based on which the competing approaches (experts) are evaluated. However, in a conversational agent scenario, there is no single appropriate answer, and the user is not expected to give feedback to all the experts, as only the agent's final answer will be presented to the user. Moreover, the authors did not show whether their approach indeed converged to the best performing criterion. Our work addresses these shortcomings by framing the problem of dynamically converging to the best answer selection criterion as a multi-armed bandits problem. This framework has the potential to be more suitable to the scenario in hand, since it does not require feedback for all the selection criteria, nor does it assume a single correct outcome.

4   Proof-of-Concept: Retrieval-Based Conversational Agent with Multi-armed Bandits

4.1   Finding the Best Answer Selection Criteria

In our scenario, an agent receives a user request and searches for an answer in a collection of interactions. We follow a *retrieve and refine* strategy[2] [22], i.e., after having retrieved a set of candidates, the agent takes advantage of a set of criteria to select a more appropriate answer. There may be several criteria available, and we may not know *a priori* which one is the best. We frame the choice of the

---

[2] However, we are not using generation and/or deep learning.

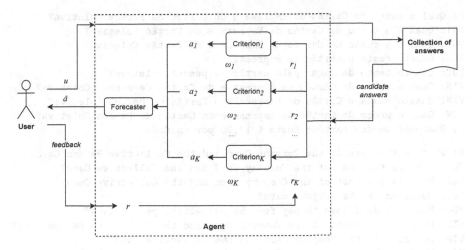

Fig. 1. Overview of the retrieval-based conversational agent scenario under the multi-armed bandits framework, for an interaction turn t.

best criterion as a multi-armed bandits problem, where each criterion is an arm associated with a weight ω_k. To learn the arms' weights, we apply the two online algorithms described in Sect. 2: EXP3 and UCB.

The learning process is shown in Fig. 1, and goes as follows: for each interaction turn t, the user sends a request u^t to the agent. The agent retrieves a set of candidate answers from its collection, and, from that set, each criterion (arm) $k = 1, \ldots, K$ chooses an answer a_k. The forecaster then chooses its answer $\hat{a}$ from the arms' answers $a_1, \ldots, a_K$, according to Eq. 1 for EXP3, and Eq. 3 for UCB. Then, the user evaluates $\hat{a}$ with a reward $r^t \in [0, 1]$. By setting each arm's loss as $\ell_k^t = -r_k^t$, the weight of the criterion k selected by the forecaster can be updated using the respective weight update rules (Eq. 2 for EXP3[3], and Eq. 4 for UCB[4]).

As our proof-of-concept scenario, we use Say Something Smart (SSS) [16], which has access to a collection of interactions (in the form of *trigger-answer* pairs) and selects an answer according to a combination of weighted criteria. In a first step (*retrieve*), given a user input, SSS selects a set of N candidate trigger-answer pairs[5] using Lucene [17]. Then, in a second step (*refine*), it applies the following criteria (which correspond to the arms in the multi-armed bandits setting):

- *Answer Frequency:* we consider the frequency of the candidate answers in the collection of interactions, following other systems based on the redundancy of the answer (such as the ones described in Lin [14] and Brill *et al.* [6]);

---

[3] For EXP3, we rounded each arm's reward to an integer value, to avoid exploding weight values, and we set η to $\sqrt{8 \log \frac{K}{T}}$, following Mendonça *et al.* [19].

[4] For UCB, we consider the estimated cost $\hat{Q}(k)$ as the "weight" for the arm k.

[5] We kept SSS's default configuration of $N = 20$ candidates.

```
P: Qual o custo do Cartão da Empresa e do Cartao de Pessoa Coletiva?
VG1: Qual é o custo do Cartão da Empresa e do Cartão Coletivo?
VG2: Qual é o custo do Cartão da Empresa e do Cartão Coletivo?
VUC: Quanto custa o cartão da empresa?
VUC: Quanto tenho de pagar pelo cartão de pessoa coletiva?
VIN: Qual o valor do Cartão da Empresa e do Cartão de Pessoa Coletiva?
VIN: Quanto custa o Cartão da Empresa e o Cartão de Pessoa Coletiva?
VIN: Qual o preço do Cartão da Empresa e do Cartão de Pessoa Coletiva?
R: Qualquer um dos cartões custa € 14,00 por unidade.

P: What is the cost of the Company Card and the Collective Person Card?
VG1: What is the cost of the Company Card and the Collective Card?
VG2: What is the cost of the Company Card and the Collective Card?
VUC: How much is the company card?
VUC: How much do I have to pay for the collective person card?
VIN: What is the value of the Company Card and the Collective Person Card?
VIN: How much is the Company Card and the Collective Card?
VIN: What is the price of the Company Card and the Collective Person Card?
R: Either of those cards costs € 14,00 per unit.
```

Fig. 2. Example entry from the AIA-BDE corpus, and its translation to English below [20].

- *Answer Similarity:* we consider that the answer can be a reformulation of the questions, following Lin [14]; thus, the similarity between the candidate answer and the user request is considered;
- *Trigger Similarity:* the similarity between the candidate trigger and the user request is considered.

Both Answer and Trigger similarity criteria use the Jaccard similarity measure. Note that, while in this experiment we use the criteria available in SSS, our approach is criterion-agnostic, thus it could be applied to any other set of criteria.

4.2   Obtaining User Feedback

We simulate user feedback using a reference corpus. At each learning step t, an interaction pair *trigger-answer* is selected from the reference corpus. The trigger tr is presented to the agent as being a user request. The agent retrieves a set of candidates from its collection of answers, and each arm k scores the different candidate answers, then choosing their highest scored answer as a_k. We simulate the user reward by measuring how well the answer $\hat{a}$ selected by the forecaster matches the reference answer, a^*, using the Jaccard similarity measure [11].

The corpus from which we built the agent's collection of interactions and the reference corpus was AIA-BDE[6] [20], a corpus of questions and answers in

---

[6] We use an updated version of the corpus reported by Oliveira *et al.* [20], which includes more question variants for each answer.

Portuguese. In AIA-BDE, for each answer (R), there are several variants (VG1, VG2[7], VUC, VIN) of the corresponding question (P), as illustrated in Fig. 2.

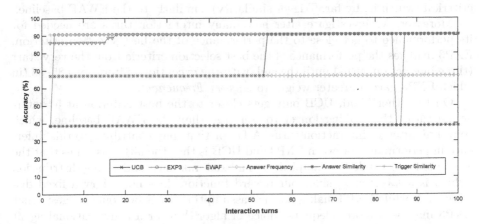

Fig. 3. Accuracy obtained by EWAF, EXP3, and UCB, as well as by each answer selection criterion.

In our experiment, we used all the pairs P-R (i.e., the gold question and answer pairs) as the agent's collection of interactions, and we used the question variations (VG1, VG2, VUC, VIN) paired with the answer R as the reference corpus. Out of these, we used 350 pairs to simulate a conversation with a user and learn the weights, and another 500 pairs to evaluate the performance of the weights learned at each iteration, in order to assess how well our online learning approach performs in the face of novel triggers (i.e., triggers that were not seen when learning the criteria's weights). We computed the accuracy, i.e., the percentage of iterations in which the agent chose the candidate answer that matched the input reference answer.

5   Experimental Results

In Fig. 3, we report the accuracy (%) of each multi-armed bandits algorithm, as well as each individual criterion, and we also compare our multi-armed bandits approach to that of Mendonça *et al.* [18,19], who used Exponentially Weighted Average Forecaster (EWAF), a popular algorithm for prediction with expert advice [7]. For clarity, we only report up to 100 learning interaction turns, since the performance for each algorithm remains the same from then on.

---

[7] VG1 and VG2 were obtained by translating P to English and back to Portuguese using the Google Translate API, once and twice, respectively [20]. Thus, duplicates, such as the one in Fig. 2, may occur.

Our first research question is whether any of the proposed multi-armed bandits approaches converges to the best criterion. As shown in Fig. 3, the performance of both EXP3 and UCB converges to that of the best answer selection criterion (which is, by far, Trigger similarity), similarly to the EWAF baseline.

Moreover, we investigate after how many interaction turns are needed for its performance to get close to the performance of the best selection criterion. EXP3 matches the performance of the best selection criteria from the very start (three interaction turns) until the end, with the exception of iterations 85–86 (in which EXP3 gave a greater weight to *Answer Frequency*).

On the other hand, UCB only gets closer to the best criterion at 54 interaction turns, thus taking longer to converge than the EWAF baseline, which converges after 18 interaction turns. A factor that may contribute to this difference in performance between EXP3 and UCB is that the latter assumes that the loss function is randomly sampled from a fixed unknown underlying distribution (which is not our case, since our reward function does not follow a fixed distribution), while EXP3 makes no such assumption. This outcome suggests that EXP3 may be a more adequate choice of algorithm for a conversational agent scenario, especially in a low-resource setting.

6 Conclusions and Future Work

In this work, we addressed a scenario where several approaches can be used and there is no gold data to properly evaluate them before deployment. We proposed an online learning approach based on the multi-armed bandits framework, and tested it on a retrieval-based conversational agent that relies on a number of criteria to select an answer. Our goal was to dynamically converge to the performance of the best answer selection criterion as the agent interacts with the user, taking advantage of their feedback, instead of evaluating each criteria *a priori*. In our experiment, in which we simulated the user feedback using a reference corpus composed of gold interaction pairs, the performance of the adversarial multi-armed bandits approach immediately matches that of the best performing selection criterion, which suggests this may be an adequate approach for a low-resource setting.

As for future work, we intend to expand this experiment by considering other answer selection criteria, as well as alternative loss functions.

References

1. Auer, P., Cesa-Bianchi, N., Fischer, P.: Finite-time analysis of the multiarmed bandit problem. Mach. Learn. **47**(2–3), 235–256 (2002). https://doi.org/10.1023/A:1013689704352
2. Auer, P., Cesa-Bianchi, N., Freund, Y., Schapire, R.E.: Gambling in a rigged casino: the adversarial multi-armed bandit problem. In: Annual Symposium on Foundations of Computer Science - Proceedings, pp. 322–331 (1995). https://doi.org/10.1109/sfcs.1995.492488

3. Banchs, R.E., Li, H.: Iris: a chat-oriented dialogue system based on the vector space model. In: Proceedings of the ACL 2012 System Demonstrations, ACL 2012, pp. 37–42. Association for Computational Linguistics, Stroudsburg (2012). http://dl.acm.org/citation.cfm?id=2390470.2390477

4. Biermann, A.W., Long, P.M.: The composition of messages in speech-graphics interactive systems. In: International Symposium on Spoken Dialogue, pp. 97–100 (1996). http://citeseerx.ist.psu.edu/viewdoc/download?doi=10.1.1.55.721&rep=rep1&type=pdf

5. Boussaha, B.E.A., Hernandez, N., Jacquin, C., Morin, E.: Deep Retrieval-Based Dialogue Systems: A Short Review. Technical report (2019). http://arxiv.org/abs/1907.12878

6. Brill, E., Dumais, S., Banko, M.: An analysis of the askmsr question-answering system. In: Proceedings of the ACL-02 Conference on Empirical Methods in Natural Language Processing - Volume 10, EMNLP 2002, pp. 257–264. Association for Computational Linguistics, USA (2002). https://doi.org/10.3115/1118693.1118726, https://doi.org/10.3115/1118693.1118726

7. Cesa-Bianchi, N., Lugosi, G.: Prediction, Learning and Games. Cambridge University Press, Cambridge (2006)

8. Chen, Q., Wang, W.: Sequential neural networks for noetic end-to-end response selection. In: Proceedings of the 7th Dialog System Technology Challenge (DSTC7) (2019). https://doi.org/10.1016/j.csl.2020.101072

9. Gašić, M., Jurčiček, F., Thomson, B., Yu, K., Young, S.: On-line policy optimisation of spoken dialogue systems via live interaction with human subjects. In: 2011 IEEE Workshop on Automatic Speech Recognition and Understanding, ASRU 2011, Proceedings, pp. 312–317 (2011). https://doi.org/10.1109/ASRU.2011.6163950

10. Genevay, A., Laroche, R.: Transfer learning for user adaptation in spoken dialogue systems. In: Proceedings of the International Joint Conference on Autonomous Agents and Multiagent Systems, AAMAS, pp. 975–983 (2016)

11. Jaccard, P.: The distribution of the flora in the alpine zone. New Phytol. $11(2)$, 37–50 (1912)

12. Lai, T.L., Robbins, H.: Asymptotically efficient adaptive allocation rules. Adv. Appl. Math. $6(1)$, 4–22 (1985). https://doi.org/10.1016/0196-8858(85)90002-8

13. Levin, E., Pieraccini, R., Eckert, W.: A stochastic model of human-machine interaction for learning dialog strategies. IEEE Trans. Speech Audio Process. 8 (2000)

14. Lin, J.: An exploration of the principles underlying redundancy-based factoid question answering. ACM Trans. Inf. Syst. $25(2)$, 6-es (2007). https://doi.org/10.1145/1229179.1229180. https://doi.org/10.1145/1229179.1229180

15. Liu, B., Yu, T., Lane, I., Mengshoel, O.J.: Customized nonlinear bandits for online response selection in neural conversation models. In: The Thirty-Second AAAI Conference on Artificial Intelligence (AAAI-18), pp. 5245–5252 (2018)

16. Magarreiro, D., Coheur, L., Melo, F.S.: Using subtitles to deal with out-of-domain interactions. In: SemDial 2014 - DialWatt (2014)

17. McCandless, M., Hatcher, E., Gospodnetic, O.: Lucene in Action, Second Edition: Covers Apache Lucene 3.0. Manning Publications Co., Greenwich, CT, USA (2010)

18. Mendonça, V., Melo, F.S., Coheur, L., Sardinha, A.: A Conversational Agent Powered by Online Learning, vol. 3, pp. 1637–1639. International Foundation for Autonomous Agents and Multiagent Systems, São Paulo, Brazil (2017). http://dl.acm.org/citation.cfm?id=3091282.3091388

19. Mendonça, V., Melo, F.S., Coheur, L., Sardinha, A.: Online learning for conversational agents. In: Oliveira, E., Gama, J., Vale, Z., Lopes Cardoso, H. (eds.) EPIA 2017. LNCS (LNAI), vol. 10423, pp. 739–750. Springer, Cham (2017). https://doi.org/10.1007/978-3-319-65340-2_60

20. Oliveira, H.G., et al.: AIA-BDE: a corpus of FAQs in Portuguese and their variations. In: Proceedings of the 12th Conference on Language Resources and Evaluation (LREC 2020), pp. 5442–5449 (2020)

21. Robbins, H.: Some aspects of the sequential design of experiments. Bull. Am. Math. Soc. **58**(5), 527–535 (1952). https://doi.org/10.1090/S0002-9904-1952-09620-8

22. Roller, S., et al.: Recipes for building an open-domain chatbot. Technical report (2020). http://arxiv.org/abs/2004.13637

23. Serban, I.V., et al.: A deep reinforcement learning chatbot. Technical report (2018)

24. Singh, S., Litman, D., Kearns, M., Walker, M.: Optimizing dialogue management with reinforcement learning: Experiments with the njfun system. J. Artif. Intell. Res. **16**, 105–133 (2002)

25. Su, P.H., et al.: On-line active reward learning for policy optimisation in spoken dialogue systems. In: Proceedings of the 54th Annual Meeting of the Association for Computational Linguistics (Volume 1: Long Papers), pp. 2431–2441. Association for Computational Linguistics (2016). https://doi.org/10.18653/v1/P16-1230, http://aclweb.org/anthology/P16-1230

26. Upadhyay, S., Agarwal, M., Bounneffouf, D., Khazaeni, Y.: A bandit approach to posterior dialog orchestration under a budget. In: 32nd Conference on Neural Information Processing Systems (NeurIPS 2018) (2018)

27. Wang, C.C., Kulkarni, S.R., Poor, H.V.: Bandit problems with side observations. IEEE Trans. Autom. Control **50**(3), 338–355 (2005). https://doi.org/10.1109/TAC.2005.844079

28. Yu, Z., Xu, Z., Black, A.W., Rudnicky, A.I.: Strategy and policy learning for non-task-oriented conversational systems. In: Proceedings of the SIGDIAL 2016 Conference, pp. 404–412 (2016)

29. Zhang, Z., Li, J., Zhu, P., Zhao, H., Liu, G.: Modeling multi-turn conversation with deep utterance aggregation. In: Proceedings of the 27th International Conference on Computational Linguistics (COLING 2018), pp. 3740–3752 (2018). http://arxiv.org/abs/1806.09102

Helping People on the Fly: Ad Hoc Teamwork for Human-Robot Teams

João G. Ribeiro[1,2]([⊠]), Miguel Faria[1,2], Alberto Sardinha[1,2], and Francisco S. Melo[1,2]

[1] INESC-ID, Lisbon, Portugal
joao.ribeiro@tecnico.ulisboa.pt
[2] Instituto Superior Técnico, Universidade de Lisboa, Lisbon, Portugal

Abstract. We present the Bayesian Online Prediction for Ad hoc teamwork (BOPA), a novel algorithm for ad hoc teamwork which enables a robot to collaborate, on the fly, with human teammates without any pre-coordination protocol. Unlike previous works, BOPA relies only on state observations/transitions of the environment in order to identify the task being performed by a given teammate (without observing the teammate's actions and environment's reward signals). We evaluate BOPA in two distinct settings, namely (i) an empirical evaluation in a simulated environment with three different types of teammates, and (ii) an experimental evaluation in a real-world environment, deploying BOPA into an ad hoc robot with the goal of assisting a human teammate in completing a given task. Our results show that BOPA is effective at correctly identifying the target task, efficient at solving the correct task in optimal and near-optimal times, scalable by adapting to different problem sizes, and robust to non-optimal teammates, such as humans.

Keywords: Ad hoc teamwork · Multi-agent systems · Human-robot collaboration

1   Introduction

As the number of robots increases in our everyday environment, many scenarios (e.g., healthcare, search-and-rescue teams, warehouse management) will require them to collaborate with humans in order to accomplish a given task. Hospitals, for example, can now count on medical robotic assistants (e.g., Terapio [11] and Robear [9]) to help nurses in tasks such as recording patients' vitals, delivering resources, and lifting patients out of bed. However, humans and robots may not be able to coordinate in advance. Hence, designing robots for these environments can be a very challenging problem, especially if you need the robot to learn how to collaborate without any pre-coordination protocol.

The research problem of collaboration without pre-coordination is known as *ad hoc teamwork* [10]. Within the robotics community, this research problem has been addressed by several robotic systems in the *drop-in player competition*

© Springer Nature Switzerland AG 2021
G. Marreiros et al. (Eds.): EPIA 2021, LNAI 12981, pp. 635–647, 2021.
https://doi.org/10.1007/978-3-030-86230-5_50

at the annual RoboCup world championships [7]. The competition served as testbed for ad hoc teamwork with robots, and highlighted several important problems that must be addressed if ad hoc teamwork is to be ported to real-world interactions. First, the ad hoc agent may not know the task it has to perform in advance, because the teammate may not explicitly communicate the task to the robot. Second, the robot may not have the capability to perceive the teammate's actions due to limited perception capabilities. Lastly, the robot may not receive any (explicit or implicit) reward signals during the interaction [6].

State-of-the-art algorithms [3,4,8] for ad hoc teamwork can, in theory, be used to allow robots to collaborate with humans on-the-fly, without any pre-coordination protocol. Unfortunately, they are not tailored for the specific challenges of human-robot collaboration identified above. For instance, PLASTIC Model [3] and PLASTIC Policy [4] rely on reward signals from the environment; other works [8] assume that a robot can observe the teammates' actions. However, these assumptions may not hold in real-world human-robot interaction settings, where the robot plays the role of "ad hoc agent" and the human plays the role of teammate.

This paper addresses the aforementioned challenges by presenting a novel approach for ad hoc teamwork. In particular, we present *Bayesian Online Prediction for Ad hoc teamwork* (BOPA), which enables a robot to learn how to collaborate on the fly with human teammates by relying only on state observations. We build on the work of Melo and Sardinha [8] but with a widely different set of assumptions. In particular, we make the following assumptions: i) there are no visible actions and the reward signals are not available; ii) the current task is described by a multi-agent Markov decision process (MMDP); iii) teammates may not always follow an optimal policy; and iv) the ad hoc agent has access to a library of possible tasks (each described as an MMDP).

In order to test our BOPA algorithm, we conducted an empirical evaluation in two different environments. The first environment is a simulation of an ad hoc robot and a human teammate in a grid world, where we evaluate the effectiveness, efficiency, scalability, and robustness of our algorithm. In the second environment, a live robot collaborates with a human teammate in order to explore uncharted areas of a map. Our empirical results, both in simulation and in a real-world scenario, show that our algorithm is not only efficient at identifying the correct task but also capable of completing all cooperative tasks without reward feedback or knowledge of human actions.

Hence, this work makes two novel contributions to the robotics community by (i) presenting the first ad hoc teamwork algorithm tailored for human-robot collaboration, together with a theoretical bound on the performance of our approach, and (ii) evaluating the ad hoc robot in order to show the effectiveness, efficiency, scalability, and robustness of our algorithm.

2 Notation and Background

We resort to a *multi-agent Markov decision process* (MMDP) framework to model our tasks. An MMDP can be described as a tuple

$$\mathcal{M} = (N, \mathcal{X}, \{\mathcal{A}^n, n = 1, \dots, N\}, \{\mathbf{P}_a, a \in \mathcal{A}\}, r, \gamma)$$

where N is the number of agents in the MMDP, $\mathcal{X}$ is the (finite) state space (we write X_t to denote the state at time step t), $\mathcal{A}^n$ is the (finite) individual action space for agent n, $n = 1, \dots, N$. $\mathcal{A}$ is the set of all *joint actions*, i.e., $\mathcal{A} = \mathcal{A}^1 \times \mathcal{A}^2 \times \dots \times \mathcal{A}^N$. We denote an element of $\mathcal{A}^n$ as a^n and an element of $\mathcal{A}$ as a tuple $a = (a^1, \dots, a^N)$, with $a^n \in \mathcal{A}^n$. Similarly, we write a^{-n} to denote a *reduced joint action*, i.e., a tuple $a^{-n} = (a^1, \dots, a^{n-1}, a^{n+1}, \dots, a^N)$, and $\mathcal{A}^{-n}$ to denote the set of all reduced joint actions. We also write A_t, A_t^{-n} and A_t^n to denote, respectively, the joint action, a reduced joint action and the individual action of agent n at time step t. $\mathbf{P}_a$ is the transition probability matrix associated with joint action a. We usually write $\mathbf{P}(y \mid x, a)$ to denote the probability $\mathbb{P}\left[X_{t+1} = y \mid X_t = x, A_t = a\right]$. Finally, $r(x)$ denotes the reward associated with a given state x. The reward is common to all agents and translates the goal of the team as a whole. γ is a scalar *discount* such that $0 \leq \gamma < 1$.

The goal of the agents in an MMDP is to select a joint policy, π, that maximizes the total discounted reward. Letting

$$v_r^\pi(x) = \mathbb{E}_\pi\left[\sum_{t=0}^{\infty} \gamma^t r(X_{t+1}) \mid X_0 = x\right],$$

the goal of the agents can be formulated as computing a joint policy, π_r, such that $v_r^{\pi_r}(x) \geq v_r^\pi(x)$ for any policy π.

3 Bayesian Online Prediction for Ad Hoc Teamwork

We now formalize ad hoc teamwork as a Bayesian prediction problem.

3.1 Assumptions

The ad hoc agent is denoted as α and the teammates as a single "meta agent", denoted as $-\alpha$. We assume the teammates know the task r and follow the corresponding MMDP's optimal policy, $\pi_r^{-\alpha}$, but the ad hoc agent does not. Additionally, and unlike [2], we do not consider a reinforcement learning setting, whereby the ad hoc agent, at each step t, is actually able to observe a reward R_t resulting from the current state X_t and joint action A_t. Instead, the ad hoc agent is only able to observe, at each step t, the current state, X_t.

Finally, we assume that the ad hoc agent knows the dynamics of the world (i.e., the transition probabilities $\{\mathbf{P}_a, a \in \mathcal{A}\}$) and that the (unknown) reward r belongs to some pre-specified library of possible rewards, $\mathcal{R} = \{r_1, \dots, r_M\}$ (which are then used to compute the MMDP's optimal policies $\pi_{r_1}, \dots, \pi_{r_M}$). By simply observing how the state evolves through time, the ad hoc agent must infer both the task and the teammate's policy.

3.2   Preliminaries

We treat the unknown MMDP reward, r, as a random variable—henceforth denoted as R to make explicit its nature as a random variable. Let $\pi_m^{-\alpha}$ denote the optimal policy for the teammates if the $R = r_m, r_m \in \mathcal{R}$, and define

$$\mathbf{P}_m(y \mid x, a^\alpha) \triangleq \mathbb{P}\left[X_{t+1} = y \mid X_t = x, A_t^\alpha = a, A_t^{-\alpha} \sim \pi_{r_m}^{-\alpha}\right].$$

We can compute $\mathbf{P}_m(y \mid x, a^\alpha)$ as

$$\mathbf{P}_m(y \mid x, a^\alpha) = \sum_{a^{-\alpha}} \mathbf{P}(y \mid x, (a^\alpha, a^{-\alpha})) \pi_m^{-\alpha}(a^{-\alpha} \mid x). \tag{1}$$

Let p_0 denote some (prior) probability distribution over $\mathcal{R}$, with $p_0(m) = \mathbb{P}[R = r_m]$. More generally, we define

$$p_t(m) = \mathbb{P}\left[R = r_m \mid \{x_0, a_0^\alpha, x_1, \ldots, x_{t-1}, a_{t-1}^\alpha, x_t\}\right]. \tag{2}$$

From Bayes theorem,

$$p_t(m) = \frac{1}{Z} \sum_{m=1}^{M} \mathbf{P}_m(x_t \mid x_{t-1}, a_{t-1}^\alpha) p_{t-1}(m),$$

where Z is a normalization constant. Finally, for $r_m \in \mathcal{R}$, we define the MDP

$$\mathcal{M}_m = (\mathcal{X}, \mathcal{A}^\alpha, \{\mathbf{P}_{m,a^\alpha}\}, r_m, \gamma), \tag{3}$$

where the transition probabilities $\mathbf{P}_{m,a}$ are defined as in (1). The optimal policy for $\mathcal{M}_m$, henceforth denoted as π_m, is the optimal "ad hoc policy" when $R = r_m$.

3.3   Bayesian Online Prediction for Ad Hoc Teamwork (BOPA)

At each time step t, the ad hoc agent selects an action A_t^α in the current state, X_t. To that purpose, it may choose to follow the action prescribed by any of the optimal policies in the set $\{\pi_1, \ldots, \pi_M\}$. The agent is only able to observe the transition between states and its own action. After observing a transition (x, a^α, y), and independently of which policy is followed,

$$\mathbb{P}[(x, a^\alpha, y) \mid R = r_m] = \mathbf{P}_m(y \mid x, a^\alpha).$$

The agent can thus update its current belief over which is the target task, p_t, using (2). Given the target reward r_m, we define the loss of policy selecting action a^α at time step t given that the target task is m as

$$\ell_t(a^\alpha \mid m) = v^{\pi_m}(x_t) - q^{\pi_m}(x_t, a^\alpha),$$

where π_m is the solution to the MMDP $\mathcal{M}_m$.

It is important to note that both $v^{\pi_m}(x_t)$ and $q^{\pi_m}(x_t, a^\alpha)$ can be computed offline when solving the MMDP $\mathcal{M}_m$. Note also that $\ell_t(a^\alpha \mid m) \geq 0$ for all a^α, and $\ell_t(a^\alpha \mid m) = 0$ only if $\pi_m(a^\alpha \mid x_t) > 0$. The action for the ad hoc agent at time step t can now be computed using our Bayesian setting as

$$\pi_t(a^\alpha \mid x_t) \triangleq \mathbb{P}\left[A_t^\alpha = a^\alpha \mid X_t = x_t\right] = \sum_{m=1}^{M} \pi_m(a^\alpha \mid x_t)p_t(m). \qquad (4)$$

We can derive a bound for the loss of our agent, when compared against an agent considering a distribution q over tasks. We use the following lemma [1].

Lemma 1. *Given a set of hypothesis $\mathcal{H} = \{1, \ldots, H\}$, for any measurable function $\phi : \mathcal{H} \to \mathbb{R}$ and any distributions p and q on $\mathcal{H}$,*

$$\mathbb{E}_{h \sim q}\left[\phi(h)\right] - \log \mathbb{E}_{h \sim p}\left[\exp(\phi(h))\right] \leq \mathrm{KL}(q \parallel p).$$

We want to bound the loss incurred by our agent after T time steps. Before introducing our result, we require some auxiliary notation. Let m^* be the (unknown) target task at time step t. The expected loss at time step t is

$$L_t(\pi_t) = \mathbb{E}\left[\ell_t(A^\alpha \mid m^*)\right] = \sum_{m=1}^{M} p_t(m)\ell_t(\pi_m \mid m^*),$$

where, for compactness, we wrote

$$\ell_t(\pi_m \mid m^*) = \sum_{a^\alpha \in \mathcal{A}^\alpha} \pi_m(a^\alpha \mid x_t)\ell_t(a^\alpha \mid m^*).$$

Let q denote an arbitrary distribution over $\mathcal{R}$, and define

$$L_t(q) = \sum_{m=1}^{M} q(m)\ell_t(\pi_m \mid m^*).$$

Then, setting $\phi(m) = -\eta\ell_t(\pi_m \mid m^*)$, for some $\eta > 0$, and using Lemma 1,

$$\mathbb{E}_{m \sim q}\left[\phi(m)\right] - \log \mathbb{E}_{m \sim p_t}\left[\exp(\phi(m))\right] \leq \mathrm{KL}(q \parallel p_t)$$

which is equivalent to

$$-\log \mathbb{E}_{m \sim p_t}\left[\exp(\phi(m))\right] \leq \eta L_t(q) + \mathrm{KL}(q \parallel p_t). \qquad (5)$$

Noting that $-2\eta\frac{R_{\max}}{1-\gamma} \leq \phi(m) \leq 0$ and using Hoeffding's Lemma,[1] we have that

$$-\log \mathbb{E}_{m \sim p_t}\left[\exp(\phi(m))\right] \geq \eta L_t(p_t) - \frac{\eta^2 R_{\max}^2}{2(1-\gamma)^2}. \qquad (6)$$

---

[1] Hoeffding's lemma states that, given a real-valued random variable X such that $a \leq X \leq b$ almost surely and any $\lambda \in \mathbb{R}$,

$$\mathbb{E}\left[e^{\lambda X}\right] \leq \exp\left(\lambda \mathbb{E}\left[X\right] + \frac{\lambda^2(b-a)^2}{8}\right).$$

Combining (5) and (6), yields

$$L_t(p_t) \leq L_t(q) + \frac{1}{\eta}\mathrm{KL}(q \parallel p_t) + \frac{\eta R_{\max}^2}{2(1-\gamma)^2}$$

which, summing for all t, yields

$$\sum_{t=0}^{T-1} L_t(p_t) \leq \sum_{t=0}^{T-1} L_t(q) + \frac{1}{\eta}\sum_{t=0}^{T-1}\mathrm{KL}(q \parallel p_t) + \frac{T\eta R_{\max}^2}{2(1-\gamma)^2}.$$

Since η is arbitrarily, setting $\eta = \sqrt{\frac{T}{2}}$ leads to

$$\sum_{t=0}^{T-1} L_t(p_t) \leq \sum_{t=0}^{T-1} L_t(q) + \sqrt{\frac{2}{T}}\sum_{t=0}^{T-1}\mathrm{KL}(q \parallel p_t) + \sqrt{\frac{T}{2}} \cdot \frac{R_{\max}^2}{(1-\gamma)^2}. \quad (7)$$

Aside from the term $\sqrt{\frac{T}{2}} \cdot \frac{R_{\max}^2}{(1-\gamma)^2}$ (which grows sub-linearly with T), the bound in (7) is similar to those reported by Banerjee for Bayesian online prediction with bounded loss [1], since

$$\sum_{t=0}^{T-1}\mathrm{KL}(q \parallel p_t) = \mathrm{KL}(\mathbf{q} \parallel \mathbf{p}_{0:T-1}),$$

where $\mathbf{q}, \mathbf{p}_{0:T-1}$ refer to distributions over sequences in $\mathcal{R}^T$.

4   Evaluation

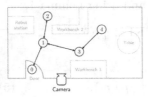  

(a) Sketch of the environment layout.   (b) RGB feed from the Intel RealSense Camera.   (c) Location using color segmentation and planar homography.

Fig. 1. Environment for ER scenario, including the environment layout, a frame where both robot and human are in position 3 (next to Workbench 1), and the segmentation and homography, used to locate the human in the environment.

We evaluate BOPA in two different environments, a simulated environment— *Panic Buttons*, or PB [5]—and a real world environment using a real robot as the ad hoc agent and a human as the teammate—*Environment Reckon*, or ER. PB is a benchmark grid-world environment where N agents must simultaneously press N buttons. ER is a real-world ad hoc teamwork scenario, where a human and a robot explore specific uncharted areas in the environment in Fig. 1a. The task is complete once all uncharted areas are visited.

We consider three different configurations for both scenarios, which correspond to the different tasks in the ad hoc agent's library.[2] Each environment/configuration is described as an MMDP with a distinct reward function. The joint optimal policies are computed using value iteration for the underlying MDP. In both environments, the ad hoc agent observes only the state of the teammate (i.e., its position in the environment) and must infer the task (i.e., configuration) and act accordingly.

4.1   Evaluation Procedure

The two scenarios are used to assess different aspects of our proposed approach. In both scenarios, the ad hoc agent can only observe the state of the MMDP, and can observe neither the teammate's actions nor any reward.

The PB scenario is used to assess the scalability, efficiency and robustness to different teammates. To the best of knowledge, our work is the first addressing ad hoc teamwork problems where the ad hoc agent has only state information available. To evaluate our approach, we compare BOPA against two baselines: an "ad hoc agent" following a random policy (named *random*), and an "ad hoc agent" following optimal policy for the task at hand (named *greedy*). The two baselines provide upper and lower bounds on the performance of BOPA.

The ER scenario, on the other hand, is used to assess the applicability of our approach in a real human-robot interaction scenario, where the state perception is not perfect, and the teammate (the human user) does not necessarily follow a pre-specified policy. We deploy our algorithm, BOPA, into a human-sized robot from our laboratory (see Fig. 1b). The position of the robot is detected using the robot localization (determined using odometry and a laser sensor). The position of the human is determined using a RealSense RGB camera (see Fig. 1b for a snapshot). The user wears high contrast shoes that are segmented from the background and used to locate the user in the room using planar homography (Fig. 1c). The human user is told beforehand the task (i.e., which locations should be visited) and asked to move between adjacent nodes at each time step and coordinate with the robot to visit the un-visited areas as quickly as possible.

4.2   Metrics

In the PB scenario, the reported values consist of averages and 95% confidence intervals over 32 independent trials, where a single trial consists of running the

---

[2] In the PB environment, different configurations correspond to different positions for the buttons; in the ER environment, different configurations correspond to different uncharted locations in the map.

three agents (greedy, BOPA, and random) against an unknown teammate. To gain some additional insight regarding the robustness of our approach, we pair the ad hoc agent with different teammates—an optimal teammate, that knows the task and acts optimally; a sub-optimal teammate, that knows the task but chooses not to act with a probability 0.3, and a teammate that acts randomly.

We report four different metrics that seek to assess effectiveness, efficiency, scalability and robustness to sub-optimal teammates. Effectiveness is measured by determining whether or not BOPA is able to identify the correct task. Efficiency is measured by evaluating whether or not the ad hoc agent is able to solve the task in near-optimal time. Scalability is assessed by observing the performance of the ad hoc agent in different problem sizes (3×3, 4×4 and 5×5 grids). Robustness is evaluated by reporting whether or not an ad hoc agent is able to cope with non-optimal teammates. In the ER scenario, we report only the first two metrics (effectiveness and efficiency).

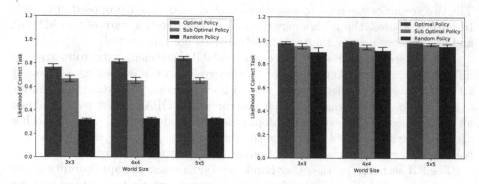

Fig. 2. Probability of correct task averaged across the whole episode, $1/T \sum_t p_t(r)$ (left) and probability of correct task, at the last step of the episode, $p_T(r)$ (right). The error bars correspond to the variability in the agent's estimate.

Table 1. Average number of steps required for task completion.

	Optimal	Sub-optimal	Random
3×3 Greedy	2.7 ± 0.5	3.4 ± 1.2	24.2 ± 23.3
3×3 Bopa	3.3 ± 0.8	4.3 ± 2.3	35.9 ± 37.7
3×3 Random	25.2 ± 27.4	26.7 ± 28.2	144.8 ± 154.1
4×4 Greedy	4.0 ± 0.8	5.2 ± 1.9	54.0 ± 56.1
4×4 Bopa	4.7 ± 0.8	6.0 ± 2.4	61.0 ± 67.0
4×4 Random	47.3 ± 50.6	56.8 ± 59.2	497.4 ± 426.3
5×5 Greedy	5.3 ± 0.9	6.7 ± 1.6	85.7 ± 97.4
5×5 Bopa	5.8 ± 0.8	8.5 ± 3.7	168.8 ± 169.5
5×5 Random	104.7 ± 106.9	103.3 ± 109.0	1120.4 ± 1003.1

5 Results

We now present and discuss the results of our experiments.

5.1 PB Scenario

The results for the PB scenario are summarized in Fig. 2 and Table 1. The plots in Fig. 2 depict the ad hoc agent's ability to identify the unknown target task, r. Figure 2 (left) presents—for the different environment sizes and teammates—the likelihood of r according to the agent's belief, averaged across the whole trial, i.e., for an episode of length T,

$$p_{\mathrm{ave}}(r^*) = \frac{1}{T} \sum_{t=1}^{T} p_t(r^*).$$

Figure 2 (right) presents the likelihood of r^* according to the agent's belief and the final step of the trial, i.e., for an episode of length T, $p_T(r^*)$.

The plots of Fig. 2 allow us to conclusively assess BOPA's effectiveness: in all environments and for all teammates, the algorithm is able to identify the target task with great certainty. The plot also shows successfully identifying the target task largely depends on the teammate's behaviors: if the teammate behaves in a misleading way (i.e., sub-optimally), this will sometimes lead to poor belief updates, hindering the algorithm's ability to identify the target task.

In terms of BOPA's efficiency (i.e., its ability to solve the target task), we can observe in Table 1 that the performance of BOPA—when playing with an optimal teammate—closely follows that of the greedy agent (i.e., the agent knowing the target task). This is in accordance with our results on effectiveness: since BOPA is able to quickly identify the target task, it performs near-optimally in all tasks.

In terms of scalability and robustness (i.e., how BOPA's performance depends on the size of the problem and the quality of the teammates), two interesting observations are in order. On one hand, the difference in performance between BOPA and the greedy agent attenuates for larger environments. This can be understood as the larger environments provide more data (i.e., teammate's action effects through state observations) for the ad hoc agent to recognize the action and immediately head to the goal. On the other hand, the negative impact of playing with sub-optimal teammates is larger for larger environments.

To conclude, and taking all results into account, we conclude that BOPA is a robust approach to the problem of ad hoc teamwork, being able to identify the unknown task in near-optimal time even with non-optimal teammates.

5.2 ER Scenario

For the ER scenario, we provide results for each of the three task configurations. In all trials, both robot and human depart from node 0 ("Door"). In the first configuration, the uncharted areas correspond to the "Door" (node 0),

"Robot station" (node 1) and the "Table" (node 4). In the second configuration, the uncharted areas correspond to nodes 1, 2, and 3 ("Robot station", "Workbench 2", and "Workbench 1", respectively). Finally, in the third configuration, the uncharted areas correspond to nodes 1, 2, and 4 ("Robot station", "Workbench 2", and "Table", respectively). The observed runs—in terms of states and agent's beliefs—are depicted in Fig. 3. No mis-detections were observed (i.e., the sensors on the robot were always able to correctly locate the robot, while the camera system always correctly located the human user).

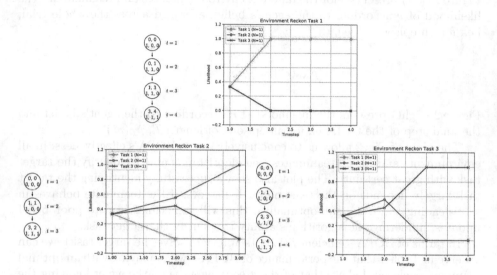

Fig. 3. Trajectories observed during the interaction with a human user (for tasks 1, 2 and 3). The diagrams on the left represent the sequence of states, (numbers on top correspond to the positions of the robot and the human, respectively, while the bits on the bottom denote whether the uncharted areas have been visited). The plots on the right depict the evolution of the robot's beliefs.

In the first run, corresponding to the first configuration, the optimal policy is for one of the agents to go towards the last unexplored node ("Table"). We can see that in the first time step, the robot had the highest uncertainty. In this turn, only the human user moved, to "Robot station". In turn 2, human proceeded to go towards the last unexplored node ("Table"), solving the task in optimal time. As the human moves towards this final node, the robot's belief on the target task goes up to 1.0. This first run enables two conclusions: first, there is no need for actual cooperation in this task, meaning if one of the agents is solving the task the other may do nothing. Second, unsurprisingly, BOPA successfully identified the correct task by observing the movement of the human user.

In the second run, corresponding to the second configuration, the optimal policy requires cooperation in order to be optimally solved. In the first timestep, the robot moved towards node 1. By observing this transition alone, we can see that the likelihood of the first task decreases to nearly 0.0, since visiting node 0 did not activate any of the three visitation bits. After this transition, BOPA still has some uncertainty on which task is the correct one, with the second and correct task having a likelihood of around 0.55 and the third task having a likelihood of around 0.44. This uncertainty is expected, since in both tasks, the observed transition is required in order to optimally solve them. After the third and last transition, however, where the robot moved towards node 3 and the human went to node 2, the state now indicates that all unexplored nodes have been explored, enabling BOPA to identify the correct task with 100% certainty. The task was also solved in its optimal number of steps.

The third run, corresponding to the third configuration, also requires cooperation in order to be optimally solved. In the optimal policy, both agents go towards node 1 first and then split up, one going towards node 2 and the other towards node 4, having to pass through node 3. This task provides ambiguity with the other two, since it needs the forth node to be explored (like the first task) and the second node to be explored (like the second task).

We can see that in the first timestep, the robot had the highest uncertainty and, once again by chance, moved towards node 1 (which is considered an optimal action for all tasks). Like with the second task, by observing this first transition alone, we can see that the likelihood of the first task decreases to nearly 0.0. After this transition, BOPA has the same uncertainty it had on the previous task (which makes sense given the exact same transition), with the second and correct task having a likelihood of around 0.55 and the third task having a likelihood of around 0.44. After the second transition, however, the robot moves towards node 2 and the human moves towards node 3. Since the flags indicating whether each node has been explored are all set to one (unlike what happened in the second task), BOPA is now able to identify the correct task with 100% certainty. This final task was also concluded in its optimal number of steps.

To conclude, taking these results into account, we can see that BOPA is not only able to identify the correct task with great certainty by inferring the teammate's behavior through state observations, but also capable of adapting to non-optimal teammates by still being able to solve the tasks.

6   Conclusion and Future Work

This paper presented and evaluated the Bayesian Online Prediction Algorithm for Ad Hoc Teamwork (BOPA), a novel approach for the ad hoc teamwork problem, where an agent had to learn to cooperate with both optimal and non-optimal teammates in solving an unknown task, without being able to observe the teammates' actions and the environment's reward signals.

Having performed both an empirical evaluation in a simulated environment following the OpenAI Gym API and a live experimental evaluation with a live robot in our laboratory running BOPA which had to assist a human teammate in solving a task, our results show that our approach is effective at identifying the correct task, efficient at solving the correct task in optimal and near-optimal times, scalable, by being able to adapt to different problem sizes, and robust, by being able to adapt non-optimal teammates, such as humans, in order to solve unknown tasks without having access to the teammates' actions and environment's reward signals.

Given that in our experimental evaluation, all sensors did not show any faulty behavior, preventing a deeper analysis of BOPA whenever the state is incorrect, our next logical line of work will be to setup a second experimental scenario where there isn't full observability of the current state (or if the current state is faultily created). In this setting we will compare BOPA against a successor which does not assume the state is fully observable, modeling the tasks as partially observable Markov decision processes instead of multi-agent Markov decision processes in order to provide yet another layer of robustness when working with real life robots and humans.

Acknowledgements. This work was partially supported by national funds through FCT, Fundação para a Ciência e a Tecnologia, under project UIDB/50021/2020 (INESC-ID multi-annual funding) and the HOTSPOT project, with reference PTDC/CCI-COM/7203/2020. In addition, this material is based upon work supported by the Air Force Office of Scientific Research under award number FA9550-19-1-0020, and by TAILOR, a project funded by EU Horizon 2020 research and innovation programme under GA No 952215. The first author acknowledges the PhD grant 2020.05151.BD from FCT.

References

1. Banerjee, A.: On Bayesian bounds. In: Proceedings of 23rd International Conference Machine Learning, pp. 81–88 (2006)
2. Barret, S., Stone, P.: An analysis framework for ad hoc teamwork tasks. In: Proceedings of 11th International Conference Autonomous Agents and Multiagent Systems, pp. 357–364 (2012)
3. Barrett, S.: Making Friends on the Fly: Advances in Ad Hoc Teamwork. Ph.D. thesis, The University of Texas at Austin (2014)
4. Barrett, S., Stone, P.: Cooperating with unknown teammates in complex domains: a robot soccer case study of ad hoc teamwork. In: Proceedings of the Twenty-Ninth AAAI Conference on Artificial Intelligence, pp. 2010–2016, January 2015
5. Brockman, G., et al.: Openai gym. arXiv preprint arXiv:1606.01540 (2016)
6. Christiano, P.F., Leike, J., Brown, T.B., Martic, M., Legg, S., Amodei, D.: Deep reinforcement learning from human preferences. In: Proceedings of the 31st International Conference on Neural Information Processing Systems, NIPS 2017, pp. 4302–4310. Curran Associates Inc., Red Hook (2017)
7. Genter, K., Laue, T., Stone, P.: Three years of the RoboCup standard platform league drop-in player competition. Auton. Agent. Multi-Agent Syst. **31**(4), 790–820 (2016). https://doi.org/10.1007/s10458-016-9353-5
8. Melo, F.S., Sardinha, A.: Ad hoc teamwork by learning teammates' task. Auton. Agent. Multi-Agent Syst. **30**(2), 175–219 (2016)
9. Pepito, J.A., Locsin, R.: Can nurses remain relevant in a technologically advanced future? Int. J. Nursing Sci. **6**(1), 106–110 (2019). https://doi.org/10.1016/j.ijnss.2018.09.013. http://www.sciencedirect.com/science/article/pii/S2352013218301765

10. Stone, P., Kaminka, G.A., Kraus, S., Rosenschein, J.S.: Ad hoc autonomous agent teams: collaboration without pre-coordination. In: Twenty-Fourth AAAI Conference on Artificial Intelligence (2010)
11. Tasaki, R., Kitazaki, M., Miura, J., Terashima, K.: Prototype design of medical round supporting robot "terapio". In: 2015 IEEE International Conference on Robotics and Automation (ICRA), pp. 829–834, May 2015. https://doi.org/10.1109/ICRA.2015.7139274

Ad Hoc Teamwork in the Presence of Non-stationary Teammates

Pedro M. Santos[1,2]([✉]), João G. Ribeiro[1,2], Alberto Sardinha[1,2], and Francisco S. Melo[1,2]

[1] INESC-ID, Lisbon, Portugal
{pedro.m.m.santos,joao.g.ribeiro}@tecnico.ulisboa.pt
[2] Instituto Superior Técnico, University of Lisbon, Lisbon, Portugal
fmelo@inesc-id.pt

Abstract. In this paper we address the problem of ad hoc teamwork and contribute a novel approach, PPAS, that is able to handle non-stationary teammates. Current approaches to ad hoc teamwork assume that the (potentially unknown) teammates behave in a stationary way, which is a significant limitation in real world conditions, since humans and other intelligent systems do not necessarily follow strict policies. In our work we highlight the current limitations of state-of-the-art approaches to ad hoc teamwork problem in the presence of non-stationary teammate, and propose a novel solution that alleviates the stationarity assumption by combining ad hoc teamwork with adversarial online prediction. The proposed architecture is called PLASTIC Policy with Adversarial Selection, or PPAS. We showcase the effectiveness of our approach through an empirical evaluation in the half-field offense environment. Our results show that it is possible to cooperate in an ad hoc manner with non-stationary teammates in complex environments.

Keywords: Multi-agent systems · Ad hoc teamwork problem · Reinforcement learning

1 Introduction

Many works on cooperative multi-agent systems (MAS) traditionally assume that the agents have some communication protocol in place or that some other coordination strategy is defined a priori (or both). These assumptions can be a problem as different types of autonomous agents (such as electronic personal

This work was partially supported by national funds through FCT, Fundação para a Ciência e a Tecnologia, under project UIDB/50021/2020 (INESC-ID multi-annual funding) and the HOTSPOT project, with reference PTDC/CCI-COM/7203/2020. In addition, this material is based upon work supported by the Air Force Office of Scientific Research under award number FA9550-19-1-0020, and by TAILOR, a project funded by EU Horizon 2020 research and innovation programme under GA N. 952215. JGR acknowledges the PhD grant 2020.05151.BD from FCT.

G. Marreiros et al. (Eds.): EPIA 2021, LNAI 12981, pp. 648–660, 2021.
https://doi.org/10.1007/978-3-030-86230-5_51

assistants and smart devices) become a ubiquitous reality in our daily lives. In many situations, these vastly different agents will have no communication or coordination protocols in place but will, nevertheless, need to cooperate effectively towards attaining some common goal (e.g., the comfort of the user). The challenge of developing autonomous agents that are capable of cooperating in a common task with unknown teammates, without explicit coordination or communication is known as the *ad hoc teamwork problem* [18].

The key challenge in ad hoc teamwork is to develop an agent (the "ad hoc agent") that is able to leverage acquired knowledge regarding the interaction with previous teammates to quickly adapt when paired with a new team. The ad hoc teamwork problem has been studied for several years in the MAS community [3,5,8,12,13,15,17]. State-of-the-art approaches, such as the PLASTIC algorithms [4], use of reinforcement learning (RL) and transfer learning techniques to successfully address ad hoc teamwork in complex domains such as *half-field offense* [9]. However, most aforementioned works assume that teammates follow stationary policies, which means that it is expected that teammates will always present the same behavior over the interaction, which is a significant limitation if ad hoc teamwork is to be extended to real world settings involving, for example, human teammates. Our work addresses the question "How can ad hoc agents successfully cooperate with non-stationary teammates in complex domains?". Our contributions are two-fold:

- We evaluate state-of-the-art algorithms—namely the PLASTIC algorithms—against non-stationary teammates. PLASTIC has only been evaluated against stationary teammates and our results show the impact that the presence of non-stationary teammates has in the performance of the method.
- We introduce an extension to PLASTIC Policy, dubbed *PLASTIC Policy with Adversarial selection*, or PPAS. This algorithm relies on the core architecture of PLASTIC Policy, but uses a teammate identification mechanism that relies on an adversarial online prediction algorithm. Such algorithm relies on milder assumptions on the process to be predicted (in our case, the teammate behavior) and is thus robust to non-stationary teammates.

We evaluate our proposed approach in half-field offense (HFO), showcasing its advantages in the presence of non-stationary teammates.

2   Related Work

Stone et al. [18] recognized the importance of having autonomous agents able to collaborate without prior coordination, which they introduced as the *ad hoc teamwork problem*. The ad hoc teamwork problem combines several different elements that set it apart from other multi-agent problems, namely: (i) the agents have no predefined coordination or communication mechanism in place; (ii) the team is not necessarily homogeneous—in particular, the ad hoc agent is often different from the other agents; (iii) the ad hoc agent should be able to leverage prior knowledge to quickly adapt to the teammates in an online manner.

A significant volume of work on ad hoc teamwork considers *stationary teammates*. In other words, the algorithms are built on the assumption that the teammates do not change their behavior throughout the interaction—for example as a result of the ad hoc agent's actions. However, in many multi-agent problems, the assumption of stationary teammates is too restrictive. Hernandez-Leal et al. [10] propose a taxonomy for agent behaviors in multi-agent settings: non adapting, slowly adapting and drastically adapting agents. We now go over relevant work in ad hoc teamwork, organizing it along the aforementioned teammate categories.

Non-adapting Teammates. These works assume that teammates follow a stationary strategy during the entire interaction. The ad hoc teamwork problem is addressed by classifying the teammates behaviour as belonging to some previouly acquired "behavior prototypes" [1,2,4,12,16]. If the prototypes are able to model the teammates' behavior correctly, then these methods can lead to fast and efficient teamwork in the absence of explicit prior coordination. This is, for example, the approach in the PLASTIC algorithms [4], which are general-purpose algorithms based on transfer learning and RL that reuse prior teammate knowledge to quickly adapt to new teammates.

Barrett et al. [4] presented both a model-based and a model-free version of PLASTIC. Both approaches were successfully in addressing the ad hoc teamwork problem. However, the model-based approach is significantly slower and had difficulty dealing with complex environments. On the other hand, the model-free version—PLASTIC Policy—was able to successfully handle complex environments and adapt fast to new teammates. In our work, we use the PLASTIC Policy architecture as a basis for our approach.

PLASTIC Policy, however, still presents some limitations. It assumes that there are similarities between the new and old teammates' behaviors, and it completely relies on finding the most suitable policy for the current team. This means that during the exploration phase the performance is low, which when dealing with critical tasks can be harmful. Also, it relies on the fact that the team follows one stationary policy, already known or very similar to past experiences. If this is not the case, the agent will keep changing between policies during the interaction, putting at risk the task. To tackle this problem, we use an adversarial approach for action selection and belief updates [13].

Slowly Adapting Teammates. These works assume that teammates adapt slowly—for example assuming that the changes in the teammates' strategy exhibits bounded variation between rounds [7,13]. Although these approaches are able to partially address non-stationary teammates, they are mostly model-based and unsuited for complex environments.

For example, Melo and Sardinha [13] proposed an online prediction approach, named *exponentially weighted forecaster for ad hoc teamwork*, able to deal with slowly adapting teammates. Their algorithm identifies the task being performed by the teammates and acts accordingly. It keeps a set of beliefs about which task is currently being performed, which are updated over time. Also, they use the prediction from "experts" to select the ad hoc agent's actions through an online prediction approach. However, their work is unable to address sequential tasks, focusing only on repeated one-shot tasks. In our work, we also adopt an online prediction approach, but use it for team identification rather than for task identification. We combine this prediction algorithm with the PLASTIC architecture [4], which allows us to deal with unpredictable teammates in complex environments—namely, teammates that are non-stationary.

Drastically Adapting Teammates. There are also a few works that assume that teammates can change between policies in a drastic manner during the interaction [11,15]. However, these algorithms are specialized to this particular setting and, for example, cannot cope with slow adaptation teammates. Additionally, they are computationally too heavy to handle complex environments such as half-field offense.

3 PLASTIC Policy with Adversarial Selection

In this section we introduce our main contribution—an algorithm for ad hoc teamwork that can handle non-stationary teammates. We dub our algorithm PLASTIC Policy with Adversarial selection, or PPAS.

Our approach extends the PLASTIC Policy architecture [4] to include an online prediction approach for teammate identification [13]—namely, the *exponentially weighted average forecaster* [6]. By combining the two, we are able to handle non-stationary teammates and deal with complex environments.

Much like the original PLASTIC Policy, our algorithm makes use of past experiences to identify, adapt and cooperate in an ad hoc manner with unknown teammates. However, in contrast with PLASTIC Policy, we do not select a single policy to follow from those previously learned, and instead use information from *all such policies*. This allows PPAS to make near-optimal predictions early in the interaction and still select good actions when facing non-stationary teammates.

3.1 Architecture

The architecture of the proposed approach can be seen in Fig. 1 and comprises three major elements. The first element corresponds to the two blocks "Team Models" and "Team Policies". These blocks contain the prior knowledge that the agent acquired, for example, by interacting with previous teams. A second element is responsible for identifying the teammates, and is performed in the "Update Weights" block. A third and final element is responsible for the selection of the actions of the ad hoc agent, and corresponds to the "Policies Predictions" and "Action Selection" blocks together.

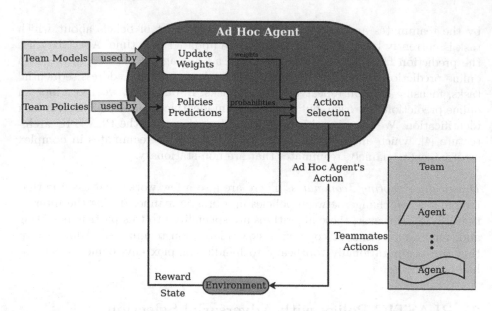

Fig. 1. Overview of PPAS. The architecture is adapted from PLASTIC Policy [4].

When faced with a new team, at each time step the ad hoc agent determines the similarity between the observed behavior of the current team and that observed in teams it previously met (stored as "Team Models"). Based on that similarity, the ad hoc agent combines the action prescribed by the "Team Policies" to determine an action to execute. The process then repeats at the next time step. In the continuation, we describe each of the above elements in detail.

Training the Team Policies and Team Models. The "Team Models" and "Team Policies" correspond to the agent's prior knowledge, acquired beforehand when the ad hoc agent interacted with different teams. In our case, they were obtained by allowing the ad hoc agent to interact with several teams of stationary teammates for a fixed number of episodes, treating the teammates as part of the environment. During such interactions, "Team Policies" are trained using model-free reinforcement learning. When interacting with a particular team k, at each step t the agent experiences a transition $\langle x(t), a(t), r(t), x(t+1) \rangle$, where $x(t)$ is the state, $a(t)$ is the action of the ad hoc agent, $r(t)$ is the resulting reward, and $x(t+1)$ is the resulting state. For each team k, the agent collects N such transitions into a set $D_k = \{\langle x_n, a_n, r_n, x'_n \rangle, n = 1, \ldots, N\}$ that is then used to learn a policy using the well-established DQN algorithm [14].

In PPAS (much like in PLASTIC Policy), policies are represented using Q-*functions*. A Q-function assigns a real value, $Q(x, a)$, to each possible state-action pair (x, a). At any state x, the action prescribed by the policy encoded by Q is the action with the maximal Q-value. In DQN, a Q-function is represented as a neural network, and the parameters θ of the network are updated to minimize

---

Algorithm 1. PLASTIC Policy with Adversarial Selection (PPAS)

1: Initialize $t = 0$, $w_k(0) = 1$ for $k = 1, \ldots, K$.
2: **for all** t **do**
3:     **for** $k = 1, \ldots, K$ **do**
4:         Get forecast vector $\xi^k(t)$
5:     $W(t) = \sum_{k=1}^{K} w_k(t)$
6:     For each action a, compute $p_a(t)$ using (1).
7:     Select action $a(t) = \arg\max_a p_a(t)$
8:     Observe new environment state $x(t+1)$
9:     **for** $k = 1, \ldots, K$ **do**
10:         Predict next state $\hat{x}_k(t+1)$
11:         $d_k = \|x(t+1) - \hat{x}_k(t+1)\|_2$
12:         $w_k(t+1) \leftarrow w_k(t) \cdot e^{-\eta d_k}$

$$L(\theta) = \frac{1}{N} \sum_{n=1}^{N} \|r_n + \gamma \max_{a'} Q_{\theta-}(x_{n+1}, a') - Q_\theta(x_n, a_n)\|^2,$$

where $Q_\theta(x, a)$ is the output of the network for the pair (x, a), γ is a scalar discount, and $Q_{\theta-}$ is a copy of the network that is held fixed during most of the training process.[1] The ad hoc agent thus learns a function Q_k for each team $k = 1, \ldots, K$, and all such functions are collected in the "Team Policies".

The "Team Models", on the other hand, consist of a collection of past experiences for each team, which are used to determine how similar the behavior of the current team is to that of the teams previously encountered.

Action Selection. In PLASTIC Policy [4], the teammate identification is conducted by maintaining a belief over the set of "Team Models". The belief is updated using the similarity between the observed behavior of the current team and that in the teams in the library. The agent then selects—from the library of Team Policies—the action prescribed by the policy for the most likely team.

In PPAS we instead follow Melo and Sardinha [13] and use an online prediction algorithm to select the action to select at each time step, based on the action predictions of *all* the policies in the "Team Policies". PPAS maintains a weight w_k for each team k in the library of "Team Policies". As the agent interacts with its current team, it will query at each time step t each policy in "Team Policies". Such query returns, for each team k, a "forecast vector" $\xi^k(t)$ indicating the most likely actions in the current state $x(t)$. The exponentially weighted forecaster then computes a distribution $p(t)$ over actions by averaging the vectors $\xi_k(t), i = 1, \ldots, K$, where

$$p_a(t) = \frac{1}{W(t)} \sum_{k=1}^{K} w_k(t)\xi_a^k(t), \tag{1}$$

---

[1] We refer to the work of Mnih et al. [14] for details on DQN.

with $\xi_a^k(t)$ indicating the probability of action a according to $\xi^k(t)$ and $W(t) = \sum_k w_k(t)$. Given the distribution $p(t)$, the action selection is greedy, which means that the action with the highest probability is the one chosen.

Teammate Identification. The teammate identification consists of determining which (if any) of the teams in the "Team Models" best matches the team that the ad hoc agent is currently facing. As seen above, PPAS maintains a weight w_k for each team in the library. The weights are initialized to 1, suggesting a uniform "initial belief" over teams—before interacting with the current team, there is no reason to believe that any one team is more likely than the other.

To update these weights, the agent observes how the behavior of its teammates affects the environment. At each time step t, as the environment transitions to a new state, $x(t+1)$, the agent calculates the similarity between the transition $(x(t), x(t+1))$ with similar transitions stored in the "Team Models" for each of the teams. Given the predicted transition for team k, $(\hat{x}_k(t), \hat{x}_k(t+1))$, PPAS computes the Euclidean distance d_k between the actual next state, $x(t+1)$, and the "predicted" next state, $\hat{x}_k(t+1)$. The weights are then updated according to the exponential weighted forecaster update rule [6], yielding

$$w_k(t) \leftarrow w_k(t-1)e^{-\eta d_k}, \tag{2}$$

for a suitable constant $\eta > 0$. PPAS is summarized in Algorithm 1.

4   Experimental Evaluation

We now describe the experimental evaluation of our algorithm. We compare PPAS against the original PLASTIC Policy, which we henceforth abbreviately denote SPP (Standard PLASTIC Policy), illustrating the advantages of our approach in the presence of non-stationary teammates.

4.1   Experimental Setup

Half-Field Offense. We evaluate our work in the HFO scenario, a complex environment that offers multiple challenges—a continuous multi-dimensional state space, real-time actions, noisy sensing and actions, and sparse rewards. In HFO there are two competing teams: the offense team and the defense team. Our agent belongs to the offense team, and the objective of our team is to score a goal (see Fig. 2 for a depiction of HFO). Both teams start without ball, and the game ends when either (1) The offense team scores goal; (2) The ball leaves the game area; (3) The defense team catches the ball; (4) The game exceeds the maximum number of steps allowed (500 steps).

NPC Agents. To create the Team Models and Policies, we used teams of agents created as part of the 2D RoboCup Simulation League competition. We use 5 teams from the 2013 competition as teammates: *aut*, *axiom*, *cyrus*, *gliders*, and *helios*. For the defense team, we use the HFO benchmark agents, the *agent2d*.

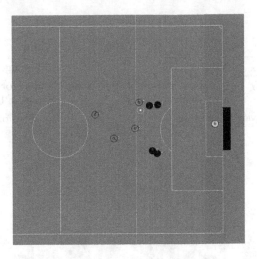

Fig. 2. Screenshot of the HFO environment. In HFO the attacking team (in yellow) tries to score against a defending team (in blue and pink). (Color figure online)

Environment Model. In order to run the DQN part of PPAS, we must describe HFO as a Markov decision problem, identifying the states, actions, reward, and dynamics (i.e., how states evolve). We consider two variations of HFO: the *limited version*, where both defense and offense teams have two players; and the *full version*, where the defense team has 5 players and the attack team has 4 players.

- The state is described by 13 features in the limited version and 23 features in the full version. These features include positions, velocities, orientations of each agent, position and velocity of the ball.
- We adopt a similar action space of Barrett et al. [4], that includes a discretized set of actions (passes to the different teammates, running towards the ball, shooting with different power. In the limited version we consider 11 discrete actions and 13 discrete actions in the full version.
- We define the reward function as follows: a goal is worth a reward of 1000; the other termination conditions are worth a reward of −1000. All other steps correspond to a reward of −1.
- The dynamics are ruled by the HFO simulator. Since our approach is model free, there is no need to specify the dynamics explicitly.

Training. Both PPAS and PLASTIC policy trained with the 5 aforementioned teams prior to the beginning of the experiment. Each ad hoc agent played each team for 100,000 episodes, collecting the necessary data data. Each episode consisted of a full HFO game. The Team Policies were trained using DQN, as described in Sect. 3, while the Team Models used a combination of KD-Trees and arrays as a model for each team, storing the transitions experienced by the agent when playing that team.

Table 1. Test scenario description.

Scenario	First	Second
Teammate type	NPC Agents	Ad hoc agents
Teammate policy	In each trial one of five teams is chosen randomly	Same algorithm as the ad hoc agent being tested
Teammate behavior	Stationary	Non-Stationary

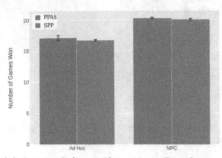
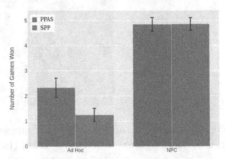

(a) Limited (2 vs 2) setting. Results are averaged over 1,000 trials.

(b) Full (4 vs 5) setting. Results are averaged over 100 trials.

Fig. 3. Number of won games out of a total of 25 games in the limited and full settings.

4.2 Results

The experiments were designed to answer the following questions: (a) When facing stationary opponents, is PPAS able to retain the state-of-the-art performance of PLASTIC Policy and (b) When facing non-stationary opponents, is PPAS able to outperform PLASTIC Policy, showcasing improved robustness?

To answer the two above questions we consider two distinct scenarios: in a first scenario, both algorithms are run against stationary teammates, corresponding to the teams already encountered during training: in each trial the agent is paired with a team randomly selected from the 5 aforementioned teams. In the second scenario, both algorithms are tested in self-play (i.e., against a team of similar ad hoc agents). Since these teammates are all adjusting their behavior simultaneously, they behave in a non-stationary manner. The different scenarios are summarized in Table 1. The results reported are averaged over a large number of trials (1,000 for the limiter version, and 100 for the full version), where a trial corresponds to 25 independent games.[2]

Limited Version (2 vs 2). We start by analyzing the performance of both ad hoc algorithms in the limited scenario (2 defenders vs 2 atackers). Figure 3(a) compares the performance of the two ad hoc agents in terms of the average number of goals scored (games won) per trial. In this simple setting, both agents

---

[2] Agents beliefs and teammate information is reset across trials.

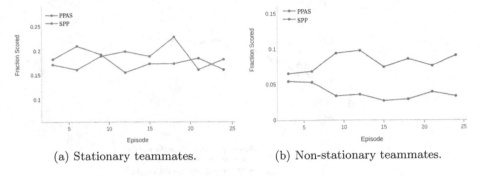

(a) Stationary teammates.   (b) Non-stationary teammates.

Fig. 4. Scoring frequency in the full HFO setting (4 vs 5) during 25 games, for the stationary and non-stationary teams. Results are averages over 100 independent trials.

attain a similar performance, both against stationary teammates (NPC) and non-stationary teammates (Ad Hoc). Although there is a slight improvement when using PPAS, this difference is not statistically significant.

This limited setting is somewhat deceiving: the fact that there are only two defenders makes it possible for a competent player to score by itself, rendering cooperation (and, thus, ad hoc teamwork) secondary. For this reason, we consider the full version, featuring 4 attackers against 5 defenders (see Fig. 2).

Full Version (4 vs 5). In the full setting—where 4 attackers try to score against 5 defenders—cooperation plays a critical role. Since there are more defenders than attackers, it is very difficult for an attacker on its own to score. Therefore, this setting provides a much clearer assessment of the team's ability to act as a team and—consequently—of the performance of the two approaches in terms of their ability to establish ad hoc teamwork.

Figure 3(b) again compares the performance of the two ad hoc agents in terms of the average number of goals scored (games won) per trial. Several observations stand out. First, the overall performance is significantly lower than in the limited case—the number of goals scored hardly exceeds 5. This is in sharp contrast with the 20 goals scored in the limited setting.

A second observation is that the difference in performance between the stationary and non-stationary teams is larger than in the limited setting. This happens since the stationary teammates have a well-defined cooperation strategy to which the ad hoc agent adapts, while the non-stationary team does not.

Finally, the third observation is that, in the full setting, PPAS attains the same score as SPP against stationary teammates, but significantly outperforms SPP against non-stationary teammates, showcasing the ability of our approach to deal with non-stationary teammates.

To further understand the comparative performance of the two ad hoc algorithms, we plot, in Fig. 4, the amount of goals scored in each of the 25 games in

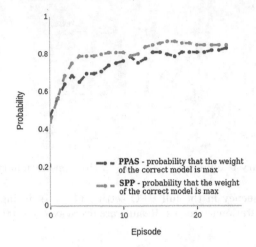

Fig. 5. Probability of the weight associated with the correct team policy being maximal when playing against stationary teammates in the full HFO setting. Results are averaged over 100 independent trials.

a trial,[3] averaged across 100 independent trials. Once again, we can observe that against stationary teammates (Fig. 4(a)), the two algorithms perform similarly, and their performance remains approximately constant across the 25 games, even if SPP exhibits more fluctuations.

However, when paired against non-stationary teammates (Fig. 4(b)), the difference between the two approaches becomes apparent. On one hand, the performance of PPAS remains approximately constant throughout the 25 games. On the other hand, the performance of SPP—which starts in a value similar to that of PPAS—steadily decreases as more games are played, suggesting that the SPP agents are unable to co-adapt.

To conclude our analysis, we depict in Fig. 5 the evolution of the probability that the correct team policy is assigned maximum weight. This is an indicator of the ability of the algorithms to identify the correct team early in the interaction. As can be seen, SPP is able to identify the correct team more quickly. However, because of the action selection mechanism in PPAS, this does not translate necessarily in a difference in performance (as seen in Fig. 3), since the action is selected based on the recommendation from *all* the teams.

Our results satisfactorily answer both our initial questions. PPAS is able to retain the state-of-the-art performance of PLASTIC Policy, whole outperforming PLASTIC Policy against non-stationary teammates. Our results also illustrate the strengths and weaknesses of both approaches. PPAS takes more time to identify the correct team, although it can select good actions even when uncertain about the team it is playing with. SPP is faster to identify the correct team, but is unable to handle non-stationary teammates.

---

[3] For ease of visualization, the results were smoothed using a 3-step running window.

5 Conclusions and Future Work

In this work, we proposed PPAS, an algorithm for ad hoc teamwork that is robust to non-stationary teammates. Our algorithm collects past experiences with different teams in the form of policy and team models. These models are then used when playing a new team through an online prediction algorithm. Even if the team is unknown and does not follow a stationary behavior, PPAS is able to select good actions and coordinate. We evaluated our algorithm in the half field offense environment, with different levels of difficulty, and illustrated the effectiveness and efficiency of our solution.

There are several interesting avenues for future research on ad hoc teamwork. For example, it would be interesting to augment our approach with parameterized agent types, instead of discrete agent types. Another interesting addition would be to investigate how to identify different levels of behavior, since teammates can display multiple behaviors.

References

1. Albrecht, S.V., Ramamoorthy, S.: A game-theoretic model and best-response learning method for ad hoc coordination in multiagent systems. In: AAMAS (2013)
2. Albrecht, S.V., Stone, P.: Reasoning about hypothetical agent behaviours and their parameters. In: AAMAS (2017)
3. Barrett, S., Stone, P.: Ad hoc teamwork modeled with multi-armed bandits: an extension to discounted infinite rewards. In: AAMAS ALA Workshop (2011)
4. Barrett, S., Rosenfeld, A., Kraus, S., Stone, P.: Making friends on the fly: cooperating with new teammates. Artif. Intell. **242**, 132–171 (2017)
5. Bowling, M., McCracken, P.: Coordination and adaptation in impromptu teams. In: AAAI (2005)
6. Cesa-Bianchi, N., Lugosi, G.: Prediction, Learning, and Games. Cambridge University Press, Cambridge (2006)
7. Chakraborty, D., Stone, P.: Cooperating with a Markovian ad hoc eeammate. In: AAMAS (2013)
8. Chen, S., Andrejczuk, E., Cao, Z., Zhang, J.: Aateam: Achieving the ad hoc teamwork by employing the attention mechanism. In: AAAI (2020)
9. Hausknecht, M., Mupparaju, P., Subramanian, S., Kalyanakrishnan, S., Stone, P.: Half field offense: an environment for multiagent learning and ad hoc teamwork. In: AAMAS ALA Workshop (2016)
10. Hernandez-Leal, P., Kaisers, M., Baarslag, T., de Cote, E.M.: A survey of learning in multiagent environments: Dealing with non-stationarity. Computing Research Repository arXiv:1707.09183 (2017)
11. Hernandez-Leal, P., Zhan, Y., Taylor, M.E., Sucar, L.E., de Cote, E.M.: Efficiently detecting switches against non-stationary opponents. Auton. Agent. Multi-Agent Syst. **31**(4), 767–789 (2017)
12. Macke, W., Mirsky, R., Stone, P.: Expected value of communication for planning in ad hoc teamwork. In: AAAI (2021)
13. Melo, F.S., Sardinha, A.: Ad hoc teamwork by learning teammates' task. Auton. Agents Multi-Agent Syst. **30**(2), 175–219 (2016)

14. Mnih, V., et al.: Human-level control through deep reinforcement learning. Nature **518**, 529–533 (2015)
15. Ravula, M., Alkoby, S., Stone, P.: Ad hoc teamwork with behavior switching agents. In: IJCAI (2019)
16. Rodrigues, G.: Ad Hoc Teamwork With Unknown Task Model and Teammate Behavior. Master's thesis, Instituto Superior Técnico (2018)
17. Stone, P.: Autonomous learning agents: layered learning and ad hoc teamwork. In: AAMAS (2016)
18. Stone, P., Kaminka, G.A., Kraus, S., Rosenschein, J.S.: Ad hoc autonomous agent teams: Collaboration without pre-coordination. In: AAAI (2010)

Carbon Market Multi-agent Simulation Model

João Bernardo Narciso de Sousa[✉], Zafeiris Kokkinogenis,
and Rosaldo J. F. Rossetti

LIACC/DEI, Faculdade de Engenharia, Universidade do Porto,
Rua Dr. Roberto Frias, 4200-465 Porto, Portugal
{up201606649,kokkinogenis,rossetti}@fe.up.pt

Abstract. Carbon Markets are a market-based tool to help the fight against climate change by reducing greenhouse gases (GHG) emissions. Corporations have to buy allowances covering the emissions they produce, being required to pay heavy penalties otherwise. It is based on the 'cap and trade' principle, meaning that there is a cap value - the maximum number of allowances being sold - providing scarcity to the market. This paper proposes a formalization of an agent-based model that replicates the context of applying a carbon auction market and other regulatory mechanisms and presents the results of various experiments of different policies to gather some intuitions regarding the functioning of carbon markets.

Keywords: Social simulation · Carbon markets · Multi-agent systems · Agent-based modelling

1 Introduction

Carbon markets are a free market-based tool that provides incentives for economic agents to reduce their emissions in a way that incorporates the environmental costs of their actions as a factor to weigh in their decisions. It is based on the allocation and trading of carbon allowances (also called carbon credits or permits) that enable the holder to emit a certain amount of emissions proportional to their number. It is usually mandatory for the economic agents to hold the needed allowances, otherwise facing hefty penalties for excess emissions that the credits do not cover. This kind of mechanism is more commonly used for regulation emissions of big corporations, but the principle can also be applied on a more personal basis - called personal carbon trading [6] - even though examples of its application are very scarce and limited [1]. There are more examples of carbon trading on a bigger scale, like the European Union Emission Trading System (EU ETS) [4]. In the following subsections, various standard features of carbon markets will be presented.

A fundamental concept characterizes carbon markets: the 'cap and trade'. The cap and trade principle means that the total number of allowances in the

© Springer Nature Switzerland AG 2021
G. Marreiros et al. (Eds.): EPIA 2021, LNAI 12981, pp. 661–672, 2021.
https://doi.org/10.1007/978-3-030-86230-5_52

market at a given time is predetermined. This mechanism allows for a more accurate target level of emissions, and the cap usually descends over time, guaranteeing an emission decline. For example, during Phase 3 (2013–2020) of the EU ETS, the cap was reduced annually by a linear factor of 1.74%. Emission caps are set according to reliable estimates on current and potential future emissions, so the regulator must have reliable information regarding firms' emission levels and their reduction potential.

Credit Allocation and Acquisition. There are different ways for participants of a given emission trading scheme to get allowances.

Free Allocation. Firstly, the scheme may include a free allocation mechanism. The regulator in charge of the scheme defines the number of free credits to give to each actor according to factors like industry sector, the dimension of the actor, emission history and risk of carbon leakage, in other words, the risk that companies transfer their production to other jurisdictions with more lenient emission regulations, ultimately reducing costs but not reducing emissions. Taking into account those factors, there are two main ways by which the credits are allocated. The first one is through benchmarking, a reference value relative to production activity. The other one is through grandfathering, the emission history of a company. The number of freely allocated credits may be higher at the beginning of the scheme to decrease its implementation costs and risks of perturbing the economy and reducing over time.

Allowance Auction Market. Most schemes adopt an auction mechanism for regulators to sell carbon permits combined with a free allocation mechanism, although there are examples that rely exclusively on free allocation to introduce allowances in the economy. That is the case, for example, of the South Korean Emission Trading Scheme - the credits on its first phase came 100% from free allocation, while on its second phase they came 97% from free allocation and 3% from auctioning [8]. Auction Markets can take several forms. In the case of EU ETS it follows a single-round, sealed-bid and uniform-price format. This means that bidders who want to buy credits can submit any number of bids during a single bidding window, and each bid must specify the number of allowances to buy and the price the bidder is willing to pay for them. When the bidding window closes, the auction platform orders the bids by price in decreasing order and determines the clearing price, in other words, the price at which the sum of volumes bid matches or exceeds the volume of allowances up for auction. All bids priced higher than the clearing price are successful, and successful bidders have to pay only the clearing price. Instead of having a uniform-price format, the auction can take a discriminatory-price format, meaning that successful bidders pay different prices for the allowances according to their bid price instead of the clearing price. Regulators also can establish ceiling or floor prices, meaning that allowances can not be sold for more than or less than a specified value.

Penalties. Polluters who do not have enough credits to cover their emissions may have to pay a fine or have some kind of punishment. In the EU ETS case, during Phase 2 and 3, there was a fine of 100€ per ton of GHG not covered by a permit. There are schemes, however, that do not apply fines. It is the case of both Tianjin and Chongqing's pilot carbon markets. In those cases, companies that do not comply are disqualified from finance subsidies and government support. In other cases, like the carbon markets of Guangdong and Hubei, the regulator not only charges fines but also deducts the double of the excessive emissions from the freely allocated allowance of the next year [11].

1.1 Carbon Tax

Carbon taxes are another tool that can be used in alternative to or alongside a carbon market. It is based on a fixed value that polluters have to pay for each pollution unit. This lack of complexity is one of its advantages as it becomes easier to legislate, implement and enforce. Another advantage over cap and trade schemes based on free-allocation and not on auctions is that it generates revenue for the regulator, as the tax has to be paid directly to the regulator instead of having allowances given for free which are then sold and bought between corporations. Another advantage is related to the signalling it provides to the economy. A carbon tax is clear: it sends a signal that pollution imposes a negative externality on society, so that cost should be internalized by the payment of a tax. Even if the polluter is willing to pay the price for its still a tax, while on a carbon market system with free allocation, polluters may receive permits to "pollute for free", and even if that does not happen, the polluters are still able to purchase the "right to pollute" [2]. That does not send the same signals as having to pay an additional cost for every polluting activity. Another critical comparison that can be made between these two tools is related to uncertainty. Cap and trade schemes may produce high levels of uncertainty regarding costs for polluters, as the price of allowances freely floats in the market, while with a carbon tax, companies know precisely how much they will have to pay if they know how much they will emit. On the other hand, cap and trade schemes can limit precisely the total number of allowances (the cap), while with a carbon tax, even though it can be adjusted, it is not possible to know beforehand how much impact it will have in terms of limiting pollution. This precision that cap and trade schemes provide may also be a disadvantage when the cost of CO_2 abatement for firms is unknown or uncertain. An excellent example of that is what happened in Phase 1 of EU ETS. In that case, the regulator did not accurately assess the capability of firms to reduce their emission, and they decided to reduce their emissions to their allocated allowance quantity without paying for additional permits. In two years, the allowances' prices were reduced to almost zero [7]. To tackle issues like the one explained, the EU created a Market Stability Reserve (MSR), a program that reserves a certain number of allowances in case of an oversupply and releases allowances in case of shortage [11].

1.2 Multi-agent Based Simulation

As we can see, market-based tools for emission mitigation like cap and trade schemes in combination with carbon taxes are complex and contain multiple moving parts. There are many possible ways to implement those kinds of regulations, and how all the different economic agents will respond to them is often impossible to predict. The uncertainty involved in this problem makes it a good candidate for applying a Multi-Agent-Based Simulation, where agents perform reasoning and make production and market decisions to get intuitions about possible results of different policies over time.

2 Model Formalization

2.1 The Model

The multi-agent system model and agents formalization will be inspired by [3]. Our model can be described as a tuple $\langle Ag, A, X, x_0, \varphi \rangle$ where:

- Ag is the set of agents of the model. In this case, Agents can only be regulators or polluters, so that $Ag \in \{Regulator, Polluter\}$. Regulators are the ones who set the regulations and goals, and polluters are all producers of the same kind of good and sell them in the same market;
- A is the action space that includes all actions possible to be executed in the system. Those actions will be presented in the next section where agents will be properly defined;
- X is the environmental state space of the system. It includes relevant state information of the system, so that

$$X = \{TotalEmissions, TotalDemand, TotalSupply, State\},$$

where, $TotalEmissions$ is the value of the polluters' total emissions, while $TotalDemand$ and $TotalSupply$ represent the demand of a certain good in the goods market and the sum of the productions of all the polluters, respectively. The $State$ variable is the stage in which the simulation is. There are four possible stages, so that

$$State \in \{ProductionStep, BiddingStep, AuctionStep,$$
$$MarketStep, OutputDecisionStep\}$$

- x_o is the initial state of the model;
- φ is the agents' capability function that describes possible actions for an agent at a given state.

2.2 The Agents

In our model, the agents are defined as a tuple $\langle T, S, g, t, s_0, U \rangle$ where:

- T is the type of the agent, so that $T \in Polluter, Regulator$.
- S is the set of internal states of the agent;

- g is the agent's state transition function;
- t is the agent's decision function that describes the action it will choose given an internal state and the state of the model;
- s_0 is the agent's initial internal state;
- U is a utility function that assigns a value to each possible internal state.

Regulators are the ones able to run the auctions, set goals like the emission trading cap (the maximum number of carbon allowances to sell at a certain time), distribute free allowances (the aforementioned "free allocation" rule), and set carbon taxes, and penalties to polluters. Each polluter must have one and only one regulator assigned to it. That means that it is possible to have several regulators establishing very different sets of rules for different polluters, creating many different "parallel" carbon markets. This aspect may be useful on certain simulation scenarios when it is intended to simulate polluters belonging to different countries or economic blocks, or in the case of hierarchical carbon markets, when for example, smaller polluters have to abide by a municipal carbon market but bigger ones are integrated on a national or supra-national one. The state of a regulator is

$$S = \{carbonTax, lastClearingPrice, cap, totalEmissions, penaltyFactor\},$$

where $carbonTax$ is the price per emission that polluters being regulated will have to pay. $lastClearingPrice$ is the clearing price of the last allowance auction. cap is the number of allowances to be introduced at a certain point in time. In other words, it is the target value of emissions. $totalEmissions$ is the sum of emissions of the polluters that being regulated by each regulator. The utility function is related to the reduction of emissions over time. Finally, $penaltyFactor$ is a multiplier so that polluters who do not have enough allowances for their emissions will have to pay

$$penaltyFactor * (emissions - allowances),$$

Polluters are companies that produce goods and emit emissions based on their productivity levels. The state if the polluter is

$$S = \{emissionsPerProduct, profitRate, costPerProduct,$$
$$regulator, producedGoods, emissions, allowances, \pi\}$$

The variable $emissionsPerProduct$ is the value of emissions that a polluter emits by a unit of production. $profitRate$ is the profit rate that the agent wants to maintain when selling its goods. $costPerProduct$ is the unitary cost of producing a good. $Regulator$ is a reference to the regulator agent that is jurisdictionally in charge of the polluter. $producedGoods$ is the number of produced goods at a certain point. $emissions$ is the number of emissions resulting from the production of goods at a certain point. $allowances$ is the number of carbon allowances that the agent possesses. π is the profit, the value of sales minus the production costs minus costs related to a carbon market or a carbon tax. The utility function is related to the increase of the profit over time.

2.3 Simulation Stages

For each period of time t, the simulation runs a sequence of several steps.

Production Step. In this stage, all polluters p calculate their $emissions_{p,t}$ for that period of time. The emissions are based on the number of goods produced and the CO2 emission values by product, following the equation:

$$emissions_{p,t} = producedGoods_{p,t} * emissionsPerProduct_p$$

Bidding Step. In this step, the polluters go to the auction market to get their needed carbon allowances. To do that, they place bids that include information on the volume of allowances to buy $bidVolume_{p,t}$ and on the intended price of those $bidPrice_{p,t}$. To calculate the number of credits to buy, each polluter calculates the difference between their emissions and the credits they already have, plus an additional marginal (for example, 2% of the difference). So, $bidVolume_{p,t} = emissions_{p,t} - allowances_{p,t} + margin_{p,t}$. To calculate the bid price, the polluter has to follow a strategy based on a certain strategy [5,9] and a reservation price. The reservation price $rp_{p,t}$ is the maximum value that a polluter is willing to pay for an allowance (one unit). It is given by the equation:

$$rp_{p,t} = \frac{sales_{p,t} - costPerProduct_{p,t} * producedGoods_{p,t}}{emissions_{p,t}}$$

There are three possible strategies for bid price definition:

- Risky strategy : $bidPrice_{p,t+1} = cp_{r,t} + \frac{3}{4}(rp_{p,t+1} - cp_{r,t})$
- Neutral strategy : $bidPrice_{p,t+1} = cp_{r,t} + \frac{1}{2}(rp_{p,t+1} - cp_{r,t})$
- Conservative strategy : $bidPrice_{p,t+1} = cp_{r,t} + \frac{1}{4}(rp_{p,t+1} - cp_{r,t})$

being $cp_{r,t}$ the last clearing price of the auction market of the regulator associated with the polluter. The clearing price is the lowest price for which an allowance was sold in the last auction. At t=0, the bid price is a random value so that $bidPrice_{p,0} \in [0, rp_{p,0}]$. The initial probability of selecting each strategy, $prob_{p,t,s}$ is 1/3, being $s_{p,t} \in \{1,2,3\}$ the strategy chosen by the polluter. Each strategy's probability is based on the propensity $prop_{p,t,s}$ towards each strategy.

$$prop_{p,t+1,s} = (1-g)prop_{p,t,s} + \psi_{p,t,s}$$

$$\psi_{p,t,s} = \begin{cases} (1-e)\pi_{p,t}, & s = s_{p,t} \\ \frac{e}{2}\pi_{p,t}, & s \neq s_{p,t}. \end{cases}$$

where $\pi_{p,t}$ denotes the agent's profit, and e and g are parameters representing experiment and recency and are experimentally set to be 0.2 and 0.1, respectively [5]. Finally, the probability for each strategy is given by:

$$prob_{p,t+1,s} = prop_{p,t+1,s} / \sum_{x=1}^{3} prop_{p,t+1,x}$$

Auction Step. After all bids have been placed, it is time for the regulators to run the auction markets. The number of carbon allowances to auction for each regulator r is equal to the emission cap previously established at the agents' initialization. It is usually a percentage of the emissions of a certain initial point in time, for example, $cap_r = \sum emissions_{p,0} * 0.9$, meaning that in that scenario, the goal is to reduce by 10% the number of current CO2 emissions. The cap can also decrease over time. Each regulator orders the bids of their polluters by price, following descending order. Credits are then allocated until there are no more credits to allocate. In this process, the last bid to which allowances are allocated can be entirely fulfilled or only partly. The last successful bid price is the new clearing price, meaning that all bids with prices higher than that one were successful too. The clearing price is an essential indicator of the calculation of the bids' prices by the polluters.

Market Step. In this step, the goods produced by the polluters are sold on a market. For the sake of simplicity, we assumed that all polluters participate in the same goods market, independently of which regulator supervises them. We also assumed that all polluters produce the same product and that they are all in competition. Selling orders are placed containing a volume to sell, $sellVolume_{p,t} = supply_{p,t}$ and a price that includes the production costs, a profit margin, and the cost of the credits bought on the previous step. It is given by the equation

$$sellPrice_{p,t} = costPerProduct_i * (1 + profitRate_p)$$
$$+ (allowancesCost_{p,t}/supply_{p,t})$$
$$+ (carbonTax_{r,t} * emissionPerProduct_{p,t})$$

After all the selling orders have been placed, they are ordered by price in ascending order. The orders are then satisfied until the market demand has been fulfilled. In our scenario, our demand follows a simple normal distribution. However, it would be interesting to utilize a different demand function that can reproduce more complex phenomena like the one proposed in [10]. Finally, the total sales of a polluter are

$$sales_{p,t} = \begin{cases} sellVolume_{p,t} * sellPrice_{p,t}, & \text{if successful sale,} \\ 0, & \text{if not.} \end{cases}$$

Output Decision Step. In this final step, the results of the operation of the polluter agents are calculated, and decisions are made based on the variation of those results over time. This is the phase when the fruits of the regulations and the carbon market materialize; that is, it is the phase when incentives and penalties result in changes in production volumes, ideally by the expansion of production by the most efficient agents and by the retraction of the biggest polluters. Firstly, the profit $\pi_{p,t}$ is calculated following the equation

$$\pi_{p,t} = salesp, t - (costPerProduct_p * producedGoods_{p,t}) - allowancesCost_{p,t}$$
$$- (penaltyFactor_{r,t} * (emissions_{p,t} - allowances_{p,t}))$$
$$- (carbonTax_{r,t} * emissionsp, t)$$

The new output, in other words, the number of goods to produce for the next cycle is

$$producedGoods_{p,t+1} =$$

$$\begin{cases} producedGoods_{p,t} * \alpha, & \text{if } \pi_{p,t} - \pi_{p,t-1} > \Delta_\pi \\ producedGoods_{p,t}, & \text{if } |\pi_{p,t} - \pi_{p,t-1}| \leq \Delta_\pi \\ producedGoods_{p,t} * \beta, & \text{if } \pi_{p,t} - \pi_{p,t-1} < -\Delta_\pi \end{cases}$$

being Δ_π the profit variation threshold for changes in output, $\alpha \in]1, +\infty[$ the output increase factor and $\beta \in]0, 1[$ the output decrease factor. Apart from the profit variation, two other factors can make an agent increase or decrease their production. If the profit variation of an agent is positive, and the demand of the previous tick goods market was not satisfied, the production will increase. If the number of sold goods by the agent in the previous tick goods market is less than 80% of the number of produced goods by it, the production will decrease.

3   Experiments and Results

For the experiments, the model's initial state will be the following, unless stated otherwise: The simulations will contain 1000 polluter agents and one regulator. Each polluter will have an initial production of 10000 items. The cost of production of each agent will be 20 for every agent, and the profit rate will be 0.1 and equal for every agent. The polluters are differentiated by their emission per product, which follows a normal distribution with mean x and variation y, and that will allow the comparison of behaviours of the most efficient companies and their worst-performing counterparts. The allowance cap will be 90% of the total emissions on the simulation's first iteration. The penalty factor will be 2. The demand of the goods market will follow a normal distribution with a mean of 90% of the initial total supply. Finally, the results presented represent the evolution of the system 2000 ticks after the start of the simulation.

3.1   Scenario 1 - Auction Market

This first scenario makes use of a carbon allowances auction market as the only emissions regulation mechanism. As we can see in Fig. 1, and for the sake of a more straightforward comparison, we have grouped the fifty more efficient, the fifty less efficient polluters, and the fifty close to average polluters supply measurement - the number of produced goods - per tick. The slow degrowth of the biggest polluters is very visible, along with a less sharp replacement of that lost supply by more efficient corporations. We used the word "replacement" because as visible in Fig. 2, the number of the products supplied in the market has just a tiny decrease to adapt to the mean of the demand, but is always above it. Until a certain point, corporations with average efficiency and high efficiency are benefited.

The replacement of less efficient productions by the more efficient ones has an apparent effect on the total amount of emissions of the system as visible in Fig. 3. This amount is reduced by about 10% after 2000 ticks (Fig. 4 and 5).

3.2   Scenario 2 - Carbon Tax

This second scenario uses a carbon tax as a regulatory mechanism without applying an auction market. The fixed value of the carbon tax used for this example scenario is 10€ per tonne of CO2.

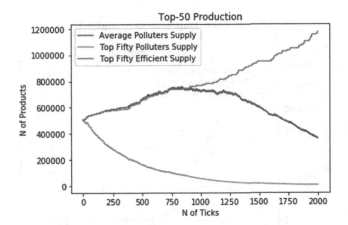

Fig. 1. Production of the top-50 more efficient, 50 average, and top-50 less efficient in scenario 1

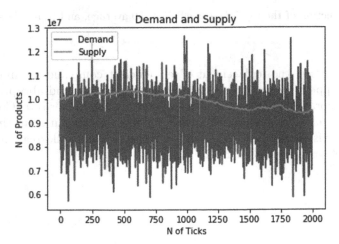

Fig. 2. Demand and supply of the goods market in scenario 1

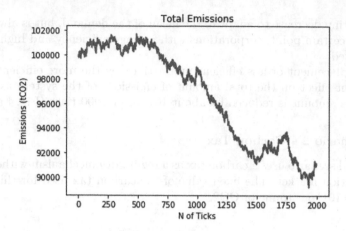

Fig. 3. Total emissions in scenario 1

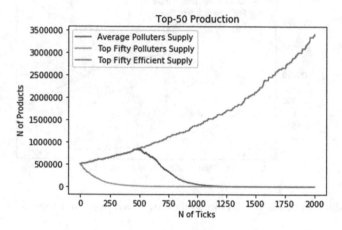

Fig. 4. Production of the top-50 more efficient, 50 average, and top-50 less efficient in scenario 2

As we can see, the replacement of less efficient companies by more efficient ones still happens with a carbon tax but is much faster and abrupt. The most efficient corporations production also grows at a much higher rate. Corporations with average efficiency do not flourish with this mechanism as in the previous scenario. As visible in Fig. 6, the results in terms of a global decrease in emissions are relatively similar to scenario 1.

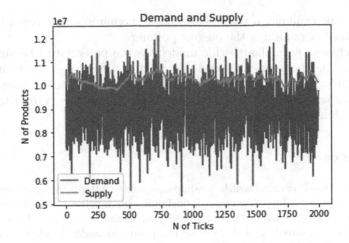

Fig. 5. Demand and supply of the goods market in scenario 2

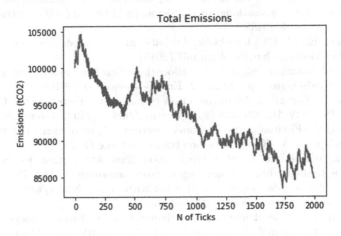

Fig. 6. Total emissions in scenario 2

4   Conclusions and Future Work

This report describes an agent-based social simulation model that can experiment with different regulatory mechanisms of carbon emissions. In the future, this model could be expanded to make it more robust, allowing for more complex experiments and a more realistic setup. Some examples: Artificial intelligence methods could be added to allow a more complex agent decision process to decide their production levels and bidding strategies. More kinds of agents could be added, for example, citizen agents that do not produce anything but consider their consumption and the carbon footprint of it. Agents that do produce goods could be differentiated by producing different goods and being engaged in different markets and supply chain relationships. More regulatory mechanisms could be added - for example, a positive incentive mechanism that rewards efficient agents instead of punishing the biggest polluters.

In conclusion, even though this model has the potential to be significantly extended by the inclusion of several new features, its current state allows for a general simulation of regulatory mechanisms and, given different parameters to the model, it is possible to learn new insights about how agents react to different carbon auction markets and carbon taxes.

References

1. Norfolk island carbon/health evaluation study. https://web.archive.org/web/20121228190331/. http://www.norfolkislandcarbonhealthevaluation.com/
2. Avi-Yonah, R., Uhlmann, D.: Combating global climate change: why a carbon tax is a better response to global warming than cap and trade. Stanford Environ. Law J. **28** (2008). https://doi.org/10.2139/ssrn.1109167
3. Centeno, R., Billhardt, H., Hermoso, R., Ossowski, S.: Organising mas: a formal model based on organisational mechanisms, pp. 740–746 (2009). https://doi.org/10.1145/1529282.1529438
4. Comission, E.: EU ETS handbook. Available at https://ec.europa.eu/clima/sites/clima/files/docs/ets_handbook_en.pdf (2015)
5. Cong, R.G.: Auction design for the allocation of carbon emission allowances: uniform or discriminatory price? Int. J. Energy Environ. **1** (2010)
6. Fawcett, T., Parag, Y.: An introduction to personal carbon trading. Clim. Policy - CLIM POLICY **10**, 329–338 (2010). https://doi.org/10.3763/cpol.2010.0649
7. Jacobsen, M.: Environmental economics lecture 6–7, ucsd econ 131 (2016)
8. Partnership, I.C.A.: Korea emissions trading scheme (2021)
9. Tang, L., Wu, J., Yu, L., Bao, Q.: Carbon allowance auction design of China's emissions trading scheme: a multi-agent-based approach. Energy Policy **102**, 30–40 (2017). https://doi.org/10.1016/j.enpol.2016.11.041. http://www.sciencedirect.com/science/article/pii/S0301421516306462
10. Thavikulwat, P.: Modeling market demand in a demand-independent business simulation. Simul. Games **20**(4), 439–458 (1989). https://doi.org/10.1177/104687818902000403
11. Zhang, M., Liu, Y., Su, Y.: Comparison of carbon emission trading schemes in the European Union and China. Climate **5**, 70 (2017)

Cloud Based Decision Making
for Multi-agent Production Systems

Hamood Ur Rehman[1,2]($\boxtimes$), Terrin Pulikottil[3,4],
Luis Alberto Estrada-Jimenez[3,4], Fan Mo[1], Jack C. Chaplin[1], Jose Barata[3,4],
and Svetan Ratchev[1]

[1] University of Nottingham, Nottingham, UK
{Hamood.Rehman,Fan.Mo,Jack.Chaplin,Svetan.Ratchev}@nottingham.ac.uk
[2] TQC Ltd., Nottingham, UK
[3] Centre of Technology and Systems, UNINOVA Instituto Desenvolvimento
de Novas Tecnologias, Caparica, Portugal
{tpulikottil,lestrada,jab}@uninova.pt
[4] NOVA University of Lisbon, Caparica, Portugal

Abstract. The use of multi-agent systems (MAS) as a distributed control method for shop-floor manufacturing control applications has been extensively researched. MAS provides new implementation solutions for smart manufacturing requirements such as the high dynamism and flexibility required in modern manufacturing applications. MAS in smart manufacturing is becoming increasingly important to achieve increased automation of machines and other components. Emerging technologies like artificial intelligence, cloud-based infrastructures, and cloud computing can also provide systems with intelligent, autonomous, and more scalable solutions. In the current work, a decision-making framework is proposed based on the combination of MAS cloud computing, agent technology, and machine learning. The framework is demonstrated in a quality control use case with vision inspection and agent-based control. The experiment utilizes a cloud-based machine learning pipeline for part classification and agent technology for routing. The results show the applicability of the framework in real-world scenarios bridging cloud service-oriented architecture with agent technology for production systems.

Keywords: Cloud computing · Multi-agent · Machine learning · Production systems

1 Introduction

The increasing demand for small batch sizes and customized products, combined with a high level of market fluctuations, is requiring manufacturing industries to change their traditional production methods. In some areas, fixed lines with centralized control are being replaced by autonomous modules with distributed

© Springer Nature Switzerland AG 2021
G. Marreiros et al. (Eds.): EPIA 2021, LNAI 12981, pp. 673–686, 2021.
https://doi.org/10.1007/978-3-030-86230-5_53

and decentralized control, with the goal of increasing their level of agility and flexibility, but uptake is slow.

To achieve this transition, several manufacturing paradigms have been suggested and have successfully showcased applications that enable adaptable and re-configurable manufacturing solutions. Examples of these emerging paradigms are the Evolvable Production Systems (EPS) [1], Bionic Manufacturing Systems [2], Holonic Manufacturing Systems (HMS) [3], and Reconfigurable Manufacturing Systems (RMS) [4]. Each takes a different approach to move traditional mass production towards an era of embedded system intelligence capable of mass customization and high product personalization.

Emerging technologies such as artificial intelligence, multi-agent technologies, service-based infrastructures, and cloud computing [5] are supporting the implementation of these new paradigms and enabling the necessary infrastructure to develop new levels of interoperability, integration, and seamless data exchange. These are critical requirements for the transition to the fourth industrial revolution where high levels of digitization of resources are expected.

However, these technological enablers are recent developments, and one of the common challenges is the lack of methodologies that showcase their implementation and integration in real scenarios, leaving such works in very theoretical and abstract terms.

This article proposes a multi-agent framework capable of reconfiguring and monitoring manufacturing operations in response to data from a cloud-based analysis pipeline. The framework was defined to be generic and useful for various environments, and here is instantiated in a specific use case based on product testing. A multi-agent infrastructure runs distributed on the shop floor and grants intelligence to products, which can hence communicate their required operations with transport elements and machines. The introduction of a monitoring entity allows the system to be constantly checking for faults. A cloud-based machine learning platform provides intelligence "as a service" that allows the product agents to store, train and predict machine learning models that support decision making and feedback.

This paper is organized as follows; Section 2 introduces the background of the related technology for this paper. Section 3 details the decision-making framework based on a cloud platform. Section 4 is about experimentation and deployment. Section 5 explains final conclusions and future works.

2   Background

Machine learning (ML) allows the software to learn over time from data and make decisions and predictions that improve over time. ML is being used to improve decision-making, improve operations and customer experiences in a wide range of sectors.

Many real-world problems have high complexity and unknown underlying models which makes them excellent candidates for the application of ML. ML can be applied to various areas of computing to design and programming explicit algorithms with high-performance output, such as in the manufacturing industry, robotics [6], e-commerce, medical applications [7], scientific visualization [8] and fault diagnosis [9].

Cloud technologies applied to manufacturing enable the conversion of manufacturing resources and capabilities into entities capable of being virtualized, combined, and enhanced [10] established the cloud concept in detail and presented a system that was service-oriented and interoperable. The system revolved around the customer/cloud user and enterprise user.

Cloud technologies often enable on-demand use of resources that follow a deployed-as-you-need model so that resources may be used with common interfaces. The cloud services can be mainly divided into Platform-as-a-service (PaaS), Infrastructure as a service (IaaS), Software as a service (SaaS). PaaS cloud-based solutions offer connectivity of a user's applications to the application resources, web services, or storage infrastructure of a cloud. IaaS, the major component in a PaaS solution, is a platform where services provided by other platform providers. While Software as a service (SaaS) is an application software delivery model. In the SaaS delivery model, the application software is delivered via the Internet to end-users over an Internet Protocol (IP) connection.

Distributed artificial intelligence (DAI) has attracted research interest because it can solve complex computing problems by breaking them into simpler tasks. DAI algorithms can be divided into three categories: parallel AI, distributed problem solving (DPS), and multi-agent systems (MAS) [11]. Parallel AI involves the development of parallel algorithms, languages, and architectures to improve the efficiency of classic AI algorithms by taking advantage of task parallelism. DPS involves dividing a task into several subtasks, and each subtask is assigned to one of a group of cooperating nodes (called computing entities). Computing entities have shared knowledge or resources and predefined communications with other entities, which limits their flexibility [12].

MAS divides the components of the system into autonomous and 'selfish' software agents, each aiming to achieve its own goals by collaborating with other agents. MAS supports complex applications where many components with conflicting objectives need to interact by breaking them into independent simpler entities. They require distributed and parallel data [13].

Agent technology is recognised as a powerful tool for the 21st century manufacturing system. Researches are on-going for utilising agent technology in manufacturing enterprises, production process planning and scheduling, workshop control, and re-configurable manufacturing systems [14].

The applications of agents in manufacturing industry have seen wider acceptance, such as: process and manufacturing control [15–18], manufacturing simulation and execution [19–21], reconfiguration and self-adaptation in manufacturing [3,22,23]. Monitoring, quality control, and diagnostics in manufacturing [24–27] can be greatly benefited by agent integration coupled with other technologies.

Machine vision and image processing techniques utilised in manufacturing applications are used for integrated inspections to detect defects and improve product quality in the process [28]. In many cases, traditional machine learning has made great progress and produced reliable results [29], but different prepossessing methods are required, including structure-based, statistical-based, filter-based, and model-based techniques. To enhance performance for quality control these techniques can be combined with expert knowledge to extract representative features [30, 31] that influence quality. Most of the previous research about manufacturing quality monitoring with agent application does not relate with cloud computing technologies and machine learning. This work addresses that area.

3   Decision Making Framework

The framework for cloud-based decision-making in manufacturing is divided into two components, the multi-agent system, and the cloud computing services. A Graphical representation of the framework is given in Fig. 1.

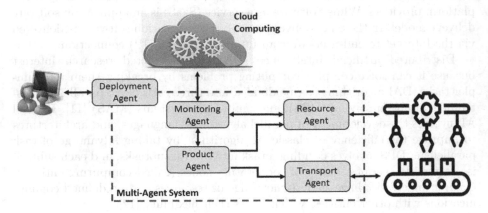

Fig. 1. Framework for MAS and cloud-intelligence integration

3.1   Multi-agent System (MAS) Component

The framework requires a set of agents with defined responsibilities that are each instantiated when required. The agents developed in PROSA [32] and PRIME [25] projects served as an inspiration for the development of this component. Some agents may each have a physical asset associated with it and provides an interface to the virtualized "skills" performed by the physical asset. The list of agents and their functionalities are given in Table 1.

The sequence diagram (Fig. 2) shows the interaction between products, transportation assets, monitoring elements, and resources. It assumes that the agents have been already launched. This means that their skills and services have been already identified by the Deployment Agents (therefore, DAs are not included in the sequence diagram).

Table 1. Agent types and their functionalities

Agent type	Functionalities
Deployment agents (DAs)	Launches and kills the agents according to the task being performed. Keeps track of the list of agents being deployed
Product agents (PAs)	Represents each product on which tasks are being performed (one agent per product). Requests skills from other agents to be performed on the product. Updates the product properties (e.g. faulty or not) as task progresses. The agent is removed when the product is finished
Transport agents (TAs)	Performs the skills of moving the product from one place to another. Performs skills monitoring the development of bottlenecks in the system. Examples include conveyors, pick & place robots, AGVs
Monitoring agents (MAs)	Collects data from other agents and provides information. Utilizes the cloud computing platform for decision making. Skills being performed includes quality prediction, prognostics
Resource agents (RAs)	Represents a resource on the shop floor. Provides the skills provided by the resource. Extracts data from the resource it is abstracting

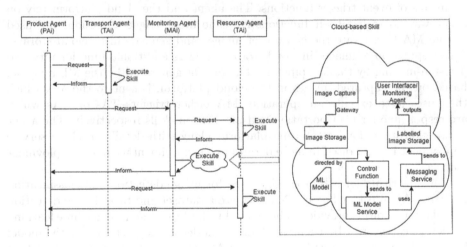

Fig. 2. Sequence diagram for the framework

Product Agents (PA) guides the sequence of the process creating a product by requesting the skills from other agents to be performed on the physical product instance. This request of skills could vary depending on the product properties and the skills required to create the product.

Transport Agents (TA) execute the skills requested by the PA to move the product to the required resources and to inform the current position of the product to PA. The TA also considers the buffers and potential bottlenecks that might arise before executing its skills.

Resource Agents (RA) represent shop-floor resources (such as machining centers, robots, sensors, cameras). RAs can provide their availability, task status info, and resource information as per request.

Monitoring Agents (MA) doesn't have a physical entity associated with it but utilizes the skills provided by RAs if required (e.g. image capturing skills from a camera RA). The MA offers the cloud computing functionality as skills if required for quality prediction and prognostics. For example, PA requests MA to perform a skill of quality prediction of the product associated with it. MA if required, requests RA to perform its skill (e.g. take a photo of the product). MA then uses a cloud platform for decision-making and informs PA about the quality of the product.

3.2   Cloud Computing Component

Cloud computing is used to enhance the capability of the multi-agent framework by bridging it with service-oriented architecture. The MA looks for certain events that act as a trigger for it to execute its functionality (requesting RAs and informing PA). Each of the services housed in the cloud can be instantiated by means of event trigger functions. The agent and the cloud platform rely on a gateway to realize their functionality. The event trigger functions are used by the MA to activate the capture of images and send them to cloud storage. This population of images in cloud storage triggers additional functionality and decision-making by the ML pipeline. The insight generated by the ML pipeline, based on the captured images in the cloud platform, is sent to the MA which then uses it to execute an operation. MA either triggers TAs or RAs which are responsible for transportation and production skills respectively. The agent interaction with cloud computing platform along with details on cloud service deployment is elaborated in more detail in the experimentation and deployment section.

The algorithm for ML processing used for image detection and classification is Neural Architecture Search (NAS) where a dataset and task (image detection and classification) is provided. This is used to find the design of machine learning model, that performs best among all other models for a given task as the model is trained under the provided dataset. NAS uses search strategy to find best model from all possible models that maximises performance (Fig. 3).

The three constituent of NAS include search space, search strategy and performance estimation. Search space defines the neural architecture selection basis like chain or multi-branch network, micro/macro-search or cell-search [33]. Search strategy and performance estimation employ multiple methods selected on the search space selected previously [33] such as random search, reinforcement learning, and evolutionary algorithms. The model derived from this approach can be used directly for the purpose. Google Cloud Platform (GCP) based its AutoML service on a novel architecture NASNET that uses NAS for image classification. NASNET redesigns the search space so best layer could be found and

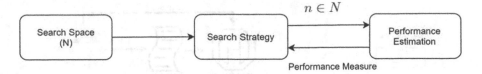

Fig. 3. NAS algorithm for determination of image detection and classification ML model

stacked multiple times in flexible manner for final network. This network was used to perform search strategy on image datasets and best learned architecture was selected for image detection and classification. More detail on the work can be found in the work done by Google Research Team [34].

4   Experimentation and Deployment

The experiment carried out in this work includes the implementation of cloud-based decision-making and the multi-agent-based simulation of the proposed shop floor. The demonstrator used as a basis for this experiment is shown in (Fig. 4) and includes conveyors, three drilling stations, and one camera module. At this point, the Factory I/O environment was used specifically to demonstrate

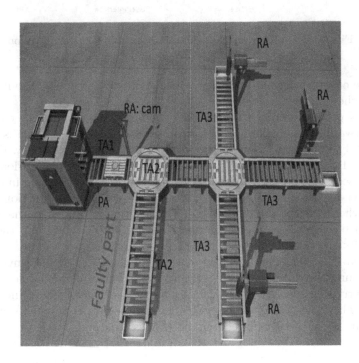

Fig. 4. Shop-floor demonstrator environment in Factory IO

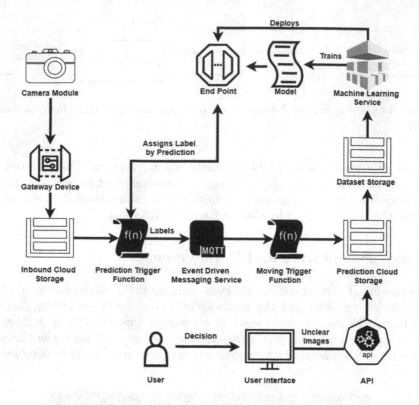

Fig. 5. Cloud based machine learning pipeline for part detection

a use case of a plant layout and to provide an objective vision of the implementation of the proposed framework.

Once a product's order has been launched into the system, the component moves forward through the first conveyor until the camera module is reached. Immediately, it takes a picture of the component and compares it with an ML cloud-based classifier. The part is labelled and routed as per decision. A conveyor is used to direct the component to the rework/reject station in case that the part is defective. In other cases, it looks for the other production resource stations where the part could be routed. This routing is decided on the condition of station busyness. The part is routed to a less busy station and the station executes its function or skill and the process is finalized.

The experimental setup includes services employed in a cloud environment, agent resources, and deployed physical resources. The camera module connected to Raspberry Pi acting as a gateway device to the Cloud-Based Machine Learning Pipeline. The functionality employed by cloud-based services is of visual quality inspection for defect-free production and process routing.

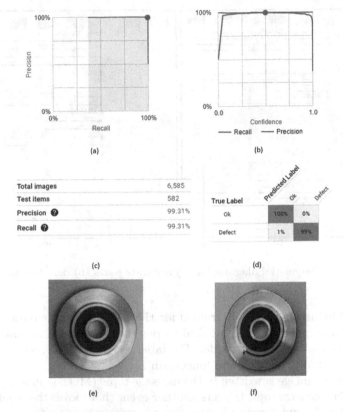

Fig. 6. ML pipeline deployment. (a) Precision vs recall against identified part labels. Precision is measurement of positive label assignment (ratio between the True Positives and all the Positives) and recall is the measure of model correctly identifying true positives. (b) Maximum confidence at Threshold = 0.5. (c) Dataset size (total and test images). (d) Confusion matrix representing true and predicted labels. (e) Accepted (OK) part. (f) Defective Part.

4.1   Cloud-Based Decision Making

Cloud-based machine learning (ML) model is trained on images and deployed for analysis on an end-point (Fig. 6). As more and more classifications take place the model is improved. The classified images are sent to the pipeline for training with every iteration. The cloud-based deployment of quality inspection for mechanical components are used as the basis for agent-based decision-making. The images for classification are taken from a public dataset [35], and are trained to a high level of confidence.

Images ingested from the gateway device obtained by the camera module are stored in the storage housed by the cloud platform. This event of image storage acts as an event trigger that executes a script sending the stored image at the machine learning service endpoint. The endpoint houses the model that is

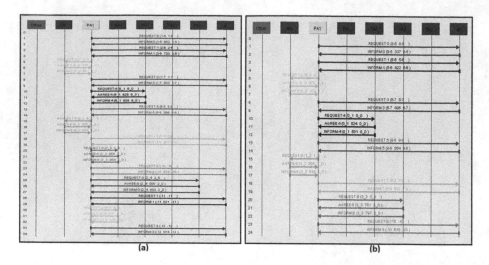

Fig. 7. Sequential diagram for (a) accurate parts (b) defective parts

determined by using NASNET, trained for the task and on the dataset in GCP. At this endpoint, the image is labelled as per the classification obtained by the trained, tested, and validated model. The label assigned to the image falls within the category of 'ok', 'defect', and 'uncertain'.

The labelled image is written to the message topic (MQTT publish/subscribe service). This message topic triggers another event that moves the labelled image to the predicted cloud storage offering separate storage services for the categories. The labelled images are moved into each respective service as per category. The uncertain image requires human intervention. An Application Protocol Interface (API) is incorporated that takes the uncertain image and inquires the accurate (ok) or defective status from the human operator. The image is then classified as per human input (Fig. 5).

4.2   Multi-agent Based Simulation

The agent-based framework presented in previous section is implemented and supported by the cloud-based platform.

Agent programming is implemented with the JADE (Java Agent Development Environment) platform. The agents deployed in JADE use cloud based classification input generated by vision model trained on the dataset, as input leading to further actions as per the proposed framework discussed above. All of the actors in the production environment are controlled by means of agents.

In the current use case, the agent execution and simulation is performed after the deployment of six agents: PA, MA, TA1, TA2, TA3 and RA. TA3 and RA represent the set of stations and their required transportation respectively. To account for similarity in resource skill and identical negotiation steps, TA3 and RA were not deployed individually rather resources 1, 2 and 3 are represented by agent RA and conveyors by the agent TA3. The simulation is performed within two variants, based on cloud based decision process, set by the MA if the part is defective (variant 1) or accurate (ok) (variant 2). The simulation process can be seen in Fig. 7. Figure 7(a) presents the sequential model generated when a part is defective. In this case the TA2 is activated routing the product to a storage place for defective parts. Finally, in Fig. 7(b) the sequential model generated starts a negotiation process with RA followed by TA3 with the aim of performing the respective job.

5   Conclusion and Future Work

The research presents an elaborate framework on the application of cloud and agent technologies on quality control by vision inspection and agent-based control in a production system. The approach developed is suitable to achieve a quality testing-driven production that compliments the 'no-faults-forwards' approach in manufacturing. It reduces the risk of accepting defective parts and rejecting good parts (Type 1 and 2 errors). This approach benefits in reducing costs as well as maintaining quality standards. Future work for this approach involves expanding the Machine Learning models on the cloud, developing inferences from structured data along vision models. This will enable integration with data generated on n shop floor for better control in production applications. The current-use case considers diverting of parts to less busy stations; however, a methodology to define an optimal routing resource has to be developed in future works. The multi-agent system capability will be enhanced to enable routing to stations having different processing capabilities. Deploying the test-driven production approach to multiple physical use-cases will also be a part of future activities.

Currently, the approach is constrained by the size of the data set i.e. a large number of pictures are required by the system to train the model for accurate prediction, which is a limitation of the service. A limitation however is a gap in proper integration of cloud services with agent technology for effective coordination and control. Future works will be looking into different ways the limitation can be overcome while keeping data set size to minimum and developing mechanism for effective service deployment and integration. Other mechanisms for deploying the cloud-based testing control will be implemented and compared with the multi-agent approach. Another limitation observed in the research is related to interoperability, common ontology, semantics, and protocols across the whole production line. Multiple APIs need to be deployed for communication between cloud pipeline, gateway device, agent system, and production system devices. A solution to this problem will be discussed in future works. Finally, future developments will include the creation of the necessary interfaces to link the simulated environment in Factory I/O with JADE and with the cloud based ML infrastructure. This will clearly showcase the advantages of the framework and will be a step ahead towards its implementation in an industrial environment.

Acknowledgement. This work is carried out under DiManD Innovative Training Network (ITN) project funded by the European Union through the Marie Sktodowska-Curie Innovative Training Networks (H2020-MSCA-ITN-2018) under grant agreement number no. 814078.

References

1. Onori, M., Barata, J.: Evolvable production systems: new domains within mecha-tronic production equipment. In: 2010 IEEE International Symposium on Industrial Electronics, pp. 2653–2657. IEEE (2010)
2. Tharumarajah, A.: Comparison of the bionic, fractal and holonic manufacturing system concepts. Int. J. Comput. Integr. Manuf. **9**(3), 217–226 (1996)
3. Van Brussel, H., Wyns, J., Valckenaers, P., Bongaerts, L., Peeters, P.: Reference architecture for holonic manufacturing systems: prosa. Comput. Ind. **37**(3), 255–274 (1998)
4. Bi, Z.M., Lang, S.Y., Shen, W., Wang, L.: Reconfigurable manufacturing systems: the state of the art. Int. J. Prod. Res. **46**(4), 967–992 (2008)
5. Leitão, P., Colombo, A.W., Karnouskos, S.: Industrial automation based on cyber-physical systems technologies: prototype implementations and challenges. Comput. Ind. **81**, 11–25 (2016)
6. Wang, L., Du, Z., Dong, W., Shen, Y., Zhao, G.: Hierarchical human machine interaction learning for a lower extremity augmentation device. Int. J. Soc. Robot. **11**(1), 123–139 (2019)
7. Wu, D., Zhang, Y., Ourak, M., Niu, K., Dankelman, J., Vander Poorten, E.B.: Hysteresis modeling of robotic catheters based on long short-term memory network for improved environment reconstruction. IEEE Robot. Autom. Lett. **6**(2), 2106–2113 (2021)
8. Torayev, A., Schultz, T.: Interactive classification of multi-shell diffusion MRI with features from a dual-branch CNN autoencoder. In: EG Workshop on Visual Computing for Biology and Medicine (2020)
9. Tang, T., Hu, T., Chen, M., Lin, R., Chen, G.: A deep convolutional neural network approach with information fusion for bearing fault diagnosis under different working conditions. In: Proceedings of the Institution of Mechanical Engineers, Part C: Journal of Mechanical Engineering Science, p. 0954406220902181 (2020)
10. Vincent Wang, X., Xu, X.W.: An interoperable solution for cloud manufacturing. Robot. Comput.-Integr. Manuf. **29**(4), 232–247 (2013)
11. Wooldridge, M.: An Introduction to Multiagent Systems. John Wiley & Sons (2009)
12. Bond, A.H., Gasser, L.: Readings in Distributed Artificial Intelligence. Morgan Kaufmann (2014)
13. Botti, V., Omicini, A., Mariani, S., Julian, V.: Multi-agent Systems. MDPI-Multidisciplinary Digital Publishing Institute (2019)
14. Adeyeri, M.K., Mpofu, K., Olukorede, T.A.: Integration of agent technology into manufacturing enterprise: a review and platform for industry 4.0. In: 2015 International Conference on Industrial Engineering and Operations Management (IEOM), pp. 1–10. IEEE (2015)
15. Li, Z., Jiang, X., Yao, S., Li, D.: Research on collaborative control method of manufacturing process based on distributed multi-agent cooperation. In: 2018 11th International Symposium on Computational Intelligence and Design (ISCID), vol. 2, pp. 41–46. IEEE (2018)

16. Li, D., Jiang, X., Wei, X.: Research on manufacturing process control based on multi-agent-system. In: 2018 IEEE 4th Information Technology and Mechatronics Engineering Conference (ITOEC), pp. 1306–1309. IEEE (2018)

17. Răileanu, S., Borangiu, T., Morariu, O.: Multi-agent solution for automated part supply in robotized holonic manufacturing. In: Rodić, A., Borangiu, T. (eds.) RAAD 2016. AISC, vol. 540, pp. 211–218. Springer, Cham (2017). https://doi.org/10.1007/978-3-319-49058-8_23

18. Vatankhah Barenji, A., Vatankhah Barenji, R.: Improving multi-agent manufacturing control system by indirect communication based on ant agents. Proc. Inst. Mech. Eng. Part I J. Syst. Control Eng. **231**(6), 447–458 (2017)

19. Gwiazda, A., Sękala, A., Banaś, W.: Modeling of a production system using the multi-agent approach. In: IOP Conference Series: Materials Science and Engineering, vol. 227, p. 012052. IOP Publishing (2017)

20. Blesing, C., Luensch, D., Stenzel, J., Korth, B.: Concept of a multi-agent based decentralized production system for the automotive industry. In: Demazeau, Y., Davidsson, P., Bajo, J., Vale, Z. (eds.) PAAMS 2017. LNCS (LNAI), vol. 10349, pp. 19–30. Springer, Cham (2017). https://doi.org/10.1007/978-3-319-59930-4_2

21. Büth, L., Broderius, N., Herrmann, C., Thiede, S.: Introducing agent-based simulation of manufacturing systems to industrial discrete-event simulation tools. In: 2017 IEEE 15th International Conference on Industrial Informatics (INDIN), pp. 1141–1146. IEEE (2017)

22. Leitao, P., Karnouskos, S., Ribeiro, L., Lee, J., Strasser, T., Colombo, A.W.: Smart agents in industrial cyber-physical systems. Proc. IEEE **104**(5), 1086–1101 (2016)

23. Barata, J., Camarinha-Matos, L.M.: Coalitions of manufacturing components for shop floor agility-the Cobasa architecture. Int. J. Networking Virtual Organ. **2**(1), 50–77 (2003)

24. Peres, R.S., Rocha, A.D., Leitao, P., Barata, J.: Idarts-towards intelligent data analysis and real-time supervision for industry 4.0. Comput. Ind. **101**, 138–146 (2018)

25. Rocha, A.D., Peres, R.S., Flores, L., Barata, J.: A multiagent based knowledge extraction framework to support plug and produce capabilities in manufacturing monitoring systems. In: 2015 10th International Symposium on Mechatronics and its Applications (ISMA), pp. 1–5. IEEE (2015)

26. Baer, S., Bakakeu, J., Meyes, R., Meisen, T.: Multi-agent reinforcement learning for job shop scheduling in flexible manufacturing systems. In: 2019 Second International Conference on Artificial Intelligence for Industries (AI4I), pp. 22–25. IEEE (2019)

27. Rokhforoz, P., Gjorgiev, B., Sansavini, G., Fink, O.: Multi-agent maintenance scheduling based on the coordination between central operator and decentralized producers in an electricity market. arXiv preprint arXiv:2002.12217 (2020)

28. Xie, X.: A review of recent advances in surface defect detection using texture analysis techniques. ELCVIA: Electronic Letters on Computer Vision and Image Analysis, pp. 1–22 (2008)

29. Neogi, N., Mohanta, D.K., Dutta, P.K.: Review of vision-based steel surface inspection systems. EURASIP J. Image Video Process. **2014**(1), 1–19 (2014). https://doi.org/10.1186/1687-5281-2014-50

30. Pernkopf, F., O'Leary, P.: Visual inspection of machined metallic high-precision surfaces. EURASIP J. Adv. Signal Process. **2002**(7), 1–12 (2002)

31. Wang, J., Ma, Y., Zhang, L., Gao, R.X., Wu, D.: Deep learning for smart manufacturing: methods and applications. J. Manuf. Syst. **48**, 144–156 (2018)

32. Wyns, J.: Reference architecture for holonic manufacture: the key to support evolution and reconfiguration. Unpublished PhD thesis, Katholieke Universiteit Leuven, Leuven (1999)
33. Elsken, T., Metzen, J.H., Hutter, F., et al.: Neural architecture search: a survey. J. Mach. Learn. Res. **20**(55), 1–21 (2019)
34. Zoph, B., Vasudevan, V., Shlens, J., Le, Q.: Automl for large scale image classification and object detection. Google AI Blog **2**, 2017 (2017)
35. Dabhi, R.: casting product image data for quality inspection. In: https://www.kaggle.com/ravirajsinh45/real-life-industrial-dataset-of-casting-product (2020)

A Data-Driven Simulator for Assessing Decision-Making in Soccer

Tiago Mendes-Neves[1,2]([✉]) [iD], João Mendes-Moreira[1,2] [iD],
and Rosaldo J. F. Rossetti[1,3] [iD]

[1] Faculdade de Engenharia, Universidade do Porto, Porto, Portugal
{up201406104,jmoreira,rossetti}@fe.up.pt
[2] LIAAD - INESC TEC, Porto, Portugal
[3] LIACC - Laboratório de Inteligência Artificial e Ciência de Computadores, FEUP,
Porto, Portugal

Abstract. Decision-making is one of the crucial factors in soccer (association football). The current focus is on analyzing data sets rather than posing "what if" questions about the game. We propose simulation-based methods that allow us to answer these questions. To avoid simulating complex human physics and ball interactions, we use data to build machine learning models that form the basis of an event-based soccer simulator. This simulator is compatible with the OpenAI GYM API. We introduce tools that allow us to explore and gather insights about soccer, like (1) calculating the risk/reward ratios for sequences of actions, (2) manually defining playing criteria, and (3) discovering strategies through Reinforcement Learning.

Keywords: Soccer simulation · Simulation · Decision-making · Reinforcement learning

1 Introduction

There are multiple approaches to simulate the game of soccer. However, it is not easy to obtain insights into the actual game from these simulators. Here we propose an alternative approach: use event stream data [4] and deep learning to build the simulator. Using data to build the simulator allows us to obtain a different representation of the game that abstracts from simulating complex physics and other details that are not relevant to analyze the game at a high-level. Having a high-level simulator can provide interesting insights to the users, like soccer analysts.

Data-driven soccer simulators have advantages over current state-of-the-art simulators. The most relevant advantage is that the high level of knowledge required to build a simulator is replaceable with data models. This advantage

This work is financed by National Funds through the Portuguese funding agency, FCT - Fundação para a Ciência e a Tecnologia, within project UIDB/50014/2020.

G. Marreiros et al. (Eds.): EPIA 2021, LNAI 12981, pp. 687–698, 2021.
https://doi.org/10.1007/978-3-030-86230-5_54

shifts the requirement of sufficient knowledge about the system to requiring sufficient data points to build the simulator accurately.

Another advantage of this approach is that it allows us to change the testing environment by altering the data used to build the simulator's model. For example, we can build a simulator that tries to replicate a team's behavior by training the models with data of a specific team. Furthermore, having a simulator allows using Reinforcement Learning (RL) algorithms to discover new patterns in the game.

Soccer is a challenging game to model because human-like physics is hard to simulate. We do not address this problem in this paper. Instead, we abstract from this problem by using high-level event data from soccer games.

Currently, the literature does not address the problem of building a soccer simulator from existing data. Physics-based simulators dominate current approaches, making it challenging to research new strategies or ask "what if" questions. Furthermore, the environments have low flexibility for adaptation, i.e., it is hard and expensive to model a team's behavior in these simulators.

This paper describes an approach to fill this gap by creating a simulator built from data. We describe a new simulator that can simulate the soccer game from a high-level perspective, oriented towards actions. We developed the simulator following the OpenAI GYM API, which facilitates experiments with compatible libraries for RL.

The simulator requires an agent to decide the best action to make according to the current state and then gives feedback in the form of a reward. We present three use cases for the simulator that offer evidence of the proposed framework's utility: comparing playing sequences, comparing playing criterion, and discovering policies using RL.

The main contributions of this work are the following: In Sect. 2 we review the related work, focusing on soccer simulators, use cases for soccer data, and RL. In Sect. 3 we describe the main contribution of the paper, the soccer simulator, presenting the flow diagram, data used, and the resulting models used to produce the simulations. In Sect. 4 we present and discuss the results of three proposed use cases for the simulator. Finally, in Sect. 5 we present our conclusions and future direction.

2   Related Work

Solutions for simulating soccer games have been available since *NASL Soccer* was launched in 1979 by *Intellivision*. In fact, soccer is widely popular as a video game. Recently, this genre is represented by the *FIFA*[1], *PES*[2] and *Football Manager*[3] franchises. Video games have become very realistic from the graphics point of view. However, this has come at the price of complexity. Moreover, behavioral realism is not adequate since entertainment is the main purpose of

---

[1] ea.com/games/fifa.

[2] konami.com/wepes.

[3] footballmanager.com.

these games, with business decisions affecting how the game is designed. This lack of focus on realism leads to problems in terms of reliability.

There are alternative solutions to video games. Robotic soccer simulation has a broad number of solutions available. RoboCup [16] has competitive leagues focused on simulation in both 2D and 3D, and there is a large community developing strategies for these simulators [1]. Still, robotic soccer does not represent the actual soccer game. Even with the field rapidly advancing, we are still decades away from robotic soccer replicating human soccer to a high-fidelity level.

Google Research Football [11] currently represents the state-of-the-art of soccer simulation. The authors present a simulator based on a physics engine used in competitions sponsored by soccer teams [9]. Due to a focus on RL tasks, this simulator represents an improvement over video game simulators in computational performance. The same problem of robotic soccer simulators is still present. This simulator cannot correctly model human body behavior and interaction with the ball, introducing errors in the simulation.

We believe that our proposal will be able to introduce novel ways to analyze the game of soccer. Currently, soccer data analytics has been experiencing a very steep growth. Data tracking systems such as GPS, optical tracking, and event annotation are being applied at the club level, increasing the quantity and quality of data available in the field.

Current use cases for soccer data focus on evaluating player performance. For example, Plus-Minus rating [10] that represent the weighted sum of the contributions of playings to goals scored/conceded in a game, and VAEP [4] that evaluates player actions by calculating the probability of an action leading to a goal in the short term.

From tactical analysis [26] to injury forecast [19], there are many use cases for soccer data. Some of these works are made in partnership with soccer teams, proving that this is a research field with high applicability.

In one of the use cases presented for our simulator, we explore RL algorithms to find policies to help decision-making in soccer. RL aims to train an agent in an environment to maximize a reward function, allowing for a model that can learn from experience without previous information about the goal or the environment.

RL is central to some of the most celebrated recent successes in machine learning. Examples of this success are the high-human ability achieved in computer games such as StarCraft II [24,25], Dota 2 [3] where they have beaten current world champions, and the Atari game library [13,20]. Outside of computer games, we have Chess, Shogi [13,22] and Go [23], with wins over world champions, and Poker [8].

One of the most common comments from the players that faced these agents is that they are innovative. These agents can learn and develop unique and previously unseen strategies to play the games [17]. Novel strategies are valuable in many fields, including soccer. If correctly implemented, these strategies can give an edge to the team, becoming an advantage on the pitch.

In this work, we explore several RL algorithms: Advantage Actor-Critic (A2C) [15], Deep Deterministic Policy Gradient (DDPG) [12], Proximal Policy

Optimization (PPO) [21], Soft Actor-Critic (SAC) [7], and Twin Delayed Deep Deterministic Policy Gradient (TD3) [6]. The main reason for testing these algorithms was that they could handle continuous state and action spaces, which is a requirement of our simulator.

The DDPG algorithm produced the best results. DDPG is built on the foundational work of previous successes in the RL world by DeepMind. This algorithm aims to provide Deep Q Networks' [14] learning environment and extend it to continuous observation and action spaces using a target policy network.

Deep Q Networks aims to approximate the action-value table, known as Q values, using a non-linear approximation. The preferred approximation technique is Deep Learning. It would be possible to use Deep Q Networks in our approach if we discretized the observation and action space. However, due to the curse of dimensionality, this approach would be time-consuming. Using an Actor-Critic approach, DDPG avoids the dimensionality problem.

3   Simulator

The simulator is available in *Python*. All the code necessary to reproduce this work is publicly available[4], alongside the code used in the use cases presented in Sect. 4.

Figure 1 shows the simulator's flow diagram. The simulator has a state that indicates the ball's current coordinates *(X, Y)*. The player chooses an action with a probability of success that depends on the current state and player intention. If the action is successful, the simulator gets into a new state. If it fails, the sequence ends. The shot action always ends the sequence and returns a reward equivalent to the probability of scoring from the current state.

Using the probability of scoring might not be the best approach to find the required solutions. For example, there are situations where it is important to minimize the chances of conceding a goal. While this work does not address it, the framework allows the user to set up their reward function as he wants.

3.1   Data

We used event data from the 2016/17 season to the 2018/19 season from the Portuguese First Division. Event data is composed of the time and location of predefined events, like passes and shots, and describes an action in detail [4]. The dataset contains 15 719 shots and 681 989 passes.

Decroos [4] defined the SPADL language for describing player actions. The goal was to standardize soccer event data from multiple providers. We used this framework to prepare our data for the simulator. Our feature set contains the following features: *type of event, player, team, success, (x, y, endX, endY)* coordinates, and *isGoal*. The only difference compared to the SPADL language is that the *BodyPart* attribute was not available on our data set.

---

[4] github.com/nvsclub/SoccerActionsSim.

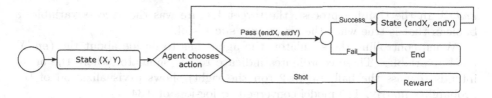

Fig. 1. Diagram showing the flow of the simulator. From a state, we can perform an action that will change our current state. In case the agent chooses the shot action, the sequence ends, and the agent receives a reward equivalent to the probability of scoring from the current state. If the sequence ends with a failed pass, the agent receives no reward.

We were unable to address a limitation in data. For passes, we need to assume that end coordinates represent the player's intention. This assumption is reasonable for successful passes, but for blocked passes, the *(endX, endY)* coordinates will represent the position where the pass was blocked, rather than player intention. This factor will introduce some errors in our simulations.

3.2 Models

To build the models, we used the MLPClassifier, from the scikit-learn Python package. We required fast prediction times, and Deep Learning algorithms allowed predictions to be quick without losing quality in the model. To define the hyperparameters, we used Optuna TPE optimizer [2]. Optuna helps us find which hyperparameter combination minimized the error of our models.

The goal of the models is to learn a representation of the underlying data. Therefore, after finding the optimal parameters on Optuna using a 50–50% train-test dataset, we use the whole dataset in the training procedure.

To adapt the environment for simulating a specific team, the user needs to change the data used to train the models, increasing the team's patterns in data. We do not want the environment to have models that generalize to all teams. Therefore we incentive a certain level of memorization on the models, i.e., models with larger architectures than what is required.

Shots. The concept of expected goals [18] inspires the model that simulates shots. The success of a shot is dependent on the state of the agent *(x, y)*. This approach is used to build other analytic frameworks in soccer such as Decroos [4], and Fernández [5]. To train the network, we used the *isGoal* feature as the target variable. *isGoal* is a boolean variable that is true when the shot leads to a goal. Figure 2 (on the left) shows a visualization of the probability matrix. The model converged to log-loss of 0.27.

Passes. To simulate passes, we followed a similar approach. The probability of success is dependent on current coordinates *(x, y)* and target coordinates *(endX,* *endY*). In the training process, the target feature was the *success* variable, a boolean that is true when the action was successful.

When controlling the simulator, the agent has to decide about the (*endX, endY*) variables. These coordinates indicate to the simulator where the agent intends to pass the ball. Figure 2 (on the right) shows a visualization of the probability matrix. The model converged to log-loss of 0.34.

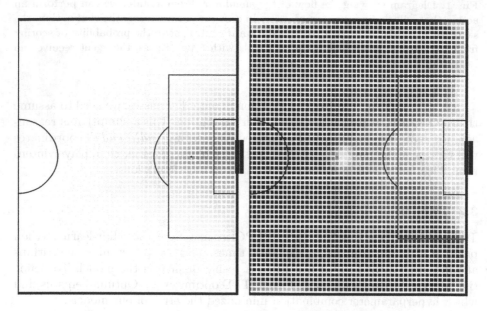

Fig. 2. On the left: a probability matrix given by the shot model for every position in the opposition's half. Darker spots indicate higher probabilities of scoring. On the right: a probability matrix given by the passing model. Predicts the success of passes with origin in the orange dot. (Color figure online)

4   Results

To demonstrate the capabilities of our simulator, we designed three use cases. First, we will present the methodology to calculate and visualize the likelihood of scoring from a specific play sequence. In this use case, we show that it is possible to compare different sequences of play among themselves to assess the efficacy of that sequence of actions.

The second use case illustrates the simulator's usage alongside action maps to assess the best actions in certain parts of the field, referred to as the playing criterion. For this, we divide the soccer field into 38 parts: first, we divide the defensive half into 12 equal-sized squares, and then we divide the rest of the pitch into areas that become smaller when closer to the opponent's goal to capture more detail in the most relevant areas. For each of these parts, we set an action. Then, we systematically evaluate this playing criterion and return information to the user. The information returned allows the user to improve the action map iteratively.

Finally, we take advantage of implementing the simulator according to the OpenAI GYM API to run RL algorithms in our simulator. We will run a set of experiments using the Stable-Baselines3 library, using the algorithms that can handle continuous state and action spaces, such as A2C, DDPG, PPO, SAC, and TD3. The goal is to find an automated way of building the playing criterion on the simulator.

4.1   Simulating Sequences of Play

The first use case that we present is the simulation of sequences of play. With this approach, we can simulate and compare different sequences of play and their outcomes. A sequence of play is a set of actions executed sequentially. By changing this set of actions, we will obtain different sequences.

Figure 3 shows an example of how to compare sequences. We calculate the outcome of three sequences. We will consider the first sequence as the baseline sequence. Then we produce two other suggestions of actions.

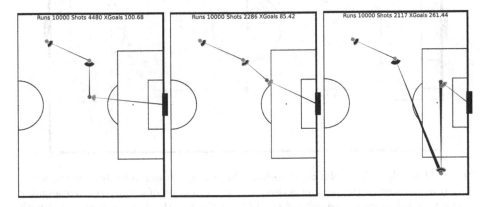

Fig. 3. The outcome of three play sequences. Comparing the first sequence with the others, we can find that the third option was the one that leads to more goals overall. Note that we obtained these results with the simulator trained with data from all teams. For specific teams, the results seen in this figure can be substantially different.

The first suggestion is to move the last pass closer to the goal, increasing the probability of scoring from the shot. However, this proposal does not increase the sequence's probability of scoring since the pass became riskier than the previous. We were able to find that an action that looked better did not result in a better outcome since it reduced the number of expected goals in 10 000 iterations from 100 to 85.

A second proposal is to move the ball wide for a cross. This approach has a better risk-reward ratio than the original sequence, scoring 261 goals in 10 000 iterations, more than doubling the baseline. With this information, we can conclude that this was the best sequence to use.

This framework allows us to judge whether an action that happened was the best option available. The reasoning behind this example that we presented applies to many other scenarios.

4.2   Building Playing Criterion

Figure 4 presents a framework that allows the user to define a playing criterion and obtain numerical feedback for the decisions made. For each marked area, the user chooses an action and, in the case of a pass, the length and direction.

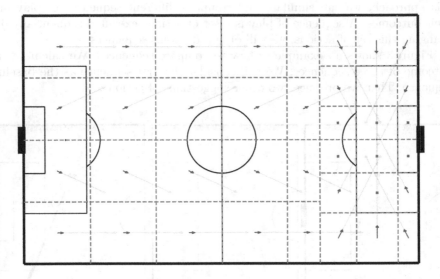

Fig. 4. Manually defined playing criterion. The orange arrows indicate that the action chosen in that area is the passing action, with the direction of the arrow corresponding to the pass's direction. Red arrows are 1/10 of the length of the actual pass length, represented in orange. Blue squares represent areas where the chosen option is to have a shot at the goal. This criterion achieves a reward of 0.0149 (for comparison: the average of 20 randomized criteria is 0.0084). (Color figure online)

This framework can quickly iterate through different criteria and test which types of actions improve or degrade the scoring probability. For example, if we replace a shot with a pass, what is the gain obtained in 10 000 simulations?

This framework allows the user to implement optimization algorithms, e.g., Genetic Algorithms, to optimize the actions. We hope to address this in future work.

4.3 Reinforcement Learning

Our approach to automatically optimize the actions taken in the simulator was to use RL. For this, we used the Stable-Baselines3 Python package. Since we used the OpenAI GYM API, it is easy to use RL libraries in our simulator.

We tested the algorithms compatible with continuous state and action spaces, namely A2C, DDPG, PPO, SAC, and TD3. We present the results of the tests for all algorithms using the default parameters from the library. For the DDPG and TD3 algorithms, we tested two types of action noise (Ornstein Uhlenbeck and Normal noise). Furthermore, since the DDPG presented a higher ceiling in preliminary tests, we also present the larger network results for both the critic and actor networks. Table 1 shows the results obtained.

Table 1. Results from the RL algorithms on the developed simulator. OU - Ornstein Uhlenbeck.

Algorithm	Parameters	Avg score	Max score
A2C	Default	0.0158	0.0169
DDPG	Default + OU noise ($\sigma = 0.3$)	0.0160	0.0272
	HiddenLayers = [400, 300] + OU noise ($\sigma = 0.3$)	0.0124	0.0318
	Default + Normal noise ($\sigma = 0.3$)	0.0108	0.0158
PPO	Default	0.0134	0.0140
SAC	Default	0.0068	0.0079
TD3	Default + OU noise ($\sigma = 0.3$)	0.0115	0.0164
	Default + Normal noise ($\sigma = 0.3$)	0.0126	0.0167

The different action noise types did not show any relevant results. Therefore we opted to maintain the Ornstein Uhlenbeck noise recommended by the authors [12]. In this problem, we are interested in obtaining the highest score possible. Although inconsistent, the DDPG algorithm presents the highest ceiling in terms of performance. Furthermore, the other algorithms have difficulties in learning a better policy than simply shooting in every position. Figure 5 presents the results obtained by running the DDPG algorithm with increased network size (400, 300) and a larger amount of timesteps (100k). The score obtained was 0.0318.

The DDPG algorithm found an interesting policy: it moves the ball towards the right side from the attacking point of view and then crosses it towards the center. In Fig. 5 we can observe a big orange cluster in the zone of the field where the agent crosses from, indicating that RL was able to find an efficient strategy in this particular environment setup.

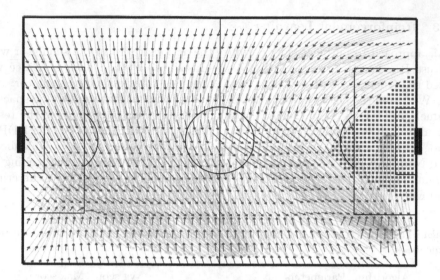

Fig. 5. Visualization of the decision making of the DDPG algorithm. The red arrows indicates that the action chosen specific coordinate is the passing action, with the direction indicating where the pass is directed to. Red arrows are 1/10 of the length of the actual pass length, represented in orange. Blue squares represent areas where the best option is to have a shot at goal. (Color figure online)

5   Conclusion

We built a soccer simulator that models the game from a different perspective. This event-driven approach enabled multiple use cases that we presented in this paper. The work presented in this paper indicates that data-driven soccer simulators can enable new ways of analyzing the game.

The use cases presented demonstrate that we can gather insights from the simulator. In the first use case, we can evaluate how a change an action affects the scenario's outcome, enabling us to improve decision making. The second use case shows how we can use the simulator to test high-level strategies. The last use case automated the discovery of these high-level strategies using RL. The strategy found by the DDPG algorithm provided a clear insight: the agent tried to explore the strategy of directing the ball for a cross from the right side.

We believe that the potential benefits from using this simulator are very relevant for improving decision-making in soccer.

5.1   Future Work

There are two main focuses for further developing this simulator. The first is to use transfer learning or data sampling techniques to adapt the simulator to specific teams' playstyles. This feature will allow us to find insights targeted towards a specific team rather than general policies. The second focus will be to expand the accuracy of the models used to build the simulator by adding positional data. We plan to launch new versions of this simulator in the future.

References

1. Abreu, M., Rossetti, R.J.F., Reis, L.P.: XSS: a soccer server extension for automated learning of high-level robotic soccer strategies. In: 2019 IEEE International Conference on Autonomous Robot Systems and Competitions (ICARSC) (2019). https://doi.org/10.1109/ICARSC.2019.8733635
2. Akiba, T., Sano, S., Yanase, T., Ohta, T., Koyama, M.: Optuna: a next-generation hyperparameter optimization framework. In: Proceedings of the 25th ACM SIGKDD International Conference on Knowledge Discovery & Data Mining. Association for Computing Machinery, New York (2019). https://doi.org/10.1145/3292500.3330701
3. Berner, C., et al.: Dota 2 with large scale deep reinforcement learning. In: arXiv (2019)
4. Decroos, T., Bransen, L., Van Haaren, J., Davis, J.: Actions speak louder than goals: valuing player actions in soccer. In: Proceedings of the 25th ACM SIGKDD International Conference on Knowledge Discovery & Data Mining. Association for Computing Machinery, New York (2019). https://doi.org/10.1145/3292500.3330758
5. Fernández, J., Bornn, L., Cervone, D.: A framework for the fine-grained evaluation of the instantaneous expected value of soccer possessions. Machine Learning (2021)
6. Fujimoto, S., van Hoof, H., Meger, D.: Addressing function approximation error in actor-critic methods. In: Dy, J., Krause, A. (eds.) Proceedings of the 35th International Conference on Machine Learning. Proceedings of Machine Learning Research, 10–15 Jul 2018, vol. 80, pp. 1587–1596. PMLR (2018)
7. Haarnoja, T., Zhou, A., Abbeel, P., Levine, S.: Soft actor-critic: off-policy maximum entropy deep reinforcement learning with a stochastic actor. In: International Conference on Machine Learning (ICML) (2018)
8. Heinrich, J., Silver, D.: Deep reinforcement learning from self-play in imperfect-information games. In: arXiv (2016)
9. Kaggle: Google research football with Manchester City f.c. https://www.kaggle.com/c/google-football/overview
10. Kharrat, T., McHale, I.G., Peña, J.L.: Plus–minus player ratings for soccer. Eur. J. Oper. Res. **283**(2), 726–736 (2020). https://doi.org/10.1016/j.ejor.2019.11.026
11. Kurach, K., et al.: Google research football: a novel reinforcement learning environment (2020)
12. Lillicrap, T.P., et al.: Continuous control with deep reinforcement learning. arXiv (2019)
13. Mnih, V., Kavukcuoglu, K., Silver, D.: Human-level control through deep reinforcement learning. Nature (2015). https://doi.org/10.1038/nature14236
14. Mnih, V., et al.: Playing atari with deep reinforcement learning. arXiv (2013)
15. Mnih, V., et al.: Asynchronous methods for deep reinforcement learning. In: Balcan, M.F., Weinberger, K.Q. (eds.) Proceedings of the 33rd International Conference on Machine Learning. Proceedings of Machine Learning Research, vol. 48, pp. 1928–1937. PMLR, New York (2016). http://proceedings.mlr.press/v48/mniha16.html
16. Noda, I., Suzuki, S., Matsubara, H., Asada, M., Kitano, H.: Robocup-97: the first robot world cup soccer games and conferences. AI Mag. **19**(3), 49 (1998)

17. OpenAI: Openai five. openai.com/projects/five/ Accessed 6 Jan 2021
18. Pollard, R., Ensum, J., Taylor, S.: Estimating the probability of a shot resulting in a goal: the effects of distance, angle and space. Int. J. Soccer Sci. **2**, 50–55 (2004)
19. Rossi, A., Pappalardo, L., Cintia, P., Iaia, F.M., Fernàndez, J., Medina, D.: Effective injury forecasting in soccer with GPS training data and machine learning. PLOS ONE **13**(7), 1–15 (2018). https://doi.org/10.1371/journal.pone.0201264
20. Schrittwieser, J., et al.: Mastering atari, go, chess and shogi by planning with a learned model. In: arXiv (2016)
21. Schulman, J., Wolski, F., Dhariwal, P., Radford, A., Klimov, O.: Proximal policy optimization algorithms. CoRR http://arxiv.org/abs/1707.06347 (2017)
22. Silver, D., Hubert, T., Schrittwieser, J.: Mastering chess and shogi by self-play with a general reinforcement learning algorithm. In: Nature (2017)
23. Silver, D., Schrittwieser, J., Simonyan, K.: Mastering the game of go without human knowledge. Nature (2017). https://doi.org/10.1038/nature24270
24. Vinyals, O., et al.: Starcraft ii: A new challenge for reinforcement learning. In: arXiv (2017)
25. Vinyals, O., Babuschkin, I., Czarnecki, W.: Grandmaster level in starcraft ii using multi-agent reinforcement learning. Nature (2019). https://doi.org/10.1038/s41586-019-1724-z
26. Warnakulasuriya, T., Wei, X., Fookes, C., Sridharan, S., Lucey, P.: Discovering methods of scoring in soccer using tracking data. KDD (2015). https://doi.org/10.1038/s41586-019-1724-z

Text Mining and Applications

CyberPolice: Classification of Cyber Sexual Harassment

Priyam Basu[✉], Tiasa Singha Roy, Soham Tiwari, and Saksham Mehta

Manipal Institute of Technology, Manipal, India
{priyam.basu1,tiasa.roy,soham.tiwari,saksham.mehta1}@learner.manipal.edu

Abstract. Online sexual harassment is defined as unwanted sexual conduct on any digital platform and it is recognised as a form of sexual violence which can make a person feel threatened, exploited, coerced, humiliated, upset, sexualised or discriminated against. With our work we contend that such content can be leveraged to create models that could automatically detect such malicious online behaviour and thereby, ban such users from posting such content in the future, without having to wait for the other users to report them and thereby, create a safe space on social media. A major attribute of our proposed model is that it focuses on how sexual harassment can be hard to classify on social media. These spaces, unlike a formal environment, have no rigid set of rules or code of conduct to adhere to and therefore it can be very difficult to draw the line between a joke and a more malicious comment. To be able to discern the differences between such analogous statements we must have a model which can read and understand the context clues to better classify. In our paper we have worked with state-of-the-art Machine Learning and Deep Learning models and conducted extensive comparison to find the most effective model to better realise this vision of fair space by achieving the most accurate predictions.

Keywords: Machine learning · Deep learning · Sentiment analysis · Natural language processing · Neural networks · Sequential models · Transformers · Classification

1 Introduction

Cyber sexual harassment (CSH) has been characterised by analysts as a range of sexually aggressive or harassing images or texts conveyed via digital media [11]. CSH occurs in high proportions particularly among the younger generation [19]. Even though face-to-face sexual harassment research and account is ever expanding, very limited research has been conducted sexual harassment in a cyber context. As a result of this, much of what is known about Internet-based sexual harassment comes from research conducted on face-to-face sexual harassment, as well as other related Internet behavior on social media [22]. Global estimates have revealed that about 77% of women worldwide have experienced verbal sexual harassment. About 41% of those women have said that they were sexually

© Springer Nature Switzerland AG 2021
G. Marreiros et al. (Eds.): EPIA 2021, LNAI 12981, pp. 701–714, 2021.
https://doi.org/10.1007/978-3-030-86230-5_55

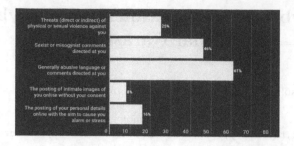

Fig. 1. Toxicity on Twitter

harassed online, receiving unsolicited graphic images, messages and comments, irrespective of any particular social media [8]. As of January 2020, the global net usage of social media rate stands at 49% (which means about 3.5 billion individuals) [26]. The percentage of adults using social media in the USA itself has increased from 5% in 2005 to 79% in 2019 [18]. About 21% of women use Twitter and 75% of women use Facebook alone. Hence, it is very important to make social media a safe space for interaction, free from predators and at the same time, giving people the liberty they deserve. Germany has created a bill which penalizes social networks that do not eliminate offensive content. However, in this matter, there is a lot of gray area to work around as there are many ways to sexually harass others on social media. Our work particularly focuses on this particular gray area and towards a more accurate system that can understand context well to allow both free and open speech and provide a safe platform to do so. An extensive comparison of Machine Learning and Deep Learning models was conducted for the specified task. The dataset worked on was curated particularly to help us delve into the context of the collected tweets. All the tweets scraped contained profanity and were then annotated based on their content into sexually harassing and otherwise. Multiple ML classifiers like Support Vector Machines, XGBoost, Random Forests etc. were implemented but did not seem to give promising results as they are unidirectional models and for the purpose of this task are unable to extract the contextual meaning. We then implemented some unidirectional (for benchmark comparison) and bidirectional deep learning models like Recurrent Neural Network (RNN)-based and Convolutional Neural Network (CNN)-based models. Finally, the best results were shown by the Transformer model BERT, with a few tweaks to its architecture, as it captured the long term dependencies and thereby, got a better understanding of the context [4].

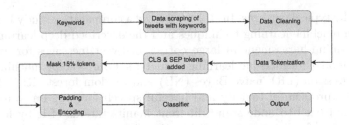

Fig. 2. Pipeline

2   Related Work

Natural language processing (NLP) fields like Sentiment Analysis can be used to make inferences about negative public sentiment based on online behaviour on different social media like Twitter, Facebook, etc. as these contain texts depicting typical moods, emotions and feelings. With the whole world having access to the internet and using it on a regular basis, acts of deviance are likely to occur at increasing rates. This along with the opportunity of remaining anonymous makes it effective to spread hateful or offensive content. One such kind of deviance is Hate Speech. A significant amount of work has already been done in Hate Speech prediction. The importance of detecting and moderating hate speech is evident from the strong connection between hate speech and actual crimes. The researchers in [13] have worked on the detection of hate speech from the tweets for sentiment analysis where they have used two different types of data to detect hate speech in machine learning and deep learning using Recurrent Neural Networks (RNNs). The authors tried to extract hate speech from tweets to find the best method to improve accuracy of multiple machine learning and deep learning methods. The paper [7] performed a systematic review of the state-of-the-art in toxic comment classification using machine learning methods. The author uses a Bag-of-words and Tf-IDF feature engineering techniques on lemmatized input text, along with Support Vector Machine and Decision Tree classifiers. For the task of classification, the Toxic Comment Classification dataset [1] is used which contains multiple classes namely - obscenity, threats, insults and identity-based hatred. The paper [21] proposed a deep convolutional neural network (DCNN) framework to improve the hate speech post detection on Twitter. The proposed DCNN model utilises the tweet text with GloVe embedding vector to capture the tweets' semantics with the help of convolution operation and achieved the precision, recall and F1-score value as 0.97, 0.88, 0.92 respectively for the best case.

Another deviant act is cyber-sexual harassment which is what we are trying to focus on this paper. Cyber-sexual harassment is any unwanted sexual conduct on any digital platform and is recognised as a form of sexual violence. The researchers in this paper [5] have proposed a pattern-based approach combined with POS tagging and text normalisation, to identify Online Harassment which is based on the detection of profane words and their links to recognized persons expressed by typical patterns. In [16] conducted a comparative study between the traditional machine learning techniques and the described deep learning models to detect online harassment in large corpus of tweet messages for which they used four models of machine learning namely: support vector machine (SVM), logistic regression (LR), naive Bayes (NB) and random forest (RF). [23] threw light on the problem of toxicity and hateful speech focusing on women as the audience and tried to understand different manifestations of it by focusing on different forms of online harassment, identify different categories of it and detect it by using different types of machine learning, deep learning, and natural language processing techniques. The authors specifically use RNNs, CNNs and word vector representations for the classification step. [6] addressed the challenge of harassment detection on Twitter posts as well as the identification of a harassment category. For a given post, they have used the transformer architecture to encode each baseline output exploiting relationships between baselines and posts. Similar work can also be found in the papers [25] and [9].

3   Dataset

Although there has been a lot of work of done before on online harassment in general, not a lot has been done on sexual harassment in specific. Privacy concerns and company policies force organisations to take down offensive content from their social media platforms. Therefore, motivated by the necessity of such data and the goal of this paper, a dataset was created by us. We propose a methodology where tweets containing keywords of abusive or harassing in nature are crawled and accordingly labelled depending on the nature of the tweet. The reason for this is that most of the times, online harassment behaviour comprises of derogatory and abusive language but, at the same time, even non-harassing statements can contain profanity like in the case of a joke, an insult etc. In this annotation process, sexual harassment was defined as unwanted sexual conduct involving the use of explicit or implicit sexual overtones causing the victim to feel threatened, exploited, coerced, humiliated, upset, sexualised or discriminated against.

3.1   Data Scraping

First, we found an open sourced harassment dataset corpus [17] on Github which contained 408 profane words which could be used in the contexts of harassment, offence or joke. Next we utilised python libraries like Tweepy to scrape those tweets from Twitter which contained at least one word from the list of offensive keywords. Twitter is an American microblogging and social networking service on which users post and interact with messages known as tweets. Registered users can post, like, and retweet tweets, but unregistered users can only read them. Violence and abuse against women on Twitter includes a variety of experiences such as direct or indirect threats of physical or sexual violence, abuse targeting one or more aspects of a woman's identity (e.g., racism, transphobia, etc.,), targeted harassment, privacy violations such as doxing – i.e. uploading private identifying information publicly with the aim to cause alarm or distress, and the sharing of sexual or intimate images of a woman without her consent.

In the list of 408 words, there were many uncommon and futile words which were removed from the list and the final shortlist consisted of 93 keywords, which were judged to be the most commonly used words. The keywords that were removed absurd terms that are not very popularly used and thus, very limited tweets can be scraped for them. Some of the keywords that were used were *balls, suck, aroused, slut* etc. Different numbers of tweets were scraped for each keyword depending on the importance of the word, based on usage frequency in current social scenario, for deciding which, discretion was used. The final dataset that we acquired had 3604 tweets based on the 93 shortlisted keywords. Table 1 depicts the form in which the raw tweets were scraped.

Table 1. Table containing scraped tweets

Tweet
@electricwit I do not like being called a whore
@TheOXGod Something in your blouse got me feeling so aroused, what you about!
@cuntasschica Long as you don't cheat you don't get beat
@Macheadlyricism suck my dick before i slap you wid it
@XlChyno @MastaPraise @DannyWalta No offense but Man your argument is so basic.
@JaqubAjmal I dunno what makes me think that, but you seem a aroused and excited

3.2 Data Cleaning and Data Labelling

The texts that were extracted from the tweets contained the original text (including emojis, numbers etc.) as well as the link to the original tweet and in some cases, link to an attached Youtube video. emojis, numbers etc.) as well as the link to the original tweet. For the task of this paper, all the external links were removed along with '@' tags. Apart from these, in case of retweets (re-posted content), the 'RT' tags (implying retweet) were also removed. Emojis were not removed as in many cases, they contained contextual meaning pertaining to the tweet. Special characters were not removed either as they are popularly used as non-graphic emoticons, thereby building on to the contextual meaning of the text. After having cleaned all the tweets, the dataset was manually annotated by the authors into two classes. Tweets that were of sexually harassing in nature we labelled as '1' and the rest were labelled as '0'. Each tweet was either sexually harassing or otherwise(could be profane, a joke etc.). The final annotated dataset is resembled by Table 2. Some of the rules followed for annotation are:

1. Text not implying sexual harassment with or without profanity is labelled as 0.
2. Text implying sexual harassment with or without profanity is labelled as 1.
3. Text implying threat but in a non-sexually harassing way is labelled as 0.
4. Text implying threat but in a sexually harassing way is labelled as 1.
5. Text implying a joke but in a non-sexually harassing way is labelled as 0.
6. Text implying a joke but in a sexually harassing way is labelled as 1.

Table 2. Final data table

Tweet	Label
I do not like being called a whore	0
Something in your blouse got me feeling so aroused, what you about!	1
Long as you don't cheat you don't get beat	0
Suck my dick before i slap you wid it	1
No offense but Man your argument is so basic	0
I dunno what makes me think that, but you seem a aroused and excited	1

In the final labelled dataset containing the cleaned tweets, about 45.26% of the tweets were labelled as 0 (i.e. not sexually harassing), and 54.74% of the tweets were labelled as 1 (i.e. sexually harassing). Thus, the dataset was quite well balanced and hence, did not cause any imbalance borne overfitting issues. For further analysis, the most frequently used words in the sexually harassing tweets and the non sexually harassing tweets were found..

4   Model Architectures

4.1   ML Classifiers

Initially, some elementary machine learning classifiers were implemented [15]. First the data was stemmed using Porter Stemmer to remove the common morphological and inflexional endings from the input tokens and then the data was vectorized using Tf-Idf Vectorizer technique with max_features equal to 5000 as it is easy to compute and it enabled picking of most descriptive terms in a document. The data was then passed through various different ML models like Linear Support Vector (SVM) Classifier, Gaussian Naïve Bayes, Logistic Regression, Random Forest Classifier, Gradient Boosting Classifier, K-Nearest Neighbor (KNN) Classifier, AdaBoost Classifier, Multi Layer Perceptron (MLP) Classifier and Stochastic Gradient Classifier.

4.2   CNN Model

Next, the model that was implemented is a simple CNN [2] architecture based model. GloVe 200d was used for obtaining vector representations of words in the tokenized input text. The first layer is an embedding layer which turns positive integers (indexes) into dense vectors of fixed size. It is then followed by a Convolution Layer of 128 neurons and a Global Max Pooling Layer. The pooled outputs from here are then passed into a Dropout Layer for regularization, to prevent overfitting, followed by two dense layers, the first having a RELU activation and the second having the final Sigmoid classification function.

4.3   LSTM Model

Long Short Term Memory (LSTM) [24] networks are a special kind of RNN, capable of learning long-term dependencies, even though computing the tokens in a serial manner. The first layer isan embedding layer with a maximum word limit of 1000, followed by an LSTM layer of 64 neurons. The third layer is a fully connected Dense layer of 256 neurons, followed by a RELU activation layer. The next layer is the usual Dropout layer to prevent overfitting. The final layer is an output Dense layer having 1 neuron, followed by Sigmoid Activation layer for final classification.

4.4   BiLSTM Model

Bidirectional Long Short-Term Memory (BiLSTM) [27] processes data in two directions since it works with two hidden layers and hence is shown to give better contextual results than a generic LSTM model. At first, the text was tokenized. The tokens were then stemmed, using Lancaster Stemmer and lemmatized using WordNet Lemmatizer. This preprocessed text was then passed into the model. The first layer is an embedding layer which turns positive integers (indexes) into dense vectors of fixed size. It is followed by a Bidirectional LSTM layer of 64 neurons followed by a dropout layer of the same dimensions for regularization to prevent overfitting. The same was again repeated two more times. The penultimate layer was a Dense layer of 64 neurons having a RELU activation function followed by a final Dense layer of 2 neurons having a sigmoid activation function for classification.

4.5   CNN-BiLSTM Model

The fifth model that was implemented is a simple CNN-BiLSTM [20] based model. The first layer is the embedding layer. It is then followed by a Convolution Layer of 32 neurons and a Max Pooling Layer with pool size equal to 2 which downsamples the input representation. The pooled outputs from here are then passed into aDropout Layer for regularization, to prevent overfitting. It is then followed by Bi-LSTM layer of 128 neurons after which the output from this layer is flattened. The outputs from here are then passed into a Dense layer having a RELU activation followed by a Dropout layer and then finally into a Dense layer having the final Sigmoid classification function.

4.6   ULMFiT Model

Universal Language Model Fine-tuning for Text Classification (ULMFiT) [12] successfully utilises transfer learning for any NLP task in order to reduce training times and achieve great results. It makes use of several novel techniques to achieves good results like discriminative fine-tuning and a different learning rate was used for each layer while fine tuning during backpropagation. It also uses Slanted triangular learning rates, i.e., first linearly increasing the learning rate and then linearly decreasing it to enable the model to converse quickly to a suitable parameter space and the fine tuning it slowly. Another factor is its gradual unfreezing, i.e., instead of fine tuning all the layers of the model at once during backpropagation, it entails unfreezing the layers of the model one by one after each epoch, starting from the last epoch. Fine tuning all layers at once could result in poor performance, by forgetting the learned weights. This method involves fine-tuning a pre-trained language model (LM), trained on the Wikitext 103 dataset, to a new dataset in such a manner that it does not forget what it previously learned. After fine tuning the language model, we need to prepare the data to then train the weights of the classification model, using the fine-tuned language model while training. After fine tuning the classification model, ULMFiT can then be used to make predictions on input data

4.7   BERT Model

The final model that was implemented was a Transformer based Bidirectional Encoder Representations from Transformers (BERT) [10] model because transformers use self-attention mechanism and process the entire input data at once instead of as a sequence to capture long term dependencies for obtaining contextual meaning. BERT tokenizes words into sub-words (using WordPiece) and those are then given as input to the model. It masks 15% of the input tokens for the model to detect the masked word. It also uses positional embeddings to replace recurrence. A pretrained bert base uncased model was used. The input text was passed through the BERT tokenizer. For every individual tokenized input, a CLS (stands for Classification) token was added at the beginning of every sentence because the training task here is sentence classification and since they need an input that can represent the meaning of the entire sentence, this tag was introduced and SEP (stands for Separator) token at the end of each text for separating each individual input for next sentence prediction. The final layer of BERT contains a token representation T and the classifier embedding C, then each T is used to predict whether the token was masked or not and the C representation to predict if the two sentences were contiguous or not. Padding was done on the tokenized text, followed by masking and obtaining the segment IDs. The pooled outputs and sequence outputs were obtained from the Bert layer, subsequently from which the classification outputs were retrieved. These were then passed through a Dense layer of 64 neurons followed by a Dropout layer for regularization to prevent overfitting, along with a RELU activation. The same was repeated again with 32 neurons in the Dense layer this time.

Lastly, a sigmoid activation function was put in a 1 neuron Dense layer for final classification.

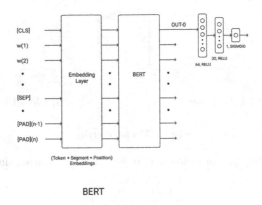

Fig. 3. BERT

5   Experiment Setup

Our work majorly focused on the comparison of the baseline forms of the above mentioned models for classification. Hence, most of the hyperparameters were kept the same. Some minor operations were performed to tune the hyperparameters depending on the model. In the Bert, CNN and CNN-BiLSTM models, Adam [14] optimizer and binary crossentropy loss function were used. For the LSTM model, RMSprop optimizer and binary crossentropy loss function were used. Finally, in the BiLSTM model, a sparse categorical crossentropy loss function was used along with Adam optimizer. The accuracy and loss progression graphs of Bert, which performed most efficiently, are shown in Fig. 4 and Fig. 4 respectively. The train-test ratio that was maintained across all the training sessions was 0.8–0.2. The models were trained on 5 epochs because the model loss increased beyond that and the batch size was varying depending on the model.

6   Results

A detailed account of performances of the machine learning models is given in Table 5 and the same for the deep learning models is given in Table 6. The benchmark test results showed that the highest model accuracy was shown by the Bert model at 83.56% with a loss of 0.727. It is evident from Table 6, that BERT is the best choice out of all the models explored by us to classify sexually harassing statements. The confusion matrix for BERT is provided in Table 3.

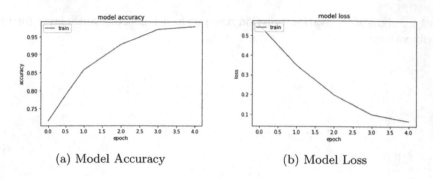

(a) Model Accuracy   (b) Model Loss

Fig. 4. Model metrics

Table 3. Confusion matrix for BERT on testing data

	P (1)	N (0)
P (1)	TP = 341	FP = 87
N (0)	FN = 46	TN = 247

While it is important that the number of false negatives of our model are minimised, it is equally important that the number of false positives are also low. A model making wrongful accusations of harassment is deleterious for the user in question. Hence, sentences falsely classified as sexually harassing by the BERT model are listed in Table 4.

Table 4. False positives by BERT

Sentence	Label
'Our boobies just wanna leave our body'	1
'i fully support my friends being sluts online, no need to apologize'	1
'Because a hot girl turns you down, she turns into a skank? Damn Mr. Rejected, shut the fuck up'	1
'Small ass world omg'	1

We would also like to highlight that our model, even though being trained only on sentences containing profane words, was also able to successfully classify sentences not containing profane words as sexually harassing. This implies that our model has been able to "understand" which words or entities in a sentence make it sexually harassing. A few such examples are provided below:

The sentence is "I gave you a promotion so you should give me some pleasure in return."

CyberPolice ALERT!! This sentence is Sexually Harassing. Call 155260 or visit https://cybercrime.gov.in to report this crime.

The sentence is "I gave you a promotion so you should give me a treat at Dominos in return."
CyberPolice says this sentence is not Sexually Harassing.

The sentence is "Your pictures make me want to do dirty things to you."
CyberPolice ALERT!! This sentence is Sexually Harassing. Call 155260 or visit https://cybercrime.gov.in to report this crime.

The sentence is "This picture has dirty cars in it."
CyberPolice says this sentence is not Sexually Harassing.

Table 5. ML algorithms

Model	Accuracy (%)	F1 score	Precision	Recall
SVM	76.83	0.768	0.768	0.768
Naive bayes	63.12	0.616	0.634	0.631
Logistic regression	76.84	0.767	0.768	0.768
Random forest	71.57	0.767	0.768	0.768
Gradient boost	76.01	0.760	0.760	0.760
KNN	70.04	0.701	0.706	0.700
Adaboost	75.31	0.753	0.754	0.753
MLP	72.68	0.727	0.726	0.728
Stochastic gradient	75.59	0.751	0.763	0.756

Table 6. DL algorithms

Model	Accuracy (%)	F1 score	Precision	Recall
BERT	83.56	0.832	0.834	0.833
BiLSTM	71.29	0.711	0.731	0.713
CNN-BiLSTM	64.63	0.647	0.658	0.642
LSTM	71.5	0.709	0.720	0.715
CNN	73.69	0.735	0.738	0.737
ULMFit	71.86	0.720	0.740	0.720

BERT takes into consideration the left-to-right and the right-to-left context of each word. Furthermore, utilising self-attention in transformer architectures while encoding these representations helps obtain deep representations for each word. Additionally, BERT has been pretrained on a large corpus of unlabelled text from Book Corpus and Wikipedia, on two NLP tasks, Masked Language Modelling (MLM) and Next Sentence Prediction (NSP). As a result, BERT's pre-trained model proves to be adept at many NLP tasks, in most cases only requiring fine-tuning of the final classification layer of the model to perform well at a particular downstream task. Hence, the cumulative effect of all aspects of BERT is easily able to capture long term dependencies in text sentences. The attention mechanism processes the entire input text at once instead of sequentially like in other networks such as RNNs, LSTSMs etc. which enables BERT to extract contextual meaning better than the other algorithms which is of primary importance for our task of detecting sexual harassment, as the model needs to differentiate between sentences having the same word distribution but completely different meaning.

The different ML models explored above along with deep learning models involving LSTMs and CNNs and even a pre-trained model like ULMFiT all failed to match the accuracy reported by BERT. Most ML models are barely able to capture and remember dependencies in any text input and as a result inherently suffer at NLP tasks. On the other hand, even though LSTMs, and CNNs are capable of capturing dependencies in input sentences, they usually aren't able to encode textual context as efficiently as BERT, which is of utmost importance in our task.

7   Conclusion

In this paper, a variety of standard models were implemented with changes made to the original architecture for the required classification task. A strict comparison of machine learning models as well as deep learning models has been done showing their performance on the given dataset. It has been concluded that BERT is the most efficient algorithm. A major problem that was faced in this project was the lack of availability of a public dataset which is specifically designed for sexual harassment and not harassment in general, for privacy reasons. Hence, the tweets had to be scraped and be manually annotated. The results obtained were promising and the model was able to distinguish between profanity and harassment, thereby giving users the right to use their freedom of speech and at the same time, preventing any predatory behaviour, which was a major aim of this paper. However, we also faced certain limitations in our work such as human error while annotating the data points as well a number of False Positive predictions made by the models as shown in Table 4. Through our project, we urge other people to further indulge into research in preventing cyber bullying and sexual harassment, and thereby, preserving internet safety and keeping it free from online predators. We will further try to improve this project by training the model on a more varied data and deploying the model as a web app to act as an automatic blocker of sexually harassing content from a website after detecting such presence thereby, making the internet a safe space for everyone. The complete code to this project is available on Github [3].

References

1. Toxic comment classification challenge. https://www.kaggle.com/c/jigsaw-toxic-comment-classification-challenge/overview
2. Albawi, S., Mohammed, T.A., Al-Zawi, S.: Understanding of a convolutional neural network. In: 2017 International Conference on Engineering and Technology (ICET), pp. 1–6 (2017). https://doi.org/10.1109/ICEngTechnol.2017.8308186
3. Basu, P.: whopriyam/Sexual-Harassment-Classification. GitHub. https://github.com/whopriyam/Sexual-Harassment-Classification
4. Basu, P., Tiwari, S., Mohanty, J., Karmakar, S.: Multimodal sentiment analysis of metoo tweets using focal loss (grand challenge). In: 2020 IEEE Sixth International Conference on Multimedia Big Data (BigMM), pp. 461–465 (2020). https://doi.org/10.1109/BigMM50055.2020.00076
5. Bretschneider, U., Wöhner, T., Peters, R.: Detecting online harassment in social networks. In: ICIS (2014)
6. Bugueño, M., Mendoza, M.: Learning to detect online harassment on Twitter with the transformer. In: Cellier, P., Driessens, K. (eds.) ECML PKDD 2019. CCIS, vol. 1168, pp. 298–306. Springer, Cham (2020). https://doi.org/10.1007/978-3-030-43887-6_23
7. Chakrabarty, N.: A machine learning approach to comment toxicity classification. CoRR http://arxiv.org/abs/1903.06765 (2019)
8. Chatterjee, R.: A new survey finds 81 percent of women have experienced sexual harassment. https://www.npr.org/sections/thetwo-way/2018/02/21/587671849/a-new-survey-finds-eighty-percent-of-women-have-experienced-sexual-harassment (2018). [Online; accessed 10-April-2021]
9. Chen, D., Smys, S.: Social multimedia security and suspicious activity detection in SDN using hybrid deep learning technique. J. Inf. Technol. Digital World 2, 108–115 (2020). https://doi.org/10.36548/jitdw.2020.2.004
10. Devlin, J., Chang, M.W., Lee, K., Toutanova, K.: Bert: pre-training of deep bidirectional transformers for language understanding (2019)
11. Ghosh Chowdhury, A., Sawhney, R., Shah, R.R., Mahata, D.: #YouToo? detection of personal recollections of sexual harassment on social media. In: Proceedings of the 57th Annual Meeting of the Association for Computational Linguistics. pp. 2527–2537. Association for Computational Linguistics, Florence (2019). https://doi.org/10.18653/v1/P19-1241. https://www.aclweb.org/anthology/P19-1241
12. Howard, J., Ruder, S.: Universal language model fine-tuning for text classification (2018)
13. Jiang, L., Suzuki, Y.: Detecting hate speech from tweets for sentiment analysis. In: 2019 6th International Conference on Systems and Informatics (ICSAI), pp. 671–676 (2019). https://doi.org/10.1109/ICSAI48974.2019.9010578
14. Kingma, D.P., Ba, J.: Adam: a method for stochastic optimization (2017)
15. Kotsiantis, S., Zaharakis, I., Pintelas, P.: Machine learning: a review of classification and combining techniques. Artif. Intell. Rev. 26, 159–190 (2006). https://doi.org/10.1007/s10462-007-9052-3
16. Marwa, T., Salima, O., Souham, M.: Deep learning for online harassment detection in tweets. In: 2018 3rd International Conference on Pattern Analysis and Intelligent Systems (PAIS), pp. 1–5 (2018). https://doi.org/10.1109/PAIS.2018.8598530
17. Mrezvan94: Mrezvan94/Harassment-Corpus. GitHub. https://github.com/Mrezvan94/Harassment-Corpus

18. Ortiz-Ospina: The rise of social media. https://ourworldindata.org/rise-of-social-media
19. Reed, E., Wong, A., Raj, A.: Cyber sexual harassment: a summary of current measures and implications for future research. Violence Against Women **26**(12-13), 1727–1740 (2020). https://doi.org/10.1177/1077801219880959. pMID: 31631815
20. Rhanoui, M., Mikram, M., Yousfi, S., Barzali, S.: A CNN-BILSTM model for document-level sentiment analysis. Mach. Learn. Knowl. Extr. **1**(3), 832–847 (2019). https://www.mdpi.com/2504-4990/1/3/48
21. Roy, P.K., Tripathy, A.K., Das, T.K., Gao, X.Z.: A framework for hate speech detection using deep convolutional neural network. IEEE Access **8**, 204951–204962 (2020). https://doi.org/10.1109/ACCESS.2020.3037073
22. Schenk, S.J.: Cyber-sexual harassment: the development of the cyber-sexual experiences questionnaire. McNair Scholars J. **12**, 8 (2008)
23. Sharifirad, S.: NLP and machine learning techniques to detect online harassment on social networking platforms (2019). http://hdl.handle.net/10222/76331
24. Sherstinsky, A.: Fundamentals of recurrent neural network (RNN) and long short-term memory (LSTM) network. Physica D **404**, 132306 (2020). https://doi.org/10.1016/j.physd.2019.132306
25. Smys, S., Basar, D., Wang, D.: Artificial neural network based power management for smart street lighting systems. J. Artif. Intell. Capsule Netw. **2**, 42–52 (2020). https://doi.org/10.36548/jaicn.2020.1.005
26. Tankovska, H.: Number of social media Users 2025. https://www.statista.com/statistics/278414/number-of-worldwide-social-network-users/ (2021). [Online; Accessed 10 April 2021]
27. Xu, G., Meng, Y., Qiu, X., Yu, Z., Wu, X.: Sentiment analysis of comment texts based on BiLSTM. IEEE Access **7**, 51522–51532 (2019). https://doi.org/10.1109/ACCESS.2019.2909919

Neural Text Categorization with Transformers for Learning Portuguese as a Second Language

Rodrigo Santos[1(✉)], João Rodrigues[1], António Branco[1], and Rui Vaz[2]

[1] NLX—Natural Language and Speech Group, Department of Informatics, Faculdade de Ciências, University of Lisbon, 1749-016 Campo Grande, Lisbon, Portugal
{rsdsantos,jarodrigues,antonio.branco}@fc.ul.pt
[2] Camões I.P. Instituto da Cooperação e da Língua,
Av. da Liberdade 270, 1250-149 Lisbon, Portugal
rvaz@camoes.mne.pt

Abstract. We report on the application of a neural network based approach to the problem of automatically categorizing texts according to their proficiency levels and suitability for learners of Portuguese as a second language. We resort to a particular deep learning architecture, namely Transformers, as we fine-tune GPT-2 and RoBERTa on data sets labeled with respect to the standard CEFR proficiency levels, that were provided by Camões IC, the Portuguese official language institute. Despite the reduced size of the data sets available, we found that the resulting models overperform previous carefully crafted feature based counterparts in most evaluation scenarios, thus offering a new state-of-the-art for this task in what concerns the Portuguese language.

Keywords: Readability classification · Language proficiency · Neural networks · Deep learning · Portuguese

1 Introduction

Learning and teaching an idiom as a second language is a challenge for students and teachers. While the former struggle with the acquisition of a new language, the latter have, among other things, to gather and create study materials that efficiently support the acquisition of that new cognitive skill.

Automatic Text Difficulty Classification, also known as Readability Assessment, can ease the work for both students and teachers as it helps to determine the level of difficulty of a text, since learning from a text that is too easy renders few benefits, and learning from a text that is to hard may frustrate the students.

Despite the usefulness of these systems for any language, most research and data is in and for English—as it is common in the field of Natural Language Processing (NLP)—leaving most languages unsupported.

With the scarcity of data for the vast majority of languages, the development of language tools for the extraction of features used on the creation of a classifiers for text difficulty level becomes an even greater challenge.

© Springer Nature Switzerland AG 2021
G. Marreiros et al. (Eds.): EPIA 2021, LNAI 12981, pp. 715–726, 2021.
https://doi.org/10.1007/978-3-030-86230-5_56

The work presented in this paper focuses on the classification of proficiency levels of Portuguese texts, a language with considerably few resources labelled according to the CEFR (Common European Framework of Reference for Languages) [19] levels, as this is the categorization used by the Portuguese official language agency Camões IP[1] in its teaching and certification activities. The CEFR levels classify text difficulty into six reference levels of increasing proficiency and difficulty, viz. A1, A2, B1, B2, C1, C2, and is widely accepted as the European standard for grading language proficiency.

Like in almost any other NLP task, automatic text classification has recently seen a boost in performance with the introduction of the neural network, deep learning architecture known as Transformer [44], more precisely through the use of gigantic deep language models that make use of this architecture and are pre-trained on very large data sets of raw text.

This unsupervised pre-training step helps the model to learn an inner representation of the language and is used to complement and alleviate the very short volume of labelled data sets that are specific for any given task, and are used for the subsequent fine-tuning of the model.

The research question of the present paper aims to answer is: while using Portuguese as an example and case study of a low-resourced language with respect to labelled data sets for language proficiency, can the new transformer based language models be shown to support a solution that over-performs the state of the art provided by feature based models for proficiency level classification on low-resource scenarios?

A positive answer to this question can benefit the low resourced languages, which are the vast majority, with few resources and that are not technologically prepared to have the tools that are required for the extraction of features for text difficulty classification.

We find that the GPT-2 [29] and RoBERTa [25] language models support very competitive scores in comparison to a feature based classifier, with GPT-2 surpassing the feature based approach and setting a new state-of-the-art performance for the Portuguese language.

Another major outcome of the research reported in this paper is the resulting classifier, which we make available as the online tool LX-Proficiency to support students of Portuguese as well as anyone interested.[2]

The remainder of this document is organized as follows: Sect. 2 presents the relevant previous work; Sect. 3 introduces the corpora used throughout our experiments; Sect. 4 summarizes the Transformer architecture and the language models used; Sect. 5 describes the implementation of the feature-based model as well as the deep language models; Sect. 6 presents and discusses the results obtained. Finally, Sect. 7 closes this document with concluding remarks.

---

[1] https://www.instituto-camoes.pt/.

[2] https://portulanclarin.net/workbench/lx-proficiency.

2   Related Work

Readability assessment has a long tradition of research on a wide range of different readability indexes (cf. overviews in [13, 18]). Recently, text difficulty classification or readability assessment has been addressed in tasks such as automatic proficiency level classification. This task aims to classify excerpts of texts in accordance to a given range of proficiency levels (typically as set up in CEFR). In addition to unsupervised readability indexes, most of the recent work has resorted to a wide range of features to train machine learning classifiers: count-based, lexical, morphological, syntactic, and semantic [24, 28].

In spite of the scarceness of data, within the paradigm of readability indexes and machine learning classifiers, a few languages have been addressed: Chinese [41], Dutch [42], Estonian [43], French [22], German [23], Italian [21, 37], Russian [30] and Swedish [34], among others.

The authors of [26] study the impact of neural networks in this task and achieve some success using BERT [17], HAN [47], and a Bi-LSTM [38] with accuracy scores ranging from 78.72% to 85.73% on three English datasets. Despite this success, they obtain good performance only for the English language, and the same type of models underperform when training on Slovenian with a smaller data set (52.77% accuracy).

Readability assessment in the Portuguese language is a research domain still largely untapped. However, it is worth mentioning the closely related work reported in [1], on a wide experimental space for Portuguese readability assessment for text simplification; in [31], on the task of automatic scoring texts produced by learners of Portuguese as a second language; and in [36], on measuring the impact of readability features to detect fake news.

Regarding the published research specifically on text difficulty assessment in Portuguese, it was reported in three papers by two teams, namely [8,9,16], which classify texts into CEFR levels and use corpora from Camões IP.

The first paper [9] makes use of a corpus with 114 labelled excerpts and four unsupervised metrics in order to classify the texts. The metrics are: the Flesch Reading Ease index [20] (27.03% accuracy); the lexical category density in the proportion of nouns (22.97% accuracy); the average word length in the number of syllables per word (29.73% accuracy); and the average sentence length in the number of words per sentence (19.09% accuracy). Their purpose was the creation of a tool to help language learners and teachers of Portuguese to assess the level of a text. Accordingly, they don't merge the features that were extracted—which could help obtain a higher performance score—as it could blur the interpretability of the tool by its users.

The second paper [8] includes a re-evaluation by human experts of the tool presented in the first paper.

Finally, the third paper [16] makes uses of a second corpus that was double in size, with 237 labelled excerpts (including the 114 excerpts used in the first two papers), and focused on extracting 52 features from the text to experiment with various machine learning models, which deliver the best performance by resorting to LogitBoost (75.11% accuracy).

Table 1. Example of the Portuguese corpus

A Célia tem 15 anos e é verdadeiramente uma pessoa da era digital. Gosta muito de informática e de novas tecnologias, mas também de viagens	A1
O Ballet Clássico alia o movimento dançado ao sentido de musicalidade, inspirando-se no universo das danças populares e palacianas	B2

3   Corpus

In its certification activities, Camões IP is responsible for running language exams on Portuguese as a second language worldwide, and thus assessing the correct difficulty level of the text excerpts for each exam is crucial.

The corpus used in the present paper was provided by Camões IP. It has 500 excerpts of Portuguese news, books and articles (including the data sets used by the three previous papers mentioned above), which are labelled with one of five CEFR levels, namely A1 (beginner), A2 (elementary), B1 (intermediate), B2 (upper intermediate), and C (advanced and proficient).

Table 1 showcases sentences from two excerpts in this corpus, separated by three levels of difficulty. We can observe that to correctly classify them, one as to take into account various factors such as sentence length or the type of vocabulary.

While this 500 texts corpus is pretty small for deep learning standards, it represents a great improvement over data sets available for previous work, doubling the 237 texts previously available to [16] and almost quintupling the 114 texts available to [8,9].

Table 2 contains the global statistics for the corpora used in this work, and Table 3 discriminates the proportion of excerpts in each class.

In order to allow for comparison to previous work, the data used was divided into 5 subsets: (i) a set that encompasses all the 500 texts that are available, termed c500 for ease of reference; (ii) a balanced set where every class has 45 texts randomly selected inside each class—capped by the size of the smallest class, B2, in c500—making a total of 225 texts, termed c225bal for ease of reference; (iii) a set that approximates the corpus of [8,9] with 114 texts, termed c114; (iv) a set with 88 texts from [8,9] consisting of a re-annotated version of subset of c114 with some texts removed due to insufficient agreement between annotators, termed c88r; and finally (v) a set that approximates the corpus used in [16] with 237 texts, which contains c114, termed c237 for ease of reference;

In Table 2, we can see that the number of sentences in each corpus closely follows the trend of number of excerpt/texts with the exception being c225bal with more sentences than c237 that has more texts.

The c225bal corpus is also the corpus with highest average of tokens and sentences per excerpt showcasing that each excerpts are in average here larger than in any other corpus.

Table 2. Corpora statistics

Corpus	Excerpts	Tokens	Av. tokens/excerpts	Sentences	Av. sentences/excerpts
c500	500	89,749	179.50	5,647	11.29
c225bal	225	49,734	221.04	2,999	13.33
c237	237	37,592	158.62	2,122	8.95
c114	114	12,875	112.94	677	5.94
c88r	88	10,793	122.65	588	6.68

Table 3. Class distribution

Corpus	A1		A2		B1		B2		C	
	Num.	Per.	Num.	Per.	Num.	Per.	Num.	Per.	Num.	Per.
c500	80	16%	135	27%	184	36.8%	45	9%	56	11.2%
c225bal	45	20%	45	20%	45	20%	45	20%	45	20%
c237	29	12.2%	39	16.5%	136	57.4%	14	5.9%	19	8%
c114	11	9.6%	11	9.6%	72	63.2%	8	7%	12	10.5%
c88r	30	34.1%	17	19.3%	23	26%	11	12.5%	7	8%

Table 3 help also to show how imbalanced c114 and c237 are, with the class with the highest percentage B1 having 63.2% and 57.4% of all texts, respectively, and the class with lowest percentage having as little as 7% and 5.9%, respectively

The last line of Table 3 presents the distribution of c88r. Given this corpus is a re-annotated version of a subset of c114, we can see that many of the texts previously classified as B1 in c114 have here a different label, with every other class growing in size with the exception of C. This can negatively affect a model trained with c114 that despite being able to achieve a good performance score, in reality the model is adjusted to data that is wrongly labeled and has a big bias towards one class. This same issue might be prevalent in c237, and it it only somewhat mitigated in c225bal, due to the balance of every class, and in c500, as its size may help mitigate the wrong classification.

4   Transformer Models

The introduction of the deep learning architecture Transformer [44] has produced a revolution in the field of Natural Language Processing (NLP). Where previously sets of rules, features, and various machine learning models were used, they have been successfully replaced with a variant of the Transformer architecture.

These Transformer variants are machine learning algorithms that obtain state-of-art performance on a wide range of Natural Language Understanding and Generation tasks. They are neural network algorithms that encapsulate a tokenizer, contextual embeddings and a task-specific prediction algorithm.

Typically the deep learning pipeline consists of string tokenization, converting raw text to a sparse index encoding, followed by a transformation to sparse indices resorting to several neural network layers (representing a contextual embedding), and finally, a head layer outputs to a task-specific prediction (e.g. language modeling, sequence classification, question answering or conditional generation among others).

In terms of architecture, the Transformer [44] extrapolates the idea underlying the Attention Mechanism [2] and creates a sequence-to-sequence encoder-decoder model that relies almost only on Attention layers, creating a model that is both better and faster at dealing with language processing tasks than the previous Recurrent Deep Networks.

In this work we use two Transformer based models, namely the GPT-2 [29] model and the RoBERTa [25] model. The tokenizers from both models rely on a statistical analysis from the training corpus using subwords units. More specifically, they use a byte-level Byte-Pair Encoding (BPE) vocabulary [39].

4.1 GPT-2

The GPT-2 is an autoregressive neural network that makes use of the decoder side of the Transformer model and its training objective is to decode the next token (word or piece of word) in a sentence.

More precisely, given an input sequence $x_{1:n-1}$, it learns by predicting the next word:

$$x_{1:n-1} \Rightarrow x_n \tag{1}$$

Internally the model uses a mask-mechanism to make sure the predictions for the target token n only use the inputs from x_1 to x_{n-1} but not the future tokens, which means that for the prediction of each token the model only has access to the tokens on the left of the target token. This means that the model is pre-trained on raw texts only, with no need for human-labeled data. While the model thrives on generation tasks, it can be used to extract features that can be used on various downstream tasks.

During fine-tuning, a classification head is added to the top of the model. The head performs a sequence classification for each input sequence $x_{1:N}$ and gives a possible output y from a class set C:

$$x_{1:N} \xrightarrow{\text{outputs}} y \in C \tag{2}$$

We implemented the GPT-2 classification model resorting to the open-source library *Transformers* [46], with a 12 layers and 12 attention-heads model architecture, totaling 124M parameters, and initializing the model with a model fine-tuned from English to Portuguese.[3]

4.2 RoBERTa

Like GPT-2, the RoBERTa model makes use of part of the Transformer model, only this time it is the encoder side on the Transformer that is used. The

---

[3] https://huggingface.co/pierreguillou/gpt2-small-portuguese.

RoBERTa model is an improvement upon the BERT model [17] as it does not use the NSP (Next Sentence Prediction) training objective, and uses more data, longer sequences, and a bigger batch size than the original BERT model.

RoBERTa has the train objective named MLM (Masked Language Model), where a word at random is masked in the sentence and the model is asked to predict what was the word that was masked. In particular, this model receives an input token sequence $x_{1:N}$ and trains the model by predicting a masked word x_n that was swapped at random by a mask token (e.g., <MASK>):

$$x_{1:N\backslash n} \Rightarrow x_n \tag{3}$$

Internally, the model has access to every word on the left and on the right of the masked word, creating a stronger context than in the GPT-2 model (only words to the left) to predict the word. Just like GPT-2 during fine-tuning, a classification head is added to the top of the model (see Eq. 2).

Since hugging face has no pre-trained RoBERTa model in Portuguese, we trained a new RoBERTa model with 6 layers and 12 attention-heads, totaling 68M parameters, on 10 million Portuguese sentences and 10 million English sentences from the Oscar corpus.[4]

5   Implementation

In order to compare with previous work, we re-implemented the classifier from [16], having gathered information from this paper, which is based on the dissertation [15], from one of the authors, and from the tool's website[5].

We trained the classifier using 10-cross fold validation, used the same features, and the same classifier LogitBoost.[6] The paper does not indicate the parameters used, so we used the default parameters. With the average of 3 runs, we found a performance score (74.12%) that is in line with the score (75.11%) reported in the reproduced paper [16], both presented in the Table 4. The difference of 0.99% in accuracy makes us confident that both the reproduced classifier and reproduced corpus are close to the ones in the original paper.

As mentioned above, in this work we make use of the GPT-2 and RoBERTa models for classifying Portuguese text into one of the five CEFR proficiency levels. We fine-tuned both models on the five corpora, with both models using a batch size of 1; 5 epochs for the c88r and c225bal, 10 epochs for c114, c237 and c500; and using a learning rate of $2e-5$ for GPT-2 and $1e-5$ for RoBERTa.

We trained/fine-tuned each model using 10-fold cross validation. While this method is not usual for neural networks, mainly because it is very time consuming, we used it in order to allow for comparison with the scores obtained in previous work. Every model is trained three times and the performance scores reported are an average of these three runs.

---

[4] https://oscar-corpus.com/.

[5] https://string.hlt.inesc-id.pt/demo/classification.pl.

[6] https://logitboost.readthedocs.io/.

Table 4. Performance (accuracy)

Model	c114	c88r	c237	c500	c225bal
Unsupervised indexes [9]	21.82%	29.73%	-	-	-
Feature-based LogitBoost [16]	-	-	75.11%	-	-
Our LogitBoost reproduction	**86,84%**	48,86%	74,12%	68,60%	59,70%
GPT-2	84,21%	55,68%	**76,23%**	**75,62%**	**65,48%**
RoBERTa	85,32%	**57,83%**	75,45%	72,50%	63,19%

6   Evaluation and Discussion

While accuracy allows for a quick and intuitive grasp of the performance, in scenarios like ours where classes are severely unbalanced, other metrics can be more sensible. Hence, we complement accuracy with macro-averaged f1 score and quadratic weighted kappa as in both these metrics all classes contribute equally regardless of how often they appear in the test set. Table 5 presents the performance scores for LogitBoost, GPT-2 and RoBERTa.

The absolute highest performance score (86.84%) is obtained for the c114 corpus using LogitBoost. While one might consider that this model trained with this corpus is the best performing model, a case can be made that in reality the high imbalance of the corpus, mainly in the B1 class, creates a heavily biased model that will performs poorly in a real world scenario. The same argument can be provided for c237. Like c114, this data set is also heavily imbalanced.

The most simplistic baseline model that always answered with the majority class (B1) would already achieve as much as 57.4% and 63.2% accuracy with c237 ans c114 respectively (cf. Table 3). Despite this, the c237 corpus is our comparison gateway to the work of [16] (scoring 75.11%), and both the GPT-2 (with 76.23%) and RoBERTa (75.45%) models achieve higher accuracy than it, with the GPT-2 model even beating the other models for c237 in all the three evaluation metrics (Table 5).

The corpus supporting the worst performance scores is c88r, which is not surprising due to its reduced size. Here no model has a clear advantage over the others, with each model being better than the other two in one of the three metrics. Both c88r and c114 are the gateway to comparison with [8,9], which are outperformed by the other models, mainly due to the unsupervised indexes and the rudimentary algorithm used, viz. linear regression.

Finally, the novel data sets presented in this work c500 and c225bal support their best performance with GPT-2, and both appear as strong candidates for a real world application.

Given its the largest balanced corpus, with all classes with equal size, the latter presents itself as a fairer model for all classes. Accordingly, it can be seen as providing the best sensible scores to compare the performance of the various models—with GPT-2 outperforming the other models—and thus the reference scores for this task for the Portuguese language given the labelled data available

Table 5. Performance (accuracy, macro-f1, quadratic weight kappa)

Model	c114			c88r			c237			c500			c225bal		
	acc	f1	qwk	acc	f1	qwk	acc	f1	qwk	acc	f1	qwk	acc	f1	qwk
LogitBoost	**86,84**	**0,737**	**0,898**	48,86	**0,429**	0,720	74,12	0,553	0,735	68,60	0,643	0,791	59,70	0,595	0,809
GPT-2	84,21	0,675	0,793	55,68	0,348	**0,736**	**76,23**	**0,556**	**0,760**	**75,62**	**0,689**	**0,859**	65,48	0,649	0,879
RoBERTa	85,32	0,615	0,792	**57,83**	0,322	0,691	75,45	0,510	0,709	72,50	0,589	0,826	63,19	0,562	0,848

at present. In turn, due to its larger size, the former has also an interesting advantage as it has seen and learned from a wider range of examples and may more closely represent the distribution of data in the real world. Here again, GPT-2 is by far the best performing model, in all evaluation metrics.

7 Conclusion

The results reported in this paper show that, despite the very small dimension of the labeled data available and the known need of neural methods for large data sets, the neural-based transformer based language models are capable of performing on par with non neural models trained on features in the task of text difficulty classification, even achieving state-of-the-art performance for the Portuguese language. These results thus demonstrate that good performance on the task can be achieved if one has a small corpus, and can thus dispense with auxiliary language tools for feature extraction needed by non neural learning approaches previously used. This comes as good news for under-resourced languages that do not have the language resources and tools needed for the extraction of the relevant features.

Moreover, we offer access to the GPT-2 model trained with the c500 corpus, as we deem it as the model that more likely follows closely the distribution of classes in the real usage scenario of the students of Portuguese as second language applying to certification from Camões IP. It underlies the online service LX-Proficiency,[7] which can be freely accessed online from the PORTULAN CLARIN Research Infrastructure for the Science and Technology of Language[8].

For future work we would like to study the impact of knowledge transfer from other languages that have more resources (e.g. English), as well as methods to synthetically increase the size of the training set.

Acknowledgements. The work leading to the research results reported in this paper were mostly supported by Camões I.P. Instituto da Cooperação e da Língua. It was also partially supported by PORTULAN CLARIN Research Infrastructure for the Science and Technology of Language, funded by Lisboa 2020, Alentejo 2020 and FCT—Fundação para a Ciência e Tecnologia under the grant PINFRA/22117/2016.

---

[7] https://portulanclarin.net/workbench/lx-proficiency.
[8] The PORTULAN CLARIN workbench comprises a number of tools that are based on a large body of research work contributed by different authors and teams, which continues to grow and is acknowledged here: [3–7,10–12,14,27,32,33,35,40,45].

References

1. Aluisio, S., Specia, L., Gasperin, C., Scarton, C.: Readability assessment for text simplification. In: Proceedings of the NAACL HLT 2010 Fifth Workshop on Innovative Use of NLP for Building Educational Applications, pp. 1–9 (2010)
2. Bahdanau, D., Cho, K.H., Bengio, Y.: Neural machine translation by jointly learning to align and translate. In: 3rd International Conference on Learning Representations, ICLR 2015 (2015)
3. Barreto, F. et al.: Open resources and tools for the shallow processing of Portuguese: the TagShare project. In: Proceedings of the 5th International Conference on Language Resources and Evaluation (LREC), pp. 1438–1443 (2006)
4. Branco, A., Henriques, T.: Aspects of verbal inflection and lemmatization: generalizations and algorithms. In: Proceedings of XVIII Annual Meeting of the Portuguese Association of Linguistics (APL), pp. 201–210 (2003)
5. Branco, A., Castro, S., Silva, J., Costa, F.: CINTIL DepBank handbook: Design options for the representation of grammatical dependencies. Technical report, University of Lisbon (2011)
6. Branco, A., et al.: Developing a deep linguistic databank supporting a collection of treebanks: the CINTIL DeepGramBank. In: Proceedings of the 7th International Conference on Language Resources and Evaluation (LREC), pp. 1810–1815 (2010)
7. Branco, A., Nunes, F.: Verb analysis in a highly inflective language with an MFF algorithm. In: Caseli, H., Villavicencio, A., Teixeira, A., Perdigão, F. (eds.) PROPOR 2012. LNCS (LNAI), vol. 7243, pp. 1–11. Springer, Heidelberg (2012). https://doi.org/10.1007/978-3-642-28885-2_1
8. Branco, A., Rodrigues, J., Costa, F., Silva, J., Vaz, R.: Assessing automatic text classification for interactive language learning. In: International Conference on Information Society (i-Society 2014), pp. 70–78 (2014)
9. Branco, A., Rodrigues, J., Costa, F., Silva, J., Vaz, R.: Rolling out text categorization for language learning assessment supported by language technology. In: Baptista, J., Mamede, N., Candeias, S., Paraboni, I., Pardo, T.A.S., Volpe Nunes, M.G. (eds.) PROPOR 2014. LNCS (LNAI), vol. 8775, pp. 256–261. Springer, Cham (2014). https://doi.org/10.1007/978-3-319-09761-9_29
10. Branco, A., Rodrigues, J., Silva, J., Costa, F., Vaz, R.: Assessing automatic text classification for interactive language learning. In: Proceedings of the IEEE International Conference on Information Society (iSociety), pp. 72–80 (2014)
11. Branco, A., Silva, J.: A suite of shallow processing tools for Portuguese: LX-suite. In: Proceedings of the 11th Conference of the European Chapter of the Association for Computational Linguistics (EACL), pp. 179–182 (2006)
12. Costa, F., Branco, A.: Aspectual type and temporal relation classification. In: Proceedings of the 13th Conference of the European Chapter of the Association for Computational Linguistics, pp. 266–275 (2012)
13. Crossley, S.A., Skalicky, S., Dascalu, M., McNamara, D.S., Kyle, K.: Predicting text comprehension, processing, and familiarity in adult readers: new approaches to readability formulas. Discourse Process. **54**, 340–359 (2017)
14. Cruz, A.F., Rocha, G., Cardoso, H.L.: Exploring Spanish corpora for Portuguese coreference resolution. In: 2018 Fifth International Conference on Social Networks Analysis, Management and Security (SNAMS), pp. 290–295 (2018)
15. Curto, P.: Classificador de textos para o ensino de português como segunda língua. Master's thesis, Instituto Superior Técnico-Universidade de Lisboa, Lisboa (2014)

16. Curto, P., Mamede, N., Baptista, J.: Automatic text difficulty classifier. In: Proceedings of the 7th International Conference on Computer Supported Education, vol. 1, pp. 36–44 (2015)
17. Devlin, J., Chang, M.W., Lee, K., Toutanova, K.: BERT: pre-training of deep bidirectional transformers for language understanding. In: Proceedings of the 2019 Conference of the North American Chapter of the Association for Computational Linguistics: Human Language Technologies, Volume 1 (Long and Short Papers), pp. 4171–4186 (2019)
18. DuBay, W.H.: The Principles of Readability. Impact Information, Costa Mesa (2004)
19. Council for Europe, Council for Cultural Co-operation, E.C., Division, M.L.: Common European Framework of Reference for Languages: learning, teaching, assessment (2001)
20. Flesch, R.: How to Write Plain English: A Book for Lawyers and Consumers. Harpercollins, New York (1979)
21. Forti, L., Grego G., Santarelli, F., Santucci, V., Spina, S.: MALT-IT2: a new resource to measure text difficulty in light of CEFR levels for Italian l2 learning. In: 12th Language Resources and Evaluation Conference, pp. 7206–7213 (2020)
22. François, T., Fairon, C.: An "AI readability" formula for French as a foreign language. In: Proceedings of the 2012 Joint Conference on Empirical Methods in Natural Language Processing and Computational Natural Language Learning, pp. 466–477 (2012)
23. Hancke, J., Meurers, D.: Exploring CEFR classification for German based on rich linguistic modeling. In: Learner Corpus Research, pp. 54–56 (2013)
24. Jönsson, S., Rennes, E., Falkenjack, J., Jönsson, A.: A component based approach to measuring text complexity. In: The Seventh Swedish Language Technology Conference (SLTC-18), Stockholm, Sweden, 7–9 November 2018 (2018)
25. Liu, Y., et al.: Roberta: A robustly optimized BERT pretraining approach. arXiv preprint arXiv:1907.11692 (2019)
26. Martinc, M., Pollak, S., Robnik-Šikonja, M.: Supervised and unsupervised neural approaches to text readability (to be published)
27. Miranda, N., Raminhos, R., Seabra, P., Sequeira, J., Gonçalves, T., Quaresma, P.: Named entity recognition using machine learning techniques. In: EPIA-11, 15th Portuguese Conference on Artificial Intelligence, pp. 818–831 (2011)
28. Pilán, I., Volodina, E.: Investigating the importance of linguistic complexity features across different datasets related to language learning. In: Proceedings of the Workshop on Linguistic Complexity and Natural Language Processing, pp. 49–58 (2018)
29. Radford, A., et al.: Better language models and their implications. OpenAI Blog (2019). https://openai.com/blog/better-language-models
30. Reynolds, R.: Insights from Russian second language readability classification: complexity-dependent training requirements, and feature evaluation of multiple categories. In: Proceedings of the 11th Workshop on Innovative Use of NLP for Building Educational Applications, pp. 289–300 (2016)
31. del Río, I.: Automatic proficiency classification in l2 Portuguese. Procesamiento del Lenguaje Nat. **63**, 67–74 (2019)
32. Rodrigues, J., Costa, F., Silva, J., Branco, A.: Automatic syllabification of Portuguese. Revista da Associação Portuguesa de Linguística (1), 715–720 (2020)
33. Rodrigues, J., Branco, A., Neale, S., Silva, J.: LX-DSemVectors: distributional semantics models for Portuguese. In: Silva, J., Ribeiro, R., Quaresma, P., Adami, A., Branco, A. (eds.) PROPOR 2016. LNCS (LNAI), vol. 9727, pp. 259–270. Springer, Cham (2016). https://doi.org/10.1007/978-3-319-41552-9_27

34. Santini, M., Jönsson, A., Rennes, E.: Visualizing facets of text complexity across registers. In: Proceedings of the 1st Workshop on Tools and Resources to Empower People with REAding DIfficulties (READI), pp. 49–56 (2020)

35. Santos, R., Silva, J., Branco, A., Xiong, D.: The direct path may not be the best: Portuguese-Chinese neural machine translation. In: Proceedings of the 19th EPIA Conference on Artificial Intelligence, pp. 757–768 (2019)

36. Santos, R., et al.: Measuring the impact of readability features in fake news detection. In: Proceedings of The 12th Language Resources and Evaluation Conference, pp. 1404–1413 (2020)

37. Santucci, V., Santarelli, F., Forti, L., Spina, S.: Automatic classification of text complexity. Appl. Sci. **10**, 7285 (2020)

38. Schuster, M., Paliwal, K.K.: Bidirectional recurrent neural networks. IEEE Trans. Signal Process. **45**, 2673–2681 (1997)

39. Sennrich, R., Haddow, B., Birch, A.: Neural machine translation of rare words with subword units. In: Proceedings of the 54th Annual Meeting of the Association for Computational Linguistics (Volume 1: Long Papers), pp. 1715–1725 (2016)

40. Silva, J., Branco, A., Castro, S., Reis, R.: Out-of-the-box robust parsing of Portuguese. In: Proceedings of the 9th International Conference on Language Resources and Evaluation (LREC), pp. 75–85 (2009)

41. Sung, Y.T., Lin, W.C., Dyson, S.B., Chang, K.E., Chen, Y.C.: Leveling l2 texts through readability: combining multilevel linguistic features with the CEFR. Mod. Lang. J. **99**, 371–391 (2015)

42. Tack, A., François, T., Desmet, P., Fairon, C.: NT2Lex: a CEFR-graded lexical resource for Dutch as a foreign language linked to open Dutch wordnet. In: Proceedings of the Thirteenth Workshop on Innovative Use of NLP for Building Educational Applications, pp. 137–146 (2018)

43. Vajjala, S., Loo, K.: Automatic CEFR level prediction for Estonian learner text. In: Proceedings of the Third Workshop on NLP for Computer-Assisted Language Learning, pp. 113–127 (2014)

44. Vaswani, A., et al.: Attention is all you need. In: Proceedings of the 31st International Conference on Neural Information Processing Systems, pp. 6000–6010 (2017)

45. Veiga, A., Candeias, S., Perdigão, F.: Generating a pronunciation dictionary for European Portuguese using a joint-sequence model with embedded stress assignment. In: Proceedings of the 8th Brazilian Symposium in Information and Human Language Technology (2011)

46. Wolf, T., et al.: Transformers: state-of-the-art natural language processing. In: Proceedings of the 2020 Conference on Empirical Methods in Natural Language Processing: System Demonstrations, pp. 38–45 (2020)

47. Yang, Z., Yang, D., Dyer, C., He, X., Smola, A., Hovy, E.: Hierarchical attention networks for document classification. In: Proceedings of the 2016 Conference of the North American Chapter of the Association for Computational Linguistics: Human Language Technologies, pp. 1480–1489 (2016)

More Data Is Better Only to Some Level, After Which It Is Harmful: Profiling Neural Machine Translation Self-learning with Back-Translation

Rodrigo Santos[✉], João Silva, and António Branco

NLX–Natural Language and Speech Group, Department of Informatics, Faculdade de Ciências, University of Lisbon, 1749-016 Campo Grande, Lisbon, Portugal
{rsdsantos,jsilva,antonio.branco}@di.fc.ul.pt

Abstract. Neural machine translation needs a very large volume of data to unfold its potential. Self-learning with back-translation became widely adopted to address this data scarceness bottleneck: a seed system is used to translate source monolingual sentences which are aligned with the output sentences to form a synthetic data set that, when used to retrain the system, improves its translation performance. In this paper we report on the profiling of the self-learning with back-translation aiming at clarifying whether adding more synthetic data always leads to an increase of performance. With the experiments undertaken, we gathered evidence indicating that more synthetic data is better only to some level, after which it is harmful as the translation quality decays.

Keywords: Machine translation · Back-translation · Synthetic corpus

1 Introduction

When compared with alternative approaches to translation, neural machine translation (NMT) is known to need a large volume of training data to unleash all its potential, which could create a bottleneck to its application to the vast majority of language pairs, for which little parallel corpora exist. Fortunately, since the seminal study of [12], the so-called back-translation technique offered a solution to alleviate this drawback and became widely used to improve NMT. It can be seen as a form of self-learning approach where the performance of a machine translation system is increased by increasing the amount of its training data with synthetic parallel texts that are produced by the previous version of that system, with inferior translation performance.

To create the synthetic data one needs (i) a monolingual corpus in the desired target language, (ii) an MT system previously trained for the target→source language direction and (iii) to translate the data in (i) with the system in (ii). As expected, the synthetic corpora produced via back-translation is of lower quality than the original parallel corpora used to train the seed system. Nonetheless,

© Springer Nature Switzerland AG 2021
G. Marreiros et al. (Eds.): EPIA 2021, LNAI 12981, pp. 727–738, 2021.
https://doi.org/10.1007/978-3-030-86230-5_57

back-translation has been used to improve NMT as the increase of translation quality with the increase of the volume of training data has been found to offset the decay of quality with the additional synthetic data.

While validating the old maxim that "there is no data as more data", this gives hope to make NMT progress dependent mostly on the availability of increasingly larger computational power, to crunch increasingly larger amounts of synthetic training data, rather than on the availability (or the scarceness) of naturally occurring, non-synthetic parallel data.

Some studies have assessed the variation in the volume of synthetic corpora, [6,10] a.o., confirming that an increase in the synthetic data volume leads to an improved NMT performance. However, to the best of our knowledge, only [4] have studied the self-learning curve provided by back-translation when the training (synthetic) data receives successive increments.

Edunovo et al. [4] resort to back-translation for the German-English and French-English language pairs. They explore various methods to obtain the back-translated sentences by experimenting with: (i) beam and greedy search; (ii) unrestricted and restricted sampling over the target vocabulary; and (iii) by inserting noise into the beam search output. The plain beam search was the worst performing method and beam with added noise (beam+noise) the best. Moreover, in the plain beam search method, a fall in quality is noticeable after some amount of synthetic data is reached, while this is not apparent for the beam+noise method in the experiments reported.

Our goal in this paper is to empirically address the question of whether there is a limit for pushing back-translation and its benefits. In particular, we investigate whether this tipping point behaviour is associated only to the beam search method, or if it is associated to back-translation in general, even if eventually with different tipping points and curve shapes for different methods and initial conditions.

We are seeking to obtain empirical evidence on whether larger synthetic data always bring better translation (lesson: "more data is better"), or rather whether larger synthetic data eventually faces a ceiling for the improvement of translation quality, and if yes, whether that ceiling is approached asymptotically ("more data is either better or not harmful") or reached as a global maximum after which performance decays ("more data is better only to some level, after which it is harmful").

Knowing the answers to these questions is important in order to understand what is the strength that can be expected from self-learning NMT with back-translation and how to make the most efficient use of this technique.

To pursue this goal, we focused on NMT self-learning curves with back-translation. We perform experiments on a highly resourced language pair, viz. German-English, and on a under resourced pair, viz. Portuguese-Chinese. This permits to study the effects of back-translation on different language pairs as well as on different scenarios concerning the availability of resources for NMT.

We found that the performance gains obtained with back-translation do not extend indefinitely, and that in fact there is a point where they peak, after which quality keeps falling. This was observed for both back-translation methods, beam and beam+noise, and also for both pairs of languages, the high-resourced and the low-resourced language pair. We found also that the beam+noise method provides better results in the highly resourced than in the under resourced scenario.

The remaining of this paper is organized as follows. Related work is presented in Sect. 2 and Sect. 3 addresses the methods of obtaining synthetic parallel corpora. Section 4 describes the setup for the various experiments carried out. Sections 5 and 6 present and discuss the results obtained. Finally, Sect. 7 closes this document with concluding remarks.

2   Related Work

Back-translation was initially proposed for Statistical MT, whose data-driven methods also benefit from additional synthetic parallel data [17]. Following this approach, [12] implemented the first NMT system that resorted to back-translated data. They compared back-translation to the mere addition of plain monolingual target data, on both source and target sides, and found that while both methods improved performance, back-translation leads to a significantly larger gain.

Motivated by this result, the usage of back-translation became common practice with NMT. In the most recent Conference on Machine Translation WMT2019 [2], nearly two-thirds of the participating systems used back-translation in some way.

Papers that followed [12] studied the impact of the variation in the quantity of synthetic data provided for training [10], as well as the better methods for obtaining synthetic data [4].

Other studies focused on filtering the synthetic corpus [6] in order to increase its average quality. [5,18], in turn, studied an iterative approach where a system trained on synthetic data is used to create an additional batch of synthetic data, which is then added to the training set and used to train the next version of the system, and so on.

While related to the results of the above mentioned papers, our research question is different from theirs. Rather than seeking to further perfect back-translation, here we are interested in gaining insight about the learning curves of NMT systems supported by back translation.

3   Methods for Back-Translation

When using synthetic parallel corpus to train NMT systems, the natural (non-synthetic) sentences are used in the target language side and their synthetic counterparts, obtained via machine translation from the natural ones, in the source side, rather than vice-versa. In this way, rather in the opposite fashion, the trained system is able to produce better sentences since the natural sentences

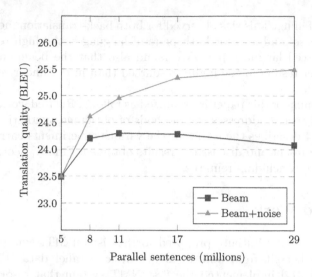

Fig. 1. Learning curves with back-translation with beam and beam+noise methods for English→German. Reproduced from [4].

are usually of good quality—even though the source sentences can be noisy at times.

The synthetic corpus produced with the seed NMT system is then concatenated with the seed parallel corpus, leading to a larger corpus, with more sentence diversity, which supports the training of a translation system with better performance than the seed one. The quality of this system is tied not only to the quantity but also to the quality of the synthetic parallel data, which is impacted by the method used to obtain the synthetic translation.

3.1   Beam Search

The most common approach used to obtain the synthetic translations involves the use of beam search [12], which eventually consists of picking, for a given source sentence, its best (i.e. most likely) translation and adding that source-translation pair to the synthetic corpus.

While, at first blush, picking the most likely translation could seem the best approach, it turns out not to be so, with other methods outperforming it substantially [4]. This happens because always picking the most likely translation leads to less varied translations, as alternative translations that are not the most likely one—though often close to it—will never be picked to integrate the synthetic parallel corpus.

Another problem found with this approach is that performance drops after a certain amount of back-translated synthetic data is added if that data has been obtained with beam search. This behaviour is visible in Fig. 1, adapted from [4]. The first data point in the figure represents the score of the seed model—for the

Monolingual sentence (German)	Der schnelle braune Fuchs springt über den faulen Hund .
Beam search output (English)	The quick brown fox jumps over the lazy dog .
Randomly delete words	The quick brown jumps over the lazy dog .
Randomly replace words with filler tokens	The quick <BLANK> jumps over the lazy <BLANK> .
Randomly shuffle words	quick <BLANK> The jumps over lazy . the <BLANK>

Fig. 2. Adding noise to the output of beam search

beam and the beam+noise methods—trained on 5 million English-German parallel natural sentences. Each subsequent point represents the addition of different amounts of synthetic parallel data.[1] A drop in quality is visible after adding 12 million synthetic parallel sentences when the synthetic corpus is obtained via beam search, but not when it is obtained with the beam+noise method.

3.2 Beam Search+Noise

Different methods have been proposed to mitigate the problem of lack of diversity in back-translated data. One of them is to inject noise [8] into the translations obtained, by randomly changing the order of words, randomly erasing words, or randomly replacing words with a filler token.

We use here the same technique as [4], and add noise to the synthetic sentences by applying the following operations in sequence: (i) deleting words with a probability of 0.1, (ii) replacing words by a filler token—we use the token <BLANK>—with a probability of 0.1, and (iii) randomly shuffling words no further than three positions apart.

Edunovo et al. [4] are not explicit concerning the exact method they used to implement the third step. We based our implementation on the description provided in [8]. Each word is initially assigned an index, $1 \ldots n$, corresponding to its position in the sentence. Next, for each word, an uniformly random real number from the range $[0; 4[$ is picked and added to the index of that word. Finally, the words are placed in the sentence following the sorting by their indexes. Figure 2 illustrates the several steps of adding noise to the beam search outputs.

From Fig. 1, [4] observe that adding noise to the output of beam search outperforms the method of using only beam search, and that no decrease in quality was found as the size of the synthetic corpus is exetended (for the amount of synthetic parallel data they resorted to).

---

[1] This model is trained on a total of 17 million sentences: 5 million of the seed corpus and 12 million of the back-translated corpus. We will use this notation throughout this work, with the first point in the plot representing the seed system, and the subsequent corpora resulting from the addition of the seed corpora with the synthetic corpora.

4   Experimental Setup

This section presents the NMT architecture we used in this paper, as well as the corpora and pre-processing steps resorted to for each experiment. This is followed by the description of the experiments carried out.

4.1   NMT Architecture

We adopt the Transformer model [16] with the "Base" settings, which consist of 6 encoder and decoder layers, 8 attention heads and embedding size of 512.

The Transformer model follows the standard sequence to sequence architecture [14] where an Encoder stack encodes the input sequence, regardless of its length, into a vector of fixed dimensionality, that is then decoded into the target sequence by a Decoder stack.

The main innovations of the Transformer model are in (i) how it relies solely on the attention mechanism [1], dispensing with any of the recurrent modules of previous architectures; and (ii) how it resorts to multiple heads of attention and self-attention, all in all ending with a model that has better performance and needs less training time.

We use the Transformer implementation in the Marian framework [7] and we train with a patience of 10 over the validation on the development corpus every 5,000 updates.

4.2   Corpora

Portuguese-Chinese. In the low-resource scenario, to create the seed system, we used the data sets used in [11]. The Portuguese-Chinese UM-PCorpus [3] has 1 million parallel sentence pairs and was used to train the seed system. The 5,000 sentence pairs of the UM-PCorpus together with the training corpus will be used as development data. The first 1,000 sentences from the News Commentary v11 corpus [15] were used as test set.

The monolingual corpus from which the synthetic parallel data will be obtained is MultiUN [15], composed of documents of the United Nations with close to 11 million sentences.

Every corpus is pre-processed with the Moses tokenizer,[2] for Portuguese, and with the Jieba segmentation tool,[3] for Chinese. Vocabularies with 32,000 sub-word units [13] are learned separately[4] for both languages of the seed corpus. We do so because for this language pair translation quality is lower when vocabularies are learned together and embedding layers are shared [11].

English-German. For the German-English experiments, we trained the seed system on the same data set as [4], that is all the WMT 2018 parallel data, with the exception of the ParaCrawl corpus. We also remove all sentence pairs where

---

[2] https://github.com/alvations/sacremoses.
[3] https://github.com/fxsjy/jieba.
[4] https://github.com/rsennrich/subword-nmt.

one of the sentences is longer than 250 words, and every pair with a length ratio between source and target larger than 1.5 or smaller than 0.5.

Differently from [4], who use newstest2012 for development and testing, we used newstest2012 corpus for development, and the newstest2019 corpus for testing.

Like in [4], the monolingual corpus from which the synthetic parallel data was obtained is the German monolingual newscrawl data distributed with WMT 2018. We filter this monolingual corpus by removing duplicates and sentences longer than 250 words, with the resulting data set having slightly more than 226 million sentences.

The corpora were pre-processed with the Moses tokenizer, and a joined vocabulary with 32,000 sub-word units was learned.

4.3   Experiments

In order to assess if back-translation always improves translation quality with the addition of new synthetic data, we carried out three experiments.

We experiment with the two methods for obtaining synthetic parallel data presented in Sect. 3 for the Portuguese→Chinese pair. For English→German, we experimented with the beam+noise method, as the learning curve with the beam method had already been shown in [4] to have a n-shape with a tipping point for this language pair, depicted in Fig. 1.

Portuguese→Chinese. The Portuguese-Chinese language pair has very few resources available for it [3] and is under-represented in the NMT literature. Back-translation appears as a promising option to improve translation quality for this pair.

The experiment with this language pair permits to study the impact of back-translation in a scenario with more demanding conditions, namely with less language resources and for languages from two very disparate language families.

For Portuguese-Chinese, and for each method (beam and beam+noise), we trained four systems with different amounts of added synthetic data, namely with 1, 3, 6 and 10 million synthetic sentence pairs obtained with the initial seed system.

English→German. The use of the English-German language pair is the natural follow-up of the experiments undertaken in [4], focusing on the beam+noise method. This permits also an experimental scenario that contrasts with the previous one in that we are dealing with one of the most researched language pair, with many more language resources to support NMT.

To study the behaviour of the beam+noise method on English-German, we trained various systems with different amounts of added synthetic parallel data. The seed model was trained with the same 5 million parallel sentences as in [4]. and was then used to produce synthetic parallel data, with which we trained six new models with 2, 5, 10, 20, 30, and finally 100 million sentences.

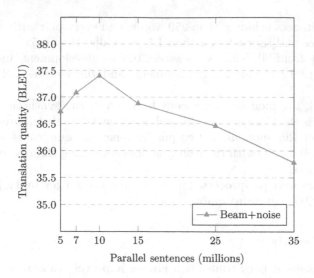

Fig. 3. Learning curve with back-translation with the beam+noise method for English→German

Note that since there are differences in the test corpus and model we are using and the ones used in [4], we cannot continue their work from their last data point, we need to redo performance scores for this experiment.

5   Results

The performance of every NMT model was evaluated with the BLEU metric [9], implemented by the `multi-bleu.perl` script, part of the Moses toolkit.[5]

5.1   English→German

The results for the English→German experiments with the beam+noise method are depicted in Fig. 3. Like with the beam method only (cf. Fig. 1), one observes also here a dip in translation quality after a certain amount of synthetic data is added, with the learning curve peaking at 37.40 BLEU points when 5 million synthetic sentences are added, an improvement over the seed model with 36.73 BLEU points.

We note that, while the Transformer "base" model may not support performance gains with back-translation as large as the Transformer "big" model used in [4], performance improvements can nevertheless still be obtained with the 'base" model.

For the largest amount of added data, 100 million synthetic sentence pairs, translation performance suffers a hard blow, with the model achieving only

---

[5] https://www.statmt.org/moses/.

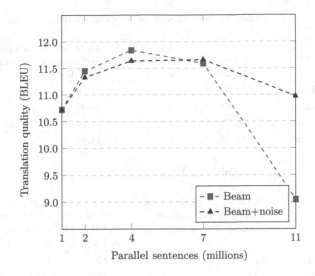

Fig. 4. Learning curves with back-translation with the beam and beam+noise methods for Portuguese→Chinese

28.65 BLEU points—the plot in Fig. 3 is not representing this data point as that would adversely impact the readability of the other points.

5.2 Portuguese→Chinese

Beam Search. As depicted in Fig. 4, back-translation for the Chinese - Portuguese language pair with the beam search method suffers also a drop in quality after a certain amount of synthetic data is added. The performance of the seed model for Portuguese→Chinese has 10.72 BLEU points. The models enriched with back-translation have improvements until 3 million synthetic sentences are added, reaching 11.84 BLEU points. After this, performance scores start falling, confirming that back-translation with beam search has a peak, after which adding more synthetic sentences only harms translation performance.

Beam+Noise. As can be observed in Fig. 4, the same behaviour occurs with the beam+noise method except that to reach the tipping point, a larger amount of synthetic data than with the beam method alone is needed.

The seed model is the same as for the beam search method, with 10.72 BLEU points. The following three data points see cumulative improvements, peaking at 11.66 BLEU points for the model trained with 6 million synthetic sentences added (7 million in total). This is also where the beam+noise method outperforms the beam method for the first time. But while the beam+noise method outperforms the beam method from that point onward, its maximum (11.66) is lower than the maximum (11.84) achieved by the beam search method. For the next model trained with the largest amount of data, 11 million, there is a drop in quality. This dip, however, is considerably smoother than what is observed for

Table 1. Seed model vs Tipping model

		Seed performance (BLEU)	Seed size (million sent.)	Tipping performance (BLEU)	Tipping size (million sent.)
En→De	Beam+noise	36.73	5	37.40	10
	Beam	23.49	5	24.30	11
Pt→Zh	Beam+noise	10.72	1	11.66	7
	Beam	10.72	1	11.84	04

Table 2. Performance gains

		Delta performance (BLEU)	Delta Size (million sent.)	Performance gain [tip. BLEU/seed BLEU] (%)	Performance gain rate [delta performance/ delta size] (BLEU points/million sent.)
En→De	Beam+noise	0.67	5	1.82%	0.13
	Beam	0.81	6	3.45%	0.14
Pt→Zh	Beam+noise	0.94	6	8.77%	0.16
	Beam	1.12	3	10.45%	0.37

the beam method, which confirms that the beam+noise method performs better than the beam method for larger amounts of data.

When comparing Figs. 1 and 4, one observes that the superiority of the beam+noise over the beam method is inverted. This is in line with similar inversion already noticed by [4] on two other methods, where the relative ranking of the beam and sampling methods depends on the amount of data used to create the seed model, with the sampling method outperforming the beam method in a highly resourced scenario, and vice-versa in an under resourced scenario.

6   Discussion

To help profiling the self-learning with back-translation, key scores and figures are combined and gathered in Tables 1 and 2.

The performance gain is larger in the under-resourced scenario (10.45% and 8.77% with the beam and the beam+noise method, respectively), illustrated by the Portuguese-Chinese language pair, than in the highly-resourced scenario (3.45% and 1.82% with the beam-noise and the beam method, respectively), illustrated by the English-German scenario. Back-translation is more effective in an under-resource scenario as it provides a better boost of translation quality when the seed system is trained with smaller amounts of data.

Back-translation is also more efficient in an under-resourced scenario as, proportionally, it requires a smaller extension of the seed data to obtain the same level of performance enhancement. The performance gain rate is larger for Portuguese-Chinese(0.37 and 0.16 BLEU points/M sentences with the beam and the beam+noise method, respectively) than for English-German(0.14 and 0.13). With the best performance gain observed (10.45%)—in the case of Pt→Zh + Beam —, the tipping performance attained is a humble 11.84 BLEU score. To attain the best tipping performance observed (37.40 BLEU score)—in the case of En→De + Beam+noise —, back-translation helps with a humble 1.82% of performance gain with respect to the seed system. Interestingly, in terms of absolute size of the volume of synthetic data necessary to be added to reach the tipping performance, that increment lies in the short range of 3M to 6M sentences, irrespective of the type of scenario at stake.

All in all, taking into account the research question in this paper, the key lesson learned when profiling NMT self-learning with back-translation is that "more data is better only to some level, after which it is harmful".

7 Conclusion

Back-translation is a widely used technique for creating synthetic parallel corpus, by translating monolingual data with a seed translation system to augment the amount of data available for training a new model. While back-translation has been found to be a valid technique for obtaining models with better performance, the evidence gathered in this paper indicates that the gains are not ever growing with the addition of more synthetic data. The performance peaks at some point, after which adding more back-translated data only hurts performance.

Our experiments addressed two methods for generating back-translated data, plain beam search and beam+noise, and were run for two language pairs representing different scenarios of resource availability, Chinese-Portuguese for a scenario of low resource availability, and English-German for a scenario of high resource availability. The finding that performance peaks before starting to drop was consistent throughout all experiments. We also confirm that the best method for generating back-translated data depends on the quality of the seed model doing the back-translation, with the beam+noise method being better suited for high resource scenarios, as this method outperforms beam search for the English-German highly resource language pair, but is outperformed by the latter for the under resourced Portuguese-Chinese language pair.

We conclude that back-translation, despite its strengths, is not an approach that should always be applied to ultimately arrive at a better system. The gains obtained from back-translation peak at some point, but the point where this peak occurs depends on various factors, such as the quality of the seed system and the method used for back-translation. As such, the use of back-translation should be carefully considered and monitored to eventually not reduce translation quality.

Acknowledgement. This research was partially supported by PORTULAN CLARIN–Research Infrastructure for the Science and Technology of Language, funded by Lisboa 2020, Alentejo 2020 and FCT–Fundação para a Ciência e Tecnologia under the grant PINFRA/22117/2016.

References

1. Bahdanau, D., Cho, K., Bengio, Y.: Neural machine translation by jointly learning to align and translate. In: Proceedings of the International Conference on Learning Representations (ICLR) (2015)
2. Barrault, L., et al.: Findings of the 2019 conference on machine translation (WMT19). In: Proceedings of the 4th Conference on MT, pp. 1–61 (2019)
3. Chao, L.S., Wong, D.F., Ao, C.H., Leal, A.L.: UM-PCorpus: a large Portuguese-Chinese parallel corpus. In: Proceedings of the LREC 2018 Workshop "Belt and Road: Language Resources and Evaluation", pp. 38–43 (2018)
4. Edunov, S., Ott, M., Auli, M., Grangier, D.: Understanding back-translation at scale. In: Proceedings of the 2018 Conference on Empirical Methods in Natural Language Processing, pp. 489–500 (2018)
5. Hoang, V.C.D., Koehn, P., Haffari, G., Cohn, T.: Iterative back-translation for neural machine translation. In: Proceedings of the 2nd Workshop on Neural Machine Translation and Generation, pp. 18–24 (2018)
6. Imamura, K., Fujita, A., Sumita, E.: Enhancement of encoder and attention using target monolingual corpora in neural machine translation. In: Proceedings of the 2nd Workshop on Neural Machine Translation and Generation, pp. 55–63 (2018)
7. Junczys-Dowmunt, M., et al.: Fast neural machine translation in C++. In: Proceedings of ACL 2018, System Demonstrations, pp. 116–121 (2018)
8. Lample, G., Conneau, A., Denoyer, L., Ranzato, M.: Unsupervised machine translation using monolingual corpora only. In: International Conference on Learning Representations (ICLR) (2018)
9. Papineni, K., Roukos, S., Ward, T., Zhu, W.J.: BLEU: a method for automatic evaluation of machine translation. In: Proceedings of the 40th Annual Meeting of the Association for Computational Linguistics, pp. 311–318 (2002)
10. Poncelas, A., Shterionov, D., Way, A., de Buy Wenniger, G.M., Passban, P.: Investigating backtranslation in neural machine translation. In: 21st Annual Conference of the European Association for Machine Translation, pp. 249–258 (2018)
11. Santos, R., Silva, J., Branco, A., Xiong, D.: The direct path may not be the best: Portuguese-Chinese neural machine translation. In: Progress in Artificial Intelligence (EPIA 2019), pp. 757–768 (2019)
12. Sennrich, R., Haddow, B., Birch, A.: Improving neural machine translation models with monolingual data. In: Proceedings of the 54th Annual Meeting of the Association for Computational Linguistics (Volume 1: Long Papers), pp. 86–96 (2016)
13. Sennrich, R., Haddow, B., Birch, A.: Neural machine translation of rare words with subword units. In: Proceedings of the 54th Annual Meeting of the Association for Computational Linguistics (Volume 1: Long Papers), pp. 1715–1725 (2016)
14. Sutskever, I., Vinyals, O., Le, Q.V.: Sequence to sequence learning with neural networks. In: Neural Information Processing Systems, pp. 3104–3112 (2014)
15. Tiedemann, J.: Parallel data, tools and interfaces in OPUS. In: Proceedings of the 8th International Conference on Language Resources and Evaluation (LREC 2012), pp. 2214–2218 (2012)
16. Vaswani, A., et al.: Attention is all you need. In: Neural Information Processing Systems, pp. 5998–6008 (2017)
17. Wu, H., Wang, H., Zong, C.: Domain adaptation for statistical machine translation with domain dictionary and monolingual corpora. In: Proceedings of the 22nd International Conference on Computational Linguistics, pp. 993–1000 (2008)
18. Zhang, Z., Liu, S., Li, M., Zhou, M., Chen, E.: Joint training for neural machine translation models with monolingual data. In: 32nd AAAI Conference (2018)

Answering Fill-in-the-Blank Questions in Portuguese with Transformer Language Models

Hugo Gonçalo Oliveira[✉]

Department of Informatics Engineering, CISUC, University of Coimbra,
Coimbra, Portugal
hroliv@dei.uc.pt

Abstract. Despite different applications, transformer-based language models, like BERT and GPT, learn about language by predicting missing parts of text. BERT is pretrained in Masked Language Modelling and GPT generates text from a given sequence. We explore such models for answering cloze questions in Portuguese, following different approaches. When options are not considered, the largest BERT model, trained exclusively for Portuguese, is the most accurate. But when selecting the best option, top performance is achieved by computing the most probable sentence, and GPT-2 fine-tuned for Portuguese beats BERT.

Keywords: BERT · Masked language model · GPT · Cloze questions · Fill-in-the-blank · Semantics

1 Introduction

Tests for language learners are suitable means of assessing Natural Language Processing (NLP), because they put developed techniques in the same scenarios as humans, thus enabling to analyse how they compare. It is thus no surprise that benchmarks have been created from such tests. Examples include the Test of English as a Foreign Language (TOEFL)[1], with 80 multiple-choice synonym questions; or Entrance Exams, a former CLEF track [20], with multiple-choice questions about a given textual document.

Suitable tests include cloze questions, i.e., sentences where a blank replaces a word and the goal is to select this word from a list of options. At a first glance, this task suits well bidirectional language models, such as BERT [5], which is based on a Transformer neural network and currently used in many NLP tasks. BERT models are pretrained in two tasks, one of which is Masked Language Modelling (MLM), where it learns precisely to predict masked words (i.e., blanks) in a text, considering both the left and the right context. This also means that such models can be used in this task without further fine-tuning. But another transformer-based model, GPT-2 [17], can also be useful in a similar scenario,

---

[1] https://aclweb.org/aclwiki/TOEFL_Synonym_Questions_(State_of_the_art).

© Springer Nature Switzerland AG 2021
G. Marreiros et al. (Eds.): EPIA 2021, LNAI 12981, pp. 739–751, 2021.
https://doi.org/10.1007/978-3-030-86230-5_58

as it generates text, given input sequences. Having this in mind, as well as the goal of language models (LMs), using BERT and GPT-2 for answering fill-in-the-blank questions for language learners seems only natural.

The present study can be seen as a benchmark on how well recent LMs actually learn about the proper usage of the Portuguese language. They are explored when answering a set of 3,890 multiple-choice cloze questions, created in the scope of REAP.PT [24], a tutoring system for teaching Portuguese to foreigners. Two experiments were performed for automatically filling in the blanks: one does not consider the options, and the other selects the best option. Methods for the previous were tested with three BERT models that cover the Portuguese language, Multilingual BERT, by the developers of BERT, and BERTimbau [25] base and large; and also a GPT-2 model fine-tuned for Portuguese.

When options are not considered, the best performance is by BERT's MLM, specifically the large model. But even though MLM adapts well to the prediction of suitable words, the test is quite challenging and, without considering the options, accuracy is low. Moreover, when the problem becomes choosing the best option, it is by far preferable to compute the most probable sentence, based on internal raw predictions of the model. Here, the best model was GPT-2, which selected the best option for 80% of the questions, which doubles the accuracy of answering the same questions by exploiting lexical knowledge bases [10].

After this introduction, we overview transformer-based LMs and their application for solving language tests, like cloze questions. Then we describe the dataset and the tested models, and present the two experiments performed, together with the approaches followed, the results achieved, and some examples. The paper ends with a brief summary of the main conclusions.

2 Background and Related Work

Transformers [26] are a neural network architecture with attention mechanisms, popularly adopted in NLP, due to its ability to capture several linguistic phenomena. There are many language models (LMs) based on this architecture, out of which we highlight GPT [17] and BERT [5].

GPT uses only the decoder blocks of the Transformer and is a one-way model that learns to predict text based on the left context. As traditional LMs, it suits well text generation. BERT uses only the encoder and is a bidirectional model, because it considers both left and right context when learning contextual representations of words and sentences.

Such models learn about general language in pretraining. BERT does this through Masked Language Modelling (MLM), where it learns to predict 15% of the (masked) tokens in a large collection of texts, and Next Sentence Prediction (NSP), where it learns whether a sentence should follow another. GPT is pretrained in the prediction of the tokens following a given sequence.

But both models may be further fine-tuned for other tasks. When first presented [5], fine-tuned versions of BERT achieved state-of-the-art in a range of downstream NLP tasks, including Named Entity Recognition, Natural Language Inference and Question Answering in the SQuAD [18] test. BERT has since then been heavily used in NLP, including in tests like RACE [13], a multiple-choice Machine Reading Comprehension test based on English exams for Chinese students. Some of the best results in RACE are achieved with ALBERT [14], a lighter BERT, e.g., by leveraging on knowledge transferred from other question answering datasets and, together with a binary classifier, computing the confidence on each option [12]. GPT is typically fine-tuned for different domains, styles or languages, and it has been shown to perform some NLP tasks (e.g., question-answering) unsupervisedly [17].

Even though fine-tuning these models is common and necessary for many tasks, pretrained models can sometimes be enough. For instance, they have been explored for analogy solving, semantic similarity and relation discovery [7]; and assessed for the presence of relational knowledge [15], when used for filling blanks ending sentences like *"iPod Touch is produced by ..."*. This suits well GPT models but, as long as the blank corresponds to a single token, BERT MLM may be used as well. But having the blank in any position is precisely what BERT MLM is trained for, considering both left and right context, whereas GPT will only consider the left. BERT was further assessed in a cloze task [8], to conclude that it performs particularly well for retrieving hypernyms (e.g., *"A robin is a ..."*), but has difficulties with negation (e.g., *"A robin is not a ..."*). There is also work on filling blanks that spread for more than one token [6], and on reformulating input examples of some tasks as cloze-style phrases, thus helping LMs to better understand the tasks [23], but both are out of the scope of this paper.

Since pretraining transformer-based LMs requires many computational resources, originally, there were only BERT models for English and Chinese. A multilingual model, covering 104 languages, included Portuguese, and it was fine-tuned for computing Semantic Textual Similarity [21,22]. BERTimbau [25], pretrained exclusively for (Brazilian) Portuguese, became available one year later and lead to improvements on the state-of-the-art of Named Entity Recognition, Sentence Textual Similarity and Recognizing Textual Entailment. As for GPT, using the most recent GPT-3 [2] requires an approval by OpenAI, but pretrained versions of GPT-2, with different sizes, are available for usage by anyone. They were pretrained in English text but, recently, the small GPT-2 was fine-tuned for Portuguese, under the name GPorTuguese-2.

To our knowledge, and despite their suitability, the aforementioned models have not been used for answering cloze questions in Portuguese. Previous attempts, on the same dataset as ours, exploited the question context and lexical knowledge bases [10]. The best approach was based on random walks on a graph of relations from three Portuguese dictionaries [11], biased on the context words (Personalized PageRank) [16]. Overall accuracy was 40.7%, higher for nouns (47%) than for verbs (37%), adjectives (36%) and adverbs (28%).

3 Experimentation Setup

It has been shown that pretrained BERT and GPT-2 models capture much syntactic and semantic knowledge on the language(s) they are trained on. Thus, our main goal is to exploit them for automatically answering cloze questions in Portuguese, originally created for learners of Portuguese as a second language. This section describes the dataset used in our experiments, presents the tested models, and adds some details on implementation.

3.1 Data

Given the nature of both BERT and GPT, we see tests made for language learners as a natural benchmark for them. We thus used a collection of cloze questions, produced in the scope of the project REAP.PT [24], a computer-assisted language learning tutoring system for teaching Portuguese to foreigners. Cloze questions include: (i) a sentence where a word (stem) is replaced by a blank; (ii) a list of three distractors. In order to answer them, one has to select the stem from a shuffled list with four options, namely the stem and the distractors.

Questions were produced from sentences of the CETEMPúblico corpus [19], and stems selected from the Portuguese Academic Word List [1], in such a way that stems [3] and distractors [4] were in accordance, i.e., all of them must have the same part-of-speech (PoS) and inflection. Moreover, distractors were automatically checked not to include synonyms of the stem. Figure 1 illustrates the dataset with its first two questions, including the sentence with the blank and the list of options, where the stem is in bold.

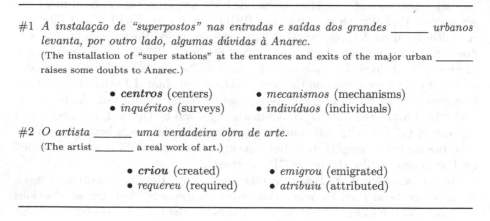

#1 *A instalação de "superpostos" nas entradas e saídas dos grandes _____ urbanos levanta, por outro lado, algumas dúvidas à Anarec.*

(The installation of "super stations" at the entrances and exits of the major urban _____ raises some doubts to Anarec.)

- ***centros*** (centers)
- *inquéritos* (surveys)
- *mecanismos* (mechanisms)
- *indivíduos* (individuals)

#2 *O artista _____ uma verdadeira obra de arte.*

(The artist _____ a real work of art.)

- ***criou*** (created)
- *requereu* (required)
- *emigrou* (emigrated)
- *atribuiu* (attributed)

Fig. 1. First two cloze questions of the dataset used.

In the example, stems are a noun and a verb, respectively for the first and second question. The full dataset has 3,890 questions, with the PoS of the stems distributed as follows: 1,769 nouns, 1,077 verbs, 809 adjectives, 235 adverbs.

3.2 Models

We tested the following transformer-based LMs that cover Portuguese:

- *BERT Base Multilingual Cased* (hereafter, BERT-ML), pretrained by the developers of BERT[2] in 104 languages, including Portuguese, with 179M parameters.
- BERTimbau [25], i.e., *BERT Base Portuguese Cased* (BERT-PT), with 110M parameters, and *BERT Large Portuguese Cased* (BERT-PT-L), with 335M parameters, both pretrained by Neuralmind, exclusively for (Brazilian) Portuguese.
- GPorTuguese-2 (GPT2-PT), with 124M parameters, the result of fine-tuning the small GPT-2 model to Portuguese[3].

All models use 768-sized vectors, except BERT-PT-L, which encodes sequences in 1,024-sized vectors. Moreover, since one of the tasks BERT is pretrained on is MLM, which has a similar goal to cloze question answering, it made sense to use the pretrained BERT versions, with no fine-tuning.

All models were loaded with the Python library *Transformers*[4] and its pipeline objects. For instance, for a mask-filling BERT model one needs only to create a *"fill-mask"* pipeline with the model's name as a parameter. Given a sentence with a masked token (e.g., the blank replaced by [MASK]), such a pipeline can be used for predicting the most suitable filling tokens.

4 Answering Fill-in-the-Blank Questions

Our first goal was to use the transformer models for predicting the most suitable word for a blank (i.e., mask). In this experiment, we assess to what extent these models can predict the correct answer, without considering the options.

4.1 Approach

For each BERT model, this experiment consists of: (i) creating a *"fill-mask"* pipeline; (ii) replacing blanks by the [MASK] token; (iii) using the model for returning a ranked-list with the top-10 most suitable words for each question.

For GPT-2, the steps were: (i) creating a *"text-generation"* pipeline; (ii) considering only the part of the questions before the blank; (iii) using the model for returning a list with 10 suitable sequences (parameter *num_return_sequences*) starting in the considered part of the question and having one more token (*max_length*). All the other parameters had the default values, including the temperature, which was set to 1.

Accuracy is given by the proportion of questions for which the prediction matches the stem (BERT), or the returned sequence ends with the stem (GPT).

---

[2] https://github.com/google-research/bert.
[3] https://huggingface.co/pierreguillou/gpt2-small-portuguese.
[4] https://huggingface.co/transformers/.

4.2   Results

Table 1 has the accuracy of the four models, considering only the first answer (#1) and also the presence of the correct answer in the top-10, overall and according to the PoS of the stem.

Table 1. Proportion of correct answers in the first and top-10 results, for each model.

Model	#1					Top-10				
	Overall	N	V	Adj	Adv	Overall	N	V	Adj	Adv
BERT-PT	14.5%	21.6%	10.2%	7.4%	5.1%	31.5%	42.3%	25.1%	18.8%	12.8%
BERT-PT-L	17.1%	25.0%	12.7%	8.8%	6.8%	34.0%	46.0%	27.3%	20.5%	14.5%
BERT-ML	3.1%	4.7%	2.0%	1.6%	0.4%	9.2%	12.6%	5.7%	4.9%	4.3%
GPT2-PT	1.9%	3.3%	0.6%	1.4%	0.0%	7.9%	11.9%	3.3%	5.6%	1.7%

We note the lowest overall performance of GPT2-PT, for which, in opposition to BERT, answers are based exclusively on the left context. Yet, even though BERT models were pretrained in the MLM task, they also struggled to correctly predict the right answer, with the best accuracy achieved by BERT-PT-ML (#1 = 17.1%). This is about 3 points higher than the accuracy of BERT-PT and more than five times the accuracy of BERT-ML, which immediately suggests that: (i) at least when the task is on a single language, it is preferable to use a model trained exclusively for that language; (ii) the large model is more powerful than the base model.

When considering the presence in the top-10, accuracy doubles for the BERT-PT models, showing that, even if not in first, many correct answers are highly-ranked. Though still lower than 10% for both, performance triples for BERT-ML and quadruples for GPT2-PT. We see also that accuracy varies depending on the PoS of the stem. It is always higher for nouns, followed by verbs, adjectives and, finally, adverbs, with a significantly lower accuracy. The only exception is GPT2-PT, where the second best accuracy is for adjectives.

4.3   Examples

Despite the apparent difficulty of predicting the correct words, generally, predictions still result in fluent sentences, especially with no context in addition to the question. In fact, when looking at some of the incorrect predictions, such as the examples in Fig. 2, we get a notion that some of the questions can be quite challenging, because they require a deep understanding of the full sentence and of syntactic rules. Also, in a minority of cases, the prediction can be used as a synonym of the correct answer (e.g., BERT-PT-L's answer in example #1743).

#1942 *Num doente com uma hemorragia intensa, a [MASK] ocorre instantaneamente e a morte será rápida.*

(In a patient with heavy bleeding, [MASK] occurs instantly and death will be rapid.)

Correct: *inconsciência* (unconsciousness)

BERT-PT	BERT-PT-L	BERT-ML	GPT2-PT
morte (death)	*infecção* (infection)	*doença* (disease)	*equipe* (team)

#1743 *A casa de campo está decorada com artefactos rurais, o que se [MASK] perfeitamente ao local onde foi construída.*

(The country house is decorated with rural artefacts, which perfectly [MASK] the place where it was built.)

Correct: *adequa* (suits)

BERT-PT	BERT-PT-L	BERT-ML	GPT2-PT
integra (integrates)	*aplica* (applies)	*dá* (gives)	*traduz* (translates)

Fig. 2. Examples of incorrectly predicted stems with the mask-filling approach.

5 Answering Multiple Choice Fill-in-the-Blank Questions

Despite being the first, we also see the previous experiment as the most challenging test to the transformer-based LMs. MLM sure has a similar goal to cloze question answering, but predictions by this task do not consider the set of options, nor by text generation. Focusing on the four options strongly restricts the search space, while avoiding issues like answering with synonyms of the right answer. In this second experiment, we explore two approaches for answering fill-in-the-blank questions, this time with the answer being one of the options.

5.1 Approaches

The result of MLM is a ranked list with the top-k predictions for the mask. One can select the top-ranked option as the answer. GPT cannot be used for MLM, but it may generate k sequences, where one may look for the top-ranked option and use it as the answer. These were the first approaches for this experiment. For BERT, we searched for the answer in the top-5,000 predictions, and for GPT, in the top-1,000 completions[5].

An alternative approach is focused exclusively on ranking the four options. More precisely, it computes the most probable sentence when the mask is replaced with each option. For BERT, we resorted to FitBERT[6], a tool that, given a masked sentence and a list of options, selects the most suitable option for the mask, based on pre-softmax logit scores, as performed by Goldberg [9]. For GPT, this is based on the loss of the model for the sequence of tokens.

---

[5] In any case, we empirically checked that, in order to have make a noticeable difference, this number would have to be at least one order of magnitude higher.

[6] https://github.com/Qordobacode/fitbert.

5.2 Results

Table 2 reports the accuracy of the tested approaches, i.e., the proportion of questions for which the selected option is the correct answer. For any approach and model, accuracy improves significantly when focusing on the four options.

Table 2. Proportion of correct answers (Accuracy) with different approaches.

	Model	Accuracy				
		Overall	Nouns	Verbs	Adjectives	Adverbs
Mask-filling	BERT-PT	40.5%	54.3%	32.7%	27.2%	17.4%
	BERT-PT-L	40.5%	54.6%	32.9%	26.9%	17.0%
	BERT-ML	15.8%	21.5%	11.0%	11.1%	11.1%
Generation	GPT2-PT	22.4%	30.3%	14.3%	19.3%	10.6%
Probability	BERT-PT	73.2%	78.5%	77.2%	60.2%	59.6%
	BERT-PT-L	76.7%	82.9%	**78.8%**	64.8%	62.1%
	BERT-ML	46.2%	51.1%	44.7%	40.0%	38.3%
	GPT2-PT	**80.3%**	**84.6%**	77.1%	**79.0%**	**67.7%**

The first conclusion is that the performance of the mask-filling approach is way below computing sentence probability. A closer inspection shows that the former is highly affected by a significant proportion of questions for which the correct answer was not among the top predictions considered, namely 29.3%, 29.2%, 57.7%, and 74.6%, respectively for BERT-PT, BERT-PT-L, BERT-ML and GPT2-PT. However, even when we doubled the number of top predictions, accuracy increased less than 1 point, suggesting that this is just not the most suitable approach in this scenario. Still, with the BERT-PT models, the overall accuracy of 40% matches previous results, based on random walks in a large lexical knowledge base [10]. And it would increase if a random option was given to answer currently unanswered questions. Improvement occur for nouns (54% vs 50%), but not for the other PoS, especially adverbs, the PoS for which more questions are left unanswered. For instance, with BERT-PT-L, about 82% of the noun questions are answered, but only 63%, 64%, and 47% of the verb, adjective and adverb questions respectively. On the other hand, with BERT-ML, accuracy is as low as 15%, lower than GPT2-PT (22.4%). This corresponds to 37% of the answered questions (43.3%), thus still higher than the random chance (25%).

However, it is by a far margin that computing the most probable sentence achieves the highest overall accuracy. Surprisingly, this rank is topped by GPT2-PT (80.3%), a model for which other approaches were not that promising. It is followed by the Portuguese BERT models. This approach not only has an answer for each question, but it takes advantage of the internal raw predictions of the models to compute the most probable resulting sentence and select

#3782 *O João disse-me que ia visitar a Carolina, mas, por [MASK] , encontrámo-la na*
rua e ficámos os três a conversar. (João told me that he was going to visit Carolina, but
for [MASK], we found her on the street and the three of us stayed there, talking.)

Options: **coincidência**, *década, norma, etiqueta*
(**coincidence**, decade, norm, ceremony)

BERT-PT	BERT-PT-L	BERT-ML	GPT2-PT
coincidência	*norma*	*etiqueta*	*coincidência*

#2657 *Muitas pessoas não arriscam uma ida à praia nos meses da Primavera, devido à*
[MASK] do tempo. (Many people do not risk going to the beach in the spring months, due
to the [MASK] weather.)

Options: **inconstância**, *reformulação, implicação, manutenção*
(**changing**, reformulation, implication, maintenance)

BERT-PT	BERT-PT-L	BERT-ML	GPT2-PT
manutenção	*manutenção*	*inconstância*	*inconstância*

#3715 *A história central do filme que vi ontem é fácil de [MASK] , o que não quer dizer*
que seja uma história simples. (The central story of the film I saw yesterday is easy to
[MASK], but this does not mean that it is a simple story.)

Options: **resumir**, *esclarecer, adaptar, declinar*
(**summarise**, clarify, adapt, decline)

BERT-PT	BERT-PT-L	BERT-ML	GPT2-PT
adaptar	*adaptar*	*declinar*	*resumir*

#70 *Já [MASK] o teu dinheiro na conta, podes levantá-lo.* (I already [MASK] your money
to the account, you can withdraw it.)

Options: **creditei**, *desanexei, rastreei, enrijeci*
(**credited**, detached, tracked, stiffened)

BERT-PT	BERT-PT-L	BERT-ML	GPT2-PT
enrijeci	*creditei*	*enrijeci*	*enrijeci*

#40 *Só numa sociedade letrada e generalizadamente [MASK] poderá surgir o impre-*
visto da grande criação cultural. (Only in a literate and generalized [MASK] society the
unexpected of great cultural creation can arise.)

Options: **culta**, *negativa, óbvia, classificada*
(**cultured**, negative, obvious, classified)

BERT-PT	BERT-PT-L	BERT-ML	GPT2-PT
negativa	*classificada*	*negativa*	*culta*

#2609 *O atleta continua a recuperar de uma intervenção cirúrgica ao perónio, com inter-*
venção [MASK] dos ligamentos. (The athlete continues to recover from a surgical intervention to the fibula, with [MASK] intervention of the ligaments.)

Options: **reconstrutiva**, *inovativa, relaxante, computável*
(**reconstructive**, innovative, relaxing, computable)

BERT-PT	BERT-PT-L	BERT-ML	GPT2-PT
reconstrutiva	*reconstrutiva*	*computável*	*relaxante*

#1427 *Falta [MASK] um mês para as eleições legislativas e tudo parece estar em aberto*
quanto ao partido que sairá vencedor. ([MASK] a month for the legislative elections and
everything seems to be open about the party that will win.)

Options: **exactamente**, *distintamente, individualmente, temporariamente*
(**exactly**, distinctly, individually, temporarily)

BERT-PT	BERT-PT-L	BERT-ML	GPT2-PT
temporariamente	*temporariamente*	*temporariamente*	*exactamente*

Fig. 3. Examples of incorrectly predicted stems with the probability approach.

the best option. It is clearly the most suitable approach for answering multiple choice cloze questions, while confirming that, internally, these models have enough knowledge for answering a large portion of challenging questions.

Overall, BERT-PT-L (76.7%) beats BERT-PT again, with BERT-ML well behind. On the performance for each PoS, the trend is still a higher accuracy for nouns, with differences in the remaining (e.g., with GPT2-PT, second best accuracy is for adjectives and, for verbs, it is beaten by BERT-PT-L).

5.3 Examples

Despite the significant increase in performance, even with the best approach and model, about 20% of the questions are answered incorrectly. We are not aware of the typical human performance on this kind of test but, as referred for the first experiment, our feeling, as native speakers, is that the test is actually very challenging, with many questions requiring not only fluency, but also deep knowledge of the language, both at the semantic and syntactic level.

Figure 3 illustrates this with questions where the best approach failed to give the right answer with some models. As expected, there are questions where the only correct answer is by GPT2-PT (#3715) or BERT-PT-L (#70), but also where BERT-PT (#3782) or BERT-ML (#2657) guessed the correct answer and the other BERT models did not. In question #2657, common-sense knowledge is necessary, i.e., that the weather in Spring is unstable. On a minority of examples, incorrect answers could make sense (e.g., BERT-PT-L in #3715 or the others in #40). Finally, in question #1427, all BERT models gave the same answer (temporarily), which is indeed related to the following sequence (a month is a period of time), but results in an odd construction with an unclear interpretation.

6   Conclusion

We have explored transformer-based LMs for automatically answering 3,890 cloze questions in Portuguese. Despite many challenging questions, these models can answer a great portion, especially when the search space is restricted to the four options. This confirms that these are powerful models, with internal representations implicitly capturing a great amount of linguistic knowledge.

We see this as one more contribution towards learning more about transformer-based LMs and how they perform for Portuguese. Among our conclusions, we note that, when options are not available, BERT is more suitable and, even when it does not guess the right answer, frequently produces fluent sentences. Moreover, in the monolingual task tackled, it is preferable to use a BERT model pretrained exclusively in Portuguese, ideally, the large version, as it leads to minor improvements.

When the goal is to select the best of four options, the best performance is achieved by computing the probability of the resulting sentences, based on the internal raw predictions of the models. Following this approach, 80% of the questions were correctly answered with GPT2-PT, beating the best BERT model almost by 4 points. This represents an expressive 40-point improvement, when compared to previous results based on random walks in lexical knowledge bases [10], i.e., this approach correctly answers twice the number of questions than the previous.

Furthermore, we take the idea that the cloze questions dataset can be useful as a benchmark for Portuguese LMs, and to help advancing the state-of-the-art. We thus made it available for anyone, from https://github.com/NLP-CISUC/ClozeQuestions, together with the source code of some of the approaches used in this paper.

Even though we see the achieved performance as promising, especially given the challenging test, there is still room for improvement. In the future, the same test can be answered with other LMs, and, possibly other approaches. We should test GPT-2 with different parameters and, of course, explore GPT-3 [2], which could improve on GPT-2 fine-tuned for Portuguese, but might also struggle for being multilingual, as BERT-ML did. Moreover, variants of BERT and of other neural LMs are expected to be released in a near future, for Portuguese, and thus suitable for attempting at improving the performance reported here.

Acknowledgement. This work was partially funded by: the project SmartEDU (CENTRO-01-0247-FEDER-072620), co-financed by the European Regional Development Fund (FEDER), through Portugal 2020 (PT2020), and by the Regional Operational Programme Centro 2020; and national funds through the FCT – Foundation for Science and Technology, I.P., within the scope of the project CISUC – UID/CEC/00326/2020 and by the European Social Fund, through the Regional Operational Program Centro 2020.

References

1. Baptista, J., Costa, N., Guerra, J., Zampieri, M., Cabral, M., Mamede, N.: P-AWL: academic word list for Portuguese. In: Pardo, T.A.S., Branco, A., Klautau, A., Vieira, R., de Lima, V.L.S. (eds.) PROPOR 2010. LNCS (LNAI), vol. 6001, pp. 120–123. Springer, Heidelberg (2010). https://doi.org/10.1007/978-3-642-12320-7_15
2. Brown, T.B., et al.: Language models are few-shot learners. arXiv:2005.14165 preprint (2020)
3. Correia, R., Baptista, J., Eskenazi, M., Mamede, N.: Automatic generation of *cloze* question stems. In: Caseli, H., Villavicencio, A., Teixeira, A., Perdigão, F. (eds.) PROPOR 2012. LNCS (LNAI), vol. 7243, pp. 168–178. Springer, Heidelberg (2012). https://doi.org/10.1007/978-3-642-28885-2_19
4. Correia, R., Baptista, J., Mamede, N., Trancoso, I., Eskenazi, M.: Automatic generation of cloze question distractors. In: Second Language Studies: Acquisition, Learning, Education and Technology (2010)
5. Devlin, J., Chang, M.W., Lee, K., Toutanova, K.: BERT: pre-training of deep bidirectional transformers for language understanding. In: Proceedings of the 2019 Conference of the North American Chapter of the Association for Computational Linguistics: Human Language Technologies, pp. 4171–4186. ACL (2019)

6. Donahue, C., Lee, M., Liang, P.: Enabling language models to fill in the blanks. In: Proceedings of the 58th Annual Meeting of the Association for Computational Linguistics, pp. 2492–2501. ACL (2020)

7. Ethayarajh, K.: How contextual are contextualized word representations? Comparing the geometry of BERT, ELMo, and GPT-2 embeddings. In: Proceedings of the 2019 Conference on Empirical Methods in Natural Language Processing and 9th International Joint Conference on Natural Language Processing (EMNLP-IJCNLP), pp. 55–65 (2019)

8. Ettinger, A.: What BERT is not: lessons from a new suite of psycholinguistic diagnostics for language models. Trans. Assoc. Comput. Linguist. 8, 34–48 (2020)

9. Goldberg, Y.: Assessing BERT's syntactic abilities. arXiv:1901.05287 (2019)

10. Gonçalo Oliveira, H.: A survey on Portuguese lexical knowledge bases: contents, comparison and combination. Information 9(2), 34 (2018)

11. Gonçalo Oliveira, H., Antón Pérez, L., Costa, H., Gomes, P.: Uma rede léxico-semântica de grandes dimensões para o português, extraída a partir de dicionários electrónicos. Linguamática 3(2), 23–38 (2011)

12. Jiang, Y., et al.: Improving Machine Reading Comprehension with single-choice decision and transfer learning. arXiv:2011.03292 preprint (2020)

13. Lai, G., Xie, Q., Liu, H., Yang, Y., Hovy, E.: RACE: large-scale reading comprehension dataset from examinations. In: Proceedings of the 2017 Conference on Empirical Methods in Natural Language Processing, pp. 785–794 (2017)

14. Lan, Z., Chen, M., Goodman, S., Gimpel, K., Sharma, P., Soricut, R.: ALBERT: a lite BERT for self-supervised learning of language representations. arXiv:1909.11942 preprint (2019)

15. Petroni, F., et al.: Language models as knowledge bases? In: Proceedings of the 2019 Conference on Empirical Methods in Natural Language Processing and 9th International Joint Conference on Natural Language Processing (EMNLP-IJCNLP), pp. 2463–2473. ACL (2019)

16. Pilehvar, M.T., Jurgens, D., Navigli, R.: Align, disambiguate and walk: a unified approach for measuring semantic similarity. In: Proceedings of the 51st Annual Meeting of the Association for Computational Linguistics, pp. 1341–1351. ACL (2013)

17. Radford, A., Wu, J., Child, R., Luan, D., Amodei, D., Sutskever, I.: Language models are unsupervised multitask learners. OpenAI Blog 1(8), 9 (2019)

18. Rajpurkar, P., Zhang, J., Lopyrev, K., Liang, P.: SQuAD: 100,000+ questions for machine comprehension of text. In: Proceedings of the 2016 Conference on Empirical Methods in Natural Language Processing, pp. 2383–2392 (2016)

19. Rocha, P.A., Santos, D.: CETEMPúblico: Um corpus de grandes dimensões de linguagem jornalística portuguesa. In: V Encontro para o processamento computacional da língua portuguesa escrita e falada, PROPOR 2000, pp. 131–140. ICMC/USP (2000)

20. Rodrigo, A., Peñas, A., Miyao, Y., Hovy, E.H., Kando, N.: Overview of CLEF QA Entrance Exams task 2015. In: Working Notes of CLEF 2015 - Conference and Labs of the Evaluation forum. CEUR-WS (2015)

21. Rodrigues, R.C., da Silva, J.R., de Castro, P.V.Q., da Silva, N.F.F., da Silva Soares, A.: Multilingual transformer ensembles for Portuguese natural language tasks. In: Proceedings of the the ASSIN 2 Shared Task: Evaluating Semantic Textual Similarity and Textual Entailment in Portuguese, vol. 2583. CEUR-WS.org (2020)

22. Rodrigues, R., Couto, P., Rodrigues, I.: IPR: the semantic textual similarity and recognizing textual entailment systems. In: Proceedings of the the the ASSIN 2 Shared Task: Evaluating Semantic Textual Similarity and Textual Entailment in Portuguese, vol. 2583. CEUR-WS.org (2020)

23. Schick, T., Schütze, H.: Exploiting cloze-questions for few-shot text classification and natural language inference. In: Proceedings of the 16th Conference of the European Chapter of the Association for Computational Linguistics, pp. 255–269. ACL (2021)

24. Silva, A., Marques, C., Baptista, J., Ferreira, A., Mamede, N.: REAP.PT serious games for learning Portuguese. In: Caseli, H., Villavicencio, A., Teixeira, A., Perdigão, F. (eds.) PROPOR 2012. LNCS (LNAI), vol. 7243, pp. 248–259. Springer, Heidelberg (2012). https://doi.org/10.1007/978-3-642-28885-2_29

25. Souza, F., Nogueira, R., Lotufo, R.: BERTimbau: pretrained BERT models for Brazilian Portuguese. In: Cerri, R., Prati, R.C. (eds.) BRACIS 2020. LNCS (LNAI), vol. 12319, pp. 403–417. Springer, Cham (2020). https://doi.org/10.1007/978-3-030-61377-8_28

26. Vaswani, A., et al.: Attention is all you need. In: Advances in Neural Information Processing Systems, pp. 5998–6008 (2017)

Cross-Lingual Annotation Projection
for Argument Mining in Portuguese

Afonso Sousa[1], Bernardo Leite[1,2] (ID), Gil Rocha[1,2] (ID),
and Henrique Lopes Cardoso[1,2(✉)] (ID)

[1] Faculdade de Engenharia, Universidade do Porto, Porto, Portugal
{ammlss,bernardo.leite,gil.rocha,hlc}@fe.up.pt
[2] Laboratório de Inteligência Artificial e Ciência de Computadores (LIACC), Porto, Portugal

Abstract. While Argument Mining has seen increasing success in monolingual settings, especially for the English language, other less-resourced languages are still lagging behind. In this paper, we build a Portuguese projected version of the Persuasive Essays corpus and evaluate it both intrinsically (through back-projection) and extrinsically (in a sequence tagging task). To build the corpus, we project the token-level annotations into a new Portuguese version using translations and respective alignments. Intrinsic evaluation entails rebuilding the English corpus using back alignment and back projection from the Portuguese version, comparing against the original English annotations. For extrinsic evaluation, we assess and compare the performance of machine learning models on several language variants of the corpus (including the Portuguese one), following both in-language/projection training and direct transfer. Our evaluation highlights the quality of the generated corpus. Experimental results show the effectiveness of the projection approach, while providing competitive baselines for the Portuguese version of the corpus. The corpus and code are available (https://github.com/ AfonsoSalgadoSousa/argumentation_mining_pt).

Keywords: Natural language processing · Argument mining · Annotation projection · Sequence tagging

1 Introduction

The ability to engage in the process of argumentation is prevalent in human communication. Humans use argumentation to convey inclinations or opinions and reason over them. With the advent of computer technology, the process of automating argumentative reasoning has seen a growing interest.

Argument Mining (AM) aims to automate the identification and extraction of inference structures and reasoning steps employed in natural language argumentation, usually expressed in written texts.

Understanding argumentative structures enables the assessment of the adopted standpoints and the opinions that sustain such positions, and is relevant in several domains, including discourse analysis, summarization, debate modeling, and law, among others [23]. As crucial as AM might be, the ambiguity of natural language

© Springer Nature Switzerland AG 2021
G. Marreiros et al. (Eds.): EPIA 2021, LNAI 12981, pp. 752–765, 2021.
https://doi.org/10.1007/978-3-030-86230-5_59

text, the different writing styles, the implicit context and the complexity of building argument structures make this research area very challenging. In AM, there are not yet many works emphasizing cross-lingual approaches [10]; approaches typically carry out a monolingual setting, mostly in English [22], but also in other languages, such as German [8], or Chinese [15]. Moreover, the expensive effort of acquiring high-quality annotated corpora for new languages, which entails hiring expert annotators or querying large crowds in crowd-sourcing experiments, makes working in AM for less-resourced languages harder. In the absence of good quality corpora, cross-lingual approaches are of utmost importance to train Natural Language Processing (NLP) systems in AM. This is in line with current trends in NLP, which increasingly recognize the possibility and the necessity to work cross-lingually [24].

In this work, we address the problem of cross-lingual AM for the Portuguese language. For that, we build a machine-translated version of one of the most popular AM datasets – the English dataset of persuasive student essays (PE) [28] – and compare the performance of machine learning models trained for the task of sequence tagging of argumentative discourse units (ADU).

In summary, the contributions of this paper are:

- We build and make available a machine-translated version of the Persuasive Essays corpus in Portuguese.
- We propose a tweak when projecting annotations to make the algorithm more resilient to the verbosity of Romance languages.
- We perform token-level sequence tagging for AM on the Portuguese version of the PE corpus, thus extrinsically evaluating its quality by comparing with versions of the corpus in other languages. The trained models and their scores also serve as competitive baselines for further work on these corpora.

The rest of the paper is organized as follows: Sect. 2 concerns visiting the current literature and highlighting the main findings that relate to this work. Section 3 explains the structure and some statistics from the Persuasive Essays corpus and its versions in other languages. Section 4 explains the proposed annotation projection pipeline and its use for generating the Portuguese version of the corpus. Section 5 evaluates the generated corpus in competition with other versions in other languages, through training models for ADU sequence tagging. Finally, Sect. 6 concludes.

2 Related Work

Existing approaches for AM focus on specific sub-tasks, such as argument unit segmentation [1], identifying different types of argument components [12,22], or recognizing argumentative discourse relations [19]); some approaches address the AM problem from an end-to-end perspective [9].

Eger et al. [9] proposed an end-to-end learning pipeline for AM, which combines component type and BIO scheme (beginning-inside-outside) prediction. Nowadays, Transformer-based models, such as BERT [6], are the best performing architectures on multiple NLP tasks, including AM. Wang et al. [30] propose a multi-scale BERT-based model that branches the prediction of each component type based on its scale dependency. As far as we know, this is the best performing solution for component tagging in the PE corpus.

In recent years, there has been an increased interest in evaluating sequence tagging models not only within individual languages [25], but also in cross-lingual settings [33, 35]. Most of the approaches for AM are specifically designed for English, and resources for other languages are scarce. For Portuguese, only a dataset built from a mixture of opinion articles has annotations according to the claim-premise scheme [26].

Cross-lingual approaches try to exploit resources in a resource-rich language when tackling with the same problem in a less-resourced language. Two common techniques to do so are *direct transfer* and *projection*. Direct transfer [18] consists of training models with annotated data in the source language, often using multi-lingual pre-trained word embedding representations feeding a neural network architecture, and employing such models directly on data in the target language. Projection [5,34] entails using parallel data to project existing annotations in the source language to the target language. Eger et al. [10] adopt this approach for AM and show a very narrow deficit from the results obtained using a machine-translated corpus, compared with the results obtained using the human-labeled corpus. Our approach is based on this work.

Parallel data can be obtained by using state-of-the-art neural machine translation (NMT) techniques, which have recently shown significant improvements [32]. Annotation projection relies on alignments between the words in each of the parallel sentences.

Alignment techniques can be employed separately, but some works pursue a multi-task approach for jointly learning to align and translate [2,11]. However, NMT requires sufficient amounts of parallel data to train high-quality machine translation systems, and their performance deteriorates when not enough data is available [20]. For that reason, statistical approaches to word alignment are still widely used, such as Giza++ [21] and fast-align [7]. SimAlign [14] leverages high quality contextualized word embeddings [3,6] to create similarity matrices that are then fed to three different proposed algorithms to create the alignments.

3   Corpora

As noted by Rocha et al. [27], for NLP tasks in a cross-language setting, argument annotated corpora are required in different languages and should ideally: (a) contain annotations of arguments in different languages, (b) follow the same argumentation theory, and (c) belong to the same genre of text and similar domains. One of the most widely used corpora for AM is the Persuasive Essays (PE) corpus [28], which follows a claim-premise model of argumentation. This corpus is composed of 402 English essays on controversial topics, such as "Advantages and disadvantages of machines over humans". Table 1 details some of the corpus statistics. Argument annotations distinguish between the *major claim* (the central position of an author with respect to the essay's topic), *claims* (controversial statements that are either *for* or *against* the major claims), and *premises*, which give reasons for claims or other premises and either *support* or *attack* them. Overall, there are 751 major claims, 1506 claims, and 3832 premises. There are 5338 relations, most of which are supporting relations (>90%) [9].

Table 1. Statistics of the persuasive essays corpus.

	Train	Dev	Test
Paragraphs	1587	199	449
Sentences	4866	586	1383
Tokens	105988	12657	29537
Unique words	7299	2199	3703

The corpus was further extended to include projected versions in German, Spanish, French, and Chinese [10]. The Spanish and German versions were used in this work (Sect. 5) as benchmarks to compare with our approach.

4 Annotation Projection

We build a Portuguese version of the PE dataset using annotation projection, relying on automatic machine translation and word alignment tools.

4.1 Input Data

For this work, the data used is the CoNLL-formatted, paragraph-level version of the PE dataset[1]. The CoNLL format scheme (see example in Fig. 1) provides token-level annotations for ADUs and their relations, following the BIO scheme notation to denote tokens as non-argumentative (**Outside**), as the start of an ADU component (**Beginning**), or as an inner token of an ADU (**Inside**). Each component can be either a claim (C), a premise (P), or a major claim (MC). This results in a total of 7 token labels: 'O', 'B-MajorClaim', 'I-MajorClaim', 'B-Claim', 'I-Claim', 'B-Premise', 'I-Premise'. ADU relations have not been projected to the language variants of PE [10] and are also out of the scope of this work; however, they are projected in our Portuguese version of the PE corpus.

4.2 Translation

For translation, we opted for automatic translation techniques. While the hand-crafted solution might be less erroneous, the literature suggests that machine translation algorithms, and more specifically transformer-based models, generate good quality context-aware translations [10,32]. To leverage the contextual capabilities of transformer-based translators, we have conducted translations at the paragraph level. We rely on a pre-trained transformer-based translation model [29] from the HuggingFace framework[2]. The specifications of the translation model are not integral to this work as these new neural machine translation models have a very good performance [32]. However, it is

---

[1] https://github.com/UKPLab/acl2017-neural_end2end_am/tree/master/data/conll/Paragraph_Level.

[2] https://huggingface.co/Helsinki-NLP/opus-mt-en-ROMANCE.

```
44      are         I-Premise:54:Support
45      watched     I-Premise:54:Support
46      closely     I-Premise:54:Support
47      and         I-Premise:54:Support
48      judged      I-Premise:54:Support
49      by          I-Premise:54:Support
50      the         I-Premise:54:Support
51      community   I-Premise:54:Support
52      .           O
53      But         O
54      during      B-Claim:For
55      our         I-Claim:For
56      childhood   I-Claim:For
```

Fig. 1. Example CoNLL-formatted snippet. Left: 1-based index of the token in the paragraph. Center: token. Right: BIO-scheme label; ADU type; first token in the ADU targeted by the current ADU; relation type (the premise containing tokens 44–51 supports the claim starting at token 54).

worth noting that this model was trained on OPUS[3], using a set of different languages, encompassing both European and Brazilian Portuguese.

4.3 Alignment

Parallel sentences, in English (EN) and Portuguese (PT), of the PE corpus were aligned using SimAlign [14], which claims superior performance over various statistically-based alignment methods for text alignment without requiring parallel training data. The authors propose three different approaches: Argmax, a fast solution which finds just local optima, with a naive solution for tied similarities; Itermax, a greedy algorithm applying Argmax iteratively; and Match, a slower solution which finds the global maximum using a bipartite weighted graph and frames alignments as an assignment problem.

We empirically test these approaches regarding the number of tokens in the source language that are left out without alignment. For the *dev* set we got 80.39%, 32.4% and 4.55% of ADUs with at least one missing token in the respective alignment, for Argmax, Itermax and Match, respectively. The Match approach was by far superior to the other approaches in this dataset. The translated *train*, *dev* and *test* sets achieved a similar percentage of ADUs with missing alignments (2.4%, 4.43% and 3.86%, respectively).

For illustration purposes, we show an example selected from the *dev* set:

- EN: $First_0$ and_1 $foremost_2$, $_3$ $email_4$ can_5 be_6 $count_7$ as_8 one_9 of_{10} the_{11} $most_{12}$ $beneficial_{13}$ $results_{14}$ of_{15} $modern_{16}$ $technology_{17}$ $._{18}$
- PT: $Primeiro_0$ e_1 $acima_2$ de_3 $tudo_4$ $,_5$ o_6 $email_7$ $pode_8$ ser_9 $contado_{10}$ $como_{11}$ um_{12} dos_{13} $resultados_{14}$ $mais_{15}$ $benéficos_{16}$ da_{17} $tecnologia_{18}$ $moderna_{19}$ $._{20}$
- EN → PT Alignment: [0-0, 1-1, 2-2, 2-3, 2-4, 3-5, 4-7, 5-8, 6-9, 7-10, 8-11, 9-12, 10-13, 11-16, 12-15, 13-16, 14-14, 15-17, 16-19, 17-18, 18-20]

---

[3] https://opus.nlpl.eu/.

The alignment algorithm creates a list of pairs of indices per sentence, where the left index corresponds to the token in the source sentence (English) that aligns with the token in the target sentence (Portuguese) identified by the right index. We can observe that the alignment algorithm was able to correctly map all the tokens to their respective translations. This includes not only the typical switched order of adjectives and nouns ("modern$_{16}$ technology$_{17}$" and "tecnologia$_{18}$ moderna$_{19}$"), but also the challenging token "foremost$_2$", which aligns to three Portuguese tokens ("acima$_2$ de$_3$ tudo$_4$"), and the expression "one$_9$ of$_{10}$ the$_{11}$ most$_{12}$ beneficial$_{13}$ results$_{14}$", where two of the tokens ("the$_{11}$" and "beneficial$_{13}$") align with a single one ("benéficos$_{16}$") in the Portuguese translation "um$_{12}$ dos$_{13}$ resultados$_{14}$ mais$_{15}$ benéficos$_{16}$", which is shorter. We can also observe that some tokens in Portuguese are not aligned with any token in English (in this particular case, token "o$_6$", which is a determinant).

4.4 Projection Algorithm

Once we have word-level alignment information, we are able to address the annotation projection task. For each ADU in each source sentence, we build $\langle start, end, component\ type \rangle$ triplets, where $start$ and end are the indices of the first and last tokens of the ADU. We map this span to the ADU in the target language by using the minimum and maximum indices of the target tokens that are aligned with any token in the source ADU, as given by the alignment of both sentences.

To account for the verbosity of Romance languages when compared with Germanic languages – more specifically, the added determinants in Portuguese (or French, as noted by Eger et al. [10]) that have no correspondence from English (see the example in Sect. 4.3) –, we propose a simple but effective heuristic: if the token to the left of the ADU in the target language has no alignment from the source language, we include it in the ADU, thus becoming its new left boundary. We dub this the "padding" heuristic. The following practical example best explains this behavior:

- EN: In$_0$ fact$_{1,2}$ [stringent$_3$ gun$_4$ control$_5$ does$_6$ not$_7$ decrease$_8$ violence$_9$ and$_{10}$ crime$_{11}$] because$_{12}$ [most$_{13}$ gun$_{14}$ violence$_{15}$ is$_{16}$ committed$_{17}$ with$_{18}$ guns$_{19}$ obtained$_{20}$ illegally$_{21}$] .$_{22}$
- PT: De$_0$ fato$_{1,2}$ [o$_3$ rigoroso$_4$ controle$_5$ de$_6$ armas$_7$ não$_8$ diminui$_9$ a$_{10}$ violência$_{11}$ e$_{12}$ o$_{13}$ crime$_{14}$] porque$_{15}$ [a$_{16}$ maioria$_{17}$ da$_{18}$ violência$_{19}$ de$_{20}$ armas$_{21}$ é$_{22}$ cometida$_{23}$ com$_{24}$ armas$_{25}$ obtidas$_{26}$ ilegalmente$_{27}$] .$_{28}$
- EN → PT Alignment: [0-0, 1-1, 2-2, 3-4, 4-7, 5-5, 6-9, 7-8, 8-9, 9-11, 10-12, 11-14, 12-15, 13-17, 14-21, 15-19, 16-22, 17-23, 18-24, 19-25, 20-26, 21-27, 22-28]

In this example, brackets show ADU limits. Neither of the Portuguese determinants "o$_3$" and "a$_{16}$" are part of the alignment; just looking at the minimum and maximum indices to bound the target ADUs' spaces would leave these tokens out. The addition of these non-aligned tokens to the left fixes the respective ADU limits.

Finally, new triplets for the target corpus are created. Algorithm 1 shows these steps.

Onto error handling, if two target components would overlap according to the above-described strategy, we shift the right component of the conflicting pair until these have a disjoint set of tokens. If the tokens in a source ADU are not aligned to

---

Algorithm 1: Building target ADUs for a sentence

Data: s_{ADU} is the set of source ADUs as triplets $\langle start, end, label \rangle$;
$sent\_align$ is the set of aligned index pairs in the sentence
Result: set of target ADUs' triplets
for $\langle start, end, label \rangle \in s_{ADU}$ **do**
$\quad align_{ADU} \leftarrow sent\_align[start, end]$;
$\quad align_{ADU}^t \leftarrow align_{ADU}.targets$;
$\quad idx_{min} \leftarrow min(align_{ADU}^t)$;
$\quad idx_{max} \leftarrow max(align_{ADU}^t)$;
$\quad$ **if** $idx_{min} > 0$ *and* $idx_{min} - 1 \notin sent\_align.targets$ **then**
$\quad\quad\lfloor\ idx_{min} \leftarrow idx_{min} - 1$;
$\quad t_{ADU} \leftarrow t_{ADU} \cup \langle idx_{min}, idx_{max}, label \rangle$;

---

any tokens in the target language, then we ignore the projection of the ADU, labeling the corresponding tokens as non-argumentative instead. However, we are not aware of the latter issue arising in this specific corpus annotation projection, most likely because the alignment method we use is based on a bipartite graph that enforces the paring of every source token. Nevertheless, the approach as a whole is very reliant on the quality of the alignments.

4.5 Intrinsic Evaluation

To assess the quality of the created Portuguese PE corpus, we perform the inverse method to recreate the original English corpus, starting with the annotations in the Portuguese one. The intuition is that by using the same algorithm with the source and target languages reversed, we should be able to obtain the original English corpus with little to no loss in annotation information. To guarantee that the very same tokens are present in the back-projected version of the English corpus, which is important to assess the token-level score against the gold standard, we abstain from back-translating and reuse the already computed translations. We then recompute the alignments (between Portuguese and English sentences) and re-apply back-projection.

This approach inherently carries some noise from recomputing alignments, now from Portuguese to English. The graph-based approach of the SimAlign (see Sect. 4.3) yielded a percentage of ADUs with missing alignments of 68.51%, 71.98% and 65.5%, respectively for *train*, *dev* and *test* sets. This is much higher than the missing alignments from English to Portuguese (see Sect. 4.3). These results suggest that the alignment algorithm is more error-prone when mapping from more tokens to fewer tokens than vice-versa.

The padding approach explained in Sect. 4.4 yielded a prevalence of 13.04%, 21.05% and 15.64% extended ADUs, respectively for the *train*, *dev* and *test* sets. In the reverse projection task, padding had a negligible effect, with such instances occurring in less than 1% of the ADUs for each set.

We evaluate the English back-projected annotations against the original ones (which are seen as the gold standard) using token-level macro-F1 score, relying on the fact that we are looking at the same exact sentences. The per-class and general macro-F1 scores can be seen in Table 2, in which we show results employing the padding approach ("w/ padding") and without it ("w/o padding").

Table 2. Token-level evaluation of the English back-aligned and back-projected corpus (*test* set). Number of tokens is computed for Gold Standard.

	# Tokens	w/ padding			w/o padding		
		Precision	Recall	F1	Precision	Recall	F1
B-Claim	1506	0.83	0.83	0.82	0.82	0.82	0.82
B-MajorClaim	751	0.81	0.81	0.81	0.81	0.80	0.80
B-Premise	3832	0.90	0.89	0.89	0.89	0.88	0.88
I-Claim	20937	0.94	0.99	0.96	0.94	0.99	0.96
I-MajorClaim	10215	0.92	0.99	0.95	0.92	0.99	0.95
I-Premise	63326	0.98	0.99	0.98	0.98	0.99	0.98
O	47615	1.00	0.94	0.96	1.00	0.94	0.96
Overall	148182	0.91	0.92	0.91	0.91	0.92	0.91

Even though the alignment quality is much worse from Portuguese to English than from English to Portuguese, we achieved an overall F1-score of 91.44%. This is because the annotation projection algorithm relies on defining the boundaries for the ADUs to project, meaning the majority of the projection errors are either in the beginning or the end of the ADUs. This claim is supported by the results in Table 2 showing a worse performance for the components at the beginning of the ADUs. Errors are scarcer at the end of the ADUs because the alignment algorithms easily correctly align full stops. The true annotation quality might be higher in practice, as this result suffers from this worse back-alignment. Furthermore, the apparently negligible gain obtained with the introduction of the padding heuristic is misleading. As shown in the example given in Sect. 4.4, many cases of ADU extensions integrate determinants that are not present in English, which in some cases complicate the back alignment process. Therefore, while from a grammatical point of view it makes sense to include such tokens within ADU boundaries (resulting a better projected corpus), this does not necessarily contribute to the intrinsic evaluation score. The following example, taken from the *dev* set, illustrates the problem:

- EN_{gold}: First$_0$ of$_1$ all$_2$,$_3$ it$_4$ seems$_5$ to$_6$ be$_7$ true$_8$ that$_9$ [if$_{10}$ there$_{11}$ is$_{12}$ gun$_{13}$ control$_{14}$ somehow$_{15}$ crime$_{16}$ has$_{17}$ to$_{18}$ decrease$_{19}$] because$_{20}$ [fewer$_{21}$ guns$_{22}$ available$_{23}$ mean$_{24}$ less$_{25}$ crime$_{26}$] .$_{27}$
- $PT_{projected}$: Em$_0$ primeiro$_1$ lugar$_2$,$_3$ parece$_4$ ser$_5$ verdade$_6$ que$_7$ [se$_8$ há$_9$ controle$_{10}$ de$_{11}$ armas$_{12}$ de$_{13}$ alguma$_{14}$ forma$_{15}$ o$_{16}$ crime$_{17}$ tem$_{18}$ de$_{19}$ diminuir$_{20}$] porque$_{21}$ [menos$_{22}$ armas$_{23}$ disponíveis$_{24}$ significa$_{25}$ menos$_{26}$ crime$_{27}$] .$_{28}$
- PT $\rightarrow$ EN Alignment: [0-1, 1-0, 2-2, 3-3, 4-5, 5-7, 6-8, 7-9, 8-10, 9-11, 10-14, 11-12, 12-13, 13-15, 15-15, <u>16-4</u>, 17-16, 18-17, 19-18, 20-6, 20-19, 21-20, 22-21, 23-22, 24-23, 25-24, 26-25, 27-26, 28-27]

- $EN_{back-projected}$: First$_0$ of$_1$ all$_2$,$_3$ [it$_4$ seems$_5$ to$_6$ be$_7$ true$_8$ that$_9$ if$_{10}$ there$_{11}$ is$_{12}$ gun$_{13}$ control$_{14}$ somehow$_{15}$ crime$_{16}$ has$_{17}$ to$_{18}$ decrease$_{19}$] because$_{20}$ [fewer$_{21}$ guns$_{22}$ available$_{23}$ mean$_{24}$ less$_{25}$ crime$_{26}$] .$_{27}$

Brackets show ADU limits and the miss-projected labels correspond to underlined tokens. This example shows the worse performance of back-alignment from Portuguese to English – while labels projected from English to Portuguese are perfect, back-projection features several tokens with the wrong label. This is due to the fact that, in the sentence alignment from Portuguese to English, token 16 is incorrectly aligned with token 4 in English. Since token 16 in Portuguese is part of an ADU, this leads the algorithm to assume that its alignment counterpart is part of the projected ADU – in this case marking its beginning.

Generally speaking, we find these projections being of good quality from the attained F1-score of 91% for the intrinsic evaluation and from empirically searching for anomalies in the generated sentence projections. This is in line with what is stated in Eger et al. [10]. This Portuguese variant of the PE corpus compares to the original one as seen in Table 3.

Table 3. Token and unique word count for the original PE corpus and our Portuguese variant.

Subset	Portuguese		English	
	Unique words	Tokens	Unique words	Tokens
Train	9081	109317	7299	105988
Dev	2502	13137	2199	12657
Test	4407	30109	3703	29537

5   Extrinsic Evaluation

We extrinsically evaluate the dataset by gauging its usefulness for sequence tagging: the problem of assigning a label to each token. The main purpose of this analysis is to compare our Portuguese corpus with other language variants of PE, for which standard model architectures have already been explored. Eger et al. [9, 10] have used a standard bidirectional LSTM followed by a CRF layer (BLCRF [13]) to address this task. Each token is represented by the corresponding word embedding. For cross-lingual settings [10], they induce bilingual word embeddings for each language pair. In addition to token-level information, Eger et al. extend this approach to account for character-level information using a Convolutional Neural Network (CNN), leading to BLCRF+Char models [16]. The character-level CNN addresses problems of out-of-vocabulary (OOV) words, which are words not seen during training.

We train and evaluate sequence tagging models on the original English (EN) PE corpus, as well as in the machine-translated versions in Portuguese (PT), Spanish (ES), and German (DE). The Spanish and German versions of the PE were made available[4] by Eger et al. [10]. German is studied in detail on prior work [10] and, therefore, we validate our implementation on the German corpus for a direct comparison. The Spanish corpus concerns the language that is closest to Portuguese, for which we expect to obtain similar scores.

5.1 Experimental Setup

To perform token-level sequence tagging, we experiment with both BLCRF and BLCRF+Char, as well as with the multilingual BERT (mBERT) pre-trained language model[5]. We adopt the sequence tagging model [17] from NeuroNLP2[6]. For BLCRF and BLCRF+Char experiments, the training process is performed with a maximum of 200 epochs, using patience of 30, and a batch size of 16. We apply a 50% dropout on the embeddings and LSTM units. We use the Adam optimizer with a learning rate of 1×10^{-3} and momentum of 0.9. We use MUSE[7] [4] multilingual embeddings (with dimension of 300), which contain pairs of translated words that are positioned in close proximity in the vector space. Different from prior work [10], we opted to employ widely used pre-trained multilingual word embeddings (MUSE) because training our own bilingual word embeddings for each language pair is out of scope for this work. For mBERT, we employ similar hyperparameters, with exception for the learning rate that we set as 2×10^{-5} (as suggested by Devlin et al. [6]). We adopt the language model provided by Transformers library [31]. Finally, we use the provided train/dev/test splits [10].

5.2 Results

The results for projection and direct transfer (EN → PT, EN → ES and EN → DE) are shown in Table 4. The results shown are averages of three experimental runs with different random seeds. To validate the potential of the PT version of the PE corpus proposed in this work, we focus our experiments on the projection approach (in which the train, dev and test set on the target language is explored by the models). Additionally, we also show the results obtained employing recent multilingual language models using direct transfer (in which only the test set on the target language is considered), which have obtained promising results on a variety of tasks [6].

Regarding the projection approach, when comparing these values with the ones previously reported by Eger et al. [10], we observe a slight improvement for sequence tagging in English: 72.49% vs 69.27% for BLCRF and 73.02% vs 70.51% for BLCRF+Char. We associate these slight improvements with the use of different embeddings and implementation details. For BLCRF+Char, Eger et al. have reported

---

[4] https://github.com/UKPLab/coling2018-xling_argument_mining/tree/master/data/AllData/ MT/PE.

[5] https://huggingface.co/transformers/pretrained_models.html,   model   id   "bert-base-multilingual-cased".

[6] https://github.com/XuezheMax/NeuroNLP2.

[7] https://github.com/facebookresearch/MUSE.

projection performance scores of 65.92% and 63.33% for Spanish and German, respectively; in our experiments we have got 69.35% and 67.76%. As reported by Eger et al., we observe similar improvements when adding char representations (from BLCRF to BLCRF+Char). For our Portuguese corpus, we obtained 68.59%, which demonstrates that the annotation projections obtained for this language yield scores similar to those reported in prior work on other languages. Employing the multilingual BERT model (mBERT+CRF) improves results for all languages.

Concerning direct transfer, Eger et al. only reported results for EN → DE. They obtained ≈50% and ≈42% for BLCRF and BLCRF+Char, respectively. We got an improved score using mBERT (≈57%). We notice that the best results were obtained for Spanish and the least good for German.

Overall, the results obtained in projection experiments are better than those obtained from direct transfer. We also observe a greater standard deviation using direct transfer compared to the results obtained using the projection approach, for all target languages. One possible explanation for this would be the increased challenge inherent to the direct transfer learning procedure – training the model in the source language (English) and evaluating it directly, without further training, in a different target language (Portuguese, Spanish, and German). Remarkably, recent multilingual language models (mBERT) employed on a direct transfer setting perform below the projection approach employing multilingual word embeddings (BLCRF and BLCRF+Char), which is a clear indicator of the potential of the projection approach. Thus, we conclude that it is worthwhile to perform projection over direct transfer sequence tagging, either using multilingual word embeddings or mBERT. Still, we consider the use of mBERT to be promising for direct transfer, which can be particularly important when machine translation underperforms for the target language.

Finally, we claim that the obtained scores for Portuguese are indicative of both the quality of this version of the PE corpus and its feasible usage in sequence tagging. The comparable results between the Portuguese and Spanish versions of the PE corpus suggest that they poses similar challenges.

Table 4. Projection and direct transfer (EN → PT, EN → ES and EN → DE) sequence tagging results on the *test* set (token-level macro-F1).

			Machine translated		
		EN	PT	ES	DE
	BLCRF + Char	73.02 ± 1.32	68.59 ± 0.77	69.35 ± 0.97	67.76 ± 0.36
Projection	BLCRF	72.49 ± 1.69	65.46 ± 0.85	66.23 ± 1.03	65.79 ± 1.43
	mBERT + CRF	75.74 ± 0.37	70.12 ± 0.97	$\mathbf{71.29 \pm 1.06}$	$\mathbf{67.89 \pm 0.56}$
Direct transfer	mBERT + CRF		63.76 ± 2.44	66.07 ± 2.49	57.12 ± 2.73

6   Conclusions

We have built a machine-translated version of the Persuasive Essays corpus for Portuguese. We have used neural network-based translation and alignment techniques and proposed an annotation projection procedure, which includes a slight tweak to cope with the verbosity of Romance languages. The final result is a CoNLL-formatted, component and BIO scheme annotated Portuguese version of the Persuasive Essays corpus, which is the main contribution of this work.

We have analyzed the quality of the Portuguese PE corpus in two ways: intrinsically through back alignment/projection, and extrinsically by training models for ADU sequence tagging in a number of language versions of the PE corpus. From both intrinsic and extrinsic evaluations, we conclude that our version of the corpus shows promising results in the projected annotations. Our sequence tagging results for the Portuguese language are in line with the ones obtained for other languages.

Future work will aim to extend the analysis to assess how different translation and alignment algorithms contribute to the corpus's intrinsic and extrinsic performances. Also, we envision employing these techniques in other NLP annotated corpora to enrich this kind of resources for the Portuguese language.

Acknowledgment. This research is supported by LIACC (FCT/UID/CEC/0027/2020) and by project DARGMINTS (POCI/01/0145/FEDER/031460), funded by Fundação para a Ciência e a Tecnologia (FCT). Gil Rocha is supported by a PhD studentship (with reference SFRH/BD/140125/2018) from FCT.

References

1. Ajjour, Y., Chen, W.F., Kiesel, J., Wachsmuth, H., Stein, B.: Unit segmentation of argumentative texts. In: Proceedings of the 4th Workshop on Argument Mining, pp. 118–128. ACL (September 2017)
2. Bahdanau, D., Cho, K., Bengio, Y.: Neural machine translation by jointly learning to align and translate. In: Bengio, Y., LeCun, Y. (eds.) 3rd International Conference on Learning Representations (Conference Track Proceedings), ICLR 2015, San Diego, CA, USA, 7–9 May 2015 (2015)
3. Conneau, A., et al.: Unsupervised cross-lingual representation learning at scale. In: Proceedings of the 58th Annual Meeting of the ACL, pp. 8440–8451. ACL (July 2020)
4. Conneau, A., Lample, G., Ranzato, M., Denoyer, L., Jégou, H.: Word translation without parallel data. arXiv preprint arXiv:1710.04087 (2017)
5. Das, D., Petrov, S.: Unsupervised part-of-speech tagging with bilingual graph-based projections. In: Proceedings of the 49th Annual Meeting of the ACL: Human Language Technologies, pp. 600–609. ACL (June 2011)
6. Devlin, J., Chang, M., Lee, K., Toutanova, K.: BERT: pre-training of deep bidirectional transformers for language understanding. In: Burstein, J., Doran, C., Solorio, T. (eds.) Proceedings of the 2019 Conference of the North American Chapter of the ACL: Human Language Technologies, NAACL-HLT 2019, Minneapolis, MN, USA, 2–7 June 2019, Volume 1 (Long and Short Papers), pp. 4171–4186. ACL (2019)
7. Dyer, C., Chahuneau, V., Smith, N.A.: A simple, fast, and effective reparameterization of IBM model 2. In: Proceedings of the 2013 Conference of the North American Chapter of the ACL: Human Language Technologies, pp. 644–648. ACL (June 2013)
8. Eckle-Kohler, J., Kluge, R., Gurevych, I.: On the role of discourse markers for discriminating claims and premises in argumentative discourse. In: Proceedings of the 2015 Conference on Empirical Methods in Natural Language Processing, pp. 2236–2242. ACL (September 2015)

9. Eger, S., Daxenberger, J., Gurevych, I.: Neural end-to-end learning for computational argumentation mining. In: Proceedings of the 55th Annual Meeting of the ACL (Volume 1: Long Papers), pp. 11–22. ACL (July 2017)
10. Eger, S., Daxenberger, J., Stab, C., Gurevych, I.: Cross-lingual argumentation mining: machine translation (and a bit of projection) is all you need! In: Proceedings of the 27th International Conference on Computational Linguistics, pp. 831–844. ACL (August 2018)
11. Garg, S., Peitz, S., Nallasamy, U., Paulik, M.: Jointly learning to align and translate with transformer models. In: Inui, K., Jiang, J., Ng, V., Wan, X. (eds.) Proceedings of the 2019 Conference on Empirical Methods in Natural Language Processing and the 9th International Joint Conference on Natural Language Processing, EMNLP-IJCNLP 2019, Hong Kong, China, 3–7 November 2019, pp. 4452–4461. ACL (2019)
12. Habernal, I., Gurevych, I.: Argumentation mining in user-generated web discourse. Comput. Linguist. **43**(1), 125–179 (2017)
13. Huang, Z., Xu, W., Yu, K.: Bidirectional LSTM-CRF models for sequence tagging. arXiv preprint arXiv:1508.01991 (2015)
14. Jalili Sabet, M., Dufter, P., Yvon, F., Schütze, H.: SimAlign: high quality word alignments without parallel training data using static and contextualized embeddings. In: Proceedings of the 2020 Conference on Empirical Methods in Natural Language Processing, pp. 1627–1643. ACL (November 2020)
15. Li, M., Geng, S., Gao, Y., Peng, S., Liu, H., Wang, H.: Crowdsourcing argumentation structures in Chinese hotel reviews. In: 2017 IEEE International Conference on Systems, Man, and Cybernetics (SMC), pp. 87–92 (2017)
16. Ma, X., Hovy, E.: End-to-end sequence labeling via bi-directional LSTM-CNNs-CRF. In: Proceedings of the 54th Annual Meeting of the ACL (Volume 1: Long Papers), pp. 1064–1074. ACL (August 2016)
17. Ma, X., Hovy, E.: End-to-end sequence labeling via bi-directional LSTM-CNNs-CRF. In: Proceedings of the 54th Annual Meeting of the Association for Computational Linguistics, Berlin, Germany (Volume 1: Long Papers), pp. 1064–1074. Association for Computational Linguistics (August 2016). https://doi.org/10.18653/v1/P16-1101. https://www.aclweb.org/anthology/P16-1101
18. McDonald, R., Petrov, S., Hall, K.: Multi-source transfer of delexicalized dependency parsers. In: Proceedings of the 2011 Conference on Empirical Methods in Natural Language Processing, pp. 62–72. ACL (July 2011)
19. Nguyen, H., Litman, D.: Context-aware argumentative relation mining. In: Proceedings of the 54th Annual Meeting of the ACL (Volume 1: Long Papers), pp. 1127–1137. ACL (August 2016)
20. Och, F.J., Ney, H.: Improved statistical alignment models. In: Proceedings of the 38th Annual Meeting of the ACL, pp. 440–447. ACL (October 2000)
21. Och, F.J., Ney, H.: A systematic comparison of various statistical alignment models. Comput. Linguist. **29**(1), 19–51 (2003)
22. Palau, R.M., Moens, M.F.: Argumentation mining: the detection, classification and structure of arguments in text. In: Proceedings of the 12th International Conference on Artificial Intelligence and Law, pp. 98–107. Association for Computing Machinery (2009)
23. Peldszus, A., Stede, M.: From argument diagrams to argumentation mining in texts: a survey. Int. J. Cogn. Inform. Nat. Intell. **7**(1), 1–31 (2013)
24. Pikuliak, M., Šimko, M., Bieliková, M.: Cross-lingual learning for text processing: a survey. Expert Syst. Appl. **165**, 113765 (2021)
25. Plank, B., Søgaard, A., Goldberg, Y.: Multilingual part-of-speech tagging with bidirectional long short-term memory models and auxiliary loss. In: Proceedings of the 54th Annual Meeting of the ACL (Volume 2: Short Papers), pp. 412–418. ACL (August 2016)

26. Rocha, G., Lopes Cardoso, H.: Towards a relation-based argument extraction model for argumentation mining. In: Camelin, N., Estève, Y., Martín-Vide, C. (eds.) SLSP 2017. LNCS (LNAI), vol. 10583, pp. 94–105. Springer, Cham (2017). https://doi.org/10.1007/978-3-319-68456-7_8

27. Rocha, G., Stab, C., Lopes Cardoso, H., Gurevych, I.: Cross-lingual argumentative relation identification: from English to Portuguese. In: Proceedings of the 5th Workshop on Argument Mining, pp. 144–154. ACL (November 2018)

28. Stab, C., Gurevych, I.: Parsing argumentation structures in persuasive essays. Comput. Linguist. **43**(3), 619–659 (2017)

29. Vaswani, A., et al.: Attention is all you need. In: Guyon, I., et al. (eds.) Advances in Neural Information Processing Systems 30: Annual Conference on Neural Information Processing Systems 2017, 4–9 December 2017, Long Beach, CA, USA. pp. 5998–6008 (2017)

30. Wang, H., Huang, Z., Dou, Y., Hong, Y.: Argumentation mining on essays at multi scales. In: Proceedings of the 28th International Conference on Computational Linguistics, pp. 5480–5493. International Committee on Computational Linguistics (December 2020)

31. Wolf, T., et al..: Transformers: state-of-the-art natural language processing. In: Proceedings of the 2020 Conference on Empirical Methods in Natural Language Processing: System Demonstrations, pp. 38–45. Association for Computational Linguistics (October 2020). https://www.aclweb.org/anthology/2020.emnlp-demos.6

32. Yang, S., Wang, Y., Chu, X.: A survey of deep learning techniques for neural machine translation. arXiv preprint arXiv:2002.07526 (2020)

33. Yang, Z., Salakhutdinov, R., Cohen, W.W.: Transfer learning for sequence tagging with hierarchical recurrent networks. In: 5th International Conference on Learning Representations (Conference Track Proceedings), ICLR 2017, Toulon, France, 24–26 April 2017. OpenReview.net (2017)

34. Yarowsky, D., Ngai, G., Wicentowski, R.: Inducing multilingual text analysis tools via robust projection across aligned corpora. In: Proceedings of the 1st International Conference on Human Language Technology Research (2001)

35. Zhang, Y., Gaddy, D., Barzilay, R., Jaakkola, T.: Ten pairs to tag - multilingual POS tagging via coarse mapping between embeddings. In: Proceedings of the 2016 Conference of the North American Chapter of the ACL: Human Language Technologies, pp. 1307–1317. ACL (June 2016)

Acceptance Decision Prediction in Peer-Review Through Sentiment Analysis

Ana Carolina Ribeiro$^{(\boxtimes)}$ [ID], Amanda Sizo [ID], Henrique Lopes Cardoso [ID],
and Luís Paulo Reis [ID]

Artificial Intelligence and Computer Science Laboratory (LIACC), Faculty of Engineering,
University of Porto, Porto, Portugal
{up201602840,up202010567}@edu.fe.up.pt, {hlc,lpreis}@fe.up.pt

Abstract. Peer-reviewing is considered the main mechanism for quality control of scientific publications. The editors of journals and conferences assign submitted papers to reviewers, who review them. Therefore, inconsistencies between reviewer recommendations and reviewer comments are a problem that the editor needs to handle. However, few studies have explored whether it is possible to predict the reviewer recommendation from review comments based on NLP techniques. This study aims to predict reviewer recommendation of the scientific papers they review (accept or reject) and predict reviewers' final scores. We used a dataset composed of 2,313 review texts from two computer science conferences to test our approach, based on seven ML algorithms on regression and classification tasks and VADER application. SVM and MLP Classifier achieved the best performance in the classification task. In the regression task, the best performance was achieved by Nearest Neighbors. One of the most interesting results is the positive classification of most reviews by VADER: reviewers present constructively written reviews without highly negative comments land; therefore, VADER cannot detect reviews with a negative score.

Keywords: Peer-review · Sentiment analysis · Machine learning algorithms

1 Introduction

The peer-review system is considered the principal mechanism for quality control of scientific publications [1], with the potential to contribute to the rigor of the work published in the academic community [2]. Journals and conferences apply this mechanism to submitted papers they receive to select those to be published. The editors of journals and conferences send submitted papers to experts (reviewers) who review them and send their evaluation report to the editors.

The evaluation report presents a summary judgment on suitability for publication, followed by comments [1, 3]. Usually, the comments introduce both the advantages and disadvantages of a submitted paper and then assign an overall score to recommend a decision status (typically accept or reject). A level of consistency is expected between these recommendations and the reviewer's comments. Previous studies [4] tried to predict

© Springer Nature Switzerland AG 2021
G. Marreiros et al. (Eds.): EPIA 2021, LNAI 12981, pp. 766–777, 2021.
https://doi.org/10.1007/978-3-030-86230-5_60

this consistency using a neural network model with a novel abstract-based attention mechanism. However, it is necessary to further research to find whether the review texts and the recommendation scores are consistent with each other [2].

Additionally, sentiment analysis is a popular topic in Natural Language Processing (NLP) research and studied for a long time. Some researchers have applied sentiment classification to an extensive range of text domains, such as product reviews, movie reviews, tweets, and news papers, among others [5]. However, there is little research on sentiment classifications of the peer-review texts, not only because a dataset of reviews is difficult to obtain but also due to the following challenges [2]:

- The reviewer's opinionated text is mixed with the non-opinionated text, making it difficult to separate them. For example, a review contains a summary of the paper's contributions, notes on writing, grammatical errors, and reviewer suggestions;
- And, the reviewer presents the pros and cons of scientific papers, making it challenging to capture the reviewers' critical points as evidence for the general recommendation.

According to these challenges, this study tries to predict the reviewer recommendation from review texts. Therefore, we carried out three tasks. (1) Paper Acceptance Classification: The first task focuses on predicting the final decision of the scientific paper, given the review text to predict whether the paper will be accepted and rejected. (2) Overall Evaluation Score Prediction: The second task corresponds to the prediction of the overall evaluation score attributed by the reviewers, i.e., given the review text, predict a continuous value between −3 and 3 (Overall Evaluation) assigned by the reviewers. (3) Sentiment Analysis: The third task corresponds to verifying whether the sentiment/polarity attributed to the review corresponds to the overall evaluation score attributed by the reviewers. Finally, we used the outputs of sentiment analysis as new features in the first task to verify any improvement in the performance of the algorithms for paper acceptance classification. For the performance of the tasks, we used data from two computer science conferences.

The remaining of this paper is organized as follows. Section 2 presents the related work in sentiment analysis approaches and related works on the topic. Section 3 presents the materials and method for conducting this research and describes the steps of the project: evaluation dataset, data pre-processing, application of machine learning algorithms, and sentiment analysis. Section 4 shows the results from the machine learning algorithms in classification and regression tasks and sentiment analysis. Section 5 discusses the results obtained. Section 6 presents the conclusions and future research directions.

2 Related Work

Sentiment analysis aims to identify and analyse the components of an individual's opinion [6, 7]. The sentiments of an aspect are classified in different categories, depending on the purpose of the sentiment classification [6], for example, positive, negative, and neutral classes for tweets.

The traditional approaches for sentiment analysis are classified into lexicon-based and machine learning (ML) approaches. The lexicon-based methods use precompiled sentiment lexicons, including different words and their polarity, to classify a given the word into positive or negative sentiment class labels [8]. Several other lexicons are proposed in the literature, for example, WordNet-Affect, SenticNet, MPQA, and SentiWordNet. This type of approach does not require a training dataset. The challenge of lexicon-based methods is developing a sentiment lexicon for unstructured data, the semantic and lexical variation, and the different senses the same word (i.e., the same string) may have.

However, ML approaches have helped to mitigate this problem. ML approaches are based on ML algorithms to classify the words into their corresponding sentiment labels [5, 8]. The main advantage of ML approaches is their capacity to represent learning. In contrast to lexicon-based approaches, ML approaches require a training dataset, which contains the examples from which the system will learn to perform a given [classification-based] task [9]. Some studies [10, 11] also show the possibility of combining the two approaches. Hybrid approaches allow the use of advantages of each approach and try to obtain the best possible results [12].

According to [6] these sentiment analysis approaches are accused of inefficient in dealing with the dynamic nature of language, increasing the amount of data, and short text structures like tweets, comments, reviews (restaurants, movies, hotels), among others. Traditional approaches find it difficult to adjust a model designed for a specific task to a new task. Deep Learning (DL) methods have been applied due to their automatic resource learning ability, where they discover exploratory and discriminative input representations from the data themselves [4, 13, 14].

There are still few studies on sentiment analysis in peer-review texts. Hua et al. [13] proposed an approach based on argument mining to understand the content and structure of peer reviews. The authors started by segmenting propositions through the methods Conditional Random Field (CRF) and bidirectional Long short-term memory (LSTM) network connected to a CRF output layer (BiLSTM-CRF), comparing with three baselines: FullSent (treating each sentence as a proposition), PDTB-conn (segmenting sentences when any discourse connective is observed) and RST-parser (segmenting discourse units by the RST parser). The authors found that BiLSTM-CRF outperforms other methods (Precision: 82.25, Recall: 79.96, F1-score: 81.09). In the classification of the propositions, they applied Support Vector Machines (SVM) and Convolutional Neural Network (CNN), and the latter presented the best performance.

Kang et al. [15] performed two different NLP tasks: (1) given a paper, predict whether the paper will be accepted in a set of conferences, and (2) predict the scores of aspects of the paper, such as novelty, substance, and meaningful comparison. In the first task, they applied different classifiers: Logistic Regression (LR), SVM, Random Forest (RF), Nearest Neighbors, Decision Tree (DT), Multilayer Perceptron (MLP), AdaBoost, and Naive Bayes (NB). In the second task, they applied the CNN algorithm, Recurrent Neural Networks (LSTM), and deep averaging networks.

The study of Habimana et al. [6] aims to present the implementation of sentiment analysis methods in scientific paper reviews as a proof of concept for future applications. The authors used the NB classifier, SVM, an unsupervised classifier in a scoring algorithm based on Part-Of-Speech tagging and keyword matching. Finally, a hybrid method using both the scoring algorithm and SVM. One of the most interesting results was the improvement obtained by combining the scoring algorithm and SVM. The score gives additional information to the SVM to facilitate the classification.

3 Materials and Methods

3.1 Evaluation Dataset

In this study, the data belong to two computer science conferences. The data of the conferences are not public; throughout this paper, they are called Artificial Intelligence Conference and Robotics Conference. Table 1 shows the data dictionary. In total, 2,313 reviews were collected, and the acceptance rate of papers is over 60% in all conferences (Table 2). In total, 661 papers were reviewed. This dataset is not open and available to the community.

Table 1. Data dictionary.

Attribute	Description	Type
paperID	ID of paper	Number
paperTitle	Title of paper	Varchar
reviewID	ID of review	Number
review	Reviewer's comment content	Varchar
Review Confidence	Reviewer's confidence: 1 (none), 2 (low), 3 (medium), 4 (high), 5 (expert)	Varchar
Overall Evaluation	Overal Evaluation of paper: -3 (strong reject), -2 (reject), -1 (weak reject), 0 (borderline paper), 1 (weak accept), 2 (accept), 3 (strong accept)	Varchar
preDecision	Preliminary Decision: Accepted, Rejected	Varchar
totScore	Total Score: $-3, -2, -1, 0, 1, 2, 3$	Number

3.2 Data Preprocessing

We applied some techniques and methods for cleaning and pre-processing text data. Firstly, HTML/XML tags, punctuation, digits, and special characters have been removed. In the text reviews, different numeric and special characters do not affect the analysis. However, they often create confusion during the conversion of the text file to a numeric vector. Then, tokenization was applied, and stopwords have been identified and removed. These steps significantly reduce the number of attributes of the dataset [8]. Also, the Snowball Stemmer algorithm was applied to all corpus words, normalizing several variants into the same form [13].

After the data cleaned, we applied formal feature extraction methods. The most basic form of weighted word feature extraction is Term Frequency (TF), where each

Table 2. Statistics for all datasets.

	Total of papers	Total of reviews	% of accepted papers	% of rejected papers
AI Conference 2013	147	598	63.27%	36.72%
AI Conference 2019	223	740	60.09%	39.91%
Robotics 2015	160	553	75.63%	24.37%
Robotics 2019	131	422	84.73%	15.27%
Total	661	2313	69.44% (459)	30.59% (202)

word is mapped to a number corresponding to the number of occurrences of that word in the whole corpora. In word weighting methods, documents are translated into a vector containing the frequency of the words in the document. The Inverse Document Frequency (IDF) is used in combination with the frequency of implicitly common words in the corpus. The IDF measures the proportion of documents in the dataset in which the word appears. This means how common or rare a word is in the entire document set. The closer it is to 0, the more common a word is. This combination of TF and IDF is known as Term Frequency-Inverse Document Frequency (TF-IDF). Also, we tested the impact of computing TF-IDF scores on n-grams of different lengths (n-gram = 2 to 13).

3.3 Machine Learning Algorithms

We apply several ML algorithms in different tasks. The Paper Acceptance Classification task used: SVM, NB, DT, Random Forest (RF), MLP Classifier, Nearest Neighbors Classification (NNC), and LR. The Overall Evaluation Score Prediction task applied: Support Vector Regression (SVR), Gradient Tree Boosting (GTB), Nearest Neighbors Regression (NNR), and MLP Regression. A brief explanation of these algorithms is presented below.

SVM algorithm is used to analyse data for classification and regression analysis by the construction of hyper-planes. In a binary classification problem, the hyper-plane separates the document vector in one class from the other [16]. The method of Support Vector Classification can be extended to solve regression problems. This method is called Support Vector Regression (SVR) [17].

NB text classification has been widely used for document categorization tasks. This algorithm is a probabilistic classifier method based on Bayes' theorem. DT is a high-speed algorithm for both learning and prediction. The main idea is to create a tree based on the attribute for categorized data points [18, 19]. RF is an ensemble learning method for text classification. The main idea of RF is generating random decision trees. NNC is a non-parametric technique used for text classification applications. Given a test document x, the NNC algorithm finds the k-nearest neighbors of x among all the documents in the training set and scores the category candidates based on the class of k neighbors. The similarity of x and each neighbor's document could be the score of the category of the

Neighbor documents [20]. Also, NNC can be extended to solve regression problems. Neighbors-based regression can be used in cases where the data labels are continuous rather than discrete variables.

One of the earliest methods of classification is LR. LR predicts probabilities rather than classes. LR classifier works well for predicting categorical outcomes. However, this prediction requires that each data point be independent, attempting to predict outcomes based on a set of independent variables [21]. GBT builds an additive model in a forward stage-wise fashion; it allows for optimizing arbitrary differentiable loss functions. GBT is an accurate and effective off-the-shelf procedure that can be used for both regression and classification problems [22]. MLP Classifier implements a multilayer perceptron algorithm that trains using backpropagation. Class MLP Regressor implements a multilayer perceptron that trains using backpropagation with no activation function in the output layer.

3.4 Sentiment Analysis

In the sentiment analysis task, the main goal is to verify whether the overall evaluation score attributed by the reviewers corresponds to the sentiment computed by Valence Aware Dictionary for Sentiment Reasoning (VADER). VADER is a lexicon and rule-based sentiment analysis tool specifically attuned to sentiments expressed in social media. VADER uses a combination of a sentiment lexicon-a list of lexical features (e.g., words)-which are generally labeled according to their semantic orientation as either positive or negative [23, 24]. VADER tells about the positivity and negativity score and how positive or negative sentiment is. The VADER returns four values such as:

- Pos: The probability of the sentiment to be positive.
- Neu: The probability of the sentiment to be neutral.
- Neg: The probability of the sentiment to be negative.
- Compound: The normalized compound score calculates the sum of all lexicon ratings and takes values from -1 (most extreme negative) to 1 (most extreme positive). A review is positive if the compound score is equal or superior to 0.05, neutral if it is between -0.05 and 0.05, and negative if it is equal or inferior to -0.05.

VADER classified the reviews according to the predominant sentiment/polarity after pre-processing data: positive, neutral, or negative. The reviewers' overall evaluation score ranges between -3 (strong reject) and 3 (strong accept). To be able to compare with the classification made by VADER, these evaluations are grouped as follows: positive (OverallEvaluation ≤ 2), ($-1 \leq$ OverallEvaluation ≤ 1), and negative (OverallEvaluation ≤ 2).

Finally, we carried out a final classification task. In this task, we used VADER outputs as new features for the classification task. The objective was to compare whether incorporating these new features improves the algorithms used in the Paper Acceptance Classification task.

4 Results

Before applying the algorithms, the Stratified K-Folds (k = 10) used the cross-validator method to split the data into training data and test data. Stratified K-Folds is a variation of k-fold that returns stratified folds: each set contains approximately the same percentage of each target class sample as the complete set. After the data is converted into numeric vectors and split into training and test data, a scaling process was applied, which helps manage the vectors and keep them in the [0, 1] range. Also, to found the most optimal parameters for each algorithm, we applied a grid search.

The ML technology selected for the study development was Scikit-Learn, which supports the Python programming language. Also, some python libraries were used: the Pandas and NumPy library for data manipulation. We also used the Natural Language Toolkit for language processing.

4.1 Paper Acceptance Classification

In this task, the classifiers presented in Subsect. 3.3 were applied. The performance evaluation of the algorithms was done through the analysis of the confusion matrix and the metrics obtained from it: precision, recall, F1-measure, and accuracy (Table 3). The algorithms with the highest percentage of correctly classified cases are the SVM and the MLP Classifier, both with an accuracy of 0.77. In contrast, the DT has the lowest rate of correctly classified instances (accuracy: 0.66).

Table 3. Results for paper acceptance classification.

Algorithm	Precision	Recall	F1-score	Accuracy
SVM	0.88	0.56	0.54	0.77
NB	0.62	0.62	0.62	0.71
DT	0.56	0.57	0.57	0.66
RF	0.37	0.50	0.43	0.74
MLP Classifier	0.69	0.68	0.68	0.77
NNC	0.37	0.50	0.43	0.74
LR	0.69	0.72	0.70	0.74

4.2 Overall Evaluation Score Prediction

In the Overall Evaluation Score prediction, we apply the regressors presented in Subsect. 3.3. The algorithm's performance was based on the coefficient of determination (R2), Mean Square Error (MSE), Root Mean Square Error (RMSE), and Mean Absolute Error (MAE) (Table 4). The algorithm with the best performance in the coefficient of determination is the Nearest Neighbors Regressor since closer to one means better. However, the algorithm has an MSE of 2.48, representing the average number of errors, the

RMSE is 1.57, and the MAE is 1.33. In this analysis of error metrics (MSE, RMSE, and MAE), the GBR algorithm presents fewer errors than the other algorithms' performance.

Table 4. Results for overall evaluation score prediction.

Algorithm	R^2	MSE	RMSE	MAE
SVM	0.67	2.25	1.50	1.23
GBR	0.78	1.64	1.28	1.05
NNR	0.84	2.48	1.57	1.33
MLP Regressor	0.81	2.68	1.63	1.34

4.3 Sentiment Analysis

From the 2,313 reviews, 1832 reviews were classified with positive sentiment, 41 reviews with neutral sentiment, and 440 reviews with negative sentiment (Fig. 1). The majority of positive reviews are related to the high percentage (above 60%) of papers accepted in the conferences.

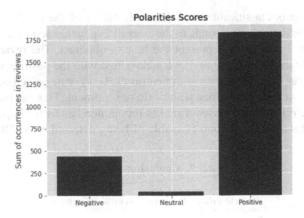

Fig. 1. Polarities for reviews.

The most positive reviews correspond to good feedbacks about the papers submitted by reviewers (Table 5). However, some errors could be found among the most negative reviews (Table 6). This is because VADER "interpretsno" as a negative word, and sometimes this word is used in a positive context.

Table 5. Highest positive sentiment reviews (Top 5).

Review	pos
The paper is written in a clear and easy…	0.488
I enjoyed reading the paper. It's an interest…	0.474
This is a solid paper, that's addresses well the…	0.444
The authors have proposed effective agent…	0.443
Interesting contribution on heterogeneous	0.430

Table 6. Highest negative sentiment reviews (Top 5).

Review	neg
No pdf was submitted, just the abstract…	0.314
The authors present a human-robot collision…	0.279
Missing the discussion of the related works…	0.268
I did not understand what was new…	0.247
The 3D digital mapping is an important problem…	0.242

After sentiments classification and the exploitation of the results, we verified if sentiments classification corresponds to the overall evaluation scores attributed by the reviewers. Table 7 and Table 8 present the results obtained. The reviews with positive overall evaluation score (-2 or 3) were classified with the positive sentiment (813 reviews). However, several reviews with neutral (1, 0, 1) or negative (-2, -3) overall evaluation score were also classified with positive sentiment. This can happen because, when papers are rejected, the reviewer makes recommendations for improvements and does not present a negative discourse capable of being detected by VADER.

Table 7. Confusion-matrix.

Predicted/Real	Positive	Neutral	Negative
Positive	813	9	46
Neutral	983	19	105
Negative	266	16	56

Table 8. Evaluation metrics VADER.

Metrics	Precision	Recall	F1-score	Accuracy
VADER	0.36	0.37	0.27	0.38

Only 19 reviews with neutral overall evaluation score were classified with neutral sentiment, and 56 reviews with negative overall evaluation score were classified with negative sentiment. Therefore, the accuracy is low (0.38). Finally, Table 8 presents the results obtained in the last task. In this classification task, the main goal is to compare the results with the Paper Acceptance Classification results and analyse whether the application of new features (VADER outputs) improves the performance of the algorithms. In Table 8, the values in parentheses correspond to the change in score relative to Table 3 for every metric.

5 Discussion

In the Paper Acceptance Classification task, the SVM and MLP Classifier algorithms have the best performance accuracy (0.77). However, the MLP Classifier (0.68) F1-score is higher than the SVM (0.54), which means that the harmonic mean of the precision and recall of the MLP Classifier is higher. Thus, the MLP Classifier can be considered the algorithm with the best performance in the final decision classification - accepted or rejected. The LR algorithm has an accuracy (0.74) slightly lower than the MLP Classifier, but its F1-score (0.70) is the highest within the set of tested algorithms. Finally, the algorithm with the most insufficient accuracy (0.66) is DT, but the NNC and RF algorithms have the lowest F1-score value (0.43). These results follow the literature, where the SVM is the algorithm with the best accuracy and the LR also with good results in binary classification. In the Overall Evaluation Score Prediction task, four regression algorithms were tested: SVR, GBR, NNR, and MLP Regressor.

According to the results and the tested algorithms, the NNR has the highest determination coefficient (R2): the built model can explain 84% (0.84) of the data. However, the error metrics (MSE, RMSE, and MAE) are high compared with the other algorithms. The same happens with the MLP Regressor algorithm, where the value of the determination coefficient is high, but the error metrics are also increased compared to the other algorithms. The GBR algorithm has a determination coefficient of 0.78, and the error metrics are the lowest compared to the different algorithms. In general, the GBR algorithm presents the best performance concerning error metrics.

VADER showed the sentiment classification of the reviews, compared with the overall evaluation score attributed by the reviewers, has an accuracy of 0.38 and the F1-score of 0.27. These values are low when compared with results from other studies. The low values of accuracy can be related to the negative evaluations attributed by the reviewers. Sometimes, VADER attributes a positive sentiment to reviewers with a negative evaluation. When papers are rejected, the reviewer makes recommendations for improvements and does not present a negative discourse capable of VADER's detection. The VADER outputs were added as new features in the Paper Acceptance Classification task. According to the results, the accuracy values increased in all algorithms, except in the NB. Unlike the first experiment (without the VADER outputs), the RF is the algorithm with the highest accuracy (0.78), followed by the SMV (0.77) and MLP Classifier, and NNC with an accuracy of 0.76. However, the F1-score values show that the MLP Classifier remains the algorithm with the highest value (0.70). Thus, the MLP Classifier remains an algorithm with distinguished performance. The NB algorithm has the lowest accuracy concerning all algorithms.

6 Conclusions and Future Work

This paper has studied the application of sentiment analysis techniques and machine learning tasks in the domain of paper reviews. One of the most interesting results is the positive classification of most reviews by VADER. This happens because the reviewers present reviews written in a constructive way and without highly negative comments and, therefore, not detectable by VADER. The dataset used is not open, and, therefore, other researchers cannot replicate or apply different techniques to these data, limiting the present study.

We have identified some opportunities for future work: longitudinal evaluation of consistency between the review and the acceptance or rejection of the paper by each reviewer. This may allow a better evaluation of papers since it would be possible to recognize whether a reviewer is strict or not; explore the application of transformers and neural language models; more advanced methods for building features such as topic models or document embeddings [14]. Finally, few other articles use the review of scientific papers as a domain of application and, therefore, the proposal of this study is an initial contribution to the field.

Acknowledgments. The first author is supported by FCT (Portuguese Foundation for Science and Technology) under grant PD/BD/2020.04698.BD. This work was financially supported by: Base Funding -UIDB/00027/2020 of the Artificial Intelligence and Computer Science Laboratory – LIACC - funded by national funds through the FCT/MCTES (PIDDAC).

References

1. Bornmann, L.: Scientific peer review. Ann. Rev. Inf. Sci. Technol. **45**, 199–206 (2011)
2. Wang, K., Wan, X.: Sentiment analysis of peer review texts for scholarly papers. In: 41st International ACM SIGIR Conference on Research and Development in Information Retrieval, pp. 175–184 (2018). https://doi.org/10.1145/3209978.3210056.
3. Fletcher, R.H., Fletcher, S.: The Effectiveness of Editorial Peer Review. BMJ Books, London (2003)
4. Socher, R., et al.: Recursive deep Models for semantic compositionality over a sentiment treebank. In: Proceedings of the 2013 Conference on Empirical Methods in Natural Language Processing, pp. 1631–1642 (2013)
5. Pang, B., Lee, L.: Opinion mining and sentiment analysis. Found Trends Inf. Retr. **2**(1), 1–135 (2008)
6. Habimana, O., Li, Y., Li, R., Gu, X., Yu, G.: Sentiment analysis using deep learning approaches: an overview. Sci. China Inf. Sci. **63**(1), 1–36 (2019). https://doi.org/10.1007/s11432-018-9941-6
7. Tang, D., Qin, B., Liu, T.: Deep learning for sentiment analysis: Successful approaches and future challenges, Wiley Interdiscip. Rev. Data Min. Knowl. Discov. **5**(6), 292–303 (2015). https://doi.org/10.1002/widm.1171
8. Ravi, K., Ravi, V.: A survey on opinion mining and sentiment analysis: tasks, approaches and applications. Knowl. Based Syst. **89**, 14–46 (2015). https://doi.org/10.1016/j.knosys.2015.06.015
9. Raza, H., Faizan, M., Hamza, A., Mushtaq, A., Akhtar, N.: Scientific text sentiment analysis using machine learning techniques. Int. J. Adv. Comput. Sci. Appl. **10**(12), 157–165 (2019). https://doi.org/10.14569/ijacsa.2019.0101222

10. Goel, A., Gautam, J., Kumar, S.: Real time sentiment analysis of tweets using naive Bayes. In: 2016 2nd International Conference on Next Generation Computing Technologies, pp. 257–261 (2016). https://doi.org/10.1109/NGCT.2016.7877424

11. Mukwazvure, A., Supreethi, K.P.: A hybrid approach to sentiment analysis of news comments. In: 2015 4th International Conference on Reliability, Infocom Technologies and Optimization ICRITO Trends and Future Directions (2015). https://doi.org/10.1109/ICRITO.2015.735 9282.

12. Yuan, J., Wu, Y., Lu, X., Zhao, Y., Qin, B., Liu, T.: Recent advances in deep learning based sentiment analysis. Sci. China Technol. Sci. **63**(10), 1947–1970 (2020). https://doi.org/10. 1007/s11431-020-1634-3

13. Kaur, M., Singh, S.: Analyzing negative ties in social networks: a survey. Egypt. Info. J. **17**(1), 21–43 (2016). https://doi.org/10.1016/j.eij.2015.08.002

14. Tang, D., Qin, B., Liu, T.: Document modeling with gated recurrent neural network for sentiment classification. In: Conference Proceedings-EMNLP 2015: Conference on Empirical Methods in Natural Language Processing, pp. 1422–1432, (2015). https://doi.org/10.18653/ v1/d15-1167

15. Kang, D., et al.: A dataset of peer reviews (PeerRead): collection, insights and NLP applications. In: NAACL HLT 2018 - 2018 Conference on North America Chapter Association Computer Linguistics Human Language Technology-Proceedings Conference, vol. 1, pp. 1647–1661 (2018). https://doi.org/10.18653/v1/n18-1149

16. Platt, J.C.: Probabilistic outputs for support vector machines and comparisons to regularized likelihood methods (1999)

17. Fan, R.E., Chang, K.W., Hsieh, C.J., Wang, X.R., Lin, C.J.: LIBLINEAR: a library for large linear classification. J. Mach. Learn. Res. **9**(2008), 1871–1874 (2008). https://doi.org/10. 1145/1390681.1442794

18. Ren, J., Lee, S.D., Chen, X., Kao, B., Cheng, R., Cheung, D.: Naive Bayes classification of uncertain data. In: Proceedings of IEEE International Conference on Data Mining, ICDM, pp. 944–949 (2009). https://doi.org/10.1109/ICDM.2009.90

19. Zhang, H.: The optimality of naive Bayes. In: Proceedings Seventeenth International Florida Artificial Intelligent Research Social Conference FLAIRS 2004, vol. 2, pp. 562–567 (2004)

20. Laaksonen, J., Oja, E.: Classification with learning k-nearest neighbors. In: IEEE International Conference on Neural Networks-Conference Proceedings, vol. 3, pp. 1480–1483 (1996). https://doi.org/10.1109/icnn.1996.549118

21. Cheng, W., Hüllermeier, E.: Combining instance-based learning and logistic regression for multilabel classification. Mach. Learn. **76**(2–3), 211–225 (2009). https://doi.org/10.1007/s10 994-009-5127-5

22. Friedman, J.H.: Greedy function approximation: a gradient boosting machine. Ann. Stat. **29**(5), 1189–1232 (2001). https://doi.org/10.1214/aos/1013203451

23. Kowsari, K., Meimandi, K.J., Heidarysafa, M., Mendu, S., Barnes, L., Brown, D.: Text classification algorithms: a survey. Information **10**(4), 1–68 (2019). https://doi.org/10.3390/inf o10040150

24. Borg, A., Boldt, M.: Using VADER sentiment and SVM for predicting customer response sentiment. Expert Syst. Appl. **162**, 113746 (2020). https://doi.org/10.1016/j.eswa.2020. 113746

Application of Data Augmentation Techniques for Hate Speech Detection with Deep Learning

Lígia Iunes Venturott$^{(\boxtimes)}$ ⓘ and Patrick Marques Ciarelli$^{(\boxtimes)}$ ⓘ

Universidade Federal do Espírito Santo, Vitória, Brazil
`patrick.ciarelli@ufes.br`

Abstract. In the past decade, there has been a great increase in the usage of social media, and with it also an increase on dissemination of online hate-speech. Some of the most advanced techniques for online hate-speech detection are based on deep learning. Unfortunately, this kind of technique requires a large amount of labeled data, which is not so easy to find. One way of trying to overcome this problem is with the use of data augmentation techniques. The present paper explores data augmentation in order to improve the performance of deep neural networks on the task of hate speech detection on a small dataset in Portuguese.

Keywords: Hate-speech · Deep learning · Data augmentation

1 Introduction

In the past decade, there has been a great increase in the usage of social media. On 2019, the social network Twitter had approximately 330 millions of active users and 500 millions of tweets posted per day [11]. These platforms make communication possible between people from different cultures, religions and interests. Combined with the false feeling of anonymity, these factors generate a fertile environment for hate speech, such as racism, sexism, xenophobia, homophobia, and others.

Most social networks explicitly forbid the dissemination of this kind of speech. Several countries consider hate speech dissemination illegal, and in some places the platform can be held responsible if the post is not removed. Unfortunately, the great amount of users and posts makes the control of content an almost impossible task [18].

In this context, there is a need for automatic tools capable of detecting hate speech. There are several works on automatic hate speech detection. Several of them use classic machine learning techniques, like Malmasi and Zampieri [10] and Davidson et al. [2], that use SVM (Support Vector Machine) and logistic regression. Recently, there is a number of works that use Deep Learning techniques for NLP (Natural Language Processing) tasks. Even though deep architectures

© Springer Nature Switzerland AG 2021
G. Marreiros et al. (Eds.): EPIA 2021, LNAI 12981, pp. 778–787, 2021.
https://doi.org/10.1007/978-3-030-86230-5_61

can perform very well on NLP tasks [17], these models require a large amount of data in order to be trained. Well-constructed datasets are resources which take a lot of time and work to be build and, unfortunately, datasets are specific to each language, so that normally a dataset made of English texts cannot be used to train an algorithm for text classification in other languages.

Although there are several works on hate-speech detection for English, there is less work done in other languages. In case of Portuguese, for example, there are few datasets [7,12], and they do not contain a large amount of examples. In addition to that, it is not always possible to apply the same methods used in language with extensive hate-speech, because models trained on small datasets are more prone to overfitting. One strategy to try to overcome this problem is using data augmentation.

Data augmentation is common in the field of computer vision, where operations such as cutting or inverting the picture, and adding noise, can substantially increase the size of the dataset. However, these same operations cannot be applied so easily in textual data, since they might change the meaning of the text.

In this paper we explore three data augmentation techniques described in Wei et al. [19] and try to improve the results of deep architectures on a small hate-speech dataset in Portuguese.

The next section presents some previous works related to the subject of automatic hate-speech detection. Section 3 describes the methodology used in this work, such as the dataset used, deep architectures, metrics, training and testing settings. Section 4 contains the results of the experiments carried out and in Sect. 5 we present our conclusions and final considerations.

2 Related Work

Some works have already tried to address the problem of hate speech or offensive language detection.

The work of Rosa et al. [14] uses deep neural networks to detect cyberbulling. In Del Vigna et al. [3], in addition to detecting the presence of hate-speech the authors also classify its intensity.

In Badjatiya et al. [1], several methods are explored: Support Vector Machines, Gradient Boosted Decision Trees, Random Forest, Logistic Regression and Deep Neural Networks. They also explore different encoding methods, such as bag-of-words vectors, TF-IDF vectors and GloVe embeddings.

Wei et al. [19] present four techniques of text data augmentation and evaluate them on benchmark text classification tasks. Two of the techniques explored do not require language-specific resources and can be applied to any language.

The majority of existing work is focused on the English language, but in 2017 de Pelle and Moreira [12] created a dataset of offensive comments in Brazilian Portuguese, containing comments taken from a news website. Fortuna et al. [7] also created a dataset for hate-speech in Portuguese. Their dataset is composed of tweets and the texts are classified in 81 hate categories in total.

Silva and Serapião [15] explore hate-speech detection in Portuguese. They use several methods for this task, including Bayes Naive Classifier, Support Vector Machine, Logistic Regression and Multi Layer Perceptron.

3   Methodology

In this section, we describe the applied methodology and the resources used in this work.

3.1   Datasets

In order to evaluate our methodology, we used OffComBR, a dataset of offensive comments on Portuguese [12]. The dataset consists of 1,250 comments found in the Brazilian news website *g1.globo.com*, where each comment was classified by 3 judges into "offensive" and "non-offensive" categories. There are two versions of this dataset, OffComBR-2 and OffComBR-3. In OffComBR-2 the label of each comment is given by the majority of votes. In this version 419 comments (32.5%) were considered offensive by at least 2 judges. OffComBR-3 only includes comments where the 3 judges agreed upon the classification. It contains 1,033 comments, of which 202 (19.5%) are classified as offensive. We chose to use OffComBR-2 because it contains more examples than OffComBR-3.

3.2   Data Pre-processing

Before applying any data augmentation we preprocessed the dataset. First, the words were lemmatized. In the lemmatization process inflexions are removed and the words are returned to their base form or dictionary form. For this, we used the NLPyPort module for Python [6]. The resulting dataset was not as good as expected, and this occurred mainly for two reasons:

- Due to the informal nature of the dataset, we are able to find several slangs and other words specific of internet vocabulary. Also, several words are spelled wrong, which makes recognition harder.
- The module has limitations and cannot recognize some verbal forms of the words.

Despite the suboptimal result, we decided to keep the lemmatized text in order to reduce the number of out-of-vocabulary words. After the lemmatization, we also removed stopwords.

3.3   Data Augmentation

In this paper, we explored the use of data augmentation techniques for texts in order to overcome small dataset problems, such as overfitting. For this, we use 3 different data augmentation techniques summarized by Wei et al. [19] and compare them to the models' performance on the original dataset.

Random Deletion. We randomly choose 1 word from the comment, this word is removed generating a new text entry. This procedure is repeated N times over the original comment, making sure that the removed word is different each time.

In the case the comment contains a number of words L, where $L < N$, the procedure is repeated L times, and not N.

Seeing that N is generally a very small number and we rarely have $L < N$, we could imply that this process generates a dataset of size approximately $N+1$ time the original.

We experimented with different values of N, $N = [1, 2, 3]$.

Random Swap. Two words are randomly chosen in the comment, and their positions in the text are swapped. The dataset generated by this method is 2 times the size of the original, containing the original comments and the comments with the swapped words.

Synonym Replacement. Like in Random Deletion, we choose a word randomly from the comment. Using a synonym dictionary, we find a synonym and replace the original word. In the case we cannot find a synonym in the dictionary, we select another word, also randomly. This procedure is repeated N times, making sure not to repeat words.

The synonym dictionary used in this work was compiled by Dias-da-Silva et al. [5] and it can be found on GitHub[1].

3.4   Sentence Encoding

We use pre-trained GloVe embeddings [13] of dimensionality 50. The embeddings were created by Hartmann et al. [8] and are available online[2].

3.5   Architectures

LSTM. The Long Short-Term Memory network is a type of recursive neural network (RNN) normally used to analyse sequential data, such as text.

Recursive architectures analyse the information along the temporal axis. When analysing the information of moment t the network possesses information of the previous analysis done for moment t-1. In this way, RNNs are able to take order in account.

In this work, we use a simple LSTM model, where we use the last state as input to the Dense Layer. The shown in Fig. 1a.

---

[1] https://github.com/stavarengo/portuguese-brazilian-synonyms.
[2] http://www.nilc.icmc.usp.br/nilc/index.php/repositorio-de-word-embeddings-do-nilc.

CNN. The Convolutional Neural Network (CNN) is a deep architecture that uses filters to extract information from the data. Although it was originally created to be applied to images in Computer Vision (CV), this architecture has shown good efficiency in Natural Language Processing tasks (NLP) [9].

We use the 1 dimensional CNN, where the kernel goes through the data along the temporal axis. Considering that the data has the shape $T \times N$ where T is the number of words in the sentence and N is the size of the representation of each word, a kernel of size k will be of shape $k \times N$. A layer of the CNN is composed of D kernels in parallel. These D kernels process the same data, and their outputs are concatenated.

We used a simple CNN, with a ReLU activation function and Max Pooling, with pooling size $p = 3$. The output of the Max Pooling is flattened and dropout is applied. The resulting vector goes through a Dense Layer.

Parallel CNN. We also test a CNN architecture based on the one described in Badjatiya et al. [1]. In this architecture, we use 2 parallel branches, each containing a CNN with kernels of different sizes. For this architecture we fixed the sizes $k = [3, 4]$.

The output of each CNN goes through a ReLU activation function and a GlobalMaxPooling and then they are concatenated. We apply dropout to the resulting vector and then it goes through a Dense Layer.

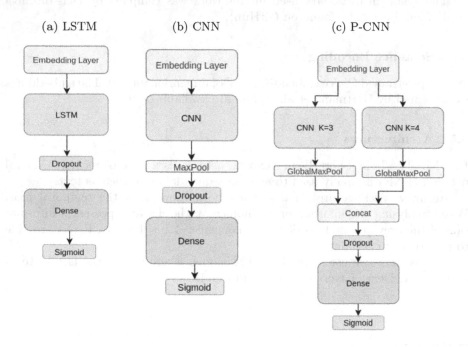

Fig. 1. Architectures used in experiments

3.6   Experimental Setup

Hyperparameters Optimization. In order to optimize the hyperparameters for each model, we used the Bayesian Optimization algorithm [16]. We fixed the Adam optimizer for all the architectures and we used the Bayesian Optimization to find the best learning rate. The best hyperparameters can be found in Table 1.

Table 1. Hyperparameters used for LSTM, CNN and P-CNN

CNN		P-CNN		LSTM	
Kernel size	3				
Filters	45	Filters	45	LSTM size	25
Learning rate	0.01	Learning rate	0.01	Learning rate	0.03
Dropout rate	0.1	Dropout rate	0.1	Dropout rate	0.1

Training-Testing Settings. We used the "best model" approach, where the model is trained for a high number of epochs and on each epoch the validation accuracy is compared to the best validation accuracy so far. The model that obtains the best validation accuracy is stored and used for testing. In our experiment the number of epochs was set to 20, but we observed that, for every architecture, the best results were achieved on the first 10 epochs.

Statistical Significance. In order to make sure our results had statistical significance, we used the Wilcoxon signed-rank test [4]. The Wilcoxon test is a non-parametric statistical hypothesis test. We chose to use this test because it does not presume any distribution, such as the normal distribution. We use the k-fold cross-validation in order to use all the dataset for training and testing, with k = 5. We run this experiment 8 times for each architecture. The Wilcoxon test is applied over these samples. The numbers shown in the results are the average of the results.

3.7   Measures

We chose to use the F1 score to evaluate our models. Due to the imbalanced datasets, we believe F1 score would be a better measure than accuracy.

4   Results

The first experiments were made to see if the data augmentation techniques would bring any improvement. For the Random Deletion and Synonym Replacement techniques, we experimented different values of N to see which would present better results.

In order to guarantee statistical significance, we used the Wilcoxon test and calculated p. We only present the results of tests where $p < 0.05$.

First, we show the results for each architecture without applying any data augmentation technique. The results are shown in Table 2. Then, we evaluate the results for each architecture individually. In Tables 3, 4 and 5, the terms [del, swap, syn] refer to the augmentation techniques Random Deletion, Random Swap and Synonym Replacement, respectively. The number after the term refers to the value of N in the case of Random Deletion and Synonym Replacement.

Table 2. Results without applying any data augmentation technique

Arch	ACC	F1
CNN	0.69133	0.64673
P-CNN	0.78078	0.77379
LSTM	0.77989	0.77117

4.1   Results with CNN

The simple CNN had worse results than other architectures. But, it also presented better relative results with the data augmentation techniques. All the augmentation methods applied presented $p < 0.05$. The F1 values and their increase are exposed in Table 3. Random Deletion with $N = 2$ presented the greatest increase.

Table 3. Results of data augmentation with CNN architecture

CNN	F1	F1 increase (%)
del1	0.67983	3.310
del2	0.69068	4.395
del3	0.68636	3.963
swap	0.68916	4.243
syn1	0.68245	3.572
syn2	0.68703	4.030
syn3	0.68676	4.002

4.2   Results with Parallel CNN

The Parallel CNN, or P-CNN, had much better results than the simple CNN. Most data augmentation methods applied showed some improvement with this architecture. Only the Synonym Replacement with $N = [1, 2]$ had $p > 0.05$, which leads to the question if a larger value of N could present more improvement. The results are shown in Table 4. Even though the Synonym Replacement method did not bring any significant boost in the results with $N = [1, 2]$, when $N = 3$ it has the best results, with almost 2.3% gain.

Table 4. Results of data augmentation with P-CNN architecture

P-CNN	F1	F1 increase
del1	0.78475	1.096
del2	0.79570	2.191
del3	0.78927	1.548
swap	0.78270	0.890
syn3	0.79678	2.298

4.3 Results with LSTM

For the LSTM architecture, the only augmentation strategies that resulted in $p < 0.05$ on the Wilcoxon test were Random Swap and Synonym Replacement with $N = 1$. Any other value for N in the Synonym Replacement generated increases too small to be considered relevant. We can see in Table 5 the results for the LSTM architecture. We chose to show the other results for Synonym Replacement in order to better observe the gradual decrease in gain with the increase of N. We can observe in Fig. 2 the increase for each technique.

Table 5. Results of data augmentation with LSTM architecture

LSTM	F1	F1 increase (%)
swap	0.78972	1.855
syn1	0.78246	1.129

(a) LSTM   (b) CNN   (c) P-CNN

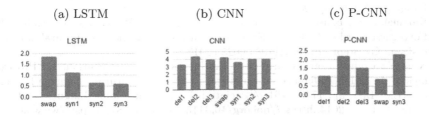

Fig. 2. F1 increase with data augmentation for each architecture (%)

5   Conclusions

In this paper, we addressed the problem of small datasets on hate-speech for Portuguese and we proposed a method to try to handle the problem. We evaluated some data augmentation techniques on a small dataset and the effects when applied to common deep neural networks. It can be observed that these techniques provide some improvement on the results.

It is important to remark that these techniques are easy to implement, with no extra cost in training besides the enlargement of the dataset itself. Therefore, they can be easily used at most applications. Synonym Replacement is the only technique that requires extra resources, a language specific synonym dictionary. The other two techniques can be applied regardless of the language.

In summary, the methods presented provide some improvement, but they leave room for more exploration. Future work might include more complex methods of data augmentation and experimenting how these methods would affect the performance of other deep architectures.

Acknowledgements. We thank the Postgraduate Program in Electrical Engineering at Universidade Federal do Espírito Santo, and FAPES for the financial support.

References

1. Badjatiya, P., Gupta, S., Gupta, M., Varma, V.: Deep learning for hate speech detection in tweets. In: Proceedings of the 26th International Conference on World Wide Web Companion, pp. 759–760. International World Wide Web Conferences Steering Committee (2017)
2. Davidson, T., Warmsley, D., Macy, M., Weber, I.: Automated hate speech detection and the problem of offensive language. In: Eleventh International AAAI Conference on Web and Social Media (2017)
3. Del Vigna, F., Cimino, A., Dell'Orletta, F., Petrocchi, M., Tesconi, M.: Hate me, hate me not: Hate speech detection on facebook (2017)
4. Demšar, J.: Statistical comparisons of classifiers over multiple data sets. J. Mach. Learn. Res. **7**, 1–30 (2006)
5. Dias-Da-Silva, B.C., Moraes, H.R.d.: A construção de um thesaurus eletrônico para o português do brasil. ALFA: Revista de Linguística (2003)
6. Ferreira, J., Gonçalo Oliveira, H., Rodrigues, R.: Improving NLTK for processing Portuguese. In: Symposium on Languages, Applications and Technologies (SLATE 2019) (June 2019) (in press)
7. Fortuna, P., da Silva, J.R., Wanner, L., Nunes, S., et al.: A hierarchically-labeled Portuguese hate speech dataset. In: Proceedings of the Third Workshop on Abusive Language Online, pp. 94–104 (2019)
8. Hartmann, N., Fonseca, E., Shulby, C., Treviso, M., Rodrigues, J., Aluisio, S.: Portuguese word embeddings: Evaluating on word analogies and natural language tasks. arXiv preprint arXiv:1708.06025 (2017)
9. Kim, Y.: Convolutional neural networks for sentence classification. In: Proceedings of the 2014 Conference on Empirical Methods in Natural Language Processing (EMNLP), pp. 1746–1751. Association for Computational Linguistics, Doha, Qatar, October 2014. https://doi.org/10.3115/v1/D14-1181, https://www.aclweb.org/anthology/D14-1181

10. Malmasi, S., Zampieri, M.: Detecting hate speech in social media. arXiv preprint arXiv:1712.06427 (2017)
11. Omnicore: Omnicore. https://www.omnicoreagency.com/twitter-statistics/ (2020). Accessed 15 Mar 2020
12. de Pelle, R.P., Moreira, V.P.: Offensive comments in the Brazilian web: a dataset and baseline results. In: Anais do VI Brazilian Workshop on Social Network Analysis and Mining. SBC (2017)
13. Pennington, J., Socher, R., Manning, C.D.: Glove: global vectors for word representation. In: Empirical Methods in Natural Language Processing (EMNLP), pp. 1532–1543 (2014). http://www.aclweb.org/anthology/D14-1162
14. Rosa, H., Matos, D., Ribeiro, R., Coheur, L., Carvalho, J.P.: A "deeper" look at detecting cyberbullying in social networks. In: 2018 International Joint Conference on Neural Networks (IJCNN), pp. 1–8. IEEE (2018)
15. Silva, A., Roman, N.: Hate speech detection in portuguese with naïve bayes, svm, mlp and logistic regression. In: Anais do XVII Encontro Nacional de Inteligência Artificial e Computacional. pp. 1–12. SBC (2020)
16. Snoek, J., Larochelle, H., Adams, R.P.: Practical bayesian optimization of machine learning algorithms. arXiv preprint arXiv:1206.2944 (2012)
17. Socher, R., Bengio, Y., Manning, C.D.: Deep learning for nlp (without magic). In: Tutorial Abstracts of ACL 2012, ACL 2012, p. 5. Association for Computational Linguistics, USA (2012)
18. Watanabe, H., Bouazizi, M., Ohtsuki, T.: Hate speech on Twitter: a pragmatic approach to collect hateful and offensive expressions and perform hate speech detection. IEEE Access 6, 13825–13835 (2018)
19. Wei, J., Zou, K.: Eda: Easy data augmentation techniques for boosting performance on text classification tasks. arXiv preprint arXiv:1901.11196 (2019)

Automated Fake News Detection Using Computational Forensic Linguistics

Ricardo Moura[1], Rui Sousa-Silva[2,3] (iD), and Henrique Lopes Cardoso[1,4](✉) (iD)

[1] Faculdade de Engenharia, Universidade do Porto, Porto, Portugal
{up201604912,hlc}@fe.up.pt
[2] Faculdade de Letras, Universidade do Porto, Porto, Portugal
rssilva@letras.up.pt
[3] Centro de Linguística da Universidade do Porto (CLUP), Porto, Portugal
[4] Laboratório de Inteligência Artificial e Ciência de Computadores (LIACC),
Porto, Portugal

Abstract. Fake news is news-like content that has been produced without following journalism principles. Fake news try to mimic the look and feel of real news to intentionally disinform the reader. This phenomenon can have a strong influence on society, thus being potentially a severe problem. To address this phenomenon, systems to detect fake news have been developed, but most of them build upon fact-checking approaches, which are unfit to detect misinformation when a news piece, rather than completely false, is distorted, exaggerated, or even decontextualized. We aim to detect Portuguese fake news by following a forensic linguistics approach. Contrary to previous approaches, we build upon methods of linguistic and stylistic analysis that have been tried and tested in forensic linguists. After collecting corpora from multiple fake news outlets and from a genuine news source, we formulate the task as a text classification problem and demonstrate the effectiveness of the proposed features when training different classifiers for telling fake from genuine news. Furthermore, we perform an ablation study with subsets of features and find that the proposed feature sets are complementary. The highest results reported are very promising, achieving 97% of accuracy and a macro F1-score of 91%.

Keywords: Fake news detection · Forensic linguistics · Natural language processing · Text classification · Disinformation · Misinformation

1 Introduction

Technology has evolved significantly in recent years, and its development and adoption have become increasingly fast and easy. One of the technologies that came to define and influence the next generations is new computer-mediated communication channels, such as social media, messaging services, and blogs. These channels made it possible for anyone to share anything about any topic at

G. Marreiros et al. (Eds.): EPIA 2021, LNAI 12981, pp. 788–800, 2021.
https://doi.org/10.1007/978-3-030-86230-5_62

any time, instantly and effortlessly. As a result, people are more connected than ever. Companies are aware of this phenomenon and try to use it for their own advantage, e.g. the media now share news on social media. In fact, studies report that people are shifting away from traditional news sources to social media and messaging services to find their news [25]. Even though these platforms have many advantages, they raise a serious problem: the so-called fake news. Because those platforms give all users the freedom to share everything they want at any time, fake news can emerge very easily and rapidly spread disinformation.

The fake news phenomenon can be defined in several different ways and be of multiple types, from satire to fabrication [20], and some of them are even permissible (i.e., satire). The definition of fake news has mutated throughout the years and began to be applied under wrong circumstances [23]. In the context of this paper, fake news is news that does not follow the journalism principles of factuality, objectivity, and neutrality [3,13]. Instead, fake news pieces try to mimic the look and feel of real news [24] with the intent to mislead the reader. Here lies the distinction between mis- and disinformation: unlike the latter, the former does not intend to mislead.

Although untruthful news accounts have always existed, their use as a way of manipulation and control has recently gained more attention, due to their fast and immediate propagation through social media, without any kind of curation or filtering. Lay people are attracted to this kind of news because of their alluring headlines (used as *clickbait*) and often give more attention to this kind of news than to truthful accounts [4].

Currently, there are two widely used methods to detect fake news: a manual alternative with human intervention and an automatic alternative with Machine Learning methods [8]. The former places the responsibility to assess the news' veracity and accuracy entirely on humans, who then have to flag it depending on their judgment. However, this is not the best option because it has a limited scalability and humans (frequently non-experts) are not sufficiently skilled to distinguish fake from genuine news. The latter alternative to detect fake news consists of using sophisticated computer systems. However, most existing systems are based on fact-checking methods, which fall short of the desired effectiveness, as these systems still lack the robustness to perform a reliable verification of which information is falsely presented [8]. Additionally, detecting fake news goes beyond identifying false information; fact-checking methods are useful when facts are manipulated, but less so when the truth in the news is distorted, exaggerated, or even decontextualized.

This paper presents a system that, contrary to fact-checking, does not depend on the veracity of the facts. Instead, we focus on how the author communicates and how the news is written. In light of this, we address the fake news phenomenon using an approach based on forensic linguistic analysis, i.e. an analysis that considers linguistic and stylistic methods which have been tried and tested in forensic contexts, e.g. to attribute authorship or detect bias in texts [22]. These include, but are not limited to: text statistics (e.g., average text, paragraph, sentence and word length, and n-gram sequences); spelling; and lexical choices (e.g., Part-of-Speech). We claim that these approaches have a significant potential to also detect fake news.

Using two corpora collected from multiple sources, we conducted a series of experiments to understand what linguistic characteristics are intrinsic of fake news. Our experiments show promising results with an accuracy of up to 97% and a macro average of F1-score of 90%.

This paper is structured as follows. Section 2 briefly presents previous work on fake news detection using methods similar to the ones applied in this paper. Section 3 introduces the resources used in our experiments, specifically the corpora (Sect. 3.1) and external resources (Sect. 3.2). Section 4 describes the process, from extracting the features to building the model. Next, in Sect. 5, we share, evaluate, and discuss our results. Finally, in Sect. 6 we draw some conclusions, give a perspective into the project's current stage, and discuss what could be the next steps and future work.

2   Related Work

Fact-checking is the predominant approach to detect fake news. Notwithstanding, there are alternative methods that seek to make a decision based on linguistic patterns present in the text. The reasoning being that, when someone writes a lie or a deceiving text, they strategically write the text in a way to avoid suspicion [12]. However, not all traces and patterns can be hidden, and hence linguistics-based approaches are often employed for detecting lies, despite being somewhat understudied in the literature.

Ahmed et al. (2017) [1] propose fake news detection using only n-gram analysis. The authors reached the best performance when using Term Frequency-Inverse Document Frequency (TF-IDF) as a feature extraction technique and a Linear Support Vector Machine (LSVM) as a classifier, with an accuracy of 92%. This accuracy is better than the results obtained by Horne and Adali (2017) [14] (see below). However, this high accuracy score can represent a Population Bias or Representation Bias [19]: as Cruz et al. (2019) [6] highlight, relying only on n-gram analysis could present a problem because the results of this feature extraction method may vary depending on media content throughout the years.

Perez et al. (2017) [21] made a set of experiments to identify linguistic properties predominating in fake content. The authors constructed two datasets: one was collected via crowd-sourcing covering six news domains; the other was obtained by scraping data from the web, and covers celebrity fake news. They built a fake news detector that achieved the best performance (78% accuracy) using LSVM. The features used were: n-grams encoded as TF-IDF values; count of punctuation characters; psycho-linguistic features, such as summary categories (e.g. analytical thinking or emotional tone), linguistic processes (e.g. function words or pronouns) and psychological processes (e.g. affective processes or social processes); and features related to readability, such as the number of characters, complex words, long words, number of syllables, word types and paragraphs, among other content features.

Differently from works that focus on the main text, Horne and Adali (2017) [14] consider solely news headlines for detecting fake news. The authors build on the assumption that fake news are targeted at audiences that are not likely to read beyond headlines. They extracted different features and arranged them into three categories: Stylistic Features (e.g. number of stopwords, number of all capital letter words, PoS tagger count on each tag, etc.); complexity features (e.g. readability scores); and psychological features (e.g. number of emotion or informal/swear words). With this set of features extracted from a corpus from 2016 US Election news (retrieved from BuzzFeed) and other scraped news websites related to US politics, the authors have built a LSVM classifier, achieving 71% accuracy.

Overall, these findings show that linguistic-based approaches are understudied. These approaches are, in fact, used but mostly in other contexts and with different goals, such as rumor detection [2], deception detection [18], or hyperpartisanship detection [6]. Such lack of research into fake news detection using approaches other than fact-checking is also evident in Portuguese. Comparing the performance between the works studied is non-trivial, because the authors target different datasets.

3   Resources

In this section, we introduce the corpora used in our experiments, as well as the external resources used to build the classifier models used to detect fake news. This project focuses on detecting fake news written in Portuguese. Although Portuguese is one of the most widely spoken languages [26], it still has limited linguistic resources available when compared to English. Due to this limitation, most tools supporting NLP show sub-optimal performance. Nevertheless, we will use tools that already have features and offer support of Portuguese to train the model.

3.1   Corpora

Given the nonexistence of an annotated dataset distinguishing fake from genuine news, we follow a silver standard approach [11] with automatically annotated data [5] when collecting news items for both classes. By using this approach, each news article is labeled (fake or not) according to the category associated with the website where it is published. URLs of the news, which were collected between November and December 2020 and included in the dataset, are made available[1].

Fake News Corpus
Although there are several online corpora of fake news[2], to the best of our knowledge none is based on Portuguese. We create a corpus by scraping websites that

---

[1]   drive.google.com/file/d/1jqiMxbcH6H4ozA3zbTnxphriQx1fKi4G/view.
[2]   https://github.com/sumeetkr/AwesomeFakeNews.

are known to publish fake news contents[3]. From those available, we have chosen five: *Bombeiros24*, *JornalDiario*, *MagazineLusa*, *NoticiasViriato*, and *Semanari-oExtra*. Some scraped news articles were deemed unusable since they were tagged, by the source, as opinion articles, which have a status that differs from regular news. Our fake news corpus contains 10 343 news pieces posted between 2017 and 2020.

Público News Corpus

We build the genuine news corpora by scraping news articles from *Público*, one of the most reputable news outlets in Portugal. Some scraped articles were deemed unusable since the authors categorized them as parody; hence, they should not be considered fake news. Thus, 110 066 news in total were collected from the same period as part of the fake news corpus.

3.2   Natural Language Processing Resources

We explored multiple resources to get the best results for processing the news articles and ended up using a mix between NLTK[4] for the Portuguese stopwords list, the pySpellChecker[5] library for spell checking, and spaCy models for Portuguese[6] for the other tasks (specifically tokenization, part-of-speech tagging, named entity recognition, and lemmatization). We also use Scikit-Learn[7] implementations of the classifiers we have trained and the function CountVectorizer, from the same library to calculate the *n*-grams.

4   System Description

Our fake news detection approach includes two phases. The first is a feature extraction phase, where we convert the news articles into a feature-based representation. Subsequently, we train several machine learning models using the representations obtained.

4.1   Feature Extraction

The main text of the news articles is converted into a set of linguistic features. These features (described in more detail in Table 1) can be divided into four categories:

---

[3]   a)   sabado.pt/portugal/detalhe/be-pede-audicao-da-erc-para-esclarecer-registo-de-sites-de-fake-news

b)   dn.pt/edicao-do-dia/11-nov-2018/fake-news-sites-portugueses-com-mais-de-dois-milhoes-de-seguidores–10160885.html.

[4]   www.nltk.org/howto/portuguese_en.

[5]   www.github.com/barrust/pyspellchecker.

[6]   www.spacy.io/models/pt.

[7]   www.scikit-learn.org.

n-grams: We calculate the vocabulary composed of all lemmatized tokens in the documents and subsequently extract a set of unigrams, bigrams, and trigrams, encoded as normalized counts and with TF-IDF. In order to avoid the influence of named entities, we adopt an approach that obfuscates them and focuses on an approach used in forensic linguistic analysis. We use spaCy's named-entity recognition to replace classified entities with their respective label – person, organization, and location (e.g. *"Cristiano Ronaldo"* becomes *"[PERSON]"*).

Frequencies: We extract a collection of relative frequencies, including the frequency for each punctuation character, the frequency for each Part-of-Speech tag, and the frequency of each type of adverb.

Text Statistics: We also obtain a set of statistical features: the number of paragraphs, sentences, tokens, stopwords, characters and syllables. From these, we also generate some average counts: average number of sentences per paragraph, words per paragraph, words per sentence and characters per word.

Readability: We compute a set of features that measure how easy it is to read a text. These include vocabulary richness (i.e., how diverse the vocabulary used by an author is), readability indices (e.g. Flesch [9], Flesch-Kincaid [15], Gunning Fog [10] and SMOG [17]), and ratios such as the percentage of long words (>12 characters), obfuscated words [16] (words with numbers or special characters, e.g. *"cr1me"*), misspelled words, and polysyllable words (>2 syllables).

4.2   Dataset Description

Figure 1 shows the distribution of the features that seem to differ the most between fake and genuine news. Feature values were normalized and outliers were hidden to facilitate understanding.

As far as *n*-gram features are concerned, (lemmatized) word sequences such as *"primeiro ministro"* (prime minister), *"presidente"* (president), *"empresa"* (company), or *"milhão"* (million), are far more frequent in genuine than in fake news. Conversely, words such as *"rede social"* (social media), *"mostrar"* (show), *"mulher"* (woman), or *"vida"* (life) are more frequent in fake news than in genuine news. The dataset also shows that genuine news tend to reference entities more often than fake news, which results in a higher count of entity-related *n*-grams.

Table 1. Features used to build the model for Fake News detection. A star (*) indicates that the feature is a feature set.

Feature	Description
Text statistics	
Num paragraphs	Number of paragraphs
Num sentences	Number of sentences [spacy]
Num tokens	Number of tokens
Num stopwords	Number of stopwords [nltk]
Num chars	Number of chars
Num of syllables	Number of syllables
Avg sents per para	Average number of sentences per paragraph
Avg words per para	Average number of words per paragraph
Avg words per sents	Average number of tokens per sentence
Avg chars per sents	Average number of characters per sentence
Avg chars per word	Average number of characters per word
Frequencies	
Freq punctuation *	Relative frequency of each punctuation character
Freq PoS tags *	Relative frequency of each PoS tag
Freq type of adverbs *	Relative frequency of each type of adverb
Readability	
Vocabulary richness *	Measures of vocabulary diversity: ratio between the total number of words and the number of unique words – with or without stopwords
Readability indices *	Measures of text reading/understanding difficulty – *flesch, fleschkincaid, gunningfog,* and *smog*
% long words	Fraction of words with 12 or more characters
% obfuscated words	Fraction of words containing punctuation or numbers
% misspelled words	Fraction of words with spelling errors
% uppercase words	Fraction of uppercase words
% polysybl words	Fraction of words eith three or more syllables
N -grams	
n-grams *	TF (counts) and TF-IDF of unigram, bigrams, trigrams. In total 600 n-grams

4.3   Classification Process

We conduct several experiments with each feature category and with multiple Machine Learning algorithms, specifically: Logistic Regression (LR), Linear Support Vector Machines (LSVM), Random Forest (RF), Decision Tree (DT), Gradient Descent (SGD), Naive Bayes (NB), and Gradient Boosting Classifier (GBC). We use Scikit-Learn's implementations of these algorithms and resort

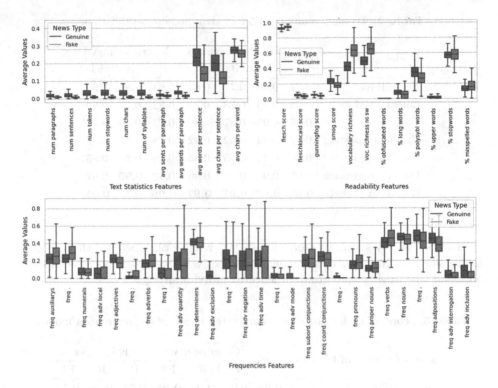

Fig. 1. Distribution values per class for each feature set.

to the default values of the hyperparameters as defined by the library, only specifying (when possible) the class_weight property to "balanced" to make the algorithms handle both classes with equal importance, and for LR the Lasso penalty (l1).

To better assess the performance of each model, we use 5-fold stratified cross-validation. In each fold, we return the following metrics: Accuracy, Precision, Recall, and F1-score. Although we pay attention to all these metrics, we mainly focus on two. The first is Accuracy, which is the metric consistently presented in the related works section (see Sect. 2). However, due to the imbalanced nature of our dataset, the second metric we focus on is the macro average F1-score. Furthermore, we collect the feature importance for every model to understand the features that each model deems more important to choose between the fake and genuine news classes.

5 Experimental Results

The results shown in Table 2 are the average performance rates for each model in the 5-fold stratified cross-validation setup. We can observe that Logistic Regression and Random Forest achieve the best results.

Table 2. Average results from 5-fold stratified cross-validation.

Model	Acc.	Weighted average			Macro average		
		P	R	F1	P	R	F1
Naive Bayes	0.77	0.93	0.77	0.82	0.63	0.85	0.64
Linear SVM	0.78	0.95	0.78	0.77	0.82	0.77	0.69
SGD	0.87	0.95	0.87	0.90	0.72	0.90	0.76
Gradient boosting	0.92	0.93	0.92	0.92	0.75	0.83	0.78
Decision tree	0.95	0.95	0.95	0.95	0.85	0.85	0.85
Logistic regression	0.95	0.96	0.95	0.96	0.82	**0.95**	0.87
Random forest	**0.97**	**0.97**	**0.97**	**0.97**	**0.96**	0.87	**0.91**

Tables 3 and 4 show, in more detail, the results obtained by the Logistic Regression and Random Forest models, respectively; we also report the results obtained when using each group of features individually.

Table 3. Scores of each feature's category fitted in a Logistic Regression model.

Features (number of features)	Acc.	Genuine news			Fake news		
		P	R	F1	P	R	F1
N-grams (600)	**0.96**	0.98	**0.98**	**0.98**	0.76	0.80	0.78
Frequencies (64)	0.88	0.98	0.88	0.93	0.39	0.81	0.53
Text Statistics (11)	0.90	**0.99**	0.90	0.94	0.46	0.90	0.61
Readability (12)	0.89	**0.99**	0.89	0.94	0.43	0.86	0.57
All Features (687)	0.95	0.65	0.94	0.77	**0.99**	**0.95**	**0.97**

Logistic Regression obtains high accuracy scores regardless of the set of features used, especially the model trained with n-grams or the one trained with all the features. The accuracy is even slightly higher when the model trained only with n-grams is used, compared to the all-features model. However, if we examine the F1-score, we can see that although the n-grams model performs well in finding genuine news, it shows a poor performance when detecting fake news. Since this a fake news detection problem, it makes sense to consider the best model trained with all the features, which achieves a macro-F1 score of 0.87 (as shown in Table 2).

The models trained with Random Forest also present very high accuracy scores, even outperforming Logistic Regression. Nevertheless, we will use the F1-score once more. The best model, in this case, is the one where all the features are used for training. Although the Random Forest model is almost perfect at identifying genuine news, the same cannot be said about fake news. Comparing the best model of each algorithm, we notice that the F1-score for fake news is

Table 4. Scores of each feature's category fitted in a Random Forest model.

Features (number of features)	Acc.	Genuine news			Fake news		
		P	R	F1	P	R	F1
N-grams (600)	0.96	0.97	0.99	0.98	0.89	0.64	0.75
Frequencies (64)	0.96	0.96	0.99	0.98	0.91	0.55	0.69
Text Statistics (11)	0.96	0.97	0.99	0.98	0.81	0.65	0.72
Readability (12)	0.95	0.96	0.99	0.97	0.77	0.53	0.62
All features (687)	**0.97**	**0.98**	**1.00**	**0.99**	**0.94**	**0.75**	**0.83**

lower in the Random Forest model. Nevertheless, the model trained with Random Forest yields the best results, achieving the highest macro-F1 score among all models (as per Table 2).

In both learning algorithms, we can also notice that the models trained using frequencies or readability properties alone result in comparatively poorer performance. Nevertheless, when combining with the remaining feature sets, the overall performance is improved. Among all feature sets, we can see that the n-grams always return the best results for both algorithms. Even though entities were obfuscated, these results may still exhibit some overfitting, as n-grams are highly reliant on the vocabulary used.

Results with Logistic Regression also indicate that with the exception of n-grams, none of the feature sets can distinguish fake news with a precision higher than 0.5. However, when all of the features are used simultaneously, the model yields an excellent precision score for the fake news class. Additionally, although each feature set performs rather well at distinguishing genuine news when all features are used, precision drops significantly.

5.1   Feature Analysis

We analyze the main features used by each model to predict the class label. For Random Forest, we use the *feature_importance_* property[8], while for Logistic Regression we use the *coef_* property[9]. Since each model has its own way of calculating feature importance, we cannot directly compare the values. Furthermore, the two classifiers make predictions in very different ways. Random Forest is a non-linear classifier composed of a multitude of decision trees, whilst Logistic Regression is based on a linear decision boundary and uses a weighted sum of the features to make predictions. This makes comparing feature importance between the models non-trivial. Nevertheless, what we can do is compare which are the top ten features each model considers the most important:

---

[8] scikit-learn.org/stable/modules/generated/sklearn.ensemble.RandomForest Classifier.

[9] scikit-learn.org/stable/modules/generated/sklearn.linear_model.LogisticRegression.

Logistic Regression	Random Forest
1. num stopwords	1. num syllables
2. num syllables	2. num chars
3. avg words per paragraph	3. num tokens
4. avg sents per paragraph	4. vocabulary richness
5. 1-gram counts 'milhão'	5. avg words per paragraph
6. 2-gram counts 'milhão euro'	6. num stop words
7. freq !	7. vocabulary richness without sw
8. freq [	8. avg chars per sentence
9. smog score	9. avg words per sentence
10. freq <<	10. 1-gram counts [ORG]

The feature analysis suggests noticeable differences in fake news articles as compared to genuine news. While Random Forest relies mainly on features from the text statistics category, the Logistic Regression model considers that all feature sets are important.

Similar to Random Forest, the Logistic Regression model places more importance on text statistics, when compared to the other categories. However, Logistic Regression also places some importance on other feature sets: first, the n-grams "milhão" and "milhão euro", which are more frequent in fake news, as mentioned in Sect. 4.2. Next, the model uses punctuation frequencies, such as "!". This frequency can represent the author's emotions, which are expected to occur more often in fake news. The other two frequencies are more related to the style chosen by the authors, which may represent overfitting. Lastly, the model uses a readability score – SMOG. This metric performs a calculation based on the number of sentences and the number of polysyllable words (both metrics are higher in genuine news) to grant a final score estimating the years of education needed to understand a text.

In addition to the features related to text statistics, the Random Forest model also uses unigram counts [ORG] and vocabulary richness features. The former means that it gives importance to the number of entities identified as organizations. The latter measures language diversity, which is unexpectedly higher in fake news, as mentioned in Sect. 4.2.

6   Conclusions

Fake news is news that does not follow the principles of journalism. Instead, the authors of such news try to mimic the look and feel of real news, and have a hidden agenda to disinform the reader. This phenomenon is a severe problem in our society, and the topic has become increasingly relevant in recent years.

For this paper, we collected a corpus of fake news and a corpus of genuine news from the same time frame using a silver standard approach. We then performed feature engineering inspired on approaches used by forensic linguistic analyses.

Although this remains understudied, we conclude that a forensic linguistics-grounded approach for classifying fake news can be applied with great success.

To the best of our knowledge, this is the first work that applies this kind of approach to solve the problem of fake news detection to Portuguese texts.

For future work, we intend to further analyze the robustness of this approach. To do so, we will investigate how our model performs on other corpora and possibly with manually annotated datasets. Furthermore, we will consider exploring the problem in a multi-class formulation exploring different text genres (e.g. fake, genuine, sensationalist news, and so on). We also believe that using neural language models, such as BERT [7], can be a promising direction, and is thus worth exploring.

Acknowledgments. This research is supported by project DARGMINTS (POCI/01/0145/FEDER/031460), CLUP (UIDB/00022/2020), and LIACC (FCT/UID/CEC/0027/2020), funded by Fundação para a Ciência e a Tecnologia (FCT).

References

1. Ahmed, H., Traore, I., Saad, S.: Detection of online fake news using n-gram analysis and machine learning techniques. In: Traore, I., Woungang, I., Awad, A. (eds.) ISDDC 2017. LNCS, vol. 10618, pp. 127–138. Springer, Cham (2017). https://doi.org/10.1007/978-3-319-69155-8_9
2. Alkhodair, S.A., Ding, S.H., Fung, B.C., Liu, J.: Detecting breaking news rumors of emerging topics in social media. Inf. Process. Manage. **57**, 102018 (2020)
3. Bender, J., Davenport, L., Fedler, F., Drager, M.: Reporting for the Media. Oxford University Press, Oxford (2012)
4. Browne, R.: 'Junk news' gets massive engagement on Facebook ahead of EU elections, study finds. CNBC (2019). https://www.cnbc.com/2019/05/21/junk-news-gets-higher-engagement-on-facebook-ahead-of-eu-elections.html. Accessed 19 Apr 2021
5. Chowdhury, M.F.M., Lavelli, A.: Assessing the practical usability of an automatically annotated corpus. In: Proceedings of the 5th Linguistic Annotation Workshop, pp. 101–109. Association for Computational Linguistics, Portland, Oregon, USA, Jun 2011. https://www.aclweb.org/anthology/W11-0412
6. Cruz, A., Rocha, G., Sousa-Silva, R., Lopes Cardoso, H.: Team Fernando-Pessa at SemEval-2019 task 4: Back to basics in hyperpartisan news detection. In: Proceedings of the 13th International Workshop on Semantic Evaluation, pp. 999–1003. Association for Computational Linguistics, Minneapolis, Minnesota, USA, Jun 2019. https://doi.org/10.18653/v1/S19-2173
7. Devlin, J., Chang, M.W., Lee, K., Toutanova, K.: BERT: pre-training of deep bidirectional transformers for language understanding (2019)
8. Álvaro Figueira, Oliveira, L.: The current state of fake news: challenges and opportunities. Procedia Computer Science (2017). https://doi.org/10.1016/j.procs.2017.11.106
9. Flesch, R.: A new readability yardstick. J. Appl. Psychol. **32**(3), 221–233 (1948)
10. Gunning, R.: The Technique of Clear Writing. McGraw-Hill, New York (1952)
11. Hahn, U., Tomanek, K., Beisswanger, E., Faessler, E.: A proposal for a configurable silver standard. In: Proceedings of the Fourth Linguistic Annotation Workshop, pp. 235–242. Association for Computational Linguistics, Uppsala, Sweden, July 2010. https://www.aclweb.org/anthology/W10-1838

12. Hancock, J.T., Curry, L.E., Goorha, S., Woodworth, M.: On lying and being lied to: A linguistic analysis of deception in computer-mediated communication. Discourse Process. **45** (2007). https://doi.org/10.1080/01638530701739181

13. Harrower, T.: Inside Reporting: A Practical Guide to the Craft of Journalism. McGraw-Hill Companies, Incorporated (2007)

14. Horne, B.D., Adali, S.: This just. In: Fake news packs a lot in title, uses simpler, repetitive content in text body, more similar to satire than real news (2017)

15. Kincaid, J.P., Aagard, J.A., O'Hara, J.W.: Development and test of a computer readability editing system (CRES). Technical report, TRAINING ANALYSIS AND EVALUATION GROUP (NAVY) ORLANDO FL (1980)

16. Laboreiro, G., Oliveira, E.: What we can learn from looking at profanity, pp. 108–113 (2014). https://doi.org/10.1007/978-3-319-09761-9_11

17. Laughlin, G.H.M.: Smog grading-a new readability formula. J. Reading **12**(8), 639–646 (1969). http://www.jstor.org/stable/40011226

18. Litvinova, O., Seredin, P., Litvinova, T., Lyell, J.: Deception detection in Russian texts. In: Proceedings of the Student Research Workshop at the 15th Conference of the European Chapter of the Association for Computational Linguistics (2017)

19. Mehrabi, N., Morstatter, F., Saxena, N., Lerman, K., Galstyan, A.: A survey on bias and fairness in machine learning. arXiv (2019). arXiv:1908.09635

20. Mourão, R.R., Robertson, C.T.: Fake news as discursive integration: an analysis of sites that publish false, misleading, hyperpartisan and sensational information. Journalism Stud. **20**(14), 2077–2095 (2019). https://doi.org/10.1080/1461670X.2019.1566871

21. Pérez-Rosas, V., Kleinberg, B., Lefevre, A., Mihalcea, R.: Automatic detection of fake news. arXiv preprint arXiv:1708.07104 (2017)

22. Sousa-Silva, R.: Computational forensic linguistics: an overview of computational applications in forensic contexts. Language and Law/Linguagem e Direito **5**(2), 118–143 (2019)

23. Sullivan, M.: What it really means when trump calls a story 'fake news'. https://www.washingtonpost.com/lifestyle/media/what-it-really-means-when-trump-calls-a-story-fake-news/2020/04/13/56fbe2c0-7d8c-11ea-9040-68981f488eed_story.html (2020). Accessed 20 Apr 2021

24. Tandoc, E., Lim, Z., Ling, R.: Defining "fake news": a typology of scholarly definitions. Digital Journalism **6** (2017). https://doi.org/10.1080/21670811.2017.1360143

25. Vorhaus, M.: People increasingly turn to social media for news. https://www.forbes.com/sites/mikevorhaus/2020/06/24/people-increasingly-turn-to-social-media-for-news/ (2020). Accessed 5 Apr 2021

26. Weber, G.: Top languages. The World's 10 (2008)

Author Index

Printed in the United States
by Baker & Taylor Publisher Services